PART 2
CONTEMPORARY THEMES AND ISSUES

BMA

CONTEMPORARY HUMAN
RESOURCE MANAGEMENT

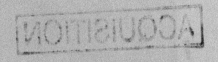

CONTEMPORARY HUMAN RESOURCE MANAGEMENT

Text and Cases

Fifth Edition

Adrian Wilkinson,
Tom Redman
and Tony Dundon

PEARSON

Harlow, England • London • New York • Boston • San Francisco • Toronto • Sydney
Auckland • Singapore • Hong Kong • Tokyo • Seoul • Taipei • New Delhi
Cape Town • São Paulo • Mexico City • Madrid • Amsterdam • Munich • Paris • Milan

PEARSON EDUCATION LIMITED
Edinburgh Gate
Harlow CM20 2JE
United Kingdom
Tel: +44 (0)1279 623623
Web: www.pearson.com/uk

First published 2001 (print)
Second edition published 2006 (print)
Third edition published 2009 (print)
Fourth edition published 2013 (print and electronic)
Fifth edition published 2017 (print and electronic)

ISBN: 978-1-292-08824-2 (print)
        978-1-292-08826-6 (PDF)
        978-1-292-17068-8 (ePub)

British Library Cataloguing-in-Publication Data
A catalogue record for the print edition is available from the British Library

Library of Congress Cataloging-in-Publication Data
Names: Redman, Tom, 1952- editor. | Wilkinson, Adrian, 1963- editor. |
   Dundon, Tony, 1962- editor.
Title: Contemporary human resource management : text and cases / [edited by]
   Adrian Wilkinson, Tom Redman and Tony Dundon.
Description: Fifth edition. | Harlow, United Kingdom : Pearson Education,
   [2017]
Identifiers: LCCN 2016023769| ISBN 9781292088242 | ISBN 9781292170688 (ePub)
Subjects: LCSH: Personnel management. | Personnel management—Study and
   teaching. | Personnel management—Case studies.
Classification: LCC HF5549.15 .C66 2017 | DDC 658.3—dc23
LC record available at https://lccn.loc.gov/2016023769

Print edition typeset in Times LT Pro 10/12 by Lumina Datamatics, Inc.

ARP Impression 98
Printed in Great Britain by Ashford Colour Press Ltd.

NOTE THAT ANY PAGE CROSS REFERENCES REFER TO THE PRINT EDITION

To Erin and Aidan
and
Rachel and Rosie
and
Diane, Liam and Kate

BRIEF OF CONTENTS

CONTENTS

CASE STUDIES AND EXERCISES

EDITORS

Adrian Wilkinson is Professor and Director of the Centre for Work, Organisation and Wellbeing at Griffith University, Brisbane, Australia. Prior to his 2006 appointment, Adrian worked at Loughborough University in the United Kingdom where he was Professor of Human Resource Management from 1998 to 2006. Adrian has also worked at the Manchester School of Management at the University of Manchester Institute of Science and Technology. He holds Visiting Professorships at Loughborough University, the University of Sheffield and the University of Durham, and is an Academic Fellow at the Centre for International Human Resource Management at the Judge Institute, University of Cambridge. Adrian has authored, co-authored and edited some 25 books, over 150 articles in refereed journals and numerous book chapters. His books (with co-authors) include *Making Quality Critical* (Routledge, 1995); *Managing Quality and Human Resources* (Blackwell, 1997); *Managing with TQM: Theory and Practice* (Macmillan, 1998); *Understanding Work and Employment: Industrial Relations in Transition* (Oxford University Press, 2003); *Human Resource Management at Work* (5th edition, Chartered Institute of Personnel and Development, 2012); *The SAGE Handbook of Human Resource Management* (Sage, 2009); *The Oxford Handbook of Participation in Organisations* (Oxford University Press, 2010); *The Research Handbook of The Future of Work and Employment Relations* (Elgar, 2011); *The Future of Employment Relations* (Palgrave, 2011); *The Handbook of Comparative Employment Relations* (Elgar, 2011) and *The International Handbook of Labour Unions* (Elgar, 2012). *Contemporary Human Resource Management* (Pearson, 2013); *The Oxford Handbook of Employment Relations* (OUP, 2014) and the *Handbook of Research on Employee Voice* (Elgar, 2014).

He is a Fellow and Accredited Examiner of the Chartered Institute of Personnel and Development in the UK and a Fellow of the Australian Human Resource Institute. Adrian was appointed as a British Academy of Management Fellow in 2010. He is an Academician of the Academy of Social Sciences and a Fellow of the Australian Academy of Social Sciences. Adrian is Joint Chief Editor of the *Human Resource Management Journal* (HRMJ).

Tom Redman was Professor of Human Resource Management. Before joining Durham Business School, Tom was a Professor of Human Resource Management at the University of Sheffield. Prior to this he was Professor of Human Resource Management at the University of Teesside. Tom also spent 10 years in industry, in quality, production and HR management positions (mainly with Royal Worcester Porcelain) prior to re-entering academic life. His books include *Managing Managers* (Blackwell, 1993) and *Managing with TQM: Theory and Practice* (Macmillan, 1998) and *The SAGE Handbook of Human Resource Management* (Sage, 2009). He was a Fellow of the Chartered Institute of Personnel and Development. Sadly, Professor Redman passed away suddenly during the production stages of this edition of the book. He will be sadly missed. His work and influence on the field of HRM continues.

Tony Dundon is Professor of Human Resource Management and Employment Relations at Alliance Manchester Business School, University of Manchester, UK, and is a visiting honorary professor at University of St Andrews and the Kemmy Business School, University of Limerick. Tony's research areas include employment relations, human resource management and organisational performance, employee voice and trade union organising. Professor Dundon is a Fellow of the Academy of Social Sciences (FAcSS), former Chief Examiner for the Chartered Institute of Personnel and Development (CIPD), joint Editor-in-Chief of the *Human Resource Management Journal* (HRMJ), Consulting Editor for the *International Journal of Management Reviews* (IJMR); International Advisory Board Member of *Work, Employment and Society* (WES). Tony has held visiting positions at Sydney University; Deakin University, Melbourne; Toulouse Business School, France; and Queensland University of Technology. His books include *Understanding Employment Relations*, (2nd edition, McGraw Hill, 2011); *Cases in Global Management: Strategy, Innovation and People Management* (Tilde University Press, 2012); *Global Anti-Unionism* (Palgrave, 2013) and *Handbook of Research on Employee Voice* (Edward Elgar, 2014).

CONTRIBUTORS

Peter Ackers	Professor of Employment Relations, Department of HRM, De Montfort University, Leicester
Deirdre Anderson	Senior Lecturer in Organisational Behaviour, School of Management, Cranfield University
Thomas A. Birtch	Associate Professor, Department of International Business and Management, University of Nottingham, China, Senior Research Fellow, Institute for Manufacturing, University of Cambridge, UK, and Director, International Centre for Incentives, Rewards, and Performance
Aline Bos	Researcher/Assistant Professor, Utrecht School of Governance Consulting, Utrecht University, The Netherlands
Paul Boselie	Professor, Utrecht School of Governance, Utrecht University, The Netherlands
Michelle Barker	Professor, Griffith Business School, Griffith University
Sara Branch	Research Fellow, Griffith Criminology Institute, Griffith University
Michelle Brown	Professor of Management (Human Resource Management), University of Melbourne
David A. Buchanan	Emeritus Professor of Organizational Behaviour, Cranfield University School of Management
Samantha Callan	Associate Director for Families and Mental Health, Centre for Social Justice – Independent UK think tank
	Honorary Research Fellow, School of Clinical Sciences and Community Health, College of Medicine and Veterinary Medicine, Edinburgh University
Catherine Cassell	Deputy Dean of Business School and Professor of Organisational Psychology, Leeds University
Jenny Chan	Lecturer and Junior Research Fellow, School of Interdisciplinary Area Studies, Kellogg College, University of Oxford.
Alistair Cheyne	Professor of Organisational Psychology and Director of Internationalisation and Accreditation, School of Business and Economics, Loughborough University
Flora F. T. Chiang	Professor, Department of Management, Hong Kong Baptist University
David G. Collings	Professor of Human Resource Management, Dublin City University
Edel Conway	Professor of Human Resource Management, Dublin City University
Michael Dickmann	Professor of International Human Resource Management and Program Director MSc in Management, Cranfield University
Tony Dobbins	Professor of Employment Studies, Bangor Business School
Elaine Farndale	Associate Professor of Human Resource Management, School of Labor and Employment Relations, and Center Director, Center for International Human Resource Studies, The Pennsylvania State University
Mark Gilman	Director, Business Improvements and Growth (BIG) Associates Ltd
Irena Grugulis	Professor of Work and Skills, Leeds University Business School
Cynthia Hardy	Laureate Professor, Department of Management and Marketing, University of Melbourne
Philip Hancock	Professor of Work and Organisation, Essex Business School
Geraint Harvey	Senior Lecturer in HRM and Industrial Relations, Birmingham Business School, University of Birmingham
Gail Hebson	Senior Lecturer in Employment Studies, Manchester Business School

Donald Hislop	Reader in Sociology of Contemporary Work, and Head of Discipline, Human Resource Management and Organisational Behaviour, School of Business and Economics, Loughborough University
Louise Hopper	Company HR Manager, Herts for Learning Ltd
Scott Hurrell	Lecturer in Management , Work and Organisation, University of Glasgow
Clare Kelliher	Professor of Work and Organisation, Cranfield School of Management, Cranfield University
Ashlea Kellner	Research Fellow, Centre for Work, Organisation and Wellbeing, Griffith University
Gill Kirton	Professor of Employment Relations, School of Business and Management, Queen Mary, University of London
Nicholas Kinnie	Associate Dean Undergraduate Taught Students, and Professor in Human Resource Management, School of Management, University of Bath
John Loan-Clarke	Former Senior Lecturer in Organisational Development, Loughborough University
Aoife M. McDermott	Senior Lecturer in Human Resource Management, Cardiff Business School, Cardiff University
Paula K Mowbray	Doctoral Student, Griffith University
Sheryl Ramsay	Senior Lecturer, Griffith Business School, Griffith University
Hugh Scullion	Formerly Professor in International Management, at the Cairnes School of Business and Economics, NUIGalway
Agnieszka Skuza	Assistant Professor, Poznan University of Economics and Business
Dora Scholarios	Professor of Work Psychology, Organisational Behaviour and Human Resource Management, University of Strathclyde
Ruth Smyth	Head of HR (Europe and Americas), Alexander Mann Solutions
Juani Swart	Associate Dean Faculty, Professor in HRM and Director, Work and Employment Research Centre (WERC), School of Management, University of Bath
Paul Thompson	Professor of Employment Studies, University of Stirling
Peter Turnbull	Professor of Management, School of Economics, Finance & Management, University of Bristol
Melissa Tyler	Professor of Work and Organisation Studies, University of Essex
Maja Vidović	Lecturer, Rochester Institute of Technology Croatia
Diane van den Broek	Associate Professor, Work and Organisational Studies, The University of Sydney Business School
Steven Vincent	Professor of Work and Organisation, and Head of Leadership, Work and Organisation, Business School, Newcastle University
Geoffrey Wood	Dean and Professor of International Business, Essex Business School, University of Essex
Xiaozheng Zhang	Senior Lecturer in Human Resource Management, Nottingham Business School, Nottingham Trent University

ACKNOWLEDGEMENTS

As with any book, the list of acknowledgements is extensive, but these are the most important. Thanks to our editor. As usual, our family and friends make a major contribution, and we are grateful to our families for their support while the book was being written.

While this book was being finalised, Tom sadly passed away. He will be missed.

Publisher's acknowledgements

Figures

Figure 2.4 from *People Management and Performance*, Oxford: Routledge (Purcell, J., Kinnie, N., Swart, J., Rayton, B. and Hutchinson, S. 2009), Figure 1.2, p. 15. Reproduced by permission of Taylor & Francis Books UK; Figure 10.2 adapted from H. De Cieri and P. Dowling, Strategic human resource management in multinational enterprises: theoretical Research in Personnel and Human Resource Management: *Strategic human resources in the twenty-first century, 4th Supplement* (Wright, P.M., Dyer, L.D. and Boudreau, J.W. (Eds.), 1999), Stamford, CT: JAI Press, © Emerald Group Publishing Limited, all rights reserved; Figure 10.4 from *Global Careers, London: Routledge* (Dickmann, M. and Baruch, Y., 2011) p. 120, Figure 5.4, permission conveyed through Copyright Clearance Center, Inc.; Figure 10.5 adapted from Expatriate selection, training and career-pathing: A review and critique, *Human Resource Management*, Vol. 26 (3), pp. 331–45 (Mendenhall, M., Dunbar, E. and Oddou, G., 1987), John Wiley & Sons; Figure 10.6 from A. Haslberger, Expatriate adjustment: a more nuanced view, in, *International Human Resource Management – A European Perspective*, 2nd ed., p. 138, Figure (Dickmann, M., Brewster, C. and Sparrow, P. (Eds.), 2008), London: Routledge. Reproduced by permission of Taylor & Francis Books UK; Figures 10.7, 10.8 from Dickmann, M. (2014), Key Trends in Global Mobility, RES Forum, UniGroup Relocation Network and Equus Software, 102 pages, London; Figure 16.1 from M. Marchington, Employee involvement: patterns and explanations, in, Participation and Democracy at Work: *Essays in honour of Harvie Ramsay* (Harley, B., Hyman, J. and Thompson, P. (Eds.), 2005), London: Palgrave; Figure 20.1 from United we stand, or else? Exploring organizational attempts to control emotional expression by, *Journal of Organizational Change Management*, Vol. 16 (5), pp. 534–46, Figure 1 (Driver, M., 2003), Emerald Group Publishing Ltd., © Emerald Group Publishing Limited, all rights reserved; Figure 21.1 from Part-time employment in *OECD Factbook 2014: Economic, Environmental and Social Statistics* – © OECD 05-05-2014. Reproduced with permission of the OECD; Figure 21.2 from Eurostat (online data code: ifsa_etpga), Eurostat, http://ec.europa.eu/eurostat/web/main/home, © European Union, 1995 – 2016; Figure 22.1 from mobbing.ca, http://www.mobbing.ca, Bobbie Osborne (Photographer) and Anton Hout (Designer), reprinted with permission of Anton Hout of Overcome Bullying Canada; Figure 22.3 from Workplace Bullying, Mobbing and General Harassment: A Review, *International Journal of Management Reviews*, Vol.15, No.3, 280–99 (Branch, S., Ramsay, S., and Barker, M 2013), Wiley. Reproduced with permission of Blackwell Scientific in the format Republish in a book via Copyright Clearance Center; Figure 22.4 from Workplace Mobbing Australia, www.workplacemobbing.com/mobbing.html, Linda Shallcross (designer). Reproduced with permission of Linda Shallcross of Workplace Mobbing Australia; Figure 23.1 from Social Media(tion) and the Reshaping of Public/Private Boundaries in Employment Relations, *International Journal of Management Reviews* (McDonald, P. and Thompson, P 2015), doi: 10.1111/ijmr.12061. Reproduced with permission of Blackwell Scientific in the format Republish in a book via Copyright Clearance Center.

Tables

Table 1.1 from *Human Resources Management: A Critical Text*, 3rd ed., Cengage (Storey, J. 2007) p. 9, © 2007, Cengage. Reproduced by permission of Cengage Learning EMEA Ltd; Table 3.1 from IDS HR Study 865, Competency Frameworks, March 2008, p. 17, www.idshrstudies.com, table reprinted by kind permission of Income Data Services; Table 3.2 from *Resourcing and Talent Planning*, Chartered Institute of Personnel Development (CIPD) (2011) p. 16, CIPD, with the permission of the publisher, the Chartered Institute of Personnel and Development, London (www.cipd.co.uk); Table 4.1 adapted from *Staffing Organizations: Contemporary practice and theory*,

3rd ed., Mahwah, N.J.: Lawrence Erlbaum Associates (Ployhart, R.E., Schneider, B. and Schmitt, N.) p. 380, Table 7.3, permission conveyed through Copyright Clearance Center, Inc.; Table 8.2 from Unitarism and employer resistance to trade unionism, *International Journal of Human Resource Management*, 25(18), 2573–90 (Cullinane, N. and Dundon, T. 2014), reprinted by permission of the publisher (Taylor & Francis Ltd; http://www.tandfonline.com); Table 10.1 from *Managing Across Borders: The transnational solution*, Random House Business Books (Bartlett, C. and Ghoshal, S., 1989), and Harvard Business School Publishing; Tables on page 283 and 284 from *Global Careers*, London: Routledge (Dickmann, M. and Baruch, Y., 2011) p. 40, , permission conveyed through Copyright Clearance Center, Inc.; Table 10.2 adapted from N.J. Adler and F. Ghadar, Strategic human resource management: a global perspective, in, *Human Resource Management: An international comparison*, p. 240, Table 1 (Pieper, R. 1990), New York: de Gruyter, © 1990 de Gruyter; permission conveyed through Copyright Clearance Center, Inc.; Table 10.4 adapted from *International Human Resource Management*, London: CIPD (Harris, H., Brewster, C. and Sparrow P. 2003) p. 146, with the permission of the publisher, the Chartered Institute of Personnel and Development, London (www.cipd.co.uk); Table 10.5a adapted from *Global Careers, London: Routledge* (Dickmann, M. and Baruch, Y 2011) p. 194, permission conveyed through Copyright Clearance Center, Inc.; Table 10.5b adapted from *Global Careers, London: Routledge* (Dickmann, M. and Baruch, Y. 2011) p. 194, permission conveyed through Copyright Clearance Center, Inc.; Table 10.6 adapted from *Global Careers,* London: Routledge (Dickmann, M. and Baruch, Y., 2011) p. 234, permission conveyed through Copyright Clearance Center, Inc.; Table 18.2 from *Diagnosing and changing organizational culture.*, 1 ed., Addison-Wesley. (Cameron, K. S., & Quinn, R. E. 1999); Table 22.1 from Bullying: From the playground to the boardroom, *Journal of Leadership and Organizational Studies,* Vol. 12 (4), pp. 1–11 (Harvey, M. G., Heames, J. T., Richey, R. G. and Leonard, N. 2006), Copyright © 2006 Baker College. Reprinted by permission of SAGE Publications.

Text

Box 4.4 from Using situational interviews to assess engineering applicant fit to work group. Job and organizational requirements, *Engineering Management Journal*, Vol. 18, pp. 27–35; Extract on pages 138–9 from Expansive learning environments: Integrating Organisational and personal development, *Workplace learning in context*, p.130 figure (Rainbird H., Fuller A and Munro A 2004), London and New York: Routledge: Routledge. Reproduced by permission of Taylor & Francis Books UK; Case Study 5.3 from The rise of the 'network organisation' and the decline of discretion, *Human Resource Management Journal*, Vol. 13(2), pp. 45–59 (2003), John Wiley & Sons; Box 10.1 from P. Almond and O. Tregaskis, *International HRM, in, Human Resource Management: A contemporary approach*, 6th ed. (Beardwell, J. and Claydon, T., 2010) p. 649, © Pearson Education Limited 2001, 2010; Box 10.2 from *The coffee-machine system: how international selection really works*, Vol. 10 (3), International Journal of Human Resource Management (Harris, H. and Brewster, C., 1999) pp. 488–500, permission conveyed through Copyright Clearance Center, Inc.; Box 11.1 from *Culture's Consequences: Comparing values, behaviors, institutions and organizations across nations, Thousand Oaks, California*, 2nd ed., Sage Publications (Hofstede, G., 2001) p. 29, ISBN 0-8039-7323-3 © Geert Hofstede B.V., quoted with permission; Case Study 11.1 from *Human resource management practice and institutional constraints: The case of Mozambique*, Vol. 27 (4), Employee Relations: An International Journal (Webster, E. and Wood, G., 2005) pp. 369–85; Case Study 14.1 from Dobbins, T. (2005), 'Irish Ferries dispute finally resolved after bitter stand-off'. European Foundation for the Improvement of Living and Working Conditions, Dublin. http://www.eurofound.europa.eu/observatories/eurwork/articles/irish-ferries-dispute; Box 14.2 from http://www.nytimes.com/2015/06/04/us/last-task-after-layoff-at-disney-train-foreign-replacements.html; Box 16.1 from *Information and Consultation of Employees (ICE) Regulations 2004*, Department for Business, Innovation and Skills, DTI 2006 (2006) © Crown copyright. Contains public sector information licensed under the Open Government Licence (OGL) v3.0. http://www.nationalarchives.gov.uk/doc/open-government-licence/version/3/; Box 23.1 adapted from Broughton, A., Foley, B., Ledermaier, S., & Cox, A. (2013). The use of social media in the recruitment process. Retrieved May, 2, 2014, Acas research paper 1.

PART 1

FUNDAMENTALS OF HUMAN RESOURCE MANAGEMENT

CHAPTER 1

HUMAN RESOURCE MANAGEMENT: A CONTEMPORARY PERSPECTIVE

Adrian Wilkinson, Tom Redman and Tony Dundon

Introduction

This book is about Human Resource Management (HRM) and is concerned with the way in which organisations manage their people. In this introductory chapter we discuss our own approach to the study of HRM and the rationale underpinning the ordering and presentation of material in the book. Our aim is to chart the broad terrain of a rapidly developing field of study in order to prepare the reader for the more finely grained treatment of specific HRM topics to be found in the individual chapters. In particular, we examine the rise of HRM, the effects of the changing context of work on HRM, the strategic nature of HRM practice, its impact on organisational performance and the changing role of the HR function. The chapter concludes with a consideration of our views on the audience at which the book is targeted and some thoughts on how it may best be used.

The development of HRM

The roots of HRM can be found in the emergence of industrial welfare work from the 1890s, as organisations driven by a mix of humanitarian, religious and business motives began to provide workplace amenities such as medical care, housing and libraries. In addition, employment offices were established to deal with hiring, payroll and record keeping. When scientific management emerged, the principles of science were also to be applied to the management of people as well as the management of production. We see here the shift from direct systems of management (personal supervision, traditional paternalism and simple piecework systems) to more technical systems of management and bureaucratic forms of employment (Gospel, 2009). From here the HRM function came to life, responsible for establishing modern personnel methods (Kaufman, 2010b), and we have seen a growing professionalisation of the role. However, it has been seen as largely an administrative function dealing with the 'labour problem' rather than contributing to strategic goals. The former welfare and personnel administrative tradition is the backcloth to the rise in HRM.

The past 20 years or so have seen the rise of what has been called the new HRM orthodoxy (Bacon, 2003; Guest, 1998; Torrington *et al.*, 2014; Wilkinson *et al.*, 2009). In the mid-1980s in the UK, and earlier in the US, the term 'HRM' became fashionable and gradually started to replace others such as 'personnel management', 'industrial relations' and 'labour relations'. The practitioners of people management are no longer personnel officers and trainers but are HR managers and human resource developers (and importantly, line managers). The 1990s saw the launch of new journals and the flourishing of university courses in HRM; many of these in the UK are now endorsed and professionally accredited by the Chartered Institute of Personnel and Development (CIPD). A new HRM bandwagon was well and truly rolling.

Early contributions on the implications of the rise of HRM were concerned to define it and to compare it with the more traditional approach to personnel management (e.g. Guest, 1987). HRM was in turn both heralded as 'a new era of humane people oriented employment management' (Keenoy, 1990: 375) and derided as a 'blunt instrument to bully workers' (Monks, 1998), especially with the decline of collective bargaining and the reduced influence of trade unions (Nolan and Wood, 2003). There has been considerable ambiguity in the use of the term, with various commentators using 'HRM' as simply a more modern label for traditional personnel management, as a 're-conceptualising and re-organising of personnel roles', or as a new and distinctive approach, attempting to develop and utilise the potential of human resources to the full in pursuit of an organisation's strategic objectives. It is the promise that is held by this latter view that has most excited practitioners and attracted the attention of management academics (Marchington and Wilkinson, 2012; Kaufman, 2015; Wilkinson and Johnstone, 2016).

There has long been a debate over whether HRM is no more than a relabelling of personnel management, the 'old wine in new bottles' critique, or something more fundamental (Legge, 1995; Kaufman, 2015). Traditionally, personnel management was characterised as having little focus on broader business links and being overly concentrated on the activities of personnel professionals, unions and a range of operational techniques. Thus personnel management was seen as a low-level record-keeping and 'people maintenance' function. The HRM stereotype, in contrast, is characterised as being much more concerned with business strategy, taking the view that HR is *the* most important organisational resource. Thus there has been much talk of an HRM 'revolution' with a transformation from administrative efficiency to the role of HRM as a fully-fledged strategic business partner. HRM, speculate Ulrich and Dulebohn (2015), has been on a journey with the purposeful singular direction which is to 'add value to the firm'.

The new HRM?

Boxall and Purcell (2011: 2) point out that defining HRM is important and should not be rushed. Definitions specify and clarify the intellectual space to be discussed and uncover the different perspectives on which to examine the subject and explain phenomenon. Some of the key defining features of HRM include 'beliefs and assumptions', 'strategic qualities', the 'critical role of managers', and finally 'key levers' (see Table 1.1). An earlier definition of HRM by Storey (1995) emphasises a particular set of policies identified with 'high-commitment management' or 'high-performance work systems':

> Human resource management is a distinctive approach to employment management which seeks to achieve competitive advantage through the strategic deployment of a highly committed and capable workforce, using an integrated array of cultural, structural and personnel techniques. *(Storey, 1995: 5)*

In contrast, a broader definition is provided by Boxall and Purcell:

> HRM includes anything and everything associated with the management of employment relationships in the firm. We do not associate HRM solely with a high-commitment model of labour management or with any particular ideology or style of management. *(Boxall and Purcell, 2000: 184)*

Bacon (2003) points out that if HRM is defined exclusively as high-commitment management then the subject marginalises itself to the discussion of a relatively small number of distinct companies since many organisations pursue a 'low-wage path'. The above 'exclusive' definition thus identifies HRM in contrast to other forms of labour management

Table 1.1 The new HRM model

---

1 Beliefs and assumptions

- That it is the human resource which gives competitive edge.
- That the aim should not be mere compliance with rules, but employee commitment.
- That therefore employees should, for example, be very carefully selected and developed.

2 Strategic qualities

- Because of the above factors, HR decisions are of strategic importance.
- Top management involvement is necessary.
- HR policies should be integrated into the business strategy – stemming from it and even contributing to it.

3 Critical role of managers

- Because HR practice is critical to the core activities of the business, it is too important to be left to personnel specialists alone.
- Line managers are (or need to be) closely involved as both deliverers and drivers of the HR policies.
- Much greater attention is paid to the management of managers themselves.

4 Key levers

- Managing culture is more important than managing procedures and systems.
- Integrated action on selection, communication, training, reward and development.
- Restructuring and job redesign to allow devolved responsibility and empowerment.

Source: Storey, 2007: 9.

(industrial relations or traditional personnel management), whereas the second inclusive definition covers all forms of labour management (Bacon, 2003: 73).

Slippage between these two differing definitions, the new HRM according to Storey and HRM as a more generic term, is the cause of considerable confusion, generating more heat than light in debates on HRM and its meaning. However, although evolution is less exciting than revolution, Torrington *et al*.'s (2014) view was that HRM is merely the next stage in the development of personnel management is persuasive. Torrington (1993), a staunch defender of 'good' personnel management, has also suggested that much of what is now labelled 'HRM' may be seen much more simply as longstanding good people management practice, while what was less effective has been relegated to remain, rather unfairly it seems, with the 'personnel management' brand.

Lewin (2008) defines HRM as the attraction, retention, utilisation, motivation, rewarding and disciplining of employees in organisations, and this connects with other contemporary definitions that see HRM as the 'management of people at work' (Marchington and Wilkinson, 2012). This seems a good approach, which is broad and less subject to fashion. The idea also conveys the shift in terms of a greater emphasis on the ways in which people are managed is as a resource which may positively contribute to organisational success and effectiveness. In discussing the importance of a broad definition, Boxall and Purcell (2011) suggest that:

> HRM refers to all those activities associated with the management of work and people in organisations . . . related terms such as 'employee relations', 'labour management' and 'people management' are used as synonymous for HRM . . . defining HRM as a particular style is obviously a legitimate way to proceed. It opens up questions such as: What practices constitute a high-commitment model. . . . [An] inclusive definition of HRM is more appropriate. *(Boxall and Purcell, 2011: 2, 9)*

In this sense HRM has an aspirational quality that connects with perspectives to elaborate on concepts such as employee motivation, performance, commitment, managerial power and legitimacy and ideology. Even an inclusive definition of HRM about the management of people can have its origins in one or more competing perspectives to the study and practice of HRM. Table 1.2 summarises four such competing approaches.

Table 1.2 Alternative approaches to the study and practice of HRM

Approach	Beliefs and Assumptions	Strategic Qualities	Role Line Mangers	Key Drivers
Matching Models				
(Hard)	Compliance	Calculative efficiency	Rule-bound	Product demand
(Soft)	Nurturing commitment	People-supportive policies	Coaching	Training and development
Organisational Performance	Performance-enhancing	Bundles of complementary HR policies	Strategic and measured KPIs	Internal and external fit (integration)
Radical (Critical) Management	Exploitation of people at work	Global business model (capitalist) sources of power	Authority agents of owners	Peer surveillance/ Control of labour process
Employee-Centric Approach	Critical of cause-and-effect assumptions	Balance of opposing interests	Significant and active agents	Integration of individual and collective orientated processes

Developed from ideas in Storey, 2007; Sisson, 2010; Kaufman, 2010b, 2015

The first can be labelled as '*Matching HR Models*'. An early and influential Matching Model was that known as the Michigan School of HRM, developed by Fombrun *et al.* (1984) and regarded as 'hard' HRM. The approach is to stress a very tight calculative (hard) fit between business needs and the way people are managed to ensure optimum employee effort and performance. The latter is measured by strict rules to select, reward, train and/ or replace employees. Hard HRM is often seen as an approach that views employees as akin to any other factor of production to be hired and fired on purely efficiency grounds. In contrast, another Matching Model was developed by Harvard Business School and became known as a 'soft' variant of HRM. Pioneered by Beer *et al.* (1985), the starting point was to consider stakeholder interests – including employee well-being – relative to business and context factors. It was known as an approach that sought to stress the word 'human' rather than the word 'resource'. While considered to be richer and more analytically fruitful than its harder variant, it was also more difficult to specify and assess such softer human attributes (Guest, 2015b).

A second perspective to the study and practice of HRM can be described as the '*Organisational Performance*' school. This will be discussed more extensively shortly, for now it is sufficient to acknowledge that for some, people management styles and HRM is 'the' key driver of sustainable competitive advantage and improved organisational performance. The *Organisational Performance* school has its roots in the Matching Models approach noted above; however, contemporary perspectives seek to present something of a universalistic and one-best-way scientific approach to quantify and measure bundles of HR practices that predict causal impact on profit, performance, productivity and employee effort (Huselid, 1995; Pfeffer, 1998). The guiding principle is that performance is first and foremost, with employee interests of lower order importance or significance (Guthrie *et al.*, 2011).

A third and long-standing stream of literature engaged with the journey concerned with the way people are managed at work is a '*Radical*' or '*Critical Management*' perspective. Scholars such as Keenoy (1997; 2014), Thompson (2011) and Willmott (1993), among others, have a suspicion of what HRM claims to be from the start, even when they differ in terms of structural or post-structural explanations. The core intellectual contribution is rather than view HRM as a particular discursive model which may be performance-enhancing for the good of the firm, and by association good for employees and society, the radical perspective is much more critical and seeks to contextualise the management of people at work within the stages of capitalist development and managerial power and authority relations. The Radical school is concerned with power relationships at the workplace and across society, often explained by a global neo-liberal economic and political agenda that engenders discrimination and unfairness and not universal performance-enhancing outcomes. Interestingly, radical scholars further question the ethos and evolution of much university business school curricula and what and how the subject of HRM is taught Thompson (2011: 364) articulates the critical agenda to HRM thus:

> Employees do not expect a 'champion', but within the constraints of the capitalist employment relationship and organisational power structure, they would prefer to not be fed crap in the name of communication and to be treated with a degree of fairness. *(Thompson, 2011: 364)*

A final perspective is the '*Employee-Centric Approach*', also summarised in Table 1.2. This perspective maybe defined as more pluralist in seeking to manage and mediate divergent interests that are both cooperative but also antagonistic when managing people at work. It recognises collective as well as individual practices to manage people (Boxall and Purcell, 2011). As a perspective it is critical of normative cause-and-effect claims about HRM leading to improved organisational effectiveness, or as a system premised on an overly simplistic view of mutual cooperation between employer and employee (Boxall, 2013; Marchington, 2015; Purcell, 1999). A key feature of the 'Employee-Centric Approach' is how employees experience work and react to management policy and action. To this end, both workers and line managers are not assumed to be passive recipients but active agents embedded in a system to balance opposing interests and objectives. As such, HRM involves a process of management–employee mutuality, or the balance of the need to both control employee effort while simultaneously seeking workforce cooperation (Boxall and Macky, 2014). At its very core, it relates back to Boxall and Purcell's (2011) extended discussion about the importance of definition, including influences such as managerial power and authority, union representation as well as non-union voice, management ideologies and societal and institutional embeddedness.

 ## The changing context of work

> Things are happening in employment that are neither a cause nor an effect of HRM but which could have some impact on it. These include the intensification of work, the choices of work location provided by technology and the divisive nature of a society in which many are idle and impoverished while many others are seriously over-worked.
> *(Guest, 1998: 51)*

Even the more 'upbeat' HRM work such as that of Storey (1992), Pfeffer (1998) or Ulrich *et al.* (2007) indicates that changes in the arena of HRM did not come from initiatives designed directly to do this. Change was driven by broader organisational initiatives, and thus personnel specialists have not been seen as the key drivers of change. Similarly, Wood's (1999) work on high-commitment practices suggests that innovations in HRM tend to accompany changes in production systems and that innovations on humanistic grounds are unrealistic. Thus in part HRM can be seen as a consequence of managing in 'uncharted territory' with new rules governing the employment relationship (Wilkinson *et al.*, 2014).

In the main, developments in HRM have been driven by large-scale organisational changes as employers adjust to a more competitive external neo-liberal global economic environment (Sisson, 2010). To meet some of the challenges posed by intense competition, organisations have been downsized, delayered and decentralised (Nolan, 2011). Organisations are now less hierarchical in nature; have adopted more flexible forms and have been subjected to continuing waves of organisational change programmes such as total quality management, business process re-engineering, performance management, modernisation, lean production, outsourcing and off-shoring of core activities resulting in a seemingly relentless pressure on employees and line managers to push through culture change initiatives (Taylor *et al.*, 2014; Townsend and Dundon, 2015).

But we need to be careful: there is a danger that, because of the economic crisis, accounts of new managerial initiatives, internal policy changes or some sort of wider organisational restructuring are portrayed as some major paradigm-shifting transformation, when the reality might be rather different. The rhetoric of organisational change often relies too heavily on hype from unrepresentative examples (Beynon *et al.*, 2002; Thompson and O'Connel Davidson, 1995). Crouch (2013), for instance, argues that the power of large corporations has remained relatively intact if not, paradoxically, increased through the financial crisis. Corporate governance models project an image that some corporations or banks are assumed to be 'too big to fail' with a power resource to shape and control their own markets, dominate supply chain networks and how smaller firms manage their workers. Managers, it seems, often perceive themselves to be in the midst of massive organisational change. Eccles and Nohira's (1992) historical account of post-Second World War management traces how it has been the norm rather than the exception for practitioners and writers to view their organisational environment as turbulent and characterised by transformative change or, as Sorge and van Witteloostuijn (2004) put it, the nature of the change hype changes regularly just as flu viruses mutate over time.

Nevertheless, it does appear that the type of staff employed and the way they are managed has also undergone change. Rubery (2015) charts four specific changes, driven in part by almost insurmountable (unstoppable) global forces which affect the way people work and how they are managed, known as the 4Fs: feminisation, flexibilisation, fragmentation and financialisation. *Feminisation* charts changes in labour market demography as to 'who' is employed. For example, the proportion of women in work has grown significantly over the last few decades. However, issues of equality in terms of gender discrimination, underrepresentation of women in higher skilled and professional occupations and ever growing gender pay differentials appear widespread in multiple areas and sectors (Muzio and Tomlinson, 2012; Rubery *et al.*, 2016).

Flexibilisation explains changes to the 'way' people work, with attendant implications for HRM. So employees are now more likely to be female, and also work part time and away from the workplace (e.g. home working and mobile working), with many jobs mediated by technology (e.g. hot desking, telework, social media) and engaged in very precarious and insecure jobs (e.g. zero hours contracts). These changes are about functional flexibility (the way workers are managed using multi-skilling and technology, etc.), numerical flexibility (how employees are employed using casual or temporary contracts) and spatial flexibility – where they work.

Fragmentation is the nature of the employee–employer relationship and who is managing whom. Flexibility has also resulted in extensive use of subcontractors, consultants, outsourcing, temporary employees and interims. The boundaries between work and home are also more fragmented (Walsh, 2009), and HR responsibilities are blurred across organisational boundaries, public–private partnerships, franchises, agencies and other forms of inter-firm contractual relations, which have a major impact on the management of people at work (Grimshaw *et al.*, 2010; Marchington *et al.*, 2011a,b). Fragmenting and blurring of HR relationships have not been restricted to the private sector, and we have seen the rise of the so-called 'new public management' with its emphasis on economy and efficiency (Pollit and Bouchert, 2011). The public sector has undergone many similar changes, with new organisational forms emerging in wake of 'marketisation', compulsory competitive tendering, 'modernisation', 'best value' and the challenges of maintaining HRM practices post-austerity (Grimshaw *et al.*, 2010; Rubery *et al.*, 2016).

Finally, *Financialisation* is about changes to the actual conduct and meaning of work. Because of market and context changes, organisations of all shapes and sizes now aim to generate surplus not necessarily through the making of goods or provision of services, even if these are their core business functions, but gains obtained from investments in de-regulated financial markets. Rubery (2015: 8) provides a little known but illustrative example using the car industry. In 2003 General Motors (GM), one of America's largest employers and iconic car manufacturers earned more than $800 million, not from the making of its cars and trucks, but from investments in mortgages and finance. Its car and truck operations earned GM just $83 million in the same year. However, in 2008 GM was declared bankrupt because of its financial investments.

Some of these context changes are seen as facilitating more discretion for staff, such as the opportunity to work part-time, while at the same time others reinforce a high degree of managerial control and are geared almost exclusively on improving corporate performance. Here the relevance of HRM comes to the fore; new forms of work and organisation demand new HRM strategies and practices. The new work context also brings new HRM challenges; not the least of these derives from the impact of such changes on the stresses and strains involved in working under such conditions.

Here the growing literature on stress at work paints a rather disconcerting picture of organisational life in the new workplace. Research from the European Agency for Safety and Health at Work (2013) reports psychosocial stress as one of the key challenges for HR. Surveying around 35,000 workers across 31 European countries, the data show work-related stress, burnout and depression to be important in the respondents' workplace, with as many as 7 in 10 people identifying job reorganisation, job insecurity, long hours, excessive workloads and bullying encounters as the main causes of stress. The importance of HR comes to the fore again when considering the costs of work-related stress and mental ill-health to business (and arguably to society as a whole). Mental ill-health is now *the* most common cause of sick absence in firms in developed economies, accounting for as much as 40 per cent of lost time (OECD, 2012). Analysts also predict that stress and ill-health at work will cost a massive US$16 trillion in lost output globally over the next two decades unless managed and addressed (Bloom *et al.*, 2011).

In reviewing the scientific analysis on stress and well-being, Sparrow *et al.* (2015: 157) outline a number of issues in which HRM is crucial. First, management style can be a powerful game-changer. For instance, managers who manage through supportive leadership styles (e.g. authentic, transformational, servant, empowering and ethical styles) are likely to engender more productive employees with less damaging effects on subordinate health, than those who manage through negative and bullying styles (e.g. toxic, abusive, authoritarian styles). Second, HRM can have an empowering effect on employees. For example, job autonomy, job involvement and self-control can engage workers in their job and support a more positive attitude and mental well-being. Third, job variety may improve (or at least not negatively impact) employee stress and well-being by better managing excessive workloads and hours. Fourth, communication and voice may give workers a sense of belonging so they understand better their role and value to an organisation. Finally, social relationships at work can affect well-being and stress, especially the nature of relationships with line managers and supervisors that use (or abuse) power resources to control employee actions.

Overall, it is thus not difficult to see the important role of HRM and the related elements of management style, line manager ideologies and beliefs, employee relations, performance objectives, or various contextual changes considered above in shaping peoples mental health, well-being or stress at their place of work.

However, despite the above aspirational role for HRM, research paints a more negative than positive landscape. While HRM practices (e.g. employee assistance programmes and workplace counselling schemes) are used in some organisations to provide a more supportive environment, there is evidence that they may only ease rather than cure the impact of workplace stress. Thus the general picture may be rather bleak. Indeed, HRM practices may have added considerably to the stresses of modern worklife with the increased use of such practices as performance management systems, contingent pay and flexibilisation (Thompson, 2011). For example, in relation to flexibility, reports from the Citizens Advice Bureau find numerous accounts of worker exploitation, with unilateral changes in contracts and forced reduction in hours and pay. It seems ironic that organisations like McDonald's or Sports Direct can implement sophisticated business systems that deliver a bread roll or pair of runners with exact timing and precision, often from suppliers in locations on the other side of the planet, yet they cannot determine what hours an employee who lives one or two miles away can work for the next few days or weeks. This is the phenomenon of 'zero hours contracts', whereby employers do not guarantee that any work will be offered, but should they require labour the employee has to be available if and when the manager demands. The impact of organisational changes on employees has been so considerable that commentators now argue that there is a need to radically reconstruct the nature of the 'psychological contract' between employer and employee. Guest (2015b) issues a call to arms for HRM, as a profession and an academic discipline, to re-introduce the importance and value of promoting a 'positive employment relationship as a means to employee well-being as the central anchor point in HRM'. The goal is for HR systems to connect first and foremost with workforce trust, justice and well-being as a path to positive employment and then organisational performance (Kougiannou *et al.*, 2015; Guest, 2015b; Heffernan and Dundon, 2016).

These concerns have led to engagement being the latest idea to take root in the world of HRM (Alfes *et al.*, 2010; MacLeod and Clarke, 2009; Grunman and Saks, 2014; Wilkinson and Fay, 2011). The CIPD define it as 'a combination of commitment to the organisation and its values, plus a willingness to help out colleagues. It goes beyond job satisfaction and is not simply motivation. Engagement is something the employee offers: it cannot be "required" as part of the employment contract' (CIPD, 2012: 1). A Watson Wyatt study (2009) indicated that a company with highly engaged employees achieves a financial performance that is four times better than those with poor engagement. The consultancy industry often predicts potential gains from engagement. For example, Gallup say that more highly engaged staff take an average of 2.5 sick days per year, whereas disengaged staff take on average 6.2 sick days per year (Harter *et al.*, 2006). The concept has not been without criticism. Welbourne (2011) observes the beauty of employee engagement is that it can be everything (positive) to everybody. As she points out, employee engagement speaks to something most managers believe, that is, when employees go 'above and beyond' the call of duty then organisations fare better.

In the UK, the Macleod report entitled *Engaging for Success* (MacLeod and Clarke, 2009) was designed to open a national discussion on the subject; however, the assumption behind this was not to debate the merits of the idea but to work out how best to implement it given a recognition that one size does not fit all. Trust in management, job satisfaction and involvement in decision making are seen as the basic building blocks for employee engagement (Purcell, 2010). In a special issue on the topic of engagement in the *International Journal of Human Resource Management*, Truss *et al.* (2013) point out that the topic is very susceptible to being stretched and bent. Engagement is, in many ways, a contested area of people management and the very ideas of contestation seem to be forgotten in a race to prove some undefined and imprecise connection to performance.

However, a stream of research evidence shows that engagement is not simple, straightforward or assured. From the UK Workplace Employment Relations Survey (WERS) data not all employees appear engaged and, indeed, the number who are 'fully engaged', defined as scoring highly on every dimension, is often less than one in five. On a scale of 1–5, where 1 is 'fully disengaged' and 5 is 'fully engaged' with 3 meaning 'neither engaged nor disengaged', the expectation would be that the bulk of employees in a well-functioning firm would be 'engaged' (i.e. score 4) and the median score would be over 3. Lower levels of engagement are also more likely to be found where there is perceived unfairness in rewards, where there is bullying and harassment and where people believe they are stuck in their jobs and feel isolated from open communications.

Nor is the international evidence very complimentary on the alleged success of engagement. In North America, reported as a region with the highest engagement scores, some 29 per cent of workers say they are 'fully engaged'. The European average is 24 per cent, and only 10 per cent of employees in China say they are engaged (BlessingWhite, 2011). Of course there are problems with such data sources, especially those originating from consultants with a commercial or market-driven agenda to sell the concept of better engaged employees improves performance. Purcell (2014: 248) argues that the search to find one measure of engagement with a simplistic view that the higher the score leads to higher performance is worrying. It is equally plausible that reverse causality may be in existence and people feel engaged because they work for successful firms. Further, the debate is often skewed so that engagement is only about its performance-enhancing benefits for the firm, which ignores other goals of social legitimacy and reciprocity for employees.

The idea of social legitimacy and the reciprocity of engagement draw attention to the idea of a psychological contract, where employee perceptions of fairness and trust are important sources of power and influence in how employees are managed (Cullinane and Dundon, 2006). One can see why managers would like to get employees working harder or smarter because they are engaged, but what is the return for employees? Or what can employers provide to support employees better? Another neglected dimension is whether engagement will always be good. Can staff be too engaged for their own good? (Marchington and Wilkinson, 2012: 352–5).

There is a danger that engagement – like other fashionable people management clichés such as talent management or knowledge management – is no more than a euphemism used to re-define or re-label the subject of HRM. Clearly, more and better designed research is needed in this area. A strong central theme of HRM in these accounts is that of linking people management practice to business strategy, and we examine this in the next section of this chapter.

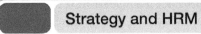

Strategy and HRM

HR scholars have been calling for a stronger focus on the human resources inside the firm and how they are managed (Boselie and Paauwe, 2009; Harley, 2015). Sparrow *et al.* (2015) call for a more integrated analysis of strategic and other business related theories into the study of HRM. They identify a number of related contextual and thematic developments, many mentioned above, that could more usefully be integrated into mainstream HRM: business innovation; customer-centric operations management; lean production; inter-firm networks and relationships; engagement, fairness and well-being; and marketing and talent. As Morris and Snell (2009: 85) point out, strategic management depends very much on what people know and how they behave, and because no other resource possessed by a firm has free will or heterogeneity of ideas, products and services often originate in individuals and by groups of employees working in collaboration. This makes the human resources within the firm, and how they are managed, a potentially unique source of competitive advantage. The increase in differentiated workforces poses added cultural, geographical and competency gaps (Marchington and Wilkinson, 2012: 5). Despite this call, it is rare for texts on strategy to pay much attention to HRM issues; for example, Johnson *et al.* (2011) devote only a handful of pages to managing human resources while Grant (2010) allocates just one page to HRM in his discussion of resources and capabilities.

Meanwhile the study of HRM has adopted a cross-functional approach and expanded its breadth of analysis beyond the staple concerns of selection, training and reward, etc. (Paauwe, 2004). In particular, one stream of research, strategic human resource management (SHRM), has emerged as being particularly influential in this respect. In essence SHRM theory posits that an organisation's human resource assets are potentially the sole source of sustainable competitive advantage. Much of the work in this area draws from the resource-based theory (RBT) of the firm (Allen and Wright, 2007; Barney, 1995; Boxall and Purcell, 2011). Here RBT suggests that competitive advantage depends ultimately on an organisation having superior, valuable, rare, non-substitutable resources at its disposal and that such resources are not easily imitated by others. The non-imitable nature of resources is a key aspect, otherwise competitors would be able to replicate and the advantage would rapidly disappear

A recurrent theme in the SHRM literature is that organisations need to 'match' their human resource strategies to their business strategies, so that the former contribute towards the successful implementation of the latter (Becker and Huselid, 2009; Boxall, 1992; Lengnick-Hall and Lengnick-Hall, 1988; Martin-Alcazar *et al.*, 2005; Miller, 1987; Schuler and Jackson, 1989). A number of sectoral and company-level studies have shown how organisations facing change in their competitive environment have responded with new business strategies, which in turn have required a transformation in the organisations' approach to the management of staff (see, for example, Boxall and Steenveld, 1999; Snape *et al.*, 1993).

This approach argues for a fit or match between business strategy and a human resource strategy, which fosters the required employee attitudes and behaviour. In this sense, human resource strategy flows from the initial choice of business strategy (Purcell, 1989). Furthermore, to the extent that changes in the corporate environment evoke a particular business strategy response, human resource strategies can also be seen as being strongly influenced by environmental change (Hendry *et al.*, 1988). As Sparrow and Hilltrop (1994: 628) argue, 'HRM strategies are all about making business strategies work'. A closely related body of work has recently called for a *configurational* approach to SHRM. Here it is argued that it is the pattern of HRM practices that supports the achievement of organisational goals and that, in line with the contingency approach, fit with strategy is vital to explaining the HR – performance nexus. The configurational approach takes the best-fit view a step further in that it argues that there are a number of specific ideal types that provide both horizontal fit between HR practices, and vertical fit between HR practices and business strategy (Ferris *et al.*, 1999). The configuration of practices which provides the tightest fit is then seen as being ideal for the particular strategy. Although this work is still in its relative infancy, there has been some theorising on the nature of the 'ideal types' of configurations for customer, operations or product-led organisations, etc. (Martin-Alcazar *et al.*, 2005; Sheppeck and Militello, 2000).

Nevertheless, there is an issue as to how far human resource strategies can simply be 'matched' with the requirements of a changing business strategy (Bacon, 2008). As Boxall (1992: 68) notes, much of the 'matching' literature has implicitly assumed that employee attitudes and behaviour can be moulded by management strategy in the pursuit of strategic fit. However, human resource outcomes cannot be taken for granted, and whatever the merits of the view that HR executives must increasingly see themselves as 'business managers', it is important to recognise that the management of people at work is about more than simply selecting the appropriate fit with a given business strategy. Thus the best-fit approach can be criticised for failing to acknowledge the importance of social norms and legal rules in the search for alignment (Paauwe and Boselie, 2007; Guest, 2015a). Indeed, the notion of fit is somewhat static and an inappropriate metaphor in a fast-changing corporate world.

Moreover, as Boxall and Purcell (2011) note, inconsistent application of well-designed HR policies often undermines their desired impact. Crucially, 'there is no such thing as *the* single HR practice of the firm. It is more accurate to imagine the HR practices of the firm as norms around which there is variation due to the idiosyncratic behaviour of line managers' (Boxall and Purcell, 2011). Truss *et al.* (2013) note the importance of 'agency' in shaping links between HR practices (such as engagement) and desired outcomes, thus we should not assume that simply having a particular human resource policy will necessarily lead to a predicted result. Problems of implementation and interpretation occur alongside people's sometimes unpredictable responses and actions.

Performance and HRM

For years, HR professionals have yearned for evidence to show that people were really the most important asset a company had and that good HR practice delivered in terms of organisational performance. By the mid-1990s their prayers appeared to have been answered in that a growing number of studies sought to demonstrate just that. For example, in research undertaken on behalf of the then Institute of Personnel and Development in the UK, the Sheffield Effectiveness Programme [based on 100 small and medium-sized enterprises (SMEs) in manufacturing] concluded that people management is not only critical to business performance but is also much more important than an emphasis on quality, technology, competitive strategy or R&D in terms of influence on the bottom line. Thus according to Patterson *et al.* (1998), this finding in one sense validates the oft-quoted claims of CEOs that people are the most important asset but is also paradoxical in that it is one aspect of business that is the most neglected:

> Overall, the results of this study clearly indicate the importance of people management practices in influencing company performance. The results are unique, since no similar study has been conducted, comparing the influence of different types of managerial practices upon performance. If managers wish to influence the performance of their companies, the results show that the most important area to emphasise is the management of people. This is ironic, given that our research has also demonstrated that emphasis on HRM practices is one of the most neglected areas of managerial practice within organisations. *(Patterson et al., 1998: 21)*

These findings have been replicated in the public sector. In a well-cited study of the NHS, UK, West *et al.* (2002) reported that practices associated with high-performance work systems (HPWS), particularly the extent and sophistication of appraisal systems, the extent of teamworking and the quality and sophistication of training, were associated with lower patient mortality. However, research studies sponsored by the Chartered Institute of Personnel Development (CIPD) have also underscored the broad scale of the implementation problems of 18 'high-commitment' practices in 237 UK companies. Only 1 per cent used more than three-quarters of the practices, 25 per cent used more than half and 20 per cent used fewer than a quarter (Guest, 2000). These findings and others have become a source of increasing concern to both HR practitioners and academics (Caldwell, 2004).

There are various terms used in these studies, for example high-performance management, high-commitment management, best practice HRM, high-involvement management, but each share a common message: the adoption of HRM practices pays in terms of where it matters most, the bottom line (Appelbaum *et al.*, 2000; see also Kinnie and Swart, Chapter 2 of this volume). The general argument is that piecemeal take-up of HR practices means that many organisations miss out on the benefits to be gained from a more integrated approach (Marchington and Wilkinson, 2012). The collection of reinforcing HR practices have begun to be referred to as a 'bundle' and the task of HR managers is to identify and implement such HR systems.

However, this appears to be rather more easily prescribed than achieved (Guthrie *et al.*, 2011; Kaufman, 2010a; Lewin, 2011). Many authors produce lists of HR practices which should be included in these bundles. Unfortunately, there is yet little consistency and we still await a definitive prescription of the best 'bundle'. Boselie *et al.* (2005), Wall and Wood (2005) and Storey (1992) identified aspects such as integrated selection systems, performance-related pay, harmonisation, individual contracts, teamworking and learning companies. Pfeffer (1998) provides a list of seven 'universal' practices: employment security, selectivity in recruitment, high levels of contingent reward, self-managed teams, extensive training and development, information-sharing and harmonisation of status differentials. These are held together under an overarching philosophy with a long-term commitment and a willingness to engage in consistent measurement of whether or not high standards are being achieved. Other studies have different bundle configurations with wide variability in the number of practices included. Dyer and Reeves (1995) counted 28 HR practices across four studies about HR-performance link, of which only one practice, formal training, was common to all. Becker and Gerhart (1996) found 27 practices, none of which was common across five studies examining the HR-performance link. Delaney *et al.* (1989) identified 10 practices, Huselid (1995) 13 and Wood (1999) 17. The range of practices must seem at the very least confusing to the practitioner but, more than this, there appear to be some quite contradictory notions in the various lists (Wall and Wood, 2005). For example, on the one hand, formal grievance systems appear in some bundles as an indicator of best practice, but are associated in others with trade unionism and seen as part of a bureaucratic older 'personnel management' approach. Yet as Guest (2015a: 53) reminds us, the MacLeod and Clarke (2009: 103) report on 'engaging for success' in the UK suggests that optimal results are achieved when direct employee engagement is combined with indirect (union or works council) participation. Thus any notion that unions are somehow dinosaurs that don't have a place in the HR-performance debate is mistaken.

Aside from the inconsistencies in the HRM bundle and the unitarist or biased view that marginalises unions or other employee representative agents from the equation, the best practice and universalistic approach has received considerable criticism for other reasons. Purcell, for example, is wary of the claim for a universal application:

> The claim that the bundle of best practice HRM is universally applicable leads us into a utopian cul-de-sac and ignores the powerful and highly significant changes in work, employment and society visible inside organisations and in the wider community. The search for bundles of high commitment work practices is important, but so too is the search for understanding of the circumstances of where and when it is applied, why some organisations do and others do not adopt HCM, and how some firms seem to have more appropriate HR systems for their current and future needs than others. It is only

one of many ways in which employees are managed, all of which must come within the bounds of HRM. *(Purcell, 1999: 36)*

Reviews of the HRM-performance relationship (Boselie *et al.*, 2005; Combs *et al.*, 2006; Guest, 2011; Lewin, 2011; Kaufman, 2010a; Paauwe, 2009; Sengupta and Whitfield, 2011) point out that there are unresolved issues of causality – largely because few studies use longitudinal data, problems of the narrow base of the work undertaken, and concerns that much of the data is self-reported by single management respondents, neglect of the actual implementation of practices, as well as doubts about measures of performance which are used. Even if the data does indicate a link, we lack understanding of the processes involved and the mechanisms by which practices translate into a desired employment climate (Cafferkey and Dundon, 2015). Equally problematic is the implicit assumption that a particular bundle of practices is feasible for all organisations. Some HR systems that were designed to engender higher performance have been shown to mediate perceptions of injustice and limited employee well-being (Heffernan and Dundon, 2016). In short, the idea of a HR system that is designed to improve performance first and foremost can result in workers feeling less committed with diminished rather than enhanced job satisfaction. The notion of a reinforcing bundle of practices cannot be fully convincing given the variation in actual practices used across firms and the often neglected consideration of employee needs and wants in the equation. It is unlikely, say, that the very act of introducing practices X, Y and Z will deliver benefits in a universal manner in different contexts and markets. Kaufman (2010b: 287) argues that 'modern (Strategic) HRM has partial explanatory power but nonetheless is fundamentally flawed by substantial specification error'. He contends that the performance effect from HRM in a competitive economy is probably zero (at best) and not always (if ever) positive. Guest (2011) concludes that after two decades of extensive research, we are still unable to answer core questions about the relationship between human resource management and performance. This is largely the result of limited longitudinal research to address the linkages between HRM and performance via the management of HR implementation. As he observes 'many of the basic questions remain the same and after hundreds of research studies we are still in no position to assert with any confidence that good HRM has an impact on organisational performance' (Guest, 2011: 11).

Because of variable adoption of practices and imprecise methodological specification, the HR-performance debate is an area of much potential. Some clarity is starting to be provided by the growing number of meta-analyses of the HR-performance linkage (e.g. Combs *et al.*, 2006; Subramony, 2009; Crook *et al.*, 2011; Jiang *et al.*, 2012). Although there are methodological and theoretical criticisms of individual studies, the weight of meta-analytical evidence is strongly suggestive of a positive linkage. Also clarity is starting to emerge on how the performance effect of HRM is transmitted and what goes on in the so-called black box (Jiang *et al.*, 2012). Godard (2004: 371) argues that the conflicts embedded in the structure of the employment relationship may limit the effectiveness of the high-performance paradigm for employers, and render it highly fragile, and it is this that may explain its variable adoption depending on workplace context. These same conflicts may also explain why high-performance practices are often implemented in ways that tend to have negative effects for workers and unions. In other words, it may be in the interests of only a minority of employers to adopt high-performance management and, even when it is adopted, it may not have positive implications for workers or their unions. Thus there is a need to recognise that there may not be a universal coincidence of interests, or the idea that 'what is good for employers will be also be good for workers and their unions' is far too simplistic and biased (Blyton *et al.*, 2011; Dundon and Dobbins, 2015). Similarly, Lewin (2011) has suggested a dual theory of HRM in which some groups of employees are best managed through what he terms high-involvement management, while others are not seen as an asset on which expenditure will yield a positive economic return and are managed via a low-involvement model. The former applies to core employees only. The key question here sees concerns over the best balance of core and peripheral staff (an answer which is likely to differ by industry), although he notes that the ratio of peripheral to core employees has grown markedly in the USA and in other developed nations over the last quarter of a century. And, as Rubery (2015) has illustrated, many of these types of peripheral jobs tend to be gender biased that discriminate disproportionately against women.

The changing role of HRM

Despite the growing recognition of the importance of effective people management for organisational success as discussed above, there are still a number of concerns about the future for HRM (Farnham, 2015; Guest and Conway, 2011; Sparrow *et al.*, 2015). At a surface level the HRM function seems to be in good health. The CIPD now claims over 140,000 members (CIPD, 2015) and WERS data show that the proportion of workplaces with personnel specialists, defined as managers whose job titles contain personnel, HR or industrial, employee or staff relations and who spend at least a quarter of their time on such matters, has been rising. The percentage of workplaces that employed a personnel specialist has remained similar for around two decades: currently 56 per cent of all private sector firms in the UK (van Wanrooy *et al.*, 2013: 53). While there has been little change in the aggregate trend, there has been substantial increase of board-level representation by those responsible for HR among smaller and medium-sized firms, rising from 39 per cent in 2004 to 60 per cent by 2011 (van Wanrooy *et al.*, 2013: 53). However, what HR professionals actually do and what influence or authority they may have on a board is a very different issue altogether, and worries about the effectiveness of the HR function linger on.

According to Peter Drucker, there has been a tendency in the past for the HR department to be seen as something of a 'trash can' function, a repository for all those tasks which do not fit neatly anywhere else:

> Personnel administration . . . is largely a collection of incidental techniques without much internal cohesion. As personnel administration conceives the job of managing worker and work, it is partly a file-clerk's job, partly a housekeeping job, partly a social worker's job and partly fire-fighting to head off union trouble or to settle it . . . the things the personnel administrator is typically responsible for . . . are necessary chores. I doubt though that they should be put together in one department for they are a hodge-podge . . . They are neither one function by kinship of skills required to carry out the activities, nor are they one function by being linked together in the work process, by forming a distinct stage in the work of the managers or in the process of the business *(Drucker, 1961: 269–70; quoted in Legge, 1995: 6)*.

Table 1.3 lists some of the key functions that HR departments now provide. In part, Drucker's critique that the HR function lacks coherence has been moderated by some recent organisational changes (Sparrow *et al.*, 2015). In particular, the practice of outsourcing saw many of the more peripheral HR responsibilities, such as catering arrangements and security, subcontracted to specialist firms. Equally, the practice of decentralising HR responsibility from corporate central departments to business-unit-level departments, shared-services, and further still to line management has seen much 'streamlining' of HR responsibilities. However, perhaps more worrying for the HR function is that these trends have also seen some traditional core personnel areas, such as recruitment, training and employee welfare management, also outsourced to HR consultants. In some accounts these trends have been seen as part of a 'crisis' as HR struggled for legitimacy and status in cost-conscious times (Parry, 2011; Sparrow *et al.*, 2015). Others have interpreted the increasing use of consultants as reflecting a sign that HR is now seen as being much more important and thus merits additional investment. Management consultants are argued to be an important conduit along which new and more sophisticated HR practices flow between organisations. However, some recent trends suggest that a 'crisis' of interpretation may be

Table 1.3 Functions performed by the HR department

HR-performance

Recruitment and selection

Training and development

Reward and performance management

Employment relations

Organisational culture

Internationalisation and globalisation

Diversity and equality

Downsizing

Organisational change

Involvement and participation

Engagement

Ethics and governance

Knowledge management

Bullying

Flexibility

Talent management

Employee well-being

Technology and HRM

more in tune with the facts. In particular, the devolution of HR appears to have been taken one step further and there is now a considerable debate on the benefits of outsourcing. In part, such changes have been driven by further cost pressures in a period of corporate downsizing and economic turbulence, but more worrying for the HR function is that outsourcing may also have been fuelled by senior management concerns about the quality and responsiveness of in-house HR functions (Greer *et al.*, 1999). There is a large gap between what HR professionals see as their role and how other managers in the organisation see it (Hird *et al.*, 2010).

The recognition that HR issues are vitally important in organisations has, paradoxically, not been all good news for the HR department given its 'Cinderella' image. It seems that many senior managers may be of the view that people management is far too important to be left to the HR department, and the HR function appears to be at a dangerous crossroads, with some suggesting ascendancy to a full 'business partner' while others predict a painful demise (Keegan and Francis, 2010). On the one hand, the ascendancy school sees the rise of HR following hard on the success of SHRM and the creation of competitive advantage for organisations. In contrast, the formula for demise often involves the failure of HR to understand the broader business agenda. The literature typically sees a need for the 'reinvention' of HR along such lines and that HR must simply evolve or die. Some suggest that HR needs to learn to manage 'beyond the organisation', which involves finding ways to incorporate innovative business models and collaborative partnership across inter-firm networks (Sparrow *et al.*, 2015). Similarly, Ulrich and Dulebohn (2015) talk of the need for the HR function to change from its current status as an 'inside-outside' approach of people management, towards a more 'outside-inside' arrangement; that is, an arrangement where external stakeholders proactively influence what HR does inside a firm, commensurate with wider contextual changes and pressures.

What then is the 'formula' for HR success? First, in addressing this question there is a real danger in slipping into unrealistic, wishful thinking – of which there is already an ample supply in the prescriptive HR literature. Second, there is rather more consistency in the literature on what the future for HR should *not* be based on, than that on what it should be. Thus Rucci (1997) has suggested that the worst-case scenario for HR survival is a department that does not promote change, does not identify leaders, does not understand the business, does not know customers, does not drive costs and does not emphasise values. According to Pfeffer (1998: 195), 'if human resources is to have a future inside organisations, it is not by playing police person and enforcer of rules and policies, nor is it likely to be ensured by playing handmaiden to finance'.

In contrast, there are a wide variety of suggestions for what the HR department should do in the future. The future agenda, according to Sparrow *et al.* (2015), is the need to design not only HR strategy but also business strategy, promoting a customer-centric culture around innovation, fairness and well-being as a source of better engagement. Long-standing arguments hold sway that HR needs a comprehensive vision and that future HR managers will require coordination skills across functions, business units and borders following the increased globalisation of business, and general management, communication leadership, creativity and entrepreneurship competencies (Beer and Eisenstat, 1996). One of the more contemporary debates is the need for HR managers to be equipped and skilled in HR analytics, drawing on big data to assess potential change in people's attitudes, behaviours and make adjustments to HR practices (Ulrich and Dulebohn, 2015; Angrave *et al.* 2016). Ulrich *et al.* (2007) reported the results of survey research on the key competencies managers believe will be necessary for future success in HR roles including understanding of business, knowledge of HR practices, ability to manage culture, ability to manage change and personal credibility.

Thus a key theme in much of the work is that HR needs to earn its place at the top, i.e. senior management (Pritchard, 2010). One danger in these accounts is that the emphasis is very much on the strategic and business aspects of the HR role. In particular, the 'bread and butter' issues of effectively managing the recruitment, selection, appraisal, development, reward and involvement of staff has been rather pushed to the periphery. There is thus a real concern that HR managers could be neglecting 'the basics' in their search for legitimacy and status with senior managers (Wright and Snell, 2005). Arguably, HR could be accused of ignoring employees. Indeed, HR 'futurologists', it seems, need to be reminded of Giles and Williams' (1991) rejoinder to accept that the HR role is to serve their customers and not their egos. In short, there is a danger that the senior management and shareholder customers will be getting rather better service than the 'employee customer' in the HR department of the future. Such a view is shared by Francis and Keegan (2006), who note that the employee champion role is shrinking because HR professionals have been encouraged to aspire to the role of strategic or business partner. Lewin (2008: 1) argues that it is not just about being a business partner:

> There are many other roles and purposes that HR functions and those who lead these functions serve in modern business enterprises including complying with human resource/labor regulation (newer and older regulation), enforcing organizational and employment policies and practices, measuring employee performance, providing services and assistance to employees, maintaining employee personnel files, monitoring workplace safety, handling employee relocation. With this menu of potential duties and responsibilities, it is understandable that many HR functions in modern business enterprises are considered to be largely operational functions rather than strategic functions. But if the claim that business enterprises increasingly compete on the basis of their intellectual capital is at all valid, then the main challenge regarding HRM in the 21st Century is for HR functions and leaders to keep their eye on the prize of a strategic role in these enterprises while also performing the necessary operational role.

Thus one of our aims in the presentation of material in this book has been to balance the discussion in terms of both employee expectations and management expectations of the HR function. For example, in accounts of topics such as downsizing, involvement and participation, performance management, reward and flexibility, the aim has been not only to examine critically HR's strategic role in the process but also to review the impact of these practices on employees. The last section of this chapter now discusses in more detail the layout of the book and some suggestions on its use.

The book

This book has been written primarily as a text for students of business and management who are studying HRM. It aims to be critical but pragmatic: we are wary of quick fixes, slogans, prescriptive checklists and bullet points of 'best practice'. The authors are all prominent researchers and draw from a considerable depth of research in their field. Each chapter provides a critical review of the topic, bringing together theoretical and empirical material. The emphasis is on analysis and insight, and areas of growing significance are also included in each chapter. At the same time we wish to look at the implications of HRM research and theory development for practice and to do so in a readable, accessible manner. The book does not assume prior knowledge on the part of the reader, but seeks to locate issues in a wider theoretical framework. It is suitable for MBAs, and for undergraduates who these days may be doing business studies as well as degrees in engineering, humanities, social sciences, etc. As such, this is appropriate for modular degree courses.

Each chapter is accompanied by a combination of case studies and/or exercises for students. The intention is that students should be actively involved in the study of HRM. We believe that in this sense the book is unique, where the trend has been for the publication of separate text and case books. Our aim in combining these elements in a single volume is to permit a smoother integration of the topic material and supporting cases and exercises. In all chapters the authors have provided both text and cases, although in some we also include additional material from other authors. The cases and exercises are of different lengths, level and type in order to serve different teaching and learning purposes, e.g. a long case study for students to read and prepare prior to seminars/tutorials as well as shorter cases and exercises which can be prepared in the session itself. The aim is to provide a good range of up-to-date, relevant material based upon actual HRM practice.

The book is divided into two parts; the first one, the 'Fundamentals of HRM', examines the core elements of HR practice (see Table 1.3 above). In this section there are chapters on the HRM-performance link; selection and recruitment, performance appraisal, employee development, reward, employment relations, line managers and corporate culture. The second half of the book, 'Contemporary Themes and Issues', addresses some key areas of importance in HRM practice. Here there are chapters on international and comparative HRM, careers, downsizing, participation, ethics, work–life balance, emotion, flexibility, bullying, knowledge management, talent management, employee well-being and the role of technology and social media in HRM.

CASE STUDY 1.1

HUMAN RESOURCE MANAGEMENT AND PRIVATE EQUITY IN A HOSPITAL

ALINE BOS AND PAUL BOSELIE

Introduction

This case focuses on the impact of private equity (PE) interventions on human resource management (HRM) in a hospital. We first set the stage about PE and HRM and then turn to the case.

Private equity firm

A private equity firm (PEF) invests money in organisations not quoted on a stock market in exchange for a periodic management fee and a share in profits. Typically, within three to seven years the firms sell their investment (Robbins et al., 2008). PEFs earn the sum of the capital gain on resale and the operating profit realised meanwhile.

PEFs roughly execute two strategies: an upward or a downward strategy (Wright and Bruining, 2008). The upward strategy represents additional investments in the organisation because of untapped resources that can contribute to organisational success. The HRM implications might be recruitment and selection of new employees and substantial training and development. The downward strategy represents cost reduction strategies. The HRM implications might be cutting employee benefits and performance-related pay linked to financial performance.

Human resource management

HRM involves management decisions related to policies and practices which together shape the employment relationship and are aimed at achieving individual, organisational and societal goals (Boselie, 2010). This definition builds on a continental European perspective in which multiple stakeholders are taken into account, such as trade unions. This is also a characteristic of the Dutch society (Paauwe, 2004). Another key characteristic of the Dutch context is the impact of institutional mechanisms (i.e. labour legislation) on HRM (Paauwe and Boselie, 2003). The incorporation of multiple stakeholders and contextual factors in studying HRM therefore makes sense.

Dominant Anglo-Saxon HRM perspectives tend to take a more unitarist view focused on shareholder value and include a limited number of stakeholders. PEFs tend to embrace Anglo-Saxon principles. This approach is very relevant in the context of semi-public organisations that differ in some respects from the private sector. First, public service organisations are in many cases partly financed by public funds. Second, services delivered by these organisations are seen as essential services, which also focus on public values such as access and transparency. Finally, public service workers are often seen as being motivated by contributing to society and not by financial aspects (Vandenabeele, 2007).

The central question in this case study is therefore: What is the impact of PE interventions on human resource management in semi-public organisations?

Sub-questions that are linked to the central research question are:

- What is the actual involvement and participation in decision making of different stakeholders?
- What is the potential impact of PE on HRM practices?
- What is the potential impact of PE on HRM outcomes?

The Case: Dutch Hospital Rembrandt Van RIJN

The general Rembrandt van Rijn hospital employs around 1,600 people including 300 medical specialists. After privatisation of the municipal Rembrandt van Rijn hospital in the late 90s, the deficits ran up to over €7 million. The Dutch Minister of Health announced the closure of the hospital but the Second Chamber in Dutch Parliament prevented the minister from doing so. By 2007 the hospital was nearly bankrupt. The two-tier board of the hospital was confronted with major financial losses. Regular financiers such as banks were no longer willing to finance the hospital. In 2007 the board members got in touch with a PEF interested in investing in the hospital on the condition that the PEF got ownership of the hospital.

The case has three phases:

1. the pre-bid phase;
2. the actual private equity intervention and direct consequences;
3. the period of two to six years after the private equity intervention.

1. The pre-bid phase: Barbarians at the gate or El Salvador?

The initial meetings between the two-tier board of the hospital and representatives of the PEF are top secret to avoid negative publicity and internal turbulence. At this stage, the two board members decide to actively involve a senior legal officer. After several secret meetings the board members make a public announcement that the hospital is investigating the possibility of PE involvement. For most employees the news is not immediately picked up and taken seriously. After a stream of negative announcements over the past two years about low performance levels, most employees are aware of the sense of urgency for a major organisational change. For them a PE intervention is too abstract and difficult to assess. From here on all members of the management team (the level below the two-tier board) are also involved in the negotiation process with the PEF. Medical specialists and the medical staff are consulted and the supervisory board is informed as well.

The HR director, as part of the management team, convinces the board that from this moment on the works council and the client council of the hospital should be informed on a regular basis. As the media picks up the story of a possible PE intervention in the hospital, this evokes a hot debate about the nature of the PEF's intentions and possible negative impact of such an intervention. From this moment on employee trust levels decline dramatically, in particular with regard to employees' trust in management. Top management response to all the commotion is putting emphasis on the sense of urgency and the opportunity a PE intervention creates for organisational renewal.

2. The actual private equity intervention

After a year of negotiations it looks like nothing is going to change. The financial performance of the hospital is even more pressing. Representatives of the PEF propose a bonus package for the top management arguing that these bonuses are necessary to retain top managers during and after the PE intervention process. As soon as the media finds out about this pay proposal the PEF is accused of bribing top managers to make the ownership change happen. While this type of bonus intervention for top management is common in PE interventions, given the healthcare context and its public values this proposal feeds scepticism about the PEF's true intentions with the hospital. Employee trust in top management decreases even further.

The two-tier board sticks to the plan and pursues the process of an actual intervention. They decide to organise road shows for all employees within the hospital, to (a) provide a platform for employees to share their emotions, frustrations and feelings of insecurity, and (b) to show leadership and emphasise the sense of urgency for a radical change. Without new investments the hospital is most likely to go bankrupt within one or two years.

The HR director's main concern at this stage of the actual PE intervention is the retention of highly motivated and qualified employees. Both medical specialists and nurses represent the human capital of the hospital. Major employee turnover rates could damage the continuity of healthcare activities.

3. The period after the private equity intervention

The PE intervention is completed. The works council involvement at an early stage in the process pays off. In the actual transition of ownership the works council's trust in top management supports creating the new deal with the PEF. Much to everybody's surprise, the first 12 months after the take-over nothing changes. Then one of the board members makes use of an early retirement arrangement. The vacancy is filled by a top manager connected to the PEF. From then on, things start to change rapidly. A new performance management system, based on General Electric's Six Sigma system, is introduced to increase efficiency, improve service quality and stimulate innovation. The HR practices linked to this new performance system include:

- training and development of nurses aimed at improving productivity (more clients per hour) and increasing customer satisfaction scores;
- individual and team scorecards with weekly and monthly outcome measures such as customer satisfaction, employee absence rates, productivity outcomes and peer evaluations of job performance;
- bonuses for excellent teams up to one additional month's pay for every team member.

At the same time, some major reorganisations are planned to make drastic cutbacks:

- all hospital volunteers are dismissed because in fact they are old and need a lot of care themselves, which distracts the medical professionals from their patients;
- the level of middle management is removed. The board now directly speaks with medical professionals;
- new and financially attractive forms of medical service are introduced, such as an influenza clinic and a stop smoking clinic;
- contracts with interim managers and external advisors are terminated;
- temporary contracts are terminated and those workers can only continue working for the hospital when they work for a special flex company that employs contingent workers in healthcare;
- multiple disciplines within the hospital are labelled as non-core business activities and are outsourced.

Conclusion

The PE intervention has led to improved organisational performance with regard to productivity and service quality levels. After six years a deficit €4.3 million is turned into an annual profit of around €5 million. The hospital jumped from place 99 in 2007 to 49 in 2011 in the Dutch hospital ranking.

1 The hospital executed an intentional strategy of involving different stakeholders involved in early phases, which fits the European stakeholder perspective and turns out to be a good strategy when the deal is actually made.
2 Concerning the HRM practices, goal setting through performance management has become a central theme. The new performance management system clarifies the linkage between organisational goals, team goals and individual employee goals. The HR function and its HR professionals have played an important role in the implementation and communication of the new performance management system.
3 The HRM outcomes are not clear yet. Employee satisfaction levels from the yearly employee surveys still show moderate scores. Employees appear reasonably satisfied about their job but less happy with their organisation. The general employee trust in management is still relatively low. Many good healthcare workers have left the organisation.

Lessons learned

The case study shows the relevance of different phases in the process of organisational change related to a PE intervention. It also reveals the importance of dynamics and the notion of time: organisational challenges are in a state of flux. In this case, upward as well as downward strategies are executed; each strategy needs specific HR interventions. This also shows us the relevance of both content and underlying processes related to HRM issues. The HRM discipline is often implicitly focused on the content of static issues. This PE intervention highlights the impact of processes and dynamics. The case study also emphasises the role of top management in the change process. The road shows are important for stressing leadership support of the organisational changes made and for employees' trust in the strategic decisions being made. The involvement of works councils and client council paid off in the later stage of the private equity process. Finally, the case highlights the relevance of perceptions and sentiments of those involved. Emotions, feelings of insecurity, employee distrust in management, turnover intentions, dissatisfaction and low commitment levels are partly inevitable in times of major organisational change. HRM can contribute to decrease these negative attitudes and perceptions with an active role of the HR function and its HR professionals in PE interventions.

Questions

1 What are the advantages and disadvantages of works council and client council involvement at an early stage of a PE intervention from the top management perspective and the individual employee perspective?

2 What kind of HR policies and practices can be applied to retain valuable employees during a process of a major organisational change?

3 Why is it important that the two board members actively participate in a road show in which they personally explain the PE situation?

4 What is the impact of a General Electric-inspired performance management system on nurses and medical specialists in a hospital?

5 How does the new performance management affect organisational commitment, occupational commitment and team commitment of employees within the hospital?

6 What is the impact of outsourcing disciplines on employees who are being outsourced and employees who may stay?

7 What kind of competencies do HR professionals need for adding value to the organisational change process caused by a PE intervention?

8 What kind of concrete HR practices can be applied to minimise the negative effects on a PE intervention on employee attitudes and perceptions? Explain why.

CASE STUDY 1.2

FIRE-FIGHTING HRM IN CHINA'S NEW GLOBAL ECONOMY

TONY DUNDON AND JENNY CHAN

Foxconn is perhaps one of the largest single employer's on the planet, with around 1.5 million workers. It has some 200 subsidiaries around the world, although the bulk of its operations and staff are employed in approximately 30 factories across China: in Chengdu, Shenzhen, Beijing and Shanghai among others. Foxconn was founded in 1974 in Taiwan and has grown as a world-leading supply chain transnational corporation. The company makes components and manufactures electronic products that feature in most people's everyday lives: iPhones, iPads, computers, cameras, games and gaming consoles and TVs (and more). Foxconn is ranked about 30th on the Fortune Global 500 list of top corporations, with annual revenues in excess of US$130 billion. The term 'factory' can be misleading when the true image of a Foxconn production facility is realised; probably more

accurately described as 'a city' or, in company speak, 'a campus'. In Shenzhen city, south China, for example, over 500,000 people live and work at the Foxconn site, many of whom are rural migrant workers who flock to these expansive industrial cities for employment. And many of these employees live on-site in factory dormitories, with six to eight people sharing bunk beds.

As a single corporation it dominates the world market for outsourced electronics, with about 50 per cent of total market share and a client list including some of the most well-known household brands: Apple, IMB, Sony, Motorola, Nokia and many others who all utilise a global supply chain network of manufacturing firms assembling production in many developing regions of the world.

Its size and scale means that Foxconn provide an extensive array of human resource support systems for staff at these 24-7 continuous production 'cities' in China. The larger sites such as that at Shenzhen contain its own on-site hospital, banks, a post office, its own fire service, and workers can access educational and schooling opportunities, there is a library, and sports ranging from soccer, swimming, tennis and basketball courts. There is a cinema/theatre, supermarkets and restaurants, and even a wedding dress shop on-site for workers seeking love and marriage. It is evident that young workers from rural provinces of China can earn much higher salaries and acquire and expand their skills and career opportunities than in their home villages.

However, considerable criticism has been levelled at Foxconn (and Apple) given reports about harsh working conditions and the way staff members are managed. There is a military style work regime because of supplier-dominated relationships. For example, when the likes of Apple or Dell issue model updates or launch a new product, production and work pressures intensify for Foxconn employees. Many employees end up working long 12-hour shifts, often with overtime going unpaid. Supervision has been reported as intensive and intimidating with workers having to take time off during low peak periods as a way to circumvent overtime

regulations and protective labour laws. Evidence points to unsafe working conditions, including fatal explosions in some factories, and other risks causing significant distress and health hazards to thousands of employees; for example, workers who polish the new, shinier and streamlined iPad inhale toxic aluminium dust. In the first five months of 2010 twelve suicides – attempted and achieved – by distraught employees who jumped from factory dormitories at Foxconn's Shenzhen sites caught the attention of the world's media. The company's response was to install safety netting between buildings. Company management and the trade union offered counselling to employees, without fully acknowledging its management responsibilities or addressing the profound anxiety faced by a young cohort in a highly unequal Chinese society marked by a deep rural-urban divide.

One anonymous employee remarked: 'The use of death is simply to testify that we were ever alive at all . . . and that while we lived, we had only despair' (Chan and Ngai, 2010). Across other Foxconn factories riots and violent altercations have broken out between workers, state police and company security personnel. In Foxconn, the image of people management is literally that of fire-fighting.

Questions

1 How do you feel after reading the short Foxconn case study?

2 Which, if any, of the four competing perspectives to HRM in Table 1.2 do you think capture the way people are managed at Foxconn?

3 What does the Foxconn case tell us about flexibility, outsourcing and work fragmentation issues discussed in Chapter 1?

4 What responsibilities and influence does or should the likes of Apple have over Foxconn's human resource strategy?

5 Is democratic unionisation on the factory floor a possibility of change?

Suggested Further Reading

Chan, J., Ngai, P. and Selden, M. (2015) 'Apple's iPad City: subcontracting exploitation to China', in van der Pijl, K. (ed.) *Handbook of the International Political Economy of Production*, Cheltenham: Edward Elgar Publishing, 76–97.

Chan, J., Ngai, P. and Selden, M. (2013) 'The politics of global production: Apple, Foxconn and China's new working class', *New Technology, Work and Employment*, Vol.28, No.2, 100–15.

Chan, J. and Ngai, P. (2010) 'Suicide as protest for the new generation of Chinese migrant workers: Foxconn, Global Capital, and the State', *The Asia-Pacific Journal*, Vol.37, No.2, 10.

Bibliography

Alfes, K., Truss, C., Soane, E.C., Rees, C. and Gatenby, M. (2010) *Creating an Engaged Workforce*, London: Chartered Institute of Personnel and Development.

Allen, M. and Wright, P. (2007) 'Strategic management and HR', in Boxall, P., Purcell, J. and Wright, P. (eds.) *The Oxford Handbook of Human Resource Management*, Oxford: Oxford University Press.

Angrave, D., Charlwood, A., Kirkpatrick, I., Lawrence M. and Stuart, M. (2016) 'HR and analytics: why HR is set to fail the big challenge', *Human Resource Management Journal*, Vol.26, No.1, 1–11.

Appelbaum, E., Bailey, T., Berg, P. and Kalleberg, A. (2000) *Manufacturing Competitive Advantage: The Effects of High Performance Work Systems on Plant Performance and Company Outcomes*, New York: Cornell University Press.

Bacon, N. (2003) 'Human resource management and industrial relations', in Ackers, P. and Wilkinson, A. (eds.) *Understanding Work and Employment: Industrial Relations in Transition*, Oxford: Oxford University Press.

Bacon, N. (2008) 'Management strategy and industrial relations', in Blyton, P., Heery, E., Bacon, N. and Fiorto, J. (eds.) *The SAGE Handbook of Industrial Relations*, Thousand Oaks, CA: Sage.

Barney, J. (1995) 'Looking inside for competitive advantage', *Academy of Management Executive*, Vol.9, No.4, 49–61.

Becker, B. and Gerhart, B. (1996) 'The impact of human resource management on organizational performance: progress and prospects', *Academy of Management Journal*, Vol.39, No.4, 779–801.

Becker, B.E. and Huselid, M.A. (2009) 'Strategic human resource management: where do we go from here?', in Wilkinson, A., Bacon, N., Redman, T. and Snell, S. (eds.) *The SAGE Handbook of Human Resource Management*, London: Sage.

Beer, M., Spector, B., Lawrence, P., Quinn Mills, D. and Walton, R. (1985) *Human Resource Management: A General Manager's Perspective*, New York: Free Press.

Beer, M. and Eisenstat, R. (1996) 'Developing an organisation capable of implementing strategy and learning', *Human Relations*, Vol.49, No.5, 597–619.

Beynon, H., Grimshaw, D., Rubery, J. and Ward, K. (2002) *Managing Employment Change, The New Realities of Work*, Oxford: Oxford University Press.

BlessingWhite (2011) *Employee Engagement Report 2011: Beyond the Numbers*, Princeton, NJ: Blessing-White Inc.

Bloom, D.E., Cafiero, E.T., Jané-Llopis, E., Abrahams-Gessel, S., Bloom, L.R., Fathima, S., Feigl, A.B., Gaziano, T., Mowafi, M., Pandya, A., Prettner, K., Rosenberg, L., Seligman, B., Stein, A.Z. and Weinstein, C. (2011) *The Global Economic Burden of Noncommunicable Diseases*, Geneva: World Economic Forum.

Blyton, P., Heery, E. and Turnbull, P. (eds.) (2011) *Reassessing the Employment Relationship*, Basingstoke: Palgrave Macmillan.

Boselie, P. (2010) *Strategic Human Resource Management. A Balanced Approach*, Berkshire: McGraw-Hill.

Boselie, P. and Paauwe, J. (2009) 'HRM and the resource based view', in Wilkinson, A., Bacon, N., Redman, T. and Snell, S. (eds.) *The SAGE Handbook of Human Resource Management*, London: Sage.

Boselie P., Dietz, G. and Boon, C. (2005) 'Commonalities and contradictions in HRM and performance research', *Human Resource Management Journal*, Vol.15, No.3, 67–94.

Boxall, P. (1992) 'Strategic human resource management: beginnings of a new theoretical sophistication?', *Human Resource Management Journal*, Vol.2, No.3, 60–79.

Boxall, P. (2013) 'Mutuality in the management of human resources: assessing the quality of alignment in employment relationships', *Human Resource Management Journal*, Vol.23, No.1, 3–17.

Boxall, P. and Macky, K. (2014) 'High-involvement work processes, work intensification and employee well-being', *Work, Employment and Society*, Vol.28, No.6, 963–84.

Boxall, P. and Purcell, J. (2000) 'Strategic human resource management: where have we come from and where should we be going?', *International Journal of Management Reviews*, Vol.2, No.2, 183–203.

*Boxall, P. and Purcell, J. (2011) *Strategy and Human Resource Management*, New York: Palgrave Macmillan.

Boxall, P. and Steenveld, M. (1999) 'Human resource strategy and competitive advantage: a longitudinal study of engineering consultancies', *Journal of Management Studies*, Vol.36, No.4, 443–63.

Cafferkey, K. and Dundon, T. (2015) 'High performance work systems, innovation and employee outcomes: embedding macro and micro perspectives', *Personnel Review*, Vol.44, No.5, 666–8.

Caldwell, R. (2004) 'Rhetoric, facts and self-fulfilling prophecies: exploring practitioners' perceptions of progress in implementing HRM', *Industrial Relations Journal*, Vol.35, No.3, 196–215.

CIPD (2012) *Annual Report*, London: Chartered Institute of Personnel Development.

CIPD (2015) *Annual Report*, London: Chartered Institute of Personnel Development.

*Combs, C., Lui Y., Hall, A. and Ketchen, D. (2006) 'How much do high performance work systems matter? A meta-analysis of their effects on organizational performance', *Personnel Pyschology*, Vol.59, No.3, 501–28.

Crook, T.R., Todd, S.Y., Combs, J.G., Woehr, D.J. and Ketchen Jr, D.J. (2011) 'Does human capital matter? A meta-analysis of the relationship between human capital and firm performance', *Journal of Applied Psychology*, Vol.96, No.3, 443.

Crouch, C. (2013) *Making Capitalism Fit for Society*, Cambridge: Polity Press.

*Cullinane, N. and Dundon, T. (2006) 'The psychological contract: a critical review', *International Journal of Management Reviews*, Vol.8, No.2, 113–29.

Delaney, J.T., Lewin, D. and Ichniowski, C. (1989) *Human Resource Policies and Practices in American Firms*, Washington, DC: US Government Printing Office.

Drucker, P. (1961) *The Practice of Management*, London: Mercury.

Dundon, T. and Dobbins, T. (2015) 'Militant partnership: a radical pluralist analysis of workforce dialectics', *Work, Employment and Society*, Vol.29, No.6, 912–31.

Dyer, L. and Reeves, T. (1995) 'Human resource strategies and firm performance: what do we know and where do we need to go?', *International Journal of Human Resource Management*, Vol.6, 656–70.

Eccles, R. and Nohira, N. (1992) *Beyond the Hype: Rediscovering the Essence of Management*, Boston, MA: Harvard Business School Press.

European Agency for Safety and Health at Work (2013), *Pan-European opinion poll on occupational safety and health*. Available at: https://osha.europa.eu/en/safety-health-in-figures.

Farnham, D. (2015) *Human Resource Management in Context: Strategy, Insights and Solutions* (4th edn.), London: Chartered Institute of Personnel and Development.

Ferris, G.R., Hochwarter, W.A., Buckley, M.R., Hamell-Cook, G. and Frink, D.D. (1999) 'Human resource management: some new directions', *Journal of Management*, Vol.25, No.3, 385–415.

Fombrun, C.J., Tichy, N.M. and Devanna, M.A. (1984) *Strategic Human Resource Management*, New York: Wiley.

Francis, H. and Keegan, A. (2006) 'The changing face of HRM: in search of balance', *Human Resource Management Journal*, Vol.16, No.3, 231–49.

Giles, E. and Williams, R. (1991) 'Can the personnel department survive quality management?', *Personnel Management*, April, 28–33.

Godard, J. (2004) 'A critical assessment of the high-performance paradigm', *British Journal of Industrial Relations*, Vol.42, No.2, 349–78.

Gospel, H. (2009) 'Human resource management: a historical perspective', in Wilkinson, A., Bacon, N., Redman, T. and Snell, S. (eds.) *The SAGE Handbook of Human Resource Management*, London: Sage.

Grant, R. (2010) *Contemporary Strategy Analysis* (7th edn.), Oxford: Blackwell.

Greer, C.R., Youngblood, S.A. and Gray, D.A. (1999) 'Human resource management outsourcing: the make or buy decision', *Academy of Management Executive*, Vol.13, No.3, 85–96.

Grimshaw, D., Rubery, J. and Marchington, M. (2010) 'Managing people across hospital networks in the UK: multiple employers and the shaping of HRM', *Human Resource Management Journal*, Vol.20, No.4, 407–23.

Grunman, J.A. and Saks, A.M. (2014) 'Being psychologically present when speaking up: employee voice and engagement', in Wilkinson, A., Donaghey, J., Dundon, T. and Freeman, R.B. (eds.) *Handbook of Research on Employee Voice*, Cheltenham: Edward Elgar.

Guest, D. (1987) 'Human resource management and industrial relations', *Journal of Management Studies*, Vol.24, No.5, 503–21.

Guest, D. (1998) 'Beyond HRM: commitment and the contract culture', in Marchington, M. and Sparrow, P. (eds.) *Human Resource Management: The New Agenda*, London: Pitman.

Guest, D. (2000) 'Piece by piece', *People Management*, 20 July, 26–31.

Guest, D. (2007) 'Human resource management and the worker: towards a new psychological contract?', in Boxall, P., Purcell, J. and Wright, P. (eds.) *Oxford Handbook of Human Resource Management*, Oxford: Oxford University Press.

Guest, D. (2011) 'Human resource management and performance: still searching for some answers', *Human Resource Management Journal*, Vol.21, No.1, 3–13.

Guest, D. (2015a) 'Voice and employee engagement', in Johnstone, S. and Ackers, P. (eds.) *Finding a Voice at Work: New Perspectives on Employment Relations*, Oxford: Oxford University Press.

Guest, D. (2015b) 'Putting the human back into HR', Paper presented to the CIPD Applied Research Conference, Warwick Business School, The Shard, London, 8th December.

Guest, D. and Conway, N. (2011) 'The impact of HR practices, HR effectiveness and a "strong HR system" on organisational outcomes: a stakeholder perspective', *International Journal of Human Resource Management*, Vol.22, No.8, 1686–702.

Guthrie, J., Flood, P., Liu, W., MacCurtain, S. and Armstrong, C. (2011) 'Big hat, no cattle? The relationship between use of high-performance work systems and managerial perceptions of HR departments', *International Journal of Human Resource Management*, Vol.22, No.8, 1672–85.

Harley, B. (2015) 'The one best way? "Scientific" research on HRM and the threat to critical scholarship', *Human Resource Management Journal*, Vol.25, No.4, 399–407.

Harter, J.K., Schmidt, F.L., Killham, E.A. and Asplund, J.W. (2006) *Q12 Meta-Analysis*, Omaha, NE: Gallup.

Heffernan, M. and Dundon, T. (2016) 'Cross-level effects of high-performance work systems (HPWS) and employee well-being: the mediating effect of organizational justice', *Human Resource Management Journal*, Vol.26, No.2, 211–31.

Hendry, C., Pettigrew, A. and Sparrow, P. (1988) 'Changing patterns of human resource management', *Personnel Management*, November, 37–41.

Hird, M., Sparrow, P. and Marsh, C. (2010) 'HR structures: are they working?', in Sparrow, P., Hird, M., Hesketh, A. and Cooper, C. (eds.) *Leading HR*, London: Palgrave Macmillan.

Huselid, M. (1995) 'The impact of human resource management practices on turnover, productivity and corporate financial performance', *Academy of Management Journal*, Vol.38, No.3, 635–72.

Jiang, K., Lepak, D.P., Hu, J. and Baer, J.C. (2012) 'How does human resource management influence organizational outcomes? A meta-analytic investigation of mediating mechanisms', *Academy of Management Journal*, Vol.55, No.6, 1264–94.

Johnson, G., Whittington, R. and Scholes, K. (2011) *Exploring Corporate Strategy* (8th edn.), London: Prentice Hall.

Kaufman, B. (2010a) *Hired Hands or Human Resources: Case Studies of HRM Programs and Practices in Early American Industry*, Ithaca, NY: Cornell University Press.

*Kaufman, B. (2010b) 'SHRM theory in the post-Huselid era: why it is fundamentally misspecified', *Industrial Relations: A Journal of Economy and Society (Berkeley)*, Vol.49, No.2, 286–313.

Kaufman, B. (2015) 'Market competition, HRM and firm performance: the conventional paradigm critiqued and reformulated', *Human Resource Management Review*, Vol.25, No.1, 107–25.

Keegan, A. and Francis, H. (2010) 'Practitioner talk: the changing text-scape of HRM and emergence of HR business partnership', *International Journal of Human Resource Management*, Vol.21, No.6, 873–98.

Keenoy, T. (1990) 'HRM: rhetoric, reality and contradiction', *International Journal of Human Resource Management*, Vol.1, No.3, 363–84.

Keenoy, T. (1997) 'Review article: HRMism and the language of re-presentation', *Journal of Management Studies*, Vol.34, No.5, 825–41.

Keenoy, T. (2014) 'Engagement: a murmuration of objects?', pp. 197–220, in Truss, C., Alfes, K., Delbridge, R., Shantz A. and Soane, E. (eds.) *Employee Engagement in Theory and Practice*, London: Routledge.

Kougiannou, K., Redman, T. and Dietz, G. (2015) 'The outcome of works councils: the role of trust, justice and industrial relations climate', *Human Resource Management Journal*, Vol.25, No.4, 458–77.

Legge, K. (1995) *Human Resource Management: Rhetorics and Realities*, Basingstoke: Macmillan.

Lengnick-Hall, C.A. and Lengnick-Hall, M.L. (1988) 'Strategic human resources management: a review of the literature and a proposed typology', *Academy of Management Review*, Vol.13, No.3, 454–70.

Lewin, D. (2008) 'HRM in the 21st century', in Wankel, C. (ed.) *Handbook of 21st Century Management*, London: Sage.

Lewin, D. (2011) 'High performance human resources', in Wilkinson, A. and Townsend, K. (eds.) *The Future of Employment Relations*, London: Palgrave Macmillan.

MacLeod, D. and Clarke, N. (2009) *Engaging for Success: Enhancing Performance through Employee Engagement*, London: Department for Business, Innovation and Skills.

Marchington, M. (2015) 'Human resource management (HRM): too busy looking up to see where it is going longer term?', *Human Resource Management Review*, Vol.25, No.2, 176–87.

Marchington, M. and Wilkinson, A. (2012) *Human Resource Management at Work* (5th edn.), London: Chartered Institute of Personnel and Development.

Marchington, M., Rubery, J. and Grimshaw, D. (2011a) 'Alignment, integration and consistency in HRM across multi-employer networks', *Human Resource Management*, Vol.50, No.3, 313–39.

*Marchington, M., Hadjivassiliou, K., Martin, R. and Cox, A. (2011b) 'Employment relations across organisational boundaries', in Wilkinson, A. and Townsend, K. (eds.) *The Future of Employment Relations*, London: Palgrave Macmillan.

Martin-Alcazar, F., Romero-Fernandez, P. and Sanchez-Gardey, G. (2005) 'Strategic human resource management: integrating the universalistic, contingent, configurational and contextual perspectives', *International Journal of Human Resource Management*, Vol.16, No.5, 633–59.

Miller, P. (1987) 'Strategic industrial relations and human resource management: distinction, definition and recognition', *Journal of Management Studies*, Vol.24, No.4, 347–61.

Monks, J. (1998) 'Trade unions, enterprise and the future', in Sparrow, P. and Marchington, M. (eds.) *Human Resource Management: The New Agenda*, London: FT/Pitman.

Morris, S. and Snell, S. (2009) 'The evolution of HR strategy: adaptations to increasing global complexity', in Wilkinson, A., Bacon, N., Redman, T. and Snell, S. (eds.) *The SAGE Handbook of Human Resource Management*, London: Sage.

Muzio, D. and Tomlinson, J. (2012) 'Researching gender, inclusion and diversity in contemporary professions and professional organizations', *Gender, Work and Organization*, Vol.19, No.5, 455–65.

Nolan, P. (2011) 'Money, markets, meltdown: the 21st-century crisis of labour', *Industrial Relations Journal*, Vol.42, No.1, 2–17.

Nolan, P. and Wood, S. (2003) 'Mapping the future of work', *British Journal of Industrial Relations*, Vol.41, No.2, 165–74.

OECD (2012) *Sick on the Job? Risks and Realities about Mental Health and Work*, OECD Publishing: Paris. Available at: DOI:10.1787/9789264124523-en.

Paauwe, J. (2004) *HRM and Performance: Achieving Long Term Viability*, New York: Oxford University Press.

Paauwe, J. (2009) 'HRM and performance: achievements, methodological issues and prospect', *Journal of Management Studies*, Vol.46, No.1, 129–42.

Paauwe, J. and Boselie, P. (2003) 'Challenging "strategic HRM" and the relevance of the institutional setting', *Human Resource Management Journal*, Vol.13, No.3, 56–70.

Paauwe, J. and Boselie, P. (2007) 'HRM and societal embeddedness', in Boxall, P., Purcell, J. and Wright, P. (eds.) *The Oxford Handbook of Human Resource Management*, Oxford: Oxford University Press.

Parry, E. (2011) 'An examination of the e-HRM as a means to increase the value of the HR function', *International Journal of Human Resource Management*, Vol.22, No.5, 1146–62.

Patterson, M., West, M., Hawthorn, R. and Nickell, S. (1998) 'Impact of people management practices on business performance issues', *Issues in People Management, No.22*, London: Institute of Personnel Management.

Pfeffer, P. (1998) *The Human Equation*, Boston, MA: Harvard Business School Press.

Pollit, C. and Bouchert, G. (2011) *Public Management Reform: A Comparative Analysis of New Public Management Governance and the Neo-Weberain State*, Oxford: Oxford University Press.

Pritchard, K. (2010) 'Becoming an HR strategic partner: tales of transition', *Human Resource Management Journal*, Vol.20, No.2, 175–88.

Purcell, J. (1989) 'The impact of corporate strategy on human resource management', in Storey, J. (ed.) *New Perspectives on Human Resource Management*, London: Routledge.

Purcell, J. (1999) 'Best practice and best fit: chimera or cul-de-sac?', *Human Resource Management Journal*, Vol.9, No.3, 26–41.

Purcell, J. (2010) *Building Employee Engagement*, ACAS policy discussion paper. Available at: www.acas.org.uk.

*Purcell, J. (2014) 'Disengaging from engagement', *Human Resource Management Journal*, Vol.24. No.3, 241–54.

Robbins, C.J., Rudsenske, T. and Vaughan, J.S. (2008) 'Private equity investment in health care services', *Health Affairs*, Vol.27, No.5, 1389–98.

Rubery, J. (2015) 'Change at work: feminisation, flexibilisation, fragmentation and financialisation', *Employee Relations*, Vol.37, No.6, 633–44.

Rubery, J., Keizer, A. and Grimshaw, D. (2016) 'Flexibility bites back: the multiple and hidden costs of flexible employment policies', *Human Resource Management Journal*, forthcoming.

Rucci, A.J. (1997) 'Should HR survive? A profession at the crossroads', *Human Resource Management*, Vol.36, No.1, 169–75.

Schuler, R.S. and Jackson, S.E. (1989) 'Determinants of human resource management priorities and implications for industrial relations', *Journal of Management*, Vol.15, No.1, 89–99.

Sengupta, S. and Whitfield, K. (2011) 'Ask not what HRM can do for performance but what HRM has done to performance', in Blyton, P., Heery, E. and Turnbull, P. (eds.) *Reassessing the Employment Relationship*, London: Palgrave Macmillan.

Sheppeck, M.A. and Militello, J. (2000) 'Strategic HR configurations and organizational performance', *Human Resource Management*, Vol.39, No.1, 5–16.

Sisson, K. (2010) *Employment Relations Matters*. Available at: https://www2.warwick.ac.uk /fac/soc/wbs/research/irru/erm/.

Snape, E., Wilkinson, A. and Redman, T. (1993) 'Human resource management in building societies: making the transformation?', *Human Resource Management*, Vol.3, No.3, 43–60.

Sorge, A. and van Witteloostuijn, A. (2004) 'The (non)sense of organizational change: an *essai* about universal management hypes, sick consultancy metaphors, and healthy organization theories', *Organization Studies*, Vol.25, 1205–31.

Sparrow, P. and Hilltrop, J. (1994) *European Human Resource Management in Transition*, London: Prentice Hall.

Sparrow, P., Hird, M. and Cooper, C. (2015) *Do We Need HR? Repositioning People Management for Success*, London: Palgrave Macmillan.

Storey, J. (1992) *Developments in the Management of Human Resources*, Oxford: Blackwell.

Storey, J. (ed.) (1995) *Human Resource Management: A Critical Text*, London: Routledge.

Storey, J. (ed.) (2007) *Human Resource Management* (4th edn.), London: Routledge.

Subramony, M. (2009) 'A meta-analytic investigation of the relationship between HRM bundles and firm performance', *Human Resource Management*, Vol.48, No.5, 745–68.

Taylor, P., D'Cruz, P., Noronha, E. and Scholarios, D. (2014) 'From boom to where? The impact of crisis on work and employment in Indian BPO', *New Technology, Work and Employment*, Vol.29, No.2, 105–23.

*Thompson, P. (2011) 'The trouble with HRM', *Human Resource Management Journal*, Vol.24, No.4, 1–13.

Thompson, P. and O'Connel Davidson, J. (1995) 'The continuity of discontinuity: managerial rhetoric in turbulent times', *Personnel Review*, Vol.24, No.4, 17–33.

Torrington, D. (1993) 'How dangerous is human resource management?', *Employee Relations*, Vol.15, No.5, 40–53.

Torrington, D., Hall, L., Taylor, S. and Atkinson, C. (2014) *Human Resource Management* (9th edn.), London: Pearson.

Townsend, K. and Dundon, T. (2015), Understanding the role of line managers in employment relations in the modern organisation', *Employee Relations*, Vol.37, No.4, 1–17.

*Truss, C., Shantz, A., Soane, E., Alfes, K. and Delbridge, R. (2013) 'Employee engagement, organisational performance and individual well-being: exploring the evidence, developing the theory', *International Journal of Human Resource Management*, Vol.24, No.14, 2657–69.

Ulrich, D., Brockbank, W., Johnson, D. and Younger, J. (2007) 'Human resource competencies: responding to increased expectations', *Employment Relations Today*, Vol.34, No.3, 1–12.

Ulrich, D. and Dulebohn, J.H. (2015) 'Are we there yet? What's next for HR?', *Human Resource Management Review*, Vol.25, No.2, 188–204.

Vandenabeele, W. (2007) 'Towards a theory of public service motivation: an institutional approach', *Public Management Review*, Vol.9, No.4, 545–56.

van Wanrooy, B., Bewley, H., Bryson, A., Forth, J., Freeth, S., Stokes, L. and Wood, S. (2013) *Employment Relations in the Shadow of Recession: Findings from the 2011 Workplace Employment Relations Study*, Basingstoke: Palgrave Macmillan.

Wall, T.D. and Wood, S.J. (2005) 'The romance of human resource management and business performance and the case for big science', *Human Relations*, Vol.58, No.4, 429–62.

Walsh, J. (2009) 'Work life balance', in Wilkinson, A., Bacon, N., Snell, S. and Redman, T. (eds.) *The SAGE Handbook of Human Resource Management*, London: Sage.

Watson Wyatt (2009) *Continuous Engagement: The Key to Unlocking the Value of Your People During Tough Times*, Work Europe Survey 2008–2009, London: Watson Wyatt.

Welbourne, T. (2011) 'Engaged in what? So what? A role-based perspective for the future of employee engagement', in Wilkinson, A. and Townsend, K. (eds.) *The Future of Employment Relations: New Paradigms, New Approaches*, London: Palgrave Macmillan.

West, M., Borrill, C., Dawson, J., Scully, J., Carter, M., Anelay, S., Patterson, M. and Waring, J. (2002) 'The link between the management of employees and patient mortality in acute hospitals', *International Journal of Human Resource Management*, Vol.13, No.8, 1299–311.

Wilkinson, A. and Fay, C. (2011) 'New times for employee voice?', *Human Resource Management*, Vol.50, No.1, 65–74.

Wilkinson, A. and Johnstone, S. (2016) *An Encyclopaedia of Human Resource Management*, Cheltenham: Edward Elgar.

Wilkinson, A., Wood, G. and Demirbag, M. (2014) 'People management in emerging market multinationals', *Human Resource Management*, Vol.53, No.6, 835–49.

Wilkinson, A., Bacon, N., Redman, T. and Snell, S. (2009) 'The field of human resource management', in Wilkinson, A., Bacon, N., Redman, T. and Snell, S. (eds.) *The SAGE Handbook of Human Resource Management*, London: Sage.

Wilkinson, A., Bacon, N., Snell, S. and Redman, T. (eds.) (2009) *The SAGE Handbook of Human Resource Management*, London: Sage.

Willmott, H. (1993) 'Strength is ignorance, slavery is freedom: managing culture in modern organisations', *Journal of Management Studies*, Vol.30, No.4, 515–52.

Wood, S. (1999) 'Human resource management and performance', *International Journal of Management Reviews*, Vol.1, No.4, 367–413.

Wright, M. and Bruining, H. (2008) 'Private equity and management buy-outs: international trends, evidence and policy implications', in Wright, M. and Bruining, H. (eds.) *Private Equity and Management Buy-outs*, Cheltenham/Northampton: Edward Elgar.

Wright, P. and Snell, S.A. (2005) 'Partner or guardian? HR's challenge in balancing value and values', *Human Resource Management*, Vol.44, No.2, 177–82.

---

*Useful reading.

CHAPTER 2
HUMAN RESOURCE MANAGEMENT AND ORGANISATIONAL PERFORMANCE: IN SEARCH OF THE HR ADVANTAGE

Nicholas Kinnie and Juani Swart

Introduction

Research into the links between HR practices and organisational performance has become one of the main areas of study in the field of Strategic Human Resource Management (Paauwe *et al.*, 2013b; Purcell and Kinnie, 2007). Indeed, Jackson *et al.* (2014: 63) claim that 'the relationship between HRM systems and financial performance has been the primary focus of strategic HRM for the past three decades'. The claims made for the impact of HR practices on business performance raised the profile of the issue among practitioners and policy makers alike. However, debate rages among academics over these claims and their theoretical, empirical and methodological underpinnings (Paauwe *et al.*, 2013b: 1). Indeed, Guest (2011: 3), in a recent review, notes that after 20 years of extensive research we are 'knowledgeable but not much wiser' about the links between HR and performance.

While some authors regard the evidence as the Holy Grail they have been searching for, others question the basis of the research (Legge, 2001). They say the research is too narrowly focused on business performance at the expense of other important measures such as employee well-being and corporate responsibility (Delaney and Godard, 2001; Janssens and Steyaert, 2009; Marchington and Grugulis, 2000; Thompson, 2011). Others warn of the risks of methodological weaknesses and confusion which cast doubt on the robustness of the relationship between HR and performance (Gerhart, 2013; Paauwe, 2009; Purcell, 1999; Wright *et al.*, 2005).

It is not difficult to see the reasons for the increased interest in the field. Senior managers were looking for ways to improve their performance by becoming more flexible and responsive in markets that became increasingly competitive because of globalisation and deregulation (Becker and Gerhart, 1996; Boxall and Purcell, 2011; Paauwe *et al.*, 2013b). The rise of the knowledge economy where firms rely almost completely on their human and intellectual capital for their competitive advantage elevated the importance of people management still further (Swart, 2007). In this context, managers of HR saw the opportunity to demonstrate their contribution to the business more convincingly than in the past (Wright *et al.*, 2005). Some researchers in the field, it has been suggested, were motivated by the desire to demonstrate the policy relevance of their research (Legge, 2001; Jackson *et al.*, 2014; Thompson, 2011).

It is against this background that we aim in this chapter to:

- position the debate on HR and performance in the wider context of strategy, structure and Human Resource Management (HRM). In particular, we consider the impact of cross-boundary working on the links between people management and performance;
- identify a suitable framework for analysing the HR and performance research;
- review the research and evidence in this field critically;
- consider the implications of cross-boundary ways of organising work for the links between HR and performance;
- provide case study examples.

 ## Strategy, structure and HRM

We first need to place the HR and performance debate in its wider context of the links between strategy, structure and HRM. These debates have consumed many person hours and we are consequently able only to scratch the surface.[1] We will first briefly discuss the various perspectives on strategy and then consider issues of organisational structure.

The adoption of HR practices is often thought to be strategic only if:

1 it contributes to organisational performance,[2] and in doing so
2 is aligned with the strategy of the organisation.

This leads us to question what strategy is and just what the variations in the alignment between the HR practices and the business strategy might be.

Boxall and Purcell (2011: 40) follow Mintzberg (1994) and differentiate between the firm's strategic plan and its strategy. They ask whether an organisation, especially a small organisation, which does not have a strategic plan and strategic objectives, can be said to have a strategy. The existence of a strategy and the ability to strategise will, of course, differ from industry to industry. In some industries the market conditions change at a faster rate than others: some are characterised by novel and complex problems while others are more predictable.

We need first to understand the ways in which HR strategy might vary (Swart *et al.*, 2004). The principal source of variation is the predictability of, and knowledge about, the environment. At one extreme, organisations will have a clear sense of how the environment may evolve. The environment in, for example, the public sector and industries with large capital costs of configuration change such as the energy industry, tends to be more stable or at least more predictable. At the other extreme, firms do not know whether their environment will change rapidly nor what may trigger a change in the environment. For example,

---

[1] Those looking for a more in-depth treatment are advised to consult Boxall and Purcell (2011) or Paauwe *et al.* (2013a).
[2] The link between HR and performance as it relates to strategy will not be discussed in this section as most of the chapter is dedicated to this exploration.

research and technology firms may not be able to predict what the next wave of scientific discovery may be. Importantly, contemporary ways of organising work in networks also mean that work environments become less predictable. Firms respond to uncertainty in demand by creating a spread of responses at as low a cost as is practicable in order to capture the demand that eventually emerges (Powell and Wakeley, 2003).

Each of these types of environment presents a different strategic paradigm and requirement for competence development (see Figure 2.1). First, the left-hand position represents the classic perspective, which views strategy as a plan or a set of strategic objectives (Ansoff, 1965; Porter, 1985). Success or failure, according to this school of thought, is determined internally through operational detail of the strategic plan (Whittington, 2001). The more stable and predictable environment allows for environmental diagnosis, scenario planning, gap analysis and forecasts with their relevant action plans. This approach to strategy has been criticised severely in recent years, mainly because of the dynamic nature of global markets which call for flexibility. This raises the further question as to whether it is possible first, to write a strategic plan and second, to implement this as planned (Boxall and Purcell, 2011).

As we move along the continuum we arrive at a point which sees strategy as process. According to this viewpoint the strategy process changes continually as a result of ongoing learning across the organisation and is therefore more adaptable throughout its enactment.

According to Pettigrew (1973) strategy as a process is influenced by individual and collective cognitions and the interplay of power and politics at every organisational level. This approach is essentially more fluid with an emphasis on the enactment of strategy, as expressed through behaviours and cognitions. It is therefore more about *seeing* strategy than *planning* strategy.

This perspective can be illustrated by taking the example of a call centre whose customer relationship processes need to change considerably because of technological development and labour market shifts. The call centre may not know exactly how this technological development could impact upon its processes, but a strategy can be enacted through developing relationships with the originators of advanced technologies (in response to technological change and in preparation for customer demands) and as customers make their decisions.

Finally, the other extreme of the continuum, often found in networked working arrangements, represents an evolutionary approach to strategy where several partners influence the strategic development process. Here organisations operate in near-chaotic environments where change is typically too fast, too unpredictable and too implacable to anticipate and pre-empt and the advice is to concentrate on day-to-day viability while trying to keep options open (Whittington, 2001: 37). The strategic responses in these environments are characterised by a random generation of a spread of responses (since prediction

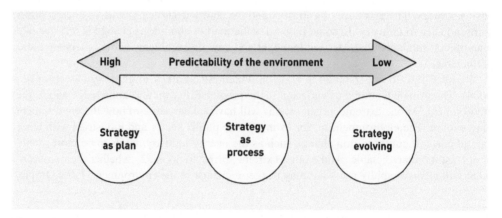

Figure 2.1 The strategy continuum

is futile), together with a cost sensitive trialling of these responses and a planned retention of knowledge gained by that trialling. If we refer to the example of the research and technology organisation (Tocris Cookson in Box 2.1 below) that develops several research innovations to an unexpected buyer demands, we can see that the organisation can 'keep its options open' through the design and initial development of several offerings. These are then exposed to developments in the market, both through professional networks, scientific partnerships and through market testing. Through the process of gauging responses to possible compounds, for example, the organisation can learn more about its environment and therefore develops an ability to enact future strategies and reinvests the knowledge gained in the development process.

Each of the points on the continuum in Figure 2.1 has implications for competence development. The key focus for the first position is on the development of core competence that will enable the enactment of the strategic plan. Competence development is, therefore, specific and relatively narrow. The focus on competence development is more broadly defined at the mid-point in the continuum where there are several options to a relatively familiar but changing environment. For example, the focus could be on customer service or technology development, but given the uncertainty it is impossible to define exactly which core competence will be needed to successfully compete in the marketplace. Finally, the right-hand position calls for a development of a more generic meta-competence that is related to multiple-offering development, trial analysis and fast response once the source of change is known. The level of the competence development is therefore higher compared with the previous two cases and the focus is even wider.

This continuum takes a knowledge-based view to strategy and represents the strategic paradigms accordingly. Several other methods of representation are possible including the strategic freedom perspective. Firms at each point along the continuum may experience various degrees of client pressure or influence upon their strategic choice. A large firm such as Toyota may not be in a position to plan for every eventuality but given its dominant position within its local network it has a greater degree of freedom of strategic choice (Kinnie *et al.*, 2005). Boxall and Purcell (2011: 50) argue it is important to steer between 'hyper-determinism' on the one hand and 'hyper-voluntarism' on the other. Firms therefore neither completely control their environment nor are they completely controlled by it. This is a general statement; we need to be aware of the varying degrees of freedom within and between industries that operate within each of the strategic paradigms. This has implications for the ways human resources are deployed and developed to achieve sustainable competitive advantage.

In this section we have so far considered the variety of forms that the links between strategy and HR might take. In particular, we have differentiated between three different links between strategy and HR by referring to a continuum based on the predictability of and knowledge about the environment. Having set the context through the consideration of strategy and HR we now turn our attention to changes taking place in organisational structure which have important consequences for how HR practices are linked to performance.

The way we work has changed significantly in the last two decades (Cappelli, 2008). Organisations in a knowledge-based economy rely not only on their own knowledge and skills to generate valuable outputs but they also draw on inter-organisational resources to create sustained competitive advantage (Fisher *et al.*, 2008; Lepak and Snell, 2007; Marchington *et al.*, 2005, 2011; Rubery *et al.*, 2003; Swart, 2011; Swart and Kinnie, 2014). Networked ways of working have developed where products and services are co-created by stakeholders who work, often in project teams, across organisational boundaries (Donnelly, 2009, 2011; Fincham, 1999). This presents challenges to linking HR practices and organisational performance which are even more profound than those in more traditional organisations where it is easier to generate commitment to the organisation (Kinnie and Swart, 2012). Firms find they employ people whom they do not manage (where they are working, for example, on client sites, as in the Alexander Mann

Solutions case study) or have to manage people whom they do not employ directly (as in the case of Marks and Spencer).

In practice, HR therefore needs to cross organisational boundaries to match the activities of human capital it is seeking to manage. This has implications at both the level of the organisation and the individual employee.

At the organisational level networked working involves the co-creation of products and services that have economic value for stakeholders extending beyond the boundaries of the firm, i.e. the network benefits from the collaborative employment arrangements. This suggests that we need to adopt a relational approach where we consider how suppliers, partners, clients and customers influence the way people are managed. This, in turn, poses significant questions about the HR practices needed at the level of the network to improve performance at the organisational and network levels. The focus of the HRM model is therefore no longer simply on seeking to manage employees within organisational boundaries. Success now depends on being able to leverage human capital (Wright and McMahan, 2011) both within and across organisational boundaries. This presents a profound challenge to both HR and line managers. In practice, they have to manage (i) staff that is employed by their firm but over which they do not have control – which is often found in a matrix context; (ii) agency and self-employed staff and (iii) staff working for partners, suppliers and clients who are collaborating on a project. For example, if the attitudes and behaviour of an employee in one organisation (for instance, an assembler of manufactured products) are affected by the actions of employees in suppliers then should the HR practices apply to both organisations?

This challenges many of the taken-for-granted assumptions about the use of traditional HR practices such as reward and performance management. In a cross-boundary environment many of these authority-based levers are simply irrelevant. Instead, HR and line managers find they have to rely on the management of lateral rather than hierarchical relationships – something for which they may be ill-equipped by traditional management training and development programmes. Similar challenges exist in organisations which rely heavily on the work of volunteers, such as charities. Again, few of the traditional HR instruments are relevant here and emphasis is placed on developing commitment to the organisation and the network through attachment to values, beliefs and principles.

Employees working across organisational boundaries interact with a series of external parties including clients, partners and suppliers. This creates the opportunity for them to become committed to these parties rather than to the organisation which employs them (Kinnie and Swart, 2012). Indeed, these parties may be competing for the commitment of these employees. Furthermore, in some cases, such as consulting, we might refer to employees occupying a liminal space where they are 'betwixt and between' organisations (Garsten, 1999: 603; Tempest and Starkey, 2004). They are at the limits of existing social structures which breed ambiguity for those spanning organisational boundaries (Tushman and Scanlan, 1981). Whereas more traditional employees could tie their identity to their organisation the 'networked citizen' anchors their identity in their 'skill' and thus puts employability before loyalty to an organisation. Employees occupying this liminal space may experience a sense of freedom but also insecurity and an absence of trust. Lacking traditional organisational ties they may find themselves floating between their firm and their client, but anchored to neither (O'Mahoney, 2007: 11). This may reduce their willingness to engage in extra role behaviour towards their employer and poses questions about the most effective HR practices for managing individual employees who occupy this liminal space (Kinnie and Swart, 2012).

Our discussion of networked working demonstrates that the network represents additional challenges to the links between HRM and performance because of the multiplicity of stakeholders that compete for the commitment and discretionary behaviour of the individual.

HR and organisational performance: our approach and some background

Our aim is not to simply describe and evaluate all the available research in the field. This is a self-defeating task because the reader will quickly become lost in a mass of detail. Indeed, there are already a number of excellent detailed reviews to be found elsewhere (Becker and Gerhart, 1996; Becker and Huselid, 2006; Boselie *et al.*, 2005; Boxall and Purcell, 2011; Combs *et al.*, 2006; Delery and Doty, 1996; Guest, 2011; Huselid and Becker, 2000; Jackson *et al.*, 2014; Kaufman, 2015; Lepak *et al.*, 2006; Paauwe, 2009; Paauwe, Guest and Wright, 2013a; Purcell, 1999; Purcell and Kinnie, 2007; Purcell *et al.*, 2009; Wall and Wood, 2005; Wright and Gardener, 2000; Wright *et al.*, 2005). One review of the research (Wall and Wood, 2004) examined the 26 most cited studies published since 1994 and identified a number of characteristic features. Half were based in the industrial sector, most used a single respondent and were cross-sectional in design. Just over half the measures of performance were self-reported and were from the same source as the HRM measures.

We take a thematic approach to the research referring to key studies as illustrations. More importantly, we use a much needed theoretical framework based on the concept of Human Resource Advantage (Boxall, 1996, 1998; Boxall and Steeneveld, 1999) to guide us through the maze of research findings. We use this framework to examine the research thematically in the following way. The next major section outlines the concept of HR advantage and explains how it will be used to structure our analysis of the impact of HR policy and practice.[3] This is followed by an examination of the research into the two forms of HR advantage referred to as Human Capital Advantage (HCA) and Organisational Process Advantage (OPA). The chapter concludes by considering the theoretical, methodological and practical implications of our discussion. Before all of this we need to give some of the background to our discussion.

Background to the research

There has been a long-standing, almost intuitive view that the performance of an organisation was affected by the way its employees are managed. Indeed, this was virtually an unstated assumption behind much of the early research into Scientific Management, the Hawthorne studies and Total Quality Management movement. However, much of this early work lacked a strategic focus (Golding, 2004; Legge, 1978).

Research in the US in the early-to-mid 1980s looked in a more focused way at the possible links between HR and performance. The texts by Beer *et al.* (1985) and by Fombrun *et al.* (1984) were thought to be particularly influential and in some ways represented a major leap forward in the area. These studies were not, however, based on empirical research and there were no attempts at this stage to measure performance in any well-defined or systematic way (Truss, 2001: 1122).

It is only relatively recently that studies have explicitly focused on the performance issue and the data has been available and shown a positive relationship between the presence of key HR practices and organisational performance. Much of the recent interest can be traced back to the work of Huselid (1995) and Pfeffer (1994; 1998) in the US [which itself can be linked back to Peters and Waterman (1982)]. The key work is that by Huselid (1995) who sought to measure the contribution of HR to performance in much more well defined and precise ways than in the past. Drawing on a survey of 968 US firms and taking financial

---

[3]Following Lepak *et al.* (2006: 221) we define HR policies as expressing the broad HR aims in particular areas, e.g. the commitment to pay for performance, whereas HR practices are the specific organisational actions designed to achieve specific outcomes, e.g. profit sharing, individual appraisal related pay.

performance (although other outcome measures were also used, for example, employee turnover and retention) as his dependent variable he used sophisticated statistical techniques to consider the impact of high performance work systems. Huselid found that 'the magnitude of the returns for investments in High Performance Work Systems is substantial'. Indeed, 'A one standard deviation increase in such practices is associated with a relative 7.05% decrease in (labour) turnover, and on a per employee basis, $27,044 more in sales and $18,641 and $3,814 more in market value and profits, respectively' (Huselid, 1995: 667). More recently, Huselid and Becker (2000: 851) claimed that 'Based on four national surveys and observations in more than 2,000 firms, our judgement is that the effect of a one standard deviation change in the HR system is 10–20% of a firm's market value.'

Research by Patterson et al. (1997) in the UK came up with similar findings. Drawing on research in 67 UK manufacturing businesses studied over time they found that 18 per cent of the variation in productivity and 19 per cent of profitability could be attributed to people management practices. These were a better predictor of company performance than strategy, technology and research and development.

Following the early research there have been over 100 studies looking at the links between HR and performance and many of these have focused on the links between HR practices and performance. Boselie et al. (2005) report that there were 104 articles on these topics in refereed journals between 1994 and 2003. Jackson et al. (2014) drawing on a review of 154 articles published between 1992 and 2013 examining HRM systems as opposed to individual practices found that 77 of them focused on the links with performance. As we have mentioned earlier, this extensive effort reveals mixed views on the nature of these links. Jackson et al. (2014: 19) express one view 'firms with coherent HRM systems outperform those without such systems on issues of financial interest to the owners and investors (e.g. return on equity, return on assets, Tobin's Q, profit growth, stock return etc.' However, Paauwe et al. (2013b: 3) note that progress has been 'modest' while Purcell and Kinnie (2007: 533) noted 'numerous review papers . . . have found this field of research often wanting in terms of method, theory and the specification of HR practices to be used when establishing a relationship with performance outcomes'. Becker and Huselid (2006: 921) put the same point in a slightly different way, 'Despite the remarkable progress the field of SHRM may be at a cross-roads.'

These studies have stimulated an intense debate surrounding the very nature, purpose and outputs of the research (Hesketh and Fleetwood, 2006; Janssens and Steyaert, 2009; Keenoy, 1997; Legge, 1995; Paauwe, 2009; Paauwe et al., 2013b; Thompson, 2011). However, before we explore the findings of this research in more detail we need to establish our framework for analysis.

Human resource advantage

Research in the field has often been criticised for an excessive emphasis on the quantitative analysis of data collected by the survey method. For example, when commenting on the early research Guest (1997: 264) noted that 'While these studies represent encouraging signs of progress, statistical sophistication appears to have been emphasised at the expense of theoretical rigour. As a result the studies are non-additive, except in a very general way.' Wood (1999: 408) in turn argued that 'The empirical work . . . has concentrated on assessing the link between practices and performance with increasing disregard for the mechanisms linking them.' Consequently, Guest argued (1997: 263) 'if we are to improve our understanding of the impact of HRM on performance, we need a theory about HRM, a theory about performance and a theory about how they are linked'.

The work by Peter Boxall and his colleagues provides a way forward with their development of the concept of Human Resource Advantage (HRA) (Boxall, 1996, 1998; Boxall and Purcell, 2011; Boxall and Steeneveld, 1999). HRA is the series of policies, practices and processes that together contribute to the competitive advantage of the organisation. This advantage is comprised of a Human Capital Advantage (HCA) and an Organisational Process Advantage (OPA). There are various forms of capital which are critical to organisational performance (including human, social, structural, organisational, client and network capital – see Figure 2.2 for further details) and our discussion focuses on the generation of HCA, which involves developing superior practices in key areas such as recruitment, selection, training and team building designed to ensure the best people are employed and these staff develop high levels of skill. However, HCA is unlikely to generate competitive advantage in the practices themselves because they are easily copied (Mueller, 1996). It is the processes and routines required to put these practices into operation as intended that are more difficult to replicate and form the OPA (Boxall, 1996: 67). These processes, such as team-based learning and cross-functional cooperation, develop over time, are socially complex and causally ambiguous (Boxall and Purcell, 2011: 103–4). It is these processes which are likely to be highly complex when work takes places across organisational boundaries (Swart and Kinnie, 2014).

Both HCA and OPA can generate competitive advantage, but they are most effective when they are combined together. The form of HR advantage is likely to change as the firm grows through the establishment, mature and renewal contexts (Boxall, 1998). Thus 'while knowledge of individual HR practices is not rare, the knowledge of how to create a positively reinforcing blend of HR philosophy, process, practice and investment *within* a particular context is likely to be very rare' (Boxall and Purcell, 2003: 86). This 'social architecture' is created and re-created at all levels in the firm and is therefore especially difficult to imitate (Mueller, 1996: 177).

For our purposes this creates a dual focus on the design and content of HR practices *and* the role of line managers and employees in putting these into action. We use this framework as a way of organising our discussion of the links between HR and performance. We look first at the research conducted into the influences shaping the HR practices that comprise the HCA. This can be broken down into two schools of thought typically referred to as 'best practice' and 'best fit'. Attention is then turned to studies of OPA looking at the role of employees and line managers.

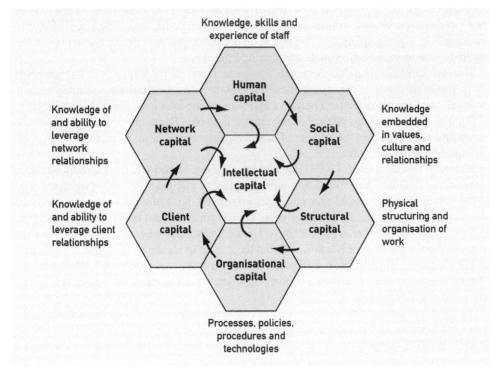

Figure 2.2
Forms of capital
Sources: Kinnie *et al.*,
2006; Swart, 2006.

Human capital advantage

Research into the impact of HR practices on performance can be divided into two groups. First, those who argue that a set of HR practices can be identified which can be applied in a wide variety of circumstances and will have a positive effect on business performance. The second view is that the effectiveness of HR practices depends on the external and internal context of the organisation. We review each of these using illustrations from the principal studies.

Best practice

There is a long history of researching individual best practices, for example psychology-based research into psychometric testing (Boxall and Purcell, 2011: 86–7). What is new is the concept of looking for a combination, system or 'bundle' of practices which need to be combined together (Guest, 1997; Huselid, 1995; Jackson *et al.*, 2014; Lepak *et al.*, 2006: 218; MacDuffie, 1995). Making changes to individual practices will, it is argued, have a very limited effect, whereas making changes together will have a more powerful effect. This suggests there is a set of practices which can and should be adopted by firms which will lead to improvements in performance. In practical terms not only must firms become aware of these practices but they also need support from top-level managers to adopt these practices. Researchers have also highlighted the need to avoid what they referred to as 'deadly' combinations, for example the introduction of individual performance pay and teamworking (Delery, 1998).

The terms for these bundles vary, indeed there is an array of acronyms used which seem designed to confuse the practitioner and the academic, including HR System, High Commitment Management (HCM), High Performance Work Systems (HPWS), High Involvement Management (HIM).

These approaches seek to identify a distinctive set of successful HR practices that can be applied successfully to all organisations irrespective of their setting. Pfeffer (1994; 1998) developed a list of 16 best practices, which were subsequently reduced to seven (1998). The seven practices are: employment security, selective hiring, self-managed teams/teamworking, high compensation contingent on organisational performance, extensive training, reduction of status differentials and sharing information.

Huselid (1995) argued that there needs to be an integrated system of work practices to fit the particular needs of the organisation. This research involved collecting data relating to the number of practices the firm employs by means of a postal questionnaire completed by a single respondent representing the company as a whole. The resulting analysis produced impressive results linking the number of practices and various forms of performance – typically profit and market value.

Research by Guest *et al.* (2003) drawing on a survey of 366 UK firms produced rather more mixed results. They found that increased use of HR practices was associated with lower labour turnover and higher profit per employee, but not with higher productivity. However, once profitability in earlier years is taken into account these associations cease to be significant (Guest *et al.*, 2003: 306). Thus the association between HR practices and organisational performance is confirmed, but there is no evidence to show that the presence of HR practices causes a change in performance (Guest *et al.,* 2003: 307). Wright *et al.* (2005) also found that virtually all of their significant correlations disappeared when controlling for past performance.

This type of research has a number of advantages because it focuses the debate on the role of HR practices but also raises various problems (Boxall and Purcell, 2011: 90–4; Purcell, 1999). Two kinds of problems have been identified: methodological and theoretical (Paauwe, 2009). Let us look at methodological problems first.

Methodological problems

Perhaps the easiest way of summarising the criticisms of this research is to pose a series of questions.

What is the direction of causation? It is possible that the direction of causation is in the opposite direction to that which is proposed since it may be only the successful firms that can afford these HCM practices (Paauwe *et al.*, 2013b: 3; Guest *et al.*, 2003: 309). Indeed, Wright *et al.* (2005: 432–3) argued for exercising 'extreme caution in inferring a direct causal impact on performance'. They suggest that dual causation provides a possible explanation for what they have observed: business units that perform well invest more in HR practices, which pay off in terms of improved performance. There is also the possibility that respondents might believe that HR practices are good simply because the performance of their organisation is good (Gerhart, 1999: 42; Wright and Gardener, 2000: 8). Moreover, it is highly likely that there will be multiple causes of any improvement in performance and it is very difficult to unpick these satisfactorily.

What measures should be used? The measures of performance are typically narrowly focused on financial criteria with very few studies examining the broader issue of employee attitudes and well-being (Janssens and Steyaert, 2009). Similarly, there are issues over the extensiveness of HR practices: should they, for example, apply to all employees or only a selection? One study may examine whether the organisation has self-managed teams (i.e. yes or no), while another may look at the proportion of employees working in a self-managed team. Linked to this is the profound problem, discussed in more detail when we look at organisational process advantage, which has either been ignored or side-stepped by much of this research that the practices that are being so carefully counted are not actually implemented in practice.

How should the data be collected, analysed and presented? Many studies rely on postal surveys where the main problem is mis-reporting by single respondents who have limited knowledge of the extent and use of the practices themselves (Gerhart, 1999). Much of the research makes use of highly sophisticated statistical techniques that produce results that are hard for the practitioner, as well as many students and academics, to understand.

Theoretical challenges

As we have mentioned, there have been strong criticisms of the lack of theoretical development. This poses another set of questions which need to be addressed. Best practice for whom? Is there room for an employee voice in this discussion or is the emphasis simply on the perspective of shareholders and managers? (Boxall and Purcell, 2011: 85–6). Marchington and Grugulis (2000: 1105–6; Thompson, 2011) consider the impact of these practices on employees and argue that these practices, such as teamwork or performance-related pay,

> which appear superficially attractive may not offer universal benefits and empowerment but actually lead to work intensification and more insidious forms of control; in other words, quite different and more worrying interpretations from that portrayed in the 'upbeat' literature – such as that by Pfeffer.

They are in short 'nice words and harsh realities'.

Ramsay *et al.* (2000) investigated the labour process explanation, which argues that improvements in productivity are the result of the intensification of work using the data from the Workplace Employee Relations Survey (Cully *et al.*, 1999). However, they could not find support for either the labour process or the high commitment management explanations.

More generally, the absence of an independent employee voice is noted (Marchington and Grugulis, 2000: 1119), reflecting a set of unitarist assumptions underpinning Pfeffer's work. Thus emphasis tends to be on the psychology-based techniques such as recruitment and selection, training, performance appraisal and pay rather than those based on pluralist assumptions, for example employee involvement practices and collective bargaining (see also in this volume: Harvey and Turnbull, Chapter 8 and Dundon and Wilkinson, Chapter 16).

Which practices should be included? It is relatively easy to spot so-called 'bad' practices, for example the use of unstructured selection interviews or a poorly conducted performance appraisal. However, it is difficult to get agreement on what the good practices are, apart from the most obvious statements such as the need for careful planning (Paauwe *et al.*, 2013b: 7). The lists of practices themselves vary (Boxall and Purcell, 2011: 90) and there is no agreement on what constitutes the best practices, such that 'studies of so-called high-performance work systems vary significantly as to the practices included and sometimes even as to whether a practice is likely to be positively or negatively related to high performance' (Becker and Gerhart, 1996: 784). Guest and Hoque (1994), for example, list 23 practices, MacDuffie (1995) has 11 items and Pfeffer has seven. Marchington and Grugulis (2000: 1114) note that employment security is included by Pfeffer but not by a number of other authors; similarly, the importance of employee voice varies: some include it but Pfeffer does in a very limited way. Arthur (1994) gives low emphasis to variable pay whereas Huselid (1995) and MacDuffie emphasise this (Truss, 2001: 1124). Consequently, both Boxall and Purcell (2011) and Youndt *et al.* (1996: 839) argue there is a need for this kind of research to be more selective in the way findings are presented.

Do you need all of these practices and are they all equally important? The argument put forward by MacDuffie (1995), based on bundles of HR practices, suggests that these practices need to be combined and just taking one or two are likely to be ineffective. Marchington and Grugulis (2000: 1112–5) argue that in practice we often find weak links between these practices or simply contradictory practices – one person's job security might be at the expense of another person's whether in the employing firm or a subcontractor.

Are all employees treated in the same way? Are these practices just reserved for a minority of supposedly core employees or are they applied to all (Marchington and Grugulis, 2000: 1117)? This is not just an issue of differences between manual and staff employees but applies more widely in times of the decline of the internal labour market and the externalisation of the workforce through sub-contracting and network relations. Early work into the 'flexible firm' suggested that employees would be treated differently based on how central they were to the core of the firm (Atkinson, 1984). More recent work by Lepak and Snell (1999), discussed below, also addresses this issue. There is also growing evidence that certain practices are more effective or at least more worthwhile for specific groups of employees (Becker and Huselid, 2011), which offers support for the contingency approach to HRM.

What is the level and unit of analysis? The question of the level and unit of analysis is an important one (Paauwe, 2009). In some cases the research has been carried out at the level of the corporate head office (Huselid, 1995) where the gap between HR practices, the employees they are intended for and performance is wide. Other research has collected data at the level of the business unit where the gap between the HR policy and performance data is narrowed (Wright *et al.*, 2003). This issue is addressed to some extent by the sectoral studies discussed below.

If these practices are so effective why are they not used more widely? Evidence from the Workplace Employee Relations Survey (Cully *et al.*, 1999) found that only 14 per cent of workplaces used HCM while in the US (Osterman, 1994) only 35 per cent of firms used two or more HCM practices, a finding confirmed by Gittleman *et al.* (1998). Guest *et al.* (2000) found that only 1 per cent of their firms used three-quarters of 18 progressive practices and 20 per cent use less than a quarter. It is possible that just putting practices in on their own does not change very much, leading to a loss of enthusiasm because of the difficulty in identifying results.

More generally, Guest *et al.* (2000) tell us that there were relatively few firms in their survey that had an HR strategy and a long tail of firms who did not. They found that while two-thirds of firms rely on people as their source of competitive advantage only about 10 per cent gave people a priority above that of marketing and finance, and in most companies people are not viewed by top managers as their most important asset.

How important is the context? Both national context where customers, laws, cultures and styles vary (Boxall and Purcell, 2011: 90–1) and organisational sectoral contexts pose questions about the suitability of these practices, although multinational companies will attempt to standardise their practices across countries (Boxall and Purcell, 2011: 92–3). There may well be circumstances where employers simply cannot afford these practices, most commonly in labour intensive organisations, where arguably the difficulty of controlling costs is greatest (Marchington and Grugulis, 2000: 1117).

To sum up, we can see from these questions that although the best practice view has gained a great deal of publicity because of the simplicity of the message it has also attracted widespread criticism. Indeed, Purcell (1999) has characterised research in this area as leading into a *cul-de-sac* where no forward progress is possible. Many of the critics argue that what works in one organisational setting, for example a small knowledge intensive firm, will be quite different to what is effective in another, for example a low cost manufacturing company, or an NHS Trust. This leads them to argue that in order to maximise performance managers must tailor their HR policies and practices to the contexts within which they are working – a view typically referred to as 'best fit'.

Best fit

This perspective is derived from the contingency view that argues that the effectiveness of HR practices depends on how closely they fit with the external and internal environment of the organisation. Business performance, it is argued, improves when HR practices mutually reinforce the choice of competitive strategy. This is the concept of vertical integration, or 'line of sight', between the competitive strategy, the objectives of the firm, the HR practices and individual objectives (Buller and McEvoy, 2012; Fombrun *et al.*, 1984; Wright *et al.*, 1994), and it helps to explain lack of diffusion because the appropriate practices will depend on the context.

There are different views on the importance of fit with particular contexts (Paauwe *et al.*, 2013c) focusing on content, process, implementation, the strength of interactions between practices and dominant goals. Some stress the stage in the life cycle, whereas others draw attention to the 'outer context' of the competitive strategy or the 'inner context' of existing structures and strategy (Hendry and Pettigrew, 1992). It is also important to note that it is not just the 'stage of growth/life cycle' which is important but also the size of the organisation. That is to say, a mature, small organisation would require a very different set of HR practices from those required by a mature multinational corporation.

Some authors (Baird and Meshoulam, 1988; Kochan and Barocci, 1985) argue that there needs to be a fit between the HR practices and the stage in the business life cycle. They suggest that the HR practices needed during the start-up phase are quite different from those needed during growth, maturity and decline. However, most organisations will have a series of products that are at different stages in their life cycles producing the situation familiar to many managers whereby certain parts of their business are growing whereas others are shrinking, producing quite different pressures on HR practices.

However, perhaps the best known examples of this perspective draw on analysis (Porter, 1980) of the sources of competitive advantage (Miles and Snow, 1978, 1984; Schuler and Jackson, 1987), which argues that HR practices work best when they are adapted to the competitive strategy. Miles and Snow (1984) identify three types of strategic behaviour and link these to various HR practices: 'Defenders' will have narrow, relatively stable products and will emphasise internal, process-oriented training and internal pay equity; 'Prospectors' have changing product lines and rely more on innovation leading to the use of external recruitment, results-oriented compensation and external pay equity; 'Analysers' have changing and stable product lines leading them to use internal and external recruitment and pay equity measures and process-oriented performance appraisal.

Schuler and Jackson (1987) and Jackson and Schuler (1995) developed these approaches where they identified the different competitive strategies of organisations and the role behaviours which were needed with each of them. They drew attention to the different kinds of behaviours needed for innovation, quality enhancement and cost reduction and the types of HR practices which are needed to achieve these. For example, a strategy based on cost leadership will result in minimal levels of investment in human capital with low standards for recruitment and poor levels of pay and training. In contrast, a strategy based on innovation calls for HR practices that encourages risk taking and cooperative behaviour. Youndt *et al.* (1996) and Delery and Doty (1996) provide some support for this perspective.

The 'best fit' approach is well illustrated in studies carried out in a single sector where most firms are operating within the same industrial context. For example, Arthur (1994) demonstrated how steel mini-mills firms pursuing cost leadership business strategies adopted cost minimisation command and control type approaches. Those seeking product and quality differentiation pursued HCM or HPWS approaches with emphasis on training, employee problem solving, teamworking, higher pay, higher skills and attempts to create a work community. Batt and Moynihan (2004) found that HR practices emphasising investment in employees were more successful in the parts of the industry that required employees to exercise their discretion when they examined call centres in the US telecommunications industry.

Thompson (2000) carried out two surveys of firms in the UK aerospace industry. In 1997 he found that establishments with higher levels of value added per employee tended to have higher penetration of innovative working practices among their non-management employees. These workplaces were more likely to engage in specialist production for niche markets and employed a richer mix of technical and professional employees. Later work in 1999 revealed 'compelling evidence that firms introducing a greater number of high performance work practices have much improved business performance' (Thompson, 2000: 10). Firms moving from less than five to more than six innovative practices made a 34 per cent gain in value added per employee.

Other research has highlighted the influence of the network of relationships within which firms especially knowledge intensive and professional service firms are working (Beaumont *et al.*, 1996; Donnelly, 2011; Kinnie and Swart, 2012; Sinclair *et al.*, 1996; Swart and Kinnie, 2003; Swart *et al.*, 2007; Swart and Kinnie, 2014). Firms form relationships with clients, suppliers and collaborators who will seek to influence the HR practices pursued by the focal firm both directly and indirectly (see Box 2.1 and Figure 2.3). These external parties influence HR practices directly, for example through shaping recruitment and selection criteria or through requiring certain types of training to be conducted, or indirectly by setting performance targets that can be reached only by adopting, for example, team-based forms of work organisation (Kinnie and Parsons, 2004; Swart and Kinnie, 2014). We explore these and other challenges emanating from this cross-boundary working in further detail below.

Box 2.1 HRM in practice   Tocris Cookson

Tocris Cookson, with 60 employees, is a specialist chemical company with experience in the synthesis of a wide variety of compounds. They employ teams of skilled chemists (mainly at post-doctoral level) and operate from one site in the UK and one site in the USA. HR practices in Tocris Cookson can be understood only in the context of the network in which they operate (see Figure 2.3 below).

Tocris Cookson's key clients are life science researchers at universities or other research institutes. In order to build these client relationships and make the compounds they need to maintain very strong ties with large pharmaceutical companies, patent lawyers and academics in the field. Pharmaceutical firms often have patents on some of the chemicals that need to be synthesised; however, these could lapse in an 8–10-year period. If a 'cool chemical is spotted' the patent rights need to be negotiated with the relevant firm. A senior manager in Tocris Cookson said, 'once our key to success was developing compounds, now it is building relationships'.

Relationships with universities also need to be maintained to:

(i) update employees' skills in the pharmacological discipline;
(ii) build client relationships, where the universities are often users of the compounds made;
(iii) build an external recruitment pool by making top performing research chemists aware of the business.

The process of building external relationships was regarded as 'an art' which could only be mastered over several years of experience: first as a doctoral chemist, then as a post-doctoral researcher and finally as a negotiator with major pharmaceutical firms.

Tocris Cookson recruits its employees during a post-doctoral placement at the company and this is often their first full-time employment. Managers regard this as a threat because of the majority of their workforce is young, highly qualified and mobile (single). The threat is managed through the strong organisational culture, which employees describe as a family or home away from home.

Most formalised HR practices originated from an elaborate HR policy, which was written by the part-time HR manager. The drive toward more formalised HR systems coincided with the company objective of 'becoming more corporate'. Within the set of formalised practices, performance management was central to other HR practices both practically, given its links to reward and development, and politically because it influenced the career development of this group of knowledge workers. Furthermore, the performance appraisal process was questioned by research chemists and there was a push to develop an in-house system because it is particularly difficult to appraise the outcome of research. This resulted in sets of HR practices evolving from formalised practices that may have originated outside the firm to sets of practices that grew from within the community of knowledge workers.

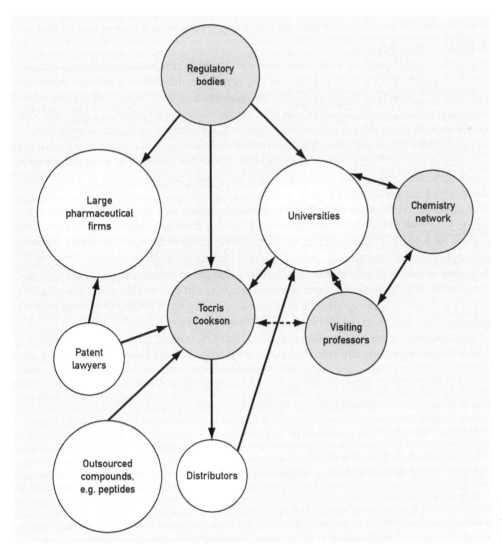

Figure 2.3
Tocris Cookson network

Labour markets are also important because firms in certain industries and geographical areas find they have to compete much more intensively than others. Tight labour markets, for example where call centres are concentrated, will put pressure on particular HR practices such as recruitment and selection and reward (Kinnie *et al.*, 2000).

Others argue that HR practices need to fit with and complement other important strategies and structures within the organisation. Organisational size will be important – larger firms will have complex internal structures often with multiple layers and more generally just the resources needed to fund certain approaches, for example a formalised salary structure or recruitment scheme. The manufacturing strategy of the firm also needs to be taken into account (Baron and Kreps, 1999; Boxall and Purcell, 2011: 83; Purcell, 1999).

The best fit approach has been subject to extensive review (see Boxall and Purcell, 2011: 71–85; Paauwe *et al.*, 2013c; Purcell, 1999: 32 for further details). Perhaps the most basic point of all is the assumption that firms have a competitive strategy with which HR practices can fit (Legge, 1995; Ramsay *et al.*, 2000). The second and related point is that it is possible to typify the firms in the way that has been suggested. Purcell (1999) suggests this is unlikely for a variety of reasons. In practice, organisations may pursue a mix of competitive strategies, for example seeking both cost leadership and differentiation, leading to confusion over the most appropriate HR practices. Even if the firm does have a strategy, this view assumes that the one they have is the most appropriate for them. This may not be the case if firms do not have sufficient knowledge of their external environment or if they have misinterpreted the information that they have gathered.

Multiple contingencies

Perhaps the biggest problem is that most firms exist within complex external environments with multiple contingencies that cannot all be isolated or identified. There are particular problems with modelling the influences, with understanding what happens if the influences do not all pull in the same direction and with coping with change (Purcell, 1999: 34). This raises the issue of the dynamic fit between policy and context: if the external environment changes should firms keep changing their practices to fit the market circumstances (Buller and McEvoy, 2012)? There are strong arguments against this because HR practices are quite slow to change. Consequently, Purcell (1999) has argued that firms seeking a best fit are effectively chasing a 'chimera'.

In response to criticisms of the best fit approach, Wright and Snell (1998) argue for the need to have both fit and flexibility (Boxall and Purcell, 2011: 84). This is not just the ability to move from one best fit to another, but to be able to adapt to the situation where the need to change is virtually continuous. 'Flexibility provides organisations with the ability to modify current practices in response to non-transient changes in the environment' (Wright and Snell, 1998: 757). In particular, there is a need to achieve fit between the HR system and the existing competitive strategy while at the same time achieving flexibility in a range of skills and behaviours needed to cope with changing competitive environments.

More broadly, there may be some characteristics of successful organisations that are impossible to model, usually referred to as idiosyncratic contingency or causal ambiguity (Purcell, 1999: 35). These are the patterns and routines of behaving or the cultural norms that have been built up slowly over a long period associated with success. It may simply not be possible to disentangle what exactly are the key factors in success when looking at a large complex organisation.

Treating employees differently

The need to respond to external pressures creates problems of treating employees with consistency of treatment especially over time (Baron and Kreps, 1999). In reality, it is likely that a combination of practices will be needed depending on external circumstances: as products grow and decline there may need to be redundancies for some employees but also the need to retain good employees and to develop them (Boxall and Purcell, 2011: 79–82).

In response to some of these criticisms we have seen the development of the HR architecture model (Lepak and Snell, 1999). This is based on the configurational view, which argues that it is unlikely that a company will use a single approach for all its employees (Becker and Huselid, 2011). It suggests that the best fit approach is too simple because there is a need to focus on combination or patterns of practices which are needed – putting horizontal fit together with vertical fit (Delery and Doty, 1996). Most organisations employ different groups of employees who will need to be treated differently and in effect there are different configurations of practices for different types of employees.

The Lepak and Snell model of HR architecture expresses these ideas in a more accessible form. They argue that,

> To date most strategic HRM researchers have tended to take a holistic view of employment and human capital, focusing on the extent to which a set of practices is used across all employees of a firm as well as the consistency of these practices across firms. We believe that the most appropriate mode of investment in human capital will vary for different types of capital. *(Lepak and Snell, 1999: 32; Lepak et al., 2011)*

Their model distinguishes between employees on the basis of the value they create for the organisation (the extent they contribute towards the creation of competitive advantage), and the extent to which their knowledge and skills are specific to that organisation (uniqueness).

This approach represents a step forward but also raises various questions. In particular, there is the issue of consistency here: if an employer wishes to pursue an inclusive culture-based approach why should they treat employees differently? If certain activities are externalised there is a danger that the core competences of an organisation will be lost. There is also a moral issue here – why should different groups be treated differently?

Purcell *et al.* (2009) has examined this is in a slightly different way looking at the attitudinal outcomes such as organisational commitment and job satisfaction for different occupational groups (see Box 2.2 for further details).

Box 2.2 HRM in practice   ### Influences on the attitudes of different occupational groups

Much of the research assumes that the set of HR practices adopted will have the same effect on all employees who work for the organisation. We investigated this, drawing on an analysis of data drawn from the *Workplace Employee Relations Survey, 2004* (Kersley, 2006). We found[4] (Purcell et al., 2009) that a different practice mix is associated with high levels of organisation commitment for different occupations. There are some practices (satisfaction with the work itself and with the level of managerial support) which seem to have a consistently positive influence on employee commitment across virtually all of the employee groups. However, there were other aspects of the work experience which were distinctively associated with particular work groups. Sales and customer service workers' commitment seemed to be closely tied to the flexibility of the job, whereas the role of line managers was unimportant. Pay satisfaction was important for skilled, personal service and elementary workers, while teamwork was important only for the commitment of skilled and personal service employees. The role of line managers was important for all employees other than sales and customer service work. Variables for job stress, career opportunities, job involvement and training were not associated with employee commitment. Further details of the most important HR practices for each group are given

---

[4]We focused on the largest occupational group in each workplace.

below (the shaded areas indicate that there are negative correlations between the HR practice and employee commitment).

Lower skill employees: elementary
Satisfaction with work itself
Satisfaction with pay
Trust managers

Lower skill employees: operatives
Expect long-term employment
Satisfaction with achievement
Relationships with managers
Job security
Satisfaction with work itself
Trust managers
Zero hours
Job sharing
Payment By Results
Selection by performance tests

Sales
Zero hours
Satisfaction with work itself
Able to reduce FT to PT hours
Job security guarantee

Skilled workers
Zero hours contracts
Satisfaction with achievement
Satisfaction with pay
Satisfaction with work itself
Teamworking
Job challenge
Trust managers
Able to work term-time only

Five days training
Satisfaction with job security
Employee unease

Professionals
Ability to change work patterns
Select via performance tests
Satisfaction with work itself
Satisfaction scope to use initiative
Trust managers
Ability to work same hours
Zero hours contracts

HRM models that fit network characteristics

As we have discussed, the development of networked ways of working poses significant and novel problems when seeking to develop a best fit. The issue of 'fit with what?' looms large in this context or put differently we need to ask how best we can understand contemporary work contexts or what is the most appropriate unit of analysis? Swart and Kinnie (2014) focus on the boundaries of work activity (Kogut and Zander, 1996) to distinguish between three types of networked working which vary according to: (i) the properties of the boundaries, (ii) the focal point of work activity and (iii) the prominent identification. These three types are: interaction (where firms interact with clients and partners but protect their firm-specific skills); interwoven (where firms collaborate in a limited way to produce network outputs) and integrated (where there is profound and sophisticated inter-firm cooperation to focus on network level outputs). Inherent in each network type is a series of structural, relational and knowledge-based tensions that exist between the network and the firms and between the firm and its employees (Donnelly, 2009, 2011; Purcell *et al.*, 2009; Phelps, 2012). Following this they developed a typology of HRM models that exist within a networked context which are used to manage the challenges associated with each network type. The first type involves buffering employees from the network by developing organisation-centric practices. These firms seek to leverage a strong set of organisational values and culture which form the foundation of the portfolio of HR practices. The example of Mother (see Case study 2.1) provides excellent insights into the way in which this is achieved. A second approach involves borrowing from the network where HR practices mainly exist at the organisation level with some practices, such as resourcing, operating at the level of, for example, an integrated project team. In order to achieve both network- and firm-level objectives professionals from individual firms, such as engineers, independent contractors and regulators, often collaborate in a network where they work as an integrated project team. One such example is where defence contractors may collaborate to build a new warship. The individual partners may work together on a shared physical site and will often share domain knowledge, such as naval engineering. The nature of this networked way of working often requires long-term commitment to the integrated project team. The advantage for the individual firm is that their employees will gain exposure to cutting-edge industry knowledge which could then be integrated into the firms. The danger is, however, that the integrated project team becomes a focal point for the professionals and their knowledge consequently becomes so specialised that it cannot be leveraged within their employing organisations. The final approach is referred to as balancing the network where there is a strong emphasis on developing network level HR practices. The professionals from the various firms will work together so closely that a separate, partly virtual, organisation will be established to direct their interaction. The Marks and Spencer case study (see Case study 2.3) provides a good example of this kind of networked activity where a series of management structures and HR practices were developed to hold the network together. Individuals would therefore identify with their employing organisation, but would also hold a very strong identification with the separate networked organisation. In this context, the cross-boundary team represents an organisation in its own right and would have sets of HR practices that exist at the level of the network and therefore ensures the sustainability of the cross-boundary organisation. The advantage of this advanced form of networking is the efficiency and the 'ease' of collaboration which it facilitates via the shared identity established. The risk is that employees may seek employment opportunities with other collaborators in the network. This may lead to a loss of human capital for the employing firm.

In summary, we have considered the best practice and best fit approaches towards the generation of human resource advantage and examined the criticisms which have been made of these. It is possible, however, that these approaches can be reconciled. Boxall and Purcell (2011: 95–6) conclude that some general principles can be established, for example on selection interviewing, but that practices themselves are likely to be influenced by best fit considerations at national, network and organisational levels. This combination of views remains, however, incomplete because it is still looking only at the formal practices and we now need to consider how these practices are actually used.

Organisational process advantage

The key theme running throughout our discussion has been that the acquisition of HR advantage depends on developing both a capital and a process advantage (Purcell, 1999: 36; Boxall and Purcell, 2011: 17). We need to therefore understand how HR practices are actually translated into operation before we can begin to thoroughly understand the links between HR and performance (Guest and Bos-Nehles, 2013; Wright and Nishii, 2013). It is important to look at the routines and processes, or using another language, both the formal and informal practices which make up the day-to-day realities of organisational life.

Studying OPA is much more difficult than looking at practices because these processes are often tacit and intangible; they are immune to data collection by postal questionnaire and analysis by sophisticated statistical packages. In fact, OPA is only seen most clearly when it is absent, when things go wrong: there is infighting between departments, poor knowledge sharing within and between project teams or people do not work to their full potential. The concept of OPA is derived from research carried out into the resource-based view (RBV) of strategy.

Resource-based view

This draws attention to the intangible assets of the firm which make up its distinctive competencies and organisational routines (Purcell, 1999: 35). The RBV has developed from business strategy literature that competitive advantage is based on what is difficult to imitate not on what can be copied. There is a need to develop an exclusive form of fit. This is particularly important for knowledge intensive firms that rely almost entirely on their human and intellectual capital for their success and is effectively rebalancing an over dependence on the Porter approach (Boxall and Purcell, 2011: 97–100). It also emphasises the importance of know-how-in-action (Swart, 2011) of human capital as a resource and re-introduces the human aspect of human resource strategy (Wright and McMahan, 2011).

The RBV involves looking at the internal resources of the firm and considering the ways in which HR can maximise their contribution to development of competitive advantage. This focuses on how human resources can become scarce, organisation specific and difficult to imitate (Barney, 1991; Barney and Wright, 1998) and draws on the research into core competencies (Hamel and Prahalad, 1994).

In particular, this view involves looking at how HR can develop the following (Barney and Wright, 1998; Golding, 2004: 51):

Value – how does the firm seek to distinguish itself from its competitors? What part does HR play in this?

Rarity – is the firm doing something with its employees that its competitors are not?

Inimitable – casual ambiguity means that the unique history of each firm makes it difficult to ascertain what causes the advantage and therefore makes it difficult to copy.

Non-substitutability – these internal resources are integrated into coherent systems so advantage is sustainable and cannot be substituted by other resources.

Research into the resource-based view tends to be associated with unpredictable environments and emphasises what is distinctive. However, we need to remember that firms also need to have the base line characteristics right before developing distinctive characteristics, what Hamel and Prahalad (1994) and Boxall (1996) refer to as 'table stakes', the resources and skills needed simply to play the game. Once these have been established it is the differences between firms which are important. Truss (2001) notes one of the problems with the RBV is its emphasis on the importance of synergy and fit between the various elements of the HR system and asks how compatible a systems-based approach is with flexibility (Becker and Gerhart, 1996: 789).

Becker and Huselid (2006: 901) note, however, that 'the attention given to the independent influence of "implementation" in the strategy literature offers an opportunity to make the theoretical HR-performance link more concrete'. Indeed, they recall that Barney (2001: 54) notes that 'the ability to implement strategies is by itself a resource that can be a source of competitive advantage'. This also relates to the original conceptualisation of the RBV which emphasises the importance of managerial enactment and decision making.

If we are to examine the implementation issues in the HR context we need to consider what has come to be known as the 'black box' research.

Application to HR: examining the 'black box'

Becker and Gerhart (1996: 793) noted the importance of examining the implementation of HR practices when they argued that 'future work on the strategic perspective must elaborate on the black box between a firm's HR systems and the firm's bottom line'. Moreover, 'more effort should be devolved to finding out what managers are thinking and why they make the decisions they do' (1996: 794). This suggests we need to understand how and why HR practices influence performance and to move away from basic input–output models which have policy inputs on the left-hand side of the model and outcomes on the right-hand side (Becker and Huselid, 2006; Wright and Nishii, 2013).

When we begin to look inside the 'black box' we find that there are differences between the espoused practices and the practices in use (Elorza *et al.*, 2011). Truss (2001) highlights the importance of the informal processes that exist alongside the formal practices drawing on her research in Hewlett Packard. There were clear gaps between what the company claimed they were doing and what was actually experienced by employees 'in areas such as appraisals and training and development the results obtained were not uniformly excellent; in fact some were highly contradictory' (Truss, 2001: 1143). Although the formal HP appraisal procedures rewarded employees' performance against targets related to the company's objectives 'informally what counted was visibility and networking if people wanted to further their careers' (Truss, 2001: 1144). Despite espousing the value of training fewer than half said they got the training they needed to do their job, fewer than half felt the appraisal system was working well and fewer than one third felt their pay was fair. 'These are all examples of a strong disconnect between the "rhetoric" of human resource management as expressed by the human resource department, and the reality as experienced by employees' (Truss, 2001: 1143). This 'highlights the importance of the informal organisation as mediator between policy and the individual' (Truss, 2001: 1144).

Similarly, a study of 12 organisations where there was a clear gap between formal HR policy statements and actual practice in areas such as performance appraisals, training, involvement and communication (Purcell *et al.*, 2003; 2009). For example, in organisations which claimed to have formal employee involvement schemes (such as team briefs) for all their employees, not all staff were aware of the existence of these initiatives and an even lower proportion of employees claimed to have been practically involved in such schemes (Hutchinson and Purcell, 2003: 36).

Research into formal and informal practices (Brown, 1972, 1973; Terry, 1977) has a long tradition in the industrial relations literature and sheds important light on contemporary concerns about the key processes involved. This makes a focus solely on formal practices inappropriate, and in particular we need to consider the role of the 'individual manager as agent, choosing to focus his or her attention in varying ways' (Truss, 2001: 1145). We consider this by looking at discretionary behaviour. However, we first need to examine the role of employees when engaging in discretionary behaviour.

Employee discretionary behaviour

The importance of employee discretionary behaviour has been highlighted by research in the US steel, clothing and medical equipment industries (Appelbaum *et al.*, 2000). Drawing evidence from shop floor employees and managers as well as a study of formal HR practices, Appelbaum and her colleagues found that the willingness of employees to engage in discretionary behaviour depended on the creation of opportunities to participate, skill development and motivation and incentives (Appelbaum *et al.*, 2000: 118–20).

Their most important finding was that the positive effects of HPWS on plant performance were felt through increased discretionary effort by employees and an improved knowledge accumulation. These practices had a different effect on performance in different industries (Appelbaum *et al.*, 2000: 227). In steel, there was evidence that quality and employment security raised 'up time' by 8 per cent, incentives by 13 per cent and work organisation by 14 per cent and HPWS as a whole by 17 per cent (Appelbaum *et al.*, 2000: 108). In clothing, modular production involving self-directed teams reduced sewing time by 94 per cent and led to substantial cost savings. In medical equipment, the opportunity to participate is closely linked to value added per dollar and profits and quality (Appelbaum *et al.*, 2000: 108). The likelihood of employees engaging in this discretionary behaviour is also influenced by the role of line managers.

Role of line managers in bringing practices to life

Recent research has examined the research looking at implementation drawing attention to the stages of implementation, the roles of different managers from senior executives to line managers (Guest and Bos-Nehles, 2013) and the need for multiple levels of analysis (Wright and Nishii, 2013). Most research has, however, examined the role of line managers and how the discretionary behaviour of these managers, especially first line managers, contributes towards the development, or absence, of an organisational process advantage.

Over the last decade numerous studies have observed how line managers have played a more prominent role in the delivery of HR practices such as performance management, team leadership and communications as an increasing number of people management activities have been devolved to them (Hutchinson and Wood, 1995; Larson and Brewster, 2003; Renwick, 2000). The important role of line managers has been identified by Marchington and Wilkinson (2002: 232–7) and earlier work on the 'forgotten supervisor' (Child and Partridge, 1982; Thurley and Wirdenius, 1973) and the role of the line manager in the emergence of informal practices (Armstrong and Goodman, 1979; Brown, 1972, 1973; Terry, 1977).

Recent studies (Guest and Bos-Nehles, 2013; Purcell and Hutchinson, 2007; Purcell *et al.*, 2003, 2009; Wright and Nishii, 2013) show that the way line managers implement and enact HR practices by 'bringing them to life' and show leadership strongly influences employees' attitudes. Employees' perceptions of line management behaviour (in terms of how they carry out their HR activities such as responding to suggestions from employees) was the most important factor in explaining variations in both job satisfaction and job discretion – or the choice people have over how they do their jobs. There is also evidence that a pattern can be traced between line manager activities, employee attitudes and the performance of comparable business units and in changes over time.

Bartel (2000) examined these issues in the banking industry in Canada and found that when controlling for environment and branch and managerial effects that the HR environment (as measured by the quality of feedback and communications) has a significant positive effect on loan sales. Although there were common HR practices, it was clear that there was discretion over how these were applied. One standard deviation increase in managerial effectiveness accounts for a 16–26 per cent increase in loan sales. Thus the discretion exercised by branch managers has a direct effect on performance through the education and motivation of branch staff.

These differences between 'espoused' and 'enacted' practices can be partly attributed to the line manager for a variety of reasons (Hutchinson and Purcell, 2003; Marchington, 2001; McGovern *et al.*, 1997; Purcell and Hutchinson, 2007). Line managers may suffer from work overload partly because of organisational restructuring and the demise of the middle manager and simply lack the time to carry out all their duties. They may have inadequate training on how to operate the practices, lack commitment to them (Marchington, 2001), be doubtful about the claimed benefits or simply be ignorant of what is expected of them.

In an attempt to analyse this role, Purcell *et al.* (2009) develop a model which places the discretionary behaviour exercised by line managers at the centre of the analysis, as shown in Box 2.3 and Figure 2.4. In particular, it sees the link between HR practices and performance as being the interaction between line manager behaviour and employee attitudes and behaviour. Line managers are important because of the key role they play in the generation of operational process advantage: most employees experience work through their contacts with their immediate team and their team leader.

The key role played by line managers opens up further lines of inquiry concerning how these line managers are themselves managed. Research (Hutchinson and Purcell, 2003) suggests that the key factors influencing line managers' commitment and job satisfaction and their willingness to engage in discretionary behaviour are their relationships with their line managers and the existence of career opportunities. In addition, work–life balance, the ability to discuss problems with their managers and job security are associated with organisational commitment, while involvement is linked with job satisfaction (Hutchinson and Purcell, 2003: 48; Hutchinson and Purcell, 2007).

More broadly, this suggests that the values and culture of the organisation can be a form of organisational process advantage. There are positive links between this form of OPA and organisational commitment; for example, employees in firms which exhibit 'strong values' or who have a clear, well established Big Idea have higher levels of commitment compared to employees in firms without these strong values (Purcell *et al.*, 2003; 2009). Box 2.4 provides more details of this. This supports the argument made by Barney (1986: 656) some

> ## Box 2.3 HRM in practice   HR causal chain model
>
> Many attempts to link HR policy and performance pay insufficient attention to the linking mechanisms. We draw on the work of Appelbaum *et al.* (2000), MacDuffie (1995) and Wright and Nishii (2004) to identify the key causal steps in the chain from intended HR practices to performance outcomes (Purcell *et al.*, 2009).
>
> The model has the following key features:
>
> - *Intended HR practices* are those designed by senior management to be applied to most or all of the employees and concern employees' ability, motivation and opportunity to participate. These practices will be influenced by the articulated values of the organisation and found in the HR manual or the appropriate web pages. These also include the ways work is structured and organised since this has an impact on employee attitudes and behaviour.
> - *Actual HR practices* are those which are actually applied, usually by line managers. There may often be a substantial difference between the espousal and the enactment of HR practices in an organisation (Hutchinson and Purcell, 2003).
> - *Experienced HR practices* require that attention is focused on how employees experience and then judge the HR practices that are applied to them. What they perceive may be different, or the same, as intended and may be judged through a lens of fairness and organisational justice.
> - *Attitudinal outcomes* include attitudes employees hold towards their job, and their employer and/or levels of morale or motivation. This especially includes employees' willingness to cooperate and their overall satisfaction with their job.
> - *Behavioural outcomes* flow in the main from these attitudinal dimensions. This can be learning new methods of working, engaging in behaviour which is beyond that required, such as organisational citizenship behaviour (OCB) (Coyle-Shapiro *et al.*, 2004), or seen in levels of attendance and remaining in the job (or their opposites).
> - *Performance outcomes* can be distal or proximal and can be restricted to short-term definitions of performance or can be expanded to include measures of effectiveness.
>
> More precisely the model draws attention to:
>
> - the need to distinguish between intended HR and actual HR practices as experienced by employees;
> - the key role played by line managers in the interpretation and implementation of HR practices;
> - the link between experienced practices and employee attitudes and behaviours;
> - the choice of performance measures that have meaning and significance for the companies and are close to the employee attitudinal data;
> - the importance of organisational culture.

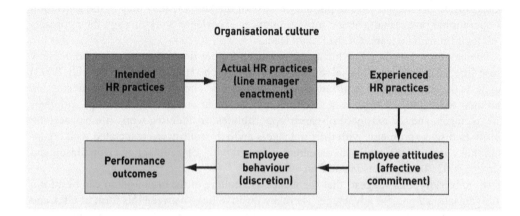

Figure 2.4
HR causal chain model
Source: Purcell *et al.*, 2009.

time ago that 'Firms with sustained superior ... performances typically are characterised by a strong set of core managerial values that define the way they conduct business.' More recent research (Alfes *et al.*, 2012) has built on this by exploring the role of trust in explaining the links between HR practices and performance. This research found that trust in the

Box 2.4 HRM in practice   The Big Idea

In some companies it is not just the senior managers but also employees at all levels who identify strongly with the values and mission of the organisation. We came to call this 'the Big Idea' since it seemed there was something simple or easy to explain that captured the essence of the firm and clearly informed or enthused HR policy and practice. The essence of this is:

'A clear sense of mission underpinned by values and a culture expressing what the firm is and its relationship with its customers and employees.'

The Big Idea had a number of attributes:

- **Embedded** – it was embedded throughout the organisation, for example quality in Jaguar.
- **Connected** – it connected, and derived from the same root, the way customers were treated and employees managed, for example, mutuality in Nationwide.
- **Enduring** – it was enduring, not a flash in the pan, not the product of a board discussion on an away day and had clear historical roots, for example a long standing commitment to 'have fun and make money' in AIT.
- **Collective** – it was encapsulated in routines about the way work was done and people behaved. In that sense it was collective, combining people in processes and routines in the sense of a taken for granted, everyday activity as seen in Nationwide.
- **Measured and managed** – it was measured and managed often using broad measures of performance as we found in Selfridges.

Source: Purcell et al., 2009.

employer has an important moderating effect in the links between perceived HR practices, task performance, turnover intentions and individual well-being. Similarly, Yalabik *et al.* (2013) found that work engagement was a mediator between affective employee commitment, job performance and intention to quit.

 Conclusions and implications

We have examined research into the links between HR and performance using the concept of HR advantage. This has highlighted the importance of gaining both a human capital and an organisational process advantage. Our discussion has implications for method, theory and practice.

The methodological debates referred to here are likely to continue. The approach based on the sophisticated analysis of quantitative data collected by questionnaires is likely to remain popular, especially where it is supported by a wider research tradition and higher education infrastructure as in the US. However, the implication of this discussion is that this approach is unlikely to gain insights into the organisational processes that are clearly crucial to successful organisations. Indeed, Becker and Huselid (2006: 915) argue that,

A clearer articulation of the 'black box' between HR and firm performance is the most pressing theoretical and empirical challenge in the SHRM literature. This requires a new emphasis on integrating strategy implementation as the central mediating variable in the HR-performance relationship.

These critical processes and routines can only be effectively examined by means of the case study approach. The case study need not be a single organisation, indeed, in some circumstances the most appropriate unit of analysis is the series of activities which take place within an inter-organisational network. However, the problems of generalisability of case study findings will remain. One possible way forward is the collection of a combination of quantitative and qualitative data perhaps within a restricted number of industries (Paauwe, 2009).

A whole series of theoretical issues are thrown up by our discussion. Perhaps the most basic issues of all revolve around questions such as: What do we mean by performance? Whose performance? How do we measure this? Delaney and Godard (2001) have argued it is time for the research to move outside the narrow confines of financial performance. Not only should the narrow measures of organisational performance be broadened but also concern should be given to wider measures such as employee well-being. This also points to the need to move away from the assumption that all employees are treated in the same way. Becker and Huselid (2006: 908) argue that research needs to focus on the level of the business process because this is where strategic value is created, not at the level of the firm. This business process may exist across organisational boundaries at the level of the network posing significant further challenges. This, in turn, means greater attention needs to be given to the differentiation of HR practices to support these business processes which again take us back to the importance of implementation since 'Designing an HR system with greater differentiation is not the problem. The challenge is motivating line managers to implement these systems' (Becker and Huselid, 2006: 919).

We also need to explore the concept of HR advantage in more detail, particularly the sources of organisational process advantage or disadvantage. We need to understand more clearly why gaps between espoused and operational policy emerge and what the consequences of this are for all parties. If line managers are critical to this, we need to know more about how they are managed and what factors influence their attitudes and behaviour. This raises the much broader issue of widening the focus of study away from human resource management to people management (Purcell and Kinnie, 2007: 543). From the tendency to study formal HR practices to a range of factors that impinge directly on the employee experience of work and which trigger discretionary behaviour. This would include the role of line managers in the operation of policy, the cultural context and work organisation and job design.

The emergence of networked based ways of working brings about its own theoretical challenges. Much of the research so far has examined the forms of human, social and organisational capital within the confines of the organisation (Swart and Kinnie, 2013). However, given that that networked based ways of working are the predominant way of working for some organisations, we have to reframe our research focus. In particular, we need to work to identify the forms of human and social capital that are needed to support the achievement of network based rather than merely organisation based objectives (Swart and Kinnie, 2014).

The policy and practice implications of our discussion are profound. The 'best fit–best practice' debate has largely been sidelined by the realisation that both fit and flexibility are needed. The most likely way of getting this is by employing staff who carry out the HR practices most closely to the way that they were intended. More generally, the implication is that simply developing the appropriate practices is not in itself going to be enough because HR advantage also depends on how these practices are implemented. Looking for a link between HR practices and performance is a misguided activity because the main focus needs to be on the links between policy, practices, processes, implementation and performance. As ever, these processes are dependent on the skills of managers in actually implementing practices. This is difficult enough where traditional authority based relationships exist but is even more challenging in a networked environment where managerial influence is exerted horizontally rather than vertically.

This focus on process has potential benefits for HR specialists because these processes have to be carefully developed internally and cannot simply be copied from a textbook in the way that practices might be. Here the HR practitioner role becomes key because the development of what we might call 'best processes' can become a core competence which is embedded within the thinking and acting of the organisation such that it cannot be imitated or outsourced.

CASE STUDY 2.1

MOTHER LONDON

NICHOLAS KINNIE AND LOUISE HOPPER[5]

Background

Mother London is a creative organisation employing around 280 people and part of Mother Holdings, which has 20 companies with around 700 people including freelancers. Established in 1996, Mother works with around 40 clients, including a number of high-profile brands. It is independently owned by its seven partners who include the three founding partners. Mother's main outputs are producing commercials for television, and cinema as well experience events and some online output. Not experienced an experience event is the actual term – highly participative marketing events. It has also developed creative ideas in addition to traditional advertising including an award winning feature film, graphic novels and various 'house projects' such as the 'uncarriable carrier bags'. It has an extremely high reputation for its creative output and was recently voted Agency of the Decade by *Campaign* magazine.

Core principles

Mother is characterised by a series of core principles which reflect the beliefs of its founders and have a profound effect on how it is managed and structured and the relationships it has with its employees and clients.

Quality of creative output

Creativity is the essence of Mother. The quality of the creative output is at the heart of everything that Mother produces. In the words of one of the founding partners, 'it's what comes out of the door that matters' while another senior manager said 'Mother stands for creativity'. Since its foundation, Mother has become the destination brand for creative people who are attracted by the opportunity to work alongside people who have a high reputation for creativity and to work with well-known clients.

Holy Trinity of values

This emphasis on the quality of output is reflected in what is referred to as the 'Holy Trinity' within Mother – essentially a statement of values which underpins how they work. It is these values which set their priorities and drive their relationships with employees and clients. These values are:

- Produce high quality creative output;
- Have fun;
- Make money.

Ways of organising

Mother have a distinct way of organising and working with clients which is unlike other creative and advertising agencies. In many other agencies there will be a group of staff known as Account Handlers or Client Services (sometimes referred to as the 'suits') which act as the 'go-between' between the creative staff (the T-shirts) and the client representatives. Mother has dispensed with this group preferring that their creative staff, their strategists and their producers have direct contact with clients.

Ways of working

Mother is characterised by a highly collaborative style of working which involves both specialists and non-specialists being involved in the creative process. In particular, there is a high degree of flexibility and permeability between the various skill groups. Staff often perform multiple roles and will move frequently between different teams. Moreover, a problem-solving approach is adopted which often involves multiple solutions being developed of which one is selected.

Joint ownership of creativity

In an industry which is often accused of pandering to the highly individualistic prima donnas who build personal portfolios at the expense of others, Mother promotes joint ownership of creative output. Rewards and recognition are attributed to Mother collectively rather than to individuals.

Brand teams

The brand teams are at the heart of the creative process and are responsible for running campaigns and managing relationships with clients. These teams are

[5]Group Head of HR, Mother Holdings Ltd.

dedicated to a particular client, brand or campaign and are typically composed of (see Figure 2.5):

- **Creatives** – these include copywriters, art directors and Creative Directors;
- **Strategists** – who are responsible for the development of strategy;
- **'Mothers'** – who coordinate the team activities;
- **'Nannies'** – who manage the relationships and logistics of the team.

These Brand Teams then work with a series of internal and external parties in order to produce work for clients. These include the television editing suite, Finance, HR and Office Management, each of which has a Discipline Head, and with a whole set of external television producers.

However, it is the way Mother works with clients which is particularly distinctive. Members of the brand teams work alongside the client representatives to focus on the problem; they see the client as part of the solution to the shared problem rather than the problem. In the words of one senior manager 'our way of working is designed to work *with* the client rather than *for* the client … agencies are often seen to be at the beck and call of clients, whereas we are not afraid to turn around and say no'.

Forms of capital

We can consider the key resources, or forms of capital, upon which Mother draws to develop its creative output. In particular, we can consider their human, social and organisational capital.

Human capital

The core principles of Mother mean that they are completely reliant upon the quality of their human capital for their success, indeed they can be said to adopt a 'talent- or people-centric approach'. The staff themselves have very high reputations in the industry built up over many years and they are highly skilled and experienced. They tend to employ staff who have gained some experience elsewhere and are attracted to work at Mother because of the people who already work there. In the words of one senior manager, 'they need to have a passion for creativity, they need to be inquisitive, be up for a challenge, have an edge about them and a conviction about what they do'. However, they also need to be 'tenacious and get stuff done. They need to be right and left brain people. And although they need to be ambitious – they also need to have humility.'

Social capital

The core principles and especially the 'Holy Trinity' of values mean that the culture of the organisation plays a key part in Mother's success. The fit with the organisation culture, which gives priority to creativity, is absolutely essential; in essence this commitment is the glue that holds Mother together. Without this it would be impossible to convert the knowledge, skills and experience of its staff into valuable client outputs. The result is a high level of emotional attachment to the work produced.

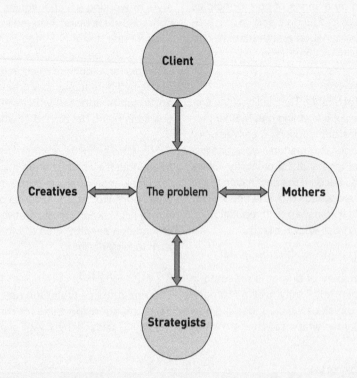

Figure 2.5 Ways of working with clients

Organisational capital

The structures, procedures and processes also reflect the core principles of Mother. The organisation structure itself is relatively flat with only three levels, but more importantly there is a high level of interaction between the partners and more junior staff. One distinctive characteristic is the way in which staff is physically located. Not only is the work space open plan but many staff are not physically located within what in a more traditional organisation would be their function or department. The Head of HR is just as likely to be sitting next to a Creative as someone from Finance. Moreover, staff is rotated between their allocated spaces every eight weeks to allow a wide range of relationships to be formed and contribute to the development of social capital.

People management practices

People management responsibilities are shared between three groups of staff: Discipline Heads; the HR team and the Partners. These practices make a direct contribution to the success of Mother.

Resourcing

External recruitment is mostly in the hands of each Head of Discipline who work with the Partners to identify suitable staff. Although some use is made of agencies, most newcomers are recruited through the extensive personal networks of senior staff. The selection process involves the Heads of Discipline and the Partners with most emphasis placed on the applicant's portfolio of work. A cultural fit is also extremely important and considered when hiring. The HR team deal with the unsolicited applications and internships.

The internal allocation of creative staff is made by the Head of Creative Resource in collaboration with the Partners. The task here is to balance the needs of the employees for interesting and challenging work and the clients who want to work with the best possible staff. Senior staff is very aware of the risk of their best staff being poached by competitors.

Training and development

There is a mix of formal and more informal training opportunities. Although a budget is set aside for formal training for each employee there are no formal, routine training programmes. Instead, bespoke training is arranged for employees as needed. Much more emphasis is placed on the opportunity for relatively junior staff to work alongside much more senior staff. Employees learn by working with other experienced people, by being challenged by new creative tasks and from clients. In particular, great care is taken to identify the training and development needs of individual staff. One of the resource managers said, 'I take great care to find out what they want to do, what are their aspirations, do they want to write a book or a blog?'

Performance management and rewards

There is an annual system for appraising performance to be carried out by the line managers. This meeting involves discussion of the previous year's performance and changes to the reward package. However, any changes in salary have to be approved by one of the Partners. The benefits package is very strong with very good provision for insurance and time off.

Questions for discussion

1 In what ways have the different forms of capital contributed to the success of Mother?

2 Explain the role of people management practices in supporting these forms of capital.

3 What risks and problems might Mother encounter in the future in the people management area and how might these be overcome?

CASE STUDY 2.2

ALEXANDER MANN SOLUTIONS

NICHOLAS KINNIE AND RUTH SMYTH[6]

Background

Alexander Mann Solutions (AMS) provides Recruitment Process Outsourcing (RPO) and consultancy services to 45 major clients. They were the first to introduce the concept of RPO in 1996 and are now the leading global provider of these services employing approximately 1,500 people. They have won a series of awards over the years, most recently the HROA Baker's Dozen Customer Satisfaction Award.

Mission and structure

AMS provides talent and resourcing capability for organisations, based on the shared belief that people are the foundation for success. They deliver this through innovative and measurable outsourcing and consulting services. In practice, the services provided can be grouped into three areas:

- Outsourced recruitment and selection services;
- Management of internal resourcing and contingent workforces;
- Consulting advice in areas such as employer branding, external and internal resourcing, talent management, executive search and outplacement and redeployment.

They provide these services to clients in various sectors including: Investment Banking, Retail Banking & Financial Services, Consulting Services, IT & Telco, Healthcare, Defence & Engineering and FMCG. The geographical breakdown of numbers of employees is as follows:

Table 2.1 Geographical location of employees

Region	Number of Employees
UK	800
Continental Europe (excluding the UK)	470
Asia–Pacific	180
Americas	50

Employees are located on one of four sites (see Figure 2.6):

- Client sites providing day-to-day recruitment and selection services, where about 40 per cent of their employees are located;
- Global Services Centres (in Krakow, UK, Manila and Cleveland, OH) providing extensive back-office services such as security checks and organising interview schedules and assessment centres (15 per cent of the workforce);
- Regional Offices providing recruitment and selection services to clients (39 per cent of the workforce);
- UK office central functions including HR, resourcing, finance, commercial, legal, marketing facilities and technology (6 per cent of the workforce).

A very high proportion of AMS staff is therefore working for clients either directly or indirectly. AMS employees based on client sites are working alongside client staff on a daily basis and are surrounded by their branding. One client-based senior manager said, *'You are pretty much totally immersed with the client. Everything about your employment, bar your pay packet, is client-focused, your business card, your laptop, your client office. My contact with the world outside of (the client) is minimal.'* The risk here is that AMS employees may become more committed to their client than to their employer. Indeed, in some instances AMS can seem very remote and abstract.

Role types

The following roles are typically found within each of the client teams:

- **Head of Client Services** – has overall responsibility for relationships and delivery of all resourcing services to one or more clients;
- **Manager** – is responsible for the day-to-day management of the client relationship and service delivery;
- **Principal Specialist** – responsible for delivering day-to-day services to hiring managers and dealing with candidates;

---

[6]Head of HR, Alexander Mann Solutions.

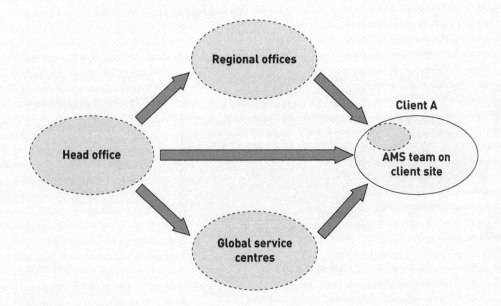

Figure 2.6 Alexander Mann Solutions – location of staff

- **Specialist** – is involved in the day-to-day resourcing activities for the client;
- **Administrator/Coordinator** – provides back-up and support to the Specialist and Principal Specialists.

Client teams can vary in size from over 100 people for a large account to just two or three for a smaller one.

People Strategy

The People Strategy seeks to make the employee value proposition of 'inspiring people' a reality for all employees. In particular, the People Capital specialists aim to support the AMS vision and mission by driving business transformation and delivering operational excellence through the provision of innovative global programmes. In particular, the key priorities are to create a high-performance culture within AMS by:

- Creating a positive and inclusive environment;
- Strengthening the leadership capability;
- Identifying and nurturing talent;
- Rewarding achievement and delivering high performance;
- Making a positive difference to global and local communities;
- Ensuring flexibility and choice.

People capital structure

There is a global team, based in six territories (UK, US, Australia, Poland, Philippines, China) of approximately 20 HR and training professionals (see Figure 2.7). The HR Business Partner (HRBP) model is adopted, with the HRBP providing specific sector or geography specific support, who are in turn supported by an HR operations team (administration, technology, reporting, etc.), as shown below. Most of the Operations support is provided from Poland and the Philippines.

Particular emphasis is given to the professional development of AMS employees. Indeed, the firm facilitates professional development by encouraging employees to move between different clients on a regular basis – typically after two years with a client. This is designed to allow employees to learn new skills, acquire knowledge about a range of sectors and add well-known brands to their CV. One client manager said, *'without ever having to jump into another organisation I am getting the exposure and contacts, and just working with clients in different industries is quite rare'.* Another more junior client-based employee said, *'I have had variety...you might work on something for 6 months and then it is something else, you always feel as if you are doing something a bit different.'* While a team manager commented that *'There is always the*

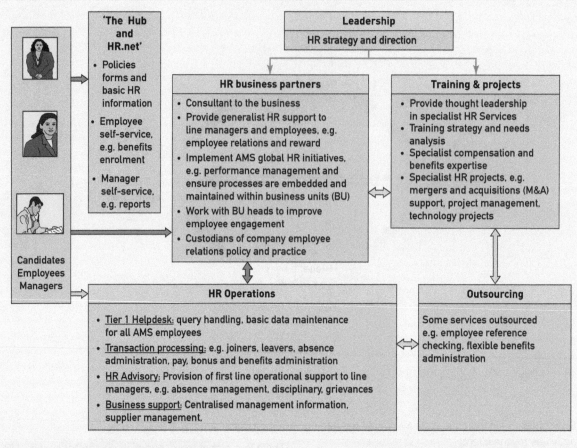

Figure 2.7 People capital structure in AMS

opportunity to take yourself off one client site and go and work another site, so that was always a big draw for me, the fact that I am part of a bigger organisation that has other opportunities.'

This also has benefits for clients because they have the benefit of staff that has a range of experiences upon which they can draw, and the staff themselves have a network of talent that they can consult if a difficult problem emerges.

Research into employee attitudes

AMS has carried out a series of surveys in order to improve their understanding of employee attitudes and behaviours. These surveys (known as Pulsepoint) have formed the basis for the development of an action plan setting targets to be achieved before the next survey.

Findings from the first survey

There were key findings in the areas of employee commitment and professional and career development.

Employee commitment

There were two important findings. First, it was found that employee commitment was positively related to

willingness to stay in the organisation. Second, the organisational commitment of employees on client sites was lower than that elsewhere.

Professional and career development

The key findings were that the satisfaction of professional development needs within the organisation was positively related to willingness to stay and managers with three to four years of experience have unmet training and development needs.

Subsequent actions that were taken and their outcomes

A series of actions were taken to improve employee commitment, communications and involvement and professional development opportunities.

Employee commitment, communications and involvement

A series of actions were taken to improve employee commitment including: first, a substantial enhancement of the corporate induction process to improve the frequency and content of the programme; second, the introduction of the knowledge exchange, an online repository of people and organisational information and finally, improved guidance to senior managers when managing communications.

In addition, various actions were taken to improve communications with and involvement opportunities for employees. This included members of the Leadership Team visiting over 400 employees on client sites in 2010; extensive in-house communications regarding AMS achievements including the Pulsepoint results through *The Point*, a hard copy in-house magazine, and CheckPoint, which involved making leadership team video webcasts available to all employees and the initiation of the Global Inspiring Teamwork award. Furthermore, all members of the Leadership Team are now measured on the results from the Pulsepoint surveys, and Heads of Client Services have to develop action plans in collaboration with the people capital team to address areas of concern ensuring a high level buy-in to these issues.

Impact of these changes

These changes contributed to a number of improvements in employee attitudes and behaviours. First, there were important changes in employee attitudes. Employee commitment (scale 1–7) increased from 4.93 (2009) to 5.27 (2011), an 8 per cent improvement and employees' intention to quit reduced from 3.20 (2009) to 2.94 (2011) an 11 per cent reduction. This contributed towards a reduction in employee turnover leading to substantial cost savings.

In terms of organisational performance more generally, there has been a substantial growth of the business following the successful acquisition of two major clients and one major client re-signing. In addition, there has been a significant increase in employment with over 500 permanent hires in 2010 and an additional 220 new employees taken on between September 2010 and February 2011. These changes also contributed to the winning of two awards: the Baker's Dozen – the main accreditation award for RPO outsourcing and the corporate partner of the year by AMS's UK Charity of the Year.

Professional development

A series of actions were taken which sought to improve opportunities for professional development within AMS. These included increasing technical and soft skills training by 15 per cent, increasing the management development programmes by 45 per cent especially in the areas of performance management and coaching and a significant increase in the number of senior managers who attended the AMS Leadership Academy. In addition, there was an improvement in the agility of HR processes in response to employee and manager feedback, which allowed localised promotion decisions and performance management decisions within accounts and functions.

The impact of these changes was an increase in the proportion of the workforce promoted internally from 10 to 15 per cent and an increased ability to move positions within AMS to improve skill development leading to 240 moves in 2010. In addition, the Investors in People Bronze Award was obtained along with the Polish Investors in Human Capital Award.

Questions

1 What are the main challenges faced by AMS when seeking to strengthen employee commitment to the organisation?

2 Consider the possible actions that AMS might have made to strengthen organisational commitment?

3 Why have AMS made the changes, as detailed in the case, to their HR practices?

4 What evidence is there that these changes have had a positive influence on organisational performance?

CASE STUDY 2.3

MARKS & SPENCER ONE TEAM

NICHOLAS KINNIE AND JUANI SWART

Marks and Spencer is a major UK-based retailer employing over 78,000 people with over 700 stores in the UK. Our detailed focus within Marks and Spencer is on the establishment of a logistical network, known as One Team, which provides a best practice example of the operation of HR practices at the level of the network. In this case the various stakeholders in the network acknowledged the need to establish network level skills, relationships and processes to improve performance. In order to do this they critically developed HR practices at the level of the network.

The network is composed of Marks and Spencer and its third party logistical and fulfillment solutions partners (referred to as the 3PLs) who supply warehousing and merchandising facilities. In 2010 Marks and Spencer, led by Jason Keegan, Head of Logistics – Strategic Network, teamed up with its 3PLs, including DHL, NDL, Wincanton, Tesam Distribution, IDS, CML and The Elite Group, to form One Team.

The shared aims of the One Team network are to work together to improve the performance of Marks and Spencer and the network by sharing knowledge and best practice between the parties. In particular, they seek to build a highly competitive retail network, achieve high levels of customer satisfaction, generate significant cost savings and establish a common culture. Although the network was instigated by Marks and Spencer, the 3PLs have participated extensively in the operation of One Team. The network has implemented a number of common practices and a shared approach to human capital management. In order to do this they have structured their decision making and created HR practices at the level of the network.

There are two key managerial structures which are integral to the operation of One Team. First, a Steering Group was established jointly by senior Marks and Spencer staff and each of the 3PLs. This group takes overall responsibility for the direction and strategy of One Team and establishes a common purpose among the members. Meetings take place face to face monthly usually at 3PL sites around the country. Second, five work-streams were established to take responsibility for particular aspects of One Team activities including Values and Behaviours, Marketing and Communications, Collaboration, Customer Focus and Developing Talent.

These involve managers below the Steering Group from Marks and Spencer and the 3PLs acting semi-autonomously, but reporting to the Steering Group regularly with plans for action to contribute to One Team. Both of these managerial structures are vital to supporting the development of shared knowledge and skills. Moreover, they also provide the infrastructure for the continuation of this cross-boundary organisation and they also offer important development opportunities for staff at all levels.

Senior Marks and Spencer managers saw the enhancement of talent management throughout One Team as one of their clear objectives and the principal responsibility of the Developing Talent work-stream. The work-stream facilitates this by advertising all relevant job vacancies across all members of One Team via the shared website, discussed below. This encourages staff to move between 3PLs and Marks and Spencer in ways they would not have done previously. Indeed, this provides Marks and Spencer with the opportunity to identify future talent and to retain this within the network. Employees have the opportunity for career development in ways that they would not otherwise have been aware.

Key internal resourcing decisions were also made over which staff would be allocated to the work-streams. Critically, these staff members were identified according to their role suitability and were drawn from a variety of levels and might just as easily include a team leader as a senior manager from a 3PL site. Once they became members of these work-streams the staff had clear opportunities to develop their personal skills and knowledge in a number of respects. First, each work-stream had a high degree of autonomy over how they achieved their objectives. Consequently, the members found they had the freedom to develop new ideas and to innovate. Second, since the members of the work-stream were drawn from multiple levels in One Team, junior staff could find themselves working alongside quite senior staff from Marks and Spencer and other 3PLs in a way they would not do normally. Apart from the knowledge and skills development opportunities, these staff had career benefits because they had a chance to 'get themselves noticed'. It is important to note that the developmental opportunities now extended beyond the boundaries of each organisation and existed at the level of the network.

Alongside these more informal development opportunities there are also a series of formal training and development activities at the level of the network. These activities are focused on One Team and not the 3PLs and aim to develop multi-level agility and to encourage the sharing of knowledge and best practices. For instance, training needs analysis within One Team showed that in order for One Team to function more effectively at the team level there was a need for members of the 3PLs to understand their inter-personal styles and managerial approaches in greater detail. A process was implemented across the network wherein which each individual's preferred communication style was identified and each team was made aware of its particular team member configuration. This enabled improved communication within the cross-boundary team as well as enhanced social relationships.

Performance management and reward practices were also established at the level of the network. Efficiency targets were established for each site and performance was measured weekly. Each site has complete knowledge of its own performance and the performance of others within the league table which was established. This provides a strong incentive to improve performance, which is highly visible throughout One Team. Once these targets were set, each local manager sought to make changes to improve their performance. Often this led to changes in working practices which led to improvements in efficiency and performance against target. These improvements could then be shared throughout the network either in the workstreams or via the website.

There were also One Team reward mechanisms to recognise the contribution of individual employees. Every month an employee was recognised for their outstanding contribution and these were then entered into a quarterly competition. The rewards linked to being the 'employee of the month' included travel and entertainment benefits; all of which were linked to personal pride in having displayed One Team values and behaviours. This network-level practice provided a financial and recognition incentive for employees to identify with the network and therefore they were willing to share rather than hoard their knowledge.

Perhaps one of the key drivers in the multi-dimensional agility model is the involvement and participation practices that exist at the level of the network. There are a series of practices designed to encourage all members to adopt a One Team perspective and to strengthen the relationships at all levels. First, six regional champions were established who meet face-to-face regularly to build relationships and share knowledge. Second, various social activities take place between members of the sites at all levels to build awareness of One Team and make contacts. Third, employees at all levels have the opportunity to contribute to the One Team suggestion scheme for efficiency savings discussed above. Fourth, the One Team website mentioned previously has multiple purposes. Not only does it allow the job vacancies to be advertised it also provides for social network and activities between members of One Team at multiple levels. Finally, all employees are encouraged to wear the One Team uniform rather than the uniform of the 3PL that they work for.

In summary, One Team provides a sophisticated example of infrastructure, managerial practices and HR practices which operate across all the member organisations at the level of the network. Critically, these practices impact upon all levels of seniority within the partners and Marks and Spencer. It is not only senior staff who are involved, junior staff also have opportunities to develop their career, improve their knowledge and exercise decision-making discretion in ways that would not be available to them within their 3PL. Moreover, these structures and practices are multi-stranded. They are not solely focused on cost savings and efficiencies and recognise that shared values and behaviours and relationships hold the key to the knowledge sharing which in turn is the life blood of productivity improvements.

It is important to understand that this HRM model, which exists at the level of the network, results in the development of flexible human capital, which can be effectively deployed across the network as well as within the individual firms. These efficiencies have resulted in very significant cost-savings, multi-stranded talent development and have generated further networked ways of working. This HRM model therefore supports a positive spiral of networked benefits.

Questions

1 What were the key forms of human, social and organisational capital generated in One Team?

2 What role did HR practices play in supporting these forms of capital?

3 In the future:

  a How might the network be developed further?

  b What obstacles might be encountered to further development?

  c How might these obstacles be overcome?

Bibliography

Alfes, K., Shantz, A. and Truss, C. (2012) 'The link between perceived HRM practices, performance and well-being: the moderating effects of trust in the employer', *Human Resource Management Journal*, Vol.22, No.4, 409–27.

Alvesson, M. (2004) *Knowledge Work and Knowledge Intensive Firms*, Oxford: Oxford University Press.

Ansoff, H.I. (1965) *Corporate Strategy*, Harmondsworth: Penguin.

Appelbaum, E., Bailey, T. and Berg, P. (2000) *Manufacturing Advantage: Why High-Performance Systems Pay Off*, Ithaca, NY: ILR Press.

Armstrong, P. and Goodman, J. (1979) 'Management and supervisory custom and practice', *Industrial Relations Journal*, Vol.10, No.3, 12–24.

Arthur, J. (1994) 'Effects of human resource systems on manufacturing performance and turnover', *Academy of Management Journal*, Vol.37, No.3, 670–87.

Atkinson, J. (1984) 'Manpower strategies for flexible organisations', *Personnel Management*, August 28–31.

Baird, L. and Meshoulam, I. (1988) 'Managing two fits of strategic human resource management', *Academy of Management Review*, Vol.13, No.1, 116–28.

Barney, J. (1986) 'Organizational culture: can it be a source of competitive advantage?' *Academy of Management Review*, Vol.11, No.3, 656–65.

Barney, J. (1991) 'Firm resources and sustained competitive advantage', *Journal of Management*, Vol.17, No.1, 99–120.

Barney, J. (2001) 'Is the resource-based theory a useful perspective for strategic management research? Yes', *Academy of Management Review*, Vol.26, No.1, 41–56.

Barney, J. and Wright, P. (1998) 'On becoming a strategic partner: the role of human resources in gaining competitive advantage', *Human Resource Management*, Vol.37, No.1, 31–46.

Baron, J. and Kreps, D. (1999) 'Consistent human resource practices', *California Management Review*, Vol.41, No.3, 29–53.

Bartel, A.P. (2000) 'Human resource management and performance in the service sector: the case of bank branches', *NBER Working Paper Series*, Cambridge, MA: National Bureau of Economic Research.

Batt, R. and Moynihan, L. (2004) 'The viability of alternative call centre models', in Deery, S. and Kinnie, N. (eds.) *Call Centres and Human Resource Management*, Basingstoke: Palgrave Macmillan, 25–53.

Beaumont, P.B., Hunter, L.C. and Sinclair, D. (1996) 'Customer-supplier relations and the diffusion of employee relations change', *Employee Relations*, Vol.18, No.1, 9–19.

Becker, B. and Gerhart, B. (1996) 'The impact of human resource management on organizational performance: progress and practice', *Academy of Management Journal*, Vol.39, No.4, 779–801.

Becker, B. and Huselid, M. (2006) 'Strategic human resource management: where do we go from here?', *Journal of Management*, Vol.32, No.6, 898–925.

Becker, B. and Huselid, M. (2011) 'Bridging micro and macro domains: workforce differentiation and strategic human resource management', *Journal of Management*, Vol.37, No.2, 421–8.

Beer, M., Spector, B., Lawrence, P., Quinn Mills, D. and Walton, R. (1985) *Human Resource Management: A General Manager's Perspective*, New York: Free Press.

Berg, P. (1999) 'The effects of high performance work practices on job satisfaction in the United States Steel Industry', *Relations Industrielles/Industrial Relations*, Vol.54, No.1, 111–34.

Berg, P., Appelbaum, E., Bailey, T. and Kalleberg, A. (1996) 'The performance effects of modular production in the apparel industry', *Industrial Relations*, Vol.35, No.3, 356–73.

Boselie, P., Dietz, G. and Boon, C. (2005) 'Commonalities and contradictions in research on human resource management and performance', *Human Resource Management Journal*, Vol.15, No.3, 67–94.

Boselie, P., Paauwe, J. and Jansen, P. (2000) 'Human resource management and performance lessons from the Netherlands', *International Journal of Human Resource Management*, Vol.12, No.7, 1107–25.

Boxall, P. (1992) 'Strategic human resource management: beginnings of a new theoretical sophistication?', *Human Resource Management Journal*, Vol.2, No.3, 60–79.

Boxall, P. (1994) 'Placing HR strategy at the heart of business success', *Personnel Management*, Vol.26, No.7, 32–5.

Boxall, P. (1995) 'Building the theory of comparative HRM', *Human Resource Management Journal*, Vol.5, No.5, 5–17.

Boxall, P. (1996) 'The strategic HRM debate and the resource-based view of the firm', *Human Resource Management Journal*, Vol.6, No.3, 59–75.

Boxall, P. (1998) 'Achieving competitive advantage through human resource strategy: towards a theory of industry dynamics', *Human Resource Management Review*, Vol.8, No.3, 265–88.

Boxall, P. (1999) 'Human resource strategy and industry-based competition: a conceptual framework and agenda for theoretical development', in Wright, P., Dyer, L., Boudreau, J. and Milkovich, G. (eds.) *Research in Personnel and Human Resource Management (Supplement 4: Strategic Human Resources Management in the Twenty-First Century)*, Stamford, CT and London: JAI Press.

Boxall, P. and Purcell, J. (2000) 'Strategic human resource management: where have we come from and where should we be going?', *International Journal of Management Reviews*, Vol.2, No.2, 183–203.

Boxall, P. and Purcell, J. (2003) *Strategy and Human Resource Management,* Basingstoke: Palgrave MacMillan.

Boxall, P. and Purcell, J. (2011) *Strategy and Human Resource Management* (3rd edn.) Basingstoke: Palgrave MacMillan.

Boxall, P. and Steeneveld, M. (1999) 'Human resource strategy and competitive advantage: a longitudinal study of engineering consultancies', *Journal of Management Studies*, Vol.36, No.4, 443–63.

Brown, W. (1972) 'A consideration of custom and practice', *British Journal of Industrial Relations*, Vol.10, No.1, 42–61.

Brown, W. (1973) *Piecework Bargaining*, Oxford: Heinemann.

Buller, P.F. and McEvoy, G.M. (2012) 'Strategy, human resource management and performance: sharpening the line of sight', *Human Resource Management Review*, Vol.22, 43–56.

Cappelli, P. (ed.) (2008) *Employment Relationships*, Cambridge: Cambridge University Press.

Child, J. (1997) 'Strategic choice in the analysis of action, structure, organizations and environment: retrospect and prospect', *Organization Studies,* Vol.18, No.1, 43–76.

Child, J. and Partridge, B. (1982) *Lost Managers*, Cambridge: Cambridge University Press.

Combs, J., Yongmei, L., Hall, A. and Ketchen, D. (2006) 'How much do high performance work practices matter? A meta-analysis of their effects on organizational performance', *Personnel Psychology*, Vol.59, 501–28.

Coyle-Shapiro, J.A.M., Kessler, I. and Purcell, J. (2004) 'Exploring organizationally-directed citizenship behaviour: reciprocity of it's my job?', *Journal of Management Studies*, Vol.42, 85–106.

Cully, M., Woodland, S., O'Reilly, A. and Dix, G. (1999) *Britain at Work: as Depicted by the 1998 Workplace Employee Relations Survey*, Abingdon: Routledge.

Delaney, J.T. and Godard, J. (2001) 'An industrial relations perspective on the high performance paradigm', *Human Resource Management Review*, Vol.11, 395–429.

Delery, J. (1998) 'Issues of fit in strategic human resource management: implications for research', *Human Resource Management Review*, Vol.8, No.3, 289–309.

Delery, J. and Doty, H. (1996) 'Modes of theorising in strategic human resource management: tests of universalistic, contingency and configurational performance predictions', *Academy of Management Journal*, Vol.39, No.4, 802–35.

Donnelly, R. (2011) 'The coalescence between synergies and conflicts of interest in a top consultancy firm: an analysis of the implications for consultants' attitudes and behaviours', *Human Resource Management Journal*, Vol.20, No.1, 60–73.

Dyer, L. and Reeves, T. (1995) 'Human resource strategies and firm performance: what do we know and where do we need to go?', *International Journal of Human Resource Management*, Vol.6, No.3, 656–70.

Dyer, L. and Shafer, R. (1999) 'Creating organizational agility: implications for strategic human resource management', in Wright, P., Dyer, L., Boudreau, J. and Milkovich, G. (eds.) *Research in Personnel and Human Resource Management (Supplement 4: Strategic Human Resources Management in the Twenty-First Century)*, Stamford, CT and London: JAI Press.

Elorza, U., Aritzeta, A. and Ayestarán, S. (2011) 'Exploring the black box in Spanish firms: the effect of the actual and perceived system on employees' commitment and organisational performance', *International Journal of Human Resource Management*, Vol.22, No.7, 1401–22.

Fincham, R. (1999) 'The consultant-client relationship: critical perspectives on the management of organizational change', *Journal of Management Studies*, Vol.36, No.3, 335–51.

Fombrun, C., Tichy, N. and Devanna, M. (eds.) (1984) *Strategic Human Resource Management*, New York: Wiley.

Fox, A. (1974) *Beyond Contract: Work, Power and Trust Relations*, London: Faber.

Gerhart, B. (1999) 'Human resource management and firm performance: measurement issues and their effect on casual and policy inferences', in Wright, P., Dyer, L., Boudreau, J. and Milkovich, G. (eds.) *Research in Personnel and Human Resource Management (Supplement 4: Strategic Human Resources Management in the Twenty-First Century)*, Stamford, CT and London: JAI Press.

Gerhart, B. (2013) 'Research on human resource management and effectiveness: some methodological challenges', in Paauwe, J., Guest, D. and Wright, P. (2013a) *HRM and Performance: Achievements and Challenges*, Chichester: Wiley.

Gittleman, M., Horrigan, M. and Joyce, M. (1998) '"Flexible" workplace practices: evidence from a nationally representative survey', *Industrial and Labor Relations Review*, Vol.52, No.1, 99–115.

Golding, N. (2004) 'Strategic human resource management', pp. 32–74, in Beardwell, I., Holden, L. and Claydon, T. (eds.) *Human Resource Management. A Contemporary Approach* (4th edn.), Harlow: Pearson Education.

Goshall, S. and Napahiet, J. (1998) 'Social capital, intellectual capital and the organizational advantage', *Academy of Management Review*, Vol.23, No.2, 242–66.

Gratton, L., Hope-Hailey, V., Stiles, P. and Truss, C. (1999a) 'Linking individual performance to business strategy: the people process model', *Human Resource Management*, Vol.38, No.1, 17–31.

Gratton, L., Hope-Hailey, V., Stiles, P. and Truss, C. (1999b) *Strategic Human Resource Management: Corporate Rhetoric and Human Reality*, Oxford: Oxford University Press.

Guest, D. (1987) 'Human resource management and industrial relations', *Journal of Management Studies*, Vol.24, No.5, 503–21.

Guest, D. (1995) 'Human resource management, trade unions and industrial relations', in Storey, J. (ed.) *Human Resource Management: A Critical Text*, London: Routledge.

Guest, D. (1997) 'Human resource management and performance: a review and research agenda', *International Journal of Human Resource Management*, Vol.8, No.3, 263–76.

Guest, D. (1999) 'Human resource management and performance: the workers' verdict', *Human Resource Management Journal*, Vol.9, No.3, 5–25.

Guest, D. (2011) 'Human resource management and performance: still searching for some answers', *Human Resource Management Journal,* Vol.21, No.1, 3–13.

Guest, D. and Bos-Nehles, A. (2013) 'HRM and performance: the role of effective implementation', in Paauwe, J., Guest, D. and Wright, P. (2013a) *HRM and Performance: Achievements and Challenges*, Chichester: Wiley.

Guest, D. and Hoque, K. (1994) 'The good, the bad and the ugly: employment relations in new non-union workplaces', *Human Resource Management Journal*, Vol.5, No.1, 1–14.

Guest D., Michie, J., Conway, N. and Sheehan, M. (2003) 'Human resource management and corporate performance in the UK', *British Journal of Industrial Relations*, Vol.41, No.2, 291–314.

Guest, D., Michie, J., Sheehan, M. and Conway, N. (2000) *Effective People Management: Initial Findings of the Future of Work Study*, London: Chartered Institute of Personnel and Development.

Hall, L. and Torrington, D. (1998) 'Letting go or holding on: the devolution of operational personnel activities', *Human Resource Management Journal*, Vol.8, No.1, 41–55.

Hamel, G. and Prahalad, C. (1994) *Competing for the Future*, Boston, MA: Harvard Business School Press.

Hendry, C. and Pettigrew, A. (1992) 'Strategic choice in the development of human resource management', *British Journal of Management*, Vol.3, No.1, 37–56.

Hesketh, A. and Fleetwood, S. (2006) 'Beyond measuring the human resources – organizational performance link: applying critical realist meta-theory', *Organization*, Vol.13, No.5, 677–700.

Huselid, M. (1995) 'The impact of human resource management practices on turnover, productivity and corporate financial performance', *Academy of Management Journal*, No.38, No.3, 635–72.

Huselid, M. and Becker, B. (2000) 'Comment on "Measurement error in research on human resource management: how much error is there and how does it influence effect size estimates?" By Gerhart, Wright, McMahan and Snell', *Personnel Psychology*, Vol.53, No.4, 835–54.

Hutchinson, S., Kinnie, N., Purcell, J., Collinson, M., Scarbrough, H. and Terry, M. (1998) *Getting Fit, Staying Fit: Developing Lean and Responsive Organisations*, London: Institute of Personnel and Development.

Hutchinson, S., Kinnie, N., Purcell, J., Rees, C., Scarbrough, H. and Terry, M. (1996) *The People Management Implications of Leaner Ways of Working, Issues in People Management No.15*, London: Institute of Personnel and Development.

Hutchinson, S. and Purcell, J. (2003) *Bringing Policies to Life*, London: Chartered Institute of Personnel and Development.

Hutchinson, S. and Purcell, J. (2007) *The Role of Line Managers in People Management*, London: Chartered Institute of Personnel and Development.

Hutchinson, S. and Wood, S. (1995) *Personnel and the Line: Developing the New Relationship: The UK Experience*, London: Institute of Personnel and Development.

Ichniowski, C., Shaw, K. and Prennushi, G. (1995) 'The impact of human resource management practices on productivity', Working Paper 5333, Cambridge, MA: National Bureau of Economic Research.

Ichniowski, C., Kochan, T., Levine, D., Olson, C. and Strauss, G. (1996) 'What works at work: overview and assessment', *Industrial Relations*, Vol.35, No.3, 299–333.

Jackson, S. and Schuler, R. (1995) 'Understanding human resource management in the context of organizations and their environments', *Annual Review of Psychology*, Vol.46, 237–64.

Jackson, S., Schuller, R. and Jiang, K. (2014) 'An aspirational framework for strategic human resource management', *Academy of Management Annals*, Vol.8, No.1, 1–56.

Janssens, M. and Steyaert, C. (2009) 'HRM and performance: a plea for reflexivity in HRM studies', *Journal of Management Studies*, Vol.46, No.1, 143–55.

Kaufman, B. (2015) 'Market competition, HRM, and firm performance: The conventional paradigm critiqued and reformulated', *Human Resource Management Review*, Vol.25, 107–25.

Keenoy, T. (1997) 'HRMism and the languages of re-presentation', *Journal of Management Studies*, Vol.34, No.5, 825–41.

Kersley, B., Alpin, C., Forth, J., Bryson, A., Bewley, H., Dix, G. and Oxenbridge, S. (2006) *Inside the Workplace: First Findings from the 2004 Workplace Employment Relations Survey*, Abingdon: Routledge.

Kinnie, N. and Parsons, J. (2004) 'Managing client, employee and customer relations: constrained strategic choice in the management of human resources in a commercial call centre', pp. 102–26, in Deery, S. and Kinnie, N. (eds.) *Call Centres and Human Resource Management*, Basingstoke: Palgrave.

Kinnie, N. and Swart, J. (2012) 'Committed to whom? Professional knowledge worker commitment in cross-boundary organisations', *Human Resource Management Journal*, Vol.2, No.1, 21–38.

Kinnie, N., Purcell, J. and Hutchinson, S. (2000) 'Human resource management in telephone call centres', in Purcell, K. (ed.) *Changing Boundaries*, Bristol: Bristol Academic Press.

Kinnie, N., Swart, J. and Purcell, J. (2005) 'Influences on the choice of HR systems: the network organisation perspective', *International Journal of Human Resource Management*, Vol.16, No.6, 1004–28.

Kinnie, N., Purcell, J., Hutchinson, S., Rayton, B. and Swart, J. (2005) 'Satisfaction with HR practices and commitment to the organisation: why one size does not fit all', *Human Resource Management Journal*, Vol.15, No.4, 9–29.

Kinnie, N., Swart, J., Lund, M., Morris, S., Snell, S. and Kang, S.-K. (2006) *Managing People and Knowledge in Professional Service Firms*, London: Chartered Institute of Personnel and Development.

Kochan, T. and Barocci, T. (1985) *Human Resource Management and Industrial Relations*, New York: Basic Books.

Kogut, B. and Zander, U. (1996) 'What do firms do?', *Organization Science*, Vol.7, No.5, 502–18.

Larsen, H.H. and Brewster, C. (2003) 'Line management responsibility for HRM: what is happening in Europe?', *Employee Relations*, Vol.25, No.3, 228–44.

Legge, K. (1978) *Power, Innovation, and Problem-solving in Personnel Management*, London: McGraw-Hill.

Legge, K. (1995) *Human Resource Management: Rhetorics and Realities*, Basingstoke: Macmillan.

Legge, K. (2001) 'Silver bullet or spent round? Assessing the meaning of the high performance commitment management/performance relationship', in Storey, J. (ed.) *Human Resource Management: A Critical Text* (2nd edn.), London: Thompson Publishing.

Leonard, D. (1992) 'Core capabilities and core rigidities: a paradox in managing new product development', *Strategic Management Journal*, Vol.13, 111–25.

Leonard, D. (1998) *Wellsprings of Knowledge: Building and Sustaining the Sources of Innovation*, Boston, MA: Harvard Business School Press.

Lepak, D. and Snell, S. (1999) 'The strategic management of human capital: determinants and implications of different relationships', *Academy of Management Review*, Vol.24, No.1, 1–18.

Lepak, D., Takeuchi, R. and Swart, J. (2011) 'How organizations evaluate and maintain fit of human capital with their needs', pp. 333–58, in Burton-Jones, A. and Spender J.C. (eds.) *The Oxford Handbook of Human Capital*, Oxford: Oxford University Press.

Lepak, D., Liao, H., Chung, Y. and Harden, E.E. (2006) 'A conceptual review of human resource management systems in strategic human resource management research', *Personnel and Human Resource Management*, Vol.25, 217–71.

Lowe, J., Delbridge, R. and Oliver, N. (1997) 'High-performance manufacturing: evidence from the automotive components industry', *Organization Studies*, Vol.18, No.5, 783–98.

MacDuffie, J.P. (1995) 'Human resource bundles and manufacturing performance: organizational logic and flexible production systems in the world auto industry', *Industrial and Labor Relations Review*, Vol.48, No.2, 197–221.

MacDuffie, J.P. and Pil, F.T. (1997) 'Changes in auto industry employment practices: an international overview', in Kochan I.A., Lansbury, R.D. and MacDuffie, J.P. (eds.) *After Lean Production: Evolving Employment Practices in the World Auto Industry*, Ithaca, NY: ILR Press.

Marchington, M. (2001) 'Employee involvement at work', in Storey, J. *Human Resource Management: A Critical Text* (2nd edn.), London: Thompson Publishing.

Marchington, M. and Grugulis, I. (2000) '"Best practice" human resource management: perfect opportunity or dangerous illusion?', *International Journal of Human Resource Management*, Vol.11, No.6, 1104–24.

Marchington, M. and Wilkinson, A. (2002) *People Management and Development*, London: Chartered Institute of Personnel and Development.

McGovern, P., Gratton, L., Hope-Hailey, V., Stiles, P. and Truss, C. (1997) 'Human resource management on the line?', *Human Resource Management Journal*, Vol.7, No.4, 12–29.

Miles, R. and Snow, C. (1978) *Organizational Strategy, Structure and Process*, New York: McGraw-Hill.

Miles, R. and Snow, C. (1984) 'Designing strategic human resources systems', *Organizational Dynamics*, Vol.13, No.1, Summer, 36–52.

Miles, R. and Snow, C. (1999) 'The new network firm: a spherical structure built on human investment philosophy', in Schuler, R. and Jackson, S. (eds.) *Strategic Human Resource Management*, Oxford: Blackwell.

Miller, D. and Shamsie, J. (1992) 'The resource-based view of the firm in two environments: the Hollywood film studios from 1936 to 1965', *Academy of Management Journal*, Vol.39, No.3, 519–43.

Millward, N., Bryson, A. and Forth, J. (2000) *All Change at Work: British Employment Relations 1980–1998 as Portrayed by the Workplace Industrial Relations Survey Series*, London: Routledge.

Mintzberg, H. (1994) 'Rethinking strategic planning part 1: pitfalls and fallacies', *Long Range Planning*, Vol.27, No.3, 12–21.

Mueller, F. (1996) 'Human resources as strategic assets: an evolutionary resource-based theory', *Journal of Management Studies*, Vol.33, No.6, 757–85.

Osterman, P. (1987) 'Choice of employment systems in internal labor markets', *Industrial Relations*, Vol.26, No.1, 46–67.

Osterman, P. (1994) 'How common is workplace transformation and who adopts it?', *Industrial and Labor Relations Review*, Vol.47, No.2, 173–88.

Osterman, P. (2000) 'Work reorganization in an era of restructuring: trends in diffusion and effects on employee welfare', *Industrial and Labor Relations Review*, Vol.53, No.2, 179–96.

Paauwe, J. (2009) 'HRM and performance: achievements, methodological issues and prospects', *Journal of Management Studies*, Vol.46, No.1, 129–42.

Paauwe, J., Guest, D. and Wright, P. (2013a) *HRM and Performance: Achievements and Challenges*, Chichester: Wiley.

Paauwe, J., Wright, P. and Guest, D. (2013b) 'HRM and performance: what do we know and where should we go?', in Paauwe, J., Guest, D. and Wright, P. (2013a) *HRM and Performance: Achievements and Challenges*, Chichester: Wiley.

Paauwe, J., Boon, C., Boselie, P. and den Hartog, D. (2013c) in Paauwe, J., Guest, D. and Wright, P. (2013a) *'HRM and Performance: Achievements and challenges*, Chichester: Wiley.

Patterson, M., West, M., Hawthorn, R. and Nickell, S. (1997) 'Impact of people management practices on business performance', *Issues in People Management No. 22*, London: Institute of Personnel and Development.

Peters, T. and Waterman, R.H. (1982) *In Search of Excellence: Lessons from America's Best-Run Companies*, New York: Harper & Row.

Pettigrew, A.M. (1973) *The Politics of Organizational Decision Making*, London: Tavistock.

Pfeffer, J. (1994) *Competitive Advantage Through People*, Boston, MA: Harvard Business School Press.

Pfeffer, J. (1998) *The Human Equation: Building Profits by Putting People First*, Boston, MA: Harvard Business School Press.

Pfeffer, J. and Salancik, G.R. (1978) *The External Control of Organizations: A Resource Dependence Perspective*, New York: Harper & Row.

Phelps, C., Heidl, R. and Wadhwa, A. (2012) 'Knowledge, networks, and knowledge networks: a review and research agenda', *Journal of Management*, Vol.38, No.4, 1115–66.

Pil, F.K. and MacDuffie, J.P. (1996) 'The adoption of high involvement work practices', *Industrial Relations*, Vol.35, No.3, 423–55.

Porter, M.E. (1980) *Competitive Strategy*, New York: Free Press.

Porter, M.E. (1985) *Competitive Advantage: Creating and Sustaining Superior Performance*, New York: Free Press.

Powell, J.H. and Wakeley, T. (2003) 'Evolutionary concepts and business economics: towards a normative approach', *Journal of Business Research*, Vol.56, 153–61.

Prahalad, C. and Hamel, G. (1990) 'The core competence of the corporation', *Harvard Business Review*, Vol.68, No.3, May–June, 79–91.

Purcell, J. (1999) 'Best practice and best fit: chimera or cul-de-sac?', *Human Resource Management Journal*, Vol.9, No.3, 26–41.

Purcell, J. (2004) 'The HRM–performance link: why, how and when does people management impact on organisational performance?', John Lovett Memorial Lecture, University of Limerick. Available from the author.

Purcell, J. and Hutchinson, S. (2007) 'Front line managers as agents in the HRM–performance causal chain: theory, analysis and evidence', *Human Resource Management Journal*, Vol.17, No.1, 3–20.

Purcell, J. and Kinnie, N. (2007) 'Human resource management and business performance', in Boxall, P., Purcell, J. and Wright, P. (eds.) *The Oxford Handbook of Human Resource Management*, Oxford: Oxford University Press.

Purcell, J., Kinnie, N., Hutchinson, S., Rayton, B. and Swart, J. (2003) *Understanding the People and Performance Link: Unlocking the Black Box*, London: Chartered Institute of Personnel and Development.

Purcell, J., Kinnie, N., Swart, J., Rayton, B. and Hutchinson, S. (2009) *People Management and Performance*, Oxford: Routledge.

Ramsay, H., Scholarios, D. and Harley, B. (2000) 'Employees and high-performance work systems: testing inside the black box', *British Journal of Industrial Relations*, Vol.38, No.4, 501–31.

Renwick, D. (2000) 'HR-line work relations: a review, pilot case and research agenda', *Journal of European Industrial Training*, Vol.24, Nos.2–4, 241–53.

Richardson, R. and Thompson, M. (1999) 'The impact of people management practices on business performance: a literature review', *Issues in People Management*, London: Institute of Personnel and Development.

Schuler, R. (1989) 'Strategic human resource management and industrial relations', *Human Relations*, Vol.42, No.2, 157–84.

Schuler, R. (1996) 'Market-focused management: human resource management implications', *Journal of Market-Focused Management*, Vol.1, 13–29.

Schuler, R. and Jackson, S. (1987) 'Linking competitive strategies and human resource management practices', *Academy of Management Executive*, Vol.1, No.3, 207–19.

Sinclair, D., Hunter, L. and Beaumont, P.B. (1996) 'Models of customer–supplier relations', *Journal of General Management*, Vol.22, No.2, 56–75.

Snell, S., Youndt, M. and Wright, P. (1996) 'Establishing a framework for research in strategic human resource management: merging resource theory and organizational learning', *Research in Personnel and Human Resources Management*, Vol.14, 61–90.

Snell, S., Lepak, D. and Youndt, M. (1999) 'Managing the architecture of intellectual capital: implications for human resource management', in Wright, P., Dyer, L., Boudreau, J. and Milkovich, G. (eds.) *Research in Personnel and Human Resources Management: Strategic Human Resource Management in the Twenty-First Century*, Stamford, CT: JAI Press.

Swart, J. (2006) Intellectual capital: disentangling an enigmatic concept, *Journal of Intellectual Capital*, 7(2), pp. 136–159.

Swart, J. (2007) 'HRM and knowledge workers', in Boxall, P., Purcell, J. and Wright, P. (eds.) *The Oxford Handbook of Human Resource Management*, Oxford: Oxford University Press.

Swart, J. (2011) 'That's why it matters. The value generating properties of knowledge', *Management Learning*, Vol.49, No.3, 319–32.

Swart, J. and Kinnie, N. (2001) 'Human resource advantage within a distributed knowledge system: a study of growing knowledge intensive firms', paper presented at ESRC Seminar: 'The Changing Nature of Skills and Knowledge'. Manchester School of Management, September 2001. Available from the authors.

Swart, J. and Kinnie, N. (2003) 'Knowledge intensive firms: the influence of the client on HR systems', *Human Resource Management Journal*, Vol.13, No.3, 37–55.

Swart, J. and Kinnie, N. (2004) *Managing the Careers of Knowledge Workers*, London: Chartered Institute of Personnel and Development.

Swart, J. Kinnie, N. and Purcell, J. (2003) *People and Performance in Knowledge Intensive Firms*, London: Chartered Institute of Personnel and Development.

Swart, J. and Kinnie, N. (2013) 'Managing multi-dimensional knowledge assets: HR configurations in PSFs', *Human Resource Management Journal*, Vol.23, No.2, 160–79.

Swart, J. and Kinnie, N. (2014) 'Re-considering boundaries: Human Resource Management in a networked world', *Human Resource Management*, Vol.53, No.2, 291–310.

Swart, J., Kinnie, N. and Rabinowitz, J. (2007) *Managing Across Boundaries*, London: Chartered Institute of Personnel and Development.

Swart, J., Price, A., Mann, C. and Brown, S. (2004) *Human Resource Development: Strategy and Tactics*, London: Butterworth-Heinemann.

Tempest, S. and Starkey, K. (2004) 'The effects of liminality on individual and organizational learning', *Organization Studies*, Vol.25, No.4, 507–27.

Terry, M. (1977) 'The inevitable growth of informality', *British Journal of Industrial Relations*, Vol.15, No.1, 76–90.

Thompson, M. (2000) 'Final Report: The Bottom Line Benefits of Strategic Human Resource Management, the UK Aerospace People Management Audit', London: Society of British Aerospace Companies.

Thompson, P. (2011) 'The trouble with HRM', *Human Resource Management Journal*, Vol.21, No.1, 355–67.

Thurley, K. and Wirdenius, H. (1973) *Approaches to Supervisory Development*, London: Institute of Personnel Management.

Truss, C. (2001) 'Complexities and controversies in linking HRM with organizational outcomes', *Journal of Management Studies*, Vol.38, No.1, 1121–49.

Tushman, M.L. and Scanlan, T.J. (1981) 'Characteristics and external orientations of boundary spanning individuals', *Academy of Management Journal*, Vol.24, No.1, 83–98.

Truss, C., Shantz, A., Soane, E., Alfes, K. and Delbridge, R. (2013) 'Employee engagement, organisational performance and individual well-being: exploring the evidence, developing the theory', *International Journal of Human Resource Management*, Vol.24, No.14, 2657–69.

Ulrich, D. (1997) 'Measuring human resources: an overview of practice and a prescription for results', *Human Resource Management*, Vol.36, No.3, 303–20.

Ulrich, D. (1998) *Human Resource Champions*, Boston, MA: Harvard Business School Press.

Wall, T. and Wood, S. (2004) 'The romance of human resource management and business performance, and the case for big science', *Human Relations*, Vol.58, No.4, 429–62.

Wall, T. and Wood, S. (2005) 'The romance of HRM and business performance, and the case for big science', *Human Relations*, Vol.58, No.4, 29–62.

Whittington, R. (2001) *What is Strategy – and Does It Matter?* (2nd edn.), London: Thompson Learning.

Wood, S. (1996) 'High commitment management and payment systems', *Journal of Management Studies*, Vol.33, No.1, 53–77.

Wood, S. (1999) 'Human resource management and performance', *International Journal of Management Reviews*, Vol.1, No.4, 367–413.

Wood, S. and Albanese, P. (1995) 'Can we speak of high commitment management on the shop floor?', *Journal of Management Studies*, Vol.32, No.2, 215–47.

Wright, P. and Gardener, T.M. (2000) 'Theoretical and empirical challenges in studying the HR practice–firm performance relationship', paper presented at the Strategic Human Resource Management Workshop, European Institute for Advanced Studies in Management, Insead, March. Available from the Center for Advanced Human Resource Studies Working Paper Series Number 00–04, Cornell University.

Wright, P. and McMahan, G. (2011) 'Exploring human capital: putting human back into strategic management', *Human Resource Management Journal*, Vol.21, No.2, 93–104.

Wright, P. and Nishii, L.H. (2004) 'Strategic HRM and organizational behavior: integrating multiple levels of analysis', paper presented at the Erasmus University Conference 'HRM: What's Next?'.

Wright, P. and Nishii, L.H. (2013) 'Strategic HRM and organizational behavior: integrating multiple levels of analysis', pp. 97–110, in Guest, D. (ed.) *Innovations in HR*, Oxford: Blackwell Publishing.

Wright, P. and Snell, S. (1998) 'Toward a unifying framework for exploring fit and flexibility in strategic human resource management', *Academy of Management Review*, Vol.23, No.4, 756–72.

Wright, P.M., Gardener, T.M. and Moynihan, L.M. (2003) 'The impact of HR practices on the performance of business units', *Human Resource Management Journal*, Vol.13, No.3, 21–36.

Wright, P., McMahan, G. and McWilliams, A. (1994) 'Human resources and sustained competitive advantage: a resource-based perspective', *International Journal of Human Resource Management*, Vol.5, No.2, 301–26.

Wright, P.M., Gardner, T., Moynihan, L.M. and Allen, M. (2005) 'The HR performance relationship: examining causal direction', *Personnel Psychology*, Vol.58, No.2, 409–46.

Wright, P., McCormick, B., Sherman, W. and McMahan, G. (1999) 'The role of human resource practices in petrochemical refinery performance', *International Journal of Human Resource Management*, Vol.10, No.4, 551–71.

Yalabik, Z., Popaitoon, P., Chowne, J. and Rayton, B. (2013) 'Work engagement as a mediator between employee attitudes and outcomes', *International Journal of Human Resource Management*, Vol.24, No.14, 2799–823.

Youndt, M., Snell, S., Dean, J. and Lepak, D. (1996) 'Human resource management, manufacturing strategy, and firm performance', *Academy of Management Journal*, Vol.39, No.4, 836–66.

CHAPTER 3

RECRUITMENT

Scott Hurrell and Dora Scholarios

Introduction

Recruitment is often neglected in the HRM literature. Most accounts combine the discussion of recruitment with selection, with greater emphasis on selection. However, the more effective organisations are at identifying and attracting a high-quality pool of job applicants, the less important the selection stage of hiring becomes. According to some, recruitment is 'the most critical human resource function for organisational survival or success' (Taylor and Collins, 2000: 304).

Barber (1998: 5) provided one of the first dedicated reviews of recruitment,[1] defining it as 'practices and activities carried out by the organization with the primary purpose of identifying and attracting potential employees'. Emphasis is usually on filling a position from outside a firm (rather than internal appointments or promotion). An important development is the greater attention devoted to how individuals become applicants – or the attraction element. Sometimes referred to as an 'applicant perspective' (Billsberry, 2007), this acknowledges a two-way relationship between organisations and applicants, where applicant decision making becomes an important factor shaping whether the recruitment process is successful or not. It is not just the efficiency of the organisation's procedures in identifying applicants that will ensure the desired outcome (a good match between the individual and the job) but also how potential applicants perceive and act on the opportunities offered.

In this chapter, we use both an organisational and applicant perspective to understand recruitment. Our approach is represented in Figure 3.1. We begin with a summary of the context within which recruitment takes place (the external environment, organisational characteristics, and the nature of the job vacancy to be filled). We often use the example of the UK for illustrative purposes, although draw widely on international research to show the pressures impacting organisations globally. We show how each of these contextual drivers impacts recruitment activities, and emphasise the reasons why many organisations now pay more attention to the applicant perspective. This is the driving force behind many recent developments such as the growth in e-recruitment, social media and 'employer branding'.

---

[1]For other reviews see, for example, Breaugh (2012) and Yu and Cable (2014).

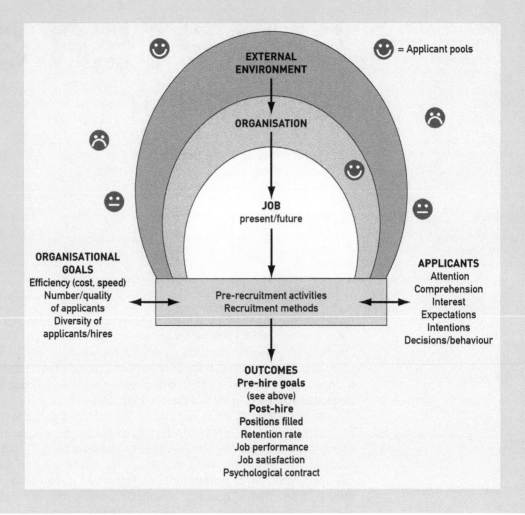

Figure 3.1
Recruitment
framework

The external environment

At one time, it was thought that the aim of recruitment was simply to maximise the size of the applicant group, which would then be reduced through a rigorous selection procedure. This assumed an abundant supply of qualified applicants and that those selected would accept the jobs offered. Although this approach may have sufficed for the job demands and labour force of the past, these assumptions are more tenuous in today's employment context. In this section, we consider how the organisation's external environment impacts recruitment.

The economy

The wider economy exerts a positive or negative effect on hiring activity through job growth and contraction. Following the global economic crisis of 2008, for example, employment levels in most advanced economies have yet to return to pre-recession levels (ILO, 2015). Southern European countries have fared especially badly, with unemployment in Greece and Spain around 25 per cent.

Even in economies that have partially recovered, problems remain. Since 2008 there has been an increase in precarious work such as zero hours, temporary and part-time contracts throughout Europe (EC, 2011). In the UK, the proportion reporting that they work in such jobs involuntarily because they cannot find more stable work has increased significantly since the recession (TUC, 2015). Even before the recession, writers in the US (Autor *et al.*, 2006) and UK (Goos and Manning, 2007) described polarised labour markets. Despite much job creation in 'lovely' high skilled/high paid technical and professional work, there was also an increasing volume of 'lousy' low skilled/low paid jobs, with a reduction in intermediate skilled jobs. In developing parts of the world, such as some regions of Asia and North Africa, this polarisation of jobs is starker still (ILO, 2015).

Labour markets and the supply of skilled job applicants

Economic conditions also affect the degree to which employers can fill job vacancies. A slow 'loose' job market creates a relative oversupply of job applicants. This allows organisations easier access to appropriate supplies of skill, and greater power to hold salaries constant and become more selective when hiring. Many job applicants, therefore, have less bargaining power relative to employers because of a large number of job applicants that are willing to work for relatively depressed wages.

In countries where employment is recovering there has been an increase in vacancies that employers report as being 'hard to fill' because applicants with the correct skills cannot be identified (skills shortages). Indeed, although only 4 per cent of UK establishments reported skills shortage vacancies (SSVs) in 2013, this had increased by a third since 2011 (Winterbotham *et al.*, 2014), indicating increasing competition for recruits. Skills shortages also disproportionately affect particular sectors, with manufacturing and business services amongst the worst affected in 2013. SSVs were also more likely in skilled trades occupations and certain specialised professional roles (ibid.). In such instances and where labour markets begin to tighten post-recession, organisations may have to become more creative in finding job applicants, for example through identifying non-traditional applicant groups or by offering additional incentives like pay and benefits.

Since 2004, many European employers have benefitted from an increase in labour mobility from Eastern Europe. Taking the case of migration to the UK, the proportion of non-native born workers increased from 9 per cent of the workforce in 2002 (ONS, 2011) to over 15 per cent in 2013 (Rienzo, 2014). The biggest proportional rise was in those from the eight Eastern European and Baltic accession states (EUA8) joining the EU in 2004 (ONS, 2011). Workers from the EUA8 states are much more likely to be found in low skill jobs, for which they are frequently over qualified and have the lowest average wages in the UK (Rienzo, 2014a). Migrants from other areas are more likely to be employed in professional occupations (ibid.). The UK Health Service, for example, has recruited skilled migrants to fill gaps in health professional roles (Department of Health, 2007).

Skill supply is also affected by levels of educational attainment. More graduates are being produced than ever before; the UK, for example, has some of the highest tertiary education attainment rates in the OECD and EU (OECD, 2013). Nevertheless, even graduates may not always satiate employer demand. Fifteen per cent of UK employers reported that graduates were not 'well prepared' for work in 2013 (Winterbotham *et al.*, 2014).

Issues with skills mismatches can also detrimentally affect workers. Even though more jobs now require a degree or higher qualification, a UK-wide skills survey conducted in 2012 revealed that 22 per cent of graduates reported being *over* qualified for their jobs (Felstead *et al.*, 2013). Despite positive evidence regarding upskilling, the same survey also reported over-qualification amongst *non*-graduates (37 per cent). Some countries report even wider skills mismatches. China has rapidly expanded university education but graduate unemployment has been estimated to range anywhere from 9 per cent (ILO, 2015) to 30 per cent (Sharma, 2014). Furthermore, the majority of Chinese graduates surveyed in 2013 expressed dissatisfaction with their jobs (ILO, 2015). Case study 3.1 explores issues related to the Chinese graduate labour market in more depth.

Recruiters thus need to be aware of various labour market trends that affect the match between workers' skills and the jobs on offer. Even where skills systems appear to be functioning relatively well (such as in the UK) difficulties still arise in certain occupations, sectors and for certain groups of workers.

Challenges of demographic and social change

The size and composition of the labour force is projected to change dramatically, with implications for employers' recruitment goals and practices. Global issues such as immigration, an ageing population and more women seeking employment mean a far more diverse workforce (ILO, 2015). Some of these changes will exacerbate skills shortages and recruitment problems (e.g. a shrinking labour force due to population ageing) whilst some changes may offset these issues (e.g. immigration). Changing retirement laws, such as the abolition of the Default Retirement Age in the UK, could also contribute to flattened recruitment levels and youth unemployment as people continue to work for longer. The future of recruitment thus faces many uncertainties.

Given continuing skill shortages in some areas, organisations will increasingly turn to candidates from 'non-traditional' talent pools, such as migrants, older workers, or women returners. This kind of targeted recruitment could be beneficial to some industries that continue to experience skill shortages, such as the European ICT sector. This youth-orientated industry has been highlighted for the implicit age discrimination in its recruitment methods, which reinforce negative stereotypes of older workers (Healy and Schwarz-Woelzl, 2007). Such stereotypes exclude suitable applicants (whilst also possibly being illegal), exacerbate skills shortages and thus harm both applicants and organisations. This situation has led to calls for the industry to re-orientate recruitment methods to encourage a more age diverse workforce (ibid.).

Another trend is the changing priorities of job candidates and what attracts them to jobs and organisations. In one survey, the top attractions to a job listed by employees were location of work (47 per cent), holiday entitlement (43 per cent), flexible working and bonuses (39 per cent), and the company's workplace culture and environment (38 per cent) (YouGov, 2006). PricewaterhouseCooper's (2010) global survey confirmed that flexible working arrangements were more valued by employees across countries, rather than other benefits such as bonuses or training and development.

This growing concern for work–life balance and flexibility has been popularly linked to the working preferences of so-called 'Generation Y' or 'millenials', born between approximately 1980 and the millennium (Ng *et al.*, 2010). This generation are seen as ambitious, impatient for advancement and eager to learn – but also much more concerned with accommodating their non-work lives, working with 'good' people in 'nurturing' work environments (ibid.) and ensuring that their employers' values (for example, on the environment) fit their own (Murray, 2008).

Ng *et al.*'s (2010) study of 23,000 Canadian undergraduates' career preferences confirmed a high degree of homogeneity within Generation Y. Nevertheless, other studies in Belgium (Dries *et al.*, 2008) and New Zealand (Cennamo and Gardner, 2008) have found similarities between Generation Y and other generations casting some doubt on the group's distinctiveness. Generation Y's increased preferences for autonomy and work–life balance did, however, remain even within these studies. Employers are taking notice. Box 3.1 illustrates how some of the most attractive global employers design their recruitment strategies with Generation Y job seekers in mind.

Employment legislation

Freedom from discrimination is generally viewed as a fundamental right. All member states of the International Labour Organization (ILO), a specialist branch of the United Nations, are obliged to 'respect, promote and realise' certain fundamental rights at work, one of

| Box 3.1 HRM in practice | Global companies' attractiveness and recruitment strategies |

The power of the brand

Many global companies follow a 'talent pipeline' recruitment strategy. This requires an attraction and employer branding strategy.

Examples of this in operation are provided by Universum's World's Most Attractive Employer rankings (www.universumglobal.com) and report on 'Building a Global Employer Brand'. In 2014, Universum surveyed over 200,000 business and engineering graduate job seekers in more than 30 countries.

Headline findings:

- The top 'business' employers were: Google, PricewaterhouseCooper (PwC) and EY (Ernst & Young).
- In IT/engineering, first again is Google, followed by Microsoft and BMW.
- Students worldwide expect creative, dynamic work environments.
- In 'western' economies, students prioritise future earnings and leadership opportunities.
- Indian students prioritise leadership opportunities, high future earnings and rapid promotion, and use by far the most communication channels to learn about employers (e.g. employer presentations, social networking, live webinars with employers).
- Russian students prioritise earnings and opportunities for performance-related bonuses.
- Chinese students prioritise 'softer' career advancement aspects, such as good references for future career.

Universum concludes that employers' attempts to attract talent globally should 'customize their value proposition more heavily in Asia and Russia', placing more emphasis on career advancement opportunities and remuneration in developing markets.

The talent pool strategy

Stahl *et al.*'s (2012) global study involving interviews with 263 HR professionals in 20 leading multinational corporations and 36 countries showed that many tend to follow a talent pool strategy – hiring the 'best' and *then* placing them in jobs. Key features of these companies' strategies are as follows:

- Recruit the best with very low selection ratios (number hired divided by number of applicants). Many hire the top 1 per cent from thousands of applicants.
- Recruit for person–organisation or person–culture fit not specific positions.
- Build relationships with potential candidates, e.g. use Internet applications, ties with international universities and internship programmes.
- Use global branding for name recognition and to understand what appeals to applicants, e.g. professional freedom, learning opportunities and work–life balance.

which is the 'elimination of discrimination' (ILO, 1998). European Union (EU) member countries must also comply with EU legislation on this matter. One example is UK legislation to comply with the 2000 EU Equal Treatment Directive (EU, 2014), which outlawed discrimination on the 'protected characteristics' of age, sexual orientation, religion or belief, as well as updating disability discrimination legislation. These developments are now included within the 2010 Equality Act alongside protection related to sex, race, gender reassignment and maternity.

Employers face legal action and employment tribunals if their recruitment practices are not compliant with legislation. The basic principle of employment legislation related to recruitment is that all individuals should be considered according to their merits and provided equality of opportunity.[2] The general principle of equality in recruitment applies both to *direct* discrimination on the basis of a protected characteristic covered by legislation (see above), and *indirect* discrimination, where there is no intentional discrimination but the practice disproportionately impacts members of a particular group. For example, recruiting through events targeted exclusively at all boys' schools would indirectly discriminate against women (for a more detailed overview of protected characteristics and types of discrimination see ACAS, 2014).

Of particular importance for recruitment is the concept of 'positive action'. Positive *discrimination* when making hiring decisions is controversial because of its acceptance of quota systems to redress existing discrimination. Positive discrimination remains illegal in the UK but is allowed in some countries to redress serious historical imbalances, for example in post-Apartheid South Africa. Positive *action* emphasises ensuring equal access to opportunity, is legal in the UK and was extended by the Equality Act.

If a group which shares a particular protected characteristic is under-represented in a job or workplace (e.g. low levels of ethnic minority police officers), or is felt to face a particular disadvantage then employers can take voluntary positive action to increase this group's participation (such as targeted recruitment activity) (ACAS, 2014). Using our earlier example of ICT occupations, if an employer recognises under-representation of women and can attribute this to hiring procedures (e.g. recruiting from undergraduate engineering courses where women are already under-represented), then positive action may be used. This action could take the form of a recruitment campaign that uses alternative channels to try to increase the number of applications from women (e.g. recruit from Master's IT conversion courses). Under the Equality Act, however, positive action could extend to the selection decision itself and involve deliberately hiring a woman over a man for the job, but *only* if they were as qualified for the job as the man.[3]

Employers may decide to take positive action to avoid legal action or to manage the risk of costly tribunals. There is some evidence to suggest that employers do act on such legislation. Woodhams and Corby (2007), for example, showed an increase in the use of monitoring or positive action in recruitment, since the introduction of disability legislation in 1995 and 2003. There are also arguments for a 'business case' in reducing discrimination during recruitment, e.g. to gain access to a wider applicant pool and harness the skills of a more diverse group of employees. In fact, examples of positive action recruitment efforts are now prominently publicised on many organisations' websites, for example Sikh recruitment by the British Army or female officers in many police forces.

Monitoring job applicants by protected characteristics when used to ensure representativeness and meritocracy in recruitment is considered good practice. However, equal opportunities policies and genuine practices to support them tend to be more common in public sector organisations, large workplaces, and those with HR specialists (Hoque and Noon, 2004). McKay and Avery (2005) recommend caution in simply seeking numerical targets to satisfy diversity goals if workplace climates are not consistent with the principles of diversity. 'Otherwise firms will be apt to default on their implied recruitment promises, minority recruits will feel misled, and some form of backlash will be probable' (335).

Other regulations affecting recruitment are more about ensuring standards or protecting the public. These apply to the employment of particular groups, for instance ex-offenders, and specify procedures, like disclosure of previous convictions, to protect vulnerable people, e.g. children (the Criminal Records Bureau, for example). High profile cases, such as the murder of British schoolgirls Holly Wells and Jessica Chapman in 2002, have revealed that if the applicant had been vetted at the recruitment stage, it may have been possible to prevent

---

[2] This is unless it can be objectively justified as legitimate, appropriate and necessary, for example because a protected characteristic is a genuine occupational requirement for a job (Wadham, *et al.*, 2010). An example of an occupational requirement may be the need to recruit a female doctor to work in a women's jail.

[3] For positive action to be applied in a selection decision, the Equality Act requires (1) that a candidate with the protected characteristic is *as qualified as* other candidates for the post, and (2) that there is evidence that people with the particular protected characteristic are under-represented or face particular difficulties in the workplace. If these are not met then any decision that takes a protected characteristic into account will in itself be unlawful. Employers must always consider the 'abilities, merits and qualifications of all the candidates (for a job)' using the protected characteristic only as a 'tie-breaker' (ACAS, 2011: 8).

a tragedy. A further piece of legislation that impacts upon recruitment practices in the UK is the 1998 Data Protection Act (DPA), which gives job applicants the right to transparency in the collection of recruitment data in terms of what is being collected and why (ICO, 2005).

The discussion so far has focused on four aspects of the outer ring presented in Figure 3.1 – the external environment. We can summarise the effects of these pressures on recruitment as follows:

External Environment	Impact on Recruitment
	Skill needs and supply of candidates
Economy	Composition of the applicant pool
Labour market	Recruitment strategy and practice
Social change	• *equity and fairness of processes*
Legislation	• *degree of selectivity possible*
	• *monitoring and targeting applicants*

The organisation

An organisation's activities, geographical location, industry sector, and stage of growth or technological development can impact upon skill needs and the availability of suitable applicants. Employers in areas of high unemployment, for instance, usually experience looser labour markets, while those in larger urban conurbations will benefit from a more heterogeneous and skilled labour force.

Some industry sectors have also been impacted more than others by globalisation, technological advances, changing business environments and/or legislation. Post-financial crisis, for example, financial service organisations have been subject to increasing regulation to reform the sector. Although all organisations will be affected in some way by external forces, some sectors, such as the public or health sector, have a relatively more stable skill demand and supply. A firm's stage in its life cycle (e.g. whether they are experiencing growth, stability or decline) will also affect their recruitment needs and demand for labour as will their business strategy. On this latter point, Phillips and Gully (2015) state how firms' recruitment strategies will be affected by whether they wish to 'make' talent internally or 'buy' it externally. These authors also highlight how firms following a low cost strategy may seek very different skills from those pursuing an innovative strategy.

Size

One feature that, perhaps, has the most significant impact on how an organisation manages recruitment is its size. Large organisations are more likely to: recruit on a regular basis; use more recruitment sources; have dedicated HR staff for recruitment; train recruiters; adopt diversity policies and practices and derive their recruitment strategy from wider organisational and HR priorities (Barber *et al.*, 1999; Hoque and Noon, 2004). Recruitment strategies in large organisations tend to be more strategically driven and formalised. As noted above, large public sector organisations are especially likely to adopt diversity policies and set recruitment targets. However, small and medium-sized enterprises (SMEs) dominate most countries' economies. In the UK, 99.3 per cent of enterprises are classified as small (employing less than 50 employees) and 0.6 per cent as medium (employing between 50 and 249 employees) (BIS, 2014). Much recruitment activity, therefore, is likely to be informal rather than guided by a formal structure or specialist HR staff.

Generally, recruitment presents greater challenges for smaller companies. SMEs have, on aggregate, a more constrained pool of resources to expand the workforce or dedicate to recruitment. Unlike larger organisations, small companies are less likely to have the resources to meet demands for a more diverse workforce in keeping with demographic changes (Gallagher and O'Leary, 2007). They are also less able to recruit from internal or national labour markets and are often thought to be disadvantaged by not having the promotional prospects which large firms can offer (Cable and Graham, 2000).

Research evidence confirms that smaller firms tend to rely on less bureaucratic and formal methods of recruitment, such as word of mouth, referrals or networking (Phillips and Gully, 2015). This can lead to several problems such as restricting the potential supply of qualified recruits, and/or reliance on unsuitable candidates, simply because they are convenient. Carroll *et al.* (1999) showed how restricting the pool of recruits for childcare jobs to mainly young women eventually resulted in problems of high turnover due to disillusionment with the job. Such a restricted pool could also be viewed as discriminatory and illegal. This same research, however, also showed that informality and the use of trusted recruitment sources were viewed as more cost effective in the short term.

Along the same lines, SMEs may be better placed to use local labour markets and informal channels to deal with recruitment problems. Lockyer and Scholarios (2004) found that small hotels could identify and match potential employees with local customer expectations using informal methods. Large hotels which were part of a chain tended to operate a more bureaucratic approach, for example relying on advertisements in national newspapers or, as we explore further in the next section, outsourcing recruitment to agencies. In many cases, this meant they were less effective at utilising local networks to fill vacancies.

Outsourcing and devolution of HRM

In larger organisations, the responsibility for recruitment has shifted over the last few decades. This has occurred alongside important broader trends in HRM including the devolution of traditional HR roles and functions to line managers and an upsurge in the number of companies claiming to implement Ulrich's HR partner model. One version of the latter sees HR as a 'three-legged stool' consisting of strategic business partners (senior HR professionals working with business leaders), shared administrative service centres, and centres of HR expertise (Ulrich and Beatty, 2001).

Forty per cent of large UK organisations have introduced the Ulrich model for their HR function (CIPD, 2013a). As a result, the recruitment function appears in various forms across organisations. In large multinationals it is often carried out by HR Partners or 'experts' as in the Ulrich model. Elsewhere it is undertaken by a shared service centre that provides routine administration and sometimes more tailored additional HR services. Shared service centres can be resourced by in-house staff or they can be outsourced to specialist third party providers, often for particular grades of staff such as executives (CIPD, 2011). An outsourcing strategy, referred to as 'Recruitment Process Outsourcing' (RPO), is viewed as a way of cutting costs, improving efficiency and attracting high-quality applicants (Belcourt, 2006). Before the recession and decline in recruitment levels, a vibrant business had emerged in RPO partnerships. Agencies can carry out the whole recruitment process on behalf of the organisation, although they may have to periodically re-tender to retain their contracts.

Some partnerships between organisations and outsourcers have developed to such a level of sophistication that they have been hailed as a template for a 'new model of recruitment' (Gallagher and O'Leary, 2007). This model combines personalised, 'high-value' approaches for high-skilled positions, with more standardised processes for low-skilled positions. However, there seems to be a decrease in the use of agencies, with many employers viewing them as unaffordable, an unnecessary expense, and stopping to use them altogether (CIPD, 2011; 2013). Some issues associated with RPO are explored in Case study 3.2.

In organisations that retain the recruitment function, this is often centralised as part of a support function for line managers. HR may have a role in providing expert help to line managers. In the case of agency partnerships, this becomes one of setting, agreeing and monitoring the standard of service provided by the agency, thus removing more routine tasks from HR. Arguably, these different roles and responsibilities enhance, or at least change, the role of HR practitioners, requiring them to become active 'players' in the business (Ulrich and Beatty, 2001).

Taking each of these organisational characteristics into account, the importance of the second layer of the model in Figure 3.1 can be summarised as follows.

The Organisation	Impact on Recruitment
Sector	Frequency of recruitment
Location	Attractiveness as an employer
Growth	Benefits package/career opportunities offered
HR strategy	Whether use a global market for recruits
Size	Strategic goals of recruitment
	Formalisation of procedures
	Responsibility for recruitment (*line manager, HR partnering, outsourcing, ad hoc*)

The job

We have already noted how the changing nature of jobs affects employer skills demand. For example, many companies are recruiting for 'motivation' or 'attitude' across different jobs (Bates *et al.*, 2008) emphasising the increasing importance of generic, transferable and customer-orientated competencies.

Employers must also make a decision about whether the job should be allocated internally to existing employees or filled using externally resourced staff – full time, subcontracted, outsourced or temporary. This depends to a large extent on the expected employment relationship. Lepak and Snell (2002) describe a rational choice process with respect to the level of human capital required to perform the job. Jobs that require high skill and unique knowledge (hence greater investment in training) are better managed as internal promotions or transfers, as these have implications for building a committed workforce. Jobs which do not require costly training, and which can be performed at a lower skill level, can be externalised with a view to a more short-term employment relationship.

Short-term employment strategies, of course, also have adverse effects. Employers' under-investment in temporary employees may affect their future employability (Kellard *et al.*, 2001) and can result in skills shortages caused by staff turnover. Furthermore, many jobs that have short tenure (and high turnover) are poor quality, not least in terms of pay, and are thus potentially unattractive to potential recruits.

The distinction between high and low quality work highlights the distinction between core and peripheral workers (Boxall and Purcell, 2003). Those viewed as core to long-term business success usually have commensurate resources dedicated to recruitment. For high-value graduate positions, for example, large companies tend to have dedicated recruitment programmes managed by in-house staff. Those of less perceived long-term value may be outsourced entirely or employed on less secure, short-term contracts. The use of peripheral (e.g. agency) workers allows the organisation to operate more flexibly in unpredictable and competitive markets, but at a potential cost to job quality and worker security. Box 3.2 interrogates the use of various types of freelance and temporary workers in the US via the use of 'on-demand' technology.

Box 3.2 HRM in practice   'There's an App for that': The immediate recruitment of freelance workers (US)

The US company 'Handy' has developed an app whereby householders can request the services of 'home helps' on demand (paid, on average, $18 an hour) to cover duties ranging from cleaning to flat-pack-furniture assembly. The app provides an extremely responsive way to match labour demand with a supply of freelance workers. Handy now covers 29 of the largest US cities as well as Toronto and Vancouver in Canada and six cities in the UK. Other similar companies provide services such as grocery delivery and laundry.

Opportunities for more highly skilled and creative workers are also being provided through similar technology. For example, Topcoder matches the services of freelance software coders to clients. Medicast provides doctors on demand within two hours in Miami, Los Angeles and San Francisco, with patients sending requests and detailing their symptoms through an app.

These arrangements have benefits for highly skilled freelancers who seek portfolio careers, moonlighters and/or students who wish to fit work around studies. However, ethical and welfare issues arise, including the precarity of work for the individual employee, (especially if this is their main source of income), and the exclusion of freelance workers from certain legal protections (Hurrell, 2015).

Source: *The Economist*, 3rd January, 2015.

Pre-recruitment activities

The previous sections illustrate the diverse recruitment conditions which organisations face. It is hard, therefore, to imagine a single, 'best practice' approach to recruitment that would be appropriate for all situations. However, there are some generalisations that can be made about how organisations should prepare for recruitment. Detailed accounts of these activities can be found in other texts (see, for example, Lees and Cordery, 2000). Here, we provide a brief review of two of the most fundamental pre-recruitment activities – producing job descriptions and person specifications.

Job descriptions

Filling a vacancy begins with job analysis. This should be 'a purposeful, systematic process for collecting information on the important work-related aspects of a job' (Gatewood and Feild, 1998: 245), and should define what is required to perform the job successfully. Data collection methods may include: interviews/surveys with job incumbents or supervisors; observation; past job descriptions and/or databases about occupational classifications. For example, a firefighter's job may involve the task of 'applying water or chemical agents to extinguish flames' but we need to know the essential worker attributes, such as situational awareness or confidence and resilience in the face of pressure, to recruit the right person to carry out this task (Department for Communities and Local Government, 2009).

Campion's (1988) multidimensional model of job analysis and design attempted to draw together many approaches to job analysis to provide the most comprehensive description possible of what a job entails. This proposed that jobs should be described using all of the following dimensions: tasks; worker characteristics (knowledge, skills, abilities, personality, motivation, perceptual–motor requirements); job context (tools/equipment; degree of social interaction); the reward structure (benefits accruing to teamwork or autonomy) and job demands (problem solving, intensity, speed).

There are at least two notable points about current thinking on describing jobs. The first is that the components of a job, whether the tasks or worker characteristics, cannot be separated from the organisational setting in which they take place; hence the position of the job at the centre of the concentric circles in Figure 3.1. The notion of skill, for example, may reflect specific product markets or organisational strategies. For example, two hotel workers may possess similar interpersonal communication skills. Different job and organisational settings, however, mean that one uses these in the context of tightly prescribed standards and a script to guide customer interactions, while the other may have more scope to use their discretion (Hurrell *et al.*, 2013). These findings have implications for job analysis methods, which some suggest should be refocused around broader work analysis rather than specific job tasks (Gatewood and Feild, 1998). There are also implications regarding matching work contexts with the preferences of potential applicant groups. Workers seeking short-term employment may be targeted for low discretion jobs, and workers seeking long-term positions for high discretion jobs.

A second key point is that job descriptions should not be static or too narrow. Descriptions should take into account how jobs may change as a result of environmental drivers (e.g. technological advances or competitive pressures), and consider the interconnections between specific jobs and other organisational roles (Sanchez, 1994). Future-orientated (or strategic) job analysis (Schneider and Konz, 1989) should intentionally include those involved in planning change in the organisation rather than relying on existing job incumbents as a source of information.

Person specifications and competency frameworks

Person specifications, which are derived from the job description, detail the personal qualities that workers require to perform the job. The exact nature of person specifications has been influenced greatly by competency profiling. This identifies the worker-based attributes (knowledge, skill, ability, personality and other traits) that are required to reach a required level of performance (or competence). The difference between this and traditional approaches is that the emphasis is on observable behaviours.

Competency profiling emerged from the work of McClelland (1976) and Boyatzis (1982). Focusing initially on managers, they identified the behaviours that differentiated high and poor performers, linking these to key underlying personal qualities. In the UK, there was an equally strong movement towards a functional competence approach based on minimum standards of observable performance outcomes rather than inferring underlying personal attributes. Today, this tradition continues in approaches that specify Key Performance Indicators (KPIs), or the behaviours the individual should achieve. Companies may purchase 'off the shelf' frameworks, which can then be amended to suit their needs, or develop their own competency frameworks in-house or with consultants. This then might feed into the compilation of a competency dictionary, which demonstrates each competency with positive

Table 3.1 Example competency statement and associated behaviours

Team Spirited	
The way we pull together in an environment, which recognises and celebrates each other's strengths and contribution.	
Positive Behaviours	**Negative Behaviours**
• Works effectively together to accomplish organisational goals. • Builds positive working relationships with other teams and individuals. • Shows consideration for the needs of the team; thinks about how colleagues will affect them. • Happy to provide support to colleagues; doesn't wait to be asked.	• Creates or tolerates an 'us and them' culture. • Relies upon others to complete their work; doesn't take ownership. • Doesn't build networks; see themselves as self-sufficient. • Avoids dealing with conflict between teams.

Source: IDS HR Studies 865, March 2008: 17.

and negative indicators (see Table 3.1 for an example related to the competency 'team spirited'). As with future-orientated job analysis, the competencies that organisations specify as the basis for recruitment and selection should be continually reviewed so that they can anticipate emerging and declining competency requirements (Robinson *et al.*, 2005).

Competency frameworks are evident in growing numbers of organisations. In 2010, two thirds of 168 UK organisations used a competency framework to target their recruitment (Suff, 2010); by 2013, 82 per cent of 462 organisations reported using competency-based interviews in selection (CIPD, 2013b). Many companies identify 'core competencies' which are applied to all employees – for instance 'customer focus' and 'communication' – as well as specific competencies that may apply to different occupational groups. Typical competencies used are teamworking, people management, results-orientation and problem solving (ibid.). These examples indicate further that organisations are interested in recruiting for personal qualities as well as for specific technical skills and qualifications.

Returning again to Figure 3.1, we can now add further detail to how job requirements are likely to shape recruitment, as follows:

The Job	Impact on Recruitment
Current demands/skills	Person specification
Core/periphery	Positions to be filled (*short term/long term, skill type/level*)
Job/work analysis	
Future job demands	Entry requirements
	Changes to competency profile
	'Future orientation' of job analysis
	Effort in targeting applicant groups

Recruitment methods

As a result of the challenges discussed so far, organisations seem to be using more creative solutions to communicate with potential applicants and targeting diverse applicant groups. Internet (e-) recruitment has become the method of choice. Table 3.2 shows the popularity of various recruitment methods in UK organisations and how this differs between sectors.

In this section, we summarise the most popular methods, moving from those which provide advantages in terms of the efficiency of recruitment (agencies, e-recruitment) to those which are directed more at attracting the attention of candidates such as social media or informal processes (referrals, networks). We conclude with a strategy borrowed from marketing which aims to solve recruitment difficulties by directly targeting applicant perceptions – employer branding.

Agencies and headhunters

Forty-nine per cent of employers, and many more in the private sector, reported using agencies (Table 3.2). As discussed above, agencies may provide efficiency gains. Forde and Slater (2006), however, argue that agency employment is also accompanied, in many cases, by low levels of organisational commitment and greater job insecurity for employees.

A specific form of agency recruitment is carried out by executive search agencies or headhunters, which identify candidates for senior roles. This involves calling targeted individuals with the intention of tempting them to apply for specific posts, but can also involve

Table 3.2 Most effective methods to attract applicants, by industry sector (%)

| | All 2013 | Sector (2013) | | | | All 2010 |
		Manuf. and Production	Private Sector Services	Public Sector	Voluntary, Community, Not-For-Profit	
Own corporate website	62	50	56	78	70	63
Recruitment agencies	49	69	56	29	35	60
Commercial job boards	38	27	47	33	33	33
Employee referral scheme	33	41	49	7	17	35
Professional networking (e.g. LinkedIn)	31	35	43	15	17	14
Local newspaper advertisements	29	29	20	33	49	36
Specialist journals/trade press	24	14	13	47	33	31
Speculative applications/ word of mouth	23	29	25	13	20	24
Apprenticeships	20	21	19	26	16	12
Jobcentre Plus	19	21	18	13	29	23
Search consultants	17	22	18	16	12	22
Links with schools/ colleges/universities	14	12	16	15	10	18
Secondments	12	4	11	23	10	11
National newspaper ads	12	3	4	32	16	16
Social networking sites (e.g. Facebook)	9	0	13	7	10	3
Alumni (previous employees)	6	8	7	5	1	5
Links with local organisations making redundancies*	6	9	6	6	1	–
Local employment partnerships	4	0	4	7	3	6
Other	6	8	3	8	7	5

Source: CIPD (2013b).
Base: 457 (2013); 464 (2010).
*New item introduced after 2010.

the development of close relationships between the agency, the client and potential job seek-ers (Finlay and Coverdill, 2000). For senior-level appointments, where both parties require discretion, headhunters are likely to remain the preferred route of recruitment.

Internet (e-) recruitment

Job information and recruitment channels are increasingly found on company websites or portals that host vacancies for a number of organisations. As shown in Table 3.2, accord-ing to a 2013 survey of almost 500 UK employers, 62 per cent of organisations regarded corporate websites as the most effective method for attracting applicants, especially in the public and non-profit sectors, surpassing more traditional methods. The most commonly reported benefits of e-recruitment are cost effectiveness, the generation of a larger candidate pool, ease of use and speed of hiring (Parry and Tyson, 2008). There are, inevitably, some drawbacks for employers. The primary problem is the time taken to filter out large numbers of potentially unsuitable applicants (ibid.), although more effective targeting may reduce this. Other problems include concern that certain applicant groups may not be reached, and the impersonal nature of e-recruitment.

For applicants, the Internet allows easier access to try and match their skills with employer needs. Employer websites are popular communication channels across countries (although less so in China, Russia and Brazil) as shown by Universum's 2014 survey of business and engineering graduates (Box 3.1), and for many graduates, the Internet may be the only job search medium. There are concerns, however, about accessibility for some groups, such as the unemployed, less IT-literate or older applicants (Searle, 2006). E-recruitment may also not be fully compliant with disability discrimination legislation. Organisations should, therefore, also use traditional methods, such as application forms and print media, to ensure equality of access to information.

Social networking websites

Social media technology is an especially relevant e-recruitment channel for young job seekers. Research consultants, the Aberdeen Group, report that 73 per cent of 18- to 34-year-olds found their last job through a social networking site (Beagrie, 2015). Employer use of social networking websites for recruitment, particularly LinkedIn, is now accepted practice to help target recruitment or raise awareness of the employer brand (CIPD, 2013b). Table 3.2 shows a steady rise in the use of such professional networking sites, more than doubling between 2010 and 2013, with especially wide use in the private sector.

A recent trend is 'viral recruitment' where companies use social media sites to target technologically literate Generation Y applicants. Some creative examples pioneered by TMP Worldwide, an international recruitment consultant, include the use of online digital music service Spotify to guide potential graduate recruits to Jaguar Land Rover's career website and the use of virtual gaming adverts to recruit graduates for jobs at the British Intelligence agency (GCHQ) (see www.tmpw.co.uk). In the latter example, games such as Tom Clancy's 'Splinter Cell: Double Agent' were chosen because of their espionage theme. GCHQ's 2013 recruitment campaign for technical talent to work in cyber security also involved a game to crack a cryptic code, which was widely publicised across news and social media, receiving 353,000 followers on Twitter. Case study 3.1 provides an example of a social media game that was used as an international recruitment tool by Marriot hotels.

More controversially, there is also increased reported use of employers using social networking sites to pre-screen applicants (as distinct from trying to attract them). Broughton *et al.* (2011) cite a US survey of over 2,600 HR professionals, 45 per cent of whom checked applicants' social network profiles prior to hiring them. A further survey of almost 600 UK managers revealed that approximately 20 per cent found information online about an applicant, which the applicant did not volunteer (Viadeo and YouGov, 2007). Almost 60 per cent of these managers stated that such information influenced their hiring decisions, with HR managers especially likely to report that decisions were negatively influenced.

In addition to some of the general implications of e-recruitment discussed above, there are specific implications for social media recruitment.

- *Legality issues and indirect discrimination.* If information on any of the characteristics covered by discrimination law are discovered through social network sites and then used to reject applicants, this would be illegal. There is also the possibility of indirect discrimination if those most likely to use social media (e.g. young people) are more likely to not be hired based on information they post online.

- *Invasion of privacy.* If information is sought covertly data protection may become an issue. The public nature of social networking sites makes data protection implications unclear; however, ethical issues regarding applicants' right to privacy remain.

Targeting applicant perceptions: referrals, networks, recruiters and incentives

Some methods are more directly focused on influencing the way that potential applicants perceive the job and their decision to apply. Table 3.2 shows that informal methods, such as employee referrals, using professional networks and word of mouth, are considered effective at attracting applicants by between approximately a quarter and a third of employers. These methods are especially popular in the private sector, for entry level jobs and small businesses. We summarise the evidence regarding their pre- and post-hire effectiveness below.

- *Pre-hire outcomes.* Building networks is intended to create relationships with potential employees. For example, employers create links with schools/colleges/universities, perhaps offering internships and work placements to students with the prospect of retaining them as permanent employees. Professional networking, especially through online sites like LinkedIn, has been used increasingly for specialist IT staff, financial services and the media; for example, to 'build pipelines of possible future recruits' amongst those not actively seeking jobs (ComputerWeekly.com, 11 June, 2010).

Also relevant at the pre-hire stage are applicant perceptions. Applicants' first impressions of the organisation, and their decision to apply, are affected by the nature of the initial contact. A large body of research on 'realistic' recruitment information shows that this can lead to more accurate expectations and better post-hire outcomes, such as reduced staff turnover (Landis *et al.*, 2014). Perceptions are also influenced by financial incentives, such as increased pay or 'golden hellos', especially for hard-to-fill vacancies, although such recruits may be less likely to feel attachment to and remain with the organisation (Taylor and Schmidt, 1983).

- *Post-hire outcomes.* Methods that build strong relationships between the applicant and organisation are thought to improve fit between employee and employer values/needs; increase future employee satisfaction/commitment; and increase retention rates (Anderson *et al.*, 2001). In some respects, methods such as referrals may enhance the quality of applicants who ultimately apply for jobs. Candidates who have already been vetted by an employee are usually a better fit with the company and job and have a better understanding of the business (Yakubovich, 2006). Realistic information communicated by the employee attracts people with more accurate expectations and better 'fit' with the role/organisation, allowing others to self-select out of the process at an early stage. Employees also may feel that their reputation is at stake with a referral, encouraging them to refer only the highest quality applicants.

Contradictory evidence, however, suggests that the high trust between referrer and applicant creates unrealistic expectations leading to lower person–organisation fit once hired (Hsieh and Chen, 2011). Informal methods also bring specific dangers. They may perpetuate existing social networks and working practices and act as barriers to change. They also often result in fewer women or minorities being hired (Breaugh, 2012) and are susceptible to 'same as me' hiring decisions (Shwed and Kalev, 2014), and thus may perpetuate discrimination.

Employer branding

Taking the applicant perspective further, there has been a surge of interest in the image of the employer and, in particular, 'branding' as a competitive attraction strategy (Collins and Kanar, 2014). In this vein, large graduate employers in the UK cited improving students' perceptions of their organisation as their biggest recruitment challenge in 2014 to 2015 (High Fliers, 2015). Branding was a feature of recruitment strategy for the top global employers we highlighted in Box 3.1.

The concept implies that organisations should think beyond recruitment for specific job vacancies, and focus on communicating information about their image and the whole employment package. This is especially important when there is competition for skilled labour, as applicant decision making may be influenced by other job offers or informal information about a company, for example negative comments on blogs. It has also been found that graduates' misperceptions of the quality of opportunities available in particular sectors may lead to recruitment difficulties. Hurrell *et al.* (2011) found such a case when examining recruitment to paid jobs in the voluntary sector.

Various sources of information such as corporate websites, word of mouth, university sponsorship or publicity events can contribute to perceptions of a brand. High profile publications are also influential. For example, more job applications are submitted to companies ranked high in US business publications, such as Fortune's *100 Best Companies to Work For* (Cable and Turban, 2003) or the UK's Sunday Times' *Best Companies to Work For.*

Many recruitment researchers now focus on the symbolic attributes of organisations (such as corporate values) as being more relevant indicators of applicant attraction than instrumental attributes (such as salary or location), especially during the early stages of recruitment. Lievens and Highhouse (2003) developed the instrumental–symbolic framework for recruitment, building on marketing concepts describing how consumers assign meaning to products to enhance self-identity. Where such attraction occurs, positive identification with an organisation's symbolic attributes can help align employees' skills with organisational requirements (Hurrell and Scholarios, 2014).

The need for an applicant perspective

The 'war for talent', when demand for applicants exceeds supply (which may become more of a concern as the economic climate improves), and the search for more engaged and committed employees has meant that an approach based purely on matching job and person characteristics is often inadequate. As examined further in the next chapter, staffing may be viewed as an interactive social process where the applicant also has power. This places greater importance on the perceptions of applicants. In some situations companies will have to work harder to attract qualified applicants, maintain their interest, and convince them that they should accept an offer of employment.

Applicant 'attraction' to organisations implies getting applicants to view the organisation as a positive place to work. A considerable amount of research has been generated on just how applicant views are formed; for instance, how applicants are affected by recruiter behaviour; what draws their attention to corporate websites and how they process and then use information to make decisions about the attractiveness of the organisation (Ehrhart and Ziegert, 2005). This has provided information on the effectiveness of alternative recruitment sources, as well as investigating which sources provide the best employees in terms of post-hire outcomes like better job performance and lower turnover. We have reviewed some of this research in our consideration of each recruitment method above. Case study 3.3 considers the issue of 'fit' between applicants and the brand.

Conclusions

There is no 'best practice' recruitment approach, although methods that comply with equality legislation are a requirement. The model shown in Figure 3.1 demonstrates the factors which will impact recruitment outcomes, and hence the range of activities which organisations may adopt. The scarcity and criticality of the skills sought, decisions concerning the permanency of jobs, and the impact on particular applicant groups are just a few of the issues discussed in this chapter, which determine how employers choose to attract job applicants. For some organisations, recruitment is planned, integrated into wider organisational and HR strategies, and a key concern of senior managers who wish to attract and retain committed people. For others, it remains low priority with ad hoc arrangements, sometimes through recruitment agencies. HR practitioners still have a role to play, but that role might range from one of simply sending out instructions in a service centre, to one of major strategic importance where specific expertise is required, as in the design and/or implementation of behavioural competency frameworks.

The 'applicant perspective' considers all recruitment methods as part of the developing relationship between applicants and organisations which take place in a changing external context. Recent interest in this approach has added considerably to earlier research and has recognised that all recruitment channels send relevant messages to potential applicants, which will affect their perceptions of the job/organisation and their intentions to apply. As well as trying to address objective recruitment goals (such as cost and diversity targets), organisations will also therefore gain from using methods that communicate attractive yet accurate images of the job and organisation to applicants. Taking all these factors into account should mean a greater chance of successful recruitment, in the short term and, in the longer term, with respect to the performance and attitudes of future employees.

CASE STUDY 3.1

RECRUITMENT ISSUES IN THE GLOBAL HOSPITALITY AND TOURISM INDUSTRY: THE PARTICULAR CASE OF CHINA

SCOTT HURRELL AND DORA SCHOLARIOS

Hospitality and tourism are important sources of economic growth for many countries. Increased labour mobility and migration have created more numerous and diverse employment opportunities. Yet, the industry often struggles to find suitable recruits, suffering from reputational issues, for example, related to status, pay, working patterns, and the precarity of work, especially for migrants. Some workers may tolerate these issues in the short term, such as students working part time, migrants from deprived areas or travelling transient workers. However, they can inhibit long-term recruitment goals and especially the recruitment of top talent (Zhang and Wu, 2004). Baum (2015) states that tourism, as an industry, has been slow to react to the leadership deficit that it faces and has fallen behind other sectors as a result.

A country in which there appears to be a particular opportunity for the attraction of highly skilled applicants who could fill leadership deficits is China. As noted in the text, China faces an over-supply of graduates and graduate unemployment following rapid expansion of the university sector. The ILO (2015) reported that the majority of Chinese graduates in a 2013 survey expressed discontent with their jobs. This 'rising joblessness' of Chinese graduates (Sharma, 2014) has been a concern for a number of years, attracting attention from around the world. In June 2014 the BBC asked the question: 'What do you do with millions of extra graduates?' specifically concerning India and China (ibid.). The BBC's report states that the official graduate unemployment rate in China was 15 per cent six months after graduation. However, experts in China believe that the real unemployment rate may be as high as 30 per cent (ibid.).

The Chinese authorities are reportedly worried about the potential for unrest and have even released proclamations that graduates should lower their initial expectations away from 'the big cities and the best work positions' to consider less prestigious jobs that can nevertheless help develop the country, such as

working in the army or in rural areas (Blanchard, 2011). Because of its Confucian routes, China remains a hierarchical country both within families and the workplace with cultural differences also apparent between urban/coastal and rural areas (Child and Warner, 2003). Young people in coastal regions, especially in cities, have been more exposed to outside influences, seeing themselves as more cosmopolitan than the 'local' Chinese in other areas (ibid.: 22). The notion of preserving 'face' (or *mianzi*) is also central to Chinese cultural principles. A graduate may feel that taking an 'inferior' job causes them to lose face with their family and peers, especially if moving from an urban to rural area.

The general issues highlighted above with hospitality and tourism employment were noted by Zhang and Wu (2004) in their roundtable discussion of issues affecting the industry in China. This study involved 17 senior hotel and travel agency managers as well as four academic representatives who taught students majoring in hospitality and tourism. Their findings are summarised below.

- Hotel managers noted that positions were becoming increasingly difficult to fill. They attributed this firstly to increased competition, as more and more hospitality establishments opened in China. They also believed that changes in the expectations and perceptions of young, well-educated potential job applicants were a key barrier to recruitment. As China has become increasingly subject to globalisation, higher-paying sectors such as IT and banking have increased graduates' salary expectations. Hotel managers felt that they could not match these raised expectations. Recruitment issues were exacerbated further by the poor reputation of the sector and the view that such jobs were a platform to something better. Managers reported that they would like to pay graduates more but are often on short-term contracts themselves and under pressure to keep costs down, and so have little authority to raise wages.
- Hotel managers also believed that where graduate trainees from hotel schools did take jobs within the

sector they quickly became dissatisfied with conditions, work relations, supervision and the fact that they did not immediately start in managerial roles. New recruits often left soon after joining. There was also a perception that young graduate entrants may feel undermined by their initial supervisors; with supervisors valuing experience and the young graduates valuing the knowledge they have gained from education (potentially an issue related to *mianzi*).

- Travel agency managers reported that it was becoming more difficult to attract graduates to international tour guide positions. They attributed this to falling wages and the increased attractiveness of sectors that could pay considerably more, such as IT and banking. The work was seen as 'low status' – routine and lacking development opportunities (even for managers) – and as a 'stepping stone to something else', inhibiting the retention of young graduates into management positions. Managers also believed that graduates feared the sector was dying out (for example, because of online travel agencies).

- University representatives affirmed that students often did not want employment in the sector once they had learned more about it. Students reportedly often initially viewed the subject as easy and providing good job prospects in 'nice' environments. In some cases university representatives reported that students' parents may have also wished them to study the subject. However, many experienced 'reality shock', especially when they learned that they would initially start in operative roles as trainees before progressing to management. University lecturers believed that it was often unnecessary to start graduates in such junior positions and that hotels should do more to aid the transition of young graduates into the workplace by providing better training and empowerment opportunities. In turn, the hotel managers believed that universities should better orientate students and that current internships offered by universities in the industry were not fit for purpose. The managers recommended that universities develop better links with hospitality and tourism organisations.

One international hotel brand, which tried to rectify the kinds of staff shortages noted above, is Marriott (Siedsma, 2011).[4] In 2011 Marriott needed to fill 50,000 jobs worldwide by the end of the year and launched a Facebook game, 'My Marriott Hotel', to aid the process. This targeted people under the age of 35. The game took 10 months to develop at an undisclosed cost. The chain wished to recruit in a variety of jobs – chefs, lifeguards, sales and marketing staff and resort and housekeeping staff. After three weeks the game had attracted players from 99 countries. The game is effectively a simulation similar to other Facebook games such as Farmville and gives potential job applicants the opportunity to 'manage' their own hotel, starting off with the kitchen and moving to other areas. Participants have budgets to spend and can hire and train employees. Points are won or lost depending on levels of customer satisfaction and, eventually, virtual profit levels. Marriott also developed a Facebook career page to run in tandem with the game and interested players could click on a link which took them to the company's careers website. The game is used for recruitment purposes only, with performance on the game not used for selection decisions. Susan Strayer, Marriott's Senior Director for Global Employer Brand and Marketing, reported that particular recruitment issues were reported in Asia and especially China. She said, 'In China we struggle in the hospitality industry. People there want their kids working in a prestigious job. They don't realise that hospitality can be prestigious.' The need to appeal to China was explicitly recognised in developing the game, which was available in Mandarin as well as English, Spanish, French and Arabic.

Marriott's actions are consistent with Baum's (2015) recommendation that tourism organisations use social media as a recruitment tool. Efforts to do so have, in part, led to global mobility and migration within the sector. The question arises as to how successful this approach could be in addressing China's skills shortages in hospitality and tourism.

Exercise

You are the group HR manager of a national hotel chain in China, employing approximately 1,000 people. You have 100 vacancies for trainee graduate managers and a further 150 vacancies for operative roles across a number of functions in both urban and rural areas. You have noticed the same recruitment issues within your organisation as hotel managers in Zhang and Wu's (2004) study and employ a similar progression route for trainee graduate managers as reported within their study. Your boss, the company HR Director, has heard about Marriott's approach to recruitment and wishes you to assess how effective such an approach may prove within your own chain and *why* it may work. She has asked you to prepare a report to cover the following points:

1. What is the theoretical basis underlying an approach like the Marriot's?
2. What factors would you have to take into account in designing such an approach for our organisation?
3. How successful do you think such an approach would be within our organisation?

---

[4]We first became aware of this example through Nickson (2013).

4. Do you think that Marriott's approach may prove more successful for some positions rather than others and/or in attracting certain kinds of candidates?

5. Are there any other approaches to recruitment that our organisation could potentially use to alleviate the recruitment issues? Explain why these could work.

6. Are there any particular factors (such as those related to our organisation and/or the national context) that may hinder *any* of the approaches that you have suggested to improve recruitment?

7. What role can we reasonably expect universities with hospitality and tourism degree programmes to play in improving the image of the sector?

8. Given the external environment, is it possible for us (or any Chinese hotel employer) to improve the reputation of the sector?

Another issue to consider …

Given graduate employment issues in China, how reasonable do you think it is that the Chinese Government has urged graduates to lower their employment expectations?

CASE STUDY 3.2

OUTSOURCING RECRUITMENT AT BLUEBERRY

SCOTT HURRELL AND DORA SCHOLARIOS

This case highlights the issues of recruitment outsourcing and methods used to recruit for scarce skills.

Blueberry is a subsidiary of a multinational IT company based in the US, Globalchip, and provides Globalchip's European technical helpdesk. Currently, the helpdesk employs 40 staff, and recruits new employees directly. New recruits need to be fluent in a European language other than English and have technical competence (computer skills, some product knowledge) and customer service skills. Finding individuals with this skills mix has been very difficult. Currently, the Customer Service Unit includes fluent speakers of Spanish, French, Italian, Finnish, Dutch, German and Greek. The majority are non-UK nationals. There is a very tight budget for salaries.

In the US, Globalchip operates a similar help desk for Asia. When this Help Desk was established the strategy adopted, after much discussion and deliberation, was to outsource recruitment to an agency (Succuro). The HR Director of Globalchip asked the HR partner responsible for liaising with the European Help Desk, Liz McDonald, to identify whether she could put a similar outsourced recruitment process in place. She was also asked to collaborate with her US colleague to determine the difficulties that Succoro currently face in recruiting suitable individuals.

Liz's enquiries have shown that Globalchip has a three-year contract with Succuro, which is due for renewal soon. A 'service-level agreement' was produced by the company, which clearly indicated what level of performance was expected of the agency, for instance time to fill vacancies.

Succoro is finding it increasingly difficult to recruit suitable people within the budget constraints. However, it is an important contract which it wants to retain. The agency has been performing well and exceeding the service-level agreement in some indicators. Succoro uses an online application form, and then screens applicants in a telephone interview. Globalchip managers are involved in the final selection decision.

Liz is a member of a local network of HR practitioners from a number of organisations. One of the other members, Jim Gray, works for an agency that runs a similar recruitment process for a mobile phone company elsewhere in the UK. Jim shared his experience of recruiting those with language and technical skills:

The main difficulty is trying to attract applicants to jobs that pay a little below the average. Our agency cannot afford to use some of the more

popular websites because they are expensive. We need to use other ways of targeting people who might be willing to live and work in the UK – almost to sell the experience. We try to use networks like websites for those who want to travel and work abroad as well as advertising on our agency's overseas websites. We target social networking sites like Facebook and Gumtree. We are having real difficulties getting speakers of, for example, Dutch and Finnish to come to work in the UK.

It takes about eight weeks to fill a vacancy, though for some of the more common languages there is sometimes a pool of applicants in our skills bank.

Liz is still investigating the implications of outsourcing for Blueberry.

Questions

1   How would outsourcing change the role of HR in the recruitment process?

2   What is a service-level agreement?

3   Which methods would you use to attract applicants to the international call centre in the UK?

4   To what extent is Jim's experience an example of 'viral' recruitment? What are the potential advantages and drawbacks of such an approach?

CASE STUDY 3.3

RECRUITMENT AND SKILLS GAPS IN FONTAINEBLEAU AND OXYGEN

SCOTT HURRELL AND DORA SCHOLARIOS

Fontainebleau and Oxygen are two leading multinational hotel chains with a strong focus on customer service. Two of their UK outlets, however, reveal contrasting fortunes in terms of workers' customer service skills.

The exact nature of the hotels' service brands differs considerably. Oxygen staff described the hotel as 'young', 'fresh' and 'stylish'. The building itself had won design awards and had a minimalist interior complemented by modern art prints. There was an emphasis on informality when serving customers with employees allowed discretion over service encounters and their appearance at work, to supplement their designer uniform. Oxygen employees were required to be 'funky' 'friendly' and 'individual'.

Fontainebleau's service brand was much more formal, and characterised as 'traditional' and 'professional'. The hotel had opulent décor, with antique-style furniture complemented by classical art prints. Employees had to adhere to rigid brand standards, reinforced through regular training. Employees were expected to interact with customers in a highly formal manner and be 'polite', 'clean' and 'tidy'. Fontainebleau provided an industry-standard uniform and had strict staff appearance guidelines.

Managers in one branch of Fontainebleau reported that a number of current staff were not fully proficient in customer service skills (known as skills *gaps*). Managers reported such gaps in approximately 25 per cent to 30 per cent of front-line service staff; rising to 60 per cent on the reception desk (although many receptionists were new). In Oxygen, no customer service skills gaps were reported. Fontainebleau had a staff turnover rate of 75 per cent in the previous year and Oxygen 42 per cent.

Both hotels used a variety of recruitment methods. Oxygen, however, relied more heavily on recruiting from university campuses and was also slightly more reliant on recommendations from current employees.

The rationale for staff recommendations also differed between the hotels. In Fontainebleau the HR manager believed that recruiting through employee recommendations fostered a happy team environment, whilst in Oxygen there was more emphasis on the fit between people and the establishment.

Formal job adverts also differed. Whilst Fontainebleau tended to emphasise details about the job and benefits of working for the company, Oxygen emphasised the brand. One advert, for example, gave a picture of the inside of the hotel alongside the words 'distinctive', 'unmistakable', and 'unique' before adding 'but enough about you' and then describing what Oxygen offered to employees. This advert mirrored a customer advertising campaign, with near identical wording. Oxygen (unlike Fontainebleau) also took applicants on an establishment tour as part of the recruitment process. The reception manager reported that he found the tour especially useful to allow candidates to assess the reality of their expectations of the hotel.

Source: Adapted from Hurrell and Scholarios, 2014

Questions

1 What factors could potentially have led to Fontainebleau experiencing higher levels of customer service skills gaps than Oxygen?

2 What perspectives on recruitment discussed in the chapter can be used to analyse Oxygen's superior performance in terms of skills gaps and staff turnover?

3 Are there any apparent contradictions in terms of the recruitment approaches of Fontainebleau and their subsequent experiences with turnover and skills gaps?

4 Are there any potential drawbacks with Oxygen's approach to recruitment?

Bibliography

ACAS (2011) *The Equality Act – What's New for Employers*?, London: ACAS.

ACAS (2014) *The Equality Act 2010 – Guidance for Employers*, London: ACAS.

Anderson, N., Born, M. and Cunningham-Snell, N. (2001) 'Recruitment and selection: applicant perspectives and outcomes', pp. 200–18, in Anderson, N., Ones, D., Sinangil, H.K. and Viswesvaran, C. (eds.) *Handbook of Industrial, Work, and Organizational Psychology: Volume 1 Personnel Psychology*, London: Sage.

Autor, D., Katz, L.F. and Kearney, M.S. (2006) *The Polarization of the US Labor Market*, Cambridge, MA: National Bureau of Economic Research.

Barber, A. (1998) *Recruiting Employees: Individual and Organisational Perspectives*, London: Sage.

Barber, A.E., Wesson, M.J., Roberson, Q.M. and Taylor, M.S. (1999) 'A tale of two job markets: organizational size and its effects on hiring practices and job search behaviour', *Personnel Psychology*, Vol.52, No.2, 841–67.

Bates, P., Johnson, C. and Gifford, J. (2008) Recruitment and Training among Large National Employers, Institute for Employment Studies and IFF Research on behalf of Learning and Skills Council.

Baum, T. (2015) 'Human resources in tourism: still waiting for change? A 2015 reprise, *Tourism Management*, Vol.50, 204–12.

Beagrie, S. (2015) 'Getting social media recruitment right', www.hrmagazine.co.uk, 26th January. Available at: http://www.hrmagazine.co.uk/hr/features/1149347/getting-social -media-recruitment.

Belcourt, M. (2006) 'Outsourcing: the benefits and risks', *Human Resource Management Review*, Vol.16, No.2, 269–79.

Billsberry, J. (2007) *Experiencing Recruitment and Selection*, Chichester: John Wiley & Sons.

Blanchard, B. (2011) 'China says graduates should lower job expectations', *Reuters*, 28th March. Available at: http://in.reuters.com/article/2011/03/28/idINIndia-55925820110328.

Boxall, P. and Purcell, J. (2003) *Strategy and Human Resource Management*, Basingstoke: Palgrave Macmillan.

Boyatzis, R.E. (1982) *The Competent Manager: A Model for Effective Performance*, New York: Wiley.

Breaugh, J.A. (2012) 'Employee recruitment: current knowledge and suggestions for future research', pp. 68–87, in Schmitt, N. (ed.) *The Oxford Handbook of Personnel Assessment and Selection* New York: Oxford University Press.

Broughton, A., Higgins, T., Hicks, B. and Cox, A. (2011) *Workplaces and Social Networking: The Implications for Employment Relations*, London: ACAS.

Cable, D.M. and Graham, M.E. (2000) 'The determinants of organizational reputation: a job search perspective', *Journal of Organizational Behaviour*, Vol.21, 929–47.

Cable, D.M. and Turban, D.B. (2003) 'The value of organizational image in the recruitment context: a brand equity perspective', *Journal of Applied Social Psychology*, Vol.33, No.1, 2244–66.

Campion, M.A. (1988) 'Interdisciplinary approaches to job design: a constructive replication with extension', *Journal of Applied Psychology*, Vol.73, No.3, 467–81.

Carroll, M., Marchington, M., Earnshaw, J. and Taylor, S. (1999) 'Recruitment in small firms. Processes, methods and problems', *Employee Relations*, Vol.21, No.3, 236–50.

Cennamo, L. and Gardner, G. (2008) 'Generational differences in work values, outcomes and person-organisation values fit', *Journal of Managerial Psychology*, Vol.23, No.8, 891–906.

Child, J. and Warner, M. (2003) 'Culture and management in China', *Research Papers in Management*, Cambridge: Judge Business School, University of Cambridge. Available at: https://www.jbs.cam.ac.uk/fileadmin/user_upload/research/workingpapers/wp0303.pdf.

CIPD (2011) *Resourcing and Talent Planning*, London: Chartered Institute of Personnel and Development.

CIPD (2013a) *HR Outlook: Winter-2012–13: Views of Our Profession*, London: Chartered Institute of Personnel and Development.

CIPD (2013b) *Resourcing and Talent Planning*, London: Chartered Institute of Personnel and Development.

Collins, C.J. and Kanar, A.M. (2014) 'Employer brand equity and recruitment research', pp. 284–97, in Yu, K.Y.T. and Cable, D.M. (eds.) *The Oxford Handbook of Recruitment*, New York: Oxford University Press.

ComputerWeekly.com (11 June, 2010) 'Will LinkedIn reshape the recruitment sector?'. Available at: http://www.computerweekly.com/news/1280097144/Will-LinkedIn-reshape-the-recruitment-sector.

Department for Business Innovation and Skills (BIS) (2014) *Business Population Estimates for the UK and Regions 2014*. Available at: https://www.gov.uk/government/uploads/system/uploads/attachment_data/file/377934/bpe_2014_statistical_release.pdf.

Department for Communities and Local Government (2009) *National Firefighter Selection Process. Development of the National Firefighter Selection Tests: Psychological Report*. Available at: www.communities.gov.uk.

Department of Health (2007) *Additionality Shortage Professions List*. Available at: http://www.dh.gov.uk.

Dries, N., Pepermans, R. and De Kerpel, E. (2008) 'Exploring four generations' beliefs about career', *Journal of Managerial Psychology*, Vol.23, No.8, 907–28.

Ehrhart, K.H. and Ziegert, J.C. (2005) 'Why are individuals attracted to organizations?', *Journal of Management*, Vol.31, 901–19.

European Commission (EC) (2011) 'EU Employment and Social Situation Quarterly Review: September', Brussels: European Commission: Employment, Social Affairs and Inclusion.

European Union (EU) (2014) 'Equal Treatment in Employment and Occupation'. Available at: http://eur-lex.europa.eu/legal-content/EN/TXT/?uri=uriserv:c10823.

Felstead, A., Gallie, D., Green, F. and Inanc, H. (2013) *Skills at Work in Britain: First Findings from the Skills and Employment Survey 2012*, London: Centre for Learning and Life Chances in Knowledge Economies and Societies, Institute of Education. Available at: http://www.cardiff.ac.uk/socsi/ses2012/[hidden]resources/1.%20Skills%20at%20Work%20in%20Britain%20-%20mini-report.pdf.

Finlay, W. and Coverdill, J. (2000) 'Risk, opportunism and structural holes: how headhunters manage clients and earn fees', *Work and Occupations*, Vol.27, No.3, 377–405.

Forde, C. and Slater, G. (2006) 'The nature and experience of agency working in Britain: what are the challenges for human resource management?', *Personnel Review*, Vol.35, No.2, 141–57.

Gallagher, N. and O'Leary, D. (2007) *Recruitment 2020. How Recruitment is Changing and Why it Matters*, London: Demos.

Gatewood, R.D. and Feild, H.S. (1998) *Human Resource Selection* (4th edn.), Fort Worth, TX: Dryden Press.

Goos, M. and Manning, A. (2007) 'Lousy and lovely jobs: the rising polarization of work in Britain', *The Review of Economics and Statistics*, Vol.89, No.1, 118–33.

High Fliers (2015) *The Graduate Market in 2015*, High Fliers Research Ltd.

Healy, M. and Schwarz-Woelzl, M. (2007) 'Recruitment policies and practices in the context of demographic change: critical issues in the ICT sector and recommendations', Report of MATURE project. Available at: www.mature-project.eu.

Hoque, K. and Noon, M. (2004) 'Equal Opportunities policy and practice in Britain: evaluating the "empty shell" hypothesis', *Work Employment and Society*, Vol.18, No.3, 481–506.

Hsieh, A.T. and Chen, Y.Y. (2011) 'The influence of employee referrals on P-O fit', *Public Personnel Management*, Vol.40, No.4, 327–39.

Hurrell, S. A. (2015) Uber labour ruling in California could send shockwaves *through the sharing economy*, The Conversation June 24th. Available at: https://theconversation .com/uber-labour-ruling-in-california-could-send-shockwaves-through-the-sharing-economy-43728.

Hurrell, S.A., Warhurst, C. and Nickson, D. (2011) 'Giving Miss Marple a makeover: graduates, skills shortages and the voluntary sector', *Non-Profit and Voluntary Sector Quarterly*, Vol.40, No.2, 336–55.

Hurrell, S.A., Scholarios, D. and Thompson, P. (2013) 'More than a "Humpty Dumpty" term: strengthening the conceptualization of soft skills', *Economic and Industrial Democracy*, Vol.34, No.1, 161–82.

Hurrell, S.A. and Scholarios, D. (2014) 'The people make the brand: reducing social skills gaps through person-brand fit and human resource management practices', *Journal of Service Research*, Vol.17, No.1, 54–67.

Incomes Data Services (IDS) (2008) *Competency Frameworks*, HR Studies, 865, London: IDS.

Information Commissioner's Office (ICO) (2005) *Data Protection: Quick Guide to Employment Practices Code*, Wilmslow: ICO.

International Labour Organization (ILO) (1998) 'The text of the Declaration and its follow-up'. Available at: http://www.ilo.org/declaration/thedeclaration/textdeclaration/lang--en /index.htm.

ILO (2015) *World Employment Social Outlook: Trends 2015*, Geneva: ILO. Available at: http:// www.ilo.org/global/research/global-reports/weso/2015/lang--en/index.htm.

Kellard, K., Walker, R., Ashworth, K., Howard, M. and Liu, W.C. (2001) 'Staying in Work; Thinking about a New Policy Agenda', DFEE Research Report No.264, Nottingham: DFEE.

Landis, R.S., Earnest, D.R. and Allen, D.G. (2014) 'Realistic job previews: past, present and future', in Yu, K.Y.T. and Cable, D.M. (eds.) *The Oxford Handbook of Recruitment*, New York: Oxford University Press, 423–36.

Lees, C.D. and Cordery, J.L. (2000) 'Job analysis and design', pp. 45–68, in Chmiel, N. (ed.) *Introduction to Work and Organizational Psychology*, Oxford: Blackwell.

Lepak, D.P. and Snell, S.A. (2002) 'Examining the human resource architecture: the relationships among human capital, employment, and human resource configurations', *Journal of Management*, Vol.28, No.4, 517–43.

Lievens, F. and Highhouse, S. (2003) 'The relation of instrumental and symbolic attributes to a company's attractiveness as an employer', *Personnel Psychology*, Vol.56, No.1, 75–102.

Lockyer, C.J. and Scholarios, D. (2004) 'Selecting hotel staff: why best practice doesn't always work', *International Journal of Contemporary Hospitality Management*, Vol.16, No.2, 125–35.

McClelland, D.C. (1976) *A Guide to Job Competency Assessment*, Boston, MA: McBer and Company.

McKay, P. and Avery, D. (2005) 'Warning! Diversity recruitment could backfire', *Journal of Management Enquiry*, Vol.14, No.4, 330–36.

Murray, S (2008) *StepStone Total Talent Report 2008: A report from the Economist Intelligence Unit.* Available at: http://www.economistinsights.com/sites/default/files /StepStoneTotalTalentReport_2008_final.pdf.

Ng, E.S.W., Schweitzer, L. and Lyon, S.T. (2010) 'New generation, great expectation: a field study of the millennial generation', *Journal of Business and Psychology*, Vol.25, No.2, 281–92.

Nickson, D. (2013) *Human Resource Management for the Hospitality and Tourism Industries*, (2nd edn.), London: Routledge.

Organization for Economic Co-operation and Development (OECD) (2013) 'Education at a Glance 2013: United Kingdom' *OECD Country Note*. Available at: http://www.oecd.org/edu /United%20Kingdom_EAG2013%20Country%20Note.pdf.

Office for National Statistics (ONS) (2011) *Non-UK born workers – 2011*. Available at: http:// www.ons.gov.uk/ons/rel/lmac/non-uk-born-workers/2011/non-uk-born-workers.html.

Parry, E. and Tyson, S. (2008) 'An analysis of the use and success of online recruitment methods in the UK', *Human Resource Management Journal*, Vol.18, No.3, 257–74.

Phillips, J.M. and Gully, S.M. (2015) 'Multilevel and strategic recruiting: where have we been, where can we go from here?', *Journal of Management*, Vol.41, No.5, 1416–45.

PricewaterhouseCooper (2010) 'Managing Tomorrow's People: Where will you be in 2020?'.

Rienzo, C. (2014) 'Migrants in the UK Labour Market: An Overview', Migration Observatory Briefing, Centre of Migration, Policy and Society (COMPAS), Oxford: Oxford University. Available at: http://www.migrationobservatory.ox.ac.uk/briefings/migrants-uk-labour -market-overview.

Rienzo, C. (2014a) 'Characteristics and Outcomes of Migrants in the UK Labour Market', Migration Observatory Briefing, COMPAS, Oxford: University of Oxford. Available at: http://www.migrationobservatory.ox.ac.uk/briefings/characteristics-and -outcomes-migrants-uk-labour-market.

Robinson, M.A., Sparrow, P.R., Clegg, C. and Birdi, K. (2005) 'Forecasting future competency requirements: a three-phase methodology,' *Personnel Review*, Vol.36, No.1, 65–90.

Sanchez, J.I. (1994) 'From documentation to innovation: reshaping job analysis to meet emerging business needs', *Human Resource Management Review*, Vol.4, No.1, 51–74.

Schneider, B. and Konz, A. (1989) 'Strategic job analysis', *Human Resource Management*, Vol.28, No.1, 51–63.

Searle, R. (2006) 'New technology: the potential impact of surveillance techniques in recruitment practices,' *Personnel Review*, Vol.35, No.3, 336–51.

Sharma, Y. (2014) 'What do you do with millions of extra graduates?', BBC News, 1st July. Available at: http://www.bbc.co.uk/news/business-28062071.

Shwed, U. and Kalev, A. (2014) 'Are referrals more productive or more likeable? Social networks and the evaluation of merit', *American Behavioral Scientist*, Vol.58, No.2, 288–308.

Siedsma, A. (2011) 'Marriott hopes to win with Facebook game', *Workforce*, 11th July. Available at: http://www.workforce.com/articles/marriott-hopes-to-win-with-facebook-game.

Stahl, G., Björkman, I., Farndale, E., Morris, S.S., Paauwe, J., Stiles, P., Trevor, J. and Wright, P. (2012) 'Six principles of effective global talent management', *Sloan Management Review*, Vol.53, No.2, 25–42.

Suff, R. (2010) 'Using competencies in HR practices: the 2010 IRS survey', *IRS Employment Review*, 23rd August.

Taylor, M.S. and Collins, C.J. (2000) 'Organizational recruitment: enhancing the intersection of theory and practice', pp. 304–34, in Cooper, C.L. and Locke, E.A. (eds.) *Industrial and Organizational Psychology: Linking Theory and Practice*, Oxford: Blackwell.

Taylor, M.S. and Schmidt, D.W. (1983) 'A process-oriented investigation of recruitment source effectiveness', *Personnel Psychology*, Vol.36, No.2, 343–54.

Trades Union Congress (TUC) (2015) *The Decent Jobs Deficit: The Human Cost of Zero-Hours Working in the UK*, London: TUC. Available at: https://www.tuc.org.uk/sites/default /files/DecentJobsDeficitReport_0.pdf.

Ulrich, D. and Beatty, D. (2001) 'From players to partners: extending the HR playing field', *Human Resource Management,* Vol.40, No.4, 293–307.

Viadeo and YouGov (2007) 'What does your NetRep say about you? A study of how your Internet reputation can influence your career prospects'. Available at: http://www.rp-net .com/online/filelink/386/ETUDE%20VIADEO_NetRep_2007.pdf.

Wadham, J., Robinson, A., Ruebain, D. and Uppal, S. (2010) *Blackstone's Guide to the Equality Act 2010*, Oxford: Oxford University Press.

Winterbotham, M., Vivian, D., Shury, J., Davis, B. and Kik, G. (2014) 'UK Commission's Employers Skills Survey 2013: UK Results', Wath upon Dearne: UKCES. Available at: https:// www.gov.uk/government/uploads/system/uploads/attachment_data/file/327492/evidence -report-81-ukces-employer-skills-survey-13-full-report-final.pdf.

Woodhams, C. and Corby, S. (2007) 'Then and now: disability legislation and employers' practices in the UK', *British Journal of Industrial Relations*, Vol.45, No.3, 556–80.

Yakubovich V. (2006) 'Passive recruitment in the Russian urban labor market', *Work and Occupations*, Vol.33, No.3, 307–34.

YouGov (2006) *Has your Business got the X Factor?* London: Croner.

Yu, K.Y.T and Cable, D.M (eds.) (2014) *The Oxford Handbook of Recruitment*, New York: Oxford University Press.

Zhang, H.Q. and Wu, E. (2004) 'Human resource issues facing the hotel and travel industry in China', *International Journal of Contemporary Human Resource Management*, Vol.16, No.7, 424–28.

CHAPTER 4

SELECTION

Dora Scholarios

Introduction

'Best practice' employee selection is usually associated with the 'psychometric' model. This recommends rigorously developed psychometric tests, performance-based or work simulation methods, and the use of multiple methods of assessment, all designed to accurately measure candidates' knowledge, skills, abilities, personality and attitudes.

This view has dominated literature on selection. Its popularity is no doubt because of its emphasis on objectivity, meritocracy and efficiency, which are all evident in the story of selection, and indeed the emergence of HRM over the last century. Industrialisation and mass manpower planning during the early twentieth century required a systematic way of matching the attributes of individuals to the requirements of jobs, and drew from psychological research on scaling individual differences (for example, the work of Alfred Binet or Raymond Cattell in the field of education). Systematic selection is now regarded as one of the critical functions of HRM, essential for achieving firm-level strategy (Ployhart and Moliterno, 2011), and a core component of what has been called a high commitment or high performance management approach to HRM (Marchington and Wilkinson, 2012; Pfeffer, 1998).

This chapter begins with a review of the principles of the psychometric model and the range of assessment methods which follow this model. The chapter then considers whether organisations have adopted these methods. This leads to a more sceptical account of 'sophisticated' selection, and the possibility of three alternative perspectives: a 'best fit' approach; an interactive decision process perspective and a discourse view, which describes selection as a contested, rather than rational, process, muddied by multiple possible interpretations and interests. We conclude by examining what these alternatives imply for selection practice and for HRM.

A brief overview of psychometric quality

How do we identify people with knowledge, skill, ability and the personality to perform well at a set of tasks we call a job? Even more difficult, how do we do this before we have ever seen that person perform on the job? (Ployhart et al., 2006: 10)

This is the problem which gives the psychometric model its alias as the 'prediction' or 'predictivist' paradigm. Decisions whether to hire someone are usually based on their performance on a test assessing their suitability for the job – hence the prediction – but how do we make sure this test does what it is intended to do? Four standards are used to make this evaluation (see Farr and Tippins, 2010 or Schmitt, 2012 for more detail).

1   The method of assessment must be *reliable*, i.e. accurate and free from contamination. Reliable methods have high physical fidelity with job performance itself, are standardised across applicants, have some degree of imposed structure and show consistency across multiple assessors. Work samples or simulations which measure performance on a structured task reflecting behaviours used in the job are likely to have high reliability. Interviews are generally thought to have low reliability, although the use of multiple decision makers and standardisation, like question–response scoring, increase their reliability (Levashina *et al.*, 2014).

2   Selection methods must also be *valid* – relevant for the work behaviours they are meant to predict. At minimum, to be valid, assessment must be designed around a systematic job analysis and person specification for the job, and be reliable. For example, introducing structure into interviews enhances their validity. A valid method, though, should also show an association between scores on the proposed selection method and desired job behaviours. This is often expressed as a correlation coefficient – known as a criterion-related validity coefficient – representing the relationship between scores on the predictor (or proposed selection method) and scores on a criterion (or proxy measure) of job performance; for example, a personality test of extraversion (the predictor) might be correlated with the number of sales made by a retail worker (the criterion). This correlation coefficient can range from 0 (chance prediction or no relationship) to 1.0 (perfect prediction). Table 4.1 summarises low, moderate or high predictive validity coefficients for a range of methods.

3   *Subgroup predictive validity* should be the same for different applicant groups, such as men and women. Members of one subgroup should not be selected disproportionately more or less often than members of another. The example of cognitive ability testing illustrates perfectly the trade-offs between predictive validity and different subgroup prediction. Tests which measure general cognitive ability provide the best predictors of future success in the workplace regardless of the specific job, with validity coefficients up to .60 (Schmidt and Hunter, 1998). However, some minority groups tend to score lower as a group on such tests, even though the tests are not inherently unfair, e.g. immigrant versus majority groups in Belgium and the Netherlands (Sackett *et al.*, 2010).

4   The selection method should have high *utility* for the organisation. Methods with high validity which are not expensive to develop or administer will have higher utility. This also is affected by the hiring context, for example, the number of applications received for a job opening and the proportion of these who will be hired (the selection ratio).

The 'what' and 'how' of selection

Each of these four psychometric standards is concerned with how we should design selection methods for determining people's suitability for jobs. Also relevant is what underlying individual characteristics we wish to capture with these methods, as a range of methods (the

Table 4.1 The psychometric quality and acceptability of alternative selection methods

Selection Method	Psychometric Quality			User Acceptability
	Predictive Validity[a]	Subgroup Differences (Race/Gender)	Utility	
Cognitive				
Ability/aptitude test	High	Large/small	High	Moderate
Achievement/job knowledge test	High	Moderate/small	High	Favourable
Non-cognitive				
Personality test	Low/moderate	Small/small	Moderate	Unfavourable
Biographical information	Moderate	Small/small	Moderate	Unfavourable
Experience	Moderate	Small/small	Low	Moderate
Performance-based				
Work sample	Moderate/High	Small–moderate/small	Moderate	Favourable
Interview-unstructured	Low	Small/small	Moderate	Low
Interview-structured	High	Small/small	Moderate	Moderate
Situational judgement test	Moderate	Moderate/small	High	Favourable
Assessment centre	Moderate	Moderate/small[b]	Moderate	Favourable

Sources: Ployhart *et al.*, 2006: Table 7.3; Schmidt and Hunter, 1998.
Notes
[a]Descriptors for criterion-related validity coefficients are based on the following accepted ranges: 0.10 = Low; 0.20 = Moderate; 0.30 and above = High.
[b]Descriptors reflect general findings. Subgroup differences tend to vary by exercise.

'how') could be used to tap into a single underlying construct (the 'what'). For example, application forms, interviews and psychometric tests could all be used to measure personality, but with varying degrees of psychometric rigour.

One useful framework distinguishes between cognitive, non-cognitive and performance-based individual differences. Cognitive characteristics reflect intellectual processes, academic achievements and knowledge; non-cognitive characteristics include personality traits, motivation, past experience and qualifications; and performance-based characteristics refer to behavioural examples of job performance. Each of these constructs represents the 'what' to be measured; the selection technique used to do this represents the 'how'.

Table 4.1 brings together the four psychometric standards and three types of individual differences to classify various selection methods. The table also indicates the general findings from research on user acceptability with respect to these methods, an issue to which we return later in the chapter. The table shows that performance-based selection methods generally have higher reliability/validity, lower subgroup differences in predictive validity and higher user acceptability, all of which has resulted in their increasing popularity.

Cognitive ability

Psychometric tests are standardised instruments designed to measure individual differences, most commonly cognitive ability or aptitude, achievement or personality. Measures of ability focus on current levels of skill in specific areas, such as arithmetic or verbal ability, while aptitude refers to one's potential to learn or acquire skill, regardless of past experience. Aptitudes may be targeted at specific occupational areas – an aptitude for making inferences from numerical data contributes to performance in financial services occupations. Tests of

Box 4.1 HRM in practice	Screening for graduate jobs

Graduate employers in the UK expected an average of 69.2 applications per vacancy in 2014, rising to over 100 for fast-moving consumer goods companies, investment banking and IT (Association of Graduate Recruiters, 2014). To deal with this number of applications, employers used minimum entry requirements – 74 per cent required a 2:1 degree classification and 38 per cent examined high school grades – and 67.4 per cent used online ability tests to screen for graduates with high potential. The most common tests were numerical reasoning (77.2 per cent) and verbal reasoning (75.6 per cent).

achievement include school examinations, typing tests, or statutory professional examinations, for example, for accountancy certification.

During the 1980s, interest centred on tests of general cognitive ability (referred to as g). Most test batteries measuring g consist of tests of numerical, verbal, reasoning and spatial ability, and emphasise future potential for learning or adapting to new situations (see Box 4.1 for an example). Research shows that tests of g provide the best way of predicting performance differences between job applicants in any type of job, with potentially high returns on investment (utility) for organisations. They are strong predictors of various measures of job success, including supervisory ratings, production quantity and quality, and training performance (Ones *et al.*, 2010). This has been shown to hold across different employment and cultural contexts (Salgado *et al.*, 2003).

There are, however, several areas of resistance to tests of g. First, performance on a test does not necessarily reflect intelligence or the test-taker's best possible performance, but may depend on whether the individual is interested in doing well, where they focus their attention and how much effort they expend. This leads to the distinction between typical and maximal performance. Some argue we should focus on finding out how a person typically performs a task in the actual job environment (Klehe *et al.*, 2015). Later, we consider personality tests as one way of predicting typical behaviour.

A second development is in tests measuring different kinds of 'intelligence'. This includes creative and emotional intelligence, which cannot be captured by linguistically based psychometric tests, but which affects many aspects of work performance (Joseph and Newman, 2010). Tacit knowledge, which represents practical knowledge of 'how' to do a job, has also received attention, especially in non-routine jobs, such as management (Sternberg *et al.*, 1995). Current thinking on the structure of ability distinguishes between tests which measure fluid intelligence, representing general reasoning ability across situations, and crystallised intelligence, representing a culturally specific view of intelligence which develops as a result of specific experiences (Carroll, 1993).

Finally, as shown in Table 4.1, cognitive ability testing suffers from high subgroup differences in predictive validity; that is, it has adverse impact on members of minority racial groups (Berry *et al.*, 2011). Even though the reliability, validity and utility of cognitive ability testing have all been shown – suggesting they are free from any bias – their use is a liability to employers who are concerned with maintaining a diverse workforce. This can lead to substantially different hiring rates, especially as organisations become more selective (i.e. hire fewer applicants or increase their cut scores on selection methods). 'Best practice' recommends careful design and validation of tests for particular groups (men/women, racial/cultural groups) to provide norm-referenced testing (Ryan and Tippins, 2009).

Personality

Personality is a non-cognitive characteristic. There is continuing debate about fakeability, generally low predictive validity (Table 4.1), and even about the very existence of such a thing as personality. Despite this, research interest and practice has focused on the

Five Factor Model or the 'Big Five' dimensions. This claims that personality differences between people can be explained by five dimensions – Extraversion, Conscientiousness, Agreeableness, Neuroticism or Emotional Stability and Openness to Experience (Costa and McCrae, 1992). One of these in particular – Conscientiousness – has emerged as a valid predictor of many aspects of work performance. This combines hard work, thoroughness, self-control and dependability, and is shown to have higher validity when used to predict pro-social aspects of work performance (also known as discretionary behaviour) such as altruism and (inversely) turnover or theft (Salgado, 2002).

Most summaries conclude that personality tests are valid and useful when developers pay attention to possible moderators, such as social desirability effects or the specific task contexts which are being predicted. Simply adding a specific context – such as the words 'at work' to questions in a personality test (e.g. 'At work, I keep my belongings neat and clean') – seems to improve significantly the validity of the Big Five for predicting job performance (Shaffer and Postlethwaite, 2012). Further context, such as type of work, helps even more. For instance, the dimensions of Extraversion, Agreeableness and Neuroticism generally predict customer service behaviours, but in sales environments (closing a deal, for example), Agreeableness may be a disadvantage (Liao and Chuang, 2004).

Another application is in the use of personality tests to predict team performance. The aggregated score of team members on some of the Big Five personality dimensions, including the score of team leaders, is related to how well the team works together. Personality explains why homogeneous groups are more cohesive, while those which are heterogeneous are better at problem-solving (Moynihan and Peterson, 2004).

Ones *et al.* (2007) summarised the findings from accumulated validity studies and showed that the Big Five personality dimensions predict performance best for customer service, sales and managerial occupations. They are most useful when used in combination with other information about the person and for specific work contexts, and have lower adverse impact for women or racial minority groups than cognitive ability tests. Procedures to detect or prevent faking include early warning messages to test-takers or monitoring eye-tracking and response latency (Ziegler *et al.*, 2011).

Debates continue about the role of personality testing in selection (e.g. Morgeson *et al.*, 2007; Tett and Christiansen, 2007), but measures based on personality and other non-cognitive psychological constructs remain popular. For example, emotional intelligence describes personal and social competence in managing one's own and others' emotions, and predicts performance in roles requiring inter-personal interaction and leadership qualities (Joseph and Newman, 2010). Another development is compound personality traits – 'custom-made' personality measures based on combinations of traits designed to predict job-relevant behaviour in a specific context. Integrity, for example, which has grown in importance (see Box 4.2), is made up of measures of hostility, impulsiveness, trust and dutifulness; these have been used to predict dishonest (or counterproductive) work behaviour with high validity (Van Iddekinge *et al.*, 2012). Other compound scales have been designed for predicting customer service, stress tolerance, violence and managerial potential (Ones *et al.*, 2007).

Box 4.2 HRM in practice   Looking for integrity in bankers

Social responsibility and client empathy have become the focus of recruitment for many investment banks dealing in trading, wealth management and securities – areas which contributed to the financial meltdown in 2008 and damaged the reputation of banking. Since 2013, the Chartered Institute for Securities and Investment requires all exam candidates in the capital markets sector in the UK, Ireland, Europe and North America to pass the *IntegrityMatters* test before taking their professional exam, to encourage them to think ethically in different situations.

Source: *Financial Times*, 23 June 2013.

Biographical information

Another non-cognitive characteristic is biographical information or biodata, where applicants describe retrospectively their past experience and work history. The assumption is that performance on past jobs predicts how someone will behave in future job situations as it reflects underlying personal qualities such as attitudes or motivation. Application forms designed to collect biodata (now commonly online) tend to be used by large organisations as their initial screening device.

Biodata has moderate to high predictive validity for predicting tenure and performance, but selectors tend to be cautious about its use (Breaugh *et al.*, 2014). 'Hard', verifiable items such as success in educational or occupational pursuits tend to be more valid and favoured than 'soft' items related to values or aspirations, which are liable to faking. Selectors also must avoid using information haphazardly without consideration of the important qualities to be judged for the job opening. The general principle behind making biodata job-relevant involves 'criterion keying' – linking desirable/undesirable responses to each item with either high- and low-performing groups of employees. Furnham (1997), for example, linked items showing applicants' financial responsibility, early family responsibility and stability to high performing insurance salesmen. Instruments known as Weighted Application Blanks or Biographical Information Blanks make the weighting of important items more objective and reduce adverse impact against protected groups (Chapman and Webster, 2003).

Biodata has other limitations. Focusing on past accomplishments is suited only to those with experience. This is why many graduate recruitment schemes assess aptitude (potential) or personal competencies rather than experience (Box 4.1). Contrary to 'criterion-keying', however, many graduate employers have increased minimum entry qualifications from non-degree to degree, even though a university degree bears no relation to the qualities actually required to do the job. This phenomenon is known as 'credential creep' or 'degree inflation'. Finally, legislation addressing age and disability discrimination places non-job-related items (e.g. age) at risk of legal challenge.

Performance-based methods

The third type of individual difference targeted by selection methods is performance itself. Performance-based tests and simulations focus on replicating a set of behaviours required on the job rather than an underlying psychological characteristic (see Box 4.3 for examples). The focus is on measuring present performance in order to predict future performance.

Work samples or job simulations are 'high-fidelity' methods which focus on assessing performance of actual tasks – what a person can actually do rather than what they 'know'. Compared to cognitive and non-cognitive measures, these methods have less adverse impact for women and minority ethnic groups. Schmitt (2003) showed that while a simulation had lower validity than a cognitive test (.36 versus .46), a higher proportion of capable minority individuals were selected using the simulation. Users (managers and candidates) are generally more favourable towards performance-based methods. Selectors tend to pay more attention to observed behavioural information about a candidate than self-report data derived from personality or biodata, and candidates benefit from a realistic preview of the job itself.

Situational judgement tests (SJTs) are 'low fidelity' simulations. These ask applicants to select from several possible behavioural responses for a question about a work situation. This is essentially a test of judgement, which emerged originally as a measure of tacit knowledge or knowledge acquired through experience to complete everyday tasks. As there is no absolute correct answer, responses may vary depending on how the questions are designed, revealing some uncertainty about what is actually being measured. Ployhart and Erhart (2003) showed that asking people what they 'would do' in a certain situation tended to tap behavioural intentions, personality and past behaviour; asking what they 'should do' tapped job knowledge and cognitive ability. SJTs have generally high validity, low subgroup differences and benefit from evolving multimedia delivery formats.

Box 4.3 HRM in practice   Increasing realism through performance-based methods

Job simulations

Schmitt (2003) describes a role-play simulation which replicates a typical day in the life of a service representative at an insurance company. Typical tasks were customer questions about insurance rates and coverage options. Candidates had 30 minutes to review background material (company policies and procedures) and examine an abbreviated version of the customer database. Two trained assessors made a series of 11 customer query calls to the applicants using detailed scripts. The assessor who was not role-playing listened and took notes.

Situational judgement tests (SJTs)

Lievens (2013) examined video-based physician–patient SJTs assessing interpersonal skills for medical school admissions in Belgium. These are based on the identification of critical incidents and use semi-professional actors, with the involvement of experienced physicians. Lievens showed their validity for predicting performance in situations involving patient interaction, both at medical school and later in general practice.

Multimedia simulation

Holland and Lambert's (2013) contact centre simulation captured core competencies (computer skills, accuracy, multitasking, customer service and sales potential) and provided a 'fun' candidate experience (the industry struggles to retain candidates through the whole hiring process). Candidates are placed in a fictitious contact centre through an interactive dashboard and are scored on role-play calls. Improvements in Average Call Handling Time, Transferred Calls and First-Call Resolution were shown one and three years after implementing the new hiring method. It was also thought to help reduce attrition.

Multimedia SJTs are used in advanced manufacturing, service and managerial selection (Fetzer, 2013). A multimedia format can be used to attract candidates. For example, one bank created a numerical reasoning test which looked like the Bloomberg business television channel with key information scrolling along the bottom of the screen ('Guide to assessment', *People Management*, 8 October 2012). Fetzer suggests that game-inspired assessment will become the standard for selection in the future. As simulations become more powerful in representing the 'reality' of work, they will provide better assessment of complex processes, such as judgement, prioritisation, decision-making or diagnostic skills and increasing candidate acceptability.

Finally, structured interviews involve situational or behaviour-based assessments and show high predictive validity (Table 4.1). Companies can significantly enhance the validity of their selection methods by adding a structured interview to their hiring process (Huffcutt, 2011). Some examples of how structure can be introduced are by using a critical incident-based job analysis for designing the questions, using multiple, trained interviewers and raters, minimising use of prior information, such as applicant test scores, or limiting prompting or elaboration (Levashina *et al.*, 2014). These authors also found that face-to-face interviews tended to use more elements of structure than either phone or video interviews, and cautioned about the lack of media richness in the latter, for instance verbal or non-verbal cues which aid communication. This is worrying given their rapidly increasing use.

Questions based on hypothetical situations (situational interviews), past behaviour/experience (behavioural interviews) or job knowledge provide the best psychometric quality, especially when tied to specific competencies identified in job analysis. Job relevance allows assessors to focus on qualities directly linked to actual performance rather than making inferences about underlying characteristics (as shown by the example in Box 4.4).

Box 4.4 HRM in practice   Situational interviews for predicting 'fit'

An engineering company developed an interview to assess entry level engineers' tendency to act in ways that 'fit' the values of the organisation. Incumbent project engineers created the following dilemma and rating criteria using a behaviourally anchored five-point scale:

Suppose that you are in charge of a large-scale equipment installation project that must be completed on time to avoid significant penalties for exceeding the expected due date. The six-month-long project is now about 75 per cent completed and your PERT analysis indicates that, at best, it will be finished about 2–3 days ahead of schedule. However, an installation supervisor who works for you has just informed you that there may be a delay in material delivery that could add 7–10 working days to the project. What would you do to deal with this situation?

1 = Poor. Ignore the situation since it is only a potential problem. Be prepared to deal with it when/if you hear that the delay is actually going to occur.

3 = Acceptable. Tell the supervisor that you expect them to deal with the problem. Remind the supervisor of the completion date and make it clear that you expect it to be met and that you want to be kept appraised of the situation.

5 = Excellent. Meet with the supervisor ASAP to determine the exact nature of the potential problem and formulate a plan for preventing or dealing with it. Set a follow-up procedure to make sure that the plan is being carried out.

Source: Maurer, 2006.

Mixed approaches

The emphasis on behaviour is also visible in the competency movement. Competencies are transferable personal qualities, such as teamworking or business awareness, which draw from a range of skills, abilities, traits, job knowledge, experience and other qualities needed to perform a job effectively. Service orientation, for example, includes personality characteristics, such as courtesy, and behaviours displayed towards customers (Baydoun *et al.*, 2001). 'Future-oriented' behavioural competencies go beyond person–job fit. A typical example is in graduate selection where leadership potential is assessed on the basis of past behaviours and achievements.

A recent trend, noticeable from hospitals to financial services companies, is to move away from behavioural competency approaches to assess motivation and 'strengths' – 'authentic' capacities for behaving or thinking in a particular way ('The rise of strengths-based recruitment', 13 May 2014, www.hrmagazine.co.uk). This is thought to be better at attracting and identifying committed candidates with qualities such as passion or empathy, and lead to performance improvements, for example generating greater revenue. Box 4.5 shows interview questions based on each approach.

An amalgam of many of these approaches is reflected in assessment centres which focus on a series of exercises (role-play, group case studies/discussions, in-tray exercise) designed to reveal various behaviour-based performance dimensions (problem solving, decision making, teamwork). With multiple methods, multiple assessors and systematic scoring procedures for integrating candidate data, they provide good validity for many occupations and have high user favourability because of their face validity (their appearance of measuring job-related factors). The range of exercises ensures lower adverse impact against underrepresented groups (Table 4.1).

There is some concern about the consistency and objectivity of assessor ratings. Brown and Hesketh (2004) described a high degree of impression management by candidates,

Box 4.5 HRM in practice   From competencies to strengths and motivation

Comment on the reliability, validity and fairness of these questions.

Behaviour-based competency interview question

Tell me about a time when you inspired others to meet a common goal?

Strengths-based interview questions

When do you feel you are most like 'yourself'?
What activities energise you?

Motivation-based interview question

Please explain why you have applied for this particular graduate programme. Why are the reasons you have stated important to you?

especially by 'players' who are able to produce 'flashes of the appropriate behavioural competencies' (2004: 173), and assessor evaluations based on opinions formed when 'watching from afar' rather than objective scores. Others believe it is possible to make a 'good tool even better' (Lievens *et al.*, 2009: 142). Assessor training in scoring and how they conduct final evaluations, as well as systematic design of the exercises, is essential for reliability and validity. Given their high cost, though, they are likely to be used only for high-level roles e.g. managers.

Summary of trends

The review so far shows several important trends in selection which build on the four indicators of psychometric quality.

- *More reliable and valid assessment tools.* This is achieved, for example, by: detailed job analyses; introducing structure and standardisation; training assessors; carrying out validation studies and making more use of statistical techniques, such as meta-analysis, across validity studies to increase the precision of the prediction task. Advances in these areas have resulted in increased confidence in the validity of many selection methods (Ryan and Ployhart, 2014).
- *Greater use of high validity/low adverse impact assessment tools.* Many selection processes use multiple methods to increase validity and lower adverse impact. For an example in call centres which combines biodata, psychometric cognitive or non-cognitive tests and situational judgement tests see Konradt *et al.* (2003).
- *Increasing importance of assessing non-cognitive qualities.* Across all types of jobs, interest has grown in a wider spectrum of behaviours, such as organisational citizenship or adaptability. Some personality tests are good predictors of this type of behaviour, and situational interviews can be designed to assess behaviours like helping colleagues (Latham and Skarlicki, 1995).
- *Increasing use of bespoke simulations.* These provide behavioural indicators of qualities relevant to a particular job or organisation, along with low adverse impact and high user acceptability. Such organisationally specific approaches reflect a growing strategic orientation which links selection to wider competencies, not just job-specific skills.

- *Technology and assessment.* Many selection methods are now delivered online or digitally. Questions remain about the security of online testing, the quality of applicants achieved with these methods, and equality. Some organisations use an unproctored Internet test for pre-screening and a second (in-person) test sitting for the actual decision (Lievens and Chapman, 2010). Video resumes introduce potential stereotyping based on social cues, such as accent or looks, which could encourage discriminatory hiring, while digital interviews may inhibit the quality of interviewer–interviewee communication (for an alternative view see Box 4.6). The use of social media for hiring decisions is also growing, raising issues for validity, legality, invasion of privacy and fairness (Roth *et al.*, 2016). Even personality testing is being re-shaped with the creation of algorithms to analyse patterns in social media data (Box 4.7).

Box 4.6 HRM in practice   Are video resumes fair?

Equality guidelines for selection usually recommend 'blind' screening when it comes to social categorisation characteristics such as gender or ethnicity. In one of the first studies of video resumes (or CVs), Hiemstra *et al.* (2012) found that ethnic minority job seekers in the Netherlands perceived pre-recorded video resumes as more face valid than paper resumes contrary to native Dutch job seekers. The positive perceptions of ethnic minorities seems counter to expectation. How might this be explained? Consider issues of language proficiency and opportunity to perform.

Box 4.7 HRM in practice   Predicting personality from social media 'big data'

The rise in the use of LinkedIn, Facebook and Twitter by employers to find new talent (2012 Social Recruiting Survey) has made personality prediction based on social media data a reality. TweetPsych provides a personality profile based on qualitative text mining of Twitter feeds. Some data suggests validity of around .40 for the prediction of Openness and Extroversion. What are the ethical and legal implications?

Source: *Psyche.* The Newsletter of the Psychometrics Forum, summer 2014 (www.psychometricsforum.org).

What do organisations actually do?

Psychometric principles of good practice in the design and administration of assessment methods are endorsed by professional psychological and HR associations across the world, but most employers tend not to pay close attention. Informal selection methods such as sifting CVs, responding to speculative applications and unstructured interviews still dominate.

Larger organisations with a dedicated HR function are more likely to adopt a psychometric approach, testing for ability, personality or competencies (Zibarras and Woods, 2010). This was shown in two global surveys of over 1,000 HR professionals (Fallow and Kantrowiz, 2013; Ryan *et al.*, 2015). In Ryan *et al.*'s survey, 43 per cent overall used combined test scores in a formal manner, mainly to test personality, ability or leadership competencies. There has been some convergence across countries, perhaps due to multinational companies applying a single selection system, but there tends to be greater cognitive test use in Europe than the US, and especially in Belgium, Britain, the Netherlands and Spain (Salgado and Anderson, 2002). Recent estimates for large UK employers place the use of personality or ability tests at 45 and 42 per cent, respectively (CIPD, 2013).

Performance-based and competency tests tend to be more common in the public rather than private sector, and for managerial and administrative/secretarial positions. Their greater use in the public sector is because this sector has tended to do more to ensure that hiring practices are non-discriminatory and encourage diversity (Wolf and Jenkins, 2006).

Explaining practice

Selection is more than the application of assessment techniques. Three other perspectives take into account the organisational and social hiring context: (1) selection as 'best fit' for the organisation (as opposed to a 'best practice' model); (2) selection as an interactive decision process involving multiple stakeholders and (3) selection as discourse, where power and interests dominate what happens more than the rigour of assessment methods.

(1) Selection as 'best fit': the organisation's perspective

In the study of HRM generally, there is often an assumption of similar needs across sectors, organisations, occupations and even countries, which leads to 'best-practice' guidelines, such as those of the psychometric model. Valid methods are held to always have high utility, but this assumes a low selection ratio (a low number hired relative to the number of applicants), that the cost of poor selection is high (as it may be in a top management or skilled position), and that the top performers can always be selected (the 'best' actually accept the job offer). The reality of staffing is that these conditions are not always met.

Table 4.2 summarises a range of factors which shape selection practice. These are organised using Klehe's (2004) distinction between economic and social pressures as a way of illustrating the effects of the wider context of selection decisions and allow us to make predictions about when psychometric approaches are likely to be adopted.

With respect to economic pressures, short-term resource considerations (e.g. the cost of more structured behavioural interviewing, training inexperienced assessors, or relieving managers for assessment days) often outweigh the longer-term potential returns. Similarly, the need to hire quickly or for fewer applicants means organisations are less likely to invest heavily in selection procedures. This describes many SMEs, organisations located in suburban or rural areas, or sectors where there are skills shortages. Responding to unsolicited correspondence and face-to-face contact may be a more rational option for attracting suitable candidates.

Social pressures are divided into two types in Table 4.2: legislative/institutional and stakeholder pressure. We consider the role of stakeholders in the next section. Employers are increasingly required by law in many countries to pay attention to psychometric principles. Public sector

Table 4.2 Factors influencing selection practice and decisions

Economic Pressures
Short-term financial impact, e.g. skills supply, labour market tightness, organisation size, ownership (multinational, single owner, shareholder pressures), time constraints, presence of HR
Long-term financial impact, e.g. high-skill (managerial/professional) occupations/ vacancies, competition, market segment/differentiation strategy

Social Pressures
Legislative/institutional, e.g. regulatory environment, accountability of organisation, national culture
Other stakeholders, e.g. users, applicants, industry, test developers

organisations are especially affected. In an examination of 400 Canadian federal selection discrimination cases, Terpstra and Kethley (2002) showed that the government sector was more likely to have had litigation brought against it than any other sector. This kind of accountability and risk encourages the use of multiple methods, greater standardisation and monitoring of selection procedures in order to ensure diversity (Jewson and Mason, 1986). US federal legislation also goes further in placing a burden on employers to justify the job-relatedness of all selection measures, and this is one of the reasons why psychometric testing is used more in some European countries (the UK, Spain and Portugal) than in the US (Salgado and Anderson, 2002). UK employers, conversely to those in the US, perceive the rigour of a testing approach as a 'precautionary measure' which can protect them from legal challenge (Wolf and Jenkins, 2006).

Box 4.8 illustrates the pressures faced in two industry examples – hotels and construction – where cost, time and recruitment crises may be more salient than reliability and validity.

Box 4.8 HRM in practice	Economic and social pressures on selection

ECONOMIC PRESSURES ➡	SELECTION	⬅ SOCIAL PRESSURES
	Example 1: HOTELS	
Labour market (competition, shortages) *Short-term pressures to fill vacancies* (casualisation, high turnover) *Market segmentation* (chain, deluxe) *Resource pressures* (only chains have centralised HR/train selectors)	*Short-termist approach* Informal methods targeted at local transient labour market/unpredictability *Longer-term approach* Strategic alignment (high quality localised approach, combines standardisation with informal networks) Emphasis on staff retention, person–culture fit	*Applicant perceptions* (low pay, poor prospects, antisocial hours, hard work, isolated locations)
	Example 2: CONSTRUCTION (Manual and skilled/technical workers)	
Workflow (project-/network-based, local site decentralisation, flexibility due to design/supply variations) *Project ownership* (network of subcontractors and professionals, local focus) *Labour market* (skill shortages, limited training, competency-based skill certification voluntary) *Resources* (working to contract, time, cost) *Change* (rapid technological change, changing markets, multiskilling)	Larger firms more formalised ('skills identity card', HR functions) Local variation even where formalised procedures existed (procedures called 'raindances') Strong emphasis on probationary days (work simulations) and site-manager local networks (time-served on other jobs) After technical ability, valued honesty, conscientiousness, adaptability	*Applicant perceptions* (dangerous work, masculine culture, antisocial hours) *Industry* (Industry Training Board common accreditation) *Customers* (pressures for improved quality, cost reduction) *Firm-specific demands* (work against industry standards) *Site manager* (autonomous at local level) *Legislation* (Health & Safety)

Sources: Lockyer and Scholarios, 2004; 2007.

(2) Selection as an interactive decision process

Social pressures can also originate from other stakeholders in the hiring process. This includes the selectors (managers, HR) who implement the procedures, institutional bodies which set guidelines for entry into occupations or for assessment (e.g. professional associations) and applicants themselves. Searle (2003) argues that test developers, whose interests are quite distinct from those of organisations and applicants, are an increasingly powerful stakeholder because of the access they have to testing data. Thus hiring involves an interactive process of information exchange and negotiation between the organisation and its wider environment. This impacts two general areas.

How methods are perceived by stakeholders

In Table 4.1, we introduced the idea of user acceptability as a counterweight to the psychometric ideals of reliability and validity. This refers to whether the method is perceived as credible, and hence whether managers or practitioners will actually use it, as well as how it is perceived by the candidates who are exposed to it. Performance-based methods are more favourable and more likely to be adopted and used appropriately than less transparent, psychometric tests. Ryan *et al.*'s (2015) survey of practitioners confirmed that the most common reason for not using tests was a preference for one's own (perhaps more credible) methods, such as interviews.

User participation in developing selection methods is also important. Millmore (2003) talks about the involvement of multiple stakeholders, including all levels of management and peers, in the design of the process (e.g. defining person specifications, panel interviews). This should lead to greater consensus about the qualities being sought and hence more reliable assessment.

Applicants also are important stakeholders. They have a right to be treated with dignity, have their privacy respected, for example, in application forms and interviews, and receive information on what is expected of them and their performance (Gilliland and Steiner, 2012). This highlights the importance of perceptions of fair treatment or procedural justice (Cropanzano and Wright, 2003). Job applicants are consistent across countries in how they rate the fairness of selection methods, with cognitive tests, interviews and work samples rated highest for respect for privacy and being given opportunity to perform (Box 4.9). Such findings are important for the design of selection systems dealing with international

---

Box 4.9 HRM in practice   **Perceived fairness of selection methods**

Job applicants across 17 countries seem to rank their most and least favourable methods consistently. These rankings are shown from (1) 'most favourable' to (10) 'least favourable' below. How does this compare with your own experiences?

1 work sample tests
2 interviews
3 CVs/resumes
4 cognitive tests
5 biographical information
6 references
7 personality tests
8 honesty/integrity tests
9 personal contacts
10 graphology

Source: Anderson *et al.*, 2010.

applicants, as their reactions are likely to be similar. Perceptions also influence whether qualified applicants maintain interest in the job for which they are applying; whether they decide to continue to the next stage of the recruitment process; or whether they accept the job if offered. Box 4.10 lists 'best practice' recommendations from a group of the most respected international experts on candidate reactions to selection systems.

How applicants perceive the job or organisation

Negative impressions may be caused by uninformative websites; disinterested recruiters; long application processes; or undesirable images of the employer brand. Conversely, early interactions encourage those who see a match with the values of the organisation to remain in the application process. In an example from a police force in a US Midwest city, the interview stage provided a realistic preview of the job and prompted some candidates to withdraw from the process (Ployhart *et al.*, 2002).

This is important for several reasons. First, if some applicant groups withdraw from the process more frequently than others, then potentially qualified candidates who are required to meet skill gaps are excluded. This seems to be the case for the hospitality industry because of the perceptions of what the job offers (Box 4.8).

Second, members of minority groups, such as women or blacks, may experience more negative perceptions. These applicants withdrew disproportionately from the US police selection process above. This harms diversity targets, an issue of some concern to police forces in many parts of the world who consider being representative of the community as essential to good policing.

Finally, in some employment situations more power lies with applicants than the organisation. The hospitality industry is often portrayed as being in competition with higher paying, 'cleaner' temporary work offered by the likes of call centres. More interactive methods of selection, such as interviews, may be more effective at tackling negative perceptions and attracting qualified applicants. Of course, problems of bias and limits on diversity which are associated with informality still have to be recognised.

A further purpose of selection is to build relationships between the organisation and future employees. The interview has high 'social validity' for both managers and candidates as it allows two-way communication and a richer environment for both to establish person–organisation 'fit' (Dipboye *et al.*, 2012). Candidates perceive interviews as fairer, allowing them to make better decisions about the organisation. Our earlier discussion about how technology may be changing the richness of the interview dynamic has important implications for the issue of social validity.

One last consequence of paying attention to social processes in selection is 'socialisation impact' (Anderson, 2001). Methods which allow both parties to establish 'fit' will lead to employees who are more likely to be satisfied in their jobs, more committed to the goals of the organisation and less likely to leave.

Box 4.10 HRM in practice   **Best practice checklist for successful candidate reactions**

Provide informative explanations to applicants.

Give applicants a chance to show what they know.

Use selection methods based on sound scientific evidence.

Give timely feedback.

Give informative feedback.

Treat applicants with due respect throughout the selection process.

Source: Bauer *et al.*, 2012.

(3) Selection as discourse

A more radical view is that selection is a process which cannot easily be reduced to the quality of assessment tools and rational decision making. The reference to discourse relates to the idea that there are many different ways of talking about (i.e. describing and understanding) selection. The choice of which discourse we focus on at a particular point in time will vary; for example, some may value meritocracy and hence use a discourse which focusses on developing neutral assessment techniques which are reliable and valid (a psychometric discourse), while others are more concerned with mutual respect, treating applicants in an ethical way and building relationships of trust (a decision interactive discourse). These two examples, in fact, are often used to describe the quite different dominant discourses which guide selection practice in North America versus Europe, respectively (de Wolff, 1993). These selection discourses have become accepted by the culture as a result of societal values and guiding principles, established, for example, through legislation. Other discourses also may develop within organisations, clusters of organisations or professions as a result of other powerful forces. This may explain why 'blue-chip' multinational companies, who project themselves as global market leaders or 'good employers', often lead the way in adopting the most sophisticated, expensive and psychometrically sound selection systems, in order to be seen to comply with 'good practice' as presented by respected external bodies (e.g. those promoting equal opportunities legislation or HR professionalism). This view goes as far as to argue that selection discourses, such as strict psychometric measurement, can be used as a way of making the management of people more explicitly controllable, for example to further particular interests (Townley, 1989).

We use two examples here to illustrate this perspective. The first questions whether job suitability can be objectively reduced to an agreed set of individual qualities.

The 'good' firefighter. A firefighter has to be able to put up with long periods of monotony and boredom, but can suddenly be faced with emotional and harrowing situations. In many ways, the job is now so procedural things rarely go wrong (for instance, virtual reality of many of the city's buildings means that firefighters no longer enter smoke-filled buildings without knowing where they are going). In fact, they have to be able to follow instructions without questioning orders in what can be a militaristic culture. As well as basic physical ability and practical tests, assessors are looking for evidence of person–culture fit (prior knowledge of the service, commitment to a career and serving the community) all of which is assessed through self-report questions on an application form (e.g. Why do you want to become a firefighter?) and interviews with senior officers. How can these complex demands be reduced to behaviours appropriate for every situation? Assessors often cannot agree on the suitability of candidates, and use other shortcuts, such as appearance, to justify their decisions, even though they all go through assessor training. 'State of the art' for firefighter selection recommends a combination of cognitive/mechanical and interpersonal/emotional skills tests, but this 'all-rounder' view may just be the latest construction of the 'good' firefighter, which contrasts to earlier beliefs that firefighters should be the 'bravest and strongest' (shown through physical ability), 'smartest' (cognitive testing), or have the 'right' person profile (personality testing). This may be just another discourse of what is 'acceptable' reflecting society, and the historical and cultural influences of those who draw up the person specifications and make final decisions. In a study of a similar profession, police work, good performance was constructed as a 'masculine crime fighting' discourse (as opposed to a service discourse, which privileges skills associated with femininity). This prevented potentially qualified women from applying (Dick and Nadin, 2006).

The second example challenges the assumption of the rational assessor, showing how the decision process involves shifting negotiations between selectors (Bolander and Sandberg, 2013).

Graduate assessment centres. Despite multiple assessors and careful exercise design, assessment centres have been portrayed as 'politically charged contexts', 'largely uncontrollable and permeated with problems of meaning', and a 'conspiracy of distortion' between assessors who rank subjectively while hiding behind a 'façade of systematic and scientific professionalism' (Knights and Raffo, 1990: 37). Brown and Hesketh's (2004) analysis of attempts to measure 'soft' competencies at graduate assessment centres showed that even after training on diversity issues, assessors were still inclined to resort to first impressions or compare people to existing management in the company. In 'washing up sessions' some opinions held more sway than others (e.g. a particularly negative view of how one candidate described what she gained from her gap year) and simplistic heuristics were used to organise the information from each exercise about the candidates. Candidates were labelled 'stars', 'geeks', 'razors' and 'safe bets'. Value was attached to 'appearance, accent and appropriate behaviour' (2004: 161) tending to favour the social capital possessed by Oxbridge candidates, while finding ways to match these to the 'objectively defined' behavioural indicators.

Conclusions and implications for HRM

'Best practice' selection encompasses measures of cognitive, non-cognitive and performance qualities. Performance-based methods, with their lower adverse impact against under-represented groups, accommodate diversity as a strategic direction, whether among multinationals or the publically accountable government sectors. Beyond this, though, different ways of understanding selection have also gained prominence. These expand on the non-rational, unplanned, informal, social and power bases of selection, leading to an alternative language for evaluating hiring processes.

Diverse contexts dictate alternative logics from that of prediction or formality, suggesting a 'best fit' approach. For instance, firms facing staffing problems will use methods which they consider will attract the 'right type' of employees. The psychometric model assumes that the number of applicants exceeds positions available, and that the best applicants will always accept job offers. This is clearly not the case.

Selection can also be judged in terms of the quality of the social exchange between organisations and other stakeholders. The treatment of applicants, and their perceptions and attitudes, play an important role. Also important is the way that selection techniques are used to further interests which are often only tenuously linked to the psychometric model's aspirations of objectivity and fairness. Each of these perspectives – 'best fit', interactive decision process and discourse – highlights the deficiencies of the psychometric model for achieving a comprehensive understanding of all aspects of the selection problem (cf. Herriot, 1993; Iles, 1999).

Within HRM, selection is viewed as a core function essential for achieving key organisational outcomes; high performance, low levels of absenteeism and turnover, and high employee well-being and commitment have all been linked with 'selective hiring' (Marchington and Wilkinson, 2012). However, the reality of HRM strategic integration and practice seldom has matched the rhetoric, and this seems equally as applicable to the adoption of 'best practice' selection. Based on 'best fit' perspectives, expensive testing and bespoke assessment may be reserved for high value employees that organisations wish to retain or those at senior levels.

From the psychometric perspective, those responsible for selection should serve a monitoring function, ensuring that methods are designed and reappraised according to practice and legislative developments, and validation programmes. This assumes, however, that HR and HR issues are afforded an appropriate status and influence. Interactive perspectives require that all stakeholders' views are accommodated, and encourage selectors to think of applicants as potentially powerful decision makers. The increased devolution of HR functions to line managers requires additional support, although in many organisations, such as SMEs, this is rarely available. These issues, nevertheless, are crucial in all contexts if we acknowledge the discourse perspective's warnings of how subjectivity and vested interests obstruct the ideal of meritocratic selection systems.

CASE STUDY 4.1

MONEYFLOW

DORA SCHOLARIOS

A financial services call centre, Moneyflow, dedicated 3 hours 20 minutes to each candidate for the position of Customer Advisor. At the time, there was a vibrant employment market in the area and this call centre was competing against 15 other companies for qualified staff. Many of those recruited often left after the two days of training. Recruitment consultants were used to pre-select candidates for the company to interview. The recruitment agency chosen seemed to understand the skill specifications required. The company also carried out a validation of the process by correlating scores at the hiring stage (predictors) with Customer Advisors' supervisory performance ratings (the criterion) after six months on the job (i.e. for those who were hired). These validity coefficients are shown in parentheses for each selection method below.

Stages of recruitment/selection

1 General register of candidates formed (few active call centre workers were available given the buoyant employment situation).
2 Ads placed locally and nationally, including in universities.
3 Candidates asked to complete work history and a financial planning questionnaire (to eliminate credit risks).
4 Customer orientation score (.30): the company designed a self-assessment application form based on critical incident methods. This captures five customer-oriented competencies (customer focus, fact finding, relating to customers, convincing, oral communication) and two related to discretionary behaviour (independent facilitation, job dedication). It also acts as a realistic job preview to inform candidates of the sales component of the job.
5 Skills test score (.58): combined scores on tests of visual accuracy; spelling; key depressions; arithmetic and alphanumeric skill.
6 Telephone role-play rating (.58): 'You are a CA in a travel service.' Two assessors looked for questioning/listening/selling skills.
7 Recruitment consultants sent a list of candidates to the company to select for one hour interview with two team leaders. Depending on need, the agencies often put all candidates forward for interview without pre-selection.
8 Interview rating (20–30 minutes with manager) based on CV/work history (.21): sales skills were explored further in the interview.

Questions

1 Based on Table 4.1 and the validity coefficients, what is the overall psychometric quality of this procedure?
2 Explain the 'balance of power' in the selection process between employers, candidates and other stakeholders.
3 What recommendations would you give the call centre on their selection process? Refer to Table 4.2.

CASE STUDY 4.2
GLOBAL OR LOCAL STAFFING?

DORA SCHOLARIOS

Case scenario

The corporate HR Director and Manufacturing Director of a US multinational with locations worldwide (including South America, Asia, the Middle East and Africa) are debating whether to implement a global selection system for engineers in all the manufacturing plants or to allow each country to develop its own system tailored to the location's special needs. The Manufacturing Director feels that a good engineer needs to have the same skills no matter where in the world you go. He wants the HR group to come up with a web-screening tool, including a standardised competency-based application form and tests, and interview protocol that can be implemented worldwide. These should be linked to the company's brand values – technology, customer value, courage, integrity and impact. The HR Director believes that different characteristics are needed to perform the engineering job in different countries, not least to fit with local management practices; e.g. communication or representation. Therefore, each region needs to come up with its own system.

The problem

This case scenario is based on the work of Ryan and colleagues who over the last two decades have studied the growing use of global staffing systems used by many multinational companies, such as Motorola and Shell. Ryan and Tippins (2009) concluded that globalisation, efficiency and technology are the main driving forces behind increasing convergence towards 'sophisticated' selection systems. Organisations are increasingly sourcing their skilled talent from across the globe and the millennial generation are more mobile (PriceWaterhouseCooper Talent Mobility 2020). This suggests more global hiring practices, but some argue for local cultural sensitivity. For example, in many countries, hiring may be based on possessing a degree from a prestigious university or having a contact in the organisation. Changing to an 'impersonal' selection procedure may even signal that the company is no longer a 'good employer' for those with elite education. Another issue is that tests or interview questions designed for Western candidates may be unfamiliar in some cultures. Maurer's situational interview designed for engineers (Box 4.4) implies a particular relationship with a subordinate which may not transcend cultures. Moreover, apart from the costs of translation and ensuring cross-cultural equivalence of methods, subsidiary locations may not have the expertise in implementing formalised selection systems or the resources for training.

Consider some of the evidence gathered by Ryan and her colleagues.

- **Cultural values do matter**
  Ryan *et al*. (1999) surveyed HR practitioners/senior managers in 959 organisations in 20 countries. Countries scoring high on the cultural value of uncertainty avoidance (feeling threatened by unknown situations), such as Belgium, Japan and Spain, made greater use of testing and standardised interviews.

- **Local autonomy matters**
  Ryan *et al*. (2003) interviewed local managers. One Motorola manager commented, 'they don't want to be compared to the US, they want to be compared locally for selection. It's their applicant pool really from which they draw.' They recommended integrating 'global tools into local systems'.

- **Applicants' preferences are converging**
  In 2008 a global sample of over 1,000 undergraduates were asked to rate their perceptions of selection tools used by a particular multinational for an entry-level management job (including biodata, cognitive, personality and situational judgement tests). There were no country differences, suggesting that cultural differences in candidates' perceived fairness are not a barrier to the global selection systems used by multinationals.

Questions

1 What is your position on the case scenario? Provide an argument making use of Ryan's evidence and the economic and social pressures impacting selection (Table 4.2).

2 Design a multi-stage process for hiring graduate engineers into this US multinational in a country of your choice. Provide an explanation for your decisions.

CASE STUDY 4.3

'YOU'RE EITHER ABERCROMBIE HOT – OR YOU'RE NOT'

DORA SCHOLARIOS

American clothing retail firm Abercrombie & Fitch has stores in the UK, Canada, Japan, Singapore and throughout Europe, and is expanding rapidly. It has been ranked 219 in Deloitte's *Global Powers of Retailing*, 2015 and is one of the 1,000 largest American companies according to revenue.

Image is central to how the company sells its four brands – Abercrombie & Fitch, Abercrombie Kids, Hollister and Gilly Hicks. Investor materials describe the flagship Abercrombie & Fitch brand as 'rooted in East Coast traditions and Ivy League heritage' and 'the essence of privilege and casual luxury'. The importance of these brand values to the company is shown in an effort to disassociate from the MTV reality show *Jersey Shore* by paying the cast not to wear its clothes. The company claim their rowdy behaviour is 'contrary to the aspirational nature of our brand' (BBC News, 17 August 2011).

As described by one of the employees in the company's recruitment video, employees are expected to be ambassadors for the brand. Job advertisements are for 'cool' and 'good looking' applicants (Human Resources News, 2010). A company spokesperson describes their advertisements as just 'aimed at attracting fun-loving and stylish people for the job' and as having no discriminatory intent.

This approach is consistent with the image they wish to portray of the company and brands they sell. The job description for sales assistants (called 'models') states: 'Models protect and project the image of the brand through personal style, providing customer service and maintaining presentation standards' (www .abercrombie.co.uk/anf/careers/model.html). Sales associates and managers reflect the 'casual, energetic and aspirational attitude of the brands'.

One manager described it as, 'You're either Abercrombie hot – or you're not.' Their 'look policy', which was revealed in a 2005 class action discrimination suit brought by 10,000 former job applicants and employees, stipulates that all employees 'represent Abercrombie & Fitch with natural, classic American style consistent with the company's brand' and 'look great while exhibiting individuality'. Workers must wear a 'clean, natural, classic hairstyle' and have nails which extend 'no more than a quarter inch beyond the tip of the finger'.

Attracting and selecting future leaders, 'models' and 'part-time impacts'

In the world of fashion retail, there is no shortage of young willing workers attracted to the brand cachet of Abercrombie & Fitch. Drawing significantly from the part-time student workforce, many potential applicants, themselves, are 'brand advocates'. In fact, this is one of the qualities which the company looks for in potential employees. Social media sites such as Facebook and Twitter are used to build a following and a potential pool of self-selected applicants. Once hired, store managers emphasise to new hires that they were selected because of their looks – 'people see us and they want to be us' – and they are also given opportunities to be 'cast' as billboard models. Mystery shoppers ensure employees are adhering to company guidelines regarding their look. This 'image management' all has a strong impact on future applicants' expectations of what an Abercrombie & Fitch employee should be like, and, in some at least, shapes the desire to be one of them.

The following extracts from online fora ('The Student Room' and 'Glassdoor') for discussing jobs and employers reveal potential applicants' perceptions of the company.

> I've had an interview for Hollister's and for Abercrombie & Fitch. I haven't heard from any of them yet. But both interviews went really well to [sic] my opinion. Also do you guys think that they hire black people? I am a model, black (chocolate skin) not too skinny and pretty. I am going to attach a picture to this but please let me know of what you think.

> This company stresses customer service, by using several different taglines, depending on where you're in the store [fitting room, front room, registers]. They clearly hire based on looks and personality. I have not seen anyone with acne or any overweight people yet.

The selection of graduates for their retail management programme is similar to most other multinational company graduate schemes. There is an emphasis on retail experience, demonstrated behavioural competencies, and a series of panel and one-to-one interviews. The Manager in Training programme is the first step towards becoming a 'store executive' (Assistant Manager and then Store Manager) and a future within the company.

We hire nice, smart, talented people who are interested in building a career at Abercrombie & Fitch. We have a strong philosophy of promotion from within. All of our District Managers, Regional Managers, Directors – even the Senior Vice President of Stores – have gone through the Manager in Training program. (www.abercrombie.co.uk/anf/careers)

TARGETjobs, an online graduate jobs forum which provides potential applicants with Employer Insights and tips on how to get hired, describes the importance of demonstrating retail experience, details of when applicants have exceeded a set target, and experience of leading and organising others. Even for these positions, the advice from independent experts is to pay attention to style: 'given that all Managers in Training will be working on the shop floor around their merchandise, having some idea of the style of the stores in which they will be working will certainly help give off the right image'. Stores Recruiting Teams target Careers Fairs at specific universities, and online recruitment media are used to project the youthful, good-looking and fun company culture. Interviews are described on online careers fora as 'laid back', often taking place in a food court or walking around a mall, and involving one or two Store/District Managers.

For sales associates, applications are taken 'in store', which presents an early opportunity to screen out those who are not 'Abercrombie hot'. Store managers approach customers to encourage them to apply as potential employees. The company has created a 'look book', a collection of images for managers to refer to when hiring. A group interview usually includes questions such as 'What is your favourite thing about Abercrombie & Fitch, and what style, in your opinion, is the style of Abercrombie & Fitch?'

The role of 'model' mainly consists of saying hello to customers rather than folding clothes, replenishing stock or working the tills as in any other retail job. This is left to the part-time 'impact team'. The person specifications for these two roles are compared in Table 4.3.

Past employees tell some interesting stories about the differences between the roles. Take for example, Luke, posting a response to a *BBC News Magazine* article on 'What is the Abercrombie look?' (26 June 2009).

Whilst at uni I worked in the stockroom and as a shop floor maintainer (tidying stock). I was told on many occasions that I was not allowed to speak to the models and they were told they were not allowed to help maintain the look of the room. The amount of flirting is sickening and the favouritism between managers and models is enough to make you gag. Every year we get an intake of models who have just come off of the program shipwrecked and every time the superiority complex was quick to kick in as the 'hotties' established themselves apart from the 'notties'.

Is this discrimination?

Direct linking of corporate and HR strategy is common in companies which reinforce a brand image through their employees. One well known example is Hooters, the American restaurant chain known for its scantily clad waitresses. The company's expectations of employees are stated up front in a written contract which all prospective employees must sign.

I hereby acknowledge and affirm that the Hooters concept is based on female sex appeal and that the work environment is one in which joking and innuendo based on female sex appeal is commonplace. I also expressly acknowledge and affirm I do not find my job duties, uniform requirements or work environment to be intimidating, hostile or unwelcome.

(*The Guardian*, 11 April 2008)

The company can claim that its hiring policies simply tailor the employee qualities they are seeking according to the market demands of a solid (mostly male) customer base.

Table 4.3 Abercrombie & Fitch sales assistant roles

Models	Part-time Impact
What you need to bring to the job	*What you need to bring to the job*
Sophistication, aspiration, sense of style, diversity awareness, integrity, applied learning, outgoing personality and communication skills	Positive outlook, diversity awareness, integrity, applied learning, passion for the brand, work ethic and communication skills
Skills you will develop on the job	*Skills you will develop on the job*
Passion for the brand, multi-tasking, adaptability/ flexibility, attention to detail, product knowledge and customer focus	Multi-tasking adaptability flexibility, attention to detail, customer focus, adhering to company guidelines in personal appearance and rules of conduct, stockroom systems, scanning systems and merchandising

Source: http://www.abercrombie.co.uk/anf/careers.

Abercrombie & Fitch may use the same argument to justify hiring based on its 'look policy'. However, it has come under legal pressure to reform its hiring practices. Class action lawsuits in the US have charged the company with discrimination against minorities and women. In *Gonzalez et al.* v *Abercrombie & Fitch* (14 April 2005), Latino, African American, Asian American and female job applicants or former employees (the plaintiffs) argued that they were either limited to low visibility, back-of-the-store type jobs or terminated because of their race or ethnicity. The settlement agreement required, among other conditions:

- that the company abide by 'benchmarks' for hiring and promotion of the affected groups;
- a prohibition on targeting (predominantly white) fraternities, sororities and specific colleges for recruitment;
- advertising in publications which targeted minorities of both genders;
- Equal Employment Opportunity and Diversity Training for all employees with hiring authority;
- that managers' performance evaluations and bonuses should be based on making progress toward diversity goals;
- marketing materials which reflect diversity.

They appointed a Vice President of Diversity and Diversity and Inclusion Team to build a culture that fosters 'personal commitment to diversity' (*Racing towards Diversity Magazine*, Spring, 2012). Recruitment pages now feature various ethnic minorities and 'diversity awareness' is a quality expected from all employees (see Table 4.3). The website advertises the company's success in embracing 'the conversation around diversity and inclusion'. For example, it cites the following facts:

- Hollister is now the number 1 brand amongst 8 to 15-year-old African American youth.

- In 2011, 50 per cent of stores associates are non-white, compared to 35 per cent in 2008 and 10 per cent in 2004.
- In 2012, the company was named Best Place to Work for GLBT equality by Human Rights Campaign.

(http://www.anfcareers.com/Page/Diversity)

Discrimination cases continue, however. In 2009 a sales assistant in London claimed she had been 'hidden' in a stockroom because of her prosthetic arm, and in 2008 a Muslim US teenager claimed she was turned down for a sales position because of her hijab (the latter case was upheld by the US Supreme Court in May 2015). In 2013 France's official human rights body, Le Défenseur des Droits, investigated the company over discriminatory hiring based on physical appearance, claiming while hiring for looks may be justified for models, the company were using their 'models' as sales staff.

With recruitment targeting of job candidates by managers, it is hard to see how any kind of diversity targets for recruitment can be monitored. Managers are clearly encouraged to make decisions based on 'image norms' as part of all selection methods, including interviews, as well as in the informal approaches to customers with 'the look'.

In a 2006 interview for Salon.com, Mike Jeffries, CEO, made the following statement about their corporate strategy:

Candidly, we go after the cool kids. We go after the attractive all-American kid with a great attitude and a lot of friends. A lot of people don't belong [in our clothes], and they can't belong. Are we exclusionary? Absolutely. Those companies that are in trouble are trying to target everybody: young, old, fat, skinny. But then you become totally vanilla. You don't alienate anybody, but you don't excite anybody, either.

Questions

1 How are each of the perspectives of selection – psychometric, best fit, interactive decision process and discourse – represented in the hiring process for (a) Managers in Training and (b) sales assistants (both 'models' and 'part-time impact' roles)?

2 Evaluate the selection process with respect to the four criteria of psychometric quality described at the start of the chapter. Can falling short on any of these criteria, in your opinion, be justified? Design a selection process for the sales associate roles in Table 4.3 using psychometric principles (start with a job analysis).

3 Identify as many examples of 'selection as an interactive decision process' in this case as you can. Should these processes be eliminated on the grounds they discriminate against particular groups, or can a case be made for retaining all or some of them?

4 How is the 'selection as discourse' perspective reflected in this case?

5 Why have the legal challenges to the company's hiring approach not eliminated the problem?

Bibliography

Anderson, N. (2001) 'Towards a theory of socialization impact: selection as pre-entry socialization', *International Journal of Selection and Assessment*, Vol.9, Nos.1–2, 84–91.

Anderson, N., Salgado, J.F. and Hülsheger, U.R. (2010) 'Applicant reactions in selection: comprehensive meta-analysis into reaction generalization versus situational specificity', *International Journal of Selection and Assessment*, Vol.18, No.3, 291–304.

Association of Graduate Recruiters (2014) 'The AGR graduate recruitment survey 2014: summer review'. Available at: http://www.agr.org.uk.

Bauer, T.N., McCarthy, J., Anderson, N., Truxillo, D.M. and Salgado, J.F. (2012) 'What we know about applicant reactions to selection: research summary and best practices', SIOP White Paper Series.

Baydoun, R., Rose, D. and Emperado, T. (2001) 'Measuring customer service orientation: an examination of the validity of the customer service profile', *Journal of Business and Psychology*, Vol.15, No.4, 605–20.

Berry, C.M., Clark, M.A. and McClure, T.K. (2011) 'Racial/ethnic differences in the criterion-related validity of cognitive ability tests', *Journal of Applied Psychology*, Vol.96, 881–906.

Bolander, P. and Sandberg, J. (2013) 'How employee selection decisions are made in practice', *Organization Studies*, Vol.34, No.3, 285–311.

Breaugh, J., Labrador, J., Frye, K., Lee, D., Lammers, V. and Cox, J. (2014) 'The value of biodata for selecting employees: comparable results for job incumbent and job applicant samples?', *Journal of Organizational Psychology*, Vol.14, No.1, 40–51.

Brown, P. and Hesketh, A. (2004) *The Mismanagement of Talent*, Oxford: Oxford University Press.

Carroll, J.B. (1993) *Human Cognitive Abilities: A Survey of Factor-Analytic Studies*, Cambridge: Cambridge University Press.

Chapman, D.S. and Webster, J. (2003) 'The use of technologies in the recruiting, screening, and selection processes for job candidates', *International Journal of Selection and Assessment*, Vol.11, Nos.2–3, 113–20.

CIPD (2013) *Resourcing and Talent Planning*, London: Chartered Institute of Personnel and Development.

Costa, P.T., Jr. and McCrae, R.R. (1992) 'Normal personality assessment in clinical practice: the NEO Personality Inventory', *Psychological Assessment*, Vol.4, 5–13.

Cropanzano, R. and Wright, T.A. (2003) 'Procedural justice and organizational staffing: a tale of two paradigms', *Human Resource Management Review*, Vol.13, 7–39.

Dick, P. and Nadin, S. (2006) 'Reproducing gender inequalities? A critique of realist assumptions underpinning personnel selection research and practice', *Journal of Occupational and Organizational Psychology*, Vol.79, No.3, 481–98.

Dipboye, R.L., Macan, T.H. and Shahani-Denning, C. (2012) 'The selection interview from the interviewer and applicant perspective: can't have one without the other', pp. 323–53, in Schmitt, N. (ed.) *The Oxford Handbook of Personnel Assessment and Selection*, Oxford University Press.

Fallow, S.S. and Kantrowitz, T.M. (2013) *2013 Global Assessment Trends Report*, SHL.

Fan, J., Gao, D., Carroll, S.A., Lopez, F.J., Tian, T.S. and Meng, H. (2012) 'Testing the efficacy of a new procedure for reducing faking on personality tests within selection contexts', *Journal of Applied Psychology*, Vol.97, No.4, 866–80.

Farr, J.L. and Tippins, N.T. (2010) *Handbook of Employee Selection*, New York: Routledge.

Fetzer, M. (2013) 'Future directions', pp. 259–64, in Fetzer, M. and Tuzinski, K. (eds.) *Simulations for Personnel Selection*, New York: Springer Science+Business Media.

Furnham, A. (1997) *The Psychology of Behaviour of Work*, Hove: Psychology Press.

Gilliland, S.W. and Steiner, D.D. (2012) 'Applicant reactions to testing and selection', pp. 629–66, in Schmitt, N. (ed.) *The Oxford Handbook of Personnel Assessment and Selection*, Oxford University Press.

Hiemstra, A.M., Derous, E., Serlie, A.W. and Born, M.P. (2012) 'Fairness perceptions of video resumes among ethnically diverse applicants', *International Journal of Selection and Assessment*, Vol.20, No.4, 423–33.

Herriot, P. (1993) 'Commentary: a paradigm bursting at the seams', *Journal of Organizational Behavior*, Vol.14, 371–5.

Hogan, R.T., Hogan, J. and Busch, A. (1984) 'How to measure service orientation', *Journal of Applied Psychology*, Vol.69, No.1, 167–3.

Holland, B. and Lambert, D. (2013) 'How to measure contact center skills using multimedia simulations', pp. 129–56, in Fetzer, M. and Tuzinski, K. (eds.) *Simulations for Personnel Selection*, New York: Springer Science+Business Media.

Huffcutt, A.I. (2011) 'An empirical review of the employment interview construct literature', *International Journal of Selection and Assessment*, Vol.19, No.1, 62–81.

Human Resources News (2010) 'Recruitment policy of Abercrombie and Fitch draws criticism'. Available at: http://www.humanresources-news.co.uk.

Iles, P. (1999) *Managing Staff Selection and Assessment*, Milton Keynes: Open University Press.

Jewson, N. and Mason, D. (1986) 'The theory and practice of equal opportunities policies: liberal and radical approaches,' *Sociological Review*, Vol.34, No.2, 307–24.

Joseph, D.L. and Newman, D.A. (2010) 'Emotional intelligence: an integrative meta-analysis and cascading model', *Journal of Applied Psychology*, Vol.95, No.1, 54–78.

Klehe, U. (2004) 'Choosing how to choose: institutional pressures affecting the adoption of personnel selection procedures', *International Journal of Selection and Assessment*, Vol.12, No.4, 327–42.

Klehe, U, Grazi, J., Mukherjee, T. and Liebig, J. (2015) 'Typical and maximum performance', pp. 228–44, in Nikolaou, I. and Oostrom, J.K. (eds.) *Employee Recruitment, Selection, and Assessment Contemporary Issues for Theory and Practice*, New York: Psychology Press.

Knights, D. and Raffo, C. (1990) 'Milkround professionalism in personnel recruitment: myth or reality?', *Personnel Review*, Vol.19, No.1, 28–37.

Konradt, U., Hertel, G. and Joder, K. (2003) 'Web-based assessment of call center agents: development and validation of a computerized instrument', *International Journal of Selection and Assessment*, Vol.11, Nos.2–3, 184–93.

Latham, G.P. and Skarlicki, D.P. (1995) 'Criterion-related validity of the situational and patterned behavior description interviews with organizational citizenship behavior', *Human Performance*, Vol.8, 67–80.

Levashina, J., Hartwell, C.J., Morgeson, F.P. and Campion, M.A. (2014) 'The structured employment interview: narrative and quantitative review of the research literature', *Personnel Psychology*, Vol.67, No.1, 241–93.

Liao, H. and Chuang, A. (2004) 'A multilevel investigation of factors influencing employee service performance and customer outcomes', *Academy of Management Journal*, Vol.47, 41–58.

Lievens, F. (2013) 'Adjusting medical school admission: assessing interpersonal skills using situational judgement tests', *Medical Education*, Vol.47, No.2, 182–9.

Lievens, F. and Chapman, D. (2010) 'Recruitment and selection', pp. 133–54, in Wilkinson, A. (ed.) *The SAGE Handbook of Human Resource Management*, London: Sage.

Lievens, F., Tett, R.P. and Schleicher, D.J. (2009) 'Assessment centers at the crossroads: toward a reconceptualization of assessment center exercises', *Research in Personnel and Human Resources Management*, Vol.28, 99–152.

Lockyer, C. and Scholarios, D. (2004) 'Selecting hotel staff: why best practice doesn't always work', *International Journal of Contemporary Hospitality Management*, Vol.16, No.2, 125–35.

Lockyer, C. and Scholarios, D. (2007) 'The "raindance" of selection in construction: rationality as ritual and the logic of informality', *Personnel Review*, Vol.36, No.4, 528–48.

Marchington, M. and Wilkinson, A. (2012) *Human Resource Management at Work* (5th edn.), London: Chartered Institute of Personnel and Development.

Maurer, S.D. (2006) 'Using situational interviews to assess engineering applicant fit to work group job and organizational requirements', *Engineering Management Journal*, 1 September.

Millmore, M. (2003) 'Just how extensive is the practice of strategic recruitment and selection?', *Irish Journal of Management*, Vol.24, No.1, 87.

Morgeson, F.P., Campion, M.A., Dipboye, R.L., Hollenbeck, J.R., Murphy, K. and Schmitt, N. (2007) 'Reconsidering the use of personality tests in personnel selection contexts', *Personnel Psychology*, Vol.60, No.3, 683–729.

Moynihan, L.M. and Peterson, R.S. (2004) 'The role of personality in group processes', pp. 317–45, in Schneider, B. and Smith, D.B. (eds.) *Personality and Organizations*, Mahwah, NJ: Lawrence Erlbaum.

Ones, D., Dilchert, S., Viswesvaran, C. and Judge, T.A. (2007) 'In support of personality assessment in organizational settings', *Personnel Psychology*, Vol.60, No.4, 995–1027.

Ones, D., Dilchert, S., Viswesvaran, C. and Salgado, J.F. (2010) 'Cognitive abilities', pp. 255–75, in Farr, J.L. and Tippins, N.T. (eds.) *Handbook of Employee Selection*, New York: Routledge.

Pfeffer, J. (1998) *The Human Equation. Building Profits by Putting People First*, Boston, MA: Harvard Business School Press.

Ployhart, R.E. and Erhart, M.G. (2003) 'Be careful what you ask for: effects of response instructions and the construct validity and reliability of situational judgment tests', *International Journal of Selection and Assessment*, Vol.11, No.1, 1–16.

Ployhart, R.E. and Moliterno, T.P. (2011) 'Emergence of the human capital resource: a multi-level model', *Academy of Management Review*, Vol.36, No.1, 127–50.

Ployhart, R.E., McFarland, L.A. and Ryan, A.M. (2002) 'Examining applicants' attributions for withdrawal from a selection procedure', *Journal of Applied Social Psychology*, Vol.32, No.11, 2228–52.

Ployhart, R.E., Schneider, B. and Schmitt, N. (2006) *Staffing Organizations: Contemporary Practice and Theory*, Mahwah, NJ: Lawrence Erlbaum.

PricewaterhouseCoopers (2012) *Talent Mobility 2020: The Next Generation of International Assignments*, New York: PwC.

Roth, P. L., Bobko, P., Van Iddekinge, C.H. and Thatcher, J.B. (2016) 'Social media in employee-selection-related decisions: a research agenda for uncharted territory', *Journal of Management*, Vol.42, No.1, 269–98.

Ryan, A.M. and Ployhart, R.E. (2014) 'A century of selection', *Annual Review of Psychology*, Vol.65, No.20, 1–20.

Ryan, A.M. and Tippins, N. (2009) *Designing and Implementing Global Selection Systems*, Chichester: Wiley–Blackwell.

Ryan, A.M., McFarland, L., Baron, H. and Page, R. (1999) 'An international look at selection practices: nation and culture as explanations for variability in practice', *Personnel Psychology*, Vol.52, 359–94.

Ryan, A.M., Wiechmann, D. and Hemingway, M. (2003) 'Designing and implementing global staffing systems: Part II—best practices', *Human Resource Management*, Vol.42, 85–94.

Ryan, A.M., Boyce, A.S., Ghumman, S., Jundt, D., Schmidt, G. and Gibby, R. (2008) 'Going global: cultural values and perceptions of selection procedures', *Applied Psychology: An International Review*, Vol.58, 520–56.

Ryan, A.M., Inceoglu, I., Bartram, D., Golubovich, J., Grand, J., Reeder, M., Derous, E., Nikolaou, I. and Yao, X. (2015) 'Trends in testing: Highlights of a global survey', pp. 136–53, in Nikolaou, I. and Oostrom, J.K. (eds.) *Employee Recruitment, Selection, and Assessment: Contemporary Issues for Theory and Practice*, New York: Psychology Press/Taylor & Francis.

Sackett, P.R., Shen, W., Myors., B, Lievens, F., Schollaert, E., Van Hoye, G. and Colleagues (2010) 'Perspectives from 22 countries on the legal environment for selection', pp. 651–78, in Farr, J.L. and Tippins, N.T. (eds.) *Handbook of Employee Selection*, New York: Routledge.

Salgado, J.F. (2002) 'The Big Five personality dimensions and counterproductive behaviors', *International Journal of Selection and Assessment*, Vol.10, Nos.1–2, 117–25.

Salgado, J.F. and Anderson, N.R. (2002) 'Cognitive and GMA testing in the European Community: issues and evidence', *Human Performance*, Vol.15, 75–96.

Salgado, J.F., Anderson, N., Moscoso, S., Bertua, C. and De Fruyt, F. (2003) 'International validity generalization of GMA and cognitive abilities: a European Community meta-analysis', *Personnel Psychology*, Vol.56, No.3, 573–605.

Schmidt, F.L. and Hunter, J.E. (1998) 'The validity and utility of selection methods in personnel psychology: practical and theoretical implications of 85 years of research findings', *Psychological Bulletin*, Vol.124, No.2, 262–74.

Schmitt, N. (ed.) (2012) *The Oxford Handbook of Personnel Selection and Assessment*, New York: Oxford University Press.

Schmitt, N. (2003) 'Employee selection: how simulations change the picture for minority groups', *Cornell Hospitality Quarterly*, Vol.44, 25–32.

Shaffer, J.A. and Postlethwaite, B.E. (2012) 'A matter of context: a meta-analytic investigation of the relative validity of contextualized and noncontextualized personality measures', *Personnel Psychology*, Vol.65, No.3, 445–94.

Searle, R.H. (2003) *Selection and Recruitment: A Critical Text*, Milton Keynes: The Open University.

Sternberg, R.J., Wagner, R.K., Williams, W.M. and Horvarth, J.A. (1995) 'Testing common sense', *American Psychologist*, Vol.50, No.11, 912–27.

Terpstra, D.E. and Kethley, R.B. (2002) 'Organizations' relative degree of exposure to selection discrimination litigation', *Public Personnel Management*, Vol.31, No.3, 277–92.

Tett, R.P. and Christiansen, N.D. (2007) 'Personality tests at the crossroads: a response to Morgeson, Campion, Dipboye, Hollenbeck, Murphy, and Schmitt (2007)', *Personnel Psychology*, Vol.60, No.4, 967–93.

Townley, B. (1989) 'Selection and appraisal: reconstituting "social relations"?', pp. 92–108, in Storey, J. (ed.) *New Perspectives on Human Resource Management*, London: Routledge.

Van Iddekinge, C.H., Roth, P.L., Raymark, P.H. and Odle-Dusseau, H.N. (2012) 'The criterion-related validity of integrity tests: an updated meta-analysis', *Journal of Applied Psychology*, Vol.97, No.3, 499–530.

Wolf, A. and Jenkins, A. (2006) 'Explaining greater test use for selection: the role of HR professionals in a world of expanded regulation', *Human Resource Management Journal*, Vol.16, No.2, 193–213.

De Wolff, C.J. (1993) 'The prediction paradigm' pp. 253–261, in Schuler, H., Farr, J.L. and Smith, M. (eds.) *Personnel Selection and Assessment: Individual and Organizational Perspectives*, Hillsdale, NJ: Lawrence Erlbaum.

Ziegler, M., McCann, C. and Roberts, R.D. (eds.) (2011) *New Perspectives on Faking in Personality Assessment*, New York: Oxford University Press.

Zibarras, L D. and Woods, S.A. (2010) 'A survey of UK selection practices across different organization sizes and industry sectors', *Journal of Occupational and Organizational Psychology*, Vol.83, No.2, 499–511.

CHAPTER 5

TRAINING AND DEVELOPMENT

Irena Grugulis

Introduction

Training, development and skills are key aspects of economic life. At the levels of the firm and the national economy, training offers the hope of increased competitiveness through raising skill levels, productivity and 'value added'. For trade unions and professional associations, training enhances members' expertise, facilitating negotiations for pay and status. While for individuals, given that life chances are still heavily influenced by the job a person does and the wages they earn, education and training can increase knowledge and opportunities, give access to more highly rewarded work and reduce the prospect of unemployment. Small wonder then, that consensus exists in this area, that governments encourage training through regulation or exhortation or that employers praise its importance in surveys. Yet despite this support, the levels and quality of vocational education and training in Britain is neither as high, nor as evenly distributed, as might be hoped. Excellent practice exists, but rarely 'trickles down' to less well-provided areas. This chapter explores the positive reasons why both firms and individuals should invest in vocational education and training (VET), before going on to review the very different practices of market-based and regulated economies. It describes current practice in the UK and the implications of the increasing emphasis on soft skills and personal qualities, and then concludes with explaining some of the disadvantages of training and development and the links between skill and performance. Throughout, it argues that, in common with other human resource practices, training should not be considered in isolation. Its effectiveness, or otherwise, hinges on the wider economic and organisational context.

Box 5.1 HRM in practice

I've actually got the convenor saying to me, 'we've got to watch this multi-skill thing because it's too interesting for them'.

Source: Managing Director, GKN Hardy Spicer; cited in Hendry, 1993: 92.

The case for training and development

The advantages of training and development are not illusory. Within organisations, it can equip workers to carry out tasks, monitor quality and manage complex products and services. Arthur's (1999) research into US steel mini-mills describes the way that switching between different types of steel or different shapes required close monitoring by melt-shop employees. The exact nature of changeover activities was difficult to predict and down-time was expensive so the quality and quantity of production relied heavily on the skills of operators and maintenance workers who had a considerable amount of discretion managing these shifts. Here, as elsewhere, quality products relied heavily on workers' expertise.

Training and development safeguards such productivity as well as supporting it by preparing employees for future jobs and insulating firms from skills shortages. When jobs can be filled internally, firms are less dependent on the outside labour market and do not risk appropriate recruits not being available (or not being available at the price the organisation wishes to pay). Such security is welcome. According to Vivian *et al.* (2011: 7), even in the midst of recession, 3 per cent of UK employers had skill-shortage vacancies and 13 per cent reported internal skills gaps (in which not all employees are fully proficient at the work that they do). The problems reported as a result of these gaps include difficulties with customer service, delays developing new products and losing business to competitors.

Within firms, training and development is a key element of human resource management, indeed, Keep (1989) argues that it is the litmus test against which other aspects of management practice should be gauged. When firms compete on the basis of quality and adopt high-commitment work practices such as employee involvement, teamworking or merit-based pay; developing employees is the key element in performance. It can raise the capacity of the individuals and groups employed, enabling them to participate meaningfully in systems where their contribution is encouraged (Keep and Mayhew, 1996). Arthur (1999) links the 'commitment'-oriented human resource practices in steel mini-mills to the strategic focus on quality and batch production, contrasting it with less developmental 'control' mechanisms in organisations where production was routine and where human resource practices focused on minimising labour costs.

Box 5.2 HRM in practice

McDonald's famously and relentlessly standardise every aspect of their product in order to eliminate the need for human input. The Operations and Training Manual (known to staff as 'the Bible') provides detailed prescriptions on every aspect of working life. Its 600 pages include full colour photographs illustrating the proper placement of ketchup, mustard and pickle on every type of burger, set out the six steps of counter service and even prescribe the arm motions that should be used in salting a batch of fries. Kitchen and counter technology reinforce these instructions as lights and buzzers tell workers when to turn burgers or take fries out of the fat, ketchup dispensers provide measured amounts of product in the requisite 'flower' pattern and lights on the till remove the need for serving staff to write out orders as well as prompting them to offer additional items.

For more information on this see Leidner, 1993; Ritzer, 1998.

In addition to these substantive factors, training and development also serves an important and very positive symbolic function. Everything that a firm does sends messages (of one kind or another) to its employees (one of the key elements of the positive side of HRM). Organisations that spend money on raising skills are, quite literally, investing in their workers.

Voluntarist and regulated approaches: international practice

While there is a consensus over the importance and value of training and development, this is not matched by any agreement on how best to encourage good practice. At a national level the two principal approaches are voluntarist (market based) and regulated (educational). Both the USA and Britain are broadly voluntarist. The principal assumption behind such systems is that organisations operate more effectively when unfettered by regulation. Market pressures (to remain competitive, produce quality goods and run efficiently) will ensure that, where training is appropriate, firms will invest in it and, in the absence of expensive and cumbersome official bureaucracy, investment can be accurately targeted to respond to market needs.

By contrast, in a regulated system, as in much of continental Europe, vocational education and training is supported by the state. Regulation may take a variety of forms. In France, employers are required to support training or pay a levy to the state while in Germany there is a system of extensive and rigorous apprenticeships for young people entering the labour market, coupled with 'licences to practice' for particular occupations. The assumption behind this approach is that vocational education and training is a public good and it is in the long-term interests of all to have a highly skilled workforce. However, left to themselves individual firms will prioritise profitability and may not invest in skills development or may fund only short-term and low-level training. Training and development is, after all, only one way of securing skilled workers and firms may choose to recruit workers trained elsewhere or de-skill production instead. By providing an appropriate infrastructure (or a system of levies or by regulating practice) the state ensures robust skills development.

Both voluntarist and regulated approaches can be successful. Silicon Valley, California provides an excellent example of the way that skills can be developed in a market-based system. Silicon Valley is famously the site of a cluster of extremely high-tech computing firms. These are supported by the proximity of universities (University of California campuses in Berkeley, San Francisco, San Diego and Los Angeles and private institutions such as Stanford, USC and CalTech) that supply expert labour, share research and stimulate start-up companies. Stanford (whose graduates include William Hewlett and David Packard) even set up the first university science park to provide fledgling firms with support services. The infrastructure is conducive to growth with good local transport, international airport and a state-of-the-art telecommunications system and the availability of venture capital, low levels of regulation and limited penalties on bankruptcy encourage start-ups. These small and often highly focused firms prosper through interdependency forming partnerships with other organisations and participating in employer groups to pursue initiatives such as improving technical training in city colleges that are to their mutual benefit. Individuals also collaborate through professional associations, continuing education courses and alumni associations. In firms there is little formal training but skills and expertise are developed through project work on cutting edge technical challenges. Even labour mobility, a point of concern elsewhere, assists knowledge diffusion here and increases personal and professional networks (Finegold, 1999).

Such an unstructured 'ecosystem' is very successful at developing and supporting the most expert who work at the cutting edge of their profession. However, the USA as a whole is far less successful in training and development for the majority and it is here that a more regulated system triumphs. The highly regarded German apprenticeship system is one of the best known routes to achieving vocational qualifications. Full apprenticeships last three years and trainees are taught technical skills in the classroom which are subsequently developed through participation in a series of problem-solving activities graded in terms of difficulty. Care is taken to ensure that apprentices are exposed to a full range of different work situations with central training centres supplementing workplace experience and providing additional workplace settings for trainees to learn in; an arrangement which gives smaller employers the capacity to offer high-level training. Technical training is supplemented with knowledge of work control and design (manufacturing qualifications involve familiarity with costs, design and planning, and administration and production) and, in addition to this, all apprentices are required to continue to participate in further education for the duration of their vocational studies (Lane, 1989; Rubery and Grimshaw, 2003).

Nor, despite pessimism, the problems of unifying East and West Germany, economic problems and the rise of the service sector (Culpepper, 1999; Kirsch *et al.*, 2000), does this system appear to be in decline. Apprentice numbers peaked in the mid-1990s but the system overall has remained both strong and popular. New programmes developed for IT occupations attracted 48,859 apprentices in 2002, half of whom already held an *Abitur* (the prestigious academic school leaving qualification taken at 18). And many apprenticeships have taken advantage of the fact that those taking them are far better educated than before to raise the standards of their theoretical components (Bosch, 2010).

The German system is made possible by close collaborative links between employers' associations, trade unions and regional governments cooperating on creating a system that works for the benefit of all. Indeed, Bosch and Charest (2010) argue that new apprenticeship programmes have only been successfully launched in countries such as Germany, Austria, Denmark, Switzerland and Norway, which have both strong trade unions and a tradition of corporatist cooperation between firms (though see Buchanan and Evesson, 2004a–b on the Australian experience). Taiwan is different; its economy is dominated by small and medium-sized enterprises (SMEs), which successfully resisted the introduction of a levy for vocational education and training in the 1970s. Yet, despite this it has managed to introduce extensive vocational skills development, increasing the amount of technical, vocational education and the numbers of scientists and engineers through the education system. Demand for education was for academic education (and this would have been cheaper to provide) but access to academic courses was officially restricted, more than half of school children were channelled into technical training and at university level more courses were made available for scientists and engineers and new Institutes of Technology launched. Student numbers, textbooks and curricula were state controlled and this meant that Taiwan succeeded in both the growing low-cost industrial products for export and also managed the transition from this to higher value-added production across many if not all sectors without significant reported skills shortages (Green *et al.*, 1999).

In China the situation is very different. In the years after 1949 the Chinese economy was state planned and state controlled with all decisions taken centrally. Since the 1970s and 1980s much has changed with considerable foreign investment encouraged and while state owned enterprises still form a considerable proportion of the economy, an increasing proportion of workers are employed in joint ventures with foreign firms, foreign owned or privately owned companies. Over the last few decades, as a result of these changes, the Chinese economy has grown dramatically, but this development has been uneven with most concentrated in the coastal and urban areas.

VET and skills are important issues in China since the country suffers from severe skills shortages and skills gaps, limiting its capacity to develop. Training within firms is erratic.

Some firms do train and do it well. Jürgens and Krzywdzinski's (2015) study of four automotive manufacturers highlights careful recruitment, ongoing skills training and career development (significantly, three of the four were joint ventures and the fourth, a Chinese-owned company, drew extensively on the German apprenticeship system), but it is not clear how widespread such good practice is. Provision itself varies. State owned enterprises provide most, followed by joint ventures (Cooke, 2012) but a widespread fear of poaching discourages many employers from training. Those that do may withhold certificates, so that employees struggle to prove qualifications to rival employers, or make employees contract to stay for a set period post-training (Li and Sheldon, 2010).

The state has made repeated attempts to raise skills. Firms that do not train are required to pay a levy of 1.5 per cent of turnover to support training and development, while those that do enjoy tax breaks to encourage VET (Kuczera and Field, 2010). The 'learning organisation' initiative worked with state owned enterprises and trade unions to encourage self-study, technological innovation, skill and performance contests in work, on the job training and problem solving teams. National standards, which are generally weak, have been set for various professional groups including trainers, HR specialists and managers and successive Five-Year Plans have set targets for skills. The eleventh (2006 to 2011) aimed to produce 500,000 senior technicians ('golden blue collar workers'), 1.9 million technicians and 7 million technical workers (Cooke, 2012).

The state also supports vocational education in schools. About half the age cohort attends vocational schools at upper secondary level on three- or four-year programmes. Students spend a year on placement in industry and vocational teachers are required to keep their expertise current by spending a month in industry every year, with some working part-time in industry and part time in vocational schools (Kuczera and Field, 2010). However, management of VET is devolved to provincial and local governments, with no set national standards and very variable access to funds. Shanghai, the highest spending region, spends around eight times more per pupil than Henan or Anhui. This effect is multiplied by the fact that students pay fees and such fees are often higher in prosperous areas. Links with employers are similarly variable. For some (as in Jürgens and Krzywdzinski's 2015 account above) the placements offer valuable opportunities for students to build skills and gain work experience, while employers are able to identify potential new recruits; for others, low quality training focuses on narrow skills which are not transferable. In marked contrast to the German apprenticeship system where work-based projects are carefully managed and clearly linked to an apprentice's area of study, Chinese vocational interns are often a source of cheap labour for the employer with no attempt made to make the experience useful for the students. Smith and Chan (2015) describe the way that Foxconn imposed exclusive contracts on vocational schools compelling them to send all of their students to work at Foxconn, regardless of subject. Their informants included students studying Chinese herbal medicine, secretarial services, hotel and tourism, English, horticulture and accounting. All were put to work on the assembly line. It is difficult to argue that extended experience of such work will enhance these students' skills.

Each system has its strengths and limitations. The 'high-skills market-based ecosystem' of Silicon Valley is highly responsive to developing new and expert skills in professionals working on cutting edge projects where qualifications rarely exist while regulation does mean that skilled workers are widely available, with two-thirds of German workers holding intermediate qualifications or above. By contrast, in unregulated systems some occupations neglect training even when this is to their detriment. After construction was de-regulated in the USA, training levels fell dramatically – as did investment in physical capital and productivity (Bosch, 2003). There, young people who do not graduate from high school have little chance of finding a decent job with a middle-class income (Bailey and Berg, 2010). But not even regulation guarantees provision. Although German apprenticeships are highly regarded, economic pressures mean that actual apprentice places are in decline and in former East Germany large numbers of young people are not integrated into the system.

Perhaps the most notable feature of these examples is that they are systemic, success here goes beyond the simple provision of high-quality training (indeed, in the US example formal training is one of the least significant elements of skills development). The high-skills eco-system of Silicon Valley is made possible by the fact that recruits are already extremely highly educated on entry (and many of them are IT experts). In Germany, the existence of employers' associations, trade unions and vocational colleges that are prepared to collaborate; and in Taiwan the government's readiness to both pay for skills development and take decisions that may be unpopular with individual students and their families, facilitate good intermediate skills training.

This is an important point and a key element of the success of each of these approaches. It also has implications for attempts to identify and transplant 'best practice', which generally focus only on one narrow element of a successful system. Korea's attempt to replicate the German apprenticeship system is a case in point (Jeong, 1995). This had government support and experienced German advisors were engaged. But little financial support was available, the firms employing the apprentices provided little training and used them as low-paid and low-skilled workers, few college tutors were sufficiently skilled to make up this deficit and seniority, rather than skill, remained the key element in promotion. As a result, the initiative failed. Since then job mobility has increased substantially and, as elsewhere, lifetime employment practices are being dismantled. Jobs are being created, but in recent years most have been in low-wage service sector jobs and many workers are over-qualified for, and frustrated by, work. Vocational training is available, particularly for those workers who are unemployed or need to be redeployed, but it is not well integrated into occupations (Yoon and Lee, 2010). It seems that the lessons of the earlier failure have not been learned.

Vocational education and training means different things in different countries. As Bosch and Charest (2010: 1) note:

> Depending on the quality of the VET, the signals vocational certificates give to employers might differ from country to country. In some countries, they might signal competency to perform complex tasks autonomously in a broad occupational field; in others, however, they might signal that the holder is a low achiever in the school system and possesses only narrowly based skills for specific jobs. *(Bosch and Charest, 2010: 1)*

In other words, vocational training is important but it needs to be understood as one part of a wider system of work and skills rather than as isolated initiatives. Training is only meaningful if it is integrated into work.

Training and development in the workplace

While there are many reasons to support training and development, and while both voluntarist and regulated approaches can work not every employer trains. Excellent provision exists, but is rather unevenly distributed and not all training is developmental. It is also unevenly distributed and training (and particularly of the duration and content of training) varies greatly according to both occupation and sector. Employees in the public sector, younger workers, people who are new to the job and those working in professional or clerical occupations are far more likely to receive training than older workers in 'blue collar' jobs (Cully *et al.*, 1999). Depressingly, despite increasing levels of government subsidy, training in the UK is in decline (Vivian *et al.*, 2011), particularly for high-skilled and professional workers (Mason and Bishop, 2010). Overall, training levels peaked at around 15 per cent in 2003, before falling to 13 per cent by 2012. Fewer people now receive training and the training they receive is shorter and of lower quality (Green *et al.*, 2013).

This is particularly significant when we step back from the data and recall what training is provided for. One of the main advantages of training and development was that it could enhance the skills base, equip workers with expertise and change the way that they worked.

Expansive and restrictive approaches to training and development

Systemic approaches to training and development can also be observed *within* firms. One manufacturer of bathroom showers, described by Fuller and Unwin (2004), took an *expansive* approach to development. It had a long-established apprenticeship programme and many ex-apprentices had progressed to senior management. Apprentices were rotated around different departments to gain wider knowledge of the business and improve their skills. They also attended college on day release, working towards knowledge-based qualifications which would give them access to higher education, went on residential courses designed to foster teamworking and were involved with local charities through the company's apprenticeship association. Contrast this with the *restrictive* environment of a small steel polishing company where apprentices had been reluctantly taken on only when managers were unable to recruit qualified staff. After less than a year, the two apprentices who had learned on the job had gained all the skills necessary for their work. There was no system of job rotation and formal training was limited to ten half-day courses on steel industry awareness (the sum total of apprentices' outside involvement) and an NVQ.

Source: Fuller and Unwin, 2004.

←Approaches to workforce development→

Expansive	Restrictive
Participation in multiple communities of practice inside and outside the workplace	Restricted participation in multiple communities of practice
Primary community of practice has shared 'participative memory': cultural inheritance of workforce development	Primary community of practice has little or no 'participative memory': no or little tradition of apprenticeship
Breadth: access to learning fostered by cross-company experience	Narrow: access to learning restricted in terms of tasks/knowledge/location
Access to range of qualifications including knowledge-based VQ	Little or no access to qualifications
Planned time off the job including for knowledge-based courses and for reflection	Virtually all on job: limited opportunities for reflection
Gradual transition to full, rounded participation	Fast – transition as quick as possible
Vision of workplace learning: progression for career	Vision of workplace learning: static for the job
Organisational recognition of and support for employees as learners	Lack of organisational recognition of and support for employees as learners
Workforce development is used as a vehicle for aligning the goals of developing the individual and organisational capability	Workforce development is used to tailor individual capability to organisational need
Workforce development fosters opportunities to extend identity through boundary crossing	Workforce development limits opportunities to extend identity: little boundary crossing experienced
Reification of 'workplace curriculum' highly developed (e.g. through documents, symbols, language, tools) and accessible to apprentices	Limited reification of 'workplace curriculum' patchy access to reificatory aspects of practice
Widely distributed skills	Polarised distribution of skills
Technical skills valued	Technical skills taken for granted

(Continued)

←Approaches to workforce development→

Expansive	Restrictive
Knowledge and skills of whole workforce developed and valued	Knowledge and skills of key workers/groups developed and valued
Team work valued	Rigid specialist roles
Cross-boundary communication encouraged	Bounded communication
Managers as facilitators of workforce and individual development	Managers as controllers of workforce and individual development
Chances to learn new skills/jobs	Barriers to learning new skills/jobs
Innovation important	Innovation not important
Multidimensional view of expertise	Uni-dimensional top-down view of expertise

Source: Taken from Fuller and Unwin, 2004: 130.

So the content of training is also important. Workplace training can cover a multitude of activities. Graduate trainee accountants with major accountancy firms spend three years on a mixture of formal courses, guided work experience and personal study, leading to a prestigious professional qualification. By contrast, call centre workers can expect far more basic workplace training. In Callaghan and Thompson's (2002) study, one call centre worker, who had let his voice drop slightly during a conversation with a customer, was sent on a training course to teach him to keep intonation even and enthusiastic. Both of these activities count as training and both may increase organisational effectiveness, but the advantages they confer on workers are very different.

Box 5.4 HRM in practice   Can organisations learn?

In theory, training also allows organisations to adapt to changes in the business environment; however, their success in this rests on their ability to learn, particularly their ability to learn from their mistakes. Unsurprisingly, perhaps, few firms are adept at this (Keep and Rainbird, 2000). Baumard and Starbuck's (2006) revealing analysis of organisational failures demonstrates that, far from admitting to errors, managers concealed large failures until discovery was certain then blamed them on unusual circumstances or external factors. Small failures were seen as inevitable because they did not fit in with the rest of the organisation or because the initiatives were only 'experiments'. Politically necessary behaviours to ensure managerial success but guaranteed to curtail organisational learning.

Reinforcing this, the two types of training most commonly funded by employers are health and safety and induction (though they are not the majority of all training provided, see Shury et al., 2010), a factor that may explain why temporary workers are more likely to receive training than their permanent colleagues. Heyes and Gray (2003), in their survey of SMEs after the introduction of the National Minimum Wage, found that training spend had risen, but that this was because employers were hiring younger (and cheaper) workers rather than up-skilling existing staff. Clearly, it is important workplaces are healthy and safe, and that new recruits receive adequate induction. However, it is highly unlikely that such forms of training will affect productivity, product quality or individual career development.

Training and development may also serve a social function, helping workers to form friendships and distracting them from alienating work. Two call centres investigated by Kinnie *et al.* (2000) used employee teams, games and spot prizes to motivate employees. These organisations also had three-week induction and technical training, but their on-going investment was in activities described by one supervisor as 'fun and surveillance'. An interesting modern variant on Adam Smith's (1776/1993) approval of publicly funded education for the working poor, who engaged only in simple, dehumanising and repetitive tasks, the better to support a 'decent and orderly' (1993: 436) society.

Personal qualities and generic skills

The type of training identified by Kinnie and his colleagues, the focus on games and the development of 'soft' or generic skills, is becoming more widespread. Indeed, soft skills were the most commonly mentioned skill needs by UK employers with management skills, customer handling, problem solving, teamworking and communication heading their list of requirements (Shury *et al.*, 2010: 138). In part, this shift to soft skills reflects attempts to alleviate repetitive work, increase commitment or foster a particular organisational culture, but it also stems from the fact that workforce skills are increasingly being defined in attitudinal terms. The Department for Education and Employment's Skills Task Force included communication, problem solving, teamworking, an ability to improve personal learning and performance, motivation, judgement, leadership and initiative in its list of skills (Department for Education and Employment, 2000: 24). The CBI's (1989) earlier suggestions included values and integrity and interpersonal skills; Whiteways Research (1995) extended this to cover self-awareness, self-promotion, political focus and coping with uncertainty. These are not isolated instances and some of the lists produced can be extremely long. In a study of managerial skills Hirsch and Bevan (1988) itemised 1,745 different qualities.

To a certain extent there is little here that is novel. Employers have always demanded appropriate qualities and attributes from their workers and work has always involved a mixture of soft and technical skills. It is, after all, not enough to know something, to be effective a worker must be able to put that into practice in their workplace. This may involve enlisting the assistance of others, negotiating for resources with line managers, fitting new processes into existing ones and considering the impact on current practice. Even when the skills demanded of workers are basic and tasks demand minimal engagement, workers are likely be required to 'get on' with one another and to 'fit in' (Steiger, 1993). Moreover, the increasing numbers of service jobs demand very different qualities of those who carry them out than manufacturing work. In services, the process of being served is as much a part of the purchase as any product being sold and customers may conflate their delight at service levels with their appreciation of the product (Korczynski, 2001; 2002). As a result, the way employees look and feel and the impressions and emotions they provoke in others are important (see, among others, Hochschild, 1983; Leidner, 1993). However, couching this in the language of skill causes a number of problems. Unlike formally accredited technical skills, it is not clear that soft skills are either transferable or give their holders power in the labour market. The communication skills needed to tell a customer which aisle the baked beans are in are very different from those needed to describe the rules of cricket or explain complex statistics. In each of these areas (just as for the exercise of judgement, leadership or problem solving), efficacy demands technical and local knowledge, a factor neglected by the compilers of generic lists. This is particularly worrying since there is some evidence that organisations attempting to train their staff in soft skills are neglecting the technical aspects of work (Grugulis and Vincent, 2009).

Then too, soft skills may be reciprocal and relational rather than individual. In his study of the skills required by US employers Lafer (2004) draws on research by Moss and Tilly (1996) in two warehouses in the same district of Los Angeles both of which employed present and past gang members. While managers in one complained of high turnover, laziness and dishonesty, in the second, which paid several dollars per hour more, managers had few complaints and turnover was a modest 2 per cent. As Lafer (2004: 117) argues:

> Traits such as discipline, loyalty and punctuality are not 'skills' that one either possesses or lacks; they are measures of commitment that one chooses to give or withhold based on the conditions of work offered. *(Lafer, 2004: 117)*

Focusing on motivation as an individual skill presupposes that people are unaffected by their conditions of work or the way that they are treated. Factors once considered the responsibility of management or personnel are individualised such that the emphasis on control systems, job design, pay rates or being a 'good employer' becomes the straightforward problem of hiring the most appropriately 'skilled' people (Grugulis *et al.*, 2004; Keep, 2001).

In workplaces it also seems to matter *who* exercises the skill, with soft skills being rated far more highly (as well as rewarded, see Dickerson and Green, 2002) when they are possessed by knowledge workers than by people with low or intermediate skills. Grugulis and Vincent's (2009) study of high-skilled IT professionals and intermediate-skilled housing benefit caseworkers revealed that, while soft skills were rhetorically valued in both workplaces, it was the IT professionals who were able to secure status and pay for their soft skills, with soft skills developed in tandem with high-level technical skills. The housing benefit caseworkers found that soft skills *replaced* much technical training and was used to allocate women to gendered and career-limiting roles, despite their protests. Ironically, the very entrepreneurial qualities that the employer valued in the young IT professionals enabled them to avoid learning the details of the local system, which was so necessary to their employers, and concentrate instead on gaining expertise in software which could and did help them to move to better paid work elsewhere.

Nor is the exercise of soft skills particularly clear. Employers value them but often judge their presence or their absence through sexual and racial stereotypes. Women are favoured for call centres and reception desks. Asian women are not considered to be career minded and men's marital status may be taken as a proxy for their reliability (Collinson *et al.*, 1990; Hebson and Grugulis, 2005; Oliver and Turton, 1982). As Ainley (1994: 80) argues, 'at rock bottom, the real personal and transferable "skills" required for preferential employment are those of whiteness, maleness and traditional middle-classness'. It is difficult to escape from the conclusion that in some environments focusing on soft skills can be used to legitimise prejudice and reinforce disadvantage.

This is a conundrum. At one level most jobs clearly require a mixture of both technical and soft skills and, given the existing lack of recognition for women's skills, rhetorical support for their importance should advantage them. At another, as Bolton (2004) argues, these skills – regardless of their complexity – seem to be the exception to the normal laws of supply and demand in the sense that, no matter how much employers require them, they are seldom highly rewarded when not accompanied by high levels of technical skill. The advantages that soft skills offer seem precariously dependent on their being noted, appreciated and rewarded by senior management (Grugulis and Vincent, 2009). In isolation they provide workers with few of the labour market advantages of technical skills (Keep, 2001; Payne, 1999; 2000).

In part, this is a systemic issue. A focus on soft skills (such as communication, loyalty or even punctuality) in low-level work confers few advantages on workers because it equips them only to perform low level tasks. Whereas an emphasis on teamworking, problem solving and responsibility for production integrated with technical skills in Thompson *et al.*'s

(1995) cross-national comparisons of vehicle production provided employees with opportunities for progression. Similarly, in NUMMI's plant in Freemont, California soft skills are combined with the development of technical skills and workers are given a great deal of discretion to address workplace problems (Rothenberg, 2003). But while integrating these generic qualities with challenging work may make them more 'skilful' and advantage those workers who possess or develop them, it does not overcome the tendency to read these virtues into gender, race, class, age or marital status.

The disadvantages of training and development

The overall picture of training and development is not clear cut. Some courses, qualifications and on-the-job training are excellent at developing workforce skills, which can then be integrated into the way work is designed and controlled. But developmental provision is set alongside narrow qualifications and training courses that serve only to entertain. At one level, such behaviour is difficult to explain. If training and development is universally believed to have a positive impact then why are so few firms training and why are the ones that do train confining much of their activity to short courses, health and safety and induction? Equally, why do individual employees not respond to this by filling the gap themselves? Such lack of activity appears, at best, irrational.

However, there is an explanation. Training and development does not occur in a vacuum, rather it is one aspect of an organisation's activities and exists to support the other activities. As Keep and Mayhew (1999) argue, training is a third-order issue, following on from decisions about competitiveness, product specification and job design. For organisations that choose to compete on the basis of quality, highly skilled workers are essential (and as Shury *et al.*, 2010 point out, firms that do compete on quality provide more, and better funded training); for ones that compete on cost, they are an unjustifiable extravagance – and large sections of the British economy still compete on cost (Bach and Sisson, 2000). The second reason, and this is related to the first, is that many jobs are designed to be tightly controlled with employee discretion (and with it skill) taken away. One employer, interviewed by Dench *et al.* (1999), said that their ideal worker had two arms and two legs. When this is what jobs demand, it is difficult to see how training will help. Job design is not set in stone and it is perfectly possible to construct skilled work from the same jobs, the same market conditions and the same strategy. Boxall and Purcell (2011) provide an interesting example from two firms competing with one another in delivering bottled gas. British Oxygen decided to compete by using delivery drivers as key staff. Drivers were trained in customer relations, cab-based information systems and product knowledge, ensuring that customers were satisfied and encouraging them to trade up wherever possible. By contrast, Air Products, a rival firm in the same industry facing the same pressures, decided to compete by outsourcing its haulage and distribution to an independent contractor. Their drivers were not expected to know anything about bottled gas beyond the standard health and safety guidelines. When large numbers of employers design jobs to be done without skill, pay low wages and workers with little purchasing power buy products of low price and low quality we have all the elements of what Finegold and Soskice describe as a 'low skills equilibrium' (1988).

Then too, it is instructive to consider the areas of job creation. In March 2015 78 per cent of UK jobs were in the service sector (ONS, 2015a). Service work includes many of the most highly skilled and knowledgeable workers such as medics, teachers and IT professionals but it also, and in far greater numbers, covers care workers, security staff and personal services, numbers of which are rising far faster. The sector as a whole is dominated by low-paid, part-time workers, few of whom are either highly skilled or allowed to exercise their skills in their work. This need not be the case (Bozkurt and Grugulis, 2011). McGauran's (2000; 2001) research into retail work in France and Ireland shows how French employers expect their workers to be experts in the products sold and French customers request advice on products and product care when shopping. However, it is not clear that this skilled variant of shop work influences behaviour elsewhere. Rather, pressure for hyper-flexibility, described by Gadrey (2000: 26) as 'tantamount to a personnel strategy based on zero competence', zero qualifications, zero training and zero career, means that retail work is dominated by poorly paid part-time workers and the flexibility demanded of them is availability for shift work at short notice. In Germany this is threatening long-established traditions of training and qualifications as employers avoid training employees, since this would make them expensive to hire, and rely instead on large numbers of low-paid staff supported by small numbers of highly skilled 'anchor' workers (Kirsch *et al.*, 2000).

At an individual level too there are good and sound reasons for not taking up vocational training. Human capital theory is neither as straightforward, nor as axiomatic as some commentators argue. While some qualifications do indeed bring high returns, others do not and it is the low-level vocational qualifications that bring least reward (see, for example, Grugulis, 2003). Then too, not all skills are equal and the status and labour market power of job holders influence the way their skills are perceived (Rubery and Wilkinson, 1994). In practice this means that women's work, even when technically and objectively more complex than men's, tends to be under-valued (Phillips and Taylor, 1986). Mechanistically assessing workers as a supply of skills neglects both this social construction and factors such as trust and motivation that are needed to put skills into practice at work (Brown, 2001). Human capital theory also individualises the responsibility for acquiring and developing skills. Nor is it clear that highly skilled workers create their own demand. As the UK skills survey consistently demonstrates, more than one third of workers report that their skills are under-utilised in employment (Felstead *et al.*, 2007).

Skill and performance

It seems, given the above, that the rewards from vocational training are neither as straightforward, nor as automatic, as some writers on human capital theory would like to believe. This is a key point and worth considering in a little more detail. After all, as noted at the start of the chapter, part of the implicit (and occasionally explicit) promise of skills development is a link with performance and productivity for individuals, organisations and nations. Skills should lead, in the words of the *Leitch Review* (2006), to prosperity for all.

In many instances, of course, they do. An expert and experienced worker performs better than an untried novice, in the US, college graduates earn more than their peers with only high school qualifications, and nations with better systems of education and vocational education and training out-do their competitors (Green, 2006; Nolan and Slater, 2003). However, these results are neither deterministic nor inevitable and it is worth considering three areas where the links are questionable: linking shop-floor and organisational performance; the varying points of analysis; and performance in the service sector (for a more detailed discussion see Grugulis and Stoyanova, 2011).

Analysing performance

There are many excellent studies of the impact that variations in skills and work design have on productivity. The National Institute for Economic and Social Research (NIESR) has specialised, over many decades, in conducting comparative case studies in the same industry and controlling for technology wherever possible but where work is organised differently and workers' skills vary dramatically (see Prais, 1995 for an overview of these). Their conclusions are clear and positive: highly skilled workers can contribute more to the production process; technology can be better integrated; less supervision is required and higher-quality goods result. So far so good.

Box 5.5 HRM in practice

Biscuits and skill: biscuit making in Britain and Germany
This is taken from a study of biscuit manufacture in ten British and eight German firms.

The type of biscuits produced varied greatly between the two countries, largely owing to national tastes and demand. In Britain, demand concentrated on relatively basic biscuits: either plain or with one simple coating of chocolate, cream or jam. In Germany, there was a much higher demand for decorated and multi-textured products (soft biscuits with jam filling in chocolate cases or layered variegated biscuits). Since this affected the type of biscuits that each firm produced, relative output figures were not easy to measure. On crude output figures, productivity per employee hour was 25 per cent higher in Britain than in Germany, largely because British firms produced large quantities of simple, low-quality biscuits. However, when these productivity figures were adjusted for quality, the British advantage disappeared with German firms 40 per cent more productive per employee hour.

In Germany 90 per cent of process workers were craft-trained bakers and could work in all of the main areas of operations (mixing, biscuit forming and oven control). This multi-skilling meant that three-person teams could be responsible for at least two oven lines at the same time. In German firms, employees were focused in areas that added value to the product. Maintenance staff was highly qualified and, in addition to undertaking regular maintenance, worked with supervisors to customise equipment and increase productivity. In Britain no process workers and few supervisors were vocationally qualified. As a result, each individual production line needed a three-person team to cover mixing and baking since workers were narrowly trained and tended to stick to their own jobs. Few firms had any regular system of machine maintenance since shift work meant that equipment was rarely scheduled to stop but breakdowns were frequent and high staffing levels in areas such as wrapping were needed to sort out problems caused by equipment breakdown and malfunction. On the line, narrow training restricted the ability of shop-floor workers to anticipate problems (such as machine malfunctioning) and take appropriate action.

Source: Mason *et al.*, 1996.

However, as Cutler (1992) points out, this is performance at the level of the shop floor and not of the organisation. Between these two levels other factors such as currency movements, accounting conventions, the performance of the salesforce and the national economy can and do influence firm performance. Shop-floor skills are important, but they are not the only, nor even the most important, element in organisational performance.

There are difficulties too in attempting to integrate positive returns for individuals, organisations and nations, not least because such returns may be mutually incompatible. Higher wages for individuals detract from organisational profits. Firm performance may be improved by the strategic implementation of a redundancy programme (to boost share price); national performance by *increasing* the number of people in work (Keep *et al.*, 2002). There is, as is frequently observed of the employment contract, only a *partial* coincidence of interest between these three parties. Some activities will indeed benefit all, but in many cases there is a zero-sum game and increasing performance in one area results in penalties elsewhere.

Finally, and most confusingly, is the issue of the service sector, where existing assumptions about performance and productivity are regularly challenged. Here quality may be increased by, for example, a four-star hotel employing more unskilled staff to attend to guests, carry bags or advise on local restaurants. But this move may damage their overall performance since economists tend to measure productivity by reckoning on the number of employees taken to 'process' a guest. Equally, investing in employees' skills in areas such as customer service may not attract the sort of returns that the marketing textbooks promise, since customers tend to use a whole range of factors, not simply excellent service levels, when making purchasing decisions. As Keep and colleagues (2002) point out, SwissAir, which won awards for its customer service, went bankrupt, while Easyjet thrives.

So, skills can have a positive effect on performance at a whole range of levels but this is by no means guaranteed and might best be described as prosperity for some, rather than prosperity for all.

 ## Re-thinking training and development

This chapter has deliberately extended the debate on training and development beyond the confines of formal courses and qualifications. These are important factors but for students of HRM they are only one aspect of a wider issue, the development of 'resourceful humans'. A knowledgeable workforce is the product, not of excellent training in isolation, but of a combination of a range of factors including training, job design, status, control systems and discretion (see also Hislop, Chapter 18 in this volume). As Cockburn (1983) and Littler (1982) argue, skill reposes in the individual, in the job and in the social setting. In practice, this means that for development to be effective, individuals need enough discretion and challenge in their work to exercise their skills.

Given this, there are some reasons for optimism in Britain. Between 1986 and 2012 skills in work have risen against almost every indicator. Employers are demanding more (and more advanced) qualifications and the amount of experience that employees need to do their work well is also rising. However, while this trajectory is encouraging, it starts from a low base and most work still demands few skills, with 23 per cent of jobs needing neither skills nor qualifications (Felstead *et al.*, 2013). *iMac* jobs have not yet entirely replaced *McJobs* (Warhurst and Thompson, 1998).

This under-utilisation of skills is apparent in Rainbird and Munro's (2003) research. Drawing on an extensive study of low-paid workers they found that rigid hierarchies, narrow job descriptions and cost constraints all acted as barriers that employees, who were often highly educated, skilled or anxious to progress, could not overcome. Nor was there any sign, despite the very significant differences that good managers could make, that this might change. Indeed, the structural innovations observed, such as contracting out by the public sector, often reduced employees' areas of influence and took away aspects of their work that were interesting or skilful.

There has also been a sharp decline in discretion employees can exercise, a trend that was particularly marked for professional workers. In 1986 72 per cent of professionals reported that they had 'a great deal' of choice over the way that they worked. By 2001 this figure had fallen to 38 per cent (Felstead *et al.*, 2002: 71; see also Evetts, 2002; Grugulis *et al.*, 2003; Felstead *et al.*, 2013). Yet discretion is a prerequisite for skills to be put into practice.

 ## Discussion and conclusions

Training is the pivotal element of a system designed to harness the talents of those it employs (through well designed jobs, teamworking, employee involvement and other human resource practices) is ensuring that employees are developed for their roles. However, the reverse also applies and human resource practices are the test of training.

There is little point in training and developing employees if the jobs they are to undertake are tightly controlled with no trust or discretion given. Skill is an aspect of jobs as well as a part of individuals and a highly skilled individual put in a job where they have little control, discretion or responsibility and which they have little power to change is likely to become frustrated. This means that just as many excellent analyses of human resource management have queried the extent to which its ambitious rhetoric has been matched by its lived reality, so training and development needs to be subjected to the same scrutiny. Good training and development has the capacity to significantly change lives. It can equip people for more interesting, better paid and more demanding work; help to mitigate the discrimination in the labour market experienced by women and members of minority groups and provide an effective route out of poverty for people working in unskilled and low-paid jobs. However, just because some forms of training can do this does not mean that all can. Training and development is not always and entirely a 'good thing' – not all training is developmental and not all development is integrated into work. Before according our approval we really do need to examine what are involved in particular training systems, the effect it has on individuals and the way it is integrated into work. If this is not the case there is a danger that effort and resources will be put into systems which simply reinforce disadvantage and equip people only for minimum-wage employment (Lafer, 2004) or horizontal movement between a range of low-skilled jobs (Grimshaw *et al.*, 2002).

CASE STUDY 5.1

DEVELOPING RESOURCEFUL HUMANS

IRENA GRUGULIS

This chapter showed the way that training and development may be systemic and linked to product strategies, job design, the way that work is controlled and the level of discretion workers can use. From the list below select three jobs, with different skill levels. For each set out:

a. how people are trained to do the job;

b. what (if any) continuing development they have on the job (remember that a challenging job provides opportunities for development, just as formal training does);

c. how much discretion they can exercise;

d. what other human resource policies you would expect (on pay rates, involvement, career ladders, etc.);

e. what would happen to these jobs if recruits received more developmental training or were more highly educated.

A secondary school teacher
A call centre worker
An anaesthetist
An accountant
A gardener
A shop assistant
A junior manager in a chain restaurant
A bank cashier
A factory worker
A cleaner

CASE STUDY 5.2

SOFT SKILLS AT WORK

IRENA GRUGULIS AND STEVEN VINCENT

Soft skills and personal qualities are an increasingly important part of work with employees expected to show them in work and assessed on them at recruitment, appraisal and promotion. However, there have also been claims that judging soft skills may simply be an expression of individual and collective prejudice with gender, race and class used to stereotype workers. This case study provides descriptions of two groups of workers in different organisations who had varying experiences of soft skills. Read the descriptions and answer the questions below.

Benefit caseworkers in TCS

Total Customer Services (TCS) was an outsourcing company with a contract with a London council to do housing benefit processing, work which required intermediate-level skills. The housing benefit caseworkers

were expected to demonstrate customer focus, attitude, flexibility and endurance with managers condemning the '9 to 5' mentality of the public sector and new staff was screened for positive attitudes. Initial technical training was dramatically reduced and instead staff was taught about punctuality, personal presentation and attitude. A reception desk was set up to deal with customer claimants. The work involved was largely unskilled and staff had difficulty returning to the skilled work of claims processing after stints on reception. Despite protests, women were preferred for this task since the manager considered them naturally better at it and 16 of the 20 reception workers were women. In claims processing, new managers were chosen for their soft skills (and particularly whether they were considered 'TCS people') rather than their occupational knowledge and some had no experience of housing benefit at all. Performance was monitored by statistics and claims staff lost their professional discretion.

IT consultants in FutureTech

FutureTech provided outsourced computing and IT services to Govco, a large government department. Its workers were highly skilled and new entrants were all graduates. Consultants were expected to be customer-focused, flexible and to actively work towards ensuring harmony in the relationship between the two firms; while graduates were hired as enthusiastic self-starters who were responsible for their own learning and development. Extensive training was provided with most time devoted to improving technical knowledge, though much of the actual work was mundane. Long hours and weekend working were common. Some expatriate US managers on the staff made efforts to introduce motivational techniques and make the British workers more emotional, including encouraging them to stand up and applaud themselves.

Graduates were very technically skilled but most avoided learning the details of Govco's internal systems which were necessary for success internally but had little market value. Instead, they became adept at creating their own developmental opportunities and competing for projects which involved new software. Turnover increased from 2 to 9 per cent overall and was described as 'dysfunctionally high' for graduates.

Questions

1 What soft skills were required in the two organisations? What sort of balance was there between soft skills and technical skills?

2 What effect did this have on (a) the workers, (b) their work and (c) their employers? Whom did the soft skills benefit?

3 How does knowing about workers' technical skills help us to understand this?

4 Think about another job that you are familiar with. What soft skills and what technical skills are required? Do they advantage the employee or the employer?

5 What effect does an emphasis on soft skills have on workers?

For further details of this case study see Grugulis and Vincent (2009).

CASE STUDY 5.3

JOBS, DISCRETION AND SKILL

IRENA GRUGULIS, STEVEN VINCENT AND GAIL HEBSON

This case study explores two 'networks', an outsourced group of housing benefit caseworkers and production workers in a specialist chemicals company, and considers the effect that each network had on employee skills.

Total Customer Services (TCS) specialise in business operations outsourcing. With a turnover of over £200 million per year and more than 3,000 employees, TCS has one of the largest players in this emerging market and had a strategy of rapid expansion. It took over the management of the housing benefits office of a London borough as a loss-leader in order to break into an expanding area of outsourcing business. This housing benefits office had previously been under-performing and was identified as one of the worst boroughs in London. Here, claim processing was outsourced to improve the quality of service provided.

Scotchem is a pigment manufacturing plant. It is one of several UK-based chemical production facilities owned by Multichem, a large European multinational that specialises in developing and producing industrial chemicals. Pigments have been produced on the site for over 75 years and Scotchem is Multichem's centre of excellence in pigment manufacture. The company employs over 650 people on its unionised site and produces around 24,000 tonnes of pigment. A regular feature of this production process was that Scotchem collaborates with customers and suppliers in order to develop both processes and products for specific orders.

Both of these networks were organised, and gained their flexibility, in slightly different ways. In TCS claims processing was contracted out for seven years and initially contact between the council and TCS (with the exception of contract negotiation at senior level) took the form of council staff monitoring claims processed by TCS caseworkers. However, the original contract also set performance levels for TCS and these were not met. As a result, the council set a new series of targets and weekly meetings were held with senior TCS staff to discuss performance.

Scotchem's network is far more flexible, at least in terms of its relations with customers and suppliers. Since it produces chemicals in bulk and can both place and fill orders on a very large scale, many of its suppliers and customers are long term, with 20- or 30-year relationships not uncommon. Formal contracts tended to be short term, with quarterly negotiations used to set prices and agree approximate levels of consumption in order to manage work in progress. However, these agreements are part of very long-term relationships. As a result, a series of alliances and friendships have built up between various staff members, with informal contacts and tacit knowledge supplementing official agreements about cooperation.

Contracts, control and the decline of discretion

In theory, outsourcing only changes the responsibility for completing a task, not the task itself. In theory too, such a change may improve efficiency and effectiveness. The organisation that outsources may gain numerical flexibility, hiring staff only when needed, or secure access to expertise that it lacks internally. Yet these theories focus on organisational experience or expectations and assume that the way work is managed does not affect the way it is carried out. In practice, in TCS, outsourcing required a change in management structure which fundamentally altered the work processes. Such adjustments might have been predicted. There are, broadly, two distinct ways of controlling staff: 'status', in which employees are trusted to perform often ill-specified or 'extra-functional' activities (and through which they may gain certain rights), and 'contract', where tasks tend to be clearly specified and tightly controlled, completed at the order of employers (Streeck, 1987). Most employment relationships tend to be a fluid mixture of both, influenced by organisational structures, individuals and contexts. According to the prescriptive literature, liberation from bureaucratic control should increase an individual's autonomy; in practice, in TCS, the reverse was the case. Here the process of contracting meant that tasks were more strictly defined

and monitored and employees were able to exercise less discretion.

Housing benefit staff had previously been responsible for seeing an entire claim through from start to finish, ensuring that the documentation was complete and correct and often exercising their professional judgement to condone minor omissions. Since forms were complicated and demanded repeated pieces of evidence, these omissions were reasonably common. Under TCS, once the work was contracted out, processing was reorganised so that caseworkers 'specialised' in one part of the claims process or worked in the newly-set-up call centre for extended periods of time (instead of part of a shift, as had been the case under the local authority). Housing benefit is a complex area and regulations are subject to change, so this specialisation not only made processing claims less pleasurable by taking away caseworkers' feelings of 'ownership' and making their work less interesting, it also meant that skills declined. Staff members were no longer aware of changes that occurred outside their own narrow remit. Their power to make decisions was also lost. Caseworkers were required only to ensure that the paperwork was complete before passing the form back to the local authority, rather than approving it as it stood.

> Under [the council] I had my own caseload, a set number of cases, surnames for a particular area; I go through all those cases from start to finish. If, during the benefit period, there was a change of circumstances it was my sole ability to do that case. I knew those cases. You could call the name and address and I could tell you what that entailed. We don't have that under [TCS]. What we have, it's even worse now . . . we come in and they give us this sheet and they say this is your work for the day. You don't really know the cases. Ten people could have touched that case since it came in before it gets to the person who finally pays the claim. So from the customer point of view it's not very helpful as they tend to receive letters from five or six different case workers – they say, who wrote to me?
>
> (TCS caseworker, female)

To a certain extent, this decline in discretion was an inevitable part of the contracting process. After all, tasks may be contracted out, but responsibility remains with the original organisation. This institutional separation of execution and authority has implications for work processes. While in-house staff might be controlled through trust, work undertaken by external bodies was regulated by 'contract'. Because local authorities must validate claims, council staff checked every detail of every form before authorising it. The in-house experts retained by the council found that the monitoring was as time-consuming and tedious for them as it was for the ex-colleagues they monitored.

Changing skills, changing workers

This decline in employees' discretion was also matched by changes in personnel. In TCS the initial work group was of skilled staff that had transferred over from the local authority, but these were supplemented by agency staff (25 from a workforce of 110) whose levels of skill and experience varied. Further, TCS itself hired and trained new recruits, but these were less qualified than the existing caseworkers and the training that they were given was greatly shortened.

Such increasingly active management was more a product of the subcontracting process than a reflection of changes in the skills base. The audit systems were imposed on all workers and even the most experienced and skilled staff, who had been accustomed to exercise discretion when working 'in-house', were subjected to higher levels of control as subcontractors. There was a reduction in the skills base that had existed prior to contracting out, but this reduction was a consequence rather than a cause of the increasing emphasis on audit. This reduction in skills was partly because the temporary nature of the agreements provided fewer incentives for organisations to develop and maintain employees' skills. TCS, which had a seven-year contract with the council, introduced a caseworker training programme, but they recruited less qualified people than the council had and their training programme then equipped workers with fewer technical skills since the redesigned work processes demanded fewer skills.

Scotchem and 'learning networks'

Scotchem's network was qualitatively different from TCS's outsourced work. Since it was one of the largest multinationals engaged in producing chemicals and pigments, several of its relationships with suppliers and customers were long term. Specific contracts for services could be short, but they were repeated and inter-firm relationships could and did last 20 or 30 years. Many of these companies were competitors, but the size of their orders and the duration of the contacts meant that, here at least, market dependency resulted in the growth of trust. Officially, contact took the form of contracts for particular services; unofficially, it came close to a contract for service, allowing trust and status to develop.

In Scotchem, individual employees held permanent contracts and staff at all levels were expected to exercise responsibility and engage in 'extra-functional' activities. When a new plant was set up, one of the operatives commented that:

> We've been left with quite a free role to prioritise ourselves and sort our own team out, what we do and who does it, left to our own responsibility for that. . . We know our responsibilities, we organise ourselves. I think the ownership has come from – because we understand the business and the needs of the business.

These expectations were extended to work with other firms. Orders for pigment would often involve developing products or improving delivery and, to achieve this, Scotchem employees at all levels were required to collaborate with customers and suppliers, a working arrangement which included shop-floor employees who would test new processes and equipment before developments were finalised. Two of the most recent results of such inter-organisational collaborations are a complex automated loading facility for part of the Scotchem site, and larger and tougher bags for the powdered chemicals. Extensive collaboration with one preferred supplier in producing bag specifications has maximised benefits for both parties by significantly reducing leakage which might foul the loading equipment.

Each of these collaborations was formally governed through contract, and the information that could be revealed to competitors was restricted. However, the long-term relations between the firms and the friendships that often existed between employees meant that contracts were honoured more in breach than in observation. Exchanges generally went beyond permitted limits and several people commented that projects would not have succeeded were it not for both sides' generosity with information. Significantly too, contracts set out the aims of each collaboration and little attempt was made to specify or monitor detailed tasks.

Source: Grugulis et al., 2003.

CASE STUDY 5.4

ADVERTISING FOR SKILLS

IRENA GRUGULIS

These are extracts from real advertisements for jobs. In your groups choose three advertisements **which require varying skill levels** and answer the following questions:

1 What skills are required in the advertisement?
2 Are these soft skills or technical skills?
3 What is the balance between soft skills and technical skills?
4 Do these reflect what the job really requires?
5 For these jobs are the soft skills or the technical skills more complex? Is it possible to have a job that requires high levels of soft skills but only low levels of technical skills?

Chief Executives

[No salary specified]
We now seek Chief Executives to lead these businesses and create value for stakeholders. Successful candidates will be corporate entrepreneurs, experienced in building successful businesses and teams, driving sales and revenues and creating great strategic relationships.

Group Accountant

London, £60 – 70,000
The role will involve general accounting and book-keeping for five corporate companies in various currencies and jurisdictions; performing the month-end processes, including the revaluation of foreign denominated balances; basic cash management and cash forecasting; consolidation of the group accounts in Oracle; assistance with budgeting and forecasting and ad hoc tasks including assistance with Board reporting. Candidates will need to be ACA qualified with post qualification experience in a Group of Financial Accounting role within the Oil and Gas industry.

Call Centre Representative

Swansea

£16,616 – £22,486 + **half yearly performance bonus + excellent benefits**

Having the chance to provide outstanding customer service. Enjoying a clear career path. Being part of a global brand. Just some of the things this role could mean for you.

As part of our Premier Customer Service team, you'll be dealing exclusively with high net-worth customers. These are people who demand exceptional levels of service. So you must be prepared to go above and beyond as you handle everything from balance enquiries to overseas payment requests.

There's no outbound calling involved. The challenge is to be able to resolve every call yourself, and to ensure the customer has an excellent experience every time.

Customer service roles don't get much more challenging. To rise to that challenge, you'll need to be able to show us where you've gone the extra mile for customers in the past. You'll also need some genuine experience of sales.

Bibliography

Ainley, P. (1994) *Degrees of Difference*, London: Lawrence & Wishart.

Arthur, J.B. (1999) 'Explaining variation in human resource practices in US steel mini-mills', pp. 11–42, in Cappelli, P. (ed.) *Employment Practices and Business Strategy*, Oxford and New York: Oxford University Press.

Bach, S. and Sisson, K. (2000) 'Personnel management in perspective', pp. 3–42, in Bach, S. and Sisson, K. (eds.) *Personnel Management*, Oxford: Blackwell.

Bailey, T. and Berg, P. (2010) 'The vocational and training system in the USA', pp. 271–94, in Bosch, G. and Charest J. (eds.) *Vocational Training: International Perspectives*, New York and London: Routledge.

Baumard, P. and Starbuck, W.H. (2006) *Is Organisational Learning a Myth?* London: The Advanced Institute of Management Research.

Bolton, S.C. (2004) 'Conceptual confusions: emotion work as skilled work', pp. 19–37, in Warhurst, C., Grugulis, I. and Keep, E. (eds.) *The Skills that Matter*, Basingstoke: Palgrave Macmillan.

Bosch, G. (2003) 'Skills and innovation – a German perspective', paper presented at The Future of Work/SKOPE/Centre for Organisation and Innovation Conference on Skills, Innovation and Performance, 31 March to 1 April, Cumberland Lodge, Windsor Great Park.

Bosch, G. (2010) 'The revitalisation of the dual system of vocational training in Germany', pp. 136–61, in Bosch, G. and Charest, J. (eds.) *Vocational Training: International Perspectives*, New York and London: Routledge.

Bosch, G. and Charest, J. (2010) 'Vocational training: international perspectives', pp. 1–26, in Bosch, G. and Charest, J. (eds.) *Vocational Training: International Perspectives*, New York and London: Routledge.

Boxall, P. and Purcell, J. (2011) *Strategy and Human Resource Management*, Basingstoke: Palgrave Macmillan.

Bozkurt, O. and Grugulis, I. (2011) 'Why retail work demands a closer look', pp. 1–21, in Grugulis, I. and Bozkurt, O. (eds.) *Retail Work*, Houndsmills: Palgrave Macmillan.

Brown, P. (2001) 'Skill formation in the twenty-first century', pp. 1–55, in Brown, P., Green, A. and Lauder, H. (eds.) *High Skills: Globalization, Competitiveness and Skill Formation*, Oxford: Oxford University Press.

Buchanan, J. and Evesson, J. (2004a) 'Creating markets or decent jobs? Group training and the future of work', *Australia National Training Authority*, Adelaide: NCVER.

Buchanan, J. and Evesson, J. (2004b) 'Redefining skill and solidarity at work: insights from group training arrangements in Australia', paper presented at 22nd International Labour Process Conference, 5–7 April, Amsterdam.

Callaghan, G. and Thompson, P. (2002) 'We recruit attitude: the selection and shaping of routine call centre labour', *Journal of Management Studies*, Vol.39, No.2, 233–54.

CBI (Confederation of British Industry) (1989) *Towards a Skills Revolution: A Youth Charter*, London: CBI.

Cockburn, C. (1983) *Brothers: Male Dominance and Technological Change*, London: Pluto Press.

Collinson, D., Knights, D. and Collinson, M. (1990) *Managing to Discriminate*, London and New York: Routledge.

Conniff, R. (1994) 'Big bad welfare: welfare reform politics and children', *The Progressive*, Vol.58, No.8.

Cooke, F.L. (2012) *Human Resource Management in China: New trends and practice*, London and New York: Routledge.

Cully, M., Woodland, S., O'Reilly, A. and Dix, G. (1999) *Britain at Work: As Depicted by the 1998 Workplace Employee Relations Survey*, London: Routledge.

Culpepper, P.D. (1999) 'The future of the high-skill equilibrium in Germany', *Oxford Review of Economic Policy*, Vol.15, No.1, 43–59.

Cutler, T. (1992) 'Vocational training and British economic performance: a further instalment of the "British Labour Problem"?', *Work, Employment and Society*, Vol.6, No.2, 161–83.

Dench, S., Perryman, S. and Giles, L. (1999) 'Employers' perceptions of key skills', *IES Report*, Sussex: Institute of Manpower Studies.

Department for Education and Employment (2000) 'Skills for all: research report from the National Skills Task Force', Suffolk: DfEE.

Dickerson, A. and Green, F. (2002) 'The growth and valuation of generic skills', SKOPE Research Paper, Oxford and Warwick: Universities of Oxford and Warwick.

Evetts, J. (2002) 'New directions in state and international professional occupations: discretionary decision making and acquired regulation', *Work, Employment and Society*, Vol.16, No.2, 341–53.

Felstead, A., Gallie, D. and Green, F. (2002) *Work Skills in Britain 1986–2002*, Nottingham: DfES Publications.

Felstead, A., Gallie, D., Green, F. and Zhou, Y. (2007) *Skills at Work 1986–2006*, Oxford: SKOPE and ESRC.

Felstead, A., Gallie, D., Green, F. and Inanc, H. (2013) *Skills at Work in Britain: First Findings from the Skills and Employment Survey 2012*, London: Centre for Learning and Life Chances in Knowledge Economies and Societies, Institute of Education.

Finegold, D. (1999) 'Creating self-sustaining, high-skill ecosystems', *Oxford Review of Economic Policy*, Vol.15, No.1, 60–81.

Finegold, D. and Soskice, D. (1988) 'The failure of training in Britain: analysis and prescription', *Oxford Review of Economic Policy*, Vol.4, No.3, 21–43.

Fuller, A. and Unwin, L. (2004) 'Expansive learning environments: integrating organisational and personal development', pp. 126–44, in Rainbird, H., Fuller, A. and Munro, A. (eds.) *Workplace Learning in Context*, London and New York: Routledge.

Gadrey, J. (2000) 'Working time configurations: theory, methods and assumptions for an international comparison', pp. 21–30, in Baret, C., Lehndorff, S. and Sparks, L. (eds.) *Flexible Working in Food Retailing: A Comparison between France, Germany, the UK and Japan*, London and New York: Routledge.

Green, F. (2006) *Demanding Work: The Paradox of Job Quality in the Affluent Economy*, Princeton, NJ and Oxford: Princeton University Press.

Green, F., Ashton, D., James, D. and Sung, J. (1999) 'The role of the state in skill formation: evidence from the republic of Korea, Singapore and Taiwan', *Oxford Review of Economic Policy*, Vol.15, No.1, 82–96.

Green, F., Felstead, A., Gallie, D. and Inanc, H. (2013) *Training in Britain: First Findings from the Skills and Employment Survey 2012*, London: Centre for Learning and Life Chances in Knowledge Economies and Societies, Institute of Education.

Grimshaw, D., Beynon, H., Rubery, J. and Ward, K. (2002) 'The restructuring of career paths in large service sector organisations: "delayering", up-skilling and polarisation', *Sociological Review*, Vol.50, No.1, 89–116.

Grugulis, I. (2003) 'The contribution of NVQs to the growth of skills in the UK', *British Journal of Industrial Relations*, Vol.41, No.3, 457–75.

Grugulis, I. and Stoyanova, D. (2011) 'Skill and performance', *British Journal of Industrial Relations*, Vol.49, No.3, 515–36.

Grugulis, I. and Vincent, S. (2009) 'Whose skill is it anyway? "Soft" skills and polarisation', *Work, Employment and Society*, Vol.23, No.4, 597–615.

Grugulis, I., Vincent, S. and Hebson, G. (2003) 'The rise of the "network organisation" and the decline of discretion', *Human Resource Management Journal*, Vol.13, No.2, 45–59.

Grugulis, I., Warhurst, C. and Keep, E. (2004) 'What's happening to skill', pp. 1–18, in Warhurst, C., Grugulis, I. and Keep, E. (eds.) *The Skills That Matter*, Basingstoke: Palgrave Macmillan.

Hebson, G. and Grugulis, I. (2005) 'Gender and new organisational forms', pp. 217–385, in Marchington, M., Grimshaw, D., Rubery, J. and Willmott, H. (eds.) *Fragmenting Work: Blurring Organisational Boundaries and Disordering Hierarchies*, Oxford: Oxford University Press.

Hendry, C. (1993) 'Personnel leadership in technical and human resource change', in Clark, C. (ed.) *Human Resource Management and Technical Change*, London: Sage.

Heyes, J. and Gray, A. (2003) 'The implications of the national minimum wage for training in small firms', *Human Resource Management Journal*, Vol.13, No.2, 76–86.

Hirsch, W. and Bevan, S. (1988) *What Makes a Manager?* Brighton: Institute of Manpower Studies, University of Sussex.

Hochschild, A.R. (1983) *The Managed Heart: Commercialization of Human Feeling*, Berkley, CA: University of California Press.

Jeong, J. (1995) 'The failure of recent state vocational training policies in Korea from a comparative perspective', *British Journal of Industrial Relations*, Vol.33, No.3, 237–52.

Jürgens, U. and Krzywdzinski, M. (2015) 'Competence development on the shop floor and industrial upgrading: case studies of auto makers in China', *International Journal of Human Resource Management*, Vol.26, No.9, 1204–25. Available at: DOI: 10.1080/09585192.2014.934888.

Keep, E. (1989) 'Corporate training strategies: the vital component?', pp. 109–25, in Storey, J. (ed.) *New Perspectives on Human Resource Management*, London: Routledge.

Keep, E. (2001) 'If it moves, it's a skill', paper presented at ESRC seminar on the Changing Nature of Skills and Knowledge, 3–4 September, Manchester.

Keep, E. and Mayhew, K. (1996) 'Evaluating the assumptions that underlie training policy', pp. 303–34, in Booth, A. and Snower, D.J. (eds.) *Acquiring Skills*, Cambridge: Cambridge University Press.

Keep, E. and Mayhew, K. (1999) 'The assessment: knowledge, skills and competitiveness', *Oxford Review of Economic Policy*, Vol.15, No.1, 1–15.

Keep, E. and Rainbird, H. (2000) 'Towards the learning organisation?', pp. 173–94, in Bach, S. and Sisson, K. (eds.) *Personnel Management: A Comprehensive Guide to Theory and Practice*, Oxford: Blackwell.

Keep, E., Mayhew, K. and Corney, M. (2002) 'Review of the evidence on the rate of return to employers of investment in training and employer training measures', SKOPE Research Paper, Universities of Oxford and Warwick, SKOPE.

Kinnie, N., Hutchinson, S. and Purcell, J. (2000) 'Fun and surveillance: the paradox of high commitment management in call centres', *International Journal of Human Resource Management*, Vol.11, No.5, 967–85.

Kirsch, J., Klein, M., Lehndorff, S. and Voss-Dahm, D. (2000) 'The organisation of working time in large German food retail firms', pp. 58–82, in Baret, C., Lehndorff, S. and Sparks, L. (eds.) *Flexible Working in Food Retailing: A Comparison between France, Germany, the UK and Japan*, London and New York: Routledge.

Korczynski, M. (2001) 'The contradictions of service work: call centre as customer-oriented bureaucracy', pp. 79–101, in Sturdy, A., Grugulis, I. and Willmott, H. (eds.) *Customer Service: Empowerment and Entrapment*, Basingstoke: Palgrave.

Korczynski, M. (2002) *Human Resource Management in Service Work*, Basingstoke: Palgrave.

Kuczera, M. and Field, S. (2010) *Learning for Jobs OECD Reviews of Vocational Education and Training: Options for China* OECD. Available at: http://www.oecd.org/education/innovation-education/learningforjobs.htm.

Lafer, G. (2004) 'What is skill?', pp. 109–27, in Warhurst, C., Grugulis, I. and Keep, E. (eds.) *The Skills That Matter*, Basingstoke: Palgrave Macmillan.

Lane, C. (1989) *Management and Labour in Europe*, Aldershot: Edward Elgar.

Leidner, R. (1993) *Fast Food, Fast Talk: Service Work and the Routinizations of Everyday Life*, Berkeley and Los Angeles, CA: University of California Press.

Leitch, S. (2006) 'Prosperity for all in the global economy – world class skills. Final report', *Leitch Review of Skills*, London: The Stationery Office.

Li, Y. and Sheldon, P. (2010) 'HRM lives inside and outside the firm: employers, skill shortages and the local labour market in China', *International Journal of Human Resource Management*, Vol.21, No.12, 2173–93. Available at: DOI: 10.1080/09585192.2010.509623.

Littler, C. (1982) *The Development of the Labour Process in Capitalist Societies*, London: Heinemann.

Mason, G. and Bishop, K. (2010) 'Adult training, skills updating and recession in the UK: the implications for competitiveness and social inclusion', LLAKES Research Paper, London: Institute of Education.

Mason, G., Van Ark, B. and Wagner, K. (1996) 'Workforce skills, product quality and econo-mic performance', pp. 175–98, in Booth, A. and Snower, D.J. (eds.) *Acquiring Skills*, Cambridge: Cambridge University Press.

McGauran, A.-M. (2000) 'Vive la différence: the gendering of occupational structures in a case study of Irish and French retailing', *Women's Studies International Forum*, Vol.23, No.5, 613–27.

McGauran, A.-M. (2001) 'Masculine, feminine or neutral? In-company equal opportunities policies in Irish and French MNC retailing', *International Journal of Human Resource Management*, Vol.12, No.5, 754–71.

Moss, P. and Tilly, C. (1996) 'Soft skills and race: an investigation into black men's employment problems', *Work and Occupations*, Vol.23, No.3, 252–76.

Nolan, P. and Slater, G. (2003) 'The labour market: history, structure and prospects', pp. 58–80, in Edwards, P. (ed.) *Industrial Relations: Theory and Practice*, Oxford: Blackwell.

Oliver, J.M. and Turton, J.R. (1982) 'Is there a shortage of skilled labour?', *British Journal of Industrial Relations*, Vol.20, No.2, 195–200.

ONS (2015a) 'EMP14 All Employees by Industry Sector', Newport: Office for National Statistics. Available at: http://www.ons.gov.uk/ons/publications/re-reference-tables .html?edition=tcm%3A77-367096#tab-Employment-tables.

ONS (2011b) 'Training statistics, labour force survey', Newport: Office for National Statistics.

Payne, J. (1999) 'All things to all people: changing perceptions of "skill" among Britain's policy makers since the 1950s and their implications', *SKOPE Research Paper No.1*, Coventry: University of Warwick.

Payne, J. (2000) 'The unbearable lightness of skill: the changing meaning of skill in UK policy discourses and some implications for education and training', *Journal of Education Policy*, Vol.15, No.3, 353–69.

Phillips, A. and Taylor, B. (1986) 'Sex and skill', in Feminist Review (ed.) *Waged Work: A Reader*, London: Virago.

Prais, S. (1995) *Productivity, Education and Training: An International Perspective*, Cambridge: Cambridge University Press.

Rainbird, H. and Munro, A. (2003) 'Workplace learning and the employment relationship in the public sector', *Human Resource Management Journal*, Vol.13, No.2, 30–44.

Ritzer, G. (1998) *The McDonaldisation Thesis*, London: Sage.

Rothenberg, S. (2003) 'Knowledge content and worker participation in environmental management at NUMMI', *Journal of Management Studies*, Vol.40, No.7, 1783–802.

Rubery, J. and Grimshaw, D. (2003) *The Organization of Employment*, Basingstoke: Palgrave Macmillan.

Rubery, J. and Wilkinson, F. (1994) 'Introduction', in Rubery, J. and Wilkinson, F. (eds.) *Employer Strategy and the Labour Market*, Oxford: Oxford University Press.

Shury, J., Winterbotham, M., Davies, B., Oldfield, K., Spilsbury, M. and Constable, S. (2010) *National Employer Skills Survey for England 2009: Main Report*, London: UKCES.

Smith, A. (1776/1993) *Wealth of Nations*, Oxford and New York: Oxford University Press.

Smith, C. and Chan, J. (2015) 'Working for two bosses: student interns as constrained labour in China', *Human Relations*, Vol.68, No.2, 305–26. Available at: DOI: 10.1177/0018726714557013.

Steiger, T.L. (1993) 'Construction skill and skill construction', *Work, Employment and Society*, Vol.7, No.4, 535–60.

Streeck, W. (1987) 'The uncertainties of management in the management of uncertainty: employers, labour relations and industrial adjustment in the 1980s', *Work, Employment and Society*, Vol.1, No.3, 281–308.

Thompson, P., Wallace, T., Flecker, J. and Ahlstrand, R. (1995) 'It ain't what you do, it's the way that you do it: production organisation and skill utilisation in commercial vehicles', *Work, Employment and Society*, Vol.9, No.4, 719–42.

Vivian, D., Winterbotham, M., Shury, J., Davies, B. and Constable, S. (2011) *UK Employer Skills Survey 2011: First Findings*, London: UKCES.

Warhurst, C. and Thompson, P. (1998) 'Hands, hearts and minds: changing work and workers at the end of the century', in Thompson, P. and Warhurst, C. (eds.) *Workplaces of the Future*, London: Macmillan.

Whiteways Research (1995) *Skills for Graduates in the 21st Century*, London: Association of Graduate Recruiters.

Yoon, J.H. and Lee, B.-H. (2010) 'The transformation of the government-led vocational training system in Korea', pp. 162–86, in Bosch, G. and Charest, J. (eds.) *Vocational Training: International Perspectives*, New York and London: Routledge.

CHAPTER 6
REWARD MANAGEMENT

Flora F. T. Chiang and Thomas A. Birch

Introduction

Managing rewards effectively is critical to organisations. Simply put, reward management can have a powerful influence on employee behaviour and performance and, hence, the achievement of an organisation's goals and objectives and ultimately its competitiveness. Moreover, unlike other activities within the human resources management function, reward management has significant implications to organisations *before* (e.g. recruitment), *during* (e.g. motivation, retention), and *after* (e.g. pension) an individual's employment. Because rewards often represent one of the most significant costs of producing goods and services, organisations are compelled to continuously seek new and cost effective ways to reward their employees. This necessitates that reward managers not only work closely and proactively with other human resources management professionals (e.g. job design, training and development, employee relations) but also with individuals across different functions (e.g. sales and marketing, R&D, manufacturing) and geographies (e.g. foreign subsidiaries) in an organisation as well as with external partners (e.g. pay trend consultants) to maximise the effectiveness of rewards. It also requires that reward managers understand how and why rewards and their efficacy are likely to vary within and between organisations, industries, and countries due to a range of factors in the business environment and differences in the reward needs and preferences of individuals (Chiang and Birch, 2006; 2007; 2012). Thus, to be effective, reward management must strike a balance between the reward capabilities and goals of the organisation, the potentially diverse set of reward needs and preferences of its workforce and a myriad of other external and internal forces in the organisation's business environment when designing and administering a total reward framework.

However, as scholars, practitioners, and the popular business press caution, reward management may not always be straightforward and can even be contentious. Evidence suggests that some of the most notable labour disputes in history are the result of employee dissatisfaction with reward practices (e.g. perceived inequalities in compensation and benefits) (Listverse, 2011). In fact, many of the world's most well-known and respected multinational corporations (e.g. Wal-Mart, McDonald's, General Electric and Cathay Pacific) have faced industrial action stemming from reward related issues (Bloomberg Business, 2015). Even in countries such as China where public protests are prohibited by law, labour disputes about pay and working conditions occur frequently (China Labor Bulletin, 2015). Some controversial reward issues are even receiving heightened attention globally. For example, intense international debate surrounds the social desirability of a large gap between CEO and average worker pay (for a review see Shaw, 2014; Patton, 2012), which has been shown to be as large as 373 to 1 in the United States, 206 in Canada, 148 in Switzerland, 147 in Germany, 127 in Spain, 110 in Czech Republic, 104 in France, 93 in Australia, 89 in Sweden, 86 in Hong Kong, 84 in the United Kingdom, 76 in Israel and in Netherlands, 67 in Japan, 58 in Norway, 53 in Portugal, 48 in Denmark, 36 in Austria and 28 in Poland (AFL-CIO, 2015a). Widespread criticism has also been levied at organisations allowing excessive pay gaps to persist between male and female employees performing identical or similar jobs.

This chapter introduces the subject of reward management. It begins by briefly defining reward management and exploring different perspectives about rewards found in the literature. Next, the major types of rewards and reward systems that comprise an organisation's total reward framework are introduced. This is followed by a closer look at important issues and decisions related to pay determination. Attention is then devoted to the strategic role of rewards (i.e. how organisations use rewards to support their business strategy), and, in particular, one of the most popular and growing forms of variable or contingent reward – *performance for pay* (PFP). Finally, issues relevant to the transferability of rewards across borders are discussed, including the implications of country differences on reward design and administration. Throughout the chapter, real life examples and cases are provided to help reinforce key concepts and improve understanding about current issues facing reward management practitioners. The chapter concludes with a case study about rewarding innovation at Huawei. Additional supplementary readings are also suggested.

Defining reward management

Reward management has been defined in different ways. Most broadly, WorldatWork (2015) suggests that it reflects the management of 'all of the employer's available tools that may be used to attract, retain, motivate, and satisfy employees'. According to Armstrong (2012: 6), it represents 'the strategies, policies and processes required to ensure that the value of people and the contribution they make to achieving organisation, departmental and team goals is recognised and rewarded. It is about the design, implementation and maintenance of reward systems (interrelated reward processes, practices and procedures) which aim to satisfy the needs of both the organisation and its stakeholders and to operate fairly, equitably and consistently'. Perkins and White (2011: 3) describe reward management as a central pillar supporting the employment relationship. They contend that it is how rewards are managed that affects the quality of the relationship and its outcomes (see also Harvey and Turnbull, Chapter 8 in this volume).

Common to all definitions is the notion that reward management reflects how rewards are designed and administered, and is critical to attracting, retaining, and motivating employees to achieve desirable outcomes. Individuals are attracted to a job because of the rewards it offers, remain with an employer because they believe that the rewards they receive are fair and equitable, and are motivated to achieve high levels of performance and other desirable behaviours for an organisation because they believe that such behaviours will be rewarded.

As the illustrations of typical reward management frameworks provided in Figure 6.1 depict and as will be elaborated throughout the chapter, reward management is shaped and defined by a range of external (e.g. competitive conditions, labour law, national culture) and internal forces (e.g. organisational goals, objectives, strategy, culture, leadership, workforce demands) in an organisation's business environment. At the same time, today's organisations are unlikely to rely on any one single type of reward or reward system. Instead, an organisation's reward management framework or reward architecture is likely to include a mix or combination of different types of rewards and reward systems that are tailored to support different performance goals and objectives. Thus reward managers must be cognisant of the interplay between a range of factors and forces when designing and administering rewards as well as how such activities are likely to impact different facets of an organisation and its strategy.

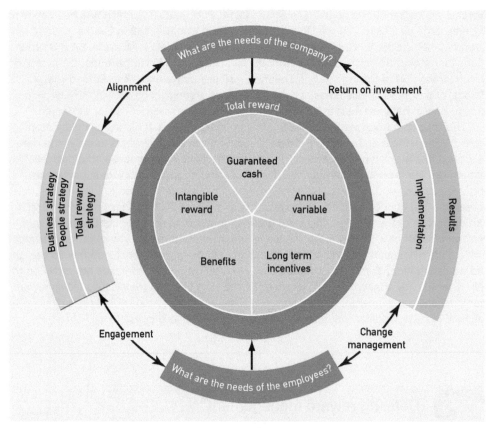

Figure 6.1 Examples of Reward Management Frameworks*: **(a)** Hay Group Total Reward Framework™

*The Hay Group. Retrieved from: http://www.haygroup.com/uk/services/index.aspx?id=10150

The conceptualisation of reward

Reward management has benefited from several different perspectives in the literature, including from economics, psychology, and management, as summarised in Table 6.1. According to the economic school, rewards (e.g. wages) serve as medium of exchange and have utility, cost, and control connotations. They are viewed as a cost of production and are provided to employees in exchange for the economic value they add to the firm. Marginal productivity theory argues that wages paid to an employee should equal the extra value of productivity that the employee contributes to total production (Sidney and Tarascio, 1971). Wage efficiency theory similarly suggests that pay should be set at a level that equates to an employee's productive efficiency. Moreover, agency theory suggests that while employers (principals) attempt to maximise return on rewards, employees (agents) are self-interested and risk-averse and if left unchecked may choose actions that maximise their rewards (pay) and minimise their work effort (shirk) (Eisenhardt, 1989). Because of information asymmetries between the principal and agent and because monitoring costs can be high, it is argued that in order to better align employer–employee interests, pay should be made conditional on performance (e.g. contingent rewards) (Jensen and Meckling, 1976). That is, financial incentives may help control the costs associated with dysfunctional and opportunistic employee behaviour (Abelson and Baysinger, 1984; Jensen and Meckling, 1976).

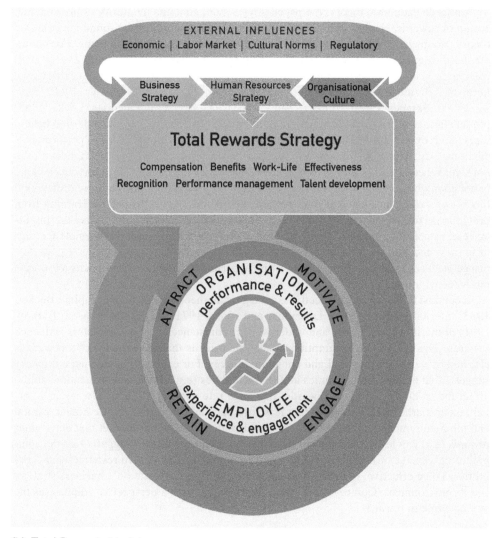

(b) Total Rewards Model

WorldatWork. Retrieved from: https://www.worldatwork.org/aboutus/html/aboutus-whatis.jsp.

Table 6.1 The conceptualisation of reward across different theoretical perspectives

Perspective	Theory	How Rewards Are Viewed
Economics	Marginal productivity Wage efficiency Agency	Labour costs; exchange for economic value; control mechanisms
Psychology	Needs	Need satisfaction
	Expectancy	Potential motivators and incentives
	Reinforcement	Reinforcers
	Equity	Exchange for a fair balance
	Goal setting	Goal setting mechanisms
Management	Human capital	Individual attributes
	Internal labour market	Organisational factors
	Resource-based	Means to gain competitive advantage

Similar to economic theory, the psychology school contains the utility or instrumental notion of rewards. However, unlike the cost and control connotations found in economic theory, the psychology school views rewards as motivational mechanisms. For example, needs theories (e.g. Maslow's 1954 hierarchy of needs model, Herzberg *et al.*'s 1959 two-factor need typology) contend that rewards are a motivational means to satisfying a range of individual needs and preferences. Expectancy (Porter and Lawler, 1968), reinforcement (Skinner, 1969), equity (Adams, 1963), and goal setting theories (Locke, 1968) provide further insights into the conditions under which rewards might elicit desired behaviours. Both expectancy and reinforcement theories explicitly link reward to performance, albeit they differ in the way that individuals are viewed to perceive this instrumental relationship. Whereas expectancy theory focuses on reward expectations (i.e. a forward-looking belief about the attainment of a reward after performance is demonstrated), reinforcement theory stresses the influence of prior reward experiences (e.g. retrospective learning from previous performance-reward outcomes). Lastly, equity theorists emphasise the importance of establishing rewards based on comparable job worth in order to promote feelings of fairness and goal setting theory helps establish the goal setting mechanisms (e.g. performance feedback) that underlie a reward's link to performance, the link that elicits a reward's motivational impact.

In contrast to the above perspectives, management theories (e.g. human capital: Becker, 1983; internal labour market: Doeringer and Piore, 1971 and resource based: Barney, 1991) primarily examine why and under what circumstances contextual factors influence rewards. The underlying assumption of such theories is that the efficacy of a reward is affected by various situational and contextual forces. For example, human capital theory suggests that employees' attributes and characteristics (e.g. experience, education, skills) affect the level and extent of rewards (i.e. wage rate and pay structure), whereas internal labour market theory stresses that it is firm demand (i.e. firm-specific human capital and job requirements) as opposed to the supply side of the labour market that determines rewards (e.g. pay level, promotion). Resource-based theory further suggests that the competitive advantage of firms is derived in part from maximising reward resources and capabilities. To be effective, rewards must be aligned with an organisation's business strategy and its environment (Gomez-Mejia and Balkin, 1992). Such a perspective emphasises the strategic role of rewards.

Types of rewards

As illustrated in Figure 6.2, there are a range of financial and non-financial types of rewards that organisations can use to compensate their employees. More specifically, financial rewards can be either direct or indirect. Direct financial rewards represent an employee's fixed and variable income. Whereas, fixed income (e.g. basic salary) is often the largest component of an employee's financial rewards and is typically provided to employees at regular predetermined time intervals (e.g. weekly, monthly) variable income represents a form of financial reward that is contingent on an employee's performance and can be either short- (e.g. merit pay, bonuses, cash awards) or long-term oriented (e.g. profit sharing, stock options). For example, merit pay may be provided in the form of an incremental increase to an employee's annual basic salary to recognise his or her past performance, while bonus pay may be provided to an employee in the form of a one-off lump sum payment and does not change or alter an employee's annual basic salary. Indirect financial rewards, on the other hand, consist of a range of benefits and services provided to employees as part of their employment, such as deferred income (e.g. pensions and medical insurance) and perquisites (e.g. paid vacations, housing allowances, company cars, and club memberships).

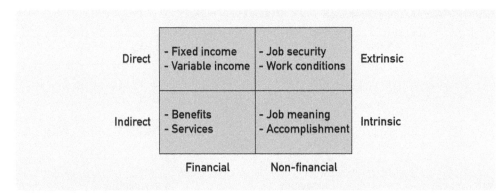

Figure 6.2
Types of rewards

By contrast, non-financial rewards consist of both extrinsic and intrinsic types of rewards and do not benefit employees in a monetary sense. Whereas extrinsic non-financial rewards are direct and tangible rewards that are externally attached to the job (e.g. job security, recognition, status, work relationships, training opportunities, and flexible work schedules), intrinsic non-financial rewards are related to the actual attributes and content of a job, accrue from the performance of the job itself and are dependent on individual experiences (e.g. job meaning, feelings of accomplishment, competency and personal growth; Hackman and Lawler, 1971; Herzberg *et al.*, 1959; Lawler and Hall, 1970). That is, extrinsic rewards are external, tangible, and direct, and intrinsic rewards are internal, psychological, and indirect.[1]

Overall, the use of financial and non-financial types of rewards can vary substantially within and between organisations, industries, and countries. At the same time, the impact of financial and non-financial rewards is often interdependent. For example, the positive feelings associated with recognition (a non-financial reward) may be strengthened by the addition of a contingent financial reward. Thus understanding the implications of different types of rewards and how they interact when mixed and combined is integral to effective reward management.

Types of reward systems

In addition to determining the types of rewards to be utilised, organisations must also decide which type(s) of reward system will be adopted to administer rewards. Reward systems can be based on non-performance (time, seniority, skill and competency) and performance related criteria (individual or collective performance), as summarised in Table 6.2. For example, a seniority-based reward system, a popular non-performance reward system, typically rewards employees based on their length of service or time on the job in an organisation. In Japan such reward systems are widely used to support the common practice of life-long employment, in which employees remain with the same organisation for the majority of their careers. Although seniority-based reward systems may increase worker loyalty and productivity as employees build up skills through on-the-job training and experience, they have been accused of impeding labour mobility and the long-term competitiveness of organisations. Other non-performance reward systems, such as skill- or competency-based reward systems, remunerate employees based on the acquisition of specific work-related skills, knowledge, and competencies and are viewed to facilitate employee learning and the development of skills necessary to the achievement of an organisation's strategic objectives, including supporting talent management process.

---

[1]For further conceptual distinctions between intrinsic and extrinsic rewards see Dermer, 1975; Dyer and Parker, 1975; Guzzo, 1979; and Kanungo and Hartwick, 1987.

Table 6.2 A comparison between types of reward systems

Criteria	Basis of Performance	
	Individual	Collective
Non-performance	Time	ESOPs
	Seniority	
	Skills	
	Competencies	
Performance	Piecework	Team/unit pay
	Commission	Profit sharing
	Individual bonus	Gain sharing
	PFP	ESOPs

By contrast, performance-based reward systems, as will be discussed in greater detail below, remunerate employees according to how well they perform their job or achieve specific performance targets and job tasks. Also commonly referred to as variable or contingent reward systems (e.g. PFP), these types of reward systems explicitly link rewards to individual or collective performance outcomes, such as units of production (piecework), sales goals, quality, customer satisfaction, profit, sales revenue, group productivity, and cost savings targets. Given that non-performance reward systems (e.g. seniority-based reward systems) are often criticised for creating a sense of entitlement and wage inflation, reward systems contingent on performance are gaining widespread popularity. In a survey of its members, WorldatWork (2012) found that 84 per cent of respondents worked for an organisation that has implemented a variable pay system, of which most used bonuses (76 per cent), individual incentives (59 per cent) and performance sharing (58 per cent). In a similar survey conducted by Aon Hewitt (2014), 91 per cent of organisations surveyed were found to use contingent rewards, which on average represented 12.7 per cent of their payroll budget.

Exercise 1   The Pros and Cons of different types of reward systems

What are some of the major advantages and disadvantages of non-performance versus performance reward systems? Discuss.

Interestingly, different types of rewards may be administered through either non-performance or performance oriented reward systems depending on their overall intent. For example, employee stock ownership plans (ESOPs), a type of reward provided to employees primarily to create a sense of ownership in the performance of an organisation, may be granted to employees after they complete a pre-determined service period (non-performance-based reward system) or alternatively after the attainment of specific performance objectives (performance-based reward system), depending on the organisation's reward strategy.

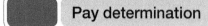 **Pay determination**

Determining the actual amount of rewards to be provided to employees for specific jobs or pay determination represents a critical stage in the reward management process and entails several interdependent and iterative steps, including calculating the average rate of pay (e.g. basic salary) for each specific type of job, determining the importance of job-versus person-based factors to a job, pricing job content and performing job evaluations, and establishing a set of pay grades and scales or bands for different job groups and categories (a job hierarchy that reflects the nature and importance of different jobs in the organisation).

As illustrated in Figure 6.3, pay determination requires consideration of a range of factors and different approaches. For example, calculating the average rate of pay for a particular job is meant to reflect its value to the organisation and requires an assessment of both internal (e.g. cost implications, importance of the job to business strategy and performance, company ability to pay, and employee needs and preferences) and external factors (e.g. competition for labour, government policies and regulations). Unionised employees, for instance, may require higher pay than non-unionised employees or when collective bargaining power is high), the market rate for pay may decline (during periods of economic recession or when labour market supply is increasing), changes in government policies and labour laws (e.g. minimum wage, hours of work, overtime pay and equal pay for equal work) are likely to impact pay levels, and individuals' reward needs and preferences should be taken into account to ensure that employees are attracted, retained and motivated.

Moreover, the manner in which pay is determined is also influenced by the emphasis an organisation places on job- versus person-based factors. When an organisation emphasises job-based factors, reward managers typically determine pay for a job based on different dimensions of its content (e.g. job tasks, duties and responsibilities), an approach that should result in employees performing the same job receiving identical or similar pay. By contrast, when person-based factors are emphasised, reward managers typically evaluate different characteristics of employees, such as knowledge, skills, abilities, competencies and performance, to determine pay. In practice, most organisations use a combination of job- and person-based criteria as part of their pay determination process.

Furthermore, pricing job content is typically accomplished by utilising a combination of internal (e.g. job evaluations) and external mechanisms (e.g. pay trend surveys). Although such a process is intended to foster both internal and external pay equity (Gupta and Jenkins, 1991), organisations often over-rely on external assessments and comparisons. Whereas internal equity refers to pay relationships between jobs within the same organisation (e.g. pay differences between the marketing and production manager), external equity refers to pay relationships between an organisation and its peers or rivals in the same industry (e.g. pay differences between a company's marketing manager versus the same position in its competitors). While the former reflects internal consistency and fairness, the latter helps to ensure competitiveness with the external labour market. In addition to internal and external equity, a third type of

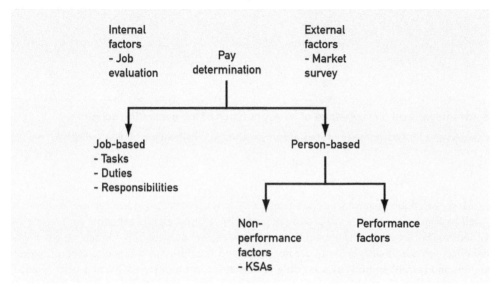

Figure 6.3

Pay determination

equity, individual equity, reflects an individual's perception of the fairness associated with his or her input (e.g. effort) versus output (e.g. pay) compared with that of his or her colleagues in the same or similar jobs in the organisation (Adams, 1963).

As the examples of non-analytical and analytical job evaluation schemes provided in Box 6.1 suggest, job evaluations represent formal and systematic processes for determining the relative worth of and assigning values to different jobs (essential to setting of pay grades and scales or bands and to creating a job hierarchy). By and large, job evaluations involve consideration of different dimensions of a job's content (e.g. job responsibilities and complexity, knowledge, skills, and competencies required) and requires the setting of minimum, mid-point, and maximum pay levels for each job category or class. They also enable different weightings or importance to be calculated and attached to different dimensions of the job content which, in turn, affect a job's relative worth (i.e. pay level).

Box 6.1 HRM in practice   Non-analytical vs. analytical job evaluation schemes

Non-analytical

Ranking of whole jobs in order of 'size', complexity or business impact is the most straightforward method of job evaluation and entails listing jobs in their order of importance according to one or multiple criteria, albeit using only one aspect of the job may distort outcomes. The process typically focuses on a handful of 'benchmark' jobs (rather than a time-consuming evaluation of all jobs in the organisation) around which other roles are placed in their assessed order of importance. Once all jobs have been listed, the job evaluators then need to make decisions about the number of grades they would like to use in their organisation and agreed break points (i.e., at points where there is perceived to be a step difference in the size of jobs).

Other types include job categorisation or job classification, which represents a more top-down approach whereby job categories, classes or grades are determined in advance and roles are slotted or placed into the category in which they are perceived to fit best and paired comparison viewed as a more rigorous approach to job ranking, which forces the employer to make a choice between two factors or two whole jobs and arrive at more objective decisions about the relative worth of a job.

Analytical

Points factor is by far the dominant form of job evaluation, the Hay job evaluation method being the leading proprietary brand of 'points factor' schemes. The points factor method is a highly analytical approach to job evaluation, breaking down jobs into a number of factors against which points are allocated. The factors are intended to be impersonal objective lenses through which a job is deconstructed into its component parts, with each part scored independently, and then the values are added together to give a total points value to the re-assembled job.

Source: Childs, 2004.

Exercise 2   The advantages and disadvantage of different types of job evaluation schemes

What are the advantages and disadvantages of non-analytical versus analytical job evaluation schemes? Discuss.

Moreover, a job hierarchy or classification system may contain either narrow bands with small pay variations between different types of jobs or broad bands that allow for larger pay variations. For example, the recent trend towards the broadening of pay ranges (i.e. broadbanding) provides managers with greater scope and flexibility to respond to labour market signals and reward employees according to variations in seniority, skills, and performance

(Heery and Noon, 2005). Broadbanding also enables career progression and lateral growth in position without requiring promotions or title changes. Companies such as IBM, Xerox and AT&T are well known for their sophisticated broadband pay structures. In terms of pay dispersion, it can reflect the size of pay differential between individuals within (horizontal or lateral dispersion) and across job categories (vertical dispersion) within an organisation (Gupta *et al.*, 2012; Shaw, 2014). Whereas horizontal dispersion refers to pay differences between individuals in the same job or at the same organisational level, vertical dispersion refers to the pay difference between the highest- (e.g. CEO) and lowest-paid positions in a firm. Horizontal pay variations within jobs usually occur because of individual differences, whereas vertical pay variations across jobs usually occur because of differences in a job's content and its strategic value to an organisation. (Gupta *et al.*, 2012). For reward managers it is important to note that the extent of pay variation in an organisation is likely to impact employee perceptions of fairness. Individuals often judge fairness by making social comparisons – either internally externally, or individually; upward or downward (vertical) or lateral (horizontal). Research has shown that pay inequities result in a wide range of organisational problems and can adversely impact employee motivation and performance (Kepes *et al.*, 2009), pay satisfaction (Sweeney and McFarlin, 2005), commitment and turnover (Shaw and Gupta, 2007).

To ensure the competitiveness of rewards, organisations typically review pay trends in the external labour market. External labour market analysis helps organisations benchmark pay and different dimensions of their reward management framework with that of competitors and industry peers. Organisations can then choose whether to adopt a reward strategy that either leads, matches, or lags the market. For example, pursuing a 'lead' reward strategy typically means that the organisation will pay higher than industry average levels of pay (e.g. pay higher wages than competitors), a strategy. (e.g. Google, Twitter, and Goldman Sachs) that often enables them to attract more highly qualified recruits and talent than low-paying firms in the same labour market (Fortune, 2015b). By contrast, organisations adopting a lag reward strategy typically pay their employees below the market rate (e.g. Walmart and McDonald's) a strategy that may be employed when an organisation's ability to pay is restricted by internal (e.g. a limited labour budget) or external (e.g. a forecasted economic downturn) constraints. Lastly, a market match reward strategy reflects the average pay that most firms offer for a similar job in the industry.

Decisions about which reward strategy to adopt (i.e. lead, lag or match) mainly depends on an organisation's overall business strategy and is likely to have significant cost and performance implications. For example, organisations that are cost-driven may opt for a lag strategy, those that use a match approach are more likely to compete on grounds other than labour costs, and those that place a high value on human resources or serve high-end customers are more likely to choose a lead reward strategy that enables them to differentiate from rivals on the basis of labour quality. Already a market leader, Google's 10 per cent across-the-board increase in compensation was an attempt not only to attract further top quality talent but also to increase existing employees' commitment (PayScale, 2011). See Box 6.2 for examples of hierarchical versus egalitarian reward cultures.

Overall, organisations use a variety of tools to determine pay, including job evaluation, pay trend surveys, and assessments of external and internal factors, the ultimate aim being to maximise return on investment whilst at the same time fostering the three forms of equity, namely internal, external and individual.

Understanding the strategic role of rewards

Increasingly, organisations are recognising that rewards can play a strategic role in cultivating change and achieving performance objectives and a range of other desirable outcomes, including fostering a strong performance culture (Fairhurst, 2008), corporate entrepreneurship (Kuratko *et al.*, 2001), innovation (Curran and Walsworth, 2014), safety (Mattson and Hellgren, 2014) and high performance work systems (HPWS) (Kessler, 2001). See Box 6.3

Box 6.2 HRM in practice   Hierarchical vs. egalitarian reward cultures

The vertical dispersion or pay gap between top management and junior front-line employees is typically wider in hierarchical (e.g. a large pay gap between the CEO and lower-level employees) versus egalitarian reward cultures (e.g. greater parity in pay across organisational levels). For example, US corporations tend to implement hierarchical pay structures [e.g. average employees at Walmart receive the minimum hourly wage versus its CEO who receives a multimillion-dollar annual compensation package (Fortune, 2015); the gap between the CEO of McDonald's pay and average store workers was 580:1 in 2011 (Bloomberg, 2012)]. However, some companies are bucking this trend by establishing more egalitarian pay systems [e.g. W.L. Gore & Associates, the maker of Gore-Tex, is known for its egalitarian organisational culture in which there are few traditional job titles and every employee becomes a shareholder of the company after one year (Fortune, 2015b)]; in April 2015 the CEO (Dan Price) of Gravity Payment, a Seattle-based credit card processing company, decided to take a USD $930,000 pay cut to provide each of his employees with a minimum wage of USD $70,000, the intention being to create income equality for his workforce (Money, 2015)).

Discussion question: What are the advantages and disadvantages of hierarchical versus egalitarian reward cultures?

Box 6.3 HRM in practice   Attracting and retaining talent through reward segmentation at Microsoft

In order to better align rewards with the goals of its One Microsoft strategy and talent management process, Microsoft made dramatic changes to its reward strategy. This began by identifying the core employee group most relevant to enhancing and sustaining its competitive advantages (i.e. Engineering and Research, which constitutes about one-third of the company's workforce). Next, efforts were made to strengthen the performance culture of this employee group by enhancing merit pay (i.e. the highest compensation is provided to the highest-performing employees) and taking a lead reward strategy relative to the external labour market to ensure that employees are rewarded at levels of remuneration closer to the top of the market.

Source: Rettenmyer, 2014.

for an example of how rewards are being used to enhance Microsoft's performance culture. Rewards signal to employees the behaviours and performance outcomes that are valued by an organisation. In particular, scholars argue (e.g. Arrowsmith *et al.*, 2010) that the achievement of specific performance goals (e.g. improving customer service quality, reducing error rates, enhancing output levels) necessitates using variable or contingent reward strategies. Chiang and Birtch (2012) provide a discussion about the performance implications of financial versus non-financial rewards and Box 6.4 provides examples of some interesting incentive schemes in practice. One type of variable or contingent reward that is gaining heightened popularity is pay for performance (PFP), as shall now be discussed.

The special case of PFP

Designing, administering and evaluating PFP

PFP is grounded in the notion that its incentive value motivates desirable behaviour and reinforces effort, especially when there is a clear, measurable and objective link between the reward and the desired performance outcome. In this sense, PFP reward systems

Box 6.4 HRM in practice   The diversity of incentive programs in practice

Incentive programs have been used by organisations to encourage a wide range of behaviours, including safety performance at Xiamen Airlines (Wu *et al.*, 2015), environmental improvement initiatives at Hotel Nikko Hong Kong (HKSAR Environmental Protection Department, 2015), weight loss (Kullgren and Norton, 2013) and pollution prevention (Berrone and Gomez-Mejia, 2009).

(i) At Johnson & Johnson a health incentive program is used to promote and reward healthy employee behaviours. In addition to promoting worker productivity, the program helped reduce costs (e.g. healthcare, sick leave). From the late 1990s to 2006, smoking declined from 12 per cent to 4 per cent, high blood pressure dropped from 14 per cent to 6 per cent and high cholesterol dropped from 19 per cent to 6 per cent in its US workforce (Johnson & Johnson, 2015).

(ii) To motivate employee engagement and continuous improvement, the Sun Hing Vision Group in Hong Kong implemented an incentive plan which is based on employees' suggestions and ideas about how to improve efficiency and productivity. The 10 best ideas are selected by a Total Improvement Committee and then filmed and presented at company-wide town hall meetings. Awardees receive a cash incentive.

Some organisations also design innovative and fun incentive plans to motivate employees.

(iii) For example, McDonald's launched the Road to Rio initiative in 2014, in which employees from the top 5 per cent of restaurants according to customer satisfaction ratings were entered into a lucky prize draw for a trip to the World Cup in Brazil, an initiative that helped boost the speed and quality of customer service (Robert, 2015).

(iv) Hewlett-Packard (HP) offers a Golden Banana Award to reward employees who come up with a new idea or a solution to a problem. As company legend has it, the award came about when a manager searched his office to find something to acknowledge an engineer's solution to a problem. The only item the manager could find was a banana. The Golden Banana Award now symbolises employee innovation at HP (Nelson, 2009).

are believed to have powerful incentive and sorting effects (Gerhart and Rynes, 2003). Moreover, their growth in popularity is said to stem from several key factors, including that (a) pay is considered a more direct and visible means to incentivise performance; (b) organisations appear to have more discretion in setting PFP than in other areas, such as pay level, which is more constrained by labour and product market parameters (Gerhart *et al.*, 2009) and (c) it offers a tangible way to assess the investment return on labour costs (i.e. ROI).

However, in spite of their popularity, contingent reward systems, such as PFP, are not free from criticism (see Gerhart and Fang, 2014 for a review) and have been argued to create dysfunctional effects and unintended consequences. For example, it has been argued that PFP may lead to the neglect of or withdrawal from behaviours that are valued by the organisation because employees believe that such behaviours are not rewarded (e.g. employees who are rewarded based on sales volume may devote less attention to service quality, employees rewarded based on individual performance may be less willing to perform group-oriented citizenship and helping behaviours, such as orienting new recruits). Adverse sorting effects may also attract and retain employees who are oriented more toward risk taking (Cadsby *et al.*, 2007). Some critics also suggest that PFP may lead to counterproductive behaviours, such as workplace bullying (Samnani and Singh, 2014). Others still argue that such reward systems may have even contributed to unethical behaviour deemed to be at the heart of the global financial crisis in 2008 (i.e. banking misconduct spanning the US, Europe, and Asia and the mis-selling of excessively risky and dubious financial products, such as sub-prime mortgages in the US, PPI in the UK, risky investment products in Australia, and Lehman mini-bonds in Hong Kong) (Lindley, 2014).

Is a financial incentive the best motivator?

A major question facing the efficacy of performance rewards, such as PFP, is whether a financial incentive is the best motivator. As studies suggest, the effectiveness of financial incentives as a motivators remains controversial. According to one view, such an incentive can actually be a dissatisfier and de-motivator (Herzberg *et al.*, 1959), undermine intrinsic work motivation (Deci *et al.*, 1999) and instil undesirable competition (Deming, 1986). It is also argued that financial incentives may only achieve short-term compliance (Pfeffer, 1998) or encourage a narrow focus on a particular task (Kohn, 1988), and, as a consequence, may not be applicable or effective in certain jobs or industries. By contrast, a more positive view suggests that a financial incentive can be a motivator (Lawler, 1981), a driver, a secondary reinforcer, a conditioned incentive or an instrument for attaining valued outcomes (Jenkins, 1986; Opsahl and Dunnette, 1972). Considerable support exists for the use of financial incentives as means of improving employee performance and achieving other desirable behaviours (see reviews by Jenkins *et al.*, 1998; Locke *et al.*, 1980; Gerhart and Fang, 2014). For example, a meta-analyses by Locke *et al.* (1980) found that among rewards financial incentives resulted in increased worker performance by as much as 30 per cent.

Moreover, whether a financial incentive is an effective motivator also depends on employee needs and preferences – that is, how the financial incentive is perceived and valued by employees is important to securing its motivational effect. Undoubtedly, a financial incentive can be a powerful motivating reward for many individuals, especially those who possess an instrumental attitude towards work (Mitchell and Mickel, 1999). Nevertheless, to more fully understand the effectiveness of financial incentives, such as PFP, requires consideration of a range of different employee attributes and characteristics. For example, employee attitudes toward risk are important to reward schemes such as PFP because risk-averse employees are normally less willing to forgo a guaranteed amount of pay (e.g. basic salary) in favour of pay contingent upon performance, especially when employees believe that performance outcomes may be beyond their control. This is in sharp contrast to individuals with less or lower risk aversion who prefer jobs in which pay is linked more closely to performance, especially when the potential performance contingent reward is significant (Cadsby *et al.*, 2007; Cable and Judge, 1994). As research suggests PFP may also be more attractive to high than low performers (Trank *et al.*, 2002).

Measuring PFP

The implementation of PFP is said to depend on whether (a) pay is the most efficacious incentive; (b) performance can be measured accurately and objectively to determine pay outcome; (c) a clear line-of-sight between pay and performance can be established; and (d) the level or amount of the pay is in proportion to the performance attained (Gerhart *et al.*, 2009). However, in practice, problems often arise for PFP reward systems at the design stage. For example, effective PFP implementation is said to be especially reliant on the ability of reward managers to measure specific aspects of job performance, a process that entails four important considerations (Gerhart *et al.*, 2009; Gupta and Shaw, 2014), including whether:

- PFP is based on individual, group/unit, or organisational performance;
- the emphasis of PFP is results – (e.g. production outputs, sales revenue targets) or behaviour-oriented (e.g. customer ratings);
- PFP is based on objective measures (e.g. piece-rate) or subjective measures (e.g. supervisor ratings);
- the pay and performance criteria are clearly specified and communicated to employees in advance.

That is, PFP plans can be based on individual or collective performance (e.g. group/unit) and while the potential pitfalls of individual-based PFP are evident, collective-based incentive plans also have potential drawbacks, including a weaker link between employee effort and performance outcomes (line of sight), potential free-riding problems (e.g. shirking) and

Table 6.3 Results- versus behaviour-based performance measures

	Results-Based	Behaviour-Based
Advantages	More credible and avoid subjectivity in evaluation	Can be used for any type of job
	Evaluation is based on more objective measures	Allow the rater to factor in variables that are not under the employee's control but influence performance
	Higher motivational intensity	Allow to rate performance using means and behaviours
	Encourage focus on desired ends and impacts/outcomes	Avoid employees to focus only on explicit job performance targets/objectives at the expense of other contextual or citizenship behaviours
Disadvantages	Not all jobs are associated with an objective outcome measure	Can be subjective, especially evaluation is made by a single rater, who can suffer from rater's problems (e.g. halo effect)
	Focus on short-term results and employees will only focus on aspects that are measured	More difficult to differentiate employees based on behaviours (vs. objective results)
	Performance or achievement of results can be influenced by external factors	Not applicable in jobs where either the opportunity to observe behaviours or the ability to judge behaviours is not feasible

Source: Gerhart *et al.*, 2009.

fairness issues. Similarly, both results- and behaviour-based PFP measures have inherent advantages and disadvantages (see Table 6.3). Whereas results-oriented measures may be more objective and reliable, objective measures are not always possible for certain jobs and, as a consequence, it may not be possible to establish viable, quantifiable and meaningful job objectives and performance measures. Hence, when it is hard to establish valid measures, performance targets are often based on what is easily measured as opposed to what is considered important (Kessler, 2001).

Moreover, the choice about which approach to adopt – whether individual or collective or results- or behaviour-based – should relate to the objectives of the organisation and the nature of the job being measured. For example, when team objectives (e.g. collaboration and cooperation) are viewed as being more important than individual performance goals, then individual-based PFP may be detrimental to such objectives. Results-based measures for PFP may also be more appropriate for sales occupations in which objective performance measures (e.g. sales quotas) are available. By contrast, behaviour-based measures may be more appropriate for jobs when results-based performance measures are more difficult to quantify.

Lastly, although performance appraisal is an essential tool for any reward system, it is especially important to PFP. Performance appraisal represents the main mechanism through which rewards can be determined and allocated in relation to PFP's pre-determined performance objectives. Thus, without a valid performance appraisal system in place to support PFP it is difficult for reward managers to accurately distinguish between good and poor performers, allocate rewards effectively, communicate performance outcomes to employees, or to take corrective action (e.g. establish an employee development plan). See also Brown and Redman, Chapter 7 in this volume.

Other characteristics of PFP

In addition to the above, the effectiveness of a PFP plan is also influenced by whether (a) the magnitude of the incentive pay is large enough to be motivating; (b) employees see a direct link between their pay and the intended performance outcome and (c) the pay is based on factors outside the control of the employee. Reward managers must therefore address additional questions such as:

- Is PFP linked only to intended performance outcomes or other outcomes?
- What proportion of employee rewards are variable or contingent on performance?
- What are the PFP differences between high and low performers?
- Is PFP applied to all types of jobs or only to certain groups of employees?

In practice, addressing such questions may be difficult. First, pay systems tend to be oriented more toward factors other than pay differentiation, such as pay equality, because managers are often reluctant to make distinctions between employees on the basis of performance (this is often reflected by the small magnitude of the incentive). As research has shown, the pay difference between high versus average performers is typically only 1.1 to 1.5 per cent, which is unlikely to be motivational (Gerhart and Fang, 2014). However, if the magnitude is too large, although the incentive effect may be higher, the risk of unintended negative consequences is also likely to increase (e.g. create potential agency costs, such as moral hazard).

Second, although PFP is considered to be a performance-based reward system, other non-performance factors may influence pay decisions (e.g. seniority), especially in public or large firms which use salary 'point' systems. While a higher performance rating usually means that one receives a higher amount of PFP, the actual increase often depends on the employee's salary relative to average pay. That is, smaller amounts of PFP may be given to employees with higher relative basic salaries versus greater amounts for individuals with below average pay, the aim being to enable lower paid employees to 'catch up' to average pay levels through higher raises. In this sense, any benefits associated with linking pay to performance may be undermined. Finally, budget constraints may also limit the potential size of incentive pay. Hence, PFP differences between high and low performers may not be significant enough to be motivating. See Boxes 6.5 and 6.6 for examples of incentive programmes in practice.

| Box 6.5 HRM in practice | A 'special blend' of incentives at Starbucks Hong Kong |

The power of incentives is said to be governed by two laws, contingent reinforcement and immediate reinforcement, the former asserting that for a reward to have maximum reinforcing value, it must be contingent upon the demonstration of desired behaviour and the latter asserting that the more immediate the delivery of a reward after the occurrence of a desirable behaviour, the greater the incentive and reinforcing value of the reward (Schermerhorn, 2010).

The Starbucks incentive program in Hong Kong reflects such principles and attempts to strengthen the reward–performance link. Unlike the traditional practice in Hong Kong to provide an annual thirteenth month bonus (i.e. an additional month's salary), Starbucks adopted a more frequent approach to incentives. That is, its performance evaluation and incentive pay distribution takes place quarterly, instead of on an annual basis. Store managers are evaluated on three key performance dimensions, namely, employee retention, sales target acheivement, and customer satisfaction using a point scale (with a maximum of 500 points). Managers who score below 100 points are not entitled to any incentive pay while those who score between 100 and 500 points are eligible to receive a 10 to 35 per cent bonus based on their basic salary.

Discussion question: The timeliness of an incentive is believed to be important to motivating desirable behaviour. What are the advantages and disadvantages of rewarding employees more frequently?

In sum, PFP implementation requires careful goal setting, performance measurement, evaluation, and pay determination to be effective (Kessler, 2001). It can be perceived by employees either positively or negatively and has no intrinsic meaning or motivating power unless it symbolises either positive information (e.g. recognition for good performance) or a controlling mechanism (e.g. pay is the reason to work, behaviour is controlled by pay). In this sense, PFP's motivational effect is tied to employee perceptions about why and how it is provided. For instance, when the contingent pay symbolises recognition and appreciation as opposed to serving as a mechanism for controlling employee behaviour, its motivating effect is likely to be stronger.

Box 6.6 HRM in practice   **Linking rewards to company values at the MTR**

The Mass Transit Railway (MTR), Hong Kong's rapid transit railway system, is one of the most profitable and efficient railway systems in the world, with a farebox recovery ratio as high as 186 per cent. Opened in 1979, the system includes 218.2 km (135.6 mi) of rail with 155 stations, is the most common mode of public transport in Hong Kong, with over five million trips made during an average weekday, and consistently achieves a 99.9 per cent on-time rating.

To reward staff for their accomplishments and behaviours significant to the corporation's vision, mission, and values (VMV) the MTR has introduced several award schemes – a 'Living the MTR Values (LV) Award' and a 'VMV Heroes' scheme that enables managers to provide more tangible and, timely recognition to staff for their accomplishments. Four criteria closely aligned with the MTR's values are used to determine the awards, as follows:

Excellent Service: Employee commitment to proactively providing safe, efficient and caring service to customers.

Mutual Respect: Working in an open team environment based on trust, joint commitment and respect. Respecting the views of the community and other stakeholders.

Value Creation: Creating profits through efficient execution, continuous improvement, and innovation in delivering products and services valued by customers.

Enterprising Spirit: Courage to question the status quo, proactively taking initiatives, and having the resourcefulness to overcome obstacles and reach new horizons.

Awards typically consist of a non-cash prize of not more than HK$400 (USD 50) in value, a personalised certificate of recognition, and a pin reflecting the corporation's values. 'Success Stories' are placed on the corporation's internal website for sharing.

Discussion question: Some organisations attempt to create incentive systems on a small budget. Is it possible to motivate employees using small awards, certificates, and other symbolic methods of recognition? Discuss.

International reward management

The proliferation of cross-border business and multinational corporations (MNCs) has necessitated the internationalisation of reward management. International reward management begins with recognising how country (e.g. economic and labour market conditions, labour legislation) and individual differences (e.g. values) are likely to vary across borders and, in turn, influence the design, administration, and effectiveness of different types of rewards and reward systems. It also requires consideration of how best to organise and structure the reward management function of a MNC as a whole (e.g. a centralised function at the parent or, authority delegated to autonomous country or regional level units). Moreover, because MNCs operating in different countries are likely to employ different types of employees, such as parent country nationals (PCNs), locals or host country nationals (HCNs), and third country nationals (TCNs), this leads to greater diversity and cross-national mobility in a workforce, which in turn places different demands on the design and administration of rewards. Such issues underscore the added complexity associated with international reward management.

For example, MNCs must determine the degree to which various country differences (e.g. economic, regulatory, social) support or constrain the design and administration of different types of rewards and reward systems. Some constraints may be rigid (e.g. minimum wage legislation) whereas others may be more normative (e.g. the influence of cultural norms and values on employee preferences for rewards). Questions that must be addressed include whether a MNC should use a consistent (uniform) or differential (customised) approach to reward management in its subsidiaries or strategic business units (SBUs) operating in different countries. Additionally, MNCs also need to consider the influence of factors such as the organisation's overall business strategy, the role of different SBUs and the types of employees (i.e. PCNs, HCNs or TCNs) they recruit. MNCs operating globally may have different business objectives for their SBUs located in different countries and regions, and, as a consequence, this needs to be reflected in their reward practices. Reward practices should also reflect whether the MNC is ethnocentric, polycentric, regiocentric or geocentric (Dowling *et al.*, 2013). For instance, a MNC with an ethnocentric approach may rely more on PCNs to manage foreign located subsidiaries (e.g. PCNs on expatriate terms), whereas a geocentric approach may recruit employees regardless of nationality, necessitating differences in the types and systems of rewards utilised.

Another fundamental challenge facing reward managers in MNCs is how to balance global integration (e.g. universal reward systems) with adaptation and responsiveness to local market situations (e.g. tailor-made local reward systems) (Ghoshal, 1987). Such a challenge involves ensuring equity across operations and among locals versus expatriates. This is important because issues related to the comparability of reward packages between the parent (headquarters) and foreign subsidiary operations may affect the effectiveness and acceptability of reward practices (i.e. perceived unfairness or dissatisfaction may weaken the motivational effectiveness of rewards). Significant differences between parent and foreign subsidiary reward practices may also involve material costs in terms of designing, administering, coordinating, and monitoring rewards.

Moreover, reward practices that are effective in one country may not always be effective in another country. For example, as cross-cultural studies have shown, financial rewards are likely to be more effective in masculine cultures because this type of culture has a high preference for achievement and material success, unlike feminine cultures, which are characterised by strong social needs, such as quality of life and personal relationships, making relationship-oriented rewards more acceptable (Chiang and Birtch, 2006; 2007; 2012). Similarly, individual performance-based reward systems may not work well in countries which value social harmony and group solidarity (Hofstede, 2001). Instead, group-based reward systems are likely to be more appropriate in such cultures. In terms of reward distribution, individualist cultures may prefer the use of the equity rule (i.e. differentiating pay based on individual performance), whereas collectivist countries may prefer equality or need-based allocation of rewards (Early and Erez, 1997).

However, as some studies suggest the influence of country differences, such as national culture, may not be as straight forward as once thought (McSweeney, 2002; Gerhart and Fang, 2005). For example, individual oriented PFP plans are gaining popularity in collectivist countries such as China, Japan and Korea. Chinese companies such as Lenovo, Huawei and Haier are now successfully using a wide range of individual oriented performance-based incentive programs to reward high-performing employees (Liu, 2010). Similar performance-based reward systems are also gaining popularity in Japan and Korea countries that traditionally relied on seniority-based pay systems and life-long employment. Honda and Fujitsu now use performance-based rewards (Pollack, 1993) and KEPCO (the largest energy firm in South Korea) and Samsung have shifted from seniority to performance-based reward systems (*Harvard Business Review*, 2011). By and large, the proliferation of performance-based reward practices can in part be explained by the influence of cost and productivity rationale. Thus, to be effective, reward managers in MNC's must also be cognisant of how reward practices and their applicability continues to evolve and change across borders.

Conclusion

Reward management is vital to organisations and represents a key constituent in the human resource management function. Rewards represent an important means through which individuals are attracted to an organisation, retained and incentivised to perform desirable behaviours. Because today's organisations are increasingly being forced to do more with less – maximise employee performance whilst simultaneously minimising costs – this necessitates more than ever before that reward managers seek new and innovative ways to improve the viability and effectiveness of different types of rewards and reward systems. The effective design and administration of an organisation's reward management framework also necessitates consideration of a myriad of internal and external factors in an organisation's business environment, a process that becomes more complex as organisations globalise. As this chapter highlighted, despite considerable advances in our understanding about what constitutes effective reward management, certain reward practices continue to be controversial. For example, although PFP continues to grow in its popularity for all types of organisations (e.g. private, public sector, not-for-profit) as a tool for aligning rewards with an organisation's strategic goals and performance objectives, it often encounters implementation problems and has a range of potential adverse effects. Thus, reward management is a complex activity that necessitates reward managers work closely and proactively with a variety of stakeholders both within and outside the organisation to ensure its effectiveness.

CASE STUDY 6.1

REWARDING INNOVATION AT HUAWEI

THOMAS A. BIRTCH AND FLORA F. T. CHIANG

Company background

Huawei is a global leader in the information and communication technology (ICT) industry. Founded in 1987, it is a private company wholly owned by its employees.[2] The company has grown from a small start-up based in Shenzhen, China to become a leading global technology company providing telecom network equipment, IT products and solutions and smart devices for telecom carriers, enterprises, and consumers in over 170 countries. In 2015 Huawei ranked 228th in the Global Fortune 500 index based on revenues of approximately CNY 288,197 million (USD$ 45 billion). It is now the largest supplier of telecom infrastructure, software, and services in the world and its, major competitors include Ericsson, Nokia, ZTE, Alcatel-Lucent and Cisco (*The Economist*, 2012, 2014; Reuters, 2014).

As illustrated in Figure 6.4, Huawei emphasises innovation relevant to customer needs and advancing its technological leadership through research and development (R&D). Over 10 per cent of the company's annual sales revenue is invested in R&D, an activity that employs more than 45 per cent of its 170,000 employees. The company openly cooperates with its industry partners to build efficient and integrated digital logistics systems that enhance interconnectivity and interactivity and strives to be the 'first choice and best partner' for telecom carriers and enterprise customers and a brand of choice for consumers. An advocate of sustainability, the company supports the development of secure and stable network operations and helps customers and industries improve efficiency and low-carbon economic growth. According to Huawei, its international growth strategy, promoting 'glocalized' operations, aims to localise its operations in the countries it operates, whilst simultaneously building a strong global value chain.

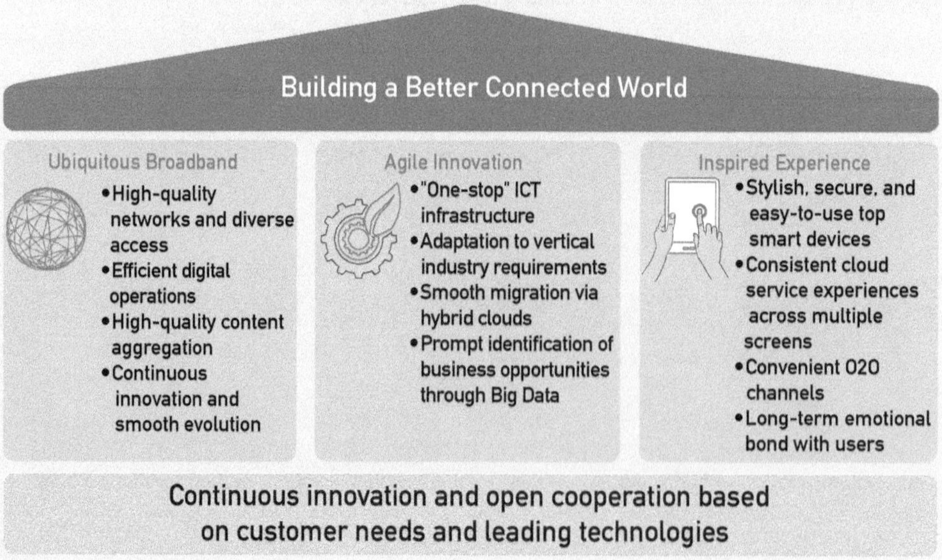

Figure 6.4 Value propositions
Source: Annual Report (2014, p.16).

[2]Although Huawei describes itself a 'collective' or 'employee owned' company, with its founder Ren Zhengfei claiming to directly own less than 1.5 per cent, its actual ownership structure is opaque and surrounded by a culture of secrecy (see McGregor, R. (2010), *The Party: The Secret World of China's Communist Rulers*).

Core values

According to Huawei, it succeeds through its 'customers' success'. Serving customers and responding to their needs represents a major driving force behind its growth and development. Moreover, the long-term value it creates for its customers is used as a yardstick to gauge its work and performance. Figure 6.5 summarises Huawei's core values.

Research & development

R&D at Huawei emphasises the development and innovation of key ICT technologies, architectures and standards. According to its 2014 Annual Report, the company employed over 76,000 product and solution R&D professionals worldwide and invested 14.2 per cent (CNY 40,845 million) of its revenues for the year into R&D. The company operates approximately 16 R&D centres, including in the US, Germany, Sweden, France, Italy, Russia, India, and China, works closely with industry partners, academia, and research institutes and has 28 joint innovation centres with leading carriers. By the end of 2014 Huawei had joined more than 177 industry standards organisations, filed 72,636 patent applications of which 38,825 had been

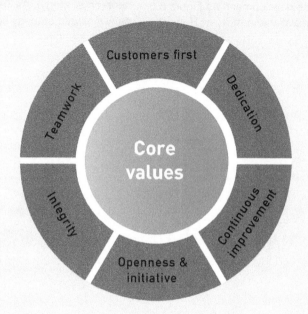

Customers first	Huawei exists to serve customers, whose demands are the driving forces behind our development. We continuously create long-term value for customers by being responsive to their needs and requirements. We measure our work against how much value we bring to customers, because we can only succeed through our customers' success.
Dedication	We win customers' respect and trust primarily through dedication. This includes every effort we make to create value for customers and to improve our capabilities. We value employees' contributions and reward them accordingly.
Continuous improvement	Continuous improvement is required for us to become better partners for our customers, improve our company and grow as individuals. This process requires that we actively listen and learn in order to improve.
Openness & initiative	Driven by customer needs, we passionately pursue customer-centric innovations in an open manner. We believe that business success is the ultimate measure of the value of any technology, product, solution or process improvement.
Integrity	Integrity is our most valuable asset. It drives us to behave honestly and keep our promises, ultimately winning our customers' trust and respect.
Teamwork	We can only succeed through teamwork. By working closely in both good times and bad, we lay the foundation for successful cross-cultural collaboration, streamlined inter- departmental cooperation and efficient processes.

Figure 6.5 Core values

Source: *The Sustainability Report* (2014, p.8), Huawei company report.

granted, had invested a total of CNY190 billion in R&D over the past decade and had become a Top 100 Global Innovator.

Human resources

Huawei considers, its employees its 'most valuable treasure' and the key to retaining competitiveness and a leadership position. Employee health, safety, and benefits are priorities. The company believes that it provides reasonable and timely rewards to dedicated employees. In 2009 the company began transforming its human resource model from a 'function-based platform' to an 'employee-centric platform', which it argues better promotes employee development. As Figure 6.6 depicts, the dominant operational activity of Huawei's workforce is R&D.

To complement its growth strategy, Huawei fosters the development of local talent in each country it operates. Its recruitment policy encourages sourcing talent locally and compliance with local labour laws and regulations. As of 2015 Huawei employed approximately 30,000 non-Chinese staff from over 160 countries and regions around the world.

Reward management

Huawei describes its reward system as competitive and aims to attract and retain high quality human resources to support and accelerate the company's development and growth (i.e. a market leading remuneration strategy). As Table 6.4 illustrates, the company's reward strategy has evolved in several phases since its founding.

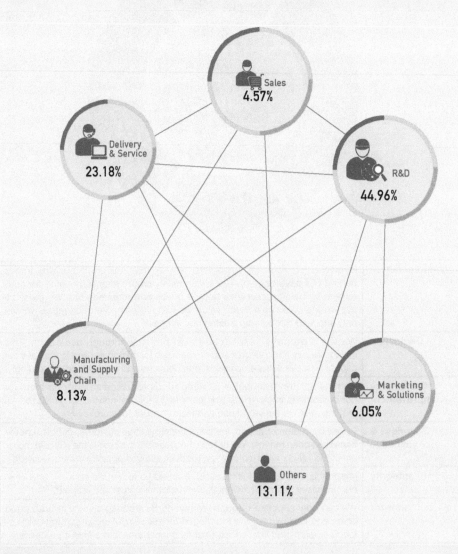

Figure 6.6 The allocation of workforce by operational field

Source: 2013 Huawei 2013 Sustainability Report, p. 53.

Table 6.4 Huawei's Remuneration Evolution

Phase 1: Non-cash remuneration strategy	Phase 2: Competitive remuneration strategy	Phase 3: Sharing remuneration strategy
– Virtual stock program launched due to lack of resources during the start- up period	– Offering high salary + high subsidies + high bonus supported by abundant internal and external resources in high-speed development period	– Hard-worker-based initiative to promote development of high level talent during steady expansion period

Source: Internal document (translated from Chinese).

Underscoring the company's reward philosophy and practices, Hu Houkun, Rotating CEO, stated that,

'In 2014, to strive for excellence, we raised salaries and incentives for operational units in the field and high-performing employees. We fully implemented the "Contribute and Share" mechanism for annual bonus. Regarding long-term incentives, we rolled out the Time-based Unit Plan (TUP) globally so that all outstanding employees, especially those at the junior and middle levels, could share in more of the benefits of the company's medium-to-long-term development. In 2015, we will continue to incentivize performance. We will step up efforts to provide more differentiated and targeted incentives to better motivate employees. While increasing monetary incentives, we will further extend the range of our non-monetary incentives, including awards such as "Whiz Kids" and "Future Stars". We must provide high-performing employees with access to fast-track promotions, with regard to both positions and job levels, so that they get more development opportunities and rewards. Opportunities and rewards will also be used to attract talented people, including outstanding former employees, to join our team. Mechanisms must be put in place to ensure outstanding people can be brought in, engaged and retained. We will continue to care for employee health and happiness, with more focus on their overall wellbeing. We will also continue to build a world-class workplace, with improved recreation and dining facilities." (5 January 2015)

Table 6.5 provides a summary of the types of rewards used by Huawei. In general, the company pays higher

Table 6.5 Types of rewards used at Huawei

Basic Composition of Remuneration

Economic Remuneration	Non-economic Remuneration
Basic salary	Sense of existence
Welfare benefits	Sense of satisfaction
Paid non-working hours	Values
Medical care	Working conditions
Life insurance	Challenging work
Pension	Learning opportunities

Source: Internal document (translated from Chinese).

than market average wages and employs major international pay and compensation specialist consulting firms to regularly monitor and advise on pay conditions and best practices in the market. For example, the HR Department utilises compensation data from the Hay Group, Mercer, Aon-Hewitt, and other consulting firms to regularly adjust employee compensation and its compensation plan in an effort to strike a balance between market competitiveness and the cost of rewards.

To develop its employees, Huawei offers a range of opportunities for learning, training, and promotion as well as two distinct career development paths – management and technical/professional. In addition to a comprehensive eLearning platform, Huawei operates 45 training centres globally that provide training services in 16 different languages, including English, Spanish, French and Russian. Both general learning and development programs and cross-functional professional capability development programs are provided to increase employee knowledge and expertise. In order to promote employees' personal growth and development, the company also regularly sends its employees overseas for further study and training and has established an internal certification system (e.g. Huawei Certified Network Engineer). Additionally, to increase employees' commitment to the development of skills, the company links training with pay and promotion. For example, the 'Huawei Science and Technology Fund' encourages researchers to innovate and start new projects and rewards the most productive researchers with promotions, better facilities and improved working conditions. In 2013 average training amounted to approximately 37.29 hours per employee.

Employee bonuses are closely linked to overall company performance, the performance of an employee's department and an employee's individual performance. A long-term incentive mechanism is used in an attempt to share benefits with employees worldwide and align the personal contributions of employees with the company's long-term development. Huawei provides non-monetary incentives that emphasise three areas (health, development and relationships), including the working environment and emotional care, and promotes work–life balance through family days and other activities. Lastly, its employee benefits system provides a safety net for all employees and includes, mandatory and commercial insurance (e.g. personal accident insurance, critical illness insurance, life insurance, medical insurance, business travel insurance) and defined contribution retirement plans.

Rewarding Performance

Huawei has implemented a results-oriented performance management system to support its business strategy. Goals are set for employees and adjusted on a regular basis. As illustrated in Figure 6.7, by continuously setting goals, coaching, appraising and communicating, managers help employees improve their performance and capabilities. As part of its performance management system, 3 to 5 per cent of Huawei's employees are laid off annually and it is common practice for the salaries of other poor performers to be reduced.

Incentives and awards

Huawei uses a variety of incentives to motivate its employees. An Award Department was established to oversee the evaluation and distribution of awards. There are two features of the awards. First, they cover a wide range of performance outcomes. For example, as long as employees make some distinctive work progress or achievement (e.g. the completion of a project, research achievements) they will obtain an award. Second, all awards are cash based and there is no set limit to the amount of awards. As a consequence, big achievements are eligible for substantial financial awards.

Long-term incentives

Huawei no longer offers direct ownership of the company to its junior and middle levels employees. Instead, it has begun to implement a profit-sharing and bonus plan based on employee performance for all eligible employees, which it labels the TUP. According to its 2014 Annual Report,

"Under the TUP, time-based units (TBUs) are granted to the recipients, which entitle the recipients to receive a cash incentive calculated based on the annual profit-sharing amount and the cumulative end-of-term gain amount. Both of the annual profit-sharing and the end-of-term gain amount are determined at the discretion of the Group. The TBUs will have an exercise period of five years, and after the first, second and third anniversary of the date of grant, each one third of the TBUs will become exercisable and recipients will receive the annual profit-sharing amount accordingly. The end-of-term gain amount will be paid to the recipients upon the expiry of the TBUs or at the date the recipients resign or are dismissed. As at December 31 2014, the valid TBUs granted were 1,051,400,894 units; liability and the corresponding personnel expenses have been recognised in respect of 385,160,827 units of the valid TBUs." (p. 79)

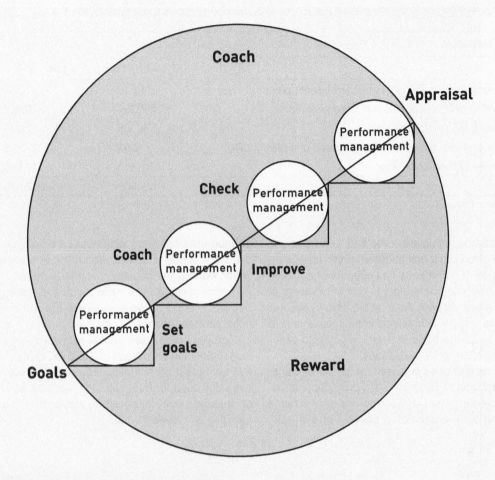

Figure 6.7 Performance management system

Source: http://career.huawei.com/career/en/i18n/images/performance.gif, accessed 14 October 2015.

Table 6.6 summarises the proportion of different types of remuneration allocated at Huawei according to position.

Huawei's annual personnel expenses by compensation type for the 2014 fiscal year are summarised in Table 6.7.

Criticism and obstacles facing Huawei

Despite its success, considerable controversy surrounds Huawei's competitive practices, organisational culture, and reward practices (*The Wall Street Journal*, 2014; *Financial Times*, 2014; *The Economist*, 2012). For example, in addition to ethical questions over its competitive practices and concerns that its products may pose national security risks (e.g. in the US).

Huawei has also been criticised for its extreme workloads and excessive employee overtime. According to employees, it is normal to work until 3 o'clock in the morning and then return to work the next day

Table 6.6 Remuneration distribution for different job classifications

	Fixed Income %	Variable Income %	Stock %
Senior management	40	20	40
Mid-level management	50	30	20
Professionals	60	25	15
Operators	90	10	0

Source: Internal document, presentation to employees, 2015.

Table 6.7 An example of Huawei's annual personnel expenses by compensation type

Personnel Expenses

	2014 CNY million	2013 CNY million
Expenses recognised in respect of defined benefit plan	1,918	1,338
Contributions to defined contribution retirement plans	7,387	6,497
Total costs on post-employment plans	9,305	7,835
Expenses recognised in respect of time-based unit plan (TUP)	963	25
Salaries, wages and other benefits	61,540	44,590
	71,808	52,450

Source: 2014 Annual Report, p. 78.

by 9:00 am. Some employees even find it necessary to sleep in the office (what has become known as a "mattress" culture). The company has even been accused of making 'overtime' mandatory (e.g. a component of performance evaluations). As a result, employees feel compelled to forgo holidays and annual leave and to work considerable periods of overtime to avoid sanction or poor performance evaluations.

Huawei has also been criticised for its lack of transparency in relation to various reward practices, including the implementation of its stock option scheme and the employee evaluation process. For example, although the company claims to be wholly employee owned, it remains unclear about the actual extent to which employees actually own the company. Moreover, employees do not have a voice in management decisions and foreign employees are not eligible to hold company shares.[3]

Lastly, as discussed above, Huawei's performance management system leads to 3 to 5 per cent of employees being laid off annually. However, the system has been criticised for targeting older employees in favour of cheaper newly-hired graduates and for adversely affecting employee morale.

Questions

1 How would you characterise the alignment between Huawei's business strategy, core values and reward practices?

2 Huawei's competitive strategy emphasises R&D and the development of innovative capabilities. What are the advantages and disadvantages of its current reward management practices in relation to such a strategy?

3 Would Huawei's reward system be appropriate if the company's business model were any different (e.g. a low cost strategy)?

4 Is Huawei's reward management framework appropriate for rewarding and incentivising its R&D professionals. What changes should be recommended, if any?

---

[3]Some employees report that they find the stock option scheme difficult to understand and receive limited information about their actual shareholdings.

Bibliography

Abelson, M.A. and Baysinger, B.D. (1984) 'Optimal and dysfunctional turnover: toward an organization-level model', *Academy of Management Review*, Vol.9, 331–41.

Adams, J.S. (1963) 'Toward an understanding of inequity', *Journal of Abnormal and Social Psychology*, Vol.67, No.5, 422–36.

AFL-CIO (2015a) 'Executive paywatch'. Available at: http://www.aflcio.org/Corporate-Watch /Paywatch-2015.

Aon Hewitt (2014) 'New Aon Hewitt survey shows 2014 variable pay spending spikes to record-high level'. Available at: http://aon.mediaroom.com/New-Aon-Hewitt-Survey-Shows -2014-Variable-Pay-Spending-Spikes-to-Record-High-Level.

Armstrong, M. (2012) *Armstrong's Handbook of Reward Management Practice: Improving Performance through Reward*, London: Kogan Page Publishers.

Arrowsmith, J., Nicholaisen, H., Bechter, B. and Nonell, R. (2010) 'The management of vari-able pay in European banking', *The International Journal of Human Resource Management*, Vol.21, No.15, 2716–40.

Barney, J.B. (1991) 'Firm resources and sustained competitive advantage', *Journal of Man-agement*, Vol.17, 99–120.

Becker, G. (1983) *Human Capital: A Theoretical and Empirical Analysis with Special Refer-ence to Education*, Chicago, IL: University of Chicago Press.

Berrone, P. and Gomez-Mejia, L.R. (2009) 'Environmental performance and executive com-pensation: an integrated agency-institutional perspective,' *The Academy of Management Journal*, Vol.52, 103–26.

Bloomberg (2012) 'McDonald's $8.25 man and $8.75 million CEO shows pay gap'. Available at: http://www.bloomberg.com/news/articles/2012-12-12/mcdonald-s-8-25-man-and-8-75 -million-ceo-shows-pay-gap.

Bloomberg Business (2015) 'Fast-food workers rally in 236 cities seeking higher pay'. Avail-able at: http://www.bloomberg.com/news/articles/2015-04-14/fast-food-workers-to-rally-in -230-u-s-cities-seeking-higher-pay.

Cable, D.M. and Judge, T.A. (1994) 'Pay preferences and job search decisions: a person-organization fit perspective', *Personnel Psychology*, Vol.47, 317–48.

Cadsby, C.B., Song, F. and Tapon, F. (2007) 'Sorting and incentive effects of pay-for-performance: an experimental investigation', *Academy of Management Journal*, Vol.50, 387–405.

*Chiang, F. and Birtch, T.A. (2007) 'The transferability of management practices: examining cross-national differences in reward preferences', *Human Relations*, Vol.60, 1293–330.

Chiang, F. and Birtch, T.A. (2006) 'An empirical examination of reward preferences within and across national settings,' *Management International Review*, Vol.46, 573–96.

Chiang, F. and Birtch, T.A. (2012) 'The performance implications of financial and non-financial rewards: an Asian Nordic comparison', Journal of Management Studies, Vol.49, No.3, 538–70.

Childs, M. (2004) 'Managing reward: job evaluation and grading. One-stop guide'. Available at: http://www.xperthr.co.uk/commentary-and-analysis/managing-reward-job-evaluation -and-grading/46896/.

China Labor Bulletin (2015) 'Wages and employment'. Available at: http://www.clb.org.hk /en/view-resource-centre-content/100206.

Curran, B. and Walsworth, S. (2014) 'Can you pay employees to innovate? Evidence from the Canadian private sector', *Human Resource Management Journal*, Vol.20, No.3, 290–306.

Deci, E.L., Koestner, R. and Ryan, R.M. (1999) 'A meta-analytic review of experiments examining the effects of extrinsic rewards on intrinsic motivation', *Psychological Bulletin*, Vol.25, 627–68.

Deming, W.E. (1986) *Out of the Crisis*, Cambridge, MA: Center for Advanced Engineering Study, MIT.

Dermer, J. (1975) 'The interrelationship of intrinsic and extrinsic reward', *Academy of Management Journal*, Vol.18, 125–9.

Doeringer, P.B. and Piore, M.J. (1971) *Internal labor markets and manpower analysis*. Lexington, MA: D.C. Health.

Dowling, P.J., Festing, M. and Engle, A.D. (2013) *International Human Resource Management: Managing People in a Multinational Context* (6th edn.), Thomson Learning.

Dyer, L. and Parker, D.F. (1975) 'Classifying outcomes in work motivation research: an examination of the intrinsic-extrinsic dichotomy', *Journal of Applied Psychology*, Vol.60, 455–8.

Eisenhardt, K.M. (1989) 'Agency theory: an assessment and review', *Academy of Management Journal*, Vol.14, 57–74.

Early, P.C. and Erez, M. (1997) *The Transplanted Executive: Why You Need to Understand How Workers in Other Countries See the World Differently*, New York: Oxford University Press.

Fairhurst, D. (2008) 'Am I "bovvered"? Driving a performance culture through to the front line', *Human Resource Management Journal*, Vol.18, No.4, 321–26.

Financial Times (2014) 'Huawei pulls back the curtain on ownership details', February 27. Available at: http://www.ft.com/cms/s/0/469bde20-9eaf-11e3-8663-00144feab7de .html#axzz3lozawjj7.

*Fitzsimmons, S.R. and Stamper, C.L. (2014) 'How societal culture influences friction in the employee–organization relationship', *Human Resource Management Review*, Vol.24, 80–94.

Fortune (2015a) 'A Wal-Mart worker making $9 an hour would have to work 2.8 million hours to match the CEO's pay'. Available at: http://fortune.com/2015/02/19/wal-mart-wage-hike -2-million-hours/.

Fortune (2015b) '100 best companies to work for: 2015'. Available at: http://fortune.com /best-companies/.

Gerhart, B. and Fang, M. (2005) 'National culture and human resource management: assumptions and evidence', *International Journal of Human Resource Management*, Vol.16, 975–90.

*Gerhart, B. and Fang, M. (2014) 'Pay for (individual) performance: issues, claims, evidence and the role of sorting effects', *Human Resource Management Review*, Vol.24, 41–52.

Gerhart, B.A. and Rynes, S. (2003) *Compensation: Theory, evidence, and strategic implications*, Thousand Oaks, CA: Sage.

Gerhart, B., Rynes, S.L. and Fulmer, I.S. (2009) 'Pay and performance: individuals, groups, and executives', *Academy of Management Annals*, Vol.3, 251–315.

Ghoshal, S. (1987) 'Global strategy: an organizing framework', *Strategic Management Journal*, Vol.8, 425–40.

Gomez-Mejia, L.R. and Balkin, D.B. (1992) *Compensation, organizational strategy, and firm performance*, Cincinnati, OH: Southwestern.

*Gupta, N., Conroy, S.A. and Delery, J.E. (2012). 'The many faces of pay variation', *Human Resource Management Review*, Vol.22, 100–115.

Gupta, N. and Jenkins, G.D., Jr. (1991) 'Job evaluation: an overview', *Human Resource Management Review*, Vol.1, 91–5.

Gupta, N. and Shaw, J.D. (2014) 'Employee compensation: the neglected area of HRM research', *Human Resource Management Review*, Vol.24, 1–4.

Guzzo, R.A. (1979) 'Types of rewards, cognitions, and work motivation', *Academy of Management Review*, Vol.4, 75–86.

Hackman, J.R. and Lawler, E.E. (1971) 'Employee reactions to job characteristics', *Journal of Applied Psychology Monograph*, Vol.55, 259–85.

Harvard Business Review (2011) 'The Globe: The paradox of Samsung's rise'. Available at: https://hbr.org/2011/07/the-globe-the-paradox-of-samsungs-rise.

Heery, E. and Noon, M. (2005) *A Dictionary of Human Resource Management*, New York: Oxford University Press.

Herzberg, F., Mausner, B. and Snyderman, B. (1959) *The Motivation to Work*, New York: Wiley.

HKSAR Environmental Protection Department (2015) 'A guide to corporate environmental performance reporting', Chapter 3: Report Framework and Contents. Available at: http://www.epd.gov.hk/epd/misc/corp-env/epd-eng/chapter3.htm.

Hofstede, G. (2001) *Culture's Consequences: Comparing Values, Behaviors, Institutions, and Organizations Across Nations*, Thousand Oaks, CA: Sage.

Huawei (2014) Annual report of Huawei. Available at: http://www.huawei.com/en/about-huawei/corporate-info/annual-report/2014/img/huawei_annual_report_2014_en.pdf.

Huawei (2014) Sustainability report of Huawei. Available at: http://www.huawei.com/en/sustainability/sustainability-report.

Japan Times (2014) 'Seniority pay on its way out?' Available at: http://www.japantimes.co.jp/opinion/2014/11/04/editorials/seniority-pay-on-its-way-out/#.VdPoCLfovGg.

Jenkins, G.D. (1986) 'Financial incentives', in Locke, E.A. (ed.) *Generalizing from Laboratory to Field Settings*, Lexington Books.

Jenkins, G.D., Jr., Mitra, A., Gupta, N. and Shaw, J.D. (1998) 'Are financial incentives related to performance? A meta-analytic review of empirical research', *Journal of Applied Psychology*, Vol.83, 777–87.

Jensen, M.C. and Meckling, W.H. (1976) 'Theory of the firm: managerial behavior, agency costs, and ownership structure', *Journal of Financial Economics*, Vol.3, 305–50.

Johnson & Johnson (2015) 'Role of incentives and rewards in remaining healthy'. Available at: https://www.jnj.com/sites/default/files/pdf/role-of-incentives-rewards.pdf.

Kanungo, R.N. and Hartwick, J. (1987) 'An alternative to the intrinsic-extrinsic dichotomy of work rewards', *Journal of Management*, Vol.13, 751–66.

Kepes, S., Delery, J. and Gupta, N. (2009) 'Contingencies in the effects of pay range on organizational effectiveness', *Personnel Psychology*, Vol.62, 497–531.

Kessler, I. (2001) 'Reward systems', in Storey, J. (ed.) *Human Resource Management: A Critical Text*, International Thomson Business Press.

Kohn, A. (1988) 'Inner & outer rewards', *Across the Board*, Vol.25, 11–3.

Kullgren, J.T. and Norton, L.A. (2013) 'Individual- versus group-based financial incentives for weight loss: a randomized, controlled trial', *Annals of Internal Medicine*, Vol.158, 505–14.

Kuratko, D.F., Ireland, R.D. and Hornsby, J.S. (2001) 'Improving firm performance through entrepreneurial actions: Acordia's corporate entrepreneurship strategy', *The Academy of Management Executive*, Vol.15, No.4, 60–71.

Lawler, E.E. III, (1981) *Pay and Organization Development*, Reading, MA: Addison-Wesley.

Lawler, E.E. III and Hall, D.T. (1970) 'Relationship of job characteristics to job involvement, satisfaction, and intrinsic motivation', *Journal of Applied Psychology*, Vol.54, 305–12.

Lindley, D. (2014) 'Risky business: the case for reform of sales incentives schemes in banks'. Available at: http://www.consumersinternational.org/media/1529404/sales-incentive-report _riskybusiness_final2_151014.pdf.

Liu, Y. (2010) 'Reward strategy in Chinese IT industry', *International Journal of Business and Management*, Vol.5, 119–27.

Listverse (2011) 'Top 10 famous strikes in recent history'. Available at: http://listverse .com/2011/11/17/top-10-famous-strikes-in-recent-history/.

Locke, E.A. (1968) 'Toward a theory of task motivation and incentives', *Organizational Behavior and Human Performance*, Vol.3, 157–89.

Locke, E.A., Feren, D.B., McCaleb, V.M., Shaw, K.N. and Denny, A.T. (1980) 'The relative effectiveness of four methods of motivating employee performance', in Duncan, K.D., Gruneberg, M.M. and Wallis, D. (eds.) *Changes in Working Life*, John Wiley & Sons Ltd.

Maslow, A.H. (1954) *Motivation & Personality, 2nd Edition*, New York: Harper & Row.

Mattson, M. and Hellgren, I.T.J. (2014) 'Effects of staff bonus systems on safety behaviors', *Human Resource Management Review*, Vol.24, 17–30.

McSweeney, B. (2002) 'Hofstede's model of national cultural differences and their consequences: a triumph of faith – a failure of analysis', *Human Relations*, Vol.55, 89–118.

Mitchell, T.R. and Mickel, A.E. (1999) 'The meaning of money: an individual-difference perspective', *Academy of Management Review*, Vol.24, 568–78.

Money (2015) 'Why this CEO pays every employee $70,000 a year'. Available at: http://time .com/money/3831828/ceo-raise-70000-dan-price/.

MTR. Available at: http://www.mtr.com.hk/archive/corporate/en/sustainability/2013rpt /MTR_SR%202013_24Jun_Final.pdf.

Nelson, B. (2009) 'Secrets of successful employee recognition'. Available at: http://www .qualitydigest.com/aug/nelson.html.

Opsahl, R.L. and Dunnette, M.D. (1972) 'The role of financial compensation in industrial motivation', in Tosi, H.L., House, R.J. and Dunnette, M.D. (eds.) *Managerial Motivation and Compensation: A Selection of Readings*.

Patton, L. (2012) 'McDonald's $8.25 man and $8.75 million CEO shows pay gap', *Bloomberg News*. Available at: http://www.bloomberg.com/news/2012-12-12/mcdonald-s-8-25-man -and-8-75-million-ceo-shows-pay-gap.html.

PayScale (2011) 'Google's HR practices explained'. Available at: http://www.payscale.com /compensation-today/2011/06/google.

Perkins, S.J. and White, G. (2011) *Reward Management* (2nd edn.), Chartered Institute of Personnel and Development.

Pfeffer, J. (1998) 'Six dangerous myths about pay', *Harvard Business Review*, May–June.

Pollack, A. (1993) 'Japanese starting to link pay to performance, not tenure'. Available at: http://www.nytimes.com/1993/10/02/world/japanese-starting-to-link-pay-to-performance -not-tenure.html.

Porter, L.W. and Lawler, E.E. III (1968) *Managerial attitudes and performance*, Homewood: Richard D. Irwin Inc.

Rettenmyer, N. (2014) 'Attracting and retaining critical talent through rewards segmentation at Microsoft'. The Human Capital Agenda in EMEA – Creating Value in Challenging Times. Available at: http://info.mercer.com/rs/mercer/images/EMEA_Anthology_2013.pdf.

Reuters (2014) 'Huawei profit jumps on smartphones, U.S. asks Hua-who?' Available at: http://www.reuters.com/article/2014/01/15/us-huawei-results-idUSBREA0E02P20140115.

Robert, C. (2015) 'McDonald's restaurants puts motivation and reward at heart of busi-ness strategy', *Employee Benefits*. Available at: http://www.employeebenefits.co.uk /benefits/total-reward/mcdonalds-restaurants-puts-motivation-and-reward-at-heart-of -business-strategy/106809.article.

Samnani, A.-K. and Singh, P. (2014) 'Performance-enhancing compensation practices and employee productivity: the role of workplace bullying', *Human Resource Management Review*, Vol.24, 5–16.

Schermerhorn, J. (2010). Management. 11th ed. New York: J. Wiley.

Shaw, J.D. (2014) 'Pay dispersion', *The Annual Review of Organizational Psychology and Organizational Behavior*, Vol.1, 521–44.

Shaw, J.D. and Gupta, N. (2007) 'Pay system characteristics and quit patterns of good, aver-age, and poor performers', *Personnel Psychology*, Vol.60, 903–28.

Sidney, R.F. and Tarascio, V.J. (1971) *Wage and employment theory*, New York: Ronald Press.

Skinner, B.F. (1969) *Contingencies of Reinforcement*, New York: Appleton-Century-Crofts.

Suff, P., Reilly, P. and Cox, A. (2007) *Paying for Performance: New Trends in Performance-Related Pay*, Institute for Employment Studies.

Sweeney, P. and McFarlin, D. (2005) 'Wage comparisons with similar and dissimilar others', *Journal of Occupational and Organizational Psychology*, Vol.78, 113–31.

Trank, C.Q., Rynes, S.L. and Bretz, R.D., Jr. (2002) 'Attracting applicants in the war for talent: differences in work preferences among high achievers', *Journal of Business and Psychology*, Vol.16, 331–45.

The Economist (2012) 'The company that spooked the world', August 4. Available at: http:// www.economist.com/node/21559929.

The Economist (2014) 'The great disrupter's new targets'. Available at: http://www. economist.com/news/business/21618861-chinese-firm-prepares-take-hp-cisco-and-other-it-giants-great-disrupters-new.

The Korea Times (2010) 'KEPCO to adopt results-based annual salary system'. Available at: http://www.koreatimes.co.kr/www/news/biz/2014/11/123_62374.html.

The Korea Times (2013) 'High labor cost risk to Korean economy'. Available at: http://www.koreatimes.co.kr/www/news/biz/2013/09/334_143439.html.

The Wall Street Journal (2014) 'The search for clarity on a key question: Who owns Huawei?', January 15. Available at: http://blogs.wsj.com/chinarealtime/2014/01/15/the-search-for-clarity-on-a-key-question-who-owns-huawei/.

Total Executive (2014) 'Does Western style pay-for-performance work in Japan?' Available at: http://totalexec.com.au/totalexec-views/2014/5/6/does-western-style-pay-for-performance-work-in-japan.html.

WorldatWork (2012) 'Compensation programs and practices 2012'. Available at: http://www.worldatwork.org/waw/adimLink?id=65522.

WorldatWork (2015) *The WorldatWork Handbook of Compensation, Benefits and Total Rewards: A Comprehensive Guide for HR Professionals*, Hoboken, NJ: John Wiley & Sons. Available at: https://books.google.nl/books?id=3zAABwAAQBAJ&pg=PT438&lpg=PT438&dq=%22all+of+the+tools+available+to+the+employer+that+may+be+used+to%22&source=bl&ots=IDJDRk4xmL&sig=87q5NQ03Vnztnlz-kr5kduMHT1M&hl=nl&sa=X&ved=0CDwQ6AEwBGoVChMI8dCpzfnUyAIVReCmCh2xXgsf#v=onepage&q=All%20of%20the%20tools%20available%20&f=false.

Wu, W., Peng, A. and Seijts, G. (2015) *Xiamen Airlines: Pay for Performance*, Ivey Publishing, W15163.

*Xavier, B. (2014) 'Shaping the future research agenda for compensation and benefits management: some thoughts based on a stakeholder inquiry', *Human Resource Management Review*, Vol.24, 31–40.

Additional resources

WorldatWork (www.worldatwork.org) is a non-profit human resources association for professionals and organisations focused on compensation, benefits, work–life effectiveness and total rewards.

Chartered Institute of Personnel and Development (http://www.cipd.co.uk) is a professional body for HR and people development, has 140,000 members worldwide and has a blog dedicated to reward issues.

Supplementary readings

References marked "*" represent good supplemental readings and further sources of information.

CHAPTER 7
PERFORMANCE APPRAISAL

Michelle Brown and Tom Redman

Introduction

Performance appraisal is a widely used tool of human resources management. Initially used as a tool for managers, it is now used to evaluate the performance of manual, secretarial and administrative staff and part-time staff in the public and private sectors. Traditionally appraisals were conducted by supervisors, though in recent years there has been an expansion in range of people who are able to provide data and make assessments of an employee's performance.

In this chapter we explain how appraisals are conducted, what they are used for and their role as a managerial control tool within broader performance management systems. We then assess how well appraisal does in identifying the 'best' performers. We then move onto a discussion of recent variations in appraisal including upward feedback systems, 360-degree systems, team appraisal and customer appraisals. We conclude the chapter with a review of some of the problems with performance appraisal.

Development of performance appraisal

Informal systems of performance appraisal have been around as long as people have worked together; it is a universal human tendency to make evaluations of our colleagues at work. Formal performance appraisals have a shorter but still lengthy history. Grint (1993) traces it back to a third-century Chinese practice. In the UK, Randell (1989) identifies its first use via the 'silent monitor' in Robert Owen's textile mills. Here a multicoloured block of wood was hung over the employee's workspace with the front colour indicating the foreman's assessment of the previous day's conduct, from white for good through to black for bad. Owen also recorded a yearly assessment of employees in a 'book of character'. Since these early developments, performance appraisal has become a staple element of HRM practice in both public and private sector organisations around the globe.

Contemporary performance appraisals are typically annual assessments of an employee's performance. Performance appraisal is used as one element of a much broader performance management system. Performance management has been defined as 'systems and attitudes which help organisations to plan, delegate and assess the operation of their services' (LGMB, 1994: 6). The outcome of an appraisal is typically a rating – a numerical (1, 2, 3, 4 or 5), letter (A, B, C, D, E) or word (e.g. average, above average) grade that can be used for administrative purposes (e.g. pay increases, promotion or dismissal) or developmental purposes (e.g. identifying training needs).

The performance rating is typically made by the employee's immediate supervisor (though as we shall see later evaluations can be made by others as well). The supervisor has been the main rater of employee performance as he/she has the opportunity to observe the performance of the employee and has knowledge of the job. Supervisors, however, are not always comfortable carrying out appraisals, a phenomenon labelled 'performance appraisal discomfort' (Saffie-Robertson and Brutus, 2014). When the supervisor is experiencing performance appraisal discomfort they are likely to put off rating their employees or inflate their ratings in order to avoid difficult conversations with their employees (Villanova et al., 1993).

Employees can be wary of appraisals. In fact, one survey suggested that one in four employees dread their performance review more than anything else in their working lives (http://www.bloomberg.com/bw/articles/2014-03-06/performance-reviews-dont-let-feedback-crush-you). The rating of their performance not only affects their employment within the organisation but also issues of face. Most employees consider themselves to be above average performers (Meyer, 1980). Employees typically attribute episodes of poor performance to factors beyond their control (e.g. 'it's not my fault: the equipment was not working'), while supervisors have a tendency to attribute poor performance to the employee (e.g. 'you did not work hard enough'). The acceptability of a performance rating to an employee is affected by the credibility of the supervisor. When employees regard their supervisor as credible they are more likely to accept the rating than when the supervisor is not a credible source.

The practice of performance appraisal

How is appraisal conducted?

There is a wide range of methods used to conduct performance appraisals, from the simplest of ranking schemes through objective, standard and competency-based systems (see below) to complex behaviourally anchored rating schemes (see Snape et al., 1994). The nature of an organisation's appraisal scheme is largely a reflection of its managerial beliefs (Randell, 1994), the amount of resources it has available to commit and the expertise it possesses. Thus smaller organisations with limited HR expertise tend to adopt simpler ranking and rating schemes while the more complex and resource-consuming systems, such as competency-based and 360° appraisal, are found mainly in larger organisations.

Most employers use only one type of appraisal scheme, often a 'hybrid form' of a number of methods, and a few companies even provide employees with a choice of methods in how they are appraised. The IRS surveys (IRS, 1994; 1999) found many organisations with more than one system of performance appraisal operating. The main reason behind multiple systems was the wish to separate out reward and non-reward aspects of appraisal, different systems for different occupational groups (e.g. managerial and non-managerial employees) and separate systems for different parts of the organisation.

What is appraisal used for?

Organisations use performance appraisal for a wide range of purposes. Surveys commonly report the use of performance appraisal for clarifying and defining performance expectations, identifying training and development needs, providing career counselling, succession planning, improving individual, team and corporate performance, facilitating communications and involvement, allocating financial rewards, determining promotion, motivating and controlling employees and achieving cultural change (Bowles and Coates, 1993; IDS, 2007; IRS, 1994, 1999; Nankervis and Compton, 2006).

These purposes have been classified into two broad categories – evaluative and developmental. Research suggests that the evaluative purposes are on the increase while the developmental purposes are on the decline (Armstrong and Baron, 1998; CIPD, 2005; Gill, 1977; IPD, 1999; Long, 1986). Thus there has been a shift in performance appraisal away from using it for career planning and identifying future potential and increased use of it for improving current performance and allocating rewards.

The developmental and evaluative purposes can be in conflict. Recording the past and influencing future performance is difficult to achieve in a single process. The danger is that appraisal concentrates on the past at the expense of the future performance, with a common analogy here being that this is rather like using the rearview mirror to drive future performance. Similarly, allocating rewards and identifying training needs are often seen as being incompatible objectives in a single appraisal scheme (Boswell and Boudreau, 2002). The openness required for meaningfully assessing development needs is closed down by the need for the employee to 'explain away' performance problems in order to gain a pay rise. However, the danger of disconnecting reward allocation from appraisal is that appraisers and appraised would not treat the process as seriously because without it appraisal lacks bite and 'fires blank bullets' (Lawler, 1994).

Do the best performers get the highest appraisal ratings?

Appraisals are intended to identify the 'best' performers (Kessler, 1994); however, ratings are not always accurate. There has been extensive research into the unintentional and intentional errors made by supervisors when rating their employees (Shields, 2007).

Unintentional errors include rating employees too positively ('leniency error') or too negatively ('strictness error'). Raters might be overly sensitive to a particular dimension of an employee's performance so that when they do well on this dimension that rate the employee highly ('halo error') or when they do poorly on this dimension lowly ('horn error'). Supervisors who are uncomfortable with distinguishing between employees might rate their employees at the midpoint of the grading scale (e.g. a 3 on a 5-point rating scale), often known as 'central tendency error'. 'Similar-to-me error' is when the supervisor favours those employees who they seen as similar to themselves. When the supervisor's rating of an employee is heavily influenced by (good or bad) performance at the end of the evaluation period, the supervisor is committing 'recency error'.

Supervisors also make intentional errors, whereby they deliberately inflate or deflate an employee's rating for political purposes (Longenecker *et al.*, 1987). Sometimes ratings are artificially deflated to show who is the boss; to prepare the ground for termination; to punish a difficult and rebellious employee; and even to 'scare' better performance out of the appraisee. A poor performer may be given an inflated (excellent) rating in order that they will be promoted up and out of the department. Managers may inflate ratings in the hope that an exemplary set of appraisals reflects favourably on the manager responsible for such a high-performing team.

When employees perceive performance ratings to be manipulated for political reasons they report reduced job satisfaction and higher intention to quit (Poon, 2004).

One way in which we can access the accuracy of ratings is by examining the ratings given to male and female employees. Women are *less* likely to get a high performance rating relative to their male counterparts (Varma and Stroh, 2001). Moreover, women are more likely to receive critical feedback: Snyder (2014) found that 58.9 per cent of the performance reviews received by men contained critical feedback, compared with 87.9 per cent for women. 'Watch your tone', 'stop being so judgmental' showed up in 2.4 per cent of the critical reviews received by men and in 76 per cent of the critical reviews received by women. The pro-male bias in performance ratings is particularly prevalent when women are in jobs traditionally carried out by men and the supervisor has strong gender stereotypes.

When a supervisor likes an employee they are more likely to get a higher performance rating from their supervisor (Sutton *et al.*, 2013). The positive relationship between liking and ratings may reflect a bias by the supervisor as they are more likely to recall positive information that is consistent with their liking of the employee when rating their performance. Even when a supervisor recalls negative information about a liked employee they are likely to attribute these episodes to factors outside the employee's control. Alternatively, the positive relationship between supervisor liking and employee rating may reflect the performance of the employee. Supervisors like employees who perform well! We are yet to determine which of these two explanations are supported by research.

What is clear is that supervisor liking matters! Employees can engage in behaviours to influence the way they are perceived by their supervisor, otherwise known as 'impression management' (Wayne and Liden, 1995). There are many impression management techniques (Jones and Pitman, 1982), including:

1 *self-promotion* involves exaggerating or highlighting one's accomplishments and abilities so as to be seen as competent;
2 *ingratiation* involves doing favours and using flattery and opinion conformity to be seen as likeable by the supervisor;
3 *intimidation* involves acting threateningly or intimidatingly to colleagues so they will view you as forceful or dangerous;
4 *supplication* involves broadcasting one's shortcomings in an attempt to be viewed as needy;
5 *exemplification* involves making others perceive your actions as exemplary and worthy of serving as a role model; going above and beyond what is expected to be seen as dedicated by the supervisor.

Impression management tactics have been shown to have an impact on performance ratings, though the tactic used can make a difference. Ingratiation has been found to have a positive impact on supervisor-performance ratings, while self-promotion has a negative impact on supervisor-performance ratings (Higgins *et al.*, 2003). The impact of impression management techniques is stronger in the hands of employees who are politically skilled (Harris *et al.*, 2007).

Performance appraisal as managerial control

With the decline of careers in the flat, delayered organisation, HRM techniques such as performance appraisal have become more important managerial tools in motivating and controlling the workforce. Appraisal is now seen by some commentators as being much more important in maintaining employee loyalty and commitment than in directly managing performance (Bowles and Coates, 1993). Its use provides managers with a major opportunity to reinforce corporate values and attitudes and thus it appeals as an important strategic instrument in the control process. Thus we find an increasing use of appraisal systems for non-managerial employees that are based on social, attitudinal and trait attributes (Townley, 1989). Employees are increasingly being appraised not only on 'objective' measures such as attendance, timekeeping, productivity and quality but also on more subjective aspects such as 'dependability', 'flexibility', 'initiative' and 'loyalty'.

Analyses of performance appraisal, based upon the work of Foucault, have given particular emphasis to the power relations implicit in performance appraisal (Coates, 1994; Townley, 1993).

For Townley, performance appraisal has the potential to act as the 'paper equivalent' of the panopticon with its 'anonymous and continuous surveillance' (1993: 232). Thus recent developments in appraisal, which have both broadened the range of and increased the number of appraisers, via 360° appraisal, upward appraisal and the use of external customers, have increased the potential for managerial control and the utilisation of the panoptical powers of performance appraisal. In such systems the employee is now continually exposed to the appraisers 'constant yet elusive presence' (Fuller and Smith, 1991: 11). Every customer, peer, subordinate and colleague is now also a potential appraiser. Thus it is hardly surprising that employees have nicknamed peer reviews of performance 'screw your buddy' systems of appraisal.

Managers are not immune from the disciplinary 'gaze' of performance appraisal. Organisations encourage managers to pay attention to appraisals by holding them accountable for both completing performance evaluations and the ratings they give their employees. Accountability is a form of monitoring (Mero *et al.*, 2007) that makes managers work harder. In order to provide accurate and/or defensible performance assessments, a manager needs to collect more data on subordinate performance and spend more time processing this information.

Developments in performance appraisal

There have been many innovations in performance appraisal practice – no longer is appraisal an interaction between a supervisor and their employee. In this section we review alternative systems that involve multiple raters.

Upward appraisal

Upward appraisal involves the employee rating their manager's performance, especially their leadership skills. Data from subordinates is valued as they have a unique perspective on the behaviour and activities of their manager. Direct reports can provide feedback that can assess the manager's ability to, for example, provide clear direction, motivate performance, coach for performance improvement and recognise accomplishments.

Upward appraisal is seen as being more in tune with the delayered organisation where managerial spans of control are greater and working arrangements much more diverse. In such situations employees are in much greater contact with their manager than the manager's manager and thus traditional top-down boss appraisal is seen as being less effective. A gap between a manager's self-assessment and a subordinates rating is intended to increase the manager's self-awareness. Upward feedback can suggest areas for improvement. It is anticipated that managers will respond to the insights by making changes (Johnson and Ferstl, 1999).

The effectiveness of upward appraisal is partially dependent on the quality of the information provided by direct reports. In most cases, direct reports provide feedback via an anonymous questionnaire. The process is anonymous to overcome employees' worries about providing honest but unfavourable feedback on managerial performance. Anonymity limits the potential for managerial 'retribution' or what is termed the 'get even' factor of upward appraisal. The effectiveness of upward appraisal is also affected by the extent to which the manager accepts the feedback as credible. When there is a lot of variability within the ratings of direct reports, managers tend to dismiss the ratings as inaccurate (London and Smither, 1995).

360° performance appraisal

The term 360° appraisal (also known multi-rater or multi-source feedback system) describes the all-encompassing direction of feedback derived from a composite rating from peers, subordinates, supervisors and occasionally customers. It is normally conducted via an anonymous survey, although some recent innovations include the use of audio and videotape to record feedback answers. Some organisations also use online computerised data-gathering systems. Three hundred and sixty degree feedback systems are used to measure behaviours and competencies, how others perceive an employee and address skills such as listening, planning and goal setting.

Three hundred and sixty degree feedback systems were intended to be a development tool (Antonioni, 1996), though increasingly organisations are linking 360° to remuneration. Some commentators argue that for 360° to be effective it must first commence as a developmental tool and only after extensive training and with employee support be extended to an evaluative tool. Others suggest that 360° appraisal is being 'overstretched' by including such broader administrative concerns and that these additions blunt its usage as a feedback tool (Toegal and Conger, 2003).

A key feature of most 360-degree systems is rater anonymity. In order to protect raters it is necessary that six to nine raters are used. Multiple raters also provide a range of coverage (high and low assessments) of the employee's behaviour (Bergmann and Scarpello, 2001). Further protection for raters is provided by tabulating the results and presenting them in an aggregated (often by rater category such as peer or direct report) format. To ensure that managers reflect on the feedback and make changes to their behaviours, organisations often employ a facilitator.

An implicit assumption in 360-degree feedback systems is that use of multiple raters can improve both the fairness and accuracy of the performance assessment. On the fairness issue, Grint (1993) notes, those 360-degree systems simply replace the subjectivity of a single appraiser with the subjectivity of multiple appraisers. On the accuracy issue, meta analyses show that inter-rater agreement in multisource rating of all types of performances is low (Conway and Huffcutt, 1997). Correlations between the assessment of managers and subordinates were 0.14. Correlations between supervisors and peers were a bit higher at 0.34.

Studies on the impact of 360-degree feedback systems are mixed. There is some evidence that 360-degree feedback brings about changes in leader behaviours. For example, when employees note an improvement in leader behaviours there is an increase in the level of employee engagement and satisfaction as well as reduced intentions to leave (Atwater and Brett, 2006). Other studies indicate that 360-degree feedback processes sometimes create no measurable change (Siefert et al., 2003) and, at times, may have negative effects. For example, individuals who received low ratings from their subordinates reduced their level of loyalty and commitment to their subordinates after receiving feedback (Atwater et al., 2000). In another study, supervisors' ratings of leader–member exchange and liking toward their subordinates decreased following negative feedback from those subordinates (Atwater et al., 2000). Moreover, when individuals receive negative feedback (i.e. ratings that were low or that were lower than expected) they do not see it as accurate or useful and it generated negative reactions such as anger and discouragement (Brett and Atwater, 2001).

Feedforward

The problem with all of the systems we have discussed so far is they focus on the past, on what has already occurred. In response to these concerns Kluger and Nir (2010) developed an alternative approach – the feedforward interview (FFI). The FFI is intended to enhance performance and improve manager–subordinate collaboration by focusing on the positive aspects of employee experiences instead of focusing on what is 'wrong'. The FFI attempts to elicit success stories from employees with a view to creating the same facilitating conditions for success in the future. There are three elements in the FFI:

1. The employee is asked to identify stories that illustrate successful performance in order to help generate new knowledge about performance;
2. The supervisor focuses the conversation on situations wherein both the employee and the organisation benefit in order to identify when the employee demonstrated extraordinary performance without compromising either their own needs or the needs of others. The supervisor puts aside their own opinions to help them fully understand the message of their employee;
3. The employee is asked to identify the discrepancy between his or her goals and the current performance. A gap between goals and the current performance can generate the motivation for behavioural change.

There have been a couple of studies assessing the impact of FFI. Budworth *et al.* (2015) found that the FFI increased performance four months later, relative to the performance appraisal where the emphasis was on the past. McDowall *et al.* (2014) reported that employee self-efficacy (belief in their capacity to produce specific performance attainments) significantly increased following FFI compared to feedback that focuses on the past and therefore assisting employees to obtains their performance goals.

Customer appraisal

Total quality management (TQM) and customer care programmes are now very widespread in both the private and public sectors. One impact of these initiatives is that organisations are now increasingly setting employee performance standards based upon customer care indicators and appraising staff against these. A mix of 'hard' quantifiable standards such as 'delivery of a customer's first drink within two minutes' and soft qualitative standards such as 'a warm and friendly greeting', as used at one roadside restaurant chain, are now used in performance appraisal systems (IRS, 1995b). The use of service guarantees, which involve the payment of compensatory moneys to customers if the organisations do not reach the standards, has also led to a greater use of customer data in performance appraisal ratings.

Customer service data for use in appraising employees is gathered by a variety of methods. First, there is the use of a range of customer surveys, such as via the completion of customer care cards, telephone surveys, interviews with customers and postal surveys. Organisations are now using such surveys more frequently and are increasingly sophisticated in how they gather customer views. Second, there is a range of surveillance techniques used by managers to sample the service encounter. Here the electronic work monitoring of factory workers is being extended into the services sector. For example, customer service managers at contact centres spend considerable time and effort reviewing staff performance by recording staff–customer conversations and giving immediate feedback, as well as using the data for the regular formal review process.

Third, and even more controversial, is the increasing use of the so-called 'mystery' or 'phantom' shopping (Anonymous, 2001). For some commentators, customer service can only be really effectively evaluated at the boundary between customer and organisation and this view has fuelled the growth of mystery shopping as a data-capturing process. Here staff employed by a specialist agency purport to be real shoppers and observe and record their experience of the service encounter. It is now commonly used in banks, pub companies, insurance companies, supermarkets and parts of the public sector. Some local authorities evaluate the quality of telephone responses by employing consultants to randomly call the authority and assess the quality of the response (IRS, 1995b).

Mystery shopping is argued to give a company a rich source of data that cannot be uncovered by other means, such as customer surveys. Such surveys, although useful for some purposes, are often conducted many months after the service encounter and thus exact service problems are difficult to recollect. Mystery shopping is also seen as being particularly useful in revealing staff performance that causes customers to leave without purchasing. In many service sector organisations a natural consequence of the use of mystery shoppers has been to utilise the data in the performance evaluations of staff (Fuller and Smith, 1991). Although as yet relatively understudied, there are a number of concerns with mystery shopping, not least the psychometric quality of data collected in comparison to customer surveys. Few studies have addressed this issue, but work by Kayande and Finn (1999) report that mystery shopping provides 'reasonably reliable ratings' of performance and that such data can be produced at considerably less cost than customer surveys. All this suggests that mystery shopping is very likely to grow in use in the future.

However, these data-gathering methods are not very popular with staff. Employees often question the ethics of introducing mystery shoppers and feel that it represents a distinct lack of managerial trust in them (Shing and Spence, 2002). Thus employees describe shoppers in terms of 'spies' and 'snoopers' and react with hostility and 'shopper spotting' to their introduction.

The introduction of mystery shopping for largely negative reasons of catching staff performing poorly only fuels such reactions. Cook (1993) advises that using them to reward staff for good performance rather than punish them for poor performance can help their acceptance. Employees who obtain good mystery shopping ratings should be rewarded and recognised, while those who obtain poor ones should use them as a source of identifying training needs.

Team-based appraisal

Work is increasingly being restructured into work teams and there is debate about when and how to evaluate team performance. The nature of the team can be important in deciding the level of performance appraisal (Scott and Einstein, 2001).When a team is formed in order to deal with a short-term matter and will be disbanded after the matter is dealt with, it is not be appropriate to evaluate the performance of the team. When teams are permanent and have responsibility for allocating work tasks, setting bonuses, selecting new staff and disciplining errant members, issues arise as to how to effectively appraise performance. On the one hand, team performance appraisal gives a team the information it needs to identify team problems and to develop team capabilities. It heightens team pride and ownership, increasing commitment and identification of members with the team. On the other hand, focusing solely on team performance can create problems. Some team members may be tempted to 'free ride' on their colleagues. Teams are encouraged to use peer pressure to solve free rider problems though this can create animosity that can limit the effectiveness of the team (Heneman and von Hippel, 1995). Team appraisal can create a problem with 'perverse sorting' as all employees will want to belong to the highest performing teams. Individual high performing employees will be unhappy with the lack of recognition for their efforts.

There are also challenges in what to assess. In individual appraisals, the focus is often on evaluating the achievement of the tasks set out for the job. For teams, some commentators (Scott and Einstein, 2001) argue that the best way to appraise performance is by focusing on the outcomes of the team (e.g. productivity, sales volume and customer complaints). Targets are set, performance measured and assessments made, and rewards allocated equally to team members. The supervisor makes no attempt to differentiate one member from another in performance terms.

But the performance of the team is affected by individual team members so there can be a need to appraise their performance. Appraisals of team members can include assessment of the quality of the interactions with other team members. The data for team member appraisals can be from peer reviews. Fellow team members have an opportunity to observe performance and they have an understanding of the work that needs to be done. Peer reviews have been called 'management by stress' (Heneman and von Hippel, 1995) because of the ambiguity of the process.

Competency-based appraisal

Interest in the concept of competency has been one of the major HR themes of recent times. Connock (1992) describes it as one of HRM's 'big ideas'. One consequence of this has been the attempt by some organisations to use the competency approach to develop an integrated human resource strategy. This has been particularly pronounced in HR practices targeted at managers but is also growing for non-managerial groups. A consequence of the development of organisational competency models has been that employers have increasingly extended their use from training and development, selection and reward into the area of appraisal. For example, the most widely reported innovation in performance appraisal systems during the recent past has been the linking of appraisals to competency frameworks (Abraham *et al.*, 2001; IRS 1999).

The assessment of competencies in the appraisal process has a number of benefits. The evaluation of competencies identified as central to a good job performance provides a useful focus for analysing the progress an individual is making in the job rather than the static approach of many ability- or trait-rating schemes. Thus competency-based assessment is especially useful in directing employee attention to areas where there is scope for improvement. The use of competencies broadens appraisal by including 'how well is it done' measures in addition to the more traditional 'what is achieved' measures. It also helps concentrate the appraisal process on the key area of performance and effectiveness and provides a language for feedback on performance problems. This latter benefit overcomes one of the problems of traditional objective-based appraisal systems in which the appraiser is often at a loss as to how to counsel an employee on what they should do differently if the appraisal objectives have not been achieved. However, these benefits must be counterbalanced against the development and running costs involved and the wider critical debate surrounding the 'competency movement' in general.

Problems of performance appraisal

Impact of appraisals

A number of high profile organisations have recently dropped their performance appraisal system. Accenture, Gap and General Electric have publicly announced that they have dropped their appraisal systems as it generates more costs than benefits. Concerns about the value of appraisals have been expressed by many of the participants over the years. People IQ (quoted in Elicker et al., 2006) reported that only 13 per cent of employees, and only 6 per cent of CEOs, believe that their organisation's current performance appraisal process is useful. Only 6 per cent of HR executives regarded the performance appraisal process as an 'excellent' use of time (Nabaum et al., 2014).

There is a body of research that suggests that appraisals do not improve employee job performance (Jawahar, 2007; Smither et al., 2005). Aguinis et al. (2011) reported that less than one third of over 5,000 employees believed that their performance appraisal had helped them improve their performance. Appraisals may have a negative effect on an employee's job satisfaction (Ferris et al., 2008). Brown et al., 2010 found that employees who had a poor experience with their appraisal were more likely to be dissatisfied with their job, and to have low organisational commitment. Similarly, in a recent four-year longitudinal study with a sample of more than 6,000 public-sector employees, Linna et al. (2012) found that a poor performance appraisal experience had a negative effect on employees' perceptions and attitudes. Particularly notable is research showing that when employee experiences are positive, appraisals still resulted in negative attitudes and lower organisational performance. Mani (2002) found that over 40 per cent of the staff in a public-sector organisation was dissatisfied with their appraisal, including those who received a 'good' or 'outstanding' rating.

There is a growing concern that performance appraisal systems, because of their focus on improving the 'bottom line', have added to the pressures of work for employees. There is increasing concern that employees are now being performance managed to exhaustion (Brown and Benson, 2003) and burnout (Gabris and Ihrke, 2001), which then has a negative impact on organisational performance.

Why appraisal does not work

Supervisors are often seen as the 'weak' link in appraisal systems. HR professionals design good systems which are rendered ineffective by the actions of the supervisors. For supervisors, appraising an employee's performance is an emotionally difficult process. Most employees regard themselves as above average performers (Meyer, 1980) so tend to react badly when a supervisor rates them as average or below average. Geddes and Baron (1997) found that 98 per cent of supervisors reported an adverse employee reaction after communicating negative feedback, including verbal aggression, low morale and sabotage.

Supervisors can regard the appraisal process as a distraction from their 'real work' of meeting sales or production deadlines. Often the paperwork used to support the system can become excessive and give rise to a considerable bureaucratic burden for supervisors, particularly as the number of employees they apprise grows. Some organisations have attempted to reduce this problem by designing paperless systems, requiring the employee to complete the bulk of the paperwork, or moving to a computer-based system.

Supervisors often come to the appraisal process with a set of existing views about what constitutes good performance, as well as making adjustments to performance standards based on the circumstances of the individual (Murphy and Cleveland, 1991). When supervisors across an organisation apply their own interpretation of an appraisal process, the results can be inconsistent (i.e. what it takes to get a high rating under one supervisor is different to what it takes to get a high rating with another supervisor) undermining employee confidence in the appraisal process. The short-hand rules that supervisors develop when appraising employees minimises their cognitive effort in searching for and arriving at decisions that are easy to justify (Mero *et al.*, 2007; Tetlock, 1992).

Organisations encourage managers to pay attention to the performance appraisal processes by holding them accountable for both completing performance evaluations and the ratings they give their direct reports (Levy and Williams, 2004). The intent of accountability is to create a link between individuals, their decisions and its consequences (Tetlock, 1985). The assumption is that managers are motivated to 'maintain the approval and the respect of those to whom they are accountable' (Tetlock, 1985: 309). Early research suggested that managers inflated their performance ratings (Mero *et al.*, 2003) when they were made accountable for their ratings. Mero *et al.* (2007) reported that when managers had to justify their ratings to someone in authority they provided more accurate ratings. The greater accuracy was the result of the manager being more diligent in collecting, recording and processing data on employee performance.

Another way in which organisations have attempted to improve performance appraisal is through the use of more objective measures of performance. However, objective-based schemes are not without difficulties. First, measurement is often difficult and, according to Wright (1991), 'there are a number of jobs where the meaningful is not measurable and the measurable is not meaningful'. The tendency is also to simplify measurement by focusing on the short rather than the long term. Second, the actions of the employee may account for little of the variability in the outcomes measured and thus the extent to which they are achievable is not within the employee's control. This has posed real problems with appraisals in industries such as financial services, where the economic climate and general business cycle arguably affect outcomes far more than individual effort.

Conclusions

Performance appraisals are a controversial tool of human resource management. As we have seen appraisal are commonly used in organisations but do not always have the support of the participants in appraisal – employees, managers and HR professionals. Nor do appraisals always generate positive outcomes for employees and organisations. As a consequence there has been experimentation with different forms of appraisal including who is able to provide performance rating data (e.g. upward appraisals and 360° appraisals).

We suggest that organisations expect a lot from appraisals but allocate insufficient resources to make them effective. Performance appraisal is hard work and consumes a lot of ongoing organisational time and resources in order to be effective (Brown and Nally, 2014). Further, organisations need to be aware of the links between performance appraisal and other HR tools, especially reward management and employee development when implementing a performance appraisal system.

CASE STUDY 7.1

PERFORMANCE APPRAISAL AT FEDERATION HOSPITAL

MICHELLE BROWN

Organisation background[1]

Federation Hospital provides healthcare services, including the full range of in-patient, day-case and out-patient services. It employs 2,200 'whole time equivalent' (WTE) staff. The hospital is struggling to meet the growing demand for medical services. With the aging of the population and the hefty costs of attending a local doctor, many patients are presenting with serious conditions which are more costly and time consuming to treat. The government, in response to pressures from the general public, has instituted performance standards for hospitals; for example, defining the amount of time it should take for patients to be treated based on their medical condition.

The history of performance appraisal at Federation Hospital

Performance appraisals at Federation Hospital were first implemented for senior managers and professional employees in 1998, principally as a development tool. This system operated until 2005 when a new CEO was appointed. The new (American) CEO believed that performance appraisals play a key communication role in an organisation. Both supervisors and employees become aware of the objectives of the organisation and work out how their job will assist with the achievement of the organisations objectives. Further, the CEO was keen to establish a 'performance culture' in the organisation. According to the CEO:

> Performance culture is at the heart of competitive advantage in the twenty-first century. With a performance culture we can derive the most from the limited funds available for health care.

Further, the CEO as of the view that in order to be effective, appraisals had to influence pay increases and had to apply to everyone in the organisation. Not all members of the senior management team were supportive of change to the appraisal system. Some senior managers argued that it would create an individualistic culture that would

be incompatible with the team-based work of the non-managerial staff in the hospital. Others managers wanted to see a developmentally focused system appraisal system. Medical technologies and health care practices are constantly evolving and the hospital needed to have a mechanism to help keep staff up to date.

The HR department at the hospital spent the next 18 months reviewing performance appraisal systems in other organisations in order to fully understand the options and their applicability to the hospital. The new appraisal policy was circulated to all hospital staff (managerial and non-managerial) in June 2007. Over the next few months, supervisors were trained how to complete the new online forms and given some tips on how to provide negative feedback to their employees.

The revised appraisal policy at Federation Hospital placed importance on setting measurable individual objectives. The policy document outlines the principles underpinning individual objective setting as following the acronym 'SMART': objectives should be specific, measurable, agreed/achievable, realistic and time-bound, with the form of measurement for each objective to be agreed at the time that they are set.

The appraisal process

Mechanics

Under the new system, Federation Hospital performance objectives cascade downward through the organisation. The business plan is formulated by December/January each year and reviews conducted during February and March for senior managers in which their performance objectives for the coming year are established. The majority of appraisals for non-managerial employees take place during April and May. Non managerial employees often complain that:

> My manager just passes down their objectives onto me. I am a lab technician so there is not much that I can do to affect the performance of the hospital.

Another frequent complaint is the high level of managerial staff turnover in the hospital because of resignations, promotions, transfers and secondments.

---

[1]This case study draws on experiences in many organisations.

This level of managerial change makes it difficult for the manager to develop a good understanding of the work of the employee and effectively assess their performance. High managerial turnover also inhibits the development of a close working relationship between manager and employee. Better quality reviews occur when both parties know each other well leading to a more open and useful discussion at the performance review.

Coverage

Experience with the pre-2007 appraisal system demonstrated that senior managers varied in their willingness to undertake appraisals of their junior managers. Senior managers would complain that:

> ... appraisals are time consuming and get in the way of good relationships with my employees.

As a result only up to a third of those whose performance was supposed to be assessed was actually assessed. The post-2007 appraisal system built in incentives for managers to undertake their appraisal responsibilities: one of the performance objectives of managers is to appraise their staff. The timely completion rates of appraisals is now near 100 per cent,

though as one HR official noted, the average rating score for employees at Federation Hospital has also increased from 3.1 to 3.9.

Documentation

The appraisal system rates employees on a 5-point scale (1 = needs improvement; 5 = outstanding). A copy of the form supplied by HR to all supervising managers is provided in Table 7.1. Reactions among managers to the form were mixed. Some managers felt that the form was a good general framework to help them assess their employee's performance. Other managers were very unclear about how they were to evaluate their employees. As one manager noted, 'what is an outstanding in conflict management?'

The appraisal meeting

Once a year the supervisor and the employee have a face-to-face meeting to review progress towards the performance goals set at the beginning of the evaluation cycle and come up with a performance rating. The younger employees regarded the appraisal meeting as a good opportunity to find out how they were doing. For the most part, younger employees were seen to be

Table 7.1 Appraisal form at Federation Hospital

Employee name:

Employee ID:

Supervisor:

Date of appraisal:

	Needs Improvement	Average	Good	Very Good	Outstanding
Effective conflict management skills	1	2	3	4	5
Meets punctuality standards	1	2	3	4	5
Quality focus	1	2	3	4	5
Completes work in a timely manner	1	2	3	4	5
Works accurately	1	2	3	4	5
Works well under pressure	1	2	3	4	5
Courteous to others	1	2	3	4	5
Follows instructions	1	2	3	4	5

Total score

Comments:

Employee signature:

more receptive to feedback so the managers tended to spend more time with them. The more experienced employees resented the appraisal meetings.

> I have been doing my job for the last 15 years. I do not need to have someone who has never done the job tell me what to do.

Managers were required to find 'areas for improvement' for each of their employees, which employees interpreted as finding fault with their work.

> I meet all of my performance objectives but my supervisor is obsessed with having a tidy desk. He dropped my performance rating from a 4 to a 3. It is insane. My job is to look after patients and that in my mind trumps a tidy desk.

Table 7.2 provides a summary of the amount of time spent in the appraisal meeting and shows that the majority of employees reported interviews of at least 30 minutes, with 47 per cent having interviews of more than an hour. Some managers like to keep the meetings short as some employees regard the meeting as an opportunity to review the manager's performance:

> Last week I had to cut a meeting short as the receptionist just went on and on about how hard it is to work here with such old technology. She said it was my fault she was not performing at an acceptable level.

Table 7.3 provides a summary of the time the supervisor and the employee spent talking during the appraisal meeting. Judging from Table 7.3, appraisers were not usually dominating the interviews: only 1 per cent of employees reported that the manager talked for more than 75 per cent of time during the appraisal meeting. Almost half of the employees said that there was equal time spent by them and their supervisor talking during the appraisal meeting.

Table 7.4 sets out the extent to which various issues were discussed during the appraisal meeting. The data in table demonstrates that managers focus on the extent to which work objectives have been met (63 per cent say thoroughly discussed) and the establishment of new objectives for the next evaluation cycle (65 per cent say thoroughly discussed). Less attention is given to the career development aspects: only 35 per cent say their skills or competences were thoroughly discussed.

While many managers supported the idea of employee development, the problems lie in the implementation. The biggest problem was in finding the funds in the training budget to pay for costly external courses. Denying staff access to training was having a negative impact on perceptions of the appraisal system.

> In order for me to move up the management ladder of the hospital I need to do a Master's degree. When I asked my supervisor during my appraisal meeting for support, she just smiled and said I wish I could assist but there is just no money. What is the point of the system if there is no money?

In Table 7.5 employees provide data on what they think was positive and negative in their supervisor

Table 7.2 How long did the appraisal interview last?

	% of employees
Less than 30 minutes	11
Between 30 minutes and an hour	43
Between one and two hours	35
More than two hours	12

Table 7.3 During the appraisal interview, approximately what proportion of the time did you and the appraiser talk?

	% of employees
Mainly me (more than 75%)	13
Approximately 60% me	26
Approximately equal	48
Approximately 60% appraiser	12
Mainly the appraiser (more than 75%)	1

Table 7.4 To what extent were the following issues covered in your appraisal?

	3	2	1
	Thoroughly Discussed	Briefly Discussed	Not Discussed at All
	%	%	%
Your achievement of work objectives	63	32	5
Your future work objectives	65	31	4
Your personality or behaviour	17	42	42
Your skills or competencies	35	52	13
Your training and development needs	45	43	12
Your career aspirations and plans	30	43	27
Your pay or benefits	3	12	85
Your job difficulties	24	57	19
How you might improve your performance	16	40	44
How your supervisor might help you to improve your performance	15	45	40
Your personal or domestic circumstances	4	20	76

appraisal behaviours. Supervisors were seen to be taking the process seriously with 61 per cent of appraises (strongly agreeing or agreeing) with the statement that 'my supervisor takes my appraisals very seriously'. About half of the appraisees (48 per cent) were 'confident that my supervisor is as objective as possible when conducting appraisals'.

Some appraisees expressed concerns about the quality of the formal feedback they were receiving with 32 per cent of appraisees disagreeing or strongly disagreeing with the statement that 'my supervisor is good at giving me feedback on my performance'. HR was particularly concerned with the data that suggested that a political element had entered into the appraisal process. About a third of appraisees agreed or strongly agreed that 'I have to keep on good terms with my supervisor in order to get a good appraisal rating' and that 'supervisors use appraisals to reward their favourites'.

Mid cycle reviews

The formal annual reviews are supported by 'mid cycle reviews'. The policy document sees these as a 'crucial element' of the appraisal process. Regular informal feedback was intended to ensure that employees did not get into difficulties between formal appraisal meetings. Informal feedback could also reduce the level of emotion at the appraisal interview as the rating of the supervisor should come as 'no surprise' to the employee. The data in Table 7.5 suggests that informal feedback is not being regularly provided with 40 per cent of appraisees disagreeing or strongly disagreeing with the statement that 'I receive

regular informal feedback from my supervisor regarding my progress towards agreed targets and objectives.' Employees with a more positive experience point out that they have requested and received, additional mid cycle review. They saw mid cycle reviews as useful to fine-tune, and often to replace, objectives that had been rendered obsolete by a rapidly changing organisational environment. Mid cycle reviews allowed for individual objectives to be kept in line with changes in business strategy.

In addition to the lack of informal feedback there was some concern about the quality of the informal feedback. For some employees, the mid cycle reviews were rushed 'corridor and canteen chats' that tended to focus on the negatives (e.g. patient complaints) rather than any positives (e.g. successfully dealing with difficult patient families). Some employees worried that this would bias their performance rating: their manager would recall only the negatives at their formal appraisal meeting.

Objective setting

The increased emphasis on work objectives and measurability promoted by the CEO is reflected in the issues covered in the appraisal process, with employees reporting that the achievement and planning of work objectives were the most thoroughly discussed issues in the appraisal process (see Table 7.4).

In Table 7.6 employees provide insights into the quality of the objective setting process. Supervisors were doing a good job at setting clear goals with 46 per cent agreeing or strongly agreeing with the statement 'the

Table 7.5 Perceived supervisor behaviour

	5	4	3	2	1
	Strongly Agree (%)	Agree (%)	Neither Agree nor Disagree (%)	Disagree (%)	Strongly Disagree (%)
POSITIVE ASPECTS					
My supervisor is good at giving me feedback on my performance.	7	38	22	25	8
I receive regular informal feedback from my supervisor regarding my progress towards agreed targets and objectives.	4	37	19	30	10
My supervisor takes my appraisals very seriously.	21	40	25	12	2
My supervisor takes my career aspirations very seriously.	5	38	36	17	4
I am confident that my supervisor is as objective as possible when conducting appraisals.	10	38	28	6	2
NEGATIVE ASPECTS					
I have to keep on good terms with my supervisor in order to get a good appraisal rating.	11	18	21	35	15
Supervisors use appraisals to reward their favourites.	13	15	16	30	26
I am not entirely happy about challenging my supervisor's appraisal of my performance.	15	18	17	37	13
I found it difficult during my performance appraisal to talk freely with my supervisor about what I wanted to discuss.	9	22	14	39	16

goals that I am to achieve are clear'. It appears that the goals were sometimes imposed on appraisees: only 42 per cent agreed or strongly agreed that 'my supervisor allows me to help choose the goals that I am to achieve'. Some managers argue that employees are often not very good at setting objectives but rather than impose objectives would provide copies of their own objectives in advance of the review process.

The imposition of objectives was a source of irritation for both supervisors and employees. Pushing employees could damage the relationship with an employee. However, the danger with imposing objectives on employees reluctant to accept them was that employees play 'lip service' to them and are not committed to their achievement. In some cases, imposing objectives was seen as

necessary as employees often tried to game the system by setting easy objectives. As one employee notes:

> What I've learnt, as time goes by, is you've got to be careful, right at the outset, how you set your objectives because you can be over optimistic, unrealistic. There's a danger of sitting down and thinking of all the things you'd love to do, or ideally should do, forgetting that you've got lots of constraints and you couldn't in a month of Sundays achieve it. So I think quite a few of us have learnt there is a skill in setting objectives which are reasonable and stand a chance of being achieved. I think that that bit is probably more important than anything else. There is nothing more demoralising

Table 7.6 Objective setting process

	5	4	3	2	1
	Strongly Agree %	Agree %	Neither Agree nor Disagree %	Disagree %	Strongly Disagree %
The goals that I am to achieve are clear.	8	38	22	24	8
The most important parts of my job are emphasised in my performance appraisal.	3	31	38	21	7
The performance appraisal system helps me understand my personal weaknesses.	5	47	19	26	3
My supervisor allows me to help choose the goals that I am to achieve.	13	29	31	18	9
The performance appraisal system helps me to understand my job better.	3	29	27	32	9
The performance appraisal system gives me a good idea of how I am doing in my job.	6	39	25	24	6

than being measured against something which you yourself have declared as being in need of being done and finding that you couldn't possibly do it.

The connection between the objectives and an employee's jobs was not clear for 32 per cent of employees. This seems to be due, in part, to the increasing emphasis on teamwork in the hospital but the emphasis on individual performance in the appraisal process. The focus on identifying and making improvements was clear to employees: 52 per cent agreed or strongly agreed with the statement: 'the performance appraisal system helps me understand my personal weaknesses'.

Accuracy of appraisal

HR encourages both supervisors and employees to collect data on performance throughout the year and then bring it along to the appraisal meeting.

I always try to get my facts right first before approaching an employee, rather than going on hearsay. Try to establish some substance towards giving that feedback, and if they say it was just hearsay, you've got evidence to back it up.

Supervisors prefer to rely on the objectives set at the beginning of the evaluation cycle.

I basically look at her performance objectives and say well you agreed to this. These sorts of performance indicators are what we agreed on prior to this. This part here I don't think you're meeting.

Employees bring along a variety of documentation to the appraisal meeting.

I took lots of things along to the appraisal meeting. One of my objectives was to set up team objectives on the ward. I copied examples of these objectives and took them along. I showed reports I had done on the empowerment of patients, and gave her copies of patients' meetings. I used information to show that I had done things. I used these things to prove to her that I had achieved them.

In Table 7.7 employees provide an assessment of the accuracy of their appraisal. A slim majority (51 per cent) agreed or strongly agreed that 'my performance appraisal for this year represents a fair and accurate picture of my job performance'. For some employees the lack of accuracy may be related to ambiguity about the 'standards used to evaluate my performance' (42 per cent disagreed or strongly disagreed). There was also some uncertainty about what constitutes good performance with 50 per cent

Table 7.7 Measuring performance

	5	4	3	2	1
	Strongly Agree %	Agree %	Neither Agree nor Disagree %	Disagree %	Strongly Disagree %
My performance appraisal for this year represents a fair and accurate picture of my job performance.	7	44	23	21	5
My supervisor and I agree on what equals good performance in my job.	6	44	29	15	6
I know the standards used to evaluate my performance.	2	29	27	35	7

agreeing or strongly agreeing with the statement: 'My supervisor and I agree on what equals good performance in my job.'

Supervisors often get frustrated with their employees when they refuse to take responsibility for their performance.

A nurse I was apprising said, 'This is why I cannot do my job. This is why I cannot achieve this objective.' And then trotted out a great list of problems with the job.

One issue that is a source of frustration for employees is the absence of a publicly available summary of the performance ratings. While each employees rating is accessible to them via the staff intranet they have no idea of how their rating fits with the overall distribution of scores.

How I can make sense of my rating when I do not know if this is high or low relative to other employees like me? And why can't the hospital share this information? What are they sacred of?

Performance payments

The CEO of Federation Hospital introduced performance payments in 2007 as part of the new appraisal system. An employee's rating was used to determine the percent increase in pay. As the budget situation of the hospital is always tight, they are unable to announce the amount of money associated with each performance rating. Over the last few years the average individual performance payment has been 3 per cent. For some employees the amounts available are not worth the effort.

I worked my tail off last year. Stayed back late and helped others when we were short staffed. And after tax all I got was a couple of hundred pounds for my efforts. Never again am I going to work so hard for so little.

For some of the longer serving members of Federation Hospital there was no need for a financial incentive. They enjoyed the work in the hospital and the patients.

I don't need someone wielding a financial stick to tell me how to do my job or push myself.

Questions

1 How effective is the appraisal system at Federation Hospital? Think about its impact on employee performance and retention.

2 Should Federation Hospital retain the current appraisal system? Why or why not?

3 What challenges do managers at Federation Hospital face when rating employee performance?

4 How effective are the managers at evaluating employee performance?

5 How would you rate the fit between the appraisal system, the objectives of the hospital and nature of the work undertaken?

6 Should the CEO of Federation Hospital include a 360-degree feedback system for all managers? Why or why not?

7 Would a feedforward system be appropriate for Federation Hospital?

Bibliography

Abraham, S., Karns, L., Shaw, K. and Mena, M. (2001) 'Managerial competencies and the managerial performance appraisal proves', *Journal of Management Development*, Vol.20, No.10, 842–52.

Aguinis, H., Joo, H. and Gottfredson, R.K. (2011) 'Why we hate performance management – and why we should love it', *Business Horizons*, Vol.54, 503–97.

Anonymous (2001) 'Using "mystery shoppers" in evaluating performance of security officers', *Hospital Security and Safety Management*, Vol.21, No.11, 1–3.

Antonioni, D. (1996) 'Designing an effective 360 degree appraisal feedback process', *Organisational Dynamics*, Vol.25, 24–38.

Armstrong, M. and Baron, A. (1998) *Performance Management*, London: IPD.

Atwater, L.E. and Brett, J.F. (2006) '360-degree feedback to leaders: does it relate to changes in employee attitudes?', *Group and Organization Management*, Vol.31, No.5, 578–600.

Atwater, L.E., Brett, J.F., Waldman, D. and Yammarino, F. (2000) *Predictors and Outcomes of Upward Feedback*, Unpublished manuscript, Arizona State University West.

Atwater, L.E., Waldman, D.A., Atwater, D. and Cartier, P. (2000) 'An upward feedback field experiment: supervisors' cynicism, reactions and commitment to subordinates', *Personnel Psychology*, Vol.53, 275–97.

Bowles, M.L. and Coates, G. (1993) 'Image and substance: the management of performance as rhetoric or reality', *Personnel Review*, Vol.22, No.2, 3–21.

Brown, M. and Benson, J. (2003) 'Rated to exhaustion? Reactions to performance appraisal processes', *Industrial Relations Journal*, Vol.34, No.1, 67–81.

Brown, M. and Heywood, J.S. (2005) 'Performance appraisal systems: determinants and change', *British Journal of Industrial Relations*, Vol.43, 659–79.

Bergmann, T.J. and Scarpello, V. (2001) *Compensation Decision Making* (4th edn.), Fort Worth, TX: Harcourt College Publishers.

Boswell, W.R. and Boudreau, J.W. (2002) 'Separating the developmental and evaluative performance appraisal uses', *Journal of Business and Psychology*, Vol.16, No.3, 391–412.

Brett, J.F. and Atwater, L.E. (2001) '360 degree feedback: accuracy, reactions and perceptions of usefulness', *Journal of Applied Psychology*, Vol.86, No.5, 930–42.

Brown, M., Hyatt, D. and Benson, J. (2010) 'Consequences of the performance appraisal experience', *Personnel Review*, Vol.39, No.3, 375–96.

Brown, M. and Nally, M. (2014) 'Performance management: poison, panacea or plain hard work?', *Insights*, Vol.15, (April), 31–7.

Budworth, M., Latham, G.P. and Manroop, L. (2015) 'Looking forward to performance improvement: a field test of the feedforward interview for performance management', *Human Resource Management*, Vol.54, No.1, 45–54.

CIPD (2005) *Performance Management*, Survey Report, London: Chartered Institute of Personnel and Development.

Coates, G. (1994) 'Performance appraisal as icon: Oscar-winning performance or dressing to impress?', *International Journal of Human Resource Management*, Vol.5, No.1, 165–91.

Connock, S. (1992) 'The importance of "big ideas" to HR managers', *Personnel Management*, Vol.21, No.11, 52–6.

Conway, J.M. and Huffcutt, A.I. (1997) 'Psychometric properties of multisource performance ratings: a meta-analysis of subordinate, supervisor, peer, and self-ratings', *Human Performance*, Vol.10, No.4, 331–41.

Cook, S. (1993) *Customer Care*, London: Kogan Page.

CPCR (1995) *The Right Angle on 360-degree Feedback*, Newcastle: CPCR.

Elicker, J.D., Levy, P.E. and Hall, R.J. (2006) 'The role of leader-member exchange in the performance appraisal process,' *Journal of Management*, Vol.32, No.4, 531–51.

Ferris, G.R., Munyon, T.P., Basik, K. and Buckley, M.R. (2008) 'The performance evaluation context: social, emotional, cognitive, political, and relationship components', *Human Resource Management Review*, Vol.18, No.3, 146–63.

Fuller, L. and Smith, V. (1991) 'Consumers' reports: management by customers in a changing economy', *Work Employment and Society*, Vol.4, No.1, 1–16.

Gabris, G.T. and Ihrke, D.M. (2001) 'Does performance appraisal contribute to heightened levels of employee burnout?', *Public Personnel Management*, Vol.30, No.2, 157–72.

Geddes, D. and Baron, R.A. (1997) 'Workplace aggression as a consequence of negative feedback', *Management Communication Quarterly*, Vol.10, No.4, 433–54.

Gill, D. (1977) *Appraising Performance: Present Trends and the Next Decade*, London: IPD.

Grint, K. (1993) 'What's wrong with performance appraisals? A critique and a suggestion', *Human Resource Management*, Vol.3, No.3, 61–77.

Harris, K.J., Kacmar, K.M., Zivnuska, S. and Shaw, J.D. (2007) 'The impact of political skill on impression management effectiveness', *Journal of Applied Psychology*, Vol.92, No.1, 278–85.

Heneman, R.L. and von Hippel, C. (1995) 'Balancing group and individual rewards: rewarding individual contributions to the team', *Compensation and Benefits Review*, Vol.27, No.4, 63–72.

Higgins, C.A., Judge, T.A. and Ferris, G.R. (2003) 'Influence tactics and work outcomes: a meta-analysis', *Journal of Organizational Behavior*, Vol.24, 89–106.

IDS (2007) *Performance Management*, HR Studies, London: Incomes Data Services.

IPD (1999) 'Training and Development in Britain 1999', IPD Survey Report, London: Institute of Personnel and Development.

IRS (1994) 'Improving performance? A survey of appraisal arrangements', *Employment Trends*, No.556, 5–14.

IRS (1995a) 'Survey of employee relations in local government', *Employment Trends*, No.594, 6–13.

IRS (1995b) 'The customer is boss: matching employee performance to customer service needs', *Employment Trends*, No.585, 7–13.

IRS (1999) 'New ways to perform appraisal', *Employment Trends*, No.676, 7–16.

Jawahar, I.M. (2007) 'The influence of perceptions of fairness on performance appraisal reactions', *Journal of Labor Research*, Vol.28, No.4, 735–54.

Johnson, J.W. and Ferstl, K.L. (1999) 'The effects of interrater and self-other agreement on performance improvement following upward feedback', *Personnel Psychology*, Vol.52, 271–303.

Jones, E.E. and Pittman, T.S. (1982) 'Toward a general theory of strategic self-presentation', pp. 231–61, in Suls, J. (ed.) *Psychological Perspectives on the Self*, Hillsdale, NJ: Lawrence Erlbaum.

Kayande, U. and Finn, A. (1999) 'Unmasking the phantom: a psychometric assessment of mystery shopping', *Journal of Retailing*, Vol.75, No.2, 135–217.

Kessler, I. and Purcell, J. (1992) 'Performance related pay: objectives and application', *Human Resource Management Journal*, Vol.2, No.3, 16–33.

Kessler, I. (1994) 'Performance related pay: contrasting approaches', *Industrial Relations Journal*, Vol.25, No.2, 122–35.

Kluger, A.N. and Nir, D. (2010) 'The feedforward interview', *Human Resource Management Review*, Vol.20, 235–46.

Lawler, E.E. (1994) 'Performance management: the next generation', *Compensation and Benefits Review*, May–June, 16–28.

Levy, P.E. and Williams, J.R. (2004) 'The social context of performance appraisal: a review and framework for the future', *Journal of Management*, Vol.30, No.6, 881–905.

LGMB (1994) *Performance Management and Performance-Related Pay. Local Government Practice*, London: Local Government Management Board.

Linna, A, Elovainio, M., Van den Bos, K., Kivimäki, M., Pentti, J. and Vahtera, J. (2012) 'Can usefulness of performance appraisal interviews change organizational justice perceptions? A 4-year longitudinal study among public sector employees', *The International Journal of Human Resource Management*, Vol.23, No.7, 1360–75.

London, M. and Smither, J.W. (1995) 'Can multi-source feedback change perceptions of goal accomplishment, self-evaluations, and performance-related outcomes? Theory-based applications and directions for research', *Personnel Psychology*, Vol.48, No.4, 803–23.

Long, P. (1986) *Performance Appraisal Revisited*, London: Institute of Personnel and Development.

Longenecker, C.O., Sims, H.P. and Gioia, D.A. (1987) 'Behind the mask: the politics of employee appraisal', *Academy of Management Executive*, Vol.1, 183–93.

Longenecker, C. (1989) 'Truth or consequences: politics and performance appraisals', *Business Horizons*, November–December, 76–82.

Mani, B.G. (2002) 'Performance appraisal systems, productivity, and motivation: a case study', *Public Personnel Management*, Vol.31, No.2, 141–59.

McDowall, A., Freeman, K. and Marshall, S. (2014) 'Is feedforward the way forward? A comparison of the effects of feedforward coaching and feedback', *International Coaching Psychology Review*, Vol.9. No.2, 135–46.

Mero, N.P., Guidice, R.M. and Brownlee, A.L. (2007) 'Accountability in a performance appraisal context: the effect of audience and form of accounting on rater response and behavior', *Journal of Management*, Vol.33, No.2, 223–52.

Mero, N.P., Motowidlo, S.J. and Anna, A.L. (2003) 'Effects of accountability on rating behavior and rater accuracy', *Journal of Applied Social Psychology*, Vol.33, 3493–515.

Meyer, H.H. (1980) 'Self-appraisal of job performance', *Personnel Psychology*, Vol.33, 291–5.

Murphy, K.R. and Cleveland, J.N. (1991) *Performance Appraisal: An Organisational Perspective*, Boston, MA: Allyn & Bacon.

Nabaum, A., Barry, L., Garr, S. and Liakopoulos, A. (2014) 'Performance management is broken: replace "rank and yank" with coaching and development'. Available at: http://dupress .com/articles/hc-trends-2014-performance-management/.

Nankervis, A.R. and Compton, R.L. (2006) 'Performance management: theory in practice?', *Asia Pacific Journal of HRM*, Vol.44, No.1, 83–101.

Poon, J.K.L. (2004) 'Effects of performance appraisal politics on job satisfaction and turnover intentions', *Personnel Review*, Vol.33, No.3, 322–34.

Randell, G. (1989) 'Employee appraisal', in Sisson, K. (ed.) *Personnel Management: A Comprehensive Guide to Theory and Practice in Britain*, Oxford: Blackwell.

Randell, G. (1994) 'Employee appraisal', in Sisson, K. (ed.) *Personnel Management: A Comprehensive Guide to Theory and Practice in Britain*, Oxford: Blackwell.

Redman, T. and Snape, E. (1992) 'Upward and onward: can staff appraise their managers?', *Personnel Review*, Vol.21, No.7, 32–46.

Saffie-Robertson, M.C. and Brutus, S. (2014) 'The impact of interdependence on performance evaluations: the mediating role of discomfort with performance appraisal', *International Journal of Human Resource Management*, Vol.25, No.3, 459–73.

Scott, S.G. and Einstein, W.O. (2001) 'Strategic performance appraisal in team-based organizations: one size does not fit all', *Academy of Management Executive*, Vol.15, No.2, 107–16.

Shields, J. (2007) *Managing Employee Performance and Rewards*, Sydney: Cambridge University Press.

Shing, M. and Spence, M. (2002) 'Investigating the limits of competitive intelligence gathering: is mystery shopping ethical?', *Business Ethics: A European Review*, Vol.11, No.4, 343–4.

Siefert, C., Yukl, G. and McDonald, R. (2003) 'Effects of multisource feedback and a feedback facilitator on the influence of behavior of managers toward subordinates', *Journal of Applied Psychology*, Vol.88, No.3, 561–9.

Smither, J.W., London, M. and Richmond, K.R. (2005) 'The relationship between leaders' personality and their reactions to and use of multisource feedback: a longitudinal study', *Group & Organization Management*, Vol.30, 181–211.

Snape, E., Redman, T. and Bamber, G. (1994) *Managing Managers*, Oxford: Blackwell.

Snyder, K. (2014) 'The abrasiveness trap: high-achieving men and women are described differently in reviews', *Fortune*. Available at: http://fortune.com/2014/08/26/performance -review-gender-bias/.

Sutton, A.W., Baldwin, S.P., Wood, L. and Hoffman, B.J. (2013) 'A meta-analysis of the relationship between rater liking and performance ratings', *Human Performance*, Vol.26, 409–29.

Tetlock, P.E. (1985) 'Accountability: the neglected social context of judgment and choice', pp. 297–32, in Staw, B.M. and Cummings, L. (eds.) *Research in Organizational Behavior*, Greenwich, CT: JAI.

Tetlock, P.E. (1992) 'The impact of accountability on judgment and choice: toward a social contingency model', *Advances in Experimental Social Psychology*, Vol.25, 331–76.

Toegel, G. and Conger, J. (2003) '360-degree feedback: time for reinvention', *Academy of Management Learning and Education*, Vol.2, No.3, 297–311.

Townley, B. (1989) 'Selection and appraisal: reconstituting "social relations"', in Storey, J. (ed.) *New Perspectives on Human Resource Management*, London: Routledge.

Townley, B. (1993) 'Performance appraisal and the emergence of management', *Journal of Management Studies*, Vol.30, No.2, 221–38.

Varma, A. and Stroh, L. (2001) 'The impact of same-sex LMX dyads on performance evaluations', *Human Resource Management*, Vol.40, No.4, 309–20.

Villanova, P., Bernardin, H.J., Dahmus, S.A. and Sims, R.L. (1993) 'Rater leniency and performance appraisal discomfort', *Educational and Psychological Measurement*, Vol.53, No.3, 798–9.

Wayne, S.J. and Liden, R.C. (1995) 'Effects of impression management on performance ratings: a longitudinal study', *Academy of Management Journal*, Vol.38, No.1, 232–60.

Wright, V. (1991) 'Performance related pay', in Neale, F. (ed.) *The Handbook of Performance Management*, London: Institute of Personnel Management.

CHAPTER 8
EMPLOYEE RELATIONS

Geraint Harvey and Peter Turnbull

Introduction

Employee relations can broadly be defined as the study of the employment relationship in all its different guises (e.g. full time, part time, temporary and casual). For any employment relationship, management and workers have some interests in common (e.g. the survival and success of the organisation) but other interests are quite distinct and frequently conflict. For example, while the employer is keen to minimise labour costs and maximise labour productivity, the worker is keen to secure a 'living wage' (and more) and feel secure at work. Security for the worker is not simply a question of protection against arbitrary dismissal (employment security) and the opportunity to build a career (job security). Security also encompasses being safe from any potential hazards or work-related ill-health (work security), as well as the knowledge that employees will be fairly treated and be able to 'speak out' (and/or have someone who can speak out on the employees' behalf) when the decisions of management have an impact on daily work routines and future employment prospects (representation security) (Standing, 1997). As a result, in any employment relationship there are questions of efficiency, equity and voice to be considered (Budd, 2004).

In a democratic society, ensuring a 'balance' between efficiency (the economic production of goods and services), equity (e.g. fair compensation and working conditions) and voice (both individual and collective) can be regarded as a 'moral imperative' (Budd, 2004). Equity and voice are fundamental employment rights (Conventions 87, 98, 100 and 111 of the International Labour Organisation, ILO), and are in fact recognised as human rights (Articles 1, 2, 7, 19, 20 and especially 23 of the United Nations Universal Declaration of Human Rights). In contrast, the imperative for efficiency stems from property rights (ownership and control of the means of production) and efficiency is means to an end (to make a profit) rather than an end in itself. The central question for any employee relations system is therefore whether the means justify the ends?

It is widely accepted that state regulation of the employment relationship is good at providing equity, while strong trade unions, works councils and the like can provide effective voice. In the UK, however, the gender pay gap for all employees was still almost 20 per cent in 2013 (Department for Media, Culture and Sport, 2014) and income inequality – the gap between rich and poor – is ever widening (Dorling, 2014). Trade union membership has fallen from over half the working population in 1979 (over 13 million members) to just a quarter in 2014 (6.4 million members) (BIS, 2015), but non-union forms of representation fail to meet the standards set by the ILO. All too often individual employees are afraid to 'speak up' or 'blow the whistle', even when the organisation is engaged in illegal business practices such as fixing interest rates or mis-selling financial products. In short, employee relations in the UK are characterised by inequity and a 'representation gap' (Marginson, 2015; Towers, 1997), with the neo-liberal penchant for 'unregulated' (free) markets tipping the balance in favour of efficiency *at the expense of* equity and voice. It is notable that much of the research in human resource management in liberal market economies such as the UK and the USA, especially that focused on the 'high performance' HR policies of 'best practice' firms, is primarily concerned with equity and voice *as an instrumental means to improve efficiency* (Adams, 2005: 116).

How, then, does management ensure that employment relationships are efficient and generate a profit? When firms hire workers, what they purchase in the labour market is the 'capacity' of women and men to work ('labour power'), whereas what the employer is actually interested in is the 'performance' of work (physical, mental, emotional and aesthetic 'labour'). Most discussions of efficiency tend to revolve around the economic or technical dimensions of the employment relationship – input versus output – but the wage-effort bargain is always indeterminate. Even if workers are paid by the piece (e.g. the number of widgets produced or telephone calls made/received) at a price agreed in advance, the quality of production or service is difficult to specify *ex ante* and can be even more difficult to determine *post hoc* (e.g. how polite was the telephone call, 'even when recorded for training purposes', or how genuine was the smile when the cabin crew welcomed you on-board your flight?) (Blyton and Turnbull, 2004: 39). Put differently, there are both quantitative and qualitative dimensions to the efficiency of any employment relationship (Gordon, 1976). The congruence between potential and performed labour will depend not only on the 'best way' of (technically) combining equipment, labour and other inputs but also the on the power and authority of the employer over the employee. There can be no employment relationship without the employer's 'power to command' and the employee's 'duty to obey', but while employees might submit to the authority of the employer they will always retain a very strong interest in the (ab)use of their labour (Blyton and Turnbull, 2004: 40).

Historically, managements' attempts to extract labour from labour power have alternated between rational and normative discourses, although both are underpinned by a desire to control (Barley and Kunda, 1992). For example, the theory of scientific management (Taylorism) assumed that streamlining production processes and appealing to the worker's self-interest was the most effective way to control the workforce. The theories of welfare capitalism and human relations, in contrast, proposed that management could more effectively regulate workers by attending not only to their behaviour but to their emotions and aspirations: 'By winning the hearts and minds of the workforce, managers could achieve the most subtle of all forms of control: moral authority' (ibid.: 364). In a nutshell, control has to be 'constructed in a fashion that also "manufactures" consent … [because] … No matter how extensive the controls, in the final analysis, management is reliant on employee co-operation' (Keenoy, 1992: 93–5).

The decisions that govern employment relationships include 'market relations' that determine the price of labour and other substantive terms and conditions of employment (e.g. hours of work, holidays, pension entitlements and the like) as well as 'managerial relations' that determine the procedural dimensions of the employment relationship such as how much work is to be performed, who defines this work, and, most crucially, how? For example, management might unilaterally determine the rules governing employment or negotiate a collective agreement with a trade union. Some conditions of work are enshrined in law by the state (e.g. maximum hours of work and the rights of whistleblowers to report wrongdoing) while an increasing array of third parties to the employment relationship campaign to persuade firms to pay a 'living wage' or respect equality and diversity.

What distinguishes the employment relationship from other forms of contractual exchange in a capitalist economy is therefore the imperative to create an economic surplus, the coexistence of cooperation and conflict, the indeterminate nature of the exchange relationship between employer and employee, and the asymmetry of power (Blyton and Turnbull, 2004: 41). In what follows we examine how different actors involved in employee relations – employers, employees and their trade union organisations, the state and other third parties – seek to influence market and managerial relations to their own and to their mutual benefit. The general context of the labour market is considered first before turning to the activities of trade unions and the employment relations policies of employers.

The labour market and the law

Countries with 'common law' (English) as opposed to 'civil law' (French or German) systems of employment regulation are characterised by weaker levels of worker protection (especially worker entitlements to overtime pay, annual leave, redundancy notice and redundancy payments) (OECD, 2013).This difference is illustrated graphically in Figure 8.1, which is based on 40 employee relations variables that are aggregated into five areas: alternative employment contracts, regulation of working time, regulation of dismissal, employee representation, and industrial action. The erosion of employment protection during the years of Thatcherism (1979–1997) is clearly visible, as is the gradual restoration of some employment protection thereafter. Nonetheless, the level of protection enjoyed by the labour force in the UK is well below that of other European Union (EU) Member States, especially EU15 countries such as France and Germany.

The common law is a strategy of social control that seeks to support private market outcomes whereas civil law seeks to replace such outcomes with state-desired outcomes (Deakin *et al.*, 2007; La Porta *et al.*, 2008). As a result, the law imposes fewer constraints on managerial prerogative under a common law system, which often results in more flexible and more precarious forms of (atypical) employment. By way of illustration, while the UK has one of the highest employment rates (almost 72 per cent of adults between the ages of 15 and 64 years in 2014) and one of the lowest unemployment rates (just over 6 per cent in 2014) in the EU,[1] more than two-thirds of the new jobs created between 2008 and 2014 were 'self-employed' people. The self-employed now constitute 15 per cent of the total workforce, higher than at any time over the last 40 years, and these people work longer hours (compared to employees) and have experienced a much more significant fall in their real income (over 20 per cent since 2008) (ONS, 2014) compared to the typical (median) UK worker (around 10 per cent) (Blanchflower and Machin, 2014; Machin, 2015).

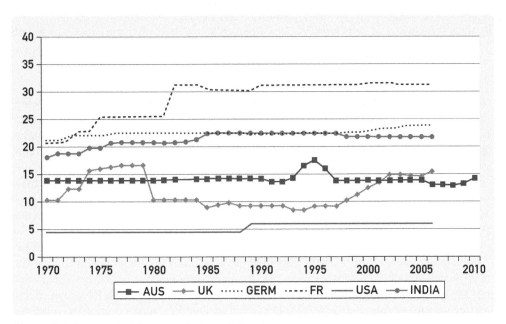

Figure 8.1 Aggregate labour market regulation index
Sources: Cooney *et al.* 2011; Deakin *et al.* 2007; Deakin and Sarkar, 2008.
Notes: AUS = Australia; UK = United Kingdom; GERM = Germany; FR = France;
USA = United States of America.

---

[1]http://ec.europa.eu/eurostat.

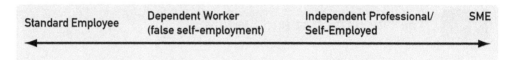

Figure 8.2 The spectrum of employment relationships
Source: Leighton and Wynn, 2011: 17.
Notes: SME = small and medium-sized enterprises (as the self-employed are independent and are covered by commercial legal norms – contracts are judged to be transactional – they are often subsumed under the SME label at the far end of the spectrum).

Whereas an employee has a contract *of* service, the self-employed have a contract *for* services, but there is no specific employment legislation that defines 'self-employment'. Figure 8.2 indicates that in between the 'standard employee' and the 'genuinely self-employed' (typically understood to include those who provide specialist services, actively market their services to the world in general, provide their own tools and other equipment, carry a level of risk, and invoice for fees) is a group of 'dependent workers'. The latter are often referred to as 'bogus' or 'false self-employed' (HM Revenue & Customs, 2014) as these people typically find themselves in complex contractual relationships, supplying their labour to the employer via a third party (e.g. a temporary work agency) or on ad hoc basis as freelancers or temps with a 'zero-hours' contract (Adams and Deakin, 2014a and 2014b). Invariably, it is much easier for the (unscrupulous) employer to minimise the costs and maximise the productivity of these precarious and unprotected workers.

In the late 1990s the legislature defined, or more accurately reinvented, a separate category of 'worker' (Employment Rights Act 1996, s.230 (3)), which 'included individuals who contracted to supply their personal services in a situation of economic dependence, but who did not have sufficient stability or regularity of work to be able to demonstrate employee status' (Adams and Deakin, 2014b: 11). This new category of 'workers', estimated to include up to 5 per cent of the workforce (Pedersini, 2002), included individuals for whom:

- there is an obligation to provide personal service;
- there is mutuality of obligation (i.e. the employer has a duty to offer work over a period of time and the employee has a duty to accept such work if it is offered);
- he or she is not carrying out a business and the other party is not a customer;
- he or she does not otherwise meet the test for being an employee.

Only certain social rights attach to this new definitional category of 'worker', the logic being that: 'norms that do not require a stable employment relationship, such as the right to the minimum wage … or the right not to be discriminated against in employment … can be applied to certain "quasi-dependent" workers, leaving employment protection rights exclusively to the domain of the "employee"' (Adams and Deakin, 2014a: 796–7). However, the operation of the 'worker' concept has not been successful in bringing casual and intermittent work within the scope of minimum wage and working time protection. As a result, a person's status as an 'employee' is still the gateway to most employment protection rights in the UK, as documented in Table 8.1.

Returning to Figure 8.1, it is clear that employment protection increased under the New Labour governments (1997–2010), principally as a result of the Employment Rights Act 1999, which introduced a statutory procedure for union recognition in organisations employing 21 or more workers, and the fact that New Labour signed up to the European social agenda (Treaty of Amsterdam, 1997). The latter resulted in a succession of amendments to UK employment law and the extension of employment rights (e.g. for part-time, fixed-term and temporary agency workers). However, both in opposition and when in government, Tony Blair made it clear that there would be no systematic strengthening of the power of organised labour, either through individual or collective employment rights. In fact, Blair made clear his view that trade unions had been responsible for some of the economic ills experienced by the UK in the past (Mayhew and Wickham-Jones, 2015). As a result, the

Table 8.1 General categories of rights and protections

Right/protection	Employee	Worker	Self-employed
Right not to be unfairly dismissed (after two years' service)	yes	no	no
Right to receive written statement of terms and conditions	yes	no	no
Itemised payslip	yes	no	no
Statutory minimum notice	yes	no	no
Statutory redundancy pay (after two years' service)	yes	no	no
Protection from discrimination in the workplace	yes	yes	?
National Minimum Wage	yes	yes	no
Protection from unlawful deduction from wages	yes	yes	no
Paid annual leave	yes	yes	no
Right to daily and weekly rest breaks	yes	yes	no
Pension auto-enrolment	yes	yes	no
Right to be accompanied at a disciplinary or grievance hearing	yes	yes	no
Rights under data protection legislation	yes	yes	yes
Whistleblowing protection	yes	yes	?
Statutory Sick Pay	yes	?	no
Statutory maternity, paternity, adoption leave and pay	yes	no	no
Unpaid time off to care for dependants	yes	no	no
Right to request flexible working	yes	no	no
Time off for antenatal care	yes	no	no
Time off for trade union activities	yes	no	no
Protection under the transfer of undertakings legislation	yes	no	no
Health and safety in the workplace	yes	yes	yes

? = possibly (determined by case law).

strengthening of employment protection has done little for employee voice or the 'balance of power' in the workplace (Smith and Morton, 2006). It has certainly not reversed the fortunes of trade unions, which once more face the prospect of a further erosion of employment protection and collective bargaining power under Conservative Government's austerity programme and proposed reform of employment law (e.g. Trade Union Bill, 2015).

Trade unions and their members

The main reason why workers join a trade union is 'support if I had problems at work' rather than improved pay and conditions, free legal advice or other services provided by the union (Waddington and Whitston, 1997: 521). However, the ability of trade unions to secure improvement in their members' terms and conditions of employment is often used as a 'proxy measure' of the strength of the labour movement. The differential in wages between union and comparable non-union members – typically referred to as the 'union mark-up' – is the most common measure. During the 1980s the union mark-up held up remarkably well, despite the adverse economic and political climate, but by the 1990s there were signs of an erosion of the union/non-union wage differential and by the turn of the century all the available evidence indicated that unions had more impact on the *process* of pay determination than the *outcome* (Turnbull, 2003: 493). Involvement in the process – having a voice at work in market relations – is, of course, an end in itself, but in recent years the process of joint regulation has been reduced to little more than consultation over the unilateral decisions of management. The result has been a marked deterioration in the wage-effort bargain for most employees.

The most common response to the financial crisis (post-2008) was to freeze wages and reorganise work (van Wanrooy *et al.*, 2013: 6–7). Around a third of the workforce experienced a wage freeze or direct (gross) pay cut and almost as many reported an increase in their workload (ibid.: 8). As wages failed to keep up with inflation, real wages suffered an unprecedented decline, with younger workers in particular suffering the 'double whammy' of greater falls in real wages and bigger rises in unemployment (Machin, 2015). Falling real wages is the principal reason why the living standards of working age households are now worse than before the crisis (ibid.). These data suggest that trade unions have been unable to protect, let alone 'mark up', their members' pay and many other conditions of employment in the face of austerity.

The latest data reveal that the percentage difference in gross hourly average earnings for union members compared to non-union members is almost 22 per cent in the public sector and over 8 per cent in the private sector (BIS, 2015: 14). However, this is more a reflection of the composition of union membership than the collective bargaining power of organised labour. If union membership was simply a function of 'need' (i.e. if the most vulnerable and lowest paid were the most likely to join a trade union) then trade union density (defined as the proportion of employees who belong to a union) would be highest in sectors such as 'accommodation and food services' and among temporary rather than permanently employed workers. In fact, union density is lowest among workers in the accommodation and food services sector at only 4 per cent union density in 2014, while less than 15 per cent of temporary workers were union members compared to almost 26 per cent of permanently employed staff in 2014 (ibid.: 10 and 26). Whereas the 'stronghold' of union membership used to be in mining and manufacturing, today it is public sector workers, professionals and more highly educated workers who are most likely to belong to a trade union (BIS, 2015). Within the ranks of the UK's trade union movement, women now constitute the majority (55 per cent of all trade union members were women in 2014 compared to 45 per cent in 1995) (ibid.: 15).

Ease of organising particular workers clearly plays an important part in union membership levels as it is more difficult for unions to recruit a geographically dispersed, highly fragmented workforce. This is illustrated by the fact that union membership is much higher in larger firms with 50 or more employees (over 33 per cent union density in 2014 compared to less than 16 per cent in establishments with fewer than 50 employees) (ibid.: 26). What also matters is the structural and associational power of the workforce. The former refers to the worker's location in the economic system (e.g. supply and demand for the worker's labour and whether she or he occupies a key position in the labour process) while the latter refers to how unions develop their own organisation (e.g. resources and recruitment strategies) and draw on available forms of institutional support for collective organisation and representation (e.g. affiliation to political parties and institutional forms of representation such as statutory works councils) (Wright, 2000: 962).

Associational power can be built 'from the grassroots' by identifying an 'issue' that is of concern to most people in a particular workplace, and most importantly is winnable. 'Organisation' is built on the back of this issue, ideally through one-to-one, face-to-face communication between union activists (full-time officials or lay representatives) and all employees in the workplace. This organisation is used to 'educate' each worker on the issue(s) in question and how, through 'unity', the workforce can redress any problems. Only when members understand the issues can they be asked to become involved in collective 'action' to

win changes at work (Blyton and Turnbull, 2004: 135). This 'organising cycle' – issue →
organisation → education → unity → action – is designed to build union consciousness,
encourage membership participation, and foster rank-and-file participation. In contrast, a
'servicing' approach focuses much more on existing union members, their 'willingness to
pay' for union services as opposed to their 'willingness to act' against the employer. The
servicing approach also relies more heavily on employer cooperation and the ability of full-
time union officials to solve members' problems (ibid.: 167).

The 'soul' of a trade union will depend on whether it is union officials (servicing) or rank-
and-file members (organising) who represent employees (Budd, 2004: 141; see also Hodder
and Edwards, 2015). The 'scope' of employee representation will depend on the extent to
which the union focuses on the (narrow) 'vested interests' of its members or what is often
called the union's 'sword of justice' (i.e. broader socio-economic, political and legal concerns that affect union and non-union workers alike). This gives rise to four (ideal) 'types'
of trade union, as depicted in Figure 8.3. Thus it is possible to have an organising approach
that focuses on the workplace (employee empowerment unionism) or broader society (social
movement unionism). Likewise, a servicing approach might focus on the vested interests
of current members (business unionism) or wider social partnerships that not only embrace
employers but also political parties and other interest organisations. In (civil law) societies
that provide universal coverage for worker entitlements, with strong(er) support for trade
unions and collective bargaining (e.g. 'extension clauses' in collective agreements that bring
non-union workers into the scope of collective bargaining), a broader strategy of representation is much easier to sustain. In the UK, unions are much more focused on the workplace
after decades of a decentralisation of collective bargaining.

The original rationale for a decentralisation of collective bargaining in the 1960s was
threefold. First, workplace bargaining, if 'properly conducted', was widely regarded as 'the
most effective means of giving workers the right to representation in decisions affecting their
working lives, a right which is or should be the prerogative of every worker in a democratic
society' (Lord Donovan, 1968: 54). Second, management could most effectively 'regain
control' of workplace employment practices and curb wage inflation by sharing power with
workplace union representatives. Third, based on the 'best practice' of the Fawley oil refinery (Flanders, 1964), greater efficiency could be fashioned through workplace productivity
bargaining. In practice, however, 'the idea of giving [workplace union reps] more by sharing power was complete anathema to [management]' (Ogden, 1981: 36). Instead of protecting voice and providing a vehicle for greater equity,[2] the decentralisation of collective

		SOUL	
		Organising	*Servicing*
SCOPE	*Broad*	Social movement unionism	Social partnership (Euro-style)
	Narrow	Employee empowerment unionism	Business unionism

Figure 8.3 The soul and scope of independent employee representation
Source: Adapted from Budd, 2004: 141.

---

[2]One of the strongest and most consistent 'union effects' is a narrowing of wage and other forms of inequality in the workplace (see Turnbull, 2003).

bargaining has resulted in a substantial reduction in the proportion of employees covered by collective agreements and a narrowing of the scope of collective agreements.

Whereas two-thirds of employees were covered by collective bargaining arrangements in the early 1980s, today that figure is less than a quarter (van Wanrooy *et al.*, 2013: 22). The UK now has the lowest level of collective bargaining coverage in Europe with the exception of Lithuania (Ewing and Hendy, 2013). By 2011 only 7 per cent of private sector workplaces bargained with unions over pay for any of their employees and just a sixth of private sector employees (16 per cent) had their pay set by collective bargaining. In the public sector, collective bargaining still takes place in the majority of workplaces (57 per cent compared to 70 per cent in 2004), but this no longer embraces the majority of public sector workers (just 44 per cent of public sector employees in 2011 compared to 68 per cent in 2004).[3] Taking the three issues included in the statutory union recognition procedure – pay, hours and holidays – a further contraction in the scope of collective bargaining is indicated by the fact that only 25 per cent of all unionised workplaces reported negotiations on these issues in the WERS 2011 survey (compared to 32 per cent in 2004). Of particular note was a significant decline in the private sector (down from 27 per cent in 2004 to 18 per cent in 2011) (ibid.: 23). This confirms the 'hollowing out' of collective bargaining that was evident in previous studies (e.g. Brown and Nash, 2008) as negotiations over 'managerial relations' (e.g. staffing) has largely disappeared (Marginson, 2015: 651).

To a significant extent, these developments reflect the preferences and HR policies of employers. While less than one in five workplace managers responsible for employee relations openly state that they are not in favour of trade union membership (van Wanrooy *et al.*, 2013: 14), the percentage who agreed that they would rather consult directly with employees rather than a trade union was 80 per cent in 2011 (compared to 77 per cent in 2004). Moreover, their preference is for direct (individual) rather than indirect (collective) consultation as only 7 per cent of establishments reported a joint consultation committee (JCC) in 2011 (ibid.: 15).[4] These developments confirm earlier prognoses (e.g. Ogden, 1981) that to achieve a balance of efficiency, equity and voice requires a change in management attitudes from a 'unitary' to a 'pluralist' frame of reference, accompanied by 'soft' rather than 'hard' HRM policies.

The management of employee relations

Managerial relations are often referred to as 'management style', which encapsulates management's 'preferred way of dealing with employees individually and collectively' (Purcell and Gray, 1986: 213). In terms of how the organisation deploys and develops the individual at work, this might involve significant investment in employee training and career progression within a well-defined internal labour market, or alternatively the treatment of employees as a cost to be minimised and a commodity to be exploited (Purcell, 1987: 536–7). While the former corresponds to contemporary accounts of 'soft HRM', the latter denotes a 'hard', if not harsh, approach to HRM. Turning to collectivism, for many observers this dimension of management style is synonymous with traditional industrial relations (i.e. collective bargaining with trade unions) where the

---

[3]A large proportion of the recent decline (around 10 percentage points) is accounted for by the decline of collective bargaining in the healthcare sector (down from 75 per cent of the workforce in 2004 to 14 per cent in 2011) in large part because the Independent Pay Review Body resumed responsibility for pay (van Wanrooy *et al.*, 2013: 22).

[4]Most JCCs operate without any trade union representatives (union reps sit on only 28 per cent of JCCs). One in ten private sector workplaces consult with appointed (as opposed to elected) employee representatives who have no connection with a trade union and who do not operate within a JCC (van Wanrooy *et al.*, 2013: 15).

key distinction is whether or not management consider it 'right and proper' for employees to participate in the decision-making processes of the organisation. The traditional (mis)conception of industrial relations conflates collectivism with conflict, presuming an adversarial relationship between management and labour. However, in more recent years a much-lauded approach – cooperative collectivism – proposes a 'partnership' between management and trade union(s). The Involvement and Partnership Association (IPA) – a not-for-profit organisation whose advisory board includes members from the Confederation of Business Industry (representing employers) and the Trades Union Congress (representing trade unions and workers) – has proposed a set of underlying principles for partnership, specifically:

- Joint commitment to the success of the organisation;
- Joint recognition of each other's legitimate interests;
- Joint commitment to employment security;
- Joint focus on the quality of working life;
- Joint commitment to operating in a transparent manner;
- Joint commitment to add value to the arrangement.[5]

Partnership is premised on the socially beneficial effects of trade unions and the potential to foster cooperation and resolve conflicts through joint regulation of the employment relationship. In some countries, partnership agreements are embedded in a wider social partnership supported by the state. In the UK, in contrast, partnership deals are company or workplace-based and are best conceived as a 'productivity coalition' between management and 'insiders' (i.e. core workers seeking to protect their job and associated terms and conditions of employment in the context of a management-led agenda for restructuring). It is telling that, as with much 'best practice' HRM, beyond a select group of well-publicised agreements (e.g. Samuel, 2014) partnership is difficult to agree and even more difficult to sustain (e.g. Evans *et al.*, 2012), not least because management cannot be relied upon to keep their promises and not renege on the agreement when times get tough (Thompson, 2003) as during the current crisis.

While the public exposition (ideology) of partnership is expressly pluralist, such agreements are often informed by unitarist values. Pluralists see conflict as inevitable and indeed legitimate in any and all employment relationships. Unitarists, in contrast, proceed from the position of one source of authority and one focus of loyalty in the organisation, where the employer's prerogative is seen as legitimate, rational and accepted and where the employee identifies unreservedly with the aims of the organisation and its management policies (Fox, 1966a: 3). The distinction between a frame of reference (how one sees the world) and an ideology (how one wants others to see the world) (Budd and Bhave, 2008: 94) highlights the possibility of actors preaching from one ideology while practising another, of saying one thing (e.g. 'people are our most important asset') while doing something else (e.g. discriminating, underpaying, and disregarding or denigrating workers' voice).

The assumption that employee interests coincide with management will no doubt appeal to management but seem unconvincing to others. As Fox (1966b: 372) noted, as an employer ideology (i.e. an instrument of legitimisation for managerial authority that demands loyalty from the workforce), it is much easier to treat conflict as 'irrational' or 'deviant' behaviour (to blame troublemakers and 'shoot the messenger'). It follows that trade unions can then be dismissed as an unwelcome 'third party' to the employment relationship, competing for the loyalty of the workforce and disturbing the harmony that would otherwise prevail. It would be unfair, however, to tar all employers with the same unitarist brush. As Cullinane and Dundon (2014: 2574) note, variations in unitarism can be discerned 'between those that are essentially apologetics for brut authoritarianism and those that emphasise, more benignly,

---

[5]http://www.ipa-involve.com/partnership-in-the-workplace/.

the value of employee loyalty and commitment in a union-free milieu'. For the latter strategy to succeed, employees must still be given a voice and to do so can help build the foundations for commitment and higher productivity. Data from the latest Workplace Employment Relations Survey (WERS 2011), for example, reveals that while only 43 per cent of employees are satisfied with the amount of involvement they have in the decisions of their firm, of those who are satisfied over 90 per cent felt loyal to their organisation and 87 per cent felt proud to work for their employer (compared to 49 per cent and 38 per cent, respectively, for those who were not satisfied with their involvement in decision making) (van Wanrooy *et al.*, 2013: 19).

The 'traditional' and 'crudely exploitative' variant of unitarism is characterised by the 'constantly asserted and enforced right of the master to demand unquestioning obedience from his servants' (Fox, 1974: 297). While such language might sound archaic it is in fact enshrined in the common law of liberal market economies such as the UK and Ireland:

> it has long been a part of our law that a servant repudiates the contract of service if he wilfully disobeys the lawful and reasonable orders of his master. (*Pepper* v *Webb, 1969, UK Court of Appeal*)

> it has long been a part of our law that a servant repudiates the contract of service if he wilfully disobeys the lawful and reasonable orders of his Master. Such a refusal fully justifies an employer dismissing him summarily. (*Berber* v *Dunnes Stores Ltd, 2009, Irish Supreme Court*)

Paternalist variants of unitarism, in contrast, are more indulgent and forgiving, with workers treated as children to be looked after, rewarded and disciplined by their employer as a parent would a child (Wray, 1996: 702). A third and more sophisticated variant of unitarism – often referred to as 'human relations' because, in the words of Lord Sieff (1984: 28), the former Chairman of Marks & Spencer, 'we are human beings at work not industrial beings' – is founded on a deeper (pluralist) understanding of the employment relationship. To be sure, management ideology is unitary but 'management thinking is effectively pluralist to the extent that management recognise the need to manage employee relations *as if* the workforce had divergent interests. In this way, management is able to identify concerns, allay fears, satisfy workers aspirations *and stay non-union*' (Blyton and Turnbull, 2004: 305, original emphasis). Table 8.2 summarises these three variants in terms of the nature of employer authority, the basis of workplace conflict, and management's attitude towards trade unionism.

In the UK today, both the state and employers project a business world that is ever more competitive, increasingly global in scope and demanding of greater flexibility, dutifulness and dedication from the workforce. It is in this context that unitarism has become a 'ubiquitous managerial ideology' (Dundon and Gollan, 2007: 1194) while the state promotes a model of 'employment-at-will' (i.e. the right to hire and fire, or take a job and quit, at any time for any reason). In what is described as the 'egoist employment relationship', where competition is assumed to create the optimal outcome, 'efficiency is the primary

Table 8.2 Variants of the unitary ideology

	Traditional	Paternalist	Human Relations
Employer authority	Autocratic	Benevolent autocracy	Sophisticated manipulation
Workplace conflict	Illegitimate due to terms of contract	Arise from employee misunderstandings	Arise from managerial failures
Trade unionism	Interferes with managerial prerogative	Disruptive of familial culture	Unnecessary because of in-house policies

Source: Cullinane and Dundon, 2014: 2577.

objective … and whatever the market bears is best' (Budd and Bhave, 2008: 103). Why else would employers request, and the state sanction, the 'right' of employees to 'opt out' of various employment protections designed, amongst other things, to protect their safety and health (e.g. regulations on maximum working time)?[6]

In a 'free market' that now extends beyond the sovereign shores of the UK and the (limited) protection offered by national employment law and/or collective agreements, competition comes from workers employed on lower conditions in other EU Member States and further afield (e.g. China and India) where goods can be produced and services provided far more cheaply. The result is an international 'race-to-the-bottom' as a result of 'social dumping', a strategy 'geared towards the lowering of wage or social standards for the sake of enhanced competitiveness, prompted by companies and indirectly involving their employees and/or home or host country governments' (Bernaciak, 2012). In their pursuit of efficiency it seems that employers are increasingly willing to ignore employee voice and only promote equity when there is a 'business case' to do so. In a democratic society the ends surely cannot justify such a mean approach to employee relations.

Conclusion

If employee relations are judged by the 'balance' that is achieved between efficiency, equity and voice (Budd, 2004), then the employment relationship in the UK is found wanting. 'Balance' in this context is not about 'equal weighting' but the search for employment arrangements that enhance one or more dimensions without undue sacrifices in other dimensions (Budd, 2005: 196). In the grip of austerity, labour productivity in the UK continues to fall behind that of our international competitors and the response is a further erosion of employee voice and an on-going failure to close equality gaps between rich and poor, men and women and different ethnic groups, which has detrimental effects in the workplace and beyond (Dorling, 2014; Wilkinson and Pickett, 2009). Alternatives are available. In fact, the clue is in the meaning of balance in employee relations – improving efficiency by enhancing voice and actively promoting equality in all aspects of our working and non-working lives.

---

[6]The WERS 2011 survey found that in a third of workplaces at least one employee had opted out of the Working Time Regulations (1998). Unsurprisingly, inside these workplaces average working hours were longer (van Wanrooy et al., 2013: 30).

CASE STUDY 8.1

IS RYANAIR THE SOUTHWEST AIRLINES OF EUROPE?

GERAINT HARVEY AND PETER TURNBULL

Between 2004 and 2013 the long-established 'legacy' airlines in Europe (e.g. Air France, Alitalia, British Airways (BA), Iberia, KLM and Lufthansa) increased their intra-European seat capacity by less than three million whereas low fares airlines (LFAs) (e.g. easyJet, Ryanair and Wizz Air) increased their capacity by almost 21 million seats. The total European market share of LFAs is now well over 40 per cent, with a dominant share (over 50 per cent) in many national markets for European flights (e.g. Hungary, Ireland, Italy, Latvia, Lithuania, Spain and the UK). This is much higher than other regional markets such as North America where the LFAs market share is around 30 per cent, despite the USA being the home of Southwest Airlines (SWA), widely acknowledged as the world's first low cost airline.[7] Not only have LFAs grown rapidly in recent years, they have also grown profitably. Or rather, the market leaders such as Ryanair, easyJet and SWA have grown profitably, unlike the legacy airlines who have struggled to cover their long-run cost of capital (Button, 2003). Between 1999 and 2008 the civil aviation industry's cumulative operating profit was a mere US$44 billion, translating into a margin of just 1.1 per cent. Over this same period, however, the world's leading LFAs recorded much higher margins – SWA just under 9 per cent, Ryanair 19 per cent and easyJet 6 per cent – and delivered US$11.5 billion in operating profit (Tarry, 2010).

On both sides of the Atlantic, the emergence of LFAs was contingent on the liberalisation of air transport services, as prior to the late 1970s in the USA and the mid-1990s in Europe the civil aviation sector was governed by strict rules on market access in the domestic market and bilateral air service agreements (BASAs) between countries that regulated international routes. BASAs typically specified the destinations (city pairs), carriers (typically the national 'flag' airline of the respective countries), flight frequency, capacity, and prices. Some BASAs even included revenue sharing. As a result, an airline only had to be as efficient as the other airline on an international route and there was little or no incentive to drive down costs or drive up productivity – after all, prices were predetermined, capacity was agreed (reducing any scope for economies of scale) and any additional revenue generated might ultimately be shared with the rival airline/state.

In the USA the domestic market was deregulated in one fell swoop in 1978, opening access to routes (city pairs) to new entrants who were free to set their own prices and offer whatever capacity the market would bear. In Europe the process of liberalisation was more gradual, with three reform packages (December 1987, July 1990 and July 1992) that changed licensing from national to EU criteria, opened access to the market and removed capacity restrictions (Kassim, 1996: 116). By April 1997 the Single European Aviation Market (SEAM) permitted full cabotage rights (i.e. the right of an airline from one Member State to offer services in another State, such that Ryanair, for example, can now offer flights from Madrid to Ibiza and Parma to Cagliari). Ryanair is now Europe's largest airline – based on scheduled air capacity within and from Western Europe (over 89 million available seats in 2013) – well ahead of easyJet (66 million seats) and the major legacy airlines such as Lufthansa (58 million seats), Air France (44 million seats) and BA (39 million).[8] In the words of Michael O'Leary, Ryanair's CEO, 'We cover all of Europe – a bit like a social disease.'[9]

The low cost business model pioneered by SWA, which is contrasted with the traditional legacy airlines model in Table 8.3, has been emulated by airlines across the globe, at least in terms of the technical and operational features of the model (Alamdari and Fagan, 2005). The well-known 'Southwest effect' is achieved

---

[7]SWA has a market share of over 70 per cent of the top 100 city-pairs in the USA and around 25 per cent of the total market.

[8]However, Ryanair fly to fewer of Europe's top 100 city-pairs than easyJet (38 compared to 49) and far fewer primary airports in the top 100 city-pairs (24 compared to easyJet's 46).

[9]New Economic Leaders Forum, Dublin 19th April 2013. Can be viewed at: https://www.youtube.com/watch?v=mKDyeN2CYsE.

Table 8.3 Airline business models

Low Fares Airlines (LFAs)	Traditional Legacy Airlines
Point-to-point	Network/hub-and-spoke
Secondary/regional airports	Primary airports
Multi-European bases	Home country hub
No interlining	Interlining and code sharing
High aircraft utilisation/quick turnaround	Lower aircraft utilisation on short-haul flights
Single aircraft type (e.g. B737-800 or A319)	Mixed fleet
Higher seat density	Mixed-class cabin
Pay for service items (e.g. checked baggage)	Inclusive service/price
One-way fares	Round-trip price discrimination
Direct selling (telesales/internet)	Travel agents

by dramatically reducing fares (on average by 65 per cent on a route), which then stimulates traffic (typically in excess of 30 per cent) (Gittell, 2005: 7–9) enabling the airline to establish a 'dense' route with high frequency between major cities that will sustain a high load factor (in excess of 80 per cent) and low fares.

A simple calculation based on just some of the variables listed in Table 8.3 serves to illustrate the cost advantages of the low cost model. For example, LFAs will pay lower airport charges at secondary/regional airports, their maintenance costs will be lower for a single aircraft type, depreciation costs per block hour will be lower with higher utilisation (which is more easily achieved on a point-to-point route using less congested airports), and their distribution costs will be lower because of direct sales via call centres and internet sales (by-passing travel agents and thereby avoiding commission). Taken together, the combined cost savings can amount to 20 to 30 per cent per trip for a LFA using an Airbus A319 or Boeing 737–800 on an intra-European route. With a higher seat density – LFAs are able to operate aircraft with around 160 seats with a single class cabin configuration, shorter seat pitch and narrower width and the removal of hot galleys, whereas most legacy airlines operate the same aircraft with 130 seats or less – and higher load factors (around 80 per cent compared to 65 to 75 per cent), costs can be reduced even further to anywhere between 30 to 50 per cent for most European short-haul operations. Ryanair, which is arguably in a class of its own when it comes to low(er) costs, enjoys a cost advantage of 60 per cent (Harvey and Turnbull, 2014: 14–15).

Popular accounts of SWA – the management books that fill the shelves of airport bookshops (e.g. Freiberg

and Freiberg, 1996) – highlight the company's strong corporate culture and the desire for all employees to '*live* the Southwest Way' (i.e. display 'a Warrior's Spirit, Servant's Heart, and Fun LUVing Attitude') and '*work* the Southwest Way' ('to focus on safety, on high customer service delivery, and low costs') (SWA, 2012: 5). SWA is a high security, high wage, high skill, high productivity airline, a textbook model of 'best practice' (soft) HRM.

Security: the airline has deliberately pursued a conservative but consistent growth strategy of around 10 to 15 per cent per annum in order to deliver on its commitment to employment and job security. The company avoids layoffs at all costs because, in the words of Herb Kelleher, co-founder and former CEO, 'Nothing kills your culture like layoffs … We could have furloughed at various times and been more profitable but I always thought that was short-sighted' (quoted by Bamber *et al.*, 2009: 92). A defining characteristic of the SWA Way is 'its willingness to forgo quick solutions to invest long term in the maintenance of relationships among managers, employees and business partners' (Gittell, 2005: 12).

Wages: SWA is one of the highest paying airlines in America and frequently appears in the list of 'best 100 US companies to work for' (Bamber *et al.*, 2009: 4–5; Freiberg and Freiberg, 1996; Gittell *et al.*, 2004; SWA, 2012).

Skills: in 2012 SWA recorded over 520,000 hours of health and safety training (over 11 hours per employee), over 17,000 hours on employees' human rights (one in five employees participated in this training), and the company's training programmes routinely cover environmental stewardship and sustainability. The airline's 'University for People' provides training and career development to help employees 'learn and grow'.

Productivity: high productivity at SWA is achieved through the 'relational coordination' of activities during aircraft turnaround at the gate, which maximises the utilisation of the company's most costly assets. This involves different employee groups – flight and cabin crew, mechanics, ramp, gate, baggage handlers, fuelling, cleaning, ticketing – working together, sharing information and solving problems in a socially complex work environment that is interdependent, uncertain and time constrained (the target aircraft turnaround is typically 20 to 30 minutes) (Gittell, 2005). Employees work 'as' a team and not simply 'in' a team, which is critical for SWA's system of relational coordination and rapid aircraft turnaround. Whenever problems arise (e.g. a flight delay or technical problems with ground handling equipment) resolution is sought within the team (bottom up) rather than via managerial fiat (top down). SWA regards employee wellbeing as an important driver of high productivity and outstanding customer service standards: 'We create a culture of LUV. After all, happy Employees equal happy Customers, and happy Customers keep flying Southwest' (SWA, 2012: 39).

Underpinning the airline's HR policies is an employee relations strategy built on cooperative collectivism. SWA is the most highly unionised airline in America – union density currently stands at around 83 per cent – and unions are treated as 'business partners', not 'third parties'. Opportunities for employees to participate in decision making (e.g. on pay and benefits) has directly enhanced the performance of the organisation as SWA leads the way in timely contract negotiations (efficient collective bargaining), and the airline has only ever experienced one strike in its 40-year history (Gittell *et al*., 2004: 171–3). Data from other US airlines indicate that efforts to avoid unions are not likely to produce a sustained improvement in either service quality or airline financial performance (ibid.: 177; see also Bamber *et al*., 2009). In a European context this conclusion on service quality certainly holds in the case of Ryanair – the airline recently came bottom in a poll of the UK's top 100 brands (*Which?*, 2013) – but union avoidance has been central to the Irish airline's unfolding business strategy and industry-leading profitability.

Ryanair is a vehemently anti-union company (O'Sullivan and Gunnigle, 2009) and has vigorously resisted organising campaigns by pilots in particular (Harvey and Turnbull, 2015). The company's reasoning is twofold: 'first that it makes it impossible for the pilot unions to have any influence over the Ryanair contract pilots, and second that it gives Ryanair far more workforce flexibility than a settled, unionised labour force would ever allow in practice'(Michael O'Leary, quoted by Learmont, 2013: 55). Ryanair's (hard) approach to HRM is based on low security, low wages, minimum skill, but high productivity.

Insecurity: Ryanair directly employs only management and a minority of aircrew (over 70 per cent of pilots and more than 60 per cent of cabin crew are hired via agencies on temporary contracts). All ground operations – check-in, baggage handling, aircraft fuelling, etc. – are sub-contracted to third parties. Cabin crew are initially employed on a short-term contract with one of two agencies (CrewLink offers three-year contracts and WorkForce International only two years) while flight crew are hired by two different agencies (Brookfield Aviation International and Storm McGinley) but are required to supply their services to Ryanair via a (limited) 'Employment Company', as illustrated in Figure 8.4. For all aircrew, therefore, there is very limited security. While there are opportunities for promotion within the company, especially for First Officers who aspire to be Captain (job security), there is very high turnover (employment insecurity). Flight and cabin crew are paid only for flying hours (income insecurity). Pilot contracts with Brookfield, for example, state that 'the services of the pilot are provided on an as required and/or casual basis', but 'there is no obligation upon Brookfield to locate or offer work' (i.e. a 'zero hours' contract). Work insecurity is indicated by the reluctance of staff to report safety concerns. For example, a recent survey of almost 1,100 pilots revealed that:

- over 78 per cent did not 'have confidence in the confidentiality of the Ryanair safety reporting channels';
- almost 90 per cent were not 'satisfied that the Ryanair safety system provides appropriate feedback on previous incidents that have occurred in Ryanair';
- almost 89 per cent did not 'consider Ryanair to have an open and transparent safety culture'.[10]

---

[10](see Parker 2013).

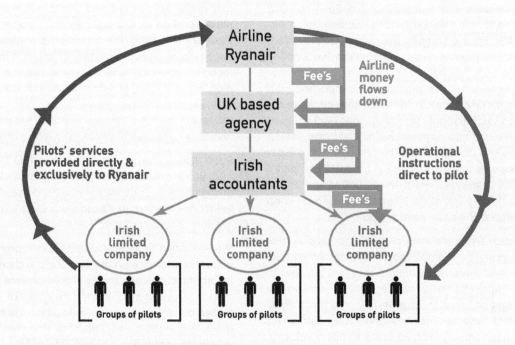

Figure 8.4 'Self-employed' pilots working for Ryanair
Source: Ryanair Pilots' Group, Press Conference, Berlin, 22 May 2014.

Low wages: cabin crew hired via an agency can expect to earn around €1,100 per month, including commission from in-flight sales of food and drinks. However, their contract stipulates three months unpaid leave (compulsory furlough) in every 12-month period between the months of November and March (Ryanair experiences much greater variation in its schedule – summer peak versus winter trough – than legacy airlines and other LFAs). Over a two-year period, therefore, their earnings are less than €20,000, but they must also pay for their own initial training (€500 to register, €1,649 for the actual training, €700 for accommodation – bed only – at the training school, and a €600 administration fee, deducted from monthly salary during the first six months of employment, if the candidate cannot afford to pay the training costs in advance) as well as hire of uniform (€30 per month). Earnings minus training costs and uniform hire leaves the cabin crew with less than €16,000 (less than €900 per month), which is less than the UK National Minimum Wage for a worker aged 18 to 20 years. Most pilots have accumulated debts of between €80,000 and €100,000 to obtain a commercial pilots licence and must then pay €28,500 (in advance) for their 'type-rate' training at Ryanair (to fly Boeing 737–800 aircraft) and a further €2,400 for initial line training. A survey of more than 1,100 members of the Ryanair Pilot Group found than 45 per cent earned between €30,000 and €60,000 per annum, the majority of whom are First Officers (new recruits) who struggle to payoff interest on their debts after living expenses away from home. Both cabin and flight crew can be assigned to any of Ryanair's seventy bases around Europe and they must cover all their own travel and accommodation costs.

Minimum skill: whereas Ryanair recruits pilots with only 200 flying hours, most airlines demand anywhere in the region of 500 to 1,500 hours[11] and the latter is now the minimum requirement set by the Federal Aviation Authority in the USA. Interviews for potential cabin crew at recruitment days run by employment agencies are rather perfunctory – lasting only 10 to 15 minutes – with most attention on the candidate's appearance, financial situation and willingness to be flexible. Training is 'compliant with regulations' rather than 'comprehensive', with emphasis on sales skills as well as safety. Shortcomings in the company's training of cabin crew were exposed in a Channel 4 *Dispatches* documentary, 'Ryanair Caught Napping'.[12]

High productivity: the most significant contribution to Ryanair's low cost base comes from high labour productivity (Barrett, 2004: 93). Ryanair's costs per

[11] http://www.flightdeckfriend.com/#!latest-pilot-jobs/c1mba.
[12] https://www.youtube.com/watch?v=zi-x_UgTTOQ.

employee were less than €50,000 in 2011 to 2012 compared to well over €106,000 at Scandinavian Airlines (SAS), Europe's highest cost legacy airline.[13] With lower wages than its rivals and an intensive working schedule concentrated over a nine-month (summer peak) period when the majority of (temporary) staff work the maximum number of hours allowed under the European flight and duty time limitations (900 hours of flying), Ryanair has very low unit labour costs (labour productivity x labour costs). The company's profit per employee was over €81,000 in 2011 to 2012 compared to €49,000 at easyJet, less than €20,000 at Aer Lingus, and less than €1,000 at the International Airlines Group (incorporating British Airways and Iberia).

Although Ryanair's workforce is dispersed across Europe, everyone is employed on an Irish contract, as the 'place of work' is an aircraft that is registered in Ireland. Thus a Bulgarian worker hired to work in the cabin might be based in Spain and fly predominantly to Italy and Greece, but Irish law governs her terms and conditions of employment. As in the shipping industry, the flag of registration is 'more convenient' (a more permissive common law system in Ireland) and crew can be hired from whichever countries are likewise 'more convenient'. 'Rule shopping' leads to 'social dumping', a situation described by the European Commission as: 'where foreign service providers can undercut local service providers because their labour standards are lower'.[14] Clearly, this would be more difficult, and certainly less profitable, if Ryanair recognised trade unions in Ireland.

Irish law provides for a form of 'company-unionism' (or what Americans call a 'yellow dog union') via an 'excepted body', defined by the Trade Unions Acts of 1941 (s.6(3)(h)) and 1942 (s.2) as 'a body all the members of which are employed by the same employer and which carries on negotiations for the fixing of wages or other conditions of employment of its own members (but no other employees)'. Ryanair operates a system of Employee Representative Committees (ERCs) in each base for cabin crew and permanently employed pilots. 'Agreements' made by ERCs often have 'conditional benefits' attached to forestall union organisation. For example, pilots at several German bases working on a five days on/four days off roster were warned that:

this roster agreement and annual allowance will remain in place for as long as Ryanair [Bremen, Hann, Weeze] pilots deal directly with the company and engage in no work stoppages. If Ryanair is forced to recognise any pilot trade union or association at [Bremen, Hann, Weeze] or if there is any industrial action of any kind at [Bremen, Hann, Weeze] then the roster will revert to 5 on 3 off with 5 on 2 off six times per annum and the annual allowance will be withdrawn.[15]

Such arrangements are contrary to ILO Convention 98, which Ireland has ratified. When a similar case involving pilots in Dublin was brought to the attention of the ILO's Freedom of Association Committee, the Committee' pointed out that:

the existence of legislative provisions prohibiting acts of interference on the part of the authorities, or by organizations of workers and employers in each other's affairs, is insufficient if they are not accompanied by efficient procedures to ensure their implementation in practice … Irish law does not ensure adequate protection against acts of interference (e.g. non-prohibition of conditional benefits) nor does it promote collective bargaining (e.g. by providing for a procedure to require an employer to recognize a trade union) (Case No.2780, C.87 and C.98).

Ryanair might claim to be the 'Southwest Airlines of Europe'[16] but its HR strategy and employment relations could hardly be more different, epitomised in the words of the respective CEOs:

When I started out, business school professors liked to pose a conundrum: Which do you put first, your employees, your customers, or your shareholders? As if that were an unanswerable question. My answer was very easy: You put your employees first. If you truly treat your employees that way, they will treat your customers well, your customers will come back, and that's what makes your shareholders happy (Herb Kelleher, co-founder and Chairman of Southwest Airlines).[17]

MBA students come out with: 'My staff is my most important asset.' Bull****. Staff is usually your biggest cost. We all employ some lazy ******* who needs a kick up the backside, but no one can bring themselves to admit it (Michael O'Leary, CEO Ryanair).[18]

[13]www.centreforaviation.com.

[14]http://www.eurofound.europa.eu/observatories/eurwork/industrial-relations-dictionary/social-dumping.

[15]https://www.ryanairpilotgroup.com/sites/default/files/press-releases/RPG%20Press%20Pack%20-%20Berlin%202022%20May%202014%20-%20Final%20-%20Copy_0.pdf.

[16]http://www.cnbc.com/id/100839583.

[17]http://www.strategy-business.com/media/file/sb35_04212.pdf.

[18]http://www.telegraph.co.uk/travel/travelnews/9522319/Michael-OLearys-most-memorable-quotes.html.

Questions

1 What is the basis of cooperation between management and labour at (a) SWA and (b) Ryanair?

2 Are Ryanair pilots genuinely or falsely 'self-employed'?

3 How would you characterise the soul and the scope of trade unionism at SWA (refer to Figure 8.3)?

4 What is the nature of employer authority and management's attitude towards trade unionism at (a) SWA and (b) Ryanair (refer to Table 8.2)?

5 Can you foresee a time/place/circumstances when/where Ryanair might recognise a trade union (either willingly or unwillingly)?

Bibliography

Adams, R.J. (2005) 'Efficiency, equity, and voice as moral imperatives', *Employee Responsibilities and Rights Journal*, Vol.17, No.3, 111–7.

Adams, Z. and Deakin, S. (2014a) 'Institutional solutions to precariousness and inequality in labour markets', *British Journal of Industrial Relations*, Vol.52, No.4, 779–809.

Adams, Z. and Deakin, S. (2014b) *Re-regulating Zero Hours Contracts*, London: Institute of Employment Rights.

Alamdari, F. and Fagan, S. (2005) 'Impact of the adherence to the original low-cost model on the profitability of low-cost airlines', *Transport Reviews*, Vol.25, No.3, 377–92.

Bamber, G.J., Gittell, J.H., Kochan, T.A. and von Nordenflycht, A. (2009) *Up in the Air: How Airlines Can Improve Performance by Engaging Their Employees*, Ithaca, NY: Cornell University Press.

Barley, S.R. and Kunda, G. (1992) 'Design and devotion: surges of rational and normative ideologies of control in managerial discourse', *Administrative Science Quarterly*, Vol.37, No.3, 363–99.

Barrett, S.D. (2004) 'The sustainability of the Ryanair model', *International Journal of Transport Management*, Vol.2, No.2, 89–98.

Bernaciak, M. (2012) 'Social dumping: political catchphrase or threat to labour standards?', Working Paper 2012.06, Brussels: European Trade Union Institute.

BIS (2015) *Trade Union Membership 2014: Statistical Bulletin*, London: Department for Business, Innovation & Skills.

Blanchflower, D. and Machin, S. (2014) 'Falling real wages', CentrePiece, London School of Economic, Spring, 19–21.

Blyton, P. and Turnbull, P. (2004) *The Dynamics of Employee Relations* (3rd edn.), Houndmills: Palgrave.

Brown, W. and Nash, D. (2008) 'What has been happening to collective bargaining under New Labour? Interpreting WERS 2004', *Industrial Relations Journal*, Vol.39, No.2, 91–103.

Budd, J.W. (2004) *Employment with a Human Face: Balancing Efficiency, Equity, and Voice*, Ithaca, NY: ILR Press.

Budd, J.W. (2005) '*Employment with a human face*: the author responds', *Employee Responsibilities and Rights Journal*, Vol.17, No.3, 191–9.

Budd, J.W. and Bhave, D. (2008) 'Values, ideologies, and frames of reference in industrial relations', pp. 92–112, in Blyton, P., Heery, E., Bacon, N.A. and Fiorito, J. (eds.) *The SAGE Handbook of Industrial Relations*, London: Sage.

Button, K.J. (2003) 'Does the theory of the "core" explain why airlines fail to cover their long-run costs of capital?', *Journal of Air Transport Management*, Vol.9, No.1, 5–14.

Cooney, S., Gahan, P. and Mitchell, R. (2011) 'Legal origins, labour law and the regulation of employment', pp. 75–97, in Berry, M. and Wilkinson, A. (eds.) *Research Handbook in Comparative Employment Relations*, Cheltenham: Edward Elgar.

Cullinane, N. and Dundon, T. (2014) 'Unitarism and employer resistance to trade unionism', *International Journal of Human Resource Management*, Vol.25, No.18, 2573–90.

Deakin, S., Lele, P. and Siems, M. (2007) 'The evolution of labour law: calibrating and comparing regulatory regimes', *International Labour Review*, Vol.146, Nos.3–4, 133–62.

Deakin, S. and Sarkar, P. (2008) 'Assessing the long-run economic impact of labour law systems: a theoretical reappraisal and analysis of new time series data', *Industrial Relations Journal*, Vol.39, No.6, 453–87.

Department for Media, Culture and Sport (2014) *Secondary Analysis of the Gender Pay Gap: Changes in the Gender Pay Gap Over Time*, London: HMSO.

Donovan, Lord (1968) Royal Commission on Trade Unions and Employers' Associations 1965–68, Report, Cmnd 3623, London: HMSO.

Dorling, D. (2014) *Inequality and the 1%*, London: Verso.

Dundon, T. and Gollan, P. (2007) 'Re-conceptualising voice in the non-union workplace', *International Journal of Human Resource Management*, Vol.18, No.7, 1182–98.

Evans, C., Harvey, G. and Turnbull, P. (2012) 'When partnerships don't "match-up": an evaluation of labour-management partnerships in the automotive components and civil aviation industries', *Human Resource Management Journal*, Vol.22, No.1, 60–75.

Ewing, K.D. and Hendy, J. (2013) *Reconstruction after the Crisis: A Manifesto for Collective Bargaining*, London: Institute for Employment Rights.

Flanders, A. (1964) *The Fawley Productivity Agreements: A Case Study of Management and Collective Bargaining*, London: Faber.

Fox, A. (1966a) *Industrial Sociology and Industrial Relations*, Royal Commission on Trade Unions and Employer Associations, Research Paper No.3, London: HMSO.

Fox, A. (1966b) 'Managerial ideology and labour relations', *British Journal of Industrial Relations*, Vol.4, No.3, 366–78.

Fox, A. (1974) *Beyond Contract Work, Power and Trust Relations (Society Today & Tomorrow)*, London: Faber & Faber.

Freiberg, K. and Freiberg, J. (1996) *NUTS! Southwest Airlines Crazy Recipe for Business and Personal Success*, New York: Broadway Books.

Gittell, J.H. (2005) *The Southwest Airlines Way: Using the Power of Relationships to Achieve High Performance*, New York: McGraw-Hill.

Gittell, J.H., Von Nordenflycht, A. and Kochan, T. (2004) 'Mutual gains or zero sum? Labor relations and firm performance in the airline industry', *Industrial & Labor Relations Review*, Vol.57, No.2, 163–80.

Gordon, D.M. (1976) 'Capitalist efficiency and socialist efficiency', *Monthly Review*, Vol.3, 19–39.

Harvey, G. and Turnbull, P. (2012) *The Development of the Low Cost Model in the European Civil Aviation Industry*, Brussels: European Transport Workers' Federation.

Harvey, G. and Turnbull, P. (2014) *Evolution of the Labour Market in the Airline Industry due to the Development of the Low Fares Airlines (LFAs)*, Brussels: European Transport Workers' Federation ETF. Available at: http://www.etf-europe.org/files/extranet/-75/44106/LFA%20 final%20report%20221014.pdf.

Harvey, G. and Turnbull, P. (2015) 'Can labor arrest the "sky pirates"? International trade unionism in the European civil aviation industry', *Labor History*, Vol.56, No.3, 308–26.

HM Revenue & Customs (2014) *Onshore Employment Intermediaries: False Self-Employment*, Summary of Responses, 13th March 2014. Available at: https://www.gov.uk/government /uploads/system/uploads/attachment_data/file/290046/Onshore_Intermediaries_False_Self _Employment_Summary_of_Responses.pdf.

Hodder, A. and Edwards, P. (2015) 'The essence of trade unions: understanding identity, ideology and purpose', *Work, Employment & Society*, Vol.29, No.9, 843–54.

Kassim, H. (1996) 'Air transport', pp. 106–31, in Kassim, H. and Menon, A. (eds.) *The European Union and National Industrial Policy*, London: Routledge.

Keenoy, T. (1992) 'Constructing control', pp. 91–110, in Hartley, J.F. and Stephenson, G.M. (eds.) *Employment Relations: The Psychology of Influence and Control at Work*, Oxford: Blackwell.

La Porta, R., Lopez-de-Silanes, F. and Shleifer, A. (2008) 'The economic consequences of legal origins', *Journal of Economic Literature*, Vol.46, No.2, 289–90.

Learmont, D. (2013) 'Pilot schemes', *Airline Business*, Vol.29, No.5, 54–7.

Leighton, P. and Wynn, M. (2011) 'Classifying employment relationships – more sliding doors or a better regulatory framework?', *Industrial Law Journal*, Vol.40, No.1, 5–44.

Machin, S. (2015) 'Real wages and living standards', Centre for Economic Performance, Paper EA024, London School of Economics.

Marginson, P. (2015) 'The changing nature of collective employment relations', *Employee Relations*, Vol.37, No.6, 645–57.

Mayhew, K. and Wickham-Jones, M. (2015) 'The United Kingdom's social model: from Labour's New Deal to the economic crisis and the Coalition', pp. 144–76, in Erik Dølvik, J. and Martin, M. (eds.) *European Social Models From Crisis to Crisis: Employment and Inequality in the Era of Monetary Integration*, Oxford: Oxford University Press.

OECD (2013) 'Protecting jobs, enhancing flexibility: a new look at employment protection legislation', in *OECD Employment Outlook 2013*, OECD Publishing.

Ogden, S. (1981) 'The reform of collective bargaining: a managerial revolution?', *Industrial Relations Journal*, Vol.12, No.4, 30–42.

ONS (2014) *Self-employed Workers in the UK – 2014*, Office for National Statistics. Available at: http://www.ons.gov.uk/ons/dcp171776_374941.pdf.

O'Sullivan, M. and Gunnigle, P. (2009) 'Bearing all the hallmarks of oppression: union avoidance in Europe's largest low-cost airline', *Labor Studies Journal*, Vol.34, No.2, 252–70.

Parker, A. (2013) Ryanair pilots raise safety concerns, ft.com (August 11th). The http address for this article is: http://www.ft.com/cms/s/0/474c27c0-0293-11e3-880d-00144feab7de.html#axzz4Gjct2SJ5.

Pedersini, R. (2002) '"Economically dependent workers", employment law and industrial relations', Dublin: Eurofound. Available at: http://eurofound.europa.eu/observatories/eurwork/comparative-information/economically-dependent-workers-employment-law-and-industrial-relations.

Purcell, J. (1987) 'Mapping management styles in employee relations', *Journal of Management Studies*, Vol.24, No.5, 533–48.

Purcell, J. and Gray, A. (1986) 'Corporate personnel departments and the management of industrial relations: two case studies in ambiguity', *Journal of Management Studies*, Vol.23, No.2, 205–23.

Samuel, P.J. (2014) *Financial Services Partnerships: Labor-Management Dynamics*, New York: Routledge.

Sieff, M. (1984) 'How I see the personnel function', *Personnel Management*, December 28–30.

Smith, P. and Morton, G. (2006) 'Nine years of New Labour: neoliberalism and workers' rights', *British Journal of Industrial Relations*, Vol.44, No.3, 401–20.

Standing, G. (1997) 'Globalization, labour flexibility and insecurity: the era of market regulation', *European Journal of Industrial Relations*, Vol.3, No.1, 7–37.

SWA (2012) *Building LUV: 2012 Southwest Airlines One Report*, Dallas, TX: Southwest Airlines.

Tarry, C. (2010) 'Low-cost commodity', *Airline Business*, Vol.26, No.2.

Thompson, P. (2003) 'Disconnected capitalism: or why employers can't keep their side of the bargain', *Work, Employment & Society*, Vol.17, No.2, 359–78.

Towers, B. (1997) *The Representation Gap: Change and Reform in the British and American Workplace*, Oxford: OUP.

Turnbull, P. (2003) 'What do unions do now?', *Journal of Labor Research*, Vol.24, No.3, 491–527.

van Wanrooy, B., Bewley, H., Bryson, A., Forth, J., Freeth, S., Stokes, L. and Wood, S. (2013) *The 2011 Workplace Employment Relations Study: First Findings*, London: Department for Business, Innovation and Skills.

Waddington, J. and Whitston, C. (1997) 'Why do people join unions in a period of membership decline?', *British Journal of Industrial Relations*, Vol.35, No.4, 515–46.

Which? (2013) 'Are you being served?', *Which? Magazine*, October, pp. 15–20.

Wilkinson, R.G. and Pickett, K. (2009) *The Spirit Level: Why More Equal Societies Almost Always Do Better*, London: Allen Lane.

Wray, D. (1996) 'Paternalism and its discontents: a case study', *Work, Employment & Society*, Vol.10, No.4, 701–15.

Wright, E.O. (2000) 'Working-class power, capitalist-class interest, and class compromise', *American Journal of Sociology*, Vol.105, No.4, 957–1002.

CHAPTER 9

ORGANISATIONAL AND CORPORATE CULTURE

Alistair Cheyne and John Loan-Clarke

Introduction

In the study of organisations and their management, the concept of culture has become increasingly important. Culture has been used to characterise an organisation or group of individuals within a social structure. It is not, however, a well-defined concept (Münch and Smelster, 1992); it describes roles and interactions that derive from norms and values in the sociological tradition, or from beliefs and attitudes in the social psychological field (Wunthow and Witten, 1988).

Differing views of culture have been incorporated into organisational theory to give rise to the concepts of organisational culture (Brown, 1998) and the similar corporate culture (Peters and Waterman, 1982). 'Organisational culture' tends to refer to a naturally occurring phenomenon that all organisations possess, whereas corporate culture is held to be more management-driven, in an attempt to increase organisational effectiveness. For organisations, Yu (2007) suggests that having an appropriate corporate culture is held as a vital element of many companies' successes, and failures.

This chapter outlines theory and research in organisational culture; it considers definitions and categorisations of culture, investigates the links between culture and human resource management (HRM), and examines how organisations might attempt to manage culture.

Organisational culture

The importance of culture stems from the notion that it provides a dynamic and interactive model of organising (Jelinek *et al.*, 1983; Smircich, 1983) and can help explain how organisational environments might be described, assessed and ultimately controlled (Deal and Kennedy, 1982; Schneider, 1990). Furthermore, a number of authors have proposed that successful organisations have a strong, positive corporate culture (Deal and Kennedy, 1982; Peters and Waterman, 1982; Yu, 2007). Culture can, therefore, imply a practical way of explaining how and why particular organisations enjoy differing levels of success (Brown, 1998; Trompenaars and Hampden-Turner, 1997). In the field of human resource management, organisational culture is increasingly held to be essential to success (see, for example, DeCenzo and Robbins, 2002). The suggestion that organisational effectiveness is influenced by corporate culture has been particularly influential for practising managers. A key influence for the formation of this assumption was the 1982 book by Peters and Waterman, *In Search of Excellence*:

> Without exception, the dominance and coherence of culture proved to be an essential quality of the excellent companies. Moreover the stronger the culture and the more it was directed towards the marketplace, the less the need there was for policy manuals, organization charts or detailed procedures and rules. *(1982: 75)*

However, some research (for example, Booth and Hamer, 2008; Kotter and Heskett, 1992) has indicated the causal link between culture and organisational effectiveness is not necessarily easy to identify. We will come back to the potential link between culture and performance.

Defining organisational culture

Schein (1985) has defined organisational culture in terms of shared values and perceptions of the organisation, beliefs about it and common ways of solving problems within the organisation. It is an ongoing process through which an organisation's behaviour patterns become transformed over time, installed in new recruits, and refined and adapted in response to change (Schein, 1985). Culture basically concerns organisational values and norms (Flamholtz, 2001) that help an organisation's members to interpret and accept their world; it highlights actions that are acceptable to the organisation (Moorhead and Griffin, 1995). It is not so much a by-product of an organisation as an integral part of it, which influences individuals' behaviours and contributes to the effectiveness of the organisation. Reviews of organisational culture (for example, Rousseau, 1990) have detailed numerous definitions that have developed over the years. Emphasis, in many cases, is on values, beliefs and expectations that are shared within the group and/or organisation, and which, in turn, can help the members make sense of their environment, and direct behaviour. These shared values may be directly related to leaders' values within the organisation (Giberson *et al.*, 2009) or be the result of manager directed learning within organisations (Van den Steen, 2010).

Layers of culture

Some (for example, Rousseau, 1990; Schein, 1985) describe culture in organisations as having a series of different layers. Schein (1985) suggests that there are three levels of culture: artefacts, values and basic assumptions. Figure 9.1 shows a representation of these layers of culture, organised from readily accessible, and therefore more easily studied, to difficult to access.

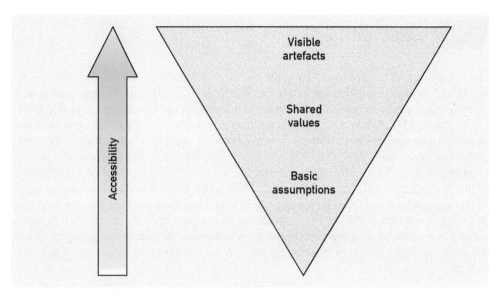

Figure 9.1 Schein's layer of organisational culture

At the most accessible level is visible artefacts, or products of cultural activity. These might include patterns of behaviour (Cooke and Rousseau, 1988) observable to those outside the culture, for example, corporate logos and the physical layout of the organisation. The middle layer relates to values and priorities assigned to organisational outcomes. Such values might be reflected in group behavioural norms, or beliefs about what is acceptable and unacceptable within the organisation. This layer can be learned about through interaction with and questioning of group members. Patterns of unconscious assumptions (Schein, 1984) are the deepest of the layers of culture, and these may not be directly known by the organisation's members. An appreciation of layers of culture could, therefore, be important when considering whether culture can be managed. Hatch (1997) has adapted Schein's (1985) original layers model to incorporate organisational symbols and processes and Hofstede *et al.* (1990) have divided the more accessible elements of culture into values, at the deepest level, through rituals and heroes, to symbols at the shallowest.

Subcultures

Culture may also have different effects in different parts of the organisation. Subcultures can develop (Trice and Beyer, 1993), which can be associated with different roles, functions and levels (Hampden-Turner, 1990). Schein (2004) agrees that cultures are found at every level of an organisation, as well as for the organisation as a whole. For example, there may also be differences in manifest culture between management and other staff (Furnham and Gunter, 1993). Adams and Ingersoll (1989) have proposed that the best way to conceive of organisational culture is in terms of its constituent subcultures. Organisations have been described as umbrellas for diffuse collections of subcultures, which may or may not cohere harmoniously (Martin *et al.*, 1985), and are nested (Pidgeon, 1991) and overlapping, being mutually influential across, and between, levels and groups. Morgan and Ogbonna (2008) suggest if organisations comprise subcultures this means that we must also accept that subgroups and individuals may have differing goals. In terms of cultural maintenance it may be, therefore, more useful to talk of 'cultural alignment'; a mechanism designed to influence and align subcultures with the overall, or 'dominant', organisational culture (Thom, 1997). As a process, alignment might involve the identification of major differences between organisational and subcultures and then, depending on the nature of those differences, the promotion of appropriate organisational values and practices throughout the subcultures.

Categorisations of culture

In addition to definitions of culture and descriptions of level, several researchers have developed classifications of organisational culture, allowing organisations to be described as different types of objective entity. Balthazard *et al.* (2006) suggest that much of the research on organisational culture has focused on describing types of cultures and producing dimensions of culture. These allow comparison and evaluation of different organisations in terms of their culture, and allow types of culture to be associated with successes and failures. There are many such categorisations; two of the better known are illustrated in Box 9.1.

Box 9.1 HRM in practice   Categorisations of culture

Deal and Kennedy

Deal and Kennedy's (1982) categorisation of corporate culture was the result of visiting hundreds of organisations and is based on two factors: the degree of risk associated with business, and the speed of feedback about the success of activities. This resulted in four distinct types:

Tough-guy macho	an organisation of risk takers who receive immediate feedback; examples include police, management consultants, media.
Work hard/play hard	a low-risk, quick-feedback culture which encourages people to maintain high levels of activity; examples include sales companies, computer companies.
Bet your company	the high-risk, slow-feedback culture, where ideas are given time to develop; examples include large multinationals engaged in research and product development.
Process	the classic bureaucracy where feedback is slow and risks are low, so individuals focus on the processes; examples might include local government and regulated industries.

Harrison

An early, influential, classification of organisational culture was suggested by Harrison (1972) [later elaborated on by others, including Handy (1978) and Williams *et al.* (1993)], and describes four main types of culture in organisations:

Power	has a single source of power. Typically these types of organisation react quickly, but success often depends on those with the power at the centre and these organisations might be small, owner-managed businesses.
Role	these types of organisations are typically described as bureaucracies, with an emphasis on functions and specialities. These organisations are good for stable environments and could include public sector organisations.
Task	the focus for these types of organisation is accomplishing goals; power is based on expertise and flexibility is important, for example management consultancies.
Person	these types of organisation exist primarily to serve the needs of their members. Individuals are expected to influence each other through example and helpfulness, and have almost complete autonomy. This type of culture may be evident in those in professional practice, such as lawyers or doctors, or collective organisations.

Some similarities are apparent from these classifications; for example, *process* and *role,* seem to be tapping into similar types of culture to some degree. However, while this is a useful starting point in describing culture, as Deal and Kennedy (1982) acknowledge, we should remember that they represent ideal situations or models for us to compare actual organisations against, and no organisation will fit the types exactly.

The influence of national culture

The consideration of culture is complicated further when the effects of societal and national cultures are considered. Hofstede (1980) studied these influences in relation to IBM operating in over 40 countries worldwide. Hofstede (1991) demonstrated that managers in different countries varied in the strength of their attitudes and values regarding various issues. Four dimensions were identified:

- **Power distance** – the extent to which members are willing to accept an unequal distribution of power, wealth and privilege.
- **Uncertainty avoidance** – the manner in which individuals have learned to cope with uncertainty.
- **Individualism** – the degree to which individuals are required to act independently.
- **Masculinity** – related to dominant values such as success and money.

A fifth dimension, 'confucian dynamism' – the degree to which long-termism or short-termism is the dominant orientation in life – was added after further analysis in an attempt to capture key aspects of Eastern cultural values. However, the core cultural values of Eastern nations have received much attention in their own right. For example, Wong *et al.* (2010) claim that there are five important values in Chinese culture, collectivism, harmony, respect for age and seniority, relationships and face; these do not correspond completely with Western views of national culture diversity.

Hofstede's work is not only deemed to be important for the identification of specific cultural differences (Hatch, 1997) but it has also shown that organisational culture is an entry point for societal influence on organisations. This notion has been developed further in the work of Fons Trompenaars (Trompenaars and Hampden-Turner, 1997). However, Gerhart and Fang (2005) have re-analysed Hofstede's original data and, using different statistical indicators, claim that organisational differences account for more variance than country differences.

It is clear from the literature examined above that there are certain consistencies in the way culture is defined. Many agree that organisational culture involves beliefs and values, exists at a variety of different levels, and manifests itself in a wide range of artefacts, symbols and processes within any particular organisation or subgroup. Culture helps to interpret meaning and understand the environment, potentially influencing individuals' behaviour and contributing to the effectiveness of the organisation. Implicit here is the notion that the more individuals identify with the key values of the organisation, the more important those values become and the stronger the culture (Booth and Hamer, 2008). Two examples of problems that can be encountered by individuals' interpretations of an organisation's culture and adherence to cultural norms are highlighted in Box 9.2.

| Box 9.2 HRM in practice | **Problems of strong culture** |

What happens when individuals feel bound to behave in a particular way?

Piper Alpha

An explosion and resulting fire destroyed the North Sea oil production platform Piper Alpha on 6 July 1988, killing 167 men. The public enquiry (Cullen, 1990) pointed out a number of managerial and organisational issues in the development of the disaster. One aspect that might give an insight into the culture in the organisation was the delay in shutting down feeds from neighbouring platforms. The Piper Alpha fire might have burnt out sooner had it not been fed new fuel from the nearby Tartan and the Claymore platforms. Both could see that Piper Alpha was burning, but, it has been suggested, felt they did not have the authority to shut down production. There may be many explanations for these actions, but they could suggest that the organisation's culture might be characterised as a role or process culture where individuals adhered to a strong hierarchy.

Japan Airlines

On 13 January 1977, a Japan Airlines DC-8 crashed shortly after take-off from Anchorage Airport, killing all on board and destroying the aircraft. The flight was captained by a 53-year-old American pilot with 23,000 hours' flying experience; his Japanese co-pilot was 31 years old, with less experience (1,600 hours). The investigation found that the captain was around three times over the legal limit for driving a car. The National Transportation Safety Board held that a contributing factor to this accident was the failure of other crew to prevent the captain flying.

Anderson and colleagues (2003) suggest that, while it is difficult to gauge exactly what happened, the incident may be related to perceptions of command relationships. Given categorisations of national cultural, we might expect a US culture to be low on power distance and individualistic, while Japan has a culture that has high power distance and is collective. As Anderson *et al.* (2003) point out, the co-pilot would have been conscious of his role and the seniority of the captain, and so might have questioned the captain in a discreet way rather than the more assertive challenge that would have been needed in this situation.

Culture and organisational performance

Of particular interest is the (assumed) link between organisational culture and performance. Much effort has gone into defining and assessing the link between culture and organisational outcomes, often in the hope of finding the 'best' culture. Pinho *et al.* (2014) hold that the likelihood of achieving goals is greater in companies with strong cultures, so we might expect a link to superior performance in those cases. Lee and Yu (2004) point out that much research on the link with performance has focused on a search for particular shared organisational traits or values that result in superior performance. Attempts have been made to link the assessment of organisational culture with financial performance; Gordon and DiTomaso (1992) suggest that the appropriate culture for achieving results in the organisations they examined may not be best described only as 'strong' in terms of consistency but also as flexible. The organisational culture related to effectiveness may, therefore, best be conceived as a combination of several characteristics, which facilitate enhanced performance.

Petty and colleagues (1995) have endeavoured to link culture with broader performance measures, including customer accounting, support services, marketing and employee health and safety in one overall measure. This study found evidence of associations between the measures of performance and organisational culture, with the strongest relationship between 'teamwork' and performance. They conclude that a culture that fosters cooperation may be the most effective. Lee and Yu (2004) studied the link between organisational culture and a number of performance outcomes in Singaporean companies. They found some evidence to suggest that the cultural strength of organisations was related to performance, but only in some of the cases. However, Wilderom *et al.* (2000) are not convinced that meaningful conclusions can be drawn. They argue that different measures of culture are used in different studies and that the operationalisation of performance is inconsistent and lack validity. Subjective measures of performance, for example as made by the chief executive of an organisation, seem to invite bias.

It may be that culture influences performance through intermediary variables. Garnett *et al.* (2008) suggest that communication has an indirect role by acting as moderator or mediator of organisational culture's influence on performance. Sackmann (2010) has emphasised the need for examining contingent, interactive relationships in order to better understand culture and performance. Taking up this theme, Kotrba *et al.* (2012) investigated whether consistent cultures (those with highly shared values) produced better market-to-book ratios; sales growth and return on assets. They found that consistent cultures interacted with higher scores on other cultural dimensions of involvement, adaptability and mission, to enhance market-to-book ratios and sales growth. Surprisingly, they found that high consistency, along with moderately low scores on the three other cultural dimensions, was associated with high profitability. This highlights that different cultural dimensions are required to deal with contradictory business challenges.

Organisational culture and human resource management

It is worth exploring the impact of culture on 'people management' practices. Human resource management and organisational culture seem to be highly intertwined concepts; Storey (1995) and Legge (2005) have articulated the centrality of organisational culture to the development and practice of human resource management. Storey (1995: 8) suggests that managing culture change coincides so much with the movement towards HRM that they 'become one and the same project'. As he observes, management does not merely seek compliance with rules and the implementation of procedures as a way of controlling employee behaviour, but seeks to develop high levels of employee commitment through the management of culture (Storey, 1995).

Some consider that culture cannot be controlled by management within the organisation, whereas others tend to believe that it is at least possible. Nevertheless, there has been something of a convergence of approach to researching and understanding culture from those who believe that there is the potential to manage organisational culture. As Barley *et al.* (1988) have noted both groups are interested in identifying how culture can be used as a mechanism to enhance performance. There have been concerns expressed regarding this approach to the management of employees. Whereas previous rational approaches overtly used rules, regulations and procedures as a way of ensuring behavioural compliance from employees, many see culture management as equally controlling but in a covert way. The difference is that culture management techniques focus much less on rational than on emotive approaches to employee management. Therefore, the winning of 'hearts and minds' and the legitimacy of seeking to manipulate employee emotions has been questioned (Casey, 1995). Assuming that culture management is possible, HRM provides one possible avenue to achieve this.

Culture management and HRM practices

It would seem logical that the human resources function ought to be centrally involved in attempting to influence organisational culture. An example where it was the case is American Express. Fairbairn (2005) has outlined the role taken by HR in culture change. The approach sought to build on aspects of the culture which were considered positive. The CEO (2005: 81) 'believed that any change must reflect the realities and expectations of stakeholder groups, including employees'. Employees were asked to envision what the organisation should be like in five years' time, and how it should get there. This approach is rather different to management-imposed culture change. The area of mergers and acquisitions, for example, is one where culture clashes between organisations have not been given enough attention by senior management who tend to concentrate on financial issues.

Ngo and Loi (2008) investigated links between certain HR practices, culture and organisational performance. Performance was assessed by HR managers in various multinationals operating in Hong Kong, comparing their organisation to the industry 'average'. They found that employee behaviour flexibility, and HR practice flexibility had positive effects on adaptability culture. This culture had a positive effect on facets of HR performance. This HR performance mediated the impact of culture on perceptions of organisational performance such as sales and profit. Chow and Liu (2009), studying 451 firms in China, found that organisational effectiveness is contingent upon linkages between appropriate cultures and HR systems, which must be aligned with business strategy. Both these studies illustrate the complexity of matching certain types of culture and HR practices in order to (potentially) influence organisational performance. However, Alvesson and Karreman (2007) suggest that even where extensive HR systems and practices exist, they may not work as effectively, or rationally, as they purport to do. They found that despite the existence of systematised performance rating systems, structured selection processes, etc., promotion decisions could still be biased in an international management consultancy firm. However, inside the organisation the prevailing beliefs were that excellent HR practices existed and the culture was one of objectivity and career progression based on performance criteria. Various facets of HR activity might be used either to reinforce the existing culture within an organisation or to support culture change efforts; some examples are discussed below.

Recruitment and selection

Traditionally, organisations have sought to match individuals' abilities to job requirements, commonly known as person–job (P–J) fit. Research has developed to focus on the fit between the person and the organisation (P–O), particularly in respect of the organisation's culture. In this sense the individual's abilities/competencies are considered less important than their attitudes/values and the match of these with the organisation's culture. Adkins and Caldwell (2004) explore whether the match of the individual with the subculture or group (P–G fit) of the organisation in which they are located may be more important to factors such as job satisfaction. They found that there were differences between groups (subcultures), even in an organisation seeking to maintain a strong overall organisational culture. This matching of the individual's values with the organisation's culture can be assessed, for potential employees, during the selection process. However, it is also important for individuals to assess whether the organisation's culture matches their own preferences. Examples of how the management of culture has been used to attract and retain employees are shown in Box 9.3.

Box 9.3 HRM in practice	Managing culture to attract staff

Madame Tussauds, which runs visitor attractions in various countries, relies on seasonal labour during peak periods. The company emphasises that it is a fun place to work as one of its mechanisms for (re)attracting staff. It uses beer and pizza evenings, Halloween balls and other events for staff to reinforce the culture it wishes to project (Arkin, 2004).

A study by Braddy et al. (2006) indicates that websites dedicated to recruitment can be useful in influencing potential applicants' perceptions of the organisation's culture. Perceptions of diversity (photos of staff from various ethnic backgrounds) and innovation (comments about how highly valued it was by the organisation) were the culture dimensions most effectively communicated. The importance of a rewards culture was also communicated through reference to organisational policies regarding bonuses and other incentives. Explicit statements about organisational values and employee testimonials regarding their work experience in the organisation were also influential.

Arnold et al. (2003) identified that some potential employees were put off by what they saw as unrealistic advertising and promotion campaigns which portrayed UK National Health Service (NHS) work as rather more positive and attractive than candidates perceived it to be, and underplayed difficulties. Therefore, key cultural values that participants wished to see associated with the NHS, such as honesty and integrity, appeared to be undermined by the recruitment campaigns which were simultaneously emphasising the high degree of expertise and professionalism expected of its staff.

Employee induction

A key opportunity for the organisation to influence employee values is during the early stages of their employment. An extensive literature has referred to the impact of the social- isation process on organisational newcomers. Harris and Ogbonna (2011) found that the greater the extent of formalised socialisation activity the greater the management-espoused cultural control over employees. In contrast, McMillan-Capehart (2005) emphasises that individualised socialisation efforts lead to a greater diversity of values and beliefs. Even if organisations commit considerable time and effort to the formalised socialisation process at the point of organisational entry, individuals will still, over time, be influenced by informal events which affect the newcomer's perspectives (for example, Ricks, 1997). Unless the formalised institutional socialisation represented by induction programmes is reinforced by the activities and contacts newcomers encounter in day-to-day organisational life, it may not necessarily achieve the desired effect (from the organisation's perspective).

Training and development

Williams *et al.* (1993) suggest that training focused on employee behaviour is likely to be necessary in seeking to change employee values and attitudes. Indeed, Kunda (1992) argues that explicit attempts to change values can lead to employees feeling manipulated or brainwashed and therefore becoming very cynical. Ogbonna and Wilkinson (1988) indicate that even behaviourally focused change efforts can lead to what they called resigned behavioural compliance. Scheeres and Rhodes (2006) have identified that in-house training programmes which are explicitly designed to inculcate managerially desired culture are unlikely to succeed where, as one training programme participant put it: 'what management would say . . . with the core values and one thing and another, is at odds with how it really is on a day-to-day basis' (2006: 232).

In terms of corporate-level organisational learning and transfer across nations, Hong *et al.* (2006) have highlighted the importance of cultural considerations. In a study of Japanese subsidiary companies operating in south China, they noted that corporate values had to be taken into account as well as technical knowledge components. The use of parent company socialisation processes, as well as open-plan factory and office designs, facilitated cross-border transfer of organisational learning systems.

Fields *et al.* (2006) studied the responses of Hong Kong Chinese and US organisations to uncertainty in the supply of qualified labour. Hong Kong organisations increased training and development activity, whereas US organisations reduced it. Fields *et al.* (2006) suggested that Hong Kong employees, in a collectivist culture, would perceive more training as both a reward, and an indication that the organisation was enhancing the value of the individual to it. In the individualistic US culture, less training occurred as, employees who have enhanced their skills, may seek a better job elsewhere.

Communication and integration activities

Communication is considered by many managers to be a central component of culture management (Williams *et al.*, 1993). Manipulation of artefacts and symbols, Schein's (1985) top or surface level of culture, is the focus here. Trice and Beyer (1993) identify two 'rites' that organisations may use to communicate culture. The rite of enhancement, for example the use of company newsletters, team briefings and employee of the month award schemes, can serve a number of purposes. It can spread good news about the organisation; equally, it could focus on individuals, and provide public recognition. At the same time this recognition of individual achievement is designed to communicate to others what is expected of them. The rite of integration uses non-work activities as a way of influencing employees' emotions. For example, organised social events can be used to try to foster a sense of binding employees to the organisation, particularly important where the organisation seeks to foster a high degree of teamworking and team commitment.

Cross-cultural integration

French (2010) reports that AXA, the insurance multinational, has attempted to overcome the potential influence of national culture in a number of ways. First, employees from various countries took part in focus groups to consider the relevance of the organisation's stated values in different cultures. Five key values were considered to best represent the organisation and potentially overcome cultural barriers. These values were then linked to behavioural traits, and staff were recruited, and appraised against these behaviours. Other research shows that national culture preferences can still prevail. Miah and Bird (2007) found that national culture in countries in South Asia (India, Pakistan and Bangladesh) was more influential in shaping HRM styles and practices in

Japanese subsidiary and joint-venture activity in those countries. Autocratic rather than participative approaches were preferred. Studying the influence of national as well as organisational culture, Engelen *et al.* (2012) have found that cross-functional integration is higher, and has positive impact on new product development, when the national culture dimension of collectivism is higher. The effect of this was enhanced when the organisation had a strong corporate culture as well.

As Froese *et al.* (2008) discuss, there are various complex factors to consider when cross-national acquisitions occur. The type of strategy adopted by the acquiring organisation (e.g. assimilation and separation), the cultural distance between the two organisations in respect of their existing organisational and national cultures, the expectations of the acquired organisation's employees in respect of degree of change, and the influence of contextual factors such as the prevailing economic conditions all need to be taken into account. Froese *et al.* (2008) found that Korean employees in firms acquired by Western organisations were more accepting of, and satisfied with, market-oriented reforms because they expected them and saw the economic necessity of them in a Korean economy that was struggling. However, changes towards individualism which clashed with Confucian values were not well received.

Payment/rewards systems

Armstrong (1999) suggests that the organisation's remuneration policy can be used as a way of communicating organisational values. Williams *et al.* (1993) stress that consistency is important if the organisation is not to send mixed messages to employees regarding management's preferred cultural values.

Lowe *et al.* (2002) studied reward practices across 10 countries. Contrary to expectations, group or organisation-based performance incentives did not occur as much in 'collectivist' societies as would have been predicted. More consistent with Hofstede's (1991) dimension of masculinity, Schneider and Barsoux (2003) found that Swedish employees are likely to prefer time off from work, rather than a financial bonus, i.e. consistent with the country's higher preference for the femininity end of the dimension.

In multinational organisations the use of expatriate managers can be considerably more expensive than employing local managers. For example, Chen *et al.* (2002) have identified that employing expatriates in China can mean that they are paid up to 50 times more than local staff. However, Bonache and Fernandez (2005) note a number of reasons, including cultural ones, why the organisation may decide to incur these extra costs, for example if host country company-specific knowledge is required, possibly combined with the need to implement a global, rather than local, strategy.

Performance management/appraisal

Investigations into performance management as a conduit for spreading organisational value tends to find some discrepancy between espoused values and short-term demands. Hofstetter and Harpaz (2011) identified that the formal performance assessment system designed by senior management was operationalised and interpreted somewhat differently by middle and junior managers in the organisation. Considering the formal system to be a reflection of senior management's espoused cultural preferences, the authors considered that the 'norms in use' by other managers in the organisation were rather different.

Williams (2002) suggests that the performance management process might be seen as a way of developing, at least in part, a 'performance culture'. However, certain advocates of performance management, e.g. Armstrong (1994), tend to associate performance management with a set of values reflecting openness, trust, employee participation, etc. in the performance management process. In contrast, a performance culture simply focuses on increasing employee productivity. For example, Fletcher and Williams (1992) identified that an organisation's performance culture placed particular emphasis on 'bottom line' results. Employees felt that fear was the driving force underpinning the performance culture rather than participation and openness.

Arkin (2007) reports an interesting example of the issues associated with seeking to introduce a standard approach to performance management in a multinational organisation. Kimberley-Clark operated in 68 countries around the world. Performance ratings were high but sales and share price were not good. There seemed reluctance to rate anyone below average. An international project team was created to develop a new approach, and a 360-degree feedback system was agreed. However, because employees in Korea, South America and Asia were concerned about giving feedback on their managers, the compromise of anonymity was made, despite the reluctance of Western countries, who wanted to encourage openness and transparency. Because of the process of consultation and adaptation, a survey of employees found that 95 per cent were confident in the new system's use.

Leadership

The importance of leaders as figureheads of, and role models for, preferred culture and values is seen as crucial. A new leader is often associated with a new approach to culture. Leaders at different levels in the organisation have influence and control over various organisational rites (Trice and Beyer, 1993). Schein (2004) identifies a number of mechanisms that leaders use to embed, and reinforce, beliefs, values and assumptions. Allocation of resources rewards and status by the leader is important. Equally, explicit role-modelling and coaching communicates what the leader considers important. Schein (2004) emphasises that formal mechanisms such as training are not necessary in order to communicate cultural values; leader behaviour, observed in normal work activity, is sufficient.

Chatman and Cha (2003) give the example of Dreyer's Grand Ice Cream. At one point in time they experienced (a) their CEO getting a brain tumour; (b) a significant rise in raw material costs and (c) the termination of a large distribution contract. Rather than panic and cut costs, they continued their normal cultural practices such as openness in communication. They introduced free-phone calls for employees to hear pre-recorded updates by the CEO. They continued to invest in training activities. As one employee put it, (2003: 30) '. . . they reassured us by calling it straight . . . they informed us of their game plan, and that they counted on us . . . you thought you'd run through a wall for this guy'.

Research conducted in China by Tsui *et al.* (2006) identifies interesting variations on leader behaviour and its interaction with organisational culture. Leaders described as 'performance builders' (mostly young, with management qualifications) focused primarily on external adaptation of the organisation to its environment. They gave little attention to internal processes to develop/reinforce values, and their organisations had relatively weak cultures. In contrast, 'institution builders' focused strongly on internal processes/systems to reinforce values but were much less charismatic as leaders. They relied on the support of other managers to reinforce culture. These organisations had stronger cultures, and used human resource systems, such as selection, reward and training, to reinforce and sustain culture.

Is culture change feasible?

There is considerable scepticism regarding the feasibility of management proactively changing organisational culture. For example, Meek (1982) suggests that those who propose that culture change is feasible do not recognise that power differentials exist within organisations that subcultures exist and that ultimately, in seeking to change culture, management is seeking to control employees. Ogbonna (1992) suggests that the espoused aim of many culture change programmes, to enhance employee commitment, is not achieved. In many senses change is focused purely on employee behaviours and achieved through compliance. Sackmann (1991) suggests that since cultures are highly complex, dynamic systems with individual and group variability within them, they are not really amenable to management.

Despite cynicism about achieving culture change, some writers have argued that culture change is feasible, albeit with difficulty. For example, Pettigrew (1990) has, on the basis of considerable research, proposed a number of factors for consideration in seeking to undertake culture change. He does note that this will be an arduous process and is more likely to affect surface levels of culture than core assumptions.

Harris and Ogbonna (1998) summarise the differing views on the feasibility of changing culture by suggesting three different perspectives: (a) culture can be managed; (b) culture cannot be managed and (c) culture can be manipulated, but only under certain conditions. They also stress that little research effort has been directed at understanding employee reactions to managerial culture change attempts. Therefore, they conducted an empirical study in two contexts, one food and one clothing company in the British retail sector. They identified that employees could respond in a range of ways and that two key determinants seemed to be at play. One was willingness to change and the second was the existing strength of the particular subculture (for example, division of the organisation). Responses could range from active rejection through to active acceptance. Particularly interesting responses were reinvention and reinterpretation. Reinvention occurs where the attributes of the existing culture are recycled so that superficially, at least, they appear to be in line with the new culture being espoused by management. Reinterpretation occurs where employee values and behaviour are modified to some extent, but in a way which is consistent with both the existing culture and the desired culture. While there appears to be some adoption of the espoused culture, this is filtered through the understanding of the existing culture and in that sense is not necessarily a predictable response. As we commented earlier, individuals can and do respond to culture change efforts in widely different ways. As Harris and Ogbonna (1998) note, there can be a range of responses between outright acceptance and rejection. This unpredictability of response makes culture change difficult to manage and attempts at culture change should not seek radical change but work incrementally.

Conclusions

Based on the evidence, what can we say about organisational culture? First, we can describe organisational culture as a phenomenon that involves beliefs, values and behaviours, exists at a variety of different levels, and manifests itself in a wide range of artefacts within any particular organisation. Furthermore, culture might provide a useful description of organisational environments, which facilitate their comprehension, interpretation, acceptance and control, and might, but only might, help explain their success. Finally, if organisational culture is to be of use to managers and organisations, they must be able to adapt and change their culture when necessary.

It is clear, however, that while culture change and the management of it by the organisation may appear feasible, there are practical problems associated with it.

- At what level is culture change occurring – is it at the artefacts level or at the level of fundamental assumptions?
- Even if behaviour is changed, is this really culture change? If employee values and assumptions have not changed, does this really matter, if management is primarily interested in employees demonstrating appropriate behaviours?
- Do organisations have unitary cultures, and, if so, is it feasible to change the culture of the whole organisation at once?
- If organisations contain subcultures, are strategies for culture change sophisticated enough to recognise the differential approaches required?

Martin (2002) has suggested that three differing perspectives can be adopted in seeking to understand culture and therefore interpret ways to approach culture change and its effectiveness. The integration perspective is most typical of management in that it assumes an organisation-wide consensus within the organisation and that consistency is feasible. The differentiation perspective assumes that there are likely to be subcultures within the organisation. These have consensus within themselves but there is likely to be conflict between subcultures. The fragmentation perspective assumes that there is such a multiplicity of views with little or no consensus, and that managing culture will be immensely complex because of its ambiguity. As Rodrigues (2006) points out, the same organisation may experience each of these perspectives at different points in time.

CASE STUDY 9.1

UNDERSTANDING THE CULTURE OF AN ORGANISATION

JOHN LOAN-CLARKE AND ALISTAIR CHEYNE

Think about an organisation you know. This could be one you have worked in full time (now or in the past), temporarily (e.g. vacation work) or during a secondment. Consider the following two questions about that organisation.

Questions

1 What do you consider the organisation's culture to be? Either use your own words to describe this or relate your understanding of the culture to one of the models we have covered in this chapter, e.g. Harrison, Deal and Kennedy.
2 Does this culture apply equally across the whole of the organisation or just to a certain part(s) of it?
  You will initially need to think through these ideas on your own. Make some brief notes to help organise your thoughts. Having done this, exchange your ideas with others.

CASE STUDY 9.2

UNDERSTANDING CULTURE IN INTERNATIONAL HIGHER EDUCATION

XIAOZHENG ZHANG

Following the trend of internationalisation in higher education, there are an increasing number of European universities setting up international business schools in China.

CBBS (Chinese-Based Business School) was co-founded by one British and one Chinese university, in 2010. The management of the school was divided between the two partner universities along administrative and academic lines. The Chinese university looks after the administration, dealing with issues such as student recruitment and registration; employing the administrative staff; providing support such as logistics and supply of equipment and facilities. The academic work is taken care of by the British university, with responsibility for matters of learning and teaching, academic staff recruitment, evaluation of student academic performance, etc.

The administration is made up of native Chinese employees, who are required to be able to speak fluent English in order to communicate with the academic staff. In order to introduce British higher education standards into China, CBBS recruited all academic staff from the UK. These included both Chinese and British academics, who obtained their higher education degrees from a British university, and who had at least five years' work experience in the British higher education sector. Working as expatriates in Shanghai, the academic employees were provided with accommodation and other assistance in settling in China.

As part of their induction to the job, academic expatriates were briefed about the structure of CBBS in China, the student entrance level and some basic Chinese cultural background knowledge. The key concepts of Confucianism were introduced, including harmony, face-saving, respect for age and hierarchy (Flynn *et al.*, 2007). Face-saving means to maintain an individual's positive self-image in front of others as much as possible (Merkin, 2006). Moreover, within the Chinese context, an individual is not only required to protect their own 'face' in society, but also to pay great attention to caring for others' 'face' (Zhang, 2012). By doing this, people maintain harmonious relationships and avoid conflict with others.

After running for a year, the CBBS management identified some communication issues between the administrative and academic teams. The CBBS management requested the human resource department to evaluate the current situation and propose some practical plans to improve it.

Questions

1 Considering the potential influence of national culture, try to identify the main problems in communication between the administrative and academic teams.

2 What should be included as key themes in cultural training programmes for the academic expatriates?

3 In terms of recruitment and selection of academic staff, what are the important criteria that need to be considered?

CASE STUDY 9.3

CULTURAL TURBULENCE: FROM 'PEOPLE FIRST' TO 'MACHO MANAGEMENT' AT BRITISH AIRWAYS

IRENA GRUGULIS, ADRIAN WILKINSON AND ASHLEA KELLNER

At the end of the 1970s and the start of the 1980s BA was performing disastrously. Its fleet was old, its productivity was below that of its competitors; it was beset by industrial disputes; and it was recording substantial losses (£140 million or some £200 a minute in 1981). Staff discontent was matched by customer dissatisfaction. By the mid-1990s this picture was reversed. Not only had BA become the world's most profitable carrier, it was also voted the company that most graduates would like to work for (Blyton and Turnbull, 1998; Corke, 1986; Warhurst, 1995). Many attribute this turnaround to BA's own cultural change, which remodelled staff attitudes and set customer care as the primary focus of activity. As Doyle (1999: 20) noted:

> In the 80s BA had been transformed from a disastrous loss-making state enterprise . . . into the world's largest and most profitable international airline. It was a triumph for management. . . Its success was the result of the process and strategy that management introduced. The process focused on creating a vision that would inspire the BA staff and gain their enthusiastic commitment.

A great deal of effort went into shaping BA's culture. At the heart of this was the 'Putting people first' training programme launched by Colin Marshall, the chief executive, in 1983. It was attended by all employees by 1986 and aimed to revolutionise attitudes. Attendees were encouraged to take a more positive attitude to themselves, taught how to set personal goals and cope with stress, and instructed in confidence building and 'getting what they wanted out of life'. The approach was self-consciously 'indoctrinative' (Bate, 1994: 195). As Colin Marshall said:

> We . . . have to design our people and their service attitude just as we design an aircraft seat, an in-flight entertainment programme or an airport lounge *to meet the needs and preferences of our customers. (Cited in Barsoux and Manzoni, 1997: 14, emphasis added.)*

One impressive aspect of BA's cultural change was the extent to which other employment policies and practices were changed to fit the 'new' culture and the continued emphasis on these practices and programmes throughout the 1980s and 1990s. Not only were team briefings and teamworking introduced, but these were developed and refined, with TQM, autonomous teamworking and multi-skilling introduced in many areas. Direct contact with all staff was considered so important that 'down route' briefings were developed to ensure that mobile and isolated staff were not neglected, and in 1996 BA became the first company to make daily television broadcasts to its staff (Colling, 1995).

'Families' of cabin crew were created to work the same shift patterns to provide mutual support, make cabin crew feel happier about their work environments and, as a result, facilitate the production of emotional labour (Barsoux and Manzoni, 1997). The importance of emotional processes was also reflected in the new appraisal and reward systems such that work was judged on the way in which it was performed as well as against harder targets (Georgiades and Macdonnell, 1998; Höpfl, 1993). Managerial bonuses were calculated on a straight 50:50 split between exhibiting desired behaviours and achieving quantitative goals. Programmes encouraged staff input. Many HR decisions were devolved to line managers and, in the first few years of the programme at least, a commitment was made to job security.

Closely following these developments, a 'Managing people first' programme targeted managers and aimed to bring their behaviours into line with four factors focused on Clarity and 'Helpfulness', 'Promoting Achievement', 'Influencing Through Personal Excellence' and 'Teamworking' and 'Care and Trust' (Georgiades and Macdonnell, 1998).

Other courses were developed to maintain the momentum created by 'Putting people first' and 'Managing people first' and, while each was different, they all shared a focus on shaping staff emotions. Twenty years after their launch, training still included a focus on understanding oneself and taking responsibility. In 1995, Bob Ayling, having newly taken over as chief executive, continued this active management of company culture and said of his staff: 'I want them to feel inspired, I want them to feel optimistic, I want them to feel that this is a good place to be' ('Dangerous Company', BBC2, April 2000).

Such change was certainly impressive, but accounts neglect structural reasons for BA's success (Anthony, 1994). The emphasis on putting people first and caring for one another had been preceded by a rule of fear. BA's first response to its problems had been a series of redundancies with staff numbers reduced by 40 per cent between 1981 and 1983. The company also had a large share of slots at Heathrow Airport and faced little competition on many of its routes. While staff numbers were cut, infrastructure was dramatically improved. BA invested in control systems, facilities and aircraft. Between 1980 and 1985 BA replaced over half its fleet (Colling, 1995). Computer reservations were introduced; a series of hub and spoke routes developed, and focused competitive pricing introduced (Blyton and Turnbull, 1996).

The true extent of the company's cultural transformation itself is open to question. While cultural change interventions seek to influence the thoughts, values, attitudes and norms of others, employees are not cultural dupes. Cooperation may reflect ambition or pride in work as much as (or instead of) a belief in the organisation itself. Despite the claims of the literature, the existence of 'culture management' does not ensure either that employees trust management, or that management trusts employees. So, in BA, 'new' practices varied in the extent that they were introduced in departments and conflict between employees and management did not cease.

Nor was job security quite as robust as it seemed. Alliances, mergers and franchising agreements with other airlines already supported what was, in effect, 'tiered' terms and conditions, with employees based at Heathrow privileged over those elsewhere. This emphasis on part-time, seasonal and subcontracted work was extended to most operations. The engine overhaul plant was sold off, data-processing work was moved overseas, and job security for existing staff questioned (Blyton and Turnbull, 1996; Colling, 1995; Warhurst, 1995). In short, BA, while putting a great deal of effort into encouraging certain behaviours from staff, did not base its employment practices around the new culture in the way suggested. Their human resource management techniques were impressive, but not everyone benefited from them.

Staff reactions to 'culture change' included enthusiasm and acceptance but also doubt, concern, opposition and open cynicism. Such individual reactions were mirrored by the collective representations and the persistence of disputes even at the height of the 'cultural success'.

The 1997 dispute

By the end of the 1990s many of the factors that had provided the basis for the company's success were under threat. Low-cost carriers were undercutting prices and alliances between rivals ensured that cross-national traffic would be less likely to transfer to BA. In response, Ayling claimed that BA needed a second revolution. BA sought its own alliances, as well as proposing £1 billion of cost savings from within the organisation, with the aim of doubling profits by the year 2000. Much of this was to come from staff savings, including 5,000 voluntary redundancies, with staff to be replaced by new employees on lower pay (Blyton and Turnbull, 1998).

Reducing costs was also extended to 'core' BA staff. In early 1997, BA attempted to change the structure of payments to cabin crew; existing employees would be 'bought out' of their allowances (petrol, overnight stay, etc.) by receiving a higher basic wage. BA offered a three-year guarantee that no crew would earn less under the new system but nothing beyond that, and it was clear that the measure was launched with the aim of saving money. When negotiations failed, the TGWU union threatened strike action. Despite 14 years of espoused policy of caring for one another and putting people first, the tactics deployed by BA's management were described as bullying (*The Economist*, 10 July 1997). Members of cabin crew were warned not to strike and staff were told that anyone taking industrial action would be summarily sacked, then sued for damages. Any who simply stayed away would face disciplinary action, be denied promotion and lose pension rights and staff discounts for three years.

The strike ballot had an 80 per cent turnout, with 73 per cent of employees voting in favour of strike action. The TGWU called a series of 72-hour strikes, with the first scheduled for July 1997. In response, temporary staff and an alternative workforce of 'volunteer managers' were given training to perform key tasks. On the eve of the first day of action cabin crew were contacted and warned that 'they had a duty to cooperate with their employer'.

These actions influenced the impact of the strike. On the first day of action fewer than 300 workers declared themselves officially on strike but more than 2,000 called in sick. Despite the company's efforts, more than 70 per cent of flights were cancelled. It seemed that BA's macho approach had ensured only that collective action took the form of collective illness. This made things worse for BA. Those employees who had called in sick tended to stay away longer than the 72-hour strike. Many employees stayed off for the full two weeks that their sick notes allowed and, throughout this period, services were cancelled and passengers turned away. When the General Secretary of the TGWU, announced that he had written to BA suggesting that they resume negotiations, BA agreed before even receiving the letter.

The TGWU promised to save £42 million over three years. Catering was sold off and sanctions against strikers were withdrawn. BA's management fared less well, despite Bob Ayling's claim that this agreement marked a 'new beginning and spirit of cooperation'. The gulf between the managerial rhetoric on culture and official actions during the strike had a predictable effect on employee morale. The agreement itself fostered further dissent. By the end of 1997, 4,000 staff had left but 4,500 more were recruited, including 2,000 in 1998. By the terms of the agreement, these new staff members were employed on new contracts. As a result, cabin crew working on the same aircraft were (increasingly) on different pay scales. The impact of this on both labour relations and teamworking was problematic and problems were fuelled by suggestions that staff on new contracts were favoured by BA in promotion.

Bob Ayling attempted to salvage the situation by placing more emphasis on managing the company's culture. He addressed staff training sessions and held forums with groups of employees. This time there were few positive reactions. The strike cost BA £125 million; morale never entirely recovered and profits suffered. Between 1998 and 1999 they fell by 61 per cent and in 2000 British Airways announced losses of £244 million on its main business; the first loss since privatisation. These failures so coloured the public perception of the chief executive that even his attempts to refocus BA on to profitable routes and new products were not entirely welcomed. On 10 March 2000, Bob Ayling resigned as chief executive.

Continuing turbulence

The next decade was characterised by ongoing disputes and continued restructuring to reduce costs. New CEO Rod Eddington faced turmoil in the industry shortly after his appointment, following the terrorist attacks on 11 September 2001. Like other airlines, British Airways suffered heavily following the attacks and their initial response was to announce 1,800 job losses, followed shortly by a further cut of 5,200 positions (Upchurch, 2010). In fact, between 2000 and 2005 the company cut 14,000 jobs, 7,000 of which were reportedly because of falling demand (Bamber et al., 2009).

The next years saw a stream of ongoing industrial disputes and negative publicity for British Airways. In 2003, around 500 customer service employees went on strike at Heathrow Airport in protest against a new automated attendance monitoring system. Although staff returned after two days, disruptions continued as the company scrambled to reposition aircraft and crew and ultimately cost £40 million. Industrial action escalated the following year when 3,000 check-in staff threatened a 24-hour strike over a busy holiday weekend. Although the strike was averted, the threat still cost the company millions.

In 2005 the 'Gate Gourmet' dispute hit British Airways with a further revenue loss of £40 million. When Gate Gourmet, the outsourced catering function formed in 1997, announced the dismissal of 670 of its 2,000 employees, 1,000 British Airways ground staff promptly followed with an illegal sympathy strike. The strike disrupted operations at Heathrow Airport for two days, saw 700 flights cancelled and caused chaos for over 100,000 passengers. Again, in 2007, flight attendants called a strike in reaction to proposed reduction in pay, pensions and sick leave. Although the strike was averted, the company's stock fell by almost £100 million.

Through the turbulence, British Airways continued to deliver the same rhetoric to employees that brought them success in the 1990s, which was cutting costs while simultaneously developing and valuing their workforce. One-third of senior management positions were shed in a bid to 'remove duplication and complexity, provide greater accountability and reduce costs', and also, likely, in a bid to change culture (British Airways Corporate Responsibility Report, 2006: 3). This cost reduction measure was supported by a range of new programmes designed towards developing improvements through HRM. The 2008/09 Annual Report (p. 34) stated that 'to create a really high performing business we need to build an inspiring and rewarding workplace where talented people can work to the best of their ability and meet our customer needs'. British Airways introduced a range of new policies and programmes and announced a renewed focus on providing extensive training.

The ongoing unrest was creating a reputation of unreliability for customers. The management style demonstrated through these disputes was influenced by a traditional perspective, recognising the involvement of unions but supplemented with strategies designed to engage staff. Although management leaned towards a more aggressive approach in some instances such as the 1997 strikes, this style became increasingly predominant and was particularly evident in their reaction to the 2010 cabin crew strikes, a response to attempts by the company to restructure pay and working requirements for cabin crew. British Airways sought to create a 'new fleet' of cabin crew, with changes from seniority to performance-based pay and restructured lines of authority. In the face of staff resistance and the overwhelming majority in favour of industrial action, the company sought an injunction from the High Court to prevent the threatened 20-day strike. Following the injunction, management sought to locate and reprimand all employees who even alluded to supporting further strike action within the company.

In the following months, British Airways suspended and disciplined over 45 cabin crew who indicated support for industrial action. According to Upchurch (2010), an indication of support was deemed to include comments on social media outlets, posts on the union website forum, text messages to colleagues, and even overheard private discussions. However, it was the notifications of suspension and dismissal which were deemed to be particularly harsh and unreasonable: employees were marched out of meetings or met on the tarmac on disembarkation from their aircraft to be informed of their suspension (Upchurch, 2010).

In its dealings with employees, British Airways have exhibited what has been termed as 'macho-management'. In the 2010 dispute, management appeared to ignore traditional disciplinary methods and pursued a more aggressive stance. The use of disciplinary action based on evidence as weak as hearsay and overheard conversations was unprecedented and has been equated with 'the worse aspects of the methods used by the Stalinist secret police' (Upchurch, 2010: 7). In early 2015, allegations surfaced that information garnered by BA during the dispute may have come from in-house investigators improperly accessing employee emails and phone calls of cabin staff, and that the union was paid £1 million to stop them from suing the company for these actions. The main union for cabin crew also reported an increase in the use of bullying and harassment designed to isolate members and undermine the dispute. There appeared to be an emerging subculture of aggressive management coming from the top down, deliberately engineered to intimidate union members.

Recent years have seen BA report improved performance and profitability despite simmering employee unrest. In early 2011 BA completed a merger with ailing Spanish airline Iberia in a bid to cut costs and improve competitiveness in the face of tough economic times in the industry. By 2015 productivity improvements and massive downsizing of the workforce saw Iberia return to profitability, and combined with BA, the new 'International Airlines Group' forecast a £1.4 billion profit by the end of the year. Customer goodwill has continued to grow for BA and recent surveys place them as the number one company for brand strength in the UK – ahead of Apple, Google and the BBC (Superbrands Survey UK 2014–15).

Meanwhile, distinctions between groups of cabin crew staff have continued to create tension and reinforce a divide both between employees and with management. Cabin crew joining BA after 2010 as part of the 'mixed fleet' arrangement were placed on revised contracts offering inferior salary and conditions to existing staff, echoing the problems of the late 1990s. In 2014 mixed fleet cabin crew were reportedly ready to strike when claims for pay increases – ongoing since the 2010 disputes – were rebuffed. The union reported that scheduling of shifts combined with reduced pay rates has seen young crew members working for as little as £12,000 per year, less than crew members at competing low-cost airlines. The contrast between senior and junior staff has even been reflected in cabin crew uniforms, where senior crew are permitted to wear trousers on board while new female recruits must wear skirts, potentially creating undesirable subcultures within the cabin staff.

In summary, British Airways have experienced a series of significant cultural shifts over the past three decades. In recent years, their management style moved from a sophisticated approach, where industrial action was avoided through high quality HR practices, to macho-management, where union involvement was avoided through threats and intimidation. It seems HRM has been applied on a piecemeal basis, with limited consideration of a long-term strategy or outcomes. The results appear to be the creation of a low-trust culture, with negative effects for staff satisfaction, morale, loyalty and commitment. Demoralised and resentful staff can be potentially disastrous to customer satisfaction.

From an organisational perspective, the extreme cost-cutting methods witnessed over the last three decades have been essential for survival of the company. British Airways' overall progress has been commendable, although there are improvements that could have been made to their management of employment relations and ultimately the firm's performance. The approach to managing employment relations appears to be non-sustainable and counterproductive to producing the culture required to achieve long-term success.

Source: Adapted from Grugulis and Wilkinson, 2002.

Questions

1 Explain employee reactions to culture change initiatives in this case.
2 What lessons can managers learn from this case about managing culture?

Bibliography

Adams, G.B. and Ingersoll, V.H. (1989) 'Painting over old works: the culture of organisations in an age of technical rationality', in Turner, B.A. (ed.) *Organisational Symbolism*, Berlin: Walther De Gruyter.

*Adkins, B. and Caldwell, D. (2004) 'Firm or subgroup culture: where does fitting in matter most?', *Journal of Organizational Behavior*, Vol.25, No.8, 969–78.

Alvesson, M. and Karreman, D. (2007) 'Unraveling HRM: identity, ceremony, and control in a management consulting firm', *Organization Science*, Vol.18, No.4, 711–23.

Anderson, M., Embrey, D., Hodgkinson, C., Hunt, P., Kinchin, B, Morris, P. and Rose, M. (2003) 'The human factors implications for flight safety of recent developments in the airline industry', *Flight Safety Digest*, Vol.22, No.3–4, 1–77.

Anthony, P.D. (1994) *Managing Culture*, Buckingham: Open University Press.

Arkin, A. (2004) 'Wax works', *People Management*, 25 November, 34–7.

Arkin, A. (2007) 'From soft to strong', *People Management*, 6 September, 30–3.

Armstrong, M. (1994) *Performance Management*, London: Kogan Page.

Armstrong, M. (1999) *Employee Reward* (2nd edn.), London: Chartered Institute of Personnel and Development.

Arnold, J., Loan-Clarke, J., Coombs, C., Park, J., Wilkinson, A. and Preston, D. (2003) *Looking Good? The Attractiveness of the NHS as an Employer to Potential Nursing and Allied Health Profession Staff*, Loughborough: Loughborough University.

Balthazard, P.A., Cooke, R.A. and Potter, R.E. (2006) 'Dysfunctional culture, dysfunctional organization: capturing the behavioral norms that form organizational culture and drive performance', *Journal of Managerial Psychology*, Vol.21, No.8, 709–32.

Bamber, G., Hoffer-Gittell, J., Kochan, T. and Von Nordenflycht, A. (2009) *Up in the Air*, New York: Cornell University Press.

Barley, S., Meyer, G. and Gash, D. (1988) 'Cultures of culture: academics, practitioners and the pragmatics of normative control', *Administrative Science Quarterly*, Vol.33, No.1, 24–60.

Barsoux, J.-L. and Manzoni, J.-F. (1997) *Becoming the World's Favourite Airline: British Airways 1980–1993*, Bedford: European Case Clearing House.

Bate, P. (1994) *Strategies for Cultural Change*, London: Butterworth Heinemann.

Blyton, P. and Turnbull, P. (1996) 'Confusing convergence: industrial relations in the European airline industry: a comment on Warhurst', *European Journal of Industrial Relations*, Vol.2, No.1, 7–20.

Blyton, P. and Turnbull, P. (1998) *The Dynamics of Employee Relations* (2nd edn.), London: Macmillan.

Bonache, J. and Fernandez, Z. (2005) 'International compensation costs and benefits of international assignments', in Scullion, H. and Linehan, M. (eds.) *International Human Resource Management*, Basingstoke: Palgrave.

Booth, S.A. and Hamer, K. (2008) 'Corporate culture and financial performance: an empirical test of a UK retailer', *International Journal of Retail & Distribution Management*, Vol.37, 711–27.

Braddy, P.W., Meade, A.W. and Kroustalis, C.M. (2006) 'Organizational recruitment website effects on viewers' perceptions of organizational culture', *Journal of Business and Psychology*, Vol.20, No.4, 525–43.

British Airways (2006) Corporate Responsibility Report 2006/07, Harmondsworth, Great Britain.

*Brown, A. (1998) *Organisational Culture* (2nd edn.), London: Financial Times/Pitman.

Casey, C. (1995) *Work, Self and Society: After Industrialization*, London: Routledge.

Chatman, J.A. and Cha, S.E. (2003) 'Leading by leveraging culture', *California Management Reviews*, Vol.45, No.4, 20–34.

Chen, C.C., Choi, J. and Chi, S.C. (2002) 'Making justice sense of local-expatriate compensation disparity: mitigation by local referents, ideological explanations, and interpersonal sensitivity in China–foreign joint ventures', *Academy of Management Journal*, Vol.45, No.4, 807–26.

Chow, I.H.S. and Liu, S.S. (2009) 'The effect of aligning organizational culture and business strategy with HR systems on firm performance in Chinese enterprises', *International Journal of Human Resource Management*, Vol.20, No.11, 2292–310.

Colling, T. (1995) 'Experiencing turbulence: competition, strategic choice and the management of human resources in British Airways', *Human Resource Management Journal*, Vol.5, No.5, 18–32.

Cooke, R.A. and Rousseau, D.M. (1988) 'Behavioural norms and expectations: a quantitative approach to the assessment of organizational culture', *Group and Organization Studies*, Vol.13, 245–73.

Corke, A. (1986) *British Airways: The Path to Profitability*, London: Frances Pinter.

Cullen, Hon. Lord (1990) *The Public Inquiry into the Piper Alpha Disaster*, London: HMSO.

*Deal, T.E. and Kennedy, A.A. (1982) *Corporate Cultures: The Rites and Rituals of Organisational Life*, Reading, MA: Addison-Wesley.

DeCenzo, D.A. and Robbins, S.P. (2002) *Human Resource Management* (6th edn.), New York: Wiley.

Doyle, P. (1999) 'From the top', *The Guardian*, 4 December.

Engelen, A.B., Brettel, M. and Wiest, G. (2012) 'Cross-functional integration and new product performance: the impact of national and corporate culture, *Journal of International Management*, Vol.18, No.1, 52–65.

Fairbairn, U. (2005) 'HR as a strategic partner: culture change as an American Express case study', *Human Resource Management*, Vol.44, No.1, 79–84.

Fields, D., Chan, A., Aktar, S. and Blam, T. (2006) 'Human resource management strategies under uncertainty: how do US and Hong Kong Chinese companies differ?', *Cross Cultural Management: An International Journal*, Vol.13, No.2, 171–86.

Flamholtz, E. (2001), 'Corporate culture and the bottom line', *European Management Journal*, Vol.19, No.3, 268–75.

Fletcher, C. and Williams, R. (1992) *Performance Appraisal and Career Development* (2nd edn.), Cheltenham: Stanley Thornes.

Flynn, B.B., Zhao, X. and Roth, A. (2007) 'The myth of the dragon: operations management in today's China', *Business Horizons*, Vol.50, 177–83.

French, R. (2010), *Cross-Cultural Management in Work Organisations* (2nd edn.), London: CIPD.

Froese, F.J., Pak, Y.S. and Chong, L.C. (2008) 'Managing the human side of cross-border acquisitions in South Korea', *Journal of World Business*, Vol.43, No.1, 97–108.

Furnham, A. and Gunter, B. (1993) *Corporate Assessment*, London: Routledge.

Garnett, J.L., Marlowe, J. and Pandey, S.K. (2008) 'Penetrating the performance predicament: communication as a mediator or moderator of organizational culture's impact on public organizational performance', *Public Administration Review*, Vol.68, No.2, 266–81.

Georgiades, N. and Macdonell, R. (1998) *Leadership for Competitive Advantage*, London: Wiley.

Gerhart, B. and Fang, M. (2005) 'National culture and human resource management: assumptions and evidence', *International Journal of Human Resource Management*, Vol.16, No.6, 971–86.

Giberson, T.R., Resick, C.J., Dickson, M.W., Mitchelson, J.K., Randall, K.R. and Clark, M.A. (2009) 'Leadership and organizational culture: linking CEO characteristics to cultural values', *Journal of Business and Psychology*, Vol.24, 123–37.

Gold, K.A. (1982) 'Managing for success: a comparison of the private and public sectors', *Public Administration Review*, Vol.42, November–December, 568–75.

Gordon, G. and DiTomaso, N. (1992) 'Predicting corporate performance from organizational culture', *Journal of Management Studies*, Vol.29, 783–98.

Grugulis, I. and Wilkinson, A. (2002) 'Managing culture at British Airways: hope, hype and reality', *Long-Range Planning*, Vol.35, No.2, 179–94.

Hampden-Turner, C. (1990) *Corporate Culture: From Vicious to Virtuous Circles*, London: Hutchinson.

Handy, C.B. (1978) *The Gods of Management*, London: Penguin.

Harris, L.C. and Ogbonna, E. (1998) 'Employee responses to culture change efforts', *Human Resource Management Journal*, Vol.8, No.2, 78–92.

Harris, L.C. and Ogbonna, E. (2011) 'Antecedents and consequences of management-espoused organizational culture control', *Journal of Business Research*, Vol.64, 437–45.

Harrison, R. (1972) 'Understanding your organization's character', *Harvard Business Review*, Vol.5, 119–28.

Harvey, G. and Turnbull, P. (2006) 'Employment relations, management style and flight crew attitudes at low cost airline subsidiaries: the case of British Airways/Go and bmi/bmibaby', *European Management Journal*, Vol.24, No.5, 330–7.

Hatch, M.J. (1997) *Organizational Theory*, Oxford: Oxford University Press.

Hofstede, G. (1980) *Culture's Consequences: International Differences in Work-related Values*, Beverly Hills, CA: Sage.

Hofstede, G. (1991) *Cultures and Organizations: The Software of the Mind*, Maidenhead: McGraw-Hill.

Hofstede, G., Neuijen, B., Daval Ohayv, D. and Sanders, G. (1990) 'Measuring organizational cultures: a qualitative and quantitative study across twenty cases', *Administrative Science Quarterly*, Vol.35, 286–316.

Hofstetter, H. and Harpaz, I. (2011) 'Declared versus actual organizational culture as indicated by an organization's performance appraisal', *International Journal of Human Resource Management*. Available at: http://www.tandfonline.com/doi/abs/10.1080/09585192.2011.561217.

Hong, J.F.L., Easterby-Smith, M. and Snell, R.S. (2006) 'Transferring organizational learning systems to Japanese subsidiaries in China', *Journal of Management Studies*, Vol.43, No.5, 1027–58.

Höpfl, H. (1993) 'Culture and commitment: British Airways', in Gowler, D., Legge, K. and Clegg, C. (eds.) *Case Studies in Organizational Behaviour and Human Resource Management*, London: PCP.

Höpfl, H., Smith, S. and Spencer, S. (1992) 'Values and valuations: corporate culture and job cuts', *Personnel Review*, Vol.21, No.1, 24–38.

Jelinek, M., Smircich, L. and Hirsch, P. (1983) 'Introduction: a code of many colors', *Administrative Science Quarterly*, Vol.28, 331–8.

Kotrba, L.M., Gillespie, M.A., Schmidt, A.M., Smerek, R.E., Ritchie, S.A. and Denison, D.R. (2012) 'Do consistent corporate cultures have better business performance? Exploring the interaction effects', *Human Relations*, Vol.65, No.2, 241–62.

Kotter, J.P. and Heskett, J.L. (1992) *Corporate Culture and Performance,* New York: Free Press.

Kunda, G. (1992) *Engineering Culture: Control and Commitment in a High-Tech Firm*, Philadelphia, PA: Temple University Press.

Lee, S.K.J. and Yu, K. (2004) 'Corporate culture and organizational performance', *Journal of Managerial Psychology*, Vol.19, No.4, 340–59.

Legge, K. (2005) *Human Resource Management: Rhetorics and Realities*, Basingstoke: Macmillan.

Lowe, K., Milliman, J., De Cieri, H. and Dowling, P. (2002) 'International compensation practices: a ten-country comparative analysis', *Asia Pacific Journal of Human Resources*, Vol.40, No.1, 55–78.

Martin, J. (2002) *Organizational Culture: Mapping the Terrain*, London: Sage.

Martin, J., Sitkin, S. and Boehm, M. (1985) 'Founders and the elusiveness of a cultural legacy', in Frost, P., Moore, L., Louis, M., Lundberg, C. and Martin, J. (eds.) *Organizational culture*, Beverly Hills, CA: Sage.

McMillan-Capehart, A. (2005) 'A configurational framework for diversity: socialization and culture', *Personal Review*, Vol.34, No.4, 488–96.

Meek, V.L. (1982) 'Organisational culture: origins and weaknesses', in Salaman, J.G. (ed.) *Human Resource Strategies*, London: Sage.

Merkin, R.S. (2006) 'Uncertainty avoidance and facework: a test of the Hofstede model', *International Journal of Intercultural Relations*, Vol.30, 213–28.

Miah, M.K. and Bird, A. (2007) 'The impact of culture on HRM styles and firm performance: evidence from Japanese parents, Japanese subsidiaries/joint ventures and South Asian local companies', *International Journal of Human Resource Management*, Vol.18, No.5, 908–23.

Moorhead, G. and Griffin, R.W. (1995) *Organizational Behavior* (4th edn.), Boston, MA: Houghton Mifflin.

Morgan, P.I. and Ogbonna, E. (2008) 'Subcultural dynamics in transformation: a multi-perspective study of healthcare professionals', *Human Relations*, Vol.61, No.1, 39–65.

Münch, R. and Smelster, N.J. (1992) *Theory of Culture*, Berkeley, CA: University of California Press.

Ngo, H.N. and Loi, R. (2008) 'Human resource flexibility, organizational culture and firm performance: an investigation of multinational firms in Hong Kong', *International Journal of Human Resource Management*, Vol.19, No.9, 1654–66.

*Ogbonna, E. (1992) 'Organisational culture and human resource management: dilemmas and contradictions', in Blyton, P. and Turnbull, P. (eds.) *Reassessing Human Resource Management*, London: Sage.

Ogbonna, E. and Harris, L.C. (2000) 'Leadership style, organizational culture and performance: empirical evidence from UK companies', *International Journal of Human Resource Management*, Vol.11, No.4, 766–88.

Ogbonna, E. and Wilkinson, B. (1988) 'Corporate strategy and corporate culture: the management of change in the UK supermarket industry', *Personnel Review*, Vol.18, No.6, 10–4.

Peters, T.J. and Waterman, R.H. (1982) *In Search of Excellence: Lessons from America's Best Run Companies*, New York: Harper & Row.

Pettigrew, A. (1990) 'Is corporate culture manageable?', in Wilson, D. and Rosenfield, R. (eds.) *Managing Organisations*, Maidenhead: McGraw-Hill.

Petty, M.M., Beadles, N.A., Lowery, C.M., Chapman, D.F. and Connell, D.W. (1995) 'Relationships between organizational culture and organizational performance', *Psychological Reports*, Vol.76, 483–92.

Pidgeon, N.F. (1991) 'Safety culture and risk management in organizations', *Journal of Cross-Cultural Psychology*, Vol.22, 129–40.

Pinho, J.C., Rodrigues, A.P. and Dibb, S. (2014) 'The role of corporate culture, market orientation and organisational commitment in organisational performance', *Journal of Management Development*, Vol.33, No.4, 374–98.

Ricks, T.E. (1997) *Making the Corps*, New York: Scribner.

Rodrigues, S.B. (2006) 'The political dynamics of organizational culture in an institutionalized environment', *Organization Studies*, Vol.27, No.4, 537–57.

Rohner, R.P. (1984) 'Towards a conception of culture for cross-cultural psychology', *Journal of Cross-Cultural Psychology*, Vol.15, 111–38.

Rousseau, D.M. (1990) 'Assessing organizational culture: the case for multiple methods', in Schneider, B. (ed.) *Organizational Climate and Culture*, San Francisco, CA: Jossey-Bass.

Sackmann, S. (1991) 'Managing organisational culture: dreams and possibilities', in Anderson, J. (ed.) *Communication Yearbook*, Beverly Hills, CA: Sage.

Sackmann, S.A. (2010) 'Culture and performance', pp. 188–224, in Ashkanasy, N., Wilderon, C. and Peterson, M. (eds.) *Handbook of Organizational Culture and Climate*, Thousand Oaks, CA: Sage.

Scheeres, H. and Rhodes, C. (2006) 'Between cultures: values, training and identity in a manufacturing firm', *Journal of Organizational Change Management*, Vol.19, No.2, 223–36.

Schein, E.H. (1984) 'Coming to a new awareness of organizational culture', *Sloan Management Review*, Vol.25, 3–16.

Schein, E.H. (1985) 'How culture forms, develops and changes', in Kilmann, R.H., Saxton, M.J., Serpa, R. and Associates (eds.) *Gaining Control of the Corporate Culture*, San Francisco, CA: Jossey-Bass.

*Schein, E.H. (2004) *Organizational Culture and Leadership: A Dynamic View* (3rd edn.), San Francisco, CA: Jossey-Bass.

Schneider, B. (1990) *Organizational Climate and Culture*, San Francisco, CA: Jossey-Bass.

Schneider, S.C. and Barsoux, J.-L. (2003), *Managing Across Cultures* (2nd edn.), Harlow: FT/Prentice Hall.

Smircich, L. (1983) 'Concepts of culture and organizational analysis', *Administrative Science Quarterly*, Vol.28, 339–58.

Storey, J. (1995) *Human Resource Management: A Critical Text*, London: Routledge.

The Economist (1997) 'British Airways: a Wapping mess', 10 July. Available at: http://www.economist.com/node/370513.

Thom, G. (1997) 'SHAPE – the future of safety in the North Sea', *International Conference on Safety Culture in the Energy Industries*, Aberdeen, September.

Trice, H.M. and Beyer, J.M. (1984) 'Studying organizational cultures through rites and ceremonials', *Academy of Management Review*, Vol.9, 653–69.

Trice, H.M. and Beyer, J.M. (1993) *The Cultures of Work Organisations*, Englewood Cliffs, NJ: Prentice-Hall.

Trompenaars, F. and Hampden-Turner, C. (1997) *Riding the Waves of Culture: Understanding Cultural Diversity in Business*, London: Nicholas Brealey.

Tsui, A.S., Zhang, Z.X., Wang, H., Xin, K.R. and Wu, J.B. (2006) 'Unpacking the relationship between CEO leadership behavior and organizational culture', *Leadership Quarterly*, Vol.17, No.2, 113–37.

Upchurch, M. (2010*) Creating a Sustainable Work Environment in British Airways: Implications of the 2010 Cabin Crew Dispute*, A Report for the Unite Union, Middlesex University.

Van den Steen, E. (2010) 'On the origin of shared beliefs (and corporate culture)', *Rand Journal of Economics*, Vol.41, 617–48.

Warhurst, R. (1995) 'Converging on HRM? Change and continuity in European airlines' industrial relations', *European Journal of Industrial Relations*, Vol.1, No.2, 259–74.

Wilderom, C.P.M., Glunk, U. and Maslowski, R. (2000) 'Organizational culture as a predictor of organizational performance', in Ashkanasy, N.M., Wilderom, C.P.M. and Peterson, M.F. (eds.) *Handbook of Organizational Culture and Climate*, Thousand Oaks, CA: Sage.

Williams, A., Dobson, P. and Watters, M. (1993) *Changing Culture: New Organizational Approaches* (2nd edn.), London: Institute of Personnel Management.

*Williams, R.S. (2002) *Managing Employee Performance: Design and Implementation in Organizations*, London: Thomson Learning.

Wong, A.L.Y., Shaw, G.H. and Ng, D.K.C. (2010) 'Taiwan Chinese managers' personality: is Confucian influence on the wane?', *International Journal of Human Resource Management*, Vol.21, 1108–23.

Wunthow, R. and Witten, M. (1988) 'New directions in the study of culture', *Annual Review of Sociology*, Vol.14, 49–67.

Yu, L. (2007) 'Corporate culture in the numbers', *MIT Sloan Management Review*, Spring, 4–6.

Zhang, X. (2012) 'Understanding Chinese and Western cultures: an exploration of the academic working environment in internationalised higher education', PhD Thesis, Loughborough University.

---

*Useful reading.

PART 2

CONTEMPORARY THEMES AND ISSUES

CHAPTER 10

INTERNATIONAL HUMAN RESOURCE MANAGEMENT – HISTORICAL DEVELOPMENTS, MODELS, POLICIES AND PRACTICES IN MNCs

Michael Dickmann

Introduction

International human resource management (IHRM) has matured substantially since Schuler *et al.* (1993) proposed an integrative framework of strategic IHRM. Dowling (1999) outlines a range of different variables that shape IHRM and provide a distinction to national people management approaches. Amongst these are primarily the higher complexity of organisations operating in diverse national cultures, embedded in distinct national business systems (Whitley, 1992), and having to cope with greater issues of distance, communication, control and coordination. In a simple form, IHRM concerns the strategies, structures, policies and processes used to manage people in organisations that operate in more than one country (Schuler and Jackson, 2005). Therefore, multinational corporations (MNCs), international governmental organisations (IGOs) and international non-governmental organisations (INGOs) and the people working within these are most often analysed. IHRM is to a large extent different from comparative HRM, which is devoted to understanding the people management approaches in different countries and to systematically analyse and compare these (Brewster and Mayrhofer, 2012). Where there are overlaps it often concerns issues such as the convergence of HRM in diverse countries as MNCs can be principal forces that diffuse standardised policies and practices. Comparative HRM issues are predominantly dealt with by Wood and Collings, Chapter 11 in this volume.

Given that IHRM is concerned with global approaches to people strategy, structure, policies and practices, this chapter will first trace the historical development of international organisations and the personnel challenges that these have faced. It will then present approaches that analyse the mindsets, strategic competitive considerations and structural consequences in MNCs. This is followed by a discussion of how organisations expand abroad and what shifts they experience in their HRM. This will lead us firmly into models of IHRM that depict the influencing factors, IHRM choices and goals of MNCs. Then the chapter will explicate a range of topics related to international working, balancing an organisational and individual perspective. In so doing we will develop a set of recommendations for the management of international workers.

Historical development of the multinational organisation

Several thousand years ago organisations operating in foreign regions existed. Some of the key international entities were armed forces – often invading other territories – and religious groups. Four thousand years ago Assyrian commercial organisations were active in several geographical regions, had overseas subsidiaries and employed foreigners. Therefore, it can hardly be said that IHRM is a recent phenomenon. And with large distances, the challenges of communication, transport, diverse norms and values, control and coordination became more stringent. The parallels to modern MNCs throughout history are quite strong, which can be seen at the example of the great trading companies.

The English and Dutch East India companies or the Hudson's Bay Company had huge economic power and huge people challenges associated with their geographical expanse. Distance created a communication and control problem. The firms reacted by sending trusted staff to manage far-flung operations. These would strive to shape operations around their home country social norms and working patterns. In effect, their influence can be described as social coordination. But there were stronger control mechanisms. Goals were set in the head office and financial incentives were developed. Key performance measures were defined and financial measures such as loss at loading of ship and ratio of capital to tonnage existed. Stringent control approaches, such as the use of pursers on ships, sending agents to control local managers and even reading private letters, were implemented while head offices resorted to administrators and experts to run the organisation. The development of control mechanisms, superior communication, normative integration approaches and the professionalisation of management has some parallels to modern MNCs (Carlos and Nicholas, 1988).

Much of the drivers of international expansion have had precursors in history. Seeking resources, new markets and increasing power has been prominent throughout history, but especially after the Second World War the numbers and geographical expansion of MNCs increased dramatically. This was aided by technological advances in transport, communication and information processing. At the same time, trade barriers have reduced and the availability of capital to finance foreign ventures increased (Caligiuri, 2013; Briscoe and Schuler, 2004).

The mindsets of senior leaders

IHRM strategies and structures are intimately linked to the wider business literature and many approaches are based on the seminal works of Perlmutter (1969) and Hennan and Perlmutter (1979). These authors developed a typology that was originally intended to add to the general strategy literature and which was then most eagerly integrated into the IHRM discourse. Their thinking was based on the premise that organisational strategic and structural forms are shaped by administrative heritage and senior management cognitions. Their four types are outlined below.

Ethnocentric – One size fits all and head office knows best.

In an ethnocentric company senior leaders are persuaded that their products and services are attractive both in domestic and foreign markets. In fact, based on their home-country values, norms and experiences they believe in their superior capabilities which lead to an export of their unadjusted corporate approaches. Overall, their way to compete is anchored to these perceived ownership advantages and the scale effects of large production runs. Examples of globally integrated product markets may be the computer hardware industry. It is common for foreign subsidiaries to be set up by a trusted and experienced expatriate from the country of origin. The ethnocentric firm will have a shared company culture and integrated IHRM strategies, structures, policies and practices. Senior career patterns are bound to have intensive connections to the head office and country-of-origin nationals are most likely to be in key positions.

Polycentric – Foreign markets work differently and locals know best.

Head office's top management is persuaded that markets around the world for their products and services vary substantially. Human food products, utilities and some professional services may be industries that can be seen as having a degree of polycentrism. Therefore, the polycentric firm tries to be as locally responsive as possible, which implies strong decision-making powers that are locally distributed. Each foreign operating unit is treated as a distinct national entity. This allows the polycentric to develop (or adapt) products and services that are locally attuned. Moreover, it can be responsive to the national environment (culture, legal context, key institutions) and its customers. Normally, foreign subsidiaries are set up and managed by locals who are rarely moved to the head office in the country of origin. In turn, only few expatriates go abroad to work in foreign affiliates and if so they tend to have a technical expert or financial control function.

Regiocentric – Geographical regions are different, professionals from diverse parts of the specific region know best; within region economies of scale are possible.

The regiocentric corporation has developed diverse management approaches in response to regional variations – it reflects the geographic structure and strategy of the globally operating entity. Within the regions (e.g. North America, Europe, Asia-Pacific, Africa) it is possible to find similar products and services so that some economies of scale are reaped. Regional managers may have driven the geographical expansion and start-ups in their regions. Talent is seen predominantly in regional confines, which may lead to expatriation to countries within the same region but not across to other regions. There is some degree of regional autonomy, but it is rare that European managers were to be promoted to, say, the US head office.

Geocentric – Worldwide approach where each part has unique contribution, ability not nationality counts, integration and scale economies where possible.

A geocentric organisation has a worldwide approach that leaves local autonomy to adapt where it is necessary and coordinates policies where it is beneficial. Therefore, it recognises both local differences and peculiarities (enabling responsiveness) as well as where product or service markets are integrated around the world (enabling efficiency through economies of scale). The geocentric recognises that each operating unit makes a unique contribution. This means that hierarchical structures are less important and that within this worldwide integrated organisation ability is more important than nationality. The 'best talents' are sourced from wherever inside and outside the corporation and these rotate through head office and foreign subsidiaries.

The dualities of integration and responsiveness

The diverse mindsets of senior executives have a strong impact on the strategies, structures, policies and practices of an organisation. A theoretical approach aiming to explore these differences has been developed by Prahalad and Doz (1987). These authors link the decisions about MNCs' structures to the pressures to coordinate corporate activities, control and at times standardise them (integration) with pressures to react to local variations (responsiveness) (see Box 10.1). If management cognitions are right then a firm operating in an ethnocentric product market would need to have high degrees of *operational integration* in order to cope with highly standardised product and strong pressures for economies of scale (e.g. automotive industry). Moreover, if the enterprise has many multinational customers which have the ability to assess and compare prices and service levels around the world its *strategic coordination* needs are high. If the company were to operate in a highly polycentric market then it needs to develop approaches to be able to *respond* successfully *to local variations*. For instance, a firm producing and distributing meats needs to be responsive to human preferences and religious implications (large scale pork sales in the Middle East or beef sales in India are difficult, etc.). Given that global firms are active in diverse industries and that they are exposed to a variety of pressures it is clear that there does not seem to be one best way to locate on Prahalad and Doz's integration–responsiveness grid.

Box 10.1 HRM in practice   **Integration and Responsiveness**

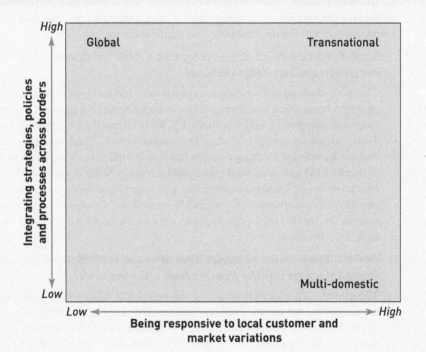

Source: Almond, P. and Tregaskis, O. (2010), Fig. 17.1, p. 649, in Beardwell, J. and Claydon, T. *Human Resource Management: A Contemporary Approach*, 6th ed., Harlow: Pearson.

Questions

Taking your own company or an organisation with which you are familiar:

a. What does it most closely resemble? What factors did you take into consideration?

b. What are the pressures that push 'your' organisation into either integration or responsiveness?

c. Are there differences between global strategy, production, finance or IHRM? If so, what are they and why do they exist?

d. Where do you think your organisation wants to go with its IHRM in future? What external pressures would exert forces for this change? What will it gain from changing its IHRM approach?

Competitive challenges and international HRM configurations

Another milestone in the discussion of business and IHRM configurations – the strategies, structures, policies and practices of organisations – has been the ideas of Bartlett and Ghoshal (1989). They base their arguments on the competitive advantage arguments of Michael Porter, the integration–responsiveness distinction of Prahalad and Doz, Perlmutter's types as well as a range of other strategic literature ideas. Bartlett and Ghoshal present nine cases of large multinational companies and analyse their worldwide strategies, structures and processes. On the one hand, the authors explore the cost advantages of highly integrated firms which suffer responsiveness challenges. On the other hand, highly responsive firms have a quality advantage because of more attractive solutions in the local market but are perceived to have a cost disadvantage. Given that many corporations experience pulls into both the integration as well as the responsiveness direction, at the core of their discussion lies how to overcome this global–local dilemma. This was the dilemma that was underlying Prahalad and Doz's discussion but Bartlett and Ghoshal expanded their ideas by introducing a further dimension – innovation. Porter (1985) had argued that competitive advantage can be derived through focus on key strengths: cost, quality or innovation. Equipped with these ideas, Bartlett and Ghoshal propose four configurations.

Multi-domestic – Polycentric strategy with a dispersed structure that has low degrees of integration and knowledge exchange.

The multi-domestic (also called multinational) has only loose links between the country of origin head office and foreign subsidiaries. Given that markets and competitive environments are seen to vary substantially, there is much autonomy for local subsidiaries. Thus integration levels, including bureaucratic control and social coordination, are low and the knowledge exchange across borders is moderate. This leads to little or no international HRM and personnel management mostly being domestic. This configuration is characterised by local responsiveness and some local innovation but little efficiency in production/management of worldwide operations. Cross-border innovation is low and outside the service sector the firm can only thrive in the long term if local national contexts are radically different.

Global – Ethnocentric strategies, structures and integrated policies and practices with strong knowledge transfer from the head office outwards.

The global corporation is based on the belief that what works in the country of origin works around the world. Products and services are highly integrated and the corporate centre has developed sophisticated coordination and clear control mechanisms. This means that foreign subsidiaries have little autonomy – instead they have the function to learn from the perceived superior experience of the head office. All key decisions, including those with regard to strategy, product development, service delivery, finance, marketing and HRM, are taken in the corporate centre. Central HRM has manifold international functions, for instance with respect to talent recruitment, selection, development, international careers or performance management. Corporate culture and communications are much more important than with the multi-domestic enterprise. The global company competes on cost efficiency through economies of scale and can have highly successful, innovative products, which were conceived and developed in the country of origin. Many companies in the IT, computer or engineering industries, e.g. Dell, General Electric, have strong global characteristics. The risks lie in the one-way innovation process that can stifle local innovation and responsiveness. This may be one of the reasons why Siemens announced in 2010 that it intends that in 2015 half of its products sold in India will be designed and produced in the sub-continent.

International – Intense focus on worldwide innovation leads to high knowledge networking activities.

The international corporation is geared to worldwide innovation and is characterised by high knowledge flows through the network of foreign affiliates and head office. The degree of integration of these firms is less defined (Dickmann and Müller-Camen, 2006). IHRM would need to build a culture that creates space for innovation in all operations and mechanisms to identify and develop product or service ideas. One firm that typifies such a culture is 3M. As such, HR's role would be to source people from anywhere in the world who have a high creative potential. In addition, the position of innovative actors within the MNC and further national and corporate factors influence how innovative HR ideas are transported and adopted within organisations (Edwards *et al.*, 2015). Control pressures may not be as strong as in the global firm since a reasonably high degree of autonomy encourages innovation. Amongst the risks of this approach are cost pressures through intense competition and the dangers of insufficient copyright protection in some countries as well as developments in knowledge exchange and focus that have led to shorter copying/reproduction times.

Transnational – An ideal, networked organisation that has simultaneously high degrees of integration where possible, responsiveness where necessary and knowledge transfer.

While the multi-domestic corporation competes on responsiveness (quality), the global firm on integration (price) and the international firm on innovation (new products or services), the fourth configuration, the transnational, achieves responsiveness, efficiency and worldwide innovation simultaneously. A central argument by Bartlett and Ghoshal is that MNCs need to achieve this ideal configuration over time if they want to survive. Going beyond Porter's argument, any firm is seen to be engaged in all three of these competitive arenas and will not prosper and thrive in the long term if it is not attractive on all these three accounts. In fact, some commentators even go beyond this nowadays in that they add other dimensions or factors such as social legitimacy and being perceived to act responsibly by customers, pressure groups and governments as a condition of survival (Porter and Kramer, 2006). In the transnational, knowledge and resource flows across borders are extensive, which includes frequent international working for staff. The transnational is a highly flexible organisation that operates in a network in which head office is *primus inter pares*, i.e. has a similar role to that of other centres of excellence in the network. Table 10.1 summarises some key strategy, structure and process considerations of the four types. One of the key roles of IHRM in a transnational is further integration through creating and sustaining a strong and shared culture. Similar to the geocentric firm, the transnational remains largely an ideal that is difficult to empirically verify. Their ideas had a tremendous impact in that many academics embarked on research looking at these configurations (e.g. Leong and Tan, 1993; Harzing, 2000) and firms proclaiming to wanting to become transnationals. Amongst the critique to the work of Bartlett and Ghoshal is that it underplays micro-political processes, power and individual agency (Edwards and Rees, 2006).

Dickmann and Müller-Camen (2006) have built on Bartlett and Ghoshal's ideas and focused not on the general configurations but on strategies, structures and processes in international HRM. In so doing they proposed that two key dimensions can be used to measure IHRM. The first, standardisation, is based on Harzing's (2000: 103) argument that there is a continuum of integration/coordination/globalisation advantages on the one side and differentiation/responsiveness/localisation advantages on the other side. In fact, this collapses the integration–responsiveness distinction into one dimension which assesses the 'uniformity' of IHRM approaches. The second dimension, knowledge networking, depicts the communication flows, including control and coordination activities, in an MNC. Sophisticated communication and coordination is important for decisions where internationally operating firms need to be responsive to the local context and where they

Table 10.1 Strategy, structure and processes in the four types of MNCs

Organisational Characteristics	Multinational	Global	International	Transnational
Configuration of assets and capabilities	Decentralised and nationally self-sufficient	Centralised and globally scaled	Sources of core competencies centralised, others decentralised	Dispersed, interdependent and specialised
Role of overseas operations	Sensing and exploiting local opportunities	Implementing parent company strategies	Adapting and leveraging parent company competencies	Differentiated contributions by national units to integrated world-wide operations
Development and diffusion of knowledge	Knowledge developed and retained within each unit	Knowledge developed and retained at the centre	Knowledge developed at the centre and transferred to overseas units	Knowledge developed jointly and shared worldwide

can standardise. In addition, it would allow worldwide innovation based on home and host country nationals' ideas. Dickmann and Müller-Camen showed that the international configuration was not sufficiently specified and proposed a type they call 'cognofederate'. Case study 10.1 in this chapter uses their ideas. A similar approach to understanding the IHRM configurations of major MNCs has been outlined by Farndale *et al.* (2010). The resulting IHRM approaches of major companies such as IBM, Samsung, Shell, Procter & Gamble or Siemens are depicted in Figure 10.1. It makes clear that companies have a choice

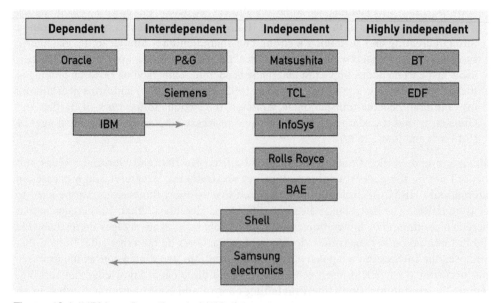

Figure 10.1 IHRM configurations in MNCs

Source: Adapted from Frandale, E. *et al.*, 2010, Context-bound configurations of corporate HR functions in multinational corporations, *Human Resource Management*, Vol.49, No.1, 45–66.

in their IHRM configurations, even if they are in the same industries, and that they move their approaches over time.

Global expansion of MNCs and international HRM implications

Adler and Ghadar's (1990) IHRM model illuminates changes in the role of culture and HRM policies and practices based on the different stages of the product lifecycle (Vernon, 1966). Much of the discussion concentrates on exploring the shifting competitive pressures and resulting expatriate effects. Moreover, the four identified stages explicate how HR activities change in response to cultural and product requirements.

Phase I: Domestic. In the domestic stage the product (or service) as well as HRM focus on the home market. Products are assumed to be novel, unique and successful in the country of origin market. This means that there is no organisational pressure to be culturally sensitive. If there are exports, the products or services will be delivered largely unadjusted. A current example could be a German bakery producing specific dark (black) bread that may be attractive to German expatriates or some highly health conscious customers in the UK precisely because of its different taste or high fibre content. HR in a domestic firm is attuned to the country of origin and there are very few international HR implications as expatriation, frequent international flying or cross-cultural seminars will not be important. Given that the head office is crucial (and foreign operations are not key), international work is not seen as good for individuals' careers. If there are international workers, product or technical competencies will be important. Further HRM implications are outlined in Table 10.2.

Phase II: International. Over time, competition increases in the home country so that foreign markets become more attractive for the firm. Overseas plants and subsidiaries may have been set up and divisional structures have been designed. Cultural sensitivity becomes more important than before because of the larger foreign workforce. However, HR approaches are designed in the corporate centre and aim to devise effective control mechanisms of the international operations. Having superior experience with the production technology and processes, the international also strives to manage knowledge transfer outwards. Therefore, seminars to increase cultural sensitivity and adaptability are introduced. There is now more expatriation to get the 'job' done but it is not integrated into general career planning so that re-entry to the country of origin is extremely difficult.

Phase III: Multinational. The multinational stage takes place when the product (service) reaches maturity and is characterised by strong competition resulting in an intensive efficiency focus. An example here could be many computer hardware firms that source standardised components from a variety of sources and compete on price. Management's focus on cultural sensitivity relaxes because the cost reduction pressures lead to a strong focus on economies of scale. Therefore the coordination of resources, production and supply-chains through integration has become paramount. HR approaches strive to establish a strong company culture and much of staff sourcing is predominantly linked to the seamless integration with the country of origin. As the foreign operations have become more important, the leadership of these is seen as more core to an individual's career. Very good performers who are culturally sensitive are selected as expatriates and 're-entry' after their global work is seen as less difficult than in earlier phases.

Phase IV: Global. The fourth stage, global, is a theoretical speculation that assumes that with increasing globalisation of business and higher competition MNCs have to operate in all three earlier phases simultaneously, finding ideal solutions to global challenges.

Table 10.2 Globalisation and human resource management

	Phase I Domestic	Phase II International	Phase III Multinational	Phase IV Global
Primary orientation	Product or service	Market	Price	Strategy
Strategy	Domestic	Multi-domestic	Multinational	Global
Worldwide strategy	Allow foreign clients to buy product/service	Increase market internationally, transfer technology abroad	Source, produce and market internationally	Gain global strategic competitive advantage
Staffing expatriates	None (few)	Many	Some	Many
Why sent	Junket	To see control or transfer technology	Control	Coordination and integration
Whom sent		'OK' performers, salespeople	Very good performers	High-potential managers and top executives
Purpose	Reward	Project 'to get job done'	Project and career development	Career and organisational development
Career impact	Negative	Bad for domestic career	Important for global career	Essential for executive suite
Professional re-entry	Somewhat difficult	Extremely difficult	Less difficult	Professionally easy
Training and development	None	Limited	Longer	Continuous throughout career
For whom	No one	Expatriates	Expatriates	Managers
Performance appraisal	Corporate bottom line	Subsidiary bottom line	Corporate bottom line	Strategic positioning
Motivation assumption	Money motives	Money and adventure	Challenge and opportunity	Challenge, opportunity, advancement
Rewarding	Extra money to compensate for foreign hardship		Less generous, global packages	
Career 'fast track'	Domestic	Domestic	Token international	Global
Executive passport	Home country	Home country	Home country, token foreigners	Multinational
Necessary skills	Technical and managerial	Plus cultural adaption	Plus recognising cultural differences	Plus cross-cultural interaction, influence and synergy

Source: Adapted from Adler and Ghadar, 1990; Beardwell and Claydon, 2010: 659.

It has, therefore, some similarities with the geocentric mindset in terms of finding the right balance of integration and responsiveness. The firm needs to build sophisticated networks internally and externally to compete successfully. HR works towards global strategic competitive advantage, which is linked to identifying, developing, deploying and performance managing the best individuals independent from their national origins. This is also seen to facilitate a rapid, globally responsive design of products and services at low costs. The global enterprise will have many expatriates from diverse countries and foreign experience becomes key for executive careers.

Adler and Ghadar's (1990) framework can be criticised as concentrating too strongly on expatriates, instead of the whole staff of the organisation or other forms of international work. Moreover, issues of creating competitive advantage through responsiveness and innovation could be explored in more depth. Further, the distinction between the international and the multinational stage could be clearer. In addition, the international expansion of knowledge-intensive firms has sometimes been extremely fast and has happened simultaneously in diverse countries. For instance, some companies conducted their initial growth phases in the US and Europe simultaneously, thereby throwing the stage approach into doubt. Lastly, Milliman and Von Glinow (1990) propose an organisational lifecycle model that takes into account that modern firms have more than just one product or service.

Strategic international HRM in MNCs

Schuler, Dowling and De Cieri (1993) have suggested the probably best-known model of IHRM. Their framework lists exogenous and endogenous factors and structural components of MNCs. It then depicts their link to strategic IHRM (SIHRM), distinguishing SIHRM, SIHRM functions, policies and practices. The strength of the framework is in its broad, descriptive conceptual approach that also takes concerns and goals of the MNC into account. While the model has been criticised because it does not explore micro-political processes between the head office and its foreign affiliates it, nevertheless, provides a very broad picture of the elements and links of SIHRM. In 1999, De Cieri and Dowling, simplified the SIHRM framework and added nuances in the areas of MNC structure and strategy (see Figure 10.2).

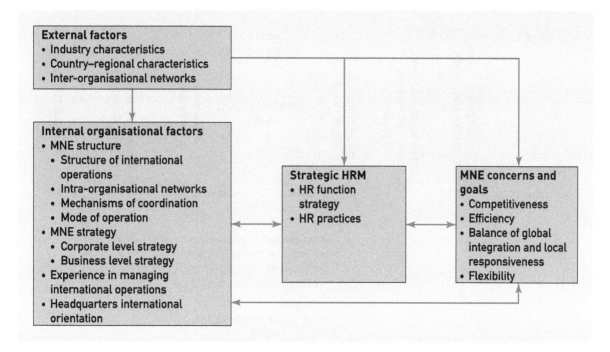

Figure 10.2 A Model of strategic HRM in MNCs
Source: Adapted from De Cieri and Dowling, 1999.

International HRM policies and practices – working abroad

Organisational and individual perspectives in international mobility

We saw that international work is not a recent phenomenon but working abroad is becoming more common and varied (Brookfield, 2014). The increasing globalisation of markets and competitive activities as well as the broad political, economic, social and technological factors underlying this have been explored elsewhere in this book.

Harris *et al.* (2003) have suggested an expatriation cycle to outline the process of international work starting from strategic considerations and ending in the return of the expatriate. Dickmann and Baruch (2011) have expanded this idea in two senses while focusing on global careers (see Figure 10.3). First, their cycle explicitly distinguishes individual and organisational perspectives, embodying the dual dependency idea. Second, their timeframe goes beyond the immediate return to cover career effects over time. This model is taken up to guide the remainder of the discussion in this chapter. In so doing, it is slightly adjusted to take account of both international mobility and global career issues.

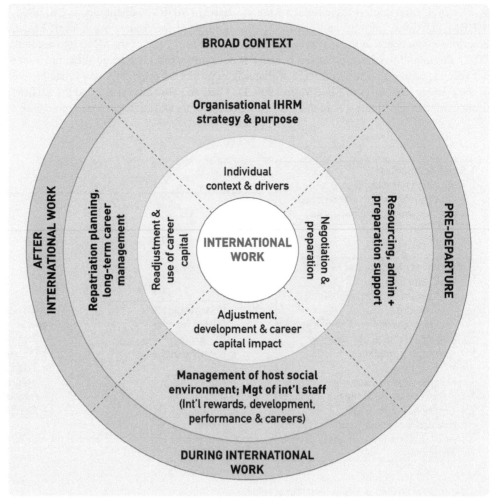

Figure 10.3 Individual and organizational areas in international work

Source: Adapted from Dickmann and Baruch, 2011.

I Dimensions and patterns of international work

Peiperl and Jonsen (2007) argue that the variations in international working can be captured by a two-dimension matrix that outlines types of global careers. One dimension is time spent away from the individual's home culture or market, and the other one the amount of interaction across cultures and markets. Baruch *et al.* (2013) propose that context should be added to time, and content, resulting in seven dimensions: time spent away, intensity of international contact (from flexpatriates to expatriates); breadth of interaction (work-related or holistic), legal context of stay (illegal, legal), international work instigator (individuals themselves, their organisations), cultural gap (size of differences) and specific role differences (work with much or little need for local sensitivity and understanding). Their distinction resulted in 20 types of international work – the dozen types probably most discussed in the literature are outlined in Table 10.3.

Much of the research about how to select, develop and manage expatriates has been conducted on traditional company-sponsored assignees and/or HRM leaders commenting on their international mobility approaches. While more insights relating to self-initiated expatriates recently emerged, the discussion below will reflect this information asymmetry.

II The broad context: drivers of international work

There are few areas at work where the dependency of individuals on their employers and, in turn, the importance of staff performance for the organisation is so high. This is why Larsen (2004) calls this relationship one of 'dual dependency'. The key strategic drivers for organisations include control and coordination considerations, global leadership development aims, skills gap filling and knowledge creation, transfer and exploitation (Edström and Galbraith, 1977; Dowling *et al.*, 2008). Above, we have explicated many of these factors in relation to corporate configurations. Below, the operational motives of quality of international resourcing (including acquisition, development and retention of talent), the speed of response to skills needs, the launching of new initiatives and the management of global careers will be discussed. But first we will explore individual drivers of working abroad.

Key antecedents include family and social background variables such as language command, friendship and familial ties with an impact on the willingness of individuals to live in geographical separation. Moreover, early experiences such as having lived or travelled overseas influences the decision about an international career (Tharenou, 2003). Lastly, personality traits such as inquisitiveness or resilience have an impact on how successful individuals may be working abroad (Bird and Osland, 2004) and may influence their viewpoints.

Table 10.3 Key types of international work

Being Abroad		
Traditional, organisation-sponsored long-term expatriation (longer than 1 year)	Short-term, organisation-sponsored expatriation (shorter than 1 year)	Self-initiated expatriation to work in an organisation, not sponsored by the employer
Inpatriation (organisation-sponsored, to the head office)	International project work	Flexpatriation (frequent business travel to different countries)
Long-term legal/illegal immigration	International sabbaticals	Virtual global work
Cross-border commuting	Short-term voluntary work and work experiences	Self-initiated foreign study (schools or universities)

Individual		Organisational	
Antecedents	*Individual motives*	*Operational considerations*	*Strategic drivers*
• Family and social background • Early experiences • Personality	• Career and development • Organisational factors and inducements • Individual interests and drivers • Family and partner considerations • National and location-specific factors	• Quality of resourcing • Speed of response • Management of global careers • Launching new initiatives	• Control • Coordination • Global leadership development • Knowledge creation transfer and exploitation

Figure 10.4 Individual and organisational drivers for international work

Source: Adapted from Dickmann and Baruch, 2011: 120.

Individual motivations to work abroad are manifold but can be discussed using five broad categories (see Figure 10.4). First, career and developmental motives are highly pertinent for foreign assignees, often being the most important driver (Hippler, 2009; Stahl and Cerdin, 2004). Often people value the chance to acquire global business acumen, cross-cultural sensitivity, gather foreign experiences and learn unusual capabilities (Tung, 1998). While these drivers appear particularly strong for company-sent expatriates, they are also important for self-initiated foreign workers (Yan *et al.*, 2002; Doherty *et al.*, 2011).

A second important driver refers to individual interests, experiences and drives. These motivations seem to be particularly strong for self-initiated expatriates (Inkson *et al.*, 1997; Andresen *et al.*, 2014). They include drivers such as a thirst for adventure, travel or life change (Richardson and Mallon, 2005), personal challenge, a quest for understanding foreign cultures or a desire to live abroad (Doherty and Dickmann, 2013).

The third, organisational, factor is sometimes key for assigned (company-sponsored) expatriates. Organisational drivers include the likely financial impact (Yurkiewicz and Rosen, 1995) but also non-financial incentives such as the expected length of stay, administrative support mechanisms and repatriation arrangements (Dickmann *et al.*, 2008; Hippler, 2009).

The fourth set of decision influences, family and partner considerations, is often perceived to be a barrier to international mobility. For instance, dual career issues – when the partner has a career of their own and does not want to suspend it – is seen to be increasingly important and so authors argue that the willingness of the partner/family to relocate should be taken into account in the assignment decision (Harvey, 1995; Sparrow *et al.*, 2004). However, family considerations can also be an incentive to expatriate as in the case when parents regard the host country education system as superior (Richardson and Mallon, 2005; Dickmann, 2013).

Fifth, national and location-specific considerations will have an impact on individuals' decisions to work abroad. The influence of host culture, history, language, climate, and security considerations has been documented (Yurkiewicz and Rosen, 1995; Black *et al.*, 1992; Haslberger, 2005). Recent studies have also outlined specific location influences when analysing particular cities. Dickmann and Mills' (2009) study of London and Haslberger and Zehetner's (2008) research in Vienna identified factors such as the tolerance of citizens or the city's reputation for business/specific sectors that were regarded as attractive by expatriates and had influenced their decision to relocate.

Table 10.4 Some advantages and drawbacks of sending home-country nationals to work abroad

Advantages	Drawbacks
• Efficient coordination	• Adaptation of expatriates uncertain
• Effective communication	• Selection procedures prone to errors
• Direct control of foreign operations	• High costs
• Diffusing central values, norms and beliefs throughout the organisation	• Difficulty in constant mentoring during stay abroad
• Broadening the view of expatriates and chance of growth for expatriates	• Complicated personnel planning procedures
• Rapid substitution of expatriates possible	• Government restrictions
• No need of well-developed international internal labour-market	• Private life of expatriates severely affected
• Appropriate for entry into international business	• Reduced career opportunities for locals
• Country-of-origin innovation	• High complexity for tax and benefits possible
• Attractiveness for home-country careerists	• High failure rates
	• Utilisation of career capital after return can be difficult
	• Potential home – host country frictions
	• Reintegration may be difficult

Source: Adapted from Harris *et al.*, 2003.

The discussion above has shown a variety of drivers why individuals go to work abroad. At times, we have distinguished self-initiated from organisation-sponsored assignees, but there are many more diverse forms of international careers. These are explored in the section below.

III Pre-departure: resourcing, admin support and preparation

Once a decision has been made to fill a position in a foreign affiliate a number of considerations should take place. Just because the job has been done by a country-of-origin expatriate hitherto does not mean that this has to continue. The above discussion of organisational drivers, especially those related to control, coordination, skills filling and knowledge transfer reasons, can give a steer as to where the new incumbent may come from and what capability set she or he needs. It has become more common for companies to task their (traditional) expatriates with identifying and developing a local successor which would in most cases be more cost-effective and would alleviate the problem of perceived 'glass ceilings' for local careers and mistrust between locals and foreigners (Hailey and Harry, 2008). Even self-initiated expatriates are suggested as a way to reduce the high costs of expatriation (as these tend to be on local contracts) and the reduction of some (mostly culture-shock related, see below) risks (Howe-Walsh and Schyns, 2010). Moreover, other forms of international work such as flexpatriation or virtual leadership may be considered.

Assuming that traditional expatriation is selected, what are the factors and organisational approaches that impact on the success of the assignment? Table 10.5 outlines a whole range of issues. In the pre-assignment phase these include job design, selection (including negotiation and contracting), administrative and logistical support as well as further preparation. In terms of job design, factors that facilitate the expatriate's adjustment to the local culture are important. As such, individuals would benefit from autonomy and discretion as well as realistic job expectations. Adjustment is also facilitated when the individual is 'on top of the job' as in the case when the position involves the use of capabilities that the person possesses and/or when the job is similar to an earlier one (Dickmann and Baruch, 2011).

The selection of expatriates has been extensively covered by the literature. Dowling *et al.* (2008) summarise the discussion on selection factors and link the decisions to the following: technical ability, cross-cultural suitability, family requirements, country/cultural

Table 10.5 Organisational activities to foster successful international adjustment

	Area	Organisational Action	Some Characteristics That Would Help
PRE-ASSIGNMENT	Design	• Give discretion in the job • Clarify job expectations and responsibilities • Gain agreement as to job objectives between individual, home and host country • Provide overlap with incumbent to facilitate 'hitting the ground running' • Align any other conflicting expectations regarding performance standards, job, working environment, etc.	*Job Design Choices:* • In most cases, choose a job that the candidate will find only a slight stretch. Adjustment to a new team and new culture is already a challenge. • For earmarked top leaders the stretch might be larger. This might include changing divisions, functions or more radical job content alterations.
	Selection and Negotiation	• Sophisticated selection factoring in personality factors, soft competencies, performance and potential • Involve partner in selection and consider extended family responsibilities • Use psychometric and other instruments and give feedback to candidate and partner regarding cross-cultural strengths and weaknesses • Match candidate's profile to inter-cultural job demands of organisation and international vacancies • Provide realistic job, local team and country previews (and also 'look–see visits')	*Individual Characteristics:* • Self-confidence • Willingness to learn about different cultures and business environments • Interpersonal orientation • Good communication skills • Willingness to critically review own values and norms • Openness
DURING ASSIGNMENT	Administrative and Logistical Support	• Provide effective administrative support in relation to the international mobility framework, compensation and benefit questions • Provide good logistical support and high quality in terms of moving abroad, accommodation (abroad and at home), health insurance, banking, schooling, return visits, etc. • Guarantee security as much as possible and provide protection in high risk areas • Monitor own and service provider activities and gain expatriate feedback for improvements	*Administrative Issues:* • Set an end-of-assignment date in order to avoid assignments that 'drag on' • Consider periodically whether the assignment objectives have been fulfilled and, therefore, keep the option of early return open • Provide support through corporate sponsor, mentors and coaches who proactively approach the assignees in regular intervals
	Social Environment	• Encourage local national employees to provide support to new assignees and families • Collect and provide information regarding social, religious, sport, cultural organisations and enable expatriates and their families to join these • Develop social support networks • Provide an Employee Assistance Programme (EAP) for people experiencing culture shock and train local manages to recognise symptoms	*Social Facilitation:* • Consider setting up local 'buddies' for expats and partners • Support partners in carving out meaningful roles for themselves • Design organisational approaches that encourage host country nationals to view expatriates as 'ingroup' rather than 'outgroup' • Brief and prepare locals with liaison roles

Area		Organisational Action	Some Characteristics That Would Help
DURING ASSIGNMENT	Training and Development	• Provide rigorous training for increased job demands; ideally linked to organisational configuration • Provide inter-cultural training (pre-departure and post-arrival) and language classes • Include partner in the training • Provide team-building initiatives together with new team • Provide (where useful) extensive briefings to local employees regarding role and function of assignee • Enable interaction with repatriates from assignment region/area	*Training and Development Considerations:* • Distinguish between local position requirements, global or international control, coordination and innovation responsibilities • Distinguish between general communication skills and development of personality of individual • Distinguish between work and social environment
	Reward Management	• Create salary transparency and avoid large pay differentials between locals and expatriates • Understand individual drivers to link compensation and incentives to these • Minimise insecurity and tax exposure to both individuals and organisations • Understand the diverse social security and taxation systems and find a solution that balances organisational and individual needs	*Design Considerations:* • Transparency if possible • Perceived equity within expatriates population • Balancing need for attracting highly capable individuals with cost saving pressures • Minimise personal risks to individuals (tax, social benefits) • Minimise organisational risks (e.g. corporate tax) • Keep administrative complexity low
	Career Issues	• Link selection to individual's long-term career plan and organisational career management (avoid 'out of sight, out of mind' syndrome) • Foster the acquisition of knowing how, knowing why and knowing whom capital • Design support mechanisms such as business sponsors, formal and informal networks, shadow career planning	*Career Planning:* • The mutual dependency of individuals and organisation is especially strong during an international assignment. There is a case for more long-term career planning which looks likely to aid retention. • Consider NOT promoting on the way out – instead, actively consider to promote upon repatriation • Consider expatriation to centres of excellence and ways how to apply insights and use social capital in the job upon return

Source: Based on Dickmann and Baruch, 2011, further developments.

requirements, language and MNC requirements. Some of these requirements (such as the MNC drivers) have been discussed above. Technical ability is highly valued by MNCs (Sparrow *et al.*, 2004) but it is clear that technical competence is not enough in a foreign context. Often it is crucial how the person adapts to local processes and customs. The cross-cultural suitability depends also on the personality of individuals. Caligiuri (2000) has linked these to the Big 5 personality theory and other authors have proposed cultural empathy, cultural intelligence, diplomacy, openness and adaptability as influencing cross-border work success (e.g. Ang *et al.*, 2007). In reality, many MNCs do not employ highly sophisticated selection criteria in relation to the international work and adjustment – instead, they seem to use predominantly technical ability, performance, language and willingness to go (Harris *et al.*, 2003; Dowling *et al.*, 2008).

Box 10.2 HRM in practice	Selection Systems	
	Formal	Informal
OPEN	• Clearly defined criteria • Clearly defined measures • Training for selectors • Open advertising of vacancy (internal/external) • Panel discussions	• Less defined criteria • Less defined measures • Limited training for selectors • No panel discussions • Open advertising of vacancy • Recommendations
CLOSED	• Clearly defined criteria • Clearly defined measures • Training for selectors • Panel discussions • Nominations only (networking/reputation)	• Selectors' individual preferences determine criteria and measures • No panel discussions • Nominations only (networking/ reputation)

Source: Adapted from Harris and Brewster, 1999.

Questions

1. What selection approach does your organisation/an organisation that you are familiar with use?
2. Why does it use it?
3. What are the advantages? What are the risks?

The international mobility selection systems can be categorised as either closed or open and either formal or informal (Harris and Brewster, 1999) (see Box 10.2).

The less formal approaches have less defined criteria and measures and are linked by the authors to a 'coffee machine system' (Harris and Brewster, 1999: 497) in which chance encounters and word-of-mouth have a strong role in candidate identification and selection. Building international management expertise and global leaders becomes more important to MNCs (GMAC, 2008), a trend that may be associated with more closed selection systems if organisations identify their high potentials and are keen to manage their global careers.

For the individual it would be important to see why she or he wants to embark on a global career and to negotiate the monetary and non-monetary conditions. Key considerations are the expatriation salary, social and tax implications (see Dickmann and Baruch, 2011, Chapters 10 and 11 for an in-depth discussion). Moreover, family support (especially for a working partner or when there are health/care issues), security, travel, as well as a range of administrative and logistical help should be defined. Lastly, further pre-departure and post-arrival developmental help should be discussed. In many cases the family of the expatriate should be integrated in the discussions and negotiations. A 'look – see' visit can help to gain more realistic expectations.

IV During international work: host environment, individual adjustment, development, careers and management of international staff

Social environment and host country national liaison role. How host country co-workers treat expatriates has an important influence on their adjustment (Huang *et al.*, 2005; Toh and DeNisi, 2007). This can be linked to the host-country national's role:

- Information-gathering role to help expatriates to understand the local organisation and local culture (Toh and DeNisi, 2007; Vance *et al.*, 2009).

- Social and emotional support role that helps expatriates to socialise and adapt to the host country's values, norms and behaviours (Toh and DeNisi, 2007).
- Training and coaching role to improve knowledge transfer (Toh and DeNisi, 2005) and to give career guidance (Vance *et al.*, 2009).
- Role of good communicator to improve communication between host-country nationals and expatriates, which may avoid conflicts (Vance *et al.*, 2009).

These roles are normally not specified in the job description of the host-country nationals and are to a large extent voluntary (Toh and DeNisi, 2007). Therefore, Templer (2010) argues that host country nationals can be unwilling to perform these roles for a range of reasons. Seeing expatriates not as members of one's own group (e.g. as outgroup) would be one of the drivers why host country nationals are not behaving in a more constructive and helpful way (Toh and DeNisi, 2007).

How can this unwillingness to help expatriates be mitigated? Toh and DeNisi suggest that organisations could draw up policies and incentives to alleviate the situation and to encourage more helpful approaches. These could include an organisational culture that values support, rewards for helping foreign assignees and a fair salary level when comparing home and host compensation. In addition, MNCs could develop cross-border coordination approaches when selecting expatriates, moderate the pay differential between expatriates and locals, use more transparent promotion processes and criteria and prepare the host country's nationals for the arrival of the foreign assignees (Bonache *et al.*, 2009; Leung *et al.*, 2009).

Training and development for international careers and expatriate work has been extensively discussed (Dowling *et al.*, 2008), and many MNCs make cross-cultural training available to their international assignees and to some extent to their families (GMAC, 2008). However, the investments in these activities remain often quite low (Doherty and Dickmann, 2012). Already in 1987, Mendenhall *et al.*, drew up a model of cross-cultural training (see Figure 10.5) that distinguished

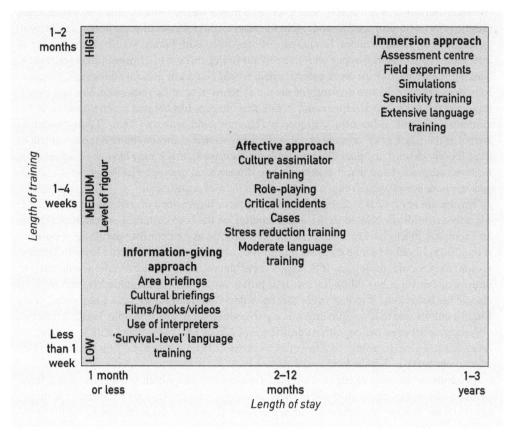

Figure 10.5 Cross-cultural training approach

Source: Adapted from Mendenhall *et al.*, 1987: 338.

training methods, their rigor and duration in relation to cultural novelty and interaction. They argue that in a situation where the cultural stretch is low and the length of stay is short *information-giving* approaches would be suitable. These would include area and cultural briefings, the use of books and films from the destination country and moderate, 'survival-level' language training. *Affective* approaches would be more suitable when there are moderate levels of cultural differences and the stay is planned to be up to one year. These could consist of role-playing, critical incident discussions, case work, culture assimilation activities, stress reduction training and more intensive, yet still moderate levels of language instruction. In these situations the training length would also be more extensive. The longest training is seen to be needed for people going into destinations which are culturally highly distinct and who would stay for long terms akin to traditional expatriation. Mendenhall *et al.* (1987) suggest an *immersion* approach that includes assessment centres, field experiments, simulations, sensitivity training and extensive language instruction.

Obviously, the expatriates openness to other cultures (see above) and her or his willingness to act upon the new insights and to attempt to adjust to the new environment have a major impact on how effective the training is likely to be. Pre-departure and post-arrival training and experience-based learning is only one step in the process of working successfully abroad. In addition, learning and cultural adaptation is a process which benefits from monitoring and feedback by others (e.g. a host national liaison person).

Adjustment to the local environment

The process of cultural learning when individuals are living in a foreign culture is called adjustment or cultural adaptation. In this sense it is akin to acculturation. The concept is key in the global mobility literature as highly adjusted individuals are seen to perform well at work (Bhaskar-Shrinivas *et al.*, 2005). Much research builds on the work of Black and colleagues (1988; 1989) who proposed a model that consists of three facets of adjustment: interaction, general and work adjustment. Socialising successfully with locals would be an element of interaction adjustment. Coping with the general living context of climate, health provision, banking, shopping, outside work entertainment would be part of general adjustment. Successfully mastering the diverse demands of the job in terms of specific responsibilities and expectations is related to work adjustment. While this concept has created much attention in the academic literature, it has been critiqued by Thomas and Lazarova (2006). Their key points were that the Black *et al.* concept is not sufficiently rooted in theory (more a measurement of three loosely defined and partially overlapping dimensions), that it may have overlooked other facets of adaptation and that it assumes a one-dimensional concept. Haslberger *et al.* (2013) pick up these points and develop a more nuanced view of adjustment.

Haslberger *et al.* (2013) distinguish between three dimensions of adjustment. The first is cognitive confidence related to the understanding of the host culture. For instance, Akpos, an expatriate in England, may experience how courteous and conflict-avoiding people are (Fox, 2005). Even when he stepped on the foot of an Englishman on the London Underground they would apologise. But Akpos' confidence level was lowered once he tried to jump a queue for a bus when he was in a hurry. Angry reactions made him rethink and change his behaviour. It took a while that he understood that fairness was a key value in the English culture and that not queuing was a grave violation of this principle. Haslberger *et al.* differentiate between the cognitive confidence of Akpos (not quite being able to explain the reactions to queue jumping) and the effectiveness of behaviour (not doing it again). Their adjustment curve is depicted in Figure 10.6.

In addition, the authors suggest a third curve of emotions which often start of in a 'honeymoon phase' (Oberg, 1960). Over time, however, the novelty and excitement of living in a foreign, maybe even exotic, country wears off and the daily 'grind' of coping with differences that one may not understand fully affects emotions. Eventually people surface from their 'culture shock' (Ward *et al.*, 2001) and both their emotions and cognitive confidence levels are likely to improve. Not everybody has to experience culture shock, in fact, if

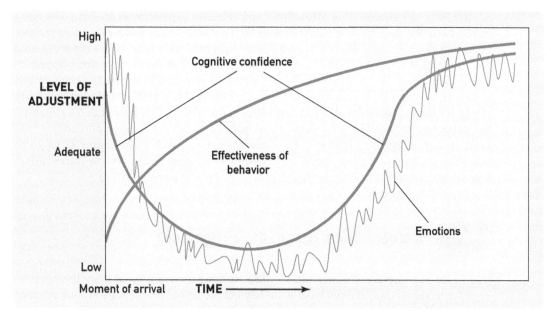

Figure 10.6 Adjustment curve with culture shock
Source: Haslberger *et al.*, 2013.

persons have had recent in-depth experience with the host culture their chances of avoiding culture shock are high (Takeuchi *et al.*, 2005). Overall, the adjustment patterns of individuals are likely to vary substantially and personal characteristics (Caligiuri, 2000), specific experiences, work and family influences and the host country context have a strong influence on the expatriate's adjustment. For instance, work adjustment is negatively influenced by role ambiguity and positively by role novelty (Kawai and Mohr, 2015).

International reward management

It is possible to have a variety of perspectives on the reward and performance elements in international mobility. In this chapter we will predominantly look at the individual and organisational issues. Employee pay and wider benefits can influence the sourcing, performance management and retention activities and outcomes of companies (Beardwell and Claydon, 2010). In order to increase the chances of international assignees being motivated and productive, Suutari and Tornikoski (2001) suggest that mobility programmes need to have well-designed rewards programmes. There is a range of choices that MNCs have when designing international compensation approaches. Organisations often want to achieve consistency, comparability and equity amongst their international staff group. Other considerations include cost-effectiveness of global transfers and ease of systems administration (Dowling *et al.*, 2008). As outlined above in the drivers of international work section, expatriates often seek financial protection, location comfort and financial advancement.

Seven international reward approaches can be identified: negotiation/ad hoc, balance sheet, localisation, lump sum, cafeteria, regional systems and global (Briscoe and Schuler, 2004). All try to balance the conflicting pressures of attempting to be efficient and to save costs versus attracting highly capable individuals to work abroad. The professional services firm Ernst and Young (2009) argues that companies increasingly tend to use either a home-based or a host-based approach. The home-based approach starts with exploring the salary, benefits and other remuneration elements of the individual in her or his country of current work. Within a spirit of not making the expatriate worse off, incentive components (such as housing allowances, hardship allowances, relocation money, educational grants) and equalisation adjustments (primarily cost-of-living adjustments, tax equalisation allowances and benefits adjustments) are being factored in to reach the foreign compensation deal. The host country-based compensation approach can also be called the 'going rate approach' as it orients itself on the host country market rates of pay and benefits. The advantages of the home-country approach are in increasing the willingness of individuals to go on an assignment as they stand to benefit financially. It can, however, be administratively complex and is often highly costly for the organisation (Doherty and Dickmann, 2012). The host-country approach has gained more popularity in recent times because of its cost-saving potential. However, it may struggle to find suitable candidates from high wage countries to go to low wage countries. A more specific discussion which models the diverse international remuneration approaches can be found in Dickmann and Baruch (2011).

Career capital during the assignment

One of the key interests for individuals when working abroad is to advance their career. In order to assess this, authors have gone beyond the actual promotions to look at modern career theory. Using a resource-based view DeFillippi and Arthur (1994) outline how to behave in order to acquire career capital. Career capital proponents such as Inkson and Arthur (2001) argue that individuals will benefit from investing in their skills, knowledge, abilities (know how), their social networks (know whom) and in mustering their inner drives and motivations (know why). International assignments have a substantial impact on these three ways of knowing with individuals and organisations devising strategies and interventions to increase career capital (Parker *et al.*, 2009; Dickmann and Doherty, 2010).

This concept is also called the intelligent career and while it is likely that individuals will acquire new skills, knowledge and abilities when working abroad and change their outlook on life (which is linked to their identity and knowing why) the social capital effects of foreign work may be less positive (Dickmann and Harris, 2005). Expatriates normally gain more international social contacts and are certain to acquire more host country connections. However, they are often 'off the radar screen' and, consequently, their home country networks may suffer. This is particularly damaging if the career system in their company is highly informal and if they are away from the head office where key promotion decisions are taken. This, then, can endanger their career path with a career wobble (Doherty *et al.*, 2008) upon return being likely. Therefore, designing support mechanisms such as business sponsors or mentors may help the expatriates to have a more positive experience and repatriation. Moreover, shadow career planning and the explicit acknowledgement and endorsement of the expatriate's need for home networking can help to reduce the risks for assignees (Harris and Dickmann, 2005).

Overall, however, the large majority of expatriates state in interviews that they have acquired career capital and that they are confident they are more valuable to the organisation. In turn, their employers devise systems so that these expatriates can add to their career capital as this is seen to be positive for current performance and long-term leadership pipelines in organisations (Dickmann and Doherty, 2010). This makes it crucial for both the individuals and the organisations that repatriates can use their expanded skills, insights and networks in their home countries.

V After international work: repatriation, retention and long-term career issues

Repatriation is sometimes seen as the 'toughest assignment of all' (Hurn, 1999). The reasons relate to the problems that some individuals and organisations face when returning from working abroad and have been captured in a range of surveys (GMAC, 2008) and articles (Lazarova and Cerdin, 2007; Stahl and Cerdin, 2004).

The organisational perspective

The employment and promotion perspective of repatriates is worse in times of economic hardship and slow growth (Huang *et al.*, 2005) so that the banking and sovereign debt crises of the early years of the third millennium decreased the positive prospects of returners. In addition, some firms have poor planning processes so that they have not assigned attractive positions for their returning assignees. This may be compounded when an enterprise is undergoing a restructuring as outlined by Dickmann *et al.* (2006) in the case of a tobacco firm that forced 40 percent of repatriates to leave. In turn, many expatriates feel that they have become more marketable and may look for new challenges outside their organisations (Dickmann *et al.*, 2006). Overall, there is a repatriation and retention challenge. In order to alleviate these problems, Caligiuri and Lazarova (2001) suggested eleven HR practices:

1 Pre-departure briefings on what to expect during repatriation.
2 Career planning sessions.
3 Guarantee/agreement outlining the type of position expatriates will be placed in upon repatriation.
4 Mentoring programs while on assignment.
5 Reorientation programs about the changes in the company.
6 Repatriation training seminars on the emotional response following repatriation.
7 Financial counselling and financial/tax assistance.
8 Lifestyle assistance and counselling on changes likely to occur in expatriates' life upon return.
9 Continuous communications with the home office.
10 Visible signs that the company values international experience.
11 Communications with the home office about the details of the repatriation process.

In fact, many organisations admit that they are not effective at repatriation planning and support and many individuals consider whether to leave their employers (Dickmann and Baruch, 2011). However, if individuals stay longer than one year after return, their retention rates over the next two years become very high with hardly any churn (Doherty and Dickmann, 2012). Companies that are seen as successful in retaining expatriates often pay attention to the eleven factors that Caligiuri and Lazarova outlined and have integrated their international mobility with a general career system, managing the acquisition and utilisation of know-how and social capital (Riusala and Suutari, 2000; MacDonald and Arthur, 2005).

The individual perspective

In an ideal scenario, repatriates look forward to 'return' and are able to apply what they have learnt abroad. Unfortunately, the reality can look very different. A common occurrence is the reverse culture shock. It arises because of changes in the home culture and context, developments in the firm (head office) they are working in and because they themselves have changed during their experiences abroad. In addition, there is often some frustration when losing some of the perks of working abroad (financial, social, kudos) and moving from being a 'big fish in a small pond' to a more normal position of being a 'small fish in a big pond'. So, what could have been a 'honeymoon' of returning and reengaging with friends and the wider context can be complicated by worries about the current job, progression opportunities, financial and social frustration. There are some parallels of how individuals cope in this phase with the culture shock when they work abroad. Some authors have identified that the 'career wobble' that may coincide with a reverse culture shock may last about one year for many persons (Doherty *et al.*, 2008).

What can individuals do to increase their chances of a successful reintegration both in their home countries as well as in the sending unit of their firm? One approach is to be attractive to one's own or other employers as well as creating realistic expectations (within oneself and in others). Dickmann and Doherty (2010) outline a range of career capital activities that increase the knowledge, skills, abilities and insights that expatriates acquire when working abroad. It is crucial to explore early (even at the pre-assignment planning stage) how these can be used upon return. For instance, trying to go to a foreign centre of excellence can make the acquired know-how more valuable for the organisation. Moreover, international workers and returnees should have a keen understanding of their social capital and consciously network with those persons that can be helpful in the process of gaining good jobs upon return. In addition, conversations before return with mentors, sponsors, HRM and other stakeholders are important for one's own realistic expectations as well as to influence the organisation's thinking towards a suitable repatriate position.

Table 10.6 outlines good practices in expatriate retention. It expands on work by Dickmann and Baruch (2011) and goes beyond the Caligiuri and Lazarova (2001) recommendations. The table is primarily based on what organisations can do and also covers individual activities to improve repatriation success.

Table 10.6 After the assignment – Good practices in expatriate retention

Area	Policies and Practices
Organisational Strategy and Structure	• Clear and attractive strategy to internationalise
	• Attractive degree of existing internationalisation
	• Little or no significant gap between statements of top management and implementation
	• Adequate organisational configuration
	• High kudos of international work
International Mobility Policies and Practices	• Staffing policies are perceived to be fair or advantageous
	• Selection looks at a range of factors, including personality factors linked into adjustment and self-adjustment upon return
	• Pre-return preparation for the job
	• On-going support for time after return
	• Long-range planning for repatriation
	• Networking opportunities
	• Continuous communication with home
Career	• Long-term career planning
	• Re-entry planning
	• Career advancement
	• Mentor system/International work sponsor system
Development	• Systematic development of professional skills
	• Systematic development of personal skills
	• Systematic development of leadership skills
	• Repatriation seminars on the emotional response
	• Financial and tax counselling, advice and help for time after return
Job Variables	• Job challenge
	• Ability to use new global capabilities
	• No reduced responsibility and autonomy

Area	Policies and Practices
Financial Impact	• Rewards for pursuing an international assignment (IA)
	• Rewards for developing an international perspective
	• Rewards for developing a worldwide network
	• Rewards for developing global skills, abilities and knowledge
	• Tie-over pay
Personal Drivers and Expectations	• Pre-return and after-return dialogues to manage expectations/build realistic pre-return expectations
	• Briefing and update regarding organisational structure, goals, politics and changes in the new locations
Family	• Help for partner to find meaningful activity such as job and career re-entry
	• Help for family to (re-)settle
Individual Activities	• Work on keeping social networks in the place of return current and useful
	• Engage in work that takes place in the location of return so that knowledge remains current and expectations realistic
	• Reflect on personal/identity changes and what that means for life after return
	• Expect financial and status changes
	• Work on acquiring transferable capabilities and/or liaise with future expatriates in order to exchange insights
	• Balance perceived career capital management/return planning deficits in your organisation and proactively address these
	• Prepare, guide and help family through the repatriation transition

Source: Based on Dickmann and Baruch, 2011: 234.

Summary

This chapter has presented key considerations in international HRM. First, it has defined IHRM, in contrast to comparative HRM, as the IHRM configurations – strategies, structures, policies and practices – that are used to manage people in international organisations, be they for-profit or not. Second, from a competitive advantage, resource-based perspective we have identified a number of types of multinational organisations that exist. The key rational was linked to creating competitive edge in a variety of dimensions, most prominently in cost (global efficiency through integration), quality (local responsiveness through product/service differentiation) and innovation (worldwide knowledge networking). Third, the chapter introduced a number of IHRM models that charted the expanse of the global people management arena. Fourth, the text shifted its perspective towards more operational aspects of international working. In so doing it has distinguished between pre-assignment, during the assignment and post-return issues of how organisations can manage their globally mobile staff. Crucially, we have also outlined the concerns, emotions, actions, and identity and capability changes of global workers on their international journeys. This has led us to a longer-term perspective than normally used. Many recommendations of how to manage international staff and how to behave as global careerists are summarised and presented in the chapter.

CASE STUDY 10.1

INTERNATIONAL HRM: AIMING TO PRACTICE TRANSNATIONAL PEOPLE MANAGEMENT, ACHIEVING COGNOFEDERATE IHRM

MICHAEL DICKMANN

InnovationCo was founded in the second half of the nineteenth century in Germany. It produces fast-moving consumer goods (FMCGs) and offers several thousand products in a variety of international markets. In the early twentieth century, the company founded its first foreign affiliate in Switzerland. In order to expand exports InnovationCo established operations in a further seven European countries before WWII. In the 1950s, production plants were founded in several countries in Europe, South America and Africa and the company started to sell in Asia. Over time, production was increasingly located abroad and the firm became more and more international in the sense of having two thirds of staff located outside Germany at the turn of the millennium.

In its production processes, InnovationCo uses a pragmatic balance of global integration and local responsiveness. Growth had mostly been achieved through the acquisition of foreign and domestic companies. This created a status quo of differentiation, which the firm wanted to shift towards more integration. The key driver to standardise production was seen to be in the increased scale effects and efficiency advantages. The diverse history of its acquired parts, their administrative heritage, different production technologies and customer insights, however, represented a chance to increase worldwide innovation.

IHRM standardisation

InnovationCo's staff is widely spread geographically. InnovationCo's HRM combines a pragmatic use of local advantages and a German approach. InnovationCo's IHRM was described by its HRM board member as wishing to harmonise the philosophy while adapting to local methods. This integrated philosophy led to standardised international leadership guidelines, created and agreed by all European HR heads. Overall, IHRM principles and broad objectives were highly standardised. In contrast, InnovationCo chose only to cooperate in a few operational areas as these were deemed to be the methods that are best developed and applied locally (see Table 1). Overall, the degree of integration depended on the perceived importance of the area, its contribution to the company's success and the determination of the head office to shape worldwide policies according to its wishes. The motto was that it wanted to give local operations freedom. This led to locally idiosyncratic HRM approaches which were tolerated by the head office.

IHRM knowledge networking

There was tight consultation and cooperation between the German head office and its subsidiaries in terms of IHRM policies and practices. This was facilitated through a conference of all HRM heads and six working meetings of all European HR top executives per year. The aim was to elicit local ideas that may be further developed and then introduced globally. The direction of knowledge exchange was multilateral and IHRM suggestions were derived from any part of the company network.

The open and intensive international communication made it hard to impose the head office view against joint resistance from foreign affiliates. In fact, a top HR manager from the head office argued that there was no intention to be the 'Vatican' – it was more seen as a heterarchical relationship that would lead to innovation on the road to transnationalism. But this had a disadvantage:

higher knowledge networking did not mean that IHRM cross-border control became easier or more efficient. In the absence of strong international control, more informal, sophisticated integration mechanisms were needed. At least in terms of IHRM, InnovationCo did not achieve the transnationalism it aimed for – instead it had become a cognofederate with some development of local solutions that some HR top managers disliked. For instance, they wanted to have a more integrated training and development policy but had encountered local resistance.

Case Study 1: Table 1 IHRM in InnovationCo: Philosophy/Principles Level

	Philosophy/Principles Level
Standardisation	
General HRM	*Leadership*: International principles and guidelines *Security*: Guidelines related to healthy work environment, job security through standard work contracts *Other – Innovation*: Principle of international cooperation to elicit best ideas and learning
Recruitment and Selection	Search for global best talent
Training and Development	Commitment to the development of staff, preference for dual vocational training to be used in local operations
Career Management	International equality of career prospects, international assignment policy
Performance Management	International principles and guidelines
Remuneration	Comparability of task and performance related compensation
Knowledge Networking	
General HRM	*Development and Review*: Concurrent international development of HR principles, multinational development of HR strategy, feedback on implementation from local units *Control and Coordination*: little international coordination of HR budgets, no local HR budgets set or reviewed in headquarters, only basic local reporting of results (e.g. headcounts), 1 global meeting, bi-national monthly regional meetings, frequent visits
Recruitment and Selection	International discussion of long-term international resourcing needs, no global committee (other than for board members)
Training and Development	Cross-nationally coordinated long-range aims for future leaders developed, cultural cornerstones defined
Career Management	Top career deciders drawn from headquarters, career principles sometimes formally discussed in European Head of HR Group
Performance Management	General international performance management principles discussed cross-border
Remuneration	Headquarters HR management set guidelines

Source: Based on Dickmann *et al.*, 2009; Dickmann and Baruch, 2011.

Case Study 1: Table 2 IHRM in InnovationCo: Operational Level

	Operational Level
Standardisation	
General HRM	Competency framework
Recruitment and Selection	Resourcing local, using diverse criteria
Training and Development	Some cross-cultural seminars and top management development integrated, dual vocational training not implemented everywhere
Career Management	Integrated approach for upper/middle management (highest four levels); database of high potentials (some local units opted out)
Performance Management	Standard processes and forms for top 4 management levels (management review and target dialogue)
Remuneration	Integration around Hay for upper five levels, lower management local; some local variation possible
Knowledge Networking	
General HRM	Explicit feedback in European HR director committee on overarching systems and instruments every two months. Global competency framework designed in international (European) cooperation. High frequency of international HR meetings and visits
Recruitment and Selection	International discussion of diverse selection instruments
Training and Development	Head office design and international review of some international management seminars; a few have explicit cultural aims
Career Management	Some cross-border exchange of data on high potentials; coordinated through more than 1% of staff abroad on international assignments
Performance Management	No international review of performance carried out
Remuneration	Central remuneration committee reviews rewards, formal cross-border discussion of experiences

Source: Based on Dickmann *et al*., 2009; Dickmann and Baruch, 2011.

Questions

1 Why do you think InnovationCo used the specific standardisation and knowledge networking approach in IHRM? What other options did it have?

2 What are the advantages and disadvantages associated with their IHRM?

3 Considering a worldwide operating organisation that you know well: how does its approach to international HRM differ?

4 What are the possible effects on global careers for managers in InnovationCo? What would international HR careers look like?

CASE STUDY 10.2

INTERNATIONAL HRM: THE CHANGING ROLE OF GLOBAL MOBILITY DEPARTMENTS

MICHAEL DICKMANN

The twenty-first century is characterised by a dramatic increase in the speed, scale and dynamics of competition between multinational firms. The work of the global mobility function supports individuals and organisations to be as effective and efficient as they can in their search for worldwide competitive advantage. Because corporations face differing contextual pressures, have varying organisational structures and compete in diverse ways, the operating model of the global mobility function, its purpose and value is highly distinct in multinationals.

The RES Forum facilitates the networking of its 600+ global mobility (GM) expert members from more than 350 MNCs. In 2014 and 2015 it explored how the role of the global mobility department was seen by the heads and senior specialists in their member organisations. While there was some large degree of inconsistency with respect to the vision of where the global mobility function should be in terms of its value proposition, four components stood out:

1 Expert on Due Diligence: Being a GM expert with respect to administrative and process knowledge to enable faultless due diligence and programme compliance. This large field may also include managing the internal and external service delivery process and quality. One member commented: 'Due Diligence . . . has to be done properly right from the start. Cross-border taxation, immigration, employment legislation, host country practices, security, medical requirements, etc.'.

2 Global People Effectiveness Expert: Running a centre of expertise that understands the mobility drivers of individuals and supports them in their international sojourns to enable them to be as effective as possible. This would include sophisticated pre-departure selection, preparation, foreign 'on-boarding' and adjustment, performance management as well as repatriation issues. One GM director explained that this would entail: 'workforce planning; make sure that the organization chooses the right (number of) people, for the right reasons, to work abroad'.

3 Global Talent Manager: Link resourcing, development and leadership ideas in global mobility work to create seamless, worldwide integrated talent management. A further director added: 'Vision that the mobility function is part of the business talent DNA, rather than mobility.'

4 Strategic Advisor: Having a broader strategic remit that would lead to the function of strategic business partner/advisor on global mobility issues. This would need the in-depth understanding of the business, its global operations, localisation and security issues as well as the link to leadership and successor issues. Global mobility metrics, analytics and return on investment (ROI) considerations would be part of the strategic considerations. A GM director explained that the function should be a 'Critical strategic tool to enable the delivery of the international business development plan'. A further RES Forum member added that the GM function should be 'responsible for analytics and reporting on value added data regards the mobile work force – ROI etc.'.

The data led Dickmann (2014) to develop a framework for the roles of Global Mobility departments that has many parallels with the work of Ulrich (1998). It is depicted in Figure 10.7.

One year later, the RES Forum conducted a follow-up survey in which it investigated how its members viewed the current role of the GM departments in their MNCs and how they would see it develop in the future. The data showed that currently GM professionals see themselves predominantly in the due diligence expert role, followed by that of strategic advisor. The talent management and global people effectiveness expert roles were comparatively less important. In future, they were working towards a much stronger emphasis on strategic advice. The due diligence role is likely to remain important. In addition, the two other roles of talent manager and global people effectiveness expert are likely to become much more important in the future (see Figure 10.8).

It has to be remarked that many GM functions are 'not there, yet'. For instance, the use of HR/GM technology remains unsophisticated in many organisations (Dickmann, 2014). The interface with talent management

Figure 10.7 The role of global mobility functions

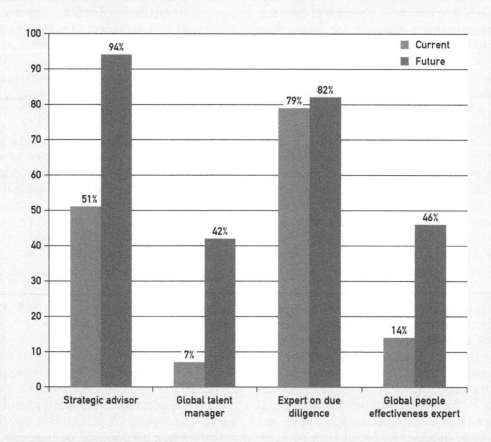

Figure 10.8 Expanding roles for GM professionals

specialists is not well defined and there are currently some role overlaps – both within these MNCs and between the different parts of the framework (Dickmann, 2015).

The case raises a raft of issues and questions. Amongst those are:

1   What role(s) do you think is most appreciated by international assignees? Why?
2   What roles may senior managers value most?
3   How can GM departments achieve to become more accepted/work more like strategic advisors?
4   How can GM professionals become better global people effectiveness experts? What might this work entail?
5   Given the parallels with the original Ulrich model – what barriers and disadvantages may the envisaged shift have?

Bibliography

Adler, N.J. and Ghadar, F. (1990) 'Strategic Human Resource Management: a global perspective', in R. Pieper *Human Resource Management: An International Comparison*, New York: de Gruyter.

Andresen, M., Bergdolt, F., Margenfeld, J. and Dickmann, M. (2014) 'Addressing international mobility confusion – developing definitions and differentiations for self-initiated and assigned expatriates as well as migrants', *The International Journal of Human Resource Management*, Vol.25, No.16, 2295–318.

Ang, S., Van Dyne, L., Koh, C., Ng, K., Templer, K., Tay-Lee, S. and Chandrasekar, N. (2007) 'Cultural intelligence: its measurement and effects on cultural judgement and decision making, cultural adaptation and task performance', *Management and Organization Review*, Vol.3, No.3, 335–71.

Bartlett, C. and Ghoshal, S. (1989) *Managing Across Borders*, London: Hutchinson Business.

Baruch, Y., Dickmann, M., Altman, Y. and Bournois, F. (2013) 'Exploring international work: types and dimensions of global careers', *The International Journal of Human Resource Management*, Vol.24, No.12, 2369–93.

Beardwell, J. and Claydon, T. (2010) *Human Resource Management: A contemporary approach* (6th edn.), Harlow: FT Prentice Hall.

Bhaskar-Shrinivas, P., Harrison, D.A., Shaffer, M.A. and Luk, D.M. (2005) 'Input-based and time-based models of international adjustment: meta-analytic evidence and theoretical extensions', *Academy of Management Journal,* Vol.48, No.2, 257–81.

Bird, A. and Osland, J. (2004) 'Global competencies: an introduction', in Lane, H.W., Maxnewski, M.L., Mendenhal, M.E. and McNett, J. (eds.) *Handbook of Global Management*, Oxford: Blackwell Publishing.

Black, J.S. (1988) 'Work role transitions: a study of American expatriate managers in Japan', *Journal of International Business Studies*, Vol.30, No.2, 277–94.

Black, J.S., Gregersen, H.B. and Mendenhall, M.E. (1992) *Global Assignments: Successfully Expatriating and Repatriating International Managers*, San Francisco, CA: Jossey-Bass.

Black, S.J. and Stephens, G.K. (1989) 'The influence of the partner on American expatriate adjustment and intent to stay in pacific rim overseas assignments', *Journal of Management*, Vol.15, No.4, 529–44.

Bonache, J., Sanchez, J. and Zárraga-Oberty, C. (2009) 'The interaction of expatriate pay differential and expatriate inputs on host country nationals' pay unfairness', *The International Journal of Human Resource Management*, Vol.20, No.10, 2135.

Brewster, C. and Mayrhofer, W. (eds.) (2012) *Handbook of Research on Comparative Human Resource Management*, Edward Elgar Publishing.

Briscoe, D. and Schuler, R. (2004) *International Human Resource Management* (2nd edn.), London: Routledge.

Brookfield Global Relocation Services (2014) 2014 Global Mobility Trends survey report.

Caligiuri, P.M. (2000) 'Selecting expatriates for personality characteristics: a moderating effect of personality on the relationship between host national contact and cross-cultural adjustment', *Management International Review*, Vol.40, No.1, 61–80.

Caligiuri, P. (2013) *Cultural Agility: Building a Pipeline of Successful Global Professionals*, John Wiley & Sons.

Caligiuri, P.M. and Lazarova, M. (2001) 'Strategic repatriation policies to enhance global leadership development', *Developing Global Business Leaders*, 243–56.

Carlos, A. and Nicholas, S. (1988) 'Giants of an earlier capitalism: the chartered trading companies as modern multinationals', *Business History Review*, Vol.62, 398–419.

De Cieri, H. and Dowling, P. (1999) 'Strategic human resource management in multinational enterprises: theoretical and empirical developments', in Wright, P.M., Dyer, L.D. and Boudreau, J.W. (eds.) *Research in Personnel and Human Resource Management: Strategic Human Resources in the Twenty-First Century,* 4th Supplement, Stamford, CT: JAI Press.

DeFillippi, R. and Arthur, M. (1994) 'The boundaryless career: a competency-based perspective', *Journal of Organizational Behavior,* Vol.15, 307–24.

Dickmann, M. (2015) 'The RES Forum Annual Report: Global mobility and the global talent management conundrum', RES Forum, UniGroup Relocation Network and Equus Software, 108 pages, London.

Dickmann, M. (2014) 'Key trends in global mobility', RES Forum, UniGroup Relocation Network and Equus Software, 102 pages, London.

Dickmann, M. (2013) 'Why do they come to London? Exploring the motivations of expatriates to work in the British capital', *Journal of Management Development*, Vol.31, No.8, 783–800.

Dickmann, M. and Baruch, Y. (2011) *Global Careers*, London: Routledge.

Dickmann, M. and Doherty, N. (2010) 'Exploring organisational and individual career goals, interactions and outcomes of international assignments', *Thunderbird International Review*, Vol.52, No.4, 313–24.

Dickmann, M., Doherty, N. and Johnson, A. (2006) 'Measuring the value of international assignments', report for PwC UK Geodesy, Cranfield School of Management, December.

Dickmann, M., Doherty, N., Mills, T. and Brewster, C. (2008) 'Why do they go? Individual and corporate perspectives on the factors influencing the decision to accept an international assignment', *The International Journal of Human Resource Management*, Vol.19, No.4, 731–51.

Dickmann, M. and Harris, H. (2005) 'Developing career capital for global careers: the role of international assignments', *Journal of World Business*, Vol.40, No.4, 399–408.

Dickmann, M. and Mills, T. (2009) 'The importance of intelligent career and location considerations: exploring the decision to go to London', *Personnel Review*, Vol.39, No.1, 116–34.

Dickmann, M. and Müller-Camen, M. (2006) 'A typology of international human resource management strategies and processes', *International Journal of Human Resource Management*, Vol.17, No.4, 580–601.

Dickmann, M., Müller-Camen, M. and Kelliher, C. (2009) 'Exploring standardisation and knowledge networking processes in transnational human resource management', *Personnel Review*, Vol.38, No.1, 5–25.

Doherty, N. and Dickmann, M. (2012) 'Measuring the return on investment in international assignments: an action research approach', *The International Journal of Human Resource Management*, Vol.23, No.16, 3434–54.

Doherty, N. and Dickmann, M. (2013) 'Self-initiated and assigned expatriates: talent management and career considerations', pp. 234–55, in *Talent Management of Self-Initiated Expatriates*, Palgrave Macmillan.

Doherty, N., Brewster, C., Suutari, V. and Dickmann, M. (2008) 'Repatriation: the end or the middle?', in Dickmann, M. Brewster, C. and Sparrow, P. (eds.) *International Human Resource Management – The European Perspective*, London: Routledge.

Doherty, N., Dickmann, M. and Mills, T. (2011) 'Exploring the motives of company-backed and self-initiated expatriates', *The International Journal of Human Resource Management*, Vol.22, No.3, 595–611.

Dowling, P. (1999) 'Completing the puzzle: issues in the field of International Human Resource Management', *Management International Review*, Special Issue No.3, 31.

Dowling, P., Festing, M. and Engle, A. (2008) *International Human Resource Management: Managing People in a Multinational Context* (5th edn.), London: Thomson Learning.

ECA (2010) *Managing Mobility Survey*, London: Employment Conditions Abroad.

Edström, A. and Galbraith, J.R. (1977) 'Transfer of managers as a coordination and control strategy in multinational organizations', *Administrative Science Quarterly*, Vol.22, No.2, 248–63.

Edwards, T., Sanchez-Mangas, R., Bélanger, J. and McDonnell, A. (2015) 'Why are some subsidiaries of multinationals the source of novel practices while others are not? National, corporate and functional influences', *British Journal of Management*, Vol.26, 146–62.

Edwards, T. and Rees, C. (2006) *International Human Resource Management: Globalization, National Systems and Multinational Companies*, London: FT/Prentice Hall.

Ernst and Young (2009) *Expatriate Policy Survey*, Zurich: Ernst & Young.

Farndale, E., Scullion, H. and Sparrow, P. (2010) 'The role of the corporate HR function in global talent management', *Journal of World Business*, Vol.45, No.2, 161–8.

Fox, K. (2005) *Watching the English: The Hidden Rules of English Behaviour*, London: Hodder & Stoughton.

GMAC (2008) *Global Relocation Trends Survey*, Woodridge, IL: GMAC Global Relocation Services.

GMAC Global Relocation Services (2009) *Global Relocation Trends: 2009 Survey Report*, Oak Brook, IL: GMAC Global Relocation Services.

Hailey, J. and Harry, W. (2008) 'Localisation: a strategic response to globalization', in Dickmann, M., Brewster, C. and Sparrow, P. (eds.) *International Human Resource Management – The European Perspective*, London: Routledge.

Harris, H. and Brewster, C. (1999) 'The coffee-machine system: how international selection really works', *International Journal of Human Resource Management*, Vol.10, No.3, 488–500.

Harris, H. and Dickmann, M. (2005) *The CIPD Guide on International Management Development*, London: Chartered Institute of Personnel and Development.

Harris, H., Brewster, C. and Sparrow, P. (2003) *International Human Resource Management*, London: Chartered Institute of Personnel and Development.

Harvey, M. (1995) 'The impact of dual-career families on international relocations', *Human Resource Management Review*, Vol.5, 223–44.

Harzing, A.-W. (2000) 'An empirical analysis and extension of the Bartlett and Ghoshal typology of multinational companies', *Journal of International Business Studies*, Vol.31, No.1, 101–20.

Haslberger, A. (2005) 'The complexities of expatriate adaptation', *Human Resource Management Review*, Vol.15, No.2, 160–80.

Haslberger, A., Brewster, C. and Hippler, T. (2013) The dimensions of expatriate adjustment, *Human Resource Management*, Vol.52, No.3, 333–51.

Haslberger, A. (2008) 'Expatriate adjustment: a more nuanced view', in Dickmann, M., Brewster, C. and Sparrow, P. (eds.) *International Human Resource Management – A European Perspective*, London: Routledge.

Haslberger, A. and Zehetner, K. (2008) 'Cosmopolitan appeal: what makes a city attractive to expatriates and how do they benefit? The example of Vienna, Austria', paper presented at 4th Workshop on Expatriation, EIASM, Las Palmas de Gran Canarias, Spain, October 2008.

Hennan, D.A. and Perlmutter, H.V. (1979) *Multinational Organizational Development*, Reading, MA: Addison-Wesley.

Hippler, T. (2009) 'Why do they go? Empirical evidence of employees' motives for seeking or accepting relocation', *The International Journal of Human Resource Management*, Vol.20, No.6, 1381–1401.

Howe-Walsh, L. and Schyns, B. (2010) 'Self-initiated expatriation: implications for HRM', *The International Journal of Human Resource Management*, Vol.21, No.2, 260–73.

Huang, T.J., Chi, S.H. and Lawler, J.S. (2005) 'The relationship between expatriates' personality traits and their adjustment to international assignments', *The International Journal of Human Resource Management,* Vol.16, No.9, 1656–70.

Hurn, B.J. (1999) 'Repatriation: the toughest assignment of all', *Industrial and Commercial Training*, Vol.31, No.6, 224–8.

Inkson, K. and Arthur, M. (2001) 'How to be a successful career capitalist', *Organizational Dynamics,* Vol.30, No.1, 48–60.

Inkson, K., Arthur, M.B., Pringle, J. and Barry, S. (1997) 'Expatriate assignment versus overseas experience: contrasting models of international human resource development', *Journal of World Business*, Vol.32, No.4, 351–68.

Kawai, N. and Mohr, A. (2015) 'The contingent effects of role ambiguity and role novelty on expatriates' work-related outcomes', *British Journal of Management*, Vol.26, 163–181.

Larsen, H.H. (2004) 'Global career as dual dependency between the organization and the individual', *The Journal of Management Development*, Vol.23, No.9, 860–9.

Lazarova, M.B. and Cerdin, J.L. (2007) 'Revisiting repatriation concerns: organizational support versus career and contextual influences', *Journal of International Business Studies*, Vol.38, No.3, 404–29.

Leong, S.M. and Tan, C.T. (1993) 'Managing across borders: an empirical test of the Bartlett and Ghoshal [1989] organizational typology', *Journal of International Business Studies*, Vol.24, No.3, 419–48.

Leung, K., Zhu, Y. and Ge, C. (2009) 'Compensation disparity between locals and expatriates: moderating the effects of perceived injustice in foreign multinationals in China', *Journal of World Business*, Vol.44, No.1, 85.

MacDonald, S. and Arthur, N. (2005) 'Connecting career management to repatriation adjustment', *Career Development International*, Vol.10, No.2, 145–159.

Mendenhall, M., Dunbar, E. and Oddou, G. (1987) 'Expatriate selection, training and career-pathing: a review and critique', *Human Resource Management*, Vol.26, No.3, 331–45.

Milliman, J. and Von Glinow, A. (1990) 'A life cycle approach to strategic international human resource management in MNCs', *Research in Personnel and Human Resources Management*, Supplement 2, 21–35.

Oberg, K. (1960) 'Cultural shock: adjustment to new cultural environments', *Practical Anthropology*, July–August, 177–82.

Parker, P., Khapova, S.N. and Arthur, M.B. (2009) 'The intelligent career framework as a basis for interdisciplinary inquiry', *Journal of Vocational Behavior*, Vol.75, No.3, 291–302.

Peiperl, M. and Jonsen, K. (2007) 'Global careers', in Gunz, H. and Peiperl, M. (eds.) *Handbook of Career Studies*, Thousand Oaks, CA: Sage.

Perlmutter, H. (1969) 'The tortuous evolution of the multinational corporation', *Columbia Journal of World Business*, Vol.4, No.1, 9–18.

Porter, M.E. (1985) *Competitive Strategy: Creating and Sustaining Superior Performance*, New York: Free Press.

Porter, M.E. and Kramer, M.R. (2006) 'The link between competitive advantage and corporate social responsibility', *Harvard Business Review*, Vol.84, No.12, 78–92.

Prahalad, C.K. and Doz, Y. (1987) *The Multinational Mission: Balancing Local Demands and Global Vision*, New York: The Free Press.

Richardson, J. and Mallon, M. (2005) 'Careers interrupted? The case of the self-directed expatriate', *Journal of World Business*, Vol.40, 409–20.

Riusala, K. and Suutari, V. (2000) 'Expatriation and careers: perspectives of expatriates and spouses', *Career Development International*, Vol.5, No.2, 81–90.

Schuler, R.S., Dowling, P.J. and Cieri, H.D. (1993) 'An integrative framework of strategic international human resource management', *International Journal of Human Resource Management*, Vol.4, No.4, 717–64.

Schuler, R.S. and Jackson, S.E. (2005) 'A quarter-century review of human resource management in the US: the growth in importance of the international perspective', *Management Revue*, Vol.11, 35.

Sparrow, P., Brewster, C. and Harris, H. (2004) *Globalizing Human Resource Management*, London: Routledge.

Stahl, G. and Cerdin, J.-L. (2004) 'Global careers in French and German multinational corporations', *Journal of Management Development*, Vol.23, No.9, 885–902.

Suutari, V. and Tornikoski, C. (2001) 'The challenge of expatriate compensation: the sources of satisfaction and dissatisfaction among expatriates', *International Journal of Human Resource Management*, Vol.12, No.3, 389–404.

Takeuchi, R., Tesluk, P.E., Yun, S. and Lepak, D.P. (2005) 'An integrative view of international experience', *The Academy of Management Journal*, Vol.48, No.1, 85–100.

Templer, K.J. (2010) 'Personal attributes of expatriate managers, subordinate ethnocentrism, and expatriate success: a host-country perspective', *The International Journal of Human Resource Management*, Vol.21, No.10, 1754.

Tharenou, P. (2003) 'The initial development of receptivity to working abroad: self-initiated international work opportunities in young graduate employees', *Journal of Occupational and Organizational Psychology*, Vol.76, 489–515.

Thomas, D.C. and Lazarova, M.B. (2006) 'Expatriate adjustment and performance: a critical review', pp. 247–64, in Stahl, G.K. and Bjorkman, I. (eds.), *Handbook of Research in International Human Resource Management,* Cheltenham: Edward Elgar.

Toh, S.M. and DeNisi, A.S. (2005) 'A local perspective to expatriate success', *The Academy of Management Executive*, Vol.19, No.1, 132–46.

Toh, S.M. and DeNisi, A.S. (2007) 'Host country nationals as socializing agents: a social identity approach', *Journal of Organizational Behavior*, Vol.28, No.3, 281–301.

Tung, R.L. (1998) 'American expatriates abroad: from neophytes to cosmopolitans', *Journal of World Business*, Vol.33, 125–44.

Ulrich, D. (1998) 'A new mandate for human resources', *Harvard Business Review*, Vol.76, 124–35.

Vance, C.M., Vaiman, V. and Andersen, T. (2009) 'The vital liaison role of host country nationals in MNC knowledge management', *Human Resource Management*, Vol.48, No.4, 649–59.

Vernon, R. (1966) 'International investment and international trade in the product cycle', *The Quarterly Journal of Economics*, 1 May, 190–207.

Ward, C., Bochner, S. and Furnham, A. (2001) *The Psychology of Culture Shock* (2nd edn.), London: Routledge.

Whitley (1992) 'Societies, firms and markets: the social structuring of business systems', in Whitley, R. (ed.) *European Business Systems: Firms and Markets in Their National Contexts*, London: Sage.

Yan, A., Zhu, G. and Hall, D.T. (2002) 'International assignments for career building: a model of agency relationships and psychological contracts', *Academy of Management Review*, Vol.27, No.3, 373–91.

Yurkiewicz, J. and Rosen, B. (1995) 'Increasing receptivity to expatriate assignments', in Selmer, J. (ed.) *Expatriate Management*, Westport: Quorum.

CHAPTER 11
COMPARATIVE HUMAN RESOURCE MANAGEMENT

Geoffrey Wood and David G. Collings

Introduction

There has been growing interest in the question as to whether HRM is becoming more alike around the world, or whether distinct differences within and between nations persist. Although convergence around a single set of best HR practices seems remote (entreaties of numerous experts notwithstanding), there are strong pressures on organisations to move towards more contingent practices in the light of both the global policy dominance of neo-liberalism, and the volatile nature of the global economy. Such contingency would centre on greater job and occupational insecurity, pay flexibility and the individualisation of contracts. However, there remains strong counter pressures for firms to continue to follow dominant recipes for people management within the countries in which they operate. This chapter explores the various explanations that have been advanced for this persistent difference.

This is not a terribly new question, of course, even in the nineteenth century scholars such as Durkheim and Marx sought to understand the nature of modernisation of societies and workplace practices, and the extent to which they were be coming more alike or diverging. Over the past two decades, the debate about globalisation – the extent to which the opening of markets, more mobile investors, and the apparent homogenisation of global consumer taste has made the planet more unified – has rekindled all this. A key underlying consideration in this debate is the extent to which globalisation is facilitating the convergence of national economies and the HR and other management practices that encompass this, and the homogenisation of the modus operandi of multinational corroborations (MNCs) operating in the global economy (Brewster and Wood, 2014; Collings *et al.*, 2011; Ferner, 2010; Vaiman and Brewster, 2015).

Indeed, a good starting point in looking at the globalisation and HRM debate is in the latter area: surely firms that operate on a global basis are the pioneers of a common HRM practice? The issue of multinational HR practices is examined by Dickmann in Chapter 10 of this volume. However, for the purposes of this chapter, it is worth noting that multinational corporations, one of the principle agents responsible for foreign direct investment (FDI) (Hirst and Thompson, 1999), are the key drivers in the internationalisation process (Ferner and Hyman, 1998). Thus these corporations can be perceived as significant in transferring practices from their country of origin with them when they establish operations in foreign countries (Almond, 2011a;

Ferner, 1997). What factors do you think might retard the convergence of management practices in different countries?

Looking specifically at human resource management (HRM), there is broad consensus that dominant modern conceptions of the field are heavily influenced by US thinking (Brewster, 2007; Brewster and Wood, 2014; Guest, 1990). Thus, there is a degree of expectation that these US models enjoy a hegemonic position in the global business contexts and that all HRM practice will converge on this US model. Writers such as Kidger (1991) and DiMaggio and Powell (1983) argue that US multinationals, business schools and consultants will contribute to global convergence on US conceptualisations of HRM, reflected in HRM practice across the world (see Brewster, 2007 for a recent review). In illuminating the convergence/divergence polemic in the context of cross-national management practice, we can point to a number of significant studies. For instance, Gunnigle *et al.*'s (2002) study found a clear variation between HRM practice in firms of different national origin (see also Gooderham *et al.*, 1998). In a similar vein, Harzing and Sorge (2003) found that while internationalisation strategy was more closely related to industry and size than other variables, the country of origin of firms was significant in explaining differences in control mechanisms utilised by firms. Thus there was continued divergence in control mechanisms utilised in firms of different national origin and they argue that, on balance, divergence remains in place. Geppert and his colleagues also pointed to differences in the change management strategies pursued by organisations of different nationalities (Geppert *et al.*, 2003). Thus, on balance, the literature suggests that management practices continue to be characterised by divergence across national borders (Brewster *et al.*, 2004; Harzing and Sorge, 2003), and indeed Hirst and Thompson (1999: 95) go as far as to suggest that 'in many ways . . . [national business] systems are being reinforced and strengthened by the internationalisation of business' (see also Hall and Soskice, 2001: 56–60; Whitley, 1999).

The debate is, however, a complex one and there are a number of theories advanced which posit a universalist (convergence) or continued divergence of business systems and management practices. These theories merit some discussion and the key debates are outlined below. Our discussion is framed in the arena of comparative human resource management, which is defined as 'about understanding and explaining what differences exist between countries in the way that human resources are managed' (Brewster, 2006: 68). Thus comparative HRM stands in contrast to international HRM, which Scullion (1995: 325) defines as 'the HRM issues and problems arising from the internationalisation of business, and the HRM strategies, policies and practices which firms pursue in response to the internationalisation of business': comparative HRM is about comparing what firms do in different national contexts, irrespective of whether they are multinational or not. While Boxall (1995: 5), writing in the mid-1990s, described comparative HR as a poorly theorised, emerging field, there is little doubt that we have witnessed significant theoretical and empirical development in the field the past two decades, and these developments inform our chapter.

There are two principal strands of literature on comparative HRM. The first draws on a range of different theoretical traditions to make assumptions as to the direction of national economies, supported by a mixture of case study evidence and macro-economic data – in short, top-down approaches. This area of study concerns itself primarily with what makes HR different from case to case, and what the general differences encountered are likely to be; in other words, the second and third questions with which we opened our chapter. In contrast, bottom-up approaches seek to shed more light on national commonalities and variations in human resource management through pragmatic empirical work. The primary focus of the latter school of thought is, hence, on cataloguing HRM practices, rather than trying to explain them in terms of a broader theoretical template. Again, it is about what distinguishes HR practices in particular national contexts. However, its bottom-up focus means that such studies often provide richer detail on precisely how HR is practiced in specific contexts – often enriched with case study evidence – although this may be at the expense of ease of comparative analysis. Finally, such studies draw on a range of different methods – be that surveys (economy, region, industry or firm wide), or more qualitative methods. This diversity makes for richness in detail but, of course, makes direct comparisons between contexts more difficult!

Convergence or divergence in HRM systems

Universalists: the convergence debate

The key underlying philosophy of the universalist is the general applicability of a common system of social and economic organisation (Rubery and Grimshaw, 2003). In other words, they assume that a specific general model is of universal worth. Inspired by Francis Fukuyama's (2000) suggestion that the ending of the Cold War saw the 'end of history', such perspectives assume that all national economies will move towards the neo-liberal ideal, which would be mirrored by similar shifts in firm-level practices (see also Friedman, 1999). Allowing space for individual self-actualisation and fair recognition in line with market incentives will unlock creativity and enterprise; firms will be able to operate without being reined in by distortions (Fukuyama, 2000: 320). While universalists do acknowledge that there may be variations between different countries, these are underscored by 'objective' economic or technological differences between societies or institutional barriers to the implementation of best practice as opposed to fundamental differences in what constitutes 'the best way' (ibid.). At an organisation-level convergence 'implies a relative degree of disembeddedness of practices and structures, overriding more regionally or nationally specific institutions or behavioural predispositions' (Harzing and Sorge, 2003: 188). Within the universalist school a number of distinct variations emerge. The most influential strand of this thinking is the so-called neo-institutionalist, a very diverse tradition of thought. In this chapter we primarily focus on those approaches that seek to categorise countries according to particular taxonomies, and, hence, provide insights not only on *why* practices may be broadly similar in particular settings but also *how* they may differ according to time and place.

The bulk of work in this genre makes the assumption that the US model of strong shareholder rights, weak unions and a heavily deregulated labour market is the optimal model to be followed: all societies will inevitably move towards this model, if institutional distortions can and are removed (ibid.); this is seen as a central prerequisite for the efficient operation of markets.

The implication for labour is quite profound and as Thelen (2001: 75) postulates, the convergence of human resource management and industrial relations systems is regarded by this school as:

> A seemingly inexorable, inevitable slide toward deregulation, as high unemployment and increased capital mobility allow employers to dispense with strategies based on accommodating labour and instead shop for the best (i.e. least restrictive, least expensive labour regime). The result is a convergence theory that sees changes in the 'strong labour' countries as moving them in the direction of the weak labour countries. *(Thelen, 2001: 75)*

In practice, attempts to apply such theories to the management of people have two key characteristics. The first is its prescriptive nature: it aims to highlight best practices, aimed at what things should be – and perhaps, inevitably will be – rather than taking account of divergences from this model that are likely to manifest themselves even within the US context (Brewster, 2007). Second, it makes some very definite assumptions as to what best-practice HRM is likely to be like (Brewster, 2007). In practice, the type of HRM this will translate into is that where the employer has a relatively free hand to set the terms and conditions of the employment contract and work organisation without the 'interference of extraneous parties such as trade unions' (ibid.). This may either translate into a type of 'soft HRM', where the firm emphasises communication and consultation – but little in the way of genuine co-determination by way of collective bargaining and works councils – or 'hard HRM' where the firm tightly monitors employee performance, tailoring pay to individual effort and outcomes, and where employees can be readily hired and fired according to day-to-day organisational needs. Such approaches, of course, ignore the fact that individual forms of communication tend to be primarily top-down – junior employees will be reluctant to express unpopular opinions or be seen as bearers of bad news, if this opens them to retaliation by the superiors. Again, weak job security may allow the firm to rapidly adjust its workforce size according to organisational needs and the relative demand for its goods or services, but it also weakens the commitment of employees to the organisation. In addition, such approaches discount the knowledge and wisdom employees may have accumulated over a time period of working for the organisation, which may be extremely difficult to accurately cost the worth of and which will be lost forever should they be arbitrarily dispensed with.

Finally, it is important to note that the dominance of particular economic models is somewhat cyclical resulting in punctuated recalibration of perceptions of successful economic models which should be replicated. For example, some might argue that while the heyday of such studies was the 1990s and early 2000s, when the US was doing rather better than many of the advanced societies of Western Europe, the tables turned in the first decade of the twenty-first century when, to many, the US model appeared to be one of speculation, insecure living standards and labour repression, rather than that of a new and better future. It was argued that the US model encouraged firms to create new jobs, which ignored the fact that in the US unemployment is a lot worse than might initially seem apparent based on national statistics. These statistics obscure the fact that 6 million US workers hold highly insecure 'contingent' jobs, 15 million only work in part-time or reduced hours jobs without benefits, 3 million unemployed are not counted as such because they fail to qualify for benefits, 1.5 million are in the armed forces, and a further 2 million are in prison (Harcourt and Wood, 2007). What about in firm HR practices? Things are, again, a lot less efficient than might first seem apparent. While acknowledging that there is a good degree of heterogeneity in the nature of US industry, with some firms displaying paternalistic attitudes underscored by supportive welfare capitalist traditions (Jacoby, 1997) there is also a more dominant tradition in the US context which is less favourable to employees. Nonetheless, US firms invest relatively large amounts in training; this is partially to compensate for an extremely poor vocational training system, and the recurring need to provide basic induction training to new staff in the case of firms that have high staff turnover rates (cf. Harcourt and Wood, 2007). Again, high levels of productivity in the US more reflect long working hours and fewer holidays: continental Western European workers appear capable of producing similar amounts in significantly shorter periods of time, and thus are able to enjoy more leisure time and have better work–life balance, which, again, is likely to make them more useful when they are at work. Clearly, the economic challenges which the European Union, and particularly the Eurozone, has faced since the recession of the latter part of the past decade have the potential to challenge the perceived superiority of the European system among some commentators.

At a theoretical level, new-institutionalism has been criticised from a number of perspectives since its emergence, most notably by 'old' or historical institutionalists, who accord particular attention to how societies evolve, and the nature of defining institutional moments (cf. Sorge and Streeck, 1988; Sorge and Warner, 1986). For example, Sorge and his colleagues pointed to the fact that in the context of the UK and Germany, factories of similar size, producing similar products with similar technology could demonstrate very dissimilar forms of organisation, reflecting long-standing differences in industrial traditions – there was no evidence that a US or US-like model was necessarily the best, or that it was driving out other models. They also pointed to the persistence of both corporate and free market models as responses to economic and technological change in different countries (see also Turner, 2006).

Divergence: the endurance of national systems

Sorge and Streeck (1988) have argued that there has been an explosive divergence in industrial relations, rather than an implosive convergence toward one central best practice. Morley *et al.*'s (1996: 652) study pointed to elements of convergence and divergence in European industrial relations (IR) but concluded that overall, any coherent move toward convergence was 'a long way off'. Indeed, Hall and Soskice's argument that variance between the types of capitalism alluded to above will reinforce differences in national institutional frameworks seems to have significant merit based on the empirical evidence. This is a view shared by Geppert *et al.* (2003), whose case-based data suggests, that the more globalised the organisational strategy pursued by a firm, the more it perpetuates and reinforces cross national specifics. Thus they posit 'from this perspective one could argue that globalisation ultimately reinforces the importance of different national contexts' (2003: 833). Indeed, local variation is also something which multinational companies exploit in the context of the international division of labour and the global 'value chain' (Edwards and Kuruvilla, 2005; Wilkinson *et al.*, 2001). Such segmented coordination of value chains is premised on exploiting local differences in the way most effective to the MNC, by, for example, locating R&D in nations with high technical capability and production in nations where costs are low and lower levels of regulation allows greater flexibility (Ferner, 2010).

The key schools which are generally associated with divergence or persistence of national difference arguments are broadly classified as cross cultural accounts (cf. Hofstede, 1980, 2001; Trompenaars, 1993) and institutional approaches (cf. Hall and Soskice, 2001; Whitley, 1999). We now look in turn at these schools.

Cultural accounts

Although there have been a number of studies which have attempted to classify different nationalities on the basis of cultural dimensions (cf. Schneider and Barsoux, 2003 for a synthesis of the literature), we focus on the work of Geert Hofstede as the underlying premise of all of the studies is broadly similar and Hofstede's work is generally considered the seminal study in the field. Hofstede (2001: 9) defines culture thus: 'the collective programming of the mind that distinguishes the members of one group or category of people from another'.

Key to this definition, he argues, is the fact that social systems exist only because human behaviour is not random, but rather to a certain extent predictable. In developing his theory, Hofstede identifies three levels of human mental programming, the individual, collective and universal (2001: 2–3). While the universal level of mental programming is, as the name suggests, shared by almost all of human kind, 'a kind of biological operating system', and the individual is unique to each individual, it is the collective level that is key to understanding national cultures. Most of our mental programming is learned at this collective level, this is illustrated by the fact that we share traits with people who have gone through the same learning processes but with different genetic makeup. This level of culture is shared by people belonging to a certain group. Examples of collective cultural similarities include language and deference shown to elders among other traits. Key to our discussion is Hofstede's (2001: 11) thesis that although societal norms reflective of the collective level of human programming originate in a variety of ecological factors, they have resulted in 'the development and pattern maintenance of institutions in society with particular structures and ways of functioning'. Examples of these institutions include the education system, political systems, legislation and the family. Hofstede continues that although the institutions may change over time, the underlying societal norms prevail, reflecting the persistent influence of the majority value system. Any new institutions which emerge over time are smoothed by these underlying norms until their structures and functioning eventually adapt to the norms.

Hofstede differentiated between national cultures on five different criteria. These criteria are outlined in Box 11.1. Hofstede's study was based on a sample of some 116,000 IBM employees in 72 countries who completed pen-and-paper questionnaires between 1967 and 1973. In the latter stage, data from ten more countries and three multicultural regions were added (see Hofstede, 2001 for further detail on the methodology of the study).

The key underlying premise of the culturist approach is that cross-national differences in industrial relations systems and in organisations and the management of human resources are rooted in strong values and beliefs of the people in a given country. Practices are sustained because people find it unappealing, unethical or even repulsive to do otherwise (Sorge, 2004; Vaiman and Brewster, 2015). For example, individuals in countries which are classified as high on the collectivist dimension are more likely to be ideologically committed to the trade union movement, conversely where individualist preferences prevail individuals are likely to be less ideologically committed to the trade union cause.

Box 11.1 HRM in practice   Hoftstede's dimensions of cultural difference

1 **Power distance**, which is related to the different solutions to the basic problem of human inequality.
2 **Uncertainty avoidance**, which is related to the level of stress in a society in the face of an unknown future.
3 **Individualism versus collectivism**, which is related to the integration of individuals into primary groups.
4 **Masculinity versus femininity**, which is related to the division of emotional roles between men and women.
5 **Long-term versus short-term orientation**, which is related to the choice of focus for people's efforts: the future or the present.

Source: Hoftstede, 2001. *Culture's Consequences: Comparing Values, Behaviors, Institutions and Organizations Across Nations*, 2nd edn., Thousand Oaks, CA: Sage Publications © Geert Hofstede, B.V. Quoted with permission.

Although quite influential, the culturalist approach has never been universally accepted and, indeed, the approach and specifically Hoftstede's work have been subject to a number of criticisms. Most notable is the argument that although the approach is useful in explaining differences between nationalities, it fails to account for heterogeneity within the citizens of a given country. Rather it represents a central tendency within a nation (Evans *et al.*, 2011). Although the culturalists point to the link between the evolution of a countries business system or institutional structures and the characteristics of a national culture, they generally fail to explore the relationship between the cultural values and the structural and institutional characteristics of national economic systems (Ferner, 2010; Ferner *et al.*, 2001). The results of Hoftstede's study have also been specifically criticised. Tayeb (1996) points to the limitation that the study is based on an attitude-survey questionnaire, which, she argues, is the least appropriate way of measuring culture. His choice of dimensions of cultural difference (see Box 11.1) has also been criticised (McSweeney, 2002). A further significant criticism is the fact that the research on which this approach is founded has strong methodological flaws: it is limited to a single organisation (IBM) and thus the sample may not be representative (McSweeney, 2002). It could also be categorised as 'pseudo-science' in that it makes very precise claims as to social and organisational life on feeble empirical foundations; the popularity of the approach could be explained by its simplicity, and the ability to alleviate the need for original or critical thought among those who deploy it.

At a theoretical level, the perspective has further been condemned as overly functionalist; in other words, it assumes not only that that national systems work but that they do so as a coherent whole (Bacharach, 1989). It assumes that the culture both corresponds with national boundaries, and that national cultures are immutable. This raises the awkward questions as to whether some cultures are more conducive to doing business than others, and whether some nations are condemned to a particular path on account of their cultural heritage. Of course, this cannot explain why nations can reinvent themselves. Prior to the Second World War, Austria was a poverty stricken and unstable backwater, characterised by authoritarian and conflictual employment relations. Today, Austria is a highly prosperous country; Austrian employment relations are upheld as a model of cooperation between managers and workers. More recently, both New Zealand and Ireland have enjoyed strong economic recoveries linked to legal reforms that have promoted cooperation and mutual dependence, rather than conflict and 'winner takes all' relations at the workplace. While the success of the Irish model was subject to criticism owing to the economy's dramatic fall from grace during the global economic recession (2008 to 2014, in particular) which were posited to highlight the fragile foundations of the 'Irish economic miracle' the Irish have rebounded exceptionally well. However, the partnership model which underscored the Celtic Tiger era has come to an end, and it remains to be seen what the long-term prospects for the re-emergence of the partnership model are.

Ferner summarises the value of cultural approaches quite eloquently:

> This is not to say that cultural value differences are irrelevant, merely that by themselves they are inadequate form of explanation; they do not capture real differences in the ways in which economic activity is organised in different countries, and throw little light on processes of changes and evolution in business systems *(Ferner, 2010: 542)*.

Institutionalist perspectives

Neo-institutionalism – sociological approaches

Within the field of business and management studies, there has been growing interest in the relationship between institutions and firm-level practice. However, the term 'neo-institutionalism' is an extremely wide ranging one, and encompasses many very different schools of thought. For many years, sociological approaches were very popular, popularised by the writings of Harbison and Myers (1959), Kerr *et al.* (1960) and, above all, DiMaggio and Powell (1983). Such approaches focused on the micro-level dynamics and consequences of institutions, seeking to explain why individual and clusters of firms tended to replicate specific patterns of practice, and the manner in which such patterns emerged and disseminated. Institutionalisation has been defined as the 'process by which social processes, obligations, or actualities come to take on a rule-like status in social thought and action' (Meyer and Rowan, 1977: 341). Organisations have a tendency to copy what is done elsewhere in an attempt to gain legitimacy or the support of external agencies within a society (Strauss and Hanson, 1997). While functional or technical criteria may be key determinants of adoptions of innovations at an early stage, the importance of these determinants become weaker over time (Tolbert and Zucker, 1996). Organisations sharing the same environment are likely to demonstrate isomorphism (in other words, experience pressures to do similar things) as they are believed to become structurally similar as they respond to like pressures (Brewster and Wood, 2014; Gooderham *et al.*, 1999). However, whilst clearly of great value in exploring internal organisational dynamics, these approaches were stronger in providing sets of analytical tools, then identifying which predominant sets of practices were likely to manifest themselves in particular national settings at particular times. As Meyer and Rowan (1977) note, organisations may not conform to a set of institutionalised practices simply because they are taken for granted or 'constitute reality' but because they are rewarded for doing so through increased legitimacy, resources or survival capabilities. In other words, there are some wider contextual and broader external incentives which inform the organisation's decision to adopt the practices.

Rational–hierarchical approaches

Within the discipline of economics, quite a different approach evolved towards institutions that focused primarily on their effects in terms of providing incentives or disincentives to rational actors, with the assumption that strong private property rights underpinned growth (North, 1990). In looking at the relative strength of property (and hence owner) rights, particular attention was accorded to the effects of law, constitutions and politics (Djankov *et al.*, 2003: 596). Roe (2003) argues that specific political contexts are likely to encourage co-determination at the workplace between managers and employees; in turn, this will make for poor managerial accountability to owners as the system will both divide supervisory boards and encourage collusion between workers and managers at the expense of owners. For example, many managers seek personal aggrandisement through running a disproportionately large organisation, which, in turn, encourages the inefficient use of labour; in turn, the workforce colludes in the myth of needed bigness.

In their work on the effects of judicial systems and corporate governance, La Porta and colleagues (2000) suggest that a country's legal tradition will determine investor rights.

In common law countries, investor rights vis-à-vis other stakeholders are likely to be stronger, at the expense of other stakeholder interests; the converse is true in civil law countries (La Porta *et al.*, 2000). La Porta *et al.* further argue that national legal systems mould the regulation of labour (Botero *et al.*, 2004: 1379). In civil law countries, employee rights are more clearly delineated, while governments are more likely to directly regulate labour markets (ibid.: 1340). Hence, industrial relations will affect the manner in which a corporation is governed in the same manner as investor rights will (Botero *et al.*, 2004: 1379–80). When worker rights are strong, those of owners will be relatively weak, resulting in the 'bottom line' not receiving the same degree of priority as it would in a common law setting.

Pagano and Volpin (2005) propose a further variation on such accounts, and focus on the effects of electoral systems; proportional representation electoral systems are likely to promote coalition building, again constraining the rights of shareholders at the expense of other interest groupings: such systems also are likely to encourage neo-corporatist arrangements, promoting co-determinism at workplace level, again at the expense of owner rights. Both of these schools of thought follow on a long tradition of 'property rights' approaches to understanding management: shareholders have ultimate authority, it is necessary for managers to follow their wishes, with owners' rights taking precedence over the interests of all other groups in the firm (Rollinson and Dundon 2007: 73).

What this literature has in common is that it sees employee and owner rights as a 'zero-sum game' (Goergen *et al.*, 2009). If employees have rights, it must be to the detriment of owners and vice versa. Hence, in contexts where owner rights are stronger, one is more likely to encounter hard HRM policies geared to the bottom line – performance-based pay, close monitoring of output, effective performance appraisals and insecure job tenure. In contrast, where employee rights are stronger, one is more likely to find strong unions, collective bargaining, high job security and, indeed, structures such as works councils that give employees a say in the organisation of work.

Comparative capitalism approaches

This broad body of literature rejects the rational actor model – individuals make decisions not always on the basis of information, but also owing to commitments and relations with other actors. Hence, the varieties of capitalism literature locate the firm within a centre of relations with stakeholders – owners, employees, community and community associations, and government. The theoretical origins of this tradition are diverse, drawing on both functionalist and radical theories. Within the North American industrial relations literature, abiding influences have been Dunlop and Bendix's essentially functionalist accounts (see Bendix, 1956): national industrial relations practices constitute a coherent and incrementally developing system. Firms within a business system tend to adopt similar HR practices in the interests of familiarity, and because they are closely fitted to wider economic, social and cultural realities. Some of the criticisms levelled at cultural accounts can also be focused on this literature.

Within Europe there are many different accounts, including Whitley (1999) and Amable (2003). However, probably the most influential account has been Hall and Soskice's (2001) 'varieties of capitalism' approach, which builds on earlier work by Dore (2000) and Lincoln and Kalleberg (1990), that pointed to the key distinctions both in firm-level HR practices and wider governance between Anglo-American liberal market economies (LMEs) and collaborative market economies (CMEs). Examples of the former would include the US and the UK, and of the latter, Germany, the Low Countries, Scandinavia and Japan. Hall and Soskice seek out national-level differences in the nature of capitalism and attempt to develop terms that classify these more generally than has previously been the case. They conceptualise political economies as terrains populated by political actors, each with a rational self-interest to advance their own interests. While acknowledging a multiplicity of actors, such as individuals, governments, trade unions, suppliers and others, firms are regarded as the critical actors in any capitalist economy. Firms are viewed relationally, in that the relationships which they develop with key internal and external actors are inextricably linked to the firms' ability to develop core competencies or dynamic capabilities for developing, producing and distributing goods or services profitably.

The most significant characteristic of firms operating in LMEs in this regard is management's unilateral right to manage. This is reflected in the principle of 'employment-at-will', which dominates the US IR landscape. This places little obligation on firms to provide employees with a guarantee of employment, and thus employees can be hired and fired 'at will' on the basis of business needs, resulting in highly fluid labour markets characterised by the ease of release or hire of labour, and the investment by employees in general transferable skills as opposed to company-specific ones. This can be linked to the nature of corporate governance and the fact that the interests of shareholders are emphasised above those of any other stakeholder in the business relationship (Almond *et al.*, 2003).

Closely linked to individuals' investment in general transferable skills is the nature of the training and education system in LMEs. Vocational training is generally provided by institutions offering formal education emphasising general skills rather than company-specific apprenticeships, as companies are unwilling to invest in specific training as there is no guarantee employees will remain with the firm. The imperative of employees gaining general training is further emphasised by the fluid nature of labour markets, where general transferable skills determine employment potential. This high investment in general training lowers the cost of company-specific training, however, as firms generally focus on providing employees with in-house training not as expensive as traditional apprenticeship-type programmes. Rather the focus is on further developing general marketable skills (Hall and Soskice, 2001).

Conversely, in coordinated market economies industrial relations systems are characterised by strong industrial relations institutions. These institutions have evolved in response to companies' dependence on highly skilled employees with substantial work autonomy who could potentially hold their employers to ransom by moving to other firms, while employees may be exploited if they share information with management. In the German system many of these problems were addressed through the development of industry-level bargaining between employer organisations and trade unions. As Jacobi *et al.* (1998: 190–1) argue, while unions and employer organisations are in legal and formal terms independent, in reality they are mutually dependent, and should be considered 'reliable partners within a network of stable cooperation'. These provisions arguably protect employees against arbitrary management decision making, including changes to working conditions and layoffs, thus encouraging employees to invest in company-specific skills and extra effort.

Hall and Soskice link these differences to different national strengths. The pluralist HRM policies found in CMEs are likely to be conducive to high quality incrementally innovative production (exemplifiers of the latter including Toyota, Volkswagen, Siemens, etc.). In contrast, the managerially dominant types of HRM found in LMEs are likely to be associated with either low-value-added service sector activity, or high technology innovation. This is likely to result in a number of key distinctions in terms of skills needs and HR practices. Incremental innovation requires good industry specific skills, high security of tenure (in order to encourage the development of firm-specific human capital) and cooperation and knowledge sharing through advanced forms of participation that genuinely empower employees (such as found through centralised collective bargaining and works councils) (Thelen, 2001). In contrast, hi-tech industry requires generic tertiary skills (e.g. university education), a mobile workforce and more individually oriented reward and incentives systems (Thelen, 2001). The low-value-added sweatshop paradigm requires little investment in people, with pay being tied to output or being held at the lowest acceptable level. The fact that clusters of HR practices continue to be found within particular regions and nations points to the importance of understanding national context.

Hence, Locke *et al.* point to the significance of the historical development of the employment relations system within a nation state, noting:

[A]lthough a particular approach to employment relations has emerged in all the advanced industrial nations . . . [in their study] . . . the particular from [of the employment relations approach] it has taken and its extent vary considerably within countries, between firms, industries and regions, and between countries with different historical traditions and institutional arrangements. *(Locke et al., 1995: 143)*

As with rational hierarchical accounts, a limitation of much of the literature on comparative capitalism is a neglect of the role of the multinational company, which, by definition, crosses national institutional domains. An exception to this is business systems theory, an approach that also differs from other approaches to comparative capitalism in the attention it accords to in-firm practices (Whitley, 1999). Business systems theory suggests that in spanning different national domains, MNCs are more lightly rooted into a particular context not only because they face competing pressures from country of origin and domicile but it is easier for them to exit from a setting not to their liking, making it easier not to compromise. However, business systems theory suggests that MNCs will seek to reap the competitive advantages accruing from a particular context, and hence have some incentive to integrate into local production regimes (Morgan, 2012). The latter is likely to entail, to at least some degree, emulating their work and employment relations policies. Given what you have studied thus far in Chapter 11, which perspective do you find more persuasive – convergence or divergence?

Empirical ways of understanding diversity

The preceding discussion has illustrated that we can see that diversity in HR practice may be understood from a range of different theoretical starting points. At an empirical level, there is a rich body of literature aimed at understanding variations in HR practices at a country level. While sometimes employing some of the above theories as a starting point, this literature is primarily concerned with documenting key HR practices within specific national contexts. Sometimes these have been consolidated into books about HRM in specific regions or continents, an example being Routledge's *Global* HRM series of edited books on HRM in specific regions, such as Europe (Holt Larsen and Mayrhofer, 2006), Central and Eastern Europe (Morley *et al.*, 2009), Africa (Kamoche *et al.*, 2003), Asia Pacific (Budhwar, 2004) and the Middle East (Budhwar and Mellahi, 2006), and the Wood and Brewster (2007) volume on industrial relations in Africa. These books have been distinguished by high-quality contributions often by locally based country experts, with the editorial team drawing out common themes and trends. A further recent innovation has been Morley *et al.*'s (2006) and Ackers and Wilkinson's (2003) contributions, which take a regional perspective on the comparison of industrial relations systems.

Similar country-study-type articles have been published in a range of academic journals, most notably *International Journal of Human Resource Management*, and *Employee Relations*. These articles tend to focus on defining features of HRM either from a functional-areas or relationship approach. Articles in the former genre seek to document and explain national or regional practices in recruitment and planning, motivation and reward, industrial relations, and/or human resource development. In contrast, articles following on the latter approach tend to focus on issues such as the degree of employer–employee interdependence and the extent of delegation to employees (Whitley, 1999). The former would include job security, and the extent to which employers will invest in their people, and employees inclined to accumulate organisation-specific skills. Meanwhile, the latter would include the degree of participation and involvement. In practice, the comparative lessons of individual national experiences are often only briefly alluded to, or presented in a highly attenuated form, it being left up to the reader to decide what the experience of a particular nation or region reveals about the practice of HRM more generally.

A variation of such approaches is sub-national studies and supra-national studies. As Boyer and Hollingsworth (1997) note, institutions are nested at supra- national and sub-national levels. In other words, although national setting heavily impacts on HR policies, institutions – be they rules (formal laws and informal conventions), training structures, development incentives and/or physical infrastructural provisions and support – may also vary within states, or may be shared between countries. For example, European Union directives governing labour standards have encouraged moves towards common continent-wide HR practices in many areas, an example being the treatment of elderly workers. This has led some commentators to suggest that a European-wide social model is emerging associated with cooperative HR policies: other, more pessimistic writers have argued that Europeanisation has been associated with the introduction of more hardline management-oriented 'Anglo-Saxon' practices that have seriously damaged more cooperative continental European forms of HRM (O'Hagan 2002; see also Morley *et al.*, 2006 section 2 for a discussion on these issues).

Within countries, regional development initiatives (and local training realities and historical legacies) have led to some regions pursuing distinct trajectories. An example of this would be the Grenoble hi-tech cluster in France: such regional concentrations of industry have encouraged firms to tailor their HR policies accordingly given specific sectoral needs and local skills realities. People management here centres on the efficient use of a relatively young incoming (from other parts of France, and abroad) workforce, with high levels of tertiary education, and the support of a number of excellent public research centres (Aniello, 2004: 314). In a 2004 edited collection by Colin Crouch *et al.* (2004), it was found that local production systems could be encountered in many countries across Europe, each bringing with them associated sets of HR policies and practices, in many respects different from national norms. More recently, the issue of sub-national governance systems has received increasing attention (see Almond, 2011b). With these issues in mind, what are the key challenges in conducting research on differences in HRM and industrial relations across border?

Conclusion

This chapter has aimed to introduce some of the major debates within the field of comparative HRM. A growing body of theoretical enquiry and empirical evidence points to the fact that individual nations and regions remain distinct in many areas, with there being many distinct paths to competitiveness. This would appear to vindicate the literature on comparative capitalism. At the same time, in studying comparative HRM, we need to be aware that even if countries and regions may not be coming more alike, they are all subject to change. In other words, in many respects we are studying a moving target. This would reflect the role of supra-national institutions such as the EU, technological advances, changes in laws and innovations in policy and firm-level practices and in some instances the impact of innovations introduced by foreign multinational companies operating in the host country (Ferner and Quintanilla, 2002; Gennard, 1974; Gunnigle, 1995). Hence, the new Irish HRM model, for example, is rather different from that encountered 20 years ago (see Collings *et al.*, 2008; Gunnigle, 1995). This makes the empirically oriented studies that formed the focus of the second part of this chapter of particular importance: keeping abreast of innovations in practice is an essential part of being an excellent HR manager, and, indeed, an excellent student in HRM.

CASE STUDY 11.1

HRM IN MOZAMBIQUE

GEOFFREY WOOD AND DAVID G. COLLINGS

After almost 500 years of a particularly exploitative form of colonial rule, a failed socialist experiment and a bloody civil war, Mozambique underwent radical economic adjustment in the late 1980s and 1990s in line with the then prevailing neo-liberal orthodoxy. While the latter had severely adverse consequences for large areas of an already fragile manufacturing sector, it also led to an – albeit limited – increase in foreign investment and a partial revitalisation of the transport and tourism industries.

A nationwide survey of HR practices in Mozambique revealed little evidence of innovation or of leading edge practices. While most firms had a specialised people management function, the techniques employed remained personal, informal, but also top-down. At the same time, HRM techniques cannot be considered to be uniformly 'bleak house' or 'low road'; the 'low road' hypothesis is thus falsified. Rather, HRM practices seem to have much in common with those noted in other African countries; this would include a reliance on personal networks for recruitment, the use of informal training structures, and poor pay and working conditions being mitigated by a willingness of management to make informal concessions to workers in the event of personal difficulties. In contrast to the 'low road' model, Mozambican managers do not make use of rigid sets of rules, little communication, fixed bare minimum wages, and an unwillingness to depart from fixed procedures (cf. Taylor and Bain, 2003). The dominant 'informal' managerial style is founded on autocratic partriarchalism, underpinned by personal ties. On the one hand, external shocks to the Mozambican economy have resulted in large-scale job shedding that must have done much to erode any sense of mutual commitment. On the other hand, managers retain close personal contact with the workforce – *inter alia*, through general meetings – and remain willing to adjust terms and conditions of service in response to individual need. The survey would thus provide further evidence to support Harrison (2000) and Pitcher's (2002) arguments that the Mozambican context is one characterised by long-term continuities, despite seemingly radical sociopolitical changes.

At the same time, the survey revealed evidence of a range of 'best-practice' techniques among a small minority of firms. While there is little doubt that the latter are likely to be best equipped to escape reverting to a low-wage, low-skill, low-value-added trajectory, it remains uncertain whether such a path is viable in a context of institutional weakness and cut-throat competition from abroad.

In summary, the survey revealed that relatively few firms make use of a full and complementary range of high-performance work practices. However, most firms have not reverted to the 'low road'/'bleak house' model that has become a feature of people management in specific sectors within advanced societies. Indeed, many firms rely on traditional patriarchal–authoritarianism, and are reluctant to concede their workers even basic benefits such as paid vacations and sick leave. On the other hand, many are willing to grant leave at short notice and/or advances on wages, in the event of individual workers experiencing personal difficulties. Contact is maintained with the workforce through irregular meetings, both scheduled and ad hoc, while the mode of firms made use informal on the job training. The dominant Mozambican paradigm of people management shares these common features with that found in many other tropical African countries; such practices represent the product of both adverse external environments, periodic systemic shocks and colonial and/or precolonial traditions.

However, in Mozambique, the ability of this highly personal/patriarchal managerial paradigm to engender any sense of mutual commitment is likely to have been eroded by episodic rounds of redundancies, while firms are unlikely to systematically invest in their people through formal training programmes or systematic career planning given a highly competitive environment. Less principled rivals may not only gain a short-term cost advantage, but are able to poach staff from those firms who provide effective training and development. The diffusion of higher-value-added production paradigms is only likely in a more supportive institutional context that encourages firms to buy into mutually advantageous sets of rules governing fair play (cf. Marsden, 1999), and which limits the rewards accruing to bad practice. While the more efficient enforcement of legislation may encourage the broader diffusion of 'high road' practices, their sustainability is, at least in part, contingent on the diffusion and reconstitution of supportive conventions (Dore, 2000); regrettably, this makes it extremely difficult to depart from the dominant existing paradigm.

Source: Webster and Wood, 2005.

Questions

1   What are the key features of HRM in Mozambique?
2   Why do you think HRM in Mozambique has been characterised by many continuities?

CASE STUDY 11.2
IRELAND AND THE MULTINATIONALS

DAVID G. COLLINGS AND GEOFFREY WOOD

Ireland is one of the most globalised countries in the world, owing to the significance of foreign owned MNCs which have established subsidiaries there. The scale of foreign direct investment (FDI) there is driven by a consistent public policy agenda, pursued by successive governments, of providing incentives to attract MNCs to invest in Ireland. This policy has proved very successful and recent research confirms that there are some 470 foreign-owned MNCs in Ireland (McDonnell et al., 2007) employing over 140,000 people. US-owned multinationals are particularly significant players there, with 226 US-owned subsidiaries. These include large high-profile firms such as IBM, Microsoft, Dell, Google, Pfizer, and the like. These firms are estimated to employ over 7 per cent of the private sector non-agricultural labour force and also contribute significantly through indirect employment through suppliers and the like and make a very substantial contribution to taxation revenues in Ireland.

Given the disproportionate significance of FDI and American FDI in particular in Ireland, combined with the expectation that HRM policies and practices are likely to converge on the US model, Ireland represents a very interesting context to study the convergence of HRM through looking at subsidiary practice in subsidiary operations. Further, if we do expect to witness convergence of HRM practice, Ireland would represent an interesting test case. The expected convergence would

be even more likely to emerge in US MNCs owing to the fact that they tend to be quite ethnocentric in managing the foreign operations and display a preference for centrally developed, standardised policies in their foreign operations.

There is a broad consensus that MNCs have been an important source of innovation in management practices in Ireland, particularly in the application of new HRM/IR approaches and in expanding the role of the specialist HR function. For example, MNCs have been associated with innovation in areas such as the diffusion of so-called 'high-commitment' work systems and performance-related pay innovations, which appear to have transferred, to a degree at least, to indigenous firms. Further, US MNCs have been particularly strong in their resistance to recognising trade unions, a trend which stands in contrast to Irish traditions, which were generally supportive of trade unions role in the workplace. Recent research reveals that over time, as the country's reliance on the FDI sector has increased, MNCs have found it easier to establish and operate subsidiaries on a non-union basis.

However, we do still see evidence of divergence between US MNCs and indigenous firms suggesting that divergence remains important in the Irish context. For example, based on Gunnigle et al.'s (2002) study, we see that US subsidiaries in Ireland put substantially more emphasis on performance appraisal and reward than did Irish organisations. Significantly, US MNCs displayed a degree of adoption of HR practice to account to local standards. This study also unearthed differences between US firms and subsidiaries of other nationalities, providing further evidence of sustained divergence. More recently, Collings *et al.* (2008) argued for elements of an essentially hybrid system with regard to industrial relations in US MNCs, reflecting some particularly 'American' practices in these firms, again suggesting divergence with indigenous firms.

Thus despite the relative power of US MNCs in the Irish context and the reliance of the Irish economy on the FDI sector, there is little evidence of complete convergence between US MNCs, other foreign MNCs and indigenous firms in the Irish context.

Questions

1 Consider the reasons why differences remain between foreign MNCs and indigenous firms in the Irish context.

2 What challenges may a heavy reliance on FDI have on a host government in terms of balancing the needs of powerful firms and employees in the host economy?

CASE STUDY 11.3

INSTITUTIONAL CHANGE, WORK AND EMPLOYMENT RELATIONS: THE CHANGING FORTUNES OF MERCEDES-BENZ IN SOUTH AFRICA

GEOFFREY WOOD

Cultural approaches to comparing HR between contexts tend to assume that countries do not readily change their defining cultural identities, and this will exert long-term effects on work and employment relations. While institutional approaches also assume some degree of embeddedness – that is that certain generally accepted ways of doing things are likely to persist – the recent literature on institutions has highlighted the manner in which institutional frameworks and associated rules can and do change. Such changes may be incremental, or they may involve significant ruptures at key historical moments from past forms of regulation and associated rules of conduct. In practical terms, this means that continuity cannot be always assumed in comparing work and employment relations within and between contexts. At the same time, major ruptures are relatively rare, and often carry over elements of the past order; changes in national systems are more commonly so incremental as to be invisible to all but a close observer.

In the 1980s, Mercedes-Benz's plant in East London, South Africa, was characterised by high levels of conflict. According to then HR Manager, Ian Russel, 'The union did not recognize management's right to manage. We had no structures to institutionalize conflict, no procedures, no recognition agreement' (quoted in Desai, 2008). Reflecting on events, then head of Mercedes-Benz South Africa (MBSA) Christoph Kopke acknowledged that 'Supervisors used to clock in and then lock themselves in their offices for the whole day. They didn't dare go out on the assembly lines.'

By the late 1990s, the situation had completely transformed. Reflecting this, in 2009, the plant was awarded the JD Power IQS gold quality award for the plant with the fewest defects and malfunctions of its product of any car plant in the world serving the US market, a feat that was repeated in 2010. 'To receive such an award despite the relentless pressure and stresses of the global recession over the past two years, points to the brilliant quality of our people and processes,' said company representative Hansgeorg Niefer. In 2011 a worker at the plant of 30 years standing, Francois Waters, received Daimler's Laureate of Quality Excellence 2011. Waters said:

> I felt honoured to receive this award, and humbled to be rewarded for coming to work every day and just trying to achieve the best that I possibly can. It really is a combined effort as teamwork is critical to quality standards and we depend heavily on each other's strengths. It is important that everyone has the same mindset regarding quality, and that our targets are clear to everyone who has any input into the production process. Our processes are benchmarked, and it is vital that each employee ensures that they work strictly according to set standards, day in, day out.

What can account for the changes that took place in the Mercedes-Benz plant in South Africa? And is this anything to do with institutions? Can we compare institutions and associated HR practices not only between countries, but also within the same country at different points in time?

So, although in looking at institutional approaches to comparing HRM, we tend to look at comparing different countries. However, it is also possible to look at how institutional changes have affected HR practices within a particular country.

South Africa underwent dramatic changes in both governmental structures and in terms of informal accepted rules of conduct as part and parcel of the end of apartheid in the early 1990s. Under apartheid, work and employment relations followed what is often called racial fordism, which may be defined as classic methods of mass production combined with institutionalised racism. Buoyed up by substantial gold revenues from the 1950s until the 1970s, the apartheid government had the financial resources to engage in both an active industrial policy and massive social engineering. Under apartheid, the South African domestic market was heavily protected. Moreover, the government provided a mass of subsidies to support sectors of manufacturing. Finally, large-scale infrastructural projects, including the electrification of the railway system and the expansion of port facilities greatly helped industry.

Apartheid was, in many respects, a contradictory system, which incorporated elements both to advance poor whites and to help big business, above all that which was Afrikaans-owned. However, the greatest contradictions concerned the usage of black labour. On the one hand, the apartheid regime had the long-term ambition of banishing the black majority to the rural periphery. On the other hand, large areas of industry and the mines were heavily dependent on cheap black labour. In practice, what happened was that the government sought to control the influx of black workers into the cities, linking temporary urban residential rights with employment. Moreover, job protection meant that many skilled trades were reserved for whites. In terms of labour legislation, blacks were denied access to the statutory industry-wide collective bargaining structures set up in the 1920s. Finally, the best universities and technical training institutions were reserved for whites. In practice, this led to the large-scale employment of black labour within inherently inefficient industries; institutionalised racism and low pay ensured that productivity generally low, and quality often poor.

Official propaganda notwithstanding, the African majority actively resisted the imposition and operation of apartheid through successive waves of resistance. There were many attempts to organise black workers in trade unions prior to the 1970s, but these failed to make much headway owing to a reliance on a few key activists and counterwaves of state repression. In the early 1970s, the situation changed dramatically. There were two reasons for this. First, the collapse of Portuguese rule in the southern African states of Mozambique and Angola led to the apartheid government seeking to wean itself off its reliance on ultra-cheap migrant labour from neighbouring states. High gold prices allowed for modest – but still significant – wage increases to entice greater numbers of black South Africans to work on the mines. This led to waves of spontaneous strikes in the urban centres of both Durban and East London, as workers sought similar wage increases for manufacturing jobs. Quite simply, after a long period of 'little hope', some change in material conditions finally seemed possible. Second, groups of liberal student activists established a number of worker services organisations, which soon developed into trade unions. Unlike earlier attempts at organising black workers, they adopted strong structures of shopfloor democracy, based on the British shop steward model.

The South African motor industry is concentrated in the Eastern Cape region. This was on account of the region's roughly equidistant location to the major urban centres of Cape Town, Durban and Johannesburg. In practice, a number of motor manufacturers set up plants to assemble knock-down kits in the Eastern Cape's port cities of Port Elizabeth and East London. As the apartheid regime gradually raised protective tariffs, most moved over to an ever-expanding of manufacturing activities. Mercedes-Benz even set up an engine manufacturing facility, at the time, the only Mercedes engine plant outside of Germany. Rather more sinisterly, its truck manufacturing facility supplied lorries and truck chassis that were used by the apartheid military. High local content helped circumnavigate sanctions.

Within the rural periphery, the apartheid government set about transforming the tribal reservations into 'independent' countries, with the ultimate aim of taking away South African citizenship from black South Africans. Adjoining East London, this involved the setting up of an 'independent' state apparatus, which transformed a particularly impoverished reserve into what ultimately became the 'country' of Ciskei, ruled with an iron fist by kleptocratic members of the Sebe family. Conveniently, for manufacturing firms in East London, a new township was established in the south-eastern tip of Ciskei within, albeit long, commuting distance of that city. Pass laws meant that workers would have to endure long hours on public transport to return to the 'homeland' every evening. And, unencumbered by the remaining judicial checks and balances and civil society organisations in South Africa, the Ciskei authorities were free to brutally 'discipline' workers seen as troublemakers; the latter included union activists.

On the one hand, the Mercedes-Benz plant in East London was relatively unusual on account of the relatively higher wages offered and the relative quality of its products (most other locally made cars could charitably be described as unreliable rust buckets up until the mid-1980s!). On the other hand, the relatively progressive reputation of management and the large workforce made it an attractive target for union activists. Soon the plant established a reputation for strike proneness, with unions using the wage increases forced at Mercedes as a bargaining chip against employers elsewhere in the region. The brutality, greed and general antics of the Sebe family, and, more generally speaking, Ciskeian 'independence', further radicalised the East London workforce at large.

Reforms tabled in 1979 by the apartheid government derecialised centralised bargaining. This was with the intention of co-opting increasingly effective unions, and drawing union leadership away from rank and file. On the one hand, this attempt generally failed: unions used centralised bargaining as a source of strength. On the other hand, workers for firms that already had a reputation for good wages naturally were suspicious of wage setting on industry lines. This led to ongoing tensions between union officials and the radicalised Mercedes-Benz workforce.

These tensions came to a head with the 1990 Mercedes-Benz strike. What happened was that groups of workers demanded that the firm withdraw from centralised bargaining, and rather bargain at plant level. Groups of workers occupied the plant, in defiance of union officials. After nine weeks, the occupiers were forcibly evicted by the police, with the overt support of management, and to the relief of the union. While spectacular, this occupation represented only one example of ongoing trench warfare between management and workers. This included threats of violence against foremen, the adoption of fake military garb (complete with fake weaponry) by sections of the workforce, and the large-scale theft of company property. Entire areas of the factory were reduced to no-go zones for management. Meanwhile, entire completed engines were going missing from the engine plant, and at least one finished motor car appears to have been mislaid.

The South African domestic market for luxury cars was not very large, and sanctions precluded sales to most other African states. Finally, during the 1980s, the South African economy experienced a deep recession. Given all this, the parent company in Germany seriously contemplated abandoning the enterprise in its entirety. However, whether because of altruism, a commitment to the region, and/or perhaps even guilt on having produced trucks employed by the apartheid military, Mercedes decided to stay in East London. In addition to further investment in workforce skills development, the somewhat disparate collection of factory buildings (interposed with public roads) was entirely enclosed into a large single walled complex. Not only did this reduce endemic theft, but it helped create a more uniform identity that was also helped through initiatives to beautify the factory environment and its surrounds. And, as growing numbers of Ciskei-based manufacturing firms collapsed (despite lavish state subsidies), jobs at Mercedes became increasingly desirable, not only owing to the good pay but also through the growing dearth of meaningful alternatives.

However, relief arrived for the Mercedes plant from an unexpected quarter. The last hardline apartheid president, the dangerously stupid and narrow-minded P.W. Botha, suffered a stroke. Tired of his incessant bullying, a cabal of cabinet ministers ousted the temporarily incapacitated president. He was replaced by F.W. De Klerk, who, although having a conservative reputation, lacked Botha's close ties to the security establishment. Exiled to the political wilderness, Botha largely recovered from his stroke just in time to see his life's work being undone. On opening parliament in February 1990, De Klerk astounded the world by ending apartheid, and starting negotiations with previously banned black resistance organisations, most notably the African National Congress (ANC). While undeniably an act of great political courage, De Klerk was prompted by the fact that weak minerals prices meant that the apartheid government was running out of money. Cautious neo-liberal reforms were accelerated when, following democratic elections, the ANC came into power in 1994. Essentially, this included the abandonment of a range of subsidies for inefficient industries, privatisations and an end of most protectionist measures. All this led to wholesale job losses in manufacturing. However, the ending of the tensions caused by apartheid and the inefficiencies imposed by largely racial divisions of labour – and the ongoing skilling of the African labour force – meant that successful manufacturing firms could have far leaner staffing. In the end, all this meant that South Africa experienced a growth without jobs.

At Mercedes, many of the tensions of the past dissipated with the end of apartheid. The skilled Mercedes workforce valued the prestige and high pay that came with the job in an area of by now very high unemployment. Freed from racial discrimination governing where one could live, many workers could enjoy comfortable middle-class lifestyles. Furthermore, significant numbers of shop stewards moved into junior management positions. While Mercedes had recognised unions for many years, employee participation and involvement had now broadened to a new level. Employees directly or via their representatives had a say in the organisation of work, the introduction of new technology and a range of quality issues. Communication was much improved, supplemented by mature, centralised collective bargaining at industry level. Productivity rates soared, with a strong mutual commitment by all parties to the future of the enterprise.

Over 20 years since the end of apartheid, Mercedes in East London are today a model plant. The quality of production and the productivity of the workforce are among the highest of any car plant in the world. So many Mercedes cars are exported from the East London plant that an entire new car terminal had to be constructed, necessitating a major expansion of East London harbour.

Questions

1 What happened at Mercedes-Benz in East London? What is the relationship between changes in the plant, and broader institutional transformation?

2 What are the limitations of cultural approaches to comparative HRM for understanding what happened at Mercedes-Benz?

3 Did the fact that the plant was owned by a large multinational have any effect on outcomes? If so, what were these?

CASE STUDY 11.4

REFLECTIVE CASE STUDY

GEOFFREY WOOD AND DAVID G. COLLINGS

Think of a company you know? Do its HR policies in any respect represent a product of the society in which it operates? And do firms of a similar size in the same sector practise roughly similar HR policies? If so why, and if not, why not?

Bibliography

Ackers, P. and Wilkinson, A. (2003) *Understanding Work and Employment: Industrial Relations in Transition*, Oxford: Oxford University Press.

Almond, P. (2011a) 'Re-visiting "country of origin" effects on HRM in multinational corporations', *Human Resource Management Journal*, Vol.21, No.3, 258–71.

Almond, P. (2011b) 'The sub-national embeddedness of international HRM', *Human Relations*, Vol.64, No.4, 531–51.

Almond, P., Edwards, T. and Clarke, I. (2003) 'Multinationals and changing national business systems in Europe: towards the "shareholder value" model?', *Industrial Relations Journal*, Vol.34, No.5, 430–45.

Amable, B. (2003) *The Diversity of Modern Capitalism*. Oxford: Oxford University Press.

Aniello, V. (2004) 'Grenoble Valley', in Crouch, C., Le Galès, P., Trigilia, C. and Voelzkow, H. (eds.) *Changing Governance of Local Economies*, Oxford: Oxford University Press.

Bacharach, S. (1989) 'Organizational theories: some criteria for evaluation', *Academy of Management Review*, Vol.14, No.4, 496–515.

Bendix, R. (1956) *Work and Authority in Industry*, New York: John Wiley.

Botero, J., Djankov, S., La Porta, R., Lopez-de-Silanes, S. and Shleifer, A. (2004) 'The regulation of labor', *Quarterly Journal of Economics*, Vol.119, No.4, 1339–82.

Boxall, P. (1995) 'Building the theory of comparative HRM', *Human Resource Management Journal*, Vol.5, No.5, 5–17.

Boxall, P. and Purcell, J. (2000) 'Strategic human resource management: where have we come from and where should we be going?' *International Journal of Management Reviews*, Vol.2, No.2, 183–203.

Boyer, R. and Hollingsworth, J.R. (1997) 'From national embeddedness to spatial and institutional nestedness', in Hollingsworth, J.R. and Boyer, R. (eds.) *Contemporary Capitalism: The Embeddedness of Institutions*, Cambridge and New York: Cambridge University Press.

Brewster, C. (2006) 'Comparing HRM policies and practices across geographical borders', in Stahl, G.K. and Björkman, I. (eds.) *Handbook of Research in International Human Resource Management*, Cheltenham: Edward Elgar.

Brewster, C. (2007) 'Comparative HRM: European views and perspectives', *International Journal of Human Resource Management*, Vol.18, No.5, 769–87.

Brewster, C. and Mayrhofer, W. (2011) 'Comparative human resource management', in Harzing, A.W. and Pinnington, A. (eds.) *International Human Resource Management* (3rd edn.), London: Sage.

Brewster, C., Mayrhofer, W. and Morley, M. (eds.) (2004) *Human Resource Management: Evidence of Convergence*? Oxford: Elsevier Butterworth Heinemann.

Brewster, C. and Wood, G.T. (2014) 'Comparative HRM and international HRM', *The Routledge Companion to International Human Resource Management*, 121.

Budhwar, P. (2004) *Managing Human Resources in Asia Pacific*, London: Routledge.

Budhwar, P. and Mellahi, K. (eds.) (2006*) Human Resource Management in the Middle East*, London: Routledge.

Collings, D.G., Gunnigle, P. and Morley, M.J. (2008) 'Boston or Berlin: American MNCs and the shifting contours of industrial relations in Ireland', *International Journal of Human Resource Management*, Vol.19, No.2, 240–61.

Collings, D.G., Lavelle, J. and Gunnigle, P. (2011) 'The role of MNEs', pp. 402–20, in Barry, M. and Wilkinson, A. (eds.) *Handbook of Research on Comparative Employment Relations*, Cheltenham: Edward Elgar.

Crouch, C., Le Galès, P., Trigilia, C. and Voelzkow, H. (eds.) (2004) *Changing Governance of Local Economies*, Oxford: Oxford University Press.

Desai, A. (2008) 'Productivity pacts, the 2000 Volkswagen strike, and the trajectory of COSATU in post-apartheid South Africa', *Mediations*, Vol.24, No.1, 25–51.

DiMaggio, P.J. and Powell, W.W. (1983) 'The iron cage revisited: institutional isomorphism and collective rationality in organizational fields', *American Sociological Review*, Vol.48, No.2, 147–60.

Djankov, S., Glaeser, E., La Porta, R., Lopez-de-Silnes, F. and Shleifer, A. (2003) 'The new comparative economics', *Journal of Comparative Economics*, Vol.31, No.4, 595–619.

Dore, R. (2000) *Stock Market Capitalism: Welfare Capitalism*, Cambridge: Cambridge University Press.

Edwards, T, and Kuruvilla, S. (2005) 'International HRM: national business systems, organizational politics, and the international diffusion of labour in MNCs', *International Journal of Human Resource Management*, Vol.16, No.1, 1–21.

Evans, P., Pucik, V. and Bjorkman, I. (2011) *The Global Challenge: Frameworks for International Human Resource Management*, New York: McGraw Hill/Irwin.

Ferner, A. (1997) 'Country of origin effects and human resource management in multinational companies', *Human Resource Management Journal*, Vol.7, No.1, 19–36.

Ferner, A. (2010) 'HRM in multinational companies', pp. 541–60, in Wilkinson, A., Bacon, N., Redman, T. and Snell, S. (eds.) *The SAGE Handbook of Human Resource Management,* London: Sage.

Ferner, A. and Hyman, R. (1998) 'Introduction', in Ferner, A. and Hyman, R. (eds.) *Changing Industrial Relations in Europe* (2nd edn.), Oxford: Blackwell.

Ferner, A. and Quintanilla, J. (2002) 'Between globalisation and capitalist variety: multinationals and the international diffusion of employment relations', *European Journal of Industrial Relations*, Vol.8, No.3, 243–50.

Ferner, A., Quintanilla, J. and Varul, M.Z. (2001) 'Country of origin effects, host country effects, and the management of HR in multinationals: German companies in Britain and Spain', *Journal of World Business*, Vol.36, No.2, 107–27.

Friedman, T. (1999) *The Lexus and the Olive Tree*, New York: Farrar and Strauss.

Fukuyama, F. (2000) 'One journey, one destination', in Burns, R. and Rayment-Pickard, H. (eds.) *Philosophies of History*, Oxford: Blackwell.

Gennard, J. (1974) 'The impact of foreign-owned subsidiaries on host country labour relations: the case of the United Kingdom', in Weber, A.W. (ed.) *Bargaining Without Boundaries*, Chicago, IL: University of Chicago Press.

Geppert, M., Matten, D. and Williams, K. (2003) 'Change management in MNCs: how global convergence intertwines with national diversity', *Human Relations*, Vol.64, No.7, 807–38.

Goergen, M., Brewster, C. and Wood, G. (2009) 'Corporate governance regimes and employment relations in Europe', *Industrial Relations/Relations Industrielles*, Vol.64, No.6, 620–40.

Gooderham, P., Nordhaug, O. and Ringdal, K. (1998) 'When in Rome, do they do as the Romans?' HRM Practices of US Subsidiaries in Europe, *Management International Review*, Vol.38, 47–64.

Gooderham, P.N., Nordhaug, O. and Ringdal, K. (1999) 'Institutional and rational determinants of organizational practices: human resource management in European firms', *Administrative Science Quarterly*, Vol.44, No.3, 507–31.

Guest, D.E. (1990) 'Human resource management and the American dream', *Journal of Management Studies*, Vol.27, No.4, 977–87.

Gunnigle, P. (1995) 'Collectivism and the management of industrial relations in greenfield sites', *Human Resource Management Journal*, Vol.5, No.3, 24–40.

Gunnigle, P., Murphy, K.M., Cleveland, J., Heraty, N. and Morley, M. (2002) 'Localisation in human resource management: comparing American and European multinational corporations', *Advances in International Management*, Vol.14, 259–84.

Hall, P. and Soskice, D. (2001) 'An introduction to the varieties of capitalism', pp. 1–68, in Hall, P. and Soskice, D. (eds.) *Varieties of Capitalism: The Institutional Foundations of Comparative Advantage*, Oxford: Oxford University Press.

Harbison, F.H. and Myers, C. (eds.) (1959) *Management in the Industrial World: An International Analysis*, New York: McGraw Hill.

Harcourt, M. and Wood, G. (2007) 'The importance of employment protection for skill development in coordinated market economies', *European Journal of Industrial Relations*, Vol.13, No.2, 141–59.

Harrison, G. (2000) *The Politics of Democratization in Rural Mozambique*, New York: Edward Mellon Press.

Harzing, A.W. and Sorge, A. (2003) 'The relative impact of country of origin and universal contingencies on internationalization strategies and corporate control in multinational enterprises: worldwide and European perspectives', *Organizational Studies*, Vol.24, 187–214.

Hirst, P. and Thompson, G. (1999) *Globalisation in Question* (2nd edn.), Cambridge: Polity.

Hoftstede, G. (1980) *Culture's Consequences.* Thousand Oaks: CA: Sage.

Hoftstede, G. (2001) *Culture's Consequences: Comparing Values, Behaviours, Institutions and Organizations Across Nations* (2nd edn.), Thousand Oaks, CA: Sage.

Holt Larsen, H. and Mayrhofer, W. (eds.) (2006) *Managing Human Resources in Europe: A Thematic Approach*, London: Routledge.

Jacobi, O., Keller, B. and Müller-Jentsch, W. (1998) 'Germany: facing new challenges', in Ferner, A. and Hyman, R. (eds.) *Changing Industrial Relations in Europe*, Oxford: Blackwell.

Jacoby, S.M. (1997) *Modern Manors: Welfare Capitalism Since the New Deal*, Princeton, NJ: Princeton University Press.

Kamoche, K., Debrah, Y., Horwitz, F. and Nkombo Muuka, G. (eds.) (2003) *Managing Human Resources in Africa*, London: Routledge.

Kerr, C., Dunlop, J.T., Harbison, F.H. and Myers, C.A. (1960) *Industrialism and Industrial Man: The Problems of Labour and Management in Economic Growth*, Harmondsworth: Penguin.

Kidger, P.J. (1991) 'The emergence of international human resource management', *International Journal of Human Resource Management*, Vol.2, No.2, 149–63.

La Porta, R., Lopez-de-Silanes, F., Shleifer, A. and Vishny, R. (2000) 'Investor protection and corporate governance', *Journal of Financial Economics*, Vol.58, 3–27.

Lincoln, J. and Kalleberg, A. (1990) *Culture, Control and Commitment*: *A Study of Work Organization in the United States and Japan*, Cambridge: Cambridge University Press.

Locke, R., Kochan, T. and Piore, M. (1995) 'Reconceptualizing comparative industrial relations: lessons from international research', *International Labour Review*, Vol.134, 139–61.

Marsden, D. (1999) *A Theory of Employment Systems*, Oxford: Oxford University Press.

McDonnell, A., Lavelle, J., Gunnigle, P. and Collings, D.G. (2007) 'Management research on multinational corporations: a methodological critique', *Economic and Social Review*, Vol.38, No.2, 235–58.

McSweeney, B. (2002) 'Hoftstede's model of national culture differences and their consequences: a triumph of faith – a failure of analysis', *Human Relations*, Vol.55, 5–34.

Meyer, J.W. and Rowan, B. (1977) 'Institutional organizations: formal structure as myth and ceremony', *American Journal of Sociology*, Vol.83, 340–63.

Morley, M., Brewster, C., Gunnigle, P. and Mayerhofer, W. (1996) 'Evaluating change in European industrial relations: research evidence on trends at organisational level', *International Journal of Human Resource Management*, Vol.7, No.3, 640–56.

Morgan, G. (2012) 'International business, multinationals and national business systems', in Wood, G. and Demirbag, M. (eds.), *Handbook of Institutional Approaches to International Business*, Cheltenham: Edward Elgar.

Morley, M.J., Gunnigle, P. and Collings, D.G. (eds.) (2006) *Global Industrial Relations*, London: Routledge.

Morley, M.J., Heraty, N. and Michailova, S. (2009) *Managing Human Resources in Central and Eastern Europe*, New York: Routledge.

North, D.C. (1990) *Institutions, Institutional Change and Economic Performance*, Cambridge: Cambridge University Press.

O'Hagan, E. (2002) *Employee Relations in the Periphery of Europe: The Unfolding of the European Social Model*, London: Palgrave.

Pagano, M. and Volpin, P. (2005) 'The political economy of corporate governance', *American Economic Review*, Vol.95, 1005–30.

Pitcher, A. (2002) *Transforming Mozambique: The Politics of Privatization*, Cambridge: Cambridge University Press.

Roe, M. (2003) *Political Determinants of Corporate Governance*, Oxford: Oxford University Press.

Rollinson, D. and Dundon, T. (2007) *Understanding Employment Relations*, London: McGraw Hill.

Rubery, J. and Grimshaw, D. (2003) *The Organization of Employment: An International Perspective*, Basingstoke: Palgrave.

Schneider, S.C. and Barsoux, J.L. (2003) *Managing Across Cultures* (2nd edn.), Harlow: Prentice Hall.

Scullion, H. (1995) 'International human resource management', in Storey, J. (ed.) *Human Resource Management: A Critical Text*, London: Thomson Learning.

Sorge, A. (2004) 'Cross-national differences in human resources and organisation', in Harzing, A.W. and van Ruyssevekdt, J. (eds.) *International Human Resource Management* (2nd edn.), London: Sage.

Sorge, A. and Streeck, W. (1988) 'Industrial relations and technological change: the case for an extended perspective', in Hyman, R. and Streeck, W. (eds.) *New Technology and Industrial Relations*, Oxford: Blackwell.

Sorge, A. and Warner, M. (1986) *Comparative Factory Organization*, Aldershot: Gower.

Storey, J. (1992) *Developments in the Management of Human Resources*, Oxford: Blackwell.

Strauss, G. and Hanson, M. (1997) 'Review article: American anti-management theories of organization: a critique of paradigm proliferation', *Human Relations*, Vol.50, 1426–9.

Tayeb, M. (1996) 'Hoftstede', in Warner, M. (ed.) *International Encyclopaedia of Business and Management*, London: Thomson Learning.

Taylor, P. and Bain, P. (2003) 'Call centre organising in adversity: from Excell to Vertex', in Gall, G. (ed.) *Fighting for Fairness at Work: Campaigns for Union Recognition*, London: Routledge.

Thelen, K. (2001) 'Varieties of labor politics in the developed democracies', in Hall, P. and Soskice, D. (eds.) *Varieties of Capitalism: The Institutional Basis of Competitive Advantage*, Oxford: Oxford University Press.

Tolbert, P.S. and Zucker, L.G. (1996) 'The institutionalisation of institutional theory', in Clegg, S. Hardy, C. and Nord, W.R. (eds.) *Handbook of Organization Studies*, London: Sage.

Trompenaars, F. (1993) *Riding the Waves of Culture* (2nd edn.), London: Nicholas Brealey.

Turner, T. (2006) 'Industrial relations systems, economic efficiency and social equity in the 1990s', *Review of Social Economy*, Vol.64, No.1, 93–118.

Vaiman, V. and Brewster, C. (2015) 'How far do cultural differences explain the differences between nations? Implications for HRM', *The International Journal of Human Resource Management*, Vol.26, No.2, 151–64.

Webster, E. and Wood, G. (2005) 'Human resource management practice and institutional constraints', *Employee Relations*, Vol.27, No.4, 369–85.

Whitley, R. (1999) *Divergent Capitalisms: The Social Structuring and Change of Business Systems*, Oxford, Oxford University Press.

Wilkinson, B., Gamble, J., Humphrey, J., Morris, J. and Anthony, D. (2001) 'The new international division of labour in Asian electronics: work organization and human resources in Japan and Malaysia', *Journal of Management Studies*, Vol.38, No.5, 675–95.

Wood, G. and Brewster, C. (eds.) (2007) *Industrial Relations in Africa*, London: Palgrave.

CHAPTER 12
MANAGING DIVERSITY AND INCLUSION

Catherine Cassell

Introduction

It is now over 25 years since human resource management writers and consultants started using the term 'managing diversity' as a way of addressing equal opportunity issues. A focus on diversity recognises that people differ in a variety of ways. Examples include gender, ethnicity, age, sexuality, religion, disability and social status. Managing diversity encompasses a number of concepts and refers to the systematic and planned commitment on the part of organisations to recruit and retain employees from diverse demographic backgrounds (Thomas, 1992). Building on the notion that all differences between groups and individuals within an organisation should be recognised and valued, managing diversity presents a business case for equal opportunities. In linking individual employee differences and equal opportunities initiatives directly with business strategy, the concept of managing diversity is inextricably linked to strategic HRM, and therefore a focus of concern for the HR practitioner (Shen *et al.*, 2009). As Theodorakapoulos and Budhwar (2015) suggest, the management of diversity and inclusion are increasingly regarded as key to the strategic agenda of a company because of the impetus of the business case.

The aim of this chapter is to outline the principles behind the managing diversity approach and examine some of the key issues and tensions around diversity debates. The chapter begins by outlining the context in which managing diversity has arisen. The principles of managing diversity strategies are then discussed, together with some of the techniques and tools that managers can use to this end. The international and cultural contexts of diversity strategies are then considered together with the challenges facing the creation of global diversity programmes. The chapter concludes by examining some of the key issues and debates within this field. These include a consideration of the evidence for the effectiveness of managing diversity initiatives, a critique of the business case within which managing diversity initiatives are located and the move towards a focus upon inclusion as a way of addressing issues of fairness and equality in the workplace.

Managing diversity and inclusion: a brief history

The management of diversity first emerged within the business literature towards the end of the 1980s. Therefore, in the history of personnel and HRM more generally, it is a relatively new concept. It is important to consider why the concept emerged when it did, and the currency that it currently has among HR academics and practitioners. By way of context, the triggers that led to a focus of attention towards diversity management are now considered. Two particular factors are important here: changing demographic trends and the emergence of the business case for the progression of equal opportunities.

Demographic trends

The development of managing diversity strategies is clearly located within the context of shifting demographic trends. The composition of the international workforce is changing dramatically. Prasad *et al.* pointed out the impact that these shifts initially had in North America:

> Few trends have received as much publicity or gained as much attention in management circles as the recent interest in managing diversity. It can be argued that much of this interest can be traced back to Johnston and Parker's [sic] [Packard] (1987) influential report, *Workforce 2000*, which alerted organizations to the dramatic demographic changes that were in the process of transforming the North American workforce . . . Confronted with the prospect of these major imminent changes, management practitioners, business educators, and organizational consultants quickly began preparing to meet the challenges of a new and diverse workforce in a number of ways. *(Prasad et al., 1997: 4)*

Kandola (1995), one of the pioneers of managing diversity initiatives in the UK and Europe, highlighted at the time that similar demographic changes to those that were occurring in North America were anticipated throughout Europe. Specifically, it was anticipated that there would be increasing numbers of women and ethnic minorities entering the labour market, and the overall age of the working population would increase. The argument was that such demographic trends had created the necessity to expand the labour pool to include those groups traditionally disadvantaged in the employment market. Roberson and Kulik (2007: 24) highlight how when these trends were first identified they were 'heralded as an opportunity for organizations to become more creative, to reach previously untapped markets, and in general to achieve and maintain a competitive advantage'. The key aim of diversity management, therefore, was for companies to turn such demographic trends to their own advantage and make the most of the talents of the new diverse workforce that were now available to them.

The concern with changing demographic trends prevails. Most notably predicted trends worldwide at the current time are the ageing workforce; the increased feminisation of the workforce; and the increased importance of migration (EFLWC, 2010; SHRM Foundation, 2014). As many experienced employees retire, others are choosing to work longer leaving a dilemma of how to engage the aging workforce whilst skilling up younger workers. As more women enter the workforce there is a greater need for more flexible working patterns and the challenges of managing the increasing number of international migrants is starting to be addressed in the HR literature (Guo and Al Ariss, 2015; Blätte, 2014). Hence these demographic indicators point to the need to include and value those in the workforce who may traditionally have been excluded or are not particularly visible.

A business case for equal opportunities and managing diversity

A distinctive feature of managing diversity initiatives is the focus upon the business case. The business case focuses on the business benefits that employers accrue through making the most of the skills and potential of all employees. The argument is that the loss or lack of recognition of these skills and potential, usually as a result of everyday discriminatory practices, is very costly. Consequently, the business case is fundamentally linked to the principles of strategic HRM where the human resource and its full utilisation are viewed as giving a company the competitive edge (Storey, 1995). Additionally, it is crucial that equal opportunities initiatives are seen to tie in with the overall strategic direction of a company. A business case positions achieving equality as essential to achieving organisational goals. Again, in the same way that HRM is linked into the general strategy of a firm, so equal opportunities pervades every aspect of business policy, rather than being an add-on. The effective management of diversity is seen to be the best utilisation of human resources and has a number of other positive advantages including a potentially improved corporate image with employees and customers and the generation of new business ideas and markets from the representation of a diverse workforce. Moreover, it offsets business costs such as the costs associated with the inefficient use of human resources such as high staff turnover; low productivity; and access to a restricted pool of talent.

These costs and benefits are linked in to the demographic trends outlined earlier. The business case has blossomed as a rationale for the effective management of diversity within the workplace and is an important, underpinning argument for furthering equality at work. For example, the British Chartered Institute of Personnel and Development (CIPD, 2011) have outlined three major benefits associated with the business case for equal opportunities and managing diversity that go beyond what is required by legislation. These relate to people issues such as drawing on a wider range of labour pool that will be more creative, innovative and happier in the work environment; market competitiveness where a diverse workforce can, for example, open up new market opportunities; and corporate reputation, where diversity and inclusion are linked into the wider issues of corporate social responsibility. Furthermore, in a report commissioned by the Association of Chartered and Certified accountants Özbilgin *et al.* (2014) suggest that the business case operates at four levels, each with its own different sets of justifications for adopting diversity practices. These levels are shareholder value where the focus is on the bottom line; stakeholder value with its focus upon the triple bottom line of profits, people, planet; regulatory context where there is a link between effective regulation and gaining the positive benefits of diversity; and the level of the global value chain. So although managing diversity and inclusion on their own may not be rated as the top priority for today's companies, linked issues such as retention and engagement are seen as highly urgent (Deloitte, 2014).

General principles and activities

A number of principles and activities characterise diversity management. Pitts (2006) provides a basic conceptualisation of diversity management that includes three inter-related components: recruitment and outreach, valuing differences, and pragmatic programmes and policies. The first: recruitment and outreach, focuses on an organisation seeking out a range of different types of employees. Examples of activities here include a strategic plan for reaching out to typically under-represented groups (Pitts *et al.*, 2010: 869). This is based upon the assumption that greater staff diversity will lead to access to a wider range of talent and ideas, plus access to potentially novel markets. The second component identified by Pitts (2006) is valuing differences. Exponents of the management of diversity perspective (Cox, 1992; Jackson and Associates, 1992; Kandola and Fullerton, 1994; Montes and Shaw, 2003; Thomas, 1990) argue that all differences must be valued including those of white males. Kandola and Fullerton

(1994: 8) provide a useful working definition of managing diversity which highlights the role of managing difference:

> The basic concept of managing diversity accepts that the workforce consists of a diverse population of people. The diversity consists of visible and non-visible differences which will include factors such as sex, age, background, race, disability, personality and work style. It is founded on the premiss that harnessing these differences will create a productive environment in which everybody feels valued, where their talents are being fully utilized and in which organizational goals are met. *(Kandola and Fullerton, 1994: 8)*

Indeed, differences are not only valued but also potentially celebrated. As Prasad *et al.* suggest:

> Diversity is celebrated with the help of evocative metaphors such as the melting pot, the patchwork quilt, the multicolored or cultural mosaic, and the rainbow. All of these metaphors evoke enormously affirmative connotations of diversity, associating it with images of cultural hybridity, harmonious coexistence, and colorful heterogeneity. *(Prasad et al., 1997: 4)*

A consideration of some organisational diversity policies highlight some of the differences that need to be valued and managed. A typical policy will include differences such as gender, race, disability, spent criminal convictions, sexual orientation, religion and beliefs, socioeconomic background, age and potentially others such as personality differences and working styles.

The third part of Pitt's (2006) model is pragmatic programmes and policies. These consist of a 'strategic set of management tools' (Pitts *et al.*, 2010: 870) that provide the means by which diverse groups can have their needs met. These could, for example, include family-friendly policies for those with dependents, or policies that enable religious minorities the opportunity to worship in the workplace.

Implementing diversity initiatives

Given the range of different objectives that HR professionals seek to achieve through effective diversity management (Shen *et al.*, 2009), it is not surprising that a whole range of projects can be subsumed under the heading of diversity initiatives. Some are designed to encourage the voices of all individuals to be heard, for example advisory councils made up of different groups that can report to top management, and the creation of support groups for minorities such as women's or cultural minorities networks. An example comes from IBM that has created network groups for LGBT (lesbian, gay, bisexual and transsexual) employees in 12 EU countries. Externally, IBM also collaborates with various LGBT organisations, demonstrating both internal and external support for the LGBT community (European Commission, 2005). A further example is Dublin Bus's intercultural working group that involves staff and bus drivers from different origins and ethnic backgrounds. In both cases, these network groups can raise key issues associated with the experiences of particular diverse groups that can then be addressed more generally at company level. Other initiatives ensure that attention is paid to the career development of particular minorities such as fast-track development programmes for targeted groups, or finding ways of rewarding managers on the basis of their record on developing those from targeted groups (Arnold, 1997: 179). For example, in Adecco – a multinational recruitment business – skills gap training is offered to candidates with disabilities with the aim of ensuring long-term employment. Many companies now outline their diversity and inclusion policies on their websites with examples of the interventions they are making to address diversity issues.

A key element in most of these interventions is some form of diversity training. This usually focuses on the importance of the successful management of diversity for achieving business benefits, and highlights how stereotypes of different groups may hinder their opportunities in the workplace. It also has the aim of seeking to enable the integration of minority groups into the workforce and providing other workers with the skills to be able to work productively alongside the members of such groups (Pendry *et al.*, 2007: 28). Increasingly common is the idea of unconscious bias training, where there is a recognition that we are all biased in different ways, and the aim of the training is to recognise those biases so they can be acted upon. For example, Asda Walmart describes these on their website as 'open mind sessions'. They talk about how they used unconscious bias workshops to 'upskill' their senior leaders on diversity and inclusion, focusing specifically on gender balance and the potential effect that unconscious bias can have on decision making, with particular reference to recruitment and succession planning. This training was then cascaded throughout the organisation with store managers running sessions with their teams to over 10,000 retail managers.

It appears that managing diversity and inclusion is becoming more professionalised within organisations and is increasingly widespread. For example, Hays-Thomas and Bendick Jr. (2013: 193) point out that 'at least half of all US companies with over 100 employees have some form of diversity and inclusion program, including more than 75% of the largest firms, with expenditures on these activities estimated to total $10 billion annually'. Hence diversity and inclusion programmes can now be seen routinely in many organisations.

International and cultural contexts

Recent reviews within the HR literature suggest that workforce diversity now has considerable currency within the HR profession and amongst those who lead organisations, including new economies (Theodorakapoulos and Budhwar, 2015). Research examining how diversity initiatives are being implemented internationally seems to indicate that much depends upon the cultural and historical context. Süβ and Kleiner (2007) outline how, in contrast to the USA, the starting point for managing diversity in Germany has been a focus on gender differences. They conducted a survey of 160 companies listed on the German stock exchange and found that 39.4 per cent had implemented diversity management; 18.2 per cent had heard of the concept but 42.4 per cent knew nothing about it. The authors conclude that in the German context 'the concept is far from being a widespread and naturally employed management concept'. Similarly, Meriläinen *et al.* (2009) in their research regarding diversity management in Finland suggest that diversity and its management are ignored on most Finnish corporate websites. Because Finland has had a long history of gender equality, there are instead many examples of gender equality discourse.

Other research has considered diversity and inclusion in different international contexts. Tang *et al.* (2015) point out that the word inclusion has had a long history in China, with its root firmly in traditional Chinese culture. However, inclusion has an additional meaning in the Chinese language of openness and tolerance but also being generous to the point of being magnanimous. In their research on inclusive management practices in China they highlight how a variety of inclusion practices are similar to those in research on the West, but that tolerance is unique to the Chinese context, where there is an emphasis on forgiving mistakes. Cooke and Saini (2012) argue that the Western definition of diversity is much broader than that found in China and India. Within India caste, religion and gender are seen as the most important sources of diversity. Haq (2012) also points out that the constitution of India includes a range of protected groups, for example scheduled caste and tribes and within the country. Their research 'reveals a clear divide between the public and private sector diversity mindset in terms of definition, implementation and impact of diversity policies' (Haq, 2012: 906). So within different international contexts there are still differences both within and between organisations. A complicating issue is the impact of increased globalisation. Individual companies may develop their own approach to diversity, but these approaches may be inappropriate within the different locations where a company is based. Global diversity management therefore has increasingly become the key challenge.

Managing diversity globally

With the increased globalisation of the workforce, managing diversity across international borders has become an important issue. Sippola and Smale (2007) suggest that we know very little about how multinational firms are responding to the increasingly globalised nature of their workforce and operations. The extent to which diversity policies focusing on managing difference translate neatly across borders has been questioned. Nishii and Özbilgin (2007: 1883) suggest that 'American' labels regarding difference are 'simply ridiculous' outside the US context. They give the example of Canada where an important difference in the workplace regardless of ethnicity or gender is whether one is primarily English or French speaking. Other challenges about whether a US or Western model of diversity is appropriate have been posed with regard to India (Wilson, 2003); Australia (Strachan et al., 2004) and New Zealand (Jones et al., 2000). Rao (2012), for instance, highlights how religion is one of the key facets of diversity within the Indian context but most firms do not record the religious affiliations of their staff. A pertinent example of these complexities comes from Fullerton (2013) who when outlining the policies for LGBT inclusion at Bank of America Merrill Lynch highlights that a key diversity challenge for global companies is their operations in countries where being gay is illegal such as Algeria or Jamaica, or even punishable by death, such as Uganda and Saudi Arabia.

In research examining the extent to which Finnish companies have adopted managing diversity initiatives, Meriläinen et al. summarise this problem neatly:

> It has been difficult to root the diversity management concept outside Anglophone countries since its development has taken place in a specific multicultural context that is not directly comparable to other cultural contexts that have different histories of diversity. (Meriläinen et al., 2009: 231)

Nishii and Özbilgin (2007: 1886) suggest that global diversity initiatives based on the 'exportation of US based diversity programmes abroad have failed due to their lack of attention to local cultural and demographic differences'. They outline a conceptual framework that examines the leadership and cultural foundations and the organisational outcomes of global diversity management. The framework also includes four important components that need to be in place for successful global diversity management. First, global units need to be included in the decision-making processes of the company. This is in line with the strategies for inclusion that underlie diversity initiatives. Second, human resource management policies need to be designed flexibly in order to take account of local context. Third, although there needs to be locally defined goals for addressing particular forms of discrimination that take into account power differences between groups within a cultural context, the overall goals of the global diversity initiative need to be unified across global units. This prevents fragmentation of the overall company approach (Nishii and Özbilgin, 2007: 1888).

There is some evidence that multinational companies are adopting the kind of approach recommended. Egan and Bendick (2003: 723) examined how US multinationals were seeking to implement global diversity initiatives in European locations. They conducted a survey of 30 large US MNCs from a range of industries and services. They concluded that although diversity management is likely to become important in human resource management practices of US MNCs located in Europe, there is no one best approach; rather 'for each company, the soundest approach is likely to be that which matches the degree of centralization that the firm applies to other important aspects of corporate operations'. They also draw attention to the issue that the business case may be different in different European contexts. Other case study evidence highlights similar approaches; for example, Ernst & Young report setting diversity and inclusion targets locally in line with specific cultural and legal contexts, and Rio Tinto also develop local diversity and inclusion plans for each of its major operational sites (Özbilgin *et al.*, 2014).

In summary, it would seem that the issues encountered with regard to global diversity management are similar to the debates about integration or national differentiation that characterise the nature of global HRM more generally (Sippola and Smale, 2007). Time will tell the extent to which global diversity initiatives manage to achieve their objectives. As Farndale *et al.* (2015) suggest, researchers need to expand their knowledge of various practices of diversity and inclusion across the world to gain a more nuanced understanding of global diversity and inclusion.

Do diversity initiatives deliver?

A key question about managing diversity initiatives is to what extent do they actually work? The search for empirical evidence to validate the success of managing diversity programmes can be a frustrating exercise. One of the problems is that many of the case studies of diversity programmes that are reported in the literature do not contain any evaluative element. Indeed, sometimes these case study reports focus more on promoting a particular company approach with evangelical zeal, rather than assessing and evaluating the success of a given programme. This in itself is not a problem, but, as highlighted earlier, there is the issue of how transferable the context is. Jones *et al.* (2000) point out the paradox that as managing diversity develops as a worldwide vocabulary for examining or celebrating difference, US cultural dominance may be reinforced by a US model of difference being applied globally.

It is notable, however, that a number of firms do claim considerable business benefits from their engagement with managing diversity. In a survey of 919 European companies conducted by the European Commission (EC, 2005), the strong message is that managing diversity does lead to business benefits. The authors suggest that the most important of these are the enhanced retention and recruitment of employees from a wider talent pool, improved corporate image and reputation, innovation and enhanced marketing. The case studies in the same report highlight some useful examples. For example, Deutsche Bank's development of networks with gay and lesbian staff has led to an increase in their marketing activities to gay and lesbians and a ten-fold return on their initial investment. Tesco's 'Everyone is welcome' initiative has led to significantly more people from an ethnic minority background joining the company and a 250 per cent increase in sales of products tailored to the needs of different ethnic, religious and cultural groups. Despite these reported successes the report also states that 'one of the key findings is the lack of systematic monitoring and evaluation of the progress and benefits of diversity' with nearly 70 per cent of companies failing to monitor their impact (EC, 2005: 6).

A number of authors have drawn attention to some of the problems that emerge in seeking to evaluate diversity initiatives in organisations, an ongoing problem in the literature. Ellis and Sonnenfeld (1994) reviewed three pioneering diversity programmes in US companies. They concluded that although it makes sense that the benefits of such programmes may translate into higher productivity and lower turnover, few organisations actually measure the transfer of the educational interventions into actual changes in human resource practices such as recruiting, management development and promotion. Other evidence that diversity programmes are not being evaluated comes from the work of Kochan *et al.* (2003: 8). They argue that there are few studies that look directly at the impact of diversity policies on objective measures of organisational performance. They attempted to conduct research with over

20 large and well-known Fortune 500 companies that had expressed an interest in being involved in diversity research. However, the research team encountered difficulties in following through the research in these firms. As the authors outline:

> After often considerable discussion of the data, confidentiality, and time commitments, all but four companies declined to participate. In some cases, the diversity advocates and professionals in the company lacked sufficient influence to convince line managers to spend the time required to collect the necessary data. In other cases, these professionals were reluctant to examine the effects of their organisation's policies, with a view that they had sufficient top management support for their current initiatives and did not need to demonstrate a business case to maintain this support.

As the authors suggest, one of the first interesting lessons from their research was that as well as managers not knowing the impact of diversity strategies on objective performance measures, few of them were interested in discovering this information. Within the four cases that were conducted the authors concluded that there was 'simply no evidence to support the simple assertion that diversity is inevitably either good or bad for business' (Kochan *et al.*, 2003: 17). Perhaps this was one of the reasons why the managers were unhappy about keeping data about the impact of their policies in this area.

More recently, research has begun to emerge that looks at the impact of a positive climate for diversity in an organisation on a range of business outcomes. For example, Choi and Rainey (2010) measured the levels of diversity in 67 US federal agencies and then analysed how diversity management affects the relationship between levels of diversity and perceptions of organisational performance. Their findings suggest that the benefits of racial diversity among staff are enhanced with higher levels of diversity management. A particularly interesting study reported by Shen *et al.* (2010) looked at the effects of diversity management on organisational citizenship behaviours in the Chinese context. The authors point out that in China the key diversity issue is household registration status, which differentiates rural peasants from urbanites, where rural peasants previously were forbidden from working in urban areas. Their results suggest that where there are effective diversity management practices in place, particularly in relation to selection and compensation, there is a greater likelihood in engagement in organisation citizenship behaviours from employees.

In their research on the implementation of diversity management programmes in public organisations, Pitts *et al.* (2010) suggest that management are the key players in ensuring that diversity management initiatives are successful, but the problem of evaluating the success of such initiatives is that diversity management is still an ambiguous concept which may be interpreted and therefore implemented differently across different companies. Other business priorities may also intervene. For example, Michielsens *et al.* (2014), from their in four organisations case studies of diversity practices in organisations, conclude that the prioritisation of business objectives can restrict a company's ability to facilitate greater diversity. Overall, then, it is hard not to agree with Klarsfeld (2009: 363) that 'the diversity–performance link advocated by respondents in organizations is a matter of belief or rhetoric more than scientific measurement'. Indeed Theodorakapoulos and Budhwar (2015: 177) conclude that: 'the evidence of the positive impact of diversity measures on performance is far from conclusive'.

Critiquing diversity initiatives

Beyond the question of the effectiveness of diversity initiatives, a number of other critiques have emerged about the managing diversity approach. Cassell and Biswas (2000) suggest that much of the literature that exists on the subject is largely atheoretical and that there is a need to examine the extent to which diversity initiatives really have delivered positive outcomes for disadvantaged groups in the workplace. Indeed, there is a need to focus on the different levels at which discrimination is experienced. Tatli (2011) suggests that single layer studies of diversity interventions which focus on, for example, organisational processes or individual career outcomes, are limited in their explanations. Indeed, Theodorakapoulos and Budhwar (2015: 178) suggest that one of the difficulties is that many of the research studies focus upon single-nation cases, which do not always easily translate to other settings. To address this Syed and Özbiglin (2009) instead propose a relational framework where account is taken of macro-level issues such as national structures and institutions; meso-level organisational processes such as rituals and routinised work behaviours; and micro-level work behaviours, such as power and motivation. Such a framework produces a contextual and multi-level approach currently missing in the literature. It also draws attention to the importance of intersectionality in considering experiences of discrimination.

There is also some concern within the literature that managing diversity initiatives may be implemented as just another management fashion. Prasad *et al.* (2011), in their case studies of the design and implementation of diversity management programmes in six Canadian organisations, highlight a high level of fashion consciousness among those who supplied diversity programmes and those who consumed them. They draw attention to some of the difficulties this creates, for example a lack of local relevance in the initiatives introduced and superficiality in programme design. Additionally, the bandwagon effect may lead to resistance from employees. As with any change initiative we would expect some resistance to managing diversity programmes. Yet this resistance is rarely addressed within the literature as managing diversity is promoted as being in the interest of all groups, regardless of their differences. Wahl and Holgersson (2003) provide research evidence of male managers' reactions to gender diversity activities in Sweden. They argue that a number of factors impact on those reactions, including the numerical gender distribution, and the nature of job segregation in the companies concerned. Indeed, Tang *et al.* (2015) suggest that the recent change in discourse from one of diversity to one of inclusion is recognition of the potential hostility that may emerge from those who do not see themselves as benefitting from diversity policies. Clearly, there needs to be further consideration of the issue of resistance, why it occurs and how it can be effectively managed, together with the consequences of that resistance for those traditionally disadvantaged groups who may be seen to gain from diversity initiatives.

A further important issue to consider is the extent to which the business case on which managing diversity is based is sustainable in the long term. The problem with a business case is that it is only persuasive within a given economic climate. Consequently, its impact in facilitating long-term change must be seriously questioned. For example, in times of national austerity, employing diverse groups may not be seen as a business priority. A further issue is put forward by Richards (2001: 29) who highlights how the difficulties with employer driven equal opportunities agendas are that the priorities they usually support are those seen as important by the employer. These tend to address the more visible aspects of equal opportunities, such as the number of women in senior positions. Therefore, as Omanivic (2009: 355) suggests, although diversity management initiatives might seem an emancipatory concept, it is, rather, 'one that reproduces an established social order'. A further concern is that the links between valuing diverse skills and business success can be problematic. For example, Adkins (1995), in her analysis of gender relations in the tourist industry, outlines how women workers were recruited to a variety of jobs at a theme park on the basis of their physical appearance. Consequently, women deemed as sexually attractive were employed in order to please the clients, 'sexual servicing' as Adkins calls it. Similarly, Biswas and Cassell (1996) outline a case study of a hotel where the work was clearly divided on gender lines. It was argued that it was crucial that receptionists were physically attractive as they were the first point of contact for the customer. In both these cases it could be argued, therefore, that accentuating the sexuality of women employees through styles of dress, etc. made business sense, hence drawing attention to some of the dilemmas that emerge when focusing upon a business case for equality alone.

A final point is that the business case may not apply equally to all diverse groups, and some groups might fit a business case more neatly than others. Woodhams and Danieli

(2000) suggest that there is very little written within the diversity literature about the business case for employing disabled people. They suggest that the rationality underlying the diversity approach falters in relation to the employment of disabled people in a number of ways. As a considerably heterogeneous group who are not segregated within the labour market, a managing diversity approach based on the identification of group-based characteristics has little to offer. Furthermore, a CIPD report on disadvantaged groups in the labour market (CIPD, 2010) highlighted that the most disadvantaged group of workers in the UK were ex-offenders. Yet, there is little, if any, mention of this group in the managing diversity literature. This discussion highlights the complicated nature of the processes through which issues of power, fairness and equality are reformulated into issues of competitive advantage. The potential for fundamental change within such an approach becomes questionable.

Conclusions

To conclude, managing diversity and inclusion is a live and important issue in the international workplace. Discrimination of particular groups based on a given set of characteristics is no longer seen as acceptable business practice and may indeed have a negative reputational impact. From an academic perspective there is clearly the need for far more research to evaluate the impact of diversity initiatives. Ideally, research should focus on the longitudinal assessment of diversity programmes, using a range of criteria from impact on economic performance to the attitudes of those groups that the interventions have been designed to address. Additionally, as stated earlier, there is a need to consider the various different levels of analysis and characteristics where discrimination can occur. Only then can the claims made for the success of managing diversity approaches be properly evaluated.

A further key question that remains is the problematic nature of universalistic notions of managing diversity. In practice, the term does not have a unitary meaning; it means different things to different people and can mean different things in different cultures or organisations in different international settings. Increasingly, there are challenges from other cultures about whether the Western model is appropriate. This is particularly important in relation to the development of global diversity initiatives and questions the international application of locally derived diversity policies. Furthermore, context is always important. It is evident that at certain times some groups may experience a rise in discriminatory actions against them as is evident in Kaifi's (2009) account of the experiences of Afghan-Americans post-9/11. There is also a literature emerging now about the experiences of international migrants, and the challenges they themselves and organisations face in integrating them into the workforce (e.g. Guo and Al Ariss, 2015).

Finally, we can see that *inclusion* is becoming more of a term of popular usage within the diversity management literature. Additionally, Roberson (2006) suggests that there is a move from diversity to inclusion within the practitioner literature. Whether this represents something new or different from managing diversity is another issue. Shore *et al.* (2011: 1268) suggest that the inclusion literature is still in its infancy and similar to the managing diversity concept there is a disparity amongst researchers about its definition. Having said that, perhaps the labelling of the debate is of little significance if, as an area of debate and intervention, managing diversity can offer hope for furthering equality in the workplace. More impetus is clearly needed to further moves for equality for those groups within the labour force who are traditionally discriminated against and those where new forms of pernicious discrimination are emerging. What managing diversity approaches do highlight is the economic costs to organisations of losing talented staff through discriminatory practices: a crucial issue for HRM policy and practice.

CASE STUDY 12.1

EUROZONE

CATHERINE CASSELL

Eurozone is a political lobbying organisation based in Brussels. Founded 15 years ago by two ex-European Members of Parliament, its aim is to draw the attention of members of the European Parliament and other influential bodies to the issues considered important by its clients. In the past, Eurozone lobbyists have sought to influence around issues such as immigration policies and the entry into the European Union of new countries; discussions around the common agricultural and fishing policies and the allocation of various pots of European funding. Their lobbyists work for a wide range of clients including business and political groups.

The success of the organisation has seen an associated expansion of the number of employees. Founded by Hans Klein, a German national, and René Mertens, a Belgian national, the company now employs ten other people. Additionally, the firm uses freelancers who are employed for specific assignments. These jobs are seen as particularly accessible for women who might want to combine the work with having a family. The relationship between the firm and its freelancers is particularly important because it enables the firm some flexibility around workload. The owners pride themselves on the effective long-term relationships they have built with some freelancers and that they will prioritise working for them above other lobbying organisations.

One of the key successful attributes of the company is that as the EU has expanded they have been successful in their ability to bring in a range of diverse clients from the different European nations. One factor that has attracted these clients has been the diverse composition of the company. Many of those involved in European politics recognise that the area is heterogeneous, and that the key issues and interests of those in Western and Northern Europe may differ from those in the east and the south. Therefore the company's strategy has focused on recruiting some new staff from Eastern Europe to deal with the increasing number of assignments that have arisen as a result of the expansion of the EU. The owners believe that there is a clear business case for this recruitment strategy in that they expect that Eastern European clients will be more at ease with these staff. Therefore, this will give them some advantage over their competitors in what is an increasingly crowded market.

The executive team of the company consists of the two owners and Angela Goossens, another Belgian national who was René's PA having previously worked with a number of other European Members of Parliament. Angela's role is to manage the firm's office whilst the two owners – together with the other regular staff – focus on lobbying and business development. The executive team have a weekly Monday morning meeting where work in progress and new assignments are reviewed and allocated. The assignments that the company deal with can roughly be divided into two types: those that are more general or issue specific, and those that are associated with particular countries or regions. In allocating work the executive team decide who they think will be best for the job, bearing in mind their individual skills and expertise and the current workload. The three have worked together for many years and feel comfortable that they have a positive working relationship. They are proud of what the company has achieved and of the positive, dynamic and diverse working environment they have created.

Recently, a couple of the more newer recruits: Andrulis Norkus from Lithuania and Aleksy Bartosz from Poland have requested the opportunity to meet with the executive team and Angela has invited them to the Monday morning meeting. As the discussion unfolds, René, Angela and Hans are surprised by what they are hearing from their staff. As Aleksy suggests:

'I was really proud to have secured a job with Eurozone. I knew the reputation of the firm and felt I could really add something to the company. I felt this would be a good move for my political career. However, increasingly I am feeling I might have made a big mistake. There is a clear hierarchy here in how the work is allocated, and those of us from the newer European states are always at the bottom of the pile. The really juicy general assignments always go to the Westerners, we Eastern Europeans are rarely considered for the best jobs. Yes, we may be useful for those jobs focusing on Eastern Europe, but I wanted more than that. You are just mirroring the lack of status we have in Brussels more generally, alongside your powerful nations,' Andrulis adds, 'There is a real bias towards the Western freelancers especially, they seem to get all the best work.'

The executive team are stunned by these suggestions and reassure Andrulis and Aleksy that this situation will be investigated. After the meeting Angela decides to do a review of how work has been allocated over the last 12 months. In doing so she finds that there is some justification in the claims made by Aleksy and Andrulis in that the more general jobs with the most senior clients tend to go to the Westerners. There are no obvious differences in the allocation of

work between men and women on the regular staff and the freelancers, but clear differences between those from Western and Eastern Europe. Angela reports back to René and Hans who are similarly surprised but all agree that they should try and do something to address the situation. As René puts it, 'I've always been proud of our reputation for being a dynamic and inclusive employer. This kind of thing could damage our reputation out there and, as we know, in this business reputation is everything.' The executive team decide that something must be done to address the situation and ask Angela to investigate advice about how to make their business more inclusive.

Questions

1 What interventions would you suggest the executive team take in order to achieve their aim of moving towards a culture where diverse groups are treated fairly?
2 What impact do you think your suggested interventions will have upon:
   a Eastern European employees;
   b Northern and Western European employees;
   c The senior management team.

CASE STUDY 12.2
CMC RETAILING
CATHERINE CASSELL

CMC is a global retailing organisation headquartered in California that buys and sells women's and men's fashion in retail outlets throughout the world. The company CEO, Caitlin Stephens, is one of the few female CEOs in the industry and is renowned for taking a pro-diversity stance and particularly for encouraging women to move to managerial positions in the company. Given her pro-female stance, she regularly features in the business pages and features sections of newspapers across the world, where CMC has retail outlets. Recently, the company has had a major reputational hit in that a group of female employees in Australia have accused the company of sex discrimination arguing that women with children have been discriminated against and are being paid less than men. Needless to say, the

high profile case in an Australian court has also meant that Caitlin's life has been investigated in depth by journalists seeking to find more 'dirt' on CMC and its seemingly exemplary feminist CEO.

Caitlin wonders how her company could possibly have got into the situation where they could have been involved in such discriminatory processes. The company values of diversity are inclusion are taken very seriously and all employees have to go through some form of diversity training as part of their induction to ensure that these values are engendered into everyday practices. She is aware that in different cultural locations diversity needs to be addressed in different ways. For example, in a recent expansion of the company into the Chinese market she has been keen to ensure that the values and commitment to diversity are promoted as being located within traditional Chinese notions of inclusion. She is aware that some policies do not easily translate. However, to be found guilty of discrimination in Australia presents her with a puzzle. Her Australian Director of Operations has suggested that the issue has arisen because of local management practices that will be dealt with, but given the significance of the incident for both the company and her own personal reputation, Caitlin decides to visit the Australian head office to meet with key staff and discover more about why the incident has occurred.

At a meeting with the Australian Director, Matt Sparkes, Caitlin asks more about how such discriminatory practices can occur. Matt expands on his view that the crucial issue is local management. At all of the retail outlets staff have the right to access work–life balance programmes that include flexible working. However, during the recent run up to Christmas, which is the busiest time of the year, Matt has been aware that different managers may be implementing these policies somewhat differently. Caitlin is committed to a no-blame culture so is keen to discuss the issues and problems with the policies openly with the managers concerned. Hence a random selection of local managers are collected together to meet with Caitlin for an open exchange of views about their experience of the policy.

During the discussion a number of issues with flexible working become apparent. First, it is clear that the commitment to flexible work arrangements can be problematic for store managers. For example, one manager reported that they had had little direction from their regional line manager about how to deal with staff who wanted a variety of flexible working arrangements. Moreover, they felt under considerable pressure to keep these arrangements to a minimum because of the impact they had on the operation of the stores. The manager described how with a variety of

women working different and flexible shifts, managing the operational needs of the business was an ongoing challenge. One female manager said that as a woman without children she felt that flexible working initiatives were often divisive and that she had to work hard to stop resentment towards women who worked flexibly in their department. In order to compensate some disgruntled male employees she had offered them extra overtime, one of the causes of the discrimination case in another outlet.

A second issue that emerged was that different managers were interpreting the flexible working policies in different ways. As the busiest time of the year the pressures of managing staff working patterns became even more challenging. In some cases this would lead to individual managers making more informal arrangements with staff to discourage the uptake of more rigid, formal, flexible working policies. However, the informal nature of these arrangements led to accusations of favouritism from other staff. Caitlin was surprised to discover that rather than flexible working policies leading to a more happy and motivated workforce, in some cases they had instead led to resentment and a confrontational culture.

Caitlin realised that despite the efforts that had been made to instil values of diversity and inclusion throughout the company internationally, what was just as important was how managers operationalised those values in practice. She realised that more thinking was needed about CMC's diversity and inclusion policies. Therefore she decided to institute a new diversity task force to evaluate the company's diversity and inclusion strategy with a view to ensuring that the positive company values are translated into practice. Her intention is that as well as evaluating the policy, the task force will produce a list of actions that will ensure that the company delivers on effective diversity management internationally.

Questions

Imagine you have been allocated the role of Chair of the new diversity and inclusion task force at CMC.

1 What steps would you take to evaluate the company's current diversity and inclusion strategy?

2 What interventions do you think might be useful in this case?

3 What plans would you make for evaluating your proposed interventions?

CASE STUDY 12.3

EXERCISE IN DIVERSITY TRAINING

CATHERINE CASSELL

You are the HR Director of a large multinational finance company. The company has a well-established diversity policy which covers all of the different regional locations of the company. Within the policy it explicitly states that discrimination against certain groups of the workforce based on particular differences will not be tolerated. However, you are concerned that there are different expectations and values across the senior management team in the different locations of the company. Therefore there is a lack of consistency in how difference and diversity are treated.

You are concerned that there needs to be more clarity around the interpretation of the policy worldwide and decide that you will take the opportunity to use the regular annual three-day meeting of the worldwide HR Directors to engage colleagues in a one-day training session about the challenges of managing diversity globally and the expressed company values in this area. Your aim is to ensure that all Directors are committed to the policy, and can cascade its importance once they return to their own country.

Task

Your task is to provide an overview of the content and delivery format of the day's training session. Some points to consider are:

- How will the day be divided up?
- What will be the content of each of the sessions?
- How will you surface different views of the policy in a culturally sensitive manner?
- What difficulties do you anticipate with the training you have suggested?
- How will you evaluate the impact and effectiveness of the training?

Bibliography

Adkins, L. (1995) *Gendered Work: Sexuality, Family and the Labour Market*, Buckingham: Open University Press.

Arnold, J. (1997) *Managing Careers into the 21st Century*, London: Paul Chapman Publishing.

Asda (2006) 'DWP recognises ASDA's continued good practice on age diversity'. Available at: http://your.asda.com/press-centre/dwp-recognises-asda-s-continued-good-practice-on-age-diversity.

Biswas, R. and Cassell, C.M. (1996) 'The sexual division of labour in the hotel industry: implications for strategic HRM', *Personnel Review*, Vol.25, No.5, 51–66.

Blätte, A. (2014) 'Managing diversity in Europe: the state of the state in migration and integration policy', *Journal of European Integration*, Vol.36, No.1, 91–8.

Cassell, C.M. and Biswas, R. (2000) 'Managing diversity in the new millennium', *Personnel Review*, Vol.29, No.3, 268–74.

Choi, S. and Rainey, H.G. (2010) 'Managing diversity in US federal agencies: effects of diversity and diversity management on employee perceptions of organizational performance', *Public Administration Review*, January/February, 109–21.

CIPD (2010) 'Focus: disadvantaged groups in the labour market'. Available at: http://www.cipd.co.uk/hr-resources/survey-reports/labour-market-outlook-focus-disadvantaged-groups.aspx.

CIPD (2011) 'Diversity in the workplace: an overview'. Available at: http://www.cipd.co.uk/hr-resources/factsheets/diversity-workplace-overview.aspx.

Cooke, F.L. and Saini, D.S. (2012) 'Managing diversity in Chinese and Indian organizations: a qualitative study', *Journal of Chinese Human Resource Management*, Vol.3, No.1, 16–32.

Cox, T., Jr. (1992) 'The multi-cultural organization', *Academy of Management Executive*, Vol.5, No.2, 34–47.

Deloitte (2014) *Global Human Capital Trends 2014: Engaging the 21st Century Workforce*, Texas: Deloitte University Press.

Egan, M.L. and Bendick, M. (2003) 'Workforce diversity initiatives of US multinational corporations in Europe', *Thunderbird International Business Review*, Vol.45, No.6, 701–27.

Ellis, C. and Sonnenfeld, J.A. (1994) 'Diverse approaches to managing diversity', *Human Resource Management*, Vol.33, No.1, 79–109.

European Commission (2005) 'The business case for diversity: good practices in the workplace'. Available at: http://ec.europa.eu/social/main.jsp?catId=370&langId=en&featuresId=25.

European Foundation for Living and Working Conditions (EFLWC) (2010) 'Demographic change and work in Europe'. Available at: http://www.eurofound.europa.eu/ewco/surveyreports/EU0902019D/EU0902019D.pdf.

Farndale, E., Biron, M., Briscoe, D.R. and Raghuram, S. (2015) 'Introduction: a global perspective on diversity and inclusion in organisations', *International Journal of Human Resource Management*, Vol.26, No.6, 677–87.

Friday, E. and Friday, S. (2003) 'Managing diversity using a strategic planned change approach', *Journal of Management Development*, Vol.22, No.10, 863–80.

Fulkerson, J.R. and Schuler, R.S. (1992) 'Managing worldwide diversity at Pepsi-Cola International', pp. 248–77, in Jackson, S.E. and Associates (eds.) *Diversity in the Workplace: Human Resource Initiatives*, New York: Guildford Press.

Fullerton, M. (2013) 'Diversity and inclusion – LGBT inclusion means business', *Strategic HR Review*, Vol.12, No.3, 121–5.

Guo, C. and Al Ariss, A. (2015) 'Human resource management of international migrants: current theories and future research', *International Journal of Human Resource Management*, Vol.26, No.10, 1287–97.

Haq, R. (2012) 'The managing diversity mindset in public versus private organizations in India', *International Journal of Human Resource Management*, Vol.23, No.5, 892–914.

Hays-Thomas, R. and Bendick, M., Jr. (2013) 'Professionalizing diversity and inclusion practice: should voluntary standards be the chicken or the egg?', *Industrial and Organizational Psychology*, Vol.6, No.3, 193–205.

Jackson, S.E. and Associates (1992) *Diversity in the Workplace: Human Resource Initiatives* New York: Guilford Press.

Johnston, W.B. and Packard, A.H. (1987) *Workforce 2000: Work and Workers for the 21st Century*, Indiana, IN: Hudson.

Jones, D., Pringle, J. and Shepherd, D. (2000) '"Managing diversity" meets Aotearoa New Zealand', *Personnel Review*, Vol.29, No.3, 364–80.

Kaifi, B.A. (2009) 'Managing diversity: Afghan-Americans and the aftermath of the twin towers tragedy', *Journal of Diversity Management*, Vol.4, No.4, 31–7.

Kandola, R. (1995) 'Managing diversity: new broom or old hat?', in Cooper, C.L. and Robertson, I.T. (eds.) *International Review of Industrial and Organizational Psychology*, Vol.10, Chichester: John Wiley & Sons.

Kandola, R. and Fullerton, J. (1994) *Managing the Mosaic: Diversity in Action*, London: Institute of Personnel and Development.

Klarsfeld, A. (2009) 'The diffusion of diversity management: the case of France', *Scandinavian Journal of Management*, Vol.25, 363–73.

Kochan, T., Bezrukova, K., Ely, R., Jackson, S., Aparna, J., Jehn, K., Leonard, J., Levine, D. and Thomas, P. (2003) 'The effects of diversity on business performance: report of the diversity research network', *Human Resource Management*, Vol.42, No.1, 3–21.

Meriläinen, S., Tierari, J., Katila, S. and Benschop, Y. (2009) 'Diversity management versus gender equality: the Finnish case', *Canadian Journal of Administrative Sciences*, Vol.26, No.3, 230–43.

Michielsens, E., Bingham, C. and Clarke, L. (2014) 'Managing diversity through flexible work arrangements', *Employee Relations*, Vol.36, No.12, 49–69.

Montes, T. and Shaw, G. (2003) 'The future of workplace diversity in the new millennium', pp. 385–402, in Davidson, M.J. and Fielden, S.L. (eds.) *Individual Diversity and Psychology in Organizations*, Chichester: John Wiley & Sons.

Nishii, L.H. and Özbilgin, M.F. (2007) 'Global diversity management: towards a conceptual framework', *International Journal of Human Resource Management*, Vol.18, No.11, 1883–94.

Omanivic, V. (2009) 'Diversity and its management as a dialectical process: encountering Sweden and the US', *Scandinavian Journal of Management*, Vol.25, 352–62.

Özbilgin, M. Tatli, A., Gulce, I. and Sameer, M. (2014) *The Business Case for Diversity Management*, London: ACCA.

Pendry, L.F., Driscoll, D.M. and Field, C.T. (2007) 'Diversity training: putting theory into practice', *Journal of Occupational and Organizational Psychology*, Vol.80, 27–50.

Pitts, D.W. (2006) 'Modeling the impact of diversity management', *Review of Public Personnel Administration*, Vol.26, 245–68.

Pitts, D.W., Hicklin, A.K., Hawes, D.P. and Melton, E. (2010) 'What drives the implementation of diversity management programs? Evidence from public organizations', *Journal of Public Administration Research*, Vol.20, 867–86.

Prasad, P., Mills, A.J., Elmes, M. and Prasad, A. (1997) *Managing the Organizational Melting Pot: Dilemmas of Workplace Diversity*, Thousand Oaks, CA: Sage.

Prasad, A., Prasad, P. and Mir, R. (2011) '"One mirror in another": managing diversity and the discourse of fashion', *Human Relations*, Vol.64, No.5, 703–14.

Rao, A. (2012) 'Managing diversity: impact of religion in the Indian workplace', *Journal of World Business*, Vol.47, 232–9.

Richards, W. (2001) 'Evaluating equal opportunities initiatives: the case for a transformative agenda', in Noon, M. and Ogbonna, E. (eds.) *Equality, Diversity and Disadvantage in Employment*, Houndmills: Palgrave.

Roberson, Q.M. (2006) 'Disentangling the meanings of diversity and inclusion in organizations', *Group and Organization Management*, Vol.31, No.2, 212–36.

Roberson, L. and Kulik, C.T. (2007) 'Stereotype threat at work', *Academy of Management Perspectives*, Vol.21, No.2, 24–40.

Ross, R. and Schneider, R. (1992) *From Equality to Diversity: A Business Case for Equal Opportunities*, London: Pitman.

Shen, J., D'Netto, B. and Tang, J. (2010) 'Effects of human resource diversity management on organizational citizenship behavior in the Chinese context', *International Journal of Human Resource Management*, Vol.21, No.12, 2156–72.

Shen, J., Chanda, A, D'Netto, B. and Monga, M. (2009) 'Managing diversity through human resource management', *International Journal of Human Resource Management*, Vol.20, No.2, 235–51.

Shore, L.M., Randel, A.E., Chung, B.G., Dean, M.A., Ehrhart, K.H. and Singh, G. (2011) 'Inclusion and diversity in work groups: a review and model for future research', *Journal of Management*, Vol.37, No.4, 1262–89.

SHRM Foundation (2014) Available at: http://futurehrtrends.eiu.com/report-2014/challenges-human-resource-management/.

Sippola, A. and Smale, A. (2007) 'The global integration of diversity management: a longitudinal case study', *International Journal of Human Resource Management*, Vol.18, No.11, 1895–916.

Storey, J. (1995) *Human Resource Management: A Critical Text*, London: Routledge.

Strachan, G., Burgess, J. and Sullivan, A. (2004) 'Affirmative action or managing diversity: what is the future of equal opportunities policies in organizations', *Women in Management Review*, Vol.19, No.4, 196–204.

Süβ, S. and Kleiner, M. (2007) 'Diversity management in Germany: dissemination and design of the concept', *International Journal of Human Resource Management*, Vol.18, No.11, 1934–53.

Syed, J. and Özbiglin, M. (2009) 'A relational framework for international transfer of diversity management practices', *International Journal of Human Resource Management*, Vol.20, No.12, 2435–53.

Tang, N., Jiang, Y., Chen, C, Zhou, Z., Chen, C.C. and Yu, Z. (2015) 'Inclusion and inclusion management in a Chinese context: an exploratory study', *International Journal of Human Resource Management*, Vol.26, No.6, 856–74.

Tatli, A. (2011) 'A multi-layered exploration of the diversity management field: diversity discourses, practices and practitioners in the UK', *British Journal of Management*, Vol.22, 238–53.

Theodorakapoulos, N. and Budhwar, P. (2015) 'Guest editor's introduction: diversity and inclusion in different work settings: emerging challenges, patterns and research agendas', *Human Resource Management*, Vol.54, No.2, 177–97.

Thomas, R.R., Jr. (1990) 'From affirmative action to affirming diversity', *Harvard Business Review*, Vol.68, No.2, 107–17.

Thomas, R.R., Jr. (1992) 'Managing diversity: a conceptual framework', pp. 306–18, in Jackson, S.E. and Associates (eds.) *Diversity in the Workplace: Human Resource Initiatives*, New York: Guildford.

Wahl, A. and Holgersson, C. (2003) 'Male managers' reactions to gender diversity activities in organizations', pp. 313–30, in Davidson, M.J. and Fielden, S.L. (eds.) *Individual Diversity and Psychology in Organizations*, Chichester: John Wiley & Sons.

Wilson, E.M. (2003) 'Managing diversity: caste and gender issues in India', pp. 149–68, in Davidson, M.J. and Fielden, S.L. (eds.) *Individual Diversity and Psychology in Organizations*, Chichester: John Wiley & Sons.

Woodhams, C. and Danieli, A. (2000) 'Disability and diversity: a difference too far?', *Personnel Review*, Vol.29, No.3, 402–17.

CHAPTER 13

WORK–LIFE BALANCE: NATIONAL REGIMES, ORGANISATIONAL POLICIES AND INDIVIDUAL CHOICES

Gill Kirton

Introduction

Paid work occupies a central place in the lives of most adults in developed countries. Paid work obviously provides the means for sustenance for the vast majority of people, but it is also said to contribute to a sense of identity, self-worth and usefulness in the context of society as a whole (Parent-Thirion et al., 2007). Indeed, government policies often reflect this idea, however ironical this may seem at a time when working lives have arguably been transformed for the worse, and incomes and jobs have become less secure (McDowell, 2004). Yet, increasingly, paid work is also seen to encroach on family and personal life to the extent that people's lives are often unbalanced with little time or energy left for other life activities beyond paid work.

Work–life balance concerns the reconciliation of work, private and family life. While many aspects of life can be included in work–life balance, such as time for leisure, community and citizenship activity, it is the decline of the nuclear family, an increase in the number of women in the labour market and an increase in the number of households in which both partners work, that have pushed work–life balance higher up the agenda for individuals, organisations and governments. Women are a key focus of the work–life balance policy debate because of the greater likelihood of their taking primary responsibility for the home and family and the need for them to have access to work arrangements that allow them to combine work and home responsibilities. Nevertheless, behind the work–life balance discourses of many institutions lies the objective of encouraging men to play a greater role in the family and to share household chores.

This chapter first considers work–life balance discourses; it then moves on to explore the national context of work–life balance, next work–life balance and the workplace and finally individual choice and work–life balance.

Work–life balance discourses

While it is widely believed that discourses can influence practice as well as represent the world, it is important to recognise that discourses and practices are not the same thing and that there can be a rhetoric–reality gap. Discourses of work–life balance, while part of national contexts are largely globalised, insofar as work–life balance has made its way onto the policy agenda of many if not all industrialised countries. Policies that were once called flexibility and later 'family friendly' are now firmly located within the work–life balance discourse internationally. The shift in discourse and policy language is interesting to note. Work–life balance discourse originated in neoliberal contexts, particularly in the USA and UK, where there was a policy focus on enhancing competitiveness through minimal regulation (Lewis *et al.*, 2007). Writing from a UK perspective, Fleetwood (2007) argues that discourses and practices of flexible working became detached from one another from around the late 1990s. In the late 1980s and 1990s, discourses and practices associated with the flexible firm model started to emerge in response to high levels of unemployment. For Fleetwood (ibid.), the kinds of flexible working practices that employers introduced in order to minimise the so-called rigidities of the labour market were employee-*un*friendly and the dominant discourses reflected this. For example, unions lobbied and campaigned against the 'casualization of labour' – the creation of temporary, fixed-term jobs and the erosion of employment security.

In the late 1990s, in the context of a tight labour market, employers began to offer part-time work as a specific means of attracting women, particularly mothers, against talk of the 'demographic time bomb' and the need for employers to engage in the 'war for talent' in order to remain competitive. Political discourses began to emphasise the employee, or more specifically the family-friendly nature of flexible working, painting a win-win scenario. Fleetwood (ibid.) argues that although the representation of flexible working through political and public discourses became positive, the actual *practices* were still largely employee-*un*friendly insofar as part-time work, for example, was not necessarily temporally flexible and did not always fit well with family commitments.

Somewhere towards the end of the 1990s, family-friendly practices and discourses morphed into work–life balance in order to confront or perhaps sidestep the criticism that family-friendly practices focused on women with children, excluding men and women without children. By now, the public discourse of work–life balance was wholly positive, while policies were more mixed with both employee-friendly and employee-*un*friendly elements, meaning that current discourses of work–life balance do not entirely match the realities. Even the unions have tended to adopt the positive discourse of work–life balance and tend to downplay the negative aspects of flexible working practices (Fleetwood, 2007).

Further, the change in language to work–life balance had the effect at the discursive level of making the policies *appear* gender-neutral when in reality practices remain highly gendered in terms of targeting and take-up. Despite the language of 'work–life balance' and the insistence of governments and employers that it is an issue 'for everyone', many of the policy initiatives (as discussed below) are implicitly aimed at women, especially mothers, and/or those with primary responsibility for children (usually women), just as 'family-friendly' policies were (Lewis *et al.*, 2007). Yet advocates of the new label argue that the language of work–life balance removes the discussion of the importance of achieving a better balance between home and work life from the ghetto of 'women's issues' associated with the now less popular family-friendly label. In this way, so the argument goes, work–life balance becomes an issue for everyone that employers will then take up more enthusiastically regardless of labour market conditions. The problem is that whilst we still have a marked gender pay gap internationally, it will continue to make rational economic sense for most households to privilege the male career, so whether the work–life balance discourse can remove family-friendly work practices from the ghetto of women's issues remains questionable. After all, work–life balance discourses and policies do not confront structural gender inequalities such as gender segregation and the gender pay gap, which produce the material inequalities that push women towards privileging family roles and men towards privileging paid work.

Contemporary political discourses of work–life balance influence not only current employer policies and practices but also popular perceptions. Pocock (2005) identifies four rationales for work–life balance:

- **the business case** – to help employers with the recruitment, retention and productivity of good staff;
- **the social case** – workers who are satisfied with their work–life balance are likely to be happier social citizens, carers, parents;
- **the political case** – industrialised countries are dependent on the paid work of women and workers with dependents;
- **the personal case** – enhancement of individual wellbeing.

These cases for work–life balance are reflected in political and popular discourses as well as in national and employer policies and practices. Political work–life balance discourses typically present a win-win scenario – employers benefit from greater employee flexibility (the business case), while workers get to organise their work, private and family lives in ways to suit their individual situations (the personal case). By extension, the demands of the social and political cases are also met when workers experience work–life balance satisfaction.

While in some respects the prominence of work–life balance discourses might seem to represent a progressive turn that heralds greater gender equality, there is a more negative reading. Family and parental leave policies and flexible work arrangements contained within work–life balance discourses and policies might make life easier for individuals at particular phases of their lives, but they do not challenge the cultural and institutional norms that keep men tied to long working hours and women juggling work and family (McDowell, 2004). Instead, work–life balance discourses incline more towards ensuring women are kept marginalised within organisations as the ones who are perceived to be in need of special arrangements in the form of work–life balance policies. As we see later, and in Case study 13.1, being seen to be the ones taking up flexible work and other work–life balance arrangements can have negative consequences for women's careers.

Political work–life balance discourses also tend to focus on the perspectives of those in full-time employment, which is still held as the desirable norm (Bonney, 2005). Bonney (ibid.), perhaps controversially, argues that flexible work arrangements for full-time employment have now taken priority over acknowledging and supporting part-time employment as a desirable solution to work–family conflict, particularly for parents (mostly mothers) of young children. He argues that part-timers and their lived experiences are often overlooked in popular discourses, which are shaped by influential people in politics, the media and academia who more commonly regard full-time employment for all as the most desirable state. However, even though part-time employment might be genuinely desired by some people, its career-limiting nature and limited financial benefits as it is currently configured in most countries (discussed below) should not be forgotten.

 ## The national context of work–life balance

There can be no doubt that national institutional settings – including welfare, employment and gender regimes – matter for work–life balance. Sources of support for work–life balance can come from the state, market or family or from a combination of sources. Broadly, the state is the main provider of work–life balance support in social democratic countries such as Sweden and in former socialist countries in Central and Eastern Europe (such as Bulgaria and Hungary). In conservative welfare states (Germany) and in southern European countries (Spain, Portugal), it is the family that provides the support, while in liberal countries (the UK), the market is considered as the main provider of work–life balance support (Abendroth and Dulk, 2011). Market (i.e. employer) policies (discussed later) are located within national regimes, and while some employers might offer provisions beyond the legal minimum, others will only do what is required by law. Nevertheless, there is evidence to suggest that state support for work–life balance policies can stimulate workplace support because the state can both sensitise employers to the issue and encourage them to offer support (Abendroth and Dulk, 2011). As important as national welfare regimes are for work–life balance, as a caveat it is important to state that there is some evidence that the variation in workplace support for work–life balance does not always correspond to Esping-Andersen's (1990) widely cited welfare regime typology. For example, despite post-communist countries having a strong tradition of state support, workplace support in Bulgaria and Hungary is found to be relatively modest (Abendroth and Dulk, 2011).

Even though 'parental choice' is the avowed policy aim of nearly all countries (OECD, 2008), individuals make their choices about how to combine work, family and personal life against the array of institutional constraints and enablers. For example, national public and employer childcare and eldercare provision, the social and workplace organisation of time, gender roles in the home and family all impact on how individuals are able to combine the work and non-work aspects of their lives. These institutional settings vary enormously from country to country and while there is not space here to go into detail, illustrative examples are given to underline the point that the work–life balance debate necessarily has to extend beyond the organisational and individual levels to the national.

National welfare and employment regimes

The main kinds of government policies that impact on work–life balance include (1) tax and benefit systems, (2) parental leave systems and (3) childcare provision.

1 Individualised tax systems (as opposed to a system that taxes couples), for example, mean that second earners (often mothers) pay a lower rate of tax than the primary earner, making it more attractive financially for them to work. In contrast, tax relief for non-employed partners or family assistance systems that count both partners' incomes potentially reduce the financial incentive to work. Most The Organisation for Economic Cooperation and Development (OECD) countries operate elements of both systems.

2 The availability of paid parental leave obviously makes a difference to how well mothers and fathers feel able to balance work and family. At one end of the spectrum some countries offer up to three years of paid support (Austria, the Czech Republic, Finland and Hungary) and at the other end others offer very little or no universal paid leave (e.g. USA) (OECD, 2008). The main explanation for these stark cross-national differences is that some countries (i.e. the liberal welfare states such as the USA, UK and Australia) see care as a private family responsibility rather than as a matter for the state to make provision for (Craig *et al.*, 2010). However, there have been some recent changes in some countries. Australia, for example, first introduced a universal paid parental leave policy in 2011. It provides assistance equivalent to the minimum wage to the primary carer of a newborn child for a maximum of 18 weeks. 'Dad and Partner Pay' also provides two weeks of leave paid at the minimum wage for partners of a primary carer (http://www.ncoa.gov.au/report/phase-one/part-b/7-6-paid-parental-leave-and-child-care.html). In 2015 the UK introduced shared parental pay/leave, enabling eligible parents the flexibility to share care in the first year after a child's birth/adoption (https://www.gov.uk/shared-parental-leave-and-pay/overview).

3 It is self-evident that greater access to formal state- or employer-subsidised childcare facilities helps parents to balance work and family and again this varies enormously from country to country. In most neoliberal social welfare regimes the costs of childcare are high (e.g. Australia, the UK) even with various tax benefits, and in these countries there is a relatively high dependence on informal childcare often provided by, for example, grandparents. Nevertheless, increasing numbers of children use formal childcare. In Australia, for example, in 1996, of all children aged three to four years 22 per cent used formal childcare. This figure rose to 46 per cent by 2005 (Craig *et al.*, 2010).

In general, there has been a move in the US and some European countries towards neoliberal social welfare regimes, which emphasise market-led provision, deregulation and the reduction of universal benefits (McDowell, 2004; Craig *et al.*, 2010). In the US, with its archetypal neoliberal welfare and employment regimes, work–life balance is certainly on the agenda of progressive 'think tanks', but minimal and patchy federal and state laws mean that employee rights are woefully inadequate for resolving work–family conflict and helping individuals achieve work–life balance. With no federal or state laws requiring that all employers even offer paid sick days (only about 50 per cent of workers in the US have access to paid sick leave), the US trails well behind the UK and the rest of Europe in guaranteeing workers at least some opportunities to balance work–life responsibilities (Boushey *et al.*, 2008). The US is the only OECD country without a national parental leave policy although some states do provide leave payments (OECD, 2011). In the light of the currently weak institutional support for work–life balance, the American think tank The Mobility Agenda recommends that policy makers and employers adopt four minimum work–life balance policies:

- guaranteed paid sick days for all workers;
- paid family and medical leave;
- right to request workplace flexibility;
- scheduling flexibility.

Some, at least, of the above policies are taken for granted in other countries – in many European countries, for example – and are legal requirements in many. Institutional support for work–life balance is certainly far greater in the European Union than in the USA and is a key area of policy debate within the European Employment Strategy. Over the last 20 years, discussions at European Union level have focused on making work more flexible and facilitating shorter working hours to enable people to achieve greater work–life balance. In a 'Roadmap' for equality between women and men, the European Union has the reconciliation of work, private and family life as one of its six priority areas of action for gender equality. The Roadmap identifies three main areas for action: (i) flexible work arrangements for women and men; (ii) increasing care services and (iii) better reconciliation policies for women and men (e.g. parental leave, part-time work) (CEC, 2006). OECD makes three recommendations for national policy – shown in Box 13.1. Not all countries measure up against these as shown by the OECD recommendations in Box 13.2 for selected countries.

Box 13.1 HRM in practice   What should governments do on work–life balance? OECD recommendations

- **Guarantee paid parental leave with employment protection**
  Policy often helps parents take time off around the birth of a baby and sometimes provides some pre-school support. But parents of older dependent children can also face significant barriers and they can require continuing support. The question for governments is whether caring for children at home should be subsidised.
- **Provide financial support for good, affordable childcare**
  In many countries, good childcare provisions already exist, but they are not always affordable and do not always match working hours. Some countries need to give greater financial support for childcare either through capital investment in childcare facilities or through direct payments to parents. In addition to pre-school provision, adequate out-of-school-hours/terms provision is also needed.
- **Grant employees the 'right to request' flexible working hours**
  This emphasises the involvement of both employer and employee in determining working hours that suit both parties. It extends access to low-income workers who usually have little flexibility or autonomy to decide their working hours.

Source: OECD (2008) *Policy Brief – Babies and Bosses: Balancing Work and Family Life*, OECD, Paris.

| Box 13.2 HRM in practice | Improving government support for work–life balance. OECD recommendations on selected countries |

Australia:

- Extend childcare support programmes.
- Help single parents to find work.

Canada:

- Strengthen investment in formal childcare.
- Improve affordability of childcare.
- Offer childcare support to help vulnerable families, especially single parents.

France:

- Encourage a more equitable division of unpaid work within households via improved paternity leave.
- Improve access to labour market of mothers of young or large families via tax benefits and parental leave policy design.

Germany:

- Bolster childcare services.
- Reform tax/benefit system to encourage second earners in families with children.

Netherlands:

- Improve childcare facilities to enable women's participation in full-time work.

New Zealand:

- Do more to help parents of the youngest children.
- Provide better parental leave payment rates.
- Support sole parents into full-time work via provision of quality childcare.

Spain:

- Strengthen policies to combine work and family life.
- Improve out-of-school-hours childcare.
- Encourage a more equitable division of unpaid work within households.

United Kingdom:

- Provide affordable and good quality local childcare.
- Provide an effective childcare supplement for working parents.

Source: OECD, 2013. Available at: http://www.oecdbetterlifeindex.org/topics/work-life-balance/.

Despite the prominence of work–life balance at European Union level, actual national care services and reconciliation policies are highly variable across Europe. Sweden, for example, has much lauded, subsidised childcare and mandated parental leave policies. On progressive parental leave policies, Norway stands out insofar as the parent on leave receives full pay in the form of social welfare benefits (Hardy and Adnett, 2002). Indeed, overall the most extensive national work–life balance policies are found in the Scandinavian countries (Abendroth and Dulk, 2011). However, following recent reforms, Germany now has the most generous parental leave among OECD countries (OECD, 2011). Worryingly, it seems that taking parental leave can have a negative effect on women's pay, which increases with the length of leave. There is evidence that Australian women returning to work after 12 months' parental leave were subject to an average 7 per cent wage penalty (known as the 'motherhood penalty'), increasing to 12 per cent over the subsequent year (Baker, 2011).

The length of the working week continues to be an issue discussed in relation to work–life balance even though weekly working hours have fallen among the full-time workforce in some European countries. In non-European OECD countries, many people work more than 50 hours per week. In Turkey, the figure is 43.3 per cent, in Mexico 28.8 per cent, in Korea 27.1 per cent, in Japan 22.6 per cent and in Israel 18.8 per cent. Against this working time context, some countries have started to legislate for flexible work arrangements. In the Netherlands, employees of enterprises with 10 or more workers can change their working hours for whatever reason (OECD, 2008). In the UK parents with children under age 17 (or 18 in the case of a disabled child) and carers of adults (living at the same address) have the legal right to request flexible work arrangements (including shifting to part-time hours) to allow them to balance work and caring responsibilities. Employers can only decline the request if there are good business reasons for doing so. It is mostly women who take up this entitlement.

One form of flexible working – part-time work – is particularly widespread. In all developed countries, women have a far greater propensity to work part-time than men do. The European average for part-time working is about 32 per cent for women compared with about 8 per cent of men. In the UK, 42 per cent of women work part-time, similar to Sweden, Norway and Austria, but significantly lower than the Netherlands where 55 per cent of women work part-time (the highest in the European Union) (EC, 2013). Although part-time working is more widespread among women with dependent children, many women never return to full-time work. Although the reasons for this are undoubtedly many and complex, it is clear that it is not always a simple matter of personal choice. Indeed, recent evidence indicates that a significant proportion of those working part-time in European Union countries do so involuntarily, rather than through choice – 39 per cent of men and 24 per cent of women working part-time would prefer a full-time job (EC, 2013).

Moreover, because part-time work is often segregated from full-time – i.e. found in specific occupations and industries, and often concentrated in low paid, low status jobs – many women end up either lacking the experience or skills for full-time jobs. This gendered employment pattern has far-reaching consequences for earnings even though it may offer a short-term solution to work–family conflict. For example, in the UK, the part-time gender pay gap – the difference between the pay rate of men working full time and women working part time – is around 42 per cent, compared with a full-time gender gap of around 10 per cent (ONS, 2013). In the Netherlands, a working mother with two adult children earns on average less than half the total working-life earnings of other female workers (OECD, 2011). Therefore, although again at the individual level and against institutional constraints that make full-time work for parents difficult, in many countries part-time work might seem like a solution to work–family conflict, it has quite dramatically negative consequences for women's pay and income equality in the short and long term. Certainly, when thinking about lifetime income, women pay in the longer term for what might seem like a temporary solution to work–life balance problems. In the US, part-time jobs usually come without the health insurance that American workers depend on (the USA offering only minimal publically funded health care). In the US, part-time work is therefore a far less attractive option, even in the short term, for dealing with work–family conflict and, consequently, is far less widespread (Lyonette *et al.*, 2011).

Gender regimes

It is argued that among the many aspects of national context that impact on work–life balance, the degree of gender equality is particularly relevant; that is, the degree to which national cultures support women's development and achievements and recognise the importance of including women in all aspects of life (Lyness and Kropf, 2005). The allocation of gender roles in the home and family are indicative of national gender regimes that provide more or less support for women's employment participation/economic independence and for women's equality. Although studies identify a general trend towards a more equal gender division of paid and unpaid work, countries start from different baselines and still differ in beliefs about appropriate roles for women and men (Craig *et al.*, 2010). In some countries women and men occupy highly sex-differentiated roles (e.g. male breadwinner and female homemaker), whereas in other countries gender roles are more similar or overlap (Lyness and Kropf, 2005). The belief systems underpinning gender regimes then go on to permeate national and organisational policies described above and below on work–life balance and more specifically on work and family.

Despite some variation and against the increasing participation of women in the labour market, the evidence worldwide confirms that the traditional division of domestic responsibilities between women and men persists to one extent or another (EOWA, 2008a; Parent-Thirion *et al.*, 2007). Working women continue to devote more time to household chores and caring (for children and elders) than do men. This is particularly the case for mothers, compared with non-mothers and men. The evidence from Europe shows that while men typically work longer hours in their paid jobs, when unpaid work in the home and paid work are combined women work longer hours than men do. Men's work is generally confined to their paid jobs while women use the time freed up by their typically shorter paid work hours to carry out work in the home (Parent-Thirion *et al.*, 2007). This unequal division of household and family work means that women are typically 'time poor' and obviously have less time to do other non-work activities including leisure or community, for example. For women, work–life balance is very much about work–*family* balance and the presence of children tends to accentuate the gender division of labour, but the picture is more complex than formerly when the male breadwinner and female homemaker model was more prevalent. For example, Craig *et al.*'s (2010) study of the total (paid and unpaid) work carried out by women and men in Australia from 1992 to 2006, revealed that the total workload of both mothers and fathers increased over the period, although for mothers the increase was greater. At the end of the period, mothers were spending more hours than at the start on paid work and on childcare and the same on domestic chores. Fathers were also spending more hours on paid work and childcare, but less on domestic chores. Obviously the presence of children creates extra domestic chores (shopping, cleaning, laundry, cooking) and it is women who generally pick up the extra.

Further, the continuation of a traditional household gender regime inevitably restricts women's availability for paid work and goes some way to explaining their over-representation in part-time jobs in some countries. Therefore, it is generally in the more gender egalitarian countries that we see lower levels of women's part-time work (e.g. the Scandinavian countries). In a survey carried out in Australia by the Equal Opportunity for Women in the Workplace Agency (EOWA), nearly a third of women reported that if their partners carried out a larger share of domestic tasks, they would work longer hours. Equally, there is evidence that men would like to spend more time with their families. Sixty per cent of Australian men in the same survey reported that their jobs caused them to miss out on some of the rewarding aspects of fatherhood. The report highlights an experience that extends beyond Australia that many men have become trapped in the main breadwinning role and women in the domestic, despite the fact that women have similar career aspirations to men and that men have similar family values to women (EOWA, 2008a). This underlines the interconnection between employment and gender regimes.

Work–life balance and the workplace

The business case

The idea that there is a business case for work–life balance policies is widely promulgated by governments in order to encourage employers to offer provisions. Before unpacking the business case, we must first ask why if there is a strong business case we would need national legislation as encouraged by the OECD and the European Employment Strategy (Hardy and Adnett, 2002). This caveat notwithstanding, employer benefits from work–life balance policies are said to include improved employee recruitment and retention, less employee ill-health/absenteeism and associated cost reductions, a more productive workforce and in turn a stronger financial/business performance (Boushey *et al.*, 2008). However, research finds that employers often introduce work–life balance policies to attract and retain workers without a clear understanding of which specific policies are most attractive to their actual and potential workers (Thompson and Aspinwall, 2009).

Evidence does indicate that increased opportunities to balance work and life might lead to greater employee satisfaction, which is likely to yield significant benefits for employers. For example, while working long hours can have a range of negative effects (including health and safety), research finds that the greatest negative effect is on work–life balance. Eighteen per cent of workers in the EU27 are not satisfied with their work–life balance (Eurofound, 2010). Nearly half of all employees in the US report conflicts between jobs and other responsibilities, more than a generation ago (Boushey *et al.*, 2008). Work–life balance satisfaction varies considerably among European countries, with workers in Norway and Austria showing the greatest satisfaction and those in Greece the lowest. The longer the hours worked, the more likely people are to report work–life balance dissatisfaction in all countries (Parent-Thirion *et al.*, 2007). There are also gender differences – men in Europe are most likely to report dissatisfaction in the middle of their careers (between ages 30 to 49) when they are most likely to have dependent children. Twenty-seven per cent of men with dependent children under 16 reported that their working hours did not fit well with family and social commitments outside work, compared with 18 per cent of women (Parent-Thirion *et al.*, 2007).

Women are generally less likely to report work–life balance dissatisfaction, but those who do experience problems do so constantly over the entire course of their working lives (Eurofound, 2010). Given that women generally continue to take primary responsibility for the home and family in conjunction with increased participation in paid work, lower reported levels of work–life balance dissatisfaction might seem counterintuitive. However, it is of course also the case that women are more likely to adapt their patterns of work to fit around domestic responsibilities. Flexible work arrangements and part-time work are the main means of doing this and employer policies on working time are therefore of critical importance to women.

Employer policies

Employers' work–life balance policies typically include arrangements such as parental and carers' leave, compressed hours, job-sharing, part-time work, flexitime, working from home, childcare assistance and services. While potentially these arrangements give greater flexibility for work–life balance to a range of people with different life situations and at different stages of their lives, they very clearly target women and in particular women seeking to combine work and family. One study of the recruitment value of employer that provided work–life balance benefits in the US found that childcare benefits influenced the willingness to accept a job offer more than did flexi-time, telecommuting or eldercare benefits. Further, childcare was most attractive to women (Thompson and Aspinwall, 2009).

Evidence suggests that it is public sector and large organisations that tend to provide the most extensive work–life balance provisions (Abendroth and Dulk, 2011; Lyness and Kropf, 2005; Pocock, 2005). However, it is significant that the fewer the national statutory requirements, the more variation there is in the work–life balance policies offered by employers within a country (Lyness and Kropf, 2005). Although many firms go beyond the minimum legal requirements, overall the international evidence suggests that where national provision is low, private sector firms do not appear to fill the gap, particularly when it comes to family leave and childcare assistance (Hardy and Adnett, 2002). On the other hand, where national provision is high (as in Scandinavia), employers seem to perceive little need to offer any additional work–life balance policies (Lyness and Kropf, 2005). In many cases, employers' declarative statements on work–life balance and its importance seemingly substitute for actual action (Pocock, 2005).

One factor that points to the business case for flexibility, if not for the whole package of work–life balance policies, is that flexibility is usually offered on the employer's terms to suit the employer's needs. Part-time work and flexible hours are obvious examples of arrangements that suit many employers' needs in terms of opening hours, covering busy periods, etc. Research in Australia finds that among by far the most commonly offered work–life balance initiatives are part-time work (offered by 95 per cent of organisations) and flexible hours (88 per cent). Less widespread are arrangements that might suit many employees, but that perhaps do not offer the same benefits to employers – working from home (offered by 59 per cent of organisations), job sharing (57 per cent) and compressed hours (40 per cent). Only 12 per cent of organisations offer the more expensive work–life balance policy of childcare assistance and services, but 97 per cent offer family and carer's leave (EOWA, 2008). In the UK, recent evidence indicates that the provision of work–life balance arrangements, especially flexible working and paid leave, has increased since the late 1990s and that a large number of employers now provide leave arrangements above the legal minimum. However, generally in the UK, latest evidence shows that flexible working arrangements are not as widely available, and nor are they as widely taken up, as the hype surrounding the importance of employers providing and employees achieving work–life balance might suggest. The latest WERS[1] reveals the following types of flexible work arrangements are available to at least some employees: reduced hours (available in 56 per cent of British workplaces); flexi-time (35 per cent); homeworking (30 per cent); compressed hours (20 per cent); job sharing (16 per cent); term-time only (16 per cent). With regard to uptake, flexitime is the most commonly used flexible work arrangements (30 per cent of employees), followed by working from home (17 per cent) (van Wanrooy *et al.*, 2013).

Walsh (2007) questions whether work–life balance arrangements in Britain genuinely cater for a diverse range of employee work and family needs. For example, leave for carers of older adults remains a relatively rare provision (offered by 6 per cent of workplaces) and workplace nurseries (3 per cent of workplaces) and childcare subsidies (6 per cent) are still relatively uncommon. Similarly, in Australia the EOWA notes the heterogeneity of employees and their different flexibility needs, for example, women who are pregnant or breast-feeding, employees with caring responsibilities, single parents, employees living in rural and remote areas, mature workers and employees with a disability. Employers are encouraged to consider this diversity in the design and implementation of their work–life balance policies in order to extend policies to a greater range of employees, but also to avoid the risk of flexible work arrangements becoming stigmatised and associated with inferior women's jobs (EOWA, 2008).

---

[1]WERS (The Workplace Employment Relations Study) 2011 is the latest of a series of surveys spanning three decades. Based on multiple, extensive data sources, it is widely regarded as representative of the state of employment relations/conditions in British workplaces.

Other evidence from the UK indicates that employers generally have positive attitudes to work–life balance practices. When asked general attitudinal questions about work–life balance, 92 per cent of employers in a government survey agreed that people work best when they can balance their work and the other aspects of their lives. Sixty-seven per cent agreed that everyone should be able to balance their work and home lives in the way that they want. However, when asked questions relating more to actual experiences at the workplace, 73 per cent of employers also agreed that employees should not expect to be able to change their working pattern if it would disrupt the business, and 67 per cent admitted that it is not easy try to accommodate employees with different patterns of working (Hayward et al., 2007).

It is not just formal employer policies that matter for helping individuals balance work and family. Supportive organisational and work *cultures* are also important for encouraging employees to access the flexible work arrangements and other provisions that are available to them (Lyness and Kropf, 2005; Callan, 2007). Many workers do not have access to work–life balance provisions (beyond the legal minimum), but there is evidence that even those who do are either unaware of their contractual rights or fear the consequences for their careers particularly of taking up flexible work arrangements (Walsh, 2007; EOWA, 2008). Employees generally understand that flexible work arrangements are a kind of special assistance to enable people (read women) who cannot conform to the inflexible and often long working hours to work (Lewis et al., 2007). Thus even seemingly generous employer policies are no guarantee that the workplace culture is sufficiently transformed to truly offer individuals all the flexibility that they appear to because they do not disrupt the dominant construction of the ideal worker (Callan, 2007).

Part of the explanation might lie in the fact that flexible work arrangements are not always introduced with work–life balance in mind, despite the fact that they are usually packaged under the work–life balance rubric. Flexibility can be imposed by employers to suit their business and operational needs as well as actively sought by individual workers to suit their personal and family needs. Workers with fixed, regular, daytime work hours tend to report the greatest work–life balance satisfaction. Imposed flexibility that takes away choice and/or undermines the predictability of working hours is generally disliked by workers (Parent-Thirion et al., 2007). We can see this reflected in the debate surrounding 'zero hours' contracts'. Unpredictable and imposed flexibility is obviously particularly problematic for those who need to make care arrangements for dependents. McDowell (2004) makes this clear by way of the example of an unofficial British Airways strike in 2003 over the introduction of new split shifts for the largely female check-in desk workers, which threatened to disrupt the women's childcare arrangements.

Flexibility that extends choices to workers (e.g. flexitime) is more favoured by workers themselves, but, paradoxically perhaps, those workers with the greatest say in theory in the organisation of their work hours report the greatest work–life balance dissatisfaction (Parent-Thirion et al., 2007). This is perhaps because those with greatest autonomy tend to work the longest hours (e.g. self-employed people and some professional occupations) so that the availability of flexitime is less relevant. Evidence from Australia indicates that non-management staff is more likely to have access to flexible work arrangements than management. The difference is particularly marked for compressed hours, job sharing and part-time work – the arrangements most likely to be taken up by those with childcare responsibilities. This hierarchical segregation of flexible and non-flexible jobs is problematic because managers need to be able to 'walk the talk' about flexible work arrangements otherwise flexibility risks being seen as, and actually becoming, damaging to career potential. The result is that flexible work arrangements remain strongly gendered. The same study found that while job seeking 83 per cent of women and 73 per cent of men valued organisations that support work–life balance, indicating that there is an appetite for a less gendered model of flexible work. However, 17 per cent of women and 21 per cent of men believed that their employer offered no flexibility whatsoever (EOWA, 2008).

Some forms of flexible work arrangements have been facilitated in recent years by technological advances, particularly the Internet, allowing some people to work from home and/or the workplace in some sort of combination that accommodates outside commitments and activities. While at the individual level such flexibility might enable, for example, parents, particularly mothers, to continue to work full time, the negative side is that improved communication technologies (email, broadband internet, mobile phones, smartphones, etc.) can also allow work to impinge on personal life in previously unimaginable ways, blurring the boundaries between work and non-work time and space. Many people, particularly managers and supervisors, have extensive out-of-hours contact with their workplace, which lengthens the working day and interrupts family and leisure time (Parent-Thirion *et al.*, 2007). There are now numerous internet blogs and even self-help books on the so-called 'crackberry' phenomenon – people addicted to checking email on their smartphones. If anything, rather than facilitating greater work–life balance, technology seems to have stimulated a greater addiction to paid work and a new kind of presenteeism involving always being contactable even outside of normal working hours. Thus despite the positive rhetoric that typically surrounds the flexible work debate, it is not always the solution to work–life balance that it is frequently held up to be.

Union action

In the UK, analysis of WERS 2004 found that unionised workplaces were more likely to have 'family friendly' policies (Kersley *et al.*, 2006). However, this association in itself does not prove that the unions have any direct involvement in work–life balance policy making. That said, despite a chequered history internationally of involvement in equality issues, in many countries unions are now regarded as playing an important role in improving work–life balance provisions at the workplace. In Australia, many unions have sought to increase paid maternity leave at enterprise level and have had some bargaining success. Other Australian unions have focused on control of working hours. The Australian Council of Trade Unions lobbied for extended unpaid parental leave of 24 months, better rights to return to part-time work, the opportunity to 'purchase' extra weeks of annual leave and a new right for parents to request a change in working hours to meet caring needs (Pocock, 2005). The UK Trades Union Congress biennial equality audit similarly offers a positive picture of union action on work–life balance. It found that 69 per cent of unions had up-to-date guidance/policy on flexible working and work–life balance, and more importantly, 36 per cent of unions reported negotiating successes on the issue. Further, 57 per cent of unions had up-to-date guidance/policy on working parents and carers, and 43 per cent reported negotiating successes here (TUC, 2012).

In the context of converging union strategies in Europe, Gregory and Milner (2009) suggest that three opportunity structures encourage a shift towards work–life balance issues in union campaigns and bargaining across the continent:

- rise in the proportion of women union members and leaders;
- national working time regime;
- union–management relations in specific organisations.

On the first opportunity structure, it is argued that traditionally male dominated unions have not seen the interface between work and family as a union issue. Female union negotiators are said to be more likely to bring issues of particular concern to women, such as work–life balance, to the table and that these issues are most likely to be pursued where women account for a significant proportion of membership (Kirton and Healy, 1999). National working time regimes – the second opportunity structure – can provide an opening for unions to bargain on flexible work arrangements, for example in the European countries where working time is regulated. Union–management relations – the third opportunity structure – relates to the possibility for work–life balance to be presented as a mutual gains issue and an area for management–union partnership. This enables unions in the present era of relatively low membership and power to make progress on an issue where management and union interests could be seen to converge (Rigby and O'Brien-Smith, 2010). However, Gregory and Milner's (2009) study reveals unions to be relatively marginal actors in the process of introducing and implementing work–life balance policies in France and the UK not least because they are forced into defensive positions by virtue of their weakened power bases. Nevertheless, the study did find instances in the UK where unions had an influence in the early stages of policy making and in France where negotiations on working time had led unions into negotiations on work–life balance. In contrast, Rigby and O'Brien-Smith's (ibid.) study located in the UK media and retail industry unions found unions to be fairly proactive on work–life balance issues. In neither sector did the unions adopt wholeheartedly a mutual gains stance and neither did they conceptualise work–life balance as positive flexibility. In the media sector, there was little expectation of mutual gains, and work–life balance was seen to be mainly concerned with the long-hour working that characterises jobs in the sector. In retail, the main work–life balance issue was flexible work arrangements and neither did this fit a mutual gains stance because of inconsistencies in the employer approach insofar as seemingly good national employer policies were often undermined by unsympathetic line-managers. Although the degree of impact unions can and do have on work–life balance policies and practices is variable, it is quite clear that unions in many countries are visible and active in the debate.

Individual choice and work–life balance

Although looking at work–life balance solely through an individual choice lens can obscure the structural and institutional constraints and enablers previously discussed, it is nevertheless worth considering how individuals seek to achieve work–life balance in order to avoid constructing individuals as nothing more than passive recipients of government and employer policies. This is particularly important given that a discourse of individual choice, autonomy and responsibility often pervades individuals' work–life balance narratives (see, for example, Lewis *et al.*, 2007; Kirton, 2011).

Although as stated previously, the contemporary work–life balance discourse goes beyond the reconciliation of paid work and family responsibilities, the focus here is on the work–family interface. There can be no doubt that for individuals, particularly women, work–life balance comes into sharp focus when they become parents. As discussed above, it is women who still largely shoulder domestic and family responsibilities and adapt their career aspirations and behaviour to reconcile work and family. In many countries, even highly qualified women in dual-career couples typically choose to prioritise the male partner's career and earnings potential once they have children (Hardill and Watson, 2004). Further, among such couples a traditional gender division of domestic labour remains strong with women overwhelmingly managing parenting arrangements (Windebank, 2001). Why is this?

There are of course in all likelihood multiple explanations, but Duncan *et al.* (2003) offer a compelling one. They argue that people make decisions about how parenting might be combined with paid work with reference to 'gendered moral rationalities': gender-based moral and socially negotiated views about what behaviour is right and proper (i.e. not just with reference to what childcare and parental leave are available) (ibid.: 10). While it is well established that gender matters for individual orientations to work–life balance, some research also finds that other aspects of identity such as class and race/ethnicity also matter. For example, research indicates that kinship and community are particularly salient for Asian communities who it is argued face a stronger sense of familial obligation that places pressures on individuals seeking work–life balance. Further, some 'migratory families' are spread around the world, which can add to the difficulties individuals face in achieving balance (Dale, 2005). Duncan *et al.*'s (ibid.) UK-based study, which included women of African-Caribbean background, found that ethnicity provided a 'major fault line' in mothers' understandings about combining motherhood and paid work. The African-Caribbean mothers, particularly those in professional and management jobs, were more likely than the white to regard substantial hours in employment as a component of good mothering, rather than of bad, neglectful mothering. On the other hand, mothers of Bangladeshi and Pakistani backgrounds are more likely to adopt a full-time homemaker model of motherhood compared with women of other ethnicities. However, it appears that generational change is also occurring insofar as highly educated British Bangladeshi and Pakistani women are much more likely to be in employment and less likely than their lower educated counterparts to marry and have children at a young age (Dale, 2005). Further, in another UK study of young people, similar proportions, and only a minority of all (ethnic) groups of girls said they would be happy to stay at home and look after children rather than have a career (Bhavnani, 2006).

There is also some evidence of *national* variation in conceptions of the 'good mother'. Based on a French case study, it is argued that underpinned by relatively strong childcare provision, French women have 'a certain ability to not feel guilty about the social norms associated with the image of the "good mother"'. Consequently, full-time paid work as a choice does not meet the same level of disapproval in France as in some other countries (Guillaume and Pochic, 2007). Further, conceptions of 'good' fatherhood are also changing. While the dominant breadwinning conception remains prevalent, there are also developing concepts of fatherhood as self-fulfilment and caring fatherliness, such that even though on average fathers work longer hours than mothers, some forgo other out-of-work activities to spend more time with their children (Bruegel and Gray, 2005). Further complicating conceptions of fatherhood, Bruegel and Gray (ibid.) identify a class effect insofar as men with more education and in managerial or professional jobs appear to spend more time on childcare than other men do. Kirton's (2011) study of young black and minority ethnic graduates in the UK highlights the continuation of a male breadwinner identity, but at the same time some male respondents saw family life (beyond the nuclear family) and religious obligations as equally central to their lives and had the hope and expectation that work would be accommodating. A critical mass of male role models working flexibly has been heralded as a particularly effective way of challenging assumptions about gender norms and of providing legitimacy to work–life balance policies. Kirton (ibid.) considers that perhaps black and minority ethnic (BME) men will lead the way in this respect, with a possibly stronger orientation in terms of obligations towards family, care and kinship.

Conclusion

The debate about work–life balance has permeated the public discourses and national/organisational level policy making of many countries. The aim of this chapter has been to highlight the myriad ways that despite there existing a somewhat globalised discourse, national context influences and impacts on employer work–life balance policies and on individual work–life balance orientations and choices. National welfare, employment and gender regimes and their interconnecting nature provide variable contexts in which people seek to combine paid work and other aspects of their lives, especially family. Gender regimes are particularly salient when it comes to work–family conflict, which is at the heart of work–life balance policy making. Despite a globalised win-win work–life balance discourse, it is not at all clear that all industrialised countries are heading towards policy and practice convergence. Individual work–life balance choices are further complicated when we consider not just the availability of such polices as parental leave and childcare, but also 'gendered moral rationalities' in relation to parenting that bring gender and ethnic/race identities and their intersections into the frame.

CASE STUDY 13.1

WORK–LIFE BALANCE POLICIES AND CULTURE IN TWO CASE STUDY ORGANISATIONS – PHARMERGER AND ENGCORP

SAMANTHA CALLAN

PharMerger is a pharmaceutical company with significant global presence in six continents and premises in 45 countries. The UK has two research and development sites, one of which is the subject of this case study, and 14 commercial and production locations. The history of this site can be framed in terms of three distinct eras and it is these which have shaped the culture of the current organisation to a great extent. Founded in the mid-1970s, the original organisation was taken over by a foreign company at the end of the 1980s and then merged with a UK-based global giant in the mid-1990s.

However, there is not a clear starting point to the organisation's adoption of family-friendly working; the most senior HR respondent described the site's family-friendly emphasis as having 'grown progressively, it's not as if it "came in" at any point'. Employees have had flexitime working arrangements since the early 1980s but specific and explicit family-friendly employment policies were not introduced until shortly after the merger with the pharmaceutical giant. These policies are perceived by employees to be indicative of the larger company's desire to control and systematise working patterns. Although employees were in agreement that PharMerger is more family-friendly than the original company, this was widely attributed to the passage of time, rather than to divergent approaches of the two companies. Any company aspiring to attract and retain the best employees (as PharMerger certainly does) now has to provide an environment which is more family-friendly than in previous decades.

Interviews with HR professionals revealed that, to some extent, competitors in the pharmaceutical industry whose employment packages include a high level of family-friendly provision provide the impetus for ongoing improvement of PharMerger's policies. (This is also seen in other industries; McKee et al. (2000) found that oil and gas industry employers compete with each other when setting policies through a process informed by knowledge gathered through both informal and formal networking within the sector.) HR professionals were representative of the corporate perspective in their commonly held view that provision was generous, went beyond statutory requirements and employees *should* be satisfied with it.

Managers tended to concur, especially those with responsibility for several members of staff, rather than just one or two. Other research has examined the role managers' play as gatekeepers to policy implementation (Bond et al., 2002; Yeandle et al., 2003; Dex and Scheibl, 2002) and this study confirmed previous findings about the decisive nature of their discretion. Respondents frequently described how it was 'down to the managers' and how they used policies and stated that the company itself had reached a limit in terms of policies that could be put in place. Managers described feeling constrained to a certain extent by policies; typically in the sense that policy provision was too generous in practice, if policies were fully implemented this threatened to affect their ability to deliver against somewhat inflexible and high targets.

Many employees were parents who needed their working patterns to fit around school hours; flexible working policies enabled them to leave the premises early and recommence work in the early evening. These opportunities, used almost exclusively by women, carried no penalty for administrative staff but it was typical for more senior staff to have to work in an officially part-time capacity if they wanted this level of flexibility. They also had to be willing to allow work to intrude in their home life outside their contracted hours (e.g. they were expected to access email remotely and be available on the telephone). Individual employees also had demanding and inflexible targets to reach and these, in some cases, prevented them from taking advantage of policies. One scientist, who occasionally needed to attend hospital appointments with a disabled child and thus required additional flexibility, reported that the pressure to reach her targets was a powerful disincentive to using policies. Her preferred option was to use annual leave instead. The pressure of targets strongly influenced her eventual decision to leave the company. This employee challenged key facets of the PharMerger culture, such as the 'ideal worker type', described elsewhere in the literature and evident in both organisations.

The ideal worker type is closely associated with beliefs about professionalism which 'sustain definitions of selfhood that elevate the workplace over home life'

(Kerfoot, 2002: 93). Employees conforming to this type did not tend to structure their working day explicitly around family responsibilities and prioritised 'getting the job done' over keeping to fairly set working hours. Respondents appeared to accept that ongoing career advancement required conforming to this type and exhibiting willingness to relocate, travel and be available at home outside working hours. In PharMerger the type was stronger (than in EngCorp), more evident and a source of workforce homogeneity but, common to both organisations, policies appeared to effect very little shift in this facet. This was because (a) organisational survival was perceived to depend on it and (b) the type is closely associated with the ideal worker *image*, how they want others to see them, and their preferred *identity*, how they see themselves (Hatch and Schultz, 1997; Whetten and Godfrey, 1998).

Significantly, female managers also contested the organisation's claim to be family-friendly on the grounds that career progression was impeded by taking up policies such as working slightly reduced hours. Career-oriented women whose working hours were routinely impacted by caring responsibilities (for example, they worked on a part-time or flexible hours basis) considered that they had to minimise family concerns in order to conform to the 'ideal worker type' referred to earlier. This indicates to what extent this construct was bound up with stereotypically 'male' characteristics – although many men in PharMerger were also in frequent need of a measure of flexibility so they could undertake albeit more limited caring responsibilities.

The other case study concerned an engineering company, EngCorp, which also had an international presence. The two business units included in the study are both sited in the town regarded as the company's global headquarters. EngCorp has a reputation in the surrounding area of being a 'caring' company which 'puts people first', and many respondents considered their jobs to be the best they had ever had because of their employment conditions. Not all employees were familiar with the phrase 'family-friendly', however, most referred to the flexibility which was integral to working for EngCorp, and gave examples of the understanding repeatedly shown by the company for their family responsibilities. Parental leave policies enabled parents to negotiate nine-day fortnight arrangements (by using unpaid days) and annualised hours arrangements gave them more time away from work during school holidays.

Respondents were aware of a strong sense of company identity and many described the presence of a definable and pervasive culture which they attributed to shared and recognised values. It is important to make a distinction here between 'root' culture and more diffuse values. The 'emic' or insider view of culture tends to conflate and confuse these two terms, whereas the role of the researcher in these case studies was to identify the unconscious and underlying assumptions that determine insiders' values about which, it is possible, few are aware. As was found in the PharMerger case study, several individuals clearly dissented to the recognisable majority view of the company. Managers and employees tended to hold somewhat different views of policy implementation and women's experiences could markedly contrast with those of their male counterparts.

The company described itself as 'male-dominated' and considered its family-friendly policies to be a significant aspect of its deliberative approach to attracting and retaining female engineers. (There is a parallel here with PharMerger's perceived need to maintain a high enough level of family-friendly employment provision to stay competitive in the global market for talent.) However, female employees who were ambitious in their careers judged their progression would be hampered, regardless of available policies, if they were not working according to the ideal worker type and following a different pattern to men in equivalent positions. The internalisation of this type was evident in interviews with women from both companies, even when work conflicted with their domestic responsibilities (and with men's who were primary carers, for example, widowers), given that work's intrusion into their home life went unchallenged, particularly if they were working part-time.

Source: Based on Callan, S. (2007) 'Implications of family-friendly policies for organizational culture: findings from two case studies', *Work, Employment and Society*, Vol.21, No.4, 673–91.

Questions

1 What cultural changes would be necessary to make the work–life balance policies in the case study organisations truly deliver all they promise?

2 In what ways do the work–life balance cultures of the two case study organisations seem at odds with their policies?

3 How does the concept of the 'ideal worker type' help to explain workplace work–life balance cultures?

4 Discuss the implications of work–life balance policies and cultures for women's and men's careers and for the redistribution of household and family labour?

Bibliography

Abendroth, A. and Dulk, L. den. (2011) 'Support for the work-life balance in Europe: the impact of state, workplace and family support on work-life balance satisfaction', *Work, Employment and Society*, Vol.25, No.2, 234–56.

Artiles, A. (2005) 'Work-life balance in collective bargaining examined', *European Industrial Relations Observatory Online*. Available at: http://www.eurofound.europa.eu/observatories /eurwork/articles/work-life-balance-in-collective-bargaining-examined.

Baker, D. (2011) 'Maternity leave and reduced future earning capacity', *Family Matters: Australian Institute of Family Studies*, No.89.

Bhavnani, R. (2006) 'Ahead of the game: the changing aspirations of young ethnic minority women', *Moving on up? Ethnic Minority Women and Work*, Manchester, Equal Opportunities Commission.

Bond, S., Hyman, J., Summers, J. and Wise, S. (2002) *Family-friendly Working? Putting Policy into Practice*, Bristol/York: Policy Press/JRF.

Bonney, N. (2005) 'Overworked Britons? Part-time work and work-life balance', *Work, Employment and Society*, Vol.19, No.2, 391–401.

Boushey, H., Moughari, L., Sattelmeyer, S. and Waller, M. (2008) 'Work-life policies for the twenty-first century economy', Washington DC, The Mobility Agenda.

Bruegel, I. and Gray, A. (2005) 'Men's conditions of employment and the division of childcare between parents', pp. 147–69, in Houston, D. (ed.) *Work-Life Balance in the 21st Century*, Basingstoke: Palgrave Macmillan.

Callan, S. (2007) 'Implications of family-friendly policies for organizational culture: findings from two case studies', *Work, Employment and Society*, Vol.21, No.4, 673–91.

CEC (2006) *A Roadmap for Equality Between Women and Men*, Brussels: Commission of the European Communities.

Craig, L., Mullan, K. and Blaxland, M. (2010) 'Parenthood, policy and work-family time in Australia 1992-2002', *Work, Employment and Society*, Vol.24, No.1, 27–45.

Dale, A. (2005) 'Combining family and employment: evidence from Pakistani and Bangladeshi women', pp. 230–45, in Houston, D. (ed.) *Work-Life Balance in the 21st Century*, Basingstoke: Palgrave Macmillan.

Dex, S. and Scheibl, F. (2002) *SMEs and Flexible Working Arrangements*, Bristol/York: Policy Press/JRF.

Duncan, S., Edwards. R., Reynolds, T. and Alldred, P. (2003) 'Motherhood, paid work and partnering: values and theories', *Work, Employment and Society*, Vol.17, No.2, 309–30.

European Commission (2013) Report on Progress on Equality Between Women and Men in 2012, Brussels: European Commission.

EHRC (2010) *How Fair Is Britain? Equality, Human Rights and Good Relations in 2010*, Manchester: Equality and Human Rights Commission.

EOWA (2008) Survey on Workplace Flexibility, Sydney: Equal Opportunity for Women in the Workplace Agency.

EOWA (2008a) *Generation F: Attract, Engage, Retain*, Sydney: Equal Opportunity for Women in the Workplace Agency.

Esping-Andersen, G. (1990) *The Three Worlds of Welfare Capitalism*, Cambridge: Polity Press.

Eurofound (2010) *Changes Over Time – First Findings from the Fifth European Working Conditions Survey*, Dublin: European Foundation for the Improvement of Living and Working Conditions.

Fleetwood, S. (2007) 'Why work-life balance now?' *International Journal of Human Resource Management*, Vol.18, 387–400.

Gregory, A. and Milner, S. (2009) 'Trade unions and work-life balance: changing times in France and the UK?', *British Journal of Industrial Relations*, Vol.47, No.1, 122–46.

Guillaume, C. and Pochic, S. (2007) 'What would you sacrifice? Access to top management and the work-life balance', *Gender, Work and Organization*, Vol.16, No.1, 14–36.

Hardill, I. and Watson, R. (2004) 'Career priorities within dual career households: an analysis of the impact of child rearing upon gender participation rates and earnings', *Industrial Relations Journal*, Vol.35, No.1, 19–37.

Hardy, S. and Adnett, N. (2002) 'The Parental Leave Directive: towards a "family-friendly" social Europe?', *European Journal of Industrial Relations*, Vol.8, No.2, 157–72.

Hatch, M.J. and Schultz, M. (1997) 'Relations between organizational culture, identity and image', *European Journal of Marketing*, Vol.31, No.5–6, 356–65.

Hayward, B., Fong, B. and Thornton, A. (2007) 'The third work-life balance employer survey', London, Department for Business Enterprise and Regulatory Reform. Employment Relations Research Series, No.86.

Kerfoot, D. (2002) 'Managing the "professional" man', pp. 81–98, in Dent, M. and Whitehead, S. (eds.) *Managing Professional Identities: Knowledge, Performativity and the 'New' Professional*, London and New York: Routledge.

Kersley, B., Alpin, C., Forth, J., Bryson, A., Bewley, H., Dix, G. and Oxenbridge, S. (2006) *Inside the Workplace: Findings from the 2004 Workplace Employment Relations Survey*, Abingdon: Routledge.

Kirton, G. (2011) 'Work-life balance: attitudes and expectations of young black and minority ethnic graduates', pp. 252–69, in Healy, G., Kirton, G. and Noon, M. (eds.) *Equalities, Inequalities and Diversity*, Basingstoke: Palgrave.

Kirton, G. and Healy, G. (1999) 'Transforming union women: the role of women trade union officials in union renewal', *Industrial Relations Journal*, Vol.30, No.1, 31–45.

Lewis, S., Gambles, R. and Rapoport, R. (2007) 'The constraints of a "work-life balance" approach: an international perspective', *International Journal of Human Resource Management*, Vol.18, No.3, 360–73.

Lyness, K. and Kropf, M. (2005) 'The relationships of national gender equality and organizational support with work-family balance: a study of European managers', *Human Relations*, Vol.58, No.1, 33–60.

Lyonette, C., Kaufman, G. and Crompton, R. (2011) '"We both need to work": maternal employment, childcare and health care in Britain and the USA', *Work, Employment and Society*, Vol.25, No.1, 34–50.

McDowell, L. (2004) 'Work, workfare, work/life balance and an ethic of care', *Progress in Human Geography*, Vol.28, No.2, 145–63.

McKee, L., Mauthner, N. and Maclean, C. (2000) '"Family friendly" policies and practices in the oil and gas industry: employers' perspectives', *Work, Employment and Society*, Vol.14, No.3, 557–71.

OECD (2008) *Babies and Bosses: Balancing Work and Family Life*, Paris: Organisation for Economic Co-operation and Development.

OECD (2011) *Doing Better for Families*, Paris: Organisation for Economic Co-operation and Development.

ONS (2013) *Women in the Labour Market*, London: Office for National Statistics.

Parent-Thirion, A., Fernandez Macias, E., Hurley, J. and Vermeylen, G. (2007) 'Fourth European Working Conditions Survey', Dublin: European Foundation for the Improvement of Living and Working Conditions.

Pocock, B. (2005) 'Work-life "balance" in Australia: limited progress, dim prospects', *Asia Pacific Journal of Human Resources*, Vol.43, No.2, 198–209.

Rigby, M. and O'Brien-Smith, F. (2010) 'Trade union interventions in work-life balance', *Work, Employment and Society*, Vol.24, No.2, 203–20.

Thompson, L. and Aspinwall, K. (2009) 'The recruitment value of work/life benefits', *Personnel Review*, Vol.38, No.2, 195–210.

TUC (2012) TUC Equality Audit 2012, London: Trades Union Congress.

van Wanrooy, B., Bewley, H., Bryson, A., Forth, J., Freeth, S., Stokes, L. and Wood, S. (2013) *The 2011 Workplace Employment Relations Study: First Findings*, London: Department for Business, Innovation and Skills.

Walsh, J. (2007) 'Equality and diversity in British workplaces: the 2004 workplace employment relations survey', *Industrial Relations Journal*, Vol.38, No.4, 303–19.

Whetten, D.A and Godfrey, P.C. (eds.) (1998) *Identity in Organizations: Building Theory through Conversations*, Thousand Oaks, CA: Sage.

Windebank, J. (2001) 'Dual-earner couples in Britain and France: gender divisions of domestic labour and parenting work in different welfare states', *Work, Employment and Society*, Vol.15, No.2, 269–90.

Yeandle, S., Phillips, J., Scheibl, F., Wigfield, A. and Wise, S. (2003) *Line Managers and Family-Friendly Employment*, Bristol: Policy Press/JRF.

CHAPTER 14
DOWNSIZING

Adrian Wilkinson, Tony Dobbins and Tom Redman

It was the best of times (for stockholders); it was the worst of times (for employees). The corporation was restructuring.

(DiFonzo and Bordia, 1998: 295)

Introduction

In this chapter we first introduce the subject of organisational downsizing by discussing its wider context, its extent and potential for causing problems when mismanaged. The breadth and depth of organisational restructuring seen in the industrialised economies has been significant in recent years, especially in the aftermath of the recent global financial crisis (GFC). Second, we review the methods by which downsizing occurs and consider a range of alternatives to its use. Third, we examine the processes involved and focus in particular on consultation, redundancy selection and support for those who are made redundant, and the survivors of downsizing. Lastly, we conclude by asking whether the costs of downsizing are worth it and whether downsizing translates simply into 'increased stress and decreased job security' (De Meuse et al., 1997: 168).

The contextual reality of downsizing

Downsizing is the 'conscious use of permanent personnel reductions in an attempt to improve efficiency and/or effectiveness' (Budros, 1999: 70). Downsizing and restructuring are often used interchangeably but organisations can restructure without shrinking in size and vice versa (Budros, 1999; Eurofound, 2013). Downsizing is a broad concept that can encompass various combinations of reductions in company assets – financial (stock or cash), physical (plants and other infrastructure), human or informational (databases) (Cascio, 2014). This chapter focuses on employment downsizing, which is often synonymous with layoffs and redundancies.

Since the 1980s, downsizing has gained widespread strategic legitimacy from organizational power-brokers, and is a firmly entrenched aspect of corporate culture in many advanced economies. Indeed, research on downsizing in the US (Baumol *et al.*, 2003; see also the American Management Association annual surveys since 1990), UK (Chorely, 2002; Sahdev *et al.,* 1999) and Japan (Ahmadjian and Robinson, 2001; Mroczkowski and Hanaoka, 1997) suggest that downsizing is being regarded by management as one of the preferred methods of turning around declining organisations, cutting costs and improving organisational performance (Mellahi and Wilkinson, 2010).

It is important to understand the broader context impacting upon employment downsizing in different countries. There is a distinction in the 'varieties of capitalism' literature between institutional contexts in 'liberal market economies' (LMEs) and 'coordinated market economies' (CMEs). LMEs refer to countries, including the UK, the US and Canada, in which (1) the economy primarily operates according to free market principles and delivering short-term shareholder value; (2) there is little engagement of employers or worker representative organisations in social pacts governing macro-economic issues; and (3) regulations promoting workplace consensus are weak. In contrast, CMEs (including Austria, Belgium, Denmark, Finland, Germany, the Netherlands, Norway and Sweden) are seen to have complementary linkages between institutions promoting cooperation across various levels, and patient longer-term collaborative relations occur between employers, workers and their representatives, and other institutions (Hall and Soskice, 2001). Employers in LME contexts are perceived to be more likely than those in CMEs to adopt a short-term 'hire and fire' approach and treat employees as commodity costs rather than long-term assets, with frequent recourse to employment downsizing as a means of increasing share prices on the stock market (Sisson and Purcell, 2010). Indeed, broader ascendant systemic forces relating to the GFC and intensified pressures for neo-liberalism and financialisation have impacted upon employment downsizing in many countries, as the power of financial actors to influence management decisions has increased (Heyes *et al.*, 2012; Appelbaum *et al.*, 2013; Thompson, 2013). Downsizing has often been seen as a sign of corporate virility in a climate of financialisation, and stock market prices have risen in the context of such activities. As Haigh (2004: 141) observes, 'it remains the case that the quickest way for a CEO to obtain an ovation is to propose eliminating a layer of managers, as though dusting a mantelpiece or scraping off a coating of rust'.

What is the role of HRM in downsizing? Cappelli (2009) rather disturbingly notes that senior HR specialists were not involved in layoff decisions during a recession in two-thirds of organisations in a US HR survey. Cascio (2014) observes that the dominant economic and business position is for employees to be viewed as disposable commodities rather than valuable resources. In view of this, examination of managerial practice over the past decade or so often finds a darker or 'harder' side to HRM in organisational downsizing, rather than a 'softer' resource-based HRM (Storey, 2007). In the UK context, for example, downsizing has long been seen as an easy way to remedy management problems or raise share prices.

The lack of labour market protection, the weakness of unions and the intense pressure on private and public sector companies alike to improve their profitability and efficiency have meant that the fashionable doctrine of downsizing has spread like a contagion. *(Hutton, 1997: 40)*

The above comment from Hutton illustrates that organisational downsizing is firmly established as a central aspect of 'harder' HRM practice in the UK, and this is linked to growing financialisation of the economy. Worrall *et al.* (2000) noted that there were over 200,000 noti-fied redundancies in the UK each year. Meanwhile, Cascio (2014) estimated that there were 8.5 million layoffs in the US during the recent economic crisis. This, however, pales in com-parison with the 25 million laid off from state-owned firms in China between 1998 and 2001. Downsizing thus is not only a Western phenomenon, and has seeped into corporate cultures else-where. As we see stakeholder orientation being replaced by shareholder values, as in Japan, there is now greater acceptability of downsizing even when cultural values suggest different terms are used. In Korea, redundancy is referred to as 'honourable retirement' (Higo and Klassen, 2015).

However, after a perusal of the growing numbers of textbooks on HRM, a reader could be forgiven for thinking that HRM practice is largely associated with a positively virtuous image within organisations. Righteous HRM managers recruit, train, devise strategies, man-age rewards and careers, involve employees, improve labour relations, solve problems, etc. for the mutual benefit of the organisation and their workforce. Most management books take an upbeat tone, with little reference to the more unpalatable aspects of downsizing and redundancy. Revitalising change is seen as an entirely positive process to do with 'root-ing out inertia', promoting efficiency and fostering innovation. Change is to be achieved not incrementally but through 'big leaps' (Hamel, 2000). Downsizing is more apparent in the Dilbert books (Adams, 1996), the Doonesbury cartoons (Anfuso, 1996) and Michael Moore's journalism (Moore, 1997). When managers do discuss downsizing it tends to be couched in very euphemistic terms (see Box 14.1).

Despite its importance and growing prominence, this aspect of HRM rarely merits treat-ment in the texts. In those few texts that recognise its existence the focus is usually on a

Box 14.1 HRM in practice — The sanitisation of dismissal: sacking goes out of fashion

Redundancy and dismissal is an area of HRM practice that particularly suffers from euphemistic jargon. Some of the terms HRM managers use include:

building down	downsizing	re-engineering
career re-appraisal	exiting	releasing
compressing	headcount reduction	resizing
decruiting	involuntary quit	re-structuring
de-hiring	lay-off	retrenchment
dejobbing	letting-go	rightsizing
de-layering	non-retaining	severance
demassing	outplacing	slimming
de-selection	payroll adjustment	streamlining
disemploying	rationalising	termination
downscoping	rebalancing	wastage

The motor industry seems especially afflicted in this respect, perhaps as a result of the large scale of workforce reductions. For example, General Motors described one plant closure as a 'volume-related production schedule adjustment', Chrysler had 'a career alternative enhancement program', while Nissan introduced a 'separation program'. Two motor industry personnel managers interviewed about the effects of lean production methods talked of 'increasing the velocity of organisational exit' and 'liberating from our organisation' those who could not accommodate the new system. One also talked of getting rid of the PUREs (previously unrecognised recruitment errors). In contrast, the language of the shop floor is much more direct and includes being sacked, canned, given your cards, axed and being sent down the road.

discussion of how to avoid the legal pitfalls when reducing the workforce, or they provide a simple attempt to quantify its use. Much rarer is any discussion that examines the nature, significance and aftermath of making people redundant. This neglect is a serious and somewhat puzzling one. As Chadwick *et al.* (2004) note, successful performance following downsizing requires HR practices to continue to promote the discretionary efforts of employees, retain valuable human capital and reconstruct valuable organisation structures.

One possible explanation for the neglect of this issue lies in the view that workforce reduction is considered to be an isolated and unpleasant element of HRM practice and one that is best hurriedly carried out and quickly forgotten: the so-called 'Mafia model' of downsizing (Stebbins, 1989). The statistics for redundancy and dismissal in Britain would, however, suggest that as unpleasant as it may be, workforce reduction is not an isolated event; rather, it has become a central aspect of HRM practice. What is particularly worrying here is the number of organisations downsizing who are actually making healthy profits. As Cascio (2002) points out, these are not sick companies trying to save themselves but healthy companies attempting to boost earnings. Organisational size is no longer a measure of corporate success. Western managers, it seems, have a propensity for sacking employees. Jack Welch, for example, was known as 'neutron Jack' for his actions in getting rid of employees and leaving only the buildings intact (Haigh, 2004; Welch, 2001). 'Chainsaw' Al Dunlap managed to terminate 11,000 staff in two months, representing around 35 per cent of the workforce. Shareholder value was often the banner under which these cuts were made (Lazonick, 2005: 594). This trend has continued in countries like the US and the UK more recently, with prominent examples of downsizing at extremely profitable large US multinationals like Walmart and Disney (see Box 14.2 below) and UK bank HSBC announced that it is to axe 25,000 jobs worldwide, including 8,000 in the UK (*The Guardian*, 2015). A broader explanation for the neglect of the consequences of downsizing on human beings is symptomatic also of Ghoshal's (2005) argument that 'bad management theories are destroying good management practices'. In so doing, Ghoshal claims that many theories emerging from business

Box 14.2 HRM in practice   Downsizing Disney style

The employees who kept the data systems humming in the vast Walt Disney fantasy fief did not suspect trouble when they were suddenly summoned to meetings with their boss. While families rode the Seven Dwarfs Mine Train and searched for Nemo on clamobiles in the theme parks, these workers monitored computers in industrial buildings nearby, making sure millions of Walt Disney World ticket sales, store purchases and hotel reservations went through without a hitch. Some were performing so well that they thought they had been called in for bonuses. Instead, about 250 Disney employees were told in late October that they would be laid off.

Many of their jobs were transferred to immigrants on temporary visas for highly skilled technical workers, who were brought in by an outsourcing firm based in India. Over the next three months, some Disney employees were required to train their replacements to do the jobs they had lost. 'I just couldn't believe they could fly people in to sit at our desks and take over our jobs exactly,' said one former worker, an American in his 40s who remains unemployed since his last day at Disney on Jan. 30. 'It was so humiliating to train somebody else to take over your job. I still can't grasp it.'

Disney executives said that the layoffs were part of a reorganization, and that the company opened more positions than it eliminated. But the layoffs at Disney and at other companies, including the Southern California Edison power utility, are raising new questions about how businesses and outsourcing companies are using the temporary visas, known as H-1B, to place immigrants in technology jobs in the United States. These visas are at the center of a fierce debate in Congress over whether they complement American workers or displace them. According to federal guidelines, the visas are intended for foreigners with advanced science or computer skills to fill discrete positions when American workers with those skills cannot be found. Their use, the guidelines say, should not "adversely affect the wages and working conditions" of Americans. Because of legal loopholes, however, in practice, companies do not have to recruit American workers first or guarantee that Americans will not be displaced.

Source: *The New York Times*, 2015.

schools in recent decades – especially those trying to mimic the 'hard sciences' – have done much to encourage bad management practices, including downsizing.

One trigger for increasing interest and attention for downsizing, above and beyond its greater extent and scale than in the past, is as Sennett (1997: 18) notes: 'downsizings and re-engineerings impose on middle-class people sudden disasters which were, under earlier capitalism much more confined to the working classes'. Effectively managing workforce reduction is thus of increasing importance in HRM practice, not least because of its greater scale and frequency but also because of the potentially serious negative effects of its mismanagement (Thornhill and Saunders, 1998; Wilkinson, 2004). The mismanagement of workforce reduction can clearly cause major damage to both the organisation's employment and general business reputation. Damage to the former can seriously affect an organisation's attractiveness with potential future employees by producing an uncaring, hire-and-fire image that affects the employer brand (Dewettinck and Buyens, 2002). Similarly, bad publicity over retrenchment can cause customers to worry that the firm may go out of business or give rise to problems in the continuity or quality of supplies and services, with associated reputational effects (Love and Kraatz, 2009).

There have also been increasing concerns about the organisational effectiveness of the post-downsized 'anorexic organisation'. The benefits which organisations claim to be seeking from downsizing centre on savings in labour costs, speedier decision making, better communication, reduced product development time, enhanced involvement of employees and greater responsiveness to customers (De Meuse *et al.*, 1997: 168). However, some writers draw attention to the 'obsessive' pursuit of downsizing to the point of self-starvation marked by excessive cost-cutting, organ failure and an extreme pathological fear of becoming inefficient. Hence 'trimming' and 'tightening belts' are the order of the day (Tyler and Wilkinson, 2007).

Research suggests that downsizing can have a negative effect on 'corporate memory' (Burke, 1997), employee morale (Brockner *et al.*, 1987; Brockner, 1992), destruction of social networks (Priti, 2000), increases in labour turnover (Trevor and Nyberg, 2008), and a loss of organisational knowledge (Littler and Innes, 2003). As a result, downsizing could 'seriously handicap and damage the learning capacity of organisations' (Fisher and White, 2000: 249). Further, given that downsizing is often associated with cutting costs, downsizing firms may provide less training for their employees, recruit less externally and reduce the research and development budget (Mellahi and Wilkinson, 2010). Consequently, downsizing could 'hollow out' the firm's skills capacity (Littler and Innes, 2003: 93).

Industrial conflict and workforce resistance (e.g. via strikes, sit-ins, work-ins, etc.) is also a potential problem that arises in instances of retrenchment and downsizing (Contrepois, 2011; Cullinane and Dundon, 2011; Gall, 2011). The dispute at Irish Ferries during 2005/6 over the redundancy of over 500 unionised workers, who were replaced by low-cost agency crew, was a high-profile conflict in European industrial relations (see Case study 14.3 below). We have recently seen the return of factory occupations and a wave of 'bossnappings' in France as organisations closed down factories (Jefferys, 2011; Peetz *et al.*, 2011). However, given the unparalleled levels of workforce reductions, the relatively low level of disputes overall is perhaps more surprising. It may reflect not only reduced trade union and worker power but also that redundancy is now so commonplace and woven into the fabric of industrial life that it is seen as an inevitable consequence of work in hyper-competitive times (Turnbull and Wass, 2004).

Cascio (2009) suggests that there are only two sets of circumstances where downsizing may be warranted. The first is when companies find themselves saddled with non-performing assets or consistently unprofitable subsidiaries. Here he states that they should consider selling these to buyers who can make better use of those assets. Then, employees associated with those assets or subsidiaries often move with them to the new buyers. The second case is when jobs rely on technology that is no longer commercially viable, for example in the newspaper industry where, after computer-based typesetting emerged, compositors were no longer required.

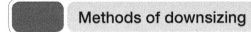

Methods of downsizing

There are a number of ways that organisations can reduce the size of the workforce. In this section we first examine the strategies employers use the most. These include natural attrition/wastage; voluntary redundancy; compulsory redundancy and early retirement. Second, we consider a range of alternatives to dismissing workers, in particular redeployment and wage reduction.

Natural attrition/wastage

Natural wastage is often preferred as the most positive and humane method of workforce reduction. It is seen as giving individuals a free choice in whether to leave or stay and thus reduces the potential for conflict and employee feelings of powerlessness. Evidence suggests that it is not the exact equivalent of normal labour turnover. It appears that in a redundancy situation both the rate and nature of labour turnover changes. Early research reported that labour turnover increases in retrenchment situations (Bulmer, 1971; Wedderburn, 1965), but this may reflect more on the nature of the labour market, with alternative jobs easier to obtain during this period. This form of workforce reduction poses problems for management in that it is unplanned and uncontrollable. Some evidence also suggests that it depresses workforce morale more than the short, sharp, shock approach of redundancy. Natural wastage is also a form of job loss that is much more difficult for employees and unions to resist because of its incremental nature.

Voluntary redundancy

This method has increasingly become most employers' preferred method of downsizing. Some common concerns are that it is expensive, as employees with long service find it attractive, and the best workers are more likely to leave because there is demand for their skills elsewhere, while poorer workers stay because they are less marketable. There is little evidence to make a judgement here, but Hardy's (1987) research suggests the reverse actually occurs in practice. Marginal performers are more likely to take up voluntary redundancy packages because of either disillusionment with the job or the fear of dismissal without any financial cushion at a later date. Savery *et al.* (1998) report that high absenteeism and low commitment are associated largely with those who have expressed an interest in voluntary redundancy. The main advantages are that at least employees are given a choice and this de-stigmatises, to some extent, the loss of the job. Although voluntary redundancy is much preferred to compulsory forms, it is sometimes seen by unions as 'selling jobs'.

Compulsory redundancy

Compulsory redundancy – where no choice is presented to the departing employee – is normally a 'last resort' strategy for employers and is usually seen as the least acceptable face of downsizing. However, as it is based on managerial decision making, it gives employers the opportunity to design and implement criteria based on business needs. Compulsory redundancy is also more common where downsizings are large scale or involve complete plant closures. According to WERS data, compulsory redundancy is also much more common in the private sector than in the public sector (van Wanrooy *et al.*, 2013). However, it has also been suggested that compulsory redundancy is rising in usage in the public sector as the potential for voluntary redundancy and early retirement has been exhausted and more generally because of doubts about the latter's effectiveness.

Retirement

Early retirement is usually utilised alongside other methods of workforce reduction, although it may often be sufficient to generate the required job cuts. It is often seen less as a method of redundancy and more as a way of avoiding it. The mechanics differ from other methods in one key respect; employees opting for early retirement are less likely to seek to re-enter the workforce. Ill-health is one cause for the increase in early retirement, but other developments at both company and national levels also lie behind the increase. There has been a major increase in the level of ill-health retirements in recent years. A commonly voiced argument is that this is a consequence of intensification of work and associated increases in stress levels, which result in more long-term sickness.

At the national level there has been a desire by governments in the US and Europe, as well as other industrialised countries, to increase work opportunities for younger workers. At the company level, the expansion of occupational pension schemes and the inclusion of standard arrangements for redundancy retirement have facilitated the use of early retirement as a method of workforce reduction (McGoldrick and Cooper, 1989). The use of enhanced early retirement benefits makes it more palatable. It would also appear that many managers, usually with little supporting evidence, associate increasing age with declining levels of productivity and poorer-quality performance. Ageism in managerial circles, it seems, is rife, and some companies even had formal 'first in first out' redundancy policies until the advent of legislation on age discrimination throughout the EU. The view that older workers have critical experience and expertise with 'seasoning', as an asset not a liability, is not widely shared (Clabaugh, 1997). The main exception here appears to be senior managers themselves. The increasing age profile of directors has caused some to question whether there should be a 'sell-by' date for such a group (Weyer, 1994).

There are a number of advantages of early retirement ('downsizing with dignity' – Barbee, 1986); in particular, it is seen as carrying less stigma than other forms of redundancy; 'retired' is a much more socially acceptable 'r' word than 'redundant'. However, there are also a number of drawbacks. The decline of the last in first out (LIFO) redundancy selection criteria, which protected older workers by virtue of seniority, has left them disproportionately vulnerable to enforced early retirement under employers' labour-shedding policies. People are now living longer and retiring earlier and thus need sound financial provision if demeaning financial dependency is to be avoided. The adequacy of early retirement benefits is increasingly being questioned. It is now clear that the past trends in early retirement will not continue, not least because of uncertainty over the capacity of pension funds to sustain the costs and the end of default retirement ages in some countries, e.g. the UK. EU-wide legislation on age discrimination and a changing policy on mandatory retirement look set to radically alter early retirement trends.

Alternatives to redundancy

Organisations do have some strategic choices in the face of falls in demand – how much labour to dismiss, how much to hoard and how much to redeploy (Peetz *et al.*, 2011). Employers may consider alternatives to redundancies, and view compulsory redundancy, especially, only as a last resort. There are wide range of possible alternatives to redundancy, including redeployment, freezing recruitment, disengaging contractors and other flexible workers, reducing overtime, secondments, career breaks, and introducing more flexible working patterns such as job sharing and part-time work.

As noted earlier, employment decisions can reflect different country contexts and approaches to human resources (Eurofound, 2013; Peetz *et al.*, 2011). For example, in the US, where they have an employment at will and 'hire and fire' philosophy, labour is more likely to be shed in contrast to some European countries, where there is more emphasis on finding alternatives. However, there is little evidence for any widespread development of redundancy alternatives in Britain. For some commentators an explanation lies in the ease with which British employers can dismiss their workers without having to consider alternatives. Turnbull and Wass (1997) argue that deregulation has made redundancy or what the European Union term 'collective dismissal', easier in the UK than other forms of workforce reduction. A consequence of a more protracted dismissal process is that it seems other countries have a much greater emphasis on avoiding redundancy. Japan and Scandinavian countries have the most developed forms of employment protection, with graded steps for cost reduction. In the case of Japan, this includes redeployment, relocation, retraining, transfer and even suspending dividends and cutting the salaries of senior managers. As Turnbull and Wass (1997) point out, this is the exact reverse of the British picture, where dividends and the bonus payments of senior managers are boosted by making workers redundant in the pursuit of short-term profit improvements.

Peetz *et al.* (2011) provide examples of macho-style behaviour such as the European automobile equipment multinational, Continental, sending a letter to 600 out of 1,120 dismissed staff offering job relocations to Tunisia for salaries of 137 Euros a month, arguing that this complied with the legal obligation to relocate staff in existing operations within the company (soyoutv.com, 2010). However, they also note many other examples of European employers using flexible reduction of working time or work sharing with partial compensation of income losses financed by public funds (e.g. at Fiat and Indesit in Italy, Scania and Volvo in Sweden, Daimler and Schaeffer in Germany, and Danfos and Grundfos in Denmark). There were others that focused on internal restructuring through redeployment of labour (e.g. Powertrain and Indesit in Italy). Some also restructured labour through training (e.g. Peugeot in France and Telecom Italia) (Glassner and Keune, 2010; see also Eurofound, 2013; Peetz *et al.*, 2011: 194–5).

In some European countries, the state has proactively intervened in the economy to forestall or prevent employment downsizing, rather than simply leaving employees fully exposed to market forces (which is more likely in liberal market economies like the US and UK). Germany's national policy responses during the most recent economic recession (and historically, well before that) are an illustrative example. A core response to the economic crisis was a *Kurzarbeit* (literally, 'short work') policy, under which companies were encouraged to temporarily place workers on reduced work schedules when demand is weak, rather than lay them off. The companies pay only for the hours worked, while the government provides up to 67 per cent of the workers' remaining wages. The program supported up to 1.5 million employees at 63,000 companies, according to the Federal Labour Agency. While the worst recession since World War II pushed up unemployment in the US to 10 per cent, a 27-year high, in Germany the rate fell to 7.5 per cent, a 17-year low and well below the 10 per cent average for the Eurozone. It is estimated that nearly half a million jobs were saved because of *Kurzarbeit* (Cascio, 2014).

Denmark is another interesting country case because it combines a seemingly liberal approach to hiring and firing with security for workers. This has been labelled as 'flexicurity'. Denmark has high social welfare benefits for workers who do lose their jobs, and invests more than other countries, as a percentage of its gross domestic product (4.4 per cent), in retraining and active labour market programmes for those who have lost jobs. The cost of this flexicurity system is covered by high tax rates, totalling 50 per cent of GDP, second only to Sweden. It is estimated that approximately two-thirds of Danes who are laid off find a new job within a year (Cascio, 2014; Janssen, 2013). Janssen (2013) argues that the real advantage of 'flexicurity' is the level of investment in active training that boosts employee adaptability, rather than employers being free to easily fire.

Research on managing in Ireland during the GFC reported that companies did not simply include 'hard' HRM policies aimed at cutting their pay roll and boosting productivity, but they also included 'soft' HRM policies aimed at maintaining employee commitment and loyalty via intensified communication and employee engagement efforts, retaining HRM initiatives and promoting fairness into their programmes to ensure that the impact is spread evenly across all groups of employees. Roche *et al.* (2011) concluded that HR managers appear to be trying to balance 'hard' and 'soft' people management policies in an effort to address short-term cost pressures while not eroding employee motivation or commitment.

Cascio (2009; 2014) points out that there is very limited research that examines the relative financial effects of these alternatives on firms, and the effects on individual employees, partly because there are few examples. He attributes this to the mental models that senior managers have about human resources. From his work he identifies two groups. One group of firms saw employees as *costs to be cut*. The other much smaller group of firms saw employees as *assets to be developed*. We can see a major difference in the approaches they took to restructure their organisations:

- **Employees as costs to be cut** – the downsizers. They constantly ask themselves, what is the minimum number of employees we need to run this company? What is the irreducible core number of employees the business requires?
- **Employees as assets to be developed** – the responsible restructurers. They constantly ask themselves, how can we change the way we do business, so that we can use the people we currently have more effectively?

As Cascio puts it, the downsizers see employees as commodities – like paper clips or light bulbs – interchangeable and substitutable, one for another. This is a 'plug-in' mentality: plug them in when you need them, pull the plug when you no longer need them. In contrast, responsible restructurers see employees as sources of innovation and renewal. They see in employees the potential to grow their businesses. However, Sisson and Purcell (2010) argue that management may often be caught between these competing views of the organisation, in terms of struggling to balance the tensions involving in being pulled towards treating employees as a cost or an asset. Any one company may use a combination of these competing approaches, and in response to variegated contextual circumstances. A key issue is if and how HR practitioners can manage these tensions and hence influence practice. Some of the main alternatives to redundancy are now briefly discussed in greater detail.

Wage reductions

Wage cuts as an alternative to job cuts tend to be sparingly used, although there have been a number of prominent examples as a method of cost reduction in the UK and elsewhere, such as in Hong Kong. A particular use has been in the introduction of US concession-style bargaining arrangements wherein employees forgo a wage increase for some form of job security agreement. In the UK, Thomas Cook in 2001 cut jobs by 1,500 and asked staff to take pay cuts of 10 per cent as business collapsed in the wake of the terrorist attacks in the US. Senior executives cut their own pay by 15 per cent and those earning more than £10,000 had their salaries cut by 3 to 10 per cent (McCallister, 2001).

Redeployment

Although employers' attempts to secure more flexible workforces have been subject to a great deal of debate, the concept of spatial flexibility and the redeployment of workers has received little attention. In the US, redeployment – or 'inplacement' – is well established. In the recession of the mid-1970s, Japanese corporations maintained as many as four million permanent employees despite the lack of work for them to do. Redeployment made this easier because of the tendency to straddle employees across several industries (Hill, 1989: 51). Even in the 1990s, when Japanese weaknesses were identified, plant closure and sell-offs were rarely carried out. While the Japanese method of labour handling during a recession makes it difficult to instigate quick turnarounds; it also means that companies still have resources at hand for a rapid expansion.

The redundancy process

Redundancy, despite the practice that managers have had in undertaking it of late, is often badly managed, with many negative consequences. In part this may stem from the rarity of formal redundancy procedures. The large majority of employers do not have an agreed and written redundancy procedure, adequately consult employees and their representatives or prepare them for the 'shock' of redundancy. Recent interest in notions of labour-management partnerships have connected with such concerns. In Spain, for example, Rodriguez-Ruiz (2015) analysed the restructuring approach followed by the highly profitable Telefónica in its 2011 redundancy plan, and explored unions' response to management strategy. Specifically, his case study tries to show how massive job cuts have been implemented through a labour-mediated downsizing strategy that mitigates contestation and industrial conflict. There is much to be gained from a humane, planned and strategic approach to downsizing (Wilkinson, 2004). According to Cameron (1994; 1998), the way downsizing is implemented is more important than the fact that it is implemented. He reports on three approaches to downsizing.

Workforce reduction strategies are focused primarily on reducing headcount and are usually implemented in a top-down, speedy way. However, the downside of such an approach is that it is seen as the 'equivalent to throwing a grenade into a crowded room, closing the door and expecting the explosion to eliminate a certain percentage of the workforce. It is difficult to predict exactly who will be eliminated and who will remain' (Cameron, 1994: 197), but it grabs the immediate attention of the workforce to the condition that exists. Because of the quick implementation associated with the workforce reduction strategy, management does not have time to think its strategy through and communicate it properly to employees. This may result in a low 'perceived distributive fairness' (Brockner *et al.*, 1987). As a result, employees may be negatively affected by the stress and uncertainty created by this type of downsizing and may react with reduced organisational commitment, less job involvement and reduced work efforts.

Work redesign strategies are aimed at reducing work (in addition to, or instead of, reducing the number of workers) through redesigning tasks, reducing work hours, merging units, etc. However, these are difficult to implement swiftly and hence are seen as a medium-term strategy.

Systematic strategies focus more broadly on changing culture, attitude and values, not just changing workforce size. This involves

> redefining downsizing as an on-going process, as a basis for continuous improvement; rather than as a programme or a target. Downsizing is also equated with simplification of all aspects of the organisation – the entire system including supplies, inventories, design process, production methods, customer relations, marketing and sales support, and so on. (*Cameron, 1994: 199*)

Again, this strategy requires longer-term perspectives than that of workforce reduction.

Sahdev (2003: 72) suggests that the main focus of HR appears to be in implementing the procedural aspects of redundancy, including fair selection and provision of outplacement services for the leavers. While this is in keeping with the organisational justice approach, the contributions need to be directed towards managing the strategic aspects of decision-making processes with a view to managing survivors effectively. He suggests that HR practitioners need to be influential at both the strategic and operational levels, in order to manage survivors effectively and thereby enable the organisation to sustain competitiveness.

To what extent is such advice heeded in reality? Many problems relate to a low level of trust between those making decisions and those receiving them, which has been a historical and enduring problem in countries like the UK where low trust work orientations by employers have often been unsurprisingly reciprocated by employees (Fox, 1974). A convincing rationale for downsizing is essential, and requires a degree of planning. 'Good HR practice' suggests that three elements of the redundancy process are often critical: consultation with employees, the selection decision and pre-post-redundancy support for those made redundant as well as those who remain. We deal with each of these in turn.

Consultation

Consultation with unions and employees is emphasised in most accounts of downsizing. Employees need to understand the rationale for downsizing and also how the process will be managed. Breaks in communication are seen as sinister and lead to rumours (Kettley, 1995). Consultation with unions over redundancies can make a difference to the nature of the redundancy process used, and occasionally the number of jobs lost (Edwards and Hall, 1999). The downsizing process is often characterised by secrecy and swiftness and is thus often poorly planned and executed with little scope for employee involvement. To some extent this reluctance to consult over workforce reduction stems from it being seen as part of a deeply entrenched managerial prerogative about the right to hire and fire and close down businesses. The case of the deputies, supervisors and correction officers dismissed by the newly elected sheriff at Clayton County, Georgia, is fortunately not that common. Staff who thought they were being invited to a swearing-in ceremony had their badges, guns and car keys removed, were then dismissed and escorted to a ride home (in police vans) under the watchful eye of rooftop snipers who were there 'just in case someone got emotional' (Younge, 2005).

Legislative restrictions on managerial prerogative in redundancy are extremely limited in the UK (CIPD, 2011). However, there is evidence that extensive consultation and employee involvement can help in smoothing implementation. US studies indicate that increased communication and participation of employees in the downsizing process were associated with improvement (Cameron, 1994; DiFonzo and Bordia, 1998).

Selection

Whatever methods are used to reach redundancy decisions, notions of fairness and 'organisational justice' are key issues. Here the process of the decision making on redundancy is equal if not more important than the outcome. Research on the perception of organisational justice by employees has been found to be related to both how the decision was made and how much 'voice' they felt they had in the process. In general, there are fewer negative attitudinal and behaviour outcomes from employees when the decision to downsize is seen as more legitimate (e.g. because of a decline in sales, increased competition, etc.), compared to a desire to increase profits, cut costs, etc. The other important factors in the selection process, which also help increase employees' perceptions of fairness, are that they should be clear and appropriate.

There are some noteworthy general trends within selection criteria. First is the distinct move away from seniority and the reduction of LIFO and towards selection based on an assessment of skills and performance (CIPD, 2011; IRS, 2004). Despite the advantages of LIFO, which according to the UK Advisory Conciliation and Arbitration Service (ACAS) is an 'objective, easy to apply, readily understood and widely accepted' criterion, it now tends to be used only as part of a wider range of selection criteria. However, with the introductions of age discrimination legislation, those with less service tend to be younger, so this makes it a risky method. There can also be problems of unfair discrimination in its application. The issue of employers using sickness absences as a criterion for redundancy has caused much concern among unions, not least because of the worry that employees will now be frightened to take time off work when genuinely sick. In the Industrial Relations Services (IRS) survey of those employers who use attendance as a criterion (60 per cent of the sample), certified absence appears to count against an employee in the selection process almost as much as unauthorised absence. Most employers (81 per cent) said that leave covered by a doctor's certificate would count against a worker, and 87 per cent said that self-certified leave would (IRS, 2004).

Despite the outwardly 'objective' nature of many of these selection criteria and mechanisms, we can also find considerable evidence of subjective manipulation of a redundancy situation by managers. In the search for 'committed' workers, employers appear to use workforce reduction for a variety of ends. Often it seems a redundancy situation is used, or in some cases even engineered, to weed out 'troublemakers' and periodically get rid of 'deadwood'. Troublemakers are variously defined as the shirkers, union activists and the non-believers in new managerial philosophies and programmes. For example, the personnel director of Co-Steel Sheerness, a British-based but Canadian-owned steel mill, described how they dealt with employees who were unhappy with the new practices of 'total team culture' and union de-recognition thus:

> When it became clear that there were employees who became increasingly dissatisfied with our new philosophies ... we bit the bullet with those employees and put in place termination programmes. About 5 to 6 per cent of employees were terminated. (*The Guardian, 6 September 1995: 19*)

Employee support

A wide variety of post-redundancy assistance can be offered to dismissed workers. There is considerable evidence to suggest that such help can have a very positive impact on the management of redundancy at a relatively low cost (e.g. Guest and Peccei, 1992). The forms of support include redeployment centres, business start-up advice, training and loans, retraining, outplacement support, pre-retirement education, financial advice, job-search help and counselling, etc.

Redundancy counselling and stress management are emphasised to help employees overcome and come to terms with some of the intense feelings of damage to self-esteem, failure, loss of confidence, decreased morale, anxiety, bitter feelings of betrayal, debilitating shock and sense of loss that accompany downsizing. Real personal, social and financial problems also stem from redundancy situations. Studies of redundancy counselling and assistance programmes report it as being valued by the recipients but somewhat unproven in its actual benefits.

The availability of support is usually much greater the more senior the redundant employee is. Thus outplacement support is more often reserved for more senior grades, and where it is provided for all employees, senior managers usually receive external specialist services while lower-grade employees have in-house services. Surveys of outplacement report that there has been considerable growth in the UK since its import from the US in the mid-1970s (Doherty, 1998). While most firms would claim expertise in wider career management advice, its main use is in downsizing situations. Its key aim is to help the redundant employee with the job-search process by providing practical services such as office support and specific counselling and advice. At more senior levels this is often provided on a one-to-one basis, involving psychometric tests and career counselling, while for other levels of employees, group programmes of CV construction and job-search strategies are provided. The most common support for operatives is the statutorily supported one of time off to look for work. The need for support in finding alternative work is a real one. Redundant workers suffer particularly in their search for a new job, the so-called 'lemon effect' (Turnbull and Wass, 1997). Here recruiters become concerned about hiring an employee who has been discarded by another employer. Employers may assume that a redundant worker is of poorer quality and potential.

Severance pay

Arguably, the acid test of support for redundant employees is the level of compensatory financial support or 'severance' pay. Some companies provide little else in the way of support for redundant workers. For example, the financially oriented Hanson Trust did not use outplacement but were said to 'use pound notes to staunch the blood' with generous severance packages. In the UK, many employers offer better severance terms than the baseline required by statute, with the main exception being public sector employers, except for senior managers. In part this reflects the paternalistic nature of some British employers, but also the pragmatic need for a form of inducement to encourage employees to volunteer. Severance is usually paid in the form of a lump sum to facilitate a 'clean break' rather than staged payments.

Survivors

The needs of those who remain post-downsizing appear to be often overlooked. For example, a survey of financial services found that 79 per cent of firms provided outplacement services for those employees who left but less than half gave support to the 'lucky' ones who remained (Doherty and Horsted, 1995). Yet we have increasing evidence that such forgotten employees are often in need of support and counselling. For example, there is considerable evidence that remaining employees feel shocked, embittered towards management, fearful about their future and guilty about still having a job while colleagues have been laid off (Devine *et al.*, 2003; Spreitzer and Mishra, 2002; Van Dierendonck and Jacobs, 2012). The effects of such feelings are not difficult to predict. Such employees are more likely to have lower morale and increased stress levels, be less productive and less loyal, with increased quit levels. Sennett describes survivors as behaving as though 'they lived on borrowed time, feeling they had survived for no good reason' (1997: 125). Indeed, the threat of further downsizing may create difficulties in that the most able seek alternative employment. Moreover, employees may be asked to do jobs they are untrained or ill qualified to do.

Conclusions

The past decade or so has witnessed unmatched levels of workforce reduction in many industrialised countries, especially in the wake of the recent GFC (Eurofound, 2013). Most organisations have undergone some form of downsizing; however, a number of key questions still remain about downsizing. These are not so much about its nature or the effects on the redundant or surviving employees, rather they centre on whether organisations, and in turn whole economies, are now in better shape post-downsizing. Are such organisations leaner and fitter or understaffed and anorexic? Has downsizing resulted in increased competitive advantage for those companies that have undergone it? What are the drivers of continuing downsizing?

An increasingly popular view is that the effects of downsizing are the equivalent of an industrial nuclear war:

> Below the chief executive and his cheerleading human resources department, a number of companies resemble nothing so much as buildings blasted by a neutron bomb. The processes and structures are all there, but no human life to make them productive.
> *(Caulkin, 1995: 29)*

There is thus mounting evidence that all is not well in the downsized organisational form. As Pfeffer states, 'downsizing may cut labour costs in the short run, but it can erode both employee and eventually customer loyalty in the long run' (1998: 192). As with all management tools, downsizing has unintended outcomes that could limit its presumed benefits such as cost reduction, removal of unnecessary layers of management and better value for shareholders. Research has shown that downsizing has mixed effects on performance (Cascio, 2002, 2014; McMahan *et al.*, 2012), showing no long-term financial payoff to downsizing, on average, while shares of downsizing companies have outperformed the stock market for six months post-downsizing, there is little evidence to suggest that long-run performance or stock prices are improved by job cuts (Hunter, 2000).

HRM clearly has a potentially important role in the process of employment downsizing. Indeed, Chadwick *et al.* (2004) confirm that downsizing is more likely to be effective in the longer term when accompanied by practices that reinforce the contribution of HR to financial success (e.g. extensive communication, respectful treatment of redundant employees and attention to survivors' concerns over job security). Trevor and Nyberg (2008) also find that supportive HRM practices buffer some of the negative employee attitudinal and behavioural consequences of downsizing.

A possible explanation for increasingly reported negative relationships between downsizing and economic performance can be found in Hamel and Prahalad's (1993) analysis of competitive advantage via resource productivity, both capital and human. They suggest that there are two ways to achieve this: first, via downsizing and second, by the strategic discipline of stretch and leverage. This latter approach seeks to get the most from existing resources. Their view is that leveraging is mostly energizing while downsizing is essentially the reverse, resulting in demoralised managers and workforces. In the jargon, it appears that to achieve economic effectiveness downsizing is far from always 'rightsizing'. Strategic decision makers seem to have forgotten the benefits of growth strategies. Stephen Roach (chief economist, Morgan Stanley), the guru of downsizing business, has now disowned the practice of slash and burn restructuring (Carlin, 1996). According to Roach, 'if you compete by building you have a future . . . if you compete by cutting you don't'.

There are undoubted variations across industries. Downsizing may be more damaging to R&D or knowledge-intensive industries where human capital is a very significant contributor to success.

Given such a grim picture of the effects of organisational downsizing, why then do managers persist in continuing with it? A number of explanations have been put forward. First, it is increasingly argued that managers have simply become addicted to downsizing because being lean and mean is now fashionable in itself. Downsizing, according to Brunning (1996), has become a corporate addiction and the 'cocaine of the boardroom'. Farrell and Mavondo suggest that:

> Managers resort to downsizing because it is simple, generates considerable 'noise and attention' in the organisation, and may be viewed by some managers as tangible evidence of their 'strong leadership'. However, managers that pursue a reorientation strategy must necessarily engage in the much more difficult intellectual task of deciding how to reorient the organisation, combined with the associated challenges of building support, generating commitment and developing a shared vision. *(Farrell and Mavondo, 2004: 396)*

Second, rather than a more 'acceptable' and appropriate use of downsizing because firms are now more productive or better organised or too bureaucratic and over-staffed, managers often feel compelled to do so by the market's demands for short-term boosts in profits. Increasingly, this is driven by intensified financialisation of economic activity (Appelbaum *et al.,* 2013; Thompson, 2013). Depressingly, it seems that downsizing acts as a reassuring signal to markets that managers are 'in control' and acting to put things right. Third, Hitt *et al.* (1994) suggest that the rage for 'mindless' downsizing (herd behaviour) is linked to the merger and acquisitions mania of the last decades as managers attempt to solve the problems associated with acquisitive rather than organic growth. Acquisition strategies are argued to promote conservative short-term perspectives among managers, hence downsizing as a solution rather than investing in human capital. Indeed, there is a case that with greater internal flexibility (e.g. wider jobs), there may be less necessity for external flexibility (e.g. via downsizing) as workers can cope more ably with adjustments and change. It is important to see security in the context of other policies. Workers are more likely to contribute ideas if they do not feel they are endangering their own colleagues' jobs, and both employer and employee are more likely to see investments in training as worthwhile.

Thus despite the sufferings of many workers in an era of redundancy there have been precious few long-term benefits to justify its level and severity, nor an overwhelming economic justification for its continuing blanket use. The redundant often find meaningful, well-paid and stable work difficult to come by, starkly illustrated by Dobbins *et al.* (2014) in their case study of Anglesey Aluminium in Wales, where workers made redundant because of closure of a large aluminium plant encountered insufficient (quality) job opportunities in the regional labour market. In picking up the pieces after redundancy many quite highly skilled workers found themselves part of an insecure labour 'precariat' with little choice but to 'make do and mend' in low-quality low-paid jobs. Meanwhile, those who remain in employment are stretched thin, worried about their security and subject to considerable work stress in anorexic organisations. Questions may well be asked of MDs and CEOs who are still rewarded with high and increasing salaries and perks (Haigh, 2004), given it is not clear that reducing headcount improves performance. Lastly, it seems that the claim of HRM that people are an organisation's most valuable resource is difficult to sustain in this context. As Guthrie and Datta (2008) argue, rather than becoming lean and mean, organisations may well become lean and lame.

Finally, as Ghoshal (2005) has observed, business school academics are also partly culpable for downsizing 'culls', given that what he calls bad management theories (like those aligning managerial interests and incentives with those of short-term shareholder value maximisation) have encouraged too much bad management practice, and poor corporate governance generally. Arguably, senior HR managers could try to do more to exert greater leverage in encouraging their organisations to champion their employees as long-term strategic assets to be developed to add value, rather than as disposable commodities to be hired and fired according to the dictate of stock prices and pressures for financialisation. However, some commentators have observed that HR as a function has moved away from this 'employee champion' role (Francis *et al.*, 2006).

CASE STUDY 14.1

THE IRISH FERRIES DISPUTE

TONY DOBBINS

A bitter industrial dispute relating to downsizing was ignited in Ireland in September 2005 when Irish Ferries sought 543 'voluntary' redundancies from its unionised Irish staff, who were to be replaced by cheaper non-union Eastern European agency-sourced labour, mainly from Latvia, on much lower wage rates and terms and conditions. While many workers accepted the redundancy terms on offer, many did not and faced a pay cut when Irish Ferries announced lower pay and conditions. In November 2005, the Labour Court issued a non-binding recommendation that Irish Ferries should continue to retain directly employed Irish staff until 2007. Irish Ferries rejected this recommendation. At the end of November, Irish Ferries brought in Eastern European agency crew to replace Irish crew and a number of Irish crew members locked themselves in the ship's boiler room. These events brought the dispute to a head and the main union (SIPTU) escalated industrial action against the company. Tens of thousands of people subsequently marched on the streets in a national day of protest in support of the Irish Ferries workers. The dispute had broader national implications because it threatened to endanger the whole model of Irish social partnership at the time. Because of the potential wider spill-over from the dispute, enormous efforts were made to reach a settlement. Finally, in December 2005, a legally binding agreement was reached during talks at the Labour Relations Commission. The settlement permitted the company to proceed with its plans to use non-union agency crews and reflag its vessels to Cyprus. A further element involved Irish Ferries conceding to paying non-Irish outsourced agency workers the Irish minimum wage rate (€7.65 per hour in 2005). Although much lower than what unionised Irish workers in the company had originally been receiving, it was significantly higher than the €3.57 rate initially proposed by the company for agency crew. Finally, the terms and conditions of employment for those remaining unionised Irish workers (a maximum of 48) were to be 'red-circled' and their terms and conditions protected. Although a settlement had been reached, the consequences of this dispute were to place issues such as a 'race to the bottom', job displacement and labour standards at the centre of Irish and, indeed, European employment relations. In the aftermath of the dispute, Irish unions successfully lobbied for a new legal framework to prevent future cases of collective redundancies and displacement of workers by employers using cheaper labour. The Protection of Employees (Exceptional Collective Redundancies and Related Matters) Act 2007 was introduced under a commitment in the then national social partnership agreement. However, uncertainty surrounding pressures for a 'race to the bottom' in labour standards remain in Irish, and European, employment relations.

Source: Dobbins, 2005.

Bibliography

Adams, S. (1996) *The Dilbert Principle*, London: Boxtree Press.

Ahmadjian, L.C. and Robinson, P. (2001) 'Safety in numbers: downsizing and the deinstitutionalization of permanent employment in Japan', *Administrative Science Quarterly*, Vol.46, No.4, 622–58.

Anfunso, D. (1996) 'Strategies to stop the layoffs', *Personnel Journal*, June, 66–99.

Appelbaum, E., Batt, R. and Clark, I. (2013) 'Implications for employment relations research: evidence from breach of trust and implicit contracts in private equity buy-outs', *British Journal of Industrial Relations*, Vol.51, No.3, 498–518.

Barbee, G, (1986) 'Downsizing with dignity', *Retirement Planning*, Fall, 6–7.

Baumol, J.W., Blinder, S.A. and Wolff, N.E. (2003) *Downsizing in America: Reality, Causes, and Consequences*, New York: Russell Sage Foundation Press.

Boone, J. (2000) 'Technological progress, downsizing and unemployment', *Economic Journal*, Vol.110, 581–600.

Brockner, J. (1992) 'Managing the effects of lay-offs on survivors', *California Management Review*, Vol.34, No.2, 9–28.

Brockner, J., Grover, S., Reed, T., DeWitt, R. and O'Malley, M. (1987) 'Survivors' reactions to lay-offs: we get by with a little help from our friends', *Administrative Science Quarterly*, Vol.32, 526–41.

Brunning, F. (1996) 'Working at the office on borrowed time', *Macleans*, 8–9 February.

Budros, A. (1999) 'A conceptual framework for analyzing why organizations downsize', *Organization Science*, Vol.10, No.1, 69–81.

Bulmer, M. (1971) 'Mining redundancy: a case study of the workings of the Redundancy Payments Act in the Durham coalfields', *Industrial Relations Journal*, Vol.26, No.15, 227–44.

Burke, W.W. (1997) 'The new agenda for organisation development', *Organizational Dynamics*, Vol.26, 6–20.

Cameron, K.S. (1994) 'Strategies for successful organisational downsizing', *Human Resource Management*, Vol.33, No.2, 189–211.

Cameron, K.S. (1998) 'Downsizing', in Poole, M. and Warner, M. (eds.) *The IEBM Handbook of Human Resource Management*, London: International Thomson Press.

Cameron, K.S., Freeman, S.J. and Mishra, A.K. (1991) 'Best practices in white-collar downsizing: managing contradictions', *Academy of Management Executive*, Vol.5, No.3, 57–73.

Cappelli, P. (2009), 'Alternatives to layoffs', *HR Executive Online*. Available at: www .hreonline.com/HRE/story.jsp?storyId=158416635.

Carlin, J. (1996) 'Guru of "downsizing" admits he got it all wrong', *Independent on Sunday*, 12 May.

Cascio, W.F. (1993) 'Downsizing: what do we know? What have we learned?', *Academy of Management Executive*, Vol.7, 95–104.

Cascio, W.F. (2002) 'Strategies for responsible restructuring', *Academy of Management Executive*, Vol.16, 80–91.

Cascio, W.F. (2009) 'Downsizing and redundancy', in Wilkinson, A., Redman, T., Snell, S. and Bacon, N. (eds.) *The SAGE Handbook of Human Resource Management*, London: Sage.

Cascio, W.F. (2014) 'Alternatives to downsizing: efforts in responsible restructuring', paper presented as part of symposium, 'Cooperative employment relations to preserve jobs: responsible restructuring practices and shared work' (D. Marschall, Chair), Labor and Employment Relations Association, Portland, OR, 29 May.

Cascio, W.F., Young, E.C. and Morris, J.R. (1997) 'Financial consequences of employment-change decisions in major U.S. corporations', *Academy of Management Journal*, Vol.40, 1175–89.

Caulkin, S. (1995) 'Take your partners', *Management Today*, February, 26–30.

Caves, R. and Krepps, M. (1993) 'Fat: the displacement of nonproduction workers from US manufacturing industries', Brookings Papers on Economic Activity, Vol.2, 227–88.

Chadwick, C., Hunter, L. and Walston, S. (2004) 'Effects of downsizing practices on the performance of hospitals', *Strategic Management Journal*, Vol.25, No.5, 405–27.

Chorely, D. (2002) 'How to manage downsizing', *Financial Management*, 6 May.

CIPD (2011) *Redundancy Factsheet*, London: Chartered Institute of Personnel and Development.

Clabaugh, A. (1997) 'Downsizing: implications for older employees', Working Paper, Perth, Australia: Edith Cowan University.

Contrepois, S. (2011) 'Labour struggles against mass redundancies in France: understanding direct action', *Employee Relations*, Vol.33, No.6, 642–53.

Cullinane, N. and Dundon, T. (2011) 'Redundancy and workplace occupation: the case of the Republic of Ireland', *Employee Relations*, Vol.33, No.6, 624–41.

Datta, D.K., Guthrie, J.P., Basuil, D. and Pandey, A. (2010) 'Causes and effects of employee downsizing: a review and synthesis', *Journal of Management*, Vol.36, No.1, 281–348.

De La Merced, M.J. (2011) 'American Airlines parent files for bankruptcy', *New York Times*. Available at: http://dealbook.nytimes.com/2011/11/29/american-airlines-parent-files-for -bankruptcy/.

De Meuse, K.P., Bergmann, T.J. and Vanderheiden, P.A. (1997) 'Corporate downsizing: separating myth from fact', *Journal of Management Inquiry*, Vol.6, No.2, 168–76.

Devine, K., Reay, T., Stainton, L. and Collins-Nakai, R. (2003) 'Downsizing outcomes: better a victim than a survivor?', *Human Resource Management*, Vol.42, No.2, 109–24.

Dewettinck, K. and Buyens, D. (2002) 'Downsizing: employee threat or opportunity? An empirical study on external and internal reorientation practices in Belgian companies', *Employee Relations*, Vol.24, No.4, 389–402.

DiFonzo, N. and Bordia, P. (1998) 'A tale of two corporations: managing uncertainty during organisational change', *Human Resource Management*, Vol.37, 295–303.

Dobbins, T. (2005) 'Irish Ferries dispute finally resolved after bitter stand-off', Dublin: European Foundation for the Improvement of Living and Working Conditions. Available at: http://www.eurofound.europa.eu/observatories/eurwork/articles/irish-ferries-dispute-finally -resolved-after-bitter-stand-off

Dobbins, T., Plows, A. and Lloyd-Williams, H. (2014) '"Make do and mend" after redundancy at Anglesey Aluminium: critiquing human capital approaches', *Work Employment and Society*, Vol.28, No.4, 515–32.

Doherty, N. (1998) 'The role of outplacement in redundancy management', *Personnel Review*, Vol.27, No.4, 343–51.

Doherty, N. and Horsted, J. (1995) 'Helping survivors to stay on board', *People Management*, 12 January, 26–31.

Edwards, P. and Hall, M. (1999) 'Remission: possible', *People Management*, 15 July, 44–6.

Espahbodi, R., John, T.A. and Vasudevan, G. (2000) 'The effects of downsizing on operating performance', *Review of Quantitative Finance and Accounting*, Vol.15, 107–26.

Eurofound (2013) *Monitoring and managing restructuring in the 21st century*, Luxembourg: Publications Office of the European Union.

Farrell, M. and Mavondo, F. (2004) 'The effect of downsizing strategy and reorientation strategy on learning orientation', *Personnel Review*, Vol.33, No.4, 383–402.

Fisher, S.R. and White, M.A. (2000) 'Downsizing in a learning organisation: are there hidden costs?', *Academy of Management Review*, Vol.25, No.1, 244–51.

Fox, A. (1974) *Beyond Contract: Work, Power and Trust Relations*, London: Faber & Faber.

Francis, H. and Keegan, A. (2006). 'The changing face of HR: in search of balance, *Human Resource Management Journal*, Vol.16, No.3, 231–49.

Gall, G. (2011) 'Worker resistance and response to the crisis of neo-liberal capitalism', *Employee Relations*, Vol.33, No.6, 588–91.

Garfield, A. (1999) 'Barclays shares soar as city welcomes job cuts', *Independent*, 21 May.

Ghoshal, S. (2005) 'Bad management theories are destroying good management practices', *Academy of Management Learning & Education*, Vol.4, No.1, 75–91.

Glassner, V. and Keune, M. (2010) *Collective bargaining responses to the economic crisis in Europe*, ETUI Policy Brief 1/2010, European Economic and Employment Policy, Brussels: European Trade Union Institute.

Guest, D. and Peccei, R. (1992) 'Employee involvement: redundancy as a critical case', *Human Resource Management Journal*, Vol.2, No.3, 34–59.

Guthrie, J.P. and Datta, D.K. (2008) 'Dumb and dumber: the impact of downsizing on firm performance as moderated by industry conditions', *Organization Science*, Vol.19, 108–23.

Haigh, G. (2004) *Bad Company: The Strange Cult of the CEO*, London: Aurum.

Hall, P. and Soskice, D. (2001) *Varieties of Capitalism: the Institutional Foundations of Comparative Advantage*, Oxford-New York: Oxford University Press.

Hamel, G. (2000) *Leading the Revolution*, New York: Harvard Business School Press.

Hamel, G. and Prahalad, C.K. (1993) 'Strategy as stretch and leverage', *Harvard Business Review*, March–April, 75–84.

Hardy, C. (1987) 'Investing in retrenchment: avoiding the hidden costs', *California Management Review*, Vol.29, No.4, 111–25.

Heyes, J., Lewis, P. and Clark, I. (2012) 'Varieties of capitalism: the state, financialisation and the economic crisis of 2007-?' *Industrial Relations Journal*, Vol.43, No.3, 222–41.

Higo, M. and Klassen, T. (2015) *Retirement in Japan and South Korea: The Past, the Present and the Future of Mandatory Retirement*, London and New York: Routledge.

Hill, S. (1989) *Competition and Control at Work*, London: Heinemann.

Hitt, M.A., Hoskisson, R.E., Harrison, J.S. and Summers, T.P. (1994) 'Human capital and strategic competitiveness in the 1990s', *Journal of Management Development*, Vol.13, No.1, 35–46.

Hunter, L. (2000) 'Myths and methods of downsizing', *FT Mastering People Management*, 2–4.

Hutton, W. (1997) *The State to Come*, London: Vintage.

Inman, P. (2004) 'Flying right in the face of logic', *The Guardian*, 28 August.

IRS (2004) 'The changing shape of work: how organisations restructure', *Employment Review*, No.794.

Janssen, R. (2013) 'Flexicurity: The model that never was', *Social Europe Journal*. Available at: http://www.social-europe.eu/2013/12/flexicurity-model-never/.

Jefferys, S. (2011) 'Collective and individual conflicts in five European countries', *Employee Relations*, Vol.33, No.6, 670–87.

Kettley, P. (1995) *Employee Morale During Downsizing*, Brighton: Institute of Employment Studies, Report No.291.

Lazonick, W. (2005) 'Corporate restructuring', in Ackroyd, S., Batt, R., Thompson, P. and Tolbert, P. (eds.) *The Oxford Handbook of Work and Organization*, Oxford: Oxford University Press.

Lee, P.M. (1997) 'A comparative analysis of layoff announcements and stock price reactions in the United States and Japan', *Strategic Management Journal*, Vol.18, 879–94.

Lepak, D.P. and Snell, S.A. (1999) 'The human resource architecture: toward a theory of human capital allocation and development', *Academy of Management Review*, Vol.24, No.1, 31–48.

Littler, C. and Innes, P. (2003) 'Downsizing and deknowledging the firm', *Work, Employment and Society*, Vol.17, No.1, 73–100.

Love, E. and Kraatz, M. (2009) 'Character, conformity, or the bottom line: how and why downsizing affected corporate reputation', *Academy of Management Journal*, Vol.52, 314–35.

McCallister, T. (2001) 'Thomas Cook cuts jobs and pay', *The Guardian*, 1 November. Available at: http://www.theguardian.com/business/2001/nov/01/travelnews.travel.

McGoldrick, A. and Cooper, C.L. (1989) *Early Retirement*, Aldershot: Gower.

McKinley, W., Zhao, J. and Rust, K.G. (2000) 'A sociocognitive interpretation of organisational downsizing', *Academy of Management Review*, Vol.25, 227–43.

McMahan, G.C., Pandey, A. and Martinson, B. (2012) 'To downsize human capital: a strategic human resource perspective on the disparate outcomes of downsizing', pp. 134–67, in Cooper, C.L., Pandey, A. and Quick, J.C. (eds.) *Downsizing: Is Less Still More?*, Cambridge: Cambridge University Press.

Mellahi, K. and Wilkinson, A. (2010), 'Slash and burn or nip and tuck: downsizing, innovation and human resources', *International Journal of Human Resource Management*, Vol.21, No.13, 2291–305.

Moore, M. (1997) *Downsize This*, New York: Harper-Collins.

Mouawad, J. (2012) 'American Airlines seeks 13,000 job cuts', *The New York Times*. Available at: http://www.nytimes.com/2012/02/02/business/american-airlines-seeks-job-cuts.html?ref=amrcorporation.

Mroczkowski, T. and Hanaoka, M. (1997) 'Effective downsizing strategies in Japan and America: is there a convergence of employment practices?', *Academy of Management Review*, Vol.22, No.1, 226–56.

Peetz D., Frost, A. and Le Queux, S. (2011) 'The GFC and employment relations', in Wilkinson, A. and Townsend, K. (eds.) *The Future of Employment Relations: New Paradigms, New Developments*, Basingstoke: Palgrave MacMillan.

Perkins, E. (2005) 'Airline downsizing means more hassles, fewer choices for travelers', http://www.smartertravel.com/travel-advice/Airline-downsizing-means-more.html?id=96416.

Peterson, B. (2012) 'The real story behind American's 13,000 job cuts', *Condé Nast Traveller*. http://www.cntraveler.com/daily-traveler/2012/02/American-Airlines-Job-Cuts.

Pfeffer, J. (1998) *The Human Equation*, Boston, MA: Harvard Business School Press.

Priti, P.S. (2000) 'Network destruction: the structural implications of downsizing', *Academy of Management Journal*, Vol.43, 101–12.

Roche, W., Teague, P., Coghlan, A. and Fahy, M. (2011) *Human Resources in a Recession: Managing and Representing People at Work in Ireland*, Dublin: Labour Relations Commission.

Rodriguez-Ruiz, O. (2015) 'Unions' response to corporate restructuring in Telefónica: locked into collective bargaining?', *Employee Relations*, Vol.37, No.1, 83–101.

Sahdev, K. (2003) 'Survivors' reactions to downsizing: the importance of contextual factors', *Human Resource Management Journal*, Vol.13, No.4, 56–74.

Sahdev, K., Vinnicombe, S. and Tyson, S. (1999) 'Downsizing and the changing role of HR', *International Journal of Human Resource Management*, Vol.10, No.5, 906–23.

Said, T., Le Lovarn, Y. and Tremblay, M. (2007) 'The performance effects of major workforce reductions: longitudinal evidence from North America', *International Journal of Human Resource Management*, Vol.18, No.12, 2075–94.

Savery, L.K., Travaglione, A. and Firns, I.G.J. (1998) 'The links between absenteeism and commitment during downsizing', *Personnel Review*, Vol.27, No.4, 312–24.

Schlangenstein, M. (2012) 'AMR unions seek arbitration in bankruptcy concession talks', *Bloomberg News*. Available at: http://www.bloomberg.com/news/2012-03-09/american-airlines-unions-seek-u-s-arbitrator-in-bankruptcy-giveback-talks.html.

Sennett, R. (1997) *The Corrosion of Character*, New York: Norton.

Sisson, K. and Purcell, J. (2010) 'Management: caught between competing views of the organization', in Colling, T. and Terry, M. (eds.) *Industrial Relations: Theory and Practice* (3rd edn.), Oxford: Wiley.

soyoutv.com (1 April 2010) 'Continental propose des postes en Tunisie rémunérés 137 euros par mois: les députés dégoûtés!'.

Spreitzer, G. and Mishra, A.K. (2002) 'To stay or to go: voluntary survivor turnover following an organizational downsizing', *Journal of Organizational Behaviour*, Vol.26, No.6, 707–29.

Stebbins, M.W. (1989) 'Downsizing with "mafia model" consultants', *Business Forum*, Winter, 45–7.

Storey, J. (ed.) (2007) *Human Resource Management: A Critical Text* (3rd edn.), London: Thomson.

The Guardian (1995) 6 September, 19.

The Guardian (2015) 'HSBC to rebrand UK high street bank as global shakeup sheds 25,000 jobs', 9 June. Available at: http://www.theguardian.com/business/2015/jun/09/hsbc-cuts-25000-jobs-globally.

The New York Times (2015) 'Pink slips at Disney: but first training foreign replacements', 3 June. Available at: http://www.nytimes.com/2015/06/04/us/last-task-after-layoff-at-disney-train-foreign-replacements.html

Thompson, P. (2013) 'Financialization and the workforce: extending and applying the disconnected capitalism thesis', *Work, Employment and Society*, Vol.27, No.3, 472–88.

Thornhill, A. and Saunders, M.N.K. (1998) 'The meanings, consequences and implications of the management of downsizing and redundancy: a review', *Personnel Review*, Vol.27, No.4, 271–95.

Trevor, C. and Nyberg, A. (2008) 'Keeping your headcount when all about you are losing theirs: downsizing, voluntary turnover rates, and the moderating role of HR practices', *Academy of Management Journal*, Vol.51, No.2, 259–76.

Turnbull, P. and Wass, V. (1997) 'Job insecurity and labour market lemons: the (mis)management of redundancy in steel making, coal mining, and port transport', *Journal of Management Studies*, Vol.34, No.1, 27–51.

Turnbull, P. and Wass, V. (2004) 'Job cuts and redundancy: managing the workforce complement', Paper presented at the BUIRA Annual Conference, University of Nottingham.

Tyler, M. and Wilkinson, A. (2007) 'The tyranny of corporate slenderness: "corporate anorexia" as a metaphor for our age', *Work, Employment and Society*, Vol.21, No.3, 537–49.

Van Dierendonck, D. and Jacobs, G. (2012) 'Survivors and victims, a meta-analytic review of fairness and organizational commitment after downsizing', *British Journal of Management*, Vol.23, 96–109.

Van Wanrooy, B., Bewley, H., Bryson, A., Forth, J., Freeth, S., Stokes, L. and Wood, S. (2013) *Employment Relations in the Shadow of Recession: Findings from the Workplace Employment Relations Study*, Basingstoke: Palgrave Macmillan.

Velotta, R.N. (2009) 'Airline downsizing shifts passengers to smaller regional jets', *Las Vegas Sun*. Available at: http://lasvegassun.com/news/2009/dec/04/airline-downsizing-shifts-passengers-smaller-regio/.

Wayhan, V.B., and Werner, S. (2000) 'The impact of workforce reductions on financial performance: a longitudinal perspective', *Journal of Management*, Vol.26, 341–63.

Wedderburn, D. (1965) *Redundancy and the Railwaymen*, Cambridge: Cambridge University Press.

Welch, J. (2001) *What I've Learned Leading a Great Company and Great People*, New York: Headline.

Weyer, M.V. (1994) 'The old men on the board', *Management Today*, October, 64–7.

Wilkinson, A. (2004) 'Downsizing, rightsizing and dumbsizing: quality, human resources and sustainability', *Total Quality Management*, Vol.16, Nos.8–9, 1079–88.

Worrall, L., Cooper, C. and Campbell, F. (2000) 'The impact of organisational change on UK managers' perceptions of their working lives', in Burke, R.J. and Cooper, C.L. (eds.) *The Organization in Crisis: Downsizing, Restructuring and Privatization*, Oxford: Blackwell.

Younge, G. (2005) 'New black sheriff sacks opponents', *The Guardian*, 11 January. Available at: http://www.theguardian.com/world/2005/jan/11/usa.garyyounge1

Zatzick, C.D., Marks, M.L. and Iverson, R.D. (2009) 'Which way should you downsize in a crisis?', *MIT Sloan Management Review*, Vol.51, No.1, 79–86.

CHAPTER 15

ORGANISATIONAL CHANGE AND HUMAN RESOURCE MANAGEMENT

Aoife M. McDermott and Edel Conway

Introduction

Strategic and operational changes are prevalent features of organisational life, pursued to ensure continued organisational success, and, in some cases, survival. It is therefore concerning that many scholarly contributions on organisational change open with the ominous assertion that approximately 70 per cent of change initiatives fail (Balogun and Hope Hailey, 2004; Worley and Mohrman, 2014). Others recognise that, while on average this may be the case, rates of failure (and success) vary across different types of change (e.g. cultural versus structural change, see Smith, 2002). The lack of consistent positive outcomes may be attributable to debate over the most appropriate way to implement change processes. This stems in part from the overwhelming scale of the literature, illustrated in a 2015 search of MetaLib, which returned 1,057,005 results for 'organisational change'. Debate also stems from the different perspectives taken by authors. Some adopt an analytical approach, seeking to understand what organisations and individuals actually do. Others adopt more prescriptive approaches, premised on guiding practitioners in implementing change (Burnes, 2009). Together, these factors have contributed to 'the lack of a valid framework of how to implement and manage organisational change' (By, 2005: 370). As the scale of the literature on change limits our capacity to comprehensively address all of the issues raised within it, the purpose of this chapter is threefold.

First, we introduce the nature of organisational change. Second, we explore the four cornerstones of change: drivers, processes, agents and recipients (see Figure 15.1). These cornerstones can also be considered as the 'why', 'how' and 'who' of change – with the 'who' consisting of those responsible for making change happen, and those affected by it. Considering why change occurs focuses our attention on our first cornerstone, the external and internal 'change drivers' responsible for prompting change in organisations. We note that these factors vary in urgency and force, with implications for the speed and scope of the resulting change. Considering how change occurs in organisations focuses attention on our second cornerstone, 'change processes'. We pay particular attention to seminal conceptions of planned change and trace evolution in thinking about how change occurs and how it should be managed. Our third cornerstone leads us to examine the 'change agents' who are responsible for bringing about change – including HR professionals. In our final cornerstone, we evaluate the potential responses of those who are affected by change, known as '*change recipients*', and how they can be supported. Potential responses range from readiness to resistance – and we emphasise the potential benefits of 'productive resistance'. Finally, to conclude the chapter, we explicate the role of HRM in building the organisation's capacity to manage change and respond to change-related challenges (cf. Ulrich, 1997). We summarise the specific potential roles that the HR function can adopt in supporting change programmes and the individuals designing, delivering and responding to them.

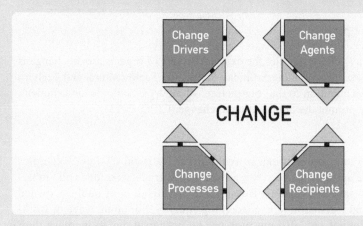

Figure 15.1
Cornerstones of change

The nature of organisational change

The basic concept of organisational change involves three ideas: (a) difference, (b) at different temporal moments, (c) between states of an organisational unit or system (Poole and Van de Ven, 2004). Ulrich (1997) identifies three forms of organisational change: *initiatives*, such as quality improvement efforts that occur regularly in many organisations and are focused on implementing new projects, programmes or procedures; *process changes* that focus on reengineering how work gets done to simplify processes and add value; and *cultural changes* that are more fundamental and premised on amending the vision and values of the organisation and how its core business is undertaken. Of course, many change processes involve a combination of all three – with culture change, process improvements and specific initiatives all drawn upon in support of overarching change goals. Using a human analogy, Ulrich (1997) suggests that culture change affects the mind and soul of an organisation; initiatives are like day-to-day nourishment, while process changes affect core bodily systems that keep the body alive (e.g. the respiratory system). Such changes can occur in a variety of ways. *Discontinuous change* occurs where rapid shifts (e.g. in strategy, structure, culture or a combination) take place, followed by periods of consolidation. However, it is often suggested that the benefits of discontinuous change do not last (By, 2009). Perceptions that a change process is 'finished' and that the associated issues have been addressed can lead to complacency – and result in further change being required in the future. This has led many authors to move away from mechanistic perceptions of change, where it is perceived as linear, disruptive, controllable and abnormal (McMillan, 2004). An alternative is *continuous change*, premised on ongoing, but still organisation-wide changes in response to external and internal drivers. A third approach is *incremental change*, which is more operationally focused, and premised on parts of the organisation dealing with smaller problems that have more limited objectives (Burnes, 2004; By, 2009). Whatever form it takes, the reasons for organisational change are many. Next we consider the first of our four change cornerstones – the external and internal drivers that explain 'why' change occurs.

First cornerstone: change drivers ('why')

External drivers of change

One of the most useful ways of considering the external drivers of organisational change is to adopt a PEST framework, incorporating *P*olitical, *E*conomic, *S*ocio-cultural and *T*echnological factors. This draws attention to the 'big picture' of an organisation's environment, including factors that may prompt the organisation to change (CIPD, 2013).

Political

Changes in the political environment can provoke organisational change. Examples include cooperative trade agreements between governments, trade sanctions and embargoes (e.g. the EU's 2014 sanctions against Russia), the privatisation of publicly owned firms (e.g. Royal Mail) and legislation (e.g. concerning equality, minimum wage or working hours). Political influence can also put pressure on organisations to increase their accountability. Examples include pressures by governments worldwide to introduce performance management systems in the public sector, such as league tables for hospitals, schools and local authorities.

Economic

The global economic environment is increasingly interconnected. The unprecedented economic crisis of 2008 resulted in government bailouts of banks worldwide as a result of reckless lending, steep rises in unemployment and a significant decrease in consumer spending (Truss *et al.*, 2012). The crisis prompted large-scale change in a variety of organisations. For example, public sector austerity measures included change programmes that radically amended employment relationships. Attempts to cut costs led to reductions in staffing levels via early retirement, substantial cuts in salaries and pensions and recruitment and promotion freezes (Giauque *et al.*, 2012; Pollitt and Bouckaert, 2011). Evidence from the UK public sector suggests that such organisational changes are linked to perceived breaches in employees' psychological contracts, which in turn are associated with lower employee contributions (Conway *et al.*, 2014).

Socio-cultural

Changes in demography and social structures have the capacity to prompt, facilitate or impede organisational change by shaping the skills, attitudes, values, expectations and behaviours available to, and within, workplaces. The ageing population, for example, has been described as perhaps *the* most defining social issue of the twenty-first century (Pitt-Catsouphes, 2007). It is estimated that people aged 65 and older will make up 28.7 per cent of the EU population by 2080, which is a substantial increase from the 2014 figure of 18.5 per cent (Eurostat, 2015). At the same time, the working age population (i.e. 15 to 64 years) is predicted to decline from its peak of 67 per cent in 2010 to 56.2 per cent in 2080. Other demographic trends prompting change include the increased participation of females in the labour force – influencing preferences for more flexible working arrangements (Senior and Swailes, 2010). There is also greater sensitivity to diversity and cultural differences given the rise in workforce mobility and diversity.

Technology

Technological change has accelerated dramatically, fuelling consumer demand and enabling information and innovation to spread across national boundaries. These developments have affected the speed and nature of work and have increased pressure on organisations to respond to competitor threats and keep pace with new technological developments. These factors have led to a focus on change as a continuous, rather than unusual, event.

Internal drivers of change

In addition to external environmental forces, internal contextual factors can prompt or shape organisational change. Examples include the appointment of a new CEO or attempts to ensure flexibility, competitiveness and longevity through the altering of human resource (HR) practices. Such internal events can lead to changes in people (workforce mix, skill levels and utilisation) and organisational processes, including strategic repositioning, cultural transformation, organisational re-structuring (including mergers and acquisitions), amendments to the manufacture of products or the provision of services, the redesign of jobs and the introduction of new technology. Changes to processes tend to affect people (though not always vice-versa), as they inevitably impact on how individuals carry out their work roles.

The force of external and internal drivers can vary, with implications for the nature, pace and scope of resultant change. For example, some changes are proactive and opportunistic (e.g. employees identify an opportunity to develop a market niche). Others are reactive and may be imposed (e.g. by law) or occur with such fast pace that they threaten a firm's viability (e.g. new technology) and require an immediate response. Other drivers are potentially threatening but slower burning, with, for example, demographic shifts prompting less urgent and radical change processes than the 2008 economic crisis and resultant austerity measures. We also note that the external and internal drivers of change can interact and are potentially iterative, such that one change driver can trigger others. For example, technology change threatens a firm's viability. This leads to the appointment of a new CEO, who attempts to change the organisation's culture to make it more dynamic, and introduces new recruitment and people management practices to support this.

Having detailed some of the reasons *why* the need for change arises, we now turn to our second cornerstone of change. We consider approaches to understanding and managing change processes, to give insight into different conceptions of *how* change takes place.

Second cornerstone: change processes ('how')

In this section we focus on our second change cornerstone, examining conceptualisations of change processes to gain insights into how they are perceived to unfold. We give a historically organised overview of the different perspectives on how change occurs, considering planned, open systems and emergent approaches to managing change processes (following By, 2005, 2009; Senior and Fleming, 2006).

1: Planned change processes

Early planned approaches

Scientific Management was one of the strongest influences on thinking about change from the late nineteenth century until the 1930s (Stickland, 1998). It considers human activity and organisation systems, including change management, as rational processes. From this perspective, the core purpose of change is to develop optimal organisational processes. It is argued that this can best be achieved by maximising individuals' behaviour through hard measurement, quantification and financial reward (Stickland, 1998). From the 1930s onwards, the Human Relations approach critiqued Scientific Management's conception of change for its over-emphasis on individuals, its one-dimensional perception of human nature (Caldwell, 2006), its neglect of external context and its failure to recognise the intangible components of organisations, such as culture (Stickland, 1998). In contrast, the Human Relations approach emphasised the need to take account of the emotional and psychological needs of workers, as well as group dynamics, in managing change (Burnes, 2009). Despite their differences, both the Scientific Management and Human Relations approaches are premised on the implementation of change without recognition of environmental dynamics, a sequential view of change and a perception that there is 'one best way' to achieve it – using rationally or psycho-socially oriented levers (Burnes, 2009; Stickland, 1998).

Organisation development

The next stage in the development of planned approaches to change was the emergence of Organisation Development (OD). This entailed an up-scaling in the scope of change, from the individual and group to organisation-wide change. OD is founded on Lewin's work on planned change (detailed later). For Beckhard (1969: 9) OD represents '*An effort (1) planned, (2) organization-wide, and (3) managed from the top, to (4) increase organization effectiveness and health through (5) planned interventions in the 'organization's processes' using behavioral-science knowledge*.' OD has a strong value base, with an orientation towards participation and consensus (Burnes, 2000). However, it has been criticised for presuming the existence of a stable environmental context (Schein, 1999) and for emphasising small-scale and incremental change (Senior and Fleming, 2006). However, from the 1980s onwards, greater attention was afforded to more radical change, prompted by an increasingly dynamic business environment (Stace and Dunphy, 1991). Burnes (2000) suggests that OD's piecemeal approach and strong orientation towards participation and consensus did not meet the needs of the market and a plethora of alternative approaches began to emerge. Burnes gives these newer approaches the broad categorisation of 'anti-OD', asserting that they embraced issues of power and politics, did not see change as straightforward and linear and instead recognised change processes as 'messy, contentious, context-dependent and open-ended' (Caldwell, 2006: viii).

Lewin's (1951) work on change processes underpinned OD, and continues to influence modern conceptions of planned change. He identified three stages in organisational change processes: unfreezing, moving and re-freezing. Unfreezing occurs when organisational members recognise that current ways of doing things are no longer useful or valid because of either new opportunities or crises. Moving is the stage where people transition to new ways of doing things. Refreezing is the stage where the change becomes embedded in practice, processes and culture (arguably to a lesser extent under 'emergent' models of change, discussed later). Lewin argued that change cannot be realised when forces in favour of the status quo outweigh those striving for change. When both are relatively equal, the status quo is not threatened because of what he termed 'quasi-stationary equilibrium'. To unfreeze established norms of behaviour, Lewin proposed that forces striving for change have to increase, or those supporting the status quo decrease – or some combination of both. He suggests that modifying forces maintaining the status quo can produce less resistance than increasing the forces for change, and will lead to a more effective change strategy.

Lewin's three-stage model of change processes has been elaborated by a number of authors. Examples include Cummings and Worley's (2001) five-stage model, Ulrich's (1998) seven-stage approach, Kotter's (1995; 1996) eight-stage approach and Burnes' (1992) nine-element approach. Figure 15.2 maps three of these prevalent change process models to Lewin (1951), to illustrate their commonality. It highlights the particular emphasis placed on unfreezing, by creating readiness for change and reducing resistance (both discussed later). The 'stage models' of planned change processes illustrated in Figure 15.2 can be helpful tools and are often used by practitioners as key success factors, or steps to be followed to ensure successful change (Cummings and Worley, 2001; Kotter, 1995). However, critics point out that these approaches are under-theorised (Buchanan, 2003), lack a

Lewin (1951)	Kotter (1995)	Cummings and Worley (2001)	Ulrich (1998)
Unfreezing	1. Establishing a sense of urgency 2. Forming a powerful guiding coalition 3. Creating a vision 4. Communicating the vision	1. Motivating change 2. Creating a vision 3. Developing political support	1. Leading change (Who is responsible?) 2. Creating a shared need (Why do it?) 3. Shaping a vision (What will it look like when we're done?)
Moving	5. Empowering others to act on the vision 6. Planning for and creating short-term wins	4. Managing the transition	4. Mobilising commitment (Who else needs to be involved?) 5. Mobilising systems and structures (How will it be institutionalised?)
Refreezing	7. Consolidating improvements and creating still more change 8. Institutionalising new approaches	5. Sustaining momentum	6. Monitoring process (How will it be measured?) 7. Making it last (How will it get started and last?)

Figure 15.2 Stage models of change processes

strong evidence base (By, 2005), fail to take account of context or culture (Fitzgerald *et al.*, 2006) and focus on planned rather than emergent change (Burnes, 2004). In addition, they are regarded as too linear because in reality change processes are less uniform and the stages may overlap in an untidy manner (Lovelady, 1984).

In considering how planned change has been conceptualised, we note transition in thinking about how change occurs – moving away from rational and linear conceptions, towards more social and iterative understandings. The next set of approaches to understanding how change occurs draw particular attention to the influence of an organisation's environment, and involve an explicit shift away from a 'one size fits all' approach to how change should be managed.

2: Open systems approaches to change processes

OD has helped to develop broad acceptance of open-systems influences on change processes (Cummings and Worley, 2001). An open system is one that is connected to, and interacts with, its environment (Open Systems Group, 1981). Accordingly, open-systems approaches to change processes emphasise the importance of environmental influences on change, the complexity and variability across different parts of organisations and the sometimes loose connections between them (Scott, 2003). The contingency and choice approaches, both examples of open-systems perspectives, are detailed below.

Since the 1960s there has been a radical shift away from a 'one best way' approach to change, leading to the emergence of contingency approaches. Contingency approaches link planned change to open-systems concepts. The contingency movement was premised on work undertaken by Lawrence and Lorsch (1967) who found that variations in the internal structures of firms were linked to their external environments. Building upon the earlier work of Burns and Stalker (1961) they proposed that organisations and their subsystems are adaptive to their environments (Jaffee, 2001). This insight led to the advent of the contingency approach, which assumes that how change should be designed and managed is influenced by organisation-specific factors such as size, strategy and technology (e.g. Miles and Snow, 1978), and also external environmental factors. The notion of 'fit' between these internal and external factors and the organisation's approach to managing change has been developed by several authors (see, for example, Stace and Dunphy, 1991), and is mirrored in the literature on HR practices.

Although the influence of the environment is recognised in the contingency approach, the dynamic nature of the environment is not. This has led to critique of the focus on planned change (Stickland, 1998), and the assumption that managers and organisations have little influence over situational variables and structures (Burnes, 1996). In contrast, the choice approach to change suggests that organisations and managers can attempt to shape their environments, and exert some influence over the approach to change that is required:

> The point is that rather than having little choice, rather than being forced to change their internal practices to fit with external variables, organisations can exercise some choice over these issues *(Burnes, 1996: 16)*.

Having established the potential influence of the environment on how change processes are designed and delivered, we turn to consider emergent approaches to managing change. This entails a shift in conceptualisation of how change occurs – from discontinuous and discrete to continuous.

3: Emergent change processes

Early approaches describe how change should be managed in ways that present it as a discrete process – with a start and end point – grounded in routine behaviours and driven from above (Beckhard, 1969). In contrast, the emergent approach to change processes advocates the need for continuous change, which emanates from the bottom of the organisation (Burnes, 2000; 2004). This approach is premised on organisations operating in dynamic environments and therefore requiring devolved and timely decision making to respond to developments. This requires readiness for change (Burnes, 1996), and the involvement of a broad range of stakeholders across levels and positions in organisations (Fitzgerald *et al.*, 2006). The dynamic nature of emergent change means that, in comparison to planned approaches to change, there is a lack of coherence and diversity in its techniques (By, 2005).

The different approaches to change discussed in this section (planned, open systems, emergent), and associated conceptions of how change processes should be managed, are summarised in Figure 15.3.

As illustrated in Figure 15.3, different approaches to understanding change processes have implications for perceptions of how change should be managed. Particular differences are evident across the approaches with regards to where change should be driven from within the organisation (top-down/bottom-up) and whether it is managed as a discrete or open-ended process. In addition, our summary has drawn attention to perceived differences in the source of change (internal/external) and the nature of change processes (linear/messy), as well as the basis on which compliance with change can be elicited (rational/psychosocial). We also note potential for the role of the HR function to vary across these approaches to delivering change – for example in whether support is oriented towards senior managers (top-down) or the broader workforce (bottom-up).

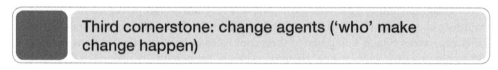

PLANNED APPROACHES TO CHANGE	OPEN SYSTEMS APPROACHES	INCREASED DYNAMISM	NEWER APPROACHES TO CHANGE
Scientific Management - Task focus - Individual orientation **Human Relations** - Group focus - Social and emotional orientation **Organisation Development** - Organisation-wide focus - Participation and consensus orientation	**Contingency approaches** - Focus on ensuring fit between the organisation's external and internal environment and its change strategy **Choice approaches** - Mitigated fit where organisation can influence situational variables and associated change strategy	Increased dynamism and competitive pressures leading to organisation change capacity **as a source of competitive advantage**	**Emergent** - Ongoing responsive change - Responsibility distributed throughout the organisation - Focus on change agents
Top-down Discontinuous Incremental	Top-down Discontinuous	**CHANGE**	Bottom-up Continuous

Figure 15.3 Summary of conceptions to change and approaches to how it should be managed

Next we consider our third cornerstone, which focuses on our first group within the 'who' of change: the change agents responsible for making it happen. In so doing, we pay particular attention to the change-agent role of HR professionals.

Third cornerstone: change agents ('who' make change happen)

Change agents are individuals (or groups of individuals), from within or outside the organisation, who champion and guide organisational members towards change. Change agency can be undertaken by a range of stakeholders including the HR function; internal or external Organisation Development consultants; strong individuals with clear vision and capacity to achieve change; or change teams/collectives dispersed throughout organisational levels (Caldwell, 2003). Early research (Ottaway, 1983) identified three categories of change agents – those who generate, implement and adopt change initiatives. More recent research has drawn attention to entrepreneurial change agents who adapt or add to planned change processes (McDermott *et al.*, 2013). Such 'adaptive' behaviour is relatively prevalent. In a study of senior staff acting as public sector change agents, Wallace *et al.* (2011) found that approximately half took responsibility for implementing government reforms, two-thirds saw a role in adapting government initiatives to fit the local context and two-thirds perceived themselves as having a role in undertaking independent change initiatives. In addition we note that change agents may take and revisit different roles during the change process (Buchanan and Storey, 1997).

The role adopted by change agents can depend, to some degree, on the nature of the change introduced. For example, major planned changes are often initially led by single change agents or 'idea champions' – typically, highly respected individuals who are willing to make the case for change, and take risks throughout the process (Kickert, 2010). On the other hand, when change is continuous, the emphasis can be less oriented towards championing the need for change and more concerned with redirecting individuals towards the changes taking place. Here, the change agent's role is concerned with managing the language and dialogue around change in order to make sense of the change and reframe it for others (Kickert, 2010; Weick and Quinn, 1999). In the case of discontinuous change, it is suggested that there is often no single change agent, but instead there may be many actors who act as a 'guiding coalition' (Kotter, 1996) and who add legitimacy to the change effort and offer emotional support to those undergoing the change (Fernandez and Rainey, 2006).

The need to deliver change and manage the ongoing work of organisations can lead to managers undertaking dual roles during change processes – i.e. undertaking their normal day-to-day managerial duties in addition to their role as change agents. A number of tensions can arise as a result (Brannick and Coghlan 2007). Often managers will not possess the required change management skills and competencies to undertake their change-related roles effectively. This may necessitate the appointment of dedicated internal change agents or external consultants who are not directly impacted by the change. A key strategic role, however, can be undertaken by the HR function and by HR professionals. They can act both as direct agents for change and as a source of support for other change agents. We now focus on important aspects of HR's change-related roles.

HR professionals as agents of change

The potential for the HR function to support and facilitate change has long been recognised. For example, Storey (1992) notes HR's role as a change-maker, assisting with the development of corporate and HR strategy. However, a broader change agency role is emphasised within Ulrich's (1997) identification of the four roles of the HR function, namely acting as an administrative expert, employee champion, strategic partner and change agent. Here the change agent role is more expansively defined as helping the organisation to adapt to new conditions. One survey of 1,200 HR managers found that over half perceived their primary role in the future as being a 'strategic partner', almost a third saw themselves as being change agents, less than five per cent perceived themselves as administrative experts in the future, and few individuals perceived themselves as employee champions (CIPD HR Survey Report, 2003). Thus HR professionals perceive the change agent role as being one of their core roles in helping organisations, managers and employees to deliver change. HR professionals can potentially undertake four change agency roles (Ulrich, 1997). First, by acting as a *catalyst* and *champion* of change, they ensure that change is part of management discussions, is integrated into formal and informal organisational agendas, and informs decision making across levels in the organisation. In support of this, Ulrich (1997) provides a set of profiling questions (premised on key success factors across the stages of change) that HR can use to diagnose the likelihood of successful change, gaps and potential supporting interventions. The second HR change agency role is acting as a *facilitator*, helping external consultants, or working internally, to create space for discussing the need for change, developing and implementing the content of the change process(es), and working with managers to develop their change management skills. Third, HR can undertake a *designer* role, focused on redesigning HR practices to support and reward the new circumstances. Last is the *demonstrator* role, where HR professionals undertake change within their own function and/or work alongside other managers to deliver change. Thus HR practitioners have potential roles across the unfreezing, moving and refreezing stages of change.

Ulrich and Brockbank (2005) later amended their description of HR's roles, such that the change agent role became subsumed within the strategic partner role. The strategic partner role is characterised as helping line managers at all levels reach their goals, by acting as a business expert, knowledge manager, consultant and change agent (Ulrich and Brockbank, 2005). Rather than de-emphasising the change agency role of HR, this typology draws attention to the need for HR to perform the role of strategic partner in conjunction with its change agent role. For Ulrich and Brockbank (2005), HR creates value by helping managers and employees, as well as external stakeholders, respond to drivers of change: identifying and delivering strategic priorities through effective change processes. This focus on HR's value creation is important. Wylie *et al.* (2014: 107) note that while change agency has been perceived as a way to reduce the occupational vulnerability of HRM, 'the prospects for HR change agency crucially depend upon the ability to demonstrate a distinctive and valued contribution'. However, the change agent role of the HR function and HR professionals is not uncontested. Some suggest that HR struggles to enact its change agency role because of scepticism among colleagues and the low status of the function (Roche and Teague, 2012; Wylie *et al.*, 2014). To successfully act as strategic partners and change agents, HR professionals need to build high-quality relationships with key organisational actors, which may be enhanced by the provision of dedicated HR support to management subunits (see Box 15.1). This can improve HR's awareness of service realities, enable the provision of tailored local support, and strengthen communication between management units and the central HR function (McDermott *et al.*, 2015). Guest and King (2004) also suggest that attracting professionals with generic managerial rather than pure people management backgrounds may enhance HR's change capacity by ensuring that change agents understand organisational processes *and* people.

In particular, it is the people element of change that is often overlooked. In this regard, HR can provide particular supports – to both managers purveying the change and employees at the receiving end of it – to deal with the challenges of creating readiness and countering resistance. Next we turn our attention to our fourth cornerstone, concerned with change recipients who are affected by change processes, and how they can be supported.

Box 15.1 HRM in practice   HR as change agent

Patricia Jenkins (pseudonym) was Head of Workforce and Organisation Development (WOD) for a Health Board division from 2013 to 2014. The role had an explicit focus on organisation development and change and included identifying: 'What is our future direction here?' and 'What is it about our workforce that will enable us, or put barriers in place, to delivering our change agenda?' Patricia had to develop strategies to address these challenges. Prior to taking the role, Patricia had undertaken workforce planning for the division and so was familiar with the day-to-day operations, challenges, and key actors in her area of work. This afforded her early credibility with colleagues. Specifically, she noted that she had been 'on the journey with them since the very early days'.

The change programme she was supporting included system redesign and brought people from different organisations together (e.g. the health board, local authorities and voluntary organisations) to help avoid unnecessary (re)hospitalisation of patients who could be supported closer to home. The HR challenge included generating an integrated workforce plan; considering how to support staff working across different organisations (including how to manage, align and sometimes gain acceptance of variation in hours of work and pay scales for similar jobs); understanding how and why team members from each organisations might do things differently and creating a shared team identity.

Interventions included structural changes (including to lines of reporting) and co-location of staff; managing culture change including amendments to HR practices; and efforts to actively promote involvement and engagement among employees, including employee representatives, through enhanced utilisation of traditional HR practices (such as appraisal), as well as additional targeted interventions. Team development was a particular focus. This included getting team members to map out their different stakeholders, leading to the identification of more than thirty different audiences for their work. This acted as a precursor to some vision-oriented work, to provide space to elaborate differences and develop a shared focus and common aims across the organisations and drawing pictures to discuss personal feelings and challenges in moving towards integrated working. It was noted that getting the teams to tell their stories was really helpful as it allowed people to acknowledge that, while personally challenging, the integration was the right way forward. Directors from participating organisations created a video to show commonality in their goals. The focus on supporting the patient emerged as a shared mobilising goal 'so there was a bit about getting people to articulate that the patient was what was important'. Patricia and the project manager believed that the provision of personal and social support for those involved in the change was an ongoing role, with attention needed to seemingly minor actions and behaviours – such as ensuring that birthday celebrations (and cake!) were shared with everyone. In addition, they worked with unions and developed joint publications and newsletters, to ensure evidence of progress. Patricia regarded her role as being 'about supporting, getting people talking, visioning what are the actions we need to take and . . . the behaviours we should see'. She also entered their work into competitions to give profile and recognition to employees' efforts, 'That's what it's about really, people being able to see the change and talk about it.' Next steps include addressing IT integration, continued investment in culturally embedding new ways of working, identifying duplication in roles, and undertaking process mapping to simplify the patient journey through the system. In reflecting on progress to date, Patricia noted that 'we did champion that piece of work really' – supporting managers and employees, and sometimes asking hard questions. However, she recognised that while the change process had progressed, it wasn't yet over.

Source: Anonymised interviews.

To consider: Which of Ulrich's (1997) four HR change agency roles (catalyst and champion; facilitator; designer; demonstrator) has Patricia undertaken?

Fourth cornerstone: change recipients ('who' is affected by change and how they can be supported?)

Reports about the high levels of failed change initiatives have given rise to some criticism regarding the perceived neglect of individual employees' reactions to change (Bartunek *et al.*, 2006; Judge *et al.*, 1999). Change recipients can display affective, cognitive and behavioural reactions that have implications for change (Oreg *et al.*, 2011). Behavioural reactions can include acceptance/compliance (Iverson, 1996), ambivalence (Piderit, 2000) and resistance (Oreg *et al.*, 2011). Here we consider how managers create preparedness for change, as well as conceptualisations of resistance and how it might be managed. We note a shift away from demonising resistance-oriented responses of change recipients, towards increasing recognition of its potential benefits (Ford *et al.*, 2008).

Creating preparedness for change: attitudinal and behavioural perspectives

Researchers have sought to better understand the people-related factors that will increase the likelihood of successful change (Rafferty *et al.*, 2013). While research has historically focused on resistance, regarded as the predominant response from employees (Sonenshein and Dholakia, 2012), an alternative wave of studies have emerged which view employees as adaptable and capable of being open to and accepting of change (e.g. Herold *et al.*, 2007). For example, studies investigating the manageability of change consider attitudes such as openness to or readiness for change, while those adopting a behavioural approach focus on reactions such as individuals' ability to cope or their commitment to change. A summary of definitions that describe these perspectives is provided in Table 15.1.

Table 15.1 Preparedness for change: attitudinal and behavioural perspectives

Focus	Definition
Readiness for change	an individual's 'beliefs, attitudes, and intentions regarding the extent to which changes are needed and the organisation's capacity to successfully undertake those changes' (Armenakis *et al.*, 1993: 681).
Openness to change	'positive affect about the positive consequences of change' (Miller *et al.*, 1994: 60).
Commitment to change	'a mindset that binds an individual to a course of action deemed necessary for the successful implementation of a change initiative' (Herscovitch and Meyer, 2002: 475). This mindset can take different forms: (1) a desire to provide support for the change based on a belief in its inherent benefits (affective commitment to change); (2) a recognition that there are costs associated with failure to provide support for the change (continuance commitment to change) and (3) a sense of obligation to provide support for the change (normative commitment to change).
Coping (with change)	'cognitive and behavioral efforts to deal with experiences that tax or exceed one's resources' (Folkman *et al.*, 1986: 993).

Armenakis and Harris (2002) propose that readiness for change comprises two cognitive components: (1) a belief that change is necessary and (2) a belief that the individual and organisation have the capacity to implement the change. They propose that readiness also incorporates the following beliefs: that there is a perceived discrepancy which makes the change necessary; that the proposed change is appropriate to fix the discrepancy; that any communications about the change promote a sense of efficacy or capability to implement the change; that there is support and resources available from principals (i.e. the organisation, managers); and that individuals assess the valence of the change in terms of their job or role which will influence their overall assessment of the change. Some individuals adapt more readily to change than others. For example, personality factors such as internal locus of control, openness to experience and a willingness to take risks are positively associated with change (Holt *et al.*, 2007; Judge *et al.*, 1999). In addition, personal resources such as general self-efficacy are positively linked to coping with change (Herold *et al.*, 2007; Holt *et al.*, 2007; Hornung and Rousseau, 2007; Judge *et al.*, 1999), and individuals who feel that they can cope with change are better equipped to make positive contributions to change processes (Cunningham, 2006). From a HRM perspective, selection processes that take into account such individual characteristics should give rise to a more adaptable workforce.

For Cummings and Worley (2001), explaining pressures for change, revealing discrepancies between the current and desired states and conveying credible positive expectations can produce sufficient dissatisfaction to create readiness for change. This is underpinned by recognition that the greater the dissatisfaction with the current situation, the greater the motivation to change. Others focus on dialogue and suggest that change results from the negotiation of meaning (Coghlan and McAuliffe, 2003; Thomas *et al.*, 2011). Some even suggest that talking in a negative way can be helpful, as it keeps the change on the agenda and allows for clarification and development (Ford *et al.*, 2008). Readiness for change is therefore facilitated by an environment supporting information and communication (Armenakis *et al.*, 2007; Holt *et al.*, 2007). These measures will influence employees' perceptions of the rationale for the change, which should give rise to personal acceptance of the need for change and better coping (Goodman and Truss, 2004). Overall, research linking change processes to change outcomes have consistently shown that high levels of participation and support, open communication, competent management and an overall sense of fairness in change implementation can influence positive reactions towards the change (Axtell *et al.*, 2002; Conway and Monks, 2008; Oreg *et al.*, 2011). It is further suggested that, when personal and organisational benefits are expected, greater readiness and commitment tends to develop (Kotter, 1996; Oreg *et al.*, 2011). However, as change is an emotional as well as a rational process, resistance to change is a natural phenomenon (Coghlan, 1993) and an integral part of change processes (Lewin, 1951). As a consequence, we consider it in our next section.

Managing resistance to change

Tichy (1983) identifies different forms of resistance at the organisational level. Technical resistance to change is based on beliefs about sunk costs in the status quo, and an unwillingness to change habitual procedures. Political resistance occurs when organisational changes threaten powerful stakeholders, such as high-ranking staff. Finally, cultural resistance can take the form of norms of behaviour and values that support the status quo. At the individual level, Kotter and Schlesinger (2008) identify four common reasons why individuals resist change. One such driver of resistance is the desire not to lose something of value. *Conservation of Resources* (COR) theory posits that individuals are motivated to gain resources in order to protect themselves against potential threat or loss (Hobfoll, 1989). According to Halbesleben *et al.* (2014), such resources can be condition-based in the form of job security, or constructive in the form of opportunities for development, supervisor support and resilience. Additional reasons for resistance include a misunderstanding of the change and its implications, a belief that the change does not make sense for the organisation and a low personal tolerance for change (Kotter and Schlesinger, 2008). Kotter and Schlesinger (2008) identify a range of strategies to manage resistance, and detail when they are appropriate. We consider these, together with related approaches identified by others, below.

Education and communication

Communication can decrease employees' anxiety and uncertainty (Ashford, 1988), especially when resistance is based on inadequate or inaccurate information (Kotter and Schlesinger, 2008). Communicating the rationale for change can therefore be helpful (Armenakis *et al.*, 1993), particularly when messages are made compelling by their links to contextual knowledge (Dutton *et al.*, 2001). Kotter and Schlesinger (2008) suggest, however, that change agents should be careful not to misrepresent the benefits of change in order to manage expectations and maintain their own credibility throughout the change process (Folger and Skarlicki, 1999; Ford *et al.*, 2008). Last, we note that as education and communication require significant time and effort, they may not be suitable when there is a lack of time and/or resources (Kotter and Schlesinger, 2008).

Participation and involvement

Involving those whom the change will affect in the change process can often prevent resistance and increase perceived readiness for change because it will create a sense of contribution and control (Armenakis and Bedeian, 1999). It can also increase the quality of the change, as employees' tacit knowledge is harnessed and used. Thus change agents need to differentiate between critical questioning and resistance. Scrutiny can help employees make sense of, and develop support for, the change (Knowles and Linn, 2004). See Dundon and Wilkinson, Chapter 16, in this volume for further information on the benefits of participation and involvement, and how they can be managed.

Facilitation and support

Being supportive can take a variety of forms. Potential interventions can include informal support from line managers, who shape employees' perceptions of their work experiences (Gerstner and Day, 1997). Alternatively, more formal interventions accessed through the HR function include job rotation, skills updates, counselling or time off. Kotter and Schlesinger (2008) suggest that such interventions are most helpful when anxiety or fear underpins employees' responses to change. However, they caution that facilitation and support can be time consuming and expensive, and may not allay employee concerns.

Negotiation and agreement

Negotiation entails offering incentives to active or potential resistors. Kotter and Schlesinger (2008) suggest that it is appropriate when stakeholders have significant capacity to impede the change process (deriving from position, influence or knowledge), and when they will be negatively affected by the change. Negotiation can be undertaken with individuals or groups (e.g. unions, or a specific set of workers such as engineers). However, scope for 'knock-on' attempts at negotiation cause Kotter and Schlesinger (2008) to deem negotiated agreements an effective, but potentially expensive way to avoid resistance.

Political approaches to managing resistance

Kotter and Schlesinger (2008) draw attention to two political strategies (manipulation and co-option) for managing resistance. This is important as the political dimensions of change are often overlooked – despite many managers perceiving political behaviour as a necessary part of their role (Buchanan, 2008; Gandz and Murray, 1980). Change agents need to be politically astute and be able to identify relevant stakeholders and power dynamics, and have political skills to influence them (Buchanan, 2008). Manipulation is a covert form of influence that aims to change the perception and behaviour of others through the way information or scenarios are presented. Co-option is a form of manipulation that involves giving a potential source of resistance a place in the design or implementation of change. However, it is their endorsement of the change, rather than participation in the process, that is sought (Kotter and Schlesinger, 2008). Additional political tactics may include developing powerful coalitions, making friends with power brokers, developing a powerful image, creating obligations, bending the rules and self-promotion (Buchanan, 2008; Gandz and Murray, 1980). Although political tactics can back-fire if actors feel they are being 'tricked' or 'used', Kotter and Schlesinger (2008) note that managers do use such approaches successfully, particularly when other tactics have failed or are not feasible.

The final strategy for managing resistance identified by Kotter and Schlesinger is an extreme form of political behaviour: *explicit* and *implicit coercion*. Coercion entails forcing people to accept a change by implicitly or explicitly threatening them, e.g. regarding their job security or promotion prospects. Coercion can entail the use of unsavoury tactics including misinformation, spreading rumours, blaming others, marginalising resisters and keeping 'dirt' files for blackmail (Buchanan, 2008).

Much attention has understandably been afforded to managing the resistance of change recipients. However, next we note recent shifts to move from managing to celebrating resistance to change.

From managing to celebrating resistance

There has been a recent and important shift in the literature from viewing resistance as a negative response, to something that can add value to a change process (Ford *et al.*, 2008; Piderit, 2000; Thomas *et al.*, 2011). Dent and Goldberg (1999: 26) suggest dispensing with the term 'resistance' and finding a phrase that reflects employees' failure to 'wholeheartedly embrace a change that management wants to implement'.

'Productive resistance' is premised on enabling change recipients to add value to change processes through conceptual expansion, innovation and the generation of new knowledge. From this perspective, deriving benefit from resistance depends on change recipients making counter-offers to the change agenda and change agents making reciprocal accommodations, leading to negotiated improvements (Thomas and Hardy, 2011). However, even this more progressive view ignores the possibility that change agents may themselves be resistant to the ideas, proposals and counter-offers submitted by change recipients (Ford *et al.*, 2008). There is particular potential for this when change recipients indicate that greater effort than originally envisaged will be required to achieve the change (Ford *et al.* 2008). Some authors note the theoretical tension created by considering behaviours beyond change acceptance as 'resistance', while simultaneously noting the need for change recipients to engage in translation and tailoring to enhance the likelihood of success (McDermott *et al.*, 2013). Next, having considered why change occurs, how change processes unfold and the actors who are involved in initiating, implementing and influencing them, we summarise the role of HR in supporting change processes, agents and recipients in more detail.

HR's role in change management

In this closing section of the chapter we summarise HR's potential roles in building organisational capacity for change, and responding to change-related challenges (cf. Ulrich, 1997). Reflecting the structure of our chapter, and as illustrated in Figure 15.4, we note potential for HR to help develop responses to change drivers, to have input into the design and delivery of change processes, to ensure the development of change agents and to support change recipients. Importantly, as previously noted, this means that HR has potential both to act as a direct agent of change and to support other change agents. However, we also note that, despite the significant rhetoric regarding the involvement of the HR function in managing the day-to-day practice of change, there is limited evidence of this occurring in a consistent and sustained way in reality (Alfes et al., 2010). As a consequence, Figure 15.5 summarises specific potential HR roles discussed within the chapter. These are organised across the unfreezing, moving and refreezing (Lewin, 1951) phases of change (although we recognise that these will be iterative). We also note roles that are likely to be ongoing.

In responding to change drivers and managing change processes, we note the potential combination of HR's strategic partner and change agent roles, reflected in the potential for input into the unfreezing, moving and refreezing stages of change.

In supporting change agents, we particularly note the importance of the selection and support of change agents to avoid individuals floundering in roles for which they feel

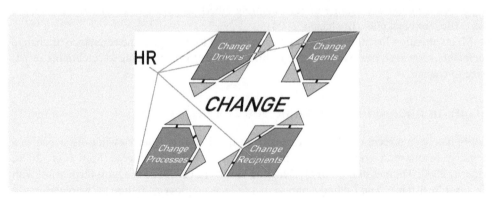

Figure 15.4 HR's role in supporting change

Potential HR contribution	Change drivers/ Change processes	Change agents	Change recipients
Unfreezing- creating readiness and preparedness for change	- Diagnosing problems/ challenges/opportunities - Embedding change in management agendas across the organisation - Developing a change strategy to adapt to new conditions - Informing, communicating and consulting with employees and employee representatives - Identifying key stakeholders and opinion leaders	- Training in building evidence-based skills for improvement - Supporting the development of material for information and consultation sessions - Providing communications training - Selecting change agents for skills, knowledge, aspirations and resilience	- Selecting employees capable of coping with change - Facilitating information, communication and consultation sessions
Moving - supporting the transition	- Using change tools to diagnose the likelihood of successful change, gaps and supporting interventions - Identifying workforce implications and appropriate supports - Developing specific interventions to deliver change - Identifying and responding to problems in the change process	- Helping to generate change-related skills, e.g. training in improvement methods - Providing change resources - Establishing of peer networks to support and spread change	- Hosting workshops to identify implications of the change for individuals and their roles - Training in new ways of doing things - Counselling - Outplacement support where required
Refreezing - helping to embed to practice	- Celebrating and promoting improvements - Recognising those involved in delivering change - Embedding structural changes and new lines of reporting - Redesigning HR processes and practices to support new status quo	- Supporting managers across levels and identifying implications of the new status quo for policies and practices	- Providing local evidence of the benefit of the change
Ongoing change - related roles	- Process mapping - Analytics to generate evidence of impact	- Support in managing workload and stress - Career and succession planning	- Support in managing workload and stress - Career planning support

Figure 15.5 Potential HR roles in change

insufficiently prepared. Change agents require a broad range of competencies including diagnostic and analytic capacity, interpersonal and communication skills, political awareness, facilitation skills, technical skills and insight (Keep, 2001). Selection can pay attention to such skills and knowledge as well as 'aspirations, resilience and adaptability' (Buchanan, 2003: 681). Systematic support, training and development and recognition are also required for individuals holding change roles (Buchanan, 2003). Further, there is potential for HR to support career planning. Buchanan (2003) notes that acting as a change agent can help individuals to develop organisational knowledge, as well as their skill set, and may provide a platform for career progression. There is also potential for HR to identify the implications of the new status quo for managerial policies and practice.

In addition to change agents requiring support because of new roles associated with making change happen, some employees may require training to enable them to develop new skills, attitudes and behaviours associated with new ways of working (Hayes, 2002). HR has a potentially ongoing role in monitoring evidence of a need for training, and deciding the level (individual, group, organisation) where this is required. In addition, as previously noted, HR may assist in supporting workers as they learn to adapt during the transition, and communicate the ongoing benefits of change, to ensure that it is sustained over time.

Conclusions

This chapter has discussed the nature of organisational change. It has also identified the four cornerstones of change, and given a succinct overview of the 'why', 'how' and 'who' of change, the reasons change occurs, conceptions of and approaches to managing change processes, the roles adopted by those responsible for delivering change and approaches to managing and supporting those affected by it. It has also noted the potential roles of the HR function and HR professionals in supporting and delivering change. In evaluating the future of organisational change management, we note that in the 1980s, the field was critiqued for having 'an unfortunate state of affairs where the waxing and waning of organisational improvement remedies are associated with limited understanding about what works and what does not and why' (Tichy, 1983: 363). Barends *et al.*'s (2013) review suggests that this remains a problem for organisational change management. However, if there is a growing consensus in the literature, it is around the need to develop and harness the full change capability of organisations and their employees. We have demonstrated the potential (and only partially exploited) contribution of the HR function and HR professionals in achieving this.

CASE STUDY 15.1

THE CARDIOLOGIST'S TALE: AN INSIDE ACCOUNT OF CHANGE LEADERSHIP

DAVID A BUCHANAN

Acknowledgements

The research underpinning this case study was funded by a grant from The Thurnham Legacy, administered by Cranfield University School of Management. As well as expressing gratitude for that funding, the author thanks the consultant cardiologist on whom this case is based, and the many other members of staff who contributed their time and shared their experiences of change, making this case account possible.

Orientation

'It is not enough for a clinician to act as a practitioner in their own discipline. They must act as partners to their colleagues, accepting shared accountability for the service provided to their patients. They are also expected to offer leadership and to work with others to change systems when it is necessary for the benefit of patients' *(Academy of Medical Royal Colleges, 2010)*.

This case records the experience of a consultant cardiologist who, as head of service, led a series of improvements to the Norwood Hospital cardiology department in 2011/12. The Cardiac Services Redesign Project produced benefits for patients, staff and the hospital as a whole, and the cardiologist won a national award. How did he achieve these successful outcomes?

Norwood was formed in 2006 by a merger of the city's two hospitals, City North and West Suburbs. Norwood had 14,000 staff, and an annual income of £760 million, caring for a population of one million. Cardiac services were provided on both campuses. There were 12 consultant cardiologists, with a cardiac assessment team that included a specialist registrar and cardiac nurses. The service had 46 beds, four cardiac catheter laboratories, inpatient echocardiography facilities, two surgical theatres, and dedicated intensive care units. The service saw around 5,000 new patients a year, and had over 12,000 follow-ups. The service had a history of improvement and change predating the merger. Achievements in the first year of this project included:

- cath lab sessions produced twice as many angiograms as before;
- the number of cath lab sessions cancelled was reduced from 27 to 5 a year;
- length of stay for patients with acute coronary syndrome was reduced from 7 to 5 days;
- specialist nurses were empowered to make triage and transfer decisions;
- the number of inpatients getting an echocardiograph within 24 hours of referral rose from 68 per cent to 90 per cent at City North, and from 82 per cent to 94 per cent at West Suburbs.

How did you become a change leader?

I joined West Suburbs in 1999 and was clinical lead from 2005 to 2006. When the hospitals merged, there was myself and the clinical lead at City North. We were interviewed for the post of head of cardiology in 2007, and I was appointed. I did that for five years, stepping down in 2012. My role involved introducing national guidelines into a general medical environment rather than a cardiology one. I was to facilitate the merger process for two to three years, and then develop the service. Once we had relocated, and dealt with the personality issues, we looked at inefficiencies in the department, hence the Cardiac Services Redesign Project.

We had a presentation from the emergency department (ED), who had done some work with the corporate transformation team. They were positive about it, so I put us forward as a department which could benefit from support. For me, it was a case of having formal administrative support to develop ideas. One of the problems was that, in addition to working as a clinician, I would be organising, going to meetings, taking on board ideas – but often being a bit ineffective in terms of finishing those tasks, partly because of time. And that's what the project gave me.

What problems did you want to solve?

We had an inefficient service. We had sessions available, but the whole team weren't available at the same times. You might have the nurses available but not the doctors and vice versa. You are in a perverse situation where waiting times are high, and you have to incentivise doctors and others to do an out-of-hours 'initiative list', to reduce the waiting list. So we had the space and the people to do the procedures, but there was no coordination between the different groups.

The system was organised around the doctors, not around the patient. It fitted with their timetables. When they turned up, things got done, and when they didn't – they didn't. The catheter list was supposed to start at nine, but they might arrive at quarter to ten because they had been in a meeting, or they dropped a child off at school. Nobody could do anything until they arrived. Lists were cancelled. The doctor was allowed, the day or the week before, to say, 'I'm not here next Wednesday'. And a nurse would contact patients to say, 'Sorry, we've had to cancel your procedure.' This behaviour was unacceptable. But there was frustration that 'we can't do anything about it because they are consultants'.

The non-medical staff were enthusiastic to put this right. I became their mouthpiece, sitting with colleagues and challenging their behaviour, gently. If you are going to challenge a consultant, your facts have to be watertight. As a group, they challenge the data; that's what you are taught in medical school – is it credible, is it relevant? And if you say, 'this is happening', they say 'I don't believe the data', 'this wasn't my patient', 'I wasn't there', 'how did you collect the data?' Finally, when you have worked through that, they'll say, 'that might be the case for ED, but not for us'.

The service redesign was about publishing the inefficiencies, and then the efficiencies as they developed. Because we had robust data, you could show it was getting better, and people were feeling better because they were doing their jobs better. The nurse turnaround time was getting better. The physiology was getting better. The number of unmanned sessions started to fall. Savings appeared. Productivity was rewarded. The harder we worked, the more we got. When I went back for resources, they'd say yes. I was able to go to staff and say, 'Remember the last time we did this, we got that machine – we can get another one.'

Why did you accept this position?

The service is relatively young. I had seen very good practice at other hospitals. Norwood had a history of warring trusts, led by two senior consultants who didn't get on, and their departments were kept separate, with suspicion on either side. It was by accident rather than design, but I found that, when I became clinical lead at West Suburbs, I achieved quite a lot within five years. The service was transformed. I enjoyed that power, being able to do that. Not power in being able to tell people what to do, but I enjoyed the interface with GPs and commissioners and trust executives saying, this is what we want to do. And the game you had to play to convince people of your service.

I was driven by the fact that the service for patients could be better, and that one way of achieving that was for me to be involved. The only way to make it better was for it to be multidisciplinary rather than just the doctors changing the way they worked, or the nurses or whatever. It was critical that everybody came on board, and I felt that I was in as strong a position to do that as anybody else. I had a senior colleague, who I have a lot of respect for, but he is more distant and hierarchical. I know from the conversations that I've had with others that there is an element of fear towards him, which I thought would not be positive in encouraging change.

I put myself forward because I thought I could do it, and do it well, and if you do it yourself, the service reflects your personality. I think I was well placed because I've done a lot of work in primary care setting up services and secondary care services. I have worked in tertiary care elsewhere. This role was to join primary, secondary and tertiary care across two trusts. Clinical leads often underestimate the amount of time that the managerial stuff will take. I think that grinds down some clinical managers because they don't have allocated, dedicated, protected time to deliver the role.

Can you describe your management style?

I have been on courses, but I haven't had any formal management training. It was learning on the job. My style is quite democratic, and I'm inclusive, not just doctor-orientated from a team approach. The service that I developed at West Suburbs was working with the nurses, the physiologists, and the doctors. Although there is a professional gap between doctors and others, I try not to have a hierarchy. I don't work well with that. I think that was advantageous. With the merger, I wasn't just merging the doctors – I was merging the nurses and the physiologists. When I realised that the doctors could be a block, it was a strategic decision on my part to merge the technicians and the nursing staff, who I had more managerial clout with. Once those disciplines came together, it was a natural progression that the doctors – to varying degrees – would come in to line.

The crux was putting in place a mechanism that allowed us to monitor everybody's behaviour. We measured everything, from the time that the patient arrived – is the patient turning up at a responsible time, when they're supposed to be here? The time for the nurse to assess the patient and sort out the investigations. The time for the porter to take the patient to where they are supposed to be. The time for the procedure, for the nurses to get the patient ready, and the doctor doing it and the aftercare. So we had all of that logged, and when I was confident it was accurate, we went public with the data.

My weakness, which I've never got to grips with – I'm not good at confrontation. There were times when taking a sterner approach would have been quicker and more efficient. But if I face an obstacle, I'll often go round it in preference to trying to smash it. There are some who go for the hard line confrontation, but . . . it's knowing when to fight the right battles. It hasn't caused a problem to date, but if I was in higher management and there was a big problem that needed me to confront somebody direct – how good would I be at it?

The thing that has fascinated me about the management process has been how much power a small group of difficult consultants can have in preventing change. It's out of proportion to the power that they ought to be able to wield. When I was first appointed as a consultant, I thought that they were all honourable men and women with a vocation and patients came first. Over time I've realised that they're human beings like everybody else, but sadly there maybe 20 to 25 per cent who are driven by other reasons – financial gain or self-interest. Most of the service operates on goodwill, the vocation, the honourable men and women, but I am alarmed at the proportion who I wouldn't categorise in that regard. That frustrates me about management in the NHS because I think that if I were chief executive of a company and I had a difficult colleague, I'd simply arrange for them to leave. But we don't have that in medicine. In some ways that's helpful, but in some ways it's not.

What challenges did you face?

I knew that within the group of 12, there would be two or three who were under-performing. But I didn't challenge them, at first. I just published the data so that every member of staff could see it. It was on a board. Everybody was emailed. We had a weekly report, published by the cath lab manager. I set up a weekly meeting with all the relevant staff; there was one medical representative but the others were from the supporting disciplines – reviewing the previous week's work to say, this is what we did, and ask is the data we collected believable before it went public.

We also organised the system six weeks in advance because if you are going to change clinics and book people in for procedures you needed a six-week time lag. People who are not performing or not turning up for their allocated sessions, the explanations they would give were, 'I didn't know about it', or 'I booked it off as leave, the secretary forgot to make a note'. We took that away by saying, 'Look, six weeks in advance, you are now locked in to this activity, ok? And unless we have a request or evidence that activity is going ahead, and if you cancel that activity, unless it's the death of a family member or something like that, it goes ahead and it's your responsibility.'

Previously, the doctor would just tell the secretary or the nurse and they would fix it. Whereas we transferred the responsibility to the consultants saying, 'look, you can still have the staff do this for you, but it's up to you to organise it and get somebody else to cover'.

'One minute they wanted to improve the performance of the cath labs and the next day they cancelled activity so that we could meet on a Monday morning. But this proved important as we wouldn't have been able to achieve as much in such a space of time otherwise. Consultants, nurses, healthcare assistants, physiologists, ward staff and radiologists got involved and it has been really effective to make a decision together and then implement it.' *(Cath lab nurse)*

We said look, this is so important, we are cancelling the activity for the morning, and we want people to attend. I spoke to the line managers and said we must have everybody here because this is what we're trying to do. And there was the usual row of consultants, arms folded, what's this all about, and various ripples of

enthusiasm as you worked your way back. There were eyes rolling as if to say, it's all very well talking about this, but a lot of it isn't achievable. We fed back on the project later, and even our consultant colleagues recognised that it had achieved something. But that was because we published their efficiency data, so it was also a reflection on them.

It proved difficult to get the time for the weekly meeting, so I cancelled a quarter of one of my sessions so that the staff could be available to come along. It was a lab session, just an hour a week first thing on a Monday morning, we would meet and then I would start my clinical work at ten. And because it was first thing on a Monday, it worked. I think staff engagement is all about making time. Often you get the response, 'Oh we've not got time to do it.' But if you explain, hang on a minute, half an hour spent doing this could save you several hours during the week, it's worth it. I think middle management in particular came to accept that, and their attendance at meetings was good.

'We stopped cath lab activity. We had sessions in the coffee room. We ordered food, and we had all-day sessions on Fridays for two weeks. I went round the wards, I went over to West Suburbs and I badgered people asking them: what do you think, what's wrong? The cath lab work was losing money, and if we carried on, we would end up in dire financial straits, and we might end up losing services and staff. So we asked, what are the issues? And we must have had two or three hundred post-its, we had emails – there was nobody backward about coming forward. And what they were saying was all true. But when we did the process mapping, we could see that it wasn't working. It took us six months to get that right. This indicates how staff had taken ownership of the process.' *(Cardiac nurse practitioner and project lead)*

And people who you had no idea had the skills came to the fore; care assistants, porters who, in their own way, were bright people with a lot to contribute. We had a guy who helped us with the collection and display of the data. He's a booking clerk, but was interested in programming and data and displays. He was fantastic. He was a real enthusiast, and he came from nowhere.

What part did organisation politics play?

I'm usually good at sussing out where people are coming from and their personalities and agendas. From that point of view, I was suited to this process.

When I took on this role, we had colleagues who were less willing to change. If I challenged them, the rest of the group would come to their support. However, over time, as others became involved, they became more isolated. So I didn't have to deal with them anymore because others would be doing it for me, which was gratifying. One colleague felt that I just had it all wrong. His view was that the new cardiac centre was a medical facility for the consultants. He said, 'You can't manage a high quality service by asking the cleaner what you should do.' I said, 'Well, I may not ask the cleaner for medical advice, but I might ask the cleaner for advice about what's the best position to put this equipment.'

You have to be able to persuade colleagues to support your service. I saw colleagues trying to get funding by saying, 'We're the best service in the trust, so you have to invest in us, and we will be even better.' And whenever they were asked for help, they would define themselves as a specialist group who needed to be treated differently. But the group that they were applying to for resources was the general pool of other doctors. The emergency department had problems with waiting times. Patients come into ED, they are dealt with by ED, then dealt with by the general on-call doctors and then by specialists. Some specialists took the view that, 'We're specialists and this isn't our problem.' But for me, actually, we're all part of this organisation, and if we as a specialist group show that we can engage with the front door, and support that part of the service, then my proposals are more likely to be supported because I've made friends in ED. And that's what happened.

I also had credibility because I was out and about in the hospital. On a Thursday I might be seeing patients as a cardiologist, and then on a Friday I'd be talking to them in a meeting about support for the development of the department. That wasn't being underhand, to see patients and deal with them well because I wanted to get them to support the department the following day. But that helped.

Most doctors are competitive beasts. You turn it into a competition, and they'll respond. They don't want to be bottom of the class, not doing enough procedures or not turning up. Those who were underperforming would know, but it became a reality for them when it was there in colour, bar charts, documentation. So we then saw behavioural change in those individuals. Out of the twelve, I had two or three close allies who . . . whatever I asked, they would do. And then I had three or four who needed more convincing. Then I had the two or three who were much more resistant. I had the very senior guy who always had to say no first. He would eventually agree, but never straight away. You always had to go through a bit of a charade. I knew that he'd say yes. But you felt like saying, 'Look, I know in two months' time you are going to say this is a great idea, so why don't you just say it's a great idea now?'

Why did you step down?

It was a busy full-on management role. Not mental stress, but physical. Having done my stint, I was tired, and needed a break. The other reason for stepping down . . . appointed to a managerial post as a young consultant, you are still developing clinically. And in cardiology, the field changes quite quickly. I was appointing junior colleagues who could undertake procedures that I was missing out on in terms of my own development. Had I decided that I was going to be a full-time clinical manager that wouldn't have been a problem, but I hadn't made that decision, and I stepped down.

I had one particularly difficult colleague. It was never meant to be personal, but he refused to engage, and took that out on me. Not a big deal, but I no longer had the energy to deal with him. I knew there was another wave of projects coming. And I knew that this guy would be difficult, and that this time around I wouldn't have the energy to cope. Three years previously, I would.

Questions

1 What *change leadership behaviours and attributes* were important to this doctor in this change leadership role?

2 What political tactics did he use?

3 What are the challenges for change agents raised by this case?

4 What are the training and development, and other HR implications, raised by this case?

CASE STUDY 15.2

AVOIDING A BOOKING SYSTEM BACKLASH: HOW TO GENERATE COMMITMENT TO CHANGE?

AOIFE M. MCDERMOTT AND EDEL CONWAY

Annie Fagan has taken up a new role as the deputy HR manager of a luxury travel agent (specialising in bespoke tours), and is responsible for supporting strategic change initiatives. Having previously had a generalist HR role, she felt ready to take on a new challenge. However, she has become involved in introducing a new booking system sooner than expected. She is concerned about her knowledge of the organisation's systems, technology, and 'ways of doing things', as well as her capacity to get people to support the change.

From: Matthew Hughes

To: Annie Fagan

Sent: 10/08/16

Subject: How are you settling in?

Hey Annie,

Missing you here – how you finding the new place?

Matt

From: Annie Fagan

To: Matthew Hughes

Sent: 17/08/16

Subject: Wish you were here . . .

Hi Matt,

I'm finding it tough. I had expected a bit of space to 'settle in', but I've been given a big job straight off and not one that plays to my strengths. I have to introduce a new IT/booking system (I'm not a techie genius, as well you know!!). I did suggest that it may not be the best job for me. Changing systems seems a bit premature when I haven't had time to get to know them – and don't know what's good and what's bad! Anyway, I obviously sold my 'process expertise' a bit too well, as my new boss doesn't see a problem . . .

How are Sylvie and the kids?

A x

From: Matthew Hughes

To: Annie Fagan

Sent: 18/08/16

Subject: RE: Wish you were here . . .

Hey Annie,

Everyone good – Jason convinced he's the next Messi. Coach not so sure!

What's prompted the change?

M

From: Annie Fagan

To: Matthew Hughes

Sent: 21/08/16

Subject: RE: Wish you were here . . .

Hey Matt,

The booking platform is very clunky (designed by two students on placement a couple of years ago!), so we really do need an update. But it will be a bit tricky getting the design right. And we'll have to transfer information, so we'll need to run the two systems in parallel for a while. I've been trying to get a heads up on what the new system should look like and potential risks during the process. But it's still early days for me here. The people seem nice, but the atmosphere is pretty formal – so I'm not sure if I'm getting real feedback, or if hierarchy is getting in the way. All advice appreciated. I can't afford to mess this up.

Anyway, it's Friday and the sun is shining . . . Have a great weekend!

Annie x

From: Matthew Hughes

To: Annie Fagan

Sent: 24/08/16

Subject: Readiness review?

Annie,

Have you thought about doing a change readiness review? You can check up on how staff are feeling about things, and get some early feedback on what might be needed/helpful. Do you remember the one we did when we moved offices? You could use that as a template. We asked staff about their understanding of the reasons for the change, their perceptions of potential benefits for the organisation (and for them). We also used it to check that we hadn't missed anything important, and to see if there was anything in particular we could do to support staff during the transition. We made it anonymous. I think that makes it easier for people to give honest opinions . . . Anyway, I've attached the template we used (we set up an online survey). The questions link to a couple of themes:

- Employees' understanding of the reasons for the change
- Employees' assessment of the need for change
- Employees' concerns about the implications of the change
- Employees' perceptions about the support available from the organisation
- Employees' commitment to the change
- Employees' intention to resist the change

We also had free text boxes for comments – and some of these threw up some helpful suggestions (and some complaints!). It could be a cheap and low-risk way to see how people are really feeling about it . . .

Gotta rush. . . . it's hard being busy and important!

M

From: Matthew Hughes
To: Annie Fagan
Sent: 08/09/16
Subject: Anybody out there. . . .

Earth calling Annie . . .

How are things going?!! I'd hate to think that you've been overthrown by hostile forces . . .

M

From: Annie Fagan
To: Matthew Hughes

Sent: 09/09/16
Subject: Not waving but drowning . . .

Mattie,

Sorry I've not been in touch – things have been a bit crazy here. I took your survey idea and ran with it across the organisation. I'm kinda wishing I hadn't! In truth, the feedback isn't positive – and I'm stuck on finding the best way forward. Edited highlights include (drum roll please) . . .

- Employees don't seem to understand the need for change – which may explain the lack of *any* perceived urgency (except among the senior management team, who have the data on lost productivity due to system crashes/incomplete sales due to customer fatigue. They are driving the whole thing . . .)
- Line managers and front-line staff seem to be worried about implications for their sales commission during the handover (they will have to double enter info into the two systems for a couple of months, which will take extra time . . .)
- Tech staff are concerned about not having enough staff and coding expertise to deliver what we need . . . (one comment said that management has '*wilfully ignored*' repeated requests to properly resource the change) . . .

And all of this means that there is pretty poor engagement with/commitment to the change across the organisation. That is a real problem . . . I've been thinking about how to fix it and a priority is to get the design team and the line managers on side. If they're negative nobody else will get behind it!! The main challenge is that very few employees seem to understand why the new system is necessary. We've got to fix that. It'll be a hard few months, even if we do manage to get people on board. If we don't, it could be a disaster. At the moment it's low-level grumbling. But it could turn into a full scale backlash.

I'm under pressure to show some progress. But I don't think it's a good idea to push forward as things stand.

Help!!!! What should I do???

Annie xx

Questions

1 What is the problem in this case?
2 What, if any, insights does Lewin's change model provide for this case?
3 What should Annie do?

CASE STUDY 15.3

UTEL: A CHANGE WORKSHOP

CYNTHIA HARDY

The premise of and process for culture change at UTEL

UTel[1] licenses technologies to makers of mobile phones and other mobile communication devices. It employs 1,500 employees, mostly at its European head office. The company was formed in 2001, when it was 'spun off' from being a division of GlobalTel. This led to a change in its customer base; moving from a focus on serving individual end-users of phones, towards serving other companies who manufacture and sell phones. As a consequence, the company required a change in culture to support its new mission 'to make our customers first, best and profitable through innovation, quality and commitment'. Senior management, together with external consultants, devised a cultural change programme premised on a three-hour workshop to be rolled out 80 times across the company, using the same format.

The workshops were organised around a 'Culture Toolkit' that aimed to support the attainment of the company's mission statement, and the development of a more customer-focused culture. The toolkit consisted of a brochure, a video and a set of instructions for conducting the workshops. The brochure was entitled 'UTel's Target Culture: Involving Every Employee'. The video took the form of a 10-minute question and answer session between the CEO and another senior manager. It explained why the new culture was needed and provided information on the drivers and values underpinning it. In the video the CEO states that 'next step [in the implementation of the change] is to involve everybody'. This was to happen through half-day workshops involving: (a) a presentation of the target culture, using the brochure and accompanying video; (b) a discussion of the relevance of the new culture to the particular group attending the workshop; and (c) exercises to build agreement on actions to be taken to implement the new culture. The aim was to secure involvement and input from employees and to bring about agreement on what the nature of the new culture should be and how it should be implemented across the company.

An overview of the workshop

The initial workshop, observed by the researchers and forming the basis of this case, was attended by three head office managers, two senior managers, managers from supporting functions such as Human Resources and Finance, and circa 30 middle managers, including software and hardware engineers (who are mainly male). Middle managers who attended the workshop were to take the toolkit back to their own units and use it 'to discuss how the new culture will affect their team, themselves as individuals, and Utel'. A senior manager opened the event, welcomed participants and gave them information about the workshop's structure and goals. Another senior manager delivered a Power-Point presentation describing his interpretation of the strengths and weaknesses of the local culture. This was followed by a general discussion about whether this interpretation was accurate. After a coffee break, the group considered the mission statement specified in the brochure. The video was then shown. Participants completed a 'stop/start/continue' exercise to identify one behaviour that was hindering cultural change and needed to be stopped, one new behaviour that needed to be started, and one existing behaviour that should be continued, the results of which were collected by the head office managers. The workshop concluded with a discussion of how to implement the change programme. Two core themes emerged during the workshop: the meaning of 'a customer focus' and discussion of how the implementation of the change process should progress. The communicative practices and forms of language used in the two discussions were quite different, despite being part of the same workshop.

Constructive communicative practices: theme 1, from a customer to a commercial focus

The meaning of having a 'customer focus', broadly described in the Culture Toolkit, was discussed by participants as they worked through the exercises, referred to the brochure and reflected on the video. At the start of the workshop, a senior manager emphasised the

---

[1]The company name and other details have been disguised.

need to achieve a *'common understanding'* of having a customer focus. A head office manager then put forward a number of suggestions about how this might be defined and understood. Another senior manager then asked who is the customer (the end user or another business)? One of the software engineers then challenged the assumption that the UK site is not already customer focused. He asserted:

> I believe that we are customer-oriented. I think we are customer focused as an organisation and we have been all the way through, even in our history. I think we're a customer-focused organisation.

Discussion transitioned between whether or not the site was customer focused, who was the customer, and the nature of the relationships. Later, the importance of a customer focus was challenged at a more fundamental level as one of the support staff argued that there was a need for a commercial focus:

> We are very driven by engineers and the technology . . . people do get caught up with developing incredible products that are fantastic with loads of features but from a commercial focus aren't really needed . . . as an organisation we're not necessarily as commercially and business focused as we need to be. *(Manager, support staff)*

This comment was followed by a long silence, and then a challenge by an engineer who suggested that sales and marketing staff were responsible for the customer, before discussion returned to the need for a customer focus. After iterative debate, and a return to the video, the stop/start/continue exercise was conducted and a need for a commercial focus re-emerged, initiated by support staff managers and

upheld by engineers. By the end of the discussion the group agreed that a customer focus was less important than a commercial focus. They developed a gradual consensus, defining a commercial focus as being financially aware and helping the company to be profitable.

The emergence of the need for a commercial focus was premised on participants using communicative practices and forms of language to engage with each other in negotiating meaning. These included inviting, proposing, building, clarifying and affirming on the part of senior managers and building, challenging and reiterating on the part of middle managers (see Table 1).

Constraining communicative practices: theme 2, implementation

The workshop participants also discussed and negotiated the meaning of implementation. These negotiations were much more polarised, with two parallel, separate discussions taking place: one involving senior managers and the other involving middle managers, with little evidence of engagement between them. Despite a head office manager initially encouraging the middle managers to identify the actions required for implementation, subsequent contributions by senior managers were all attempts to fix the meaning of implementation around their predetermined programme. Senior managers defined implementation in terms of the continuation of the workshops to create awareness of the existing culture, with further specific implementation activities to be decided by head office. In contrast, engineers and support staff tried to fix the meaning of implementation in terms of local actions,

Table 1 Customer focus

Language	Used by	Description
Inviting	Senior managers	Statements that encourage participation by other actors in negotiation of meanings
Affirming	Senior managers	Statements that agree with alternative meanings proposed by other actors
Clarifying	Senior managers	Questions that open up negotiation of meanings
Building	Senior and middle managers	Statements that engage with, elaborate and develop alternative meanings proposed by other actors
Reiterating	Middle managers	Statements that return to and repeat meanings
Proposing	Senior managers	Statements that introduce a new meaning
Challenging	Middle managers	Statements that reject or critique alternative meanings proposed by other actors

which required 'clear direction', 'road maps' and 'timelines'.

Senior managers used communicative practices and forms of language premised on dismissing, reiterating, deploying authority, invoking hierarchy, and reification, especially towards the end of the workshop. Middle managers attempted to resist senior management's meaning through challenging, reiterating, holding to account and undermining (see Table 2). However, rather than build on the alternative meanings of implementation proposed by middle managers, senior managers continually reinforced their preferred meaning. For example, a headquarters manager held up a copy of the brochure and, referring to the video and the exercise templates in the Culture Toolkit, shouted at all the middle managers:

> You should have . . . the video . . . I will email you the slides that we presented today [and] the agenda for the three-hour meeting that you'll have with your staff; going through the stop start in the workshops, that'll be in your slides; instructions on how to run the discussions; and also the template for the stop start workshops. The templates that we want you to work on are template two and template four, those two templates once you've conducted the workshops with your staff. I need them in by the end of August. At the end of August I will send all my information to [head office] who will make a presentation to [the CEO].

It matters what you say and how you say it: theme 3, language, power, resistance and change

The communicative practices and forms of language in the discussions around customer focus produced a relational engagement, where both parties took active responsibility for the joint tasks in which they were involved. This, in turn, helped to produce generative dialogue, which enabled new meanings to emerge collaboratively, insofar as a range of middle and senior managers contributed to identifying the need for a commercial focus, which was not part of the original change initiative. The dialogue was also characterised by constrained novelty as participants made small modifications at each dialogue turn. Interventions followed from the initial meaning of customer focus but, at the same time, helped to construct another meaning (i.e. the need for a commercial focus), which was both novel – different to the original meaning – and familiar in that it emerged incrementally by building on what went before. Power–resistance relations were facilitative insofar as middle managers engaged in communicative practices that might be construed as 'resistance to change' in that they challenged senior managers' meanings. However, it was this resistance that led to the emergence of the need for a commercial focus, i.e. it was the willingness of middle and senior managers to engage with each other, which gave rise to conceptual expansion, combination and reframing. From these

Table 2 Implementation

Language	Used by	Description
Dismissing	Senior managers	Statements that serve to rebuff or ignore alternative meanings proposed by other actors
Reiterating	Senior and middle managers	Statements that return to and repeat meanings
Deploying authority	Senior managers	Statements that contain directives that eliminate alternative meanings proposed by other actors
Invoking hierarchy	Senior managers	Statements that refer to superiors in order to justify the elimination of alternative meanings proposed by other actors
Reifying	Senior managers	Statements that invoke the Culture Toolkit to represent a particular, non-negotiable meaning
Challenging	Middle managers	Statements that reject or critique alternative meanings proposed by other actors
Undermining	Middle managers	Statements that criticise other actors in order to discredit their proposed meanings
Holding to account	Middle managers	Statements that demand action from other actors (or question lack of action) to undermine or discredit their proposed meanings

facilitative power–resistance relations came a break-through in the form of new knowledge about the need for the creation of a commercial focus – and not just a customer focus – as part of the change programme.

In contrast, the discussion around implementation was associated with calculated engagement and degenerative dialogue, with polarised reproduction of two sharply contrasting meanings of implementation. Here, there was evidence of a defensive standoff with both senior and middle managers reiterating their preferred meanings time and time again as they take their turn in the dialogue. These power–resistance relations were oppositional – with a

process that might be described as conceptual closure. With neither side willing to engage in the communicative practice of building, there was no way to bring the two meanings together or to use one to inform the other. Conceptual sterility arose with the dialogue losing momentum as senior managers engaged increasingly in coercive communicative practices. The number of interventions by middle managers started to decline around the two-hour mark. The result was a standoff as both sides steadfastly refused to acknowledge each other's ideas concerning implementation. See Figure 15.6 for a comparison of the two forms of resistance.

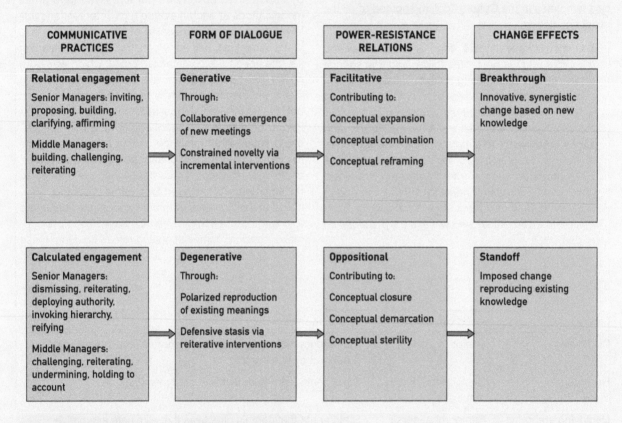

Figure 15.6 Dynamics in the negotiation of meaning
Source: Thomas *et al.*, 2011.

Questions

1 What are the practical implications arising from the forms of dialogue evident in this case?

2 Under what circumstances, if any, might it be appropriate to use communicative practices and forms of language to constrain employees' influence on change processes?

3 What, if anything, should have been done differently? Why?

Bibliography

Alfes, K., Truss, C. and Gill, J. (2010) 'The HR manager as change agent: evidence from the public sector', *Journal of Change Management*, Vol.10, No.1, 109–27.

Armenakis, A.A. and Bedeian, A.G. (1999) 'Organizational change: a review of theory and research in the 1990's', *Journal of Management*, Vol.25, No.3, 293–315.

Armenakis, A.A., Bernerth, J.B., Pitts, J.P. and Walker, H.J. (2007) 'Organizational change recipients' beliefs scale development of an assessment instrument', *The Journal of Applied Behavioral Science*, Vol.43, No.4, 481–505.

Armenakis, A.A., Harris, S.G. and Mossholder, K.W. (1993) 'Creating readiness for organizational change', *Human Relations*, Vol.46, No.6, 681–703.

Armenakis, A.A. and Harris, S.G. (2002) 'Crafting a change message to create transformational readiness', *Journal of Organizational Change Management*, Vol.15, No.2, 169–83.

Ashford, S.J. (1988) 'Individual strategies for coping with stress during organizational transitions', *The Journal of Applied Behavioral Science*, Vol.24, No.1, 19–36.

Axtell, C., Wall, T., Stride, C., Pepper, K., Clegg, C., Gardner, P. and Bolden, R. (2002) 'Familiarity breeds content: the impact of exposure to change on employee openness and well-being', *Journal of Occupational and Organizational Psychology*, Vol.75, No.2, 217–31.

Balogun, J. and Hope Hailey, V. (2004) *Exploring Strategic Change*, Harlow: FT/Prentice.

Barends, E., Janssen, B., ten Have, W. and ten Have, S. (2013) 'Effects of change interventions: what kind of evidence do we really have?', *The Journal of Applied Behavioral Science*, Vol.50, No.1, 5–27.

Bartunek, J.M., Rousseau, D.M., Rudolph, J.W. and DePalma, J.A. (2006) 'On the receiving end: sensemaking, emotion, and assessments of an organizational change initiated by others', *Journal of Applied Behavioral Science*, Vol.42, No.2, 182–206.

Beckhard, R. (1969) *Organization Development: Strategies and Models*, Reading, MA: Addison-Wesley.

Brannick, T. and Coghlan, D. (2007) 'In defense of being "native": the case for insider academic research', *Organizational Research Methods*, Vol.10, No.1, 59–74.

Buchanan, D. (2003) 'Demands, instabilities, manipulations, careers: the lived experience of driving change', *Human Relations*, Vol.56, No.6, 663–84.

Buchanan, D. (2008) 'You stab my back, I'll stab yours: management experience and perceptions of organisation political behaviour', *British Journal of Management*, Vol.19, No.1, 49–64.

Buchanan, D.A., Addicott, R., Fitzgerald, L., Ferlie, E. and Baeza, J.I. (2007) 'Nobody in charge: distributed change agency in healthcare', *Human Relations*, Vol.60, No.7, 1065–90.

Buchanan, D. and Badham, R. (1999) 'Politics and organizational change: the lived experience', *Human Relations*, Vol.52, No.5, 609–29.

Buchanan, D. and Boddy, D. (1992) *The Expertise of the Change Agent: Public Performance and Backstage Activity*, London: Prentice Hall.

Buchanan, D., Claydon, T. and Doyle, M. (1999) 'Organization development and change: the legacy of the nineties', *Human Resource Management Journal*, Vol.9, No.2, 20–37.

Buchanan, D.A. and Storey, J. (1997) 'Role taking and role switching in organizational change: the four pluralities', in McLoughlin, I. and Harris, M. (eds.) *Innovation, Organizational Change and Technology*, London: International Thomson.

Burnes, B. (1992) *Managing Change: A Strategic Approach to Organizational Development and Renewal*, London: Pitman.

Burnes, B. (1996) 'No such thing as . . . a "one best way" to manage organizational change', *Management Decision*, Vol.34, No.10, 11–8.

Burnes, B. (2000) *Managing Change: A Strategic Approach to Organizational Dynamics* (3rd edn.), London: Pitman.

Burnes, B. (2004) *Managing Change: A Strategic Approach to Organisational Dynamics* (4th edn.), Harlow: Prentice Hall.

Burnes, B. (2009) *Managing Change* (5th edn.), England: Pearson Education.

Burns, T. and Stalker, R. (1961) *The Management of Innovation*, London: Tavistock.

By, R.T. (2005) 'Organisational change management: a critical review', *Journal of Change Management*, Vol.5, No.4, 369–80.

By, R.T. (2009) 'Organisational change management: a critical review', pp. 46–58, in Price, A. (ed.) *The Principles and Practices of Change*, Hampshire: Palgrave Macmillan.

Caldwell, R. (2003) 'Models of change agency: a fourfold classification', *British Journal of Management*, Vol.14, No.2, 131–42.

Caldwell, R. (2006) *Agency and Change*, Oxon: Routledge.

Cameron, E. and Green, M. (2012) *Making Sense of Change Management: A Complete Guide to the Models and Techniques of Organisational Change* (3rd edn.), London: Kogan Page.

Campbell, D. (2012) 'Public managers in integrated services collaboratives: what works is workarounds', *Public Administration Review*, Vol.72, No.5, 721–30.

Chanlat, J.F. (1997) 'Conflict and politics', pp. 472–80, in Sorge, A. and Warner, M. (eds.) *Handbook of Organizational Behaviour*, London: Thomson.

Choi, M. (2011) 'Employees' attitudes toward organizational change: a literature review', *Human Resource Management*, Vol.50, No.4, 479–500.

CIPD HR Survey Report (2003) 'Where we are, where we're heading'. Available at: http://www.cipd.co.uk/subjects/hrpract/hrtrends/hrsurvey.htm?IsSrchRes=1.

CIPD (2013) 'PESTLE analysis factsheet'. Available at: http://www.cipd.co.uk/hr-resources/factsheets/pestle-analysis.aspx.

Coghlan, D. (1993) 'A person centred approach to dealing with resistance to change', *Leadership & Organization Development Journal*, Vol.14, No.4, 10–4.

Coghlan, D. and McAuliffe, E. (2003) *Changing Healthcare Organisations*, Dublin: Blackhall.

Conway, E. and Monks, K. (2008) 'HR Practices and commitment to change: an employee-level analysis', *Human Resource Management Journal*, Vol.18, No.1, 70–87.

Conway, N., Kiefer, T., Hartley, J. and Briner, R.B. (2014) 'Doing more with less? Employee reactions to psychological contract breach via target similarity or spillover during public sector organisational change', *British Journal of Management*, Vol.25, No.4, 737–54.

Cummings, T.G. and Worley, C.G. (2001) *Organization Development and Change*, Cincinnati, OH: South Western: College Publishing.

Cunningham, G.B. (2006) 'The relationships among commitment to change, coping with change, and turnover intentions', *European Journal of Work and Organizational Psychology*, Vol.15, No.1, 29–45.

Dent, E. and Goldberg, S. (1999) 'Challenging "resistance to change"', *Journal of Applied Behavioral Science*, Vol.35, No.1, 25–41.

Dutton, J.E., Ashford, S.J., O'Neil, R. and Lawrence, K.A. (2001) 'Moves that matter: issue selling and organizational change', *Academy of Management Journal*, Vol.44, No.4, 716–36.

Eurostat (2015) Population Projections. Available at: http://ec.europa.eu/eurostat/statistics -explained/index.php/Population_structure_and_ageing.

Fernandez, S. and Rainey, H.G. (2006) 'Managing successful organizational change in the public sector', *Public Administration Review*, Vol.66, No.2, 168–76.

Fitzgerald, L., Lilley, C., Ferlie, E., Addicott, R., McGivern, G., Buchanan, D., Baeza, J., Doyle, M. and Rashid, A. (2006) *Managing Change and Role Enactment in the Professional-ized Organization*, London: SDO Board.

Folger, R. and Skarlicki, D.P. (1999) 'Unfairness and resistance to change: hardship as mis-treatment', *Journal of Organizational Change Management*, Vol.12, No.1, 35–50.

Folkman, S., Lazarus, R.S., Dunkel-Schetter, C., DeLongis, A. and Gruen, R.J. (1986) 'Dynamics of a stressful encounter: cognitive appraisal, coping, and encounter outcomes', *Journal of Personality and Social Psychology*, Vol.50, No.5, 992–1003.

Ford, J.D., Ford, L.W. and D'Amelio, A. (2008) 'Resistance to change: the rest of the story', *Academy of Management Review*, Vol.33, No.2, 362–77.

Gandz, J. and Murray, V.V. (1980) 'The experience of workplace politics', *The Academy of Management Journal*, Vol.23, No.2, 237–51.

Giauque, D., Ritz, A., Varone, F. and Anderfuhren-Biget, S. (2012) 'Resigned but satisfied: the negative impact of public service motivation and red tape on work satisfaction', *Public Administration: An International Quarterly*, Vol.90, No.1, 175–93.

Gerstner, C.R. and Day, D.V. (1997) 'Meta-analytic review of leader-member exchange theory: correlates and construct issues', *Journal of Applied Psychology*, Vol.82, 827–843.

Goodman, J. and Truss, C. (2004) 'The medium and the message: communicating effectively during a major change initiative', *Journal of Change Management*, Vol.4, No.3, 217–28.

Guest, D. and King, Z. (2004) 'Power, innovation and problem solving: the personnel managers' 3 steps to heaven', *Journal of Management Studies*, Vol.41, No.3, 401–24.

Halbesleben, J.R.B., Neveu, J.P., Paustian-Underdahl, S.C. and Westman, M. (2014) 'Getting to the "COR": understanding the role of resources in conservation of resources theory', *Journal of Management*, Vol.40, No.5, 1334–64.

Hayes, J. (2002) *The Theory and Practice of Change Management*, Basingstoke: Palgrave Macmillan.

Herold, D.M., Fedor, D.B. and Caldwell, S.D. (2007) 'Beyond change management: a multilevel investigation of contextual and personal influences on employees' commitment to change', *Journal of Applied Psychology*, Vol.92, No.4, 942–51.

Herscovitch, L. and Meyer, J.P. (2002) 'Commitment to organizational change: extension of a three-component model', *Journal of Applied Psychology*, Vol.87, No.3, 474–87.

Hobfoll, S.E. (1989) 'Conservation of resources: a new attempt at conceptualizing stress', *American Psychologist*, Vol.44, No.3, 513–24.

Holt, D.T., Armenakis, A.A., Field, H.S. and Harris, S.G. (2007) 'Readiness for organisational change: the systemic development of a scale', *Journal of Applied Behavioural Science*, Vol.43, No.2, 232–55.

Hornung, S. and Rousseau, D.M. (2007) 'Active on the job-proactive in change: how autonomy at work contributes to employee support for organizational change', *Journal of Applied Behavioral Science*, Vol.43, No.4, 401–26.

Iverson, R. (1996) 'Employee acceptance of organisational change: the role of organisational commitment', *International Journal of Human Resource Management*, Vol.7, No.1, 122–49.

Jaffee, D. (2001) *Organization Theory: Tension and Change*, New York: McGraw-Hill.

Judge, T.A., Thoresen, C.J., Pucik, V. and Welbourne, T.M. (1999) 'Managerial coping with organizational change: a dispositional perspective', *Journal of Applied Psychology*, Vol.84, No.1, 107–22.

Keep, J. (2001) 'The change practitioner: perspectives on role, effectiveness, dilemmas and challenges', pp. 13–8, in Hamlin, B., Keep, J. and Ash, K. (eds.) *Organizational Change and Development: A Reflective Guide for Managers, Trainers and Developers*, Harlow: Pearson Education.

Kickert, W.J. (2010) 'Managing emergent and complex change: the case of Dutch agencification', *International Review of Administrative Sciences*, Vol.76, No.3, 489–515.

Knowles, E.S. and Linn, J.A. (eds.) (2004) 'Resistance and persuasion', *Psychology Press*.

Kotter, J.P. (1995) 'Leading change: why transformation efforts fail', *Harvard Business Review*, Vol.73, No.2, 59–67.

Kotter, J. (1996) *Leading Change*, London: Harvard Business Review Press.

Kotter, J.P. and Schlesinger, L.A. (2008) 'Choosing strategies for change', *Harvard Business Review* (reprint of 1979 article), Vol.86, Nos.7–8, 130–9.

Lawrence, P. and Lorsch, J. (1967) *Organization and Environment*, Cambridge, MA: Harvard University Press.

Lewin, K. (1951) *Field Theory in Social Science*, New York: Harper & Row.

Lovelady, L. (1984) 'The process of organisation development: a reformulated model of the change process, Part I', *Personnel Relations*, Vol.13, No.2, 8–11.

McDermott, A.M., Fitzgerald, L. and Buchanan, D. (2013) 'Beyond acceptance and resistance: entrepreneurial change agency in policy implementation', *British Journal of Management*, Vol.24, No.S1, S93–S115.

McDermott, A.M., Fitzgerald, L., Van Gestel, N.M. and Keating, M.A. (2015) 'From bipartite to tripartite devolved HRM in professional service contexts: evidence from hospitals in three countries', *Human Resource Management*, Vol.54, No.2, 813–831.

McMillan, E. (2004) *Complexity, Organizations and Change*, London: Routledge.

Miles, R. and Snow, C. (1978) *Organisational Strategy, Structure and Process*, New York: McGraw-Hill.

Miller, V.D., Johnson, J.R. and Grau, J.G. (1994) 'Antecedents to willingness to participate in a planned organizational change', *Journal of Applied Communication Research*, Vol.22, 59–80.

Open Systems Group (1981) *Systems Behaviour* (3rd edn.) London: Harper & Row, in association with the Open University Press.

Oreg, S., Vakola, M. and Armenakis, A. (2011) 'Change recipients reactions to organizational change: a 60-year review of quantitative studies', *The Journal of Applied Behavioral Science*, Vol.47, No.4, 461–524.

Ottaway, R.N. (1983) 'The change agent: a taxonomy in relation to the change process', *Human Relations*, Vol.36, No.4, 361–92.

Piderit, S.K. (2000) 'Rethinking resistance and recognizing ambivalence: a multidimensional view of attitudes toward an organizational change', *Academy of Management Review*, Vol.25, No.4, 783–94.

Pitt-Catsouphes, M. (2007) *Testimony to the Senate Special Committee on Aging*. Available at: http://www.aging.senate.gov/imo/media/doc/hr169mc.pdf.

Pollitt, C. and Bouckaert, G. (2011) *Public Management Reform*, Oxford: Oxford University Press.

Poole, M. and Van de Ven, A. (eds.) (2004) *Handbook of Organizational Change and Innovation*, Oxford: Oxford University Press.

Rafferty, A.E., Jimmieson, N.L. and Armenakis, A.A. (2013) 'Change readiness: a multilevel review', *Journal of Management*, Vol.39, No.1, 110–35.

Roche, W.K. and Teague, P. (2012) 'Business partners and working the pumps: human resource managers in the recession', *Human Relations*, Vol.65, No.5, 1333–58.

Schein, E.H. (1999) *Process Consultation Revisited: Building the Helping Relationship*, Reading, MA: Addison-Wesley.

Scott, W.R. (2003) *Organizations: Rational, Natural and Open Systems* (5th edn.), New Jersey: Prentice Hall.

Senior, B. and Fleming, J. (2006) *Organizational Change*, Essex: Pearson.

Senior, B. and Swailes, S. (2010) *Organizational Change* (4th edn.), Essex: Pearson.

Smith, M.E. (2002) 'Success rates for different types of organizational change', *Performance Improvement*, Vol.41, No.1, 26–33.

Sonenshein, S. and Dholakia, U. (2012) 'Explaining employee engagement with strategic change implementation: a meaning-making approach', *Organization Science*, Vol.23, No.1, 1–23.

Stace, D. and Dunphy, D. (1991) 'Beyond traditional paternalistic and developmental approaches to organisational change and human resource strategies', *The International Journal of Human Resource Management*, Vol.2, No.3, 263–83.

Stickland, F. (1998) *The Dynamics of Change: Insights into Organisational Transition from the Natural World*, New York: Routledge.

Storey, J. (1992) *Developments in the Management of Human Resources: An Analytical Review*, Oxford: Blackwell.

Thomas, R., Sargent, L.D. and Hardy, C. (2011) 'Managing organizational change: negotiating meaning and power-resistance relations', *Organization Science*, Vol.22, No.1, 22–41.

Thomas, R. and Hardy, C. (2011) 'Reframing resistance to organizational change', *Scandinavian Journal of Management*, Vol.27, No.3, 322–31.

Tichy, N. (1983) *Managing Strategic Change: Technical, Political and Cultural Dynamics*, New York: Wiley.

Truss, C., Mankin, D. and Kelliher, C. (2012) *Strategic Human Resource Management*, Oxford: Oxford University Press.

Ulrich, D. (1997) *Human Resource Champions*, Boston, MA: Harvard Business School Press.

Ulrich, D. (1998) 'A new mandate for human resources', *Harvard Business Review*, Vol.76, No.1, 124–34.

Ulrich, D. and Brockbank, W. (2005) *The HR Value Proposition*, Boston, MA: Harvard Business School Press.

Wallace, M., O'Reilly, D., Morris, J. and Deem, R. (2011) 'Public service leaders as "change agents" – for whom?', *Public Management Review*, Vol.13, No.1, 65–93.

Weick, K.E., and Quinn, R.E. (1999) 'Organizational change and development', *Annual Review of Psychology*, Vol.50, No.1, 361–86.

Worley, C.G. and Mohrman, S.A. (2014) 'Is change management obsolete?', *Organizational Dynamics*, Vol.43, No.3, 214–24.

Wylie, N., Sturdy, A. and Wright, C. (2014) 'Change agency in occupational context: lessons for HRM', *Human Resource Management Journal*, Vol.24, No.1, 95–110.

CHAPTER 16
EMPLOYEE INVOLVEMENT AND PARTICIPATION

Tony Dundon and Adrian Wilkinson

Introduction

Employee involvement and participation (EIP) has long been a central pillar of human resource management, with various practices often shaped by the different political, economic and legal context found in different countries. Contextual factors also influence the demand (among employees and unions) for participation as well as the desire (by managers and employers) for the types of mechanisms used. In different countries, the terms employee participation and involvement can mean very different things, often with a lack of clarity surrounding the terms and practices used. The confusion of the terms 'involvement, participation or communication' is made worse as some methods (such as team briefings or quality circles) tend to coexist and overlap with other techniques (such as joint union–management consultative committees or collective bargaining). In a European context, collective participation remains significant in certain countries, notably Germany and Sweden. However, participation is not exclusive to union-only channels and in many countries non-union employee representation (NER) has grown in popularity: in Britain 18 per cent of private sector employees work in establishments with the presence of a non-union representative (van Wanrooy et al., 2013: 60).

In considering these issues, the chapter first defines participation and considers the context in which participation has changed over time. We then review a framework against which to evaluate employee participation, and this is followed by an explanation of the types of schemes used in practice. Fourth is a consideration of the meanings and possible impacts on organisational performance and employee well-being. Finally, we review some of the current influences and policy choices in the area of employee involvement and participation.

Defining participation

EIP is something of an elastic term which can mean different things to different people (Wilkinson *et al.*, 2014). Some authors refer to involvement as participation while others use empowerment or communications, often without fully extracting the key conceptual meanings or differences that are used in practice (Wilkinson *et al.*, 2010). There are further complications when considering EIP in international terms. In European countries, for example, government policy and legislation provides for a statutory right to participation in certain areas, among both union and non-union establishments. In other countries, however, such as the US or Australia, there is less emphasis on statutory provisions for employee involvement with a greater tendency to rely on the preferences of managers and unions, resulting in a complex web of individual and collective forms of EIP in many organisations. At the same time employees encounter participation at different levels, even within the same company (Wilkinson and Dundon, 2010). Differences can be further complicated depending on the presence or absence of a trade union (Benson and Brown, 2010). It is not uncommon for non-unionised companies to use the terms 'empowerment' or 'communications', even when they utilise representative forums such as European Works Councils (Ackers *et al.*, 2005). In Britain, the WERS surveys indicate that the majority of managers generally prefer to consult with workers in more direct than indirect ways: only 10 per cent of all workplaces use a combination of both representative and direct forms of EIP, while 37 per cent of establishments use neither of these methods (van Wanrooy *et al.*, 2013: 66).

One way of making sense of the elasticity of the terms is to see EIP as an umbrella term covering all initiatives designed to engage employees. However, there are two separate underlying ideologies behind the nature of participation. First, the concept of industrial democracy (which draws from notions of industrial citizenship) sees participation as a fundamental democratic right for workers to extend a degree of control over managerial decision making in an organisation. Second, the economic efficiency model argues that it makes sense for companies to encourage greater participation. By allowing employees an input into work and business decisions can help create more understanding and hence commitment. Although these are two different perspectives towards employee participation they are not polar opposites; as Cressey *et al.* (1985) usefully reminded us, no one wants a 'democratic bankruptcy'. Such issues raise questions about what certain practices actually mean to the participants and whether EIP schemes can improve organisational effectiveness and employee well-being (Dundon *et al.*, 2004). We define employee participation in a similarly broad way, following Boxall and Purcell (2011), as incorporating a range of mechanisms 'which enable and at times empower employees directly and indirectly, to contribute to decision making in the firm'. As this chapter is also concerned with clarifying what is meant by different participation schemes, we will evaluate the extent to which various practices allow workers to have a say in organisational decisions. At times the extent of such a voice can be marginal, superficial and subject to managerial control; at other times it may be more extensive and embedded within an organisation. Informal dialogue between employees and their front-line manager is significant for effective participation. Indeed, informal communications can be the glue that holds formal participation schemes together (Marchington and Suter, 2013).

The context for employee participation

Employee participation has a long history in most westernised economies. Notwithstanding oversimplification, a number of distinct phases can be traced to help place the role of participation in a contemporary and international context. The 1960s was often preoccupied with a search for job enrichment and enhanced worker motivation. Managerial objectives tended to focus on employee skill acquisition and work enrichment, particularly in Britain and the US. In the UK, exemplar industries such as ICI and British Coal included semi-autonomous workgroups to promote skill variety and job autonomy (Roeber, 1975; Trist *et al.*, 1963). In the US participatory management schemes were similarly concerned with employee motivation as an outcome, rather than as a system that allowed workers to have a say about organisational decisions (see Budd *et al.*, 2010).

The 1970s witnessed a shift in focus towards industrial democracy, which emphasised worker rights. Participation reached its high point in the UK with the 1977 Bullock Report on Industrial Democracy, which addressed the question of how workers might be represented at board level (Bullock, 1977). This report emerged in a period of strong union bargaining power and the Labour government's 'Social Contact' of inclusion. The Bullock Report was partly union-initiated, through the Labour Party, and based on collectivist principles with employee rights established on a statutory basis (Ackers *et al.*, 1992). Experiments with worker directors were initiated in the Post Office and the British Steel Corporation, although along with the Bullock Report itself, soon abandoned with the neoliberal agenda of the Thatcher government in 1979. Earlier, in the US, collective voice through unionisation gained some legitimacy with the Wagner Act (1935), designed to protect employees who sought union representation. However, in practice, employers would go to extraordinary lengths to avoid collective participation, often by employing the services of union-busting consultants in order to by-pass collective participation channels with managerial-led initiatives (Logan, 2013). Recent studies have traced similar anti-collective traits that espouse an overtly individualistic and even anti-worker interpretation of EIP, drawn from Organisational Behaviour (OB) perspectives; in particular, a dominant Industrial and Organisational (I&O) psychological strain of OB that tends to ignore broader stakeholder interests (Kaufman, 2015; Barry and Wilkinson, 2015).

The 1980s saw a very different agenda for participation. Indeed, the vocabulary changed almost overnight. The term 'involvement' became more fashionable and associated with managerial initiatives designed to elicit employee commitment. During the 1980s the political climate was one of reducing union power and promoting individualistic and anti-collectivist philosophy akin to the I&O psychological school of OB that was gaining prominence in (some) HRM teachings and research agendas (Godard, 2014). Public policy, inspired by a global shift to neo-liberal economics, similarly found relevance in individualised and especially voluntary rather than legally mandated forms of EIP (Dobbins and Dundon, 2014a). Out went any idea of statutory support for greater industrial democracy and in came a new wave of financial deregulation, privatisation and managerial self-confidence for direct employee involvement rather than union-centred participation channels. The period witnessed a shift from large-scale manufacturing industry to private services, which shaped the preferences for more management-sponsored forms of employee participation. This wave of direct involvement was neither interested in or allowed employees to question managerial power (Marchington *et al.*, 1992). In effect, this was a period of employee involvement on management's terms.

The 1990s saw a consolidation in the use of employee participation techniques. Tapping into employee ideas and drawing on their tacit knowledge was seen as one solution to the problems of managing in an increasingly competitive marketplace, in part because of globalisation and market liberalisation by governments, and also because of increasing customer demand for more choice, quality and design. Many of the specific mechanisms to tap into such a labour resource became crystallised in models of best-practice HRM and high-commitment management developed in the US (Becker and Huselid, 1998; Pfeffer, 1998). In this way the objectives for EIP can be seen as unitarist in approach, often moralistic in tone, and predicated on the assumption that 'what is good for the business must be good for employees' (Marchington and Wilkinson, 2012).

The twenty-first century witnessed another phase, strengthened by the rise of individualistic EIP articulated in an increasingly unitarist OB approach to HRM (Godard, 2014; Kaufman, 2015). Alongside the 1990s flavour for managerial-led employee involvement, the twenty-first century also saw the emergence of increasing state regulation, particularly at a European level. According to Wilkinson *et al.* (2014), the significance of this has resulted in a continuing (and often complicated) policy dialectic that shapes management choice for employee participation. The broader environment now is more sympathetic to individual employment rights, alongside collective-type regulations such as the European Directive on Employee Information and Consultation. Arguably, the twenty-first century has ushered in a period of 'soft' regulation, which, at the same time, appears to leave intact the voluntarist arrangements in many liberal economies which afford managers a high degree of choice and self-control over workers (Gollan *et al.*, 2014).

A framework for analysing employee participation

Before outlining various participation schemes, the purpose of this section is first to explain a framework that can be used to analyse the extent to which various schemes genuinely allow employees to have a say in matters that affect them at work. What is important here is to be able to unpick the purpose, meaning and subsequent impact of employee participation (Dundon *et al.*, 2004). To this end, a fourfold framework can be used, including the 'depth', 'level', 'scope' and 'form' of various participation schemes in actual practice (Marchington and Wilkinson, 2012).

First is the 'depth' to which employees have a say about organisational decisions (Wilkinson *et al.*, 2012). A greater depth may be when employees, either directly or indirectly, can influence those decisions that are normally reserved for management. The other end of the continuum may be a shallow depth, evident when employees are simply informed of the decisions management have made (see Figure 16.1). Second is the 'level' at which participation takes place. This can be at a work-group, department, plant or corporate level. What is significant here is whether the schemes adopted by an organisation actually take place at an appropriate managerial level. For example, involvement in a team meeting over future strategy would, in most instances, be inappropriate given that most team leaders would not have the authority to redesign organisational strategy. Third is the 'scope' of participation, that is, the topics on which employees can contribute. These range from relatively minor and insignificant matters, such as car-parking spaces, to more substantive issues, such as future investment strategies or plant relocation. Finally is the 'form' that participation takes, which may include a combination of both direct and indirect schemes. *Direct* schemes typically include individual techniques such as written and electronic communications, face-to-face meetings between managers and employees (e.g. quality circles

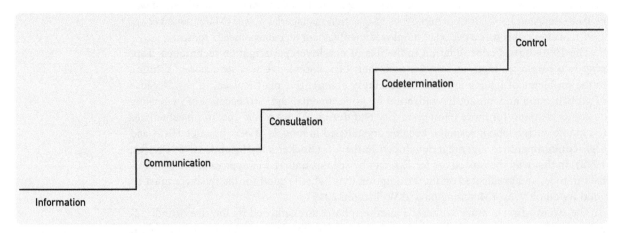

Figure 16.1 The depth of employee participation
Source: Wilkinson *et al.*, 2013: 270.

or team briefing). *Indirect* participation, in contrast, is via employee representatives, either union stewards or employee works council representatives in consultation with management. Another form of participation is task-based (or problem-solving) participation, where employees contribute directly to their job, either through focus groups or attitude surveys. There is also financial participation through variable pay and/or bonus schemes, such as profit sharing.

Taken together, this framework allows for a more accurate description not only of the type of involvement and participation schemes in use, but also the extent to which they may or may not empower employees (Marchington and Wilkinson, 2012). Figure 16.1 is more than a straightforward continuum from no involvement (information) to extensive worker participation (control). It illustrates the point that schemes can overlap and co-exist. For example, the use of collective bargaining and joint consultation does not mean that management abandon communication techniques. Central to this understanding of participation is power within the employment relationship, differentiated by the methods used (direct or indirect classifications), the level at which participation takes place (individual to boardroom level), and the extent to which any particular technique is employee- or management-centred (Wilkinson and Dundon, 2010).

Employee participation in practice

The use of various direct employee involvement initiatives speeded up during the latter part of the 1980s, and appears to have become more embedded and integrated with organisational practices across a number of leading market economies such as UK, Australia, Ireland and New Zealand (Marchington, 2015). One of the most systematic forms of communication is via the management chain of command. For example, regular meetings between managers and employees had grown over the last decade, as did suggestions schemes and newsletters (van Wanrooy *et al.*, 2013). Evidence shows that direct employee involvement is typical through face-to-face meetings between management and employees, either as a general worksite meeting or a team-briefing with supervisors: around 90 per cent of all UK workplaces had such a communication channel in 2011; while suggestion schemes were found in 25 per cent of establishments; email information sharing was found in 49 per cent of firms; with 69 per cent saying they utilise two-way written communications (van Wanrooy *et al.*, 2013: 64). Only eight per cent of British establishments had a workplace level joint consultative committee (van Wanrooy *et al.*, 2013: 62).

For the purpose of explanation and subsequent analysis, it is useful to break down the range of schemes in use into five broad classifications: communications, upward problem solving, task participation, teamworking and representative participation.

Communication is a weak form of participation but is a means by which management share information with employees, ranging from written memos, email or informal face-to-face communications. These have increased substantially in recent years, and are often regarded as a precursor to deeper forms of employee participation (Marchington and Wilkinson, 2012). Of course, communication practices vary in frequency and intensity. Some companies rely on their own internal newsletter to report a range of matters, from profits, new products to in-house welfare and employee development topics. Newer and technically sophisticated techniques include what has been termed 'E-voice', including the likes of social media, text messaging and other information technologies as a tool for employee communication (Balnave *et al.*, 2014).

The main problem with communications as a form of EIP is a lack of objectivity. Given that information is often political and power-centred, the messages managers seek to communicate to workers may be used to reinforce managerial prerogatives. The way information is communicated can also be ineffective as many line managers responsible for disseminating corporate messages lack effective communication skills, or information is conveyed in an untimely manner (often when bad news has already passed to the media before employees are told).

Upward problem-solving techniques seek to go one step further than communications by tapping into employee ideas for improvements. As with communication methods, problem-solving practices have increased, often inspired by Japanese work systems which encourage employees to offer ideas (Wilkinson *et al.*, 2013). Upward problem-solving practices are designed to increase the stock of ideas available to management as well as encourage a more cooperative industrial relations climate. Specific techniques can be either individual or collective, and range from employee suggestions schemes, focus groups or quality circles to workforce attitude surveys (Wilkinson, 2002). The fundamental difference between these practices and communication methods is that they are upward (from employees to managers) rather than downward (managers disseminating information to workers).

In relation to the framework for analysing EIP in the previous section, it is clear that upward problem-solving techniques do offer more depth than managerial communications alone. However, they have also been highly criticised as being inherently unitarist in nature (Sewell and Wilkinson, 1992). For example, the feedback given by workers in an attitude survey is essentially based on a managerial agenda as the information asked for tends to be set by employers.

The third category of practices is *task-based participation*. The objective here has been to focus attention on the actual job rather than the managerial processes for EIP. These practices have a longer pedigree in seeking to counter the degradation of work and associated employee alienation (Proctor and Benders, 2014), of which many schemes formed part of a series of work psychology experiments in the 1960s and 1970s (e.g. Tavistock Institute, Quality of Work Life Programmes in the US and Sweden). Task-based participation is often celebrated as a root to sustained organisational performance, embracing the principles of 'lean' production and efficiency, which is based on employee discretion and autonomy in the job, which in turn can lead to enhanced worker commitment and motivation. The types of practices include job enlargement and job enrichment whereby employees perform a greater range of tasks with a greater degree of job autonomy. The criticisms levelled at task-participation are that outcomes often result in work intensification rather than job enrichment. Arguably, devolving more and more responsibilities to employees can increase stress levels with workers (and line managers) who end up working harder and longer rather than smarter (Proctor and Benders, 2014; Delbridge *et al.*, 1992).

The fourth category is *teamworking*. Much of the literature around High Performance Work Systems (HPWS) or High-Commitment Management (HCM) include team-based structures as integral to achieving better organisational effectiveness through people (Harley, 2014). However, teamworking is one of the most imprecise of all the involvement and participation practices, and is often portrayed in an upbeat and uncritical way (Proctor and Benders, 2014). For example, in one of the earlier WERS surveys (Cully *et al.*, 1999), it was reported that 65 per cent of managerial respondents indicated they have teamworking in their organisation. The researchers probed deeper and asked supplementary questions that tapped into the features of what makes for a self-managed team, such as deciding how tasks would be performed and appointing team leaders, and the results then found that only three per cent of establishments utilise autonomous teams (Cully *et al.,* 1999: 43). Other commentators have reported a more subversive side to the effects of teamworking that result in forms of peer surveillance and control (Barker, 1993; Sinclair, 1992). For example, the pressure to conform to group norms and meet production targets is often policed by co-workers while simultaneously monitored by management (Geary and Dobbins, 2001).

The final category is *representative participation*, which can include joint consultation either via trade unions or, as is more typical these days, through forms of non-union employee representation (NER). Trade union participation in particular has experienced the most significant decline across most of the westernised world in recent years. In Britain, for example, union density has declined considerably, with just 26 per cent of all employees being union members (Brownlie, 2012). Union participation is more common in larger workplaces that employ over 50 employees (50 per cent). In the public sector, 92 per cent of workplaces in the UK have a recognised trade union (van Wanrooy *et al.*, 2013: 59). The figure for union density is much lower in the US, with around 12 per cent of the workforce being union members and even less, 6.8 per cent of US private sector employees enjoying union forms of participation (OECD, 2015). Importantly, the use of joint consultation often varies by company size and particular organisational context factors, such as market pressure or technologically intensive industries. There are very few enterprises with fewer than 25 employees that have workplace-level joint consultative forums (van Wanrooy *et al.*, 2013: 62).

It is often acknowledged that collective bargaining indicates a deeper form of *representative* participation in organisational decision making through the act of negotiation between management and employee (union) representatives (Kaine, 2014). However, the reality can be very different, as managers involve unions less and less as a legitimate participatory channel. This may indicate that *representative participation* is not necessarily dependent on the existence of a trade union, but mediated through alternative NER systems (Dobbins and Dundon, 2014b). Dual or multiple mechanisms for representative participation point to a complex web of employer motives; in particular, the simultaneous use of both union and non-union systems within the same organisation (Willman *et al.*, 2014). Research shows that non-union consultative committees are now much more common than they were a decade ago (van Wanrooy *et al.*, 2013). In addition, NER forums consider a range of organisational issues including working conditions, capital investment expenditure and disciplinary procedures. At the same time, others have commented that NER arrangements are often weak on power and shallow in depth (Dundon and Rollinson, 2004; Gollan, 2007).

However, debate remains concerning the efficacy of NER in relation to union-only channels and whether or not they function as a complement or a substitute to union methods of participation (Gall and Dundon, 2013). While some scholars argue that managerial motives for participation is based around the desire to control employee actions (e.g. Ramsay, 1977), NERs may actually function for other reasons (Dundon *et al.*, 2015). Indeed, it is probably wrong to view non-union employee voice as a single homogenous category of participation predicated only on the use of management power.

Evidence indicates that NERs can be quite diverse in scope and coverage (Dobbins and Dundon, 2014b). One area of dual voice that has received relatively little scrutiny but appears to be on the increase is that of *double-breasting* employee participation (Cullinane *et al.*, 2012). The antecedents of double-breasting can be traced to the construction industry in the US (Lipsky and Farber, 1976). The practice was designed to marginalise union influence by having a unionised plant compete against a non-union site for work contracts. The objective was to award work to the plant with the lowest labour costs, typically the non-union plant (Donaghey *et al.*, 2012). Research indicates that double-breasting participation has increased globally and especially among multinational organisations operating in different industries and countries, for example in manufacturing and transportation in the US (Verma and Kochan, 1985), Canada (Rose, 1986), Australia (Bamber *et al.*, 2009), Britain (Beaumont and Harris, 1992) and Ireland (Lavelle *et al.*, 2010). Dundon *et al.* (2015) conclude that the organisational politics associated with double-breasting as a motive for managers to avoid union participation will generate a 'spill-over dynamic' between union and non-union worker demands, resulting in contestation with a limited durability to double-breasting EIP.

Inevitably, there are always dangers in seeking to locate discrete boundaries between certain practices. Some schemes are often unclear and ambiguous, ranging from the mechanistic descriptions of structures and procedures to more organic techniques that shape attitudes and behaviours. Other techniques limit participation to formal institutions and procedures, such as bargaining, a particular NER committee or joint consultation, while day-to-day interactions between employee and management may engender more informal dimensions to participation, particularly within the smaller workplace devoid of many formalised HR systems (Wilkinson *et al.*, 2007). At the same time, there are questions about whether informality can survive as a viable mechanism for independent employee participation in the absence of formal structures, especially if market conditions or senior management philosophies change (Wilkinson *et al.*, 2014). It is these uncertainties that warrant a consideration of the meanings and interpretations of how EIP can impact organisational stakeholders.

The meanings and impact of participation

There are a number of problems with the meanings and definitions of the schemes outlined above. For example, in some organisations the full range of mechanisms – both direct and indirect – may be used simultaneously, while in other companies one or two techniques may be employed. There is no reason to assume that more is somehow better. It is also quite common for a particular label to be ascribed to very different practices (Wilkinson *et al.*, 2004). For example, a joint consultative committee which takes place on a monthly basis at plant level, involving senior managers and shop stewards, may have a more significant impact on decision making than a European Works Council that meets once a year, even though both are consultative and indirect in nature. There is the possibility that the latter is regarded by participants as 'bolted on' to other organisational practices, with little substance or meaning in reality (Marchington and Wilkinson, 2012).

Arguably, the extrapolation of survey evidence about the use of various involvement and participation schemes tells us very little about the forces shaping EIP or the extensiveness of various techniques over time and space (Marchington, 2015). Nor does this imply that certain schemes are an unwelcome intrusion into the lives of employees. For example, Proctor and Benders (2014) suggest that while teamworking and lean production techniques may facilitate a degree of employee autonomy, they do not remove tensions that arise from management exerting control. Donaghey *et al.* (2010: 63) examine not necessarily how much influence or voice workers may have but explaining why employees appear to remain silent. They highlight that management, through agenda-setting and manipulation of NER mechanisms, can engender a climate of silence, which effectively manages employees out of the participation channel. Of course, management do not interpret employee participation schemes in a vacuum. Dietz *et al.* (2009) show that when employees view involvement as little more than managerial rhetoric, then trust and other so-called benefits soon diminish in the eyes of employees. In many respects, employee participation can become disjointed from other HR strategies and seen as something that is bolted on, often depending on management latest fad or fashion.

The ambiguity and lack of trust about the meaning of involvement and participation schemes is evident in relation to the impact such techniques are claimed to have on enhanced organisational performance (Dundon *et al.*, 2004). First, it is practically impossible to isolate cause and effect and demonstrate that participation can lead to better organisational performance given the whole range of other contextual influences. For example, labour turnover is likely to be influenced by the availability of other jobs, by relative pay levels and by the presence, absence or depth of particular participation schemes. Second is the unease associated with the reference to benchmarking: of assessing the date at which to start making 'before and after' comparisons. Should this be the date at which the new participative mechanisms (say, a quality circle or consultative committee) is actually introduced into the organisation, or should it be some earlier or later date? For example, the claim that a quality circle saves money through a new work practice does not take into account that such ideas may have previously been channelled through a different and even better-established route. This also leads on to a third concern: that of evaluating the so-called impact and on whose terms. Should assessments be made in relation to workers having some voice (i.e. the process) or in terms of how things may be changed because of participation (i.e. the outcomes)? If it is the latter, then who gains? It remains the case that it is usually managers who decide what involvement and/or participation schemes to employ, at what level, depth and over what issues (Wilkinson *et al.*, 2010).

Employee participation and the EU

A more recent issue with regard to employee participation is the influence of European social policy. As noted earlier, the trend has been predominantly for employer-led schemes of a 'direct' nature. However, the European Commission is beginning to promote what seems to be a favoured 'indirect' (i.e. more collectivist) route to employee participation. For example, the European Works Council Directive is re-cast to enable employee representatives in organisations of 1,000 or more employees (with 150 or more in two EU member countries) the right to consult with management. Further, the European Company Statute (ECS) sets out a two-tier channel of participation for those companies that wish to avail of the EU statute (which grants companies tax advantages), including works council-type forum along with an employee representative at board level. These are similar to a range of employee participation schemes that are currently more common in other EU countries such as Germany, Denmark, Sweden and the Netherlands. Of particular significance is the European Directive (2002/14/EC) on Employee Information and Consultation, recently transposed in Britain through the 2004 Information and Consultation of Employees (ICE) regulations.

These European regulations set out the requirements for member states to have in place permanent and statutory arrangements for employee information and consultation. The net effect is that workers in European countries will have a legal right to be informed and consulted on a range of business and employment issues. In countries such as Britain and Ireland, this marks a significant departure from the traditional voluntarist system of industrial relations (Gollan and Wilkinson, 2007). In Britain there is an important caveat here: the legal right is not automatic or universal. It excludes employees in establishments with less than 50 workers, and for those in defined organisations (e.g. 50+), employees 'have to trigger' the mechanism by requesting that management implement an information and consultation system.

The scope of the directive defines 'information' as the transmission, by the employer to employee representatives, of data in order to enable them to acquaint themselves with the subject matter and to examine it. 'Consultation' means the exchange of views and establishment of dialogue between the employees' representatives and the employer, with a view to reaching agreement. Significantly, the explicit reference to 'employee representatives' in the directive is a clear indication of a preference for indirect (i.e. collectivist) forms of involvement and participation. However, the transposed ICE regulations allow for direct employee information and consultation practices, such as team meetings. Nor do the participation mechanisms have to incorporate or include unions, as the representative is defined as an 'employee' elected from and by the workforce (who may or may not be a union steward). Where the ICE regulations are likely to be contentious is among organisations that are either partly unionised, or have low union density levels. In all probability, companies that are highly unionised already have in place joint consultation arrangements that will suffice under the regulations. Similarly, in completely non-union companies, management and employees have the scope to design and implement information and consultation mechanisms in line with the regulations without a union/non-union dichotomy. More problematic is in organisations with partial union membership as it is unclear whether there have to be duplicate union and non-union employee forums, particularly if existing union representatives find it unacceptable to represent the interests of non-members. The regulations also state that organisations will have to inform and consult with employee representatives (union and/or non-union) on three general areas: the economic situation of the organisation; the structure and probable development of employment (including any threats to employment) and to inform and consult on decisions likely to lead to changes in work organisation or contractual relations (see Box 16.1 for a summary of the main features of the ICE regulations).

There are currently a range of debates and issues associated with employee participation contained in the regulations (Gollan and Wilkinson, 2007; Hall *et al.*, 2013). Article 6(1) of the EU directive ensures confidentiality in that employee representatives (and experts that may assist them) cannot disclose commercially sensitive information provided to them. Article 7 stipulates that each of the EU countries has to ensure that employee representatives have adequate protection from managerial reprisals when carrying out their duties. This is likely to be particularly important given that employee representatives may not have the support and protection of a recognised trade union. Under the ICE regulations in Britain, the Central Arbitration Committee (CAC) is charged with ensuring company compliance and has powers to impose penalties for non-compliance, amounting to fines up to £75,000. Under the regulations, management and employee representatives have the opportunity to define and negotiate their own voluntary arrangements that can vary from a statutory fall-back model; a principle that is not too dissimilar to voluntary arrangements contained in the European Works Council Directive.

Box 16.1 HRM in practice — Information and consultation of employees (ICE) Regulations 2004

- The regulations apply to undertakings in Great Britain (and Ireland) with 50 or more employees. Equivalent legislation will be made in respect of Northern Ireland.
- The legal requirement to inform and consult employees is not automatic. A formal request has to be made by employees, or by an employer initiating the process (an employer notification).
- An employer must establish information and consultation procedures where a valid request has been made by employees.
- Such a request must be made in writing by 10% of employees in an undertaking (subject to a minimum of 15 and a maximum of 2,500 employees).
- Where the employees making the request wish to remain anonymous, they can submit the request to an independent body (such as the Central Arbitration Committee).
- The employer would have the opportunity to organise a ballot of employees to endorse or reject the initial request.
- An employer can continue with pre-existing information and consultation arrangements, provided that such arrangements have been agreed prior to an employee written request and:
  - (i) the agreement is in writing, including any collective agreements with trade unions;
  - (ii) the agreement covers all employees in the undertaking;
  - (iii) the agreement sets out how the employer is to provide the information and seek employee views for consultation;
  - (iv) the arrangements have been agreed by the employees.
- Where a valid request (or employer notification) has been made, but no agreement reached, standard information and consultation provisions based on ICE Regulation 18 would apply.
- Where the standard information and consultation provisions apply, the employer shall arrange for a ballot to elect the employee representatives. Regulation 19 states that there shall be 1 representative per 50 employees, or part thereof, with a minimum of 2 and maximum of 25 representatives.
- Consultation should take place with a view to reaching agreement on decisions.
- Information must be given in such time, and in such fashion and with such content as are appropriate to enable the information and consultation representatives to conduct an adequate study and, where necessary, prepare for consultation.
- The maximum penalty for failing to comply with a declaration made by the CAC is £75,000.
- ICE Regulations 25 and 26 provide for the confidentiality of sensitive information given to I&C representatives.
- I&C representatives, and employees making a request, are protected against discrimination/unfair dismissal for exercising their rights under the ICE Regulations.
- I&C representatives are to be afforded paid time-off to carry out their duties.

Source: DTI, 2006 (see http://webarchive.nationalarchives.gov.uk/20121212135622/http://www.bis.gov.uk/files/file25934.pdf).

The ICE regulations differ from the original EU directive in a number of fundamental respects (Dundon and Rollinson, 2011). First, what the European directive defines as information and consultation is not the same as those contained in the ICE regulations. The former is a clearer indication for 'indirect' employee participation via elected employee representatives, whereas the language of the ICE regulations implies that direct information and communication channels are acceptable. Second, and referring back to the framework to analyse the depth of employee participation earlier in the chapter, the EU directive points towards a deeper and wider form of participation than the ICE regulations imply. It has been suggested that trade unions may become further marginalised because the ICE regulations apply to employee representatives, and consciously exclude any reference to recognised union officials (Gollan and Wilkinson, 2007). Third, the trigger mechanism for employees to avail of these new participation rights could result in fear or intimidation for those workers in non-union companies who do not have access to an independent trade union, employees who request these new rights might face managerial reprisals such intimidation was found in a study by Cullinane et al (2015).

As a result, employers, employees and unions have been adapting and reacting to what is an increasingly regulated environment for employee participation. It appears that these sorts of regulations have led to what Hall *et al.* (2013) term 'legally prompted' forms of employee participation. In this scenario it is suggested that the law may encourage employers to be more creative by devising their own schemes for employee information and consultation, rather than rely on a legally imposed model of employee participation under the ICE regulations. A further possibility is that managers seek to avoid an extension of employee participation by following a minimalist strategy, supported by a soft regulatory regime which imposes very little constraint on employer choice about the type and extent of EIP adopted (Dobbins, 2010; Gollan *et al.*, 2014).

Conclusions

In this chapter we have outlined the context of employee participation over the last few decades in different countries and pointed towards future directions at a European level through a continuation of regulation. We have also considered the changing contours of management choice, public policy and that the adoption of various participation schemes is often uneven and complicated. While employee participation varies by context and across different countries, it is evident that a range of schemes often co-exist within an organisation and different forms of employee participation can be either complementary or contradict other management strategies and actions. A lot depends on the extent and depth of participation schemes and whether they are viewed as embedded or bolted on to existing arrangements. Moreover, we have stressed that the meanings and interpretations of such schemes are much more important than the type or number of techniques adopted. What is important is the depth to which participatory mechanisms are integrated with other organisational practices, the scope to which workers have a genuine say over matters that affect them, and the level at which participation occurs.

These factors are now influenced and shaped by management choices as well as (in the context of Europe) increasing regulations for employee participation. The case for industrial democracy in the 1960s and 1970s gave way to a neoliberal ideology dominated by global economic pressures, with an assumption that the state would remain largely absent from the employment relationship. The impact of such influences can be complex and uneven, belying simplistic dichotomies between state regulation and management choice for certain involvement schemes. Public policy neither represents a continuation of management-led involvement evident during the 1980s, nor a rolling-back to ideals premised on industrial democracy.

At one level, the current practices of EIP appear more embedded and less fragmented than they did a decade ago (Wilkinson *et al.*, 2013). Attempts have been made to consolidate and integrate different involvement and participation mechanisms over time and various forces and pressures have shaped EIP in liberal economic regimes (Marchington, 2015). In some situations, the adversarial nature of shop-floor relations appears to have partially diminished, with a new generation of union representatives willing and able to sit alongside non-union employee representatives on joint consultative forums. In other situations, particularly among multinational organisations, plans for dual or double-breasted participation have marginalised and by-passed unions (Dundon et al., 2015). The dualism in 1980s, of separated direct (individual) and indirect (union) involvement channels seems to be more intermingled with a range of schemes that overlap and co-exist at different levels.

Where union participation exists it is highly likely to do so as part of some sort of dual or hybrid regime involving non-union communication channels. Assuming HRM professionals are becoming dominated by I&O psychologists, especially among larger organisations seeking more and more sophisticated control strategies, the future trajectory for EIP is not necessarily warming as a renewed emphasis seems geared towards further marginalising collective representation owing to a highly unitarist managerial bias.

Taken together, these developments suggest that the current policy environment holds at best a mixed trajectory for engagement and social dialogue, partly as a result of greater (soft) regulation, but also owing to continued voluntarism means there are few constraints on management choice. What remains problematic is that many managers find the European language of employment rights unpalatable and even alien to newer organisational cultures shaped by flatter and lean work regimes and neoliberal market forces. These tensions are significant as managers play a key part in interpreting legislative requirements into practice in the workplace. In this regard, employee participation is best understood not in terms of particular techniques or discrete typologies located along a static either/or continuum, but rather as a set of complex and uneven meanings and interpretations shaped by external regulation as well as internalised power resources mobilised to shape choice for voice (Dundon et al., 2014). This incorporates informal dialogue as much as formalised structures and mechanisms. The challenges that lie ahead are how such a dynamic will be played out in practice, and whether existing multiple schemes for participation will be integrated or whether a new policy framework will result in another 'missed opportunity' for many managers (Wilkinson et al., 1992).

CASE STUDY 16.1

REDESIGNING EMPLOYEE INVOLVEMENT IN A SMALL FAMILY-RUN BUSINESS

TONY DUNDON

Peninsula Lodge is a small boutique hotel close to the Great Barrier Reef in Queensland; a short distance from a national rainforest and within easy reach of beautiful beaches. It is a three-star hotel with 85 rooms, a restaurant, bistro and banqueting and conferencing facilities. Peninsula Lodge currently employs 70 employees (full time and part time), comprising three senior managers, 16 function supervisors (such as housekeeping, catering, weddings, bistro, etc.) and operational staff. Employees are not represented by a trade union.

The hotel is family-owned, and two years ago a decision was made to add a leisure centre and market the hotel as a boutique wedding venue, offering a complete package and service to the wedding market. The addition of the leisure centre was described by a family owner as 'traumatic'. It was built at the same time as a new HR plan was rolled out, which sought to engage and involve staff. However, when the family owner attempted to introduce a new system to 'professionalise' supervisors and inject a new culture of customer service among employees, many quit, including long-service supervisors who were resistant of the changes. Further, a rebranded large hotel chain in the area intensified competition, resulting in growing economic pressure for Peninsula Lodge to compete in a wedding and leisure market dominated by large corporate hotels.

After observing other boutique hotels internationally, the senior management team decided to compete by offering a unique and differentiated service rather than on price alone. This involved the design and introduction of a new employee participation and engagement plan. Four 'core' elements to the engagement strategy were implemented. First, new communication channels were introduced that gave employees information about training possibilities in leisure, tourism and hotel activities. Employees were made aware and encouraged to apply for competency and work-related qualifications. Second, staff briefings were introduced so all employees were informed about work schedules, any changing shift patterns and particular special events coming up in the hotel or in the local vicinity. Third, new standard operating procedures were introduced, and a weekly log of faults, guest comments and employee ideas were fed back up the management chain. Finally, important information was attached to individual pay slips.

Additional systems were developed around each of the four core participation elements. One of the most significant was functional area meetings and briefings which were used as a two-way communication channel. These were held every week and because staff worked different shift patterns, minutes of the meeting were posted on bulletin boards. Employees who were not in attendance at a meeting had to sign to say they had received and read the minutes.

Senior management also introduced a system of 'self-directed' teamworking across seven key areas: customer service, human development, maintenance, cost control, quality, technology and the environment. Employees from all functional areas could select to be part of a team responsible for one of the key seven areas, with management ensuring all areas were represented by staff. The team would then meet to discuss ideas and improvement. Prizes would be awarded on a monthly basis for the best ideas from staff. Half-day workshops were introduced on a bi-monthly basis so ideas of one group could be reported and proposed to the senior management team. Examples of employee ideas implemented included new gluten-free restaurant and bistro menus; new environmentally friendly technologies to help clean rooms; an information card issued to staff on weekly basis that provided up-to-date information for guests on local excursions or events.

The owners and senior managers of Peninsula Lodge feel they started to promote a new culture of participation and engagement that was absent among staff previously. Business has picked up and, anecdotally, it appears new business has emerged from word-of-mouth recommendations. However, take-up of new training schemes by employees has been minimal. Furthermore, while there have been plenty of new ideas from staff, few have been implemented by senior managers. For employees, there has been a long tradition of informal dialogue and communication and some staff feel the new strategy is too structured for a small family-run hotel.

Questions

1 Why do you think some employees feel negative about the move to more formal types of employee participation initiatives at Peninsula Lodge?

2 How would you describe employee participation at Peninsula Lodge in terms of the framework explained in the chapter (e.g. depth, level, scope, form)?

3 Do you think the size of the Peninsula Lodge is an important factor in the nature of employee participation?

4 From reading the Peninsula Lodge case, why is it difficult to establish a relationship between employee participation and organisational performance?

CASE STUDY 16.2

THE MEANING OF PARTICIPATION TO MANAGERS

PAULA K. MOWBRAY

DairyProductsInc is a milk and cream processing facility located near one of Australia's largest capital cities, employing approximately 250 staff. The facility is approximately 60 years old and in need of capital expenditure. However, the site's new owners are reluctant to spend money on capital upgrades as the site's future is uncertain, with one major supply contract recently lost and another supply contract up for renewal. In the past six months, the entire senior leadership team has been replaced, with many of the previous managers moving to a nearby dairy processing company. Many of DairyProductsInc's employees have also left and been employed by the competitor. Given the production downturn, the senior managers from the site were in discussions with staff regarding redundancies.

Understandably, many of the employees are concerned about their job security. The new senior management team have held a number of forums to discuss the redundancies with staff and have invited staff to ask questions at the forums. Staff has been told that they can ask their line managers any further questions, and the line managers have been directed to discuss those questions with senior management. Senior management are conscious that the right information is provided to employees and so they want to provide the line managers with the correct response to give their employees.

The new senior leadership team is also trying to improve the organisational culture to reflect the culture of the organisation that owns DairyProductsInc. The previous senior managers had a dictatorial leadership style and employees were used to being told what to do, whereas the new leaders are trying to instil an achievement culture into the business and to encourage their employees to contribute to continuous improvement initiatives and to speak up with their ideas to improve DairyProductsInc. To enable this, a lean manufacturing process has been implemented, with employees working in self-managed teams and expected to be involved in problem-solving issues and finding solutions. One strategy senior leaders is using to encourage employees to speak up and be involved in the process is to walk the shop floor regularly, which they believe helps develop trusting relationships with their employees.

However, many of the staff are dissatisfied with the lean manufacturing process and don't believe it is their job to make suggestions. It also appears that many of the line managers feel this way and they are not supportive of implementing the lean manufacturing process or encouraging their employees to speak up. The line managers rarely walk the factory floor and, in fact, in some instances it seems that they are afraid to do so. Other line managers appear to engage in horse-play with their employees, modelling what senior managers consider 'bad behaviour'. Therefore, senior managers see that the interaction and relationships between line managers and their employees seem to be an issue. It has also come to the attention of the senior management that there is a 'no dobbing' culture, which means that grievances about other employees are rarely raised and there is reluctance by employees to formalise any grievances.

The majority of employees are employed under an Enterprise Bargaining Agreement (EBA), with the exception of middle and senior leaders and some specialist staff, including engineers. The union is mainly involved in negotiations regarding the EBA and issues concerning penalty rates, for example. There is a consultative committee comprised of union representatives and management, which was in existence long before the new owners bought DairyProductsInc. According to senior management, this channel is not being used effectively and there is a lack of alignment in how the senior management would like the committee to be used and the type of content raised. Senior managers believe that the employee representatives on the consultative committee have been using the mechanism to push their own individual agenda, and to discuss union-related issues, rather than issues related to the site. Accordingly, there was an effort by senior managers to change the content placed on the consultative committee agenda to include more significant and bigger site issues, such as discussing the ramifications of losing the grocery contract. Senior managers also believe there is a lack of understanding of the participation processes by line managers and employees, and knowing which channel should be used to raise particular issues. This meant that the processes were duplicating each other, rather than being used for their specific purpose and to deal with specific content and issues.

The senior managers are considering setting up a roster committee to involve the employees on the floor in designing the roster shift patterns, to cope with the drop in volume. The senior managers hope that this will provide a structured way to get input from employees, but they also want to ensure that any suggestions made are in alignment with the objectives of the business. Therefore, any changes to the roster shift pattern have to be win-win. Given that the viability of the site is in doubt, senior managers want to make sure that this committee is successful but are concerned that line managers and employees will not use this channel as management intended.

Questions

1 Why do you think the employees have been reluctant to speak up and to make suggestions to improve DairyProductsInc?

2 Do you think that senior managers are using the participation channels as a form of management control or are they trying to provide employee autonomy and discretion for the benefit of employees?

3 How could the lean manufacturing process be implemented better so that employees and line managers are more satisfied working in autonomous teams?

4 What should the senior managers do to ensure that the new roster committee is successful and a win-win for both management and employees?

CASE STUDY 16.3
THE DURABILITY OF 'DOUBLE-BREASTING' VOICE IN A MULTINATIONAL ORGANISATION

TONY DUNDON

Introduction

Employee participation has retained a central role in HRM over the last two decades. It can be seen as a key component of best-practice HRM and high-commitment management leading to improved organisational performance. At the same time there has been a decline in union channels of participation and an increase in NER. The mix of dual union and non-union voice has also received widespread attention from scholars and researchers. Some view NERs as a form of union-avoidance, that is, a mechanism intent on by-passing unions and removing any demand among employees for a trade union to represent their interests. On the other hand, arguments abound that NERs may function as a complement to union channels that may coexist in tandem. This case study reports on double-breasting in one large multinational organisation, adapted from Cullinane et al. (2012).

The company and its context

BritCo is a former public utility that was initially privatised in Britain in the 1980s. It is now a multinational organisation with operations in over 170 countries. The case described here is the story of how BritCo entered the Irish market and proceeded to implement a double-breasting strategy for employee participation. BritCo entered the market in the Republic of Ireland through a process of commercial acquisition, which included the purchase of a non-unionised firm. Once established in the market place, BritCo management decided the company should operate on an all-island basis. This meant merging its operation in Northern Ireland (NI) (highly unionised, centralised and part of the UK management structure) with those in the south (exclusively non-unionised, decentralised and based on newer acquired operations).

The decision to structure BritCo on an all-island basis was not without its difficulties. To begin with, BritCo (NI) has a deep history of collective representation and was a former state monopoly. There are two recognised trade unions in BritCo (NI) with over 90 per cent density, primarily operating through a UK industrial relations system with collective negotiations conducted centrally in London. In contrast, BritCo in the republic is non-union and relations are locally rather than centrally based. The merger of BritCo across the island of Ireland resulted in negative repercussions as some functions moved from the south to the north. Significantly, redundancy caused problems as terms and conditions were much lower in the south than those that had been collectively negotiated for staff in the north. Indeed, no compulsory redundancy agreement exists for unionised staff from BritCo (NI); a legacy that remained post-nationalisation. Because of what appeared to be superior employment conditions for BritCo (NI) employees, a trade union organising campaign was instigated by some workers in BritCo in the south. Unlike UK law, there is no comparable statutory trade union legislation in the Republic of Ireland. In response to the union recognition campaign in the Republic of Ireland, management instigated a double-breasting strategy with union representation in BritCo (NI) and exclusively non-union participation channels for BritCo in the republic.

Worker participation in BritCo Northern Ireland

In Northern Ireland BritCo has a long history and tradition of collective participation through centralised negotiation and joint consultation and two separate trade unions are recognised for these purposes. At the same time, the company has several other *direct* forms of employee involvement, including staff/team briefings, weekly newsletters from management, regular use of the company's intranet for communications and an annual company-wide survey. These direct employee participation techniques have increased at BritCo NI in recent years, with the CEO supportive of direct and transparent management communications. The newsletter, for example, provides staff with information on new business developments and how the company is performing. In addition, the intranet provides employees with direct access to a wide range of human resource policies (e.g. pension information and other company procedures, such as discipline). Two recent employee engagement initiatives are also noteworthy. One is a weekly public 'phone call' in which all employees can listen in 'live' to the CEO talking about business developments. Employees can respond or just listen. Another engagement initiative is an annual 'engagement survey', which asks a series of questions about employee satisfaction and commitment on a company-wide basis. The results can then be compared between regions and different business units.

In addition to the above are other *indirect* collective forms of participation, which have a much longer and deeper history across Northern Ireland operations. There is a company joint consultative committee (JCC), which includes the CEO, several functional heads (such as the HR, IT, Finance, Engineering Directors), local line managers and shop stewards, along with the full-time union official for each of the two unions. At these JCC meetings financial matters and company strategy, as appropriate to NI operations, are considered. Union officials or stewards do not have any input in terms of setting the agenda for the JCC, and typically do not know what issues will be discussed in advance of the annual meeting. However, union reps can and often do raise matters under 'any other business'. Other collective mechanisms that occur on a more regular basis include bi-monthly meetings between union stewards and senior managers to discuss any emergent issues of concern to employees. Running alongside the formal JCC and bi-monthly meetings is 'informal union–management dialogue', which tends to occur on a more regular albeit ad hoc basis. Issues pertaining to matters such as discipline, sickness or employee grievance representation will often be discussed informally or 'off the record' between union reps and managers before matters are progressed through the formal participation mechanisms.

While BritCo NI utilises both direct and indirect channels of employee participation at its NI operations, relations have not always been easy or smooth. Indeed, management say they have had to 'redefine' the union role so it can add value to the company (as well as its members). Newer roles have included how to deal with changes to work patterns in order to be more flexibly responsible to customer demands. Yet employees report a high degree of trust in management because they know that their union officials can and do call management to account when necessary.

Employee voice at BritCo in the Republic of Ireland

As in the north, employee participation at BritCo in the republic includes both 'direct' and 'indirect' mechanisms for workers to have a say. For the most part, direct employee participation converges across both BritCo NI and BritCo in the republic (e.g. company intranet, newsletters, etc.). Regarding indirect employee voice, however, things are very different in the republic with NER mechanisms used instead of union channels. These include, primarily, what is known as '*BritCo Vocal*': a non-union employee forum covering the whole of the Republic of Ireland. In addition, there is a '*Southern Works Committee*' (SWC), which is a collective employee council for Dublin-based engineers to deal with issues particular to that work group and location.

The NER arrangements at BritCo Republic had been established a couple of years ago in response to European information and consultation regulations. The NER system became inactive because of a lack in managerial support combined with little employee interest. However, the forum was relaunched as BritCo Vocal in response to a union recognition campaign at BritCo in the Republic of Ireland. Employee reps were 'elected' when they were previously 'selected' by management. Within this, electoral constituencies exist for different business units so the forum represents all occupational groups. Furthermore, employee reps have an input into issues and agenda items, and afforded the opportunity to report back to their employee constituents (using email, intranet messaging and notice boards). The separate SWC emerged at the behest of management because of that group of engineers dominating the agenda of BritCo Vocal, and because management wanted to isolate what they saw as a potentially militant and union supportive group of workers. In short, the SWC marginalised union sympathisers from the rest of the non-union workforce across Britco in the south.

While the existence of formal NER structures is important, it is necessary to assess the scope and depth of such employee participation in terms of the matters available for consultation. Perhaps the most immediate and significant issue was that of inferior redundancy conditions for employees in the republic compared to those offered to workers in Northern Ireland. The discrepancy may be explained by long-established union agreement in the north that was not available to employees in the south. In response, management used the BritCo Vocal forum to review the situation and allow non-union employee reps considerable scope in redrafting the redundancy arrangements. The outcome was a revised policy handbook that incorporated key elements of the Northern Ireland redundancy scheme in the republic.

While managers and employees were initially satisfied with BritCo Vocal, and the amount of say employee reps had in changing policy and practice, over time things started to feel very different. Employee reps on the Vocal committee felt that once management attempted to resolve an issue, interest waned. In particular, management appeared to offer greater support and enthusiasm for the Vocal forum when the union

organising campaign was at its peak. Consequently, some employee reps lost interest and dropped out of participating in BritCo Vocal forum meetings when management support waned. The way the SWC operated in practice was very similar. While it was initially active and dealt with concerns about performance management and the use of company vehicles for specific engineers at the Dublin South facility, activity diminished after about two years and when the union-organising campaign failed to secure recognition rights for workers in the republic, employee reps felt that issues had declined in importance and management allowed minor, or what they called 'tea and toilet roll issues', to be dealt with at SWC meetings.

Summary: the durability of double-breasting employee participation

Employee participation in large, complex and multinational and global organisations such as BritCo are far from straightforward. The strategy for employees to have a say across the different sites and jurisdictions of BritCo Northern Ireland and BritCo Republic has been uneven and at times contradictory. With a new CEO and a belief in a culture of engagement and voice, direct employee mechanisms started to have a stronger and deeper hold. Yet, at the same time, union channels of voice were supported and tolerated in the north, but actively discouraged in the republic. To some extent this was because management could get away with such a strategy because of different employee participation regulations. Indeed, there is no comparative union recognition legislation in the south to that in the north. Likewise, both Irish and UK governments adopted a minimalist interpretation of European regulations for employee information and consultation that effectively downgraded collective voice in favour of direct involvement channels. Double-breasting employee participation at BritCo suited a managerial agenda of seeking to redefine (diminish) the trade union role for participation. How durable and extensive such a double-breasting strategy will be in the long run is of course a matter of some debate.

Questions

1   In the BritCo case, to what extent would you say that NER forms of employee representation are deep or shallow?

2   Does a strategy of double-breasting (union and non-union) participation serve managerial or worker interests?

3   Imagine you have been asked for your professional advice and opinion from the BritCo Ireland Board of Directors. They would like you to make a short presentation about the feasibility of a strategy of double-breasting voice in which one or two plants are unionised, and other sites have exclusive non-union employee participation mechanisms. What would you include in the presentation and why?

4   Given what has been described at BritCo, should trade unions be worried about the introduction of employee information and consultation regulations?

5   What implications are there from the BritCo case for the meaning of employee participation?

Bibliography

Ackers, P., Marchington, M., Wilkinson, A. and Goodman, J. (1992) 'The use of cycles? Explaining employee involvement in the 1990s', *Industrial Relations Journal*, Vol.23, No.4, 268–83.

Ackers, P., Marchington, M., Wilkinson, A. and Dundon, T. (2005) 'Partnership and voice, with or without trade unions: changing UK management approaches to organisational participation', in Stuart, M. and Martinez Lucio, M. (eds.) *Partnership and Modernisation in Employment Relations*, Abingdon: Routledge.

Balnave, N., Barnes, A., MacMillan, C. and Thornthwaite, L. (2014) 'E-voice: how network and media technologies are shaping employee voice', in Wilkinson, A., Donaghey, J., Dundon, T. and Freeman, R. (eds.) *Handbook of Research on Employee Voice*, Cheltenham: Edward Elgar.

Bamber, G.J., Gittel, J.H., Kochan, T.A. and Van Nordenflycht, A. (2009) *Up in the Air: How Airlines Can Improve Performance by Engaging Employees*, New York: Cornell University Press.

Barry, M. and Wilkinson, A. (2015) 'Pro-social or pro-management? A critique of the conception of employee voice as a pro-social behaviour within organisational behaviour, *British Journal of Industrial Relations*. Available for early viewing at: DOI: 10.1111/bjir.12114.

Barker, J. (1993) 'Tightening the iron cage: concertive control in self-managing teams', *Administrative Science Quarterly*, Vol.38, 408–37.

Beaumont, P.B. and Harris, R.I.D. (1992) '"Double-breasted" recognition arrangements in Britain', *International Journal of Human Resource Management*, Vol.3, No.2, 267–83.

Becker, B.E. and Huselid, M.A. (1998) 'High performance work systems and firm performance synthesis of research and managerial implications', in Ferris, G.R. (ed.) *Research in Personnel and Human Resources*, Vol.16, Stamford, CT: JAI Press.

Benson, J. and Brown, M. (2010) 'Employee voice: does union membership matter?', *Human Resource Management Journal*, Vol.20, No.1, 80–99.

Boxall, P. and Purcell, J. (2011) *Strategy and Human Resource Management* (3rd edn.), London: Palgrave.

Brannen, P. (1983) *Authority and Participation in Industry*, London: Batsford.

Brewster, C., Croucher, R., Wood, G. and Brookes, M. (2007) 'Collective and individual voice: convergence in Europe?', *International Journal of Human Resource Management*, Vol.18, No.7, 1246–62.

Brownlie, N. (2012) *Trade Union Membership 2011*, London: Department for Business, Innovation and Skills.

Bryson, A., Willman, P., Gomez, R. and Kretchmer, T. (2007), 'Employee voice and human resource management: an empirical analysis using British data', *PSI Research Discussion Paper No 27*, London: Policy Studies Institute.

Budd, J.W., Gollan, P. and Wilkinson, A. (2010), 'New approaches to employee voice and participation in organizations', *Human Relations*, Vol.63 (March), 303–10.

Bullock, A. (Lord) (1977) *Report of the Committee of Inquiry on Industrial Democracy*, London: HMSO (Cmnd. 6706).

Collard, R. and Dale, B. (1989) 'Quality circles', in Sisson, K. (ed.) *Personnel Management in Britain*, Oxford: Blackwell.

Cox, A., Zagelmeyer, S. and Marchington, M. (2006) 'Embedding employee involvement and participation at work', *Human Resource Management Journal*, Vol.16, No.3, 250–67.

Cressey, P., Eldridge, J. and MacInnes, J. (1985) *Just Managing: Authority and Democracy in Industry*, Milton Keynes: Open University Press.

*Cullinane, N., Donaghey, J., Dundon, T. and Dobbins, T. (2012) 'Different rooms, different voices: double-breasting, multi-channel representation and the managerial agenda', *International Journal of Human Resource Management*, Vol.23, No.2, 368–84.

Cullinane, N., Hickland, E., Dundon, T., Dobbins, T and Donaghey, J. (2015), 'Triggering employee voice under the European Information and Consultation Directive: A non-union case study', *Economic and Industrial Democracy*, on-line early [10.1177/0143831X15584085]: 1–27.

Cully, M., O'Reilly, A., Woodland, S. and Dix, G. (1999) *Britain at Work: As Depicted by the 1998 Workplace Employee Relations Survey*, Abingdon: Routledge.

Delbridge, R., Turnbull, P. and Wilkinson, B. (1992) 'Pushing back the frontiers: management control and work intensification under JIT/TQM factory regimes', *New Technology, Work and Employment*, Vol.7, No.2, 97–106.

Department of Trade and Industry (DTI) (2006) *The Information and Consultation of Employees Regulations 2004: DTI Guidance* (January 2006). Available at: http://webarchive .nationalarchives.gov.uk/20121212135622 and http://www.bis.gov.uk/files/file25934.pdf.

Diamond, W. and Freeman, R. (2001) 'What workers want from workplace organisations', *Report to the TUCs Promoting Unionism Task Group*, London: Trades Union Congress.

Dietz, G., Wilkinson, A. and Redman, T. (2009) 'Involvement and participation', pp. 243–66, in Wilkinson, A., Bacon, N., Redman, T. and Snell, S. (eds.) *The SAGE Handbook of Human Resource Management*, London: Sage.

Dobbins, T. (2010) 'The case for beneficial constraints: why permissive voluntarism impedes workplace cooperation in Ireland', *Economic and Industrial Democracy*, Vol.31, No.4, 497–519.

Dobbins, T. and Dundon, T. (2014a) 'The European information and consultation directive in voluntarist economies', in Ackers, P. and Johnstone, S. (eds.) *Finding a Voice? Employee Representation in the New Workplace: Concepts, Models and Possible Futures*, Oxford: Oxford University Press.

Dobbins, T. and Dundon, T. (2014b) 'Non-union employee representation', in Wilkinson, A., Donaghey, J., Dundon, T. and Freeman, R. (eds.) *Handbook of Research on Employee Voice*, Cheltenham: Edward Elgar.

Donaghey, J., Cullinane, N., Dundon, T. and Wilkinson, A. (2010) 'Reconceptualising employee silence: problems and prognosis', *Work, Employment and Society*, Vol.25, No.1, 51–67.

Donaghey, J., Cullinane, N., Dundon, T. and Dobbins, A. (2012) 'Non-union employee representation, union avoidance and the managerial agenda', *Economic and Industrial Democracy*, Vol.33, No.2, 163–83.

Dundon, T. and Rollinson, D. (2004) *Employment Relations in Non-Union Firms*, Abingdon: Routledge.

Dundon, T. and Rollinson, D. (2011) *Understanding Employment Relations* (2nd edn.), London: McGraw Hill.

*Dundon, T., Wilkinson, A., Marchington, M. and Ackers, P. (2004) 'The meanings and purpose of employee voice', *International Journal of Human Resource Management*, Vol.15, No.6, 1150–71.

*Dundon, T., Wilkinson, A., Marchington, M. and Ackers, P. (2005) 'The management of voice in non-union organisations: managers' perspectives', *Employee Relations*, Vol.27, No.3, 307–19.

Dundon, T., Dobbins, T., Cullinane, N., Hickland, E. and Donaghey, J. (2014) 'Employer occupation of regulatory space for the Employee Information and Consultation (I&C) Directive in Liberal Market Economies', *Work, Employment and Society*, Vol.28, No.1, 21–39.

Dundon, T., Cullinane, N., Donaghey, J., Wilkinson, A., Dobbins, T. and Hickland, E. (2015) 'Double-breasting voice systems: an assessment of motive, strategy and sustainability', *Human Relations*, Vol.68, No.3, 489–513.

Gall, G. and Dundon, T. (eds.) (2013) *Global anti-unionism: nature, dynamics, trajectories and outcomes*, London: Palgrave Macmillan.

Geary, J. and Dobbins, A. (2001) 'Teamworking: a new dynamic in the pursuit of management control', *Human Resource Management Journal*, Vol.11, No.1, 3–23.

Godard, J. (2014) 'The psychologisation of employment relations?', *Human Resource Management Journal*, Vol.24, No.1, 1–18.

Gollan, P. (2007) *Employee Representation in Non-Union Firms*, London: Sage.

Gollan, P. and Wilkinson, A. (2007) 'Implications of the EU Information and Consultation Directive and the regulations in the UK: prospects for the future of employee representation', *International Journal of Human Resource Management*, Vol.18, No.7, 1145–58.

Gollan, P., Patmore, G. and Xu, Y. (2014) 'Regulation of employee voice', in Wilkinson, A., Donaghey, J., Dundon, T. and Freeman, R. (eds.) *Handbook of Research on Employee Voice*, Cheltenham: Edward Elgar.

Hall, M., Purcell, J., Terry, M., Hutchinson, S. and Parker, J. (2013) 'Trade union approaches towards the ICE regulations: defensive realism or missed opportunity?', *British Journal of Industrial Relations*, Vol.53, No.2, 350–75.

Harley, B. (2014) 'High performance work systems and employee voice', in Wilkinson, A., Donaghey, J., Dundon, T. and Freeman, R. (eds.) *Handbook of Research on Employee Voice*, Cheltenham: Edward Elgar.

Kaine, S. (2014) 'Union voice', in Wilkinson, A., Donaghey, J., Dundon, T. and Freeman, R. (eds.) *Handbook of Research on Employee Voice*, Cheltenham: Edward Elgar.

*Kaufman, B. (2015) 'Theorising determinants of employee voice: an integrative model across disciplines and levels of analysis', *Human Resource Management Journal*, Vol.25, No.1, 19–40.

Lavelle, J., Gunnigle, P. and McDonnell, A. (2010) 'Patterning employee voice in multinational companies', *Human Relations*, Vol.63 (March), 395–418.

Lewis, P., Thornhill, A. and Saunders, M. (2003) *Employee Relations: Understanding the Employment Relationship*, Harlow: Prentice Hall.

Lipsky, D.B. and Farber, H.S. (1976) 'The composition of strike activity in the construction industry', *Industrial and Labor Relations Review*, Vol.29, No.3, 401–28.

Logan, J. (2013) 'Employer opposition to unionisation and labour law reform in the United States', in Gall, G. and Dundon, T. (eds.) (2013) *Global Anti-unionism: Nature, Dynamics, Trajectories and Outcomes*, London: Palgrave Macmillan.

*Marchington, M. (2015) 'Analysing the forces shaping employee involvement and participation (EIP) at organisation level in liberal market economies (LMEs)', *Human Resource Management Journal*, Vol.25, No.1, 1–18.

Marchington, M. and Suter, J. (2013) 'Where informality really matters: patterns of employee involvement and participation in a non-union firm', *Industrial Relations*, Vol.52, No.S1, 284–313.

Wilkinson, A., Dundon, T. and Marchington, M. (2013) 'Employee involvement and voice', pp. 268–89, in Bach, S. and Edwards, M. (eds.) *Managing Human Resources* (5th edn.), Chichester: Wiley-Blackwell.

Marchington, M. and Wilkinson, A. (2012) *Human Resource Management at Work* (5th edn.), London: Chartered Institute of Personnel and Development.

Marchington, M., Goodman, J., Wilkinson, A. and Ackers, P. (1992) 'New developments in employee involvement', Research Paper No.2, London: Employment Department.

Northrup, H.R. (1995) 'Doublebreasted operations and the decline of construction unionism', *Journal of Labor Research*, Vol.16, No.3, 379–85.

OECD (2015) 'Trade union density: selected countries 2013 stats extracts', Organisation for Economic Development and Cooperation. Available at: https://stats.oecd.org/Index .aspx?DataSetCode=UN_DEN.

Pfeffer, J. (1998) *The Human Equation: Building Profits by Putting People First*, Boston, MA: Harvard Business School Press.

Piore, M. and Sabel, C. (1983) *The Second Industrial Divide*, New York: Basic Books.

Proctor, S. and Benders, J. (2014) 'Task-based voice: teamworking, autonomy and performance', in Wilkinson, A., Donaghey, J., Dundon, T. and Freeman, R. (eds.) *Handbook of Research on Employee Voice*, Cheltenham: Edward Elgar.

Ramsay, H. (1977) 'Cycles of control: worker participation in sociological and historical perspective', *Sociology*, Vol.11, No.3, 481–506.

Roeber, J. (1975) *Social Change at Work*, London: Heinemann.

Rose, J.B. (1986) 'Legislative support for multi-employer bargaining: the Canadian experience', *Industrial and Labor Relations Review*, Vol.40, No.1, 3–18.

Sewell, G. and Wilkinson, B. (1992) 'Empowerment or emasculation? Shopfloor surveillance in a total quality organisation', in Blyton, P. and Turnbull, P. (eds.) *Reassessing Human Resource Management*, London: Sage.

Sinclair, A. (1992) 'The tyranny of a team ideology', *Organization Studies*, Vol.13, No.4, 11–26.

Tebbutt, M. and Marchington, M. (1997) 'Look before you speak: gossip and the insecure workplace', *Work Employment and Society*, Vol.11, No.4, 713–35.

Trist, E., Higgin, G., Murray, H. and Pollock, A. (1963) *Organisational Choice: Capabilities of Groups at the Coalface under Changing Technologies*, London: Tavistock Institute.

Verma, A. and Kochan, T. (1985) 'The growth and nature of the non-union sector within a firm', in Kochan, T. (ed.) *Challenges and Choices Facing American Labor*, Boston, MA: MIT Press.

*Wedderburn, K.W. (Lord) (1986) *The Worker and the Law* (3rd edn.), Harmondsworth: Penguin.

Wilkinson, A. (2002) 'Empowerment', in Poole, M. and Warner, M. (eds.) *International Encyclopaedia of Business and Management Handbook of Human Resource Management*, London: ITB Press.

Wilkinson, A. and Dundon, T. (2010) 'Direct employee participation', in Wilkinson, A., Gollan, P., Marchington, M. and Lewin, D. (eds.) *The Oxford Handbook of Participation in Organizations*, Oxford: Oxford University Press.

Wilkinson, A., Dundon T. and Grugulis, I. (2007) 'Information but not consultation: exploring employee involvement in SMEs', *International Journal of Human Resource Management*, Vol.18, No.7, 1279–97.

Wilkinson, A., Dundon, T. and Marchington, M. (2012) 'Employee involvement and voice', in Bach, S. and Edwards, M. (eds.) *Managing Human Resources*, Oxford: Blackwell.

Wilkinson, A., Dundon, T., Marchington, M. and Ackers, P. (2004) 'Changing patterns of employee voice', *Journal of Industrial Relations*, Vol.46, No.3, 298–322.

Wilkinson, A., Dundon, T., Donaghey, J. and Freeman, R. (2014) 'Employee voice: charting new terrain', in Wilkinson, A., Donaghey, J., Dundon, T. and Freeman, R. (eds.) *Handbook of Research on Employee Voice*, Cheltenham: Edward Elgar.

Wilkinson, A., Gollan, P., Marchington, M. and Lewin, D. (2010) 'Conceptualizing employee participation in organizations', in Wilkinson, A., Gollan, P., Marchington, M. and Lewin, D. (eds.) *The Oxford Handbook of Participation in Organizations*, Oxford: Oxford University Press.

Wilkinson, A., Marchington, M., Goodman, J. and Ackers, P. (1992) 'Total quality management and employee involvement', *Human Resource Management Journal*, Vol.2, No.4, 1–20.

Willman, P., Bryson, A., Gomez, R. and Kretschmer, T. (2014) 'Employee voice and the transaction cost economics project', in Wilkinson, A., Donaghey, J., Dundon, T. and Freeman, R. (eds.) *Handbook of Research on Employee Voice*, Cheltenham: Edward Elgar.

van Wanrooy, B., Bewley, H., Bryson, A., Forth, J., Freeth, S., Stokes, L. and Wood, S. (2013) *Employment Relations in the Shadow of Recession: Findings from the 2011 Workplace Employment Relations Study*, Basingstoke: Palgrave.

---

*Useful reading.

CHAPTER 17
EMPLOYEE ENGAGEMENT

Elaine Farndale and Maja Vidović

Introduction

Employee engagement is a hot topic amongst managers, consultancies, governments and academics alike and is considered crucial for successful management of a productive workforce in organisations. Firms view employee engagement as a means to improve their performance and increase competitiveness. From a behavioural perspective, compared to less engaged workers, engaged employees put in more hours, and work with greater intensity (higher productivity) and direction (focus on the organisational priorities) (MacCormick et al., 2012). Engaged employees also demonstrate signs of higher levels of job satisfaction, commitment and organisational citizenship behaviour (Kelliher et al., 2013). In short, engagement is considered beneficial, both for organisations and often for individual employees themselves (Bakker and Demerouti, 2008).

Employee engagement is of special interest for multinational corporations (MNCs) managing a diverse workforce, and for organisations doing business in emerging economies with highly dynamic labour markets. Interest does not stop there, however. Organisations globally are faced with the challenge of new generations of employees, well known for their job-hopping behaviour, who are expected to represent half of the workforce by 2020.

Considering the importance of employee engagement for organisational success, this chapter provides an introduction to this construct and how it is measured, as well exploring the 'dark side' of engagement, and how engagement might differ from other well-known positive employee attitude and behaviour constructs. An overview of what helps to create employee engagement leads to an exploration of the outcomes we might expect from having engaged employees. Finally, we explore the meaning and practice of employee engagement in different contexts around the world.

Definition

Although employee engagement is a popular term used throughout organisations worldwide, under closer observation it becomes apparent that there are many different ways in which this construct can be observed and defined. These range from engagement being described as a positive employee attitude towards the organisation and its values (Robinson *et al.*, 2004), through employee attentiveness to role performance (Saks, 2006) to employees expressing vigour, dedication and absorption in work (Schaufeli *et al.*, 2006) and having high energy levels and professional efficacy (Maslach *et al.*, 2001). Engaged employees are said to be optimistic, highly focused on their work, enthusiastic and willing to go the extra mile to contribute to sustainable organisational success on a long-term basis (Jose and Mampilly, 2012). In brief, engagement is about employees being positive about their work and the organisation, with energy, passion and hard work often being cited as keywords describing the construct (Farndale *et al.*, 2014a).

The term 'employee engagement' originates from the psychology literature and research on how people apply themselves to the roles they perform. Kahn (1990) was the first to conceptualise engagement, identifying that people use varying degrees of their personal selves – cognitive, emotional and physical – in the roles they perform at work. This implies that employees devote varying degrees of personal engagement or disengagement while at work. Kahn (1990) reported three psychological conditions that are critical in influencing engagement: 'meaningfulness', 'safety' and 'availability'. *Meaningfulness* ('How meaningful is it for me to bring myself into this performance?') is a sense of return on investment of a person's effort in his or her work, and can be connected to the concept of job security. *Safety* ('How safe is it for me to bring myself into this performance?') is a sense of being able to employ oneself without fear of negative consequences to self-image, status or career. *Availability* ('How available am I to bring myself into this performance?') means possessing the physical, emotional and psychological resources necessary for investing oneself in role performance. The latter can also be divided into two dimensions: *personal* resource availability, such as energy, competence and family support (Rothbard, 2001) and *job* resource availability, such as social support and job control (Mauno *et al.*, 2007) with limited job demands requiring excessive physical or mental effort (Demerouti *et al.*, 2001).

Building on this groundwork, Saks (2006: 604) relates the employee engagement construct to the science of organisations, describing it as: 'the extent to which an employee is psychologically present in a particular organizational role'. Organisational roles are described as being related to a specific job or task or, in more general terms, as an organisation member. This distinction highlights our first real insight into the different types of employee engagement: work (or job) engagement and organisation engagement (Kelliher *et al.*, 2013). Commentators also refer to organisation engagement as 'behavioral engagement' (Guest, 2014; Purcell, 2014) or 'employee engagement' (Truss, 2014). To date, most attention in the academic literature has been paid to work engagement.[1]

Alongside the distinction between work and organisation engagement, Macey and Schneider (2008) take a different perspective, focusing on differences in employee characteristics. They distinguish three components that shape employee engagement: 'trait engagement', 'psychological state engagement' and 'behavioural engagement'. *Trait engagement* emphasises personal-level attributes such as personality, *psychological state engagement* is characterised by affect and feelings of energy, while *behavioural engagement* focuses on the actions of employees. Empirical studies supporting this conceptual framework are limited because of multicollinearity issues between the constructs (Harter and Schmidt, 2008), but they indicate initial support for a distinction between state and behavioural engagement (Farndale *et al.*, 2011).

Combining the types of employee engagement (work and organisation) with the dimensions of engagement (trait, state, behaviour), Table 17.1 summarises what we might define as the core components of employee engagement.

---

[1] It is important to note that the literature frequently uses the terms 'work engagement' and 'employee engagement' synonymously (Jeve *et al.*, 2015), resulting in a certain degree of confusion around the topic.

Table 17.1 Core components of employee engagement

	Work-Focused	Organisation-Focused
Trait	Work trait engagement	Organisation trait engagement
State	Work state engagement	Organisation state engagement
Behaviour	Work behavioural engagement	Organisation behavioural engagement

Work trait engagement occurs when employees have a personality that enables them to devote themselves completely to their daily tasks at work. For example, research suggests that high extraversion and low neuroticism (Langelaan *et al.*, 2006), and high extraversion and conscientiousness (Handa and Gulati, 2014) are related to higher work engagement. For organisation trait engagement, we might expect a similar scenario to occur, whether as a result of matching employee characteristics to the organisation (achieving person–organisation fit; Hamid and Yahya, 2011; Memon *et al.*, 2014) or purely as a result of the employee's natural propensity to devote him or herself when agreeing to be part of a larger group or organisation. For future research, it will be interesting to explore empirically whether person–organisation fit facilitates both work and organisation trait engagement.

Work state engagement refers to affect, and denotes employees loving their job, having great enthusiasm to get out of bed each morning and do their daily tasks. This can lead to individuals talking passionately about their work, but not necessarily having loyalty to the organisation for which they work (although the two can, of course, be highly correlated). Organisation state engagement, on the other hand, is about employees loving the organisation irrespective of their job role. Their personal values are aligned with the organisational values, and these employees make great ambassadors for spreading the corporate brand.

Behavioural engagement focuses not on the affect that employees display, but instead on their activities in the workplace. This is evidenced by employees going the extra mile and applying extra effort to complete their work. Work behavioural engagement includes employees taking the initiative in their daily work and actively seeking development opportunities. Organisation behavioural engagement is about employees being proactive in highlighting problems and suggesting improvements that may benefit the organisation as a whole.

Arguably, behavioural engagement may be more beneficial to firms from a productivity perspective, whereas state engagement creates a pleasant environment for people to work in. Ultimately, it is important to know what type of engagement is being measured, to communicate about the types of engagement a firm desires, and to understand what action plans might help to create the necessary engagement to achieve firm performance (Farndale *et al.*, 2011).

Measuring work and organisation engagement in research

One of the best ways to understand a construct is by looking at ways in which it has been empirically captured. For employee engagement, although the term is well known in the organisational psychology literature (Macey and Schneider, 2008), and is becoming well known in current everyday working life (Vance, 2006), in the human resource management (HRM) field research is still somewhat limited (Farndale *et al.*, 2011).

The employee engagement measure most commonly applied across the psychology literature, and increasingly in the HRM literature, is that of the Utrecht Work Engagement Scale (UWES) (Schaufeli *et al.*, 2002). This work engagement scale comprises 17 items to capture vigour, dedication and absorption in work. Items include: 'At my work, I feel bursting with energy', 'Time flies when I am working', 'I am enthusiastic about my job', and

'My job inspires me'. There is also a shorter nine-item version of the scale developed for application across different cultural contexts (Schaufeli *et al.*, 2006).

The attempts to measure organisation (rather than work) engagement started with Saks's (2006) study, which included items such as: 'Being a member of this organisation is very captivating', 'One of the most exciting things for me is getting involved with things happening in this organisation', and 'Being a member of this organisation is exhilarating for me'. Farndale *et al.* (2014b) build upon this framework, creating a new scale more closely aligned with the three components of the work engagement construct (vigour, dedication, absorption). They suggest items such as: 'Being a member of this organisation gives me energy,' 'Overall, I feel very dedicated to this organisation,' and 'Being a member of this organisation is very captivating.' These items capture the extent to which employees align themselves with the organisation, are emotionally attached to the organisation, show dedication and are willing to raise difficult issues and make suggestions for improvements (Camman *et al.*, 1979; Tsui *et al.*, 1997; Saks, 2006).

Types of engagement

Distinguishing between work and organisation engagement helps us to understand how employees relate to different aspects of their working life; however, it does not paint the full picture. In line with research on commitment (Cohen, 2003) and theorising based on the target similarity model (Lavelle *et al.*, 2007), it has been observed that employees hold differing perceptions about the range of people and situations they encounter in the workplace, resulting in, for example, potentially high loyalty to a supervisor, yet simultaneously a high intention to quit an organisation. It is therefore reasonable to expect that multiple foci of engagement might exist: an employee can be not only engaged with a job or an organisation, but also towards a team or profession (see, for example, Cohen, 2003; Welbourne, 2011).

Between the level of 'job' and 'organisation', we might consider the extent to which employees are engaged with their work team. For example, an employee may be deeply engaged with his or her team, while simultaneously either not being particularly happy with the organisation as a whole or even not enjoying daily tasks. Engagement may also occur related to a specific supervisor, with employees being highly engaged in working for this individual but not for others in the organisation. An additional type of engagement may occur at the level of the profession. For example, a nurse may be highly engaged with the medical profession, but may feel less engaged with specific daily tasks or the healthcare employer. Research on team engagement, supervisor engagement and profession engagement is still in its infancy but can help inform our understanding of the broader employee engagement construct.

The possible types of employee engagement discussed here start to form a clear hierarchy (see Figure 17.1). It is possible that one type of engagement may be used to reinforce another, or they may occur independently; future research in this field is required to explore this further.

Conversely, we might argue against distinguishing between these various types of engagement. Instead, perhaps our focus should be on attempting to reach consensus on a unified definition of the notion of employee engagement as a whole, rather than to dissect it further into its narrower constituent types. However, exploring the different types of engagement allows us to understand better how the construct operates in practice. This benefit has been demonstrated through the growth of research on both work and organisation engagement. For example, as Guest (2014) highlights, while work engagement has emerged as being related particularly to issues of employee health and well-being, organisation engagement is more commonly linked with organisation-level performance outcomes. We are thus able to understand more about engagement and its outcomes by breaking it down into work and organisation types. Decomposing the construct further into other different types (e.g. team, supervisor, profession) may also help to enhance our understanding further.

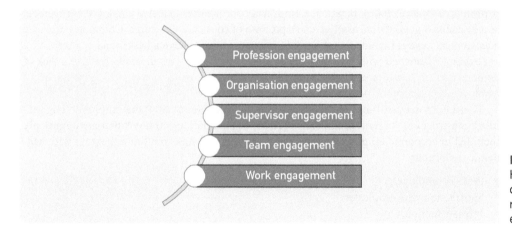

Debates and disagreements

Despite growing insights, not everyone is as enthusiastic about the concept of engagement as we have so far implied. For example, Purcell (2014: 244) argues that 'work engagement provides a distorted and misleading mirror on the world of work and the experience of workers in employment'. Given the definition of work engagement as an employee being so engrossed in his or her work at any moment of any day, this concept can only ever relate to a minority of employees. Guest (2014) also questions whether it is feasible or desirable that all employees in an organisation want or need to be fully engaged. Non-engaged staff are portrayed largely as people who have 'checked out', yet we do not know why they have disengaged from work, which may be because of organisational factors. Hence, Purcell (2014) notes that conflict is largely ignored in the engagement literature, despite potentially creating the fundamental difference between engaged and non-engaged employees. He describes this largely as a 'psychologisation of employment relations' (2014: 244), dominated by the positive psychology literature, which is hiding underlying conflict.

Guest (2014; 2015) is similarly sceptical regarding the engagement construct. Conceptually, he argues that the definition of organisation engagement (rather than work engagement) is particularly unclear; limiting the ability to develop organisational policies that can help link engagement to performance. Methodologically, Guest (2014) also argues that measures of organisation engagement tend to have a weak grounding in theory, with a concomitant lack of evidence-based management in this field.

Despite these debates and disagreements, as we have seen, advances are being made in both research and practice. As Wefald and Downey (2009) highlight, engagement is unlikely to be a passing fad given the attention it has received, and continuing research will help us address these emergent concerns.

Measuring employee engagement in practice

The more attention we pay to the diversity of definitions and types of employee engagement, the more we witness disconnect in the field between what is happening in practice compared with the academic literature. As Guest (2014: 142) highlights: 'a distinctive feature of employee engagement is that work engagement and organizational engagement seem to exist in two parallel and rather separate worlds, those of academia and industry'. Employee engagement has moved centre stage in organisations, being the focus of many corporate programs to improve performance (Vance, 2006). In practice, firms and consultancies perceive employee engagement as a desirable organisational asset given its promise of considerable returns. Corporate employee engagement surveys include a vast array of measures from 'I have a best friend at work', to 'I am extremely satisfied with my company as a place to work'. This diversity leads to a lack of homogeneity of measurement, which also hinders drawing conclusions regarding the impact of employee engagement on performance (Guest, 2014).

There is, however, emergent consensus in practice about how the employee engagement construct can be measured. Vance (2006: 6) summarises 10 items that are commonly included in corporate employee engagement surveys that link to a limited extent with academic definitions:

- Pride in employer;
- Satisfaction with employer;
- Job satisfaction;
- Opportunity to perform well at challenging work;
- Recognition and positive feedback for one's contributions;
- Personal support from one's supervisor;
- Effort above and beyond the minimum;
- Understanding the link between one's job and the organisation's mission;
- Prospects for future growth with one's employer;
- Intention to stay with one's employer.

The Gallup organisation has been highly influential in determining how a large number of organisations measure employee engagement worldwide. Gallup developed a 12-item questionnaire (the Q12) that has been widely implemented by firms globally. From an organisation perspective, having a broad base of other organisations using the same instrument to measure engagement facilitates corporate benchmarking. The Q12 explores such items as 'I have the materials and equipment I need to do my work right', 'In the last seven days, I have received recognition or praise for doing good work', and 'This last year, I have had opportunities at work to learn and grow'. In a meta-analysis, Harter *et al.* (2002) demonstrate that this Q12 measure of engagement has positive relationships with performance outcomes such as customer satisfaction, productivity and profitability.

We propose, however, that both the Q12 and many corporate engagement surveys including items described here, do not purely measure engagement, but include many of its drivers in the measurement instrument. Compared with the UWES measure of work engagement (Schaufeli *et al.*, 2002), which focuses on vigour, dedication and absorption, many of the corporate surveys include elements that relate to receiving feedback, having the opportunity to perform well either through resource or development availability, receiving support from superiors or peers and having room for growth in the job. As we describe later, many of these items have been identified in research as 'job resources' (Demerouti *et al.*, 2001) that are drivers of engagement rather than engagement itself.

Engagement and related constructs

Employee engagement in its broadest sense has been recognised as a significant field of research. There are those as we have noted, however, who are somewhat sceptical regarding the utility of this new construct, either in practice or in academic research (e.g. Guest, 2014; Welfald and Downey, 2009). We attempt to address some of these concerns here by explaining how engagement is related to but distinct from a number of other employee-level attitudinal and behavioural constructs.

Work engagement has been presented as the positive antipode to employee *burnout* (e.g. Demerouti *et al.*, 2010), but it is also argued that burnout and engagement are actually independent but related constructs (e.g. Schaufeli *et al.*, 2002). In other words, it is possible to be both highly engaged and burned out simultaneously. The high-performance work systems' literature highlights this 'dark side' of engagement, explaining how implementing HRM practices that are focused on achieving high performance outcomes can come at the expense of employee well-being (Van de Voorde *et al.*, 2012). The burnout literature has reached similar conclusions; for example, Hakanen *et al.* (2006) found that job demands lead to burnout, which leads to ill-health.

Another construct commonly discussed alongside engagement is *affective commitment*. Affective commitment represents the extent to which employees align themselves with an organisation, feel a sense of belonging and are emotionally attached to an organisation (Allen and Meyer, 1990). This represents an affective state, clearly incorporating the dedication element of engagement. However, it does not represent the whole engagement construct and is empirically distinct (Farndale *et al.*, 2014b). In line with this, work engagement has been found to be positively correlated with affective commitment, as it is expected that employees who are more energized, absorbed and dedicated will demonstrate loyalty (Christian and Slaughter, 2007; Hakanen *et al.*, 2006; Hallberg and Schaufeli, 2006; Meyer *et al.*, 2012; Wefald *et al.*, 2011). Similarly, engagement is also associated with another affective state: *job satisfaction*. There is evidence, however, that employee engagement is considered an 'emotional connection' with the organisation, as distinct from a more 'rational connection such as job satisfaction' (Kelliher *et al.*, 2013: 186).

As we have highlighted, employee engagement is not only a question of affect; it also has a behavioural component (Macey and Schneider, 2008). At this level, comparisons can be drawn with *organisational citizenship behaviour* (OCB). OCB at the organisational level describes the extra-role behaviour of employees in proactively making suggestions and being active in improving the overall efficiency and effectiveness of the organisation (Tsui *et al.*, 1997). Rather than employee engagement being synonymous with OCB, Soieb *et al.* (2013) argue that OCB is an antecedent of engagement, as it focuses on employee involvement and secures their engagement. Conversely, Rurkkhum (2010) finds support for the notion that OCB is an outcome rather than an antecedent of work engagement – employees who are more engaged are more likely to go the extra mile. Aside from this antecedent or outcome debate, the evidence does indicate that engagement and OCB are clearly related but independent (behavioural) constructs.

An important take-away from this discussion is that engagement is strongly related to each of the constructs described, but represents more than any one of these constructs alone. This is largely because engagement incorporates both attitudinal and behavioural components, representing not only how the employee feels about his or her work or the organisation, but also what they actually do on a daily basis.

Drivers of employee engagement

Organisations cannot force their employees to be actively engaged, but employee engagement can be enhanced by the actions of people within organisations (Rurkkhum, 2010). The possibility that organisations can foster (or even reduce – see Purcell, 2014) employee engagement is an important incentive to understand better the drivers (or antecedents) of employee engagement.

Derived largely from Western research, the mechanism that explains employee engagement is based in the tenets of social exchange theory (Zhang *et al.*, 2008). Social exchange theory (Blau, 1964) proposes that employees will feel obliged to reciprocate with positive attitudes and behaviours when they have a positive experience in the workplace: 'social relationships are viewed as exchange processes in which people make contributions for which they expect certain outcomes' (Thurston and McNall, 2010: 204). For example, if employees believe that a newly implemented work–life balance policy is going to be beneficial to them, they are more likely to increase their level of engagement potentially both with their job and the organisation as a whole (depending on to what they attribute the positive policy being introduced). Individuals provide benefits to others when they expect to receive something in return (Cropanzano and Mitchell, 2005), maximising benefits and minimising costs (Soieb *et al.*, 2013).

Another important framework that helps explain the antecedents of engagement is the *Job Demands-Resources Model* (JD-R) (Demerouti *et al.*, 2001). This model explains how job resources can help achieve work goals or reduce job demands and, as a result, employees feel more engaged. Examples of job resources include financial rewards (Demerouti, 1999), an integrated team climate (Bakker *et al.*, 2006a), receiving performance feedback (Demerouti, 1999) and the opportunity to participate in decision making (Karasek, 1979; Spector, 1986). This model is useful for organisations as it suggests that appropriate conditions can be created that stimulate engagement through providing appropriate job characteristics (Robinson *et al.*, 2004). While excessive job demands (e.g. too high a workload) are related to burnout, high levels of job resources are associated with engagement (Crawford *et al.*, 2010).

Job resources as drivers of employee engagement can be analysed at the organisational, interpersonal, job and task levels (Bakker *et al.*, 2004). At the organisational level, research has demonstrated that the most important drivers are management practices and monetary incentives. Interestingly, it has been found that organisations that adhere to Fayol's (1949) 14 principles of management exhibit higher levels of employee engagement (Medlin and Green, 2014). Other examples of organisations with higher levels of engagement are those that offer development opportunities and welfare for employees (Farndale *et al.*, 2011), empowerment enhancing practices (Gardner *et al.*, 2001) and a positive work climate (Greenberg, 1990; Macky and Boxall, 2007).

Albrecht and colleagues (2015) provide a detailed discussion of how engagement relates to a range of traditional HRM practices. As part of this discussion, performance appraisal has been found to demonstrate a positive association with employee engagement (e.g. Mone *et al.*, 2011; Robinson *et al.*, 2004) and, more specifically, the frequency of appraisal, outcomes of appraisal, involvement in target setting and performance feedback (Farndale *et al.*, 2011). As an outcome of the appraisal process, financial rewards have been found to motivate employees in exchange for labour (i.e. base salary) as well as monetary premiums for good performance (Demerouti, 1999). Performance appraisal allows employees to feel involved in the organisation because of the attention they receive in the process. According to the norms of reciprocity, this leads to positive feelings in employees, such as engagement.

An important step in this process of reciprocity is the role of the supervisor (Therkelsen and Fiebich, 2003). An HR department may attempt to implement an appraisal process that is designed to enhance engagement, but the outcomes depend on how supervisors implement that process. Ultimately, employees experience what the supervisor enacts, which is not necessarily what the HR department had intended (Nishii and Wright, 2008). When this alignment is not present, unanticipated outcomes may occur; for example, perceived unfairness in the performance appraisal process has been shown to diminish employee attitudes and performance (Latham and Mann, 2006).

At the interpersonal level, the relationship between an employee and his or her supervisor is extremely important, since trust is a key driver of engagement (Agarwal, 2014). Face-to-face communication with the supervisor promotes employee engagement (Mishra *et al.*, 2014), as does leader-empowering behaviour (Mendes and Stander, 2011). In addition to supervisors, interpersonal relationships with colleagues are also significant drivers of engagement. Team climates create resources through the extent to which their members 'construe themselves as interrelated to others rather than as independent and unique' (Bakker *et al.*, 2006a: 240). When the team climate is positive, i.e. members feel empathy towards their co-workers, emotional involvement occurs, resulting in employee engagement (Bakker *et al.*, 2006a; Bakker *et al.*, 2006b). Overall, these interpersonal-level relationships, including support from the line manager, colleagues and senior management, play a critical role in creating employee engagement (Farndale *et al.*, 2011).

At the job level, there are several ways to evoke employee engagement, the most common and significant being regular, frequent, and meaningful feedback. Feedback provides employees with information on their performance from superiors, colleagues or through the work process (Demerouti, 1999). Providing regular feedback triggers the reciprocity response in employees, and leads to employee engagement. Role clarity and psychological empowerment also predict work engagement (Mendes and Stander, 2011) in terms of receiving supervisor support (Saks, 2006) and having job autonomy (Farndale *et al.*, 2011). Job crafting may also be employed to enhance employee performance and improve engagement by achieving a better match between task demands and individual personality (Handa and Gulati, 2014).

Finally, at task level, variety is found to be important for engagement (Farndale *et al.*, 2011), as job enrichment and task variety have long been acknowledged as ways to increase employee motivation (Herzberg, 1968; Hackman and Oldham, 1976). By experiencing greater task variety, employees exhibit greater job satisfaction and, consequently, higher engagement. Also, participation in decision making allows employees to experience decision latitude (Karasek, 1979), enabling them to affect directly their working environment (Spector, 1986).

In summary, as Gruman and Saks (2011) argue, several models have been developed in the literature describing how to improve employee engagement; the most commonly applied being the JD-R model (Demerouti *et al.*, 2001). However, the research on how specific HRM practices might affect engagement still requires further studies (Wollard and Shuck, 2011).

Outcomes of employee engagement

Intensifying interest in employee engagement is largely the result of the perceived association with valuable performance outcomes such as a firm's financial performance, and its contribution to the retention of high-potential individuals (Harter *et al.*, 2002; Rich *et al.*, 2010; Vance, 2006). To support this, there is a growing body of research suggesting benefits of employee engagement at both the individual and organisational level.

Table 17.2 presents an overview of many of the studies that have provided support for these claims at the employee-outcome level of analysis, for both work and organisation engagement. In brief, studies[2] have demonstrated that both work and organisation engagement are significant predictors of commitment, intention to quit, OCB, burnout, innovative work behaviour and employee well-being. In addition, work engagement is also related to task and job performance, and readiness to change, while organisation engagement is related to job satisfaction. One study that did not distinguish between work and organisation engagement but instead applied a general measure of employee engagement also demonstrates its relationship with innovative work behaviour (Slatten and Mehmetoglu, 2011).

At the organisational outcome level, research is much more limited. Initial studies indicate that work engagement is positively associated with organisational performance in its broadest sense. One study that supports this relationship was conducted by Blessing-White (2011) in MNCs in India. Given the specific context of this research, its generalisability is unknown. Farndale *et al.* (2014b) did find similar results, however, using a perceived organisation performance outcome variable. In a further study, Harter and colleagues (2002)

---

[2]Note that many of the studies exploring engagement and performance outcomes are cross-sectional in nature, and therefore the direction of causality cannot be confirmed (Guest, 2014).

Table 17.2 Employee-level outcomes of work and organisation engagement

	Work Engagement	Organisation Engagement
Active learning	Farndale *et al.* (2014b)	Farndale *et al.* (2014b)
Burnout	Bakker and Demerouti (2008) Cole *et al.* (2012) Schaufeli and Bakker (2004)	Bakker and Demerouti (2008)
Commitment	Christian and Slaughter (2007) Farndale *et al.* (2014b) Hakanen *et al.* (2006) Hallberg and Schaufeli (2006) Mangundjaya (2012) Meyer *et al.* (2012) Moussa (2013) Saks (2006) Wefald *et al.* (2011)	Farndale *et al.* (2014b) Moussa (2013) Saks (2006)
Initiative	Farndale *et al.* (2014b)	Farndale *et al.* (2014b)
Innovative work behaviour	Slatten and Mehmetoglu (2011)	Slatten and Mehmetoglu (2011)
Intention to quit	Halbesleben (2010) Hallberg and Schaufeli (2006) Mendes and Stander (2011) Saks (2006) Schaufeli and Bakker (2004) Shuck *et al.* (2011) Wefald *et al.* (2011)	Moussa (2013) Saks (2006)
Job performance	Christian *et al.* (2011)	
Job satisfaction		Farndale *et al.* (2014b) Moussa (2013) Saks (2006) Shuck *et al.* (2011)
OCB	Babcock-Roberson and Strickland (2010) Farndale *et al.* (2014b) Rich *et al.* (2010) Saks (2006)	Farndale *et al.* (2014b) Saks (2006)
Readiness to change	Mangundjaya (2012)	
Task performance	Dalal *et al.* (2012) Rich *et al.* (2010)	
Well-being	Bakker and Demerouti (2008)	Bakker and Demerouti (2008)

found work engagement to be associated with customer satisfaction and loyalty, profitability, productivity, employee turnover and employee safety.

As these research findings indicate, compelling evidence (particularly for work engagement) is emerging that is driving organisations to explore employee engagement strategies. As we have seen, engaged employees provide many positive outcomes for the organisation. Reinforcing this further, it has also been demonstrated that the opposite (i.e. disengaged employees) can exhibit a passionless and uninterested attitude towards work thereby bringing about a damaging impact on self, peer and organisational performance (Pati, 2012).

Employee engagement in context

Employee engagement, almost irrespective of how we might define or measure it, is largely considered as positive by both employees and organisations, but does this view, which has been established predominantly within Western research contexts, extend to other regions of the world? As Purcell (2014: 247) highlights: 'The lack of context is a problem with much of the current work, and practice, in engagement'. In support of a universal engagement construct, cross-national studies have established the validity of common tools used to measure employee engagement (such as UWES: Schaufeli *et al.*, 2006), enabling comparisons across countries. In contrast, however, extant cross-cultural and cross-national research leads us to expect different attitudinal and behavioural responses from employees in different countries to experiences in the workplace (Farndale *et al.*, 2011).

Khatri and colleagues (2012) raise the questions of whether engagement is simply a Western construct, and whether strategies to promote higher levels of engagement can be used across operations in different countries. These are valid questions as research has found that related constructs of commitment and trust, for example, vary significantly across countries (Chen and Francesco, 2000; Gales and Barzantny, 2006; Glazer *et al.*, 2004; Huang and Van de Vliert, 2006; Hui *et al.*, 2004; Wong *et al.*, 2006). More specifically, affective commitment, job satisfaction and turnover intention have been found to be different in collectivist as opposed to individualist societies (Wang *et al.*, 2002; Wong *et al.*, 2001).

We might, therefore, expect certain cultural and institutional differences between countries to affect the meaning of employee engagement, its drivers and its outcomes (Schuler and Rogovsky, 1989). In other words, the process of facilitating employee engagement in order to achieve certain positive outcomes is affected by the context of the organisation (see Figure 17.2). Broadly speaking, research evidence suggests that differences in employee engagement between countries can be explained by aspects of national culture, frameworks of local institutions and current economic conditions (Kelliher *et al.*, 2013).

National culture is a dominant factor that affects the outcomes of HRM practices (Schuler and Rogovsky, 1989), and can therefore be expected also to influence employee engagement. Culture explains the values that drive attitudes and behaviours at the individual level, and as such may be an important explanatory mechanism in understanding engagement in different country contexts (Farndale and Murrer, 2015). The most widely used representation of national cultures is Hofstede's framework of cultural dimensions: power distance, individualism/collectivism, masculinity/femininity and uncertainty avoidance (for further details on these dimensions, see Hofstede, 1980). For example, collectivist societies are more likely than individualist societies to foster an environment in which employees have a natural propensity to feel part of a group and develop a sense of belonging. In such a context, we might therefore expect target setting or reward practices that are more focused on the group than on the individual to lead to higher levels of engagement through the norms of reciprocity. In support of this, one study found that the involvement of employers in community-based activities played a more important role in influencing engagement in

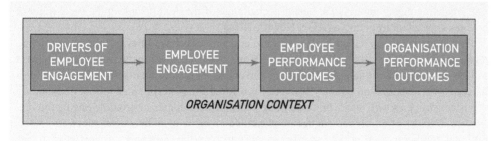

Figure 17.2
A model of employee engagement in context

India than in European countries (Farndale *et al.*, 2011), reflecting higher levels of in-group collectivism in this nation.

In order to examine the extent to which the meaning of employee engagement and the drivers of engagement differ across national contexts, Farndale and colleagues (2011) explored employee engagement in MNCs based in Europe, but operating in India and China. This research setting allowed a comparison of within-company results across different countries. Based on interviews with managers and survey data collected from employees, the results demonstrate that there is little difference in the way in which employee engagement is defined and understood across the countries involved: words such as 'passion', 'commitment', 'motivation' and 'happy' were frequently used by interviewees in all locations. Specifically, both work engagement and organisational engagement were seen by all organisations to be important. The differences that the study did highlight, however, were found in the factors that drive levels of engagement across countries. Although some of the differences observed could be explained by differences in national culture, others were because of the conditions in the local/regional labour market, the economic context and the expectations of different groups of employees. For example, in China and India, employees were more willing to engage with the organisation if extra pay was involved, while in the Netherlands the more powerful incentive to evoke engagement was work–life balance (Kelliher *et al.*, 2013).

In another multi-country study, BlessingWhite (2011) found explicit differences in engagement levels of employees across countries. The study implies that Indian workforces exhibit the highest levels of engagement worldwide, with 37 per cent of employees reporting themselves as engaged. In contrast, reporting across Europe, the same study found just under 30 per cent of employees were engaged, but with little variation across gender, organisation size or structure.

Although still in their infancy, what we can conclude from these initial cross-national studies is that employee engagement might indeed be a universal construct, although how it is engendered varies considerably. Employees across national boundaries demonstrate their engagement in the same or similar ways, and managers have the same or similar expectations of employees: that they demonstrate engagement both towards the job and the organisation. National context is, however, of critical importance for understanding the drivers that can maintain or increase employee engagement.

Conclusion

Employees have been widely recognised as one of the most valuable resources firms possess to build competitive advantage; the imperative being on having the right employees (with the right knowledge, skills and abilities) in the right place at the right time. As the practices applied to manage these employees are transferred within and across organisations, and within and across national borders, organisations need a deep understanding of which HRM policies and practices will be effective in attracting, retaining, rewarding and developing this vital organisational resource. Employee engagement has therefore moved centre stage in explaining what makes contemporary organisations stand out in terms of their performance. Successful organisations of the future will need not only to have the right employees in the right positions at the right time but to insure that these employees are also highly engaged. In brief, realising engagement is *the* business challenge of the next decade and a focal point of the emerging talent imperative (AON Hewitt, 2014).

This chapter has provided both academic and practice-based definitions of employee engagement, as well as sketching an outline of options available for measuring engagement in both domains. Recognising appropriate drivers of employee engagement (especially in different organisation and country contexts) is critical for fostering a deeper understanding of this construct, as well as for implementing successful strategies to promote engagement in practice. Drivers of employee engagement include an array of policies, practices and activities that can be applied at the organisational, interpersonal, job and task levels, with the ultimate aim of creating passionate, loyal, motivated and happy employees. Although cultural and institutional differences between countries undoubtedly influence the drivers that shape employee engagement, engagement itself has a similar meaning and is considered equally important across the globe. As for the outcomes of employee engagement, there is considerable research evidence for its association with various positive employee-level outcomes (such as commitment or task/job performance). At the organisational level, however, such evidence is still more limited but some promising first steps have been taken.

In conclusion, for both practice and academic research, a better understanding of employee engagement (and in particular its multiple types, including work and organisation engagement) can lead to a clearer expectation of potential outcomes, as well as indications of the required strategies and practices to help achieve these outcomes. Theories such as social exchange theory and the JD-R model help to explain why putting appropriate activities in place will result in higher levels of engagement. Although a relatively new construct in the HRM field, and despite some critics, the majority of evidence to date indicates that engagement is a valuable addition to positive employee attitude and behaviour constructs being studied in organisations.

CASE STUDY 17.1

ENGAGING WITH A GLOBAL IDENTITY IN A MAJOR MULTINATIONAL CHEMICALS FIRM

ELAINE FARNDALE

As a major producer of specialty chemicals and related consumer products based in Western Europe, this firm supplies industries and consumers worldwide with innovative products. Operations are based in more than 80 countries, involving over 50,000 employees worldwide.

Despite previous success, the firm is now operating in a very difficult market, where significant organisation change and downsizing is a business reality. Jobs are therefore no longer secure for employees. There are also very few opportunities for alternative employment currently because of a downturn in the economy. Therefore, despite necessary downsizing across the company, there are few employees leaving the firm voluntarily. On a more positive note, employees enjoy a very generous employment package, including substantial severance payments should they be laid off. The latter is in part because of local legislation setting minimum requirements for payments, and in part because of the efforts of the trade unions recognised by the firm. Although trade union membership is low,

influence is high as they work in partnership with the firm to ensure employees are supported.

The firm's history is one of focusing on individual product brands that are well-known across Europe. The emphasis in recent years to deal with increased competition, however, has been on shifting the values and culture from the product brand level to the level of the identity of the firm as a whole. Global corporate brand recognition is increasing, but it is not yet as high as for many of the traditional product brands. Because of the product brand history, different parts of the business operate quite independently, despite some co-location. Employee moves across business units are therefore rare.

Employee engagement in this firm is defined as a combination of devotion, working hard, being optimistic and constructive and being a team player. It is also seen as a two-way process in which employees expect something in return for their engagement, such as work–life balance. Levels of work engagement are reported as being moderately high, with an equal focus on behavioural willingness to take initiative and learn on the job, and on emotional attachment to the work. In general, workload levels are relatively low. Organisation engagement (defined here at the product brand business unit level) is somewhat higher than work engagement, particularly from a behavioural perspective, including willingness to put in extra effort to see the product brand succeed.

Various HRM practices can stimulate engagement, such as providing development opportunities and constructive performance management. Communication and involvement have also been seen as key ways to increase employee engagement in the past, as well as intrinsic motivation being considered essential. In general, once a person joins this firm, they are likely to stay for a very long time, with the majority of the workforce having over twenty years' service. This is largely facilitated by the generous employment package, alongside strong product brand loyalty. However, because of the long tenure, most employees have already reached the top of their salary scale (set by a collective bargaining agreement), so financial incentives are difficult to offer to improve performance.

Questions

1. What job resources and job demands can be identified in this case that may be contributing to engagement levels?

2. As the firm transforms its focus from multiple product brands to a single global corporate brand, how might it go about ensuring levels of employee engagement are maintained or increased at both work and organisation level?

3. How might a firm such as this increase engagement amongst employees when there is no room to offer additional financial incentives?

4. What do you think will be the effect on the engagement of remaining employees when their colleagues are laid off involuntarily across the organisation because of downsizing requirements? How might any negative effects be minimised?

CASE STUDY 17.2

MEASURING EMPLOYEE ENGAGEMENT

ELAINE FARNDALE

Imagine you are an HR manager based at the headquarters of a large domestic corporation, tasked with measuring levels of employee engagement across all of your operations. You have the support of senior management for this initiative, but must gain the buy-in of HR managers across the different business units and locations where the firm operates. You will be relying on these local HR managers to roll out your employee engagement survey, as well as they being critical to implementing potential changes as a result of the survey outcomes.

Senior management would like to receive a report from you explaining:

a. what questions you would include in your employee engagement survey;

b. why you think these questions are important;

c. any challenges you would anticipate in gaining buy-in for the survey from HR managers across the company;

d. what boundaries you might set for the engagement initiative, e.g. is the aim that all employees should be fully engaged, and is it possible for engagement of individuals to reach too high a level?

CASE STUDY · 17.3

ENGAGEMENT IN A SHARED SERVICE CENTRE IN INDIA

ELAINE FARNDALE

The Shared Service Centre (SSC) is the global services arm based in India for a major global retailer, providing information technology, business and finance services to retail operations across Europe, Asia and the Americas. Having only been established five years prior, the SSC already has over 3,000 employees, and is continuing to grow even through difficult economic times.

Engagement levels amongst employees within the SSC are reported to be high, both for work engagement and organisation engagement. In this case, organisation engagement refers to the retailer brand (rather than the SSC in particular) because of its dominant global reach. The high levels of engagement are positive news for the firm, as it sees these resulting in higher productivity, increased employee satisfaction and motivation and a willingness to be developed and grow independently.

Importantly, engaged employees are considered critical to business success because of the extremely dynamic external labour market in India. Here, turnover levels can be as high as 45 per cent in industries where five per cent in developed Western economies is more the norm. There is, therefore, constant pressure for the firm to focus on engaging and retaining its high-value employees. A combination of national culture values and economic opportunities together determine how long an employee will stay with the firm; if people are offered more money by a competitor, the natural tendency is to grasp those opportunities and move on. However, a strong driver of employee engagement in the Indian context is building a close connection between employer and employee. In this firm, senior management in the SSC, as well as line managers are seen by employees as highly supportive.

As part of an initiative to retain employees, the SSC established a corporate program to encourage employee engagement. This program is led by the HR Director, and receives direct support from the SSC's senior management. The program is implemented through the HR function in partnership with the different business units. HR supports line managers directly to ensure that employees can function and perform well, as well as helps to manage employee learning and development. HR is also responsible for delivering transparent and fair performance management processes. The SSC places great emphasis on training as an important outcome of performance appraisal; hence it offers a work environment where employees can learn, develop personally and be innovative.

Questions

1 What are the antecedents and outcomes of engagement described in this case?

2 How do you think the location of this firm in India is affecting how engagement is managed, compared to if this firm were located in a developed Western economy?

3 Why might it be either beneficial or detrimental for the firm to launch an initiative to increase levels of engagement with the local (SSC) operations, potentially challenging the already high organisation engagement with the global retailer brand?

4 What role do you think the different parties in the SSC (e.g. HR, senior management, line management, colleagues) play in supporting employee engagement? What activities might they undertake to carry out these roles?

Bibliography

Albrecht, S.L., Bakker, A.B., Gruman, J.A., Macey, W.H. and Saks, A.M. (2015) 'Employee engagement, human resource management practices and competitive advantage. An integrated approach', *Journal of Organizational Effectiveness: People and Performance*, Vol.2, No.1, 7–35.

Allen, N.J. and Meyer, J.P. (1990) 'The measurement and antecedents of affective, continuance and normative commitment to the organization', *Journal of Occupational Psychology*, Vol.63, No.1, 1–18.

Agarwal, U.A. (2014) 'Linking justice, trust and innovative work behaviour to work engagement', *Personnel Review*, Vol.43, No.1, 41–73.

AonHewitt (2012) '2012 Trends in Global Employee Engagement'. Available at: http://www.aon .com/attachments/human-capital-consulting/2012_TrendsInGlobalEngagement_Final_v11.pdf.

Babcock-Roberson, M. and Strickland, O. (2010) 'Leadership, work engagement, and organizational citizenship behaviors', *The Journal of Psychology*, Vol.144, No.3, 313–26.

Bakker, A.B. and Demerouti, E. (2008) 'Towards a model of work engagement', *Career Development International*, Vol.13, No.3, 209–23.

Bakker, A.B., Demerouti, E. and Verbeke, W. (2004) 'Using the Job Demands Resources model to predict burnout and performance', *Human Resource Management*, Vol.43, No.1, 83–104.

Bakker, A.B., Schaufeli, W.B., Demerouti, E. and Eeuwema, M.C. (2006a) 'An organizational and social psychological perspective on burnout and work engagement, pp. 229–52, in Hewstone, M., Schut, H., de Wit, J., van den Bos, K. and Stroebe, M. (eds.) *The Scope of Social Psychology: Theory and Applications*, Andover: Psychology Press.

Bakker, A.B., Van Emmerik, H. and Eeuwema, C. (2006b) 'Crossover of burnout and engagement in work teams', *Work and Occupations*, Vol.33, No.4, 464–89.

Blau, P.M. (1964) *Exchange and Power in Social Life*, New York: John Wiley.

BlessingWhite (2011) 'Employee engagement report 2011', Research report. Available at: http://www.nine-dots.org/documents/Blessing%20White%202011%20%20Employee%20 Engagement%20Report.pdf.

Camman, C., Fichman, M., Jenkins, D. and Klesh, J. (1979) 'The Michigan organizational assessment questionnaire', Unpublished manuscript, Ann Arbor, MI: University of Michigan.

Chen, Z.X. and Francesco, A.M. (2000) 'Employee demography, organizational commitment, and turnover intentions in China: do cultural differences matter?', *Human Relations*, Vol.53, No.6, 869–87.

Christian, M.S., Garza, A.S. and Slaughter, J.E. (2011) 'Work engagement: a quantitative review and test of its relations with task and contextual performance', *Personnel Psychology*, Vol.64, No.1, 89–136.

Christian, M.S. and Slaughter, J.E. (2007) 'Work engagement: a meta-analytic review and directions for research in an emerging area', *Proceedings from the Academy of Management meeting*, 3–8 August, Philadelphia, PA.

Cohen, A. (2003) *Multiple Commitments in the Workplace: An Integrative Approach*, Mahwah, NJ: Lawrence Erlbaum Associates.

Cole, M.S., Walter, F., Bedeian, A.G. and O'Boyle, E.H. (2012) 'Job burnout and employee engagement: a meta-analytic examination of construct proliferation', *Journal of Management*, Vol.38, No.5, 1550–81.

Crawford, E.R., LePine, J.A. and Rich, B.L. (2010) 'Linking job demands and resources to employee engagement and burnout: a theoretical extension and meta-analytic test', *Journal of Applied Psychology*, Vol.95, No.5, 834–48.

Cropanzano, R. and Mitchell, M.S. (2005) 'Social exchange theory: an interdisciplinary review', *Journal of Management*, Vol.31, No.6, 874–900.

Dalal, R.S., Baysinger, M., Brummel, B.J. and LeBreton, J.M. (2012) 'The relative importance of employee engagement, other job attitudes, and trait affect as predictors of job performance', *Journal of Applied Social Psychology*, Vol.42, No.1, 295–325.

Demerouti, E. (1999) *Burnout: eine folge konkreter arbeitsbedingungen bei dienstleistungs-und produktionstätigkeiten* [Burnout: a consequence of working conditions among service workers and industrial workers], Oldenburg: Lang.

Demerouti, E., Bakker, A.B., Nachreiner, F. and Schaufeli, W.B. (2001) 'The job-demands resources model of burnout', *Journal of Applied Psychology*, Vol.86, No.3, 499–512.

Demerouti, E., Mostert, K. and Bakker, A.B. (2010) 'Burnout and work engagement: a thorough investigation of the independency of both constructs', *Journal of Occupational Health Psychology*, Vol.15, No.3, 209–22.

Farndale, E. and Murrer, I. (2015) 'Job resources and employee engagement: a cross-national study', *Journal of Managerial Psychology*, Vol.30, No.5, 610–26.

Farndale, E., Beijer, S.E. and Kelliher, C. (2014a) 'Employee engagement in emerging markets, pp. 271–92, in Horwitz, F. and Budhwar, P. (eds.) *Handbook of Human Resource Management In Emerging Markets*, Cheltenham: Edward Elgar.

Farndale, E., Beijer, S.E., Van Veldhoven, M.J.P.M., Kelliher, C. and Hope-Hailey, V. (2014b) 'Work and organisation engagement: aligning research and practice', *Journal of Organizational Effectiveness: People and Performance*, Vol.1, No.2, 157–76.

Farndale, E., Hope Hailey, V., Kelliher, C. and van Veldhoven, M. (2011) 'A study of the link between performance management and employee engagement in Western multinational corporations operating across India and China', Research report. Available at: http://www.shrm.org/about/foundation/research/Documents/Farndale%20Final%20Report%2010-11.pdf.

Fayol, H. (1949) *General and Industrial Management*,' London, UK: Pittman & Sons.

Gales, L. and Barzantny, C. (2006) 'A cross-cultural test of Colquitt's four-factor justice model: United States, Taiwan and the PRC', *Proceedings from the Academy of Management meeting*, 14–16 August, Atlanta, GA.

Gardner, T.M., Moynihan, L.M., Park, H.J. and Wright, P.M. (2001) 'Beginning to unlock the black box in the HR firm performance relationship: the impact of HR practices on employee attitudes and employee outcomes', Working Paper 01–12, Cornell University, NY: CAHRS.

Glazer, S., Daniel, S.C. and Short, K.M. (2004) 'A study of the relationship between organizational commitment and human values in four countries', *Human Relations*, Vol.57, No.3, 323–45.

Greenberg, J. (1990) 'Organizational justice: yesterday, today, and tomorrow', *Journal of Management*, Vol.16, No.2, 399–432.

Gruman, J.A. and Saks, A.M. (2011) 'Performance management and employee engagement', *Human Resource Management Review*, Vol.21, No.2, 123–36.

Guest, D. (2014) 'Employee engagement: a sceptical analysis', *Journal of Organizational Effectiveness: People and Performance*, Vol.1, No.2, 141–56.

Guest, D. (2015) Voice and employee engagement, pp. 44–66, in Johnstone, S. and Ackers, P. (eds.) *Finding a Voice at Work? New Perspectives on Employment Relations*, Oxford: Oxford University Press.

Hackman, J.R. and Oldham, G.R. (1976) 'Motivation through the design of work: test of a theory', *Organizational Behavior and Human Performance*, Vol.16, No.2, 250–79.

Halbesleben, J.R.B. (2010) 'A meta-analysis of work engagement: relationships with burnout, demands, resources, and consequences', pp. 102–17, in Bakker, A.B. and Leiter, M.P. (eds.) *Work Engagement: A Handbook of Essential Theory and Research*, New York, NY: Psychology Press.

Hakanen, J.J., Bakker, A.B. and Schaufeli, W.B. (2006) 'Burnout and work engagement among teachers', *Journal of School Psychology*, Vol.43, No.6, 495–513.

Hallberg, U.E. and Schaufeli, W.B. (2006) '"Same same" but different? Can work engagement be discriminated from job involvement and organizational commitment?', *European Psychologist*, Vol.11, No.2, 119–27.

Hamid, S.N.A. and Yahya, K.K. (2011) 'Relationship between person-job fit and person-organization fit on employees' work engagement: a study among engineers in semiconductor companies in Malaysia', *Annual Conference on Innovations in Business and Management*, London, UK.

Handa, M. and Gulati, A. (2014) 'Employee engagement: does individual personality matter', *Journal of Management Research*, Vol.14, No.1, 57–67.

Harter, J.K. and Schmidt, F.L. (2008) 'Conceptual versus empirical distinctions among constructs: implications for discriminant validity', *Industrial and Organizational Psychology*, Vol.1, 36–9.

Harter, J.K., Schmidt, F.L. and Hayes, T.L. (2002) 'Business-unit-level relationship between employee satisfaction, employee engagement and business outcomes: a meta-analysis', *Journal of Applied Psychology*, Vol.87, No.2, 268–79.

Herzberg, F. (1968) 'One more time: how do you motivate employees?', *Harvard Business Review*, Vol.46, No.1, 53–62.

Hofstede, G. (1980) *Culture's Consequences. International Differences in Work-Related Values*. Thousand Oaks, CA: Sage.

Huang, X. and Van de Vliert, E. (2006) 'Job formalization and cultural individualism as barriers to trust in management', *International Journal of Cross Cultural Management*, Vol.6, No.2, 221–42.

Hui, C., Lee, C. and Rousseau, D.M. (2004) 'Employment relationships in China: do workers relate to the organization or to people?', *Organization Science*, Vol.15, No.2, 232–40.

Jeve, Y.B., Oppenheimer, C. and Konje, J. (2015) 'Employee engagement within the NHS: a cross-sectional study', *International Journal of Health Policy and Management*, Vol.4, No.2, 85–90.

Jose, G. and Mampilly, S.R. (2012) 'Satisfaction with HR practices and employee engagement: a social exchange perspective', *Journal of Economics and Behavioral Studies*, Vol.4, No.7, 423–30.

Kahn, W.A. (1990) 'Psychological conditions of personal engagement and disengagement at work', *Academy of Management Journal*, Vol.33, No.4, 692–724.

Karasek, R.A. (1979) 'Job demands, job decision latitude and mental strain: implications for job redesign', *Administrative Science Quarterly*, Vol.24, No.2, 285–308.

Kelliher, C., Hope-Hailey, V. and Farndale, E. (2013) 'Employee engagement in multi-national organizations', in Truss, K., Alfes, K., Delbridge, R., Shantz, A. and Soane, E. *Employee Engagement in Theory and Practice*, UK: Routledge.

Khatri, N., Ojha, A.K., Budhwar, P., Srinivasan, V. and Varma, A. (2012) Management research in India: current state and future directions', *Indian Institute of Management Bangalore Management Review*, 1–12.

Langelaan, S., Bakker, A.B., Schaufeli, W.B. and Van Doornen, L.J.P. (2006) 'Burnout and work engagement: do individual differences make a difference?', *Personality and Individual Differences*, Vol.40, No.3, 521–32.

Latham, G.P. and Mann, S. (2006) 'Advances in the science of performance appraisal: implications for practice', pp. 295–337, in Hodgkinson, G.P. and Ford, J.K. (eds.) *International Review of Industrial and Organizational Psychology, Volume 21*, Hoboken, NJ: Wiley.

Lavelle, J.J., Rupp, D.E. and Brockner, J. (2007) 'Taking a multi-foci approach to the study of justice, social exchange, and citizenship behavior: the target similarity model?', *Journal of Management*, Vol.33, No.6, 841–66.

MacCormick, J.S., Dery, K. and Kolb, D.G. (2012) 'Engaged or just connected? Smarthpones and employee engagement', *Organizational Dynamics*, Vol.41, No.3, 194–201.

Macey, W.H. and Schneider, B. (2008) 'The meaning of employee engagement', *Industrial and Organizational Psychology*, Vol.1, No.1, 3–30.

Macky, K. and Boxall, P. (2007) 'The relationship between "high-performance work practices" and employee attitudes: an investigation of additive and interaction effects', *International Journal of Human Resource Management*, Vol.18, No.4, 537–67.

Mangundjaya, W.L.H. (2012) 'Are organizational commitment and employee engagement important in achieving individual readiness for change?', *Humanitas*, Vol.9, No.2,185–92.

Maslach, C., Schaufeli, W.B. and Leiter, M.P. (2001) 'Job burnout', *Annual Review of Psychology*, Vol.52, No.1, 397–422.

Mauno, S., Kinnunen, U. and Ruokolainen, M. (2007) 'Job demands and resources as antecedents of work engagement: a longitudinal study,' *Journal of Vocational Behavior*, Vol.70, No.1, 149–71.

Medlin, B. and Green, K.W. (2014) 'Impact of management basics on employee engagement', *Academy of Strategic Management Journal*, Vol.13, No.2, 21–35.

Memon, M.A., Salleh, R., Baharom, M.N.R. and Harun, H. (2014) 'Person-organization fit and turnover intention: the mediating role of employee engagement', *Global Business and Management Research: An International Journal*, Vol.6, No.3, 205–09.

Mendes, F. and Stander, M.W. (2011) 'Positive organization: the role of leader behavior in work engagement and retention', *SA Journal of Industrial Psychology*, Vol.37, No.1, 1–13.

Meyer, J.P., Stanley, L.J. and Parfyonova, N.M. (2012) 'Employee commitment in context: the nature and implication of commitment profiles', *Journal of Vocational Behavior*, Vol.80, No.1, 1–16.

Mishra, K., Boynton, L. and Mishra, A. (2014) 'Driving employee engagement: the expanded role of internal communications', *International Journal of Business Communication*, Vol.51, No.2, 183–202.

Mone, E., Eisinger, C., Guggenheim, K., Price, B. and Stine, C. (2011) 'Performance management at the wheel: driving employee engagement in organizations', *Journal of Business Psychology*, Vol.26, No.2, 205–12.

Moussa, M.N. (2013) 'Investigating the high turnover of Saudi nationals versus non-nationals in private sector companies using selected antecedents and consequences of employee engagement', *International Journal of Business and Management*, Vol.8, No.18, 41–52.

Nishii, L.H. and Wright, P. (2008) 'Variability within organizations: implications for strategic human resource management', pp. 225–48, in Smith, D.B. (ed.) *The People Make the Place*, Mahwah, NJ: Lawrence Erlbaum Associates.

Pati, S.P. (2012) 'Development of a measure of employee engagement', *The Indian Journal of Industrial Relations*, Vol.48, No.1, 94–104.

Purcell, J. (2014) 'Disengaging from engagement,' *Human Resource Management Journal*, Vol.24, No.3, 241–54.

Rich, B.L., LePine, J.A. and Crawford, E.R. (2010) 'Job engagement: antecedents and effects on job performance', *Academy of Management Journal*, Vol.53, No.3, 617–35.

Robinson, D., Perryman, S. and Hayday, S. (2004) 'The drivers of employee engagement', Report No. 408, Brighton, UK: Institute for Employment Studies.

Rothbard, N. (2001) 'Enriching or depleting? The dynamics of engagement in work and family roles, *Administrative Science Quarterly*, Vol.46, No.4, 655–84.

Rurkkhum, S. (2010) 'The relationship between employee engagement and organizational citizenship behavior in Thai organizations', Doctoral dissertation, University of Minnesota, Minneapolis.

Saks, A.M. (2006) 'Antecedents and consequences of employee engagement', *Journal of Managerial Psychology*, Vol.21, No.7, 600–19.

Schaufeli, W.B. and Bakker, A.B. (2004) 'Job demands, job resources, and their relationship with burnout and engagement: a multi-sample study', *Journal of Organizational Behavior*, Vol.25, No.3, 293–315.

Schaufeli, W.B., Bakker, A.B. and Salanova, M. (2006) 'The measurement of work engagement with a short questionnaire: a cross-national study', *Educational and Psychological Measurement*, Vol.66, No.4, 701–16.

Schaufeli, W.B., Salanova, M., Gonzalez-Roma, V. and Bakker, A.B. (2002) 'The measurement of engagement and burnout: a two sample confirmatory factor analytic approach', *Journal of Happiness Studies*, Vol.3, No.1, 71–92.

Schuler, R.S. and Rogovsky, N. (1998) 'Understanding compensation practice variations across firms: the impact of national culture', *Journal of International Business Studies*, Vol.29, No.1, 159–77.

Shuck, B., Reio, T.G. Jr. and Rocco, T.S. (2011) 'Employee engagement: an examination of antecedent and outcome variables,' *Human Resource Development International*, Vol.14, No.4, 427–45.

Slatten, T. and Mehmetoglu, M. (2011) 'Antecedents and effects of engaged frontline employees: a study from the hospitality industry', *Managing Service Quality*, Vol.21, No.1, 88–107.

Soieb, A.Z.M., Othman, J. and D'Silva, J.L. (2013) 'The effects of perceived leadership styles and organizational citizenship behavior on employee engagement: the mediating role of conflict management', *International Journal of Business and Management*, Vol.8, No.8, 91–9.

Spector, P.E. (1986) 'Perceived control by employees: a meta-analysis of studies concerning autonomy and participation at work', *Human Relations*, Vol.39, No.11, 1005–16.

Therkelsen, D.J. and Fiebich, C.L. (2003) 'The supervisor: the linchpin of employee relations', *Journal of Communication Management*, Vol.8, 120–9.

Thurston, P.W., Jr. and McNall, L. (2010) 'Justice perceptions of performance appraisal practices', *Journal of Managerial Psychology*, Vol.25, No.3, 201–28.

Truss, K. (2014) 'The future of research in employee engagement, pp. 80–7, in Robinson, D. and Gifford, J. (eds.) *The Future of Engagement Thought Piece Collection, Engage for Success Peer-Reviewed Thought Leadership Series*, London, UK: Engage for Success.

Tsui, A.S., Pearce, J.L., Porter, L.W. and Tripoli, A.M. (1997) 'Alternative approaches to the employee-organization relationship: does investment in employees pay off?', *Academy of Management Journal*, Vol.40, No.5, 1089–121.

Van de Voorde, K., Paauwe, J. and Van Veldhoven, M. (2012) 'Employee well-being and the HRM-organizational performance relationship: a review of quantitative studies', *International Journal of Management Reviews*, Vol.14, No.4, 391–407.

Vance, R.J. (2006) *Employee Engagement and Commitment: A Guide to Understanding, Measuring and Increasing Engagement in Your Organization*, Alexandria, VA: SHRM Foundation.

Wang, L., Bishop, J.W., Chen, X. and Scott, K.D. (2002) 'Collectivist orientation as a predictor of affective organizational commitment: a study conducted in China', *International Journal of Organizational Analysis*, Vol.10, No.3, 226–239.

Wefald, A.J. and Downey, R.G. (2009) 'Job engagement in organizations: fad, fashion, or folderol?', *Journal of Organizational Behavior*, Vol.30, No.1, 141–5.

Wefald, A.J., Reichard, R.J. and Serrano, S.A. (2011) 'Fitting engagement into a nomological network: the relationship of engagement to leadership and personality', *Journal of Leadership and Organizational Studies*, Vol.18, No.4, 522–37.

Welbourne, T. (2011) 'Engaged in what? So what? A role-based perspective for the future of employee engagement', pp. 85–100, in Wilkinson, A. and Townsend, K. (eds.) *The Future of Employment Relations: New Paradigms, New Developments*, Basingstoke, UK: Palgrave Macmillan.

Wollard, K.K. and Shuck, B. (2011) 'Antecedents to employee engagement: a structured review of the literature', *Advances in Developing Human Resources*, Vol.13, No.4, 429–46.

Wong, C-S., Wong, Y-T., Hui, C. and Law, K.S. (2001) 'The significant role of Chinese employees' organizational commitment: implications for managing employees in Chinese societies', *Journal of World Business*, Vol.36, No.3, 326–40.

Wong,Y-T., Ngo, H-Y. and Wong, C-S. (2006) 'Perceived organizational justice, trust, and OCB: a study of Chinese workers in joint ventures and state-owned enterprises', *Journal of World Business*, Vol.41, No.4, 344–55.

Zhang, A.Y., Tsui, A.A., Song, L.J., Li, C. and Jia, L. (2008) 'How do I trust thee? The employee–organization relationship, supervisory support, and middle manager trust in the organization', *Human Resource Management*, Vol.47, No.1, 111–32.

CHAPTER 18

KNOWLEDGE MANAGEMENT AND HUMAN RESOURCE MANAGEMENT

Donald Hislop

Introduction

The subject of knowledge management is arguably developing into a relatively mature academic topic, as there has now been a sustained interest in it since the mid-1990s. The focus of this chapter is on the linkages between knowledge management and the broad topic of human resource management. This is not an insignificant task; a large body of literature now exists on both the sociocultural factors which shape workers' attitudes to knowledge management initiatives and also how HRM practices can be utilised to encourage workers to share their knowledge and participate in knowledge management initiatives. The importance of sociocultural factors to the success of knowledge management activities is visible from studies which show how levels of knowledge sharing are linked to team performance (Lee *et al.*, 2010), and levels of knowledge hoarding are negatively linked to levels of team performance (Evans *et al.*, 2015).

The objective of this chapter is to illustrate why HRM issues are of central importance to the topic of knowledge management, and to give an overview of the way that the topics have been linked thus far in the literature. In doing so, the chapter will give a flavour of the many active debates and disagreements which still exist. Before proceeding any further, however, it is necessary to define the term 'knowledge management'. At one level this is a simple task. Putting to the side the difficulties of defining such ambiguous terms as 'knowledge' and 'management', knowledge management can be defined as the attempt by an organisation to explicitly manage and control the knowledge of its workforce. However, the issue becomes more complex when it is recognised that there are a myriad number of ways by which this can be done. This can be illustrated by the number of typologies of knowledge management strategies that have been developed. One of the simplest and most widely known is Hansen *et al.*'s (1999) distinction between personalisation and codification strategies, with a personalisation strategy focused on sharing knowledge between people, linked to a business strategy of knowledge creation. On the other hand, a codification strategy is focused on the codification of knowledge, linked to a business strategy of knowledge re-use. Hunter *et al.* (2002) and Alvesson and Karreman (2001) develop more complicated typologies, both of which produce four general knowledge management strategies. Of central significance to this chapter is that, as will be discussed in more detail later, the HRM implications of these different knowledge management strategies are quite distinctive.

The chapter begins by briefly examining the broad social context within which the growth of interest in knowledge management has occurred. Following this, subsequent sections consider how knowledge work is defined, why human motivation is key to making knowledge management initiatives successful, what general factors affect the willingness of workers to participate in knowledge management initiatives, and what specific HRM practices can be used to help persuade workers to participate in such initiatives.

Social context: the growing importance of knowledge

The growth of interest in knowledge management that occurred in the mid-1990s can be, to some extent, explained by the growing significance of knowledge in contemporary economies. This has led many, both with and without the knowledge management literature, to claim that we now live in a knowledge society. Thus Littler and Innes (2003) suggest that the 'knowledge capitalism thesis' was one of the two dominant academic discourses during the 1990s, and Tam *et al.* (2002) argue that such a belief has become 'conventional wisdom'.

Empirical evidence, to some extent, backs up this claim. However, as will be seen later, this is one area of debate. The growing importance of knowledge to contemporary economies and organisations can be illustrated in a number of ways. First, since the 1950s there has been a growth in the proportion of knowledge workers in many economies. Reich (1991) showed that in the US, between the 1950s and the 1990s, 'symbolic analysts' (his term for what contemporary writers call knowledge workers) grew from 8 per cent to 20 per cent of the workforce. Contemporary evidence from other economies also supports this (Khatri *et al.*, 2010).

Critics, however, suggest that such claims and evidence provide only a partial and distorted view of the changes in the nature of work, neglecting the extent to which there has been a simultaneous growth in other types of work, such as low-skilled, routine service work (Littler and Innes, 2003; Mansell and Steinmueller, 2000; Thompson *et al.*, 2001). These writers suggest it is more accurate to talk of a bimodal trajectory in the contemporary evolution of work, with there being a simultaneous growth in highly skilled knowledge work, and low-skilled, routine service work. Thus even if a sceptical perspective is taken to the 'knowledge society' rhetoric, it is undeniable that, to some extent, there has been a growth in the importance of knowledge in contemporary economies.

Arguably, the enormous numbers of organisations which have been attempting to develop and implement knowledge management initiatives are inspired by the idea that their competitiveness and innovativeness is derived and sustained from the way they manage, facilitate and control their knowledge base, and that neglecting to do so is likely to have negative consequences for organisational performance.

Defining knowledge work

An enormous amount has been written on knowledge workers, and their growing importance is tied closely to the knowledge society perspective just discussed. Specifically, it is argued that for those societies that are evolving into knowledge societies, the number and importance of knowledge workers will increase significantly. Thus, as outlined, one of the key indicators used to establish whether a society can be characterised as being knowledge based is the proportion of knowledge workers employed in it. However, defining the types of work that can be considered to constitute knowledge work is by no means easy. This section therefore presents two contrasting definitions of the term.

The mainstream definition in the knowledge literature is that a knowledge worker is someone whose work is primarily intellectual in nature and which involves extensive and regular use of established bodies of formal, codified knowledge. From this perspective, knowledge workers represent an occupational elite: those workers who are in the vanguard of the knowledge economy, and whose work contributes significantly to the performance of their employers. Thus, as will be discussed later, they are typically regarded by their employers as workers who are worth retaining.

Based on such definitions, the ranges of occupations that are typically classified as knowledge work include:

- Lawyers (Hunter *et al.*, 2002);
- Consultants (Empson, 2001; Morris, 2001; Robertson and Swan, 2003);
- IT and software designers (Swart and Kinnie, 2003; Horowitz *et al.*, 2003);
- Advertising executives (Beaumont and Hunter, 2002);
- Scientists and engineers (Beaumont and Hunter, 2002, Benson and Brown, 2007);
- Artists and art directors/producers (Beaumont and Hunter, 2002).

Definitions of knowledge workers, therefore, overlap with and include the classical professions (such as lawyers, architects, etc.) but also extend beyond them to include a wide variety of other occupations (such as consultants, advertising executives, IT developers, etc.). Sometimes the term 'knowledge intensive work' is used to refer to such occupations because of the extent to which they involve the creation, and use of knowledge. However, the term 'knowledge intensive' has been criticised for being somewhat vague, making it open to interpretation which work constitutes knowledge intensive work (Alvesson, 2000).

However, embedded in such definitions of knowledge work is the privileging of certain forms of knowledge (abstract, theoretical, scientific knowledge) over other types of knowledge (tacit, contextual knowledge). Critics of the mainstream definition of knowledge workers, which ring-fences the term to refer to an elite range of occupations, argue that such definitions downplay, if not ignore, the extent to which all forms of work involve the application and use of knowledge to some extent (Hislop, 2008; Thompson *et al.*, 2001). Thus a second perspective on the definition of knowledge work is that in many ways all work can be defined as knowledge work.

Hislop (2008) outlines such a perspective through reconceptualising Frenkel *et al.*'s (1995) framework on knowledge work. Frenkel *et al.*'s (1995) framework provides a way of conceptualising all forms of work through taking account of three dimensions: knowledge, skills and level of creativity. The knowledge dimension takes account of the predominant form of knowledge used in work, with knowledge being characterised as being either theoretical or contextual, with theoretical knowledge representing codified concepts and principles, which have general relevance, whereas, by contrast, contextual knowledge is largely tacit and non-generalisible – being related to specific contexts of application. The skill dimension takes account of three types of skill: intellective, social and action based. Action-based skills relate to physical dexterity, social skills with the ability to motivate and manage others, while intellective skills are defined as the ability to undertake abstract reasoning and synthesise different ideas. Finally, the dimension of creativity (which is defined as a process of *original problem-solving*, from which an original output is produced (Frenkel *et al.*, 1995: 779)) considers the level of creativity in work as varying on a sliding scale from low to high.

Using these dimensions, Frenkel *et al.* (1995) define a knowledge worker as anyone who first has a high level of creativity in their work, secondly makes extensive use of intellective skills and finally also makes use of theoretical rather than contextual knowledge. Thus conceptualised, this framework is compatible with the mainstream, elitist professional knowledge work perspective. However, Hislop (2008) suggests that because it takes account of both contextual and theoretical knowledge, as well as the skill involved in work it can easily be reconceptualised to fit with the 'all work is knowledge work' perspective through defining knowledge work as any form of work involving the use of a reasonable amount of theoretical or contextual knowledge. This framework is illustrated at the end of the chapter through applying it to understand the character of two occupations, one of which fits the mainstream, elitist definition of knowledge work (management consultants) and one of which doesn't (office equipment service engineers).

Why worker motivation is key to achieving participation in knowledge management initiatives

As the knowledge management literature has evolved and developed there has been a growing awareness that taking account of sociocultural factors is key to the success of any knowledge management initiatives. For example, a plethora of evidence shows how sociocultural factors such as levels of interpersonal trust, personality, national cultural values and organisational culture can play a crucial role in shaping the attitudes of workers to participating in knowledge management initiatives (Holste and Fields, 2010; Lam, 2005; Matzler *et al.*, 2011; O'Dell and Hubert, 2011; Paroutis and Al Saleh, 2009; Teo *et al.*, 2011; Tong and Mitra, 2009) (see Box 18.1).

Part of the explanation for why workers cannot be assumed to be automatically willing to participate in knowledge management initiatives is because of structural factors which transcend individual organisations, including the power and status workers can typically derive from possessing specialist knowledge, the nature of employment relationship, and the potential for interpersonal/group conflict that exists in all organisations. First, not only is much organisational knowledge tacit and personal in character,

---

Box 18.1 HRM in practice   **Factors influencing knowledge sharing via Web 2.0 technologies**

Paroutis and Al Saleh examined the factors that influenced people's decisions regarding whether to codify and share knowledge via Web 2.0 technologies within a single multinational corporation. They interviewed both users and non-users to understand their different rationales. In terms of the non-users, one of the main barriers which explained why they didn't use the Web 2.0 platform for knowledge-sharing was a lack of time, with it being perceived that using the Web 2.0 system could distract people from their main work activities. Second, they also had concerns about both the quality ('*it could come from a non-reliable source*') and quantity ('*too much information*') of knowledge that existed on the Web 2.0 system. Finally, people's unfamiliarity with the technology meant that they felt more comfortable sharing knowledge via traditional methods that they had always used.

In terms of the users of the Web 2.0 platform, a number of different benefits from using the system were articulated. First, it was regarded as both an effective way to communicate knowledge to other people, and also as a useful way of recording people's understanding and experiences (such as on a blog). Second, it was also regarded as a useful means by which to keep in touch with other people's latest ideas. Finally, it was felt that it could help people build and develop their social networks ('*I've built professional connections world-wide that would not otherwise exist*') and their status ('*it's helping to build a level of credibility*').

Source: Paroutis and Al Saleh, 2009.

being acquired and built up by workers over time, but the possession of knowledge can also be a significant source of power and status in organisations (Hislop, 2008; Lam, 2005). This fact alone means that workers may be unwilling to participate in organisational knowledge management initiatives if they feel this involves 'giving away' a source of their power and/or status (Martin, 2006; Oltra, 2005).

Another structural factor affecting the willingness of workers to participate in knowledge management initiatives is the nature of the employment relationship, which results in the interest of workers and management not always being totally compatible. Thus, in relation to knowledge workers, there is potential conflict between workers and their employers over both who owns the knowledge of the worker, and how it is used. For example, Cushen and Thompson (2012) found that in the Irish knowledge intensive firm they studied workers were unhappy with various ways in which their company operated, including the difference between the rhetoric and reality of the corporate culture, and the low levels of job security which existed (see also Cheyne and Loan-Clarke, Chapter 9, this volume).

The potential for conflict in organisations also emanates from another structural factor: the real (and/or perceived) differences of interests between different workers and groups within organisations that inevitably exist (Marshall and Brady, 2001). In relation to knowledge management initiatives, the fact that, as discussed above, power and knowledge are closely inter-related, means that knowledge management initiatives can be used to play out what Storey and Barnett (2000) refer to as 'micro-political battles'. Thus the attitudes towards and participation (or not) by workers in organisational knowledge management initiatives are shaped by the way such behaviours affect, and link into the political battles that are a part of the fabric of organisations.

This section has therefore shown how the participation of workers in organisational knowledge management initiatives cannot be taken for granted. The following two sections look at more specific factors within organisations, which affect the attitudes of workers to knowledge management initiatives, and considers what HRM policies can be utilised to encourage the participation of workers in such initiatives.

The organisational climate and workers' attitudes to knowledge management initiatives

This section continues with the themes discussed in the previous section, why human motivation is key to the success of knowledge management initiatives, and why the participation of workers in knowledge management initiatives cannot be guaranteed. However, the focus here shifts from structural factors, which are to some extent beyond the control of organisational management, to factors affecting the general climate within organisations that are within the control of management. As outlined earlier, a lot of evidence shows sociocultural factors to be key in shaping the attitudes of workers to knowledge management initiatives. This section provides an abbreviated summary of this literature, highlighting the diversity of factors that influence workers attitudes to such activity (see Table 18.1).

The overall, somewhat general, conclusion from this evidence is that workers are most likely to be willing to participate in organisational knowledge management initiatives when the general organisational climate/culture is fair and positive; for example, where people feel their efforts are fairly rewarded and interpersonal relations between workers, and also between workers and managers, are based on trust. The following section looks at the type of HRM practices which can be used to create such a climate, and which are thus likely to help facilitate organisational knowledge management initiatives.

Table 18.1 Research data on organisational factors affecting the attitudes of workers to organisational knowledge management initiatives

Factors Affecting Workers' Attitude Towards Participation in Knowledge Processes	Study	Conclusions
Interpersonal trust and positive relations between workers	Hsu and Chang (2014)	Study of telecommunications workers which found a positive relationship between levels of interpersonal trust and levels of knowledge sharing
	Zhou et al. (2010)	Study of Chinese people which found that trust was positively related to knowledge sharing
	Holste and Fields (2010)	Study of managers within a not-for-profit organisation which found that trust was positively related to both the sharing and use of tacit knowledge
	Paroutis and Al Saleh (2009)	Knowledge sharing via Web 2.0 technologies found to be positively related to levels of organisational support
	Cabrera et al. (2005)	Survey of a Spanish IT company which found that perceptions of support from colleagues was one of three key factors positively influencing workers' attitudes to knowledge sharing
Interpersonal conflict between workers	Chen et al. (2011b)	Study of workers in Chinese software company which found task conflict to have a positive impact and relationship conflict to have a negative impact on knowledge sharing
	Wiewiora et al. (2013)	Study of Australian project-based organisations which found that character of organisational culture shaped level of inter-project knowledge sharing
	Li (2010)	IT-based knowledge sharing among US and Chinese workers positively related to the culture of knowledge sharing within the company
Positive organisational culture	Fong and Kwok (2009)	IT-based knowledge sharing among US and Chinese workers positively related to the culture of knowledge sharing within project teams
	Lam (2005)	Case study of a failed KM initiative in an Indian IT consultancy company which showed workers were unwilling to codify and share knowledge because of the competitive, individualistic culture which existed
	Cabrera et al. (2005)	Analysis suggests one key way to develop positive attitude to knowledge sharing is through developing a culture which regards knowledge sharing as a norm
	Tasselli (2015)	Study of healthcare professionals showing how inter-professional knowledge sharing was shaped by the character of people's networks as well as their personal characteristics
Group identity	Lauring and Selmer (2012)	Study of workers in three Danish universities found that knowledge sharing was positively linked to international differences between people, but not differences in age or gender
	Rosendall (2009)	Study which found that people's willingness to share knowledge with others in their work team was positively related to the strength of their identity to the team

(Continued)

Table 18.1 Research data on organisational factors affecting the attitudes of workers to organisational knowledge management initiatives (cont.)

Factors Affecting Workers' Attitude Towards Participation in Knowledge Processes	Study	Conclusions
Group identity	Ravishankar and Pan (2008)	Study of an Indian IT consultancy company which found that people's willingness to share knowledge with colleagues was negatively related to the extent to which they identified with the clients they worked with
Levels of recognition and reward for knowledge management activities	Teo *et al.* (2011)	Case study of one division of Hewlett Packard which found that one key factor shaping participation in a knowledge management was recognition for knowledge sharing efforts
	Han *et al.* (2010)	Study of workers in Taiwan which found that knowledge sharing was positively linked to participation in decision-making processes

HRM practices to support knowledge management initiatives

Before considering the way HRM practices can be used to help motivate workers to participate in organisational knowledge management initiatives, it is necessary to take account of the diversity of ways that organisations can manage their knowledge. As discussed earlier, a number of writers have developed typologies to categorise the range of knowledge management strategies that exist (Alvesson and Karreman, 2001; Hansen *et al.*, 1999; Hunter *et al.*, 2002). Each particular approach to knowledge management requires different behaviours from workers. Thus, using Hansen *et al.*'s (1999) framework, a codification-based strategy requires workers to focus their knowledge management activities around the use of IT systems, where they should codify their own knowledge and use IT-based knowledge repositories (such as searchable databases) to search for any knowledge they do not possess. On the other hand, a personalisation strategy requires workers to be willing to share their tacit knowledge directly with other people. Therefore, as each knowledge management strategy requires different behaviours, their HRM implications are distinctive.

The diversity of knowledge management strategies that exist means that it is impossible to develop a 'one best way' checklist of ways that HRM practices can be used to allow an organisation to effectively manage its knowledge. Ultimately, the way HRM practices are used requires account to be taken of the particular approach to knowledge management adopted by particular organisations (Haesli and Boxall, 2005).

HRM practices to facilitate knowledge management

In this subsection, consideration is given to how particular HRM practices can be used to motivate workers to actively participate in knowledge management initiatives.

Recruitment and selection

One way in which HRM practices can be used to underpin knowledge management initiatives is through using recruitment and selection processes to try and ensure that new staff have appropriate attitudes to organisational knowledge processes. The literature suggests there are two ways in which this can be done. First, recruitment and selection processes can be used to find people whose values and attitudes fit those of an organisation's existing culture and norms. For example, both Swart and Kinnie (2003) and Robertson and Swan (2003) found that the success of the knowledge-intensive firms they examined was partly related to their ability to recruit people who fitted in with the existing values of knowledge sharing and collegiality. Chen *et al.* (2011a) reached similar conclusions in relation to the Taiwanese R&D engineers they examined (see also Chapter 3 by Hurrell and Scholarios and Chapter 4 by Scholarios, in this volume).

How personality relates to knowledge sharing attitudes is a topic that is significantly under-researched. However, a number of studies in this area have concluded that certain personality traits do appear to be positively related to knowledge sharing attitudes. Thus the second way in which recruitment and selection processes could be used to facilitate organisational knowledge management efforts is through using personality tests to identify people who are likely to have positive attitudes to knowledge sharing. While all the studies in this area (Cabrera and Cabrera, 2005; Matzler *et al.*, 2011; Mooradian *et al.*, 2006) use the five-factor personality model, they come to different conclusions about which personality traits are related to positive knowledge sharing attitudes. Thus Cabrera and Cabrera's (2005) research, which is based on a survey of a single Spanish organisation, found that the 'openness to change' personality variable was related to a positive knowledge sharing attitude. By contrast, Mooradian *et al.*'s (2006) study, which was also based on a survey of a single organisation, found a link between 'agreeableness' and positive knowledge sharing attitudes. Finally, Matzler *et al.*'s (2011) study found that both agreeableness and conscientiousness were positively related to knowledge sharing attitudes. Thus research in this area is in its infancy and does not come to firm conclusions regarding how personality is related to knowledge sharing attitudes. Therefore, the use of personality tests to identify positive knowledge sharing attitudes needs to be treated with caution.

Creating/sustaining appropriate cultures

One of the most common ways the literature suggests that HRM practices can be used to support knowledge management initiatives is through creating, developing and supporting an organisational culture that is conducive to knowledge sharing/use/development (Cabrera *et al.*, 2005; Robertson and O'Malley Hammersley, 2000). The general features of such a culture are that knowledge sharing is regarded as a norm and that people's knowledge sharing efforts will be well supported by colleagues, that staff have a strong sense of collective identity, that organisational processes are regarded as fair and, finally, that staff have high levels of trust in and commitment to management.

A number of studies have used Cameron and Quinn's (2006) organisational culture typology (see Table 18.2) to identify which type of organisational cultures facilitate and/or inhibit knowledge management activities. These studies, which have been done in a diversity of organisational contexts, have found that a culture of adhocracy most strongly facilitates knowledge management activities, while hierarchical cultures are most likely to inhibit knowledge management activities (Liao *et al.*, 2011, Sanz-Valle *et al.*, 2011).

Job design

In the area of job design, there is virtual unanimity in the knowledge management literature about the best way to structure jobs to facilitate appropriate knowledge sharing attitudes. Fundamentally, work should be challenging and fulfilling, providing opportunities for workers both to utilise existing skills and knowledge, while also able to continuously develop their knowledge and skills (Robertson and O'Malley Hammersley, 2000; Swart and Kinnie, 2003). Thus in Horowitz *et al.*'s (2003) survey of Singaporean knowledge workers and their managers, providing challenging work was ranked as the most important factor by managers for helping to retain their knowledge workers.

Table 18.2 Cameron and Quinn's four culture types

Culture Type	Culture Characteristics	Character of Most Suitable Environment
Clan	Flexible, internally focused culture, concerned with developing strong sense of collective identity	Dynamic
Adhocracy	Flexible culture focused on being adapted to changing character of external business environment	Dynamic
Hierarchy	An internally focused organisation with limited adaptability, focused on compliance with well-established rules and norms	Stable
Market	Externally focused culture concerned with consistency and standardisation in stable environments	Stable

Further, as well as having work that is intrinsically interesting, the available evidence suggests that knowledge workers also typically regard having high levels of autonomy at work as important (Khatri *et al.*, 2010). For example, in the scientific consultancy examined by Robertson and Swan (2003), autonomy was found to be important to the consultants, and extended to areas as diverse as the projects they worked on (the consultants were free to pick and choose, so long as they reached their annual revenue targets), the selection of the training and development activities they undertook (it was the responsibility of the consultants to identify their own development needs, and funding was available to support this), work clothing and work patterns (a wide diversity of work patterns, personalities and clothing styles were apparent, and a culture of heterogeneity rather than conformity was developed and encouraged).

Finally, Cabrera and Cabrera (2005) suggest that if work is designed to allow the development of social capital between colleagues this can provide another way to facilitate interpersonal knowledge sharing within organisations. Two ways they suggest this can be done are through promoting and utilising team-based working (particularly cross-functional, interdisciplinary teams) and through encouraging the development of communities of practice.

Training

The previous section outlined the positive role that providing opportunities for self-development in work can play in motivating workers to participate in organisational knowledge management processes. While this can be done through the way jobs are organised, it can also be achieved through providing adequate and appropriate opportunities to undertake formal training. Research evidence suggests that knowledge workers regard the provision of such opportunities by their employers to be a crucially important way to help both motivate and retain them (Hunter *et al.*, 2002; Robertson and O'Malley Hammersley, 2000).

Various writers have suggested a number of more specific ways that particular types of training can facilitate appropriate knowledge behaviours. Thus Hansen *et al.* (1999) suggest that the type of training provided should reflect the particular approach to knowledge management an organisation adopts, for example with IT-based training being suitable for those pursuing a codification-based strategy, whereas training to develop interpersonal skills and team-working being appropriate for organisations pursuing a personalisation knowledge management strategy. Further, Cabrera *et al.* (2005), whose study of a Spanish company found that self-efficacy (a person's belief in and confidence about their ability to perform a particular task) was related to positive knowledge sharing attitudes, suggest that investments in training focused on developing workers, self-efficacy levels may also benefit their knowledge management efforts.

Reward and performance appraisal

There is general agreement in the knowledge management literature that rewarding people for appropriate knowledge-related behaviours and embedding knowledge-related attitudes and behaviours in performance appraisal processes represents a potentially important way to use HRM practices to underpin organisational knowledge management efforts (Cabrera and Cabrera, 2005; Oltra, 2005). Further, it is also agreed that such reward systems should reflect the particular knowledge management strategy adopted by an organisation and the type of knowledge processes associated with it. For example, Hansen *et al.* (1999) argue that if a codification strategy is pursued, the pay and reward systems should acknowledge employee efforts to codify their knowledge, and search for the knowledge of others, while with a personalisation strategy, pay and reward systems should recognise the efforts of workers to share their tacit knowledge with each other.

However, at a more detailed level there is disagreement about exactly how reward systems can be used to facilitate positive attitudes and behaviours with respect to knowledge processes. Some research suggests that individually focused financial rewards can play a positive role. For example, Horowitz *et al.*'s survey of Singaporean knowledge workers found that providing a 'highly competitive pay package' (2003: 32) was ranked as the second most effective way to help retain knowledge workers, with the lack of one being cited as the primary reason underlying the turnover of knowledge workers.

However, others suggest that such individually focused rewards can inhibit knowledge sharing through creating an instrumental attitude to knowledge sharing, and also through the way such reward mechanisms may undermine people's sense of team or community spirit and reduce the likelihood that people will share knowledge where the primary benefits of doing so are to the community or group (Fahey *et al.*, 2007). Such writers thus suggest that the best way to develop group-focused knowledge sharing is through making knowledge-related rewards group, rather than individually focused (Cabrera and Cabrera, 2005; Chen *et al.*, 2011a; Lam, 2005) (see Box 18.2). Further, these writers suggest that non-financial rewards such as recognition can play an equally if not more important role in facilitating and encouraging appropriate knowledge behaviours in people (Robertson and O'Malley Hammersley, 2000; Paroutis and Al Saleh, 2009; Teo *et al.*, 2011).

| Box 18.2 HRM in practice | Integrating HRM practices to facilitate knowledge management |

Chen *et al.* (2011a) investigated how a range of different HRM practices affected the willingness of people within R&D teams in Taiwan to share knowledge. All the R&D teams surveyed were in high-technology industries (electronics, communications, precision machinery, semiconductors and optoelectronics). They analysed the surveys of over 200 employees from over 50 separate R&D teams. Overall, they found that most of the HRM practices examined did affect people's knowledge-sharing behaviours. First, they found that recruiting people who fitted with the existing culture and values of the teams promoted knowledge sharing. Second, they also found that people's willingness to share knowledge was also positively related to the extent to which they perceived that their employer paid attention to their long-term career development. Finally, they found that performance appraisals, which were focused on the individual, inhibited people's willingness to share knowledge within teams. Thus in the type of team-based contexts that they examined, team-focused, rather than individually focused performance appraisals are likely to facilitate knowledge sharing.

Source: Chen *et al.*, 2011a

Retention: preventing knowledge loss through developing loyalty

Developing the loyalty of workers to their organisations represents another potentially important way for organisations to facilitate their knowledge management efforts. Having a high turnover rate of knowledge workers is a potentially significant problem for the organisations that employ them, because of some of the characteristics of knowledge workers outlined earlier (Alvesson, 2000; Beaumont and Hunter, 2002; Flood *et al.*, 2001). First, their knowledge is typically highly tacit. As outlined, one key source of knowledge possessed by knowledge workers is social capital, their knowledge of key individuals in client firms. Thus when such workers leave there is a risk for their employer that they will lose their clients as well. Second, low retention rates may be a problem for knowledge intensive firms as the knowledge possessed by knowledge workers is often a crucial element in organisational performance. This is because the tacit and embodied nature of much organisational knowledge means that when employees leave an organisation, they take their knowledge with them. As Byrne (2001: 325) so succinctly puts it, 'without loyalty knowledge is lost'. Thus retaining workers who possess valuable knowledge should arguably be as important an element of an organisation's knowledge management strategy as motivating workers to participate in knowledge activities.

However, analyses suggest that many organisations have high turnover rates and find retaining knowledge workers difficult. This is to a large extent because labour market conditions, where the skills and knowledge of knowledge workers are typically relatively scarce, create conditions for knowledge workers which favour their mobility (Flood *et al.*, 2001; Horowitz *et al.*, 2003). Benson and Brown (2007) present data from a counter-example where a large Australian research organisation did not suffer from such retention problems (see Box 18.3 on the next page).

Alvesson (2000) argues that one of the best ways to deal with the turnover problem is to create organisational loyalty in staff, particularly through developing their sense of organisational identity. Alvesson identifies two broad types of loyalty: instrumental-based loyalty and identification-based loyalty. Alvesson argues that the weakest form of loyalty is instrumental-based loyalty, which is when a worker remains loyal to their employer for as long as they receive specific personal benefits, with one of the most effective ways of developing such loyalty being through pay and working conditions. This conclusion is reinforced by the findings of Horowitz *et al.* (2003), which appear to present a general picture of knowledge workers displaying limited levels of organisational loyalty and being motivated to move jobs primarily by pay-related factors.

For Alvesson, the second and stronger form of loyalty is identification-based loyalty, which is based on the worker having a strong sense of identity as a member of the organisation, and where the worker identifies with the goals and objectives of their organisation. There are three strategies for developing identification-based loyalty. First, there is an institutionally based strategy, where the organisation develops a particular vision or set of values that the knowledge worker identifies with. Second is what Alvesson refers to as a communitarian-based strategy, where workers develop a strong sense of being part of a cohesive team, which is achieved partly through the use of social events which allow bonding and the development of good social relations between workers. Finally, there is the socially integrative strategy, which is a combination of the institutionally based and communitarian strategies. Joo's (2010) study on commitment and turnover intention with a large Korean firm provides support for the role that identification-based loyalty can play in facilitating commitment, as it found that people's levels of organisational commitment was positively related to the organisation's learning culture. This thus suggests that knowledge workers will be committed to their employers if they perceive that their organisation has an appropriate culture which supports knowledge and learning.

Box 18.3 HRM in practice   Loyalty and commitment among knowledge workers in Australia

Benson and Brown (2007) report the findings of research on a large Australian organisation, which compared both the commitment levels and its antecedents of some knowledge workers and routine workers. In contrast with their expectations, and with the findings of other studies into the loyalty of knowledge workers, they found that, when compared to the routine workers, the knowledge workers investigated had higher levels of attitudinal commitment.

Benson and Brown conceptualise commitment into two elements, attitudinal and behavioural commitment, with attitudinal commitment being related to a person's identification with their employer, while behavioural commitment relates to their loyalty and the extent to which they remain working for their employer. The literature on organisational commitment suggests that one of the consequences of workers having high commitment levels is that they are much less likely to leave their employer than workers with lower commitment levels. Thus high levels of commitment aid retention.

Benson and Brown define knowledge workers in terms of three characteristics of the work they do. First, knowledge work involves variety and is typically non-routine. Second, knowledge work is highly interdependent, typically involving close collaboration with a number of work colleagues. Finally, knowledge workers typically have high levels of autonomy.

Based on the findings of existing published research they hypothesise that, first, knowledge workers will have lower levels of attitudinal commitment than routine workers and, second, that knowledge workers will have a higher intention to quit (lower level of behavioural commitment) than routine workers.

Benson and Brown's research was carried out in a large Australian 'semi-governmental, scientific research organisation' (2007: 128), which employed almost 7,000 staff. Its primary aim was to aid Australian industry and to encourage the development and application of scientific knowledge in industry.

Their analysis found that neither of the hypotheses tested were supported and they found the opposite of what they expected. Thus in relation to their first hypothesis they found that 'knowledge workers had a significantly higher attitudinal commitment than routine-task employees', (2007: 132), and in relation to their second hypothesis that knowledge workers had a lower intention to quit (higher levels of behavioural commitment) than routine workers.

Benson and Brown also investigated the antecedents of the knowledge workers' and routine workers' commitment, and found that there were different antecedents for each group. Of the four work organisation variables they examined, three (role ambiguity, co-worker support and supervisory support) were significant determinants of the attitudinal commitment of the knowledge workers, while only two were significant for the routine workers (role ambiguity and supervisory support).

To explain the unexpected finding that the commitment levels of the knowledge workers were higher for the knowledge workers than the routine workers, they argue that this may be because of one specific feature of the case study organisation: the prestigious international reputation that it had. Finally, the findings of their investigation into the antecedents of organisational commitment suggest that positive relations and support from co-workers crucially affected the knowledge workers' level of organisational commitment. Thus developing good relations among colleagues represents one potential way to develop the commitment of knowledge workers.

Conclusion

As knowledge management is a (relatively) new academic discipline, there are many ongoing debates around how to define core concepts such as knowledge management, knowledge work and knowledge-intensive firms. In giving an introduction to the topic, the chapter has provided some brief insights into these issues. However, the main focus of the chapter has been on how HRM practices can be used to facilitate and support knowledge management initiatives within organisations. Broadly, HR practices can support such initiatives in two distinct, but inter-related ways. First, HR practices can be utilised to persuade, recognise and reward workers for engaging in knowledge management activities. Motivating workers to do so is key, primarily because the highly tacit and embodied nature of worker knowledge means that organisations can only gain access to this knowledge when workers are willing to share it with others. That workers are often unwilling to do so because of factors such as a lack of trust, unsupportive organisational cultures, or interpersonal conflict means that the task of motivating workers to engage in knowledge management activities is often fundamental to their success. As has been shown, such HR-related motivation can be provided through diverse means such as recruitment and selection, designing supportive cultures, designing jobs in particular ways, providing appropriate training and embedding knowledge management activities into reward and appraisal processes. The second way in which HRM practices can be used to support knowledge management initiatives is through developing employee loyalty. The importance of employee loyalty to the management of organisational knowledge also flows from the tacit and embodied nature of much employee knowledge, which means that when employees leave they often take a crucial store of organisational knowledge with them. Thus developing employee loyalty provides a means to protect the organisational knowledge base.

Questions

1 Is the potential for conflict between workers and their employers over how the workers knowledge is used unavoidable? From a managerial perspective, what, if anything, can be done to minimise such potential conflict?

2 The dominant perspective in the knowledge worker literature is that to motivate and retain them their employers need to provide them with specific and privileged working conditions. Do the benefits of doing so outweigh the potential disadvantages that may occur, for example, in creating resentment among other workers?

CASE STUDY 18.1

DOMESTIC-POWERCO: SUPPORTING KNOWLEDGE SHARING AND USE AMONG DISTRIBUTED WORK TEAMS

DONALD HISLOP

This case study examines the way management and HRM practices are used to support the work and knowledge activities in an organisation whose workers are geographically dispersed and isolated, with few opportunities to interact and meet on a face-to-face basis.

Organisational context

Domestic-Powerco is a UK-wide company whose main business is installing, repairing and servicing heating equipment in the homes of private individuals. During the 1990s, Domestic-Powerco management implemented a large-scale cost-cutting and restructuring programme, as such changes were believed necessary to allow the company to remain commercially competitive.

The research this case study is based on was carried out during the first half of 2003, with two colleagues of the author from Sheffield's Institute of Work Psychology. The research looked into the characteristics, knowledge sharing and communication dynamics of work that could be described as mobile telework, where people make extensive use of information and communication technologies as a central part of their work, and whose work requires geographic mobility between sites. The research study was small scale, and exploratory in nature and, in Domestic-Powerco, involved extended, semi-structured interviews with six people who worked in the service, repair and installation division, in Lincolnshire and South Yorkshire.

Before the restructuring process it would have been inappropriate to describe the service engineers as mobile teleworkers, as while their work required them to be geographically mobile, the engineers were not required to use ICTs, and they all operated out of central depots, from which they started and finished their daily activities. During this period, while the engineers were required to work in customers' houses on their own, the fact that they began and finished work each day from a central depot, and had to return to the depot if they needed particular spare parts, meant that there were extensive opportunities to interact with, and share knowledge between engineers. This can be illustrated by the following quote, from one of the engineers interviewed,

> I can remember just before the depot shut, we had some outside assessors come in to look at our training, and . . . the best training they saw was the informal training, with everyone stood around the locker, you know, and someone's got a part in their hand, and it's 'oh, don't take the right side off, do it from the left, it's a lot easier'.

The transformation of service engineers into mobile teleworkers

The changes involved in the restructuring project were extremely radical in nature, and involved reducing the workforce from approximately 10,000 to 4,000. Further, there was also a programme to close an enormous number of the 450 depots that existed in the UK at that time, with offices and depots being rationalised into regional centres. As part of this process, the service engineers lost their bases in local depots. These workers no longer had any physical location at which they

were based. While historically they had gone to the depot to be allocated jobs, under the new system this process was no longer necessary. Instead, each engineer, who had their own van and set of equipment, laptop and mobile phone, received their work instructions electronically. Thus, in terms of knowledge sharing, this change in working practices significantly reduced the opportunities for the type of interaction and knowledge sharing among peers illustrated by the first quote. This was summed up as follows by one of the engineers interviewed,

> [Isolation] can be an issue. I think the one thing we have lost is the word-of-mouth to engineers, the group gathering in the morning. It is like taking a part of the social life off you . . . A lot of the engineers would say the main thing they have lost is the contact with other engineers [about] this job.

As will be seen in the following section, Domestic-Powerco have recognised the consequences of these changes and have dealt with the loss of this informal means of knowledge sharing relatively successfully, through a number of mechanisms. However, among the engineers interviewed it was apparent that the organisational means to support interaction, communication and knowledge sharing did not totally satisfy their needs, and many of them developed their own informal means of doing this out of working hours, as illustrated in the following quotation,

> We all go . . . to pick up our parts, and there's a canteen there and there's often four or five of us in the morning, so we'll go up and have a cup of tea and a chat, so we've gone together – we still do meet each other, you know go in half an hour before the shift starts.

Managerial and HRM-related support for Domestic-Powerco's service engineers

Domestic-Powerco was relatively successful at providing support for its service engineers. Despite the fact that many of the engineers felt their work did not give them adequate formal opportunities to interact with colleagues, which were substituted for by the type of informal meeting described above, those interviewed were relatively happy with their work. Further, there was no evidence that they were unwilling to do their work, utilise their knowledge and share their knowledge with colleagues where appropriate.

Categorising Domestic-Powerco's strategy for managing the knowledge of its workers is difficult, as it doesn't fall neatly into any of the categories developed by the academic literature. For example, in terms of Hansen *et al.*'s (1999) framework, as will be seen, there are elements of both a codification-based strategy, where electronic means are used to collect and disseminate codified knowledge, and a personalisation-based strategy, where means are used to facilitate and encourage interpersonal knowledge sharing.

There are three broad knowledge processes that Domestic-Powerco's engineers are required to utilise in order to be able to effectively do their job. First, they need to utilise and apply their acquired knowledge. For example, the diagnosis of problems is one important task they carry out, going into customers' homes with a vague description of a problem, which requires them to identify the precise problem and sort it out. Second, they need to continually acquire new knowledge, for example learning how to install and repair new types of equipment. Finally, as with the photocopy engineers studied by Orr (1996), there is a need for engineers to search for and share knowledge with their peers. The following section outlines the range of processes Domestic-Powerco management utilised to facilitate and support these activities.

Training

There were a number of aspects to the training provided by Domestic-Powerco that supported the work activities and knowledge processes of their service engineers. First, there was a formal apprenticeship scheme, which was the basic training programme that new recruits with no previous experience were put on to learn the basic skills and knowledge of the job. This programme ran for a year with half of it being classroom-based, and half of it being on-the-job training in the region where the apprentices would finally be working. For the on-the-job part of the training apprentices went out with specific engineers and learned through both observing the engineers at work, and also by being allowed to do some tasks themselves.

The second aspect of Domestic-Powerco's training scheme, a buddy system, follows on immediately from the formal training programme, and is an extension and continuation of the engineers' on-the-job training with new engineers working full time with experienced engineers. Thus in this period, new engineers do not visit any customers' homes without a more senior engineer with them. This process serves two purposes. First, it helps the new engineers develop their diagnostic skills in applying their formal learning to specific domestic situations. Second, it also allows new engineers to develop good working and social relations with a number of more experienced engineers, which helps them develop a network of people they can contact if they require support and advice in the future, as most engineers do.

Third, to provide the engineers with opportunities to update their skills and knowledge when necessary, there are a number of mobile training centres that tour the country, which groups of engineers take turns to go to. These centres are customised, articulated lorries of which there are eight in the UK. For example, when a manufacturer launches a new piece of equipment, the mobile training centres may be used for this, as it allows the engineers to get hands-on experience looking at and working with the new equipment.

Finally, there is a system for providing staff with regular technical updates, in the form of codified knowledge and information that can be uploaded onto their laptops. This is discussed more below in the section on codified knowledge.

Managerial support

An intrinsic element of the support system for the service engineers is provided by their managers. Groups of engineers are organised into geographically based teams of between 30 and 60, with one area manager being responsible for all the engineers in a particular area. For the 'small' areas that have only 30 to 40 engineers, the area manager is likely to have sole responsibility. For larger areas with over 50 engineers, the area manager will usually also have a supporting assistant manager working for them. With these supervisory ratios, the managers interviewed emphasised the importance of trust. Managers support and supervise their engineers through a combination of phone calls, team meetings (see below) and face-to-face meetings (close to customers' homes or when they are picking up parts from distribution depots). However, supervisory ratios mean that managers are only typically able to see and/or contact each of their engineers once a week. Therefore, a hands-off style of management is a necessity rather than a positive choice by managers. The day-to-day performance of engineers can be examined by managers via the performance management system that exists, which requires engineers to complete weekly, electronic activity sheets detailing what jobs they have been working on (see below).

Team meetings/social events

Another mechanism used to bring teams of engineers together, which offers the manager an opportunity to interact with them face to face and allows the engineers to share relevant knowledge and information, and retain a sense of team spirit, is monthly team meetings. These are coordinated by the area manager and are typically relatively informal and ad hoc in nature, providing engineers with a forum to raise and discuss issues they regard as important. The staff interviewed also attended regular, team-based social events, organised outside working hours, but these were not a formal part of the management system and were organised at the discretion of area managers.

Codified knowledge

A lot of codified knowledge was also used to support the engineers in their work. For example, their laptops had extensive step-by-step lists of instructions supported by relevant diagrams for how to do most types of repair, on most types of equipment. Thus, theoretically, whatever model of equipment the customer had (with the exception of very old and outdated equipment) the engineers had, through their laptops, the resources to help them repair them. There were also regular (quarterly) updates of technical information sent to engineers on CD-roms. Finally, engineers also received some technical information as paperwork, via the postal system.

Technical support

The final form of support provided to the engineers 'in the field' was access to a 'technical helpline', which they could call up at any time if they found problems that they were unfamiliar with, or the information on their laptops did not cover. Thus, a lot of formal mechanisms existed to support the service engineers in their work, which acknowledged the isolated nature of their work, and provided mechanisms to search for and share knowledge and ideas when necessary.

Pay/performance management

The final issue examined is the pay and performance management system that the service engineers had. While searching for, sharing and effectively utilising knowledge were key aspects of their work, there were no direct pay-related incentives or rewards for doing so. These activities were assumed to be an intrinsic element of the engineers' work, and it was therefore not deemed appropriate to provide bonuses for conducting such activities. The main aspect of variability in pay that existed was where extra pay was available for working weekends or holidays and where engineers had to work overtime. The main way their performance was measured and monitored was on the quality of their work and on their work-rate. Thus each engineer had to complete a weekly activity sheet detailing all the jobs they had done. Every type of job they could do was allocated an amount of time to complete, and engineers had to ensure that they carried out enough jobs so that the time allocated to the total number of jobs they had done added up to the amount of hours they were meant to work in a particular week.

Questions

1 Is there more that Domestic-Powerco could have done with its payment and reward system to encourage/reward appropriate knowledge sharing behaviours among engineers?

2 What would be the benefits and disadvantages of Domestic-Powerco providing formal support, within work time, for the informal pre-work meetings that many engineers used to organise? Is it better to leave these meetings to be managed by staff informally or by management?

3 Is the ratio of managers to engineers adequate, or too high? Reflect on the benefits and disadvantages of either increasing or decreasing this ratio, for both managers and engineers. Is changing this ratio significantly likely to have any impact on the knowledge sharing behaviours of the engineers?

CASE STUDY 18.2

OFFICE EQUIPMENT SERVICE ENGINEERS AND CONSULTANTS AS KNOWLEDGE WORKERS

DONALD HISLOP

Introduction

Hislop (2008) reconceptualised Frenkel *et al.*'s knowledge work framework to make it compatible with the 'all work is knowledge work' perspective. The utility of the revised framework was illustrated by using it to describe and understand the skills and knowledge involved in two different jobs: management consultants and office equipment service engineers.[1] Data on the engineers was collected via conducting interviews in three small office equipment servicing companies based in the same city in the English Midlands, while data on the consultants was collected via conducting interviews in two small HRM-focused management consultancies, from the north-west and south-west of England. Both these groups of workers were classified as knowledge workers, with the skills, knowledge and level of creativity involved in their work being summarised in Table 1.

Office Equipment Service Engineers

The day-to-day work of the engineers involved visiting customers within a particular geographic area to repair, service and install office equipment such as copiers, fax machines, printers and scanners. The number of clients visited per day typically varied from between two to seven dependent upon the complexity of particular jobs. For the service engineers, the level of creativity typically involved in their work was relatively low. This was because the majority of the jobs they did were relatively repetitive and required little diagnostic analysis, with most repair and service work involving dealing with similar types of repairs and tasks. In terms of the skill dimension of the framework, there was a reasonable need to make use of all three skill types. First, action-based skills were needed as most jobs involved some amount of physically disassembling and reassembling equipment. Thus one engineer compared such work to carrying out a routine service on a car. Social skills were also necessary to allow effective communication not only with clients, but also with colleagues. The individualised nature of their work, which involved travelling to clients and working alone, required much of this communication work to be done by mobile phone.

The apparent simplicity of most jobs undertaken by the engineers was a little deceptive as it disguised the extent to which intellective skills were used. This was

Case Study 2: Table 1 Characterising the work of management consultants and service engineers

		Management Consultant	Service Engineer
	Action-Based	Low	Medium
Skills	Social (including aesthetic and emotional)	Medium	Medium
	Intellective	High	Medium
Knowledge	Contextual	Important	Medium–Important
	Theoretical	Very important	Low
Degree of creativity		High	Low–Medium

Source: From Hislop, 2008: 587, Table 2.

---

[1] All the quotations presented in this case study are taken from Hislop, 2008.

largely because these skills were relatively tacit, having been developed through experience. This process was summed up by one engineer as follows:

> You do the training course and they show you how the machine works: you take it apart. But when you get to that machine [on a job] it is when you start learning and obviously the first time you have a fault it might take you a couple of hours to figure out what it is and then the next time you go, because you have had it before, you are straight in and sort it.

In terms of knowledge, the engineers made little if any use of theoretical knowledge, but their work did involve developing and utilising contextual knowledge. This consisted of an understanding, developed over time, of what the business needs of their client's office equipment were (the engineers covered specific geographic areas and over time visited the same clients many times), and how this impacted on the type of problems that typically developed. One engineer described this as follows,

> You get to know what they expect from the machine, which might be quite different from what someone else with an identical machine expects.

Thus, the way their clients used their office equipment affected the type of faults that their equipment developed, and having an understanding of this constituted contextual knowledge for the engineers. They drew on this knowledge and combined it with the action-based and intellective skills they possessed in diagnosing and repairing these faults and carrying out their work.

Management Consultants

In contrast to the engineers, the work of the consultants involved a high level of creativity. The consultancy firms that were examined provided HRM-related advice to clients, primarily in the area of recruitment and selection. In the consultant interviews, one of the features of their work that provided the most job satisfaction was the level of variety involved in their work. For the consultants, no two clients' needs and requirements were ever the same, thus every project the consultants worked on was different and involved developing a particular solution to the specific needs of each client.

In the skill dimension of the framework, while the consultants had negligible need to develop and use action-based skills, their work involved the frequent use of both social and intellective skills. As with the engineers, there were two features of their work which required them to use social skills, first in dealing with clients and second in dealing with colleagues. The consultants needed to spend a significant amount of their time interacting with clients, face to face, by phone

and email, as they needed to first work out what their requirements were, and then once they had developed a proposed solution they had to present it to their client, and if they were happy with this, they would help implement their solution. As with the engineers, the consultants spent much of their working day away from colleagues, thus colleague-facing communication was mainly conducted by phone and email.

In understanding the nature of their intellective skills and how the consultants drew on them in their work it is useful to link them to the knowledge involved in their work. This is because all three were used simultaneously by the consultants in the key task their work involved: designing solutions to meet the specific needs of their various clients.

The work of the consultants involved the use of both theoretical and contextual knowledge. The need for theoretical knowledge and the intellectual character of the consultants' work can be seen in the fact that all the consultants are educated to at least degree level, with most having postgraduate qualifications. The contextual knowledge developed and used by the consultants related to the needs and requirements of their clients. Each client was different, and typically had diverse needs, thus with each project that the consultants worked on they had to develop their contextual knowledge of their client, largely through speaking to them and reading relevant documentation. The need for intellective skills in the work of the consultants involved bringing together their theoretical knowledge with the contextual knowledge they had developed of their client's needs to design bespoke solutions for each client. Thus intellective skills were required in synthesising these two types of knowledge. This practical application of theoretical knowledge was another feature of their work they typically found rewarding. This process of using intellective skills to apply theory to particular situations was described by one consultant as follows:

> I believe abstract theories are all very well but actually really what you want is something that applies. It's good to actually put into practice theory and hopefully make a difference to some people.

Conclusion

From the perspective of the mainstream, professionally focused definition of knowledge work outlined earlier, only the management consultants would be labelled as knowledge workers. However, by taking account of both the contextual knowledge and intellective skills involved in the work of the engineers those adopting the 'all work is knowledge work' perspective consider it legitimate to label the work of both groups as constituting knowledge work.

Questions

1 Do you agree with the analysis that is presented, that because of the requirement of the service engineers to utilise contextual knowledge that they can be classified as knowledge workers?

2 If a knowledge worker is defined as anyone whose work involves the use of a reasonable amount of theoretical or contextual knowledge can you think of any occupations that it isn't appropriate to label knowledge work?

Bibliography

Alvesson, M. (2000) 'Social identity and the problem of loyalty in knowledge-intensive companies', *Journal of Management Studies*, Vol.37, No.8, 1101–23.

Alvesson, M. and Karreman, D. (2001) 'Odd couple: making sense of the curious concept of knowledge management', *Journal of Management Studies*, Vol.38, No.7, 995–1018.

Beaumont, P. and Hunter, L. (2002) *Managing Knowledge Workers*, London: Chartered Institute of Personnel and Development.

Benson, J. and Brown, M. (2007) 'Knowledge workers: what keeps them committed; what turns them away', *Work, Employment and Society*, Vol.21, No.1, 121–41.

Byrne, R. (2001) 'Employees: capital or commodity?', *Career Development International*, Vol.6, No.6, 324–30.

Cabrera, E. and Cabrera, A. (2005) 'Fostering knowledge sharing through people management practices', *International Journal of Human Resource Management*, Vol.16, No.5, 720–35.

Cabrera, A., Collins, W. and Salgado, J. (2005) 'Determinants of individual engagement in knowledge sharing', *International Journal of Human Resource Management*, Vol.17, No.2, 245–64.

Cameron, K. and Quinn, R. (2006) *Diagnosing and Changing Organisational Culture Based on the Competing Values Framework*, Reading, MA: Addison-Wesley.

Chen, W.-Y., Hsu, B.-F. and Lin, Y.-Y. (2011a) 'Fostering knowledge sharing through human resource management in R&D teams', *International Journal of Technology Management*, Vol.53, Nos.2–4, 309–30.

Chen, Z., Zhang, X. and Vogel, D. (2011b) 'Exploring the underlying processes between conflict and knowledge sharing: a work-engagement perspective', *Journal of Applied Social Psychology*, Vol.41, No.5, 1005–33.

Currie, G. and Kerrin, M. (2003) 'Human resource management and knowledge management: enhancing knowledge sharing in a pharmaceutical company', *International Journal of Human Resource Management*, Vol.14, No.6, 1027–45.

Cushen, J. and Thompson, P. (2012) 'Doing the right thing? HRM and the angry knowledge worker', *New Technology, Work and Employment*, Vol.27, No.2, 79–92.

Empson, L. (2001) 'Fear of exploitation and fear of contamination: impediments to knowledge transfer in mergers between professional service firms', *Human Relations*, Vol.54, No.7, 839–62.

Evans, J., Hendron, M. and Oldroyd, J. (2015) 'Withholding the ace: the individual- and unit-level performance effects of self-reported and perceived knowledge hoarding', *Organization Science*, Vol.26, No.2, 494–510.

Fahey, R., Vasconcelos, A. and Ellis, D. (2007) 'The impact of rewards within communities of practice: a study of the SAP online global community', *Knowledge Management Research and Practice*, Vol.5, 186–98.

Flood, P., Turner, T., Ramamoorthy, N. and Pearson, J. (2001) 'Causes and consequences of psychological contracts among knowledge workers in the high technology and financial services industries', *International Journal of Human Resource Management*, Vol.12, No.7, 1152–65.

Fong, P. and Kwok, C. (2009) 'Organisational culture and knowledge management success at project and organisational levels in contracting firms', *Journal of Construction Engineering and Management*, Vol.135, No.12, 1348–56.

Frenkel, S., Korczynski, M., Donohue, L. and Shire, K. (1995) 'Re-constituting work: trends towards knowledge work and info-normative control', *Work, Employment and Society*, Vol.9, 773–96.

Haesli, A. and Boxall, P. (2005) 'When knowledge management meets HR strategy: an exploration of personalization–retention and codification–recruitment configuration', *International Journal of Human Resource Management*, Vol.16, No.11, 1955–75.

Han, T.-S., Chiang, H.-H. and Chang, A. (2010) 'Employee participation in decision making, psychological ownership and knowledge sharing: mediating role of organizational commitment in Taiwanese high-tech organizations', *International Journal of Human Resource Management*, Vol.21, No.12, 2218–33.

Hansen, M., Nohria, N. and Tierney, T. (1999) 'What's your strategy for managing knowledge?', *Harvard Business Review*, Vol.77, No.2, 108–16.

Hislop, D. (2008) 'Conceptualizing knowledge work utilizing skill and knowledge-based concepts: the case of some consultants and service engineers', *Management Learning*, Vol.39, No.5, 579–97.

Hislop, D. (2009) *Knowledge Management in Organizations: A Critical Introduction*, Oxford: Oxford University Press.

Holste, J. and Fields, D. (2010) 'Trust and tacit knowledge sharing and use', *Journal of Knowledge Management*, Vol.14, No.1, 128–40.

Horowitz, F., Heng, C. and Quazi, H. (2003) 'Finders, keepers? Attracting, motivating and retaining knowledge workers', *Human Resource Management Journal*, Vol.13, No.4, 23–44.

Hunter, L., Beaumont, P. and Lee, M. (2002) 'Knowledge management practice in Scottish law firms', *Human Resource Management Journal*, Vol.12, No.2, 4–21.

Hsu, M.-H. and Chang, C.-M. (2014) 'Examining interpersonal trust as a facilitator and uncertainty as an inhibitor of intra-organizational knowledge sharing', *Information Systems Journal*, Vol.24, 119–42.

Joo, B.-K. (2010) 'Organizational commitment for knowledge workers: the roles of perceived organizational learning culture, leader–member exchange quality, and turnover intention', *Human Resource Development Quarterly*, Vol.21, No.1, 69–85.

Khatri, N., Baveja, A., Agarwal, N. and Brown, G. (2010) 'HR and IT capabilities and complementarities in knowledge intensive services', *International Journal of Human Resource Management*, Vol.21, No.15, 2889–909.

Lam, W. (2005) 'Successful knowledge management requires a knowledge culture: a case study', *Knowledge Management Research and Practice*, Vol.3, 206–17.

Lauring, J. and Selmer, J. (2012) 'Knowledge sharing in diverse organizations', *Human Resource Management Journal*, Vol.22, No.1, 89–105.

Lee, P., Gillespie, N., Mann, L. and Wearing, A. (2010) 'Leadership and trust: their effects on knowledge sharing and team performance', *Management Learning*, Vol.41, No.4, 473–91.

Li, W. (2010) 'Virtual knowledge sharing in a cross-cultural context', *Journal of Knowledge Management*, Vol.14, No.1, 38–50.

Liao, S.-H., Chang, W.-J., Hu, D.-C. and Yueh, Y.-L. (2012) 'Relationships among organizational culture, knowledge acquisition, organizational learning and organizational innovation in Taiwan's banking and insurance industries', *International Journal of Human Resource Management*, Vol.23, No.1, 52–70.

Littler, C. and Innes, D. (2003) 'Downsizing and deknowledging the firm', *Work, Employment and Society*, Vol.17, No.1, 73–100.

Mansell, R. and Steinmueller, W. (2000) *Mobilizing the Information Society: Strategies for Growth and Opportunity*, Oxford: Oxford University Press.

Marshall, N. and Brady, T. (2001) 'Knowledge management and the politics of knowledge: illustrations from complex product systems', *European Journal of Information Systems*, Vol.10, 99–112.

Martin, J. (2006) 'Multiple intelligence theory, knowledge identification and trust', *Knowledge Management Research and Practice*, Vol.4, No.3, 207–15.

Matzler, K., Renzl, B., Mooradian, T., von Krogh, G. and Mueller, J. (2011) 'Personality traits, affective commitment, documentation of knowledge and knowledge sharing', *International Journal of Human Resource Management*, Vol.22, No.2, 296–310.

McDermott, R. and O'Dell, C. (2001) 'Overcoming cultural barriers to sharing knowledge', *Journal of Knowledge Management*, Vol.5, No.1, 76–85.

Mooradian, T., Renzl, B. and Matzler, K. (2006) 'Who trusts? Personality trust and knowledge sharing', *Management Learning*, Vol.37, No.4, 523–40.

Morris, T. (2001) 'Asserting property rights: knowledge codification in the professional service firm', *Human Relations*, Vol.54, No.7, 819–38.

O'Dell, C. and Hubert, C. (2011) 'Building a knowledge sharing culture', *Journal for Quality and Participation*, Vol.34, No.2, 22–6.

Oltra, V. (2005) 'Knowledge management effectiveness factors: the role of HRM', *Journal of Knowledge Management*, Vol.9, No.4, 70–86.

Orr, J. (1996) *Talking About Machines: An Ethnography of a Modern Job*, Ithaca, NY: ILR Press.

Paroutis, S. and Al Saleh, A. (2009) 'Determinants of knowledge sharing using Web 2.0 technologies', *Journal of Knowledge Management*, Vol.13, No.4, 52–63.

Ravishankar, M. and Pan, S. (2008) 'The influence of organizational identification on organizational knowledge management (KM)', *Omega*, Vol.36, 221–34.

Reich, R. (1991) *The Work of Nations: Preparing Ourselves for 21st-Century Capitalism*, London: Simon & Schuster.

Renzl, B. (2008) 'Trust in management and knowledge sharing: the mediating effects of fear and knowledge documentation', *Omega*, Vol.36, 206–20.

Robertson, M. and O'Malley Hammersley, G. (2000) 'Knowledge management practices within a knowledge-intensive firm: the significance of the people management dimension', *Journal of European Industrial Training*, Vol.24, Nos.2–4, 241–53.

Robertson, M. and Swan, J. (2003) '"Control – what control?" Culture and ambiguity within a knowledge intensive firm', *Journal of Management Studies*, Vol.40, No.4, 831–58.

Rosendall, B (2009) 'Sharing knowledge, being different and working as a team', *Knowledge Management Research and Practice*, Vol.7, 4–14.

Sanz-Valle, R., Naranjo-Valencia, J., Jimenez-Jimenez, D. and Perez-Caballero, L. (2011) 'Linking organizational learning with technical innovation and organizational culture', *Journal of Knowledge Management*, Vol.15, No.6, 887–1015.

Storey, J. and Barnett, E. (2000) 'Knowledge management initiatives: learning from failure', *Journal of Knowledge Management*, Vol.4, No.2, 145–56.

Swart, J. and Kinnie, N. (2003) 'Sharing knowledge in knowledge-intensive firms', *Human Resource Management Journal*, Vol.13, No.2, 60–75.

Swart, J. and Kinnie, N. (2010) 'Organisational learning, knowledge assets and HR practices in professional service firms', *Human Resource Management Journal*, Vol.20, No.1, 64–79.

Tam, Y., Korczynski, M. and Frenkel, S. (2002) 'Organizational and occupational commitment: knowledge workers in large corporation', *Journal of Management Studies*, Vol.39, No.6, 775–801.

Tasselli, S. (2015) 'Social networks and inter-professional knowledge transfer: the case of healthcare professionals', *Organization Studies*, Vol.36, No.7, 841–72.

Teo, T., Nishant, R., Goh, M. and Agarwal, S. (2011) 'Leveraging collaborative technologies to build a knowledge sharing culture at HP analytics', *MIS Quarterly Executive*, Vol.10, No.1, 1–18.

Thompson, P., Warhurst, C. and Callaghan, G. (2001) 'Ignorant theory and knowledgeable workers: interrogating the connections between knowledge, skills and services', *Journal of Management Studies*, Vol.38, No.7, 923–42.

Tong, J. and Mitra, A. (2009) 'Chinese cultural influences on knowledge management practice', *Journal of Knowledge Management*, Vol.13, No.3, 49–62.

Wiewiora, A., Trigunarsyah, B., Murphy, G. and Coffey, V. (2013) 'Organisational culture and willingness to share knowledge: a competing values perspective in Australian context', *International Journal of Project Management*, Vol.31, 1163–74.

Zhou, S., Siu, F. and Wang, M. (2010) 'Effects of social tie content on knowledge transfer', *Journal of Knowledge Management*, Vol.14, No.3, 449–63.

CHAPTER 19
EMPLOYMENT ETHICS

Peter Ackers

Ethics – the philosophical study of the moral value of human conduct and the rules and principles that ought to govern it.

(Collins Dictionary, emphasis added)

Introduction

Employment ethics, as a subdivision of business ethics (see Fryer, 2015; Crane and Matten, 2010; Chryssides and Kaler, 1993), involves the application of general moral principles to the management of employees' wages and conditions. In the same way as, say, sports or medical ethics, it begins with a concern about human relationships and how we treat other people. There are two dimensions to this: personal ethical issues at work, and broader questions of business social responsibility. The first addresses the way you or I should behave, as responsible individuals, towards other employees and our employer. This might include questions like personal honesty in completing expenses forms, using the work telephone or Internet facilities, resisting the temptation of bribes or simply kindness and consideration towards our workmates. Without a culture of personal ethics high standards of business ethics are inconceivable. For this reason, many organisations now have an ethical code of practice to guide employee behaviour. The focus of this chapter, however, is on the second category, where you act as a management agent for the business organisation. In this case, while there is still scope for personal discretion, your approach to other employees will be heavily circumscribed by business policy. For instance, if 'the company' decides to close an entire factory or shop or make a group of employees redundant, you will be left, as an individual manager, to implement a decision whether or not you agree with it.

In this light, the chapter aims to guide the student through employment ethics as it applies to real business management practice, particularly in Britain, past and present. As we shall see, this opens up a highly controversial, global public policy debate about the role and responsibilities of business in society, illustrated by recent political arguments about the pay and bonuses of 'bankers' and other senior business executives (see Peston, 2008). Following some discussion of the complexities of applying ethics to business, various ethical theories are introduced by applying them to a real-life ethical problem. An employment ethics agenda is then established, contrasting, in broad economic policy terms, a right-wing emphasis on the free market with a centre-left stress on social regulation. These are then linked to two competing unitarist and pluralist conceptions of management as an ethical agent in employment relations. The next section explores the institutions and agencies that can shape an ethical employment approach, followed by an assessment of a critical development of recent decades, the advent of HRM as a new way of talking about labour management. The chapter closes by advocating an 'internal' stakeholder view of employment ethics as an antidote to three fallacies of recent HRM theory and practice (see Flanders, 1970).

To begin with, however, the process of translating ethics from personal behaviour to business practice is not straightforward. As we have seen, one initial complication to business ethics is that decisions about right and wrong are made by an impersonal organisation, rather than a single identifiable individual, as in some other spheres of moral decision making. A further apparent difficulty, compared this time to other fields of management activity, is that ethics is about what *ought* to be, rather than what is. In short, it involves value judgements and differences of opinion rather than just technical decisions. In truth, the same is true of almost all organisational policy affecting human beings; only elsewhere these value judgements are hidden behind technical-sounding words such as 'efficiency'. As Fox (1966) has argued, employment relations are always viewed through competing frames of reference, leading to different interpretations of the situation. In this sense, 'ethics' should be seen as part and parcel of everyday personnel policy, not some entirely different realm of activity.

Employment ethics is still a highly problematic issue, for two further reasons. While modern business seeks the moral high ground, often for public relations purposes, sceptics retort that business ethics in general is an oxymoron – a contradiction in terms. Is not the main goal of business, after all, to maximise profits, with all other considerations, including the treatment of employees, coming a poor second? On the other hand, the employment relationship, between employer and employee, can become an especially deep-rooted and durable bond, evoking ethical notions of trust and loyalty. Paid work occupies many of our working hours and shapes our life chances, while HRM theory suggests that employees are a crucial *human resource* to be nurtured, developed and retained by the business organisation (see Beardwell and Thompson, 2014; Legge, 1995; 2004). Some argue that good ethics is, in fact, good business and, therefore, that no serious conflict exists between doing the right thing towards employees and improving business performance. This may be true for some businesses, some of the time. But more often 'being ethical' involves a real dilemma, whether you're making a difficult choice between business expedience (profits, efficiency, cost) and a moral principle, or between two conflicting ethical pressures.

While all ethics starts with common-sense claims about what is 'right' and 'fair', we soon find there are very different views about what these words mean. For this reason, we cannot say whether some employment policy is ethical or unethical, without referring back to which ethical theory we are applying. One central employment issue is how much we should pay people. At the lowest levels, this is often a responsibility of the state, as with the 2016 British 'National Living Wage', which extends existing minimum wage provision (see Ruddick, 2015; Pratley, 2015). But for the most part, this is decided by the business, acting by itself, unilaterally, or through negotiations with trade unions. So here there is great scope for ethical agency. Let me imagine for a moment that I am the main shareholder and senior manager of a business organisation. A group of manual workers have asked for a 20 per cent wages increase, to provide 'a fair day's pay for a fair day's work'. Their language asserts an ethical claim. I want to act 'ethically', but how can I decide whether their claim is a just one? To take the matter further, we must enter what is popularly known as a 'moral maze'. While the detailed facts of the case are always important, the way we interpret them will be shaped by which ethical theory we choose to follow as the road to truth (see Chryssides and Kaler, 1993: 79–107; Winstanley and Woodall, 1999).

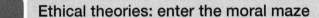

Ethical theories: enter the moral maze

Managing *reward* is one central role of HRM. So one common-sense starting point for employment ethics is to look to the costs and benefits of awarding a pay rise and then to enter the passage into the maze marked '*Consequentialism*' (see Table 19.1). Almost immediately, I begin to wonder how to weigh and measure these consequences. For instance, a pay increase will benefit these workers, but may cut into my income as owner, perhaps reducing the amount I invest in new plant and machinery, spend on myself or give to charity. How do I know which consequence is more beneficial? By now, however, my path has branched into another fairly wide thoroughfare entitled '*Utilitarianism*', which claims to answer this question. Accordingly, whichever action gives the greatest happiness or utility is to be preferred. Since my employees are more numerous than me and on lower incomes, it may seem that a wage increase would be the most ethical course. But what of the broader consequences for happiness in society, if higher labour costs raise the cost of living for customers or cut the incentive of entrepreneurs, like me, to establish business and create jobs? Another problem is that I do not know what the actual consequences will be, and can only guess. For instance, higher wages may benefit the business in the long run by improving employee performance and reducing labour turnover. Alternatively, higher labour costs may reduce competitiveness and lead to job loss. Thus, utilitarianism can nearly always provide good ammunition for both sides in an employment argument. More worrying, perhaps, it seems to provide a ready rationale for any employer seeking to wriggle out of social responsibility – which, of course, I am not.

A little discouraged, I retrace my steps to another, narrower passage, with the strange off-putting title of '*Deontology*'. On closer inspection, however, we discover that this merely means that I should act out of duty and choose to 'do the right thing' irrespective of consequences. Indeed, this way purports to lead to a 'kingdom of ends' with two cardinal principles to guide my sense of duty. One is that I should be prepared to generalise or *universalise* my decision. So if I give these manual employees an increase, we will also have to consider the situation of office workers and whether they are being treated consistently. The second principle is that we must show a *respect for persons*, by treating them as an end in themselves and not a means to an end. In practical terms, this could mean that I should not sacrifice my present duty towards these employees – by rejecting their wage claim – in order to pursue the long-term best interests of my business and society. Indeed, one path branches off, called '*Human Rights*', announcing that all employees have a 'right' to a decent 'living wage' and so on. In this way, Kant's ethic of duty can appear so high-minded that it prevents business management from even considering economic factors, which may affect the long-term viability of the firm. Moreover, the assumption that we must act out of a sense of duty to be genuinely ethical appears to outlaw any considerations of economic self-interest. What happens, for instance, if my motive is disinterested, but I am also aware that granting an increase will solve the firm's labour turnover problems? Am I still acting ethically?

But how do I know that my primary duty lies towards these employees? Suddenly I notice two less obvious paths leading in diametrically opposite directions, each also departing from the deontological mainstream. The first '*Shareholder*' way states boldly, 'Your primary duty is to the shareholders who own and invest in the company' (see Friedman, 1993). Indeed, it turns out that their property rights can only be protected by keeping costs to a minimum, maximising profits and returning the best possible dividend. It is hard to see how a pay increase for employees can match these goals, unless it has a sound economic basis such as labour shortages or increased productivity. In this view, business efficiency must serve the shareholder, first and foremost. An alternative '*Stakeholder*' way argues that shareholders or investors are just one of several interest groups represented in the business corporation, including employees, customers, suppliers and the wider community. Accordingly, my ethical duty is to balance the needs of these different groups. Hence, if the pay and conditions of employees have been neglected in recent years, a pay award may be a justifiable piece of 'rebalancing'. On the other hand, if pay is already very high compared to elsewhere, and has been passed on in high prices to customers – as in Premier League football – this will not be the right thing to do. The general problem remains of how to adjudicate ethically between the claims of the competing stakeholders. By this point, many passages have begun to merge and overlap, as stakeholding and shareholding each blur into utilitarianism on the one side, and human rights on the other, at some point on the way. As I have already begun to understand, the path to employment ethics is rarely easy.

At a clearing in the maze, however, a broad new passage begins, called '*Theories of Justice*'. Yet within a few feet, this has divided in two completely different directions. The first route, '*Justice as Entitlement*', eventually runs into the shareholder path on which we travelled earlier (see Nozick, 1993). This argues that human beings have a right to acquire and transfer property freely, providing they follow due process and avoid fraud and theft. Neither the government, nor any other organised pressure group, has a right to interfere in this free, and therefore fair, exchange. Seen in this light, my employees should conclude individual deals with me over wages and conditions, and accept whatever is the commercial going rate. Although I may pay them more, through kindness and charity – to borrow Kant's language – this is an 'imperfect duty' or an act of gratuitous generosity and it remains quite just to pay them the bare market rate. If, by banding together in a trade union, my employees are trying to 'force' me to pay a higher rate than I would from free choice, this is unjust and I would be right to resist their efforts. This view of justice, pushed to its full logical conclusion, neglects power inequalities in the employment relationship (see Colling and Terry, 2010), places little social responsibility on the business to protect the wages and conditions of employees and can lead to great economic inequality. It also demonstrates how far some ethical theories can depart from common-sense notions of fair treatment.

The other path, '*Justice as Fairness*', leads to a table and chairs, where we all sit down, don blindfolds and think about what sort of society we would like to live in, without knowing what position we would occupy in it (see Rawls, 1993). The conclusion drawn is that we would choose equal treatment except where differences work to the benefit of the worst off. We would not choose justice as entitlement for fear that we might be born without talent or resources, and end up penniless and sleeping in the streets. Applied to my situation, this suggests that if the claimants are substantially poorer than I, or other shareholders and white-collar employees, I must either demonstrate that they benefit from these inequalities, or allow the pay claim. In defence, my unique skill and responsibility may be an adequate justification. Maybe to stay within the spirit of this social contract, I should give employees some 'Voice' in the running of the business (Johnstone and Ackers, 2015). This might involve establishing a consultation committee, including union representatives, having 'worker directors' or even turning the business into some sort of cooperative owned by the entire workforce, similar to the John Lewis Partnership. These options, if taken, lead into a common passage, shared with stakeholding. One linking way is '*Communitarianism*' (see Etzioni, 1995), whereby we ponder not just the distribution of economic resources in terms of poverty and inequality but also the impact on social cohesion. In short, will high manual pay contribute to a more tightly knit workforce and community?

Table 19.1 Fitting the ethical theories together

Consequentialist	Non-Consequentialist
Utilitarianism	Kantianism
Happiness of the greatest number	Human dignity an end in itself
The end justifies the means	Universal moral rules
Language of economic utility	Language of human rights

After all this wandering in the moral maze, it is easy to become confused and disheartened. And there are three wide avenues radiating from a clearing, each promising a quick route to a satisfactory ethical conclusion. One, termed '*Divine Judgement*', invites us to abandon all this confusion and buy a tried-and-tested set of moral rules, usually off the religious shelf. My problem is that rules like the Ten Commandments were devised long before the genesis of modern business, and are too general to tell me what to do in this precise situation. So while an ethical approach may be grounded in a religious tradition, this does not mean that there are easy, ready-made solutions to complex human problems. In a diverse modern society or workplace there is also the problem of appealing to others who have different religious beliefs or none, since employment ethics is also about dialogue and persuasion (see Fryer, 2011). In short, many of my employees have very different religious and ideological backgrounds, so I am searching for a broad language of ethics that will win their assent.

Another path, '*Ethical Relativism*', runs in precisely the opposite direction, reassuring me that such diversity of opinion is unavoidable in our global, postmodern society, multicultural world and recommending that I avoid the sort of universal claims made by the deontologists earlier (see Smith and Johnson, 1996). Far better to follow the shared opinion of my particular subculture, this approach suggests. I belong to many social circles, however, each with different ethical views, while my business friends simply press a shareholder view that is quite unacceptable to my employees. Finally, I encounter '*Enlightened Self-Interest*', a way that reassures me that I worry too much (see Pearson, 1995). In the long term, good wages and conditions create loyal, productive, well-trained trustworthy employees, who, in turn, produce great rewards for all the stakeholders at the same time. This is the familiar *Business Case* for good HRM, to which we return below. Yet still I wonder, how does this pay award help or hinder and what about the short term?

An employment ethics agenda: six central issues

While the various ethical theories offer plenty of clues for what an ethical employment policy might look like, there are no straightforward and easy solutions that can be drawn from them. Moreover, most general ethical theories can be interpreted in very divergent ways. This said, the big debate in employment ethics concerns how far the state and social agencies, like trade unions, should be allowed to regulate the free market in order to protect workers' wages and conditions. And we can quickly see two main sides lining up and drawing together different elements from the above ethical theories (see Table 19.2).

The first, *right-wing economic position* stresses the utilitarian benefits of free market capitalism, duty to the shareholder, justice as the entitlement to own and freely dispose of property, and a paternalist version of enlightened self-interest which renders state regulation unnecessary. The second, *centre-left economic position* emphasises the disutilities of short-term, free market capitalism for society, employee rights, stakeholding, justice as fairness and a sceptical view of enlightened self-interest which presupposes the need for some state regulation to ensure good employment practices. In the US, this division runs quite close to the right–left political and economic argument between Republican 'Conservatives' and Democratic 'Liberals', whereas Europe, with its Social Democratic and Christian Democratic political traditions, leans more towards the second view. In these terms, the question of what is ethical employment practice transmutes into the question: how should employment be regulated and to what ends? But first, what sort of employment issues are we talking about?

Business ethics in general is already a major preoccupation of most large companies. Many corporate mission statements and ethical codes pay lip service to virtues such as integrity, fairness and loyalty and envision a variety of stakeholders, including employees. In some cases, this enthusiasm for ethics has been prompted by a scandal, which damaged a company's or industry's reputation, as with criticism of the banks for mis-selling pensions or endowment mortgages, the Enron case in the US, or Shell's bad publicity over human rights in Nigeria. We can only imagine the *corporate social responsibility* (CSR) initiatives that will follow the 2015 Volkswagen diesel emissions controversy. In other cases, ethics has been used as a marketing tool in a more proactive way. Hence, the Body Shop launched itself around a strong opposition to testing on animals for cosmetic purposes and has campaigned for fair trade with the Third World, while the Co-operative Bank has responded to customer objections to fur farming and investment in oppressive regimes. By and large, these companies have concentrated their attention on external public relations and the customer as a stakeholder, with the often undeclared assumption that stakeholding will work directly to improve the position of the shareholder. In all this, employees often appear as a poor relation in the family of stakeholders, such that companies can flaunt their ethics to customers while paying low wages and making thousands of workers redundant. Any distinctively employment ethics agenda will revolve around the damage caused to workers' wages and conditions by unregulated, flexible, free market capitalism. In so far as customers and shareholders benefit from this regime – high dividends and low prices at the expense of low wages, for instance – it may reflect a clash of stakeholder interests. As a consequence, employment ethics tends to deploy centre-left economic and ethical arguments against neo-liberal free market capitalism. Let us briefly rehearse six of these.

1 **Reward:** This relates to fair pay and the enormous gap that has opened up between executive salaries and perks, on the one hand, and those of people in low-paid, temporary jobs on the other. This links to wider contemporary concerns about rising economic inequality, even in mature Western economies (Piketty, 2014; Pickett and Wilkinson, 2010). Internal HRM decisions about the management of reward are clearly central to this. In deciding whether these are 'just' rewards we can apply Rawls' test – for example, senior management salaries are much lower in Europe and Japan than in Britain and the US – and explore issues of 'merit' and 'need'. Likewise, the British and German national minimum wage initiatives have been prompted by an ethical assessment that the 'market rate' is not always a fair rate and that the state has to intervene to regulate bad employers. On a global scale, this 'fair trade' argument applies not just to the price of fruit and vegetables, but to the wages and conditions of workers in the supply chain of large multinationals. And, while much of the public debate has centred on the gap between the rich and the poor, at the top and bottom of the remuneration system, there is also the question of relatively fair pay for comparable middle income groups, such as doctors, nurses and physiotherapists in the health system, and between individuals doing the same job (see Chiang and Birtch, Chapter 6, this volume).

2 **Exit and employment protection:** Vulnerable employees are as concerned with job security as much as wages. For instance, without stable employment it is impossible to obtain a mortgage and buy a house. This relates to concerns about the flexible labour market as it impacts individual and family welfare. Through HRM policies such as 'zero-hour contracts', some workers today are trapped in such sporadic, part-time and temporary work that they find it hard to support themselves, let alone a family. In most advanced economies, employees have some legal protection against redundancy and unfair dismissal – though this is not true of the US, with its free market ethos that employment contracts can be terminated 'at will' by either side. Going beyond the minimum laws of the land, clearly there are moral responsibilities on the business in relation to the employment security of

Table 19.2 Capitalism and theories of justice – an interpretation

	Theory of Justice	Corporate Responsibility	Employment Policies
Right Wing	Nozick (entitlement)	Shareholder (unitarist)	Free market
Centre-Left	Rawls (fairness)	Stakeholder (pluralist)	Regulated market

employees and the terms on which their jobs can be terminated (see Wilkinson, Dobbins and Redman, Chapter 14 on downsizing, this volume).

3 **Work–life balance and family-friendly policies:** Even better-paid salaried workers find it hard to draw boundaries between work and home life, such that they suffer stress and their relationships and children suffer neglect (see Ackers and El-Sawad, 2006). In all these cases, as communitarians argue, the price for society may be family and community breakdown (see Ackers, 2002). Thus the European Union (EU) Working Time Directive, laying down a maximum 48-hour working week and minimum holiday provisions, rests on the assumption that in certain circumstances the free market can fail employees and society. Recent British governments have encouraged firms to adopt family-friendly policies. The growing employment of married women with children – displacing the old male breadwinner/female housewife model – has increased these pressures, as have the caring pressures of an ageing population (see Kirton, Chapter 13, this volume).

4 **Equal opportunities and diversity:** Most modern economies are increasingly diverse, in terms of their gender, ethnic and other demographics. Some groups, such as women, black, disabled, older and gay employees have experienced discrimination in the past and may still do today. Equal opportunities policies are designed to ensure that everybody has the same chance, at every stage in the employment relationship, from recruitment through promotion to termination. At the same time, they often attempt to redress past inequalities. In extreme cases, such as slavery in the US, the Indian caste system or South African apartheid, the mechanism for helping the disadvantaged group is some form of positive discrimination. However, such policies raise interesting ethical debates, since they are in tension with the category-blind principle of the original notion of equal opportunity (see Cassell, Chapter 12 on managing diversity, this volume).

5 **Employee voice:** The entitlement of workers (and the local community in cases of major plant closure) to have some 'Voice' in the running of their business organisation, relates to broader issues of corporate governance, and whose interests the business organisation should serve. Full-blown stakeholding or organisational pluralism demands some sort of representative structure by which workers can influence company decision making (see Ackers, 2010; Johnstone and Ackers, 2015). In the past, trade unions played this role, and in many cases they still do. But this still begs the question of what happens across more than half of the economy where trade unions are completely absent. Within the EU, the European Social Chapter and various directives have tried to entrench certain minimum standards for employee representation, information and consultations (see Dundon and Wilkinson, Chapter 16 on employee participation, this volume).

6 **Individual liberty at work:** In addition to such positive rights, there is the issue of negative rights or civil liberties. For public sector workers in the EU these are now enshrined in the Human Rights Act. If centre-left thinking has often underestimated the threat of the state to individual freedom, right-wing thinkers are equally blind to the threat posed by the large business. As we have seen, equal opportunities issues around race, gender, disability, age and sexuality are already established in law and public policy. But can an employer dismiss someone because they are obese, smoke, wear an earring, have a tattoo or have eccentric religious or political views? In short, how far can a business, seeking to mould corporate culture, invade the private self of the individual employee or potential employee? This conundrum links to the question of whistleblowers or workers who expose unethical practices in their company. Does the business own their conscience because it pays the wages, or do they have a higher obligation to society?

Once more, a pluralist or stakeholding view of the corporation demands forms of external regulation to underpin these employee claims. Enlightened companies may address these issues of their own accord, through voluntary agreements, procedures and codes of practice. But, from this perspective, business as a whole cannot be trusted to do so. And firms with bad employment practices may gain short-term cost advantages and undermine the high standards elsewhere. In several of the above examples, recent British government or

EU regulation has been prompted by the decline of trade unions and collective bargaining, leaving many employees exposed to the full power of the employer. Moreover, employers *in general* have failed to fill this 'ethical gap' by voluntary action. This said, the state can only secure minimum standards, still leaving great scope for companies and managers to pioneer exemplary wages and conditions. Today, these may also include well-resourced efforts to train and involve workers, as well as 'family-friendly' policies such as extended maternity and paternity provision, flexitime or nursery facilities.

Shaping an ethical workplace

If employment ethics is to mean anything in practice, we need to identify institutions or agencies capable of implementing it. Individual virtue is necessary, but not sufficient. Rarely does one person alone have the capacity to resolve an employment ethics dilemma, as in the wages scenario earlier. Economic life is highly complex and often beyond the scope of personal acts of goodwill. Only the state or substantial social institutions, such as professional associations (Ackers, 2015) can impress some ethical pattern on the relationships that ensue. As Clegg's (1979) rule-making framework for employment relations suggests, three agencies can help to build an ethical approach into the very structure and process of economic life: from above, companies through their HRM or CSR policies and managers; from below, employees through their own self-help organisations, most notably trade unions; and, finally, from without, through the state as an expression of society's collective moral conscience. More recently, HRM academics have explored new forms of social regulation – beyond the state and trade unions – by charities and civil society pressure groups (Williams *et al.*, 2011), usually operating in concert with the three mentioned above.

Let us turn now to the most pervasive rule-making agent in most contemporary employment relationships: employers and the professional managers who act on their behalf. Even where the state and trade unions play a central part in framing the employment relationship, the chosen *management style* of employers and their managers is crucial in defining the experience of work. While some good practices can be imposed from outside – as with racial and sexual discrimination or minimum wages – the devil is in the detail, and 'company culture' may become a major obstacle to the full realisation of an ethical workplace. Corporate HRM policy is potentially central to employment ethics. But first we need to understand what management is and what real capacity it has to shape the ethical tone of the enterprise.

Today, employer regulation is only rarely exercised by the single owner in person, except in the small business. Management is the collective name for a stratum of specialist, technical workers who act as the employer's (or shareholders') agents in day-to-day dealings with the workforce. As businesses grow in size, and as the personality of the individual owner fragments into the thousands of anonymous individual and institutional shareholders of the modern public limited company, managers become the visible hands and face of employer power. This management specialism is reinforced by some professional organisation and identity as is the case with groups like accountants, or more pertinently for us, HRM or personnel managers. And there is considerable controversy over who exactly managers are answerable to, and what their social responsibilities are. What we expect of managers in the business organisation depends largely on our chosen frame of reference and this is likely to dovetail with one of the competing ethical theories discussed above. For the *Unitarists*, differences of management function and level are a purely technical issue, subordinate to their single purpose as the unquestioning agents of the shareholder owners. This 'stockholder' conception is enshrined in Anglo-American company law, though not in continental European stakeholder traditions. As the right-wing economist Milton Friedman (1993) argues, once managers or companies take on goals and responsibilities which do not serve their ultimate aim of higher profits, they betray their ultimate employers and endanger the whole future of the enterprise, indeed of capitalism itself. In short, absolute adherence to market principles outside the business and to the single line of authority within it, are but two sides of the same unitarist coin.

By contrast, *Pluralists* are likely to perceive and welcome much greater diversity of allegiance and objectives among modern managers, for two main reasons. First, from a purely sociological point of view, this conforms to their image of the business as fractured by competing interest groups, including various management levels and functions. Thus senior company directors often belong to the Institute of Directors, while line managers may join supervisory trade unions. Personnel specialists seek professional status and accreditation through CIPD courses and exams – modelled on other professional bodies such as the British Medical Association and the Law Society. Second, from a more normative perspective, this view of managers also provides them with some scope to exercise independent ethical action, as is implied in the ethical codes of bodies like the CIPD. They are no longer just servants of the shareholders, at their every beck and call. Rather, they hold responsibilities to all the stakeholders in the organisation, including workers, customers and the local community and to society as a whole. Thus the ethical role of management must be closely related to the responsibilities of business and the way in which society defines these.

The greatest burden of pluralist hopes lay upon the shoulders of personnel – now HRM – the company function and department that specialises in dealing with employees and their representatives. This aspiring management profession seemed to personify the broader social concerns of management, as in the old conception of personnel managers as enlightened umpires, bringing management and workers together, and creating industrial relations concord. But the management of people has never been the exclusive mandate of personnel. So it is important to set personnel's fluctuating role in the broader context of the overall management style adopted by the business towards employees, from the senior managers who attempt to shape the culture of the organisation, down to the line managers who actually conduct most relations between management and ordinary workers (see Fox, 1974).

Ethical HRM policy

What makes for an ethical HRM policy? This is not a simple technical question, but the start of a highly charged debate about who the business organisation and its managers are responsible to. This connects with the right-wing/centre-left divide in economic philosophy outlined above. Should the business manage labour as an economic commodity, to be bought on the market at the cheapest possible price or seek a long-term social relationship with their employees that transcends instant economic calculation? In most cases, the solution is a compromise between market and managerial relations, for while labour may be hired in an outside marketplace, it can only be put to work in the social context of the workplace. HRM reflects this need to control and motivate the workforce as a social group.

Modern personnel management emerged from large-scale Victorian paternalist capitalism, as direct personal contact between master and servant declined, and the employer families sought more institutional expressions of their ethical calling. According to Torrington and Hall (1991), social reformers were the first on the scene, notably the Quaker chocolate manufacturer's wife, Elizabeth Fry, who conducted social work outside the factory and campaigned for legislation to protect health and safety. Next, during the full flowering of Christian paternalism, on the Cadbury's Bournville scale, came the welfare officer, again usually a woman, who conducted industrial social work within the workplace. This brought social concern in line with the modern management division of labour then emerging in large factories. Thus, in 1913, the Institute of Welfare Officers was formed at Rowntree's York chocolate factory. In this respect, personnel began with the same high ideals of caring for employees as the best representatives of paternalist capitalism, and travelled with them from a personal to a professional and institutional expression of these values (see Ackers, 1998).

Today, the ethical rhetoric of HRM is everywhere in contemporary business and society. Some variation on the phrase – 'this business regards employees as its number one resource' – has become part of the ritual of company reports and briefings, tripping easily from the lips of chief executives. The sleek new HRM model is boldly contrasted with the 'bad old days' of personnel past, much as born-again Christians sometimes celebrate their new creation by darkening their own past. Before labour was a cost to be controlled; now, a resource to be nurtured. Before personnel was a routine administrative activity; now, a strategic champion of people management for heightened business performance. Before the old industrial relations was adversarial and arm's length; now, founded on consensus and employee consent. Before the personnel department coveted all people management for itself; now, a human relations gospel for all managers. Yet, in academic social science circles, there are serious doubts about these claims, and many point to the gap between 'rhetoric' and 'reality' (Legge, 2004).

Sceptics associate the trend of HRM policies in free market economies, such as the UK and US, with the right-wing view of labour, as a commodity in the external market and a cost within the firm (see Kaufman, 2015). As a result, they identify a relatively low-skilled, low-waged and poorly trained labour force, in contrast to the best continental practice in economies like Germany. Many draw on Hall and Soskice's (2001) 'varieties of capitalism' framework to distinguish between 'co-ordinated' economies that invest heavily in labour and 'liberal market' economies that tend not to (see Colling and Terry, 2010). Arguably, too, this latter mentality has denied personnel its proper status in the business organisation, and stymied the development of distinctively ethical employment policies. Sisson's (1994: 42) summary of the survey and case study evidence on the Conservative free market experiment in Britain, concludes that 'personnel management in many organisations in Britain is locked into a vicious circle of low pay, low skill, and low productivity'. In this view, little has improved today, even after a further decade of 'New Labour' governments (Sisson and Purcell, 2010). This is surprising, since the 'new' HRM had promised exactly the opposite, and raises the question of whether there is any substance to claims of a new 'ethical' approach to employment policy.

Arguably, this broad-brush dismissal of HRM obscures a more complex reality. A large proportion of employees in a rich economy, such as the UK, are professionals or 'knowledge workers' and its seems likely that these 'core' employees are managed very differently to those 'peripheral' workers, stuck at the bottom of labour market — as Atkinson's (1984) 'flexible firm' model predicted. Indeed, these divisions have been accentuated in recent years by the global availability of low-cost labour. Yet, even a liberal-market economy with large areas of low wage employment has major sectors of well-paid, high-skill and high-productivity employees, such as professional and financial services, and high-value manufacturing, where HRM policy can take a more resource-based view. In Britain, for instance, many large, blue-chip companies have partnership relations with trade unions (see Ackers, 2014; Johnstone, 2015). On the other side, co-ordinated market economies, like Germany, now have large low-pay, low-skill, and low-productivity service sectors (Gold and Artus, 2015). So in assessing the scope for ethical employment management, we need to delve beyond general statements about HRM in general, to explore the specifics of different sectors and companies. As always, there are good employers and bad and this is true almost everywhere in the world. This means that many companies and managers do still have the ethical choice of pursuing the 'high road' of good wages and conditions.

Conclusion: three fallacies of HRM ethics

On the flip side, there are two problems with most HRM theory as a basis for employment ethics. First, it is too prone to facile general rhetoric about 'valuing people', when real businesses operate within markets and have to make tough choices. Overblown claims merely play into the hands of the sceptics. Second, there is the question of whether a narrow focus of employees as 'resources' is a sound basis for an ethical employment philosophy. This brings us back to the Kantian heart of the matter: how should we treat fellow human beings? Do we regard employees and thus the employment relationship as something of intrinsic human value, even when this operates within a necessary economic framework of efficiency and competitiveness; or do we regard workers like machines, as simply means to an economic end. Here the normative language of HRM matters as much as its practical consequences – though the two are never unrelated. The danger is that once we peel away the layers of HRM hyperbole, we reach a hollow core: an impoverished ethical vision of the employment relationship. This rests upon three ethical fallacies.

1 **The golden calf fallacy** assumes that all human values should be subordinated to business considerations and calculations. At the heart of the HRM worldview stands the claim that the human resource is a business's most valued asset. This appears, at first glance, a noble belief, even if it flies in the face of the manner in which many employers actually treat their workers. In particular, it suggests a culture in which companies invest in workers' long-term development, instead of regarding them as merely costs, to be cut and controlled. Yet, there is a dangerous flaw in this ethical vision, and this relates to the broader stream of right-wing, free market economic thinking, which redefines human beings, with their complex social, spiritual and material needs, as mere rational economic categories, be these consumers or human resources. Such language assumes that business and its economic terminology should shape human aspirations, and not the other way round. From a practical management point of view, enlightened employment policies will always require a *partial* business case, to show that they will not unduly damage the organisation. Ethics should not be a recipe for economic suicide or ridicule. But to have a long-term competitive advantage at the back of your mind is not to subordinate every decision to short-term economic calculus, as HRM implies. For workers, the choice is between being a most valued economic asset and being a rounded human being whose dignity should be respected by all – in Kant's terms, a subject that should never become an object. This has grave implications for the role of HRM and other managers. They too are required to treat their subordinates as merely a means to economic ends, to count the cost of every act of kindness.

2 **The enlightened self-interest or 'business case' fallacy** takes the heresy a stage further, by pretending that business considerations alone are sufficient for companies to look after their employees, without outside regulation from the state or trade unions. As Pearson (1995) argues, a business needs to build long-term trust relationships with employees, customers and other companies in order to thrive, and therefore it needs to behave with integrity towards all these groups. Thus too often HRM theory fosters the seductive economic idea that it is in the self-interest of business to treat workers well, and that, for this reason alone, they no longer need to fear for their own protection. Yet numerous businesses, large and small, from farming to the high street, thrive on cheap, disposable labour. The significance for workers' pay and conditions is that their entitlements are entirely contingent upon what makes business successful. If profitability demands investment in the human resource, employers will undertake this; if it entails exploiting cheap disposable labour, and breaking trade unions to this end, they will do the same. These are the dangers of a one-sided economic theory that makes the treatment of human beings entirely conditional on business convenience.

3 **The happy family fallacy** assumes that the state and trade unions are unwelcome intrusions into a fundamentally harmonious, unitarist employment relationship. Most American-style HRM theory is unitarist in outlook and either silent about or actively hostile to trade unions as representative bodies (Kaufman, 2015). This approach to HRM claims to place the happy paternalist conjunction of self-interest and employee well-being on a new, harder, more calculative footing. The way we live now, in increasingly globalised, individualist and impersonal societies, talk of company loyalty can be as

specious and insincere as easy appeals to 'community' and calls for street parties to mark national anniversaries. Enlightened management can still make a central contribution in the creation of a more cooperative and cohesive employment system, through active policies like partnership (Johnstone, 2015). However, it will not do so by pretending that one exists already, if only we could see it.

The sheer ambiguity of HRM may pose the biggest ethical problem, leading to charges of misrepresentation and bad faith. What so often sounds like a species of centre-left ethical thinking, promising something extra for employees, often turns out, on closer examination, to be a sugar-coated edition of right-wing moral and economic philosophy. Milton Friedman (1993), from the latter perspective, suggests that such spurious claims to added 'social responsibility' are better left unsaid and merely detract from the strong, unvarnished case for capitalism. And it is true that right-wing ethical thinking has a firm grounding in certain business, economic and social realities. Most of us recognise, to some degree, the utilitarian benefits of a capitalist economic system, wherein countless selfish, individual market transactions produce unprecedented living standards for most people. In our personal lives, we expect this 'hidden hand' (Smith, 1993 [1776]) to be allowed considerable freedom, in order to ensure that our pensions keep pace with inflation and our food, shelter and holidays are affordable. We also want to be free to use our own money and property as freely as possible without undue interference from the state. We probably regard this economic freedom from state control (including the freedom to change job when we wish) as one essential freedom in a liberal democratic society. For all these reasons, any framework of leftist employment ethics which, like 'actually-existing-socialism' in the Soviet Union and Eastern Europe, threatens to destroy prosperity and liberty, is also likely to be unacceptable to us (Applebaum, 2013). The problem with right-wing ethical thinking is that it forces these genuine concerns to an extreme, so that only the most minimal, individual ethics, such as honesty and trust in contracts, is deemed either necessary or possible. By denying the reality of a long-term employment relationship and presenting the labour contract as a spot-market transaction, like buying a bag of apples, right-wing employment ethics sends HRM managers into the workplace naked.

Perhaps the crucial distinction here, then, is between employment ethics as a public relations façade and rationalisation for what business already does out of short-term economic self-interest, and employment ethics as an active commitment to employees above and beyond this. Behind the necessary pragmatics of economic life lie deeper ethical questions about how we treat other human beings, which can never be simply 'set aside' so that managers can concentrate on business. Take, for instance, the everyday problem of whether a parent is entitled to 'time off' to take a child to a hospital appointment. In this view, managers can and should play a crucial role in constructing socially responsible business organisations at the heart of a decent society. This would require, however, what I have termed a *neo-pluralist* approach, which places the long-term employment relationship and the wages and conditions of employees, alongside other stakeholders, at the heart of the business organisation (Ackers, 2002; 2014). In these circumstances, we could speak meaningfully of social partnership, loyalty and commitment. Within a framework of relationship capitalism, managers could regain their professional autonomy and integrity, as public servants with a stakeholder ethos, rather than simply the handmaidens of private capital. In communitarian language, the workplace would become a genuine 'moral community' responsive to society as a whole.

HRM presents us with a paradox because it talks of developing people, while considering its subjects as human resources. The reversion to economic language and the decline of company-led welfare capitalism (see Jacoby, 1997) fosters the suspicion that when push comes to shove, the calculator will always take priority over the human being. Although the rhetoric of HRM contains elements that appeal to ethical employment principles, too often practice falls short of promise on two counts. First, the optimistic rhetoric obscures features of contemporary employment relations, such as low wages and zero-hour contracts; second, many versions of HRM abdicates any autonomous, ethical role for management, beyond doing what makes shareholders and senior executives richer.

CASE STUDY 19.1

EMPLOYMENT ETHICS AT BRITISHSTORES

PETER ACKERS

Introduction

Britishstores is a chain of department stores selling clothes, food and hardware. It employs 10,000 UK workers in retail, distribution and office positions, mostly on permanent, full-time contracts. In addition, around 1,000 manufacturing workers, employed by its main subcontractor, are highly dependent on Britishstores' success and employment policy. This case study presents an opportunity to assess the ethics of the business at all stages in its development (was it doing the 'right thing' towards employees?), and to address a major contemporary dilemma between remaining competitive as a business and retaining a reputation as an ethical employer. It allows you to explore various ethical theories and to consider this business dilemma as a choice between different ethical frames of reference.

In the beginning

Britishstores was founded in 1900 as a small store in a medium-sized Scottish town by an austere, very religious Presbyterian (with his elder brother as a 'sleeping partner'). In the early days, the founder knew all his employees by their first name and exercised a strong 'fatherly' influence over their lives in and out of work. This had both benign and harsh aspects. The paternalist company was generous at times of family sickness, with the founder often visiting in person, though sometimes employees wondered if he was really checking up on them. And any employees who were caught with the smell of alcohol on their breath at work, or even drunk outside work, were summarily dismissed. The founder also promoted a strong sense of family values, organising (alcohol-free) works picnics and providing a free hamper every Christmas and at the birth of any child (up to two in number) and 200 cigarettes to the 'employee of the month'. Christian prayers were compulsory before each morning's work began. He also initiated and contributed towards various 'self-help' savings and mortgage schemes. Wages were generally slightly above the industry norm, according to the discretion of the founder, who liked to quote the parable of 'The Workers in the Vineyard' and reward those whom he thought deserved and needed most. Women employees who married were required to leave, in order to fulfil their family

duties, and all managerial positions were reserved for men with families. The firm promised lifetime job security for male employees and encouraged children to follow their parents into the trade. For many years, jobs were only rarely advertised externally.

Growth

The founder died in 1940 and ownership and control passed completely into the hands of his two sons. The boys had been educated at an English public school and lived in the Home Counties. But the founder's personal control had declined long before, as the company grew first into a British chain in the interwar years. The founder had always strongly opposed trade unions as inimical to the family atmosphere of the firm, and in 1923 the firm fought off an organising campaign by the shop workers' union which was already well established in the stores of the strong Scottish cooperative movement. As a result, 20 'ringleaders' were dismissed. During the economic depression of the 'hungry' 1930s, Britishstores gained a good reputation for maintaining employment when other businesses were laying people off. This was partly because of good business performance, but it was also widely believed that the owning family accepted lower profits in order to continue both to keep the loyal workforce and invest in the expansion of the firm.

The workforce was now counted in thousands rather than tens, so it was impossible for senior managers to retain personal, face-to-face contact – though local store managers were encouraged to do so. In response, the company developed a professional personnel department to create a more systematic set of provisions and policies. These included a non-union, representative company council that operated monthly at store level, and biannually across the whole company. Representatives were elected from every work group, and both negotiated with management over wages and consulted over any issues affecting the welfare of the workforce. There was also a welfare and sports society, which was heavily subsidised by the company and provided local Britishstores social clubs – initially on a strict temperance basis. These organised competitions for football, cricket, ballroom dancing and so on. Company developments and these social activities were reported in *Voice of Britishstores*, a monthly company newspaper produced by the personnel department. The firm also pioneered a number of other welfare benefits, including a contributory pension scheme for all employees, and a seniority and promotion system called 'Growing our own', which meant that nearly all middle and senior managers were recruited from the shop floor. Following one year's service, all employees joined the company profit-sharing scheme, which, in most years, added a further 10 per cent to their income.

Public limited company

In 1965, Britishstores became a public limited company (PLC), and within a few years family shareholdings had been dwarfed by those of pension funds and other outside investors. No senior managers now belonged to the original family, and many were being recruited from outside the business, rather than rising through its lower ranks as they had in the past. A new graduate recruitment programme had short-circuited the old seniority systems, though most middle managers had still risen from below. The business had also had to adapt to outside social trends, such as legislation for sexual and racial equality, and relaxed social mores – leading, among other things, to the serving of alcohol in Britishstores clubs. Britishstores was still perceived by workers, customers and the general public as a family-run paternalist business with a strong ethical commitment to fair play. This was reflected in the trust and loyalty of long-service employees (and very low labour turnover), and of customers who repeatedly told surveys that they would not buy their clothes anywhere else. Britishstores continued to play a high-profile public charitable role, both in the town of its origin, where the head office remains, and in the wider community. In the latter case, the company sponsored a City Technology College in inner-city Glasgow during the 1980s and actively supported 'Business in the Community'. It also funded a professorship in Business Ethics at a leading British business school.

Britishstores now has a global supply chain, with 40 per cent of its output sourced abroad. However, the company had developed another long-term business relationship since its first major expansion in 1920, with a large high-quality clothing manufacturing firm based in the town where the founder was born and Britishstores originated. Although Makeit & Co. is an independent firm, 70 per cent of its output is contracted to Britishstores – whose letters also prefix the name of the local football team. The Britishstores founder had presented to the town a park and art gallery, as well as a row of cottages for long-service company pensioners, while his wife played a prominent charitable role in the interwar town, including organising youth clubs and holidays for children of the local poor and unemployed. Still today Britishstores and Makeit & Co. together employ 800 people in the town, equally divided between them.

Britishstores' personnel policy has remained fairly stable since the main structures were set in place in the 1930s. In line with 1960s and 1970s labour law and 'best practice', however, the company council system has been supplemented by a more formal (but still non-union) grievance and disciplinary procedure. Employees have shown no further interest in union membership, partly because wages and conditions are as good as those of most comparable unionised firms, and partly because they know Britishstores senior management are strongly anti-union and fear they might lose existing benefits if they push the issue. A new company interest in equal opportunities for women was partly inspired by the national policy mood, but also by labour shortages and recruitment difficulties in the post-war retail labour market. As a result, there has been a small influx of women graduates into managerial and supervisory roles, and the old distinction between 'men's' and 'women's' jobs has been replaced by a formally non-discriminatory, A–G grading system. Equally, criticism that internal recruitment reproduced an 'all white' workforce, even in cities with large ethnic minorities, has led the company to advertise all vacancies in job centres and local newspapers, followed by a formal interview. Once again, outside policy influences have dovetailed with business concerns that its workforce should reflect the stores' potential customer base. Notwithstanding these developments, personnel policy still cultivates a long-term relationship with both the directly employed workforce and the manufacturing subcontractor. In the latter case, Britishstores has insisted on exercising substantial 'quality control' over the subcontractor's production process, while offering Makeit & Co. employees access to its social clubs and welfare provisions (though wages and conditions are handled separately). The company's long-standing commitment to high-quality British-made products has been a major attraction for its traditional customer base.

Until recently, Britishstores has interpreted the new wave of HRM thinking as largely an extension of its existing personnel practices. For instance, it has added team briefings, quality circles and a modest element of performance-related pay to its existing communications, consultation and reward structures. In some respects, like profit sharing, the firm was already a pioneer. Today, however, major changes in the retail market are forcing the company to reassess all elements of its activities. After years as a market leader, with steadily rising profits, Britishstores is now in some commercial difficulty. In particular, it faces competition from a new generation of fashion shops, which threaten its core clothing market. These firms source their products entirely from low-cost Third

World suppliers and are happy to switch these where and when the market justifies. They also employ a raw, if enthusiastic UK workforce of students and young people, almost entirely on zero-hour contracts. Their wages are close to the national minimum, often about 25 per cent less than Britishstores, and they spend far less on training and welfare. Britishstores has already responded to this threat by shedding 10 per cent of its workforce through natural wastage, early retirement and voluntary redundancy, while terminating one major contract with Makeit & Co.

The ethical and business dilemma

A new managing director has been appointed to 'turn around' Britishstores. He has asked all the main functional directors to present a root-and-branch analysis of how the business can regain its market position and restore stock market confidence. These papers will be presented to and discussed at a 'Retail 2050: Future Directions' seminar, the outcome of which will determine the new business strategy to be presented to the next company AGM.

The recently appointed head of marketing has already stolen a march on the others by circulating radical plans for a new, marketing-led, customer-focused, flexible firm that breaks almost completely with the traditional shape of the business, including its much-vaunted ethical employment policies. She proposes a new 'culture of entrepreneurship' which will withdraw the 'comfort zone' and 'time-serving' of current employment practices. Using a cricket metaphor, she argues that the point is 'not to occupy the crease but to score runs'. This will include establishing specialist boutiques and other facilities (including restaurants) within the stores, run on a franchise basis, using external subcontractors wherever possible, transferring all remaining direct employees to part-time contracts, except for a core of 'enterprise managers and supervisors' who, in future, will be paid largely according to performance. In addition, she moots the closure of the Scottish company headquarters and complete withdrawal from the town to smaller, more convenient facilities in an English new town; and the ending of the contract

with Makeit & Co. to enable Britishstores to buy on the open market and benefit fully from low labour costs in Southeast Asia. In the marketing director's view, the traditional paternalist approach is now completely archaic and untenable in the fast-moving retail market.

To further complicate matters, a whistleblower within either senior management or the marketing department has leaked these plans to the media. Rumours are circulating that Britishstores has been negotiating with a military dictatorship for access to its labour force. Concerns about the abandonment of existing employees and the exploitation of Third World 'cheap labour' have been tabled by the founder's family for the company AGM. There have been demonstrations by employees in the original 'company town', addressed by outside trade union leaders, who called for union recognition for Britishstores employees and an effective European works council. A petition has been presented to the Scottish Assembly by local MPs and church leaders, describing Britishstores as 'the unacceptable face of capitalism' and urging a consumer boycott of stores nationwide.

Historically, the personnel function, now renamed HRM, has been seen as the custodian of the company's ethical employment policies. As we have seen, these centre on a long-term relationship with a stable workforce. Concerned at the bad publicity the business is attracting, the managing director has asked you, as personnel director, to frame an explicitly ethical employment policy which overcomes the difficulties you are facing and draws on some of the business' existing strengths. There are signs that the adverse publicity is affecting customers and undermining their trust and loyalty towards the company. No options are barred, but the managing director has asked you to consider specifically the following questions.

Note: While Britishstores is a fictional ideal-type company, it incorporates many real-life elements from a number of leading British manufacturing and retail organisations. These all began as paternalist family firms with their own ethical ideas about how employment should be managed and adapted, and developed these as they grew into large, modern businesses.

Questions

1 How far was Britishstores' original employment policy 'ethical' in modern terms? What sort of ethical principles did it draw upon? Which elements would be acceptable today, and which would not?

2 How justified was the decision to prevent trade union organisation and is it still appropriate today? Consider the arguments *for* and *against* and the principles involved.

3 Construct an ethical case in favour of the flexible firm solution proposed by the director of marketing, explaining which principles you draw on.

4 Devise an alternative, HRM-driven business and ethical case for maintaining the existing long-term relationship with employees, customers and subcontractors.

5 Which stakeholder groups should take priority when push comes to shove? What duty, if any, does the company owe to its employees and shareholders in a modern free market society?

6 Design an up-to-date and realistic, *ethical employment code of practice* consistent with your answers to the above questions, which can be issued by the personnel department to all employees and used for external public relations purposes. Begin with some general principles and then identify key areas of business and employee rights and responsibilities.

CASE STUDY 19.2
ETHICAL HRM POLICIES IN A GLOBAL WORLD

PETER ACKERS

The ethical and business dilemma

Five years ago, the Global Business School (GBS) of a leading American university opened a new overseas campus near the capital city of a large developing economy. The venture has been a great financial and reputational success, creating major new income flows and raising the global profile of the university. Although more than 30 local tutors have been recruited in the country where the campus is based, the undergraduate and MBA programmes are overseen by academics at the home university and lecturers travel from the US to contribute to teaching. GBS and its university are located in a large, multicultural American city and have an outstanding reputation for ethical HRM in their home country, including awards for Equal Opportunities, Family-Friendly and Diversity policies.

The developing country is very different from the US. While there is now a substantial rich elite, most of the population live in conditions of absolute poverty by Western standards and depend on their families for welfare support. When the new GBS opened there was an elected government, but two years ago a military coup took place. This is also a very religious society, with one dominant conservative faith, which 90 per cent of the population adhere to. Other faiths are not strictly illegal, but it is hard to practice in public without harassment, including, in some cases, serious violence. The society is also strongly patriarchal, with very few women working in senior positions. Homosexuality is illegal and the country has an 'out of sight, out of mind' attitude to disability, which excludes disabled people from public life. There are also high degrees of nepotism and patronage, whereby the rich and powerful secure the best positions for their family and friends, which also extends to obtaining places at the best academic institutions regardless of merit. Lower class groups and ethnic minorities are also routinely excluded from well-paid careers and usually restricted to hereditary low-paid work.

You are the new female head of HRM at GBS, based on the American campus but with responsibility for global ethical employment policy. Your family originally came from the country where the new campus is based. A number of complaints are reaching you from the overseas campus and from American academics who have travelled to work there. One industrial relations lecturer complained that he was put under pressure by local university managers not to teach about trade unions and the liberal democratic theory of pluralism. A Business Ethics lecturer was told to focus on the dominant national religion. Letters have been received from both members of poorer social classes and religious minorities, with excellent qualifications, to say that they were rejected for admission with no explanations given. You have established that all the senior academics on the new campus are male and one American women lecture who taught there has complained of sexual harassment. The on-site head of HRM, a local man, has visited the US recently and when you raised these concerns and suggested that he applied GBS Equality and Diversity policy to address these issues, he said: 'You can't impose American values on our culture.' On the other hand, a gay rights charity has approached you informally to point out that students from the overseas campus have posted recordings on their website of lecturers making crudely homophobic comments and threatening to report gay students to the police.

Questions

How would you approach this problem? What are the major practical obstacles you face? Consider three options and decide which is best, in *your own view*.

1 *Universal*: Insist that universal standards of HRM behaviour, following the existing GBS HRM policy, are applied on the overseas campus.

2 *Relativist*: Devise a separate code of employment ethics for the overseas campus consistent with local cultural and ethical values.

3 *Pragmatic*: Recognise that 'only so much can be done' and try to encourage the local manager to avoid the more extreme violations of GBS HRM policy, while hoping that the worse practices don't come to the attention of American public opinion.

Explain which ethical theories your approach is based upon and consider the 'business case' for the policy you have chosen. Is there any other option?

Bibliography

Ackers, P. (1998) 'On paternalism: seven observations on the uses and abuses of the concept in industrial relations, past and present', *Historical Studies in Industrial Relations*, Vol.6, 173–93.

Ackers, P. (2002) 'Reframing employment relations: the case for neo-pluralism', *Industrial Relations Journal*, Vol.33, No.1, 2–19.

Ackers, P. (2010) 'An industrial relations perspective on employee participation', Chapter 3, in Wilkinson, A., Gollan, P.J., Marchington, M. and Lewin, D. (eds.) *The Oxford Handbook of Participation in Organizations*, Oxford: Oxford University Press.

Ackers, P. (2014) 'Rethinking the employment relationship: a neo-pluralist critique of British Industrial Relations orthodoxy', *International Journal of Human Resource Management*, Vol.25, No.18, 2608–25.

Ackers, P. (2015) 'Trade unions as professional associations', pp. 95–126, in Johnstone, S. and Ackers, P. (eds.) *Finding a Voice at Work? New Perspectives on Employment Relations*, Oxford: Oxford University Press.

Ackers, P. and El-Sawad, A. (2006) 'Family-friendly policies and work-life balance', pp. 331–55, in Redman, T. and Wilkinson, A. (eds.) *Contemporary Human Resource Management: Text and Cases* (2nd edn.) London: Pearson.

Applebaum, A. (2013) *Iron Curtain: The Crushing of Eastern Europe*, London: Penguin.

Atkinson, J. (1984) 'Manpower strategies for flexible organizations', *Personnel Management*, August, 28–31.

Beardwell, J. and Thompson, A. (2014) *Human Resource Management: A Contemporary Approach*, London: Pearson.

Chryssides, G.D. and Kaler, J.H. (eds.) (1993) *An Introduction to Business Ethics*, London: Chapman & Hall. (Reviewed by this author in *Human Resource Management Journal*, Vol.5, No.1, 103–5.)

Clegg, H.A. (1979) *The Changing System of Industrial Relations in Great Britain*, Oxford: Blackwell.

Colling, T. and Terry, M. (2010) *Industrial Relations: Theory and Practice* (3rd edn.), Chichester: Wiley. (See this author's review in *Work, Employment and Society*, Vol.26, No.5, 879–82.)

Crane, A. and Matten, D. (2010) *Business Ethics,* Oxford: Oxford University Press.

Etzioni, A. (1995) *The Spirit of Community: Rights, Responsibilities and the Communitarian Agenda*, London: Fontana.

Flanders, A. (1970) *Management and Unions: The Theory and Reform of Industrial Relations*, London: Faber.

Fox, A. (1966) 'Industrial sociology and industrial relations', Royal Commission on Trade Unions and Employers' Associations, Research Paper No.3, London: HMSO.

Fox, A. (1974) *Beyond Contract: Work, Power and Trust Relations*, London: Faber.

Friedman, M. (1993) 'The social responsibility of business is to increase its profits', reprint of 1973 article in Chryssides, G.D. and Kaler, J.H. (eds.) (1993) *An Introduction to Business Ethics*, London: Chapman & Hall.

Fryer, M. (2011) *Ethics and Organizational Leadership: Developing a Normative Model*, Oxford: Oxford University Press.

Fryer, M. (2015) *Ethical Theory and Business Practice*, Sage: London.

Gold, M and Artus, I. (2015) 'Employee partnership in Germany: tensions and challenges', pp. 193–217, in Johnstone, S. and Ackers, P. (eds.) *Finding a Voice at Work? New Perspectives on Employment Relations*, Oxford: Oxford University Press.

Greene, A.M. (2015) 'Voice and workforce diversity', pp. 67–94, in Johnstone, S. and Ackers, P. (eds.) *Finding a Voice at Work? New Perspectives on Employment Relations*, Oxford: Oxford University Press.

Hall, P. and Soskice, D. (2001) *Varieties of Capitalism*, Oxford: Oxford University Press.

Jacoby, S.M. (1997) *Modern Manors: Welfare Capitalism Since the New Deal*, Princeton, NJ: Princeton University Press. (Reviewed by this author in *Historical Studies in Industrial Relations*, Vol.8, 188–94.)

Johnstone, S. (2015) 'The case for workplace partnership', pp. 153–76, in Johnstone, S. and Ackers, P. (eds.) *Finding a Voice at Work? New Perspectives on Employment Relations*, Oxford: Oxford University Press.

Johnstone, S. and Ackers, P. (eds.) (2015) *Finding a Voice at Work? New Perspectives on Employment Relations*, Oxford: Oxford University Press.

Kaufman, B. (2015) 'The future of employee voice in the USA: predictions from an employment relations model of voice', pp. 265–77, in Johnstone, S. and Ackers, P. (eds.)

Finding a Voice at Work? New Perspectives on Employment Relations, Oxford: Oxford University Press.

Legge, K. (1995) 'Morality bound', *People Management*, 19 December, 34–6.

Legge, K. (2004) *Human Resource Management: Rhetorics and Reality*, London: Macmillan.

Nozick, R. (1993) 'Anarchy, state and utopia' (extract), in Chryssides, G.D. and Kaler, J.H. (eds.) *An Introduction to Business Ethics*, London: Chapman & Hall.

Pearson, G. (1995) *Integrity in Organisations: An Alternative Business Ethic,* London: McGraw-Hill. (Reviewed by this author in *Employee Relations*, Vol.18, No.6 (1996), 97–8.)

Peston, R. (2008) 'A crash as historic as the end of communism', *The Times*, Tuesday, 9 December.

Piketty, T. (2014) *Capital in the Twenty-First Century*, Boston, MA: Harvard Business School Press.

Pickett, K, and Wilkinson, R. (2010) *The Spirit Level: Why Equality Is Better for Everyone*, London: Penguin.

Pratley, N. (2015) 'Minimum pay sense', *The Guardian*, Friday, 11 September.

Rawls, J. (1993) 'A theory of justice' (extract), in Chryssides, G.D. and Kaler, J.H. (eds.) (1993) *An Introduction to Business Ethics*, London: Chapman & Hall.

Ruddick, G. (2015) 'Prices must rise to pay for £9 wage', *The Guardian*, Friday, 11 September.

Sisson, K. (ed.) (1994) *Personnel Management* (2nd edn.), Oxford: Blackwell.

Sisson, K. and Purcell, J. (2010) 'Management: caught between competing views', pp. 83–105, in Colling, T. and Terry, M. (2010) *Industrial Relations: Theory and Practice* (3rd edn.), Chichester: Wiley.

Smith, A. (1993 [1776]) 'The wealth of nations' (extract), in Chryssides, G.D. and Kaler, J.H. (eds.) (1993) *An Introduction to Business Ethics*, London: Chapman & Hall.

Smith, K. and Johnson, P. (eds.) (1996) *Business Ethics and Business Behaviour*, London: International Thomson. (Reviewed by this author in *Human Resource Management Journal*, Vol.8, No.2 (1998), 97–8.)

Torrington, D. and Hall, L. (1991) *Personnel Management: A New Approach*, Hemel Hempstead: Prentice Hall.

Williams, S., Abbott, B. and Heery, E. (2011) 'Civil regulation and HRM: the impact of civil society organizations on the policies and practices of employers', *Human Resource Management Journal*, Vol.21, No.1, 45–59.

Winstanley, D. and Woodall, J. (eds.) (1999) *Ethical Issues in Contemporary Human Resource Management*, London: Macmillan.

CHAPTER 20

EMOTION AT WORK

Philip Hancock and Melissa Tyler

Introduction

Consider the following extract from a recent job advertisement:

> You will need to be full of energy and want to add to the fun . . . if you want to start work with a great cast of characters then telephone . . .

You might be forgiven for assuming that this advert is for a job in what Robin Leidner (1993) calls 'interactive service provision' – work involving direct contact with customers or clients. In fact, it is advertising vacancies for warehouse staff at a distribution centre; for workers who handle 'things' rather than 'people'. Why is it important, then, for applicants to want to 'add to the fun', and why are potential colleagues and co-workers described as 'a great cast of characters'? It would seem that emotion is now thought of as central to business success, whether that business is selling fast food or sorting boxes. Indeed, there is now a vast body of managerial literature dedicated to the management of emotion at work, with titles such as *It's Always Personal: Navigating Emotion in the New Workplace* (Kreamer, 2013) and *Emotional Intelligence: 10 Self-control Secrets You Didn't Know* (Tran, 2015) appearing on a regular basis. Alongside this expansive literature advocating emotional self-control and the effective harnessing of emotional intelligence (EI), a growing interest has emerged in the promotion and management of happiness at work (Rao, 2010; Stewart, 2013), repackaging themes championed by the Human Relations school of management since the 1930s onwards as the new 'holy grail' of corporate success.

So why emotion, and why now? And what exactly are emotions? Can they be managed, and if so, how and with what consequences? As Simon Williams (2001: 132) observed, 'emotion is a moving and slippery target':

> Emotion is a complex, multidimensional, multifaceted human compound, including irreducible biological and cultural components, which arise or emerge in various socio-relationship contexts.

Broadly speaking, emotions are human responses to how we feel; they are how we express and make sense of feelings, either individually or socially, and so are largely intersubjective and communicative. They are often complex and contradictory – we might hear people saying that they have 'laughed until they cried' or 'wept tears of joy', for instance. As sources of (sometimes simultaneous) pleasure and pain, they are clearly central to who and what we are. Emotions can operate at many different levels, and can be highly reflexive or calculated strategies; they can be habitual or routine practices, as well as unconscious or involuntary responses, varying across time, place and culture.

Traditionally the province of psychology – with its emphasis on studying emotions largely as psychosomatic responses – it has been sociology that has dominated debates on the social nature of emotions in recent years, considering their expression and function, and also the way in which emotions are socially shaped and experienced. In this sense, sociologists have argued that no emotion is ever an 'entirely unlearnt response' (Elias, 1991), and that our emotional experiences – our ability to think about, feel and express emotions (relating to what sociologists call 'agency') – are linked to enduring social institutions and arrangements such as power and status (what sociologists call 'structure'). In this sense, emotions represent something of a juncture between society and ourselves as individuals. They also straddle both the physical and mental realms of our existence. That emotions act as something of a 'pivot' in this respect, between the individual and the structural, the personal and the social, and the corporeal and the cognitive explains, at least in part, why management theorists and practitioners have taken such an interest in emotions, focusing on emotion as central to understanding and controlling organisations, respectively.

Because of their complexity, emotions are often thought about and expressed metaphorically – as if they were fluids in a container that might spill out or overflow at any moment. This fluid metaphor has been a strong theme in organisation and management studies, in which the workplace is often talked about as if it were an 'emotional cauldron' (Albrow, 1992) beneath the surface of which a toxic brew is thought to bubble away. Tracy and Tracy (1998: 390) in their study of a US 911 Emergency Centre use the metaphor of an emotional landscape to describe 'the organization's emotion rules, and the communicative devices call-takers use to manage their emotion'. In a more recent study of the Samaritans in the UK, McMurray and Ward (2014) extend Hughes' (1958) earlier typology on taint to emphasise the presence of what they describe as 'emotional dirt' in the work undertaken by those whose job it is to handle particularly difficult emotional situations. Others have thought of emotions with reference to a weaving metaphor, arguing that emotions are 'woven' into the very fabric of organisational life (Fineman, 1994). This metaphor in particular emphasises that, rather than being a recent managerial 'fad', emotions are a fundamental part of organisational life.

The emotional turn: key concepts and issues

Although the presence of emotion within organisations has long since been recognised by management practitioners and academics, it seems to be only relatively recently (in the last three decades or so) that sustained attention has been paid to the management of emotion, and particularly to harnessing emotion as an organisational resource. As Sharon Bolton (2000) noted some 15 years ago, emotions now seem to be 'here, there and everywhere'. Several reasons can be identified for this relatively recent, and growing, turn to emotion.

Much of the academic interest in emotion was inspired by Arlie Russell Hochschild's book *The Managed Heart*, published in 1983. As Bolton and Boyd (2003: 292) have put it, 'there is little that has been written concerning the subject of emotions and organizations . . . that does not take *The Managed Heart* as a reference point'. Crucially, Hochschild's intervention into the study of service work and its management in the early 1980s provided a conceptual framework within which to understand the nature and commercial value of social interactions involved in the delivery of interactive service work, 'debunking the assumption that "real work" only takes place within manufacturing' (Lewis and Simpson, 2009: 56). Hochschild's (1983) introduction of the term 'emotional labour' to describe the ways in which emotions are incorporated into the labour process illuminated an aspect of paid work that has since been recognised as central to the lived experience of many workers, but that had been relatively obscured by dominant theoretical approaches both to management and to the study of management. Conceptualising some of the distinctive aspects of work in this way opened up fruitful avenues of investigation and analysis, and facilitated the ongoing reformulation of both academic and managerial conceptions of work necessary to keep pace with transformations in the nature of work, and in the economy in general.

One such transformation is that increasingly 'people's working lives are shaped over-whelmingly by the experience of delivering a service' (Allen and Du Gay, 1994: 255). This increase, over the past few decades, in the proportion of jobs in which people are employed specifically to work as front-line, customer-facing service providers has meant that sustained managerial attention has been paid to customer relations as a vital contributor to competi-tive advantage. This recognition has increased the importance accorded to emotion and its management, particularly for those employees in direct contact with customers. Johansson and Näslund (2009) document this process in their research on the design and management of customer experiences on board a cruise ship. Their study highlights the extent to which working in the so-called 'experience industry' places high levels of emotional demands on employees as the perceived freedom of the passengers to enjoy the experience on board the ship is dependent upon stringent managerial control of the emotional displays of service workers, and particularly of their interactions with customers and of the spaces in which these interactions take place. Similarly, Sheane's (2011) study of hairdressers in Canada emphasises the importance of workers developing skills in 'emotional and aesthetic literacy' in order to communicate effectively with customers who expect a high-quality customer service interaction.

Certainly in contemporary managerial discourse emotion has come to be viewed as an important resource that managers should harness in the pursuit of organisational per-formance. In their book *A Passion For Excellence*, Peters and Austin (1985: 287) set the scene for this, arguing that organisational emotions (the feelings, sensations and affective responses to organisation) 'must come from the market and the soul simultaneously'. As we will now reflect, however, it is not the case that management and emotion have always been seen as ideal business partners.

Emotion in management theory and practice

Emotion, bureaucracy and scientific management

Rationality can be defined as the exercise of human reason in order to make decisions geared towards an optimal resolution of a problem or ambition. As such, it is largely considered to be the opposite of following our feelings or instincts. Modern organisations have been hailed since their inception as models of rationality and instruments of rationalisation. Bureaucracy – as the typically modern form of organising – has been defined largely according to an imper-sonal and procedural rationality that has no place for emotion. What Rosabeth Moss Kanter (1977: 22), in her now classic critique of bureaucracy, refers to as 'the passionless organisa-tion', one that strives to exclude emotion from its boundaries, is an organisation that believes that efficiency should not be sullied by the 'irrationality' of personal feelings.

In her critique of the bureaucratic organisation, Kanter (1977) argues that the 'corporation' began to emerge as the dominant organisational form in the late nineteenth century, when what she calls the 'administrative revolution' (the successor to the industrial revolution) took place. By this she means that an increasing number of organisational functions were brought together and merged into a single corporate administration in order to gain control over a range of disparate activities that would otherwise have continued to be subject to uncertainty. Hence, the need to coordinate complex operations made management a specialised occupation and, as she notes, managerial skills began to be more rewarded in business than technical ones. However, as man-agers were neither owners nor a traditional 'ruling class', they were required to establish their legitimacy and did so through evoking rationality.

Control by managers was therefore presented as the most 'rational' way to run a corporate enterprise. Early twentieth-century management theory – such as Taylor's (1911) 'principles of scientific management' – enshrined rationality and defined it as the special province of managers. As Kanter (1977: 22) notes in this respect, 'the very design of organisations thus was oriented toward and assumed to be capable of suppressing irrationality, personality and emotionality'.

For Max Weber, whose sociological analysis focused largely on a critique of rationalisation, the suppression of emotion gave bureaucracies their advantage over other organisational forms. Indeed, Weber built his critical account of the spirit of capitalism – 'that attitude which seeks profit rationally and systematically' (Weber, 1989 [1904]: 64) – on the belief that it is anchored in deeply held religious and emotional attitudes of affect control. It would be incorrect, however, to say that Weber's ideal type of bureaucracy is based on a total exclusion of emotion (Albrow, 1992). As the following passage from his book *Economy and Society* indicates, Weber's account does allow for emotions within modern organisations, but only in so far as their rational calculation is perceived as an intrinsic aspect of their constitution. It is not emotion per se that Weber admits into the organisation, then, but rationalised emotion, ensuring

> That everything is rationally calculated, especially those seemingly imponderable and irrational, emotional factors – in principle, at least, calculable in the same manner as the yields of coal and iron deposits. (*Weber, 1978 [1921]: 1150*)

In sum, then, emotion was seen as irrational and unreasonable in Taylorism and bureaucracy, as the antithesis of organisation and in need either of exclusion or rational calculation on the part of managers, as the personification of rationality.

Emotion and human relations

Yet, from the 1930s onwards management theorists and practitioners began to realise that even within the confines of organisational life, emotions cannot be excluded or controlled as if they were coal or iron. In management terms, this meant a significant shift from a view of 'ideal' organisations as based on the exclusion or rational calculation of emotion to an emphasis on the idea that work is meaningful and motivating only if it offers security and opportunities for achievement and self-actualisation (Herzberg, 1974; Maslow, 1943). In what came to be known as the Human Relations School of management, emotion therefore became 'in', so to speak, as affectivity began to be recognised as being of central importance to organisational performance. Increasingly emphasised was that the management of work organisations should be based on 'articulating and incorporating the logic of sentiments' (Roethlisberger and Dickson, 1939: 462, emphasis added).

Elton Mayo (1933), in particular, emphasised the importance of primary, informal relations among workers and developed the concept of the 'informal organisation' to include the emotional, non-rational and sentimental aspects of organisational behaviour. For Mayo, workers were controlled by their sentiments, emotions and social instincts – a phenomenon that he argued needed to be taken into account when devising, executing and evaluating management strategies. As Kanter (1977) notes in her critique, however, Human Relations continued to rely on a relatively simplistic formula according to which managers were viewed as capable of controlling their own emotions as well as those of their workers. According to a management training manual written in 1947, for instance,

> He [the manager] knows that the master of men [sic] has physical energies and skills and intellectual abilities, vision and integrity, and he knows that, above all, the leader must have emotional balance and control. The great leader is even-tempered when others rage, brave when others fear, calm when others are excited, self-controlled when others indulge. (*Cited in Bendix, 1956: 332*)

While the Human Relations emphasis on informal social factors may appear to diverge from scientific management, therefore, both approaches shared a similar conception of the role of heroism vis-à-vis emotion. This meant that in the HR movement management education continued to be thought of largely as a vehicle for learning how to master, not unleash, emotion. In other words, Human Relations may have 'modified the idea of rationality but preserved its flavour' (Kanter, 1977: 22), often in highly gendered terms. As feminist writer Rosemary Pringle notes in this respect,

> While the Human Relations theorists added an informal dimension, they did not challenge the theorising of the formal bureaucratic structures. In some ways they reinforced the idea of managerial rationality: while workers might be controlled by sentiment and emotion, managers were supposed to be rational, logical and able to control their emotions. The division between reason and emotion was tightened in a way that marked off managers from the rest. *(Pringle, 1989: 87, original emphasis)*

HRM: Management gets emotional

Subsequently, management theorists have begun to emphasise that effective emotional management is a prerequisite for organisational success (Marks, 2006). In practice, this means that many current management techniques focus on the emotions of service providers and consumers simultaneously, as well as those of managers. The McDonald's 'I'm lovin' it' advertising campaign is a notable example of this. Launched in 2003, and translated into several languages across the world, the aim of the campaign was to focus on the whole McDonald's 'experience' rather than simply its product range, and in doing so, to convey 'warmth' and 'passion' (according to the description on the McDonald's website at the time). More recently, throughout 2014, Walmart established a marketing campaign, disseminated through in-store radio and social media, particularly its Facebook page, that explicitly sought to make strong emotional connections between producers, suppliers, workers and shoppers. Championed under the theme of 'Made in America' and articulated through references to empowerment and sustainability, the scheme was designed explicitly to promote a strong emotional bond as the basis of working for and shopping at Walmart.

Examples such as these shift the managerial focus to harnessing emotion as a human and therefore commercial resource, emphasising the view that

> emotions, properly managed, can drive trust, loyalty and commitment and many of the greatest productivity gains, innovations and accomplishments of individuals, teams and organisations. (Cooper, 1998: 48)

This produces what Vincent (2011: 1370) has described as 'an economy of feelings', a term emphasising that while our emotions are highly personal, they are also 'affected by managerial design and control systems that are intended to shape emotions displayed towards 'higher' organisational interests, such as increasing productivity, profitability and performance'.

According to Cooper (1998: 48) 'the ability to sense, understand and effectively apply the power and acumen of emotions as a source of human energy, information, trust, creativity, connection and influence' represents that 'really crucial ingredient' for organisational success in the contemporary era, or as Jack Welch (former chair of General Electric) put it: 'soft stuff with hard results' (cited in Cooper, 1998). The 'proper' management of emotions, in this context, is often framed in terms of the deployment of EI.

The term 'emotional intelligence' is associated most notably with the work of Harvard psychologist Daniel Goleman (2009a, b) who has argued that the effective management of EI involves:

- knowing one's emotions (emotional self-awareness);
- controlling one's emotions (emotional self-regulation);
- recognising emotions in others (social awareness);
- controlling emotions in others (relationship management);
- self-motivation.

With the correct training and development, he argues, emotionally intelligent managers can achieve a high level of emotional competence, which he defines as 'a learned capability based on emotional intelligence that results in outstanding performance at work' (Goleman, 2009b: 24). Goleman argues that EI matters more to organisational performance than cognitive abilities or technical skills and impacts particularly, he argues, at the top of the 'leadership pyramid'.

Goleman and his colleagues emphasise that 'great leadership works through the emotions' (Goleman *et al.*, 2002: 3). Echoing Mayo's earlier writing on the importance of managing the informal organisation, he distinguishes between leaders who drive emotions positively (achieving 'emotional resonance') and those who spawn emotional dissonance, 'undermining the emotional foundations that let people shine'. Here management is redefined as 'the emotional art of leadership' (Ibid.: 13) and emotionally intelligent management is deemed to make effective use of the EI competencies outlined above. The development of emotional intelligence skills has not simply been seen as the province of managers, however. Prati and Karriker (2010), in their recent study of a large US-based retail organisation, argue that emotional intelligence skills can be highly effective in moderating the relationship between an emotionally demanding work environment and voluntary turnover. Describing emotional intelligence skills as 'invaluable coping mechanisms' to defeat the adverse effects of organisational demands for a particular emotional display, they argue that 'emotional intelligence abilities can be useful resources in jobs where demands for the regulation of emotional display are excessive' (Prati and Karriker, 2010: 332). Similarly, Greenidge and Coyne (2014), in their study of private and public sector workers in the Caribbean, argue that developing skills in emotional intelligence can significantly reduce counterproductive workplace behaviours that would otherwise result in stress and burnout.

Not that the development and deployment of EI is thought to be entirely without risk, however. Peter Frost (2003), for instance, has warned of the dangers of what he terms 'toxic emotions' and, in particular, the threat they pose to emotionally engaged managers whom he refers to as 'toxin handlers' (see also Glasø and Vie, 2009). This concept refers to those who possess high levels of EI, and are able to 'recognize the emotional pain in other people and in a situation' and as a result either absorb or deflect it 'so that people can get back to their work' (Frost, 2003: 1). Yet such individuals can themselves suffer from the absence of adequate support mechanisms or organisational recognition. Thus, as Frost (2003) observes, they are highly vulnerable to personal burnout unless they develop their own coping strategies or are provided with appropriate support.

This concern notwithstanding, however, underpinning the championing of EI is the broader perception that 'without an actively engaged heart, excellence is impossible' (Harris, 1996: 18). In this respect, contemporary approaches share much in common with the earlier advocates of Human Relations and their concern to conflate what are perceived as artificial (and unprofitable) boundaries between the corporation and the individual. They have emphasised, perhaps most notably, that organisational stability comes at the price of losing originality, flexibility and creativity. Passionate commitment to organisational goals, to co-workers and to the organisation itself is seen to be lost in the unemotional organisation, a theme that underpins the recent managerial preoccupation with the promotion of workplace fun (Barsoux, 1993; Stewart and Simmons, 2010) as a way of managing emotion.

In a recent study, Tews *et al.* (2015) have highlighted the importance of four inter-related dimensions of fun at work: fun activities; managerial support for fun; opportunities for co-worker socialisation and a range of fun-related job roles and responsibilities. They argued that each of these dimensions is crucial to embedding fun into the work environment in a way that encourages the development and display of emotional commitment, including during the early stages of applicant attraction in recruitment and selection processes (Tews *et al.*, 2012). However, critical accounts of workplaces in which fun is promoted emphasise the high levels of ambivalence engendered by HRM techniques designed to encourage employees to have fun at work (Fleming and Sturdy, 2009; Hunter *et al.*, 2010; Warren and Fineman, 2007). In their research on DIY Co., for instance, Redman and Mathews (2002) found that many staff experienced the compulsion to have fun as oppressive and overwhelming, with participants commenting 'sometimes you just don't feel like having fun', 'it's not really right that you should be told by management to have fun' and 'there is a limit to how much fun you can stomach sometimes'.

Critical perspectives on emotion

Critical perspectives on the management of emotion have drawn attention largely to their alienating, degrading and objectifying effects. They have focused particularly on the control mechanisms and surveillance techniques used by organisations to prescribe and monitor the expression of emotion, and the ways in which the negation of the skills involved in the performance of emotional labour, and the techniques used to manage it, violate the right to dignity at work (Bolton, 2007). As Vincent (2011: 1383) has argued, the high commitment HRM techniques used to manage emotion, and fun, 'may simply intensify managerial control, rendering the experience of work more, rather than less, oppressive and alienating'. Also drawn attention to within the critical literature on the management of emotion at work are its potentially discriminatory effects. Nath (2011: 709), for instance, has highlighted how the emotional demands of identity management in an offshored Indian call centre resulted in customer-instigated racial abuse, resulting in 'stress, role ambiguity and work alienation', and an overwhelmingly high demand for the performance of what Hochschild (1979; 1983; 1990) calls 'emotional labour'.

Emotional labour

'Emotional labour' refers to the commodification of emotions within the labour process. In *The Managed Heart*, Hochschild (1983) made a fundamental distinction between two conceptually different if empirically related ways of managing emotions: emotion work and emotional labour. Emotion work describes the act of attempting to change an emotion and how it is displayed in everyday life. Emotion work is governed by what Hochschild (1983: 268) calls 'feeling rules' – 'a set of shared albeit often latent, rules' that define what is emotionally appropriate in any given situation. The effort involved in conforming to these rules is what she means by emotion work. So when we laugh at someone's unfunny joke, or express gratitude for an unwanted gift, we are engaging in emotion work. Emotional labour, however, is what occurs when a profit motive underpins the performance of emotion work within the context of the employment relationship – when someone pays us to manage our own emotions and those of others. As she puts it,

> By 'emotion work' I refer to the emotion management we do in private life; by 'emotional labour' I refer to the emotion management we do for a wage. *(Hochschild, 1990: 118)*

According to Hochschild, emotional labour 'requires one to induce or suppress feeling in order to sustain the outward countenance that produces the proper state of mind in others' (1983: 7). Drawing on Goffman (1959), Hochschild argues that producing the 'proper state of mind in others' involves 'surface' and 'deep' acting. Surface acting involves pretending to experience emotions that are not genuine; 'faking it', in other words. In their study of a nursing home and a department store, Wessel and Steiner (2015) have recently argued that surface acting is particularly emotionally demanding for workers because it requires a constant 'performance'. Yet, deep acting involves something more sustained and arguably more intrusive – actually changing what we feel.

Hochschild argues that 'just as we may become alienated from our physical labour in a goods-producing society, so we may become alienated from our emotional labour in a service-producing society' (1979: 571). This alienation may cause emotional labourers to feel false and estranged from their own 'real' feelings, an experience Hochschild (1983: 90) terms 'emotive dissonance'.

Example

In her classic study of the emotional labour undertaken by hospice nurses, Nicky James (1989) outlined the various skills involved in the performance of emotional labour. These include:

- being able to understand and interpret the needs of others;
- being able to provide a personal response to those needs;
- being able to juggle the delicate balance of individual and group needs;
- being able to pace work, and take account of other responsibilities.

Try to list other occupations in which these skills might be particularly important. Why might these occupations (and the skills they require) result in what Hochschild calls 'emotional dissonance'?

A wide range of organisational contexts exists in which employees are required to perform emotional labour, and its gendered aspects have been well documented by sociologists of work. In her study of police work, Susan Martin (1999), for instance, has highlighted the extent to which women police officers are often assumed to be inherently skilled at the more emotional aspects of police work, such as providing support to victims of crime, for instance, while men are assumed to be more suited to the 'real' police work of solving crime. Other research on emotional labour includes studies of fast-food workers at McDonald's (Leidner, 1993; 1999), of flight attendants (Hochschild, 1983; Tyler and Abbott, 1998), nurses (James, 1989; Pisaniello *et al.*, 2012), waiters and waitresses (Hall, 1993; Paules, 1996), hair stylists (Chugh and Hancock, 2009; Cohen, 2010), Santa Claus performers (Hancock, 2013) and many others (see Fineman, 2008). Recent studies of customer service work and in call centres in particular have highlighted the extent to which the intense demand for emotional labour, combined with the effects of identity management and working conditions, result in high levels of 'emotional burnout' (Agrawal and Sadhana, 2010; Nath, 2011; Surana and Singh, 2009).

In management journals the concern has largely been with highlighting the importance of effective recruitment, selection, socialisation and supervision in order to increase product or service quality and hence raise profitability. Notable examples include studies of supermarket and convenience store cashiers (Rafaeli, 1989; Sutton and Rafaeli, 1988) and of ride operators at Disneyland (Van Maanen and Kunda, 1989). These studies emphasise that the successful performance of emotional labour typically requires 'a complex combination of facial expression, body language, spoken words and tone of voice' (Rafaeli and Sutton, 1987: 33). This combination seems to be achieved through a range of core HRM techniques, including recruitment and selection, training, supervision and monitoring of employee presentation and performance. Critical approaches emphasise how this creates a central tension: between legal and ethical commitments to the promotion of diversity and inclusivity on the one hand, and the instrumental pursuit of commercial imperatives associated with the demands of emotional and aesthetic forms of labour on the other. HR practitioners work at the heart of this tension, and are often required to mediate its worst excesses. Williams and Connell (2010) emphasise this in their study of the recruitment, selection, training and supervision of sales-service workers in high-end retail, highlighting how employability was largely dependent upon the capacity to demonstrate 'emotional capital' during the recruitment process.

HRM practitioners are not solely the agents of emotional management, however. As O'Brien and Linehan (2014) have observed, they are also often required to undertake a large amount of emotional labour themselves. This is frequently a consequence of them needing to negotiate the kinds of tensions identified above. Variously aligned with what are often the competing expectations placed upon them, by employees as advocates and guarantors of fair play, and by senior managers, as functionaries of the strategic vision and management of the organisation, HR practitioners frequently find themselves having to manage their own emotional responses. In some cases, this is in order to win employees over to the demands of senior management through, for example, 'achieving control through an insincere but effective display of caring, or genuinely feeling empathy yet displaying neutral emotions' (2014: 1278). Alternatively, this may involve hiding negative emotional responses to managerial actions that HR practitioners themselves personally feel undermine employee welfare and dignity.

Managing emotional labour

The importance accorded to emotion and particularly to emotional labour in recent years means that considerable efforts have been made to control both its experience and expression. Hence, emotional labour is subject to a complex range of direct and indirect management control techniques and contractual obligations.

The rationalisation of emotion has been highlighted, particularly through the use of scripts and routines (Leidner, 1993; 1999). Leidner's research suggests that employers introduce a variety of strategies aimed at reducing unpredictable elements, in order to standardise the behaviour of workers and service recipients. To overcome resistance to mass-produced service, for example, employees are often required to find ways to personalise routines, or to appear to do so. Further, where too much unpredictability remains to make it possible to dispense with worker flexibility entirely, employers often undertake what Leidner (1993) calls 'routinization by transformation' – changing workers into the kinds of people who will make decisions and interact with customers in ways that management desire and approve of. Indeed, the organisations in her research (McDonald's and Combined Insurance) paid 'close attention to how their workers looked, spoke and felt, rather than limiting standardization to the performance of physical tasks' (Leidner, 1993: 18).

In her account of stories collected from members of various organisations in the US following the terrorist attacks on 11 September 2001, Michaela Driver (2003) highlights several related themes in the management and study of emotion. First, she emphasises the importance of employee perceptions of the relationship between emotional control and organisational culture. As she puts it,

> if organizational members view organizational control behaviours as indicators of their organization's culture, then the selection of control behaviours may be a critical process.
> *(Driver, 2003: 543)*

Furthermore, such measures may be an important means by which employees assess whether they 'fit' with the values and culture of the organisation, and hence are important in terms of recruitment, selection and retention (this illustrates the point made above that emotions often act as a 'pivot' between the individual and the social or organisational).

Second, employees seemed not only to accept but to expect some level of organisational control of emotional expression – 'none of the stories indicated that the storytellers resented their organizations for attempting to control their emotions' (Driver, 2003: 544). Finally, her analysis emphasised the importance of developing a contingency approach to understanding the ways in which different employees respond to organisational controls in different circumstances and across different levels of organisational and occupational hierarchies.

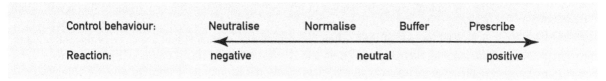

Figure 20.1
Source: Driver, 2003: 542, fig. 1. Republished with permission, Emerald Group Publishing Limited (http://www.emeraldinsight.com/).

Developing this contingency theme, Sloan (2004) highlighted the importance of occupational status for those who experience workplace frustration, noting how individuals in highly esteemed occupations are more likely than lower-status employees to deal with anger directly, and hence experience less anger-induced, work-related stress. A similar finding has emerged from recent research on the relationship between emotion, management and learning, which has emphasised the tensions that can exist between individual and organisational learning. Vince and Saleem (2004), for example, have highlighted the tensions created through repeated patterns of caution and blame within organisations. Their study shows how these tensions actually inhibit emotional processes of reflection and communication, undermining the implementation and further development of strategies explicitly designed for organisational learning.

Such contingencies, status inequalities and tensions are relatively neglected themes in the highly functionalist literature on emotional intelligence, which tends to emphasise that the successful harnessing of emotion leads unproblematically to increased identification, commitment, productivity and manageability. Yet recent research on service work has suggested that managerial efforts to secure employee identification and commitment through training, in the use of scripted and set-piece dialogue techniques, for example, can actually have the opposite effect, engendering emotional dissonance and disharmony (Lashley, 2002).

Many of the more critical studies of emotional labour also highlight the ways in which it is managed through the design of systems and routines ('scripts', for instance – see Leidner, 1993), and through particular supervisory practices (Johansson and Näslund, 2009; Van Maanen and Kunda, 1989), often involving self and peer surveillance (Tyler and Abbott, 1998).

Example

Consider the following instructions given to flight attendants during a training course at an international airline:

> Always walk softly through the cabin, always make eye contact with each and every passenger, and always smile at them. This makes for a much more personal service, and is what First Class travel and [we] as a company are all about. It's what we're here for. (Cited in Hancock and Tyler, 2001b: 31)

- Why might these instructions have been given – what were the management team and the trainers trying to achieve?
- How might the performance of emotional labour (through making eye contact, smiling and so on) have conflicted with other aspects of the flight attendant's job?
- How might the flight attendants manage (or avoid) this potential conflict?

When combined with the various demands of the work involved, techniques used to manage emotional labour can result in its performance becoming especially problematic for the individual. Such demands can involve, for instance, the requirement that a particular emotional display – such as smiling for the entire duration of a long flight – be maintained over long periods of time, often in working environments that are entirely unconducive to maintaining such displays (Bain and Boyd, 1998). Similarly, emotional labourers tend to be required to maintain an appropriate emotional display to customers who are being rude or offensive (Filby, 1992; Hochschild, 1983), or who may be experiencing extreme emotional distress (McMurray and Ward, 2014), resulting in the need for emotional labourers to deploy various coping strategies.

Coping strategies

At their simplest level, coping strategies may involve employees making use of 'back stage' areas (where customers and possibly co-workers are not present) to let off steam or simply 'switch off' (Van Maanen and Kunda, 1989: 67). Whereas managerial approaches to coping with the demands of emotional labour tend to highlight the importance of HRM techniques such as enriching job engagement through career planning and redesign of work systems (see Agrawal and Sadhana's 2010 study of employee engagement in Indian call centres), more sociological approaches tend to focus on the development of what Korczynski (2003) describes as 'communities of coping', based upon the deployment of collective forms of emotion work. Participants in Bolton and Boyd's (2003: 298) study of flight attendants, for instance, emphasised the importance of camaraderie in coping with the emotional demands of service work. According to one flight attendant in their research:

> The other crew are the best thing about this job and the only thing that keeps me going. We always manage to have a laugh during flights and that's what makes the long hours, annoying passengers and terrible working conditions bearable.

Åsa Wettergen (2010), in her study of workers involved in the processing of applications for asylum at the Swedish Migration Board, found that the men and women who took part in her research coped with the emotional demands of their work by developing interaction rituals that sustained an 'emotional regime', emphasising procedural correctness and professionalism. Similarly, in their study of 911 call-takers in a city-based Emergency Center in the US, focusing on the different ways in which feelings are understood, expressed and managed in an emotionally charged organisational setting, Tracy and Tracy (1998) emphasise the importance of communication in enabling co-workers to offer each other mutual support.

Humour also appears to be a particularly important mechanism for diffusing the potentially negative aspects of emotional labour – when police officers have to deal with major disasters, for instance, humour may be a way in which they can deal with the emotional impact of their work on themselves and their colleagues (Alexander and Wells, 1991). In her account of humour as a coping strategy in the sex industry, for example, Teela Sanders (2004) argues that sex workers consciously manipulate humour as a social and psychological distancing technique; humour contributes to a range of defence mechanisms that are necessary to protect the personal and emotional well-being of sex workers. She identifies six types of humour among sex workers that probably apply to many other forms of interactive service work that require a range of emotional management skills and coping strategies. These are:

- private jokes used to ridicule clients;
- coded jokes that flow between sex workers in the presence of clients;
- stories and anecdotes of personal disclosure framed in terms of jocularity and jest;
- humour as a strategy to resist harassment and verbal aggression from community harassers and protesters;
- humour as a source of communication with professionals (healthcare workers and police officers, for instance);
- humour as a signifier of conflict and group membership.

An alternative strategy is to retreat into the routine. Leidner (1993; 1999) suggests that sales-service workers resort to their scripts as a way of separation and that scripting is not more alienating therefore, but less so, because 'routines may actually offer interactive service workers some protection from assaults on their selves' (Leidner, 1993: 14). Another strategy identified involves a more empathetic form of deflection. For instance, in dealing with situations involving emotional conflict, Hochschild (1983: 105–8) reports that flight attendants are trained to perceive difficult or offensive passengers as people who are experiencing problems in their personal lives or who are afraid of flying, and to manage their emotions accordingly. Underlying this aspect of their training, however, is the requirement for attendants to respond positively to emotional conflicts and to manage them in such a way as to always 'think sales' and so, essentially, to rationalise an otherwise 'irrational' organisational interaction by undertaking further deep acting.

Emotional labour: Beyond Hochschild

In her critique of Hochschild's use of the term emotional labour – a concept she suggested some time ago 'has now been stretched to its very limits' – Sharon Bolton (2000) has offered a typology that distinguishes four distinct types of emotion management:

- *presentational* (emotion management according to general, social 'rules' – Hochschild's (1983) 'emotion work', see Bolton and Boyd, 2003);
- *philanthropic* (emotion management given as a 'gift');
- *prescriptive* (emotion management according to organisational/professional rules of conduct, but not necessarily in the pursuit of profit);
- *pecuniary* (emotion management for commercial gain – Hochschild's 'emotional labour', see Bolton and Boyd, 2003).

Bolton emphasises that emotional labour can be a source of pleasure as well as pain, and that many opportunities exist to engage in what Ackroyd and Thompson (1999) have called 'organisational misbehaviour'. For Yiannis Gabriel (1995), affective aspects of work are a fundamental part of what he calls 'the unmanaged organisation' – those spaces for resistance that are ultimately beyond the reach of managerial control. This may suggest, as Bolton argues, that an over-concentration on the 'pecuniary' category of emotional labour can lead to the neglect of vital parts of organisational life, in particular of 'the emotional management skills organizational actors possess' (Bolton and Boyd, 2003: 289, emphasis added), and of the potential for pleasure and job satisfaction in the performance of emotional labour.

Hence, despite its widespread and enduring influence, Bolton and Boyd (2003) note three central weaknesses in Hochschild's account of emotional labour. First, they argue, Hochschild over-emphasises the divide between public and private performances of emotional self-management, and tends to use the terms 'public' and 'commercial' interchangeably, creating an oversimplified dichotomy. Bolton and Boyd argue that here (and elsewhere) Hochschild operates according to the assumption that there is no room for 'emotion work' within organisational life.

Second, they argue that Hochschild mistakenly equates a physical labour process with an emotional one. However, Bolton and Boyd argue that unlike the factory workers in Marx's critique of capitalism, for instance, interactive service workers such as airline cabin crew 'own' the means of production (their bodies and emotions) and, therefore, ultimately control the capacity to present a 'sincere' or 'cynical' performance. What Hochschild fails to recognise, they argue, is that the indeterminacy of labour, and of managerial attempts to control it, is further exacerbated within the contested terrain of the emotional labour process as a result.

Third, Bolton and Boyd argue that 'Hochschild's concern with management attempts to seduce employees into "loving" the company, its product and its customers, creates an illusion of emotionally crippled actors' (Bolton and Boyd, 2003: 290). In contrast, they conclude that emotional labourers such as airline cabin crew demonstrate high levels of emotional dexterity as they are able to draw on different sets of feeling rules (commercial, professional, organisational and social) in order to match feeling to situation, thus rendering them multi-skilled emotional managers who are able to 'balance conflicting demands and still . . . effect polished performances' (Bolton and Boyd, 2003: 295).

Despite Bolton's critique, what remains the case, however, is that emotional labour is relatively low-paid, low-status work. One of the main reasons for this is that it is predominantly carried out by women because women are deemed to be inherently skilled in its performance (McDowell, 2009); in other words, the skill involved is 'essentialised'. This theme is explored in O'Brien's study of the UK nursing profession, which emphasises that the skills possessed by nurses are often thought to derive 'not from the qualities of being a nurse, but from the qualities of being a woman' (O'Brien, 1994: 399). Indeed, a growing body of research has focused on the gendering of emotional labour and its management, emphasising links between essentialism and the relatively low status and low pay accorded to emotional and aesthetic forms of labour (Sanders *et al.*, 2013). The extent to which this perpetuates the gender pay gap has been emphasised, as has the ways in which these continued associations serve to discriminate against men who undertake emotional labour.

Pullen and Simpson (2009) have highlighted the challenges faced by men working as nurses and primary school teachers, and Hancock *et al.* (2015) have emphasised how men who perform intimate labour have to continually negotiate the expectation that a close bond will be nurtured between service providers and customers, at the same time as maintaining an appropriate distance because of their gender. Sargent (2004: 179) sums this up when arguing that the gendering of emotion at work is premised on the assumption that while 'women's laps are places of love, men's laps are places of danger'. We explore the implications of this for men who perform emotionally intimate labour (Hancock *et al.*, 2015) in Case study 20.3 below.

Conclusions

In discussing emotion in organisations we have endeavoured to identify the various factors underpinning its emergence as an increasingly significant concern within HRM theory and practice. In sum, while traditionally emotion has largely been perceived as a relatively undesirable appendage to organisational rationality and, as such, to be excluded from organised life, in more recent approaches, particularly those associated with HRM, emotions have become increasingly valued as organisational resources. A prime example of this can be found in the idea of 'emotional intelligence'. Yet, as Fineman has noted, although HRM 'aims to harness positive emotion as a "success" ingredient' (1994: 86), emotion is still regarded as being in need of careful managerial rationalisation. As he goes on (Fineman, 1994: 545), the dominant belief continues to be that

> Cool, clear, strategic thinking is not to be too sullied by messy feelings. Efficient thought and behaviour tame emotion. Accordingly, good organisations are places where feelings are managed, designed out or removed. *(Fineman, 1994: 545)*

In the latter part of the chapter, we also outlined the insights of a range of more critical approaches to understanding organisations as 'emotional arenas' that demand the performance of emotional labour. Here, we drew largely on the work of those who have sought to understand organisational emotions in terms of their commodification. This approach has emphasised the extent to which the emotions of employees are considered fair game for employer intervention when self-presentation and interactive service style are integral parts of the labour process. As Simon Williams (2001: 112) has put it, the contemporary era is one in which emotions appear to be 'managed if not manipulated, and marketed if not manufactured, to an unprecedented degree'. Hence, the '(re)discovery' of the emotional has provided an important lever in terms of management practice and critique.

This led us to pay particular attention to the idea of emotional labour. While the definition first proposed by Hochschild over 20 years ago has endured, we acknowledged how subsequent research has not only demonstrated how the contours and experiences of emotional labour are now thought to be more complex than those described in her account, but how much more widespread it is becoming across the contemporary organisational landscape. For as Steinberg and Figart (1999: 23) noted in this regard,

> As our economy moves increasingly toward the provision of services and as the public–private distinction further blurs, the skills, effort and responsibilities associated with emotional labour will become more central to our understanding of what it means to work. *(Steinberg and Figart, 1999: 23)*

In this chapter, then, we have tried to think critically about emotion in work organisations in terms of the management of emotion and the performance of emotional labour. In Case study 20.1 (based on Russell and Tyler, 2002), we consider some of the concepts, ideas and debates introduced here with reference to the lived experience of emotion in the workplace, and reflect on some of the issues this raises for HRM theory and practice. In Case study 20.2, we examine the demand for emotional intelligence amongst HR practitioners, and in our final Case study, 20.3, we explore the management and experience of so-called 'toxic emotions' and the impact this has on working practices.

CASE STUDY 20.1

EMOTION MANAGEMENT AT GIRLIE GLITTER CO.

PHILIP HANCOCK AND MELISSA TYLER

The Girlie Glitter Co. concept and design

Girlie Glitter Co. is a UK-based chain of retail outlets whose products and services are marketed primarily at 3- to 13-year-old girls. The idea was to develop a retail store that stocked not only a range of (largely dressing up and party) clothes, hair-styling products, cosmetics and fashion accessories but also that provided the opportunity for girls to have a 'make-over' in store. The aim, as one of the co-founders of the company described it, was to create 'a girl friendly . . . pleasurable space . . . in which young girls could enjoy shopping together, and . . . mothers could enjoy shopping with their daughters'. In short, as the design team put it, the idea was to develop a retail experience that 'lets little girls live a dream'.

With this in mind, a distinct design was developed – the stores are loud, bright and have a discernible colour and style theme that clearly differentiates them from other retail outlets in the shopping centres in which they are located. Indeed, colour was considered to be a vital component of their aesthetic and the design team decided that everything should be 'pink . . . and glittery, with lots of hearts'. This helped to bring to life the idea that the presentation of the products and services on offer should be a 'magical experience'. Much like other retail outlets and theme parks marketed particularly at children and families, the emphasis was upon the creation of an atmosphere of 'clean, wholesome, family fun'.

The Girlie Glitter Co. experience

Customers are enticed into the stores largely through a combination of music, abundant use of glitter, bright lighting and white flooring, combined with distinctive chrome fittings, pink lettering and iconography (hearts and stars), as well as rows of sparkly costumes and make-up. Sales staff performs dance routines at the front of stores at regular intervals throughout the day creating 'an atmosphere of excitement', as one store manager put it. This reflects a broader performance ethos throughout the company that, at least in part, differentiates Girlie Glitter Co. from other retail outlets

selling similar products. It has important implications for the recruitment, selection, training and monitoring of sales staff. As one of the co-founders of the company put it, 'staff don't see themselves as sales assistants but as performers'.

In this respect, the marketing team developed a number of other features designed to differentiate the Girlie Glitter brand from other retail 'experiences'. As the store's publicity puts it, 'not only does Girlie Glitter stock all things feminine and girlie, it provides its young customers with the opportunity to be transformed into a fairy princess in store'. At the front of the stores are located spaces called 'Princess Studios'. These are hair-styling and make-up areas where customers can have their hair and nails done, as well as a range of themed make-overs.

Because of this aspect of their work, sales assistants (or 'performers') function not only as dancers but also as hairdressers, make-up artists and nail technicians. Instructed to 'have fun while thinking sales', they are also told to just 'do what comes naturally'. This means that sales assistants 'need to look right because we are there for the girls [customers] to copy'. In this sense, 'standard presentation is important because they are like role models, they influence the kids, much like characters in kids' cartoons or TV programmes, really', as one area sales manager said.

Aware of the potential pitfalls of standardisation and thematic repetition, however, the aim was to 'customise' the service provided, and to recruit staff capable of making individual customers feel special. Crucially, as the Girlie Glitter Co. marketing officer put it, 'this shop was not to be seen as an exploitation of children: it had to represent their dreams, and every girl who visited Girlie Glitter had to feel as though she had walked into a shop that was there just for her'. He goes on to say that this is because

customers are no longer willing to accept that the shops they visit are just places to buy goods. They demand drama and deserve to be delighted by the experience. Shops have become destinations in themselves – not only a place to purchase, but as a place to be entertained, inspired and, in the case of Girlie Glitter Co., to have loads of fun. This means that the staff we select to work here, particularly on the shop floor, are absolutely crucial.

Recruitment, selection and training at Girlie Glitter Co.

Recruitment at Girlie Glitter Co. can be likened to the formation of an all-girl pop group; potential employees are asked to sing and dance. Recruitment sessions are described not as interviews but as auditions. When a number of sales staff are being recruited for a new store, group interviews (or 'auditions') are held, followed by individual ones. As the HR officer responsible for recruitment and selection put it, 'group auditions allow you to see who shines through above the rest . . . and that's what we're looking for, people who really shine through'. Applicants, even those with relevant work experience, are often rejected because they do not look, sound or perform right. This is largely because 'personality is so important to what we do. It is vital for staff to really believe in the concept, so we recruit the personality not just the person.'

There is no specific training as such for sales staff, more an informal process of socialisation that involves, for those not skilled in hair-styling and make-up techniques, learning largely from each other. The makeovers are taught and practised much like 'painting by numbers', according to colour-coded charts and a pre-determined make-up palette. Dance routines are taught by store managers who act as choreographers, and are practised by staff mainly before and after store opening hours. All staff is encouraged to socialise together and it is routine practice for staff at new stores or new staff at established ones to be taken out to a local bar by the store or area manager on group social events.

The sales and marketing director at Girlie Glitter Co. likens her role to that of a theatre director or a stage manager: 'responsible for managing the performers who work together like a cast'. She also suggested that she sees herself very much as a scriptwriter involved in the production of Girlie Glitter Co. as a performance. This theatre metaphor carried through into other aspects of the format – store managers were likened to floor or 'front of house' managers, whose primary role is to stage manage those aspects of the store that are visible to the 'audience' [customers], and the storerooms were described as 'backstage'. The opening of the store each day was called 'curtain call', and sales staff reported feeling 'stage fright' before the store opened and the 'performance' became subject to public scrutiny.

Emotional labour at Girlie Glitter Co.

Despite their nerves, staff were told it was 'more important to smile, and to look happy, than to be step perfect' in the dance routines. For many staff, this meant either faking it or as one described it, 'going into robot':

Sometimes I just look in the mirror, smile, and remind myself to hold that position during the day. At other times, when we've got the music on and we're dancing, I start thinking about messing around with my mates the night before and then I start to smile anyway. So I daydream quite a lot. It looks like I am really enjoying myself there and then, and the customers don't know any different, so there's no harm done really. At other times you don't really have to try, because it is such good fun. You see these really cute little girls come in and do their hair and make-up and they look so pretty, really cute and it's just great. I think how much I would've loved that when I was their age, all the dressing up and stuff. Some days I really love it here. Other days, if we're busy, or there are kids that are playing up, or older girls are in here just messing about and being a pain then it's not so great and you have to just put it on because that's what we're being paid for . . . that's what we're selling, big smiles and loads of fun.

Some sales assistants coped with the embarrassment or 'stage fright' of the dance routines by relying on each other, and by 'having a laugh': 'It is scary when you're out there and it's a really busy day and you maybe see someone you know going by, or people are pointing and laughing and you just look at each other and giggle. I couldn't do it out there on my own, but at least together we can have a bit of a laugh, and I mean, to be dancing about with your mates and getting paid for it, you can't really complain can you?'

Many of the staff are conscious that they are role models for their young customers, and realise the extent to which their uniform appearance (all shop floor staff wear fitted pink T-shirts with the Girlie Glitter logo on them – for sale in children's sizes in store, and black trousers) helped them to identify together as a group. The uniform appearance of staff is thought to be particularly important by the Girlie Glitter management team.

Music is also particularly important to the management of Girlie Glitter Co., especially in terms of fostering employee and customer identification. Particular types of music (mainly by all-girl pop groups) or even specific songs come to be associated with the store, and these tend to provide a continuous soundtrack to the 'front stage' areas and, of course, to the dance routines performed at the store entrances. One particular store manager summed up the general effect of this when she said: 'Every time I hear one of the songs we play, I am immediately reminded of the company, wherever I am or whatever I'm doing.'

Some sales assistants had experienced really rude or aggressive customers – either children playing up, or their parents shouting and being abusive. When this happens

You just think, 'Oh well, they're paying for it I suppose.' It's their kid's birthday or whatever,

or maybe they're divorced Dads and this is their only day with the children and so you think, 'Just let them get on with it.' But it can be hard, sometimes. Some days when I've finished work all I can hear is the same music over and over in my head, and screaming, whining children saying 'I want this . . .' I don't think I'll ever have kids of my own, thanks very much. I've seen enough tantrums to last me a lifetime!

Questions

1 In what ways is gender relevant to the performance and management of emotional labour at Girlie Glitter Co.?

2 How might the concepts of 'surface acting' and 'deep acting' (Hochschild, 1983) be applied to the experiences of sales assistants?

3 What HRM techniques have the management team devised to encourage sales assistants to perform emotional labour?

4 What coping strategies do staff members adopt to alleviate the negative consequences of the emotional labour aspects of their work?

5 Draft a recruitment advertisement for sales assistants at Girlie Glitter Co. What key issues might you need to consider in recruiting, selecting and training new staff?

CASE STUDY 20.2
EMOTIONAL INTELLIGENCE AT CALL CO.

PHILIP HANCOCK AND MELISSA TYLER

Daljeet is a section manager at Call Co. He is responsible for managing 34 staff, who between them, work across three shifts covering a 24-hour period, seven days a week. Daljeet's team is employed in the home insurance section of an offshore call centre that handles customer service enquiries on behalf of a US-based bank. They are well-educated and IT-literate, but many are aware that their salaries are considerably lower than their US-based counterparts. Daljeet's managers are concerned because of high levels of voluntary staff turnover in his section. Staff exit interviews have suggested that the use of scripts and anglicised names make them feel 'fake', and that dealing with difficult, abusive, angry and cynical customers is a particularly demanding aspect of the job.

Combined with the stresses associated with undertaking shift work in a high-volume call centre, the emotional burnout experienced by staff is causing them to seek employment elsewhere. One of the main problems seems to be that many staff members within his team do not feel that Daljeet really understands the emotional demands of their work, or that he listens to them. Few report being encouraged to seek promotion or to consider staff development opportunities. Daljeet and his line manager have reached the conclusion that while Daljeet is coping well with the logistical and technical aspects of his role, he would benefit from developing his skills in managing people. The HR Director has identified a training consultancy that runs courses on recognising and nurturing emotional intelligence and has asked Daljeet to outline his staff development needs, and to explain how developing his own emotional intelligence might help him to manage staff more effectively.

CASE STUDY 20.3
EMOTION AND AUTHENTICITY AT THE HO HO HO AGENCY

PHILIP HANCOCK AND MELISSA TYLER

The Ho Ho Ho Agency supplies male Santa Claus performers to department stores, shopping malls, and corporate and private events across the UK during the Christmas period. Selecting its performers largely from those with theatrical backgrounds, the agency sets the highest standards, aiming to provide a professional service to its customers and clients. Not only is each performer interviewed and vetted, they are trained in a host of Santa-related skills and attributes. Training includes learning to work with children, and about the myths and stories surrounding the Santa Claus character. It also includes guidance on how to behave in a way that cannot be construed as 'inappropriate' in an adult–child relationship.

Despite the importance of the agency and its role in both preparing the performers for their work and securing contracts with clients, for most of the men concerned, the role of Santa Claus is something they perceive to be a personally significant undertaking. Many of them will tell you that in order to perform the role one has to invest emotionally in the character, fully embracing the ideals and stories associated with it. While many of the performers are paid relatively well, few would consider financial remuneration as a significant motivation for the work that they do.

Managing pain and threat in the grotto and beyond

While for the majority of the time many of the performers find their work to be both personally fulfilling and

underpinned by a genuine desire to embody the virtues and esteem of the character of Santa Claus, it is not a role without its darker side. Often, by virtue of the belief and trust children place in them the performers find themselves party to stories and expectations that are emotionally difficult. For example, one performer was clearly shaken by the request of one child for a photograph of him with the child's dead sibling's teddy bear. Others recount stories of meetings with children with severe disabilities, or life-limiting illnesses, which challenge their own self-belief and emotional control. Often this requires that they take 'time out', sometimes in the company of other performers:

> 'You know, you just say "Give me five minutes before the next one . . . there's a back door you can go outside and stand in the winter sunshine if there is any amongst the trees and just have two or three minutes and quite often you'll see there's another Father Christmas from the hut further up and he's also listening to the birdsong, you know, and sometimes you shuffle over and say "How's it going?" "Oh, okay. I've just had one of those." "Oh, right,"'

Perhaps most surprisingly, however, is the risk many of the performers feel they run from those who might wish to do harm either to the integrity of the character or to the performers themselves. Much of the time, this fear is based upon the possibility of a mistake or misunderstanding in relation to their interactions with the children who visit them. The Ho Ho Ho Agency puts many safe-guards in place in this respect – for example ensuring that there is always a third party present during any encounter between Santa and a child. The wearing of white gloves is also prescribed, both to prevent any suggestion of skin to skin contact and also to render the performers hands visible at all times. Nonetheless, what is perceived to be the current high degree of suspicion surrounding the relationship between adults and young children, still leaves many of the performers feeling continually anxious.

Perhaps even more alarming are reports of both deliberate attempts to portray the performers in a negative light, for example through children being sent in to make inappropriate requests to a performer, as well as the experience of physical abuse and violence. Such experiences range from simple jeering and beard and hat pulling by teenage gangs, to one tale of an attempted mugging while the performer sat in an open sleigh based in an out-of-town shopping mall. What is significant, however, is that common to almost all these kinds of stories is that the performers insist that they deal with the situations while remaining firmly in character, so as not to risk appearing inauthentic to any of the children who might witness these kinds of occurrences.

Questions

1 Why might the working environment of these Santa performers be described as an 'emotional cauldron'? What does this mean for the performers, agency management and customers?

2 How might the Santa performers' experience and management of emotions such as fear and anxiety be understood?

3 How do these emotions impact on the ways in which the men manage their performance and interactions with clients?

4 From an HR perspective, what measures might be introduced to make the working environment less stressful?

Bibliography

Ackroyd, S. and Thompson, P. (1999) *Organizational Misbehaviour*, London: Sage.

Agrawal, R.K. and Sadhana, J. (2010) 'Emotional labour and employee engagement in call centres: a study in Indian context', *International Journal of Work, Organisation and Emotion*, Vol.3, No.4, 351–67.

Albrow, M. (1992) 'Sine ira et studio – or do organizations have feelings?' *Organization Studies*, Vol.13, No.3, 313–29.

Alexander, D. and Wells, W. (1991) 'Reactions of police officers to body handling after a major disaster', *British Journal of Psychiatry*, Vol.159, 547–55.

Allen, J. and Du Gay, P. (1994) 'Industry and the rest: the economic identity of services', *Work, Employment and Society*, Vol.8, No.2, 255–71.

Bain, P. and Boyd, C. (1998) 'Once I get you up there where the air is rarefied: health, safety and the working conditions of airline cabin crews', *New Technology, Work and Employment*, Vol.13, No.1, 16–28.

Barsoux, J. (1993) *Funny Business: Humour, Management and Business Culture*, London: Cassell Publications.

Bendix, R. (1956) *Work and Authority in Industry: Ideologies of Management in the Course of Industrialization*, New York: Wiley.

Bolton, S. (2000) 'Emotion here, emotion there, emotional organizations everywhere', *Critical Perspectives on Accounting*, Vol.11, 155–71.

Bolton, S. (2004) *Emotion Management in the Workplace*, London: Palgrave.

Bolton, S. (ed.) (2007) *Dimensions of Dignity at Work*, London: Palgrave.

Bolton, S. and Boyd, C. (2003) 'Trolley dolly or skilled emotion manager? Moving on from Hochschild's managed heart', *Work, Employment and Society*, Vol.17, No.2, 289–308.

Chugh, S. and Hancock, P. (2009) 'Networks of aestheticization: the architecture, artefacts and embodiment of hairdressing salons', *Work, Employment and Society*, Vol.23, No.3, 460–76.

Cohen, R.L. (2010) 'When it pays to be friendly: employment relationships and emotional labour in hairstyling', *The Sociological Review*, Vol.58, No.2, 197–218.

Cooper, R. (1998) 'Sentimental value', *People Management*, April, 48–50.

Crossley, N. (1998) 'Emotions and communicative action', in Bendelow, G. and Williams, S. (eds.) *Emotions in Social Life: Critical Themes and Contemporary Issues*, London: Routledge.

Driver, M. (2003) 'United we stand, or else? Exploring organizational attempts to control emotional expression by employees on September 11, 2001', *Journal of Organizational Change Management*, Vol.16, No.5, 534–46.

Elias, N. (1991) 'On human beings and their emotions: a process sociological essay', in Featherstone, M., Hepworth, M. and Turner, B.S. (eds.) *The Body: Social Process and Cultural Theory*, London: Sage.

Filby, M. (1992) 'The figures, the personality and the bums: service work and sexuality', *Work, Employment and Society*, Vol.6, No.1, 23–42.

Fineman, S. (1994) 'Organizing and emotion: towards a social construction', in Hassard, J. and Parker, M. (eds.) *Towards a New Theory of Organizations*, London: Routledge.

Fineman, S. (ed.) (2008) *The Emotional Organization: Passions and Power*, Oxford: Blackwell.

Fleming, P. and Sturdy, A. (2009) 'Bringing everyday life back into the workplace: just be yourself!', in Hancock, P. and Tyler, M. (eds.) *The Management of Everyday Life*, Basingstoke: Palgrave Macmillan.

Frost, P. (2003) *Toxic Emotions at Work: How Compassionate Managers Handle Pain and Conflict*, Boston, MA: Harvard Business School Press.

Gabriel, Y. (1995) 'The unmanaged organization: stories, fantasies and subjectivity', *Organization Studies*, Vol.16, 477–502.

Glasø, L. and Vie, T. (2009) 'Toxic emotions at work', *The Scandinavian Journal of Organizational Psychology*, Vol.2, No.1, 13–6.

Goffman, E. (1959) *The Presentation of Self in Everyday Life*, Harmondsworth: Penguin.

Goleman, D. (2009a) *Working with Emotional Intelligence*, New York: Bantam Books.

Goleman, D. (2009b) *Emotional Intelligence: Why It Can Matter More Than IQ*, London: Bloomsbury.

Goleman, D., Boyatzis, R. and McKee, A. (2002) *Primal Leadership: Realizing the Power of Emotional Intelligence*, Boston, MA: Harvard Business School Press.

Greenidge, D. and Coyne, I. (2014) 'Job stressor and voluntary work behaviours: mediating effect of emotion and moderating roles of personality and emotional intelligence', *Human Resource Management Journal*, Vol.24, 479–95.

Hall, E.J. (1993) 'Waitering/waitressing: engendering the work of table servers', *Gender and Society*, Vol.17, No.3, 329–46.

Hancock, P. (2013) 'Being Santa Claus: the pursuit of recognition in interactive service work', *Work, Employment and Society*, Vol.27, No.6, 1004–20.

Hancock, P., Sullivan, K. and Tyler, M. (2015) 'A touch too much: negotiating masculinity, propriety and proximity in intimate labour', *Organization Studies*, Vol.36, No.12, 1715–39.

Hancock, P. and Tyler, M. (2001a) *Work, Postmodernism and Organization: A Critical Introduction*, London: Sage.

Hancock, P. and Tyler, M. (2001b) 'The look of love: gender and the organization of aesthetics', in Hassard, J., Holliday, R. and Willmott, H. (eds.) *Body and Organization*, London: Sage.

Harris, J. (1996) *Getting Employees to Fall in Love With Your Company*, New York: Amacom.

Harvard Business Review (2015) *Top 10 Must-Reads on Emotional Intelligence*, Harvard, MA: Harvard Business Review Press.

Herzberg, F. (1974) *Work and the Nature of Man*, London: Crosby Lockwood Staples.

Hochschild, A.R. (1979) 'Emotion work, feeling rules and social structure', *American Journal of Sociology*, Vol.85, No.3, 551–75.

Hochschild, A.R. (1983) *The Managed Heart: Commercialization of Human Feeling*, Berkeley, CA: University of California Press.

Hochschild, A.R. (1990) 'Ideology and emotion management: a perspective and path for future research', in Kemper, T. (ed.) *Research Agendas in the Sociology of Emotions*, New York: SUNY Press.

Hughes, E. (1958) 'Work and the self', in Rohrer, J.H. and Sherif, M. (eds.) *Social Psychology at the Crossroads*, New York: Harper.

Hunter, C., Jemielniak, D. and Postula, A. (2010) 'Temporal and spatial shifts within playful work', *Journal of Organizational Change Management*, Vol.23, No.1, 87–102.

James, N. (1989) 'Emotional labour: skill and work in the social regulation of human feeling', *Sociological Review*, Vol.37, No.1, 15–42.

Johansson, M. and Näslund, L. (2009) 'Welcome to paradise: customer experience design and emotional labour on a cruise ship', *International Journal of Work, Organisation and Emotion*, Vol.3, No.1, 40–55.

Kanter, R.M. (1977) *Men and Women of the Corporation*, New York: Basic Books.

Korczynski, M. (2003) 'Communities of coping: collective emotional labour in service work', *Organization*, Vol.10, No.1, 55–79.

Kreamer, A. (2013) *It's Always Personal: Navigating Emotion in the New Workplace*, London: Random House.

Lashley, C. (2002) 'Emotional harmony, dissonance and deviance at work', *International Journal of Contemporary Hospitality Management*, Vol.14, No.5, 255–7.

Leidner, R. (1993) *Fast Food, Fast Talk: Service Work and the Routinization of Everyday Life*, Berkeley, CA: University of California Press.

Leidner, R. (1999) 'Emotional labour in service work', *Annals of the American Academy of Political and Social Sciences*, Vol.561, 81–95.

Lewis, P. and Simpson, P. (2009) 'Centring and engendering emotions in service work: Hochschild's managed heart and the valuing of feelings in organizational research', *International Journal of Work, Organisation and Emotion*, Vol.3, No.1, 56–64.

Marks, N. (2006) 'Happiness is a series business', *Reflections on Employee Engagement*, London: Chartered Institute of Personnel and Development.

Martin, S. (1999) 'Police force of police service? Gender and emotional labour', *Annals of the American Academy of Political and Social Science*, Vol.5, No.1, 111–26.

Maslow, A.H. (1943) 'A theory of human motivation', *Psychological Review*, Vol.50, 372–96.

Mayo, E. (1933) *The Human Problems of Industrial Civilization*, New York: Macmillan.

McDowell, L. (2009) *Working Bodies: Interactive Service Employment and Workplace Identities*, Oxford: Wiley-Blackwell.

McMurray, R. and Ward, J. (2014) 'Why would you want to do that? Defining emotional dirty work', *Human Relations*, Vol.67, No.9, 1123–43.

Nath, V. (2011) 'Aesthetic and emotional labour through stigma: national identity management and racial abuse in offshored Indian call centres', *Work, Employment and Society*, Vol.25, No.4, 709–25.

Neck, C.P. and Milliman, J.F. (1994) 'Thought self-leadership: finding spiritual fulfillment in organizational life', *Journal of Managerial Psychology*, Vol.9, No.6, 9–16.

O'Brien, M. (1994) 'The managed heart revisited: health and social control', *Sociological Review*, Vol.42, No.3, 393–413.

O'Brien, E. and Linehan, C. (2014) 'A balancing act: emotional challenges in HR role', *Journal of Management Studies*, Vol.51, No.8, 1257–85.

Paules, G. (1996) 'Resisting the symbolism of service', in Macdonald, C. and Sirianni, C. (eds.) *Working in the Service Society*, Philadelphia, PA: Temple University Press.

Peters, T. (1989) *Thriving on Chaos*, London: Pan Books.

Peters, T. and Austin, N. (1985) *A Passion For Excellence*, New York: Random House.

Pisaniello, S.L., Winefield, H.R. and Delfabbro, P.H. (2012) 'The influence of emotional labour and emotional work on the occupational health and wellbeing of South Australian hospital nurses', *Journal of Vocational Behavior*, Vol.80, No.3, 579–91.

Prati, L.M. and Karriker, J.H. (2010) 'Emotional intelligence skills: the building blocks of defence against emotional labour burnout', *International Journal of Work, Organisation and Emotion*, Vol.3, No.4, 317–35.

Pringle, R. (1989) 'Bureaucracy, rationality and sexuality: the case of secretaries', in Hearn, J., Sheppard, D., Tancred-Sheriff, P. and Burrell, G. (eds.) *The Sexuality of Organization*, London: Sage.

Pullen, A. and Simpson, R. (2009) 'Managing difference in feminized work: men, otherness and social practice', *Human Relations*, Vol.62, No.4, 561–87.

Rafaeli, A. and Sutton, R.L. (1987) 'Expression of emotion as part of the work role', *Academy of Management Review*, Vol.12, 23–37.

Rafaeli, A. (1989) 'When cashiers meet customers: an analysis of the role of supermarket cashiers', *The Academy of Management Journal*, Vol.32, No.2, 245–73.

Rao, S.S. (2010) *Happiness at Work: Be Resilient, Motivated, and Successful – No Matter What*, London: McGraw-Hill.

Redman, T. and Matthews, B. (2002) 'Managing services: should we be having fun?', *The Service Industries Journal*, Vol.22, No.3, 51–62.

Roethlisberger, F.J. and Dickson, W.J. (1939) *Management and the Worker*, Cambridge, MA: Harvard University Press.

Russell, R. and Tyler, M. (2002) 'Thank heaven for little girls: "girl heaven" and the commercial context of feminine childhood', *Sociology*, Vol.36, No.3, 619–37.

Sanders, T. (2004) 'A continuum of risk? The management of health, physical and emotional risks by female sex workers', *Sociology of Health and Illness*, Vol.26, No.5, 557–74.

Sanders, T., Cohen, R.L. and Hardy, K. (2013) 'Hairdressing/undressing: comparing labour relations in self-employed body work', in Wolkowitz, C., Cohen, R.L., Sanders, T. and K. Hardy (eds.) *Body/Sex/Work: Intimate, Embodied and Sexualized Labour*, London: Palgrave.

Sargent, P. (2004) 'Between a rock and a hard place: men caught in the gender bind of early childhood education', *Journal of Men's Studies*, Vol.12, No.3, 173–92.

Sheane, S. (2011) 'Putting on a good face: an examination of the emotional and aesthetic roots of presentational labour', *Economic and Industrial Democracy*, Vol.33, No.1, 145–58.

Sloan, D. (2004) 'Emotion regulation in action: emotional reactivity in experiential avoidance', *Behaviour Research and Therapy*, Vol.42, 1257–70.

Steinberg, R. and Figart, D. (1999) *Emotional Labour in the Service Economy*, London: Sage.

Stewart, D. and Simmons, M. (2010) *Business Playground: Where Creativity and Commerce Collide*, London: FT/Prentice Hall.

Stewart, H. (2013) *The Happy Manifesto: Make Your Organization a Great Workplace*, London: Kogan Page.

Surana, S. and Singh, A.K. (2009) 'The effects of emotional labour on job burnout among call-centre Customer Service Representatives in India', *International Journal of Work, Organization and Emotion*, Vol.3, No.1, 18–39.

Sutton, R. and Rafaeli, A. (1988) 'Untangling the relationship between displayed emotions and organizational sales: the case of convenience stores', *The Academy of Management Journal*, Vol.31, No.3, 461–87.

Taylor, F.W. (1911) *Principles of Scientific Management*, New York: Harper and Row.

Tews, M., Michel, J. and Bartlett, A. (2012) 'The fundamental role of workplace fun in applicant attraction', *Journal of Leadership and Organization Studies*, Vol.19, No.1, 105–14.

Tews, M., Michel, J., Xu, S. and Drost, A. (2015) 'Workplace fun matters . . . But what else?', *Employee Relations*, Vol.37, No.2, 248–67.

Tracy, S. and Tracy, K. (1998) 'Emotional labour at 911: a case study and theoretical critique', *Journal of Applied Communication Research*, Vol.26, No.4, 390–411.

Tran, A. (2015) *Emotional Intelligence: 10 Self-control Secrets You Didn't Know*, Create Space Independent Publishing Platform.

Tyler, M. and Abbott, P. (1998) 'Chocs away: weight watching in the contemporary airline industry', *Sociology*, Vol.32, No.3, 433–50.

Van Maanen, J. and Kunda, G. (1989) 'Real feelings: emotional expressions and organizational culture', 11, pp. 43–103, in Straw, B. and Cummings, L.L. (eds.) *Research in Organizational Behaviour*, Greenwich, CT: JAI Press.

Vince, R. and Saleem, T. (2004) 'The impact of caution and blame on organizational learning', *Management Learning*, Vol.35, No.2, 133–54.

Vincent, S. (2011) 'The emotional labour process: an essay on the economy of feelings', *Human Relations*, Vol.64, No.10, 1369–92.

Warren, S. and Fineman, S. (2007) '"Don't get me wrong, it's fun here, but . . .'": ambivalence and paradox in a "fun" work environment', in Westwood, R. and Rhodes, C. (eds.) *Humour, Work and Organization*, London: Routledge.

Weber, M. (1978) *Economy and Society*, Berkeley, CA: University of California Press (First published in 1921.).

Weber, M. (1989) *The Protestant Ethic and the Spirit of Capitalism*, London: Unwin Hyman (First published in 1904.).

Wessel, J. and Steiner, D. (2015) 'Surface acting in service: a two-context examination of customer power and politeness', *Human Relations*, Vol.68, No.5, 709–30.

Wettergen, A. (2010) 'Managing unlawful feelings: the emotional regime of the Swedish migration board', *International Journal of Work, Organization and Emotion*, Vol.3, No.4, 400–19.

Williams, C. and Connell, C. (2010) 'Looking good and sounding right: aesthetic labour and social inequality in the retail industry', *Work and Occupations*, Vol.37, No.3, 349–72.

Williams, S. (2001) *Emotion and Social Theory*, London: Sage.

CHAPTER 21
FLEXIBILITY

Clare Kelliher

Introduction

Flexibility is a term which has become ubiquitous in business and political discourse in recent decades. However, it has been used in a number of different, albeit related, ways and in different contexts. First, it has been used to refer to labour market flexibility, concerned with the extent to which governments impose restrictions on employers (Lallement, 2011), second, as organisational flexibility, where organisations are able to respond to changes in their environment (Legge, 2007) and third, as flexibility in the organisation of labour (Kalleberg, 2003). Since this text is concerned with human resource management, the main focus here will be on flexibility in the way in which labour is organised. However, even within this context the term has been used in different ways, which can broadly be divided into types of flexibility which serve the interests of the employer and those which serve the interests of the employee (Alis *et al*., 2006; Zeytinoglu *et al*., 2009). This chapter will examine these two different forms of flexibility and whilst, to date, they have generally been discussed as separate activities and in different areas of the organisation and management literature, it will briefly explore the extent to which there may be potential for some synergy between the different approaches. The chapter begins with an overview of flexibility and examines the factors which have influenced the growth in flexible working practices and the calls for increased flexibility from governments, employers and employees in recent years. It then discusses the different approaches to flexibility in the organisation and management of labour in some detail and examines some of the consequences of organising labour in different ways. Finally, the chapter will explore the potential for the different interests in flexibility to be matched.

Background

Increased competitive pressure is commonly cited as the principal reason why organisations have sought to become more flexible in recent years (Kelliher and Richardson, 2012; Olsen and Kalleberg, 2004). Flexibility as a response to competitive pressure is primarily concerned with an organisation's ability to respond to changes in their external and internal environments. This may involve different ways of operating and speed of response may be important in determining whether an organisation is able to adapt to such changes. This might, for example, relate to taking advantage of a new market opportunity, or containing costs in response to difficult economic circumstances. Many changes of this nature will also have implications for the way in which labour is managed (Kalleberg, 2001). In order to be able to accommodate a short-term increase in demand, an organisation may need a corresponding short-term increase in the number of staff employed. If an employer does not have the ability to increase staff numbers for the short term only, they will need to weigh up the benefits of responding to the business opportunity, against the continuing costs of employing the additional staff when demand levels reduce.

Employers may also seek greater flexibility in the way in which labour is managed in times of more intense competition to allow them to reduce costs by managing labour more efficiently (Coe *et al.*, 2007). Organisations that experience variation in demand levels for their products or services may be able to increase efficiency by matching the supply of and demand for labour more closely. This is likely to be especially relevant for organisations that are labour intensive and where there is limited opportunity to store their product, as is the case for many services (Boxall, 2003; Korczynski, 2005). For example, in the case of businesses with predictable peaks and troughs in demand, such as retail or hospitality, employers typically increase the numbers of employees in the periods of high demand to cope with the peak and decrease the numbers in periods of lower demand.

One of the primary factors influencing the intensification of competitive pressures in recent times has been greater global integration (Marquardt, 2005). Organisations in the developed world increasingly face competition from countries in the developing world, where the cost of labour is often lower. Consequently, this has put pressure on them to look for ways of containing costs. Competing on the basis of wage rates in developing economies is unlikely to be a realistic or attractive option for them and therefore they need to look at other means of competing such as innovation, enhanced management practices, including efficiency in the use of labour. Especially in those industries which are labour intensive, flexible work practices can open up a number of ways to use labour more efficiently, by, for example, employing labour only at the times, in the locations and in the quantities needed. Efficiency may also be improved by deploying labour more flexibly and moving away from traditional job boundaries. Increased global integration has resulted in the need for greater flexibility over when work is carried out, since organisations may need to accommodate working with colleagues and clients in different time zones.

Developments in information and communication technology (ICT) have also made a significant contribution to enabling more flexible approaches to work, in particular spatial, or location flexibility (Van Dyne *et al.*, 2007). The growth in digital communication and the availability of cloud computing has allowed some types of work to be carried out away from the workplace, for example, where employees can access data and resources remotely and work in a similar way as if they were in the workplace. Furthermore, the pervasiveness of ICT into work and non-work life has also changed expectations associated with communication. In particular, the use of mobile technologies has increased expectations about the availability of people and speed of response to communications (Matusik and Mickel, 2011) since they do not need to be physically present in a particular location to receive, or respond to communications (Barley *et al.*, 2011; Besseyre des Horts *et al.*, 2012).

Whilst flexibility is often considered as an organisational issue, it also has more general relevance for how economies operate. Governments may take steps to promote labour flexibility by means of deregulating the labour market. A lightly regulated or more flexible labour market, which places fewer legal obligations on employers, it is argued, will allow for greater managerial freedom, increased attractiveness to inward investors and economic growth (Countouris and Freedland, 2013; Legge, 2007; Whitley *et al.*, 2005). Flexibility in this context may go beyond the regulation of how labour is employed (e.g. fixed term, part time), or deployed (multi-tasking and skilling) and may include employers' obligations in relation to issues such as health and safety, recognition and consultation with trade unions. In recent years, there is some evidence that governments in Europe have responded to the global financial crisis by attempting to make their labour market more flexible, deregulating working conditions and reducing employment rights (Countouris and Freedland, 2013; ETUI, 2012). For example, in Greece employment protection for temporary workers has been reduced, since it has been seen to impede the employment of young workers and the re-entry of the long-term unemployed into the labour market. Similarly, in Germany and Italy there have been moves to decentralise collective bargaining over terms and conditions of employment.

At the same time as these developments in the business environment requiring organisations to become more flexible, we have seen a number of social and demographic changes, which have resulted in employees expecting greater flexibility and choice in the way in which they work. In many countries employees seek greater flexibility over where, when and how much they work in order to achieve a better work–life balance (Bloom and Van Reenen, 2006; Eurofound, 2015; Hooker *et al.*, 2007; Yanadori and Kato, 2009). As such, employers seeking to be competitive in the labour market are likely to respond to employees desires for flexibility, to enable them to recruit high calibre employees (Rau and Hyland, 2002; Richardson, 2010). In circumstances where labour and/or skill shortages exist, employers may be particularly keen to offer flexible working options to increase their attractiveness to new recruits and to retain existing employees (see Case Study 21.2 for an example of how a company in India has approached this). In addition, offering flexible options is seen to be an important tool in recruiting generation Y who are known to place high value on the ability to achieve a satisfactory work–life balance (Gerdes, 2009) and also for older workers who otherwise might not remain in paid employment (Eurofound, 2015; Loretto and Vickerstaff, 2015). Furthermore, in some countries (e.g. Australia, the Netherlands, UK) governments have introduced a legal right to request flexible working arrangements. In a similar vein, in 2014 a Presidential Memorandum was issued in the US supporting workplace flexibility and giving Federal Government employees the right to request flexible working. The European Union has developed policy on promoting better jobs, which includes the ability to combine work and non-work activities effectively (Eurofound, 2010).

Approaches to flexibility

The discussion about and study of flexible working in organisations can be broadly divided into employer- and employee-driven flexibility, or the so-called flexibility *of* and *for* employees (Alis *et al.*, 2006). Flexibility *of* employees enables organisations to meet their needs for flexibility by using labour in non-standard ways. Flexibility *for* employees allows employees to exercise some degree of choice over how they work, to help them balance their work and non-work lives more effectively. Below each type is discussed in more detail.

Flexibility *of* employees

Flexibility of employees may include, for example, the use of temporary and part-time contracts, shift working, annual hours' contracts, and/or deployment of staff across a range of tasks, crossing traditional job boundaries. This is normally used by organisations to help them to match the supply of and demand for labour more closely and assist with the management of uncertainty (Bryson, 1999).

Back in 1985 John Atkinson developed the model of the flexible firm, which has been influential in shaping the debate about this approach to flexibility (Atkinson, 1985). The model identifies various labour use strategies which employers might use in order to achieve organisational flexibility and is based on the idea of maintaining a stable core of employees, who are supplemented by a flexible periphery. In this debate a number of broad categories of flexibility are identified, most notably numerical and functional flexibility (Kalleberg, 2001) and more recently greater attention has been given to spatial and temporal flexibility.

Numerical flexibility allows for labour to be utilised at times when needed and disposed of when not needed and might involve using part-time employment or the use of temporary staff, either employed directly or through a temporary employment agency.

Functional flexibility allows for staff to be deployed across different activities according to demand levels and might involve multi-skilling and multitasking.

Temporal flexibility involves the time at which labour is employed. Traditionally this has tended to involve shift working, designed to allow labour input for a longer period of time than a standard working day, or to allow for continuous operation on a 24/7 basis as in, for example, a hospital environment.

Spatial flexibility is associated with the location of work and enables employers to deploy labour in different locations.

These labour use strategies are likely to be of greatest use to employers who experience fluctuations in demand levels which have direct consequences for labour. Demand may vary on a predictable basis such as seasonal (in the tourism industries), weekly, daily or even within the working day (e.g. restaurants and fast food outlets), or may be unpredictable and influenced by factors such as the weather or media communication. We now examine each in more detail.

Numerical flexibility

Using numerical flexibility employers might choose to employ staff on part-time or temporary contracts, or to vary the number of hours worked by staff according to business patterns. Varying hours in line with demand levels may involve increasing and decreasing the number of hours worked by part-time staff, or alternatively may involve a longer-term arrangement for full-time staff, such as an annual hours contract (see Case Study 21.3 for an example of this).

In response to the global financial crisis, some employers have chosen to reduce employees' working hours instead of making layoffs. In countries, such as Germany this approach has been supported by government who have paid the remainder of the employee's salary from public funds (Eurofound, 2012). This is seen as a less expensive alternative to unemployment, since the employer still pays for some of the employee's time. Similarly, in the US in some states unemployment benefits were pro-rated for employees whose working hours were reduced because of economic circumstances (Abraham and Houseman, 2014). On-call working, or what is sometimes known as a zero-hours contract, has also become more common in recent years in a number of countries, notably Ireland, Italy, the Netherlands, Sweden and the UK. Here a continuous employment relationship exists between the employer and the employee, but there is no obligation on the employer to provide a minimum amount of work. The use of these arrangements has tended to be concentrated in low-skill service work such as retail and care work.

Employers who choose to use temporary staff may either employ them directly or may develop a labour supply relationship with a temporary employment agency. Temporary employment may be used to align staffing levels with fluctuations in demand, but may also be used to cope with uncertainty. For example, organisations developing a new product, or entering a new market may use temporary staff to reduce their risks until they feel able to forecast demand levels more accurately.

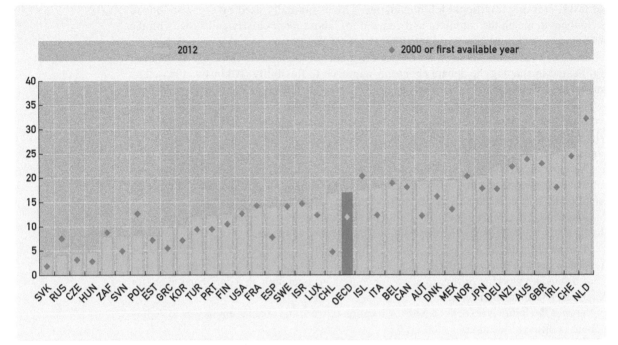

Figure 21.1 Incidence of part-time employment (as a percentage of total employment)

Source: OECD Factbook 2014: Economic, Environmental and Social Statistics - © OECD 05-05-2014.

Figure 21.1 shows the incidence of part-time work across the OECD countries. In Switzerland, Australia, Ireland and the UK, part-time employment represents in the region of a quarter of total employment and in the Netherlands part-time employment represents more than a third (37.1 per cent) of total employment. By contrast, in countries such as Russia, Hungary and the Czech and Slovak republics part-time employment is much less common and represents less than five per cent of total employment. The figure also shows that in many countries there has been a marked increase in the incidence of part-time employment since 2000.

Figure 21.2 shows the proportion of employees with a temporary contract, or contract of limited duration across the European Union member states. Poland, Spain and Portugal

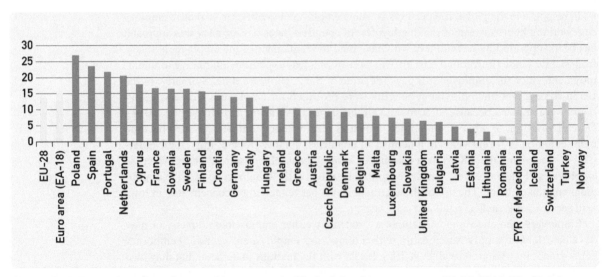

Figure 21.2 Proportion of employees with a contract of limited duration, age group 15–64, 2013 (% of total employees)

Source: Eurostat (online data code: lfsa_etpga).

all made relatively high use of this type of numerical flexibility, with in the region of one quarter of the workforce having a temporary contract. By contrast, in Romania, Lithuania and Estonia the proportion was less than five per cent. In the EU as a whole the number of employees with a contract of limited duration was 13.9 per cent. Differences in the use of flexible labour practices between member countries may reflect a number of factors, but are likely at least in part to be because of the ease with which employers can terminate the contracts of employment of permanent employees.

Functional flexibility

Functional flexibility refers to the deployment of employees across a range of tasks according to demand levels. Employees may be deployed across existing job boundaries, suggesting a more fluid approach to the management of labour than traditional approaches where staff are engaged for a particular job. Redeployment of staff may take place on an ad hoc basis, or in line with business cycles, which may occur, for example, on a seasonal, weekly or daily basis. The idea of redeploying staff across areas of work rests on the assumption that there will be variations in the nature of demand for different work tasks (Desombre *et al.*, 2006). Thus, if staff are fully occupied in the normal course of their work, little scope exists to improve efficiency by deploying them to other tasks. However, where variations in demand level do occur this can create both periods of 'idle time' for staff and also times when there is insufficient capacity to meet all demand. Redeploying staff that are multiskilled from areas of low activity to areas of high activity may reduce the need to hire additional staff and may also allow for greater speed of response to short-term and/or unpredictable fluctuations in business.

It is also argued that the use of functional flexibility can enhance quality in the provision of services. The use of trained multifunction staff can reduce the number of people a service user has contact with, thereby enabling a more holistic approach to be employed. For example, based on a study of nurses and nursing support staff, Desombre *et al.* (2006) suggest that using multiskilled staff that perform several tasks for the patient allows the experience to be more client- or user-centred, as opposed to a more traditional approach of being process- or specialism-centred.

In practice, functional flexibility can be implemented in a number of different ways and can be examined in terms of 'breadth' and 'depth' (Kelliher *et al.*, 2002). Breadth is concerned with the number of additional tasks an employee can be deployed to do. This could range from a small number closely related to their main role, to being deployed across a wide range of activities requiring diverse skills. Depth is concerned with the extent to which redeployed staff are able to take on an additional role. They may be expected and be able to take the role on fully, or may be able to only provide assistance with certain aspects of the role.

Evidence on the extent to which functional flexibility is used by organisations is less widely available than for some forms of flexibility (e.g. part-time or temporary contracts), which in part is because of the difficulty in measuring it accurately as a result of the varied nature of activities grouped under this term. The Workplace Employment Relations Survey (WERS11) shows that in the UK 65 per cent of employers report that some core employees are trained to be functionally flexible (Department for Business, Innovation and Skills, 2011), suggesting fairly widespread usage of the practice, even though it may only involve small numbers of employees in each organisation.

Temporal and spatial flexibility

Whilst the above distinctions remain relevant, in a changing world these distinctions may not be sufficient to cover all types of flexibility that employers look for, or how they interact with the types of flexibility employees may seek themselves. Developments in technology have had an important part to play in changing the way in which work is carried out (Kelliher and Richardson, 2012; Zammuto *et al.*, 2007). Through the use of ICT many employees can carry out work away from the workplace, and it is argued that in some cases the boundaries between work and non-work activities have become blurred (Tietze and Musson, 2005). It is important, however, not to lose sight that some roles still require employees to be physically present at the workplace and at designated times. For example, a doctor needs to be physically present to perform a surgical procedure and a call centre operator needs to be available during operating hours.

Changes brought about by increasing global integration have also resulted in employers looking for different forms of flexibility. Although it has always been commonplace for some employees to work outside of normal working hours (e.g. maintenance, security and cleaning staff), often on a shift basis, employers who operate in different parts of the world and in different time zones may require employees to be available to work at different times to accommodate this. For example, Sunday is a normal working day in the United Arab Emirates (UAE), therefore employees in other parts of the world who work closely with the UAE may sometimes have to work on Sunday to accommodate these different patterns. Similarly, people in Europe or the Americas who collaborate with Asia or Australia may have to alter their working time to ensure an overlap in the working day with colleagues in these locations. This might involve regular working at different times or being available for additional, short periods of time to accommodate real-time communication (Kelliher and Anderson, 2010). The use of ICT often means that this additional, short-time availability can be carried out from a remote location, without the need for the employees to be present at the workplace. Research on virtual teams who are geographically distributed, however, suggests that communication needs to be managed carefully to avoid negative outcomes, both in terms of business outcomes and employee well-being, which may stem from too much connectivity. Collins and Kolb (2012) argue that an optimal balance between connection and disconnection needs to be achieved in order to secure benefits such as team creativity.

Notably, temporal flexibility has traditionally been subject to contractual arrangements (e.g. shift work, annual-hours contracts). However, these more recent forms may be subject to rather subtler arrangements and expectations, which may effectively amount to an intensification of work (Kelliher and Anderson, 2010). The act of giving an employee a smart phone may imply expectations of availability outside of work times and away from the work place (Barley *et al.*, 2011; Perlow, 2012). For example, employees may be expected to engage in communication (phone calls, email, SMS messages, etc.) with clients outside of designated working time and on non-work days. Wireless technologies, which enable employees to stay 'in touch', have also created expectations of 'ever-availability' (Besseyre des Horts *et al.*, 2012; Matusik and Mickel, 2011).

In addition, where ICT enables work to be done remotely, this may also yield cost advantages for employers, since this may allow them to reduce the amount of work space required. If employees work remotely for all or part of the time then the need for accommodation is likely to be reduced, either because no office space is required, or systems such as 'hotdesking' may be used, which will allow higher occupancy rates for accommodation.

It is worth noting that although the above forms of flexibility have tended to be distinguished as separate activities, they may also be combined in the context of one job. For example, part-time workers may also be shift workers as is sometimes the case in retail or cleaning work. Temporary employment may also be combined with spatial flexibility, for example with locum pharmacists or supply teachers.

In recent years there have been attempts to capture other new forms of work and employment which increase flexibility (Cappelli and Keller, 2013; Eurofound, 2015). These include changes to the traditional relationship between the employer and the employee and to patterns of work. In the first category, employee sharing has emerged in some countries where several employers form a network which then hires staff that can then be deployed across any of the organisations in the network. This type of arrangement has become more common in France, with in the region of 4,400 employer groups jointly hiring staff, mostly found in agriculture. There is also evidence of more ad hoc employee sharing, where employees are reassigned to another employer on a temporary basis, when their employer does not have sufficient work for them. In Poland this has been used as a response to the economic crisis (Eurofound, 2015). In the second category, ICT-based mobile workers or e-nomads, where work is done away from the workplace and involves changes of workplace, have become increasingly common both amongst employees and self-employed workers. Whilst in some ways similar to teleworking, mobile workers differ in that they have no fixed work location. The way in which temporary employment is used has also undergone some change. Whilst temporary contracts have traditionally been used to cope with uncertainty, and/or known fluctuations in demand, more recently there has been an increased trend towards the organisation of work in project form, which has resulted in a corresponding increase in the use of temporary work. Staff are employed for the duration of a project, rather than on a permanent basis. Although this approach has long been used in industries such as construction, this has grown in the creative industries and in manufacturing (Packendorff, 2002).

The chapter now turns to examine flexibility to meet employees' needs.

Flexibility for employees

Flexibility for employees covers arrangements where the employee is able to exercise some degree of control over where, when and how much they work. Typically, this might involve reducing their hours, working remotely for all or part of their working time, or altering the time at which they work. In this context organisations offer employees the opportunity to work flexibly in order to assist them in achieving a more satisfactory balance between their work and non-work activities. Many organisations have flexible working policies which allow employees to make a request to change their working arrangements. In addition to accommodating individual requests, some organisations have standardised arrangements such as flexitime, where employees can vary their working time within certain limits. Offering flexible working options to employees has traditionally been seen as being a means to assist working parents and carers. However, in a number of countries employers increasingly offer flexible working options to all employees (CBI/Harvey Nash, 2011). Offering flexible working options to all employees may be based on a desire to be equitable, but is also likely to be based on business reasoning (CIPD, 2005). Many studies have shown that where employees have access to flexible working there are positive organisational outcomes, such as higher levels of job satisfaction (Gajendran and Harrison, 2007; Hooker *et al.*, 2007), organisational commitment (Chow and Keng-Howe, 2006; Harris and Foster, 2005), employee well-being (Redman *et al.*, 2009) and enhanced performance (Cranfield School of Management, 2008; Gajendran and Harrison, 2007). Over and above formalised arrangements, which are initiated through organisational policies, there is much evidence that informal arrangements for flexible working are prevalent in organisations (Healy, 2004; Kelliher and Anderson, 2010) and under these circumstances uptake of flexible working arrangements can be as high amongst men as women (Cranfield School of Management, 2008).

Remote working normally involves employees working from a different location for some, or all of their working time. This is often also frequently referred to as teleworking, since in practice many employees remain connected to their workplace by means of some form of information and communications technology. Remote working often takes place at home, but may also include other locations, such as coffee shops and business centres.

Working at different times, or flexitime, is where employees are able to exercise some degree of discretion over the time they work. This may be as an individual arrangement about working time, or as part of a flexitime scheme. Flexitime schemes are normally based around a framework of 'core' time, when all employees are required to be at work. Thus, essentially, they offer some discretion over starting and finishing times, although some also allow employees to 'bank' additional time worked, which can be taken as time off at a later period. Altering start and finish times may allow employees to accommodate the demands of their non-work lives more easily (e.g. the school run, healthcare appointments, participating in sports activity) and may also help employees avoid the stresses of congestion at peak travel times.

Compressed working time also changes when work is done and involves employees working their contracted working hours over a shorter period of time from what is normal in the workplace. This might involve a four-day week, or a nine-day fortnight instead of the more normal five or ten days. This type of arrangement may suit businesses with hours of operation which extend beyond a standard eight-hour working day, for example, a retail outlet operating from 10am till 8pm each day may allow employees to work 4×10-hour days, in place of 5×8-hour days.

Reduced working hours represents a different type of change to working arrangements, since in these circumstances a change to the contract of employment is made and will have implications for the employees, pay and may influence their entitlement to benefits. As such, this type of flexibility will always be subject to a formalised arrangement.

It is important to note that in practice, there may be considerable variation in how flexible working arrangements are actually enacted (De Menezes and Kelliher, 2011) and as a result it may be difficult to make generalisations about implementation and outcomes. For example, they may take the form of a regular arrangement, such as an employee who always starts work at a different time on certain days of the week, or they may be more ad hoc, such as the employee who works remotely according to the demands of their work (e.g. when they need uninterrupted concentration to complete a complex task) or non-working lives (they want to be at home to accept a delivery). There may also be considerable variation in the percentage of full time that a part-timer works for example 50 per cent or 90 per cent. Notably, again these different forms are not mutually exclusive and an employee might, for example, work reduced hours partially from home and at different times from those that are normal for the workplace.

Implementation and outcomes

Changes to working arrangements, whether driven by the needs of employers or by employees, raise a number of issues for implementation. Looking first at those arrangements which allow employees to exercise a degree of choice over where, when and how much to work, the development of policy alone is insufficient to bring about change in the way in which work is carried out and for any benefits linked to their use to be gained. Employers also need to create an environment in which these policies are accepted and can be implemented without too many obstacles (Kossek and Ruderman, 2012). For example, in a workplace where there had been a traditional approach to work organisation and where employees would normally be expected to be physically present in the workplace during designated working hours, then unfamiliarity with different working arrangements may result in reluctance on the part of managers to agree to them (Beham *et al.*, 2015). In other cases, employees who are aware that their manager is hostile to changes to working arrangements may be discouraged from making a request. Furthermore, in some organisations it may tacitly be seen as more acceptable for certain groups of employees (e.g. parents, employees in less responsible jobs) to request flexible working arrangements than others and so might deter others (e.g. senior employees, non-parents) from applying. As such, it may be important to consider the context in which they are offered, since the mere existence of a policy may have little effect on attitudes and feelings. Thus not only does policy need to be developed, but organisations need to create an environment where employees believe they are accessible to them. Perceptions of availability have been shown to be significant in relation to reaping the benefits associated with flexible working (Eaton, 2003) and the impact of this is potentially more widespread, since staff who have not taken advantage of flexible working arrangements may still place value on the availability, as they may foresee circumstances where they would like to have the opportunity to exercise some degree of choice over their working arrangements in the future.

In practical terms, a workplace that operates with traditional working arrangements may need to consider what support is required to accommodate employees working according to different arrangements, at different times or in different locations. For example, security arrangements may need to be reviewed to allow employees to access and leave the workplace at different times. The provision of support services such as IT and catering facilities may also need to be reviewed. Remote workers and those in distributed teams may need to be managed in different ways (MacDuffie, 2007) and for mechanisms to be set up to assist effective communication and maintenance of social relationships within the work environment (Mann *et al.*, 2000). Furthermore, it may be helpful to provide some training to help employees, their managers and co-workers with the transition to alternative working arrangements.

In some jobs, arrangements such as compressed working time and reduced hours may be more difficult to implement. In jobs where employees are employed to fulfil a set of responsibilities, rather than just work for specific hours (as in many professional jobs), the question arises over what is being compressed into fewer working periods, or less working time. Is it the time that the employee actually works in the week or is it their contractual hours?

There has been much debate about the outcomes of offering employees some degree of choice over when, where and how much they work. In particular, there has been much interest in the question of whether or not a business case for flexible working exists. A business case needs to be judged in the light of why a policy was put into place. If the primary objective is to ensure that the organisation fulfils its legal obligations, it might be judged on whether legal cases are taken by employees and whether the organisation has had to pay compensation and/or suffered any damage to its reputation as an employer. However, if the objective of the policy goes beyond this and is designed to contribute to greater diversity and/or organisational performance by creating favourable employee attitudes, then it needs to be judged in this context.

Whilst individual studies and particularly those conducted in recent years do present convincing evidence for a business case, in terms of organisational performance, meta-analyses and reviews of the range of evidence suggest that an unequivocal business case for the offering of flexible working policies cannot be made (De Menezes and Kelliher, 2011). The diverse body of available evidence which exists makes drawing general conclusions difficult, since many studies fail to distinguish between different degrees or frequency of flexible working. For example, it is likely that the experience of working on a 50 per cent contract will be markedly different from on a 90 per cent contract. Similarly, the employee who works remotely on an occasional or ad hoc basis is likely to have a different experience from one who works remotely all of the time. It is perhaps not surprising that these different arrangements are likely to raise different implementation issues. As such, care needs to be exercised in considering what has been examined in each case.

Furthermore, unlike many other HR policies which are effectively implemented by managers and may be imposed on employees (e.g. a pay policy linking pay levels to performance), this type of policy simply makes something available to employees and lays down a process for implementation. As a result the relationship between this type of policy and performance outcomes may not be the same as those described in the HRM and performance literature (Paauwe, 2004). In addition, as these of types of policies become more commonplace in organisations and come to be considered as normal working conditions, then any positive effects on employee attitudes may be eroded by a growing sense of entitlement (Lewis and Smithson, 2001) where employees no longer see it as something that requires reciprocation (Kelliher and Anderson, 2010).

Turning to look at employer-driven approaches, such as numerical and functional flexibility, a number of issues are raised when they are introduced. An overriding concern is that, in order to be able to reap the benefits from these forms of flexibility, employers need to be able to forecast their labour requirements accurately. If the intention is to improve efficiency in the use of labour, then employers need to monitor closely their business patterns and be able to translate these into labour requirements. They also need to be able to move sufficiently quickly to respond to unforeseen changes to demand. For example, in the case of part-time staff, employers need to be able to match the number and timing of hours with business activity at short notice. With temporary staff, if they are employed directly, employers need to decide on the appropriate length of contract to be offered. If temporary staff are employed via a temporary employment agency, then there needs to be regular communication with the agency to agree the number of staff needed.

It is noteworthy that temporary employment by its very nature promotes insecurity for staff (Legge, 2007). Many people that takes on temporary employment may be seeking the security of permanent employment and if permanent opportunities become available may leave in order to reduce job insecurity. As such, in some cases employers will pay temporary employees an enhanced rate of pay to compensate. A number of observers have noted the potential issues of equity which may arise when temporary and permanent employees are employed side by side, but with different relationships with their employer.

In the case of functional flexibility, employers need to make decisions about the breadth and depth of their approach as discussed above. The use of functional flexibility raises questions about the skill requirements and the need for training for employees who are to be redeployed, which will be determined, at least in part, by the actual way in which functional flexibility has been implemented. There are clear implications for training, but other factors which need to be considered may include whether employees who possess a greater number of skills and can be redeployed should receive some form of reward enhancement. There are also a range of issues which need to be decided upon in the day-to-day management of these multi-function staff, especially if they are redeployed within a working shift. (Kelliher and Riley (2002) document details about how uniform changes and break times need to be accommodated.)

A number of studies have attempted to investigate the relationship between various forms of numerical and functional flexibility and organisational outcomes (see, for example, Whyman et al., 2015). For human resource management outcomes, such as job satisfaction, organisational commitment and employee well-being, the evidence on numerical flexibility suggests that this type of flexibility often results in lower quality jobs (Green et al., 2010; Kalleberg et al., 2000). Employees subject to temporary contracts in particular generally report lower levels of job satisfaction and well-being as a result of the job insecurity associated with this type of contract (see, for example, Aletraris, 2010; De Cuyper and De Witte, 2008; Mauno et al., 2005). Part-time and shift working have also been found to be linked to higher rates of injury and ill-health (Robinson and Smallman, 2006). Since factors such as job satisfaction, organisational commitment and well-being have been shown to contribute to organisational performance (Boxall and Purcell, 2003; Paauwe, 2004), although numerical flexibility practices are designed to use labour more efficiently, in the longer term these practices may have the effect of indirectly inhibiting organisational performance.

In recognition of the consequences of using certain flexible labour practices for job security, the European Union has attempted to reconcile the objectives of increased competitiveness and job security by introducing a policy of flexicurity. Flexicurity attempts to combine flexibility and mobility of labour, alongside strong social security support, including unemployment benefits, pensions and healthcare (European Commission, 2007).

In contrast to the so-called 'low road' approach to HRM, which numerical flexibility is often seen as contributing to, functional flexibility is more commonly associated with a 'high road' approach since it offers employees the opportunity to develop a greater range of skills and may increase job variety (Kalleberg, 2003) and can be seen as a way of humanising work (Friedrich et al., 1998). The use of functional flexibility has been found to be associated with opportunities for learning (Lopez-Cabrales et al., 2011) organisational commitment (Van der Velde and Van den Berg, 2003) and higher retention (Kelliher et al., 2002). However, functional flexibility has also been shown to be linked to the intensification of work (Kahn, 1999; Kelliher and Gore, 2006) and in some cases increased stress has been reported (Allan, 1998; Kelliher and Desombre, 2005).

Conclusion: matching employer and employee needs

The debates concerned with flexibility of and for employees have largely taken place in isolation and as separate areas of study (Zeytinoglu *et al.*, 2009). This separation has been reflected in practice also. In many organisations flexibility of employees is the concern of operations managers seeking to increase efficiency. Flexibility for employees tends to be led by the human resources department, or sometimes those responsible for diversity and inclusion. However, studies of implementation of these practices would suggest that, as described earlier, employers can gain benefits from employee-friendly practices, such as through increased organisational commitment (Chow and Keng-Howe, 2006; Harris and Foster, 2005) and job satisfaction (Gajendran and Harrison, 2007; Hooker *et al.*, 2007) and directly on performance (Kelliher and Anderson, 2010). Equally, studies have shown employees may sometimes perceive what are intended as employer-friendly approaches as being beneficial to them. Kirkpatrick and Hoque (2006) report findings from a study of social workers who voluntarily opted for temporary employment in order to increase their direct pay, acquire a greater range of skills and experience and to accommodate lifestyle preferences. However, it is noteworthy that this was generally considered a short-term approach and many indicated that they would look for permanent employment in the future. Kelliher and Gore's (2006) study of implementing functional flexibility in retail, healthcare and hospitality environments found that employees responded positively to functional flexibility, since although it often resulted in an intensification of work, it also resulted in them gaining new skills and experiences.

Ultimately, it may be who controls access to flexibility which determines whether benefits accrue to the employer, the employee or are mutual. Furthermore, in reality some of these practices may look similar (e.g. reduced hours), although they may be being used for different purposes. As a result it is not always easy to ascertain from published statistics whether the practice being reported is employee or employer driven (Zeytinoglu *et al.*, 2009).

Where different forms of flexible working look similar in practice, this raises the question over whether there may be scope for the interests of employers and employees to be matched in the way in which these practices are enacted (De Menezes and Kelliher, 2011). It could be argued that, at least in some organisations, there may be scope to match employer and employee interests. In large organisations it may be possible to match up employee preferences over working time with the needs of the organisation to have people working at different times. For example in the stroke unit of Falu Hospital in Sweden an electronic system for planning work schedules allows the needs of the organisation to be met, whilst at the same time allowing employees to exercise influence over their own work schedule (Eurofound, 2008). The use of working time accounts may allow both employers and employees to exercise some influence over when extra work is undertaken and when that time is taken off by employees. See Case Study 21.1 as an attempt to do this. Practices such as allowing teams to self-roster around organisational requirements may help balance the needs of the organisation with those of individual team members. Given the pressure on organisations to be flexible in the face of growing competitive pressures, coupled with increased social pressures (in some countries backed up with legislative provisions), there is a real need for both researchers and practitioners to explore this possibility for a win-win situation further.

More recently, in some countries governments have been proactive in encouraging employers to think about how employer and employee's needs can be matched. In the Netherlands this has taken the form of 'New Ways of Working' (Peters *et al.*, 2009) and in the UK Agility (Agile Future Forum, 2013; CIPD, 2014).

CASE STUDY 21.1

MEETING EMPLOYER AND EMPLOYEE NEEDS FOR FLEXIBILITY AT ENGCOPLC: THE CASE OF SMART WORKING

CLARE KELLIHER AND DEIRDRE ANDERSON

EngCoPLC is a large UK-headquartered engineering company which operates on a worldwide basis. It is structured into four main divisions and employs in the region of 39,000 people, located in 50 countries across the globe. Approximately 60 per cent of their workforce are located in the UK and are distributed across eight main sites. The company's workforce is predominantly male (only about 15 per cent of the workforce is female) and most are employed on a full-time, permanent contract. The majority of employees work a traditional 39-hour week, based around standard working times. Many employees have long service records and a significant proportion have never worked for any other employer. Here we examine the implementation of a new policy on flexibility, Smart Working, at one of the UK workplaces.

In recent years the company has become more concerned with the diversity of the workforce and has introduced a number of policies designed to attract a broader spectrum of employees. There has also been a growing recognition of the importance of work–life balance to employees and the need for the company to respond to this. As such they introduced a flexible working policy a few years ago, allowing employees to request flexible working arrangements (reduced hours, remote working, different hours, etc.) in order to help them deal with the needs of their work and non-work lives more effectively.

The nature of the company's business means that there are 'ebbs and flows' over time in the level of activity throughout the company. Historically, this had tended to mean that the company used significant amounts of overtime working, in order to accommodate the 'peaks' in activity. (Beyond this, some commentators suggested that evening and weekend overtime had become institutionalised in parts of the company and this represented a significant cost for the business.) However, in addition to the peaks, there were also 'troughs' in activity and during these quieter times employees, although present during normal

working hours, were less occupied and therefore less productive. In an attempt to reconcile these variations in workload and reduce the cost of overtime, the company developed a new policy, Smart Working, which was also designed to give employees more control over their working time and help them improve their work–life balance.

The principal aim was to achieve greater flexibility and efficiency by moving from an environment which was attendance driven, to one with an emphasis on performance delivery. This was seen as central to the company's strategy and acceptance of this new way of working was tied to future investment at the UK sites. The policy had been agreed with the trade unions representing the workforce and was being rolled out across the UK.

It was designed to reduce overtime costs by scheduling employees to work additional time at peak periods, but rather than paying them for this time, they would be able to recoup it at other less busy times. TOIL (time off in lieu) accounts were set up for employees so that a record would be maintained of time owing to each employee and which could be taken off at a later date. Recognising that the end of regular overtime would result in an income loss for some employees, the policy was introduced alongside a six per cent pay increase. This was seen by some as effectively incorporating overtime into basic pay.

In essence, Smart Working allows managers to match the supply of labour more closely with current workload. In practice, managers agree output targets with employees or in some areas with self-directed work groups, for a set period of time. The thinking behind this was to move from a system which was time based to one which is performance based. The employee or work group then decide how the time resources available to them need to be used in order to achieve these targets. If in peak times employees need to work longer than their normal hours and/or needed to come in at weekends, this additional time can then be 'banked' and taken off when the workload is less high. In addition, a flexitime system was introduced which removed the traditional starting and finishing times. Symbolically, this resulted in removal of the buzzer which signified the start and end of the working day across the workplace. The flexitime system is built around core hours (11.30am to 2.30pm) when all employees are required to be at work, but outside of that employees can choose start and finish times and these can be varied according to individual employee preferences.

In order to launch this new approach to working a series of training events was set up both for managers and for employees to help them understand the working of the scheme and how it was being implemented. On the whole, employees reported that they understood the scheme and that the regulations governing how it worked were clear. There was also a general view that it had been implemented fairly. The trade unions, who were involved in negotiating the agreement, also monitored its implementation to ensure that it was being run fairly.

Smart working in practice

Flexibility over working time

Perhaps inevitably, views about how well it had worked in practice varied across the workplace. Many employees indicated that the opportunity to stagger start and finish times had been very useful to them. They welcomed the opportunity to accommodate non-work activities in their lives more easily by exercising some flexibility over working time. In essence, this type of scheme made it legitimate not to be at work outside of the core hours. In addition, the workplace was located close to a busy road network and there was often considerable congestion in the area. Having some flexibility over working time meant that employees could choose to travel at different times and avoid the stress of being stuck in traffic and not knowing whether they would make it to work on time.

Some work teams at this workplace liaised closely with their counterparts in North America and in India on a regular basis. Managers in these business areas indicated that they had encouraged employees to adopt different working times, since it meant they then had greater overlap with colleagues in different time zones – those who started earlier had a longer overlap with the working day in India and those who worked later had a greater overlap with North America. However, as a result it was acknowledged that internal meetings had to be concentrated into core hours, in order to secure maximum participation.

Nevertheless, some employees did suggest that in spite of the introduction of the new policy, many managers in the company had retained a traditional view of working time. Although in theory Smart Working made it legitimate not to be at work during traditional working hours, it was reported that some managers and co-workers, particularly those with long service records were still in a 'nine to five mindset' and had not adjusted to the new approach. This resulted in some people feeling uncomfortable if, for example, they left the workplace early. One employee reported that if he wanted to leave work early he felt more comfortable leaving at 3pm, rather than, say, 4.30pm because at 3pm many people assumed that he would be going to an off-site meeting rather than going home. This mindset of nine to five working was felt to be unattractive to younger recruits and would impact on their retention.

Some managers reported that they preferred having their employees work a regular working pattern, even if they worked at different times. As one manager explained variation in hours could make planning more difficult,

> If you come in at half eight and then you come in at half eleven the next day, you might work your hours, but for someone trying to manage the team, there is a three hour difference between the two.

Working extra time and banking hours

For some employees the Smart Working policy worked well and they were able to take TOIL at times that suited them, often for family and home related activities. However, in certain parts of the business, the greatest concern expressed by employees was the lack of opportunity to take back any additional hours they had worked, since, as they saw it, the troughs never happened. Some indicated that their contracted hours were insufficient to achieve the required workload and as a result there few opportunities for employees to take back time and attend to non-work activities. The seemingly constant number of 'rush jobs' meant that arrangements for greater flexibility could not always be honoured. In the longer term, some employees reported that this discouraged people from putting in extra hours when workload was high, since they did not see the opportunity to take the time back. Managers acknowledged that there were some employees who had a large number of banked hours.

Although described by a senior director of the company as 'delivering a better work-life balance for employees and higher productivity levels when workload drops', there was some cynicism about whether or not the scheme really contributed to work–life balance in practice.

Where employees were able to take back time it was observed that Friday was a very popular day. Several years ago working time at this site had been adjusted to allow for the working day to finish one hour earlier on Fridays. Thus, Friday was attractive, not only because it extended the weekend but also because employees needed to spend less of their banked time to take a day off. Lower staffing levels, together with people using flexitime to leave early on Fridays was seen to be problematic in those parts of the business that worked extensively with North America.

There was some debate over how working beyond normal hours was, or should be agreed. It was felt that any additional hours should be sanctioned when there was work pressure, or where it made sense to carry on working to complete a job in the working day, but not necessarily agreed when an employee just wanted the opportunity to finesse or 'gold plate' a piece of work.

There was also discussion about the detail of recording hours and how this worked in the spirit of Smart Working. In some departments there was little formal recording of hours, but rather if extra work hours were needed, then they were done, and then employees took other time away from the workplace to compensate. However, in other situations additional hours were recorded and taken back rigorously. As one employee put it, 'Every minute is recorded and every extra minute is taken off.' The general feeling was that this was not in the spirit of the policy since the six per cent pay increase linked to the implementation of Smart Working was seen to be compensation for flexibility over time. Success of implementation was seen as being largely attributable to how individual line managers worked the policy with their staff.

The introduction of Smart Working at this site had therefore met with some success, but there were some concerns over its implementation. The company was determined to build on what had been achieved, recognising the need to balance efficiency with a focus on work–life balance and employee well-being.

Questions

1 To what extent do you think employer and employee desires for flexibility can be reconciled by a scheme such as this one?
2 Are there certain circumstances that might make this more likely?
3 As a manager reviewing the introduction and implementation of this policy, what recommendations would you make to move the policy forward?

CASE STUDY 21.2

SECOND CAREERS INTERNSHIP PROGRAMME: THE TATA GROUP'S ATTEMPTS TO ENTICE PROFESSIONAL WOMEN BACK INTO EMPLOYMENT IN INDIA

CLARE KELLIHER

A major challenge facing companies in developing economies is coping with the lack of skilled staff. In rapidly developing economies, such as India, companies have an immediate need for highly qualified talent. Whilst investment in education by governments can produce a workforce with the right skills for the future, companies facing skills shortages may need to look for other ways of accessing skills. One way may be to try and attract people who are not currently in the labour force back into work. The Tata Group, one of India's largest conglomerate companies (their activities span IT, engineering, services, chemicals, energy and consumer products), has developed a scheme designed to persuade professional women to re-engage with employment following a career break, by offering an alternative to full-time, permanent employment – flexible, project-based work.

In India, although women increasingly participate in higher education and well-qualified female graduates enter employment on graduation, in the region of 40 per cent leave employment within the first 10 years, normally to take on family responsibilities. The Tata Group scheme, the Second Career Internship Programme, was launched on International Women's Day in 2008. It is set up as a career transition management programme for women professionals who have taken not more than eight years out of employment. The scheme is designed to bring professional women back into work, but on a flexible basis. The scheme engages women to work on live business projects, but they can work on a flexitime basis and some projects may also be amenable to be being done partly from home. The projects typically involve approximately 500 hours of work input over a five- to six-month period for companies in the Tata Group. Details of when and where work is done are agreed with the project lead. Participants in the scheme go through an induction programme to help them back into work and to update their skills. They are also provided with mentors for the project. This scheme is not designed to provide full-time, permanent job opportunities, but rather to provide opportunities for professional women to work in alternative ways, on a short-term, project basis. Participants may, however, subsequently explore full-time, permanent employment with the company. Approximately 30 per cent of the women who have participated in the scheme are now working for the group on a full- or part-time basis.

Sources: Tata company website http://www.tatasecondcareer.com/aboutscip.aspx.
Financial Times, 'Flexible work deals lure mothers from home to ease India's skills shortage', 27 May 2011.
The Telegraph, 'Home is where the work is', 8 March 2013.
Afternoon Despatch and Courier, 'A second chance', 7 March 2013.

Questions

1 How well do you think a scheme like this actually helps in solving problems of skills shortage for large companies like Tata? Would it work for all companies?

2 What are likely to be the important factors influencing the successful implementation of a scheme like this?

3 Are there groups, other than women, who might be attracted by a scheme like this?

CASE STUDY 21.3

LUFTHANSA: USING PART-TIME STAFF TO HELP MANAGE SEASONAL DEMAND

CLARE KELLIHER

The German airline, Lufthansa, one of Europe's largest airlines, employs some cabin crew on part-time contracts to help them deal with the seasonal nature of their business. In 2013 they launched a new scheme to hire up to 500 cabin crew on part-time contracts designed to cover the peaks in demand over the summer months more effectively.

They now offer two types of part-time contract – one which approximates to 83 per cent of full-time working and the other 50 per cent of full-time working. What is unusual about these part-time contracts is that they are part-time across the working year, rather than across a working week.

The first type, the seasonal contract, is a permanent contract of employment. However, the member of cabin crew alternates between working full-time and part-time at different times of the year. In practice, under this arrangement, the member of staff works full time from March to October and part time from December to February. The pay the employee receives, however, does not vary according to whether they are working full or part time. They are paid the same amount each month and likewise their social insurance is paid by the company throughout the year. Additional payments such as disturbance allowances, which are linked to being away, are only earned when the member of staff is actually flying. The second type of part-time contract offered for cabin crew is the 'summer-season contract' and is targeted at students and young professionals who may only want to work as cabin crew for a limited amount of time. These contracts are fixed term (18 or 24 months) which can be extended one time only for a further two years. In this case employees work half time in either three- or six-month periods, followed by either three or six months non-working time. As with the seasonal contract, they are paid throughout the year in equal instalments, whether they are working or not, but shift allowances and daily 'absence money' are only paid when working.

In both the above cases these cabin crew undergo the normal 12-week training period. Like full-time, permanent members of staff they enjoy access to other company benefits such as support for further education, reduced priced air tickets and discounts with hotels and car rental companies. Holiday entitlement and vacation bonuses are paid on a pro-rata basis.

Prior to these new arrangements being introduced, Lufthansa and their largest trade union, Unabhaengige Flugbegleiter Organisation, signed an agreement allowing different compensation models for new employees. It is also noteworthy that the use of temporary staff are capped at 15 per cent of total cabin crew numbers (in the region of 19,000).

Sources: Be-Lufthansa.com.
https://www.be-lufthansa.com/en/jobs-und-ausbildung/flight-attendant-mf/.
'Lufthansa hires temporary staff as cabin crew for new aircraft', Bloomberg Business, 4 September 2013.

Questions

1 What do you think the risks might be for Lufthansa in employing staff in this way?
2 Why do you think the new 50 per cent contracts are offered as temporary contracts with a one-time only extension?
3 Apart from these 50 per cent and 83 per cent contracts, are there other models that might be useful for businesses such as airlines which experience seasonality in their demand patterns?

Bibliography

Abraham, K.G. and Houseman, S.N. (2014) 'Short-time compensation as a tool to mitigate job loss? Evidence on the U.S. experience during the recent recession', *Industrial Relations*, Vol.53, No.4, 543–67.

Agile Future Forum (2013) 'Understanding the economic benefits of workforce agility', Agile Future Forum.

Aletraris, L. (2010) 'How satisfied are they and why? A study of job satisfaction, job rewards, gender and temporary agency workers in Australia', *Human Relations*, Vol.63, No.8, 1129–55.

Alis, D., Karsten, L. and Leopold, J. (2006) 'From Gods to Godesses', *Time and Society*, Vol.15, No.1, 81–104.

Allan, C. (1998) 'The elasticity of endurance: work intensification and workplace flexibility on the Queensland public hospital system', *Journal of Organisational Change Management*, Vol.23, No.3, 133–51.

Atkinson, J. (1985) 'Flexibility: planning for an uncertain future', *Manpower Policy and Practice*, Vol.1, 26–9.

Barley, S.R., Meyerson, D.E. and Grodal, S. (2011) 'E-mail as a source and symbol of stress', *Organization Science*, Vol.22, No.4, 887–906.

Beham, B., Baierl, A. and Poelmans, S. (2015) 'Managerial telework allowance decisions – a vignette study among German managers', *The International Journal of Human Resource Management*, Vol.26, No.11, 1385–406.

Besseyre des Horts, C.H., Dery, K. and MacCormick, J. (2012) 'Paradoxical consequences of the use of Blackberrys? An application of the Job Demand-Control-Support Model', pp. 16–29, in Kelliher, C. and Richardson, J. (eds.) *New Ways of Organizing Work: Developments, Perspectives and Experiences*, New York: Routledge.

Bloom, N. and Van Reenen, J. (2006) 'Management practices, work-life balance and productivity: a review of some recent evidence', *Oxford Review of Economic Policy*, Vol.22, 457–82.

Boxall, P. (2003) 'HR strategy and competitive advantage in the service sector', *Human Resource Management Journal*, Vol.13, No.3, 5–20.

Boxall, P. and Purcell, J. (2003) *Strategy and Human Resource Management*, Basingstoke: Palgrave Macmillan.

Bryson, C. (1999) 'Managing uncertainty or managing uncertainly?', pp. 63–88, in Leopold, J., Harris, L. and Watson, T. (eds.) *Strategic Human Resourcing*, London: Financial Times/ Pitman Publishing.

Cappelli, P. and Keller, J.R. (2013) 'Classifying work in the new economy', *Academy of Management Review*, Vol.38, No.4, 575–96.

CBI/Harvey Nash (2011) 'Navigating choppy waters: CBA/Harvey Nash employment trends survey 2011', London: CBI.

Chartered Institute of Personnel and Development (2005) 'Flexible working: impact and implementation an employer survey', London: Chartered Institute of Personnel and Development.

Chartered Institute of Personnel and Development (in association with the Agile Future Forum) (2014) *HR: Getting Smart About Agile Working*, Wimbledon, London: CIPD.

Chow, I.H. and Keng-Howe, I.C. (2006) 'The effect of alternative work schedules on employee performance', *International Journal of Employment Studies*, Vol.14, 105–30.

Coe, N.M., Johns, J.L. and Ward, K. (2007) 'Mapping the globalization of the temporary staffing industry', *Professional Geographer*, Vol.59, No.4, 503–20.

Collins, P. and Kolb, D. (2012) 'Innovation in distributed teams: the duality of connectivity norms and human agency', pp. 140–59, in Kelliher, C. and Richardson, J. (eds.) *New Ways of Organizing Work: Developments, Perspectives and Experiences*, New York: Routledge.

Countouris, N. and Freedland, M. (2013) 'Labour regulation and the economic crisis in Europe: challenges, responses and prospects', pp. 66-94, in Heyes, J. and Rychly, L. (eds.) *Labour Administration in Uncertain Times. Policy, Practice and Institutions*, Cheltenham: Edward Elgar.

Cranfield School of Management (2008) *Flexible Working and Performance: Summary of Research*, Working Families, London.

De Cuyper, N. and De Witte, H. (2008) 'Volition and reasons for accepting temporary employment: associations with attitudes, well-being, and behavioural intentions', *European Journal of Work and Organizational Psychology*, Vol.17, No.3, 363–87.

De Menezes, L. and Kelliher, C. (2011) 'Flexible working and performance: a systematic review of the evidence for a business case', *International Journal of Management Reviews*, Vol.13, No.4, 452–74.

Department for Business, Innovation and Skills, Workplace Employee Relations Survey (2011) Available at: https://discover.ukdataservice.ac.uk/catalogue/?sn=7226&type=Data%20catalogue.

Desombre, T., Kelliher, C., Macfarlane, F. and Ozbilgin, M. (2006) 'Re-organizing work roles in health care: evidence from the implementation of functional flexibility', *British Journal of Management*, Vol.17, No.2, 139–51.

Eaton, S. (2003) 'If you can use them: flexibility policies, organizational commitment and perceived performance', *Industrial Relations*, Vol.42, No.2, 145–67.

ETUI (2012) *How Has the Crisis Affected Social Legislation in Europe?* No. 2/2012, ETUI Policy Brief, ETUI, Brussels.

European Commission (2007) *Towards Common Principles of Flexicurity: More and Better Jobs Through Flexibility and Security*, Luxembourg: Office for Official Publications of the European Communities.

European Foundation for the Improvement of Living and Working Conditions (2015) *New Forms of Employment*, Luxembourg: Publications Office of the European Union.

European Foundation for the Improvement of Living and Working Conditions (2012) *Eurofound Yearbook 2011: Living and Working in Europe*, Luxembourg: European Commission.

European Foundation for the Improvement of Living and Working Conditions (2010) *European Company Survey 2009. Flexibility Profiles of EuropeanCcompanies*, Luxembourg: Publications Office of the European Union.

European Foundation for the Improvement of Living and Working Conditions (2008) 'Towards a balanced flexibility'. Available at: http://www.eurofound.europa.eu/observatories /eurwork/case-studies/attractive-workplace-for-all/falu-hospital-sweden-towards-a -balanced-flexibility.

Friedrich, A., Kabst, R., Weber, W. and Rodehuth, M. (1998) 'Functional flexibility: merely reacting or acting strategically?', *Employee Relations*, Vol.20, No.3, 504–23.

Gajendran, R.S. and Harrison, D.A. (2007) 'The good, the bad, and the unknown about telecommuting: meta-analysis of psychological mediators and individual consequences', *Journal of Applied Psychology*, Vol.92, No.6, 1524–41.

Gerdes, L. (2009) 'Bad economy hasn't changed Gen Y's desire for work/life balance'. Available at: http://www.businessweek.com/managing/blogs/first_jobs/archives/2009/09 /bad_economy_has.html.

Green, C., Kler, P. and Leeves, G. (2010) 'Flexible contract workers in inferior jobs: reappraising the evidence', *British Journal of Industrial Relations*, Vol.48, No.3, 605–29.

Harris, L. and Foster, C. (2005) *Small, Flexible and Family Friendly – Work Practices in Service Sector Businesses*, Employment Relations Research Series No.47, London: Department of Trade and Industry.

Healy, G. (2004) 'Work-life balance and family friendly policies – in whose interest?', *Work, Employment and Society*, Vol.18, No.1, 219–23.

Hooker, H., Neathey, F., Casebourne, J. and Munro, M. (2007) 'The third work-life balance employee survey: main findings', Brighton: Institute for Employment Studies.

Kahn, P. (1999) 'Gender and employment restructuring in British National Health Service manual work', *Gender, Work and Organization*, Vol.6, No.4, 202–12.

Kalleberg, A. (2001) 'Organising flexibility: the flexible firm in a new century', *British Journal of Industrial Relations*, Vol.39, No.4, 479–504.

Kalleberg, A.L. (2003) 'Flexible firm and labor market segmentation', *Work and Occupations*, Vol.30, No.2, 154–75.

Kalleberg, A.L., Reskin, B.F. and Hudson, K. (2000) 'Bad jobs in America: standard and nonstandard employment relations and job quality in the United States', *American Sociological Review*, Vol.65, 256–78.

Kelliher, C. and Anderson, D. (2010) 'Doing more with less? Flexible working practices and the intensification of work', *Human Relations*, Vol.63, No.1, 83–106.

Kelliher, C. and Desombre, T. (2005) 'Breaking down boundaries: functional flexibility and occupational identity in health care', in Zeytinoglu, I. (ed.) *Flexibility in Workplaces: Effects on Workers, Work Environments and Unions*, Geneva: IIRA/ILO.

Kelliher, C. and Gore, J. (2006) 'Functional flexibility and the intensification of work: transformation within service industries', pp. 93–102, in Askenazy, P., Cartron, D., de Connick, F. and Gollac, M. (eds.) *Organisation et Intensite du Travail* [*Organization and Work Intensity*], Toulouse: Octares.

Kelliher, C., Gore, J. and Riley, M. (2002) 'Functional flexibility: implementation and outcomes', International Industrial Relations Association Conference, 25–28 June, Toronto, Canada.

Kelliher, C. and Richardson, J. (2012) 'Recent developments in new ways of organizing work', pp. 1–15, in Kelliher, C. and Richardson, J. (eds.) *New Ways of Organizing Work: Developments, Perspectives and Experiences*, New York: Routledge.

Kelliher, C. and Riley, M. (2002) 'Making functional flexibility stick: an assessment of the outcomes for stakeholders', *International Journal of Contemporary Hospitality Management*, Vol.14, No.5, 237–42.

Kirkpatrick, I. and Hoque, K. (2006) 'A retreat from permanent employment? Accounting for the rise of professional agency work in UK public services', *Work, Employment and Society*, Vol.20, No.4, 649–66.

Korczynski, M. (2005) 'Service work and skills: an overview', *Human Resource Management*, Vol.15, No.2, 1–12.

Kossek, E. and Ruderman, M. (2012) 'Work-family flexibility and the employment relationship', pp. 223–53, in Shore, L.M., Coyle-Shapiro, J. and Tetrick, L. (eds.) *Understanding the Employee-Organization Relationship: Advances in Theory and Practice*, New York: Taylor and Francis.

Lallement, M. (2011) 'Europe and the economic crisis: forms of labour market adjustment and varieties of capitalism', *Work, Employment and Society,* Vol.25, No.4, 627–41.

Legge, K. (2007) 'Putting the missing H into HRM: the case of the flexible organisation', pp. 115–36, in Bolton, S.C. and Houlihan, M. (eds.) *Searching for the Human in Human Resource Management*, Basingstoke: Palgrave Macmillan.

Lewis, S. and Smithson, J. (2001) 'Sense of entitlement to support for the reconciliation of employment and family life', *Human Relations*, Vol.55, No.11, 1455–81.

Loretto, W. and Vickerstaff, S. (2015) 'Gender, age and flexible working in later life', *Work, Employment and Society*, Vol.29, No.2, 233–49.

Lopez-Cabrales, A., Valle, R. and Galan, J. (2011) 'Employment relationships as drivers of firm flexibility and learning', *Personnel Review*, Vol.40, No.5, 625–43.

MacDuffie, J.P. (2007) 'HRM and distributed work', *The Academy of Management Annals*, Vol.1, 549–615.

Mann, S., Varey, R. and Button, W. (2000) 'An exploration of the emotional impact of tele-working via computer-mediated communication', *Journal of Managerial Psychology*, Vol.15, Nos.7–8, 668–91.

Marquardt, M. (2005) 'Globalisation: the pathway to prosperity, freedom and peace', *Human Resource Development International*, Vol.8, No.1, 127–9.

Matusik, S.F. and Mickel, A.E. (2011) 'Embracing or embattled by converged mobile devices? Users' experiences with a contemporary connectivity technology', *Human Relations*, Vol.68, No.8, 1001–30.

Mauno, S., Kinnunen, U., Makikangas, A. and Natti, J. (2005) 'Psychological consequences of fixed-term employment and perceived job insecurity among health care staff', *European Journal of Work and Organizational Psychology*, Vol.14, No.3, 209–37.

Olsen, K. and Kalleberg, A. (2004) 'Nonstandard work in two different employment regimes: the United States and Norway', *Work, Employment and Society*, Vol.18, No.2, 321–48.

Paauwe, J. (2004) *HRM and Performance: Unique Approaches for Achieving Long-Term Viability*, Oxford: Oxford University Press.

Packendorff, J. (2002) 'The temporary society and its enemies: projects from an individual perspective', pp. 39–58, in Sahlin-Andersson, K. and Soderholm, A. (eds.) *Beyond Project Management: New Perspectives on the Temporary-Permanent Dilemma*, Malmo: Liber.

Perlow, L.A. (2012) *Sleeping With Your Smartphone: How to Break the 24/7 Habit and Change the Way You Work*, Boston: Harvard Business Review Press.

Peters, P., Den Dulk, L. and Van Der Lippe, T. (2009) 'The effects of time-spatial flexibility and new working conditions on employees' work-life balance: the Dutch case', *Community, Work and Family*, Vol.12, No.3, 279–98.

Rau, B.L. and Hyland, M.A. (2002) 'Role conflict and flexible work arrangements: the effects on applicant attraction', *Personnel Psychology*, Vol.55, No.1, 111–36.

Redman, T., Snape, E. and Ashurst, C. (2009) 'Location, location, location: does place of work really matter?', *British Journal of Management*, Vol.20, No.S1, 171–81.

Richardson, J. (2010) 'Managing flexworks: holding on and letting go', *Journal of Management Development*, Vol.29, No.2, 137–47.

Robinson, A.M. and Smallman, C. (2006) 'The contemporary British workplace: a safer and healthier place?', *Work, Employment and Society*, Vol.20, No.1, 87–107.

TATA. Available at: www.tatasecondcareer.com.

Tietze, S. and Musson, G. (2005) 'Recasting the home-work relationship: a case of mutual adjustment', *Organization Studies*, Vol.26, No.9, 1331–52.

Van der Velde, M. and van den Berg, P. (2003) 'Managing functional flexible in a passenger transport firm', *Human Resource Management Journal*, Vol.13, No.4, 45–55.

Van Dyne, L., Kossek, E. and Lobel, S. (2007) 'Less need to be there: cross-level effects of work practices that support work-life flexibility and enhance group processes and group-level OCB', *Human Relations*, Vol.60, No.8, 1123–53.

Whitley, R., Morgan, E. and Moen, E. (2005) *Changing Capitalisms? Internationalisation, Institutional Change and Systems of Economic Organization*, Oxford: Oxford University Press.

Whyman, P.B., Baimbridge, M.J., Buraimo, B.A. and Petrescu, A.I. (2015) 'Workplace flexibility practices and corporate performance: evidence from the British private sector', *British Journal of Management*, Vol.26, No.3, 347–64.

Yanadori, Y. and Kato, T. (2009) 'Work and family practices in Japanese firms: their scope, nature and impact on employee turnover', *The International Journal of Human Resource Management*, Vol.20, No.2, 439–56.

Zammuto, R.F., Griffith, T.L., Majchrzak, A., Dougherty, D.J. and Faraj, S. (2007) 'Information technology and the changing fabric of organization', *Organization Science*, Vol.18, No.5, 749–62.

Zeytinoglu, I., Cooke, G. and Mann, S. (2009) 'Flexibility: whose choice is it anyway?', *Industrial Relations*, Vol.64, No.6, 555–74.

CHAPTER 22

WORKPLACE BULLYING

Sara Branch, Sheryl Ramsay and Michelle Barker

Introduction

As a complex and costly phenomenon, workplace bullying presents significant challenges to the development and maintenance of vital, diverse and productive workplaces. Ongoing theoretical development and empirical research are important for improving the conceptual clarity of workplace bullying, identifying its processes and behaviours, reducing its many negative facets and developing effective prevention strategies. This chapter offers a comprehensive insight into these areas.

Research consistently shows workplace bullying to be a significant issue for organisations particularly because of its relatively high rate of occurrence (see Branch et al., 2013). In the management field, workplace bullying has been presented as an 'alarming issue' (De Cieri and Kramar, 2008: 625) that requires comprehensive understanding and management if the costs to individuals and organisations are to be alleviated. These costs include the significant emotional impacts on people and the associated economic losses that mount up (Einarsen et al., 2011b; McCarthy and Mayhew, 2004). This chapter aims first to present a conceptual overview of workplace bullying, including its associated behaviours, impacts, risks and antecedents, and second, to discuss prevention and management strategies of relevance to the field of management. It includes examples of research findings to help explain particular aspects of workplace bullying and to demonstrate the type of research being conducted in the area.

Research into workplace bullying began in the late 1970s, largely growing out of Scandinavian investigations into schoolyard bullying (e.g. Olweus, 1978). Indeed, links between schoolyard and workplace bullying are evident. For instance, a study of 5,288 adults in Great Britain found that children who had been targets or perpetrators of schoolyard bullying were more likely to be targets of workplace bullying (Smith et al., 2003). Moreover, the nature of bullying is similar across school and work. For instance, verbal abuse and harassment represent the most common types of schoolyard bullying, followed by exclusion and social manipulation (Rigby, 2001), which is similar to the type and pattern of bullying behaviours identified in workplace research (Einarsen et al., 2011a; Keashly and Harvey, 2005; O'Moore et al., 1998). However, the formal power of the bully presents an important difference between schoolyard and workplace bullying because 'children are bullied for the most part by peers who have no formal organisational power over them, whereas adults are ... likely to be bullied by managers and supervisors [and] others who are lacking such authority' (Rigby, 2001: 5). Interestingly, recent research into upwards bullying (i.e. a staff member bullying a supervisor or manager) supports the notion that those who lack formal sources of power within the workplace can bully individuals in positions of authority through various means, such as strengthening informal power bases (Branch *et al.*, 2007a, b).

A complication arises because throughout the world a range of terms are often used interchangeably to refer to negative social behaviours at work (including mobbing, workplace aggression, workplace incivility, workplace harassment, workplace deviance, social undermining, emotional abuse and abusive supervision) (Einarsen *et al.*, 2011a; Zapf, 2004), as highlighted in the poster from mobbing.ca (see Figure 22.1). Workplace bullying has been described as an 'umbrella' term as it can incorporate harassing, intimidating and aggressive or violent behaviours (Branch, 2008; Fox and Stallworth, 2005). The term 'mobbing', introduced by the late Heinz Leymann (1990) to reflect the group-based and cumulative nature of negative impacts towards the target, is commonly used interchangeably with workplace bullying, particularly within Scandinavian countries (Einarsen, 2000). Others differentiate between the terms (e.g. Shallcross *et al.*, 2011; 2013) by highlighting that the mobbing process encompasses the inter-relationships of perpetrators' actions and the resultant exclusion of the target from the workplace. In the US, researchers often incorporate bullying behaviours in the term 'emotional abuse' (Keashly and Jagatic, 2011), which is usually characterised as a persistent and enduring form of 'workplace aggression' (Baron and Neuman, 1996, 1998; Keashly and Jagatic, 2011). Researchers within Australia and Great Britain (including Branch, 2008; Hoel and Cooper, 2001; Rayner, 2007) tend to use the term 'workplace bullying', which is used throughout this chapter.

Figure 22.1 Poster highlighting the issue of workplace bullying

Source: mobbing.ca – http://www.mobbing.ca. Acknowledgements: Bobbie Osborne (Photographer) and Anton Hout (Designer).

How is workplace bullying defined?

Despite increased research focus on workplace bullying in recent decades, considerable confusion exists as to what it actually is and how it differs from, or is similar to, other forms of counter-productive work behaviours, such as harassment (see Figure 22.1). Especially given the range of terms in use, and the complex nature of workplace bullying, debate over the definition continues (Saunders *et al.*, 2007). However, agreement generally exists about the inclusion of, and importance placed upon, several of its characteristics (Branch, 2008; Nielsen *et al.*, 2008).

First, workplace bullying behaviours are often defined as *inappropriate* or *unreasonable behaviours* (Einarsen and Raknes, 1997; Einarsen *et al.*, 2011a; Hoel and Cooper, 2001; Saunders *et al.*, 2007). Examples of such behaviours include ridiculing people, keeping a constant eye on another's work, unreasonably questioning another's professional ability, spreading damaging rumours and explosive outbursts and threats (Rayner and Hoel, 1997; Zapf and Einarsen, 2001). However, because of different patterns and intensities of behaviours, as well as contextual factors, consistent agreement as to what exactly represents a bullying behaviour has proven difficult (Rayner, 1997). A further complicating factor is that a person's 'subjective perception of being bullied' can vary markedly from one target (as well as a perpetrator and witness) to another (Agervold, 2007: 163). The difficulty of identifying the true nature of workplace bullying behaviours will be discussed later in this chapter.

Second, definitions of workplace bullying emphasise that inappropriate *behaviours occur persistently or regularly over a period of time* (Einarsen *et al.*, 2011a; Keashly and Jagatic, 2011), which essentially excludes 'one-off' incidents or periods of short duration. According to Hoel and Cooper (2001: 4), 'the long-term nature of the phenomenon is one of the most salient features of the problem', with researchers often using a duration of six months as a guide. Furthermore, some researchers have explained workplace bullying as a form of conflict escalation in which the intensity of the attacks increase over time, with increasingly negative effects on the target (Einarsen and Skogstad, 1996; Keashly and Jagatic, 2011; Zapf and Gross, 2001). An important variation to the idea of persistent and possibly escalating behaviour is the notion of 'ongoing threat' (Zapf, 2004). For example, one verbal attack on someone may induce a long-lasting fear that it could re-occur. This variation is still open to debate.

Third, the existence of a *power imbalance* between the two parties (Keashly and Jagatic, 2011) is often regarded as an essential definitional component. However, power is complex and, while it can be formally derived (e.g. role differences of manager and employee), power can also be informal and subtle. Commonly, a prime reason cited for a power imbalance developing is the target's dependency on the perpetrator, which reduces self-defence capacities of targets. For example, workplace bullying can relate to misuse of formal, hierarchical power and/or informal power, such as access to information, influence or specific expertise. Notably, the process of being bullied can reduce a person's capacity to respond effectively, suggesting the power imbalance can develop over time.

In summary, the important defining and agreed upon characteristics of workplace bullying are the persistent use of inappropriate behaviours, coupled with the inability of targets to adequately defend themselves because of a power imbalance (Einarsen *et al.*, 2011a). Elements of these characteristics can be seen in the following widely accepted academic and practical definitions.

Example of an academic definition of workplace bullying

Bullying at work means harassing, offending, socially excluding someone or negatively affecting someone's work tasks. In order for the label bullying (or mobbing) to be applied to a particular activity, interaction, or process, it has to occur repeatedly and regularly (e.g. weekly) and over a period of time (e.g. about six months). Bullying is an escalating process in the course of which the person confronted ends up in an inferior position and becomes the target of systematic negative social acts. A conflict cannot be called bullying if the incident is an isolated event or if two parties of approximately equal 'strength' are in conflict.
(Einarsen et al., 2011a: 22)

Example of a practical definition of workplace bullying

Workplace bullying is: Persistent, unacceptable 'offensive, intimidating, malicious, insulting or humiliating behaviour, abuse of power or authority which attempts to undermine an individual or group of employees and which may cause them to suffer stress'. (*UNISON, 2003*)

However, notably, the general public may reflect somewhat different perspectives (Rayner *et al.*, 2002). For example, one study that examined individual perceptions of workplace bullying found that 14.7 per cent of 1,095 laypersons identified the repeated nature of inappropriate behaviour as part of the definition, contrasting with academic definitions that portray this as a central element (Saunders *et al.*, 2007). Rather, respondents commonly identified concepts such as fairness and respect, which is of course also a legitimate perspective.

You might like to explore the workplace bullying definition used by the university at which you are studying or organisation in which you are working. Consider how their definition of workplace bullying is similar or different to the definitions provided here, and what elements are included in the definition.

The importance of power and dependency in workplace bullying

Power and its use constitutes a central concept when discussing relationships in organisations, and is especially relevant to any discussion of workplace bullying (Branch *et al.*, 2007b; Hoel and Salin, 2003; Salin and Hoel, 2011). As identified previously, power imbalances can include the relative defencelessness of targets (Keashly and Jagatic, 2011). The concept of *dependency* is closely related to power. Importantly, the target's dependency on the perpetrator produces the power imbalance necessary for bullying to occur (Branch *et al.*, 2007b; Einarsen *et al.*, 2011a; Keashly and Jagatic, 2011). Despite dependency (and power) occurring in multiple directions (up, down and horizontally), research initially focused on 'top-down' bullying, often linked to organisational structures and the misuse of authority or formal power (Roscigno *et al.*, 2009: 1562). We now know that bullying is a far more complex interaction of formal and informal sources of power (Branch *et al.*, 2007b), as well as organisational and social structures (Hutchinson *et al.*, 2006). For example, Shallcross *et al.*'s (2010) qualitative study identified inappropriate behaviours such as gossip, rumours and false accusations of bullying that had the effect of publicly humiliating targets. The authors concluded that 'informal sources of power are not to be underestimated in their capacity to deliberately perpetrate bullying' (Shallcross *et al.*, 2010: 29). Moreover, Branch *et al.* (2007a: 275) found that a 'lack of a legitimizing agent from the organization during change may result in staff perceiving the manager as lacking legitimate power', which may lead to the manager being vulnerable to upwards bullying. As a result, workplace bullying should no longer be considered an interpersonal conflict, but rather a complex organisational phenomenon that includes the use of informal sources of power.

Vulnerability to workplace bullying has also been linked to the characteristics of individuals or marginalised groups within society and workplaces (Ramsay *et al.*, 2010). Einarsen and his colleagues (2011a), for example, suggest that being a member of a group that is considered to be outside the accepted dominant culture may be the only reason some people are bullied. Indeed, Zapf (1999) proposed that some group processes (e.g. scapegoating) are also related to workplace bullying. Ramsay and her colleagues (2010) expanded on this perspective using social identity theory (Tajfel and Turner, 1986) and social rules theory (Argyle *et al.*, 1985). The authors proposed that 'groups with negative social rules based on aggressive or anti-social behaviour (Gini, 2006) are more likely to promote and condone bullying within the group, particularly if it has a strong identity' (Ramsay *et al.*, 2010: 10). Group characteristics such as ethnicity (Fox and Stallworth, 2005), gender (Djurkovic *et al.*, 2004) and age (Zapf, 1999, cited in Zapf and Einarsen, 2011) have been found to be related to workplace bullying.

Identifying workplace bullying behaviours

While a number of specific behaviours that may contribute to workplace bullying have been identified, there are several complicating factors to consider. For example, in terms of the particular work environment and roles, Djurkovic *et al.*'s (2004) study of 150 undergraduate students found the most commonly experienced bullying behaviours to be unjustified criticism, monitoring of performance, unfair pressure and comments or sarcasm; compared with isolating the target, obstructing their work and blocking career advancement, which Pietersen (2007) identified among staff of an academic institution. There is also an indication that in managerial ranks, where greater competition and significant work pressures prevail (Salin, 2001), work-related bullying behaviours (e.g. withholding of information) are more common than non-work related behaviours (e.g. insulting remarks). Labelling bullying behaviours can also be problematic because, although some are observable (such as irrational outbursts towards others), others can be more covert and difficult to observe (e.g. gossip). Furthermore, despite the common assumption that bullying is physical in nature, it tends to be psychologically based. For instance, in a classic study of 460 male shipyard workers in Norway, threats of physical abuse and actual physical abuse were rarely reported (2.4 per cent), compared to the more covert behaviours of withdrawal of information (51.7 per cent) and dismissing a person's opinion (53.6 per cent) (Einarsen and Raknes, 1997). Moreover, workplace bullying is not only about what someone does to another, but can also include what is not done (Rayner *et al.*, 2002), for example the withholding of important information, or excluding the target from a relevant or significant work-related event (Einarsen and Raknes, 1997). As a result, workplace bullying behaviours are not always easy to recognise or identify, especially when individual behaviours are integrated within a pattern of behaviours and particular work environments.

Furthermore, identifying bullying behaviours is also complicated by the fact that perceptions by individuals can differ. For example, recipients of workplace bullying may not label it as such (Hadikin and O'Driscoll, 2000). The lack of recognition of particular behaviours as bullying may be the result of such behaviours becoming normalised in some workplaces (Hadikin and O'Driscoll, 2000; Rayner, 1997; 1999), as found by Lewis (2004) in his interview study within the UK higher education context where bullying appeared to have become an expected behavioural norm. From another perspective, Branch and Murray (2015) explored the perceptions of a wide range of bullying behaviours with a sample of 1,014 respondents. Respondents were classified as either a *target* or a *non-target* of workplace bullying. Those classified as *non-targets* identified overt and aggressive actions as the most severe behaviours (e.g. threats of violence or actual physical abuse), while *targets* reported the most severe behaviours as those that prevented them from performing their work (e.g. withholding information). Interestingly, the worst behaviour identified by *non-targets* (i.e. threats of violence or actual physical abuse) was perceived to be only moderately severe, which was lower than any rating provided by *targets* for any behaviour. Importantly, *non-target* managers rated bullying behaviours as the least severe overall, which has significant ramifications for prevention and management interventions, as managers are often responsible for implementing such programmes.

Additionally, given advances in technology, researchers and practitioners alike have turned their attention to cyberbullying, which is defined as 'an aggressive intentional act carried out by a group or individual, using electronic forms of contact, repeatedly and over time against a victim who cannot easily defend him or herself' (Smith *et al.*, 2008: 376). Thus definitions of cyberbullying also identify the repeated and enduring nature of workplace bullying as well as a power imbalance. Furthermore, cyberbullying tactics, such as unwanted e-mails, text messages, phone calls, videos or pictures and threats (Grigg, 2012), are similar to traditional bullying tactics although they are sent using online or mobile technology. Most of the research surrounding cyberbullying has focused on children or youth within contexts like schools. In comparison, there have been relatively few studies researching cyberbullying in the workplace. In one study in Australia, 10.7 per cent of respondents had experienced cyberbullying at work, with many of these targets also experiencing face-to-face bullying (Privitera and Campbell, 2009). Interestingly, a recent study that investigated perceptions of bullying of 156 students (aged between 10 and 17 years; 117 female, 45 male), found that face-to-face (traditional) bullying was considered more hurtful than cyberbullying (Corby *et al.*, 2015). It is expected that cyberbullying will require ongoing examination for some time to come.

Prevalence of workplace bullying behaviours and risk groups

Research indicates between 10 to 15 per cent of people are exposed to persistent inappropriate behaviours in the workplace (Zapf *et al.*, 2011). However, statistics on the frequency of workplace bullying can vary quite dramatically because of the various approaches to measuring it. To demonstrate, Mikkelsen and Einarsen (2001) found bullying occurred between 2.7 per cent to 8 per cent. This may be due possibly to their use of a strict criterion of experiencing two inappropriate behaviours per week during a six-month period. They also found 17.7 per cent of respondents stated they had witnessed bullying behaviours within the workplace. The authors concluded that the higher rates of witnessing may indicate that 'the real prevalence of bullying is higher than shown by the data' (Mikkelsen and Einarsen, 2001: 404).

> You might like to consider if a strict criterion of experiencing two bullying behaviours per week for six months is a practical criterion for organisations to adopt? What criterion applies in your organisation?

While workplace bullying can be found in most organisations (Lewis and Gunn, 2007), research suggests that particular individuals, groups and industries may be especially vulnerable. Zapf and Einarsen (2005) suggest most studies indicate that, of those targeted, the majority are women. For example, Lewis and Gunn (2007) found that women in the public sector (24 per cent) were bullied more than men (17 per cent). In addition, they found a higher occurrence of workplace bullying amongst non-white groups in the public sector in South Wales. Indeed, 35 per cent of non-white respondents indicated an experience of workplace bullying, compared with only nine per cent of white respondents (Lewis and Gunn, 2007). This research may reflect the group processes introduced earlier.

The effect of workplace bullying on targets

For targets of workplace bullying, the effect on their health can range from physical harm through to an increase in psychological stress (Hogh *et al.*, 2011). In a study that demonstrates the severe impact that workplace bullying can have on an individual, Mikkelsen and Einarsen (2002: 98) found that 80.5 per cent of participants reported 'no other event in their life affected them more negatively than the bullying'. This was despite the reporting of experiences such as accidents, divorce, bereavement and serious illness. Indeed, for the individual experiencing workplace bullying, the impacts can be so pervasive they may negatively affect not only their ability to function at work but other areas of life as well (Keashly and Harvey, 2006).

Examples of the wide-ranging effect workplace bullying can have on a person's life is demonstrated in its links to the occurrence of stress-related symptoms (Mikkelsen and Einarsen, 2001), depression (Niedhammer *et al.*, 2006) and post-traumatic stress disorder (PTSD) (Matthiesen and Einarsen, 2004; Mikkelsen and Einarsen, 2002). For instance, researchers have found that as exposure to bullying increases so too does the risk of depressive symptoms (Niedhammer *et al.*, 2006). Of further concern, researchers found that 76 per cent of 118 targets of workplace bullying displayed PTSD symptoms, with 29 per cent fulfilling the full diagnostic criteria of PTSD (Mikkelsen and Einarsen, 2002). Workplace bullying has also been associated with other psychological symptoms such as a higher risk of suicide attempts (O'Moore *et al.*, 1998), clinical levels of anxiety (Quine, 1999), and the long-term health risks of increased stress-related behaviours such as smoking, drinking and excessive eating (Quine, 1999). Thus bullying in the workplace can have severe and enduring physical and psychological health consequences for those who experience it.

The effect of workplace bullying on witnesses

The complexity of workplace bullying is also reflected in the web of those drawn into incidents of bullying. In a British study of 761 public sector trade union members, 73 per cent of witnesses of workplace bullying reported an increase in their stress levels, and 44 per cent of respondents were concerned about becoming the next target (Rayner, 1999). Indeed, those who witness workplace bullying and violence can be affected almost as severely as the actual target, which has vital implications for the loyalty of staff and productivity of organisations (Mayhew *et al.*, 2004). Understandably, such a *climate of fear* (Rayner, 1999) could flow on to an increase in absenteeism (Kivimaki *et al.*, 2000), which could place additional work demands on those who remain. Lowered work morale, increases in workplace conflict and stress generated as a direct consequence of workplace bullying, are also seen as affecting others' well-being through the creation of an abusive work environment and culture (Hoel *et al.*, 2011; Hogh *et al.*, 2011; Parzefall and Salin, 2010). Thus workplace bullying can have direct and indirect effects on targets and witnesses, as well as others who experience the workplace climate more generally.

You might like to think of how you would react if you witnessed a colleague of yours being bullied – keeping in mind the climate of fear that can be created when bullying occurs. What action (if any) do you think you would take? What avenues of support are there in your organisation for witnesses of bullying?

The effect of workplace bullying on the organisation

As would be expected, when the physical and psychological health effects begin to be felt by targets and witnesses of workplace bullying, an individual's ability to function at work will also be affected (Bowling and Beehr, 2006). In general, bullying can affect an organisation through loss of productivity, an increase in absenteeism and intention to leave, as well as the cost of intervention programmes (Einarsen, 2000; Hoel *et al.*, 2011; McCarthy and Barker, 2000). For instance, a classic questionnaire study of 1,100 employees of a National Health Service Community Trust in the UK revealed that targets of workplace bullying not only had higher levels of job-induced stress, including higher levels of depression and anxiety, but also had lower levels of job satisfaction, and higher intention to leave than other workers

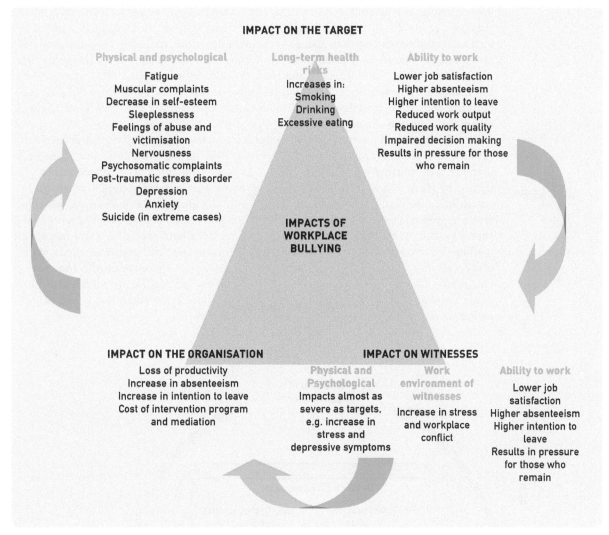

Figure 22.2 The impacts of workplace bullying

(Quine, 1999). In terms of absenteeism, Kivimaki *et al.*'s (2000) study of 5,655 hospital employees found a link between workplace bullying and an increase in sick leave. As well as the direct costs to the hospital, the financial impacts of lower motivation, impaired patient care, and the potential of staff leaving the workplace show the ongoing negative impacts of workplace bullying (Kivimaki *et al.*, 2000). Indeed, the cost of workplace bullying to organisations is staggering. Kivimaki *et al.*, (2000) estimated that absenteeism because of bullying was costing the two hospitals that participated in the study £125,000 a year (see Hoel *et al.*, 2011 for a summary of the financial costs of workplace bullying). In conclusion, workplace bullying can have severe negative impacts on targets, witnesses and the organisation as a whole, as summarised in Figure 22.2.

Antecedents of workplace bullying

In an attempt to examine how the effects of workplace bullying could be reduced for individuals and organisations, researchers have explored its antecedents. Research has examined individual factors, such as personality traits of the target or the bully (Coyne *et al.*,

2000; Douglas and Martinko, 2001; Zapf, 1999), and bullying as an interpersonal conflict (Einarsen *et al.*, 2011a). In addition, others have emphasised that bullying is a multifaceted and complex phenomenon and, as such, multiple causes, including organisational and group-related factors, need to be considered along with individual factors (Branch *et al.*, 2013; Harvey *et al.*, 2006; Heames and Harvey, 2006; Salin and Hoel, 2011; Zapf, 1999). For instance, Salin and Hoel (2011) suggest that because of the complexity of workplace bullying, the actions and reactions of the target and perpetrator can only be understood within the context in which they occur.

In a further demonstration of the complexity of workplace bullying, Harvey *et al.* (2006) note the characteristics of the perpetrator, target and environment interact together in supporting workplace bullying processes. This interplay of elements is highlighted by Heames and Harvey (2006) who propose a cross-level approach where bullying stretches beyond the perpetrator and target to the group and organisation, which in turn can provide feedback to the actors that could potentially perpetuate or, alternatively (but less likely), halt the behaviour. Thus interactions between bullies and targets as well as the environment are all involved in the occurrence and continuation of workplace bullying. Recently, Branch and her colleagues (2013) introduced a framework (see Figure 22.3) that highlights the interactive and cyclical nature of individual, group, organisational and societal factors that can all contribute to the antecedents (and continuation) of workplace bullying.

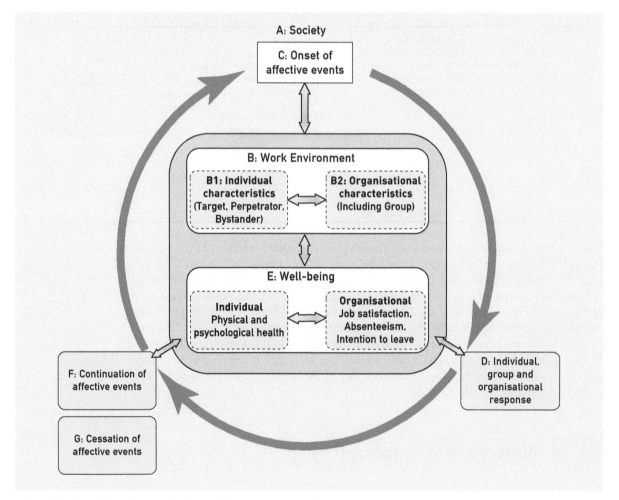

Figure 22.3 Cyclical framework of workplace bullying

Source: Branch *et al.*, 2013.

Individual level

In the main, researchers have conceptualised and investigated workplace bullying as an individual phenomenon, through research into the personality of targets and perpetrators or as an interpersonal phenomenon (Einarsen *et al.*, 2011a). For instance, an Irish study found targets of workplace bullying were identified by the researchers as introverted, conscientious, neurotic and submissive (Coyne *et al.*, 2000). Caution must be taken, however, when considering results that indicate targets of workplace bullying have particular personality traits or characteristics (Rayner *et al.*, 2002). Some researchers argue that results that identify personality traits could actually be describing profiles that have occurred as a consequence of the bullying process (see Quine, 1999). Indeed, in a recent study, Nielsen and Knardahl (2015: 128) concluded 'that personality traits may function as both predictors and outcomes of workplace bullying'. Others have warned that researching the target's personality may be perceived as 'blaming the victim', rather than reflecting a more balanced approach to understanding the circumstances of the situation (Zapf and Einarsen, 2011). Interestingly, Lind *et al.* (2009: 231) concluded that differences in personality were too small to 'differentiate targets of workplace bullying from nontargets', thus supporting the view that additional factors are at play. However, Keashly and Harvey (2006) suggest that because conflicts such as workplace bullying can relate to a hostile relationship between target and perpetrator, exploring individual factors, including characteristics of the target, is a valid approach.

The personality of the perpetrator has also been investigated, although much less so, due mainly to the reluctance of perpetrators to come forward (see Zapf and Einarsen, 2011 for summary). Despite research into the personality of workplace bullying targets and perpetrators, Rayner and her colleagues (2002) suggest that using personality screening would not be useful in identifying potential targets and bullies as there is lack of clarity about whether personality features are a cause or effect of bullying. Also, bullying is associated with a complex array of factors well beyond personality alone. Thus while personality tests may be seen as an 'easy fix', in essence this can do little to address or manage the phenomenon.

Interactions between bullies and targets

Research suggests that the reactions of targets may also play a part in the occurrence of workplace bullying (Keashly and Harvey, 2006). For instance, Zapf and Gross (2001) argue that the response of targets may further escalate the conflict with the perpetrator(s). They found that targets who successfully coped with workplace bullying were more able to recognise and avoid escalating behaviour by using less directly active strategies to defuse the situation (Zapf and Gross, 2001). Moreover, Tehrani (2011: 280) suggests that the target–perpetrator relationship is not always straightforward, and that instead, an accusation of bullying is often 'triggered by the individual's responses to a series of interactions that are built up over a period of time'. In fact, Tehrani (2003) proposes that during times of high stress and when a relationship is perceived as negative, what may otherwise be considered a minor issue (e.g. not saying hello) may be interpreted as an aggressive act. Furthermore, it has been proposed that 'prolonged exposure to abuse' may result 'in the target behaving in a hostile and aggressive manner' (Keashly and Harvey, 2006: 98).

Group and environmental level

There have also been calls for researchers to move beyond the individual and dyadic levels of analysis to consider group factors (previously discussed) and organisational factors in workplace bullying (Einarsen *et al.*, 2011a; Liefooghe and Davey, 2001;

Table 22.1 Organisational factors likely to be related to an increase in workplace bullying

Rate of change resulting in a high levels of uncertainty in the workplace

Lack of time to achieve tasks

Growing rate of diversity in the workplace

Downsizing/rightsizing resulting in concern for future longevity of survivors

Reduction of middle management resulting in an increased gap between management and workers

Lack of clearly outlined cultural norms within today's organisations

Source: Harvey *et al.*, 2006: 4.

Ramsay *et al.*, 2010; Rayner *et al.*, 2002; Samnani and Singh, 2015). Organisational factors, such as destructive and laissez-faire leadership, a negative social environment, poor job design, job insecurity, organisational change resulting in role conflict and job insecurity, high workloads, workgroup disharmony and acceptance of inappropriate behaviours (as norms) have been associated with the occurrence of workplace bullying (see Hoel *et al.*, 2011). For instance, Astrauskaitė's (2014: 31) study of a Lithuanian sample found that workplace bullying was related to 'more challenges when dealing with changes, higher pace and amount of work, more ambiguities at work, less independence in work and less transformational leadership style'. Importantly, the author found that 23 per cent of variance was explained by organisational factors, while individual factors explained 12 per cent. In addition to these factors, Harvey *et al.* (2006) proposed a number of environmental factors that appear to be increasingly linked to workplace bullying (see Table 22.1).

Importantly, it has been suggested that in a work environment of 'continuous change the potential for employees to project their fears and resentments into the construction of managers as bullies, whether deservedly or not, is high' (McCarthy *et al.*, 2002: 536). In other words, a 'victim-mentality' environment can be created (McCarthy, 1999). Interestingly, it has even been proposed that staff may actually be using the term bullying as a way of voicing their dissatisfaction with organisational issues (Liefooghe and Davey, 2001). Similarly, McCarthy (2004: xv) suggests the term '"bullying at work" has become a new signifier of distress that has acted as a solar collector of resentments'. With a complex array of factors contributing to the development and perpetuation of workplace bullying, prevention and reduction of its occurrence is clearly needed.

Prevention and management of workplace bullying

As noted by De Cieri and Kramar (2008), it is vital that the field of management comprehends and strives to address the very serious issues related to bullying in the workplace. Solutions, however, are not easy to identify. Given the complex and multidimensional nature of workplace bullying, no single approach is likely to provide organisations with the answer to solving the problem. As such, a number of researchers and practitioners have suggested a range of interrelated responses to prevent and manage bullying in the workplace. McCarthy and his colleagues (2002: 528) suggested that any effective response to workplace bullying needs to include 'prevention, redress/resolution and support'. However, until recently the effectiveness of proposed interventions to address workplace bullying has been under-researched (Saam, 2010). This may be because of a lack of a suitable theoretical model explaining workplace bullying (Einarsen, 2000) or the complexity of the phenomenon. Nonetheless, the lack of research into this area means that relatively little is known about the success of proposed interventions. With this limitation in mind, the following section will now expand upon the framework proposed by McCarthy and colleagues (2002).

Prevention

Policy

Typical methods of preventing workplace bullying include a clearly articulated 'no bullying' policy, training which includes information about responsibilities and obligations of employers and employees alike, as well as an effective risk identification and system for complaints (McCarthy *et al.*, 2002; Vartia and Leka, 2011; Vartia *et al.*, 2003). Salin's (2008) research with HR practitioners indicates their support for the incorporation of formal anti-bullying policies. However, later research by Salin (2009) suggests that the existence of formal anti-bullying policies neither increased nor decreased the reported likelihood of personnel managers taking action to address workplace bullying (i.e. reconciliation, transfer or punitive measures). Further research into this area is needed to clarify the efficacy of policies in either preventing or facilitating the management of workplace bullying.

Training and development

As suggested by McCarthy *et al.* (2002), a training programme that includes information on the responsibilities and obligations of employers and employees is one measure to prevent workplace bullying (see example in Figure 22.4). Awareness-raising about

Figure 22.4 Workplace intervention poster

its characteristics and impacts as well as what interventions can occur, are vital steps in preventing workplace bullying and should take place throughout the whole organisation (McCarthy *et al.*, 2002). Awareness training should outline the importance of clear objectives, roles and processes within the workplace, as well as the causes, impacts and handling of bullying in the workplace (Vartia *et al.*, 2003), including practical training for managers on how to deal with cases of bullying (McCarthy *et al.*, 2002; Richards and Daley, 2003; Vartia and Leka, 2011). The importance of consistent and clear training and the development of appropriate approaches across an organisation are also highlighted by Woodrow and Guest's (2014) case study research. They caution that, even when suitable policies exist, managers can be perceived by employees as lacking in skills, motivation and time for effective implementation of approaches, and managers themselves can experience uncertainty when advice from more senior staff appears to conflict with formal policies (Woodrow and Guest, 2014).

Furthermore, given the consistent research findings that link certain leadership styles (including autocratic and laissez-faire) with workplace bullying (Hoel *et al.*, 2010), it is very important to implement leadership training and development programmes. Such programmes need to include active learning in areas such as communication, team skills and the complexities of workplace bullying (Lutgen-Sandvik and Tracy, 2012). Upskilling in these areas should have a 'ripple effect' into building a positive culture that can inhibit the development of workplace bullying. This perspective is supported by Escartín *et al.*'s (2013) group-level case study research, which indicates that positive group norms (that are endorsed and enforced by leaders and managers) reduce the likelihood of workplace bullying occurring.

Developing workforce capacity and skills

Building capacity and skills based on accurate information is also suggested as essential in assisting targets and witnesses to handle workplace bullying experiences (McCarthy *et al.*, 2002; Bartlett and Bartlett, 2011; Branch *et al.*, 2012). In an early study, McCarthy *et al.* (1995) found that training in interpersonal skills, conflict resolution and stress management assisted targets of workplace bullying to manage the behaviours of perpetrators more effectively. In support of this approach, Keashly and Neuman (2009) designed an intervention that emphasised the modelling of collaborative and respectful communication in order to improve communication skills and workplace norms and reduce the occurrence of inappropriate behaviour. Vartia and Leka (2011) suggest this type of training can be directed to all members of the organisation or targeted towards managers. Bystander training is also another approach being taken (see Mentors in Violence Program; Katz, 1995). Furthermore, the importance of emotional skills training relates to findings that the emotional reactions of targets can partly mediate the relationship between workplace bullying and job satisfaction and intention to leave (Glasø *et al.*, 2011). Moreover, training of this type could link into the broader organisational context, where a positive climate of justice could ultimately reduce the prevalence of workplace bullying (Parzefall and Salin, 2010), such as the Civility, Respect and Engagement in the Workplace (CREW) initiative, which aims to develop a civil work environment (see Osatuke *et al.*, 2009).

Redress or resolution

Because of the potential of workplace bullying to intensify, especially if not dealt with early, the provision of early intervention measures is vital (McCarthy *et al.*, 2002). Early intervention is important not just in terms of reducing the harm to targets, witnesses and the organisation but also in sending a clear message that inappropriate behaviours will be addressed within the organisation (McCarthy *et al.*, 2002). Redress can include informal (e.g. a contact officer's network to provide advice) and formal measures (e.g. a timely investigation process) (Richards and Daley, 2003). According to McCarthy and his colleagues (2002), it is crucial that perpetrators of workplace bullying, whether their behaviour is intentional or unintentional, are made aware of their inappropriate behaviours. This can occur at the time of the inappropriate behaviour or through a performance review (McCarthy *et al.*, 2002). An important suggestion for managers is to adopt a problem-solving, rather than punitive approach when approaching the perpetrator (McCarthy *et al.*, 2002).

If a formal complaint is lodged, Richards and Daley (2003: 254) advise that clear and specific information be provided, including information on 'dates, times, and witnesses to incidents with direct quotes; factual description of events; indication of how each incident made the complainant feel; documentary evidence; details of any action the complainant or others have already taken'. Complaints of workplace bullying should be treated seriously and investigated in a timely manner while maintaining confidentiality (Victorian Work-Cover Authority, cited in McCarthy *et al.*, 2002). However, because of the subtle nature of workplace bullying, a no-blame resolution approach is recommended as a first intervention, when appropriate (McCarthy *et al.*, 2002).

Support

It is recommended that support via employee assistance schemes and human relations systems, such as counselling, be provided to both parties (McCarthy *et al.*, 2002; Richards and Daley, 2003; Tehrani, 2011). Indeed, 'support at work may function as a buffer against stress by providing resources to enable [targets] to cope' (Quine, 1999: 231). Other research suggests that high levels of perceived organisational support 'offset the effects of workplace bullying on intention to leave' (Djurkovic *et al.*, 2008: 415). Indeed, support, or lack thereof, is central to the ability or inability of targets to cope (Lewis and Orford, 2005; Matthiesen *et al.*, 2003). Seeking support, however, usually requires a proactive action, which is unlikely to be within the behavioural repertoire of someone who is feeling helpless and victimised, especially if they are worried this could damage their position further (Branch *et al.*, 2007b). For instance, by seeking help, individuals may be concerned they will appear incompetent, which may be especially relevant for managers who have been bullied by a subordinate (Branch *et al.*, 2007b).

Conclusion

Workplace bullying is a complex phenomenon which has increasingly become the focus of global research. Research has explored the behaviours, prevalence, vulnerable groups and the factors that contribute to the occurrence of workplace bullying. Detrimental consequences for those who are targeted, those who witness it, and the organisations in which it occurs have been consistently found, with negative effects flowing through to the wider society. Management processes, leadership styles, development of positive organisational norms and training and development are all of utmost importance in articulating, managing and ultimately preventing workplace bullying. Commonly, a 'no bullying' policy, along with training and support, are considered essential starting points in the ongoing development of useful interventions in deterring and managing bullying in the workplace. Clearly, this is an area which demands urgent, on-going attention by researchers and practitioners alike.

CASE STUDY 22.1

IS THIS A CASE OF BULLYING?

SARA BRANCH, SHERYL RAMSAY AND MICHELLE BARKER

Paul: Have you noticed how Jane keeps making those odd comments during meetings whenever I am talking?

Denise: Yes I had. At first I thought she was being funny but now it seems to be constant. What do you think her problem is?

Paul: I don't know, but it is starting to bother me. She isn't just making snide comments anymore, she has recently started talking over me during meetings with clients and 'egging' others on to make smart comments directed at me. I am starting to really hate going to meetings I know Jane will be at or just being around her. Then, the other day she came into my office and yelled at me because I hadn't got an assessment to her. I tried to explain it wasn't due for another couple of days and that she would have it, but all she could do was tell me how much work *she* had to do and that I didn't understand how busy *she* was. As if she is the only one who is busy round here. When she left, she slammed the door with such force it shook the whole office, or at least it felt like it did. I am starting to think Jane has it in for me but I don't know why. Plus, what can I do? Each thing she does may seem minor on its own. I am not sure Andrew [their manager] will take any notice. He'll probably laugh and say 'suck it up' when I say Jane slammed my door and made snide comments. It sort of looks like I'm being petty, but I'm not – it really affects me badly.

As time went on, things did not improve between Jane and Paul. The snide comments continued, with smart comments now coming increasingly from a number of other members of staff. A couple of weeks later, Denise told Paul how Jane tried to 'bad mouth' him to her, and that she thought Jane was criticising him to other staff too. Then the messages started. Paul began receiving abusive e-mails from Jane (accusing Paul of not doing his job and stating he was useless). When Paul started receiving abusive texts as well as e-mails, he went to Andrew for help. Andrew said he would have a chat with Jane. After that things settled down a bit. At least the e-mails and texts stopped, although tension between the two persisted.

Despite Paul trying to put things behind them and be pleasant, Jane would often ignore him. Sometimes she gave Paul the feeling she was looking right through him, as if he didn't exist. Then came the Facebook incident. Someone using Paul's name posted extremely rude comments and messages to a number of his friends. The only way Paul thinks it could have happened was that he left his Facebook page open one day and someone used his profile to post the comments. Over this time Paul's health started to deteriorate; he wasn't sleeping well, experienced headaches regularly and was starting to display signs of panic attacks at work. Paul had reached breaking point. He simply couldn't face going to work any longer. He took sick leave to consider his options.

Questions

1 Do you have the full picture of what is going on in the workplace?
2 What else would help you to have a greater understanding of the case?

What other people in the workplace think:

Kate: Look, Jane can be difficult at times, but she gets thing done. Really, let's face it – we've all been carrying Paul for ages. Actually, I'm happy Jane is standing up to him now because it's what we have all wanted to do for some time now.

Marian: I know everybody around here seems to think Paul is useless and that Jane is fantastic.

On the face of it, it looks that way, but Jane is only nice to you if she likes you. I am happy I have somehow kept my head down and stayed on her good side. I am not sure why she has started picking on Paul because we all used to get along before things got really busy. I am not sure if I would call it bullying though. I tried talking to Paul, but he just seems in such a bad place now, he is not making sense.

Andrew: As Paul's boss I take his sick leave seriously. Up until recently he was one of my best staff members. I was even thinking of promoting him to team leader. I know there seems to be tension between Paul and Jane, but Jane reassures me everything is okay and, until Paul makes a formal complaint, my hands are tied. It is hard to know which way to go with this type of stuff; in a way you are dammed if you do something and dammed if you do nothing.

Questions

1 Imagine you are a HR professional employed by this organisation. You have been asked to provide a development programme for staff (in relation to the above scenario).

  a Where would you start?

  b What are the main issues you need to clarify before getting started?

  c Indicate the aims of such a programme and outline the most important elements that need to be addressed within the programme.

  d How would you evaluate such a programme?

CASE STUDY 22.2
REFLECTIVE EXERCISES

SARA BRANCH, SHERYL RAMSAY AND MICHELLE BARKER

Exercise 1

- In pairs, reflect on the inter-personal conflicts you may have experienced, witnessed or heard about in the workplace and make a list of anti-social behaviours that occur in the workplace.
- Consider if gender contributed to this conflict.
- Consider if power played a role in the conflict. If yes, then what power sources were being used?
- What is the potential effect on witnesses and what could they say or do?

Exercise 2

- Within small groups, reflect on the contributing factors to workplace bullying and brainstorm three strategies at each level (i.e. individual, group and organisational) that you could use to address, and potentially reduce or prevent, workplace bullying.

Exercise 3

Judy receives a call from her old university friend Jan, who is now working as a support worker. Jan, in tears, relates to Judy the mean things her boss Nigel had been doing to her. He was nice enough when she first arrived at her job last year, but now he has become unbearable. Jan listed some of the things Nigel had done that week: 'On Monday, he came in to work and told me in front of everyone that I was too slow and that I dragged down the whole department. The rest of the week he spent glaring at me each time he passed me in the hall. Then, Nigel threw a huge temper tantrum when I did not have a report ready two days before it was due. I snapped back because I thought he was being totally unreasonable. Unfortunately, that seemed to inflame the situation. I found out later that there had been a meeting involving all the support workers that he failed to tell me about. I even heard a horrible rumour that I was sleeping with a client. I am certain Nigel started it. I just don't know what to do and who to turn to. Everyone at work just seems to keep their heads down. My partner and friends are getting fed up with me complaining about Nigel all the time. What can I do Judy?'

- Discuss how the issues raised in this scenario could be addressed using the strategies discussed in Exercise 2.

Bibliography

Astrauskaitė, M. (2014) 'Potential antecedents of workplace bullying: the importance of individual and situational factors', *Management of Organizations: Systematic Research*, Vol.71, 17–31.

Agervold, M. (2007) 'Bullying at work: a discussion of definitions and prevalence, based on an empirical study', *Scandinavian Journal of Psychology*, Vol.48, 161–72.

Argyle, M., Henderson, M. and Furnham, A. (1985) 'The rules of social relationships', *British Journal of Social Psychology*, Vol.24, 125–39.

Bartlett, J.E. and Bartlett, M.E. (2011) 'Workplace bullying: an integrative literature review', *Advances in Developing Human Resources*, Vol.13, No.1, 69–84.

Baron, R. and Neuman, J. (1996) 'Workplace violence and workplace aggression: evidence on their relative frequency and potential causes', *Aggressive Behavior*, Vol.22, No.3, 161–73.

Baron, R. and Neuman, J. (1998) 'Workplace aggression: the iceberg beneath the tip of workplace violence: evidence on its forms, frequency, and targets', *Public Administration Quarterly*, Vol.21, No.4, 446–64.

Bowling, N. and Beehr, T. (2006) 'Workplace harassment from the victim's perspective: a theoretical model and meta-analysis', *Journal of Applied Psychology*, Vol.91, No.5, 998–1012.

Branch, S. (2008) 'You say tomatoe and I say tomato: can we differentiate between workplace bullying and other counterproductive behaviours?', *International Journal of Organisational Behaviour*, Vol.13, No.2, 4–17.

Branch, S. and Murray, J. (2015) 'Workplace bullying: is the lack of understanding the reason for inaction?', *Organizational Dynamics*, Vol.44. 287–95.

Branch, S., Murray, J. and Ramsay, S. (2012) 'Workplace bullying: what can be done to prevent and manage it?', pp. 181–96, in Benscoter, B. (eds.) *The Encyclopaedia of Human Resource Management, Volume III: Critical and Emerging Issues in Human Resource Management*, San Francisco, CA: Pfieffer/Jossey-Bass.

Branch, S., Ramsay, S. and Barker, M. (2013) 'Workplace bullying, mobbing and general harassment: a review', *International Journal of Management Reviews*, Vol.15, No.3, 280–99.

Branch, S., Ramsay, S. and Barker, M. (2007a) 'Managers in the firing line: contributing factors to workplace bullying by staff: an interview study', *Journal of Management & Organization*, Vol.13, 264–81.

Branch, S., Ramsay, S. and Barker, M. (2007b) 'The bullied boss: a conceptual exploration of upwards bullying', pp. 93–112, in Glendon, A.I., Thompson, B.M. and Myors, B. (eds.) *Advances in Organisational Psychology*, Bowen Hills: Australian Academic Press.

Corby, E., Campbell, M., Spears, B., Slee, P., Butler, D. and Kift, S. (2015) 'Students' perceptions of their own victimization: a youth voice perspective', *Journal of School Violence*, Vol.00, 1–21. Available at: DOI: 10.1080/15388220.2014.996719

Coyne, I., Seigne, E. and Randall, P. (2000) 'Predicting workplace victim status from personality', *European Journal of Work and Organizational Psychology*, Vol.9, No.3, 335–49.

De Cieri, H. and Kramar, R. (2008) *Human Resource Management in Australia* (3rd edn.), North Ryde: McGraw Hill Irwin.

Djurkovic, N., McCormack, D. and Casimir, G. (2004) 'The physical and psychological effects of workplace bullying and their relationship to intention to leave: a test of the psychosomatic and disability hypotheses', *International Journal of Organization Theory and Behavior*, Vol.7, No.4, 469–97.

Djurkovic, N., McCormack, D. and Casimir, G. (2008) 'Workplace bullying and intention to leave: the moderating effect of perceived organisational support', *Human Resource Management Journal*, Vol.18, No.4, 405–22.

Dooley, J.J., Pyzalski, J. and Cross, D. (2009) 'Cyberbullying versus face-to-face bullying: a theoretical and conceptual review', *Journal of Psychology*, Vol.217, No.4, 182–8.

Douglas, S. and Martinko, M. (2001) 'Exploring the role of individual differences in the prediction of workplace aggression', *Journal of Applied Psychology*, Vol.86, No.4, 547–59.

Einarsen, S. (2000) 'Harassment and bullying at work: a review of the Scandinavian approach', *Aggression and Violent Behavior*, Vol.5, No.4, 379–401.

Einarsen, S. and Raknes, B. (1997) 'Harassment in the workplace and the victimization of men', *Violence and Victims*, Vol.12, No.3, 247–63.

Einarsen, S. and Skogstad, A. (1996) 'Bullying at work: epidemiological findings in public and private organizations', *European Journal of Work and Organizational Psychology*, Vol.5, No.2, 185–201.

Einarsen, S., Hoel, H., Zapf, D. and Cooper, C. (2011a) 'The concept of bullying and harassment at work: the European tradition', pp. 3–40, in Einarsen, S., Hoel, H., Zapf, D. and Cooper, C. (eds.) *Bullying and Harassment in the Workplace: Developments in Theory, Research, and Practice* (2nd edn.), London: Taylor & Francis.

Einarsen, S., Hoel, H., Zapf, D. and Cooper, C. (eds.) (2011b) *Bullying and Harassment in the Workplace: Developments in Theory, Research, and Practice* (2nd edn.), London: Taylor & Francis.

Escartín, J., Ullrich, J., Zapf, D., Schlüter, E. and van Dick, R. (2013) 'Individual- and group-level effects of social identification on workplace bullying', *European Journal of Work and Organizational Psychology*, Vol.22, No.2, 182–93.

Fox, S. and Stallworth, L. (2005) 'Racial/ethnic bullying: exploring links between bullying and racism in the US workforce', *Journal of Vocational Behavior*, Vol.66, 438–56.

Gini, G. (2006) 'Bullying as a social process: the role of group membership in students' perception of inter-group aggression at school', *Journal of School Psychology*, Vol.44, No.1, 51–65.

Glasø, L., Vie, T., Holmdal, G. and Einarsen, S. (2011) 'An application of Affective Events Theory to workplace bullying: the role of emotions, trait anxiety, and trait anger', *European Psychologist*, Vol.16, No.3, 198–208.

Grigg, D. (2012) 'Definitional constructs of cyber-bullying and cyber-aggression from a triangulatory overview: a preliminary study into elements of cyber-bullying', *Journal of Aggression, Conflict and Peace Research*, Vol.4, No.4, 202–15.

Hadikin, R. and O'Driscoll, M. (2000) *The Bullying Culture: Cause, Effect, Harm Reduction*, Melbourne: Books for Midwives.

Harvey, M.G., Heames, J.T., Richey, R.G. and Leonard, N. (2006) 'Bullying: from the playground to the boardroom', *Journal of Leadership and Organizational Studies*, Vol.12, No.4, 1–11.

Heames, J. and Harvey, M. (2006) 'Workplace bullying: a cross-level assessment', *Management Decision*, Vol.44, No.9, 1214–30.

Hoel, H. and Cooper, C. (2001) 'Origins of bullying: theoretical frameworks for explaining workplace bullying', pp. 3–20, in Tehrani, N. (ed.) *Building a Culture of Respect: Managing Bullying at Work*, London: Taylor & Francis.

Hoel, H. and Salin, D. (2003) 'Organisational antecedents of workplace bullying', pp. 203–18, in Einarsen, S., Hoel, H., Zapf, D. and Cooper, C. (eds.) *Bullying and Emotional Abuse in the Workplace: International Perspectives in Research and Practice*, London: Taylor & Francis.

Hoel, H., Glasø, L., Hetland, J., Cooper, C. and Einarsen, S. (2010) 'Leadership styles as predictors of self-reported and observed workplace bullying', *British Journal of Management*, Vol.21, No.2, 453–68.

Hoel, H., Sheehan, M., Cooper, C. and Einarsen, S. (2011) 'The organisational effects of workplace bullying', pp. 129–48, in Einarsen, S., Hoel, H., Zapf, D. and Cooper C. (eds.) *Bullying and Harassment in the Workplace: Developments in Theory, Research, and Practice* (2nd edn.), London: Taylor & Francis.

Hogh, A., Mikkelsen, E. and Hansen, A. (2011) 'Individual consequences of workplace bullying/mobbing', pp. 107–28, in Einarsen, S., Hoel, H., Zapf, D. and Cooper C. (eds.) *Bullying and Harassment in the Workplace: Developments in Theory, Research, and Practice* (2nd edn.), London: Taylor & Francis.

Hutchinson, M., Vickers, M., Jackson, D. and Wilkes, L. (2006) 'Workplace bullying in nursing: towards a more critical organisational perspective', *Nursing Inquiry*, Vol.13, No.2, 118–26.

Katz, J. (1995) 'Reconstructing masculinity in the locker room: the mentors in violence prevention project', *Harvard Educational Review*, Vol.65, No.2, 163–74.

Keashly, L. and Harvey, S. (2005) 'Emotional abuse in the workplace', pp. 201–35, in Fox, S. and Spector, P. (eds.) *Counterproductive Work Behavior: Investigations of Actors and Targets*, Washington, DC: American Psychological Association.

Keashly, L. and Harvey, S. (2006) 'Workplace emotional abuse', pp. 95–120, in Kelloway, E.K., Barling, J. and Hurrell Jr, J. (eds.) *Handbook of Workplace Violence*, Thousand Oaks CA: Sage Publications.

Keashly, L. and Jagatic, K. (2011) 'North American perspectives on hostile behaviors and bullying at work', pp. 41–71, in Einarsen, S., Hoel, H., Zapf, D. and Cooper, C. (eds.) *Bullying and Harassment in the Workplace: Developments in Theory, Research, and Practice* (2nd edn.), London: Taylor & Francis.

Keashly, L. and Neuman, J. (2009) 'Building constructive communication climate: the U.S. Department of Veterans Affairs Workplace Stress and Aggression Project', pp. 339–62, in Lutgen-Sandvik, P. and Sypher, B. (eds.) *The Destructive Side of Organizational Communication: Processes, Consequences and Constructive Ways of Organizing*, New York: Routledge/LEA.

Kivimaki, M., Elovainio, M. and Vahtera, J. (2000) 'Workplace bullying and sickness absence in hospital staff', *Occupational and Environmental Medicine*, Vol.57, No.10, 656–60.

Lewis, D. (2004) 'Bullying at work: the impact of shame among university and college lecturers', *British Journal of Guidance & Counselling*, Vol.32, No.3, 281–99.

Lewis, D. and Gunn, R. (2007) 'Workplace bullying in the public sector: understanding the racial dimension', *Public Administration*, Vol.83, No.3, 641–65.

Lewis, S. and Orford, J. (2005) 'Women's experiences of workplace bullying: changes in social relationships', *Journal of Community & Applied Social Psychology*, Vol.15, 29–47.

Leymann, H. (1990) 'Mobbing and psychological terror at workplaces', *Violence and Victims*, Vol.5, 119–26.

Liefooghe, A. and Davey, K. (2001) 'Accounts of workplace bullying: the role of the organization', *European Journal of Work and Organizational Psychology*, Vol.10, No.4, 375–92.

Lind, K., Glasø, L., Pallesen, S. and Einarsen, S. (2009) 'Personality profiles among targets and nontargets of workplace bullying', *European Psychologist*, Vol.14, No.3, 231–7.

Lutgen-Sandvik, P. and Tracy, S. (2012) 'Answering five key questions about workplace bullying: how communication scholarship provides thought leadership for transforming abuse at work', *Management Communication Quarterly*, Vol.26, 3–47.

Matthiesen, S. and Einarsen, S. (2004) 'Psychiatric distress and symptoms of PTSD among victims of bullying at work', *British Journal of Guidance & Counselling*, Vol.32, No.3, 335–56.

Matthiesen, S., Aasen, E., Holst, G., Wie, K. and Einarsen, S. (2003) 'The escalation of conflict: a case study of bullying at work', *International Journal of Management and Decision Making*, Vol.4, No.1, 96–112.

Mayhew, C., McCarthy, P., Chappell, D., Quinlan, M., Barker, M. and Sheehan, M. (2004) 'Measuring the extent of impact from occupational violence and bullying on traumatised workers', *Employee Responsibilities and Rights Journal*, Vol.16, No.3, 117–34.

McCarthy, P. (1999) 'Strategies between managementality and victim-mentality in the pressures of continuous change', pp. 22–3, in Fraser, C., Barker, M. and Martin, A. (eds.) *Organisations Looking Ahead: Challenges and Directions*, Logan Campus: Griffith University.

McCarthy, P. (2004) 'Costs of occupational violence and bullying', in McCarthy, P. and Mayhew, C. (eds.) *Safeguarding the Organization Against Violence and Bullying*, Basingstoke: Palgrave Macmillan.

McCarthy, P. and Barker, M. (2000) 'Workplace bullying risk audit', *Journal of Occupational Health and Safety: Australia and New Zealand*, Vol.16, 409–18.

McCarthy, P. and Mayhew, C. (2004) *Safeguarding the Organization against Violence and Bullying*, New York: Palgrave MacMillan.

McCarthy, P., Henderson, M., Sheehan, M. and Barker, M. (2002) 'Workplace bullying: its management and prevention', *Australian Master OHS and Environment Guide 2003*, Sydney: CCH Australia, 519–49.

McCarthy, P., Sheehan, M. and Kearns, D. (1995) *Managerial Styles and Their Effects on Employees' Health and Well-Being in Organisations Undergoing Restructuring*, Brisbane: School of Organisational Behaviour & Human Resource Management.

Mikkelsen, E. and Einarsen, S. (2001) 'Bullying in Danish work-life: prevalence and health correlates', *European Journal of Work and Organizational Psychology*, Vol.10, No.4, 393–413.

Mikkelsen, E. and Einarsen, S. (2002) 'Basic assumptions and symptoms of post-traumatic stress among victims of bullying at work', *European Journal of Work and Organizational Psychology*, Vol.11, No.1, 87–111.

Niedhammer, I., David, S., Degioanni, S. and 143 occupational physicians (2006) 'Association between workplace bullying and depressive symptoms in the French working population', *Journal of Psychosomatic Research*, Vol.61, 251–9.

Nielsen, M. and Knardahl, S. (2015) 'Is workplace bullying related to the personality traits of victims? A two-year prospective study', *Work & Stress*, Vol.29, No.2, 128–49.

Nielsen, M., Matthiesen, S. and Einarsen, S. (2008) 'Sense of coherence as a protective mechanism among targets of workplace bullying', *Journal of Occupational Health Psychology*, Vol.13, No.2, 128–36.

O'Moore, M., Seigne, E., McGuire, L. and Smith, M. (1998) 'Victims of bullying at work in Ireland', *Journal of Occupational Health and Safety: Australia and New Zealand*, Vol.14, 569–74.

Olweus, D. (1978) *Aggression in the Schools: Bullies and Whipping Boys*, New York: Wiley.

Osatuke, K., Moore, S., Ward, C., Dyrenforth, S. and Belton, L. (2009) 'Civility, respect, engagement in the workforce (CREW): nationwide organization development intervention at Veterans Health Administration', *The Journal of Applied Behavioral Science*, Vol.45, No.3, 384–410.

Parzefall, M. and Salin, D. (2010) 'Perceptions of and reactions to workplace bullying: a social exchange perspective', *Human Relations*, Vol.63, No.6, 761–80.

Pietersen, C. (2007) 'Interpersonal bullying behaviours in the workplace', *SA Journal of Industrial Psychology*, Vol.33, No.1, 59–66.

Privitera, C. and Campbell, M. (2009) 'Cyberbullying: the new face of workplace bullying?', *CyberPsychology and Behavior*, Vol.12, No.4, 395–400.

Quine, L. (1999) 'Workplace bullying in NHS community trust: staff questionnaire survey', *British Medical Journal*, Vol.318, No.7178, 228–32.

Ramsay, S., Troth, A. and Branch, S. (2010) 'Workplace bullying through the lens of social psychology: a group level analysis', *Journal of Occupational and Organizational Psychology*, Vol.84, No.4, 799–816.

Rayner, C. (1997) 'The incidence of workplace bullying', *Journal of Community & Applied Social Psychology*, Vol.7, 199–208.

Rayner, C. (1999) 'From research to implementation: finding leverage for prevention', *International Journal of Manpower*, Vol.20, Nos.1–2, 28–38.

Rayner, C. (2007) 'Preparing for dignity: tackling indignity at work', pp. 176–90, in Bolton, S.C. (ed.) *From Dimensions of Dignity at Work*, Oxford: Elsevier.

Rayner, C. and Hoel, H. (1997) 'A summary review of literature relating to workplace bullying', *Journal of Community and Applied Social Psychology*, Vol.7, No.3, 181–91.

Rayner, C., Hoel, H. and Cooper, C. (2002) *Workplace Bullying: What We Know, Who Is to Blame, and What Can We Do?*, London: Taylor & Francis.

Richards, J. and Daley, H. (2003) 'Bullying policy: development, implementation and monitoring', pp. 247–58, in Einarsen, S., Hoel, H., Zapf, D. and Cooper, C. (eds.) *Bullying and Emotional Abuse in the Workplace: International Perspectives in Research and Practice*, London: Taylor & Francis.

Rigby, K. (2001) 'Bullying in schools and in the workplace', pp. 1–10, in McCarthy, P., Rylance, J., Bennett, R. and Zimmermann, H. (eds.) *Bullying: From Backyard to Boardroom* (2nd edn.), Sydney: The Federation Press.

Roscigno, V., Lopez, S. and Hodson, R. (2009) 'Supervisory bullying, status inequalities and organizational context', *Social Forces*, Vol.87, No.3, 1561–89.

Rylance, J., Bennett, R. and Zimmermann, H. (eds.) *Bullying: From Backyard to Boardroom* (2nd edn.), Sydney: The Federation Press.

Saam, N. (2010) 'Interventions in workplace bullying: a multilevel approach', *European Journal of Work and Organizational Psychology*, Vol.19, No.1, 51–75.

Salin, D. (2001) 'Prevalence and forms of bullying among business professionals: a comparison of two different strategies for measuring bullying', *European Journal of Work and Organizational Psychology*, Vol.10, No.4, 425–41.

Salin, D. (2003) 'Bullying and organisational politics in competitive and rapidly changing work environments', *International Journal of Management and Decision Making*, Vol.4, No.1, 35–46.

Salin, D. (2008) 'The prevention of workplace bullying as a question of human resource management: measures adopted and underlying organizational factors', *Scandinavian Journal of Management*, Vol.24, No.3, 221–31.

Salin, D. (2009) 'Organisational responses to workplace harassment: an exploratory study', *Personnel Review*, Vol.38, No.1, 26–44.

Salin, D. and Hoel, H. (2011) 'Organisational causes of workplace bullying', pp. 227–44, in Einarsen, S., Hoel, H., Zapf, D. and Cooper, C. (eds.) *Bullying and Harassment in the Workplace: Developments in Theory, Research, and Practice* (2nd edn.), London: Taylor & Francis.

Samnani, A. and Singh, P. (2015) 'Workplace bullying: considering the interaction between individual and work environment', *Journal of Business Ethics*, 1–13.

Saunders, P., Huynh, A. and Goodman-Delahunty, J. (2007) 'Defining workplace bullying behaviour professional lay definitions of workplace bullying', *International Journal of Law and Psychiatry*, Vol.30, No.4–5, 340–54.

Shallcross, L., Ramsay, S., and Barker, M. (2010) 'A proactive response to the mobbing problem: a guide for HR managers', *New Zealand Journal of Human Resources Management*, Vol.10, No.1, 27–37.

Shallcross, L., Ramsay, S. and Barker, M. (2011) 'The power of malicious gossip', *Australian Journal of Communication*, Vol.38, No.1, 45–68.

Shallcross, L., Ramsay, S. and Barker, M. (2013) 'Severe workplace conflict: the experience of mobbing', *Negotiation and Conflict Management Research*, Vol.6, No.3, 191–213.

Smith, P.K., Mahdavi, J., Carvalho, M., Fisher, S., Russell, S. and Tippett, N. (2008) 'Cyberbullying: its nature and impact in secondary school pupils', *Journal of Child Psychology and Psychiatry*, Vol.49, No.4, 376–85.

Smith, P., Singer, M., Hoel, H. and Cooper, C. (2003) 'Victimization in the school and the workplace: are there any links?', *British Journal of Psychology*, Vol.94, 175–88.

Tajfel, H. and Turner, J. (1986) 'The social identify theory of intergroup behavior', pp. 7–24, in Worchel, S. and Austin, W. (eds.) *The Psychology of Intergroup Relations* (2nd edn.), Chicago, IL: Nelson-Hall Publishers.

Tehrani, N. (2003) 'Counselling and rehabilitating employees involved with bullying', pp. 270–84, in Einarsen, S., Hoel, H., Zapf, D. and Cooper, C. (eds.) *Bullying and Emotional*

Abuse in the Workplace: International Perspectives in Research and Practice, London: Taylor & Francis.

Tehrani, N. (2011) 'Workplace bullying: the role for counselling', pp. 381–96, in Einarsen, S., Hoel, H., Zapf, D. and Cooper, C. (eds.) *Bullying and Harassment in the Workplace: Developments in Theory, Research, and Practice* (2nd edn.), London: Taylor & Francis.

UNISON (2003) 'Bullying at work: guidelines for UNISON branches, stewards and safety representatives', London: UNISON.

Vartia, M. and Leka, S. (2011) 'Interventions for the prevention and management of bullying at work', pp. 359–80, in Einarsen, S., Hoel, H., Zapf, D. and Cooper, C. (eds.) *Bullying and Harassment in the Workplace: Developments in Theory, Research, and Practice* (2nd edn.), London: Taylor & Francis.

Vartia, M., Korppoo, L., Fallenius, S. and Mattila, M. (2003) 'Workplace bullying: the role of occupational health services', pp. 285–98, in Einarsen, S., Hoel, H., Zapf, D. and Cooper, C. (eds.) *Bullying and Emotional Abuse in the Workplace: International Perspectives in Research and Practice*, London: Taylor & Francis.

Woodrow, C. and Guest, D. (2014) 'When good HR gets bad results: exploring the challenge of HR implementation in the case of workplace bullying', *Human Resource Management Journal*, Vol.24, No.1, 38–56.

Zapf, D. (1999) 'Organisational, work group related and personal causes of mobbing/bullying at work', *International Journal of Manpower*, Vol.20, Nos.1–2, 70–85.

Zapf, D. (2004) 'Negative social behaviour at work and workplace bullying', paper presented at the Fourth International Conference on Bullying and Harassment in the Workplace, Bergen, Norway.

Zapf, D. and Einarsen, S. (2001) 'Bullying in the workplace: recent trends in research and practice: an introduction', *European Journal of Work and Organizational Psychology*, Vol.10, No.4, 369–73.

Zapf, D. and Einarsen, S. (2005) 'Mobbing at work: escalated conflicts in organizations', in Fox, S. and Spector, P. (eds.) *Counterproductive Work Behavior: Investigations of Actors and Targets*, Washington, DC: American Psychological Association.

Zapf, D. and Einarsen, S. (2011) 'Individual antecedents of bullying: victims and perpetrators', pp. 177–200, in Einarsen, S., Hoel, H., Zapf, D. and Cooper, C. (eds.) *Bullying and Harassment in the Workplace: Developments in Theory, Research, and Practice* (2nd edn.), London: Taylor & Francis.

Zapf, D. and Gross, C. (2001) 'Conflict escalation and coping with workplace bullying: a replication and extension', *European Journal of Work and Organizational Psychology*, Vol.10, No.4, 497–522.

Zapf, D., Escartín, J., Einarsen, S., Hoel, H. and Vartia, M. (2011) 'Empirical findings on prevalence and risk groups of bullying in the workplace', pp. 75–106, in Einarsen, S., Hoel, H., Zapf, D. and Cooper, C. (eds.) *Bullying and Harassment in the Workplace: Developments in Theory, Research, and Practice* (2nd edn.), London: Taylor & Francis.

CHAPTER 23

HRM AND TECHNOLOGY: FROM SOCIO-TECHNICAL SYSTEMS TO SOCIAL MEDIA

Diane van den Broek and Paul Thompson

Introduction

International trends reflect the pervasive use of computer technologies, reshaping new business models and the way employees engage with work on a day-to-day basis. In 2010 the global 'digital economy rankings', which ranked consumers, businesses and governments use of ICT in seventy countries, placed Australia and the United Kingdom ninth and fourteenth, respectively. This shows the high reliance these countries have on ICT technologies (Unit, 2010). This greater accessibility, and reduced costs of new technologies has also led to considerable advances being made in how human resource management use ICT, particularly within areas like HR planning, job design, recruiting, training and development, reward and performance as well as measuring the overall impact of human resources on business outcomes. However, while many organisations may be adopting technological advances in the operational aspects of HRM, very few appear to be taking a more strategic and holistic approach by moving beyond operational efficiency, and using data to develop a better understanding of the overall effectiveness and impact of HR on firm activities, including a consideration of issues such as employee engagement and well-being.

Taking a more reflective and conceptual view of the relationship between technology and work, this chapter also discusses the long history of rival optimistic and pessimistic accounts of the effects of technological change on the employment relationship, most particularly, whether technology has facilitated greater job autonomy or alternatively increased managerial control. This chapter will begin by examining the history of these debates that highlight the tensions between technology and work with some particular attention paid to the call centre industry as this is where some of these issues are posed in their sharpest form.

In the second half of the chapter we will provide a more detailed examination of the contemporary issues that arise from the rapid spread of social media. Whilst some of the attention focuses on attempts by companies to incorporate social media into traditional HR functions such as HR planning, performance and reward management, the main concerns of this part of the chapter include the tensions and expectations between social media and recruitment processes and the nexus between private and public lives. For example, there have been an increasing number of legal disputes around the alleged unauthorised use of technologies or sackings when organisations feel that employees have brought the firm into disrepute on Facebook, Twitter or other sites. In these cases social media has pushed human resource management into previously unchartered territories that are on the periphery of the employment relationship. At the same time, employees bring social media into work, or use it to comment on their employment and employers. As outlined in the next section, this opens up a set of 'digital disruption' issues of considerable interest to human resource managers and employees alike that have their roots in much older debates.

 ## Technology and social relations at work: issues and debates

Technology has always influenced how we undertake and understand work and employment. In the 1960s sociological and organisational theories promoted automation as something that would improve the *quality* of work. For example, Blauner (1964) argued that technologies were evolving to the point where the worker was believed to 'regain a sense of control over his [sic] technological environment that is usually absent in mass production factories' (1964: viii). Another well-known study by Woodward (1958) focused on the relations between technology and management organisation, identifying the relationship between technological complexity and spans of control. Though emphasising the strong impact of technology, recognition was given to a degree of managerial choice, meaning that production systems required both a technological organisation (that includes equipment and process layout) but also a work organisation that shapes how tasks are actually carried out – that is a social dimension.

However, this social dimension tended to get a little lost in more optimistic accounts of how technology shaped work, which verged on a technological determinist argument, suggesting that technology was the central driver for (positive) change. Whilst it has been associated with post-industrial discourses amongst academics and business thinkers for a long time, the idea was given a boost by the emergence of a new generation of information and communication technologies (ICT) and the Internet. It wasn't long before many were claiming that societies and companies were accelerating down the information superhighway to a new economy where work would be transformed and voice of employees and citizens would prevail over traditional corporate, government and collective interests (Webster, 2002: 4). Prominent social scientists such as Castells (1996; 2001) promoted optimistic ideas of informational capitalism, where an on-line economy and e-business would encourage self-programmable labour and horizontal networks rather than vertical hierarchies involving one-way top-down control. The twin themes of ICT producing better quality work and employee discretion and job controls can be seen at micro-level in Guiliano's (1982) depiction of a move from pre-industrial, to industrial and then the information age office where close relations between boss and employees and self-direction were highlighted.

 ## Alternative, control and surveillance-based arguments

In contrast to the above optimism, another approach suggested that technology was socially shaped (Mackenzie and Wajcman, 1999). As Badham (2005: 1155) notes in his overview of the debates:

> scholars increasingly view technological change at work as social (and managerial) processes in which social agency – in the form of workplace cultures, structures, and politics – shapes how technology is designed, implemented, and used. *(Badham, 2005: 1155)*

There are a number of perspectives emphasising different aspects of such social shaping. This chapter will view the relations between HRM and technology through labour process theory (LPT) as this approach best illustrates tensions and debates in managing people at work and reflects the core themes of this chapter – technology, human resource management and the employment relationship.

Labour process theory identified the importance of the social relationships that people engage in at the workplace. For example, over time we have seen that machinery has been designed and used in ways that reduced worker skills and extended managerial control. When Braverman (1974) wrote his influential book we saw a renewed interest in the way Taylorism (or Scientific Management), was applied in modern workplaces. The idea with Taylorism was that all possible brain-work by workers should be removed from the shop floor and placed in the hands of planners and managers. On his factory visits, Noble found that management used numerical control systems to extend control by transferring authority from workers to the programming office. Of equal importance, he also showed that a rival efficient method of automating machine tools that kept operator skills and control had been trialled but excluded (see Wilkinson, 1985, for a similar UK study). When Braverman was writing in the early 1970s we were at the early stages of the phase of new technology based on the microchip. However, he believed that managerially influenced software design would have similar negative effects on office workers – from secretaries to draughtsmen and women – as had been already experienced in the factory. Further pessimistic social shaping arguments were later found in studies by Sewell and Wilkinson (1992) who analysed technologies associated with the introduction of Japanese style just-in-time systems into car plants in northern England as a form of 'electronic eye' that allows management to monitor production processes and discipline workers' actions. This perceived lack of trust between employee and management has important implications for human resource management within contemporary firms.

Whilst software can reduce employee autonomy and enhance surveillance of work roles, this view tends to neglect the monitoring of collective performance though information *systems*, and the fact that managers themselves are also monitored. This works at two levels. Across the corporation, the increasing transparency of 'decentralised' units such as profit centres in networked organisations is dependent on sophisticated ICT systems and regular audits. Within the organisation, performance management through key performance indicators (KPIs) is a pervasive feature and manifest in a diverse range of cascading targets. For example, in his study of the introduction of new technology in the air traffic sector, Hallier notes that, 'With this new emphasis on unit performance . . . managers were now to be assessed on how well they controlled budgets, increased traffic movements, delivered controller validations, and reduced headcount' (2004: 54). As such, the monitoring aspects of workplace technologies affect managers, as well as workers.

Nor is ICT-enabled monitoring confined to routine work. Studies of the spread of knowledge management (KM) indicate that information systems are increasingly used to collect, convert and codify the practices of expert workers, such as those working in biotech or pharmaceuticals, 'Stretching management control back through the development phase and deepening control in the documentation process has become critical to corporate competitiveness' (McKinlay, 2002: 78). These trends have developed despite the fact that the mainstream position on KM is that it is about knowledge and people not information and tools (see Thompson and McHugh, 2009). Part of the explanation for the discrepancy can be found in how KM systems have been introduced into organisations. For example, social shaping perspectives emphasise the importance of human agency, or action, rather than technological determinism and studies also show IT specialists have tried to 'own' the new initiatives and use them to advance their occupational interests.

While the technological potential for management control and de-skilling does exist, such effects have often been exaggerated. The fact that software, for example, can be programmed to reduce skills or track performance doesn't mean that it always does. Even when management, particularly human resource managers, enable this capacity, they may not use it for fear of eroding goodwill or expending too much time and resources, or employees may resist or find ways around it. McKinlay's (2002) research on pharmaceuticals shows that it is not all about surveillance. At the same time as the information systems are codifying and standardising, the senior management of the companies are also encouraging sharing of knowledge and practice, facilitated by 'electronic cafes'. As such, the way technology shapes work is by no means predictable. However, the call centre industry has developed a reputation in this respect.

The call centre as socio-technical system

When a customer rings a call centre he or she will normally hear, 'This call may be recorded for training purposes.' This is something of a gloss on the primary purpose of surveillance. The technology is based on and Automatic Call Distribution system. Telephone and computer technologies are integrated as a means of accessing and retrieving data to manage the service interaction (for both inbound and outbound calls). Detailed statistics are collected and analysed to assess individual and team performance. These are used to set targets and timings for the calls. Only after the surveillance through remote monitoring, do we see the 'training' – the evaluation, discipline and coaching of employees. Furthermore, the alignment of the technological and human aspects of this socio-technical system was explicitly designed with control and surveillance in mind:

> The supervisor can be in full control of the daily business within the call centre by closely monitoring all activities through real time windows. Call Centre performance statistics presented in report format provide valuable input for short and long-term planning. Business plans based on reliable and accurate information on call centre performance result in better planning, better control and better business . . . CCM allows the user to define thresholds and set alarms to signal when these thresholds have been exceeded. The call centre manager will be alerted by the change in colour of the threshold value on the real-time display, a written message and optionally, an alarm will sound and a red bell icon will blink. *(Ericsson Dynamic Network Administration statement)*

There is, of course, a degree of variety in call centre work, depending on the segment of the market being serviced, complexity and variability of the product, and the depth of the knowledge required to handle the service interactions (Batt and Moynihan, 2002; van den Broek, 2008). However, most call centres involve work that is relatively standardised and scripted interactions and, unsurprisingly, such work has generated largely negative descriptions like an 'electronic sweatshop' and an 'assembly line in the head' (Taylor and Bain, 1993).

However, such views are misleading and underestimate in particular the HR issues in operating a call centre. As a number of studies have highlighted, the market strategy and associated production systems throw up a number of tensions; for example, the tensions between quantity–quality output (Taylor and Bain, 1999), low discretion–high employee commitment (Houlihan, 2002) and fun-surveillance (Purcell *et al.*, 2000). One of the main reasons for call centres to emphasise these practices is the need to promote identification with organisational culture through 'fun' events. Further, it is a characteristic feature of call centres that they rely heavily on teamwork, even though the work is highly individualised (van den Broek *et al.*, 2004). Human resources also has motivational tensions arising from the relatively widespread view of a flat structure within call centres with limited career opportunities beyond supervisor or team leader. All of these factors raise concerns about how HR might manage employee careers.

Furthermore, as extensive evidence shows, surveillance does not wholly eliminate worker resistance or misbehaviour (see Taylor and Bain, 1999; Callaghan and Thompson, 2002; van den Broek, 2003). Employees can find 'blind spots' in, and work around, the system, manipulate the procedure of putting in codes so as to get out of the queue of calls, try and guess when they are being listened to and act accordingly, challenge management interpretation of monitoring data and withhold or give off their emotions as they see fit rather than according to the potential organisational script. The ultimate way workers resist work is through 'exit', that is resigning and if there is one persistent HR problem in the call centre industry it is large-scale labour turnover. Wallace *et al.*, (2000) argue that the apparent acceptance of this as the consequence of being unwilling or unable to resolve the above tensions is a 'sacrificial HR strategy', though this has been complicated by two recent trends. First, some companies have begun to use voice recognition software to automate some of the more routine interactions, particularly for outbound, telemarketing. Second, more organisations have sought to retain their low discretion–high commitment model, but relocate their operations to lower cost India or the Philippines. This is a different facet to the technological reach of the new systems. But as Taylor and Bain (2005) show, such outsourcing has not been without problems. Labour may be cheaper but it is not necessarily easily substitutable, because of cultural and linguistic differences, as well as customer complaints and potential security issues.

The key conclusion to be drawn is that the dominant call centre model inverts the logic of a socio-technical system. As Thompson, Callaghan and van den Broek argue,

> Reference to the term socio-technical system normally refers to attempts by management and other actors in the employment relationship to construct mutually supportive and jointly optimised relations between the technical and social dimensions of work systems. Within the dominant pattern of call centre practice management have indeed created a closely aligned set of arrangements, but that integration results in perverse and negative outcomes for employees and to some extent the organisations that employ them. *(Thompson et al., 2004: 149)*

As the accompanying case study highlights, there are a number of challenges that are presented to firms that relate to how technologies are managed in the workplace and what measures should, or could, be used to balance firm needs for control and assessment and employees' desire for workplace autonomy and privacy, and customer/client desire for quality service interactions. As we discuss below, these issues are also particularly pertinent in relation to how firms store their data.

Electronic HRM

Many firms have adopted IT-enabled Human Resource Information Systems (HRIS) to acquire, store, analyse, retrieve and distribute important information relating to an organisation's human resource environment that includes within it a combination of hardware, software, people, policies, procedures and data (Bondarouk and Ruël, 2009). However, the range of engagement around electronic HRM (eHRM) varies widely. Some firms may restrict themselves to just storing wage data in relatively basic systems, while others might expand their data analysis to design job evaluations, salary surveys and salary planning that might include international benchmarking and benefits management in much more complex programs (Lowe *et al.*, 2002). The advantage of using more developed systems and analysing the data that is collected is that more proactive and preventative measures can be taken by management to pre-empt potential problems. For example, developing more detailed information on reward policies may avoid the potentially unequal distribution of compensation levels that result in high attrition rates. Other practices that can be improved through the use of eHRM could also include more targeted and effective succession planning strategies, by predicting staffing needs; undertaking workforce profile and dynamics analysis. As already discussed in the call centre industry, HRIS are also widely reported in the context of performance management where employee output can be measured both quantitatively and qualitatively against key performance indicators (Frenkel *et al.*, 1998; van den Broek, 2002). Using the call centre example, again an important question might be: what particular aspects of employee performance drive business outcomes; how should this shape other HR practices and policies and how might this knowledge elevate HR to a more strategic position within the firm. Unfortunately, the evidence seems to suggest that many firms fail to respond to these challenges and stop short of using more strategic and sophisticated approaches to eHRM (Dery *et al.*, 2013).

Similarly, HR analytics are most likely to work when HR managers work with others in the firm to identify and follow through ways to meet the immediate challenges facing the firm. One widely cited example involves Google, who developed a system to track relations between management and retention and team performance. They conducted double-blind interviews to identify what the key behaviours of their best managers were, and identified eight behaviours that made a good manager and five pitfalls that should be avoided. These are now incorporated into their manager-training programmes and coaching sessions, and teams provide feedback to managers on these behaviours to help them understand where they're doing well and where they can improve (Gardner *et al.*, 2011).

These examples suggest that advances in technology can create opportunities for senior business and HR leaders to open a dialogue between organisations and their staff. While eHRM is used in a variety of areas, such as employee learning and development, and workplace health and safety, the most widely cited HR areas that we find contemporary technologies applied in the workplace (most particularly, the use of social media) is in the area of recruitment and selection. However, again, an important question here is what are the implications of these changes on relations between employees and firms and how might technologies help HR to become a more strategic business partner by escalating the HR function from routine tasks towards a more sophisticated approach?

Social media at work

This chapter began by stating that computer technologies are reshaping the way employees engage the world around them and with the organisations they work for. Six out of seven people in the world have access to internet technologies, one in four using social networking sites. While there has been an 18 per cent increase in social network users in the past year alone, it is particularly in the emerging markets in China and India where growth is strongest. Reflecting this greater coverage and take-up, most companies have incorporated some aspects of social networking and internet technologies into their HR functions through a range of portable devices and websites (such as those listed in Box 23.1). However, as elaborated below, many firms are unsure about how to manage these technologies effectively. Most particularly, firms are concerned about, and often ignorant of, the legal and managerial implications of embracing social networking technologies.

Whilst social media is often discussed within the context of traditional HR functions such as recruitment and selection, there are numerous other important managerial and legal issues at stake here. As noted below, legal disputes between employees and firms are on the increase (Thornthwaite, 2013; 2015), representing a major example of a mismatch between the expectations of firms and their employees about how social media should be managed within the workplace. This mismatch is identified in three major areas in Figure 23.1, developed by McDonald and Thompson (2015). As the following sections indicate, tensions arise within the areas where social media is most apparent. These areas include how firms use social media in recruitment and selection; how social media blurs the lines between public and private lives and finally, how potential cyber-loafing, (that is employees accessing personal social media sites while at work), by employeesis managed by firms.

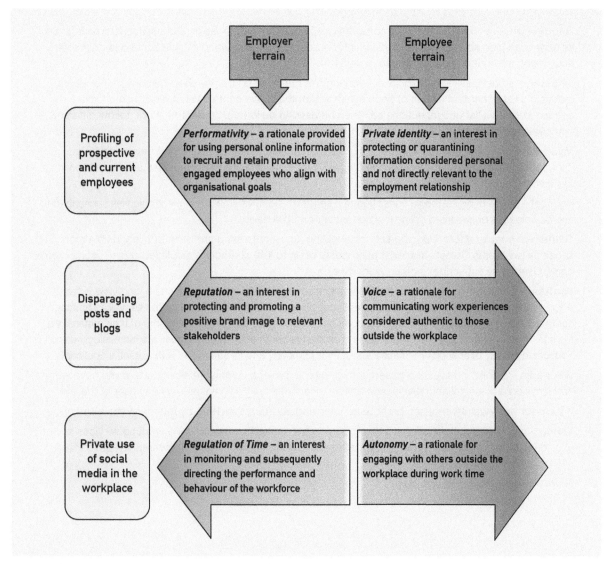

Figure 23.1 Areas of contention in the use of social media at work
Source: McDonald and Thompson, 2015.

Box 23.1 HRM in practice   **Examples of social networking sites and tools**

Blog – a discussion or informational site published on the Internet that consists of entries ('posts') typically displayed in reverse chronological order, i.e. the most recent post appears first. Until 2009 blogs were usually the work of a single individual, occasionally of a small group, and often covered a single subject. More recently 'multi-author blogs' have developed, with posts written by large numbers of authors and professionally edited. Blogs consist of regular entries of commentary and descriptions of events (*blogging*). The content of a microblog is simply smaller in size.

Facebook – a social networking service where users create personal *profiles*, add other users as *friends* and exchange messages, including automatic notifications when they update their own profile. Additionally, users may join common-interest user groups, organised by common characteristics (e.g. workplace). Users can instant message each other through the website.

Google – an American multinational corporation specialising in internet-related services; most famously, its core search engine but also a large chain of products including Google+, the second largest social networking site in the world (as of January 2013).

LinkedIn – a business-related social networking site mainly used for professional networking. Users maintain a list of contact details of people with whom they have some level of relationship, called *connections*. This list of connections can then be used to build up a contact network, follow different companies and find jobs, people and business opportunities.

MySpace – an online community of users' personal profiles. These typically include photographs, information about personal interests and *blogs*. Users send one another messages and socialise within the MySpace *community*.

Podcast – a type of digital media consisting of a series of audio, video, PDF or electronic files subscribed to and downloaded or streamed online to a computer or mobile device.

Twitter – a popular *micro-blogging* service enabling its users to send and read publicly visible messages called *tweets*. Tweets are text-based posts of up to 140 characters displayed on the user's profile page. Users may subscribe to other users' tweets.

YouTube – a (Google-owned) video-sharing website on which users can upload, share, and view videos. A wide variety of *user-generated* video content is displayed, including film and TV clips as well as amateur content such as *video blogging*. Media corporations including the BBC also offer some of their material via the site. Most videos enable users to leave and exchange comments. Organisations are increasingly using YouTube as a way of sharing information about their company and its vacancies with potential applicants.

Wikipedia – a collaborative web-based encyclopaedia project; volunteers around the world have written its 18 million articles collaboratively, and almost all articles are freely editable by any user of the site.

Whirlpool – an Australian-based broadband user website started in 1998 by founder Simon Wright.

Yahoo – an American multinational internet corporation known for its social-networking services and user-generated content, including online discussion boards (Yahoo! Groups), community-driven Q&A site (Yahoo! Answers) and photo sharing (Flickr).

Source: Adapted from Broughton *et al.*, 2011.

Recruitment and selection

There are many advantages for firms to use social networking sites for recruitment and selection. For example, companies such as Microsoft have created a dedicated website for recruitment, using job-blogs and life-at-work videos to provide useful information to those passive job seekers as well as those actively looking for work (Joos, 2008). Similarly, Deloitte regularly post YouTube videos showing employee testimonials to provide an inside view of what a job at the firm might provide new recruits. The sites involved in recruitment offer business account holders various services including the management of job postings, sending of private messages to users on career opportunities and potential employees' profile management, etc., while Facebook offers an effective medium for communicating recruitment advertisements and messages, including simple text and blogs, videos and pictures.

There is also now much evidence that HR managers are actively profiling prospective employees by looking at recruits' social networking profiles to access more detailed information about candidates. As long ago as 2008, a survey for the US Society for Human Resource Management (SHRM) found that the number of organisations accessing social networking profiles as an HR tool had grown from 21 per cent in 2006 to 44 per cent in

2008 with 13 per cent using them as a screening tool (Broughton *et al.*, 2013: 8; Davison *et al.*, 2011). Other surveys by Rowell (2010) report that 70 per cent of HR managers say they have rejected a job applicant for his or her internet behaviour.

Given the increasing take-up of these technologies, there has been considerable debate over the use of social media in recruitment and selection. Various issues emerge here. Most particularly, much of the information posted on these sites has little bearing on the suitability of an applicant to a job position. How people are portrayed on social media sites often has little to do with what individuals maybe like as an employee. In most cases people use their personal sites to have fun or joke with friends, which might include various levels of embellishment about the activities they pursue outside work. Pictures and posts may be taken out of context or intended to be provocative or humorous with the applicant unknowingly giving a misleading impression to potential employers. Similarly, information on these sites may also be old and irrelevant to the status of the applicant at the time when they are applying for positions. Furthermore, job applicants may be unaware that their application was rejected based on information accessed through social media (Ollington *et al.*, 2013).

While accessing social media profiles may be a cost effective way to gather personality and other data, HR managers must be aware of the 'due diligence' that comes with these activities, including ethical, legal, fairness as well as privacy issues (Slovensky and Ross, 2012; Allen *et al.*, 2007). They should also be aware that selection processes that rely heavily on cyber-vetting also run the risk of infringing candidate privacy. According to a Deloitte's 2009 Ethics and Workplace survey, 60 per cent of business executives thought they have a right to know how workers profile themselves and their organisations on social networks, with 30 per cent admitting to informally monitoring social networking sites. By contrast, 53 per cent of employees felt that their social networking activities are not an employer's concern, with 63 per cent of 18- to 34-year-old respondents asserting that employers have no business monitoring their online activity (Deloitte, 2009).

As a growing collection of legal cases show, there have been several invasive practices including requests for job applicants to provide passwords and login information during a job interview (Neylon O'Brien, 2011; Suddath, 2012). Also some managers are asking potential employees to allow them to become their Facebook 'friend' (Floyd and Spry, 2013). While such practices contravene Facebook's requirement to not share passwords with others, it also raises concerns about what criteria firms are basing their hiring decisions on. For example, in most countries, hiring should not be based on individual's demographic characteristics unrelated to the job requirements or performance, such as age, gender, race, religion, physical features, marital status and sexual orientation. As such, HR need to think very carefully about how personal information gleaned from social media sites might consciously or subconsciously bias the recruitment and selection process and how these activities my adversely influence relationships between candidates and recruiting firms.

Technological reach/changing boundaries

The second issue that HR need to consider is that social media offers firms unparalleled opportunities to extend their technological reach into private spheres that operate on the margins of the traditional employment relationship. Digital technologies provide unprecedented connectivity to work, greater flexibility and an increase in productivity and efficiency; however, this integration of work and home life can lead to a blurring of boundaries between these two aspects of an employee's life.

The widespread provision by companies of laptop computers, email and mobile phones provide enormous convenience and accessibility; however, many workers report that they now find it difficult to 'get away' from their work, with expectations that many professional workers are always available 'on call'. This was a trend that pre-dated Facebook and other new social media. Fraser's (2001) *White Collar Sweatshop* is full of examples of late nights at the office and the invasion of private time at home facilitated by the new communication technologies. One detailed examination of the enhanced use of time/space surveillance is Collinson and Collinson's (1997) case study of a large insurance company. Noting that, 'there was also a technological basis to the time–space surveillance of managers and salespeople' (1997: 389), they too reported how mobile phones, pagers, answerphones and modems created expectations that staff could be contactable at all times. In this case, staff was instructed never to switch off their mobile and car phones. For other managers and professionals, email is the main mechanism of compulsory contact ability. Many firms are starting to draw up codes of conduct that specify a time period during which employees can be available. This is a trend that better clarifies expectations of both firms and employees (Thomas, 2014).

While there are many advantages, new social media can accelerate this trend of electronic surveillance and entrench the inability of employees to disconnect from work. One result from these trends is the increasing debate, legal discussion and changing expectation about what employees are able to post on social media platforms in their private time. Disparaging posts made by employees about the organisations they work for are increasingly commonplace, such as the 'Good Guys' case detailed below. In this case, the national employment tribunal in Australia, Fair Work Australia, ruled on the case of Mr Damian O'Keefe's application for unfair dismissal at his workplace. His employer, the electrical and home appliance chain, The Good Guys, sacked O'Keefe after he had posted negative comments about his workplace and colleagues on Facebook. For example, the post included '"Damien O'Keefe wonders how the f . . . work can be so f . . . ing useless and mess up my pay again. C . . . ts are going down tomorrow."' The target of Mr O'Keefe's pay issues was the operations manager responsible for payment to employees, Kelly Taylor. These comments were made on a private Facebook setting but were accessible to other employees because some of his colleagues were also his Facebook 'friends'. While an employee handbook stated that 'staff, customers and suppliers . . . must be courteous and polite', there was no specific policy dealing with employee's use of social media.

While there is no question that O'Keefe's words were inappropriate and undignified; he argued unfair dismissal on the basis that he posted these views while at home, while out of business hours, and on maximum privacy settings with no explicit connection noted to the his employer. Despite these protestations, the Commission President determined that because 'the separation between home and work is now less pronounced than it was in the past' the dismissal was lawful.

'Cyberloafing' (employees accessing personal social media sites while at work) is another aspect of social media use that is challenging traditional boundaries of employment regulation and the role of HRM. According to some sources, the loss is not insignificant. One survey by America Online and Salary.com reported that the average worker wastes just over two hours per eight-hour workday, with personal internet use constituting nearly 45 per cent of the waste (Malachowski, 2005). Indeed, cyberloafing appears to be more prevalent among the higher levels within organisations than at lower levels (Garrett and Danziger, 2008), perhaps because of the greater opportunities provided by access to IT and a degree of time and task autonomy. However, these issues are not straightforward, and like all management policies and practices they require some forethought about the implications for employee relations. For example, many employees believe that they are more productive when able to access such sites freely. For example, a University of Melbourne study found that when firms allowed their employees access to social media for up to 20 per cent of each workday, 70 per cent of employees' overall productivity output increased by nine per cent (Gorman, 2013). This, and other research, suggests that short breaks on social media allow the mind to reset itself, generating higher net concentration as well as reducing employee burnout and increasing job satisfaction (Gorman, 2013; Charoensukmongkol, 2015).

Managing social media

As technology continues to diversify the range of tools available for organisations, management should ensure that they think through the repercussions of using particular technologies, and recognise the need for policies to protect both the organisation and the employees that work there. As is often the case, many firms introduce new types of technologies before considering the policy and practical implications. This chapter highlights how workplace technologies can breach the trust and impair the employment relationship by compromising the legal as well as the psychological contracts that are built up between firms and their employees. However, as set out at the beginning of this chapter, it is not the technologies per se that undermine relations between staff and management, but rather the relations between the social and the technical; that is, how relationships are developed and managed around the particular workplace technologies.

As outlined in this chapter, there are numerous ethical questions related to privacy and the extent to which it is appropriate for employers to collect information about workers' private lives. There is also an increasing body of evidence that shows a major reason for not shortlisting and for rejecting candidates was based on 'lifestyle-' rather than employment-related information (Broughton *et al.*, 2013: 2). This is of concern given the potential accuracy of the information gained by the use of social media tools. Also, there are issues that relate to the depth of the applicant pool that social media tools can access, giving rise to potential problems around diversity and discrimination. Given the, often random, array of information about individuals available on social networking sites, it is difficult to see how this information could be fairly compared.

By contrast, social media plays an important role in disseminating and acquiring information for interaction with potential employees, clients and other stakeholders. In many ways social media is integral to the maintenance of a firm's reputation, both internally to their staff and externally to clients and the wider community. However, firms must undertake an important balancing act, particularly with respect to how they manage organisational trust and employee privacy. 'Without privacy, individuals are denied physical and symbolic spaces for moral reflection as well as the resources needed to build and maintain their reputation' (Oravec, 2012: 100). These sentiments are also reflected in employment tribunals such as the Australian Fair Work Ombudsman's guidelines on best practice use of workplace technologies. For example, they suggest that firms adopt a consultative process to increase employees' awareness of the possible risks to business associated with the use electronic communications. Best practice involves clearly discussing what policies might involve; what is appropriate use of email and internet at work; detailing what information is logged and who in the organisation has rights to access this information; how the business intends to monitor or audit employee compliance with the policies and reviewing policies with employees on a regular basis (Fair Work Ombudsman, 2014).

Such initiatives not only improve managerial communication with their staff but also work towards developing positive relationships with both current and future employees and other stakeholders. For example, when job applicants are aware that organisations have viewed their social media profile, they are less likely to perceive the hiring process as fair, regardless of whether they were offered the position. This is particularly the case with respect to the perceptions of skilled knowledge employees, who have greater autonomy to pick and choose where they work. As such, we return to the central message of this chapter: that the tensions and expectations over technology, control and the nexus between private and public lives will not go away. While social media will continue to offer employers unprecedented opportunities to manage their staff through a range of managerial functions, the nature and implications of this 'digital disruption' will depend heavily on how both firms and employees perceive and negotiate around these developments.

Conclusion

This chapter has argued that workplace technologies do not necessarily facilitate greater job autonomy or increase managerial control. Indeed, while there has, and always will be, tensions around the management of workplace technologies, this chapter has emphasised how social relations shape the consequences of workplace technologies. This is as true with the use of human resource information systems as it is with other forms of eHRM.

There is also little doubt that organisations will increasingly use social networking sites to attract and select staff, and to promote their brand. The adoption of new technologies brings many advantages, to both the organisations and individuals that use these tools. However, this chapter has suggested that along with this greater accessibility and reduced costs come some important decisions and negotiations. These negotiations include discussions between firms and their staff about what potential impact these technologies will have on supporting or undermining job autonomy and managerial–employee relations.

The legal and organisational disputes that can develop around (mismatched) expectations over the use of social media have also become increasingly important. Three areas where we have identified such digital 'disruption' include: how firms use social media in recruitment and selection; how social media shapes distinctions between public and private lives and, finally, how alleged employee cyberloafing is managed within organisations. The chapter has also highlighted that whether workplace technologies, has a negative or positive influence on organisational culture will depend in large part on the transparency and integrity of HR policies, practices and processes within individual firms.

Although the legal contract of employment is formally regulated, it remains indeterminate. The psychological contract (that is, the unwritten set of expectations of the employment relationship) is also continually renegotiated and more subconsciously dependent on mutual trust and understanding between employees and their organisations. The legal cases cited above, and many other cases now appearing in employment tribunals, indicate a mismatch between the expectations between organisations and their employees about how workplace technologies, including social media, are managed. In many of these cases, a mutually agreed upon formal social media policy has been absent and because of differing expectations between employees and firms around what constitutes appropriate use of social media, the psychological contract was severely damaged. As such, a potential solution to many of these tensions could be devising more comprehensive and inclusive social media policies as part of broader discussions about the effective implementation and management of workplace technologies.

CASE STUDY 23.1

AUSTRALIAN FIRE FIGHTERS CAUGHT IN THE NET – CYBERLOAFING AND HOW HR MIGHT PRE-EMPT LEGAL ACTION

DIANE VAN DEN BROEK

The case

Fire fighters have a hell of a job. Literally! One minute they are relatively deskbound at the fire station and the next minute they are scaling a twenty-story inner-city apartment complex to extinguish a fire that has already destroyed half the building. Their day-to-day work involves intense and unpredictable bouts of physical exhaustion, smoke inhalation and danger; many fire fighters run the risk of heart attack. It's certainly not a job for the faint hearted!

The shift work also disrupts their usual body rhythms so that, for fire fighters, it is often a case of 10 days on 24-hour call, followed by five days off work. This might be a common shift pattern that unfolds until the next shift cycle is repeated. With this work routine it's hard to develop continuity in personal relationships with partners and children. But despite these shortcomings, most fire fighters love their job!

On occasions, however, this dedication and commitment is questioned. For example, fire fighters lodged a grievance (through their trade union) to the Fair Work Commission in the Australian state of Victoria against the Metropolitan Fire and Emergency Services Board (MFESB). The grievance was raised when the MFESB ruled that fire fighters use of social media (including Facebook and Twitter) and non-business internet be restricted to one hour per day.

This case, like many other similar cases, has been lodged with employment tribunals overseas and reflects growing discontent in how workers' use of social media is being restricted in the workplace. These cases also highlight what role human resource policies and practices can play in managing and potentially averting the grievances that can develop around the use of social media in the workplace.

During this particular case the trade union provided evidence to the tribunal from fire fighters that, aside from a ban on pornographic and other inappropriate sites, personal internet use had not been time-restricted before this restriction was applied. Fire fighters also argued that the restriction was applied too broadly. For example, access to sites used for peer group support and health and well-being information that was greatly appreciated by fire fighters would also be denied. Further, the union argued that the restriction had other unintended consequences, arguing that community safety messages from the emergency control centre had also been blocked. This was a big concern given that fire fighters doing MFESB projects were required to seek management approval to maintain internet access beyond 60 minutes.

The fire fighters and their union also claimed that given the nature of their work, fire fighters often had to be 'out the door in 90 seconds', and as such would not have time to turn their computers off to comply with the restriction.

Background to the case

The use of social media in the workplace has placed considerable pressure on the relationship between firms and their employees. It has also has disrupted many of the boundaries between employees' work lives and their non-work lives However, despite the growing tensions over these work and non-work boundaries, many organisations fail to develop effective human resource policies that take into account the nature of the work undertaken in the firm, and the need for mutual agreement over policies that are proposed and subsequently implemented.

As outlined in the chapter, while there are a number of areas where tensions arise, most social media policies are concerned with monitoring employees' use of social media sites while at work via restrictions on employees' private use of social media during work time. Because contemporary workplace technologies disrupt and reform the boundaries between public and private spheres, there is much disagreement between firms and their employees over what is considered 'fair and reasonable' use of social media sites while at work. On the one hand, there is recognition in employment tribunals that an employer is entitled to have a policy in place which makes clear that excessive use of social media by employees may have consequences. There is also recognition that employers have a protectable interest in regulating social media by prohibiting employees from engaging in certain behaviours via social media, including breaching confidentiality, harassment or disparagement of other employees or disparagement of the company, or posting comments that might be discriminatory on the basis of age, ethnicity, gender, disability or any other protected characteristic.

Why the need for social media policies in emergency services and fighting fires

There is little doubt that most organisations have changed the way they communicate with their customers, their employees and the community around them. As contemporary firms rely on more complex technological arrangements that support strategic and operational activities, there is a greater need for workplace policies to regulate their use. For example, when electronic email was first introduced within organisations many firms introduced policies to regulate its use. However, policies are not the only way that firms can manage their employee's use of social media. Organisational practices which consider the nature of the technology and the nature of employees work, as well as organisational culture are also important in how these issues play out. As such, in order for social media policy to build capacity for harmonious working environments, policies must be influenced by the nature of organisational structure, the nature of the work undertaken as well as established workplace cultures.

For example, most emergency response organisations remain very hierarchical in structure, where command and control is often top-down in nature, including the flow of information from managers to employees. Also, as indicated above, fire fighters undertake a very stressful job. On the one hand, they deal with life threatening situations that require immense courage and resolve to endure what might be before them on any given day. Many situations may require debriefing to allow workers to cope with extreme physical and psychological stress. By contrast, in any given 24-hour shift there may be many hours of 'down time' where little activity is required. Though the number of incidents and the occupational demands may be low at times, the peak periods can lead to excessive physical and mental fatigue.

Emergency management agencies have also recognised the need to provide the public with fast, credible and useful information to avoid or minimise risk to the communities they serve. For example, fire officials often provide fire and life-safety advice to help citizens avoid home fires and reduce the threat of wildfire to homes,

and explain how to prepare for any potential large-scale emergencies. In the past, emergency managers provided critical information during a crisis, which often reflected the government departments' requirement of accountability and control of information. Through the use of these official channels to deliver critical safety information, however, social media has also been an important immediate word-of-mouth network, where information is shared freely and instantly. As such, social media's networking potential is very helpful in providing important stakeholder information before during and after large-scale emergencies. For example, social media has allowed for community members to initiate emergency messaging helping organise relief efforts, reunite lost family members and communicate with vulnerable populations, such as senior citizens, the disabled and those with special needs. As such, the role of social media in organisations such as the Fire Brigade is extremely complex.

Questions

1 How could the Human Resources Department at the Metropolitan Fire and Emergency Services Board have averted this grievance reaching the Fair Work Commission? In your discussions, consider social media policies that favour specificity over generalities by tailoring any policy recommendations specific to the nature of the work at the Metropolitan Fire and Emergency Services.

2 What privacy issues should HR consider in developing and monitoring an effective social media policy, and how might HR best filter the availability of internet and social media sites?

CASE STUDY 23.2

A CASE[1] OF SURVEILLANCE AND HR PRACTICES IN A CALL CENTRE

PAUL THOMPSON

Tele-BankCo is a financial services typical call centre based in central Scotland, handling mostly low-end queries and transactions, and using automatic call distribution (ACD) software. It is a surveillance-intensive environment:

> The ACD allows you to have any size team you like and on the screens you can actually see right down to the person on the phone, you can see it in teams, in management groups, and so on. You can produce macros every day of the different levels of management, either down at rep level to site level. So you

can if you want to, compare the performance of teams across the sites, site against site or individual against individual. *(Manager)*

Like many call centres, it suffers from high turnover and a degree of burnout. Some managers seem to welcome this, one commenting that:

> To me attrition is very healthy in a call centre, very costly, but very healthy. Because of the stressful nature of the job and because you want these people

---

[1]The material in this case draws primarily from Callaghan and Thompson, 2002.

to keep constant energy and enthusiasm, it does the organisation some good if you can pump in some fresh blood. *(Manager)*

However, this was not the dominant view of how management should handle the tensions between quantity and quality in a low discretion–high commitment environment (see previous section). There was a strong focus on standard HR tolls of recruitment, selection and training as a partial 'solution'. Matching the job to the people was seen primarily in terms of recruiting particular types of people – those with bubbly personalities, or as one manager put it:

> The vast majority of these people in customer services centres, we are talking 99 per cent, are not bankers, they've been recruited for their personalities and communication skills.

The perceived centrality of social skills and competencies has led management at Tele-BankCo to use rigorous selection and training procedures more usually associated with high discretion jobs. As part of the recruitment process Tele-BankCo utilises telephone interviews, role plays and two-person structured interviews. Less than 10 per cent of those who apply are selected for a place on the six-week full-time training programme. Though there is some emphasis on technical skills such as navigating screens and product knowledge, the vast amount of time is spent on social competencies. At the heart of this is a conversation cycle to teach customer service representatives (CSRs) how to build rapport with people. Not only does this include managing a conversation but 'managing yourself'. Essentially, employees are taught rudimentary techniques associated with emotional labour – scripted interactions (via 'cookery cards'), voice and tone control and elicitation of responses from customers. This is backed up by a set of 19 core standards of behaviour, such as 'maintaining appropriate standards of behaviour, dress and appearance'; 'pleasant and enthusiastic with customers' and 'welcoming feedback and apologising when mistakes have been made'. Not only are these core standards continually present throughout training (with each of the 19 printed on laminated cards and pasted to the walls and doors of the training room) they are often used in evaluating performance.

However, interviews with CSRs revealed major discrepancies with how management saw the role. CSRs were much more likely to associate job requirements with surviving stressful and repetitive work, rather than applying a particular set of personality characteristics to the enthusiastic pursuit of customer service:

> I can see it [building rapport] is important, but most customers just want to come on and get their query dealt with, they don't really care whether you're they're best friend with them at the end of the call. *(CSR)*

They also consistently raised the surveillance through statistics as an obstacle to high-quality customer service:

> What they don't tell you when you come to the interview is the emphasis they put on stats. They are very statistics oriented – how long your average call is, your average wrap time . . . the emphasis in the call centre and other call centres is on the number of calls, the quality of the calls, yes, but not this rapport thing. *(CSR)*

This led to some CSRs either considering quitting, 'closing down', or going 'off script':

> They [CSRs] are all different personalities, but they're trying to mould them into a Tele-BankCo person. Like robots, and they're always pushing, pushing, and if they keep pushing, I'll be out of the door soon.
>
> My way of handling it is coming in and saying to myself, 'I do my shift from 2 to 10, it's not a career; it's a job. I answer the phone and that's it'. By not looking for anything more than that, that's my way of handling it. When I first came in, I thought it was maybe just me, but speaking to other people it's the same.
>
> We get a lot of people who are on their own, they're pensioners. They ask for a balance, and then they will want a chat – 'what's the weather like?' I'm quite happy to chat to them, but it's always in the back of your mind, got to watch my average handling time. I think you're setting a better example for the bank. *(CSR)*

What can be seen from the case is that the sociotechnical system used in call centres tends to reproduce rather than resolve the quality–quantity, low discretion–high commitment tensions, limiting the effectiveness of the investment in sophisticated HR tools.

Questions

1 As the senior HR manager at Tele-BankCo, you are asked by the bank's call centre executive to evaluate whether it would be more rational to drop the investment in sophisticated recruitment and selection and accept the current rate of attrition. Set out your response by presenting a short memo to senior management.

2 What kind of measures could be made to redesign the socio-technical system to put less emphasis on surveillance and statistics? (refer back to the previous section on call centres).

Bibliography

Please note references that are related to Case 23.1 are marked with * and references that are related to Case 23.2 are marked with **.

Allen, M.W., Coopman, S.J., Hart, J.L. and Walker, K.L. (2007) 'Workplace surveillance and managing privacy boundaries', *Management Communication Quarterly*, Vol.21, No.2, 172–200.

Badham, R. (2005) 'Technology and the transformation of work', in Ackroyd, S., Batt, R., Thompson, P. and Tolbert, P. (eds.) *The Oxford Handbook of Work and Organization*, Oxford: Oxford University Press.

Bain, P., Watson, A., Mulvey, G., Taylor, P. and Gall, G. (2002) 'Taylorism, targets and the pursuit of quantity and quality by call centre management', *New Technology, Work and Employment*, Vol.17, No.3, 170–85.**

Ball, K.S. and Margulis, S.T. (2011) 'Electronic monitoring and surveillance in call centres: a framework for investigation', *New Technology, Work and Employment*, Vol.26, No.2, 113–26.**

Batt, R. (2002) 'Managing customer services: human resource practices, quit rates, and sales growth', *Academy of Management Journal*, Vol.45, No.3, 587–97.**

Batt, R. and Moynihan, L. (2002) 'The viability of alternative call centre production models', *Human Resource Management Journal*, Vol.12, No.4, 14–34.

Blauner, R. (1964) *Alienation and Freedom*, Chicago: University of Chicago Press.

Bondarouk, T.V. and Ruël, H.J.M. (2009) 'Electronic human resource management: challenges in the digital era', *International Journal of Human Resource Management*, Vol.20, No.3, 505–14.

Braverman, H. (1974) *Labor and Monopoly Capital*, New York and London: Monthly Review Press.

Broughton, A., Higgins, T., Hicks, B. and Cox, A. (2009) 'Workplaces and social networking: the implications for employment relations, ACAS research paper 11/11.

Broughton, A., Foley, B., Ledermaier, S. and Cox, A. (2013) 'The use of social media in the recruitment process', an ACAS research publication. Available at: http://www.acas.org.uk/media/pdf/0/b/The-use-of-social-media-in-the-recruitment-process.pdf.

Cain, J. (2011) 'Social media in health care: the case for organizational policy and employee education', *American Journal of Health-System Pharmacy*, Vol.68, No.11, 1036–40.

Callaghan, G. and Thompson, P (2002) '"We recruit attitude": the selection and shaping of call centre labour', *Journal of Management Studies*, Vol.39, No.2, 233–54.

Callaghan, G. and Thompson, P. (2001) 'Edwards revisited: technical control in call centres', *Economic and Industrial Democracy*, Vol.22, No.1, 13–37.**

Castells, M. (1996) *The Rise of the Network Society: The Information Age Economy, Society and Culture*, Oxford: Blackwell, Vol. 1.

Castells, M. (2001) *The Internet Galaxy: Reflections on the Internet, Business, and Society*, Oxford: Oxford University Press.

Charoensukmongkol, P. (2015) 'Mindful Facebooking: the moderating role of mindfulness on the relationship between social media use intensity at work and burnout', *Journal of Health Psychology*. Available at: DOI: 10.1177/1359105315569096.

Collinson, D.L. and Collinson, M. (1997) 'Delayering managers: time-space surveillance and its gendered effects', *Organization*, Vol.4, No.3, 375–407.

Cullinane, N. and Dundon, T. (2006) 'The psychological contract: a critical review', *International Journal of Management Reviews*, Vol.8, No.2, 113–29.*

Davison, H., Maraist, C. and Bing, M. (2011) 'Friend or foe? The promise and pitfalls of using social networking sites for HR decisions', *Journal of Business Psychology*, Vol.26, No.2, 153–9.

Deloitte (2009) 'Ethics & workplace survey examines the reputational risk implications of social network'. Available at: http://www.slideshare.net/PingElizabeth/deloitte-2009-ethics-workplace-survey.

Dery, K., Hall, R., Wailes, N. and Wiblen, S. (2013) Lost in translation? An actor-network approach to HRIS implementation', *The Journal of Strategic Information Systems*, Vol.22, No.3, 225–37.**

Doyle, C. and Bagaric, M. (2005) *Privacy Law in Australia*, Federation Press.

Dutta, S. (2010) 'What's your personal social media strategy', *Harvard Business Review*, Vol.88, No.11, 127–30.*

Fair Work Australia (2011) *Damien O'Keefe* v *Williams Muir's Pty Ltd T/A Troy Williams The Good Guys*, Fair Work Australia, 5311, 11 August 2011.

Fair Work Ombudsman (2014) *Best Practice Guide to Workplace Privacy*, 08, Commonwealth of Australia.

Floyd, L. and Spry, M. (2013) Four burgeoning IR issues for 2013 and beyond: adverse action; social media & workplace policy; trade union regulation (after the HSU affair); and the QANTAS aftermath', *Australian Bar Review*, Vol.37, 153–74.

Fraser, J.A. (2002) *White-Collar Sweatshop: The Deterioration of Work and its Rewards in Corporate America*, W.W. Norton & Company.

Frenkel, S.J., Tam, M., Korczynski, M. and Shire, K. (1998) Beyond bureaucracy? Work organization in call centres', *International Journal of Human Resource Management*, Vol.9, No.6, 957–979.**

Gardner, N., McGranahan, D. and Wolf, W. (2011) 'Question for your HR chief: are we using our 'people data' to create value?', *McKinsey Quarterly*, March.

Garrett, R.K., Danziger, J.N. (2008) 'On cyberslacking: workplace status and personal internet use at work,' *CyberPsychology and Behavior*, Vol.11, No.3, 287–92.

Gilmore, A. (2001) 'Call centre management: is service quality a priority?', *Managing Service Quality: An International Journal*, Vol.11, No.3, 153–9.**

Gorman, A. (2013) 'Tweeting while you work helps productivity. Employer policies that ban social media miss that these breaks help workers reset', *Newsday*: combined editions, Long Island, NY.

Guiliano, V.E. (1982) 'The mechanisation of office work', *Scientific American*, Vol.247, No.3, 148–64.

Hallier, J. (2004) 'Embellishing the past: middle manager identity and informality in the implementation of new technology', *New Technology, Work and Employment*, Vol.19, No.1, 43–62.

Houlihan, M. (2002) 'Tensions and variations in call centre management strategies', *Human Resource Management Journal*, Vol.12, No.4, 67–85.**

Husin, M. and Hanisch, J. (2011) 'Social media and organisation policy (Someop): finding the perfect balance', ECIS 2011 proceedings, Paper 253. Available at: http://aisel.aisnet.org/ecis2011/253.*

Hytten, K. and Hasle, A. (1989) 'Fire fighters: a study of stress and coping', *Acta Psychiatrica Scandinavica*, Vol.80, Nos.355, 50–5.*

Jacobson, W. and Tufts, S. (2013) 'To post or not to post employee rights and social media', *Review of Public Personnel Administration*, Vol.33, No.1, 84–107.

Joos, J.G. (2008) Social media: new frontiers in hiring and recruiting', *Employment Relations Today*, Vol.35, No.1, 51–9.

Kane, G., Palmer, D., Nguyen Philips, A., Kiron, D. and Buckley, N. (2014) 'Moving beyond marketing: generating social business value across the enterprise. Findings from the 2014 Social Business Global Executive Study and Research Project. Available at: http://sloanreview.mit.edu/projects/moving-beyond-marketing, Reprint No. 56180.*

Kaplan, A.M. and Haenlein, M. (2010) 'Users of the world, unite! The challenges and opportunities of social media', *Business Horizons*, Vol.53, No.1, 59–68.*

Lowe, K.B., Milliman, J., Cieri, H. and Dowling, P.J. (2002) 'International compensation practices: a ten-country comparative analysis', *Asia Pacific Journal of Human Resources*, Vol.40, No.1, 55–80.

Mackenzie, D. and Wajcman, J. (eds.) (1999) *The Social Shaping of Technology* (2nd edn.), Milton Keynes: Open University Press.

Malachowski, D. (2005) 'Wasted time at work costing companies billions', *San Francisco Chronicle*. Available at: http://www.systemsdynamics.net/aeprod/articles/05092.pdf.

Kelly, W. (2014) 'Social media: an effective tool for risk and crisis communication? Master's thesis.

McDonald, P. and Thompson, P. (2015) 'Social media(tion) and the reshaping of public /private boundaries in employment relations', *International Journal of Management Reviews*, Vol.18, No.1, 69–84.

McKinlay, A. (2002) 'The limits of knowledge management', *New Technology, Work and Employment*, Vol.17, No.2, 76–88.

Mumford, E. (2006) 'The story of socio-technical design: reflections on its successes, failures and potential', *Information Systems Journal*, Vol.16, No.4, 317–42.**

Neylon O'Brien, C. (2011) 'The first Facebook firing case under Section 7 of the National Labor Relations Act: exploring the limits of labor law protection for concerted communication on social media', *Suffolk University Law Review*, Vol.45, 29–66.

Noble, D. (1984) *Forces of Production*, New York: Monthly Review Press.

Ollington, N., Gibb, J. and Harcourt, M. (2013) 'Online social networks: an emergent recruiter tool for attracting and screening', *Personnel Review*, Vol.42, No.3, 248–65.

Oravec, J. (2012) 'Deconstructing "personal privacy" in an age of social media: information control and regulation management dimensions', *International Journal of Academic Business World*, Vol.6, No.1, Spring.

Orlikowski, W.J. (2000) 'Using technology and constituting structures: a practice lens for studying technology in organisations', *Organisation Science*, Vol.11, No.4, 404–26.

Purcell, J., Hutchinson, S. and Kinnie, N. (2000) 'Fun and surveillance': the paradox of high commitment management in call centres', *International Journal of Human Resource Management*, Vol.11, No.2, 967–85.

Rice, A.K. (1958) *Productivity and Social Organisation*, London: Tavistock.

Rose, E. and Wright, G. (2005) 'Satisfaction and dimensions of control among call centre customer service representatives', *The International Journal of Human Resource Management*, Vol.16, No.1, 136–60.**

Rousseau, D. (2001) 'Schema, promise and mutuality: the building blocks of the psychological contract', *Journal of Occupational and Organizational Psychology*, Vol.74, No.4, 511–44.*

Rowell, E.D. (2010) 'Didn't get hired because of Facebook? You're not alone', EzineArticles, 10.

Scarbrough, H. and Swan, J. (2001) 'Explaining the diffusion of knowledge management: the role of fashion', *British Journal of Management*, Vol.12, 3–12.

Sewell, G. and Wilkinson, B. (1992) 'Someone to watch over me': surveillance, discipline and the just-in-time labour process', *Sociology*, Vol.26, No.2, 271-89.

Slovensky, R. and Ross, W.H. (2012) 'Should human resource managers use social media to screen job applicants? Managerial and legal issues in the USA', *info*, Vol.14, No.1, 55–69.

Smith, W.P. and Tabak, F. (2009) 'Monitoring employee e-mails: is there any room for privacy?', *Academy of Management Perspectives*, Vol.23, No.4, 33–48.

Suddath, C. (2012) 'Big brother wants your Facebook password', *Bloomberg Businessweek*. Available at: http://www.bloomberg.com/bw/articles/2012-03-27/big-brother-wants-your-facebook-password.

Taylor, P. and Bain, P. (1999) '"An assembly line in the head": work and employee relations in the call centre', *Industrial Relations Journal*, Vol.30, No.2, 101–17.**

Taylor, P. and Bain, P. (2005) 'India calling to the far away towns: the call centre labour process and globalization', *Work, Employment & Society*, Vol.19, No.2, 261–82.

Thomas, K. (2014) 'Workplace technology and the creation of boundaries: the role of VHRD in a 24/7 work environment, *Advances in Developing Human Resources*, Vol.16, No.3, 281–95.

Thompson, P. (2003) 'Fantasy Island: a labour process critique of the "Age of Surveillance"', *Surveillance and Society*, Vol.1, No.2, 138–51.

Thompson, P. and McHugh, D. (2009) *Work Organisations* (4th edn.), Basingstoke: Palgrave.

Thompson, P., van den Broek, D. and Callaghan, G. (2004) 'Keeping up appearances: recruitment, skills and normative controls in call centres', in Deery, S. and Kinnie, N. (eds.) *Human Resource Management in Call Centres*, Basingstoke: Palgrave.

Thornthwaite, L. (2013) Social media, unfair dismissal and the regulation of employees' conduct outside work,' *Australian Journal of Labour Law*, Vol.26, No.2, 164–84.

Thornthwaite, L. (2015) Chilling times: social media policies, labour law and employment relations', *Asia Pacific Journal of Human Resources*. Available at: http://onlinelibrary.wiley.com/journal/10.1111/(ISSN)1744-7941/earlyview.

Unit, E.I. (2010) 'Digital economy rankings 2010 beyond e-readiness', *The Economist*, June.

van den Broek, D. (2002) 'Monitoring and surveillance in call centres: some responses from Australian workers', *Labour & Industry*, Vol.12, No.3, May.

van den Broek, D. (2003) 'Call to arms? Collective and individual responses to call centre labour management', pp. 267–83, in Deery, S. and Kinnie, N. (eds.) *Call Centres and Human Resource Management: A Cross-National Perspective*, London: Palgrave.

van den Broek, D. (2004) 'We have the values: customers, control and corporate ideology in call centre operations', *New Technology, Work and Employment*, Vol.19, No.1, 2–13.**

van den Broek, D. (2008) "Doing things right", or "doing the right things"? Call centre migrations and dimensions of knowledge', *Work, Employment and Society*, Vol.22, No.4, 601–13.

van den Broek, D., Callaghan, G. and Thompson, P. (2004) 'Teams without teamwork? Explaining the call centre paradox', *Economic and Industrial Democracy*, Vol.25, No.2, 197–218.

Wallace, C.M., Eagelson, G. and Waldersee, R. (2000) 'The sacrificial HR strategy in call centres', *International Journal of Service Industry Management*, Vol.11, No.2, 174–84.**

Webster, F. (2002) *Theories of the Information Society* (2nd edn.), London: Routledge.

Wilkinson, B. (1985) *The Shopfloor Politics of New Technology*, London: Heinemann.

Woodward, J. (1958) *Management and Technology*, London: HMSO.

Zuboff, S. (1988) *In the Age of the Smart Machine: The Future of Work and Power*, London: Heinemann.

CHAPTER 24

TALENT MANAGEMENT: CONTEMPORARY ISSUES

Agnieszka Skuza and Hugh Scullion

Introduction

The work environment today is characterised by outsourcing, increasing mobility, looser psychological contracts between organisations and their employees, less predictable and more fluid career paths and more focus on self-directed learning (Nilsson and Ellstrom, 2011; Vaiman et al., 2011; D'Amato and Herzfeldt, 2008). From the organisational perspective, these new workplace characteristics lead to new challenges in securing retention of the most valuable and unique employees. This coincides with the fact that talent scarcity and competition for highly skilled labour is growing and this trend is expected to continue (Manpower Group, 2013; CIPD, 2012; Ernst and Young, 2010; Human Capital Institute, 2008; Boston Consulting Group, 2007). While companies continue to experience problems with attracting and retaining talents, they increasingly realise that knowledge, skills and abilities of their key employees is a major source of the competitive advantage, which highlights the importance of talent management (TM) practices to attract, select, develop and manage employees in a more strategic way (Scullion and Collings, 2011; Garavan et al., 2012; Sparrow et al., 2014a).

Although talent management is not a new concept (see Patton, 1967), most of the literature on talent management is not well grounded in research and is still dominated by practitioner or consultancy-based contributions despite the recognition of the strategic importance of talent management initiatives (e.g. Bryan et al., 2006; Guthridge et al., 2006). Also, the weakness of established theoretical foundations in the area persists, and there are continuing concerns over the definition, overall goals and conceptual boundaries of talent management (Sparrow et al., 2014a; Collings and Mellahi, 2009). For example, Lewis and Heckman (2006) identify three main views on the nature of talent management. The first view largely replaces the label talent management for human resource management. The second view emphasises the development of talent pools focusing on managing the progression of employees through positions in the organisation. The third view focuses on the management of talented people, and argues that all roles within the organisation should be filled with 'A performers', referred to as 'top-grading' (Smart, 1999) and emphasises the management of 'C players', or consistently poor performers, out of the organisation (Michaels et al., 2001). Recently, Collings and Mellahi (2009) added a fourth dimension that concentrates on the identification of key positions which have the potential to differentially contribute to the competitive advantage of the firm. In this chapter we adapted the definition proposed by Scullion *et al.* (2010), which states that TM includes all organisational activities for the purpose of attracting, selecting, developing and retaining the best employees in the most strategic roles (those roles are necessary to achieve organisational strategic priorities).

In this chapter we aim to:

- Explain factors behind the growth of the interest in talent management;
- Review the organisational dilemmas around the word 'talent';
- Present recent classification of approaches to talent management;
- Consider some empirical evidence on the nature of talent management in MNCs.

 Factors influencing the growth of talent management

Talent management has emerged in recent years as a key strategic issue for MNCs. The growth of TM is attributed to a number of factors, which are outlined below (see also Scullion and Collings, 2011; Sparrow *et al.*, 2014a):

- Competition between employers for talent has shifted from the country level to the regional and global levels, and MNCs increasingly need to manage talent on a regional or global basis to be competitive (Sparrow *et al.*, 2014a; Farndale *et al.*, 2014).
- There is a growing recognition of the critical role played by global talents in ensuring the success of MNCs and a growing understanding that the success of global business depends on the quality of leadership in the MNC (Scullion and Starkey, 2000). MNCs increasingly need highly mobile elites of management that are capable of developing new markets and perform boundary spanning roles to help build social networks and facilitate the international leaning and innovation to support globalisation (Farndale *et al.*, 2010; Sparrow *et al.*, 2014a). However, shortages of leadership talent have emerged as a key HR problem for many MNCs and they are often a major barrier to many companies seeking to internationalise their operations (Scullion and Brewster, 2001; Scullion *et al.*, 2007).
- The rapid growth of the emerging markets increased the demand for managerial and professional talent which can operate effectively in these markets. For example, Brazil, Turkey and two former Central and Eastern Europe (CEE) countries – Bulgaria and Romania experience particular difficulties in filling vacancies because of the lack of locally available talent, while availability of talented managers and professionals is recognised as critical to the long-term success of those countries. A recent survey conducted by Manpower Group (2012; 2013) revealed that almost 70 per cent of managers in Brazil, 60 per cent in Turkey and 50 per cent in Romania and Bulgaria reported difficulties in filling jobs, which place these countries well above the global average (35 per cent). The rapid economic, social and political transformation in these countries makes understanding of the culture more challenging and while economic development may be considerably advanced, the managerial practices are still in a period of change and are far from converging with Western models. This results in a significant demand for a distinctive type of managerial talent which can operate effectively in these culturally complex and economically turbulent markets (Li and Scullion, 2006, 2010; Tymon *et al.*, 2010; Skuza *et al.*, 2013).
- Demographic trends also influence the nature of talent management. Declining birth rates and increasing longevity are key demographic trends in developed countries which will have 'significant implications for how to manage workforce quantity, quality and costs' (World Economic Forum, 2011) and will significantly impact corporate recruitment strategies (Stahl *et al.*, 2007; Stahl *et al.*, 2012). While external recruitment is becoming more

challenging because of talent shortages, the role of talent management will increase, enhancing the attractiveness of internal talent identification, development and learning, and intensifying efforts to minimise the loss of key human capital and maximise retention of valuable talent (Echols, 2007). A second key demographic trend relates to generational differences in the workplace. As generational cohorts differ in their behaviour and attitudes in the workplace, they will respond differently to talent management practices. Analysing the influence of psychological contracts on talented employees, Festing and Schafer (2014) noticed that talent management practices do not influence the psychological contract of all talented employees in the same way and that new generation's distinct preferences and expectations will lead to the increase of interest in TM. For example, Millennials (also called Generation Y) are less loyal and more mobile; they value frequent feedback, high level of empowerment, independence, freedom to make their own decisions, and learning and self-development opportunities which make them more employable. Growing attention to TM practices results from increased necessity to fulfil individual expectations, to increase commitment and to retain the most valuable yet less loyal young employees (Festing and Schäfer, 2014).

- The growth of knowledge-based economies is a further factor impacting on talent management. The shift from product-based to knowledge-based economies and the dominance of the service sector (in developed economies reaching even 70 per cent of all jobs) resulted in a growing need by companies to hire high value workers in more complex roles which require higher levels of cognitive ability.
- The growing demand for alternative forms of international assignments such as short-term assignments or commuter assignments which together with the globalisation of a number of professional labour markets (such as Health Care and Information Technology) creates new patterns of international working (Collings *et al.*, 2007; Mayrhofer *et al.*, 2012). This offers the opportunity to both foreign-owned and indigenous companies to use differentiated expertise and potential wherever it is located, and creates a challenge of identifying and deploying highly diverse international talents.

Despite the global recession, talent management will continue to be a high priority issue for the majority of multinational corporations in the future (CIPD, 2012; PricewaterhouseCoopers, 2012; Ernst and Young, 2010; Sparrow *et al.*, 2014a; Sonnenberg *et al.*, 2014; Farndale *et al.*, 2010). Practitioner's publications such as PricewaterhouseCoopers' (2012) study of 1,250 CEOs from 60 countries demonstrate that strategies for managing talent remain a top priority for CEOs, and not having the right talent in the right place continues to be seen as a leading threat to the profitability and growth for most of the surveyed companies. A recent Manpower Group report (2013), based on almost 40,000 employers, shows that difficulties to identify and retain talent significantly constrain the ability of many companies to remain competitive, and to service clients effectively. The number of practitioners reporting those concerns was higher in 2013 than in 2012 and the highest since 2007. Similarly, an Ernst and Young report (2010) argues that TM correlates strongly with enhanced business performance, and TM programmes properly aligned with business strategies deliver a return on investment on average, 20 per cent higher than that of rival companies where TM and business strategies where not aligned.

However, measuring the effectiveness of TM and its real impact on performance remains a challenge for most companies. Part of the problem is a clear disagreement about what metrics should be used to measure TM effectiveness. A recent report by Human Capital Institute and Hewitt Associates (2008) shows that companies are often not strategic about what they measure. In addition, they often focus on practices rather than outcomes, and many companies take an ad hoc approach to TM measurement, tracking mainly a number of low-impact metrics with limited predictive value. Also, very few companies (seven per cent) consistently use metrics to align TM with business results (2008: 25). However, given the increasing pressure on revenues and returns, companies will need to apply a more strategic approach to justify expenditure on TM and prove a link between TM and business results (Boudreau and Ramstad, 2007).

Talent management versus human resource management

Another critique of TM comes from the notion that TM is not essentially different from HRM and as such is a simple rebranding or relabelling of HRM showing its 'fashionability' and adding little value to existing practice (Lewis and Heckman, 2006; Iles, *et al.*, 2010). Some research therefore challenges the distinctiveness of the concept of TM from HRM. For example, Adamsky (2003) comments that TM is simply a repackaging of old ideas under a new name and could be seen as another attempt by HR to increase its legitimacy. Cappelli (2008) points to the need to demonstrate the TM value-added over strategic human resource management. While there is some continuity between HRM and TM in terms of similar areas covered together with the link with business strategy, recent research, however, highlights significant differences between TM and HRM. For example, workforce differentiation is seen as a key feature of talent management and increasingly the importance of differentiated talent development architecture is highlighted by researchers (Boudreau and Ramstad, 2005a). This approach is based on the idea that you should invest in those human resources where you expect the best return (Gandz, 2006; McDonnell, 2011; Iles *et al.*, 2010; Collings and Mellahi, 2009; Chuai *et al.*, 2008). In contrast, HRM is more egalitarian in its approach and in this 'inclusive' approach the focus is on all employees in the organisation (Collings and Mellahi, 2009). Iles *et al.* (2010) also emphasise that, while HRM focuses more on management functions, TM concentrates more on people with the particular focus on the attraction, retention and development of talented individuals who are high on value and uniqueness. Dries (2013), on the other hand, reviewing the literature on educational psychology, states that TM is to HRM what gifted education is to general education, implying that the needs of talents are different from those of the 'average' employees (see also Gagné, 2004). Therefore TM may offer a new and different approach to people management with a focus on segmentation, where TM is seen as 'integrated HRM with a selective focus' (Iles *et al.*, 2010: 187).

The meaning of talent

Current debates highlight the increased importance of talent management in the organisational context, yet the definition of talent is still far from clear and organisations differ widely in their perspective on talent (Dries, 2013). Common distinctions that organisations make concern whether:

1 talent is a specific group of employees or all employees;
2 talent is innate or acquired;
3 talent is evaluated based on potential or performance.

The first perspective places a significant emphasis on whether approaches to talent should be exclusive or inclusive. An exclusive approach is based on the notion of workforce differentiation, which uses a differentiated HR architecture (Becker *et al.*, 2009) and assumes that investing in employees with valuable and unique skills will generate higher returns than investing in employees that lack these skills (Lepak and Snell, 1999). It is argued that this approach is more cost effective and efficient and has a greater impact on organisational performance, and that the management of employees should vary according to their contribution to competitive advantage (Collings and Mellahi, 2009; Sonnenberg *et al.*, 2014; Boudreau and Ramstad, 2007; Collings, 2014). It has been suggested, however, that the exclusive approach may undermine teamwork and the morale of the majority of employees who are not identified as talent. In addition, there are a number of critiques of the exclusive approach based on the lack of objectivity of both evaluations of performance and potential (Gallardo-Gallardo *et al.*, 2013; Sparrow *et al.*, 2014a; Guthridge *et al.*, 2008). Yet the evidence suggests that the exclusive approach is more prevalent both in the literature and in practice (CIPD, 2012). For those advocating the inclusive approach, which is egalitarian in the sense that everybody should be seen as talent and that all employees can potentially add value, the key question is: should an organisation provide all employees with the same opportunity to succeed in the organisation? In this inclusive approach talent management should be about that set of HR practices that enables identification, exploitation and optimisation of the generic capabilities of all employees (Sparrow *et al.*, 2014a).

The second perspective builds on the nature versus nurture debate and is focused upon the degree to which talent can be acquired (Meyers *et al.*, 2013; Gallardo-Gallardo *et al.*, 2013). Innate perspectives imply that talent is a mix of inborn cognitive abilities and personality which are stable and difficult to develop (Davies and Davies, 2010; Buckingham and Vosburgh, 2001). In contrast, acquired perspectives advocate that talent is a mix of knowledge, skills and abilities that are capable of being developed and imply a focus on practice, education and learning. The assumption is that talent emerges mainly through effort and experience (Ericsson *et al.*, 2007; Pfeffer and Sutton, 2006; Tsay and Banaji, 2011). The former view suggests a greater emphasis on talent identification and selection, while the latter implies more focus on talent development. Adopting the innate perspective impacts the talent selection, assessment and identification process, which is a complex multi-level process aimed at identifying those with extraordinary abilities and personality. Therefore more diagnostic instruments are used (psychological and cognitive tests, personality tests, assessment centres) which help to identify innate gifts that will allow individuals to display extraordinary skills in a specific domain and achieve above-average results. Focusing on the acquired perspective, on the other hand, allows a shift from the key-people approach (focus on a handful of key people) towards more focus on strategic competencies (knowledge, skills, abilities and personal characteristics) that contribute to the organisation's strategic intent. It also implies more focus on the talent development process based on building experiences, competencies, relationships and the learning capabilities needed to achieve organisational goals (instead of developing individual talents). This allows TM to be much more aligned with the business strategy (Sparrow *et al.*, 2014b).

The third perspective concerns the degree to which talent should be operationalised through high performance or high potential. High performance is measured through realised outputs such as achievements, results and performance (Martin and Schmidt, 2010; Silzer and Church, 2009). High potential, on the other hand, is defined through input factors and implies that 'an individual has the qualities (e.g. characteristics, motivation, skills, abilities, and experiences) to effectively perform and contribute in broader or different roles in the organisation at some point in the future' (Silzer and Church, 2009: 380). As there are relatively few empirical studies on the construct of high potential and characteristics of high potential individuals in organisations, there are a number of questions that need to be addressed empirically (see also Silzer and Church, 2009): What should be the mix of dimensions/key characteristics of high potential, and to what extent will it depend on industry, function, profession, gender, cultural or specific organisational context? What should be the level of each characteristics so an individual can be considered as high potential? Does the high potential model change when the strategy changes? Can line managers evaluate potential properly since this evaluates skills needed in the future to perform effectively in broader or different roles? Empirical research shows that high potential and performance are often used to identify talent, but the absence of the clear definition of the construct of high potential contributes to misunderstandings and misuses, and it is not uncommon that in the same organisation different managers use different definitions, which may conflict with the corporate standards (Silzer and Church, 2009).

The understanding of talent through the categories above has important implications for the talent management process. For example, it influences whether organisations focus their TM agenda more on talent identification and the selection process or on talent development process, which may also have important implications for strategic alignment of talent management practices with corporate strategy and business models. And while a universal definition for talent may not be beneficial as it is highly dependent on the specific organisational context, it is important that within an organisation various actors adopt the same perspective to talent (Sonnenberg *et al.*, 2014). Discrepancies between talent perceptions within the same organisation may result in negative consequences for organisations in terms of losing talent, nominating wrong individuals, decreased motivation of those not recognised as talent, and lack of desired effects of TM practices on those included in the talent pool.

Approaches to talent management

The four approaches to talent management identified by Collings and Mellahi (2009) is the most influential work on the approaches to talent management (Collings and Mellahi, 2009; Sparrow *et al.*, 2011; Sparrow *et al.*, 2014b). These are:

- People approach: talent management as a categorisation of people.
- Practices approach: talent management as the presence of key HRM practices.
- Position approach: talent management as the identification of pivotal positions.
- Strategic pools approach: talent management as internal talent pools and succession planning.

Those approaches are often used as alternative or even competing approaches, although in organisational practice they are often used interchangeably. Organisations with more mature talent management systems tend to use a combination of those approaches which varies according to business needs and corporate strategy.

The first people philosophy is based on the notion of the centrality of people with extraordinary abilities and unique skills that are hard to find and replace. They add a disproportionate amount of value to the organisation compared to other employees and therefore require much more investment and attention. As value creators and an inimitable source of competitive advantage they need a different set of development and retention practices.

This philosophy came to prominence in the late 1990s following the publication of the report 'The War for Talent' by a group of McKinsey consultants (Michaels *et al.*, 2001). The notion of the 'war for talent' reflected the view that human capital had emerged as the most important source of competitive advantage in a period when tight labour markets made attracting and retaining leadership and professional talent more challenging. The typical focus of talent management in this period was on differentiated individual employee performance, and therefore high potentials and high performers became the main focus of attention. Although this differentiation was captured in TM philosophy by the 'war for talent' narrative, Sparrow *et al.* (2014b) and later Sparrow and Makram (2015) argue that this approach was underpinned by the two-dimensional model of performance versus potential known as human resources portfolio matrix. Recommended by Odiorne (1984), it used the Boston Consulting Group strategic product matrix to categorise people in four categories – in terms of stars, problem children, work horses and deadwood. This categorisation was used in early 1990s by the HR function mainly for identification of high potentials and succession–management practices. Later it was developed into the more advanced nine-box model of performance–potential used also to identify deployment and development recommendations for talent. The matrix approach sends a clear signal that people should be categorised according to their proved performance and future potential for broader or new roles. Based on this approach the people perspective has attracted much criticism. First, people categorisation can diminish the value of teamwork and collaboration. Second, categorisation to 'A', 'B', and 'C' categories, which is often advocated within this perspective, can be not only discouraging for those in the 'B' or 'C' category but can also be risky because of the easiness of imitability and high risk of losing talents to competitors. Third, performance of 'star' individuals is not enough to create organisational capabilities which are highly dependent on available resources, systems, processes and networks. Fourth, people perspective on talent suggests that individual ability is a fixed trait which is not supported by empirical evidence. Finally, the people approach can be only valid when the level of business model change is low, and people have a chance to prove their superior performance and potential with regard to known and predictable business problems (Sparrow *et al.*, 2014b).

The second practice approach focuses on talent management practices required to effectively manage talent in organisations. Key talent management practices typically revolve around (Scullion *et al.*, 2010; Stahl *et al.*, 2007):

- talent identification practices – identification and selection of internal talents and external recruitment (attracting talents to the organisation, creating employee value propositions and employer brand, recruiting ahead of curve);
- talent development practices – formal programmes, relationship-based development experiences, job-based development experiences, informal/non-formal development activities (Conger, 2010; McCall *et al.*, 1988; Byham *et al.*, 2002; Garavan *et al.*, 2012);
- talent evaluation and deployment (effective succession systems, career management, internal mobility);
- talent retention (exit interviews, talent satisfaction monitoring, personalised retention strategies, building communication bridges with talents that left).

The differentiated architecture of TM practices that form 'a part of a broader system driven by the business strategy' (Sparrow *et al.*, 2014b) may not only increase strategic role of TM but also contributes to creating unique and inimitable competitive advantage deeply rooted in organisational contexts.

The third perspective, called the position approach, picks up on the strategic role of talent management that focuses on 'activities and processes that involve the systematic identification of key positions which differentially contribute to the organisation's sustainable competitive advantage' (Collings and Mellahi, 2009: 304). While an influential stream of research of talent management emphasises the idea that employees can contribute to the firm's strategic goals with their value and uniqueness (Michaels *et al.*, 2001; Lepak and Snell, 1999), a growing number of publications advocates a focus on the identification of key positions. This derives from the notion that while not all strategic processes are highly dependent on human resources, differentiation should involve jobs not the individual employees (Becker and Huselid, 2006). Human capital is recognised as having important value only when it is deployed in the implementation of organisational strategy and objectives (Boxall and Purcell, 2008). Collings and Mellahi (2009) underlie that while differentiating between strategic and non-strategic positions, organisations should change the way they think about role and job evaluation. Moving from job differentiation based on inputs (skills, efforts, abilities and working conditions) towards outputs or the potential for roles that contribute to organisational strategy becomes fundamental for this approach. The value of the position approach grows with the high level of strategic uncertainty and business model change as it facilitates the development of TM systems which are more aligned to changes in strategy and can deliver value to the business. The position approach also de-links TM strategy from leadership development as it concentrates on core strategic and operational positions, and also limits the problem of loss of motivation of those not included in the talent pool as it departs from a focus on people classification thus reducing emotional reactions to the exclusion from the talent pool.

There are, however, a few problems with this approach. First, the assessment of how valuable is a specific position is complex and highly dependent on the evaluating party. Also, the impact of specific positions on value to the organisation requires decision science that organisations typically lack (Boudreau and Ramstad, 2005a, b). Second, TM is a long-term process based on development of talented individuals for specific positions or roles. What happens with those individuals when rapid environmental changes influence business model change and the priority of specific positions will change?

The fourth approach to TM is based on strategic talent pools where investment in human capital makes the biggest difference to strategic success (Sparrow *et al.*, 2014b). Based on this notion Boudreau and Ramstad (2005a, b) introduced the term 'pivotal talent pools' and state that decisions with regard to each talent pool should consider three elements: impact, effectiveness and efficiency. Impact can be defined in terms of the level of dependence of strategic success of a particular talent pool and answers the question: 'How much will strategic success increase by improving the quality or availability of a particular talent pool?' Effectiveness concerns HR programmes and processes and their effect on the capacity and actions of employees in talent pools, and efficiency refers to the amount of HR programme and process activity that is captured from organisational investment (resources used to deliver HR practices). Strategic talent pools philosophy derives both from human capital theory in that the cost of developing and retaining talent should be viewed as investments on behalf of firm, and expectancy theory, which explains individual behavioural directions when individuals are recognised as of a special importance to the organisation (Sparrow and Makram, 2015). The key value of the strategic talent pools approach lies in identifying labour pools of strategic value that contributes to organisational success and increasing the organisational interest in optimising the use of metrics with regard to both identification of value of labour pools and the effectiveness and efficiency of HR practices. TM based on the strategic talent pool philosophy might therefore increase the confidence between management and HR and increase the role of HR as a strategic partner and value-adding function, which is still not the case in most organisations. As reported in Global Leadership Forecast (Howard and Wellins, 2009) less than one-fourth of leaders have high confidence in HR and only one-third of CEOs believe that HR is truly a strategic partner in the business.

Having examined approaches to talent and talent management the following section will seek to examine some evidence on the nature of talent management in organisations.

Application of TM: recent empirical research review

Although talent management has been a rapidly growing field, surprisingly, the research base on talent management is rather descriptive and until recently there was a dearth of empirical studies in this field. The need to understand the conceptual boundaries of the topic has resulted in academic publications of a mainly conceptual nature, although recently there has been a growth of empirical research on talent management with an increasingly important contribution coming from Europe (see Dries and Pepermans, 2008; Boussebaa and Morgan, 2008; Sheehan, 2012; Hoglund, 2012; Gallardo-Gallardo *et al.*, 2013; Bjorkman *et al.*, 2013; Festing *et al.*, 2013; Skuza *et al.*, 2013; Tansley and Tietze, 2013; Valverde *et al.*, 2013; Farndale *et al.*, 2014; Sonnenberg *et al.*, 2014). Review of the empirical research identifies three key streams of focus on TM:

- The conceptualisation of talent and talent management.
- Deployment of talent management activities and practices.
- The intended outcomes and effects of talent management.

The first stream of research draws on the psychological contract perspective based on social exchange theory. For example, Hoglund (2012) in his study of Finnish, Swedish and Norwegian multinationals examined both the direct and indirect effect of HRM practices on human capital from a talent management perspective using the psychological contract perspective to assess employee perceptions of TM. The study highlighted that while the direct effect of skill-enhancing HRM practices on human capital was insignificant, in contrast, the total indirect effect of skill-enhancing HRM practices on human capital through talent inducements turned out to be significant, highlighting the positive consequences that talent management may have on employees' attitudes and psychological contract obligations. Therefore, in summary, Hoglund's study confirmed that differential treatment of employees based on criteria constituting talent can have positive effects on employee motivation. Another study of 11 Nordic MNCs by Bjorkman *et al.* (2013) demonstrated that informing talented individuals of their status has a positive motivational effect on those individuals, supporting the general logic of talent management. Those who perceive that they are identified as talent were more likely to display positive attitudes than those who were not identified as talent. Their research also highlighted that informing individuals that they are not talent has little negative effect (Bjorkman *et al.*, 2013). Sonnenberg *et al.*'s (2014) study of 21 European MNCs also confirmed the importance of making talent management practices explicit. Their most important finding was that although many organisations favour an inclusive approach to talent identification, in practice they all differentiate between employees, although often this was not communicated to employees. However, they highlight that talent management practices which lack clear and uniform communication are more open to misinterpretation and negative outcomes. Finally, it was also suggested that well-targeted talent management programmes have a significant positive effect on psychological contract fulfilment, which is seen as a good predictor of important talent management outcomes (Sonnenberg *et al.*, 2014).

The second stream of research on talent management focuses on talent management processes. The recent study by Tansley and Tietze (2013) illustrates how talent progression through successive levels of the talent management process can be explained through a series of rites of passage (such as passing professional exams, meeting with top management, etc.). They highlight how talent advancement is contingent on the development of appropriate identities and they track the experiences of individual talent in three different talent pools – 'Rising Talent', 'Emerging Leaders' and 'Next Generation Leader' in a consulting organisation. Their findings suggest that talent advancement is based on the development of technical expertise and the emergence of particular dispositions and work orientations in this context. The study presents an interesting perspective on the dynamism of work identities, which requires a constant readjustment while the individual is going through different rites of passage. They suggest that talent has to develop to be able to quickly connect and disconnect from locations, relationships and work groups to be able to progress through the talent pools. Boussebaa and Morgan (2008) take a different approach to TM processes. They adapt an institutionalist approach to explain the deployment of common talent management systems across borders and explore how differences between the British and French institutional contexts result in different approaches to TM. Their study highlights tensions which emerge in the utilisation of a framework of talent management developed in the UK and France, which resulted in the complete failure to implement a common talent management system. While identifying high potential, UK managers assumed equality of opportunity for all managers based on meritocracy, meaning that talent identification and career progress depended on proven performance. In France, however, talent was assessed externally through the *Grandes Ecoles* system, the top tier of the higher education system and potential in France is identified at the point of entry. Graduates of those universities become the elite (*cadres*) that run French organisations and it is extremely rare for *non-cadres* to advance to the highest positions in the organisation. The study also highlighted a strong British preference for a pragmatic approach in contrast to the French preference towards intellectualism and abstract thinking. This reflected significant cultural differences between France and the UK leading to contrasting approaches to talent development in the two countries. The lack of understanding of the institutional contexts in the different countries was a major reason for the failure to implement common talent management programmes across borders.

The importance of the institutional context for the deployment of talent management practices is also highlighted in the context of SMEs, a previously neglected area of study. Festing *et al.*'s (2013) study of talent management in German SMEs highlighted that talent management in SMEs is more inclusive, which reflects both the nature of the German national education system, which promotes equality and the longer-term business orientation which operates in Germany. The results of their study provide interesting insight on the talent management process in SMEs, which is highly dependent on the CEO/owner both in talent recruitment and development, and has a strong focus on retaining talents through training and development activities which are accessible to a majority of the employees. Their study also highlighted the distinctive nature of talent issues in SMEs. Larger SMEs placed much more emphasis on talent management than smaller SMEs and are more active with cooperating with others (universities, other companies) in their talent management activities. Building effective networks and combining resources was a key challenge for SMEs in their attempt to overcome limited resources and staff shortages (Festing *et al.*, 2013).

Skuza *et al.* (2013) made an important contribution to our understanding of talent management deployment challenges in CEE countries through their empirical study of multinationals in Poland.

There is a dearth of empirical research on talent management in CEE countries (Vaiman and Holden, 2011), in spite of the increasing significance of the CEE region in the European economy. Skuza *et al.* (2013) highlight the need for organisations to understand the institutional and cultural context in which they are operating, and they identified several key challenges to talent management deployment specific to the CEE region. For example, in CEE countries appointment to talent pools is still largely based on individual technical abilities rather than leadership or personal skills, the latter not being considered important for managerial effectiveness. Also because of the culture of the region, the lack of recognition of individual successes was the norm, which often acted as disincentive for individuals to go forward for a talent role. In addition, the continued reliance on personal relations and private networks in management decisions acted as a barrier to effective talent management, and high potentials were often seen as a threat to the position of established senior managers. Further cultural barriers identified by the Skuza *et al.* (2013) study were the unwillingness to include employees in the decision-making process, a low level of innovativeness and willingness to learn, short-termism and lack of transparency in the evaluation process, all of which make it difficult to transfer Western talent management practices directly (Vaiman and Holden, 2011). The issues of talent management in CEE countries have only recently attracted the attention of organisations, and it has been argued that the strategic approach to HRM is still in the infancy stage of development in the region (Vaiman and Holden, 2011).

The issue of intended outcomes and effects of talent management is the third important stream in talent management research. First, a number of researchers have focused on the careers of high potentials. For example, recent research highlighted the career issues both from the perspective of high potentials and their organisations in the Belgian context and provided some important insights on the applicability of boundaryless career theories (in which employees often change employers aspiring freedom and flexibility) and employability in the European context (Dries and Pepermans, 2008). While the trend towards the boundaryless career is seen as common, Dries and Pepermans (2008) argue that this assumption does not fit with the expectations of high potentials, who continue to prefer more traditional career practices such as upward mobility and low inter-organisational mobility. This approach also fits with organisational efforts to promote talent from within and to invest in the development and retention of high potential internal talent. It is also suggested that non-core employees learn more through lateral moves than high potentials, acquiring the employability needed to be attractive for other organisations, while allowing high potentials to move up in the organisation. Overall, the study contributes to our understanding of how workforce segmentation might affect organisational career structures – from boundaryless orientation of non-core employees whose employability is key to progress with inter-organisational career path, to non-boundaryless career opportunities for high potentials and experts (Dries and Pepermans, 2008).

Second, research has also focused on the link between talent management and performance. A study conducted in 143 UK-owned MNCs examined the association between talent management (specifically management development) and perceived subsidiary performance (Sheehan, 2012). The study highlighted that investing in managerial talent has a positive influence on perceived subsidiary performance, but also pointed to the importance of the national context for the final returns. Specifically, the research highlighted the economic environment and the national quality of human capital will impact this relationship, which was confirmed when Czech Republic, Hungary and Poland were considered. Indeed, Poland, achieving the highest scores in both national characteristics, showed the positive and highly significant positive interaction between managerial development and perceived subsidiary performance, while Hungary achieved the lowest scores. Therefore, the study provides evidence for the argument that investing in managerial development may yield positive returns even in uncertain and volatile economic environments suggesting that the economic environment and the national quality of human capital is indeed important. Bethke-Langenegger *et al.* (2011) analysed the effect of different types of talent management strategies on organisational and individual level outcomes among Swiss corporations. Taking a broader approach to talent management outcomes in the European context, they tested four strategies – talent management focused on (a) corporate strategy and corporate goals; (b) succession planning; (c) attracting and retaining talents; and (d) developing talents. First, they found that talent management practices with a strong focus on corporate strategies and the alignment to overall corporate goals had an important impact on organisational outcomes such as company profit, the achievement of business goals and customer satisfaction, as well as on individual outcome of performance motivation. It is interesting to note that the focus on corporate strategy had much higher impact on corporate profit than any other talent management strategy. The research also highlighted that talent management focused on succession planning had an impact on corporate profit, and some individual outcomes such as performance motivation, work quality, and trust in leaders. The study also highlighted that talent management strategy was correlated to customer satisfaction and individual outcomes – performance motivation, commitment, work quality and trust in leaders, yet there was no significant effect on company profit. Finally, strategy focused on talent development showed positive correlations with all organisational and individual outcomes revealing the significance of focusing on employee development needs and expectations.

Conclusion

Recent reviews highlight the rapid increase in the number of publications on talent management during the last 10 years (Dries, 2013; Thunnissen *et al.*, 2013). However, Dries (2013) shows that only a small minority of articles that appeared in the period were published in academic journals, which highlights the slowness of the academic community to engage with research on talent management. It has been argued that this reflects concerns about the ambiguity of the theoretical and intellectual foundations of talent management and the lack of clarity of definitions of talent and talent management (Lewis and Heckman, 2006; Festing and Schäfer, 2014; Scullion and Collings, 2011). While our understanding of TM has developed considerably over the last decade, more empirical research is needed to understand the potential contribution of TM to organisational performance. Thunnissen *et al.* (2013) highlight the limitations of the one-dimensional approach to TM and advocate the benefits of a pluralistic approach which draws on multiple perspectives. There is growing recognition of the need to take account of the organisational and environmental context as well as the individual–organisational relationship to help explain how TM systems can be applied to balance employee well-being and organisational performance. As shown in the previous section, recent studies increasingly apply psychological contract perspectives (see Hoglund, 2012; Bjorkman *et al.*, 2013; Sonnenberg *et al.*, 2014) and highlight the importance of the institutional and cultural context for the deployment of talent management (see Tansley and Tietze, 2013; Boussebaa and Morgan, 2008; Festing *et al.*, 2013; Skuza *et al.*, 2013) which contributes to the development of a broader and more balanced perspective to TM. However, still much more empirical contributions are needed to prove multi-value advantage of TM systems.

Recent theoretical contributions (Sparrow *et al.*, 2014; Sparrow and Makram, 2015; Collings and Mellahi, 2009) show that in the value creation process organisations need to match TM system architecture to TM approaches, which will help them to make more informed strategic choices about their focus on people, positions, practices and strategic talent pools. They also need to consider people challenges associated with talent perception. First, they need to build a consensus around the organisational perception of talent – 1. whether to focus on an elite group of exceptional employees or all employees; 2. consider talent as a mix of inborn cognitive abilities and personality which are stable and difficult to develop or a mix of knowledge, skills and abilities that are capable of being developed; and 3. the degree and priority of potential versus performance. Second, they need to address the potential challenges of TM, such as an over emphasis on individual performance leading to diminished teamwork and internal competition instead of collaboration; unmet expectations and disillusion with organisational support of those excluded from talent pools; extensive dependence on monetary incentives; or potential development of an elitist arrogant attitudes (Collings and Mellahi, 2009; Pfeffer, 2001).

CASE STUDY 24.1

TALENT MANAGEMENT IN ELECT CO

AGNIESZKA SKUZA AND HUGH SCULLION

Introduction

This case explores some of the key talent management issues and challenges faced by a European-based electronics multinational enterprise (MNE). The company has grown rapidly through a strategy of international acquisitions and international joint ventures. The case will highlight links between the business strategy and talent management and particular attention will be paid to the management of talent internationally in both developed and emerging markets. Particular attention will be paid to the challenges of managing talent in the growing emerging markets in Central and Eastern Europe and Asia. There is a significant demand for managerial talent which can operate effectively in these markets and talent management challenges are more acute in these regions because of greater cultural and institutional differences (Skuza et al., 2013a).

Context

Elect Co[1] is a large European MNE operating in the electronics industry, and the global business environment facing the firm has been described as dynamic, complex and turbulent (company sources). The industry has been a strong contributor to economic development, but was adversely affected by the global recession, which led to restructuring and downsizing in the developed markets. However, the emerging markets are increasingly driving future global economic growth. The company faces tensions between global integration and local responsiveness. Traditionally, pressures for local responsiveness included market structure – where local companies are important and differences exist in consumer needs. On the other hand, the pressures for global integration included global competition, growing dependence on multinational customers and pressures for cost reduction.

By the early 2000s Elect Co operated on a global scale with over 20 subsidiaries; however, we suggest that Elect Co was not, in strategic terms, a global company. The company pursued a multi-domestic or country-centred strategy where national subsidiaries were responsible for their domestic markets. There was little coordination of activities in different countries. However, this strategy was becoming increasingly out of date by the mid-2000s because of changes in the world's electronic industry, particularly the globalisation of the market and the emergence of global competitors from Asia, and new patterns of industry competition through strategic alliances (company sources).

As a result, Elect Co adopted a more global orientation to global markets and restructured product development away from local markets to global markets. This involved the establishment of international production centres (IPCs) as manufacturing centres for products aimed at world markets. This shift from a multi-domestic strategy to a more globally integrated strategy also involved far reaching organisational restructuring including the establishment of a global talent management and management development programme.

Elect Co had achieved leadership positions in key markets, and increasingly would be regarded as a leader in the industry. The company has a strong commitment to leadership development and talent management combined with a growing emphasis on Corporate Social Responsibility (company sources).

In general terms, Elect Co seeks to achieve high performance through effective talent management and leadership practices, with a strong emphasis on recruitment and effective management of high calibre people. The company operates with an experienced management team and draws on mainly host country national managers (i.e. grass-roots local managers), highly qualified professionals, and a small number of expatriate managers who are used in the early stages of operation in new foreign markets mainly for the transfer of knowledge about company systems. Expatriates are rarely used beyond the early stages of operation in a new market and local managers are developed to take over the management of the subsidiary as soon as possible. The company seeks to secure a good mix and depth of skills and backgrounds and encourages both individual responsibility and a strong team orientation. The company is increasingly thinking global and

[1]This is a pseudonym to protect the company's identity.

seeks to maximise development opportunities across the group to retain top talent and develop broad experience (company sources).

In the traditional markets Elect Co seeks to maintain and build on leading market positions which have been established through innovative new products and strong leadership. The company is increasingly seeking to develop leaders who are capable of running more than one country or region and who can identify and deliver on global opportunities. In the higher growth emerging markets the company is seeking to build new businesses through partnerships and alliances with diverse cultures and to operate effectively in conditions of economic volatility. To develop these markets the company needs adaptable high calibre leaders who can build new positions in the market and can also develop the talent pool in the local market. The localised nature of the industry required that Elect Co develop strong management sensitive to the local market and cultural context, and local managers were allowed a high degree of autonomy to develop the business (company sources).

Elect Co has developed rapidly over the past 30 years from a business with modest international presence to a global enterprise with operations in more than 20 countries with a global workforce in excess of 60,000 employees. A major presence has been developed in mature markets in Western Europe and North America which accounts for approximately 60 per cent of the business. More recently, there has also been considerable growth in key emerging markets including Central and Eastern Europe, South America and Asia, with particularly rapid growth in the Chinese and Indian markets. Over the past 20 years the company have achieved impressive growth rates largely based on a highly successful foreign market entry strategy based on international acquisitions and international joint ventures, which has led to the emergence of the company as a global leader in the industry.

Decentralised approach to HR

Elect Co operated with a highly decentralised HR approach. A small team of corporate HR staff based at headquarters undertakes a relatively narrow range of functions than would be expected in global firms. This reflected the lean, highly decentralised corporate structure which has been in place at the company. The culture of decentralisation required that HR policies and practices are devolved to the business unit level to support the business strategy. Senior management sought to attract and retain high quality local management who are able to respond effectively to changing conditions in each host environment. The role of the corporate HQ was limited to senior management

development, support services and coordination. The recent shift to a more integrated global approach will pose new challenges for the corporate HR function, and the need to ensure the balance between global integration and local responsiveness will become even more critical for Elect Co as the changing business environment is increasingly driving the structure of the business and the HR agenda.

The talent management agenda

Recent research argues that MNEs increasingly need to manage talent on a global basis to remain competitive, and that talent can be located in different parts of their global operations (Sparrow *et al.*, 2014a). Shortages of managerial and professional talent have emerged as a key HR challenge facing Elect Co; the growing difficulty of recruiting and retaining managerial talent has been a significant constraint on the successful implementation of global strategies. Elect Co recognised the importance of having a sufficient level and calibre of talent to implement the international growth strategy, and talent management was a major strategic element of the company's human resources strategy.

In practice, Elect Co operates with a number of different leadership programmes for high potential staff at different levels in the organisation to ensure there is a talent pipeline which will deliver the leadership capability to run the business in the future (company sources). However, a significant talent management challenge facing Elect Co was problems relating to the willingness of leadership talent to move to the new strategic markets which are perceived to be higher risk locations (e.g. Russia, Africa and China), and, more generally, dual career and family issues could limit the international career plans of the company.

Elect Co: emerging talent management challenges

In the developed markets Elect Co's acquisition strategy involved targeting high performing companies in the local markets. A key element of the talent management strategy was acquiring and retaining top managerial and leadership talent and to retain and incentivise the high quality local management teams. In practice, the acquired firm's management were allowed a high degree of autonomy to run the subsidiary operation so long as they reached the performance targets set by company headquarters. A weakness of this approach, however, was the very limited mobility of managers between the HQ and the subsidiary which limits international management development opportunities and the ability to develop talent at the global or regional levels. However, as the company increasingly looks to the emerging markets as the high potential areas for business growth, there may be a greater need in the short term to use more expatriates to establish new business in the foreign markets and to move managers between different regions of the world. Some key talent management challenges in the emerging markets are discussed below.

The changing balance of power from developed to emerging markets in Elect Co's global operations had major implications for approaches to human capital and talent management. The talent management challenges for Elect Co were more complex in emerging markets such as India and China, which experienced high growth rates but also involved higher risk. These markets are very different to the traditional foreign markets developed by Elect Co in Europe and North America, and often joint ventures were used to enter the market to reduce the risks of developing business in these markets.

The rapid growth in Elect Co's business in the emerging markets created huge challenges in the attraction, development and retention of talent, and talent shortages continued despite the recession in many sectors. The retention of managers and professionals in the emerging markets was a key talent challenge for Elect Co because of the high turnover of staff in many sectors, and the severe nature of the competition for scarce managerial and leadership talent which can move to other MNCs or to domestic organisations.

The CEE region is an area of growing strategic importance for the company and expatriates have been used in this region to develop the market. However, more recently, a new talent strategy has emerged which involves moving high potential managers between the different countries of the region; a new pattern of international mobility that suggests some progress towards an international talent strategy. However, in Elect Co,

in practice, mobility of managers between different regions of the world was still highly limited and was far away from the development of a more integrated global talent management strategy. In practice, some of Elect Co's divisions still operated with a silo mentality, and was very reluctant to release high potential talent to other parts of the organisation which was linked to the highly decentralised culture of the company.

Managing talent in the recession

The initial response to the recession was for Elect Co to undertake a strategic review of portfolios and structures, to focus on cost reduction and to rely on experienced managers to run the business. A major casualty of the recession was the postponement of the graduate recruitment programme as well as significant redundancies and restructuring across the group. However, core leadership development and international mobility programmes were maintained, reflecting the strategic importance of leadership development to future business success. Despite the recession, shortages of key staff persisted in many sectors across the emerging markets and the retention of key leadership and high potential talent was a priority HR issue. In addition, the key role of international mobility in leadership development was increasingly recognised. Key HR challenges were to leverage opportunities for learning transfer across divisions to improve integration across businesses, to build creative management competences across the business, and to create further opportunities for international managers as well as improving talent retention and increasing the ability of managers to perform at the global level. Finally, a key challenge was to develop the capability of divisional talent by ensuring their exposure to varied challenges throughout their career.

Questions

1   What are the advantages and disadvantages of Elect Co operating with a decentralised management approach to business in general?

2   What were the main talent management challenges facing Elect Co as a result of the switch away from a multi-domestic strategy towards a more globally integrated strategy?

3   Discuss some of the main talent management challenges faced by the company in developed markets.

4   Discuss some of the main talent management challenges faced by the company in the emerging markets.

5   Why does Elect Co generally prefer to use local managers to run its subsidiary operations?

Bibliography

Adamsky, H. (2003) 'Talent management: something productive this way comes', *ERE Recruiting Intelligence*, April 22.

Becker, B.E. and Huselid, M.A. (2006) 'Strategic human resources management: where do we go from here?', *Journal of Management*, Vol.32, No.6, 898–925.

Becker, B.E., Huselid, M.A. and Beatty, R.W. (2009) 'The differentiated workforce: transforming talent into strategic impact', Boston: Harvard Business Press.

Beechler, S. and Woodward, I.C. (2009) 'The global war for talent', *Journal of International Management*, Vol.15, No.3, 273–85.

Bethke-Langenegger P., Mahler P. and Staffelbach B. (2011) 'Effectiveness of talent management strategies', *European Journal of International Management*, Vol.5, No.5, 524–39.

Bjorkman, I., Ehrnrooth, M., Makela, K., Smale, A. and Sumelius, J. (2013) 'Talent or Not? Employee reactions to talent identification', *Human Resource Management*, Vol.52, 195–214.

Boston Consulting Group (2007) *The Future of HR: Key Challenges Through 2015*, Dusseldorf: Boston Consulting Group.

Boudreau, J.W. and Ramstad, P.M. (2007) *Beyond HR: The new science of human capital*, Boston, MA: Harvard Business School Press.

Boudreau, J.W. and Ramstad, P.M. (2005a) 'Talentship, talent segmentation, and sustainability: a new HR decision science paradigm for a new strategy definition', *Human Resource Management*, Vol.44, No.2, 129–36.

Boudreau, J.W. and Ramstad, P.M. (2005b) 'Talentship and the new paradigm for human resource management: from professional practices to strategic talent decision science', *Human Resource Planning*, Vol.28, No.2, 17–26.

Boussebaa, M. and Morgan, G. (2008) 'Managing talent across national borders: the challenges faced by an international retail group', *Critical Perspectives on International Business*, Vol.4, No.1, 25–41.

Boxall, P. and Purcell, J. (2008) *Strategy and human resource management* (2nd edn.), Basingstoke: Palgrave Macmillan.

Bryan, L., Joyce, C. and Weiss, L. (2006) 'Making a market in talent', *McKinsey Quarterly*, Vol.2, 98–109.

Buckingham, M. and Vosburgh, R.M. (2001) 'The 21st century human resources function: it's the talent, stupid!, *Human Resource Planning*, Vol.24, No.4, 17–23.

Byham, W.C., Smith, A.B. and Paese, M.J. (2002) *Grow Your Own Leaders: How to Identify, Develop, and Retain Leadership Talent*, Upper Saddle River, NJ: Development Dimensions International & Prentice Hall.

Cappelli, P. (2008) *Talent on demand: Managing Talent in an Age of Uncertainty*, Boston: Harvard Business Press.

Chartered Institute of Personnel Development (2012) *Learning and Talent Development*, London: CIPD.

Chartered Institute of Personnel Development (2013) *Resourcing and Talent Planning*, London: CIPD.

Chuai, X., Preece, D. and Iles, P. (2008) 'Is talent management just "old wine in new bottles"? The case of multinational companies in Beijing', *Management Research News*, Vol.31, No.12, 901–11.

Cohn, J.M., Khurana, R. and Reeves, L. (2005) 'Growing talent as if your business depended on it', *Harvard Business Review*, Vol.83, No.10, 62–71.

Collings, D.G. (2014) 'Towards mature talent management: beyond shareholder value', *Human Resource Development Quarterly*, Vol.25, No.3, 301–19.

Collings, D.G. and Mellahi, K. (2009) 'Strategic talent management: a review and research agenda', *Human Resource Management Review*, Vol.19, No.4, 304–13.

Collings, D.G., Scullion, H. and Morley, M.J. (2007) 'Changing patterns of global staffing in the multinational enterprise: challenges to the conventional expatriate assignment and emerging alternatives,' *Journal of World Business*, Vol.42, No.2, 198–213.

Conger, J.A. (2010) 'Developing leadership talent: delivering on the promise of structured programmes', pp. 281–312, in Silzer, R.I. and Dowell, B.E. (eds.) *Strategy-Driven Talent Management*, San Francisco, CA: Jossey-Bass.

D'Amato, A. and Herzfeldt, R. (2008) 'Learning orientation, organizational commitment and talent retention across generations: a study of European managers', *Journal of Managerial Psychology*, Vol.23, No.8, 929–53.

Davies, B. and Davies, B.J. (2010) 'Talent management in academies', *International Journal of Educational Management*, Vol.24, No.5, 418–26.

Doh, J., Smith, R., Stumpf, S. and Tymon, W.G. (2014) 'Emerging markets and regional patterns in talent management: the challenge of India and China', in Sparrow, P., Scullion, H. and Tarique, I. (eds.) *Strategic Talent Management: Contemporary Issues in International Context*, Cambridge: Cambridge University Press.

Doh, J., Smith, R., Stumpf, S. and Tymon, W. (2011) 'Pride and professionals: retaining talent in emerging economies', *Journal of Business Strategy*, Vol.32, No.5, 35–42.

Dries, N. (2013) 'The psychology of talent management: a review and research agenda', *Human Resource Management Review*, Vol.23, No.4, 272–85.

Dries, N. and Pepermans, R. (2008) '"Real" high potential careers: an empirical study into the perspectives of organizations and high potentials', *Personnel Review*, Vol.37, No.1, 85–108.

Dundon, T. and Wilkinson, A. (2009) 'Human resource management in small and medium sized enterprises', in Wood, G. and Collings, D. (eds.) *Human Resource Management: A Critical Introduction*, London: Routledge.

Echols, M.E. (2007) 'Learning's role in talent management', Chief Learning Officer, October, 36–40.

Ericsson, K.A., Prietula, M.J. and Cokely, E.T. (2007) 'The making of an expert', *Harvard Business Review*, Vol.85, Nos.7–8, 115–21.

Ernst and Young (2010) *Managing Today's Global Workforce: Evaluating Talent Management to Improve Business*, London: Ernst and Young.

Farndale, E., Pai, A., Sparrow, P. and Scullion, H. (2014) 'Balancing individual and organizational goals in global talent management: a mutual-benefits perspective', *Journal of World Business*, Vol.49, No.2, 204–14.

Farndale, E., Scullion, H. and Sparrow, P. (2010) 'The role of the corporate HR function in talent management', *Journal of World Business*, Vol.45, No.2, 161–68.

Festing, M. and Schäfer, L. (2014) 'Generational challenges to talent management: a framework for talent retention based on the psychological-contract perspective', *Journal of World Business*, Vol.49, No.2, 262–71.

Festing, M., Schäfer, L. and Scullion, H. (2013) 'Talent management in medium-sized German companies: an explorative study and agenda for future research', *International Journal of Human Resource Management*, Vol.24, No.9, 1872–93.

Fugate, M., Kinicki, A.J. and Ashforth, B.E. (2004) 'Employability: a psycho-social construct, its dimensions, and applications', *Journal of Vocational Behavior*, Vol.65, 14–38.

Gagné, F. (2004) 'Transforming gifts into talents: the DMGT as a developmental theory', *High Ability Studies*, Vol.15, No.2, 119–47.

Gandz, J. (2006) 'Talent development: the architecture of a talent pipeline that works', *Ivey Business Journal*, Vol.1, 1–4.

Gallardo-Gallardo, E., Dries, N. and González-Cruz, T.F. (2013) 'What is the meaning of 'talent' in the world of work?', *Human Resource Management Review*, Vol.23, No.4, 290–300.

Garavan, T.N., Carbery, R. and Rock, A. (2012) 'Mapping talent development: definition, scope and architecture', *European Journal of Training and Development*, Vol.36, No.1, 5–24.

Gelens, J., Dries, N., Hofmans, J. and Pepermans, R. (2013) 'The role of perceived organizational justice in shaping the outcomes of talent management: a research agenda', *Human Resource Management Review*, Vol.23, No.4, 341–53.

Guthridge, M., Komm, A.B. and Lawson, E. (2006) 'The people problem in talent management', *McKinsey Quarterly*, Vol.2, 6–8.

Guthridge, M., McPherson, J.R. and Wolf, W.J. (2008) 'Upgrading talent', *McKinsey Quarterly*, 1–8 (December).

Hoglund, M. (2012) 'Quid pro quo? Examining talent management through the lens of psychological contracts', *Personnel Review*, Vol.41, No.2, 126–42.

Howard, A. and Wellins, R. (2009) *Global Leadership Forecast 2008/2009*, pp. 1–70.

Human Capital Institute (2008) 'Talent management strategy – a profit & loss perspective for real-world business impact', Vermont: Human Capital Institute Analyst.

Human Capital Institute and Hewitt Associates (2008) *Analytics to Improve HR Alignment and Drive Efficiency*, Cincinnati, OH, USA.

Iles, P., Preece, D. and Chuai, X. (2010) 'Is talent management a management fashion in HRD? Towards a research agenda', *Human Resource Development International*, Vol.13, No.2, 125–45.

Lawler, E.E. (1994) 'From job based to competency-based organizations', *Journal of Organizational Behavior*, Vol.15, 3–15.

Lepak, D.P. and Snell, S.A. (1999) 'The human resource architecture: toward a theory of human capital allocation and development', *The Academy of Management Review*, Vol.24, 31–48.

Lewis, R.E. and Heckman, R.J. (2006) 'Talent management: a critical review', *Human Resource Management Review*, Vol.16, No.2, 139–54.

Li, S. and Scullion, H. (2006) 'Bridging the distance: managing cross border knowledge holders', *Asia Pacific Journal of Management*, Vol.23, 71–92.

Li, S. and Scullion, H. (2010) 'Developing the local competence of expatriate managers for emerging markets: a knowledge-based approach', *Journal of World Business*, Vol.45, No.2, 190–6.

Manpower Group (2012) *Talent Shortage Survey 2012*, 1–36.

Manpower Group (2013) *Talent Shortage Survey 2013*, 1–47.

Martin, J. and Schmidt, C. (2010) 'How to keep your top talent', *Harvard Business Review*, Vol.88, No.5, 54–61.

Mayrhofer, W., Reichel, A. and Sparrow, P. (2012) *Alternative Form of International Working. Handbook of Research on International Human Resource Management*, London: Sage Publications.

McCall, M., Lombardo, M. and Morrison, M. (1988) *The Lessons of Experience: How Successful Executives Develop on the Job*, Lexington, MA: Lexington Books.

McDonnell, A. (2011) 'Still fighting the "war for talent"? Bridging the science versus practice gap', *Journal of Business and Psychology*, Vol.26, 169–73.

Meyers, M.C., van Woerkom, M. and Dries, N. (2013) 'Talent — Innate or acquired? Theoretical considerations and their implications for talent management', *Human Resource Management Review*, Vol.23, No.4, 305–21.

Michaels, E., Handfield-Jones, H. and Beth, A. (2001) *The War for Talent*, Boston, MA: Harvard Business School Press.

Morton, L. (2005) *Talent Management Value Imperatives: Strategies for Execution*, New York: The Conference Board.

Nilsson, S. and Ellstrom, P.E. (2011) 'Employability and talent management: challenges for HRD practices', *European Journal of Training and Development*, Vol.36, No.1, 26–45.

Odiorne, G.S. (1984) *Human Resources Strategy: A Portfolio Approach*, San Francisco, CA: Jossey-Bass.

Patton, A. (1967) 'The coming scramble for executive talent', *Harvard Business Review*, Vol.45, No.3, 155–71.

Pfeffer, J. (2001) 'Fighting the war for talent is hazardous to your organization's health', *Organizational Dynamics*, Vol.29, No.4, 248–59.

Pfeffer, J. and Sutton, R.I. (2006) 'Hard facts, dangerous half-truths, and total nonsense: profiting from evidence-based management', Boston, MA: Harvard Business School Press.

PricewaterhouseCoopers (2012) *15th Annual Global CEO Survey*, London: PWC.

Ready, D.A. and Conger, J.A. (2007) 'Make your company a talent factory', *Harvard Business Review*, Vol.85, No.6, pp. 68–77.

Ready, D.A., Conger, J.A. and Hill, L.A. (2010) 'Are you a high potential?' *Harvard Business Review*, June, 78–84.

Scullion, H. and Brewster, C. (2001) 'Managing expatriates: message from Europe,' *Journal of World Business*, Vol.36, 346–65.

Scullion, H., Collings, D.G. and Gunnigle, P (2007) 'International HRM in the 21st Century: emerging themes and contemporary debates', *Human Resource Management Journal*, Vol.17, 309–19.

Scullion, H. and Collings, D.G. (2011) *Global Talent Management*, London: Routledge.

Scullion H., Collings, D.G. and Caliguiri, P. (2010) 'Global talent management', *Journal of World Business*, Vol.45, 105–08.

Scullion, H. and Starkey, K. (2000) 'In search of the changing role of the corporate HR function in the international firm', *International Journal of Human Resource Management*, Vol.11, 1061–81.

Sheehan, M. (2012) 'Developing managerial talent: exploring the link between management talent and perceived performance in multinational corporations (MNCs)', *European Journal of Training and Development*, Vol.36, No.1, 66–85.

Silzer, R. and Church, A.H. (2009) 'The pearls and perils of identifying potential', *Industrial and Organizational Psychology*, Vol.2, 377–412.

Silzer, R.F. and Church, A.H. (2010) 'Identifying and assessing high-potential talent. Current organizational practices', pp. 213–279, in Silzer, R.F. and Dowell, B.E. (eds.) *Strategy-Driven Talent Management: A Leadership Imperative*, San Francisco, CA: Jossey-Bass.

Skuza, A., Scullion, H. and McDonnell, A. (2013) 'An analysis of the talent management challenges in a post-communist country: the case of Poland', *The International Journal of Human Resource Management*, Vol.24, 453–70.

Skuza, A., McDonnell, A. and Scullion, H. (2013a) 'Talent management in the emerging markets', in Horwitz, F. and Budwhar, P. (eds.) *Handbook of Human Resource Management in the Emerging Markets*, Cheltenham: Edward Edgar Publishing.

Smart, B.D. (1999) *How Leading Companies Win by Hiring, Coaching and Keeping the Best People*, New York: Prentice Hall.

Sonnenberg, M., van Zijderveld, V. and Brinks, M. (2014) 'The role of talent-perception incongruence in effective talent management', *Journal of World Business*, Vol.49, No.2, 272–80.

Sparrow, P., Hird, M. and Balain, S. (2011) 'Talent management: Time to question the tablets of stone?,' White paper 11/01, October, Lancaster University Management School.

Sparrow, P. and Makram, H. (2015) 'What is the value of talent management? Building value-driven processes within a talent management architecture', *Human Resource Management Review*, Vol.25, No.3, 249–63.

Sparrow, P., Scullion, H. and Tarique, I. (2014a) *Strategic Talent Management: Contemporary Issues in International Context*, Cambridge: Cambridge University Press.

Sparrow, P., Scullion, H. and Tarique, I. (2014b) 'Multiple lenses on talent management: definitions and contours of the field', in Sparrow, P., Scullion, H. and Tarique, I. (eds.) *Strategic Talent Management: Contemporary Issues in International Context*, Cambridge: Cambridge University Press.

Stahl, G., Bjorkman, I., Farndale, E., Morris, S., Paauwe, J., Stiles, P., Trevor, J. and Wright, P. (2012) 'Six principles of effective global talent management', *MIT Sloan Management Review*, Vol.53, No.2, 25–32.

Stahl, G.K., Bjorkman, I., Farndale, E., Morris, S.S., Stiles, P. and Trevor, J. (2007) 'Global talent management: how leading multinationals build and sustain their talent pipeline', Faculty & research working paper, Fontainebleau, France: INSEAD.

Strack, R., Caye, J.M., von der Linden, C., Haen, P. and Abramo, F. (2013) 'Creating people advantage 2013: lifting HR practices to the next level', London: BCG. Available at: https://www.bcgperspectives.com/content/articles/human_resources_organization_design_creating_people_advantage_2013/#chapter1.

Tansley, C. (2011) 'What do we mean by the term "talent" in talent management?,' *Industrial and Commercial Training*, Vol.43, No.5, 266–74.

Tansley, C. and Tietze, S. (2013) 'Rites of passage through talent management progression stages: an identity work perspective', *The International Journal of Human Resource Management*, Vol.24, No.9.

Thunnissen, M., Boselie, P. and Fruytier, B. (2013) 'Talent management and the relevance of context: towards a pluralistic approach', *Human Resource Management Review*, Vol.23, No.4, 326–36.

Tsay, C. and Banaji, M.R. (2011) 'Naturals and strivers: preferences and beliefs about sources of achievement', *Journal of Experimental Social Psychology*, Vol.47, 460–5.

Tymon, W.G., Stumpf, S.A. and Doh, J.P. (2010) 'Exploring talent management in India: the neglected role of intrinsic rewards,' *Journal of World Business*, Vol.45, No.2, 109–21.

Vaiman, V. and Holden, N. (2011) 'Talent management's perplexing landscape in Central and Eastern Europe', pp. 178–93, in Scullion, H. and Collings, D. (eds.) *Global Talent Management*, Abingdon: Routledge.

Vaiman, V., Lemmergaard, J. and Azevedo, A. (2011) 'Contingent workers: needs, personality characteristics, and work motivation', *Team Performance Management*, Vol.17, Nos.5–6, 311–24.

Valverde, M., Scullion, H. and Ryan, G. (2013) 'Talent management in Spanish medium-sized organizations', *International Journal of Human Resource Management*, Vol.24, No.9, 1832–52.

World Economic Forum (2011) *Global Talent Risk – Seven Responses*, Geneva: World Economic Forum.

Yost, P.R. and Chang, G. (2009) 'Everyone is equal, but some are more equal than others', *Industrial and Organizational Psychology*, Vol.2, No.4, 442–5.

Zuboff, S. (1988) *In the Age of the Smart Machine: The Future of Work and Power*, New York: Basic Books.

INDEX